THE HISTORIC PARISH OF ENGLAND AND WALES

An Electronic Map of Boundaries before 1850 with a Gazetteer and Metadata

ROGER J. P. KAIN
and
RICHARD R. OLIVER

Colchester
History Data Service, UK Data Archive
2001

First published 2001 by
History Data Service, UK Data Archive
University of Essex
Wivenhoe Park
Colchester CO4 3SQ

© Roger J P Kain and Richard R Oliver

ISBN 0 9540032 0 9

Designed and typeset by Sue Rouillard
Printed and bound in England by Sandford Turner, Exeter

The front cover shows an extract of the electronic boundary map of the area around Stamford in Lincolnshire. To access the electronic map please contact :

History Data Service, UK Data Archive,
University of Essex, Wivenhoe Park, Colchester CO4 3SQ.
Telephone: +44 (0)1206 872326; Fax: +44 (0)1206 872003;
Email: hds@essex.ac.uk;
URL: http://hds.essex.ac.uk

The rear cover is a key to the counties of England and Wales identified on the electronic map and in the gazetteer/metadata.

The inside rear cover is a key to the 115 boundary overlay sheets of the electronic boundary map in relation to Ordnance Survey New Popular Edition, one inch to one mile sheet lines.

CONTENTS

	Page
List of Figures	4
List of Tables	5
Preface	6
Introduction	
1 The value of a map of the 'historic parishes' of England and Wales	7
2 Parishes, townships, hamlets, tithings and other local areas	12
3 The inadequacy of existing published maps of 'historic parish' boundaries	17
4 Context: previous work on local area boundaries at Exeter	20
(i) *Tithe surveys (Leverhulme Trust 1987-92)*	
(ii) *Government-sponsored, large-scale mapping of England and Wales before the Ordnance Survey (ESRC 1993-98).*	
5 Sources of parish boundary information for the electronic map	22
6 A topographic underlay for the boundary mapping	25
7 Compiling the electronic map of boundaries	26
(i) *Producing a manuscript compilation.*	
(ii) *Scanning, rectifying and adding reference numbers, braces and tie lines.*	
(iii) *Compiling the gazetteer/metadata*	
8 The system of reference numbers	31
9 Defining counties	32
10 The gazetteer/metadata	34
11 Tabular summary of the boundary content	38
Abbreviated Gazetteer/Metadata	41

LIST OF FIGURES

		Page
Fig. 1:	The regional pattern of local administration in England and Wales, after Dorothy Sylvester, 1969.	13
Fig. 2:	Parishes, townships and divisions of townships as mapped by the Ordnance Survey on the 1:10,560 Yorkshire Sheet 203, surveyed 1847 and published 1851.	14
Fig. 3:	Detached parts of parishes and townships west of Kingston-upon-Hull, Yorkshire created as a result of enclosure in 1824-37.	16
Fig. 4:	An example of how enclosure maps can supply otherwise elusive boundaries: Farndish and Podington, Bedfordshire.	23
Fig. 5:	A printed extract of the electronic boundary map of the area around Stamford, Lincolnshire, with key (note that the electronic map is in colour).	26-7
Fig. 6:	Stages in compiling the boundary map.	28
Fig. 7:	An urban enlargement: Stamford, Lincolnshire	30
Fig. 8:	Key to the counties of England and Wales (& *outside rear cover*).	33
Fig. 9:	Key to the 115 boundary overlay sheets in relation to Ordnance Survey New Popular sheet lines (& *inside rear cover*).	36

LIST OF TABLES

		Page
Table 1:	Examples of sources collected by, or related to, the 'historic parishes' of England and Wales, 1086-1866	9
Table 2:	Numbers of 'census parishes' in various censuses, 1801-1881 for seven counties	10
Table 3:	Numbers of local administrative areas and sources of information for boundaries	38-9

PREFACE

This book introduces an electronic map of the historic (mainly pre-1850) parishes, townships, and other local administrative areas of England and Wales now available from the History Data Service, UK Data Archive, University of Essex. The electronic map uses as a base the 115 sheets of the Ordnance Survey one inch to one mile (1:63,360) New Popular Edition maps (1945-8) with National Grid. It contains the boundaries of about 18,240 places and is arranged as three electronic 'layers'. The first is a scan of the Ordnance Survey maps stored as grey tone sheet images. This enables the Ordnance Survey physical, cultural and place-name content to be readily visible in the background for orientation and general location purposes, while not obscuring the added boundary and reference number material. The second layer consists of the boundaries, stored as solid red lines and the third layer contains (in green) tie lines to join detached parts of parishes and the reference numbers which link places on the map to the gazetteer/metadata. A dataset of metadata accompanies the maps and contains information about the provenance of the boundaries. In this book we describe the data, the method of compilation and how the boundaries and associated metadata can be accessed. We also include an abbreviated version of the full gazetteer/metadata which serves as a hard copy index to the places located on the electronic maps.

We wish to acknowledge the support of the Leverhulme Trust and the Economic and Social Research Council which funded the research and the History Data Service for their help in mounting and maintaining the electronic records on the internet and for publishing this explanatory handbook. A number of people have helped us in our work. We would like to mention particularly Cressida Chappell and Hamish James of the History Data Service, Dr Humphrey Southall and his Great Britain Historical GIS team at Portsmouth University, Professor Margaret Spufford of the Roehampton Institute, and Dr Nicholas Coney of the Public Record Office with whom we have collaborated by supplying boundary information to assist their own research projects and Dr Roger Hellyer for kindly allowing us to copy numerous original maps. County archivists and librarians, too numerous to record individually, provided much assistance to Richard Oliver on his visits to track down the elusive last few boundaries. Sarah Wilmot conducted part of the primary research on tithe maps between 1987 and 1989. Our work has benefitted from the technical help and expertise of a number of colleagues at Exeter University and especially that of Rodney Fry and, latterly, Helen Jones and Sue Rouillard who worked on the boundary maps, Terry Bacon who assisted with scanning base maps and our draft boundary drawings, and Barry Phillips and Andrew Teed for photographic services. Sue Rouillard designed the cover and typeset the text. We are grateful to you all and are pleased to associate each of you with the published work.

15 January 2001   Roger Kain and Richard Oliver

INTRODUCTION

1

The value of a map of the 'historic parishes' of England and Wales

A major lacuna militating against the effective exploitation of many post-medieval to mid-Victorian historical sources collected by local administrative areas is the lack of information on the boundaries of those administrative areas: the so-called 'historic' or 'ancient' parishes of England and Wales. It is known that these districts came into being during the Middle Ages as the units in which the pastoral and spiritual care of the church was delivered, that the map of these ecclesiastical parishes was essentially complete by the fifteenth century, that these ecclesiastical boundaries were adopted during the early modern period for secular and judicial purposes, and that boundaries remained essentially unchanged until a number of reforms from the mid-nineteenth century onwards reorganised the local administrative geography of the country.[1] That is not the same as saying that everything remained totally unaltered in the seventeenth and eighteenth centuries but rather that the amount of change was small. In the second half of the nineteenth century, the pace of change was an order of magnitude greater. Some places were divided, others were amalgamated, some new administrative areas were created, and some others disappeared.

The structure of parish and township boundaries which formed the basis of local administration at the time of the first decennial census of population in 1801 was one which had been almost unchanged for at least three hundred years. The considerable changes in this system which occurred during the nineteenth century can be traced to the advent of the New Poor Law and secular registration in the 1830s.[2] The first boundary reforms, in 1843-4, were only permissive parliamentary acts, which enabled the division of large parishes into either smaller ecclesiastical parishes or wards.[3] The Counties (Detached Parts) Act, 1844 eliminated those detached parts of counties which were wholly surrounded by a single other county.[4] The most striking result of this was the transfer of Norhamshire, Islandshire and Bedlingtonshire from Durham to Northumberland. In theory this tidying up of county boundaries did not affect parish boundaries but in practice a number of parishes had previously been split between counties,

---

[1] See for example: J. Blair (ed,) *Minsters and Parish Churches. The Local Church in Transition 950-1200*, Oxford, Oxford University Committee for Archaeology, Monograph No. 17, 1988; J. Blair, 'The making of the English parish', *Medieval History*, 2 (1992), pp. 13-19; and O. T. Edwards, 'How many Sarum antiphonals were there in England and Wales in the middle of the sixteenth century?', *Revue Benedictine*, 99 (1989), pp. 155-80.

[2] There is a useful summary of the details of this legislation in J. R. S. Booth, *Public Boundaries and the Ordnance Survey 1840-1980*, Southampton, Ordnance Survey, 1980, pp. 75-113.

[3] New Parishes Act, 1843 (6 & 7 Vict., c.37), s.9; Poor Law Amendment Act, 1844 (7 & 8 Vict., c.101), s.19.

[4] 7 & 8 Vict., c.61, ss 1,2.

for example Lea in Herefordshire, which had included a detached part of Gloucestershire, and Catworth in Huntingdonshire, which had included several small detached parts of Northamptonshire. The Extra-Parochial Places Act, 1857 enabled some extra-parochial areas to be absorbed into adjoining parishes, although little use seems to have been made of these provisions beyond eliminating a number of areas which had nebulous boundaries anyway.[5] The same applies to the Poor Law Amendment Act, 1868 which required that extra-parochial places with no overseer should be amalgamated with adjoining civil parishes.[6]

The first Act to affect detached portions of parishes was the Divided Parishes and Poor Law Amendment Act, 1876, which permitted, but did not compel, the Local Government Board to order that detached parts of parishes could either be separate parishes in their own right, or else amalgamated with other parishes.[7] The Poor Law Act, 1879 provided for parts of parishes cut off by municipal boundaries and rivers to be treated as detached for the purposes of the 1876 Act.[8] As an early result of this, the 'fen lots' in the East, West and Wildmore Fens in Lincolnshire were completely reorganised in 1880, and about forty detached 'fen lots' of parishes and extra-parochial areas were transferred to seven compact civil parishes, thereby saving the Ordnance Survey considerable time and expense when conducting the 1:2500 survey a few years later.[9]

The next Act was the one which had the most dramatic effect: the Divided Parishes and Poor Law Amendment Act, 1882 provided that from 25 March 1883 detached parts of parishes wholly surrounded by another parish were to be amalgamated with that parish.[10] Whilst this removed large numbers of detached areas literally overnight, and numerous people went to bed in one parish and woke up in another, the Local Government Board was kept busy throughout the 1880s transferring detached areas from one parish to another using the 1876 Act. The Local Government Act, 1894, which created parish councils, effectively completed the rationalisation process by providing first, that every parish was to be within a single administrative county (this brought about a number of localised changes to county boundaries, for example at Broomhill, formerly divided between Kent and Sussex, but all in Sussex from 1895); second, that parishes straddling urban and rural district council boundaries were to be split (with the result that parishes with names such as 'Sandridge Rural' became common in the early twentieth century); and third, that other changes could be made within two years of passing the Act.[11]

---

[5] 20 Vict, c.19, ss 1, 4, 8.

[6] We infer this from the evidence of Ordnance Survey 1:10,560 first edition maps as compared with the 1851 census. The Act was the Poor Law Amendment Act, 1868 (31 & 32 Vict., c.122), s.27. This Act also extended the boundaries of parishes and townships across the foreshore to low water mark.

[7] 39 & 40 Vict., c.61, s.1.

[8] 42 & 43 Vict., c.54, ss 4, 6.

[9] There is a useful summary of these changes appended to the 1891 census returns: British Parliamentary Papers (House of Commons Series) [C.6948-I], CV, 1.

[10] 45 & 46 Vict., c.58, ss 2, 4.

[11] 56 & 57 Vict., c.73, ss 36.1.i, 36.2.

With very few exceptions, the published maps of the Ordnance Survey were produced too late to capture the historic parish boundaries which were affected by the above legislation and no other published maps are available to use as a source for the whole country. However there are two sets of manuscript, large-scale parish and township maps which together can provide some 85 per cent of ancient parish boundaries for England and Wales. These are the tithe maps of *circa* 1840 and parliamentary enclosure maps, mainly of the late eighteeenth and early nineteenth centuries. As a result of the completion of a Leverhulme Trust funded project which examined all 11,785 parish tithe maps and an ESRC-funded project on pre-Ordnance Survey large-scale parish mapping, a timely and probably once-only opportunity was provided of completing the map of historic parishes of England and Wales at relatively modest cost by utilising the physical and intellectual capital accumulated by these two related projects. Recent interest in the historical social sciences in creating a long-term, local area GIS rendered it intellectually opportune as well.[12] Our map of the boundaries of historic parishes will be of relevance to a wide range of historians and historical geographers using the kinds of local-area-based source material summarised in Table 1.

Table 1: Examples of sources collected by, or related to, the 'historic parishes' of England and Wales, 1086-1866.

Date	*Source*
1086	Domesday Book
1279	The Hundred Rolls: incomplete attempt to repeat Domesday
1291	The Pope Nicholas IV Taxation; provides first comprehensive list of parishes
1216ff	Inquisitiones Post Mortem
1327, 1332, 1334	Lay Subsidies: statistics for over 13,000 taxpaying vills
1341-2	Nonarum Inquisitiones [tax on output of corn, wool and lambs]
1377-81	Poll Tax: some detailed population lists
1440s-1490s	Reliefs from Lay Subsidies [records of tax reductions by parishes]
1524-5, 1544	Tudor Subsidies
1538ff	Start of Ecclesiastical Parish Registers
1563	Diocesan Returns of Households
1603	Diocesan Returns of Communicants, by parishes
1662-6, 1669-74	Hearth Tax Returns: survey of population and wealth, by parish
1676	Compton Census: of religious adherence, by parish
c.1792-c.1832	The Land Tax Returns, by parish
1801ff	Decennial Population Censuses, by enumeration districts
1801	The Acreage Returns: agricultural statistics, by parish
1815	Published Assessments to Property Tax, by parish
1842-3, 1859-60	Published Assessments to Income Tax, by parish
1815ff	Assessments to County Rates, by parish.
1837ff	Compulsory secular registration of births, marriages and deaths
1851	Census of Religious Worship, by parish
1854, 1866ff	Agricultural Statistics, by parish

Table 2: Numbers of 'census parishes' in various censuses, 1801-1881 for seven counties

County	1801	1831	1851	1881
Bedfordshire	143	152	153	140
Leicestershire	331	356	362	302
Lincolnshire	710	750	771	766
Nottinghamshire	258	273	294	287
Rutland	58	57	58	57
Surrey	160	165	183	171
Westmorland	109	122	118	115

Source: Published Census Reports

The maps will be of especial interest to researchers analysing the decennial censuses of population. Indeed, it was the census that introduced the regular systematic collection of statistical data by small local areas. It was of course far from being the first such national data-gathering exercise, as Table 1 indicates, but it was accompanied by an increasing interest in gathering statistical information, both for the abstract pursuit of knowledge and as an aid to national administration and policy-making. The establishment of the New Poor Law and a system of Registration Districts and Sub-Districts created a new geographical and administrative framework, even though almost all the boundaries were defined by pre-existing ones for parishes and their divisions. The notes to the published parish-level tables of the 1851 Census indicate that it was only at this date that this administrative geography achieved something like definitive shape.[13] Thus the 1851 Census can serve as a useful check-list of 'historic mother parishes' and their divisions. Table 2 demonstrates that, in terms of numbers, parish and sub-parish divisions achieved an apogee of complexity c.1851.

Over the second half of the nineteenth century, a series of acts of parliament modified the boundaries of parishes and townships in England and Wales. In and around London and occasionally elsewhere, there are a few examples of new parishes created by act of parliament in earlier times, but these are exceptional.[14]

---

[12] In 1996 the ESRC funded a workshop on Historical GIS convened by Humphrey Southall, in 1998 the Social Science History Association's Annual Meeting contained sessions on Historical GIS convened by Anne Knowles, and the Electronic Cultural Atlas Initiative based at the University of Berkeley in California intends to develop world-wide mapping.

[13] *Census of Great Britain, 1851 – Population Tables.* British Parliamentary Papers (House of Commons Series) 1852-53 [1632], LXXXV, 1, LXXXVI, 1.

[14] For example, Covent Garden, created in 1645 out of a 'precinct' of St Martins-in-the-Fields; St George Bloomsbury, created in 1729 out of St Giles-in-the-Fields; St Luke Finsbury, made a parish in 1733; West Hackney and South Hackney, created out of Hackney parish in 1824 (see 1851 census, Division I, pp 14-15, 14, 17); Bellingham, Falstone, Greystead, Thorneyburn and Wark, all created out of Simonburn by Act, 51 Geo. III, c.194 (see 1851 census, Division X, p.31).

It is also well-known that in parts of England the 'deserted village' phenomenon led to a number of amalgamations of parishes in the fourteenth and fifteenth centuries, often indicated by 'cum' or 'with' in the parish name (e.g. Wyham-cum-Cadeby in Lincolnshire), but thereafter there is little evidence of either new parishes being created, or existing ones being divided.[15] A partial exception to this generalisation is that an Act of 1662 provided that townships rather than parishes could be used for administering the poor law, though this was a change of function rather than the creation of new boundaries.[16] If boundary changes did take place independently of the creation or amalgamation of parishes, then such changes have left no documentary evidence. By contrast, the reconstruction of pre-Conquest boundaries by W. G. Hoskins and others implies a high degree of continuity.[17] Further, although in the later eighteenth century a number of parish boundary changes were brought about by dividing common lands between two or more parishes formerly enjoying grazing or other rights thereon, boundary changes between adjoining parishes were unlikely to take place unless both parishes were being enclosed simultaneously, which was unusual.[18] Multiple enclosures were most common in Norfolk, but the scope for boundary change was limited by the restricted areas which remained unenclosed, and thus parish boundary changes due to enclosure are no more common in Norfolk than they are in any other county. Changes such as the straightening of the formerly very sinuous boundary between Corringham and Springthorpe in Lincolnshire when these two were enclosed as a single operation in 1848-52 are indeed unusual. Therefore, a map of parish boundaries as they were in the first half of the nineteenth century should be of value for at least the whole of the modern period, i.e. *circa* 1500 onwards, and, given the presumption of continuity rather than change in boundary alignments, such a map should also form a useful starting point for the reconstruction of earlier boundaries.

---

[15] Compare, for example, the list of parishes in the Diocesan Return of 1563 for Lincolnshire printed in Gerald A. J. Hodgett, *Tudor Lincolnshire* (History of Lincolnshire, VI), Lincoln, History of Lincolnshire Committee, 1975, pp. 189-99 with the parishes included in the 1851 census.

[16] Poor Relief Act, 1662 (14 Chas II, c.12).

[17] W. G. Hoskins, *Fieldwork in Local History*, London, Faber & Faber, 1967, pp. 34-40. For a modern example see Della Hooke, 'Saxon conquest and settlement' in Roger Kain and William Ravenhill (eds), *Historical Atlas of South-West England,* Exeter, University of Exeter Press, 1999, pp. 95-104.

[18] See W. E. Tate & M. E. Turner, *A Domesday of English Enclosure Awards,* Reading, University of Reading Press, 1978.

2
Parishes, townships, hamlets, tithings and other local areas

Post-medieval England and Wales has been characterised by two main levels of local administration. The upper level consisted of parishes and extra-parochial places. The latter lay outside the parish system, and were not subject to parish rates; often they represented former monastic lands, for example Kirkham in the East Riding of Yorkshire, Orford in Lincolnshire and Waverley in Surrey. Extra-parochial areas were very rarely subdivided (Brinkburn in Northumberland was unusual in this), but parishes very often were. Although it is usual to refer to these sub-parish divisions as 'townships', there were regional variations both in the extent to which parishes were divided and in the terminology for these divisions.[19] Figure 1, based on the work of Dorothy Sylvester, indicates the broad regional variations in terminology.[20] Division of parishes was the usual pattern in north-east Wales and parts of mid-Wales, and in most of England north-west of a line from the Severn to the Lower Trent. North of the Mersey and the Humber and in Cheshire the undivided parish is exceptional. In the south-east half of the country it was generally unusual for parishes to be divided, but there are localised exceptions, for example in parts of Berkshire, Hampshire and Oxfordshire.

Similarly, terminology for these divisions varies. To the north-west of a line from the Severn to the Wash, they are almost invariably known as 'townships'. To the south-east, they are most commonly known as 'hamlets', though in some counties, notably Berkshire, Cornwall, Dorset, Gloucestershire, Hampshire, Somerset, Surrey and Wiltshire, they are often known as 'tythings' or 'tithings'.[21] Other terms are occasionally found; Mildenhall in Suffolk, for example, was divided into four 'wards', a term more usually reserved for urban divisions, particularly for electoral purposes from the 1830s onwards. In Wales, divisions of parishes were usually known as townships in the north and simply as 'divisions' further south. The use of these divisions of parishes as 'census parishes' in 1851 indicates a certain contemporary administrative status, but not all survived to be recorded by the Ordnance Survey later in the century as 'civil parishes'. At Newent in Gloucestershire, for example, the 1851 census notes that the boundaries of the constituent tythings were 'ill-defined', a conclusion endorsed by the present writers

---

[19] Angus J. L. Winchester, 'Parish, township and tithing: landscapes of local administration in England before the nineteenth century', *The Local Historian,* 27 (1997), pp. 3-17.

[20] Dorothy Sylvester, *The Rural Landscape of the Welsh Borderland,* London, Macmillan, 1969, pp. 167 and 169.

[21] David Harvey reports that there were 308 tithings in Cornwall in 1284 compared with 200 parishes: 'Territoriality and the territorialisation of West Cornwall', unpublished University of Exeter PhD thesis, 1996, p. 95; A. Winchester, *Discovering Parish Boundaries*, Princes Risborough, Shire Publications, 1990, p. 22..

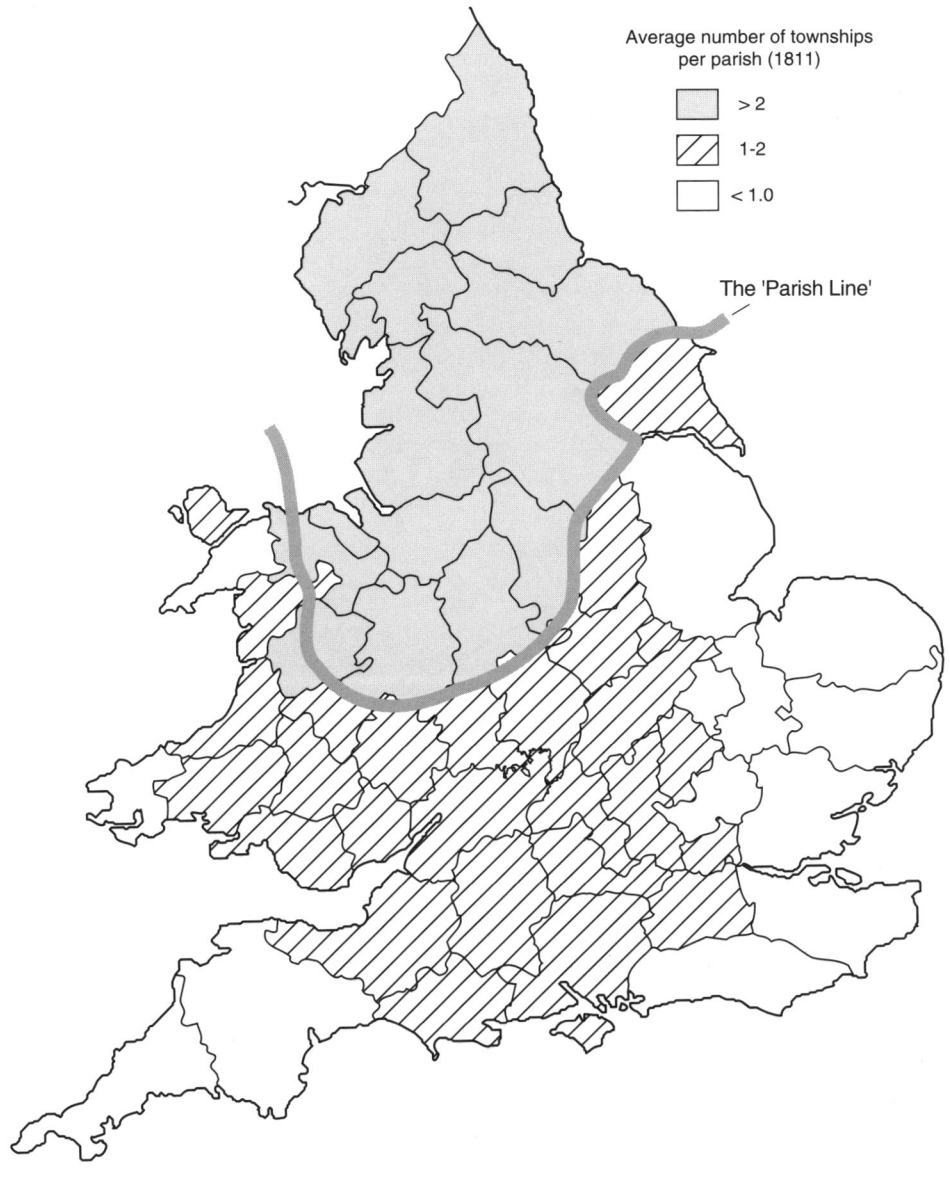

Fig:1 The regional pattern of local administration in England and Wales, after Dorothy Sylvester, 1969. From an analysis of the 1811 census, Sylvester identifies a 'parish line' dividing southern counties characterised by single township parishes from the northern counties with much larger, multi-township parishes.

Fig: 2 Parishes, townships and divisions of townships as mapped by the Ordnance Survey on the 1:10,560 Yorkshire Sheet 203, surveyed 1847 and published 1851. The upright open block names 'Thorner' and 'Barwick in Elmet' denote parishes; the solid sloping names 'Shadwell' and 'Barwick in Elmet' denote townships; the open sloping names 'Roundhay Grange' and 'Morwick' denote divisions of townships.

when they investigated the matter at Gloucestershire Record Office.[22] One might add that the term 'census parish' is a rather unfortunate one, as it adds to the confusion of 'mother parishes' and 'civil parishes', but it is too well-established to be changed.

When the Ordnance Survey started systematic mapping of administrative boundaries in 1841 with the introduction of the 1:10,560 scale, they simplified the system slightly by treating all divisions of parishes as 'townships' but introduced what can be regarded as either a refinement or a complication in the form of 'divisions of townships' and even sub-divisions of townships (see Fig.2). In 1854, the Ordnance Survey decided not to map these divisions of townships, but by that time the information had been gathered for Lancashire, Yorkshire and Durham, and we have included it in our database.[23] It is to be noted that the purposes for which these sub-township units were established are usually obscure, and that they rarely appear on the nearly contemporary tithe maps. Some were for highway administration, such as the three divisions used by the Census for the parish of Chapel-en-le-Frith in Derbyshire.[24] After 1879, the Ordnance Survey abandoned entirely the distinction between parishes and townships and from that date onwards treated all townships, tithings, hamlets etc along with all parishes which had not been so divided, as 'civil parishes', although the old system of recording both mother parishes and townships was retained in counties such as Derbyshire and Staffordshire where the 1:2500 scale survey was already under way by 1879.

Detached areas of parishes and townships fall into two broad categories: those whose origins are unknown, and those which were created intentionally between *circa* 1750 and 1850 as part of the parliamentary enclosure process. Sometimes, as around Butsfield and Satley in Lanchester parish in County Durham, enclosed in 1773-81, or west of Kingston upon Hull in Yorkshire (Fig. 3), enclosed in 1824-37, the enclosure commissioners created a pattern of numerous detached parts of townships and parishes in order to distribute equitably the various grades of land being enclosed. Elsewhere practice differed: when the East, West and Wildmore Fens in Lincolnshire were enclosed in 1801-20, geography dictated that many detached parts of parishes would be created, as communal grazing rights of 'upland' parishes were replaced by 'fen lots', but few parishes had more than one 'fen lot'. The last detached area to be deliberately created as a result of enclosure also seems to have been in Lincolnshire, at Lissingley, completed in 1851. In general the Lincolnshire and other midland enclosures usually avoided creating detached areas when land formerly common to several abutting parishes or townships was enclosed, as at Caistor Moor, Lincolnshire, in 1811-14.

---

[22] 1851 Census, Division VI, p.21.

[23] The decision is recorded in Ordnance Survey, *Administrative Boundaries in Great Britain 1951* (unpublished: copy in British Library Map Library Maps 207.aaa.14), p. 37.

[24] 1851 Census, Division VII, p.79.

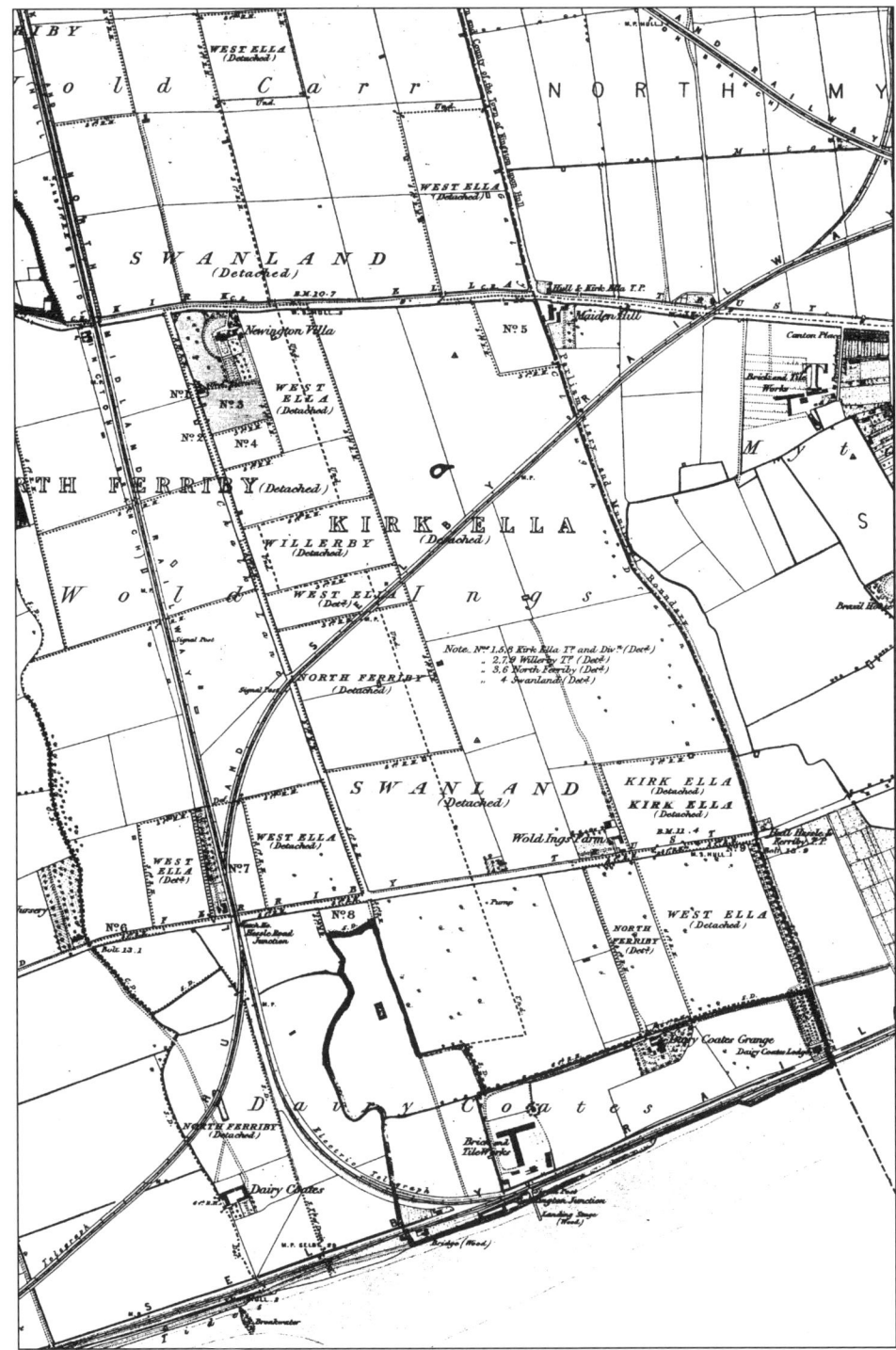

Fig: 3 Detached parts of parishes (upright open capitals) and townships (sloping closed capitals) and divisions of townships (sloping open capitals) west of Kingston-upon-Hull, Yorkshire created as a result of enclosure in 1824-37. From Ordnance Survey 1:10,560 Yorkshire Sheet 240, surveyed 1853, published 1856.

3

The inadequacy of existing published maps of 'historic parish' boundaries

This is not the first time that mapping 'historic' parish boundaries has been attempted. In 1984 *The Phillimore Atlas and Index of Parish Registers* was published under the auspices of the Institute of Heraldic and Genealogical Studies. This aimed to show both parish boundaries as they were before 1832, and the date at which each parish's registers of baptisms, marriages and burials began. Its primary aim was to serve as a finding tool for genealogists.[25] As a basis for historical GIS work it has three shortcomings. First, the scale of the mapping varies, but is invariably too small to show smaller detached areas. Second, only ecclesiastical parishes are shown; this deficiency is particularly apparent in the north-west half of the country, where almost every parish was sub-divided into townships. Third, the 'situation date' for the mapping is unclear. As an example, the map of Lincolnshire shows the parish of Habrough in its post-1888 form, with the large detached area at Habrough Marsh shown as part of Immingham parish. Similarly, there is no hint of the complicated intermixing of the Saltfleetbys and Theddlethorpes or, on the East Riding map, of the similar complexities at Mappleton and Holmpton.[26] In short, the basis on which these *Phillimore Atlas* maps were compiled is not at all clear. Although they may be perfectly adequate for their immediate purpose of providing a visual index to the location of parish registers, they are unsuited to historical geographical work, and in particular, to the rigorous demands of GIS.

Given, then, that there is no suitable modern mapping, one naturally asks whether any earlier published mapping might be adopted. There are four main genres of nineteenth century maps which contain local boundaries. These are first, 'county maps', mostly at a scale of one inch to one mile (1:63,360) or larger, by the map-makers Christopher and John Greenwood and A. Bryant, *circa* 1817-35.[27] A second source of boundary maps is the so-called 'Index to Tithe Survey' edition of the Ordnance Survey's one inch to one mile (1:63,360) Old Series maps, published *circa* 1850-70. These maps purport to include nearly all the boundaries which appear on the tithe survey maps prepared from 1837 onwards. Thirdly, there are Ordnance Survey one-inch to one mile 'New Series' maps and their parent six inches to one mile (1:10,560) and twenty-five inches to one mile (1:2500) map series of *circa* 1841-88. These maps include practically all 'mother parish' boundaries and civil parish boundaries south of Lancashire and Yorkshire. Finally, there are the revised Ordnance Survey New Series maps published

---

[25] Cecil R. Humphery Smith (ed), *The Phillimore Atlas and Index of Parish Registers*, Chichester, Phillimore, 1984, introduction, n.p. [p.vii].

[26] Humphery Smith (1984), maps 21A, 21B, 39.

[27] The extremes of scale are represented by the Greenwoods' Yorkshire at 1:84,480, and their Middlesex, at 1:31,680. It should be noted that the parish boundaries do not appear on the well-known derived county maps at 1:190,080, issued by the Greenwoods as an atlas in 1833. See Catherine Delano-Smith and Roger J. P. Kain, *English Maps: a History*, London, The British Library, 1999, especially chapter 3.

between 1893 and 1898 which include all rural civil parish boundaries current at the time that the maps were prepared.

All of these published map series have limitations of one kind or another. The Bryant and Greenwood maps are notable in providing the first extensive mapping of parish, township and similar local boundaries, but have two principal drawbacks. First, coverage is incomplete; whereas a few counties were mapped by both Greenwood and Bryant, neither mapped Cambridgeshire, and only two Welsh counties were mapped (Glamorgan and Monmouth, both by Greenwood).[28] Second, in comparison with later Ordnance Survey mapping, these county maps are all planimetrically deficient, both in absolute geometric terms, and sometimes in showing boundaries incorrectly in relation to other detail.[29]

The 'Index to Tithe Survey' edition of the Ordnance Survey Old Series one-inch maps covers England and Wales south of Lancashire and Yorkshire. It is something of a misnomer, as it does not indicate the full extent of tithe mapping (this is particularly marked in localities, such as much of the midlands, where tithe mapping only covered part of a parish).[30] Its drawbacks are mostly similar to those of the Greenwood and Bryant maps. Geographical coverage is incomplete, the mapping is planimetrically deficient, and there is no boundary information at all for tithe-free parishes or for northern England, or for parishes where tithe mapping was not completed until after 1850. In total about a third of the area of England and Wales is not covered by this map series. Further, the planimetric accuracy of the base-mapping, though generally better than that of Greenwood and Bryant, is still not particularly good.

Ordnance Survey one-inch to one mile scale maps of England north of a line passing close to Preston, Leeds and Hull were derived from six-inch (1:10,560) and larger scale mapping after 1840. These maps approach absolute standards of planimetric accuracy and they are a geodetic known quantity. They became the 'New Series' maps after 1872 by the simple expedient of renumbering. This mapping in northern England includes the boundaries of 'mother parishes', but not of any of their divisions, which only appear on the parent larger-scale maps. The remainder of the first edition of the New Series was published between 1874 and 1896 and was based on the 1:2500 and 1:10,560 resurvey of England and Wales south of Lancashire and Yorkshire which was begun in the mid-1850s. It is a far more complete source of boundary information than are either Greenwood and Bryant or the Index to Tithe Survey: geographical coverage is complete, it is planimetrically reliable, and boundary information is almost complete, except in heavily built-up areas, notably London. Only on the earliest sheets, which are all in the south-east of England where division of parishes was unusual anyway, are

---

[28] Elizabeth M. Rodger, *The Large Scale County Maps of the British Isles 1596-1850: a Union List*, Oxford, Bodleian Library, second edition 1972.

[29] See, for example, the comments on the windmill by the Harmston-Waddington boundary in Robert Wheeler and Joan Mills, 'On the reliability of farm names on Bryant's map of Lincolnshire', *Lincolnshire Past and Present* 37 (1999), pp. 7-9.

[30] See Roger J. P. Kain and Richard R. Oliver, *The Tithe Maps of England and Wales: a Cartographic Analysis and County-by-County Catalogue*, Cambridge, Cambridge University Press, 1995, pp. 827-30.

sub-parish boundaries omitted. The one substantial drawback of these maps south of Lancashire and Yorkshire is that they show civil parish boundaries as they were at the time that the 1:63,360 mapping was being prepared. While in south-east England it is an impressive record at the 1:63,360 scale of detached areas of parishes - far more so than the Index to Tithe Survey - elsewhere the record is usually of boundaries as they were after the changes brought about by the Acts of 1876 and 1882. For example, the early states of New Series sheet 301 (published 1880) are a far more comprehensive record of detached areas of parishes in north-west Sussex than is the corresponding Index to Tithe Survey mapping. On the other hand, sheet 104 (published 1891) shows the area north-west of Mablethorpe in Lincolnshire after boundary changes in the 1880s, whereas the Index to the Tithe Survey shows an intricate pattern of detached areas around the Saltfleetbys and Theddlethorpes. Although the New Series mapping is extremely useful as a starting point, and was used by us as a base for the work presented here, it needs to be supplemented from other sources.

Between 1895 and 1899 the New Series was republished in a revised edition. South of Lancashire and Yorkshire this has the disadvantage that it shows parish boundaries as they were at the time of compilation, which usually means as they were after the changes brought about by the Local Government Act of 1894. Whilst this drawback applies over the whole country, in the north of England, townships, in the guise of civil parishes, appear on Ordnance Survey 1:63,360 maps for the first time, and in general the boundary cover is fairly complete. However, particularly in parts of Cumberland, a number of civil parishes which had been separate civil parishes at the time of the 1:2500 survey in the early 1860s had disappeared by the 1890s. Once again, the mapping is useful as a starting-point, but falls short of completeness.

Thus none of the nineteenth-century 1:63,360 published maps constitutes a definitive record of parish or sub-parish boundaries as they were before the changes of the second half of that century.

―――――― 4 ――――――
Context: previous work on local area boundaries at Exeter.

At Exeter the authors in collaboration with Rodney Fry and Sarah Wilmot have been concerned with two types of boundary mapping in recent years: of tithe districts c.1840, and of areas covered by enclosure and similar public maps of the seventeenth, eighteenth and nineteenth centuries.

(i)   *Tithe surveys (Leverhulme Trust 1987-92)*

This study was published in 1995 by Cambridge University Press as: *The Tithe Maps of England and Wales: a Cartographic Analysis and County-by-County Catalogue.* Our method was to compile a database of the cartographic characteristics and topographic and other content of the whole body of 11,785 tithe maps of England and Wales. This database was analysed to provide material for writing a narrative account of the mapping and map characteristics and was also edited into a catalogue. We collected boundary information so that we could compile index maps of tithe surveys on a county basis. Our original boundary compilation maps are held at Exeter; the tithe district boundaries which they contain have been replotted for each county and are published in our book at a scale of about 1:400,000.

(ii)   *Government-sponsored, large-scale mapping of England and Wales before the Ordnance Survey (ESRC 1993-98)*

This project was concerned with analysing all large-scale parish or township maps which derived from parliamentary statute or were produced for some official or public purpose. As with the tithe maps, our objective was to compile a database that could be analysed to reveal cartographic and similar trends to enable us to write a narrative history of the mapping process. About 85 per cent by number of these parish maps were produced under the terms of private and general acts for the enclosure of open field, common, or waste mostly dating from c.1750 to c.1850. The remainder are a miscellany of rating maps, drainage maps and sanitary maps. The database is now complete and is available from History Data Service, UK Data Archive at the University of Essex.[31] We prepared a set of coverage diagrams, indicating the area of cover of each map and these have been integrated into this electronic map/metadata of English and Welsh historic parishes. Our enclosure and related map boundary data cover about 25 per cent of England and Wales; much of it covers areas for which tithe surveys are not extant.

Although the data held at Exeter from tithe, enclosure, and other parish map projects had been gathered in order to illustrate coverage of these particular historical mapped surveys to facilitate their use as sources by historians, the

---

[31] History Data Service, UK Data Archive, University of Essex, Wivenhoe Park, Colchester CO4 3SQ. Telephone: +44 (0)1206 872326; Fax: +44 (0)1206 872003; Email: hds@essex.ac.uk; URL: http://hds.essex.ac.uk

boundary maps that we had compiled provided a valuable basis for compiling a complete map of the nation's 'historic' or 'ancient' parishes and townships and their subdivisions. It became evident at an early stage in our work that there was not, as earlier studies implied, a close relationship between places mapped for tithe commutation and those mapped for enclosure. The one distribution is not a simple mirror-image of the other such that places mapped for tithe commutation were not mapped for enclosures and vice versa. Far from the one set of surveys perfectly complementing the other to produce a virtual 100 per cent map of local administrative districts, there is some overlap of the two types of mapping and a significant shortfall of places not mapped by either process. Combining both sources provided us with local area boundary information for about 87 per cent of England and Wales by area for dates up to the mid-nineteenth century, ie. before all the later nineteenth century changes (see Table 3). Our investigations revealed considerable regional variation within this overall figure from as little as 45 per cent in Westmorland and Leicestershire to 98 per cent plus for Essex, Kent, Norfolk, and Suffolk.

5

Sources of parish boundary information for the electronic map.

Notwithstanding their incomplete geographical cover, by far the most important of our sources are the tithe maps, which cover about 75 per cent of England and Wales. These were mostly produced between 1837 and 1851 as a record of the process of tithe commutation. A minority, mostly in the midland counties, are of little use because they only cover a small part of a parish, but in practice almost all these maps with fragmentary cover are duplicated by enclosure maps which depict the parish completely. Extant tithe maps are of considerable value for supplying boundaries: they were exhibited publicly to enable those interested to draw attention to errors, and when, a few decades later, the Ordnance Survey conducted its 1:2500 survey, tithe maps were used wherever possible to supply boundaries, as they were known to be reliable and unlikely to need further detailed investigation.[32]

As noted above, the tithe maps were used to provide the boundary information published as the *Index to Tithe Survey* Ordnance Survey maps. What appears to be either the original compilation for this or else a fair copy survives in the Public Record Office, as class IR 105. This manuscript version has the advantage over the published version of including a number of incomplete boundaries, reflecting districts with fragmentary tithe mapping.

About 25 per cent of England and Wales was covered by enclosure mapping, mostly prepared between circa 1760 and 1860. Although enclosure was often accompanied by commutation of tithe this was not always the case, and most enclosure after 1835 was of common grassland or moorland, often in upland areas, which was also mapped for tithe purposes. As a result, only about half the enclosure mapping is not duplicated by tithe mapping, and so it adds boundary information for about 12-13 per cent of England and Wales. Its characteristics and virtues are much the same as for tithe mapping, except that the boundary information has never been abstracted for publication at 1:63,360.[33] Although much of the useable enclosure mapping is of midland and eastern England, where there were relatively few census parishes for which boundaries are not available from Ordnance Survey sources, there are instances, for example the boundaries between Brocklesby and Newsham in Lincolnshire and between Farndish and Podington in Bedfordshire, where the limit of enclosure mapping supplies an otherwise elusive boundary (Fig. 4).

---

[32] Roger J. P. Kain and Hugh C. Prince, *Tithe Surveys for Historians,* Chichester, Phillimore, 2000, p. 75; Sir Henry James, *Account of the Methods and Processes... of the Ordnance Survey...* ,London, HMSO, 1875, pp. 40 and 57.

[33] See Roger J. P. Kain, John Chapman and Richard R. Oliver, *The Enclosure Maps of England and Wales,* (in preparation for publication by Cambridge University Press). As part of the preparatory work, all the boundary information included on the enclosure maps was transcribed on to Ordnance Survey 1:63,360 New Series base maps.

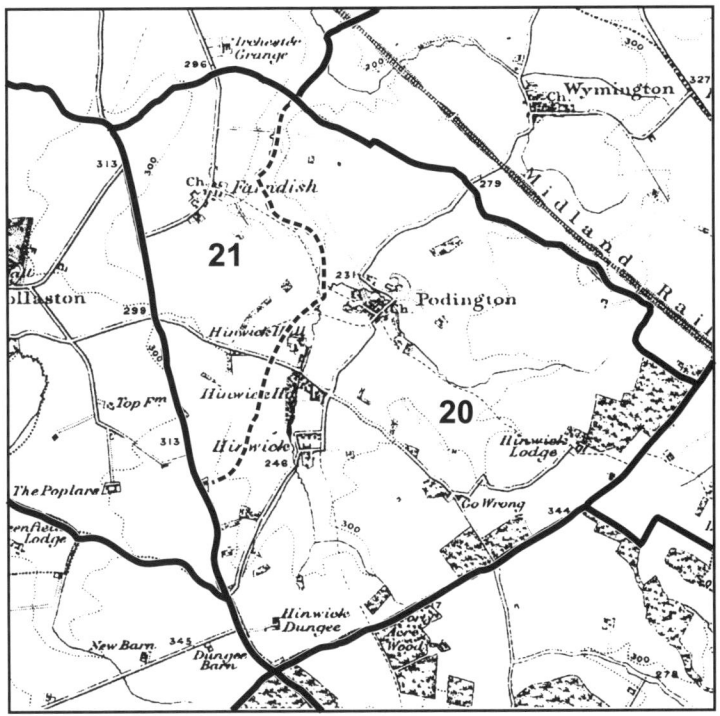

Fig:4 An example of how enclosure maps can supply otherwise elusive boundaries. Those shown solid are taken from the Ordnance Survey 1:10,560 first edition of Bedfordshire surveyed in the early 1880s; that shown broken which divides Farndish (21) and Podington (20) is taken from the enclosure mapping of these two parishes.

Tithe and the enclosure maps are 'cadastral' in the broad sense, in that the planimetric information is accompanied by separate documents setting out the ownership, area, and other details of each land parcel. Less well-known than either of these series are large-scale, local maps prepared for parochial assessment, drainage, sanitary, and other public purposes, which are also accompanied by written cadasters. Almost all of these maps date from the first two-thirds of the nineteenth century. Parochial assessment maps and other large-scale parish maps are very similar to tithe maps, and indeed some were reused for tithe purposes and vice-versa.[34] Drainage and sanitary mapping is usually restricted to the immediate area concerned, but can still be of value in providing boundaries unobtainable from other maps.[35]

---

[34] See Ralph Hyde, 'The "Act to Regulate Parochial Assessments", 1836 and its contribution to the mapping of London', *Guildhall Studies in London History* 11 (1976), pp. 54-68; Richard R. Oliver and Roger J.P. Kain, 'Maps and the assessment of parish rates in nineteenth-century England and Wales', *Imago Mundi* 50 (1998), pp. 156-73.

[35] See, for example, the record of detached areas on the mapping of 1835 for the Commissioners of Sewers for the Lower Level (Upper Division) of the River Severn: Gloucestershire Record Office D.272/9/1-3.

Taken together, tithe, enclosure and similar maps can provide boundary information for about 88 per cent of England and Wales, leaving boundaries for the remainder to be sought elsewhere. By far the most important supplementary sources are the Ordnance Survey 1:10,560 first edition maps, which together with the earlier 'cadastral' mapping supplies all but about 4 per cent of boundaries of 1851 'census parishes'. In Lancashire, Yorkshire and the counties to the north it has the twofold advantage that it is either contemporary with, or only slightly later than, the tithe surveys (1841-63), and covers areas not mapped in the *Index to Tithe Survey*.

Estate maps and similar private maps can occasionally be useful, particularly where an estate coincided with a subdivision of a parish. Also sometimes useful are the Greenwood and Bryant county maps, mostly at 1:63,360. Although as a comprehensive source they are untrustworthy, they can be useful *in extremis* when all other sources have been exhausted, particularly for some otherwise elusive extra-parochial areas. Finally, written descriptions of boundaries can also help, or may be the only record. The description of a division of the parish of Newchurch in the Isle of Wight found in a trade directory is exceptional, but a number of census divisions of urban parishes, particularly in London, are recorded in the notes to the parish-level returns of the 1851 census.

―――― 6 ――――
A topographic underlay for the boundary mapping

We have used the Ordnance Survey one-inch to one mile (1:63,360) New Popular Edition maps which carry the National Grid to supply a topographic underlay for our boundary mapping. The history of the New Popular Edition has been described in some detail by Richard Oliver, but a summary of its development and characteristics may be useful.[36] Preparation of the mapping began in 1938, but was interrupted in 1941, and initial publication took place between 1945 and 1947. Fifty of the sheets (132-7, 143-50, 155-90) were published in the style contemplated in 1938-40, based on or in the style of the 1:63,360 Fifth Edition; the remaining sheets (64, 71, 75-8, 82-6, 88-131, 138-42, 151-4) used mapping originally prepared for the 1:63,360 Popular Edition.[37] The Fifth Edition-style mapping was relatively up to date, having been fully revised between 1928 and 1939; the Popular Edition-style mapping mostly derived from revision of 1913-23. Subsequent revision of roads and built-up areas was incorporated on all sheets.

The New Popular Edition is not just a mixture of mapping styles and revision epochs; it is also a mixture of two different types of mapping, some on the Transverse Mercator projection as used for the National Grid but some is on the Cassini projection. To convert this last to the Transverse Mecator for the New Popular Edition, the original copper plates were photographed and the prints cut up and reassembled on New Popular Edition sheetlines inside a standard border and marginalia. We have not been able to investigate how far in practice some sheets of the New Popular Edition are planimetrically compromised by this process, though we would caution users to bear this history in mind if using our data in conjunction with other, more recent National Grid referenced data.

In order to assimilate the Popular Edition-derived mapping to that derived from the Fifth Edition, the Ordnance Survey made several cosmetic changes and, more importantly in our context, parish boundary information was reinstated. Whereas on the Fifth Edition style mapping parish boundaries are shown by the long-established convention of black dots, on the Popular-based sheets they are shown by continuous grey lines. The source for these boundaries is unknown: it would presumably have been either current 1:10,560 mapping, or else 1:126,720 administrative diagrams. Whichever was used, the planimetric quality of the work is very poor indeed: where boundaries on the original Popular Edition mapping do not follow features such as roads and streams, positional errors of 100 to 200 metres are commonplace, and errors of 400 to 500 metres are not unknown.[38]

---

[36] Richard Oliver, *A Guide to the Ordnance Survey One-Inch New Popular Edition*, London, Charles Close Society, 2000.

[37] See Richard Oliver, *A Guide to the Ordnance Survey One-Inch Fifth Edition*, London, Charles Close Society, 2000, and Yolande Hodson, *Popular Maps*, London, Charles Close Society, 1999.

[38] The worst example we can recall is on sheet 94, east of Ward's Stone, in grid squares 6058 and 6059: compare with the successor Seventh Series mapping.

———— 7 ————
Compiling the electronic map of boundaries

Work fell into three main stages:

(i) Producing a manuscript compilation.

(ii) Scanning, rectifying and adding reference numbers, braces and tie lines.

(iii) Compiling the gazetteer/metadata.

(i) *The manuscript compilation* was prepared using the Ordnance Survey 1:63,360 New Series map sheets as a base. The choice of edition was determined by the relative completeness of boundary depiction, as explained in Section 3 above. South of Lancashire and Yorkshire we used the sheets of the first edition, published 1874-96, and for the remainder we used the sheets of the revised edition, published 1895-9. This is an extremely useful series for such work, as the sheets are of a convenient size (A2, easily photocopied in halves as A3s), and as they were originally printed in black from copper plates, they photocopy well. This mapping was supplemented by 1:10,560 or larger scale mapping of some towns and cities, notably London, where 1:63,360 was too small a scale for compilation work. This was particularly useful for those census parishes which were not mapped by the Ordnance Survey, but for which the published returns of the 1851 census give a detailed written description of the boundaries, in terms of streets and landmarks. These enlargements were subsequently drawn at either 1:25,000, 1:10,560 or 1:5280, following a similar procedure to that for the 1:63,360 mapping.

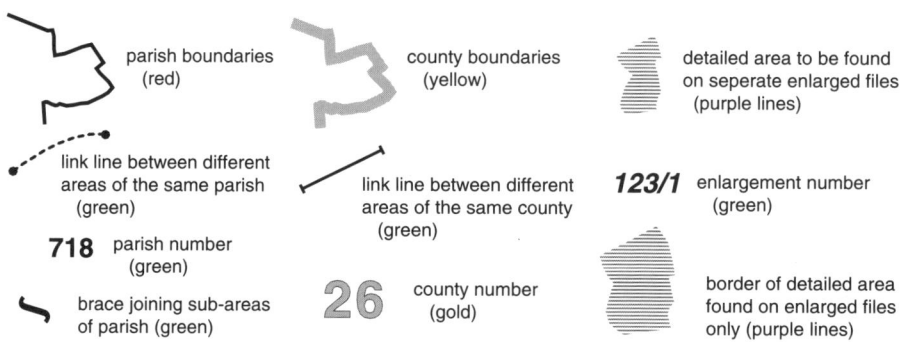

Fig.5 Above: key for the boundary maps, with an explanation of colours used. Right: a printed extract of the electronic boundary map of the area around Stamford, Lincolnshire. See also the front cover colour version.

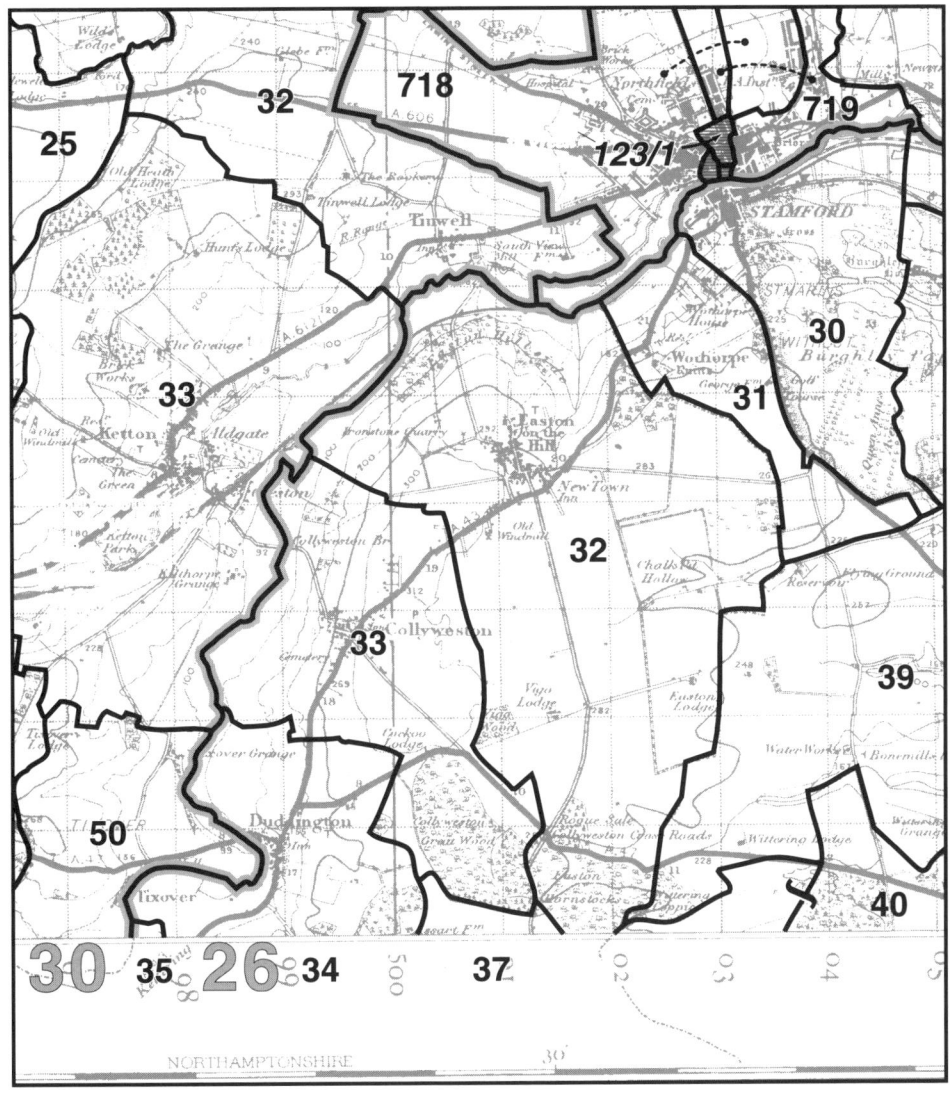

Once base maps had been obtained, a first task was to add the numbers of all the 'census parishes' from the detailed published *Census of Great Britain, 1851 – Population Tables*, which focussed our attention on those census parishes for which no boundaries appeared on the Ordnance Survey base-maps. The next stage was to compare this compilation with our *Index to Tithe Survey* maps which supplied some of the missing boundaries. These were tagged for the metadata to indicate their provenance as from tithe maps. The comparison also supplied a number of other boundaries which sub-divided 1851 census parishes. The procedure was then repeated using our enclosure coverage diagrams, with boundaries supported by enclosure mapping again tagged for the metadata.

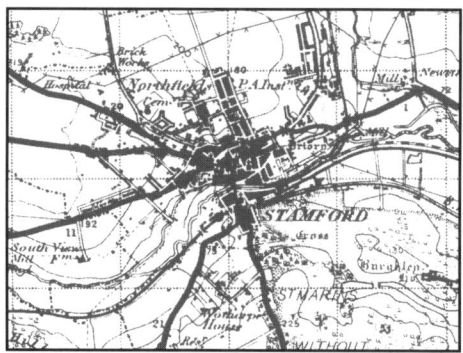

Fig.6a The topographic underlay scan of the New Popular Edition map.

Fig.6b The boundary layer, depicted by red lines on screen.

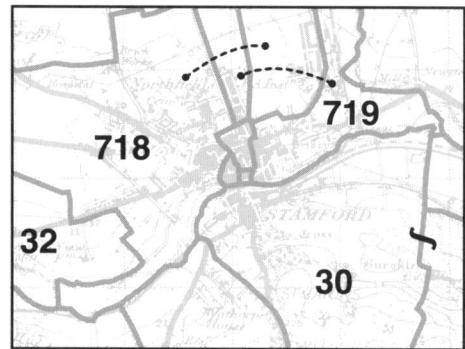

Fig.6c The parish reference number, dashed link lines and braces are shown in green.

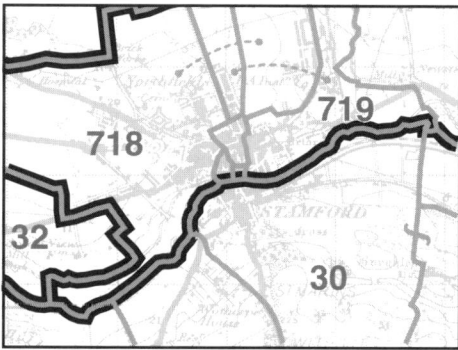

Fig.6d The county boundary is added as a broad yellow line beneath the red parish boundary.

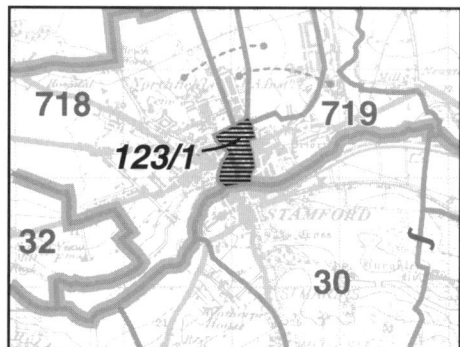

Fig.6e Highly detailed areas selected for enlargements are filled with horizontal purple lines and numbered obliquely in green.

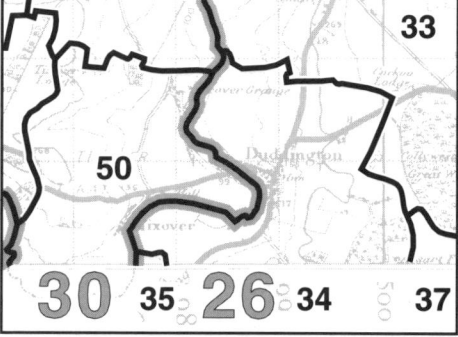

Fig. 6f County numbers are shown as large gold numbers where they cross the edges of the sheet. Parish numbers found in the margins indicate that the bulk of that parish will be found on the adjoining sheet.

The compilations were next compared with Ordnance Survey 1:10,560 first edition maps where (as particularly was the case north of the Mersey and Humber) these are substantially earlier than the derived 1:63,360 New Series mapping. Once again, this supplied both many of the remaining missing census parishes and, particularly in Durham, Lancashire and Yorkshire, divisions and subdivisions of townships. The 1:10,560 mapping was particularly valuable for urban parishes, which otherwise were rarely mapped as a whole. In the 1880s parish boundaries within cities were often omitted where parishes were small (as, for example, at Exeter) so it was sometimes necessary to refer to the larger-scale 1:2500 maps.

By this point, we had almost all the boundaries required of a map seeking to include all 1851 census parishes. We sought to fill remaining gaps by searching the map indexes in county record offices and by reference to the published county maps of Greenwood and Bryant. As mentioned before, by this means we were left with less than three per cent of boundaries missing (all but a few of which are parish sub-divisions). We generated reference numbers for each area, as described in more detail later. Boundaries of mother-parishes and county boundaries were also added. It should be noted that we have attempted to depict the coastline as it was in the early nineteenth century, and that we have followed pre-1868 practice in showing boundaries only above high water mark. Although changes to boundary patterns resulting from coast erosion are of limited extent, and mostly confined to parts of the east coast, changes resulting from reclamation are much more significant. This is especially apparent at the mouth of the river Nene, at the boundaries of Cambridgeshire, Lincolnshire and Norfolk, which was reclaimed from about 1800 onwards.

(ii) Scanning, rectifying and adding reference numbers, braces and tie lines. The compilation complete, we turned to the fair drawing. Boundary compilation maps were scanned to constitute a boundary overlay on the New Popular Edition base map. Area numbers, link lines, county boundaries etc. were then added (see Figs 5, 6 and 7).

(iii) Compiling the gazetteer/metadata. The gazetteer/metadata were compiled from the base-maps and our tithe and enclosure map databases. The main objects of the gazetter/metadata are to provide: (1) a National Grid centroid; (2) the modern form of the place-name and some nineteenth-century variants; (3) the source of the boundary information; and (4) the nature of the district (parish, township, etc) and the name of the mother parish, if applicable. Gazetteer and metadata are deposited with the History Data Service at the University of Essex and can be accessed on request to History Data Service, UK Data Archive, University of Essex, Wivenhoe Park, Colchester CO4 3SQ. Telephone: +44 (0)1206 872326; Fax: +44 (0)1206 872003; Email: hds@essex.ac.uk; URL: http://hds.essex.ac.uk The fields are described in detail below. Included in the deposited gazetteer/metadata but omitted from the hardcopy abbreviated version published in this book, are the sources of information for each boundary and some notes, such as differences between our sources as to the status of a few districts, for example, whether a place is a parish in its own right or a chapelry within another parish.

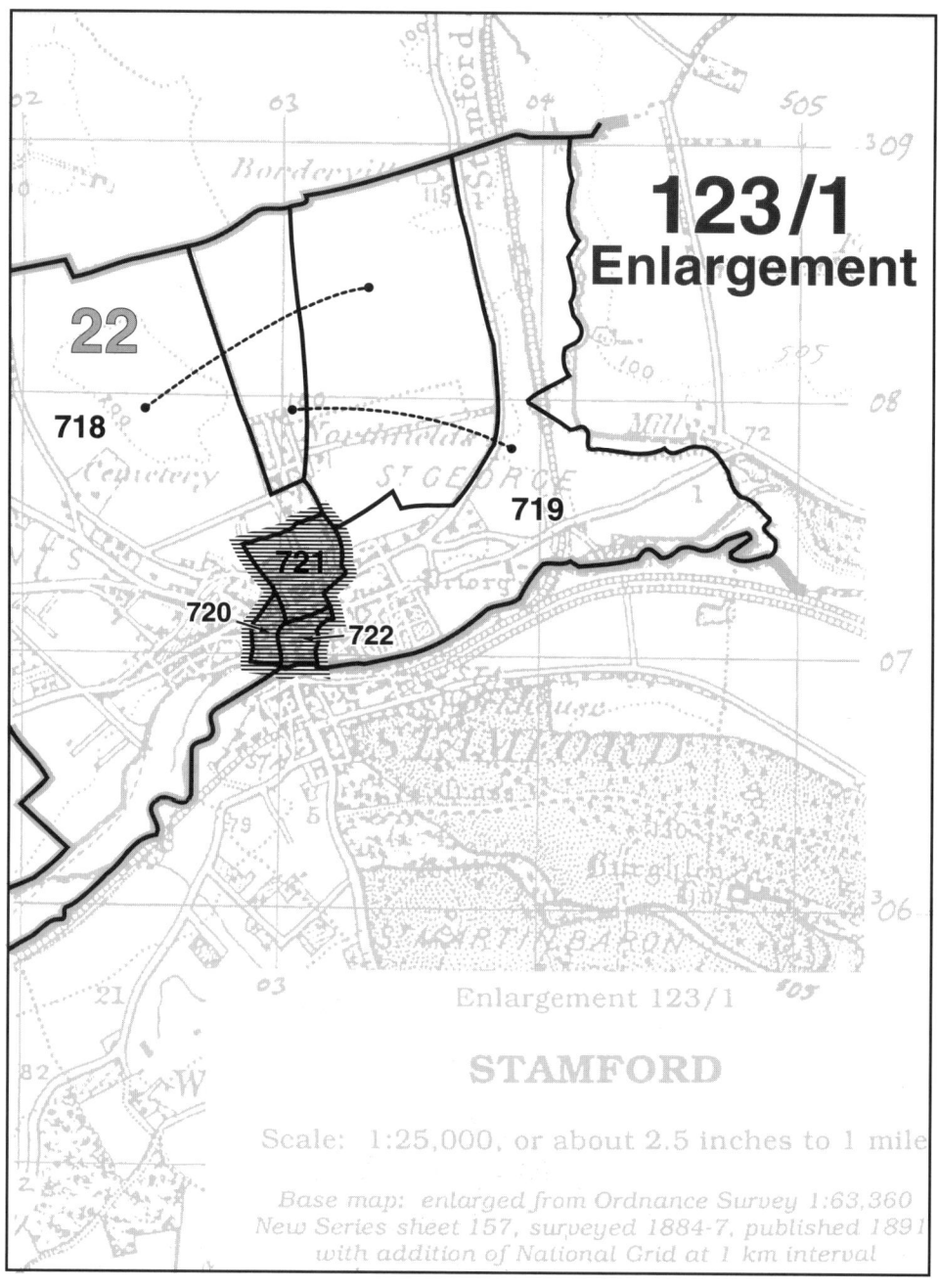

Fig.7 An urban enlargement: Stamford, Lincolnshire. Note that at this scale the purple horizontal shading denoting the area of interest, is limited to its edges. These lines relate directly to the area covered by continuous horizontal lines found on the full sheets. The enlargement number is always shown in the top right corner.

8

The system of reference numbers

Various numbering systems were considered. One was to relate our numbers to those of the 1851 census but this would have had at least three drawbacks. First, the numbers would have been inconveniently long for placing in some smaller districts, the blocks of numbers used cut across parish and county boundaries, and they would have needed suffixes where census parishes were subdivided. A second possibility was to imitate the practice of the Ordnance Survey when supplying parcel numbers for the National Grid 1:2500, of using a grid centroid for each district. This, too, would have had similar disadvantages: the numbers would be inconveniently long (two letters and six figures), and they would not have indicated hierarchical relationships. We therefore decided on a simple system of a two-digit county number with a one-, two- or three-digit district number, sometimes with a letter suffix. In order to reduce congestion on the map, county numbers are shown only in the map border and sea areas. The usual principle is that a consecutive run of numbers is used for each parish, township, and division within a township. The practical operation of this is illustrated by the parish of Sheffield in the West Riding of Yorkshire:

43/822-833 - parish of Sheffield
    822 - Intermixed lands belonging to Eccleshall Bierlow, Sheffield and Upper Hallam townships
    823 - Eccleshall Bierlow township
    824-825 - Nether Hallam township, divided into
        824 - Nether Hallam division
        825 - Heeley division
    826 - Upper Hallam township
    827-831 - Sheffield township, divided into
        827 - Sheffield West division
        828 - Sheffield North division
        829 - Sheffield South division
        830 - Sheffield Park division
        831 - Park division
    832 – Attercliffe-cum-Darnall township
    833 - Brightside Bierlow township

―――― 9 ――――

Defining counties (see Fig.8 and outside rear cover)

Although terms such as 'historic county' and 'geographical county' are commonly used, not least as a response to local government reorganisation in 1974, we have been unable to find an accurate definition of either term.[39] The authoritative Ordnance Survey definition of a 'geographical county' notes that it has never been defined by statute, and as in practice the boundaries would be affected by changes to administrative boundaries, cannot be regarded as sufficiently stable for our purpose.[40] The same authority makes no mention at all of the term 'historic county', which in the popular imagination stands for a state of things 'way back when', which includes Rutland and Middlesex, and definitely excludes Avon and Humberside, but which otherwise lacks precision.

Our definition of a county is based on the county boundaries as they were between 1844, when many detached areas of counties were abolished, and 1888, when the Local Government Act which created county councils also caused some boundary changes, most notably the creation of a whole new county of London out of parts of Kent, Middlesex and Surrey.[41] This definition has the following advantages:

1   It corresponds to the counties as shown on the first editions of the OS 1:10,560 and larger scale mapping, and the 1:63,360 mapping derived therefrom.

2   It presents a geography which includes Rutland and Middlesex, but it treats those detached parts of County Durham which were transferred in 1844 to Northumberland and Yorkshire as parts of the latter counties.

3   It is correct for the 1851 census, which we used as our checklist.

4   It avoids the difficulty that the boundaries of nineteenth-century 'registration counties' do not correspond to any reasonable definition of 'historic' counties.

The following county identification numbers are used:

01	Bedfordshire	10	Dorset	19	Kent
02	Berkshire	11	Durham	20	Lancashire
03	Buckinghamshire	12	Essex	21	Leicestershire
04	Cambridgeshire	13	Gloucestershire	22	Lincolnshire
05	Cheshire	14	Hampshire	23	City of London
06	Cornwall	15	Herefordshire	24	Middlesex
07	Cumberland	16	Hertfordshire	25	Norfolk
08	Derbyshire	17	Huntingdonshire	26	Northamptonshire
09	Devonshire	18	Isle of Wight	27	Northumberland

---

[39] We are grateful to everyone who took the trouble to read and respond to our posting on this subject on the History-GIS e-mail list on 7 September 2000.

[40] Booth (1980), p. 379 (see note 2).

[41] Kain, Chapman and Oliver, *The Enclosure Maps of England and Wales* (see note 33); Richard Oliver, *Ordnance Survey Maps: a Concise Guide for Historians*, London, Charles Close Society, 1993.

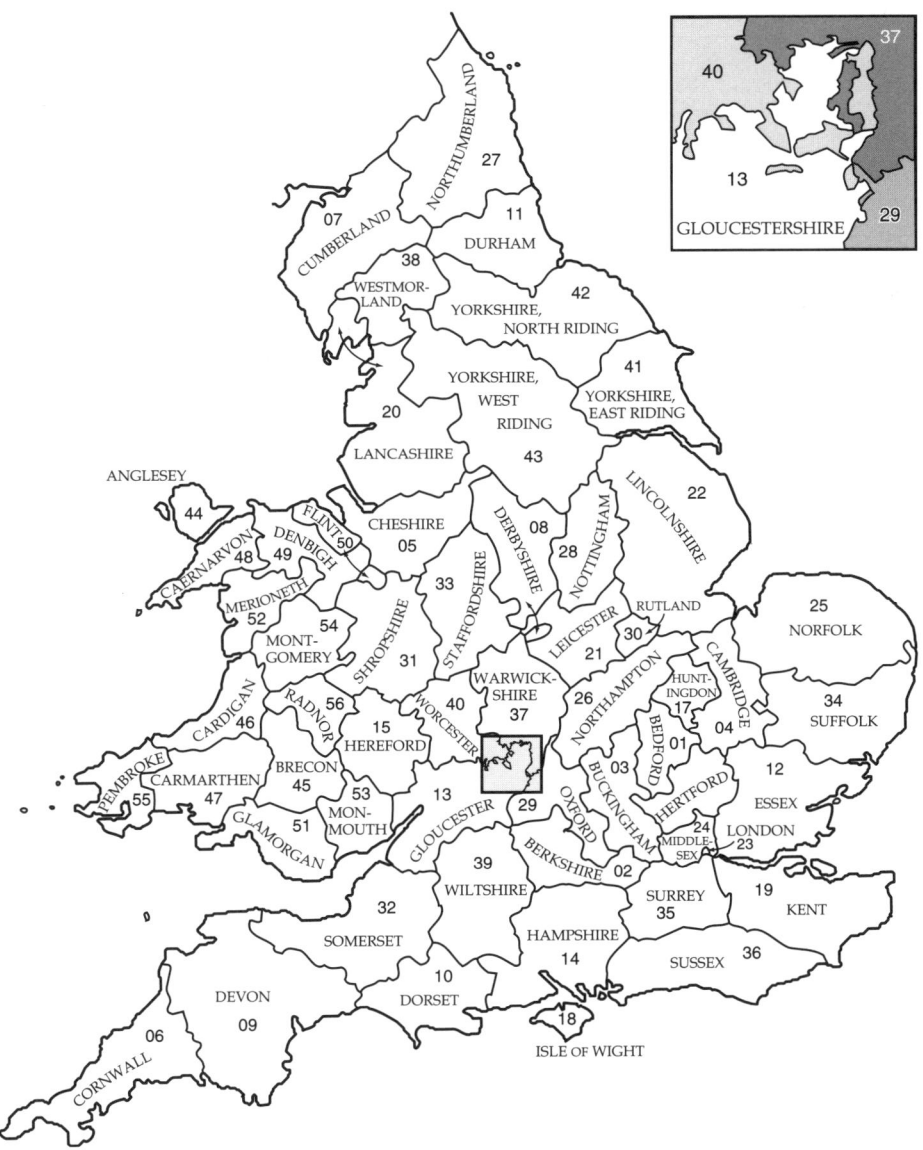

Fig.8 Key to the counties of England and Wales. County numbers are explained opposite and below.

28	Nottinghamshire	38 Westmorland	48 Caernarvonshire
29	Oxfordshire	39 Wiltshire	49 Denbighshire
30	Rutland	40 Worcestershire	50 Flintshire
31	Shropshire	41 Yorkshire, East Riding	51 Glamorganshire
32	Somerset	42 Yorkshire, North Riding	52 Merionethshire
33	Staffordshire	43 Yorkshire, West Riding	53 Monmouthshire
34	Suffolk	44 Anglesey	54 Montgomeryshire
35	Surrey	45 Brecknockshire	55 Pembrokeshire
36	Sussex	46 Cardiganshire	56 Radnorshire
37	Warwickshire	47 Carmarthenshire	

10
The gazetteer/metadata.

There are 11 fields arranged as a text format database containing entries as follows:

1 NUM

This is the unique reference for each district, consisting of a two-figure county identifier, followed by a stroke and a one-, two- or three-figure number (sometimes with a letter suffix) for each district. Thus 09/278 is Heavitree parish in Devon.

2 PLA

This is the name of the district in its modern form. It should be noted that for a number of small districts this name may not have been recorded since the later nineteenth century, and that a few detached or divided parts of parishes or townships do not appear to have had a formal name.

3 CAT

Category of district:

B	Borough
C	Chapelry
D	Division or district
EP	Extra-parochial
H	Hamlet
M	Manor
P	Parish
T	Township
X	Uncategorised, uncertain, or lands common to more than one district
Y	Tithing (or 'tything')

These categories are derived from first edition Ordnance Survey 1:10,560 maps, the 1851 census returns and tithe surveys. When these sources differ, particularly as to whether a district is a parish in its own right or is a division within a parish, priority has been accorded to the sources in the order given above, on the grounds that the Ordnance Survey made thorough investigations, that the census recurred decennially, and that for tithe commutation purposes the boundary of a tithe district, the ownership of land parcels and tithe payment apportioned to them were of more importance than the administrative status of the tithe district itself. As explained above, all these categories except P and EP are divisions of parishes, and 'hamlet', 'township' and 'tithing' are used according to region rather than according to function: the Ordnance Survey categorised all these divisions as 'townships', but the 1851 census returns use the local designations.

4 PAR

Mother parish. This is given both where a district is also a parish in its own right, and where it is part of a parish.

5 APL

Alternative place name. This records differences from the modern name (field 2) recorded by the first edition of the Ordance Survey 1:10,560, the 1851 census returns, the tithe surveys and enclosure maps and also, occasionally, the Ordnance Survey 1:63,360 Seventh Series and the current Ordnance Survey 1:50,000 where these names appear to be recent official versions of an established name, e.g. Appleby-in-Westmorland. Not systematically recorded are the several thousand instances where the 1851 census form of the name is distinguished only by the use of a hyphen (e.g. George-Nympton, Devon in the 1851 census, George Nympton on the Ordnance Survey 1:10,560 first edition). This should enable users to identify most variations in place names current in the nineteenth and twentieth centuries. In the gazetteer/metadata, the alternative name is followed by the source(s), using the same codes, (C51, O6, etc) as in field 9 SCE. [Note: this information is omitted from this abbreviated, printed gazetteer/metadata].

6 NGR

National Grid centroid of district. Grid references are provided for undivided parishes but not for divided ('mother') parishes, for which grid references for the undivided parts only will be found. The same principle applies to divided townships within mother parishes. The way that this works out can be illustrated by reference to the subdivisions of Sheffield parish listed on page 31 above. Grid references are given for the following within the mother parish of Sheffield: Intermixed lands; Eccleshall Bierlow, Upper Hallam, Attercliffe-cum-Darnall and Brightside Bierlow townships; and Nether Hallam, Heeley, Sheffield West, Sheffield North, Sheffield South, Sheffield Park and Park divisions, but not for Sheffield parish (the mother parish itself), nor for Nether Hallam and Sheffield townships, as these are divided. We have tried to follow this rule consistently such that grid references are available for what we have identified as the lowest divisions within the parish/township hierarchy of England and Wales.

7 ONP

Sheet(s) of the Ordnance Survey New Popular Edition in which the district will be found. Enlargements are numbered with the addition of a stroke and a number: thus the city of Exeter is 176/1. It should be noted that whereas the original New Popular Edition sheets included some extensive overlaps between sheets, there are no overlaps in the boundary overlay. Figure 8 is an index map of the boundary overlay in relation to New Popular Edition sheet lines.

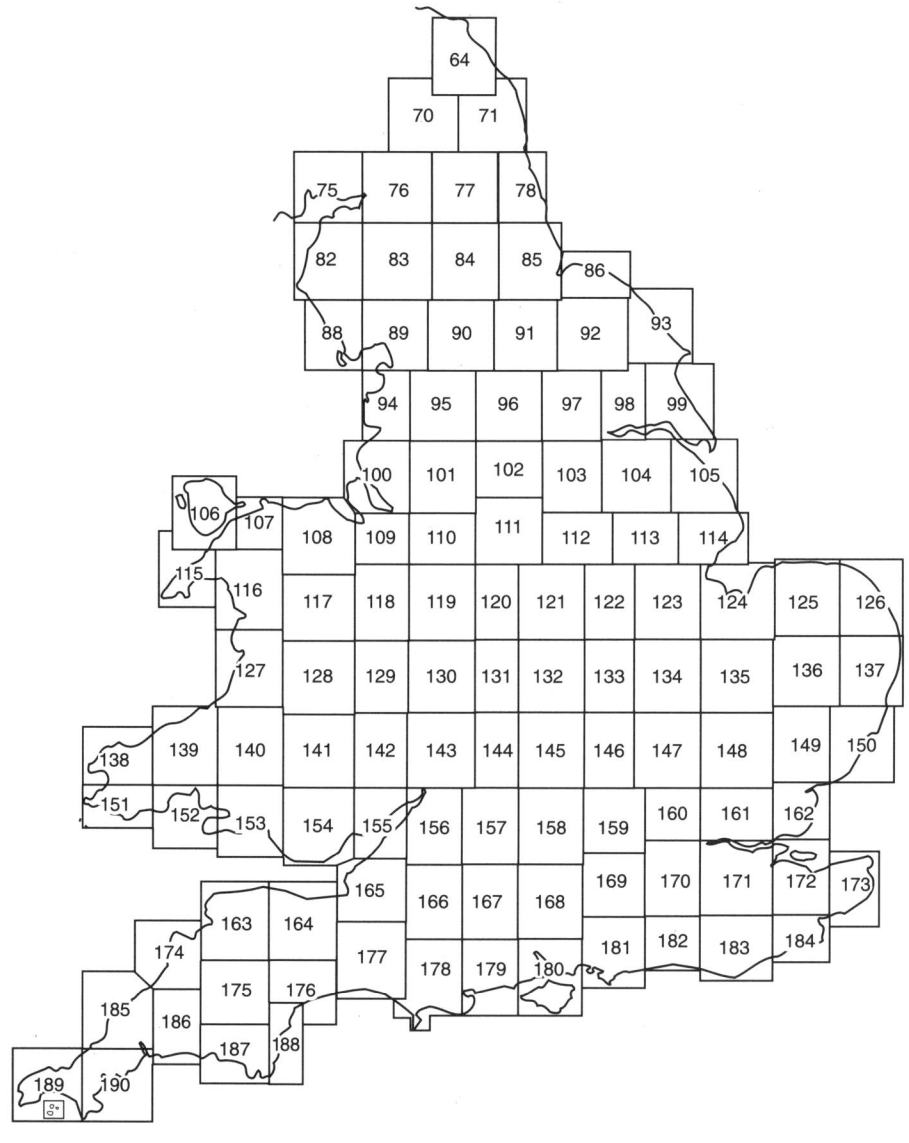

Fig.9 Key to the 115 boundary overlay sheets in relation to Ordnance Survey New Popular sheet lines (repeated on inside rear cover).

8 CEN

1851 census parish number. [Note: this information is omitted from this abbreviated, printed gazetteer/metadata]

9 SCE

Source of boundary information. [Note: this information is omitted from this abbreviated, printed gazetteer/metadata] These codes are also used in fields 5 -APL, and 11 - COM.

Bryant	County mapping by A. Bryant
C51	Published returns of the 1851 census
D	Drainage map
E	Enclosure map
Greenwood	County mapping by Christopher and John Greenwood
L	Estate or other miscellaneous maps or descriptions
O1-2	Ordnance Survey 1:63,360 New Series, revised edition (1895-9)
O1-3	Ordnance Survey 1:63,360 New Series, Third Edition (1903-13)
O1-7	Ordnance Survey 1:63,360 Seventh Series (1952-74)
O6	Ordnance Survey first edition of 1:10,560 or larger scale mapping.
R	Parochial assessment or 'rating' map
S	Sanitary map
T	Tithe map

Where a boundary is supported by several authorities, only one is cited: preference is given to tithe, enclosure, parochial assessment, Ordnance Survey mapping, and other maps, in that order.

10 REF

Archive reference for source cited in field 9, SCE. This is invariably given for manuscript maps and for what we judge to be 'unusual' printed mapping, but is unnecessary and is systematically omitted for Bryant, Greenwood, 1851 census and Ordnance Survey material. [Note: this information is omitted from this shortened, printed gazetteer/metadata]

11 COM

Comments on the entries in the preceding fields. This may include notes where, for example, sources differ on the status of a district, or on peculiarities of alternative place names. [Note: this information is omitted from this shortened, printed gazetteer/metadata]

11
Tabular summary of the boundary content

Table 3 summarises by county the numbers of places for which boundaries have been located and recorded on the electronic map and the sources from which the boundaries are derived. The counties in the table are geographical, not registration, counties. For example, the registration county of Norfolk includes a number of parishes in Cambridge and Suffolk, and many Shropshire census parishes are recorded in adjoining registration counties. The fact that the total of places for which our maps contain boundaries (18,240) is 17 per cent greater than the total number of census parishes (15,601) reflects the fact that for many counties we have boundaries for subdivisions of census parishes. Our map contains boundaries for 97.1 per cent of census parishes. Table 3 shows that for some counties 100 per cent boundary discovery has been achieved. Others have a significant proportion of missing boundaries. The Welsh cases are all to do with divisions of parishes which appear in the 1851 census; the English cases are almost all at the sub-parish level. All the missing Cambridgeshire boundaries and very many of those for Oxfordshire are the result of the census counting Oxbridge Colleges separately. The concentration in Staffordshire is almost all in the north west around Stoke. The Middlesex ones are all in central London. In every instance these places were separate for the 1851 census but had ceased to exist as separate units by the time of the Ordnance Survey 1:2500 survey in the 1870s and 1880s, and several (notably many of those in London) only ever seem to have been separate for registration purposes.

Table 3. Numbers of local administrative areas and sources of information for boundaries

Key to the Table
1 **County:** county identifier number.
2 **Tithe:** source of boundaries from tithe maps
3 **Encl:** source of boundaries from enclosure maps. Where a district is covered by both tithe and enclosure, only tithe is cited; enclosure map cover is therefore under-stated.
4 **OS:** source of boundaries from Ordnance Survey sources (mostly six-inch first edition)
5 **Cty:** source of boundaries from printed, large scale, county maps, mostly Greenwood and Bryant
6 **Rate:** source of boundaries from rating and similar maps
7 **Other:** all other maps or sources (e.g. written descriptions in the 1851 census returns)
8 **Fail:** districts for which boundaries have not been found.
9 **Total:** total of local administrative districts for which boundaries have been found

	1	2	3	4	5	6	7	8	9
	County	Tithe	Encl	OS	Cty	Rate	Other	Fail	TOTAL
Bedfordshire	01	37	66	34	0	1	0	14	152
Berkshire	02	124	46	62	0	0	10	13	255
Buckinghamshire	03	90	47	94	2	2	6	4	245
Cambridgeshire	04	66	82	46	0	1	0	19	214
Cheshire	05	469	0	58	0	0	0	0	527
Cornwall	06	198	0	32	0	0	0	0	230
Cumberland	07	3	0	309	0	0	4	12	328
Derbyshire	08	206	33	107	0	3	3	9	361
Devon	09	464	0	52	0	0	2	12	530
Dorset	10	272	0	26	3	0	3	14	318
Durham	11	0	0	348	0	0	0	5	353
Essex	12	393	11	37	1	0	0	0	442
Gloucestershire	13	178	41	159	19	2	18	41	458
Hampshire	14	234	6	96	3	0	24	9	372
Herefordshire	15	243	0	22	18	0	6	7	296
Hertfordshire	16	106	17	24	0	2	7	3	159
Huntingdonshire	17	27	58	34	0	0	0	2	121
Isle of Wight	18	28	0	4	0	0	3	0	35
Kent	19	370	0	78	0	0	13	1	462
Lancashire	20	142	0	561	0	0	0	2	705
Leicestershire	21	112	45	183	2	4	4	16	366
Lincolnshire	22	317	300	267	12	1	10	27	934
London	23	0	0	67	0	31	0	0	98
Middlesex	24	23	17	72	0	1	56	21	190
Norfolk	25	634	28	99	6	0	17	11	795
Northamptonshire	26	70	91	194	7	2	8	4	376
Northumberland	27	0	0	658	0	0	0	0	658
Nottinghamshire	28	119	78	108	0	1	2	3	311
Oxfordshire	29	114	61	144	5	2	2	30	358
Rutland	30	27	15	18	0	0	0	0	60
Shropshire	31	584	0	24	2	0	1	9	620
Somerset	32	470	3	32	0	0	12	3	520
Staffordshire	33	200	3	110	1	2	13	56	385
Suffolk	34	469	14	34	8	0	8	12	545
Surrey	35	102	6	52	2	2	17	8	189
Sussex	36	297	3	47	0	0	5	0	352
Warwickshire	37	149	8	141	3	3	1	1	306
Westmorland	38	25	0	112	0	0	0	0	137
Wiltshire	39	239	9	106	3	7	32	34	430
Worcestershire	40	150	26	80	0	2	4	9	271
Yorks, East Riding	41	8	80	374	0	0	0	2	464
Yorks, North Riding	42	0	8	695	0	1	2	0	706
Yorks, West Riding	43	91	45	828	17	0	2	9	992
Anglesey	44	73	0	4	0	0	0	2	79
Brecnoockshire	45	40	6	20	0	0	0	35	101
Caernarvonshire	48	65	0	15	0	0	0	0	80
Cardiganshire	46	104	0	2	5	0	0	6	117
Carmarthenshire	47	80	0	5	0	0	0	13	98
Denbighshire	49	124	0	22	0	0	0	4	150
Flintshire	50	7	0	140	0	0	0	0	147
Glamorganshire	51	130	0	35	0	0	13	10	188
Merionethshire	52	32	0	5	0	0	0	2	39
Monmouthshire	53	129	0	25	0	0	0	12	166
Montgomeryshire	54	197	0	4	0	0	1	6	208
Pembrokeshire	55	145	0	18	0	0	4	0	167
Radnorshire	56	25	0	25	0	0	0	24	74
TOTALS		9001	1253	6948	119	70	313	536	18240

THE HISTORIC PARISHES OF ENGLAND AND WALES

Abbreviated
Gazetteer and Metadata
of Boundaries before 1850

To access the electronic map please contact :

History Data Service, UK Data Archive, University of Essex, Wivenhoe Park, Colchester CO4 3SQ. Telephone: +44 (0)1206 872326; Fax: +44 (0)1206 872003; Email: hds@essex.ac.

URL: http://hds.essex.ac.uk

A

Ab Kettleby (parish), 21/80-81; NP 122
Ab Kettleby (township in Ab Kettleby), 21/81; SK723230; NP 122
Abbas and Templecombe (Temple Coombe, Abbas Combe) (parish), 32/381; ST714226; NP 166
Abbas Combe (parish), 32/381; NP 166
Abberley (parish), 40/100; SO750680; NP 130
Abberton (parish), 12/177; TL999191; NP 149
Abberton (parish), 40/140; SO996533; NP 143, 144
Abberwick (township in Edlingham), 27/190; NU133135; NP 71
Abbess Roding (Abbotts Roothing, Abbots Roothing) (parish), 12/254; TL566114; NP 149, 161
Abbey (extra-parochial), 22/473; TF341480; NP 114
Abbey (hamlet in St Dogmaels), 55/2; SN154469; NP 139
Abbey (parish), 39/30B; ST933876; NP 157
Abbey Dore (parish), 15/217; SO395325; NP 142
Abbey Halton (township in Burslem), 33/23; SJ902492; NP 110
Abbey Lands (township in Alnwick), 27/198; NU185158; NP 71
Abbey Street (township in St Mary [Carlisle]), 7/96; NY391561; NP 76/1
Abbey Within (Eaglesfield Abbey) (extra-parochial), 7/99; NY399559; NP 76
Abbey-Cwmhir (parish), 56/2A-B; NP 128
Abbeystead (division in township of Over Wyresdale in Lancaster), 20/126; SD551557; NP 94
Abbots Bickington (Abbotts Bickington) (parish), 9/56; SS378134; NP 174
Abbots Bromley (Abbots Bromley and Bromley Hurst) (parish), 33/195; SK100240; NP 120
Abbots Langley (parish), 16/138; TL085012; NP 160
Abbots Leigh (parish), 32/3; ST542741; NP 155
Abbots Lench (Hob Lench) (hamlet in Fladbury), 40/188; SP012518; NP 144
Abbots Morton (Abbotts Morton) (parish), 40/138; SP034546; NP 130, 144
Abbots Ripton (hamlet in Abbots Ripton), 17/62A; TL235775; NP134
Abbots Ripton (parish), 17/62A-B; NP 134
Abbots Roothing (parish), 12/254; TL566114; NP 149, 161
Abbotsbury (parish), 10/257; SY584845; NP 177, 178
Abbotsham (parish), 9/46; SS418272; NP 163
Abbotside Common [east part] (undivided Moor common to High Abbotside and Low Abbotside in Aysgarth), 42/130; SD893932; NP 90
Abbotside Common [west part] (undivided Moor common to High Abbotside and Low Abbotside in Aysgarth), 42/129; SD820960; NP 90
Abbotside Common, 42/129-130; NP 90
Abbotskerswell (parish), 9/417; SX859635; NP 188
Abbotsley (parish), 17/112; TL233568; NP 134
Abbotts Ann (parish), 14/87; SU326430; NP 168
Abbotts Bickington, 9/56; NP 174
Abbotts Morton (parish), 40/138; NP 130, 144
Abbotts Roothing (parish), 12/254; TL566114; NP 149, 161
Abdon (parish), 31/512; SO560960; NP 129
Abenbury Fawr (Abenbury Vawr) (township in Wrexham [Wrecsam]), 49/59; SJ360495; NP 109
Abenbury Fechan (Abenbury Vechan) (township in Wrexham [Wrecsam]), 50/130; SJ352492; NP 109
Abenbury Vechan, 50/130; NP 109
Aber (Abergwyngregyn) (parish), 48/24; SH670710; NP 107
Aberavan (parish), 51/101; NP 153
Aberavon (Aberavan) (parish), 51/101; SS753903; NP 153
Aberbechan (township in Llanllwchaiarn), 54/166B; SO142943; NP 128
Aberdare [Aberdar] (parish), 51/68; SO001029; NP 154
Aberdaron (parish), 48/74; SH175280; NP 115
Aberedw (parish), 56/46; SO090490; NP 141
Abererch (Abereirch) (parish), 48/53; SH395380; NP 115
Aberfafesp (parish), 54/161; SO061948; NP 128
Aberffraw (parish), 44/55; SH370713; NP 106
Aberford (parish), 43/421-423; NP 97
Aberford (township in Aberford), 43/421; SE430383; NP 97
Abergavenny [Y Fenn] (hamlet in Abergavenny [Y Fenn]), 53/37; SO298163; NP 142

Abergavenny [Y Fenn] (parish), 53/36-38; NP 141, 142
Abergele (parish), 49/7; SH945775; NP 108
Abergwaun (parish), 55/31; SM962362; NP 138
Abergwili (Abergwile) (parish), 47/33; SN460230; NP 139
Abergwyngregyn (parish), 48/24; NP 107
Aberhale (township in Tregynon), 54/111; SO063986; NP 117
Aberllunvey (parish), 45/4; NP 141
Aberllynfi (Aberllunvey) (parish), 45/4; SO175377; NP 141
Abernant (parish Abernant), 47/42; SN345235; NP 139
Aberporth (parish), 46/99; SN244504; NP 139
Abertawe (parish), 51/23-26; NP 153
Aberteifi, 46/104; NP 139
Aberwheeler (Aberwhiler) (township in Bodfari [Bodfary]), 49/31; SJ110700; NP 108
Aberwhiler, 49/31; NP 108
Aberyscir (Aberyskir) (parish), 45/59; SN993312; NP 141
Aberyskir (parish), 45/59; NP 141
Aberystruth (parish), 53/68; SO200080; NP 154
Aberystwyth (township in Llanbadarn fawr), 46/13; SN586808; NP 127
Abingdon St Helen (parish), 2/14-19; NP 158, 158/1
Abingdon St Nicholas (parish), 2/20; SU500971; NP 158, 158/1
Abinger (parish), 35/166; TQ118422; NP 170
Abinghall (parish), 13/149; SO672173; NP 143
Abington (parish), 26/223; SP777620; NP 133
Abington Pigotts (Abington-in-the-Clay) (parish), 4/168; TL305448; NP 147
Abington-in-the-Clay (parish), 4/168; NP 147
Ablington (tithing in Bibury), 13/233; SP110090; NP 144, 157
Abney and Abney Grange (township in Hope), 8/26; SK196796; NP 111
Above Coniston (division in township of Church Coniston in Ulverston), 20/10; SD322986; NP 89
Above Sawdde (hamlet in Llangadock), 47/23; SN725275; NP 140
Above Town (division in township of Above Town in Dalton in Furness township in Dalton in Furness), 20/24; SD222771; NP 88
Above Town (township in Dalton in Furness), 20/24-25; SD246760; NP 88
Abram (township in Wigan), 20/581; SD615010; NP 100, 101
Abthorpe (parish), 26/320; SP822566; NP 132, 145
Aby with Greenfield (Aby) (parish), 22/321; TF423783; NP 105
Acaster Malbis (division of Acaster Malbis township in Acaster Malbis), 41/61; SE612432; NP 97
Acaster Malbis (parish), 41/61-62, 43/57; NP 97
Acaster Malbis (township in Acaster Malbis), 43/57; SE583447; NP 97
Acaster Selby (township in Stillingfleet), 43/58; SE572417; NP97
Acklam (division in township of Acklam with Barthorpe in Acklam), 41/133; SE786615; NP 92
Acklam (parish), 41/132-134; NP 92, 98
Acklam in Cleveland (parish and township), 42/282; NP 85
Acklam with Barthorpe (township in Acklam), 41/133-134; NP 92, 98
Ackley (township in Forden), 54/97A; SJ254106; NP 117
Acklington (township in Warkworth), 27/233; NU227017; NP 71
Acklington Park (township in Warkworth), 27/234; NU209012; NP 71
Ackton (township in Featherstone), 43/614; SE410230; NP 97
Ackworth (parish), 43/630; SE447174; NP 103
Acle (parish), 25/459; TG402100; NP 126
Acol (Wood) (parish), 19/126; TR325677; NP 173
Acomb (parish), 43/46-47; NP 97
Acomb (township in Acomb), 43/46; SE572513; NP 97
Acomb, 27/451B; NP 77
Aconbury (parish), 15/184; SO515334; NP 142
Acrise (parish), 19/387; TR202429; NP 173
Acton (parish), 5/282-297; NP 109, 118, 119
Acton (parish), 24/101; TQ202812; NP 160, 170
Acton (parish), 34/413; TL892464; NP 149
Acton (township in Acton), 5/290; SJ631526; NP 110
Acton (township in Weaverham), 5/166; SJ593753; NP 100, 101, 109, 110

43

Acton (township in Lydbury North), 31/375; SO310850; NP 129
Acton (township in Wrexham [Wrecsam]), 49/55; SJ342526; NP 109
Acton and Old Felton (township in Felton), 27/287; NU185025; NP 71
Acton Beauchamp (parish), 40/163; SO698501; NP 143
Acton Burnell (Acton Burnell and Acton Pigott) (township in Acton Burnell), 31/440; SJ537020; NP 118
Acton Burnell (parish), 31/438-440; NP 118
Acton Burnell and Acton Pigott, 31/440; NP 118
Acton Grange (township in Runcorn), 5/149; SJ588854; NP 100
Acton Round (parish), 31/458; SO637958; NP 130
Acton Scott (parish), 31/425; SO456890; NP 129
Acton Trussell and Bednall (Acton Trussel and Bednall) (township in Baswich), 33/183; SJ942178; NP 119
Acton Turville (parish), 13/345; ST812807; NP 156
Acton, 5/90-91; NP 101
Adbaston (parish), 33/159-162; NP 119
Adbaston with Knighton (township in Adbaston), 33/161; SJ760278; NP 119
Adbolton (township in Holme Pierrepont), 28/259; SK604384; NP 121
Adderbury (parish), 29/32-36; NP 145
Adderley (parish), 31/6-7; NP 119
Adderley (township in Adderley), 31/6; SJ662388; NP 119
Adderstone (Adderston) (township in Bamburgh), 27/96; NU131306; NP 64, 71
Addingham (parish), 7/178-180; NP 83
Addingham (parish), 43/336-337; NP 96
Addingham (township in Addingham), 43/336; SE074494; NP 96
Addington (parish), 3/107; SP749288; NP 146
Addington (parish), 19/181; TQ651590; NP 171
Addington (parish), 35/45; TQ370636; NP 170, 171
Addle (parish), 43/393A-398; NP 96
Addlestrop, 13/101; NP 144
Addlethorpe (parish), 22/490; TF547690; NP 114
Adel (Addle) (division in township of Adel cum Eccup in Adel), 43/398; SE268398; NP 96
Adel (parish), 43/393A-398; NP 96
Adel cum Eccup (township in Adel), 43/395-398
Adforton, Stanway, Paytoe and Grange (township in Leintwardine), 15/10; SO403711; NP 129
Adisham (parish), 19/281; TR225539; NP 173
Adlestrop (Addlestrop) (parish), 13/101; SP243275; NP 144
Adlingfleet (parish), 43/952-955; NP 104
Adlingfleet (township in Adlingfleet), 43/955; SE825205; NP 98, 104
Adlington (township in Prestbury), 5/33; SJ918804; NP 101
Adlington (township in Standish), 20/383; SD598130; NP 100, 101
Admaston (township in Blithfield), 33/193; SK048241; NP 120
Admergill (division in township of Brogden with Admergill in Barnoldswick), 43/310; SD853426; NP 95
Admington (hamlet in Quinton), 13/17; SP198458; NP 144
Admiston (parish), 10/214; NP 178
Adstock (parish), 3/90; SP744308; NP 146
Adstone (hamlet in Canons Ashby), 26/274; SP595515; NP 145
Advent (parish), 6/26; SX126825; NP 185, 186
Adwell (parish), 29/272; SU698998; NP 159
Adwick le Street (parish), 43/654-655; NP 103
Adwick le Street (township in Adwick le Street), 43/654; SE542081; NP 103
Adwick upon Dearne (parish), 43/866; SE463011; NP 103
Affpuddle (parish), 10/206; SY808925; NP 178
Agden (Acton) (division of Agden township in Rostherne), 5/91; SJ716856; NP 101
Agden (Acton) (township in Bowdon), 5/90; SJ720870; NP 101
Agden (township in Bowdon and Rostherne), 5/90-91; NP 101
Agden (township in Malpas), 5/322; SJ510440; NP 118
Agglethorpe (division in township of Agglethorpe with Coverham in Coverham), 42/157; SE084867; NP 90
Agglethorpe with Coverham (township in Coverham), 42/156; NP 90, 91

Aglionby (township in Warwick), 7/42; NY446570; NP 76
Aighton (division in Aighton, Bailey and Chaigley township in Mitton), 20/233; SD690390; NP 95
Aighton, Bailey and Chaigley (township in Mitton), 20/231-233; NP 95
Aikbar, 42/196; NP 91
Aike (division of Aike township in Lockington), 41/290; TA052461; NP 99
Aike (division of Aike township in St John Beverley), 41/291; TA044463; NP 99
Aike (township in Lockington and St John Beverley), 41/290-291; NP 99
Aikton (parish), 7/118-119; NP 75
Aikton (township in Aikton), 7/119; NY274534; NP 75
Ailesworth, 26/23; NP 123, 134
Ailsby (parish), 22/96; NP 105
Ailsworth (Ailesworth) (hamlet in Castor), 26/23; TF118928; NP 123, 134
Ainderby Mires (division in township of Ainderby Mires with Holtby township in Hornby), 42/198; SE260934; NP 91
Ainderby Mires with Holtby (township in Hornby), 42/197-198; NP 91
Ainderby Quernhow (township in Pickhill), 42/248; SE352808; NP 91
Ainderby Steeple (parish), 42/217-220; NP 91
Ainderby Steeple (township in Ainderby Steeple), 42/219; SE332922; NP 91
Ainsdale (division in township of Formby in Walton on the Hill), 20/677; SD305118; NP 100
Ainstable (parish), 7/170; NY529455; NP 83
Aintree (township in Sefton), 20/685; SJ378985; NP 100
Airmyn (Armin) (township in Snaith), 43/962; SE722240; NP 97
Airton (township in Kirkby Malhamdale), 43/235; SD882593; NP 90, 95
Airyholme with Howthorpe and Baxter Howe (township in Hovingham), 42/629; SE676729; NP 92
Aisholt (Asholt) (parish), 32/270; ST195356; NP 164, 165
Aiskew (township in Bedale), 42/213B; SE278899; NP 91
Aislaby (division of Aislaby township in Egglescliffe), 11/343; NZ401124; NP 85
Aislaby (township in Middleton), 42/442; SE773858; NP 92
Aislaby (township in Whitby), 42/382; NZ857086; NP 86
Aismunderby with Bondgate (township in Ripon), 43/177; SE312686; NP 91
Aisthorpe (parish), 22/232; SK951802; NP 104
Akebar (Aikbar) (township in Finghall), 42/196; SE199911; NP 91
Akeld (township in Kirknewton), 27/67; NT954291; NP 64, 71
Akeley (Akeley cum Stockholt) (parish), 3/15; SP704381; NP 146
Akenham (parish), 34/394; TM156493; NP 150
Alberbury (division in Alberbury Lower Quarter township in Alberbury), 31/299; SJ363143; NP 118
Alberbury (parish), 31/295-309; NP 118
Alberbury Lower Quarter (township in Alberbury), 31/295-305; NP 118
Alberbury Upper Quarter (township in Alberbury), 31/306-309; NP 118
Alberbury (parish), 31/295-309, 54/87-90; NP 117, 118
Alborough (parish), 25/132; NP 126
Albourne (parish), 36/104; TQ257164; NP 182
Albrighton (parish), 31/471; SJ810040; NP 119
Albrighton (township in St Mary Shrewsbury), 31/249; SJ497181; NP 118
Alburgh (parish), 25/632; TM274872; NP 137
Albury (hamlet in Albury), 29/257; SP658051; NP 158
Albury (parish), 16/65; TL442250; NP 148
Albury (parish), 29/256B-257; NP 158
Albury (parish), 35/138; TQ055457; NP 169, 170
Alby (parish), 25/134; TG203335; NP 126
Alcester (division in Shaftesbury, St James), 10/5B; ST851227; NP 166, 178
Alcester (parish), 37/188; SP070590; NP 131
Alciston (parish), 36/324; TQ498054; NP 183

44

Alconbury (parish), 17/60; TL183771; NP 134
Alconbury Weston (parish), 17/59; TL182780; NP 134
Aldborough (Alborough) (parish), 25/132; TG173345; NP 126
Aldborough (parish), 34/264; NP 137, 150
Aldborough (division in township of Aldborough and Etherwick in Aldborough), 41/375; TA250383; NP 99
Aldborough (parish), 41/375-382; NP 99
Aldborough and Etherwick (township in Aldborough), 41/375-376; NP 99
Aldborough (parish), 42/577-578, 43/128-133; NP 91
Aldborough, 42/33A; NP 85
Aldborough (parish), 42/577-578, 43/128-133; NP 91
Aldborough (township in Aldborough), 43/130; SE405658; NP 91
Aldbourne (Aldburn) (parish), 39/102; SU244762; NP 157, 158
Aldbrough (Aldborough) (township in Stanwick St John), 42/33A; NZ206116; NP 85
Aldbury (parish), 16/143; SP948122; NP 146, 147
Aldcliffe (township in Lancaster), 20/107; SD464602; NP 89
Aldeburgh (Aldborough) (parish), 34/264; TM459570; NP 137, 150
Aldeby (parish), 25/625; TM447938; NP 137
Aldenham (hamlet in Aldenham), 16/129; TQ153981; NP 160
Aldenham (parish), 16/129-130; NP 160
Aldenham Abbey (extra-parochial), 16/131; TQ139995; NP 160
Alderbury (division in Alderbury), 39/360; SU190265; NP 167
Alderbury (parish), 39/360-362; NP 167
Alderford (parish), 25/347; TG122188; NP 125
Alderholt (Aldershott) (division in Cranborne), 10/69; SU119127; NP 179
Alderley (parish), 5/67-69; NP 101, 110
Alderley (parish), 13/341; ST775910; NP 156
Aldermaston (parish), 2/158; SU596645; NP 158, 168
Alderminster (parish), 40/257; SP241495; NP 144
Aldersey (township in Coddington), 5/356; SJ462563; NP 109
Aldershot (Aldershott) (parish), 14/31; SU862515; NP 169
Aldershott, 10/69; NP 179
Alderton (hamlet in Alderton), 13/42; SO999326; NP 143, 144
Alderton (parish), 13/42-43; NP 143, 144
Alderton (Aldrington) (parish), 26/312; SP742472; NP 146
Alderton (township in Great Ness), 31/131; SJ382173; NP 118
Alderton (township in Myddle), 31/154; SJ492241; NP 118
Alderton (parish), 34/439; TM340416; NP 150
Alderton (parish), 39/42; ST844826; NP 156
Alderwasley (township in Wirksworth), 8/157; SK331522; NP 111
Aldfield (township in Ripon), 43/186; SE263693; NP 91
Aldford (parish), 5/363-366; NP 109
Aldford (township in Aldford), 5/365; SJ422586; NP 109
Aldgate (division in St Mary Whitechapel), 24/60A; TQ342808; NP 160/1
Aldham (parish), 12/139; TL911256; NP 149
Aldham (parish), 34/532; TM043451; NP 149
Aldingbourne (Aldingbourn) (parish), 36/279; SU934054; NP 181
Aldingham (division in township of Aldingham in Aldingham), 20/31; SD280715; NP 88
Aldingham (parish), 20/31-34; NP 88
Aldingham (township), 20/31-35; NP 88
Aldington (parish), 19/397; TR072364; NP 172, 184
Aldington (parish), 40/202; SP063443; NP 144
Aldon (township in Stokesay), 31/417; SO433796; NP 129
Aldridge (parish), 33/300-301; NP 120, 131
Aldridge (township in Aldridge), 33/300; SK058008; NP 120, 131
Aldringham with Thorpe (parish), 34/263; TM460605; NP 137
Aldrington (parish), 26/312; NP 146
Aldrington (parish), 36/311; TQ273050; NP 182
Aldsworth (parish), 13/231; SP160104; NP 144, 157
Aldwark (township in Bradbourne), 8/163; SK226580; NP 111
Aldwark (township in Alne), 42/585; SE470640; NP 91
Aldwarke (Aldwark) (division in township of Ecclesfield in Ecclesfield), 43/844; SK450949; NP 103
Aldwinkle All Saints (parish), 26/78; TL008812; NP 134
Aldwinkle St Peter (parish), 26/77; SP989826; NP 134
Aldworth (parish), 2/120; SU549800; NP 158
Alethorpe (extra-parochial), 25/114; TF950310; NP 125
Alfold (division in Alfold), 35/162; TQ036347; NP 169, 170

Alfold (division in Alfold), 36/345; TQ031323; NP 181, 182
Alfold (parish), 35/162, 36/345; NP 181, 182
Alford (Alford with Tothby) (parish), 22/404; TF453760; NP 105, 114
Alford (parish), 32/349; ST608318; NP 166
Alfreton (parish), 8/142; SK419537; NP 111, 112
Alfrick (township in Suckley), 40/166; SO748526; NP 143
Alfriston (parish), 36/326; TQ509026; NP 183
Algarkirk (division in Algarkirk), 22/770A; TF301342; NP 123
Algarkirk (parish), 22/770A-B; NP 113, 114, 123
Algarkirk - Holland Fen (division in Algarkirk), 22/770B; TF218465; NP 113, 114, 123
Alkborough (parish), 22/15; SE883211; NP 98, 104
Alkerton (tithing in Eastington), 13/270B; SO773153; NP 156
Alkerton (parish), 29/324; SP381428; NP 145
Alkham (parish), 19/379; TR251422; NP 173
Alkington (tithing in Berkeley), 13/319; ST707965; NP 156
Alkington (township in Whitchurch), 31/32; SJ528392; NP 118
Alkmere (township in St Chad Shrewsbury), 31/273B; SJ501092; NP 118
Alkmonton (township in Longford), 8/233; SK198374; NP 120
Alkrington (township in Oldham), 20/485; SD872048; NP 101
All Cannings (parish), 39/161-164; NP 157, 167
All Cannings (tithing in All Cannings), 39/161; SU083637; NP 157, 167
All Fours, 9/164; NP 164, 176
All Hallows (division in Wallingford, All Hallows), 2/66A; SU606906; NP 158
All Hallows (parish), 2/66A-B; NP 158
All Hallows Bread-street (parish), 23/69; TQ323811; NP 160/2
All Hallows Honey-lane (parish), 23/42; TQ324812; NP 160/2
All Hallows Lombard-street (parish), 23/59; TQ330810; NP 160/2
All Saints Poplar (parish), 24/70; TQ378798; NP 161, 171
All Saints and St Peters, Cockley Cley (parish), 25/533; NP 125
All Saints (district in All Saints), 27/273; NZ255645; NP 78/1
All Saints (parish), 27/273, 282-284; NP 78/1
All Saints (township in All Saints), 27/282; NZ267642; NP 78/1
All Saints South Elmham (parish), 34/37A; NP 137
All Saints, Wandsworth (parish), 35/25; NP 170
All Saints or The Pallast (parish), 36/261; SU851046; NP 181/1
All Saints (All Saints North Street) (parish), 43/33; SE599518; NP 97/1
All Saints (Pavement) (parish), 43/31; SE604517; NP 97/1
All Saints (Peaseholme) (parish), 43/13; SE608518; NP 97/1
All Saints North Street, 43/33; NP 97/1
All Souls (division in St Marylebone), 24/45F; TQ291816; NP 160/1
Allendale (parish), 27/587-594); NP 77, 84
Allendale Common (area in Allendale), 27/587; NY820500; NP 77, 84
Allendale Town (township in Allendale), 27/592; NY840560; NP 77
Allensmore (parish), 15/193; SO544357; NP 142
Aller (parish), 32/306; ST393300; NP 165, 177
Allerston (parish), 42/421; SE890890; NP 92
Allerthorpe (township in Barmby Moor), 41/91; SE778477; NP 97, 98
Allerthorpe (division in Swainby with Allerthorpe township in Pickhill), 42/252B; SE333867; NP 91
Allerton (township in Childwall), 20/651; SJ402865; NP 100
Allerton (township in Bradford), 43/530A; SE112339; NP 96
Allerton Bywater (township in Kippax), 43/471; SE425276; NP 97
Allerton Mauleverer (division in township of Allerton Mauleverer with Hopperton in Allerton Mauleverer), 43/114; SE418582; NP 97
Allerton Mauleverer (parish), 43/113-115; NP 91, 96, 97
Allerton Mauleverer with Hopperton (township in Allerton Mauleverer), 43/114-115; NP 97
Allerwash (township in parochial chapelry of Newbrough in Warden), 27/603A; NY865670; NP 77
Allesley (parish), 37/97; SP282812; NP 131, 132
Allestree (parish), 8/211; SK353401; NP 121

Allexton (Alexton) (parish), 21/282; SP814996; NP 122, 133
Allhallows (parish), 7/221; NY191424; NP 82
Allhallows (parish), 19/43; TQ838777; NP 172
Allhallows (All Hallows Bread-street) (parish), 23/69; TQ323811; NP 160/2
Allhallows (All Hallows Honey-lane) (parish), 23/42; TQ324812; NP 160/2
Allhallows (All Hallows Lombard-street) (parish), 23/59; TQ330810; NP 160/2
Allhallows (Allhallows London Wall) (parish), 23/14; TQ329815; NP 160/2
Allhallows Barking (parish), 23/91; TQ334807; NP 160/2
Allhallows London Wall (parish), 23/14; TQ329815; NP 160/2
Allhallows Staining (parish), 23/97; TQ333809; NP 160/2
Allhallows the Great (parish), 23/81; TQ326807; NP 160/2
Allhallows the Less (parish), 23/82; TQ327807; NP 160/2
Allington (parish), 10/230; SY458939; NP 177
Allington (tithing in South Stoneham), 14/259; SU472161; NP 180
Allington (parish), 19/172; TQ742573; NP 171, 172
Allington (parish), 34/142; NP 137
Allington (parish), 39/308; SU206393; NP 167
Allington (tithing in All Cannings), 39/162; SU081650; NP 157, 167
Allington (township in Gresford), 49/70; SJ381569; NP 109
Allonby (township in Bromfield), 7/127; NY091435; NP 82
Allostock (township in Great Budworth), 5/130; SJ743718; NP 110
Alltmawr (parish), 45/11; SO065475; NP 141
Alltyblaca (hamlet in Llanwenog), 46/78; SN516456; NP 140
Almeley (parish), 15/52; SO337520; NP 129
Almer (Almer and Mapperton) (parish), 10/188; SY903992; NP 178, 179
Almington (Tyrley) (township in Drayton in Hales), 33/158A; SJ700340; NP 119
Almond Park, Great and Little Berwick and Newton, 31/252; NP 118
Almondbury (township in Almondbury), 43/767; SE156138; NP 102
Almondbury), 43/760-764, 767-776; NP 102
Almondsbury (parish), 13/367-372; NP 155, 156
Almondsbury (tithing in Almondsbury), 13/367; ST607842; NP 155, 156
Almsford (parish), 32/351; NP 166
Alne (parish), 42/580-585; NP 91
Alne (township in Alne), 42/582; SE503663; NP 91, 92
Alnham (parish), 27/161-164; NP 71
Alnham (township in Alnham), 27/161; NT957136; NP 71
Alnmouth (township in Lesbury), 27/206; NU250110; NP 71
Alnwick (parish), 27/196-201; NP 71
Alnwick (township in Alnwick), 27/196; NU160120; NP 71
Alnwick South Side (township in Alnwick), 27/197; NU161085; NP 71
Alphamstone (parish), 12/94; TL878354; NP 149
Alpheton (parish), 34/409; TL884508; NP 149
Alphington (parish), 9/314; SX899911; NP 176
Alpington (parish), 25/573; TG296015; NP 126, 137
Alpraham (township in Bunbury), 5/304; SJ587604; NP 109, 110
Alresford (parish), 12/171; TM068205; NP 149
Alrewas (parish), 33/222A-C; NP 120
Alrewas (township in Alrewas), 33/222A; SK170150; NP 120
Alrewas Hayes (Alrewas Hays) (extra-parochial), 33/223; SK143148; NP 120
Alsager (township in Barthomley), 5/240; SJ794555; NP 110
Alsop en le Dale and Eaton (Alsop le Dale) (township in Ashbourne), 8/175; SK155563; NP 111
Alsop le Dale, 8/175; NP 111
Alston (division in township of Alston and Hothersall in Ribchester), 20/223; SD610650; NP 94, 95
Alston, 7/175-177; NP 77, 83, 84
Alston (township in Alston), 7/175; NY720460; NP 77, 83, 84
Alston Sutton (division in Weare), 32/164; ST421512; NP 165
Alstone (hamlet in Overbury), 13/2; SP983328; NP 143

Alstone and Apeton (division in Bradley), 33/244; SJ852192; NP 119
Alstonfield (parish), 33/81-89; NP 110, 111
Alstonfield (township in Alstonfield), 33/89; SK130565; NP 111
Altarnun (Alternan, Alternon) (parish), 6/39; SX203798; NP 186
Altcar (parish), 20/679; SD338058; NP 100
Altham (township in Whalley), 20/294; SD768316; NP 95
Althorne (parish), 12/360; TQ910990; NP 162
Althorp (extra-parochial), 26/239; SP683652; NP 132, 133
Althorpe (hamlet in Althorpe), 22/8; SE828102; NP 104
Althorpe (parish), 22/7-10; NP 104
Altofts (township in Normanton), 43/610; SE380240; NP 96
Alton (Alveton) (parish), 33/106-109; NP 111, 120
Alton (Alveton) (township in Alton), 33/107; SK073420; NP 120
Alton (division in township of Idridgehay and Alton in Wirksworth), 8/153; SK281502; NP 111
Alton (parish), 14/127; SU708394; NP 168, 169
Alton Barnes (parish), 39/204; SU109633; NP 157, 167
Alton Head (division in township of Kirkby Overblow with Swindon in Kirkby Overblow), 43/385; SE311503; NP 96
Alton Pancras (parish), 10/151; ST730029; NP 178
Alton Priors (tithing in Overton), 39/168; SU118622; NP 167
Altrincham (township in Bowdon), 5/82; SJ768883; NP 101
Alvanley (township in Frodsham), 5/411; SJ498739; NP 100, 109
Alvaston (township in Nantwich), 5/249; SJ664543; NP 110
Alvaston (township in Derby St Michael), 8/269B; SK392333; NP 121
Alvechurch (parish), 40/48; SP040737; NP 130, 131
Alvediston (parish), 39/345; ST974233; NP 167
Alveley (parish), 31/481-482; NP 130
Alveley (township in Alveley), 31/481; SO770860; NP 130
Alverdiscott (district in Alverdiscott), 9/43A; SS515250; NP 163
Alverdiscott (parish), 9/43A-B; NP 163
Alverstoke (division in Alverstoke), 14/292; SU605008; NP 180
Alverstoke (parish), 14/292-293; NP 180
Alverthorpe (division in township of Alverthorpe with Thornes in Wakefield), 43/601; SE308218; NP 96
Alverthorpe with Thornes (township in Wakefield), 43/601-604; NP 96, 102
Alverton (township in Kilvington), 28/204; SK792418; NP 122
Alvescot (Alvescott) (parish), 29/165; SP270048; NP 157
Alveston (parish), 13/363; ST642863; NP 156
Alveston (parish), 37/217; SP228547; NP 131, 144
Alvingham (parish), 22/189; TF363916; NP 105
Alvington (parish), 13/169; SO600012; NP 155, 156
Alvington, 9/47; NP 163, 174
Alwalton (parish), 17/4; TL136958; NP 134
Alwent and Selaby (division in township of Gainford in Gainford), 11/302; NZ147187; NP 85
Alwington (Alvington) (parish), 9/47; SS404246; NP 163, 174
Alwinton (parish), 27/176-184, 188C; NP 70, 71
Alwinton (township in Alwinton), 27/180; NT917069; NP 71
Alwoodley (township in Harewood), 43/403; SE298407; NP 96
Amaston (division in Alberbury Lower Quarter township in Alberbury), 31/305; SJ373111; NP 118
Ambaston (township in Elvaston), 8/295; SK431321; NP 121
Amberley (township in Marden), 15/143; SO547479; NP 142
Amberley (hamlet in Amberley), 36/79; TQ035130; NP 181, 182
Amberley (parish), 36/79-80; NP 181, 182
Amble (township in Warkworth), 27/226; NU262038; NP 71
Amblecote (Amblecoat) (township in Old Swinford), 33/340; SO906861; NP 130
Ambleside (township in Grasmere), 38/79; NY387071; NP 83, 89
Ambleside (township in Windermere), 38/80; NY390044; NP 83, 89
Ambleside above Stock, 38/79
Ambleside below Stock, 38/80
Ambleston (parish), 55/50; SN005256; NP 138
Ambrosden (hamlet in Ambrosden), 29/111; SP601191; NP 145
Ambrosden (parish), 29/111-113; NP 145

Amcotts (township in Althorpe), 22/10; SE840140; NP 104
Amersham (Agmondesham) (division in Amersham), 3/200; SU960970; NP 159
Amersham (Agmondesham) (parish), 3/4, 200; NP 159
Amesbury (parish), 39/263; SU152416; NP 167
Amington and Stonydelph (township in Tamworth), 37/6; SK236041; NP 120
Amlwch (parish), 44/8; SH429934; NP 106
Amotherby (township in Appleton-le-Street), 42/639; SE750735; NP 92
Ampleforth (parish), 42/613-616; NP 92/1
Ampleforth Birdforth (township in Ampleforth), 42/615; SE571787; NP 92/1
Ampleforth Oswaldkirk (township in Oswaldkirk), 42/613; SE581782; NP 92/1
Ampleforth St Peter (township in Ampleforth), 42/614; SE582787; NP 92/1
Ampney Crucis (parish), 13/282; SP068037; NP 157
Ampney St Mary (Ashbrook) (parish), 13/284; SP081026; NP 157
Ampney St Peter (Easington) (parish), 13/285; SP090007; NP 157
Amport (parish), 14/82; SU293441; NP 167, 168
Ampthill (parish), 1/82; TL033383; NP 147
Ampton (parish), 34/524; TL864712; NP 136
Amroth (parish), 55/125; SN159081; NP 152
Amwell (division in St James Clerkenwell), 24/47B; TQ311826; NP 160/1
Ancaster (parish), 22/603-604; NP 113, 123
Ancroft (parochial chapelry in Holy Island), 27/18-20; NP 64
Ancroft (township in Ancroft parochial chapelry in Holy Island), 27/20; NT992457; NP 64
Anderby (parish), 22/408; TF539755; NP 105, 114
Anderson (parish), 10/185; SY879988; NP 178
Anderton (township in Great Budworth), 5/138; SJ648757; NP 101, 110
Anderton (township in Standish), 20/384; SD622127; NP 101
Andover (division in Andover), 14/71; SU368481; NP 168
Andover (parish), 14/71-72; NP 168
Andwell (extra-parochial), 14/106; SU690525; NP 169
Angersleigh (parish), 32/424; ST197194; NP 164, 177
Angerton (Moss-houses and Waltham-Hill) (extra-parochial), 20/8; SD222838; NP 88
Angle (parish), 55/155; SM869021; NP 151
Anglezarke (Anglezark) (township in Bolton le Moors), 20/388; SD631166; NP 101
Angmering (division in Angmering), 36/295; TQ070060; NP 182
Angmering (parish), 36/295-296; NP 182
Angram (division in township of Muker in Grinton), 42/123; SD859998; NP 90
Angram (township in Long Marston), 43/66; SE521489; NP 97
Angram Grange (township in Coxwold), 42/553; SE515762; NP 91
Anick (township in St John Lee), 27/452; NY953654; NP 77
Anick Grange (township in St John Lee), 27/453; NY957650; NP 77
Anlaby (division in Anlaby township in Hessle), 41/317; TA040280; NP 99
Anlaby (township in Kirk Ella and Hessle), 41/310, 317; NP 99, 99/1
Anlaby (township in Kirk Ella), 41/310; TA040291; NP 99, 99/1
Anmer (parish), 25/97; TF738297; NP 124, 125
Annesley (parish), 28/170; SK502522; NP 112
Ansford (Almsford) (parish), 32/351; ST644335; NP 166
Ansley (parish), 37/58; SP290927; NP 131, 132
Anslow (township in Rolleston on Dove), 33/211; SK210250; NP 120
Anstey (parish), 16/20; TL407327; NP 148
Anstey (parish), 37/105; NP 132
Anstey (township in Thurcaston), 21/131; SK552086; NP 121
Anstey Pastures (extra-parochial), 21/187; SK552073; NP 121
Anston (township in Anston cum Membris and Dinnington), 43/904-906; NP 103

Anston cum Membris (parish), 43/903-905; NP 103
Ansty (Anstey) (parish), 37/105; SP403831; NP 132
Ansty (parish), 39/381; ST948256; NP 167
Anthony (Anthony in the East) (parish), 6/110; SX401545; NP 186, 187
Anthorn (township in Bowness-on-Solway), 7/112; NY200588; NP 75
Antingham (Antingham St Mary and Antingham St Margaret) (parish), 25/137; TG254334; NP 126
Antrobus (township in Great Budworth), 5/114; SJ646806; NP 101
Anwick (parish), 22/591; TF126508; NP 113
Apethorpe (parish), 26/45; TL014951; NP 134
Apley (parish), 22/264; TF117754; NP 104, 113
Apperley (hamlet in Deerhurst), 13/53B; SO860280; NP 143
Apperley (township in Bywell St Peter), 27/636; NZ063586; NP 77
Appleby (parish), 8/336, 21/4; NP 121
Appleby (parish), 22/41-43; NP 104
Appleby (township in Appleby), 8/336; SK312107; NP 121
Appleby (township in Appleby), 22/43; SE958138; NP 104
Appleby (township in St Lawrence Appleby), 38/40; NY683203; NP 83
Appleby Parva (township in Appleby), 21/4; SK318088; NP 121
Appledore (parish), 19/433; TQ954303; NP 184
Appledram (parish), 36/266; SU842024; NP 181
Appleford (chapelry in Sutton Courtney), 2/61B; SU527933; NP 158
Appleshaw (parish), 14/75; SU305487; NP 168
Applethorpe (parish), 28/43; NP 104
Applethwaite (township in Windermere), 38/82; NY407994; NP 83, 89
Appleton (parish), 2/4A-B; NP 158
Appleton (township in Appleton), 2/4A; SP433011; NP 158
Appleton (township in Great Budworth), 5/111; SJ632840; NP 101
Appleton (parish), 25/172; TF713276; NP 124
Appleton (township in Catterick), 42/75; SE233952; NP 91
Appleton Roebuck (Appleton) (township in Bolton Percy), 43/59; SE553422; NP 97
Appleton Wiske (township in Great Smeaton), 42/60; NZ395056; NP 85, 91
Appleton, 43/59; NP 97
Appleton-le-Moors (township in Lastingham), 42/466; SE740880; NP 92
Appleton-le-Street (division in township of Appleton-le-Street in Appleton-le-Street), 42/636; SE736736; NP 92
Appleton-le-Street (parish), 42/636-641; NP 92
Appleton-le-Street (township in Appleton-le-Street), 42/636-637; NP 92
Appletree (hamlet in Aston le Walls), 26/270; SP480498; NP 145
Appletreewick (township in Burnsall), 43/207; SE075635; NP 90, 91, 96
Arborfield (parish), 2/193; SU753668; NP 169
Arbury (division in township of Houghton, Middleton and Arbury in Winwick), 20/605; SJ611924; NP 101
Archdeacon Newton (township in Darlington), 11/318; NZ253177; NP 85
Arclid (township in Sandbach), 5/217; SJ785618; NP 110
Arddynwen (Arddynwent) (township in Mold), 50/114; SJ219618; NP 108
Arddynwent, 50/114; NP 108
Ardeley (Yardley) (parish), 16/27; TL310270; NP 147
Arden with Ardenside (township in Hawnby), 42/500; SE505925; NP 91, 92
Ardingly (Ardingley) (parish), 36/60; TQ339300; NP 182, 183
Ardington (parish), 2/86; SU432882; NP 158
Ardleigh (parish), 12/119; TM048288; NP 149
Ardley (parish), 29/82; SP536263; NP 145
Ardsley (township in Darfield), 43/857; SE382057; NP 103
Ardwick (township in Manchester), 20/520; SJ861972; NP 101

47

Areley Kings (Kings Areley) (parish), 40/72; SO794802; NP 130
Argam, 41/167; NP 93
Argham (Argam) (parish), 41/167; TA112707; NP 93
Argoed (township in Mold), 50/110; SJ261647; NP 108, 109
Argoed-ystrad (township in Caron), 46/38A; SN670590; NP 140
Arkendale (division in Farnham and Knaresborough), 43/138-139; NP 91, 96
Arkendale (division in Farnham), 43/138; SE385605; NP 91, 96
Arkendale (township in Knaresborough), 43/139; SE383603; NP 91, 96
Arkengarthdale (parish), 42/102; NY975055; NP 84, 90
Arkesden (parish), 12/17; TL480348; NP 148
Arkholme with Cawood (township in Melling), 20/84; SD573722; NP 89
Arlecdon (parish), 7/258; NY045190; NP 82
Arlescott (Arlscott) (township in Barrow), 31/460; SJ646006; NP 119
Arlesey (Arlsey) (parish), 1/97; TL199370; NP 147
Arley (parish), 33/342; NP 130
Arley (parish), 37/71; SP288901; NP 131, 132
Arlingham (parish), 13/268; SO720105; NP 143, 156
Arlington (parish), 9/14; SS624406; NP 163
Arlington (tithing in Bibury), 13/234; SP108062; NP 157
Arlington (parish), 36/188; TQ546078; NP 183
Arlscott, 31/460; NP 118
Arlsey (parish), 1/97; NP 147
Armeringhall (parish), 25/483; NP 126
Armin, 43/962; NP 97
Arminghall (Armeringhall) (parish), 25/483; TG246052; NP 126
Armitage (parish), 33/226; SK083161; NP 120
Armley (township in Leeds), 43/498; SE268338; NP 96
Armston (hamlet in Polebrook), 26/68; TL068859; NP 134
Armthorpe (parish), 43/932; SE638047; NP 103
Arncliffe (parish), 42/314-315; NP 91
Arncliffe (parish), 43/224-228; NP 90
Arncliffe (township in Arncliffe), 43/225; SD925705; NP 90
Arncott (hamlet in Ambrosden), 29/112; SP614176; NP 145
Arne (parish), 10/289; SY963872; NP 179
Arnesby (parish), 21/328; SP614926; NP 132
Arnold (division in township of Arnold in Swine), 41/394; TA127423; NP 99
Arnold (division in township of Arnold in Long Riston), 41/395; TA120410; NP 99
Arnold (hamlet in Swine and Long Riston), 41/394-395; NP 99
Arnold (parish), 28/183; SK590473; NP 112, 121
Arnside (division of Beetham township in Beetham), 38/135; SD455775; NP 89
Arram (division in parish and township of Atwick), 41/360; TA163489; NP 99
Arras (division in township of Market Weighton and Arras in Market Weighton), 41/193B; SE922419; NP 98
Arrathorne (township in Hornby), 42/201; SE204934; NP 91
Arrathorne (township in Patrick Brompton), 42/204; SE201931; NP 91
Arreton (parish), 18/18; SZ524863; NP 180
Arrington (parish), 4/122; TL323509; NP 147
Arrow (hamlet in Arrow), 37/189; SP069561; NP 131, 144
Arrow (parish), 37/189-190; NP 131, 144
Arrow, 5/469; NP 100
Arrowe (Arrow) (township in Woodchurch), 5/469; SJ268863; NP 100
Arscott (township in Pontesbury), 31/291; SJ435135; NP 118
Arthington (division in township of Arthington in Adel), 43/393A; SE275447; NP 96
Arthington (division in township of Arthington in Adel), 43/393B; SE264434; NP 96
Arthington (township in Adel), 43/393A-394; NP 96
Arthingworth (parish), 26/124; SP750819; NP 133
Arthuret (parish), 7/14-17; NP 76
Artillery (parish in Christchurch Spitalfields), 24/61C; TQ335816; NP 160/1
Artington (tithing in Guildford St Nicholas), 35/130B; SU984486; NP 169

Arundel (parish), 36/221; TQ005079; NP 181
Asby (parish), 38/46-48; NP 83
Asby Coatsforth (township in Asby), 38/48; NY696123; NP 83
Asby Winderwath (township in Asby), 38/46; NY665114; NP 83
Ascot (Ascott) (hamlet in Great Milton), 29/254; SU613989; NP 158
Ascot under Wychwood (parish), 29/148; SP302188; NP 145
Ascott, 29/254; NP 158
Asenby (township in Topcliffe), 42/239; SE397750; NP 91
Asfordby (parish), 21/71; SK707194; NP 122
Asgarby (division in Asgarby), 22/441A; TF328668; NP 114
Asgarby (parish), 22/441A-B; NP 114
Asgarby (parish), 22/588; TF126454; NP 113, 123
Asgarby - West Fen (division in Asgarby), 22/441B; TF302587; NP 114
Ash (Ash next Wingham) (parish), 19/132; TR294605; NP 173
Ash (division in Ash), 35/73; SU898513; NP 169
Ash (parish), 19/76; TQ603644; NP 171
Ash (parish), 35/72-74; NP 169
Ash (township in Sutton on the Hill), 8/237B; SK257332; NP 120
Ash Magna (township in Whitchurch), 31/30; SJ568398; NP 118
Ash Parva (township in Whitchurch), 31/29; SJ580392; NP 118
Ash Priors (parish), 32/294; ST150294; NP 164
Ash, Ashe, 11/148; NP 85
Ashampstead (parish), 2/124; SU570764; NP 158
Ashbocking (parish), 34/361; TM173545; NP 150
Ashbourn, 8/179; NP 111
Ashbourne (Ashbourn) (township in Ashbourne), 8/179; SK179468; NP 111
Ashbourne (parish), 8/175, 177-185; NP 111, 120
Ashbrittle (parish), 32/272; ST047218; NP 164
Ashbrook (parish), 13/284; NP 157
Ashburnham (parish), 36/175; TQ680150; NP 183
Ashburton (parish), 9/407; SX754716; NP 175, 187
Ashbury (parish), 2/103-106; NP 157, 158
Ashbury (parish), 9/202; SX514962; NP 175
Ashbury (tithing in Ashbury), 2/103; SU264850; NP 157, 158
Ashby (parish), 25/391A; TG425158; NP 126
Ashby (parish), 25/577; NP 126, 137
Ashby (parish), 34/10; TM492996; NP 137
Ashby (township in Bottesford), 22/28; SE894084; NP 104
Ashby by Partney (Ashby juxta Partney) (parish), 22/424A-B; NP 114
Ashby by Partney (Ashby juxta Partney) (division in Ashby by Partney), 22/424A; TF431667; NP 114
Ashby by Partney - East Fen (division in Ashby by Partney), 22/424B; TF411603; NP 114
Ashby cum Fenby (parish), 22/173; TA253007; NP 105
Ashby de la Zouch (parish), 21/8-9; NP 121
Ashby de la Zouch (township in Ashby de la Zouch), 21/9; SK361172; NP 121
Ashby de la Launde (Ashby de la Laund) (parish), 22/575; TF041507; NP 113
Ashby Folville (parish), 21/122; NP 121, 122
Ashby Folville (township in Ashby Folville), 21/122; SK710129; NP 122
Ashby juxta Partney (parish), 22/424A-B; NP 114
Ashby Magna (parish), 21/331; SP567906; NP 132
Ashby Parva (Little Ashby) (parish), 21/240; SP530886; NP 132
Ashby Puerorum (parish), 22/391; TF331717; NP 114
Ashby St Ledgers (parish), 26/183; SP573682; NP 132
Ashby St Mary (Ashby) (parish), 25/577; TG330019; NP 126, 137
Ashchurch (parish), 13/46-47; NP 143
Ashcombe (parish), 9/393; SX922789; NP 176, 188
Ashcott (parish), 32/179; ST436370; NP 165
Ashdon (hamlet in Ashdon), 12/2; TL583410; NP 148
Ashdon (parish), 12/2-3; TL583410; NP 148
Ashe (parish), 14/58; SU537495; NP 168
Asheldham (parish), 12/355; TL972014; NP 162
Ashen (Esse) (parish), 12/34; TL755435; NP 148, 149
Ashendon (Ashenden) (parish), 3/153; SP703132; NP 146

Ashfield (Ashfield cum Thorpe) (parish), 34/250; TM210625; NP 137
Ashford (Echelford) (parish), 24/122; TQ073712; NP 170
Ashford (parish), 9/24; SS533349; NP 163
Ashford (parish), 19/324; TR004429; NP 172
Ashford Bowdler (parish), 31/416; SO515705; NP 129
Ashford Carbonell (parish), 31/527; SO530710; NP 129
Ashford in the Water (Ashford) (township in Bakewell), 8/100; SK194693; NP 111
Ashford, 8/100; NP 111
Ashill (parish), 25/537; TF888043; NP 125, 136
Ashill (parish), 32/434; ST326176; NP 177
Ashington (Ashingdon) (parish), 12/368; TQ868938; NP 162
Ashington (township in Bothal), 27/320; NZ265870; NP 78
Ashington (parish), 32/396; ST562215; NP 177
Ashington (Ashington cum Buncton) (parish), 36/90; TQ129161; NP 182
Ashleworth (parish), 13/120; SO816257; NP 143
Ashley (parish), 14/212; SU394300; NP 168
Ashley (parish), 26/97; SP799908; NP 133
Ashley (parish), 33/152; SJ760370; NP 119
Ashley (parish), 39/20; ST932945; NP 156, 157
Ashley (township in Bowdon), 5/86; SJ777840; NP 101
Ashley cum Silverley (parish), 4/149; TL700610; NP 135
Ashley Walk (extra-parochial division in New Forest extra-parochial), 14/302A; SU200150; NP 179
Ashleyhay (township in Wirksworth), 8/156; SK303517; NP 111
Ashmanhaugh (parish), 25/366; TG316203; NP 126
Ashmansworth (parish), 14/5; SU413572; NP 168
Ashmore (parish), 10/11; ST907174; NP 166
Asholme (township in Lambley), 27/572; NY695570; NP 76
Asholt (parish), 32/270; NP 164, 165
Ashover (parish), 8/124-126; NP 111
Ashover (township in Ashover), 8/126; SK341640; NP 111
Ashow (parish), 37/205; SP314704; NP 132
Ashperton (parish), 15/166; SO642420; NP 143
Ashprington (parish), 9/439; SX814573; NP 187, 188
Ashreigney (Ringsash) (parish), 9/119; SS622139; NP 163, 175
Ashstead (parish), 35/57; TQ184584; NP 170
Ashton (division in township of Ashton with Stodday in Lancaster), 20/105; SD469565; NP 94
Ashton (division in township of Lea, Ashton, Ingol and Cottam in Preston), 20/215; SD512303; NP 94
Ashton (hamlet in Oundle), 26/63; TL066884; NP 134
Ashton, 9/386; SX855842; NP 176
Ashton (parish), 26/299; SP768500; NP 146
Ashton (township in Tarvin), 5/385; SJ513695; NP 109
Ashton (township in Ufford), 26/27; TF107048; NP 123
Ashton in Makerfield (Ashton within Makerfield) (township in Winwick), 20/610; SD570003; NP 100, 101
Ashton Keynes (division in Ashton Keynes), 39/14A; SU048948; NP 157
Ashton Keynes (parish), 39/14A-B; NP 157
Ashton Town (division in township of Ashton under Lyne in Ashton under Lyne), 20/536; SJ936988; NP 101
Ashton under Hill (parish), 13/38; SO999380; NP 143, 144
Ashton under Lyne (township and parish), 20/538; NP 101
Ashton upon Mersey (division in Ashton upon Mersey township in Ashton upon Mersey and Bowdon), 5/77-78; NP 101, 101/1
Ashton upon Mersey (division in Ashton upon Mersey township in Bowdon), 5/78; SJ772909; NP 101/1
Ashton upon Mersey (parish), 5/76-77; NP 101
Ashton upon Mersey (township in Ashton upon Mersey), 5/77; SJ769918; NP 101/1
Ashton with Stodday (township in Lancaster), 20/105-106; NP 94
Ashton within Makerfield, 20/610; NP 100, 101
Ashurst (parish), 19/201; TQ513387; NP 171
Ashurst (parish), 36/93; TQ178157; NP 182
Ashurst Walk (division in Eling), 14/299C; SU353087; NP 180
Ashwater (parish), 9/192; SX397982; NP 175

Ashwell (parish), 16/1; TL263394; NP 147
Ashwell (parish), 30/3; SK862137; NP 122
Ashwellthorpe (parish), 25/608; TM151978; NP 136, 137
Ashwick (parish), 32/137; ST635486; NP 166
Ashwicken (parish), 25/284; TF701188; NP 124
Ashworth (township in Middleton), 20/474; SD843137; NP 101
Aske (township in Easby), 42/91; NZ167031; NP 91
Askern (township in Campsall), 43/645; SE564136; NP 103
Askerswell (parish), 10/227; SY536932; NP 177
Askerton (township in Lanercost), 7/27; NY550720; NP 76
Askham (parish), 28/64; SK741753; NP 103, 104, 112
Askham (parish), 38/20-21; NP 83
Askham (township in Askham), 38/21; NY503235; NP 83
Askham Bryan (parish), 43/55; SE553482; NP 97
Askham Richard (parish), 43/54; SE536480; NP 97
Askrigg (township in Aysgarth), 42/136; SD953921; NP 90
Askwith (township in Weston), 43/375; SE170497; NP 96
Aslackby (hamlet in Aslackby), 22/671; TF074298; NP 123
Aslackby (parish), 22/671-673; NP 123
Aslacton (parish), 25/750; TM155903; NP 136, 137
Aslocton (township in Whatton), 28/215; SK749407; NP 122
Aspall (parish), 34/247; TM172652; NP 137
Aspatria (parish), 7/222-224; NP 82
Aspatria and Brayton (township in Aspatria), 7/222; NY149321; NP 82
Aspeden (parish), 16/56; NP 147, 148
Aspenden (Aspeden) (parish), 16/56; TL350289; NP 147, 148
Aspley (hamlet in Wootton Wawen), 37/180; SP108693; NP 131
Aspley (township in Eccleshall), 33/139; SJ812329; NP 119
Aspley Guise (parish), 1/77; SP941367; NP 146, 147
Aspley Heath (division in Wavendon), 3/60; SP927349; NP 146
Aspull (township in Wigan), 20/583; SD617073; NP 100, 101
Asselby (township in Howden), 41/2; SE717279; NP 97
Assington (parish), 34/496; TL938383; NP 149
Astbury (parish), 5/228-238; NP 110
Asterby (parish), 22/336; TF264791; NP 105
Asterleigh (division in Kiddington), 29/90; SP400224; NP 145
Asterton (township in Norbury), 31/367; SO401906; NP 129
Asthall (Asthal) (parish), 29/152; SP290106; NP 144, 145, 157, 158
Astley (parish), 37/70; SP313878; NP 132
Astley (parish), 40/71; SO792680; NP 130
Astley (township in Leigh), 20/577; SJ700990; NP 101
Astley (township in St Mary Shrewsbury), 31/248; SJ531186; NP 118
Astley Abbots (Astley Abbotts) (parish), 31/491; SO707964; NP 130
Aston (Aston by Sutton) (township in Runcorn), 5/163; SJ556786; NP 100
Aston (parish), 15/2; SO465720; NP 129
Aston (parish), 16/51; TL278219; NP 147
Aston (parish), 37/32-41; NP 131
Aston (township in Hope), 8/18; SK188842; NP 102, 111
Aston (township in Oswestry), 31/103; SJ323262; NP 118
Aston (township in Wem), 31/42; SJ535287; NP 118
Aston (township in Wrockwardine), 31/220; SJ621096; NP 118, 119
Aston (township in Mucklestone), 33/153; SJ756416; NP 119
Aston (township in Aston), 37/34; SP079893; NP 131
Aston (township in Hawarden), 50/9; SJ310670; NP 109
Aston (township in Lydham), 54/195; SO290910; NP 128, 129
Aston Abbots (parish), 3/139; SP843201; NP 146
Aston Blank (Cold Aston) (parish), 13/102; SP135199; NP 144
Aston Botterell (parish), 31/563; SO636841; NP 130
Aston by Budworth (Aston) (township in Great Budworth), 5/124; SJ684797; NP 101
Aston by Sutton, 5/163; NP 100
Aston Cantlow (parish), 37/200; SP152594; NP 131
Aston Clinton (parish), 3/175-176; NP 146, 159
Aston Clinton (township in Aston Clinton), 3/175; SP879123; NP 146, 159
Aston Eyre (township in Morville), 31/493; SO650940; NP 130
Aston Flamville (parish), 21/227A-228; NP 132

Aston Flamville (township in Aston Flamville), 21/228; SP464926; NP 132
Aston Grange (township in Runcorn), 5/164; SJ563778; NP 100
Aston Ingham (parish), 15/250; SO681232; NP 143
Aston juxta Mondrum (Aston) (township in Acton), 5/296; SJ649572; NP 110
Aston le Walls (hamlet in Aston le Walls), 26/269; SP498511; NP 145
Aston le Walls (parish), 26/269-270; NP 145
Aston Magna (Aston) (hamlet in Blockley), 40/247; SP205358; NP 144
Aston on Carrant (hamlet in Ashchurch), 13/47; SO946344; NP 143
Aston Pigot (Aston Pigott) (township in Worthen), 31/324; SJ337057; NP 118
Aston Rogers (township in Worthen), 31/323; SJ348062; NP 118
Aston Rowant (parish), 29/269; SU720998; NP 158
Aston Sandford (parish), 3/185; SP770072; NP 159
Aston Somerville (parish), 13/35; SP045383; NP 144
Aston Subedge (Aston Underhill) (parish), 13/23; SP137418; NP 144
Aston Tirrold (parish), 2/75; SU558850; NP 158
Aston Underhill (parish), 13/23; NP 144
Aston upon Trent (parish), 8/293-294; NP 121
Aston upon Trent (township in Aston upon Trent), 8/294; SK412301; NP 121
Aston Upthorpe (division in Blewbury), 2/77; SU547857; NP 158
Aston with Aughton (parish), 43/895-896; NP 103
Aston with Aughton (township in Aston with Aughton), 43/896; SK464856; NP 103
Aston, 5/124; NP 101
Aston, 5/296; NP 110
Aston, 40/247; NP 144
Aston, Burston, Stoke and Little Aston (township in Stone), 33/51; SJ915317; NP 119
Astrope (division in Long Marston), 16/152; SP901180; NP 146
Astwell (hamlet in Wappenham), 26/323; SP615436; NP 145
Astwick (parish), 1/96; TL214393; NP 147
Astwood (parish), 3/39; SP952475; NP 146, 147
Aswarby (parish), 22/649; TF076404; NP 123
Aswardby (parish), 22/398; TF378703; NP 114
Atch Lench (hamlet in Church Lench), 40/192; SP038512; NP 144
Atcham (parish), 31/238-242; NP 118
Atcham (township in Atcham), 31/238; SJ546093; NP 118
Athelampton (Admiston, Athelhampstone) (parish), 10/214; SY769937; NP 178
Athelhampstone (parish), 10/214; NP 178
Athelington (Allington) (parish), 34/142; TM212708; NP 137
Atherington (parish), 9/66; SS591232; NP 163
Atherstone (parish), 37/304; NP 144
Atherstone (township in Mancetter), 37/59; SP312979; NP 132
Atherstone upon Stour (Atherstone) (parish), 37/304; SP208513; NP 144
Atherton (township in Leigh), 20/574; SD670030; NP 101
Atlow (township in Bradbourne), 8/167; SK236489; NP 111
Attenborough (parish), 28/250-252; NP 121
Attenborough (township in Attenborough), 28/251; SK519343; NP 121
Atterby (township in Bishop Norton), 22/153; SK993936; NP 104
Attercliffe cum Darnall (township in Sheffield), 43/832; SK383884; NP 102
Atterley and Walton (township in Much Wenlock), 31/453; SO640980; NP 130
Atterton (township in Witherley), 21/218; SP353982; NP 132
Attington (extra-parochial), 29/270; SP701017; NP 159
Attleborough (Attleburgh) (parish), 25/664; TM041953; NP 136
Attlebridge (parish), 25/350; TG135168; NP 125, 126
Attleburgh (parish), 25/664; NP 136
Atwick (division in parish and township of Atwick), 41/359B; TA189351; NP 99
Atwick (parish), 41/359A-360; NP 99
Atworth (tithing in Great Bradford), 39/124; ST866659; NP 156, 166

Aubourn (Auborn) (township in Aubourn), 22/539; SK930620; NP 113
Aubourn (parish), 22/538-539; NP 113
Auburn (township in Carnaby), 41/258; TA166627; NP 99
Auckley (division in Finningley), 28/1; SK654996; NP 103
Auckley (division of Auckley township in Finningley), 43/929; SE652007; NP 103
Auckley (township in Finningley), 28/2, 43/929; NP 103
Audenshaw (division in township of Ashton under Lyne in Ashton under Lyne), 20/535; SJ914984; NP 101
Audleby, Fonaby, Hundon (division in Caistor), 22/104; TA117036; NP 104
Audlem (parish), 5/270-274, 281; NP 110, 119
Audlem (township in Audlem), 5/271; SJ663437; NP 110, 119
Audley (parish), 33/42A-G; NP 110
Audley (township in Audley), 33/42E; SJ800510; NP 110
Aughton (parish), 20/363; SD398068; NP 100
Aughton (parish), 41/32, 34, 36-38
Aughton (township in Halton), 20/98; SD552673; NP 89
Aughton (township in Aughton), 41/36; SE724382; NP 97
Ault Hucknall (parish), 8/67; SK457646; NP 112
Aunby (hamlet in Castle Bytham), 22/699; SK018148; NP 123
Aunsby (parish), 22/646; TF040393; NP 123
Aust (tithing in Henbury), 13/374; ST572888; NP 155
Austerfield (township in Blyth), 43/927; SK660963; NP 103
Austerson (township in Acton), 5/284; SJ662498; NP 110
Austhorpe (division in township of Austhorpe in Whitkirk), 43/477; SE375343; NP 96
Austhorpe (township in Whitkirk), 43/476-477; NP 96
Austin Ward (division in parish and township of Holy Tinity Kingston upon Hull), 41/332; TA099105; NP 99/1
Austonley (township in Almondbury), 43/775; SE110075; NP 102
Austrey, 37/3; SK296084; NP 121
Austwick (township in Clapham), 43/277; SD780700; NP 90
Authorpe (parish), 22/295; TF398807; NP 105
Avebury (parish), 39/160; SU101704; NP 157
Aveley (parish), 12/420; TQ565805; NP 161, 171
Avenbury (parish), 15/154; SO651521; NP 143
Avening (parish), 13/306; ST872980; NP 156
Averham (parish), 28/153; NP 112
Averham (township in Averham), 28/153; SK759552; NP 112
Aveton Gifford (parish), 9/447; SX691485; NP 187
Avington (parish), 2/142; SU366700; NP 158
Avington (parish), 14/190; SU535302; NP 168
Avon (division in Christian Malford), 39/64; ST961766; NP 157
Avon (extra-parochial), 39/87; ST954760; NP 157
Avon (in Christian Malford and Avon), 39/64, 39/87; NP 157
Avon Dassett (parish), 37/266; SP410500; NP 145
Awbery Street, 2/153; NP 158, 168
Awliscombe (parish), 9/226; ST130026; NP 176
Awre (Blakeney) (parish), 13/172; SO690080; NP 156
Awsworth (township in Nuthall), 28/178; SK480441; NP 121
Axbridge (parish), 32/162; ST431547; NP 165
Axford (tithing in Ramsbury), 39/180A; SU235700; NP 157
Axminster (district in Axminster), 9/231; SY299985; NP 177
Axminster (parish), 9/231, 10/301; NP 177
Axmouth (parish), 9/295; SY285915; NP 177
Axton (township in Llanasa), 50/43; SJ108803; NP 108
Aycliffe (parish), 11/272-278; NP 85
Aydon (township in Corbridge), 27/475; NZ001993; NP 77
Aydon Castle (township in Corbridge), 27/474; NZ002668; NP 77
Aylburton (tithing in Lydney), 13/170; SO608024; NP 155, 156
Aylesbeare (parish), 9/283A-B; NP 176
Aylesbeare (tithing in Aylesbeare), 9/283A; SY039910; NP 176
Aylesbury (parish), 3/168; SP820135; NP 146
Aylesby (Ailsby) (parish), 22/96; TA198070; NP 105
Aylesford (parish), 19/173; TQ731595; NP 171, 172
Aylestone (parish), 21/205-207; NP 121, 132
Aylestone (township in Aylestone), 21/205; SP579999; NP 121, 132
Aylmerton (parish), 25/36; TG182401; NP 126
Aylsham (parish), 25/210; TG195263; NP 126
Aylton (parish), 15/282; SO663377; NP 143

Aymestrey (parish), 15/18A-B; NP 129
Aymestry (division in Stratford Hundred in Aymestrey), 15/18B; SO398648; NP 129
Aymestry (Wigmore Hundred in Aymestrey), 15/18A; SO404660; NP 129
Aynho (parish), 26/365; SP522329; NP 145
Ayot St Lawrence (Ayott St Lawrence) (parish), 16/87; TL202165; NP 147
Ayot St Peter (Ayott St Peter) (parish), 16/86; TL220148; NP 147
Aysgarth (parish), 42/129-143; NP 90
Aysgarth (township in Aysgarth), 42/139; SD997881; NP 90
Ayston (parish), 30/44; SK860010; NP 122
Aythorpe Roding (Aythorp Roothing) (parish), 12/206; TL596149; NP 148
Ayton (parish), 42/328-331; NP 85, 86
Azerley (division in township of Azerley in Kirkby Malzeard), 43/196; SE260740; NP 91
Azerley (township in Ripon and Kirkby Malzeard), 43/195-198; NP 91

B

Babcary (parish), 32/368; ST574287; NP 165, 177
Babingley (parish), 25/94; TF761263; NP 124
Babington (parish), 32/118; ST704505; NP 166
Babraham (parish), 4/134; TL511512; NP 148
Babworth (parish), 28/33; SK670805; NP 103
Bach-y-graig (township in Tremeirchion), 50/82; SJ073716; NP 108
Bachaethlon (township in Kerry [Llanfihangel-yng-Ngheri]), 54/184; SO217892; NP 128
Bache (township in St Oswald Chester), 5/506; SJ400683; NP 109
Bacheldre (township in Church Stoke), 54/191; SO248913; NP 128
Backford (parish), 5/491-495
Backford (township in Backford), 5/493; SJ398723; NP 109
Backwell (parish), 32/14; ST495680; NP 155, 165
Backworth (township in Earsdon), 27/488; NZ298723; NP 78
Baconsthorpe (parish), 25/63; TG137382; NP 125
Bacton (parish), 15/218; SO373327; NP 142
Bacton (parish), 25/47; TG333337; NP 126
Bacton (parish), 34/186; TM050670; NP 136
Bacup (division in township of Newchurch in Rossendale in Whalley), 20/280; SD870240; NP 95
Badby (parish), 26/250; SP553594; NP 132
Baddesley Clinton (parish), 37/89; SP203715; NP 131
Baddesley Ensor (parish), 37/23; SP271982; NP 131, 132
Baddiley (parish), 5/299; SJ604508; NP 109, 110
Baddington (township in Acton), 5/285; SJ643493; NP 110
Badger (parish), 31/476; SO769998; NP 119, 130
Badgeworth (parish), 13/202; SO913177; NP 143
Badgworth (parish), 32/167; ST390523; NP 165
Badingham (parish), 34/168; TM307678; NP 137
Badlesmere (parish), 19/149; TR019543; NP 172
Badley (parish), 34/530; TM065561; NP 136, 149
Badsey (parish), 40/201; SP080425; NP 144
Badshot and Runfold (tithing in Farnham), 35/146; SU868475; NP 169
Badsworth (parish), 43/662-664; NP 103
Badsworth (township in Badsworth), 43/664; SE459153; NP 103
Badwell Ash (parish), 34/188; TM006690; NP 136
Bag Enderby (parish), 22/395; TF352722; NP 114
Bagby (division in township of Bagby with Islebeck in Kirby Knowle), 42/524; SE460802; NP 91
Bagby with Islebeck (township in Kirby Knowle), 42/524-525; NP 91
Bagendon (parish), 13/239; SP007070; NP 157
Baggrave (township in Hungerton), 21/261; SK693084; NP 122
Bagillt Fawr (division in Bagillt township in Holywell), 50/29; SJ208752; NP Bagillt (township in Holywell), 50/28-29; NP 108
Bagillt Fechan (division in Bagillt township in Holywell), 50/28; SJ214743; NP 108
Baginton (parish), 37/156; SP352744; NP 132
Baglan (parish), 51/46-47; NP 153

Baglan Higher (hamlet in Baglan), 51/47; SS780940; NP 153
Baglan Lower (hamlet in Baglan), 51/46; SS753919; NP 153
Bagley (township in Hordley), 31/91; SJ401268; NP 118
Bagley Wood (extra-parochial), 2/9; SP512019; NP 158
Bagnall (division in Stoke-on-Trent), 33/24; SJ931506; NP 110
Bagthorp (parish), 25/103; NP 125
Bagthorpe (Bagthorp) (parish), 25/103; TF796323; NP 125
Baguley (township in Bowdon), 5/84; SJ808887; NP 101
Bagworth (township in Thornton), 21/136; SK444080; NP 121
Baildon (township in Otley), 43/365; SE149399; NP 96
Bailey (township in Bewcastle), 7/1; NY525815; NP 76
Bailey, 20/232; SD680380; NP 95
Bainbridge (township in Aysgarth), 42/135; SD913863; NP 90
Bainton (Baynton) (hamlet in Stoke Lyne), 29/66B; SP580272; NP 145
Bainton (parish), 26/18; TF099067; NP 123
Bainton (parish), 41/229-230; NP 98
Bainton (township in Bainton), 41/229; SE959521; NP 98
Bakewell (parish), 8/83-107; NP 111
Bakewell (township in Bakewell), 8/94; SK215685; NP 111
Balby with Hexthorpe (township in Doncaster), 43/937; SE569009; NP 103
Balcombe (parish), 36/61; TQ309311; NP 182
Baldersby (township in Topcliffe), 42/245; SE360778; NP 91
Baldersdale (division in township of Cotherstone in Romaldkirk), 42/7; NY945975; NP 84
Balderstone (township in Blackburn), 20/320; SD631322; NP 95
Balderton (parish), 28/149; SK772507; NP 113
Baldock (parish), 16/7; TL247338; NP 147
Baldon Marsh (parish), 29/245; NP 158
Baldwinholme (township in Orton), 7/140A; NY344529; NP 75, 76
Bale (parish), 25/73; TG010368; NP 125
Balk (township in Kirby Knowle), 42/523; SE477810; NP 91
Balkholme (division in township of Balkholme in Howden), 41/14A; SE787273; NP 98, 98/1
Balkholme (township in Howden), 41/14A-B; NP 98, 98/1
Balking (Baulking) (chapelry in Uffington), 2/21; SU324912; NP 158
Ballam (sub-division of Westby division in Westby with Plumptons township in Kirkham), 20/182; SD33303; NP 94
Ballidon (township in Bradbourne), 8/164; SK205560; NP 111
Ballingdon cum Brunden (parish), 12/44; TL864405; NP 149
Ballingham (parish), 15/179; SO574318; NP 142
Balne (township in Snaith), 43/965; SE592182; NP 103
Balsall (hamlet in Hampton in Arden), 37/84; SP223755; NP 131
Balscott (chapelry in Wroxton), 29/22; SP391418; NP 145
Balsham (parish), 4/137; TL570510; NP 148
Balterley (township in Barthomley), 33/43; SJ755502; NP 110
Baltonsborough (parish), 32/205; ST552348; NP 165
Bambrough (parish), 27/88-111; NP 64, 71
Bambrough Castle, 27/110; NP 71
Bambrough, 27/111
Bambrough (Bambrough) (township in Bamburgh), 27/111; NU185345; NP 71
Bamburgh (parish), 27/88-111; NP 64, 71
Bamburgh Castle (Bambrough Castle) (township in Bamburgh), 27/110; NU183351; NP 71
Bamford (division of Bamford township in Hathersage), 8/40A; SK210835; NP 102, 111
Bamford (division in Heap township in Bury), 20/426-427; NP 101
Bamford (sub-division of Bamford division in township of Heap in Bury), 20/426; SD856122; NP 101
Bamford (sub-division of Bamford division in Heap township in Bury), 20/427; SD868127; NP 101
Bamford (township in Hathersage), 8/40A-B; NP 102, 111
Bamford Moor (division of Bamford township in Hathersage), 8/40B; SK213850; NP 102, 111
Bampton (parish), 9/130; SS972220; NP 164
Bampton (parish), 29/168-173; NP 158
Bampton (parish), 38/19; NY489173; NP 83
Bampton (township in Bampton), 29/168; SP320030; NP 158
Banbury (parish), 29/16-18; NP 145

Banbury (township in Banbury), 29/16; SP456407; NP 145
Bangley (township in Tamworth), 33/285B; SK175028; NP 120
Bangor (Bangor Teifi) (parish), 46/87; SN389407; NP 139
Bangor (Bangor-is-y-coed) (parish), 49/78-81, 50/135; NP 109, 118
Bangor (parish), 48/27; SH562700; NP 106
Bangor on Dee, 50/135
Bangor Teifi (parish), 46/87; NP 139
Bangor, 50/135
Bangor-is-y-coed (Bangor, Bangor on Dee) (division in Bangor parish), 50/135; SJ396447; NP 109, 118
Banhadla (township in Llanrhaeadr-ym-Mochnant [Llanrhaiadr ym Mochnant]), 49/136; SJ169251; NP 117
Banhadla (township in Llanrhaeadr-ym-Mochnant [Llanrhaiadr ym Mochnant]), 49/137; SJ168228; NP 117
Banham (parish), 25/737; TM066880; NP 136
Banhaola (township in Llanrhaeadr-ym-Mochnant [Llanrhaiadr ym Mochnant]), 49/133; SJ147269; NP 117
Bank Head (division in township of Northallerton in Northallerton), 42/264; SE410924; NP 91
Bank Moor (district in Crosby Ravensworth), 38/33; NY641126; NP 83
Bank Newton (township in Gargrave), 43/229; SD898533; NP 95
Banks (district in townships of Burtholme and Waterhead in Lanercost), 7/31; NY585655; NP 76
Bannel (township in Hawarden), 50/13; SJ297620; NP 109
Banningham (parish), 25/213; TG220291; NP 126
Banstead (parish), 35/91; TQ245585; NP 170
Banwell (parish), 32/66; ST388608; NP 165
Bapchild (parish), 19/455; TQ927629; NP 172
Barbon (township in Kirkby Lonsdale), 38/124; SD652825; NP 89
Barby (hamlet in Barby), 26/180; SP504708; NP 132
Barby (parish), 26/180-181; NP 132
Barcheston (hamlet in Barcheston), 37/287; SP276402; NP 144, 145
Barcheston (parish), 37/287-288; NP 144, 145
Barcombe (parish), 36/127; TQ426168; NP 183
Barden (township in Hauxwell), 42/189; SE142948; NP 91
Barden (township in Skipton), 43/331; SE053582; NP 96
Bardfield Saling (parish), 12/80; TL690270; NP 148
Bardley and Harcourt (township in Stottesden), 31/573; SO691813; NP 130
Bardney (hamlet in Bardney), 22/359; TF135710; NP 113
Bardney (parish), 22/359-360; NP 113
Bardon (extra-parochial), 21/30; SK455130; NP 121
Bardsea (division in township of Great Urswick in Urswick), 20/40; SD296751; NP 88, 89
Bardsey (parish), 43/407-410; NP 96
Bardsey cum Rigton (township in Bardsey), 43/408; SE368434; NP 96
Bardsey Island (Ynys Enlli) (extra-parochial), 48/75; SH120218; NP 115
Bardwell (parish), 34/126; TL943748; NP 136
Bare (division in Poulton, Bare and Torrisholme township in Lancaster), 20/115; SD453651; NP 89
Baresby, 21/123
Barford (extra-parochial), 26/135; SP858827; NP 133
Barford (parish), 25/558; TG110077; NP 125
Barford (parish), 37/224; SP282609; NP 131, 132
Barford St John (chapelry in Adderbury), 29/36; SP445335; NP 145
Barford St Michael (parish), 29/40; SP430324; NP 145
Barford St Martin (parish), 39/326; SU052324; NP 167
Barforth (division in township of Barforth in Gilling), 42/38; NZ160160; NP 85
Barforth (division in township of Caldwell in Stanwick St John), 42/37; NZ168152; NP 84
Barfreston (Barfrestone) (parish), 19/348; TR266499; NP 173
Barham (parish), 17/58; TL138753; NP 134
Barham (parish), 19/343; TR202492; NP 173
Barham (parish), 34/358; TM137515; NP 150
Barholm (parish), 22/714; TF088107; NP 123

Barkby (parish), 21/126-128; NP 121
Barkby (township in Barkby), 21/126; SK642100; NP 121
Barkby Thorpe (township in Barkby), 21/127; SK635087; NP 121
Barkestone (Barston, Barkeston) (parish), 21/87; SK783346; NP 122
Barkham (parish), 2/24; SU780664; NP 169
Barking (hamlet in Barking), 34/291; TM075527; NP 149
Barking (parish), 12/316-319; NP 161
Barking (parish), 34/291-293; NP 149, 150
Barking Town (division in Barking), 12/316; TQ440842; NP 161
Barkisland (township in Halifax), 43/570; SE055195; NP 96, 102
Barkston (parish), 22/622; SK940420; NP 122, 123
Barkston (division of Barkston township in Sherburn in Elmet), 43/433; SE489356; NP 97
Barkston (division of Barkston township in Saxton), 43/434; SE492361; NP 97
Barkston (township in Sherburn in Elmet and Saxton), 43/433-434; NP 97
Barkway (hamlet in Barkway), 16/16; TL380380; NP 148
Barkway (parish), 16/16-17; NP 148
Barlaston (parish), 33/63; SJ895389; NP 119
Barlavington (Barlton) (parish), 36/75; SU972165; NP 181
Barlborough (parish), 8/58; SK475776; NP 103
Barlby (township in Hemingbrough), 41/49; SE634340; NP 97
Barlestone (township in Market Bosworth), 21/166; SK434061; NP 121
Barley (division in Barley with Wheatley Booth township in Whalley), 20/256; SD808407; NP 95
Barley (parish), 16/18; TL399389; NP 148
Barley with Wheatley Booth (township in Whalley), 20/256-257; NP 95
Barleythorpe (division in Oakham), 30/17; SK845096; NP 122
Barling (parish), 12/378; TQ930899; NP 162
Barlings (parish), 22/354; TF077748; NP 104, 113
Barlow (township in Brayton), 43/451; SE645288; NP 97
Barlton, 36/75; NP 181
Barmby Dun (parish), 43/943; NP 103
Barmby Dun, 43/943; NP 103
Barmby Moor (Barmby upon the Moor, Barmby on the Moor) (township in Barmby Moor), 41/90; SE775495; NP 97, 98
Barmby Moor (Barmby upon the Moor, Barmby on the Moor) (parish), 41/90-92; NP 97, 98
Barmby on the Marsh (township in Howden), 41/3; SE698281; NP 97
Barmby on the Moor (parish), 41/90-92; NP 97, 98
Barmby on the Moor, 41/90
Barmby upon the Moor (parish), 41/90-92; NP 97, 98
Barmby upon the Moor, 41/90
Barmby upon Dun (parish), 43/943; NP 103
Barmby upon Dun, 43/943; NP 103
Barmer (parish), 25/104; TF813337; NP 125
Barmoor (township in Lowick), 27/43; NT986398; NP 64
Barmpton (township in Haughton le Skerne), 11/334; NZ320186; NP 85
Barmston (township in Washington), 11/18; NZ330563; NP 78
Barmston (parish), 41/352-353; NP 99
Barmston (township in Barmston), 41/352; TA157599; NP 99
Barnack (parish), 26/28; NP 123
Barnack (township in Barnack), 26/29A; TF078056; NP 123
Barnacre with Bonds (township in Garstang), 20/150; SD518458; NP 94
Barnard Castle (township in Gainford), 11/297; NZ058177; NP 84
Barnardiston (parish), 34/330; TL715495; NP 148
Barnards Inn (extra-parochial), 24/11; TQ312815; NP 160/1
Barnborough, 43/869; NP 103
Barnbow (division in township of Barwick in Elmet in Barwick in Elmet), 43/418; SE393348; NP 96
Barnburgh (Barnborough) (township in Barnburgh), 43/869; SE489028; NP 103
Barnby (division in township of Bossall in Bossall), 42/662; SE726610; NP 92
Barnby (parish), 34/23; TM482908; NP 137

Barnby (township in Lythe), 42/378; NZ822138; NP 86
Barnby Dun (Barmby upon Dun, Barmby Dun, Barnby upon Don) (parish), 43/942A-943; NP 103
Barnby Dun (Barmby upon Dun, Barmby Dun, Barnby upon Don) (township in Barnby Dun), 43/943; SE623095; NP 103
Barnby in the Willows (parish), 28/148; SK855527; NP 113
Barnby Moor (township in Blyth), 28/23; SK659846; NP 103
Barnby upon Don (parish), 43/943; NP 103
Barnby upon Don, 43/943; NP 103
Barnes (parish), 35/28; TQ224768; NP 170
Barnes Green (division in township of Ecclesfield in Ecclesfield), 43/789; SK336959; NP 102
Barnetby le Wold (parish), 22/65; TA072090; NP 104
Barney (parish), 25/117; TF995325; NP 125
Barnham (parish), 34/103; TL860780; NP 136
Barnham (parish), 36/281; SU960035; NP 181
Barningham Norwood (parish), 25/61; NP 125, 126
Barningham Parva (parish), 25/129; NP 125, 126
Barningham Winter (parish), 25/62; NP 125, 126
Barningham (Barnington) (parish), 34/128; TL968768; NP 136
Barningham (parish), 42/17-20; NP 84
Barningham (township in Barningham), 42/19; NZ077097; NP 84
Barnington (parish), 34/128; NP 136
Barnoldby le Beck (parish), 22/89; TA239032; NP 105
Barnoldswick (Barnoldswick or Gill) (township in Barnoldswick), 43/311; SD870460; NP 95
Barnoldswick (parish), 43/309-313; NP 95
Barnsley (parish), 13/283; SP075050; NP 157
Barnsley (township in Silkstone), 43/696; SE339063; NP 102
Barnstaple (parish), 9/26; SS569334; NP 163
Barnston (township in Woodchurch), 5/467; SJ281827; NP 100
Barnston (parish), 12/209; TL650195; NP 148
Barnton (township in Great Budworth), 5/139; SJ633753; NP 101, 110
Barnwell All Saints (parish), 26/72; TL066829; NP 134
Barnwell St Andrew (parish), 26/73; TL056849; NP 134
Barnwood (parish), 13/199; SO859178; NP 143
Barony (division in township of Barony and Evenwood in St Andrew Auckland), 11/195; NZ149279; NP 85
Barony and Evenwood (township in St Andrew Auckland), 11/195-196; NP 85
Barrasford (township in Chollerton), 27/440; NY922749; NP 77
Barrett Ringstead (parish), 25/2; TF686402; NP 124
Barrington (parish), 4/163; TL416480; NP 148
Barrington (hamlet in Chipping Campden), 13/27B; SP170380; NP 144
Barrington (division in Barrington), 32/437B; ST392190; NP 177
Barrington (parish), 32/407, 437B; NP 177
Barrons Park (township in Desford), 21/175; SK502041; NP 121
Barrow (parish), 5/383; SJ475696; NP 109
Barrow (parish), 31/459; NP 119, 130
Barrow (parish), 34/220; TL770640; NP 135, 136
Barrow (township in Holystone), 27/186; NT901051; NP 70, 71
Barrow (township in Cottesmore), 30/5; SK895155; NP 122
Barrow (township in Barrow), 31/459; SO661983; NP 119, 130
Barrow Gurney (Barrow) (parish), 32/16; ST527678; NP 165
Barrow upon Trent (parish), 8/263-265; NP 121
Barrow upon Trent (township in Barrow upon Trent), 8/265; SK353288; NP 121
Barrow upon Soar (parish), 21/46-51; NP 121
Barrow upon Soar (township in Barrow upon Soar), 21/45; SK587178; NP 121
Barrow upon Humber (parish), 22/48; TA071212; NP 99, 104
Barrowby (parish), 22/628; SK861362; NP 122
Barrowby (division in township of Austhorpe in Whitkirk), 43/476; SE 391337; NP 96
Barrowden (parish), 30/51; SK947003; NP 122, 123, 133, 134
Barrowford (township in Whalley), 20/262; SD857397; NP 95
Barry (parish), 51/173; ST100672; NP 154

Barsby (Baresby) (chapelry in Ashby Folville), 21/123; SK693113; NP 121, 122
Barsham (parish), 34/27; TM397899; NP 137
Barston (parish), 21/87; NP 122
Barston (parish), 37/83; SP202791; NP 131
Bartherton, 5/261; NP 110
Barthomley (parish), 5/240-242, 33/43; NP 110
Barthomley (township in Barthomley), 5/241; SJ767530; NP 110
Barthorpe (division in township of Acklam with Barthorpe in Acklam), 41/134; SE771646; NP 92, 98
Bartington (township in Great Budworth), 5/118; SJ599770; NP 100, 101
Bartle (division in township of Woodplumpton in St Michaels on Wyre), 20/162; SD497335; NP 94
Bartlestree (chapelry in Dormington), 15/170; SO570411; NP 142
Bartlow (parish), 4/155; TL591455; NP 148
Bartlow End (hamlet in Ashdon), 12/3; TL598422; NP 148
Barton (division in Abingdon St Helen), 2/18; SU503969; NP 158, 158/1
Barton (division in township of Downholland in Halsall), 20/356; SD350090; NP 100
Barton (parish), 4/108; TL402562; NP 135, 148
Barton (parish), 38/23-28; NP 83
Barton (township in Farndon), 5/352; SJ447542; NP 109
Barton (township in Preston), 20/209; SD525375; NP 94
Barton (township in Whittingham), 27/169; NU082128; NP 71
Barton (township in Gilling), 42/51; NZ239082; NP 85
Barton (township in Stanwick St John), 42/33B; NZ226093; NP 85
Barton and Eastleigh (Barton and Eastley) (tithing in South Stoneham), 14/261; SU455190; NP 168, 180
Barton Bendish (parish), 25/513; TF727051; NP 124
Barton Blount (parish), 8/239; SK212350; NP 120
Barton Hartshorn (parish), 3/85; SP635304; NP 145
Barton in the Clay (parish), 1/120; NP 147
Barton in the Beans (township in Nailstone), 21/148; SK393063; NP 121
Barton in Fabis (parish), 28/275; SK531327; NP 121
Barton Mills (Little Barton) (parish), 34/208; TL719728; NP 135
Barton on the Heath (parish), 37/296; SP257325; NP 144
Barton Seagrave (parish), 26/157; SP897774; NP 133
Barton St Mary (parish), 13/190; SO838174; NP 143/1
Barton St Michael (hamlet in Gloucester, St Michael), 13/188B; NP 143/1
Barton St David (parish), 32/343; ST542326; NP 165
Barton Stacey (parish), 14/143; SU430403; NP 168
Barton Turf (parish), 25/368; TG351224; NP 126
Barton upon Irwell (division in township of in Eccles), 20/552; SJ769979; NP 101
Barton upon Irwell (township in Eccles), 20/541-554; NP 101
Barton upon Humber, St Mary (parish), 22/47B; TA045215; NP 99, 104
Barton upon Humber, St Peter (parish), 22/47A; TA015215; NP 98, 99, 104
Barton, Bradnor and Rushock (township in Kington), 15/41D; SO290585; NP 128, 129
Barton-le-Clay (Barton in the Clay) (parish), 1/120; TL088306; NP 147
Barton-le-Street (parish), 42/633-635; NP 92
Barton-le-Street (township in Barton-le-Street), 42/634; SE724745; NP 92
Barton-le-Willows (township in Crambe), 42/654; SE710653; NP 92
Barton-under-Needwood (township in Tatenhill), 8/323; SK204166; NP 120
Barton-under-Needwood (township in Tatenhill), 33/219; SK188186; NP 120
Barton-Westcott (parish), 29/88; NP 145
Barugh (township in Darton), 43/709; SE321078; NP 102
Barughs Ambo township (Great and Little Barugh) (township), 42/448-449
Barwell (parish), 21/215-217; NP 132

53

Barwell (township in Barwell), 21/216; SP437973; NP 132
Barwick (parish), 25/84; TF807351; NP 125
Barwick (parish), 32/474; ST563138; NP 177
Barwick in Elmet (division in township of Barwick in Elmet in Barwick in Elmet), 43/420; SE401375; NP 96, 97
Barwick in Elmet (parish and township), 43/415-420
Baschurch (parish), 31/141-147; NP 118
Basford (parish), 28/242; SK559428; NP 121
Basford (township in Wybunbury), 5/255; SJ718523; NP 110
Basford (township in Chadderton), 33/74B; SJ995515; NP 110, 111
Bashall Eaves (township in Mitton), 43/288; SD700440; NP 95
Basildon (parish), 2/123; SU603776; NP 158
Basildon (parish), 12/397; TQ715898; NP 161
Basing (parish), 14/45; SU670533; NP 168, 169
Basingstoke (division in Basingstoke), 14/47; SU625515; NP 168
Basingstoke (parish), 14/46-47; NP 168
Basingthorpe, 22/687; NP 122, 123
Baslow (township in Bakewell), 8/83; SK274725; NP 111
Bassaleg (Bassalleg) (parish), 53/118-120; NP 154, 155
Bassenthwaite (parish), 7/277; NY237311; NP 82
Bassingbourn (Bassingborne, Bassingbourne) (parish), 4/172-173; NP 147, 148
Bassingbourn (Bassingborne, Bassingbourne) (hamlet in Bassingbourn), 4/172; TL337437; NP 147, 148
Bassingfield (township in Holme Pierrepont), 28/260; SK619373; NP 121
Bassingham (parish), 22/551; SK927591; NP 113
Bassingthorpe (Basingthorpe) (hamlet in Bassingthorpe), 22/687; SK961283; NP 122, 123
Bassingthorpe (parish), 22/686-687; NP 122, 123
Bassington (township in Eglingham), 27/145; NU142162; NP 71
Baston (parish), 22/711; TF123153; NP 123
Baswich (parish), 33/183-185; NP 119
Baswich, Milford and walton (township in Baswich), 33/185; SJ952211; NP 119
Batchcott, 31/339B; NP 129
Batcombe (parish), 10/97; ST618047; NP 178
Batcombe (parish), 32/188; ST686394; NP 166
Bath, St James (parish), 32/37; ST751645; NP 156/1
Bath, St Michael (parish), 32/35; ST750650; NP 156/1
Bath, St Peter and St Paul (division in Bath, St Peter and St Paul), 32/36A; ST750648; NP 156/1
Bathampton (parish), 32/32; ST776660; NP 156, 166
Bathealton (parish), 32/318; ST072244; NP 164
Batheaston (parish), 32/29; ST774681; NP 156
Batherton (Bartherton) (township in Wybunbury), 5/261; SJ662500; NP 110
Bathford (parish), 32/31; ST792665; NP 156, 166
Bathley (township in North Muskham), 28/130; SK771594; NP 112
Bathwick (parish), 32/33; ST762651; NP 156, 166
Batley (parish), 43/585-588; NP 96
Batley (township in Batley), 43/585; SE236248; NP 96
Batsford (parish), 13/85; SP193336; NP 144
Battersby (township in Ingleby Greenhow), 42/326; NZ601075; NP 86, 92
Battersea (division in Battersea), 35/22A; TQ279760; NP 170
Battersea (parish), 35/22A; NP 170, 171
Battisford (parish), 34/534; TM052542; NP 149
Battle (parish), 36/172; TQ749160; NP 183, 184
Battle (parish), 45/58; SO009322; NP 141
Battleburn (township in Kirkburn), 41/233; SE981562; NP 98
Battlefield (parish), 31/245A-B; NP 118
Battlefield (township in Battlefield), 31/245A; SJ511178; NP 118
Battlesden (parish), 1/113; SP967284; NP 147
Baughurst (parish), 14/15; SU575601; NP 168
Baulking, 2/21; NP 158
Baumber (parish), 22/367; TF218741; NP 105, 113, 114
Baunton (parish), 13/240C; SP030050; NP 157
Bausley (township in Alberbury), 54/88; SJ334150; NP 118
Baverstock (parish), 39/291; SU028329; NP 167

Bawburgh (parish), 25/494; TG160090; NP 125, 126
Bawdeswell (parish), 25/265; TG046206; NP 125
Bawdrip (parish), 32/217; ST337395; NP 165
Bawdsey (parish), 34/440; TM349399; NP 150
Bawsey (parish), 25/286; TF664204; NP 124
Bawtry (township in Blyth), 43/928; SK655937; NP 103
Baxby (division in township of Thornton-on-the-Hill-cum-Baxby in Coxwold), 42/559; SE508747; NP 91
Baxterley (parish), 37/22; SP272966; NP 131, 132
Bay Fell (area common to Lowick and Subberthwaite townships in Ulverston), 20/15; SD268852; NP 88
Baybush, 36/112; NP 170, 182
Baydon (parish), 39/101; SU284778; NP 157, 158
Bayfield (parish), 25/69; TG060410; NP 125
Bayford (parish), 16/121; TL310090; NP 147, 160
Baylham (Baytham) (parish), 34/357; TM102515; NP 149, 150
Baynton, 29/66B; NP 145
Baysdale Moor (division in township of Westerdale in Stokesley), 42/306A; NZ630050; NP 86, 92
Baytham (parish), 34/357; NP 149, 150
Bayton (parish), 40/76; SO693732; NP 130
Bayvil (parish), 55/21; SN108412; NP 139
Beachampton (parish), 3/18; SP779367; NP 146
Beachamwell All Saints (parish), 25/512; NP 124, 125
Beaconsfield (division formerly in Hertfordshire in Beaconsfield), 3/5; SU952926; NP 159
Beaconsfield (division in Beaconsfield), 3/218; SU945898; NP 159
Beaconsfield (parish), 3/5, 218; SU945898; NP 159
Beadlam (township in Helmsley), 42/490; SE643862; NP 92
Beadnell (township in Bamburgh), 27/102; NU227295; NP 71
Beaford (parish), 9/112; SS553151; NP 163, 175
Beaksbourne (parish), 19/282; NP 173
Beal (township in Kellington), 43/639; SE533246; NP 97
Beal and Lowlin (township in Kyloe parochial chapelry in Holy Island), 27/23; NU055425; NP 64
Beaminster (parish), 10/126; ST488023; NP 177
Beamsley (division in township of Beamsley in Skipton), 43/334; SE093523; NP 96
Beamsley (division in township of Beamsley in Addingham), 43/335; SE080520; NP 96
Beamsley (township in Skipton and Addingham), 43/334-335; NP 96
Beanfield Lawns (extra-parochial), 26/94; SP858877; NP 133
Beanley (township in Eglingham), 27/140; NU084184; NP 71
Bear Park (division in township of Elvet in St Oswald), 11/123; NZ230440; NP 85
Beard (township in Glossop), 8/10B; SK012849; NP 102, 111
Bearl (township in Bywell St Peter), 27/627; NZ068641; NP 77
Bearley (parish), 37/208; SP181603; NP 131
Bearsted (parish), 19/220; TQ798553; NP 172
Bearstone (township in Muckleston), 31/4; SJ712400; NP 119
Bearwardcote (township in Etwall), 8/255; SK282339; NP 120, 121
Beauchamp Roding (Beauchamp Roothing) (parish), 12/253; TL598102; NP 148, 161
Beauchief (extra-parochial), 8/53; SK333818; NP 111
Beaudesert (parish), 37/230; SP158675; NP 131
Beaulieu (parish), 14/328; SU390000; NP 180
Beaumanor (division in Barrow upon Soar), 21/48; SK533167; NP 121
Beaumaris (parish), 44/67; SH593760; NP 106, 107
Beaumont (parish), 7/102; NY343598; NP 76
Beaumont cum Moze (Beaumont) (parish), 12/114; TM191253; NP 150
Beaumont Chase (extra-parochial), 30/43; SP846996; NP 122, 133
Beaumont Leys (extra-parochial), 21/188; SK563077; NP 121
Beausale (hamlet in Hatton), 37/171; SP250688; NP 131
Beauworth (Beaworth) (parish), 14/336; SU569251; NP 168
Beaworth (parish), 14/336; NP 168
Beaworthy (parish), 9/190; SX477967; NP 175
Bebington (parish), 5/438-442; NP 100

Bebside (township in Horton parochial chapelry in Woodhorn), 27/479; NZ272809; NP 78
Beccles (parish), 34/26; TM430908; NP 137
Beck Row (division in Mildenhall), 34/110C; TL690770; NP 135
Beckbury (parish), 31/475; SJ769017; NP 119
Beckenham (parish), 19/64; TQ377690; NP 170, 171
Beckett (tithing in Shrivenham), 2/42; SU259894; NP 157
Beckford (hamlet in Beckford), 13/39; SP981360; NP 143
Beckford (parish), 13/40-41; NP 143, 144
Beckingham (parish), 12/231; NP 149, 162
Beckingham (Beckingham and Sutton) (parish), 22/544; SK883534; NP 113
Beckingham (parish), 28/11; SK780900; NP 104
Beckington (parish), 32/97; ST813522; NP 166
Beckley (hamlet in Beckley), 29/230; SP570130; NP 145, 158
Beckley (parish), 29/230-232; NP 145, 158
Beckley (parish), 36/143; TQ855238; NP 184
Bedale (parish), 42/209-214; NP 91
Bedale (township in Bedale), 42/212; SE265880; NP 91
Beddingham (parish), 36/322; TQ450065; NP 183
Beddington (division in Beddington), 35/49; TQ300640; NP 170
Beddington (parish), 35/49-50; NP 170
Bedfield (parish), 34/253; TM227664; NP 137
Bedfont (parish), 24/123; NP 170
Bedford (township in Leigh), 20/578; SJ675985; NP 101
Bedford, St Cuthbert (parish), 1/45; TL063497; NP 147
Bedford, St John (division in Bedford Eastern Ward in Bedford, St John), 1/49A; TL053493; NP 147
Bedford, St John (division in Bedford Western Ward in Bedford, St John), 1/49B; TL051494; NP 147
Bedford, St John (parish), 1/49A-B; NP 147
Bedford, St Mary (division in Bedford Eastern Ward in Bedford, St Mary), 1/48A; TL045490; NP 147
Bedford, St Mary (division in Bedford Western Ward in Bedford, St Mary), 1/48B; TL054484; NP 147
Bedford, St Mary (parish), 1/48A-B; NP 147
Bedford, St Paul (division in Bedford Eastern Ward in Bedford, St Paul), 1/47A; TL042507; NP 147
Bedford, St Paul (division in Bedford Western Ward in Bedford, St Paul), 1/47B; TL052498; NP 147
Bedford, St Paul (parish), 1/47A-B; NP 147
Bedford, St Peter (division in Bedford Eastern Ward in Bedford, St Peter), 1/46A; TL052512; NP 147
Bedford, St Peter (division in Bedford Western Ward in Bedford, St Peter), 1/46B; TL048503; NP 147
Bedford, St Peter (parish), 1/46A-B; NP 147
Bedgellert (division in Bedgellert), 48/34; SH605515; NP 106, 107, 116
Bedgellert (parish), 48/34, 52/1; NP 106, 107, 116
Bedhampton (parish), 14/281; SU702080; NP 181
Bedingfield (Bedingfeld) (parish), 34/174; TM183683; NP 137
Bedingham (parish), 25/630; TM289920; NP 137
Bedlington (parish), 27/428-433
Bedlington (township in Bedlington), 27/432; NZ259821; NP 78
Bedminster (division in Bedminster), 32/1A; ST583714; NP 155
Bedminster (division in Bedminster), 32/1B; ST583697; NP 155, 156, 165
Bedminster (parish), 32/1A-B; NP 155, 156, 165
Bedw-syth (township in Carno), 54/117; SN974985; NP 128
Bedwas (parish), 51/132, 53/154-155; NP 154
Bedwas Lower (hamlet in Bedwas), 53/154; ST178899; NP 154
Bedwas Upper (hamlet in Bedwas), 53/155; ST163921; NP 154
Bedwellty (parish), 53/69A-C; NP 154
Bedworth (parish), 37/69; SP350870; NP 132
Beeby (parish), 21/125; SK663082; NP 121, 122
Beech (township in Stone), 33/54; SJ851382; NP 119
Beech Hill (tithing in Stratfield Saye), 2/190; SU701644; NP 169
Beechamwell All Saints (Beachamwell All Saints) (parish), 25/512; TF761059; NP 124, 125
Beechamwell St John (parish), 25/511; NP 124, 125
Beechamwell St Mary (Beachamwell St Mary and Beechamwell St John) (parish), 25/511; TF762074; NP 124, 125
Beechingstoke (parish), 39/206; SU097589; NP 167

Beeding (parish), 36/110-113; NP 170, 182
Beedon (parish), 2/116; SU480781; NP 158
Beeford (parish), 41/349-351; NP 99
Beeford (township in Beeford), 41/349; TA130540; NP 99
Beeley (parish), 8/82; SK285680; NP 111
Beeley Wood (division in township of Ecclesfield in Ecclesfield), 43/800B; SK316928; NP 102
Beelsby (parish), 22/93; TA210020; NP 105
Beenham (Beenham Valence) (parish), 2/159; SU598687; NP 158
Beer (tithing in Seaton), 9/297; SY222897; NP 177
Beer Crocombe (parish), 32/415; ST324198; NP 177
Beer Hackett (parish), 10/38; ST604118; NP 177, 178
Beerhall (division in Axminster), 10/301; ST356016; NP 177
Beesby (parish), 22/312; TF458799; NP 105
Beesby in the Marsh (Beesby) (parish), 22/312; TF458799; NP 105
Beeston (Beeston next Mileham) (parish), 25/332; TF905157; NP 125
Beeston (hamlet in Sandy), 1/59; TL172478; NP 147
Beeston (parish), 28/253; SK535365; NP 121
Beeston (township in Bunbury), 5/302; SJ537592; NP 109
Beeston (township in Leeds), 43/495; SE288307; NP 96
Beeston Regis (parish), 25/35; TG170420; NP 126
Beeston St Andrew (parish), 25/403; TG257142; NP 126
Beeston St Lawrence (parish), 25/367; TG329221; NP 126
Beetham (division of Beetham township in Beetham), 38/134; SD495790; NP 89
Beetham (parish), 38/130/135; NP 89
Beetham (township), 38/134-135
Beetley (parish), 25/269; TF265188; NP 125
Begbroke (Begbrooke) (division in Begbroke), 29/123; SP469138; NP 145
Begbroke (parish), 29/123, 196B; NP 145
Begelly (division in Begelly), 55/128; SN108085; NP 151, 152
Begelly (parish), 55/127-128; NP 151, 152
Beighton (parish), 8/56; SK424832; NP 102, 103
Beighton (parish), 25/458; TG385082; NP 126
Bekesbourne (Beaksbourne) (parish), 19/282; TR195555; NP 173
Belaugh (parish), 25/363; TG292186; NP 126
Belbank (Bellbank) (township in Bewcastle), 7/4; NY530760; NP 76
Belbank (Bellbank) (township in Stapleton), 7/5; NY510740; NP 76
Belbroughton (Bellbroughton) (parish), 40/37; SO942768; NP 130
Belby (township in Howden), 41/6; SE772283; NP 98
Belchalwell (Bellchalwell) (parish), 10/86; ST797091; NP 178
Belchamp Otton (parish), 12/38; TL802419; NP 149
Belchamp St Paul (parish), 12/36A; TL789435; NP 149
Belchamp Walter (parish), 12/438; TL823408; NP 149
Belchford (parish), 22/333; TF293759; NP 105, 114
Belfield (subdivision in Butterworth Lord's Side division in Butterworth township in Rochdale), 20/465; SD918132; NP 101
Belford (parish), 27/78-85; NP 64
Belford (township in Belford), 27/85; NU095335; NP 64
Belgrave (parish), 21/189-191; NP 121
Belgrave (township in Belgrave), 21/191; SK605067; NP 121
Belgrave, 24/36A
Belgravia (Belgrave) (division in St George Hanover Square), 24/36A; TQ283800; NP 160/1
Bellasis (township in Stannington), 27/425; NZ189782; NP 78
Bellasize (division in township of Bellasize in Eastrington), 41/20A; SE826673; NP 98/1
Bellasize (township in Eastrington), 41/20A-21; NP 98/1
Bellbank, 7/4, 7/5; NP 76
Bellbroughton (parish), 40/37; NP 130
Bellchalwell (parish), 10/86; ST797091; NP 178
Belleau (township in Belleau), 22/320; TF399789; NP 105
Bellerby (township in Spennithorne), 42/188; SE110930; NP 90, 91
Bellingham (parish), 27/276-281; NP 77

Bellingham (township in Bellingham), 27/280; NY840835; NP 77
Bellister (township in Haltwhistle), 27/578; NY693622; NP 76
Belmont (division in township of St Giles in St Giles), 11/112; NZ300440; NP 85
Belpher (township in Duffield), 8/191; SK352481; NP 111
Belsay (township in Bolam), 27/394; NZ083785; NP 77
Belstead (parish), 34/511; TM127410; NP 150
Belstone (parish), 9/426; SX621940; NP 175
Belton (Belton in Axholme) (parish), 22/6; SE782081; NP 104
Belton (parish), 21/23; SK450200; NP 121
Belton (parish), 22/620; SK937398; NP 122, 123
Belton (parish), 30/42; SK813012; NP 122, 133
Belton (parish), 34/7; TG485023; NP 126, 137
Belvoir (extra-parochial), 21/91; SK818343; NP 122
Bemersley (township in Norton in the Moors), 33/16; SJ883543; NP 110
Bempton (division in parish and township of Bempton), 41/246; TA200727; NP 93
Bempton (parish and township), 41/246-247; NP 93
Benacre (parish), 34/58; TM517841; NP 137
Benefield (parish), 26/55A-B; NP 133, 134
Benenden (parish), 19/410; TQ810329; NP 172, 184
Benfieldside (township in Lanchester), 11/158; NZ099524; NP 77, 84, 85
Bengeo (parish), 16/78; TL326152; NP 147, 148
Bengeworth (St Peters, Bengeworth) (parish), 40/205; SP050430; NP 143
Benhall (parish), 34/272; TM371619; NP 137
Beningbrough (township in Newton upon Ouse), 42/588; SE526487; NP 97
Beningholme and Grange (Benningholme and Grange) (township in Swine), 41/391; TA123385; NP 99
Benington (Bennington) (parish), 16/52; TL298232; NP 147
Benington (division in Benington), 22/759A; TF400460; NP 114, 124
Benington - East Fen (division in Benington), 22/759B; TF361565; NP 114
Benington, 22/759A-B; NP 114, 124
Bennetland (common to Hive and Gilberdyke divisions in township of Gilberdyke in Eastrington), 41/19E; SE854303; NP 98/1
Bennetland (division in township of Bellasize in Eastrington), 41/20B; SE827286; NP 98/1
Bennington (parish), 16/52; NP 147
Bennington Grange (extra-parochial), 22/613; SK835408; NP 122
Benningworth (parish), 22/342; NP 105
Benniworth (Benningworth) (parish), 22/342; TF210816; NP 105
Benridge (township in Mitford), 27/407; NZ167877; NP 78
Bensington, 29/301; NP 158
Benson (Bensington) (hamlet in Benson), 29/301; SU624921; NP 158
Benson (Bensington) (parish), 29/301-302; NP 158
Bentfield (hamlet in Stanstead Mountfitchet), 12/71; TL504257; NP 148
Benthall (division in Alberbury Lower Quarter township in Alberbury), 31/296; SJ392140; NP 118
Benthall (parish), 31/466; SJ661026; NP 119
Bentham (parish), 43/267-274; NP 89, 90
Bentham (township in Bentham), 43/267-270; NP 89, 90
Bentley (hamlet in Shustoke), 37/74; SP278950; NP 131, 132
Bentley (parish), 14/116; SU790449; NP 169
Bentley (parish), 34/513; TM118375; NP 150
Bentley (township in Wolverhampton), 33/316; SO985995; NP 119, 130
Bentley (township in Rowley), 41/218; TA022360; NP 99
Bentley Pauncefoot (township in Tardebigge), 40/52; SO988658; NP 130, 131
Bentley with Arksey (parish), 43/934; SE572062; NP 103
Bentley, 8/231; NP 120
Bentworth (parish), 14/130; SU666400; NP 168, 169
Benwell (township in St John), 27/648; NZ211643; NP 78
Benwick (hamlet in Doddington), 4/16; TL342905; NP 134, 135

Beoley (parish), 40/47; SP065705; NP 131
Bepton (parish), 36/16; SU859183; NP 181
Berden (parish), 12/66; TL475295; NP 148
Bere Ferrers (Beerferris) (parish), 9/360; SX452658; NP 187
Bere Regis (division in Bere Regis), 10/202; SY856953; NP 178
Bere Regis (parish), 10/202-204; NP 178
Berechurch (parish), 12/178; TL990217; NP 149
Bergh Apton (parish), 25/576; NP 126, 137
Berghill (township in Whittington), 31/87; SJ354304; NP 118
Berkeley (borough in Berkeley), 13/320; ST683992; NP 156
Berkeley (parish), 13/316-322; NP 156
Berkeswell (parish), 37/95; SP249788; NP 131
Berkhampstead St Mary (parish), 16/141; SP969081; NP 147, 159
Berkhampstead St Peter (parish), 16/142; SP989091; NP 147, 159
Berkhamstead (Berkhampstead St Peter) (parish), 16/142; SP989091; NP 147, 159
Berkley (parish), 32/125; ST810496; NP 166
Berkswell (Berkeswell) (parish), 37/95; SP249788; NP 131
Berners Roding (Berners Roothing) (parish), 12/252; TL606096; NP 148, 161
Berrick Salome (parish), 29/295; SU621942; NP 158
Berrier and Murrah (township in Greystoke), 7/209; NY390304; NP 83
Berriew (parish), 54/104; SJ170010; NP 117, 128
Berrington (Berringtonlaw, Berrington Law) (township in Kyloe parochial chapelry in Holy Island), 27/22; NT989438; NP 64
Berrington Law, 27/22; NP 64
Berringtonlaw, 27/22; NP 64
Berrington (parish), 31/280-284; NP 118
Berrington (township in Berrington), 31/281; SJ529069; NP 118
Berrington (township in Tenbury), 40/83; SO569669; NP 129
Berrow (parish), 32/171; ST303536; NP 165
Berrow (parish), 40/232; SO787345; NP 143
Berry Pomeroy (parish), 9/428; SX835616; NP 188
Berrynarbor (parish), 9/3; SS565450; NP 163
Bersham (township in Wrexham [Wrecsam]), 49/52; SJ305505; NP 109
Berwic (Berwick) (hamlet in Llanelli), 47/83E; SS545995; NP 153
Berwick (parish), 36/325; TQ523054; NP 183
Berwick (township in Atcham), 31/239; SJ540107; NP 118
Berwick Bassett (parish), 39/107; SU098735; NP 157
Berwick Hill (township in Ponteland), 27/521; NZ176756; NP 78
Berwick Street (division in St James Westminster), 24/37C; TQ295810; NP 160/1
Berwick St James (parish), 39/297; SU066397; NP 167
Berwick St John (parish), 39/343; ST958215; NP 167, 179
Berwick St Leonard (parish), 39/281; ST924342; NP 166, 167
Berwick upon Tweed (parish), 27/1; NT969545; NP 64
Berwick, 47/83E; NP 153
Bescaby (extra-parochial), 21/100; SK824260; NP 122
Besford (chapelry in St Andrew Pershore), 40/176; SO912466; NP 143
Besford (township in Shawbury), 31/162; SJ552252; NP 118
Bessels Leigh (parish), 2/22; SP458013; NP 158
Bessingby (parish), 41/249; TA164664; NP 93
Bessingham (parish), 25/59; TG168369; NP 126
Besthorpe (parish), 25/665; TM078961; NP 136
Besthorpe (township in South Scarle), 28/124; SK833642; NP 113
Bestwood (extra-parochial), 28/182; SK564576; NP 112, 121
Beswick (division in township of Beswick in Kilnwick), 41/287A; TA020480; NP 98, 99
Beswick (township in Manchester), 20/515; SJ865985; NP 101
Beswick (township in Kilnwick), 41/287A-B; NP 98, 99
Betchcott (Batchcott) (township in Smethcott), 31/339B; SO432984; NP 129
Betchton (township in Sandbach), 5/218; SJ786589; NP 110
Betchworth (parish), 35/118; TQ206495; NP 170
Bethecar Moor (division in township of Colton in Colton), 20/56; SD308908; NP 89

Bethersden (parish), 19/404; TQ926405; NP 172
Bethnal Green (parish), 24/63A-D; NP 160/1
Betley (parish), 33/44; SJ759483; NP 110
Betteshanger (Betshanger) (parish), 19/273; TR321531; NP 173
Bettiscombe (parish), 10/129; ST401001; NP 177
Bettisfield (township in Hanmer), 50/140; SJ461362; NP 118
Betton (township in Drayton in Hales), 31/8; SJ682368; NP 119
Betton (township in St Chad Shrewsbury), 31/273A; SJ512091; NP 118
Betton Abbots (township in Berrington), 31/280; SJ520080; NP 118
Bettws (Bettws Cedewain, Bettws Caederven) (parish), 54/105-108; NP 117, 128
Bettws (parish), 47/26; NP 153
Bettws (parish), 51/63; NP 153, 154
Bettws (parish), 53/121; ST288908; NP 154, 155
Bettws Abergele (parish), 49/5; NP 108
Bettws Bledrws (Bettws Bleddrws) (parish), 46/71; SN591524; NP 140
Bettws Caederven (parish), 54/105-108; NP 117, 128
Bettws Cedewain (parish), 54/105-108; NP 117, 128
Bettws Clyro (township in Clyro), 56/55B; SO225465; NP 141
Bettws Disserth (parish), 56/41; SO105578; NP 128
Bettws Evan (parish), 46/95; NP 139
Bettws Gwerfil Goch (parish), 52/15; SJ022483; NP 108
Bettws Ifan (Bettws Evan) (parish), 46/95; SN302477; NP 139
Bettws Leiki, 46/51; NP 140
Bettws Newydd (parish), 53/50; SO365063; NP 155
Bettws y Coed, 48/19; NP 107, 116
Bettws-y-crwyn (parish), 31/402-404; NP 128
Bettws-yn-Rhos (parish), 49/5; NP 108
Bettwsgarmon (parish), 48/35; NP 106, 107
Betws (Bettws) (parish), 47/26; SN995115; NP 153
Betws (Bettws) (parish), 51/63; SS895895; NP 153, 154
Betws Garmon (Bettwsgarmon, Bettws Garmon) (parish), 48/35; SH557562; NP 106, 107
Betws-y-Coed (Bettws y Coed) (parish), 48/19; SH780570; NP 107, 116
Betws-yn-Rhos (parish), 49/5; SH888728; NP 108
Bevercotes (Bevercoates) (parish), 28/72; SK698717; NP 112
Beverley Parks (division in township of Woodmansey and Beverley Parks in St John Beverley), 41/297; TA044371; NP 99
Beverston (Beverstone) (parish), 13/334; ST858940; NP 156
Bevill's Wood (extra-parochial), 17/61; TL204794; NP 134
Bewaldeth and Snittlegarth (township in Torpenhow), 7/234; NY219347; NP 82
Bewbush (Baybush) (division in Upper Beeding tithing in Beeding), 36/112; TQ231349; NP 170, 182
Bewcastle (parish), 7/1-4; NP 76
Bewcastle (township in Bewcastle), 7/3; NY580770; NP 76
Bewdley (borough in Ribbesford), 40/74; SO772749; NP 130
Bewerley (township in Ripon), 43/159; SE130650; NP 91
Bewholme and Nunkeeling (township in Nunkeeling), 41/358; TA156504; NP 99
Bewick (division in township of Bewick and East Newton in Aldborough), 41/379; TA238398; NP 99
Bewick and East Newton (township in Aldborough), 41/379-380; NP 99
Bexhill (division in Bexhill), 36/178; TQ728087; NP 183, 184
Bexhill (parish), 36/178-179; NP 183, 184
Bexley (parish), 19/17; TQ477742; NP 171
Bexton (township in Knutsford), 5/106; SJ746773; NP 101
Bexwell (parish), 25/524; TF635025; NP 124
Beyton (parish), 34/233; TL938632; NP 136
Bibury (parish), 13/232-235; NP 144, 157
Bibury (tithing in Bibury), 13/232; SP125075; NP 157
Bicester (parish), 29/79-80; NP 145
Bicester, King's End (township in Bicester), 29/80; SP570223; NP 145
Bicester, Market End (township in Bicester), 29/79; SP593217; NP 145
Bickenhall (parish), 32/432; ST288186; NP 177
Bickenhill (parish), 37/78; SP193835; NP 132

Bicker (parish), 22/737; TF212381; NP 123
Bickerstaffe (township in Ormskirk), 20/364; SD450040; NP 100
Bickerston (Bickerstone) (hamlet in Burnham Broome), 25/557; TG090093; NP 125
Bickerton (township in Malpas), 5/336; SJ511535; NP 109
Bickerton (township in Rothbury), 27/259; NY999996; NP 71
Bickerton (township in Bilton), 43/77; SE450506; NP 97
Bickington (parish), 9/408; SX802722; NP 175, 188
Bickleigh (parish), 9/156; SS944060; NP 176
Bickleigh (parish), 9/364; SX518627; NP 187
Bickley (township in Malpas), 5/332; SJ532486; NP 109
Bickmarsh and Little Dorsington (hamlet in Welford), 37/213; SP110488; NP 144
Bicknoller (parish), 32/256; ST113390; NP 164
Bicknor (parish), 19/166; TQ859584; NP 172
Bicton (parish), 9/304; SY059858; NP 176
Bicton (township in Clun), 31/399; SO292828; NP 129
Bicton and Calcott (township in St Chad Shrewsbury), 31/270; SJ444147; NP 118
Bidborough (parish), 19/204; TQ568436; NP 171
Biddenden (parish), 19/406; TQ849382; NP 172, 184
Biddenham (parish), 1/50; TL023500; NP 147
Biddestone St Nicholas (parish), 39/116A; ST860740; NP 156
Biddestone St Peter (parish), 39/116B; ST866734; NP 156
Biddick Waterville, 11/52; NP 78
Biddisham (parish), 32/160; ST385540; NP 165
Biddlesden (parish), 3/9; SP620390; NP 145
Biddleston (Biddlestone) (township in Alwinton), 27/179; NT953085; NP 71
Biddulph (parish), 33/1; SJ885575; NP 110
Bideford (parish), 9/44; SS460260; NP 163
Bidford (parish), 37/193; SP100520; NP 144
Bidston (parish), 5/447-450; NP 100
Bidston cum Ford (township in Bidston), 5/448; SJ282902; NP 100
Bielby (township in Hayton), 41/98; SE792439; NP 98
Bierton with Boughton (parish), 3/169; SP842152; NP 146
Bieston (Breston) (township in Wrexham [Wrecsam]), 49/58; SJ364526; NP 109
Bigbury (parish), 9/473; SX667470; NP 187
Bigby (parish), 22/64; TA039074; NP 104
Biggar (division of Isle of Walney Sub-Division of Hawcoat Division of Dalton township in Dalton in Furness), 20/30; SD195645; NP 88
Bigges Quarter (township in Longhorsley), 27/293; NZ145965; NP 71, 78
Biggin (division in Newton and Biggin township in Clifton upon Dunsmore), 37/120; SP539782; NP 132
Biggin (township in Wirksworth), 8/155; SK262482; NP 111
Biggin (township in Church Fenton), 43/446; SE542344; NP 97
Biggleswade (parish), 1/67; TL203440; NP 147
Bighton (parish), 14/169; SU619349; NP 168
Biglands and Gamelsby (Gamblesby) (township in Aikton), 7/120; NY253534; NP 75
Bignall End (township in Audley), 33/42F; SJ810520; NP 110
Bignor (division in Bignor), 36/77; SU985141; NP 181
Bignor (parish), 36/19, 77; NP 181
Bilborough (parish), 28/243; SK527422; NP 121
Bilbrough (parish), 43/65; SE528468; NP 97
Bilby (township in Blyth), 28/24; SK639831; NP 103
Bildeston (Bildestone) (parish), 34/354; TL995495; NP 149
Biley cum Yatehouses, 5/194; NP 110
Bilham (division of Bilham township in Barnburgh), 43/870; SE486059; NP 103
Bilham (division of Bilham township in Hooton Pagnell), 43/871; SE489068; NP 103
Bilham (township in Barnburgh and Hooton Pagnell), 43/870-871; NP 103
Billericay (hamlet in Great Burstead), 12/334B; TQ673943; NP 161
Billesdon (parish), 21/284-285; NP 122, 133
Billesdon (township in Billesdon), 21/285; SK720035; NP 122
Billesley (parish), 37/198; SP151568; NP 131

Billingborough (parish), 22/659; TF128338; NP 123
Billinge Chapel End (township in Wigan), 20/592; SJ529999; NP 100
Billinge Higher End (township in Wigan), 20/591; SD521017; NP 100
Billingford (parish), 25/267; TG011212; NP 125
Billingford (Pierleston) (parish), 25/760; TM174793; NP 137
Billingham (parish), 11/258-261; NP 85
Billingham (township in Billingham), 11/260; NZ468228; NP 85
Billinghay (hamlet in Billinghay), 22/572; TF166562; NP 113, 114
Billinghay, 22/571-573B; TF166562; NP 113, 114
Billingley (township in Darfield), 43/860; SE434043; NP 103
Billingshurst (parish), 36/66; TQ097261; NP 182
Billingside (township in Lanchester), 11/156; NZ136527; NP 78, 84, 85
Billingsley (parish), 31/554; SO715845; NP 130
Billington (hamlet in Leighton Buzzard), 1/139; SP940219; NP 146, 147
Billington Langho (township in Blackburn), 20/311; SD711354; NP 95
Billockby (parish), 25/390A; TG431135; NP 126
Bilsborough, 20/152; NP 94
Bilsborrow (Bilsborough) (township in Garstang), 20/152; SD527403; NP 94
Bilsby (parish), 22/406; TF479765; NP 105, 114
Bilsdale Kirkham (division in township of Bilsdale Midcable in Helmsley), 42/484; NZ570010; NP 92
Bilsdale Low Midcable (division in township of Bilsdale Midcable in Helmsley), 42/482; SE595975; NP 92
Bilsdale Midcable (township in Helmsley), 42/482-485; NP 92
Bilsdale West (Bilsdale West Side) (township in Hawnby), 42/502; SE560914; NP 91
Bilsdale West (sub-division of Bilsdale Midcable division in township of Bilsdale Midcable in Helmsley), 42/483; SE553970; NP 92
Bilsington (parish), 19/400; TR039347; NP 172, 184
Bilsthorpe (parish), 28/137; SK649595; NP 112
Bilston (township in Wolverhampton), 33/319; SO951965; NP 119
Bilstone (township in Norton juxta Twycross), 21/143B; SK362051; NP 121
Bilton (division in township of Bilton in Bilton), 43/79; SE471503; NP 97
Bilton (parish), 37/127; SP490737; NP 132
Bilton (parish), 43/77-80; NP 97
Bilton (township in Lesbury), 27/205; NU221107; NP 71
Bilton (township in Swine), 41/388; TA153323; NP 99
Bilton (township in Bilton), 43/78-79; NP 97
Bilton with Harrogate (township in Knaresborough), 43/142; SE318562; NP 96
Binbrook, St Gabriel (parish), 22/165B; TF225935; NP 105
Binbrook, St Mary (parish), 22/165A; TF205925; NP 105
Binchester (township in St Andrew Auckland), 11/208; NZ212325; NP 85
Bincombe (parish), 10/254; SY686847; NP 178
Binderton (parish), 36/231; SU842115; NP 181
Binegar (parish), 32/111; ST623498; NP 166
Binfield (parish), 2/128; SU850720; NP 159, 169
Bingfield (township in St John Lee), 27/446; NY983725; NP 77
Bingham (parish), 28/223; SK709392; NP 122
Bingley (division in township of Bingley in Bingley), 43/359; SE102392; NP 96
Bingley (parish), 43/358-361; NP 96
Bingley (township in Bingley), 43/358-360; NP 96
Binham (parish), 25/22; TF975400; NP 125
Binley (parish), 37/155; SP388777; NP 132
Binnington (township in Willerby), 41/159; TA000780; NP 93
Binsey (parish), 29/204A; SP492076; NP 145
Binstead (Binsted) (parish), 14/117; SU788412; NP 169
Binstead (parish), 18/17; SZ546893; NP 180
Binsted (Binsted) (parish), 36/283; SU986062; NP 181
Binton (parish), 37/197; SP148544; NP 131, 144
Bintree (Bintry) (parish), 25/196; TG010234; NP 125

Bintry (parish), 25/196; NP 125
Binweston (township in Worthen), 31/326; SJ299045; NP 117, 118
Birch (Great and Little Birch) (parish), 12/182; TL941198; NP 149
Birch (township in Baschurch), 31/143; SJ401239; NP 118
Bircham Newton (parish), 25/100; TF770345; NP 125
Bircham Tofts (parish), 25/101; TF782318; NP 125
Birchanger (parish), 12/69; TL509228; NP 148
Birches (township in Great Budworth), 5/133; SJ699728; NP 110
Birchington (parish), 19/125; TR298691; NP 173
Bircholt (parish), 19/329; TR075414; NP 172
Birchover (township in Youlgreave), 8/118; SK244619; NP 111
Birdbrook (parish), 12/31; TL713412; NP 148
Birdforth (township in Coxwold), 42/557; SE485762; NP 91
Birdham (parish), 36/267; SU822001; NP 181
Birdingbury (parish), 37/234; SP432672; NP 132
Birdsall (parish), 41/143; SE822643; NP 92
Birk Dale (division in township of Muker in Grinton), 42/125; NY830020; NP 84, 90
Birkbeck Fells (township in Orton), 38/72; NY592060; NP 83
Birkbeck Fells (township in Orton), 38/73B; NY590070; NP 83
Birkbeck Fells Common (undivided common in Orton), 38/73A; NY575075; NP 83
Birkby (division in township of Shadwell in Thorner), 43/413; SE369394; NP 96
Birkby (parish), 42/64-66; NP 91
Birkby (township in Birkby), 42/65; NZ343012; NP 91
Birkdale (township in North Meols), 20/354; SD326147; NP 100
Birkdale Fells (district in Crosby Ravensworth), 38/30; NY582092; NP 83
Birkenhead (chapelry in Birkenhead), 5/443; SJ312890; NP 100
Birker and Austhwaite (township in Millom), 7/319; SD201999; NP 88
Birkin (parish), 43/456-460; NP 97
Birkin (township in Birkin), 43/460; SE528274; NP 97
Birkrigg Common (common to townships of Urswick and Aldingham in Urswick), 20/35; SD286745; NP 88
Birley (parish), 15/62; SO454538; NP 129, 142
Birley Carr (division in township of Ecclesfield in Ecclesfield), 43/800A; SK328922; NP 102
Birling (parish), 19/178; TQ679610; NP 171
Birling (township in Warkworth), 27/222; NU250071; NP 71
Birlingham (Nafford and Birlingham) (parish), 40/218; SO933430; NP 143
Birmingham (parish), 37/43-52; NP 131
Birmingham All Saints (division in Birmingham), 37/52; SP052880; NP 131
Birmingham Ladywood (division in Birmingham), 37/43; SP057867; NP 131
Birmingham Ladywood (division in Birmingham), 37/44; SP041871; NP 131
Birmingham Ladywood (divisions in Birmingham), 37/43-44; NP 131
Birmingham St George (division in Birmingham), 37/51; SP066885; NP 131
Birmingham St Martin (division in Birmingham), 37/46; SP065859; NP 131
Birmingham St Mary (division in Birmingham), 37/50; SP074876; NP 131
Birmingham St Paul (division in Birmingham), 37/49; SP061876; NP 131
Birmingham St Peter (division in Birmingham), 37/47; SP077867; NP 131
Birmingham St Philip (division in Birmingham), 37/48; SP070870; NP 131
Birmingham St Thomas (division in Birmingham), 37/45; SP063863; NP 131
Birstal (parish), 43/536-545; NP 96
Birstall (chapelry in Belgrave), 21/189; SK592091; NP 121
Birstwith (township in Hampsthwaite), 43/155B; SE231586; NP 91, 96
Birthorpe (hamlet in Sempringham), 22/662; TF100339; NP 123

Birtle (division in township of Birtle cum Bamford in Middleton), 20/473; SD822141; NP 101
Birtle cum Bamford (township in Middleton), 20/472; SD833119; NP 101
Birtle cum Bamford (township in Middleton), 20/472-473; NP 101
Birtles (township in Prestbury), 5/52; SJ864742; NP 101, 110
Birtley (parochial chapelry in Chollerton), 27/366-368; NP 77
Birtley (township in Chester le Street), 11/40; NZ275558; NP 78
Birtley (township in parochial chapelry of Birtley in Chollerton), 27/366; NY885795; NP 77
Birtsmorton (parish), 40/231; SO796359; NP 143
Bisbrooke (parish), 30/53; SP888998; NP 122, 133
Biscathorpe (Biskathorpe) (parish), 22/276; TF228849; NP 105
Biscot, 1/122; NP 147
Bisham (parish), 2/208; SU850833; NP 159
Bishampton (parish), 40/190; SO993511; NP 143, 144
Bishop Auckland (Bondgate in Auckland) (township in St Andrew Auckland), 11/201; NZ198293; NP 85
Bishop Burton (parish), 41/221; SE982392; NP 98, 99
Bishop Middleham (parish), 11/226-229; NP 85
Bishop Middleham (township in Bishop Middleham), 11/229; NZ331318; NP 85
Bishop Monkton (township in Ripon), 43/170; SE325663; NP 91
Bishop Norton (parish), 22/152-153; NP 104
Bishop Norton (township in Bishop Norton), 22/152; SK988924; NP 104
Bishop Thornton (township in Ripon), 43/165-166; NP 91
Bishop Wearmouth (division in township of Bishop Wearmouth in Bishop Wearmouth), 11/77; NZ402572; NP 78
Bishop Wearmouth (parish), 11/70-79; NP 78
Bishop Wearmouth (township in Bishop Wearmouth), 11/73-75, 77; NP 78
Bishop Wearmouth North (division in township of Bishop Wearmouth in Bishop Wearmouth), 11/74; NZ388571; NP 78
Bishop Wearmouth Pans (township in Bishop Wearmouth), 11/76; NZ400574; NP 78
Bishop Wearmouth South (division in township of Bishop Wearmouth in Bishop Wearmouth), 11/75; NZ386558; NP 78
Bishop Wilton (parish), 41/110-113; NP 98
Bishop Wilton with Belthorpe (township in Bishop Wilton), 41/110; SE802556; NP 98
Bishop's Caundle (Caundle Bishop) (parish), 10/48; ST695130; NP 178
Bishop's Cleeve (hamlet in Bishop's Cleeve), 13/60; SO951276; NP 143
Bishop's Cleeve (parish), 13/58-62; NP 143, 144
Bishop's Castle (borough and township in Bishop's Castle), 31/382; SO321886; NP 129
Bishop's Castle (parish), 31/378-382; NP 129
Bishop's Hull (division inside Taunton borough in Bishop's Hull), 32/327A; ST219245; NP 177
Bishop's Hull (division outside Taunton borough in Bishop's Hull), 32/327B; ST204248; NP 164, 177
Bishop's Hull (parish), 32/327A-B; NP 164, 177
Bishop's Itchington (parish), 37/253; SP392566; NP 132, 145
Bishop's Nympton (parish), 9/75; SS766255; NP 163, 164
Bishop's Offley (township in Adbaston), 33/159; SJ778298; NP 119
Bishop's Palace (extra-parochial), 22/507; SK978717; NP 113/1
Bishop's Sutton (parish), 14/170; SU612319; NP 168
Bishop's Stortford (parish), 16/67; TL486214; NP 148
Bishop's Tawton (parish), 9/36; SS582287; NP 163
Bishop's Tachbrook (hamlet in Bishop's Tachbrook), 37/225A; SP308608; NP 132
Bishop's Tachbrook (parish), 37/225A-B; NP 132
Bishop's Waltham (parish), 14/255; SU556172; NP 168, 180
Bishopdale (township in Aysgarth), 42/141; SD967828; NP 90
Bishoper (division in Hankerton), 39/23C; ST943911; NP 157
Bishopley (division in Newlandside and Bishopley township in Stanhope), 11/175; NY026361; NP 84
Bishops Cannings (Bishops Cannings, Horton, Bourton and Easton) (division in Bishops Cannings), 39/132A; SU048654; NP 157, 167

Bishops Cannings (pariash), 39/132A-133; NP 157, 167
Bishops Frome (Froome Bishop) (township in Bishops Frome), 15/156; SO667481; NP 143
Bishops Hatfield (parish), 16/105; NP 147, 160
Bishops Lavington (parish), 39/224-225; NP 167
Bishops Lavington, 39/224
Bishops Lydeard (parish), 32/296; ST172295; NP 164, 165
Bishopsbourne (Bishopsbourn) (parish), 19/284; TR181519; NP 173
Bishopsteignton (parish), 9/397; SX907754; NP 188
Bishopstoke (parish), 14/257; SU490188; NP 168, 180
Bishopstone (parish), 15/116; SO418432; NP 142
Bishopstone (Bishopston) (parish), 36/334; TQ471014; NP 183
Bishopstone (parish), 39/100; SU252826; NP 157
Bishopstone (parish), 39/350; SU072158; NP 167
Bishopston (Bishopstone) (parish), 51/44; SS578902; NP 153
Bishopstone (parish), 51/44; NP 153
Bishopstrow (parish), 39/237; ST908452; NP 166
Bishopthorpe (parish), 43/56; SE590473; NP 97
Bishopton (parish), 11/267-269; NP 85
Bishopton (township in Bishopton), 11/267; NZ367211; NP 85
Bishopton (hamlet in Old Stratford), 37/204; SP183572; NP 131
Bishopton (township in Ripon), 43/181; SE299711; NP 91
Bishton (parish), 53/138; ST392876; NP 155
Biskathorpe (parish), 22/276; NP 105
Bisley (parish), 13/274; SO897052; NP 156, 157
Bisley (parish), 35/78; SU950591; NP 169
Bispham (division in township of Bispham with Norbreck in Bispham), 20/178; SD316398; NP 94
Bispham (parish), 20/177-179; NP 94
Bispham (township in Croston), 20/348; SD486129; NP 100
Bispham with Norbreck (township in Bispham), 20/177-178; NP 94
Bistre (township in Mold), 50/118; SJ277627; NP 108, 109
Bitchfield (parish), 22/685; SK989285; NP 123
Bitchfield (township in Stamfordham), 27/456; NZ099774; NP 77
Bittadon (parish), 9/19; SS546427; NP 163
Bitterley (parish), 31/529-532; NP 129
Bitterley (township in Bitterley), 31/531A; SO570775; NP 129
Bitterne (Bittern and Pollack) (tithing in South Stoneham), 14/260; SU443137; NP 180
Bitterscote (township in Tamworth), 33/285E; SK200035; NP 120
Bittesby (township in Claybrooke), 21/237; SP501856; NP 132
Bitteswell (parish), 21/239; SP529868; NP 132
Bitton (hamlet in Bitton), 13/402; ST688707; NP 156
Bitton (parish), 13/402-404; NP 156
Bix (parish), 29/307; SU725865; NP 159
Bixley (parish), 25/482; TG260050; NP 126
Blaby (parish), 21/247-248; NP 132
Blaby (township in Blaby), 21/247; SP575964; NP 132
Black Bourton (parish), 29/166; SP303062; NP 145
Black Callerton (township in Newburn), 27/534; NZ176698; NP 78
Black Carts and Rye Hill (extra-parochial), 27/609; NY898712; NP 77
Black Heddon (township in Stamfordham), 27/457; NZ077761; NP 77
Black Notley (parish), 12/191; TL759202; NP 148, 149
Black Torrington (parish), 9/106; SS455052; NP 175
Blackawton (parish), 9/481; SX812502; NP 187, 188
Blackborough (parish), 9/150; ST096097; NP 164, 176
Blackburn (parish), 20/303-325; NP 94, 95, 101
Blackburn (township in Blackburn), 20/308; SD685280; NP 95
Blackden (township in Sandbach), 5/211; SJ788704; NP 110
Blackford (parish), 32/376; ST660262; NP 166
Blackfordby (township in Ashby de la Zouch), 21/8; SK331181; NP 121
Blackhall High Quarter, 7/81; NP 76
Blackhall Low Quarter, 7/82; NP 76
Blackland (parish), 39/375; SU016685; NP 157
Blackley (Blakeley) (township in Manchester), 20/510; SD855035; NP 101

59

Blackmanstone (parish), 19/426; TR075293; NP 184
Blackmore (parish), 12/297; TL602017; NP 161
Blacko (township in Whalley), 20/261; SD864415; NP 95
Blackrod (township in Bolton-le-Moors), 20/407B; SD620100; NP 100, 101
Blackthorn (hamlet in Ambrosden), 29/113; SP620200; NP 145
Blacktoft (parish), 41/23-24; NP 98, 98/1
Blacktoft (township in Blacktoft), 41/23; SE841260; NP 98, 98/1
Blackwall (township in Kirk Ireton), 8/159B; SK254492; NP 111
Blackwell (parish), 8/139; SK442586; NP 112
Blackwell (township in Bakewell), 8/106; SK120720; NP 111
Blackwell (township in Darlington), 11/324; NZ283125; NP 85
Blackwell (hamlet in Tredington), 40/255; SP240433; NP 144
Blackwood and Crowborough (township in Horton), 33/2B; SJ930570; NP 110
Blacon cum Crabhall (township in Holy Trinity Chester), 5/520; SJ384685; NP 109
Bladon (hamlet in Bladon), 29/194; SP449146; NP 145
Bladon (parish), 29/194-195; NP 145
Blaen-Aeron (township in Caron), 46/38F; SN660640; NP 127, 140
Blaen-caron (township in Caron), 46/38C; SN680600; NP 140
Blaengwrach (chapelry in Glyncorrwg), 51/55; SN890050; NP 153
Blaenhonddau (hamlet in Cadoxton Juxta Neath), 51/14; SN670003; NP 153
Blaenpennal (Blaenpenal) (township in Llandewi-Brefi), 46/41; SN625655; NP 127, 140
Blaenporth (parish), 46/96; SN268488; NP 139
Blagdon (parish), 32/71; ST502580; NP 165
Blagdon (township in Stannington), 27/427; NZ221763; NP 78
Blagrave (tithing in Lambourn), 2/107A; SU310760; NP 158
Blainey with Duffryn (township in Llangynidir), 45/75A; SO150190; NP 141
Blaisdon (parish), 13/147; SO705174; NP 143
Blakeley, 20/510; NP 101
Blakemere (Blakemore) (parish), Preston on Wye (parish), 15/200; SO363409; NP 142
Blakeney (parish), 25/26; TG028434; NP 125
Blakeney, 13/172; NP 156
Blakenhall (township in Wybunbury), 5/265; SJ730479; NP 110
Blakesley (hamlet in Blakesley), 26/317; SP632510; NP 145
Blakesley (parish), 26/317-318; NP 145
Blandford Forum (parish), 10/165; ST887066; NP 178
Blandford St Mary (parish), 10/181; ST874045; NP 178
Blankney (parish), 22/562-563; NP 113
Blankney (township in Blankney), 22/562; TF064602; NP 113
Blankney Walk (division of East Dean township in Trinity, Forest of Dean), 13/154; SO655103; NP 143, 156
Blaston (parish), 21/299-300; NP 133
Blaston St Giles (St Giles in Blaston) (township in Blaston), 21/300; SP800956; NP 133
Blaston St Michael (St Michaels in Blaston) (township in Blaston), 21/299; SP807955; NP 133
Blatchinworth (division in township of Blatchinworth and Calderbrook in Rochdale), 20/462; SD959174; NP 101
Blatchinworth and Calderbrook (township in Rochdale), 20/461-2; NP 101
Blatherwyke (Blatherwycke) (parish), 26/47; SP979955; NP 134
Blawith (township in Ulverston), 20/12; SD281896; NP 88
Blaxhall (parish), 34/370; TM360570; NP 137, 150
Blaxton (township in Finningley), 43/930; SE682020; NP 103
Blayney (township in Llanfihangel Cwm-du), 45/82A; SO200260; NP 141
Bleadon (parish), 32/158; ST344574; NP 165
Bleakedgate cum Rough (subdivision in Butterworth Lord's Side division in Butterworth township in Rochdale), 20/470; SD980140; NP 101
Blean (Sts Cosmos and Damien in the Blean) (parish), 19/142; TR124615; NP 173
Bleasby (hamlet in Legsby), 22/270; TF128847; NP 104
Bleasby (parish), 28/195; SK711499; NP 112
Bleasdale (township in Lancaster), 20/135; SD571478; NP 94
Bleddfa (Blethvaugh) (parish), 56/11; SO219682; NP 128

Bledington (parish), 13/93; SP240231; NP 144
Bledlow (division in Bledlow), 3/192A; SP780020; NP 159
Bledlow (division in Bledlow), 3/192B; SU800980; NP 159
Bledlow (parish), 3/192A-B; NP 159
Blencogo (township in Bromfield), 7/131; NY191477; NP 82
Blencow, 7/193
Blendworth (parish), 14/248; SU719130; NP 181
Blenheim Park (parish), 29/125; SP433169; NP 145
Blenkinsopp (township in Haltwhistle), 27/584; NY668646; NP 76
Blennerhasset and Kirkland (township in Torpenhow), 7/232; NY181409; NP 82
Bletchingdon (Bletchington) (parish), 29/118; SP509176; NP 145
Bletchingley (parish), 35/110; TQ333500; NP 170
Bletchington (parish), 29/118; NP 145
Bletchley (hamlet in Bletchley), 3/68; SP844332; NP 146
Bletchley (parish), 3/66-68; NP 146
Bletchley (township in Moreton Say), 31/15; SJ626334; NP 119
Bletherston (Bletherstone) (parish), 55/79; SN075215; NP 138, 139
Blethvaugh, 56/11; NP 128
Bletsoe (parish), 1/15; TL027591; NP 134
Blewbury (division in Blewbury), 2/76; SU524847; NP 158
Blewbury (parish), 2/76-78; NP 158
Blickling (parish), 25/206; TG179288; NP 126
Blidworth (parish), 28/165; SK578551; NP 112
Blindbothel (township in Brigham), 7/270; NY120270; NP 82
Blindcrake, Isell and Redmain (township in Isell), 7/237; NY148350; NP 82
Blisland (parish), 6/50; SX124744; NP 185, 186
Blisworth (parish), 26/305; SP729537; NP 133, 146
Blithfield (parish), 33/193-194; NP 120
Blo Norton (parish), 25/743; TM019798; NP 136
Blockley (hamlet in Blockley), 40/243; SP135350; NP 144
Blockley (parish), 40/243-248; NP 144
Blodwel (township in Llanyblodwel), 31/116; SJ252235; NP 117
Blofield (parish), 25/453; TG330105; NP 126
Blore (parish), 33/92C, 94; NP 111
Blore (township in Drayton in Hales), 33/158B; SJ720350; NP 119
Blore with Swinscoe (Blore with Swainscoe) (township in Blore), 33/94; SK131493; NP 111
Blowty (township in Llangadfan), 54/29; SJ019113; NP 117
Bloxham (division in Bloxham), 29/30; SP435363; NP 145
Bloxham (parish), 29/30-31; NP 145
Bloxholm (parish), 22/583; TF067530; NP 113
Bloxwich (township in Walsall), 33/295; SK002030; NP 119, 120
Bloxworth (parish), 10/201; SY884946; NP 178
Blubberhouses (township in Fewston), 43/380; SE150550; NP 96
Blundeston (parish), 34/13; TM512967; NP 137
Blunham (hamlet in Blunham), 1/40; TL148518; NP 147
Blunham (parish), 1/40-41; NP 147
Blunsden St Andrew (parish), 39/52; NP 157
Blunsden St Andrew (Blunsden St Andrew) (parish), 39/52; SU135897; NP 157
Bluntisham (parish), 17/73-74; NP 134, 135
Bluntisham (township in Bluntisham), 17/73; TL363742; NP 134, 135
Blurton and Lightwood Forest (township in Trentham), 33/68; SJ904417; NP 119
Blyborough (parish), 22/148; SK933942; NP 104
Blyford (parish), 34/527; TM420773; NP 137
Blymhill (parish), 33/246; SJ817129; NP 119
Blyth (parish), 28/18-24, 43/927-928
Blyth (township in Blyth), 28/20; SK628873; NP 103
Blythburgh (parish), 34/156; TM447741; NP 137
Blyton (parish), 22/125; SK846941; NP 104
Boarhunt (parish), 14/278; SU609095; NP 180
Boarstall (parish), 3/150; SP625142; NP 145
Bobbing (parish), 19/449; TQ884652; NP 172
Bobbington (division in Bobbington), 31/579; SO828928; NP 130
Bobbington (parish), 31/579, 33/337; NP 130
Bobbington (division in Bobbington), 33/337; SO815900; NP 130

Bobbingworth), 12/273; TL533049; NP 161
Bockenfield (township in Felton), 27/290; NZ175975; NP 71
Bocking (parish), 12/128; TL765261; NP 149
Bockleton (parish), 15/77, 40/85; NP 129
Bockleton (division in Bockleton), 40/85; SO591626; NP 129, 130
Boconnoc (parish), 6/98; SX156600; NP 186
Bod-hyddon (township in Llanfyllin), 54/18; SJ115209; NP 117
Bodaioch (township in Trefeglwys), 54/134; SN988902; NP 128
Boddicot, 29/32
Boddicott, 29/32
Boddington (parish), 13/115; SO897246; NP 143
Bodean (parish), 48/58
Bodecton (parish), 36/73; NP 181
Bodedern (parish), 44/27; SH345802; NP 106
Bodelwyddan (township in St Asaph [Llanelwy]), 50/69; SJ003754; NP 108
Bodengan (township in St Asaph [Llanelwy]), 50/76; SJ053743; NP 108
Bodenham (division in Bodenham), 15/145; SO550510; NP 142
Bodenham (parish), 15/144-145; NP 142
Bodewryd (parish), 44/7; SH400906; NP 106
Bodfach (township in Llanfyllin), 54/13; SJ143208; NP 117
Bodfaen (parish), 48/58
Bodfari (parish), 49/31, 50/84; NP 108
Bodfari (township in Bodfari), 50/84; SJ096708; NP 108
Bodfary (parish), 49/31, 50/84; NP 108
Bodferin (parish), 48/73; SH178312; NP 115
Bodfuan (parish), 48/58
Bodham (parish), 25/64; TG123392; NP 125
Bodiam (parish), 36/51; TQ778261; NP 184
Bodicote (Boddicote, Boddicot) (chapelry in Adderbury), 29/32; SP467387; NP 145
Bodingen (township in Ysceifiog), 50/95; SJ152700; NP 108
Bodmin (district in Bodmin), 6/76B; SX040670; NP 185, 186
Bodmin (parish), 6/76A-B; NP 185, 186
Bodmin - Borough (district in Bodmin), 6/76A; SX072667; NP 185, 186
Bodney (parish), 25/685; TL850980; NP 136
Boduan (Bodean, Bodfuan, Bodvean, Bodfaen) (parish), 48/58; SH324384; NP 115
Bodulltin, 49/94; NP 109, 118
Bodvean (parish), 48/58
Bodwrog (parish), 44/30; SH405787; NP 106
Bodylltyn (Bodulltin) (township in Ruabon), 49/94; SJ291444; NP 109, 118
Bodynwydog and Bryn Tanger (township in Bryneglwys), 49/45; SJ167496; NP 108
Bognor (Bognor Regis) (township in South Bersted), 36/278; SZ938991; NP 181
Bolam (parish), 27/387-394; NP 77
Bolam (township in Gainford), 11/307; NZ194223; NP 85
Bolam (township in Bolam), 27/389; NZ084821; NP 77
Bolam Vicarage (township in Bolam), 27/390; NZ099828; NP 77
Bolas Magna (parish), 31/175; NP 119
Bold (township in Prescot), 20/627; SJ540900; NP 100
Bolderwood Walk (division in Minstead), 14/304C; SU247100; NP 179, 180
Boldon (parish and township), 11/8A-9; NP 78
Boldre (division in Boldre), 14/326A; SZ339985; NP 179, 180
Boldre (parish), 14/326A-B; NP 179, 180
Boldron (township in Startforth), 42/12; NZ023150; NP 84
Bole (parish), 28/39; SK792872; NP 104
Bolehall and Glascote (township in Tamworth), 37/7; SK220034; NP 120
Bollam (Bollam and Moorgate) (township in Clarborough), 28/49; SK710826; NP 103
Bollin Fee (township in Wilmslow), 5/72; SJ862806; NP 101
Bollington (division of Bollington township in Bowdon), 5/88; SJ732864; NP 101
Bollington (division of Bollington township in Rostherne), 5/89; SJ727867; NP 101
Bollington (township in Bowdon and Rostherne), 5/88-89; NP 101

Bollington (township in Prestbury), 5/38; SJ930773; NP 101
Bolney (parish), 36/96; TQ257231; NP 182
Bolnhurst (parish), 1/13; TL080588; NP 134
Bolsover (parish), 8/62-63; NP 112
Bolsover (township in Bolsover), 8/62; SK477717; NP 112
Bolsterstone (sub-division in Westnall with Waldershaigh division in township of Bradfield in Ecclesfield), 43/819; SK274971; NP 102
Bolstone (Bolston, Boulstone) (parish), 15/181; SO546327; NP 142
Boltby (township in Felixkirk), 42/537; SE492870; NP 91, 92
Bolton (parish), 7/217-218; NP 82
Bolton (township in Edlingham), 27/195; NU118144; NP 71
Bolton (township in Morland), 38/10; NY635231; NP 83
Bolton (township in Bishop Wilton), 41/111; SE773520; NP 98
Bolton (township in Calverley), 43/511; SE168357; NP 96
Bolton Abbey (township in Skipton), 43/332; SE062545; NP 96
Bolton by Bowland (Bolton by Bolland) (parish), 43/295; SD770510; NP 95
Bolton High Hide Quarter, 7/217; NP 82
Bolton Low Quarter, 7/218; NP 82
Bolton Percy (division in township of Bolton Percy in Bolton Percy), 43/60; SE533414; NP 97
Bolton Percy (parish), 43/59-64; NP 97
Bolton Percy (township in Bolton Percy), 43/60-62; NP 97
Bolton upon Dearne (division in township and parish of Bolton upon Dearne), 43/865; SE447029; NP 103
Bolton upon Dearne (parish and township), 43/864-865; NP 103
Bolton with Adgarley (sub-division of Little Urswick division of Great Urswick township in Urswick), 20/37; SD252720; NP 88
Bolton Wood, 7/218; NP 82
Bolton-le-Moors (parish), 20/387-407B; NP 100, 101
Bolton-le-Sands (parish), 20/91-96; NP 89
Bolton-le-Sands (township in Bolton-le-Sands), 20/93; SD482679; NP 89
Bolton-on-Swale (Bolton-upon-Swale) (township in Catterick), 42/84; SE256992; NP 91
Bolton-upon-Swale, 42/84; NP 91
Bonby (parish), 22/59; TA002154; NP 104
Bonchurch (parish), 18/24; SZ578783; NP 180
Bondgate (division in township of Darlington in Darlington), 11/320; NZ269106; NP 85
Bondgate in Auckland, 11/201; NP 85
Bondleigh (parish), 9/182; SS655043; NP 175
Bonehill (township in Tamworth), 33/285C; SK193206; NP 120
Bongate (parish), 38/38, 41-43
Bongate (township in St Michael Appleby or Bongate), 38/41; NY699207; NP 83
Bongate and Langton, 38/41
Boningale (Bonninghall) (parish), 31/583; SJ810028; NP 119
Bonninghall (parish), 31/583; NP 119
Bonnington (parish), 19/399; TR059343; NP 172, 184
Bonsall (parish), 8/122; SK266584; NP 111
Bonvilston (Bonvilstone) (parish), 51/155; ST070738; NP 154
Bonwick (township in Skipsea), 41/357; TA165529; NP 99
Boothby (parish), 22/553-554; NP 113
Boothby Graffoe (Boothby) (parish), 22/553-554; NP 113
Boothby Graffoe (Boothby) (township in Boothby Graffoe), 22/554; SK987592; NP 113
Boothby Pagnell (parish), 22/634; SK972308; NP 123
Boothby, 22/421; NP 114
Boothen (township in Stoke-on-Trent), 33/36B; SJ872440; NP 110
Boothorpe (division in Seal), 21/7; SK318172; NP 121
Boothstown (division in township of Worsley in Eccles), 20/558; SJ721992; NP 101
Bootle (parish), 7/316; SD094893; NP 88
Bootle cum Linacre (township in Walton on the Hill), 20/673; SJ342955; NP 100
Booton (parish), 25/262; TG121222; NP 125
Boraston (division in Burford), 31/543; SO613708; NP 129, 130
Boraston and Whatmore (township in Burford), 31/538, 543; NP 129, 130
Borden (parish), 19/448; TQ876624; NP 172

61

Bordesley (township in Aston), 37/38; SP099858; NP 131
Bordley (division in township of Hetton with Bordley in Burnsall), 43/214; SD938656; NP 90
Boreatton (township in Baschurch), 31/142; SJ413223; NP 118
Boreham (parish), 12/217; TL745102; NP 148, 149, 161, 162
Boresford and Pedwardine (township in Brampton Bryan), 15/14; SO355702; NP 129
Borley (parish), 12/43; TL848429; NP 149
Borough Fen, 26/13; TF216070; NP 123
Borough Road (division in St George the Martyr Southwark), 35/9B; TQ316798; NP 170
Boroughbridge (township in Aldborough), 43/131; SE396667; NP 91
Borras Hovah (township in Wrexham [Wrecsam]), 49/56; SJ377534; NP 109
Borras Riffre (township in Gresford), 49/65; SJ370529; NP 109
Borrowby (township in Leake), 42/519; SE428893; NP 91
Borrowby (township in Lythe), 42/371; NZ773160; NP 86
Borrowdale (township in Crosthwaite), 7/287; NY260140; NP 82
Borrowden, 27/182; NP 71
Borwick (township in Warton), 20/70; SD532730; NP 8
Bosbury (parish), 15/159; SO695435; NP 143
Boscobel (extra-parochial), 31/474; SJ830077; NP 119
Boscombe (parish), 39/309; SU209381; NP 167
Bosden (division in Handsforth cum Bosden township in Cheadle), 5/25; SJ952878; NP 101
Bosham (parish), 36/248; SU818038; NP 181
Bosherston (Stackpole Bosher, Bosherton) (parish), 55/160; SR962941; NP 151
Bosley (township in Prestbury), 5/57; SJ921661; NP 110
Bossall (division in township of Bossall in Bossall), 42/661; SE712605; NP 92, 97
Bossall (parish), 42/659-665; NP 92
Bossall (township in Bossall), 42/661-662; NP 92
Bossington (parish), 14/334; SU328305; NP 168
Bostock (township in Davenham), 5/189; SJ674688; NP 110
Boston (division in Boston), 22/753A; TF322447; NP 114, 123
Boston (parish), 22/753A-D, 753F; NP 114, 123
Boston - East Fen (division in Boston), 22/753F; TF391593; NP 114
Boston - West Fen (division in Boston), 22/753C; TF332492; NP 114
Boston East (division in Boston), 22/753B; TF349462; NP 114, 123
Boston West (division in Boston), 22/753D; TF300450; NP 114, 123
Botchardgate, 7/86
Botcherby (township in St Cuthbert [Carlisle]), 7/85; NY425564; NP 76
Botchergate (Botchardgate) (township in St Cuthbert [Carlisle]), 7/86; NY408552; NP 76
Botesdale (hamlet in Redgrave), 34/91; TM059755; NP 136
Both Hergests (township in Kington), 15/41B; SO265555; NP 128, 129, 141
Bothal (parish), 27/312-320; NP 78
Bothal Demesne (township in Bothal), 27/318; NZ239870; NP 78
Bothamsall (parish), 28/77; SK675738; NP 112
Bothel and Threapland (township in Torpenhow), 7/231; NY177385; NP 82
Bothenhampton (parish), 10/232; SY475917; NP 177
Botley (parish), 14/274; SU506124; NP 180
Botley (tithing in Cumnor), 2/3A; SP483060; NP 158
Botley (tithing in North Hinksey), 2/6B; SP489062; NP 158
Botolphs (Buttolphs) (parish), 36/109; TQ187094; NP 182
Bottegir-bach (extra-parochial), 49/22; SJ001476; NP 108
Bottesford (parish), 21/89; SK807352; NP 122
Bottesford (parish), 22/28-32; NP 104
Bottesford (township in Bottesford), 22/29A; SE898074; NP 104
Botteslow (township in Stoke-on-Trent), 33/27; SJ891466; NP 110
Bottisham (parish), 4/99; TL542616; NP 135
Botton (division in township of Wray with Botton in Melling), 20/88; SD650615; NP 89, 95

Botus Fleming (parish), 6/106; SX400620; NP 186, 187
Botwnnog (Botwnog) (parish), 48/69; SH262318; NP 115
Botwnog (parish), 48/69; NP 115
Boughrood (parish), 56/61; SO139396; NP 141
Boughton (parish), 25/529; TF705025; NP 124
Boughton (parish), 26/227; SP752657; NP 133
Boughton (parish), 28/74; SK677686; NP 112
Boughton Aluph (parish), 19/291; TR029476; NP 172
Boughton Malherbe (parish), 19/296; TQ877481; NP 172
Boughton Monchelsea (parish), 19/301; TQ777498; NP 172
Boughton Street (parish), 19/454; NP 172
Boughton under Blean (Boughton Street) (parish), 19/454; TR050588; NP 172
Bouldon (township in Holdgate), 31/499; SO542839; NP 129
Boulge (parish), 34/386; TM254530; NP 150
Boulmer and Seaton House (township in Longhoughton), 27/160; NU263143; NP 71
Boulsdon and Kilcot (tithing in Newent), 13/127A; SO705253; NP 143
Boulston (parish), 55/83; SM985135; NP 151
Boulstone (parish), 15/181; NP 142
Boultham (parish), 22/524; SK960695; NP 113
Boulton (parish), 8/277; SK383330; NP 121
Boundary (Boundary or Burton Road) (extra-parochial), 8/308; SK336189; NP 121
Boundary or Burton Road (extra-parochial), 8/308; NP 121
Bourn (parish), 4/113; TL329575; NP 134, 147
Bourne (Bourn) (parish), 22/709A-C; NP 123
Bourne (Bourn) (township in Bourne), 22/709A; TF100200; NP 123
Bournmoor (township in Houghton-le-Spring), 11/58; NZ315516; NP 78
Bourton (Bourton (Great and Little)) (hamlet in Cropredy), 29/13; SP459449; NP 145
Bourton (chapelry in Gillingham), 10/2; ST768301; NP 166
Bourton (hamlet in Buckingham), 3/79A; SP710330; NP 146
Bourton (parish), 32/15; NP 155, 165
Bourton (tithing in Shrivenham), 2/41; SU228872; NP 157
Bourton (township in Much Wenlock), 31/457; SO601964; NP 129, 130
Bourton and Draycote (parish), 37/132; SP443702; NP 132
Bourton Hold (hamlet in Buckingham), 3/79B; SP720340; NP 146
Bourton on the Hill (division in Tewkesbury Hundred in Bourton on the Hill), 13/83; SP156326; NP 144
Bourton on the Hill (division in Westminster Hundred in Bourton on the Hill), 13/84; SP184323; NP 144
Bourton on the Hill (parish), 13/83-84; NP 144
Bourton on the Water (parish), 13/100; SP168201; NP 144
Boustead Hill (township in Burgh by Sands), 7/108; NY291583; NP 75
Boveney (Lower Boveney) (hamlet in Burnham), 3/223; SU940780; NP 159
Boveridge (division in Cranborne), 10/68B; SU060150; NP 179
Bovey Tracey (parish), 9/404; SX811787; NP 175, 176, 188
Bovingdon (parish), 16/136; TL020037; NP 159, 160
Bow (Nymet Tracey) (parish), 9/208; SX725996; NP 175
Bow Brickhill (parish), 3/63; SP904346; NP 146
Bowden Edge (division in Chapel en le Frith), 8/13C; SK080820; NP 111
Bowdon (parish), 5/78-88, 90; NP 101
Bowdon (township in Bowdon), 5/87; SJ757866; NP 101
Bower Stanford (division in Alberbury Lower Quarter township in Alberbury), 31/304; SJ347125; NP 118
Bowerchalke (parish), 39/348; SU011222; NP 167
Bowers Gifford (parish), 12/391; TQ756872; NP 161, 162
Bowes (parish), 42/10-11; NP 84
Bowes (township in Bowes), 42/10; NY950130; NP 84
Bowforth and Southfield (division in township of Kirkbymoorside in Kirkbymoorside), 42/469; SE693830; NP 92
Bowland Forest (Higher Division) (township in Slaidburn), 43/283; SD650530; NP 90, 95

Bowland with Leagram (township in Whalley), 20/238-239; NP 95
Bowling (township in Bradford), 43/533; SE141310; NP 96
Bowling Green (extra-parochial), 35/133; SU493997; NP 169/1
Bowness-on-Solway (parish), 7/109-112; NP 75
Bowness-on-Solway (township in Bowness-on-Solway), 7/111; NY218612; NP 75
Bowood (extra-parochial), 39/112; ST967698; NP 157
Bowscale (Bowscale and Mossdale) (township in Greystoke), 7/208; NY336325; NP 82, 83
Bowsden (Bowsdon) (township in Lowick), 27/44; NT988420; NP 64
Bowsdon, 27/44; NP 64
Bowthorpe (parish), 25/492; TG180090; NP 126
Bowthorpe (division in township of Menthorpe in Hemingbrough), 41/52; SE698335; NP 97
Box (parish), 39/120; ST828684; NP 156
Boxford (hamlet in Boxford), 34/484; TL960399; NP 149
Boxford (parish), 2/135; SU433720; NP 158
Boxford (parish), 34/483-484; NP 149
Boxgrove (parish), 36/244; SU911083; NP 181
Boxley (parish), 19/171; TQ774595; NP 171, 172
Boxted (Boxtead) (parish), 12/100; TL999325; NP 149
Boxted (parish), 34/533; TL820505; NP 149
Boxwell with Leighterton (Boxwell and Leighterton) (parish), 13/339; ST823917; NP 156
Boxworth (parish), 4/67; TL344632; NP 134, 135
Boycott (hamlet in Stowe), 3/2; SP662361; NP 145
Boyleston (Boylston) (parish), 8/240; SK182359; NP 120
Boylston (parish), 8/240; NP 120
Boynton (division in parish and township of Boynton in Boynton), 41/245; TA135690; NP 93
Boynton (parish), 41/244-245; NP 93
Boysnope (division in township of Barton upon Irwell in Eccles), 20/544; SJ731963; NP 101
Boythorpe (division in township of Foxholes with Boythorpe in Foxholes), 41/175; SE997720; NP 93
Boyton (hamlet in Boyton), 6/12; SX308925; NP 174
Boyton (parish), 6/12, 09/196; NP 174
Boyton (parish), 34/437; TM380470; NP 150
Boyton (parish), 39/271-272; NP 166, 167
Boyton (tithing in Boyton), 39/271; ST942383; NP 167
Bozeat (parish), 26/370; SP913585; NP 133
Brabourne (parish), 19/330; TR093420; NP 172, 173
Braceborough (parish), 22/717; TF072129; NP 123
Bracebridge (parish), 22/523; SK975675; NP 113
Braceby (parish), 22/639; TF016355; NP 123
Bracewell (parish), 43/308; SD857483; NP 95
Bracken (township in Kilnwick), 41/285; SE982511; NP 98
Brackenborough (parish), 22/190; TF331904; NP 105
Brackenfield (Brackenfield and Woolley) (township in Morton), 8/135; SK372594; NP 111
Brackenholm (division in parish and township of Kirby Underdale), 41/138B; SE836592; NP 98
Brackenholme (division in township of Brackenholme with Woodhall in Hemingbrough), 41/46; SE692303; NP 97
Brackenholme with Woodhall (township in Hemingbrough), 41/45-46; NP 97
Brackenthwaite (township in Lorton parochial chapelry in Brigham), 7/274; NY169212; NP 82
Brackley Hatch (hamlet in Brackley St Peter), 26/346; SP655415; NP 145
Brackley St James (parish), 26/349; SP589378; NP 145
Brackley St Peter (hamlet in Brackley St Peter), 26/348; SP575385; NP 146
Brackley St Peter (parish), 26/346-348; NP 145
Bracon Ash (parish), 25/605; TM185997; NP 137
Bradborne (parish), 8/162-167; NP 111
Bradborne, 8/165; NP 111
Bradbourne (Bradborne) (parish), 8/162-167; NP 111
Bradbourne (Bradborne) (township in Bradbourne), 8/165; SK212526; NP 111

Bradbury (division in township of Bradbury in Sedgefield), 11/237; NZ315275; NP 85
Bradbury (township in Sedgefield), 11/237-238; NP 85
Bradden (parish), 26/319; SP652485; NP 145
Braddock (Broadoak) (parish), 6/71; SX155633; NP 186
Bradenham (parish), 3/194; SU828976; NP 159
Bradeston (parish), 25/473; NP 126
Bradfield (parish), 2/165; SU595728; NP 158
Bradfield (parish), 12/106; TM144299; NP 150
Bradfield (parish), 25/51; TG268302; NP 126
Bradfield Combust (parish), 34/306; TL893573; NP 136, 149
Bradfield St Clare (parish), 34/305; TL914579; NP 136, 149
Bradfield St George (parish), 34/304; TL919593; NP 136
Bradfield (division in township of Bradfield in Ecclesfield), 43/807-814; NP 102
Bradfield (sub-division in Bradfield division in township of Bradfield in Ecclesfield), 43/811; SK267926; NP 102
Bradfield (township in Ecclesfield), 43/803-821; NP 102
Bradfield Dale (sub-division in Bradfield division in township of Bradfield in Ecclesfield), 43/814; SK200920; NP 102
Bradford (parish), 9/105; SS430055; NP 175
Bradford (township in Manchester), 20/516; SJ872986; NP 101
Bradford (township in Bamburgh), 27/95; NU159323; NP 71
Bradford (township in Bolam), 27/393; NZ064795; NP 77
Bradford (parish), 32/326; NP 164
Bradford (parish), 43/516-535; NP 95, 96
Bradford (township in Bradford), 43/516-517; NP 96
Bradford - East End (division in township of Bradford in Bradford), 43/516; SE175335; NP 96
Bradford - West End (division in township of Bradford in Bradford), 43/517; SE160335; NP 96
Bradford Abbas (parish), 10/35; ST584153; NP 178
Bradford on Avon (borough in Great Bradford), 39/151A-B; NP 166
Bradford on Avon (division in Bradford North-Western Registration Subdistrict of borough of Bradford on Avon in Great Bradford), 39/151B; ST820610; NP 166
Bradford on Avon (division in Bradford South-Eastern Registration Subdistrict of borough of Bradford on Avon in Great Bradford), 39/151A; ST830610; NP 166
Bradford Peverell (parish), 10/224; SY649921; NP 178
Bradford-on-Tone (Bradford) (parish), 32/326; ST177232; NP 164
Bradgate Park (extra-parochial), 21/33; SK532105; NP 121
Brading (parish), 18/21; SZ592863; NP 180
Bradle (tithing in Church Knowle), 10/292C; SY930805; NP 178, 179
Bradley (division in township of Wolsingham in Wolsingham), 11/182; NZ102360; NP 84
Bradley (division in Bradley), 33/245; SJ845220; NP 119
Bradley (division in township of Huddersfield in Huddersfield), 43/746; SE158201; NP 96, 102
Bradley (parish), 8/174; SK228461; NP 111, 120
Bradley (parish), 14/131; SU640420; NP 168
Bradley (parish), 22/90; TA246055; NP 105
Bradley (parish), 33/243-245; NP 119
Bradley (tithing in Cumnor), 2/3B; SP467031; NP 158
Bradley (township in Malpas), 5/323; SJ510459; NP 109, 118
Bradley (township in Bradley), 33/243; SJ880180; NP 119
Bradley Field, 38/94
Bradley in the Moors (parish), 33/111; SK055415; NP 120
Bradleys Both (township in Kildwick), 43/347; SE011488; NP 95, 96
Bradmore (parish), 28/273; SK592313; NP 121
Bradninch (parish), 9/223; SS993046; NP 176
Bradnop (township in Leek), 33/10; SK015545; NP 110, 111
Bradpole (parish), 10/229; SY476942; NP 177
Bradshaw (township in Bolton le Moors), 20/396; SD739131; NP 101
Bradshaw Edge (township in Chapel en le Frith), 8/13B; SK040810; NP 111
Bradstone (parish), 9/349; SX382809; NP 175, 186
Bradwall (township in Sandbach), 5/215; SJ752634; NP 110

Bradwell (parish), 3/52; SP834399; NP 146
Bradwell (township in Hope), 8/21; SK158809; NP 111
Bradwell (Bradwell-next-Coggeshall) (parish), 12/188; TL816220; NP 149
Bradwell (parish), 34/2; TG506042; NP 126
Bradwell Abbey (extra-parochial), 3/53; SP811391; NP 146
Bradwell Juxta Mare (parish), 12/353; NP 162
Bradwell near the Sea (parish), 12/353; NP 162
Bradwell-on-Sea (Bradwell near the Sea, Bradwell Juxta Mare) (parish), 12/353; TM010070; NP 162
Bradworthy (parish), 9/53; SS312147; NP 174
Brafferton (division in township of Aycliffe), 11/277; NZ302218; NP 85
Brafferton (township in Aycliffe), 11/272-278; NP 85
Brafferton (parish), 42/568-570; NP 91
Brafferton (township in Brafferton), 42/569; SE453717; NP 91
Brafield on the Green (parish), 26/287; SP822587; NP 133
Braggington (division in Alberbury Lower Quarter township in Alberbury), 31/302; SJ336138; NP 118
Brailes (parish), 37/289; SP312398; NP 145
Brailsford (parish), 8/222; SK249418; NP 120
Braintree (parish), 12/192; TL759230; NP 148, 149
Braiseworth (parish), 34/181; TM131719; NP 136
Braithwaite (township in Crosthwaite), 7/282; NY220227; NP 82
Braithwell (parish), 43/890-891; NP 103
Braithwell (township in Braithwell), 43/890; SK522942; NP 103
Brakes (township in Leintwardine), 15/5; SO435758; NP 129
Bramall, 5/23; NP 101
Bramber (parish), 36/108; TQ176098; NP 182
Bramble Hill (division in Bramshaw), 14/305B; SU254147; NP 179
Bramcote (parish), 28/248; SK510380; NP 121
Bramcote (hamlet in Bulkington), 37/101; SP413883; NP 132
Bramcote Hall (township in Polesworth), 37/16; SK272048; NP 120, 121
Bramdean (parish), 14/185; SU622286; NP 168
Bramerton (parish), 25/479; TG298048; NP 126
Bramfield (parish), 16/82; TL292150; NP 147
Bramfield (parish), 34/153; TM399733; NP 137
Bramford (division inside the Ipswich municipal boundary in Bramford), 34/424B; TM140472; NP 150
Bramford (division outside Ipswich municipal boundary in Bramford), 34/424A; TM119468; NP 150
Bramford (parish), 34/424A-B; NP 150
Bramhall (Bramall) (township in), 5/23; SJ994859; NP 101
Bramham (division in township of Bramham cum Oglethorpe in Bramham), 43/88; SE427425; NP 96, 97
Bramham (parish), 43/88-90; NP 97
Bramhope (township in Otley), 43/370; SE246430; NP 96
Bramley (parish), 14/50; SU654595; NP 168
Bramley (parish), 35/140; TQ008412; NP 169
Bramley (township in Leeds), 43/499; SE241350; NP 96
Bramley (township in Braithwell), 43/891; SK495925; NP 103
Brampford Speke (district in Brampford Speke), 9/250A; SX924982; NP 176
Brampford Speke (parish), 9/2250A-B; NP 176
Brampton (parish), 7/52-54
Brampton (township in Brampton), 7/52; NY524602; NP 76
Brampton (parish), 8/78; SK327717; NP 111
Brampton (parish), 17/84; TL202705; NP 134
Brampton (township in Torksey), 22/237; SK846803; NP 104
Brampton (parish), 25/209; TG219239; NP 126
Brampton (parish), 26/101; NP 133
Brampton (parish), 34/68; TM427821; NP 137
Brampton (township in Long Marton), 38/7B; NY676230; NP 83, 84
Brampton Abbotts (parish), 15/247; SO602265; NP 142, 143
Brampton Ash (Brampton) (parish), 26/101; SP785867; NP 133
Brampton Brian, 15/13; NP 129
Brampton Bryan (Brampton Brian) (township in Brampton Bryan), 15/13; SO364721; NP 129
Brampton Bierlow (township in Wath upon Dearne), 43/853; SK410997; NP 102, 103
Brampton Bryan (parish), 15/13-14, 56/15; NP 129

Brampton en le Morthen (township in Treeton), 43/892; SK490880; NP 103
Bramshall (parish), 33/118; SK060339; NP 120
Bramshaw (division in Bramshaw), 14/305A; SU268150; NP 179
Bramshaw (division in Bramshaw), 39/374; SU278157; NP 179, 180
Bramshaw (parish), 14/305A-C, 39/375; NP 179, 180
Bramshott (division in Bramshott), 14/84; SU843329; NP 169, 181
Bramshott (parish), 14/84, 36/342; NP 169, 181
Bramshott (division in Bramshott), 36/342; SU822312; NP 181
Brancaster (parish), 25/8; TF793443; NP 125
Brancepeth (division of Brancepeth township in Brancepeth), 11/138; NZ181389; NP 85
Brancepeth (division of Brancepeth township in Brancepeth), 11/139; NZ192382; NP 85
Brancepeth (division of Brancepeth township in Brancepeth), 11/140; NZ235375; NP 85
Brancepeth (parish), 11/135-146; NP 85
Brancepeth (township in Brancepeth), 11/137-140; NP 85
Brancepeth Common (division of Brancepeth township in Brancepeth), 11/137; NZ189396; NP 85
Brandesburton (Brands Burton) (parish), 31/346-347; NP 99
Brandesburton (Brands Burton) (township in Brandesburton), 41/346; TA111484; NP 99
Brandeston (Brandiston, Bradeston) (parish), 25/473; TG335086; NP 126
Brandeston (parish), 25/259; NP 125
Brandeston (parish), 34/282; TM246607; NP 137
Brandiston (Brandeston) (parish), 25/259; TG139219; NP 125
Brandiston (parish), 25/473; NP 126
Brandon (parish), 34/107; TL752850; NP 135, 136
Brandon (township in Eglingham), 27/136; NU047178; NP 71
Brandon and Byshottles (township in Brancepeth), 11/136; NZ217412; NP 85
Brandon and Bretford (township in Wolston), 37/138; SP405765; NP 132
Brandon Parva (parish), 25/550; TG066086; NP 125
Brands Burton, 41/346; NP 99
Brandsby (division in township of Brandsby-cum-Stearsby in Brandsby), 42/609; SE594718; NP 92
Brandsby (parish), 42/608-609; NP 92
Brandsby-cum-Stearsby (township in Brandsby), 42/608-609; NP 92
Brandwood Higher End (subdivision of Whitworth division in Spotland township in Rochdale), 20/451; SD877221; NP 95
Brandwood Lower End (subdivision of Whitworth division in Spotland township in Rochdale), 20/450; SD851205; NP 95, 101
Brankin Moor (division in township of Darlington in Darlington), 11/323; NZ302130; NP 85
Bransby (hamlet in Stow), 22/234B; SK889799; NP 104
Branscliff (township in Wolstanton), 33/17A; SJ860570; NP 110
Branscombe (parish), 9/298; SY185896; NP 176, 177
Bransdale West (Bransdale West Side) (township in Kirkdale), 42/481; SE618956; NP 92
Bransford (chapelry in Leigh), 40/160; SO797515; NP 143
Branston (parish), 21/95; SK808304; NP 122
Branston (parish), 22/521; TF030670; NP 113
Branston (township in Burton upon Trent), 33/215; SK217217; NP 120
Brant Broughton (parish), 22/543; SK909549; NP 113
Brantham (parish), 34/514; TM116341; NP 150
Branthwaite (township in Dean), 7/261; NY054246; NP 82
Brantingham (area common to townships of Brantingham and Thorpe Brantingham in Brantingham), 41/209; SE931288; NP 98
Brantingham (parish), 41/207-210; NP 98
Brantingham (township in Brantingham), 41/208; SE942297; NP 98
Branton (township in Eglingham), 27/137; NU049152; NP 71
Branxton (parish), 27/77; NT897368; NP 64
Brascote (township in Newbold Verdon), 21/169B; SK442022; NP 121
Brassington (township in Bradbourne), 8/162; SK229552; NP 111

Brasted (parish), 19/195; TQ472528; NP 171
Bratoft (parish), 22/487; TF483640; NP 114
Brattleby (parish), 22/230; SK948809; NP 104
Bratton (tithing in Westbury), 39/231; ST911516; NP 166
Bratton Clovelly (parish), 9/201; SX471936; NP 175
Bratton Fleming (parish), 9/12; SS656381; NP 163
Bratton Seymour (parish), 32/362; ST680297; NP 166
Braughing (Braughin) (parish), 16/64; TL402255; NP 148
Brauncewell (parish), 22/577; TF032519; NP 113
Braunston (parish), 26/182; SP548663; NP 132
Braunston (parish), 30/20; SK828608; NP 122
Braunstone (township in Glenfield), 21/180; SK555028; NP 121
Braunstone Frith (extra-parochial), 21/181; SK549047; NP 121
Braunton (parish), 9/22; SS487376; NP 163
Brawby (township in Salton), 42/454; SE734787; NP 92
Brawdy (parish), 55/71; SM849248; NP 138
Braworth (division in township of Skutterskelfe in Rudby in Cleveland), 42/296; NZ508076; NP 85
Bray (division in Bray), 2/212; SU901775; NP 159
Bray (parish), 2/211-212; NP 159
Braybrooke (parish), 26/103; SP765845; NP 133
Braydon (hamlet in Purton), 39/51B; SU040883; NP 157
Brayton (parish), 43/450-455; NP 97
Brayton (township in Brayton), 43/450; SE600300; NP 97
Breadsall (parish), 8/210; SK374406; NP 121
Breadstone (tithing in Berkeley), 13/318; SO708008; NP 156
Breage (parish), 6/196; SW606297; NP 189
Bream (hamlet in Newland), 13/164; SO609152; NP 155, 156
Breamore (parish), 14/311A; SU152183; NP 167, 179
Brean (Breane) (parish), 32/170; ST304573; NP 165
Brearton (township in South Stainley), 43/145; SE323612; NP 91, 96
Brearton, 11/252; NP 85
Breaston (chapelry in Wilne), 8/286; SK460338; NP 121
Brechfa (parish), 47/9; SN515299; NP 140
Breckles (parish), 25/722; TL945945; NP 136
Breckonhill Quarter, 7/16; NP 76
Brecon, St David - Lower Division (Llanfaes) (division in Brecon, St David), 45/51A; SO033281; NP 141
Brecon, St David - Upper Division (division in Brecon, St David), 45/51B; SO035265; NP 141
Brecon, St John the Evangelist (parish), 45/46-48; NP 141
Brecon, St John the Evangelist - upper division (division in Brecon, St John the Evangelist), 45/47; SO042295; NP 141
Brecon, St Mary (Lower Division) (chapelry in Brecon, St John the Evangelist), 45/46; SO060280; NP 141
Breconhill (Breckonhill Quarter) (township in Arthuret), 7/16; NY438700; NP 76
Bredbury (township in Stockport), 5/13; SJ952914; NP 101
Brede (parish), 36/153; TQ828193; NP 184
Bredenbury (Bridenbury) (parish), 15/272; SO618563; NP 130, 143
Bredfield (parish), 34/385; TM268528; NP 150
Bredgar (parish), 19/165; TQ876598; NP 172
Bredhurst (parish), 19/445; TQ798622; NP 172
Bredicot (Bredicote) (parish), 40/152; SO905548; NP 130
Bredon (hamlet in Bredon), 40/241; SO922362; NP 143
Bredon's Norton (hamlet in Bredon), 40/240; SO932393; NP 143
Bredwardine (parish), 15/202; SO329448; NP 142
Breedon on the Hill (parish), 21/10-12; NP 121
Breedon on the Hill (township in Breedon on the Hill), 21/12; SK429222; NP 121
Breightmet (township in Bolton le Moors), 20/398; SD746097; NP 101
Breighton (division in township of Breighton and Gunby in Bubwith), 41/30; SE718337; NP 97
Breighton and Gunby (township in Bubwith), 41/29-30
Breinton, 15/195; SO471402; NP 142
Bremhill (parish), 39/88; ST982755; NP 157
Bremilham (parish), 39/35; ST904859; NP 156
Brenchley (parish), 19/311; TQ674423; NP 171
Brendon (parish), 9/10; SS766463; NP 163
Brenkley (township in Dinnington), 27/515; NZ217751; NP 78

Brent Eleigh (parish), 34/407; TL939489; NP 149
Brent Knoll (South Brent) (parish), 32/172; ST330518; NP 165
Brent Pelham (parish), 16/60; TL436304; NP 148
Brentor (parish), 9/339; SX468820; NP 175
Brentwood (hamlet in South Weald), 12/330; TQ589936; NP 161
Brenzett (parish), 19/431; TR001271; NP 184
Brereton cum Smethwick (parish), 5/221; SJ789642; NP 110
Bressingham (parish), 25/744; TM082822; NP 136
Breston, 49/58; NP 109
Bretby (township in Repton), 8/310; SK299229; NP 120, 121
Bretforton (parish), 40/200; SP090440; NP 144
Bretherdale (township in Orton), 38/74; NY573047; NP 83, 89
Bretherton (township in Croston), 20/344; SD476204; NP 94, 100
Brettenham (parish), 25/728; TL925845; NP 136
Brettenham (parish), 34/349; TL963539; NP 149
Bretton (township in Hawarden), 50/2; SJ353638; NP 109
Brewhouse Yard (extra-parochial), 28/236; SK571395; NP 121/1
Brewood (parish), 33/249; SJ881082; NP 119
Brices Lodge (extra-parochial), 29/147; SP340152; NP 145
Bricett (parish), 34/355; NP 149
Brickendon (division in Hertford, All Saints), 16/109; TL327099; NP 147, 160
Bricklehampton (chapelry in St Andrew Pershore), 40/180; SO981434; NP 143
Bridekirk (parish), 7/238-244; NP 82
Bridekirk (township in Bridekirk), 7/239; NY121337; NP 82
Bridell (parish), 55/7; SN177410; NP 139
Bridenbury, 15/272; NP 130, 143
Bridestowe (Bridestow) (parish), 9/332; SX506876; NP 175
Bridestowe and Sourton Common (common to Bridestowe, Sourton), 9/331; SX550880; NP 175
Bridford (parish), 9/384; SX807866; NP 175, 176
Bridge (parish), 19/285; TR173536; NP 173
Bridge Hewick (Bridge Howick) (township in Ripon), 43/179; SE347707; NP 91
Bridge Howick, 43/179; NP 91
Bridge Sollers (Bridge Sollars) (parish), 15/115; SO421419; NP 142
Bridge Trafford (township in Plemstall), 5/420; SJ453716; NP 109
Bridge Ward (division in Walsall), 33/297; SP033979; NP 131
Bridgehampton (tithing in Yeovilton), 32/399; ST561243; NP 177
Bridgemere (Bridgmere) (township in Wybunbury), 5/268; SJ718450; NP 110, 119
Bridgend (hamlet in St Dogmaels), 55/4; SN170448; NP 139
Bridgerule (parish), 9/98-99; NP 174
Bridgerule East (district in Bridgerule), 9/98; SS284029; NP 174
Bridgerule West (West Bridgerule) (district in Bridgerule), 9/99; SS267020; NP 174
Bridgham (parish), 25/727; TL958862; NP 136
Bridgmere, 5/268; NP 110, 119
Bridgnorth St Leonard (parish), 31/488; SO710932; NP 130
Bridgnorth St Mary Magdalene (parish), 31/487; SO722923; NP 130
Bridgwater (parish), 32/266; ST308370; NP 165
Bridlington (parish), 41/250-257; NP 93, 99
Bridlington (township in Bridlington), 41/255; TA173692; NP 93
Bridport (parish), 10/231; SY465927; NP 177
Bridstow (parish), 15/263; SO582246; NP 142
Briercliffe (division in township of Briercliffe with Entwistle in Whalley), 20/272; SD895355; NP 95
Briercliffe with Entwistle (township in Whalley), 20/272-273; NP 95
Brierley (township in Leominster), 15/67; SO449559; NP 129
Brierley (township in Felkirk), 43/682; SE415100; NP 103
Briershurst (township in Wolstanton), 33/17B; SJ846560; NP 110
Brierton (Brearton) (township in Seaton Carew), 11/252; NZ472300; NP 85
Briestfield (division in township of Whitley Lower in Thornhill), 43/720; SE228172; NP 102

Brigg (Glanford Brigg) (township in Wrawby), 22/63; SE999072; NP 104
Brigham (parish), 7/264-276; NP 82
Brigham (township in Brigham), 7/265; NY095302; NP 82
Brigham (township in Foston on the Wolds), 41/268; TA086537; NP 99
Brighouse (division in township of Hipperholme cum Brighouse in Halifax), 43/546; SE144231; NP 96
Brighstone (Brixton) (parish), 18/10; SZ433827; NP 180
Brighthampton (hamlet in Bampton), 29/172; SP384031; NP 158
Brighthelmstone (parish), 36/314A-C; NP 182
Brightholmlee (sub-division in Westnall with Waldershaigh division in township of Bradfield in Ecclesfield), 43/818; SK286949; NP 102
Brightling (parish), 36/137A; TQ689212; NP 183
Brightlingsea (parish), 12/170; TM083177; NP 149, 150
Brighton (Brighthelmstone) (parish), 36/314A-C; NP 182
Brighton - Kemp Town (Brightelmstone - Kemp Town) (division in Brighton), 36/314C; TQ324038; NP 182
Brighton - St Peter (Brighthelmstone - St Peter) (division in Brighton), 36/314A; TQ323051; NP 182
Brighton - The Palace (Brightelmstone - The Palace) (division in Brighton), 36/314; TQ304041; NP 182
Brightside Bierlow (township in Sheffield), 43/833; SK363893; NP 102
Brightwalton (Brightwaltham) (parish), 2/112; SU432800; NP 158
Brightwell (parish), 2/64; SU575905; NP 158
Brightwell Baldwin (parish), 29/294; SU652942; NP 158
Brightwell (parish), 34/445; TM249437; NP 150
Brignall (parish), 42/16; NZ063124; NP 84
Brigsley (parish), 22/87; TA265016; NP 105
Brigstock (parish), 26/87; SP945850; NP 133, 134
Brikby (township in Crosscanonby), 7/227; NY060375; NP 82
Brill (parish), 3/151; SP659142; NP 146
Brilley (parish), 15/47; SO261492; NP 141, 142
Brimfield (parish), 15/21; SO528670; NP 129
Brimington (township in Chesterfield), 8/72; SK405735; NP 111, 112
Brimpsfield (parish), 13/246; SO935124; NP 143
Brimpton (parish), 2/156; SU563645; NP 158, 168
Brimstage (township in Bromborough), 5/437; SJ302827; NP 100
Brind (division in township of Newsholme and Brind in Wressle), 41/41; SE743310; NP 97, 98
Brind Leys (extra-parochial), 41/40; SE740320; NP 97
Brindle (parish), 20/326; SD600243; NP 94, 95
Brindley (township in Acton), 5/289; SJ585541; NP 109, 110
Brindley Heath (township in Cannock), 33/228A; SK003157; NP 120
Bringhurst (parish), 21/304-306; NP 133
Bringhurst (township in Bringhurst), 21/305; SP842919; NP 133
Brington (parish), 17/46; TL084768; NP 134
Brington (parish), 26/240; SP661644; NP 132, 133
Briningham (Brinningham) (parish), 25/120; TG030340; NP 125
Brinkburn (extra-parochial), 27/268-270; NP 71
Brinkburn High Ward (township within Brinkburn extra-parochial), 27/268; NU114002; NP 71
Brinkburn Low Ward (township within Brinkburn extra-parochial), 27/269; NZ136988; NP 71
Brinkburn South Side (township within Brinkburn extra-parochial), 27/270); NZ127980; NP 71
Brinkhill (parish), 22/396; TF372738; NP 114
Brinkley (parish), 4/141; TL613552; NP 135, 148
Brinklow (parish), 37/141; SP428790; NP 132
Brinkworth (parish), 39/50-51; SU026823; NP 157
Brinkworth (tithing in Brinkworth, 39/49; SU020853; NP 157
Brinkynalt, 49/97; NP 118
Brinningham (parish), 25/120; NP 125
Brinnington (township in Stockport), 5/14; SJ909919; NP 101
Brinsley (township in Greasley), 28/171; SK459492; NP 112
Brinsop (parish), 15/118; SO441451; NP 142
Brinsworth (township in Rotherham), 43/840; SK415905; NP 103
Brinton (parish), 25/122; TG038356; NP 125

Brisco (township in St Cuthbert [Carlisle]), 7/80; NY427514; NP 76
Brisley (parish), 25/271; TF953212; NP 125
Brislington (parish), 32/19; ST620707; NP 156, 165
Bristol, All Saints (parish), 13/418; ST588730; NP 155/1
Bristol, Castle Precinct (extra-parochial), 13/424; ST593731; NP 155/1
Bristol, Christchurch (parish), 13/421; ST589731; NP 155/1
Bristol, St Augustine-the-Less (parish), 13/429; ST582727; NP 155/1
Bristol, St Ewin (parish), 13/419; ST588731; NP 155/1
Bristol, St George (parish), 13/410; ST625736; NP 156
Bristol, St James (parish), 13/409A-B, 427; NP 155/1
Bristol, St James - In-Parish (division in Bristol, St James), 13/427; ST588735; NP 155/1
Bristol, St James and St Paul ('united parishes'), 13/409A-B; NP 155
Bristol, St James and St Paul - Out-Parish (division in Bristol, St James and St Paul), 13/409B; ST592746; NP 155
Bristol, St John (parish), 13/420; ST587732; NP 155/1
Bristol, St Leonard (parish), 13/417A; ST588728; NP 155/1
Bristol, St Mary le Port (parish), 13/422; ST590730; NP 155/1
Bristol, St Mary Redcliff (parish), 13/412; ST591723; NP 155/1
Bristol, St Michael (parish), 13/428; ST583734; NP 155/1
Bristol, St Nicholas (parish), 13/415; ST588727; NP 155/1
Bristol, St Paul (parish), 13/409A-B, 426; ST594736; NP 155/1
Bristol, St Paul - In-Parish (division in Bristol, St Paul), 13/426; ST594736; NP 155/1
Bristol, St Peter (parish), 13/423; ST591731; NP 155/1
Bristol, St Philip and St Jacob (parish), 13/411, 425; NP 155/1
Bristol, St Philip and St Jacob - In-Parish (division in Bristol, St Philip and St Jacob), 13/425; ST596731; NP 155/1
Bristol, St Philip and St Jacob - Out-Parish (division in Bristol, St Philip and St Jacob), 13/411; ST603731; NP 155/1
Bristol, St Stephen (parish), 13/416; ST587726; NP 155/1
Bristol, St Thomas (parish), 13/414; ST591728; NP 155/1
Bristol, St Werbergh (parish), 13/417B; NP 155/1
Bristol, Temple (parish), 13/413; ST595725; NP 155/1
Briston (parish), 25/126; TG067321; NP 125
Britford (parish), 39/358; SU146279; NP 167
Brithdir (hamlet in Gelligaer), 51/75A; ST120990; NP 154
Brithdir (township in Llanidloes), 54/145; SN934968; NP 128
Briton Ferry (parish), 51/50; SS748943; NP 153
Britwell Priory (Britwell Prior) (chapelry in Newington), 29/290; SU671930; NP 158, 159
Britwell Salome (parish), 29/291; SU674937; NP 158, 159
Brixham (parish), 9/436; SX910536; NP 188
Brixton (parish), 9/466; SX552528; NP 187
Brixton (parish), 18/10; NP 180
Brixton Deverill (parish), 39/379; ST866383; NP 166
Brixworth (parish), 26/193; SP750702; NP 133
Brize Norton (parish), 29/167; SP300080; NP 144, 145, 157, 158
Broad Blunsdon (tithing in Highworth), 39/6; SU155810; NP 157
Broad Campden (hamlet in Chipping Campden), 13/27C; SP160480; NP 144
Broad Chalke (parish), 39/349; SU042250; NP 167
Broad Clyst (Broadclist) (parish), 9/245; SX999985; NP 176
Broad Hinton (division in Hurst), 2/197; SU808739; NP 169
Broad Hinton (division in Broad Hinton), 39/92; SU108773; NP 157
Broad Hinton (parish), 39/91-92; NP 157
Broad Lane (township in Hawarden), 50/11; SJ320648; NP 109
Broad Marston (hamlet in Pebworth), 13/12; SP194464; NP 144
Broad Somerford (parish), 39/46; NP 156, 157
Broad Town (tithing in Broad Hinton), 39/91; SU083787; NP 157
Broadclist, 9/245; NP 176
Broadfield (extra-parochial), 16/24; TL322309; NP 147
Broadhembury (parish), 9/225; ST094049; NP 176
Broadhempston (parish), 9/424; SX801665; NP 187, 188
Broadholme (township in Thorney), 28/122; SK895735; NP 113
Broadmayne (parish), 10/253; SY722061; NP 178
Broadnymett (Broadnymet) (district in North Tawton), 9/207; SS703008; NP 175

Broadoak, 6/71; NP 186
Broadwall (hamlet in Broadwall), 29/159A; SP254036; NP 157
Broadwall (parish), 29/159A-160; NP 157
Broadward (township in Leominster), 15/68; SO510585; NP 129
Broadwas (parish), 40/108; SO765558; NP 130, 143
Broadwater (parish), 36/304-305; NP 182
Broadwater (township in Broadwater), 36/304; TQ142053; NP 182
Broadway (parish), 10/268; NP 178
Broadway (parish), 32/433; ST312149; NP 177
Broadway (parish), 40/204; SP100375; NP 144
Broadwell (parish), 13/91; SP206274; NP 144
Broadwey (Broadway) (parish), 10/268; SY667835; NP 178
Broadwindsor (parish), 10/108; ST422047; NP 177
Broadwood Kelly (parish), 9/184; SS612059; NP 175
Broadwoodwidger (parish), 9/199; SX402922; NP 174, 175, 186
Brobury (parish), 15/112; SO345443; NP 142
Brockdish (parish), 25/766; TM209801; NP 137
Brockenhurst (division in Brockenhurst), 14/327; SU313007; NP 180
Brockenhurst (parish), 14/327A-C; NP 179, 180
Brockhall (parish), 26/241; SP639632; NP 132, 133
Brockhampton (division in Buckland Newton), 10/155; ST715062; NP 178
Brockhampton and Knoll (tything in Buckland Newton), 10/155-156; NP 178
Brockhampton (division in Brockhampton), 15/85; SO688557; NP 130, 143
Brockhampton (parish), 15/85-86; NP 130, 143
Brockhampton (parish), 15/178; SO688557; NP 143
Brockholes (Brockhole) (division in Grimsargh with Brockholes in Preston), 20/220; SD579308; NP 94
Brocklebank (township in Westward), 7/147A; NY290430; NP 82
Brocklesby (parish), 22/69; TA132112; NP 104, 105
Brockley (parish), 32/491; ST474671; NP 165
Brockley (parish), 34/311; TL822557; NP 136, 149
Brockthorp (parish), 13/254; NP 143
Brockton (township in Lydbury North), 31/374; SO330861; NP 129
Brockton, 31/496; NP 129
Brockton, 33/184; NP 119
Brockworth (parish), 13/203; SO893160; NP 143
Brocton (Brockton) (township in Baswich), 33/184; SJ970193; NP 119
Brodsworth (division in parish and township of Brodsworth), 43/879; SE514075; NP 103
Brodsworth (parish and township), 43/879-880; NP 103
Brogden (division in township of Brogden with Admergill in Barnoldswick), 43/309; SD852462; NP 95
Brogden with Admergill (township in Barnoldswick), 43/309-310; NP 95
Brokenborough (parish), 39/22; ST915895; NP 156, 157
Brokenheugh (township in parochial chapelry of Haydon in Warden), 27/602B; NY826693; NP 77
Bromborough (Bromborow, Bromborrow) (parish), 5/436-437; NP 100
Bromborough (Bromborow, Bromborrow) (township in Bromborough), 5/436; SJ351823; NP 100
Bromborow (parish), 5/436-437; NP 100
Bromborow, 5/436; NP 100
Bromby, 22/27; NP 104
Brome (parish), 25/617; NP 137
Brome (parish), 34/85; TM145765; NP 136, 137
Bromehill (Broomhill) (division in Weeting), 25/705; TL804884; NP 136
Bromeswell (parish), 34/382; TM310485; NP 150
Bromfield (parish), 7/127-132; NP 75, 82
Bromfield (parish), 19/224; NP 172
Bromfield (parish), 31/421-424; NP 129
Bromfield (township in Bromfield), 31/422; SO481773; NP 129
Bromfield, Crookdake and Scales (township in Bromfield), 7/130; NY190450; NP 82
Bromham (parish), 1/31; TL009515; NP 147

Bromham (parish), 39/130; ST975650; NP 157, 167
Bromley (parish), 19/63; TQ418688; NP 171
Bromley (township in Eccleshall), 33/148; SJ784351; NP 119
Bromley St Leonard (parish), 24/71; TQ381817; NP 161
Bromlow (township in Worthen), 31/327; SJ322016; NP 118, 129
Brompton (division in Kensington), 24/39B; TQ260787; NP 170
Brompton (township in Berrington), 31/283; SJ550076; NP 118
Brompton (township in Church Stoke), 31/363; SO251938; NP 129
Brompton (parish), 42/415-419; NP 92, 93
Brompton (township in Brompton), 42/415; SE947823; NP 93
Brompton (township in Northallerton), 42/266; SE376981; NP 91
Brompton Ralph (parish), 32/276; ST084322; NP 164
Brompton-on-Swale (Brompton-upon-Swale) (township in Easby), 42/89; NZ218018; NP 91
Brompton-upon-Swale, 42/89; NP 91
Bromsberrow (parish), 13/131; SO744339; NP 143
Bromsgrove (parish), 40/38; SO970730; NP 130, 131
Bromyard (parish), 15/88-92; NP 130, 143
Bromyard (township in Bromyard), 15/90; SO655542; NP 130, 142
Bromyhurst (division in township of Barton upon Irwell in Eccles), 20/550; SJ751962; NP 101
Bron-y-garth (township in St Martin), 31/78; SJ272368; NP 117, 118
Broncastellan (township in Llanbadarn fawr), 46/11C; SN631841; NP 127
Broncoed (township in Mold), 50/113; SJ238628; NP 108
Broncote (extra-parochial), 33/79; SK014611; NP 111
Broncroft (township in Diddlebury), 31/507B; SO544866; NP 129
Brongwyn (parish), 46/94; SN296438; NP 139
Bronington (Bronnington) (township in Hanmer), 50/141; SJ503398; NP 118
Bronllys (parish), 45/5; SO150356; NP 141
Bronnington, 50/141; NP 118
Brook (Brooke) (parish), 18/8; SZ389843; NP 180
Brook (Brooke) (parish), 19/331; TR066444; NP 172
Brook (parish), 30/21; NP 122
Brooke (Brook) (parish), 30/21; SK846057; NP 122
Brooke (parish), 25/598; TM285989; NP 137
Brookesby (parish), 21/118; NP 121, 122
Brookhampton (township in Holdgate), 31/498A; SO560900; NP 129
Brookland (parish), 19/438; TQ983255; NP 184
Brooksby (Brookesby) (parish), 21/118; SK673155; NP 121, 122
Brookthorpe (Brockthorp) (parish), 13/254; SO841118; NP 143
Broom (Broome) (parish), 40/3; SO902785; NP 130
Broom (division in township of Broom in St Oswald), 11/132A; NZ253417; NP 85
Broom (division in township of Broom in St Oswald), 11/132B; NZ242419; NP 85
Broom (hamlet in Southill), 1/92; TL173428; NP 147
Broom (township in St Oswald), 11/132A-B; NP 85
Broom-Park, 27/194; NP 71
Broome (Brome) (parish), 25/617; TM348925; NP 137
Broome (parish), 40/3; SO902785; NP 130
Broome Park (Broom-Park) (township in Edlingham), 27/194; NU108125; NP 71
Broomfield (parish), 12/245; TL702102; NP 148, 161
Broomfield (Bromfield) (parish), 19/224; TQ835517; NP 172
Broomfield (parish), 32/298; ST226327; NP 164, 165
Broomfleet (township in South Cave), 41/205; SE880272; NP 98
Broomhall (township in Wrenbury), 5/276; SJ633472; NP 110
Broomhaugh (township in Bywell St Andrew), 27/624; NZ026611; NP 77
Broomhill (division in Broomhill), 19/441; TR000192; NP 184
Broomhill (parish), 19/441, 36/148; NP 184
Broomhill (Roomhill) (division in Broomhill), 36/148; TQ981186; NP 184
Broomhill, 25/705; NP 136
Broomhope (township in parochial chapelry of Birtley in Chollerton), 27/368; NY892833; NP 77

67

Broomley (township in Bywell St Peter), 27/633; NZ042593; NP 77
Broomsthorpe (hamlet in East Rudham), 25/168; TF849278; NP 125
Broomy Walk (extra-parochial division in New Forest), 14/302C; SU210110; NP 179
Broseley (parish), 31/464; SJ688016; NP 119
Brothertoft (township in Kirton), 22/766; TF271461; NP 114, 123
Brotherton (parish), 43/464-466; NP 97
Brotherton (township in Brotherton), 43/466; SE481264; NP 97
Brotherwick (township in Warkworth), 27/221; NU229058; NP 71
Brotton (township in Skelton), 42/355; NZ689206; NP 86
Brough (parish), 38/54-57; NP 84
Brough (township in Brough), 38/55; NY799146; NP 84
Brough (township in Elloughton), 41/211; SE937266; NP 98
Brough (township in Catterick), 42/82; SE215985; NP 91
Brough and Shatton (township in Hope), 8/20; SK192818; NP 111
Brough Sowerby (township in Brough), 38/57; NY803127; NP 84
Brough under Stainmore, 38/55
Broughall (township in Whitchurch), 31/35; SJ572413; NP 118
Brougham (parish), 38/2; NY570280; NP 83
Broughton (parish), 3/58; SP907402; NP 146
Broughton (division in Broughton), 14/151; SU308336; NP 167, 168
Broughton (parish), 14/151-152; NP 167, 168
Broughton (parish), 17/67; TL282778; NP 134
Broughton (township in Preston), 20/211; SD540340; NP 94
Broughton East (township in Cartmel), 20/60A; SD399703; NP 89
Broughton in Furness (West Broughton) (township in Kirkby Ireleth), 20/2; SD220890; NP 88
Broughton with Kersall (township in Manchester), 20/507; SD829011; NP 101
Broughton Astley (parish), 21/244A-C; NP 132
Broughton Astley (township in Broughton Astley), 21/244A; SP521925; NP 132
Broughton (parish), 22/40; SE965087; NP 104
Broughton (parish), 26/162; SP843761; NP 133
Broughton (parish), 29/19-20; NP 145
Broughton (township in Broughton), 29/19; SP420393; NP 145
Broughton Poggs (parish), 29/175; SP221046; NP 157
Broughton (parish), 31/158-159; NP 118
Broughton (township in Bishop's Castle), 31/381; SO310910; NP 129
Broughton (township in Broughton), 31/159; SJ498244; NP 118
Broughton (township in Eccleshall), 33/147; SJ763340; NP 119
Broughton Gifford (parish), 39/126; ST881638; NP 156, 166
Broughton Hackett (Hacketts-Broughton) (parish), 40/153; SO926555; NP 130
Broughton (township in Appleton-le-Street), 42/641; SE770729; NP 92
Broughton (township in Kirkby), 42/323-324; NP 86, 92
Broughton (township in Wrexham [Wrecsam]), 49/53; SJ308520; NP 109
Broughton (township in Hawarden), 50/1; SJ333632; NP 109
Broughton (parish), 43/318-319; NP 95
Broughton (township in Broughton), 43/318; SD938518; NP 95
Brown Candover (parish), 14/136; SU575398; NP 168
Brown Moss (sub-division of Westby division in Westby with Plumptons township in Kirkham), 20/181; SD375300; NP 94
Brownside, 8/12; NP 102, 111
Brownsover (township in Clifton upon Dunsmore), 37/122; SP510776; NP 132
Browsholme (division in township of Forest of Bowland (Lower Division) township in Whalley), 43/286; SD674452; NP 95
Broxa (township in Hackness), 42/393; SE945915; NP 93
Broxbourne (Broxborne) (hamlet in Broxbourne), 16/114; TL350069; NP 160, 161
Broxbourne (Broxborne) (parish), 16/114-115; NP 160, 161
Broxfield (township in Embleton), 27/156; NU203167; NP 71
Broxholme (parish), 22/244; SK917773; NP 104
Broxted (parish), 12/435; TL579260; NP 148

Broxton (township in Malpas), 5/339; SJ488545; NP 109
Bruen Stapleford (township in Tarvin), 5/389; SJ492645; NP 109
Bruern (extra-parochial), 29/139; SP244173; NP 145
Bruisyard (parish), 34/257; TM331666; NP 137
Brumby (Bromby) (township in Frodingham), 22/27; SE882096; NP 104
Brumstead (Brunstead) (parish), 25/233; TG369268; NP 126
Brundall (parish), 25/474; TG321085; NP 126
Brundish (parish), 34/170; TM268697; NP 137
Brunstead (parish), 25/233; TG369268; NP 126
Brunstock (township in Crosby upon Eden), 7/23; NY422601; NP 76
Brunthwaite (division in township of Silsden in Kildwick), 43/343; SE070460; NP 96
Bruntingthorpe (parish), 21/333; SP607893; NP 132
Brunton (High and Low Brunton) (township in Embleton), 27/148; NU202248; NP 71
Brushfield (township in Bakewell), 8/102; SK163720; NP 111
Brushford (parish), 9/121; SS671078; NP 175
Brushford (parish), 32/284; SS904251; NP 164
Bruton (parish), 32/197A-198; NP 166
Bruton (tithing in Bruton), 32/197A; ST682446; NP 166
Bryanston (Bryanstone) (parish), 10/164; ST865064; NP 178
Bryher (district in Isles of Scilly), 6/220; SV877150; NP 189
Brymbo (township in Wrexham [Wrecsam]), 49/51; SJ283539; NP 108, 109
Brympton (Brympton D'Everey) (parish), 32/470B; ST524157; NP 177
Bryn-ellyn (township in Llanfyllin), 54/12; SJ154194; NP 117
Bryn-glas (township in Llanfair Caereinion), 54/46; SJ086096; NP 117
Bryn-llefrith (hamlet in Llanwenog), 46/82B; SN479471; NP 139, 140
Brynbuga (parish), 53-63-64B; NP 155
Brynbychan (township in Rhuddlan), 50/65; SJ037783; NP 108
Bryncroes (parish), 48/68; SH220315; NP 115
Bryneglwys (parish), 49/44-45; NP 108
Bryneglwys (township in Bryneglwys), 49/44; SJ145483; NP 108
Brynford (township in Holywell), 50/31; SJ190742; NP 108
Bryngwyn (township in St Asaph [Llanelwy]), 50/77; SJ044737; NP 108
Bryngwyn (township in Tremeirchion), 50/80; SJ101753; NP 108
Bryngwyn (Bryngwin) (parish), 53/25; SO392092; NP 142, 155
Bryngwyn (parish), 56/50; SO177495; NP 141
Bryngwyn Isaf (township in Caerwys), 50/86; SJ120751; NP 108
Bryngwyn Ucha (township in Caerwys), 50/85; SJ109742; NP 108
Brynhaugh (hamlet in Llanwenog), 46/85; SN474495; NP 139, 140
Brynhedydd (township in Rhuddlan), 50/58; SJ026817; NP 108
Brynheilyn (township in Llanfair Caereinion), 54/57; SJ131070; NP 117
Bryning with Kellamergh (township in Kirkham), 20/198; SD402295; NP 94
Brynkinalt (Brinkynalt) (township in Chirk), 49/97; SJ301392; NP 118
Brynllywarch (township in Kerry [Llanfihangel-yng-Ngheri]), 54/173; SO152890; NP 128
Brynuchel with Tafolog (township in Cemmes), 54/122; SH870080; NP 116, 117
Brynywal (township in Rhuddlan), 50/60; SJ031800; NP 108
Bubbenhall (parish), 37/157; SP366721; NP 132
Bubnell (Bubnel) (township in Bakewell), 8/84; SK241727; NP 111
Bubwith (parish), 41/26-31, 33, 35; NP 97, 98
Bubwith (township in Bubwith), 41/28; SE723364; NP 97
Buckabank (township in Dalston), 7/143; NY377495; NP 76, 83
Buckden (parish), 17/93; TL194677; NP 134
Buckden (township in Arncliffe), 43/228; SD895795; NP 90
Buckenham (parish), 25/470; TG359058; NP 126
Buckenham Parva (parish), 25/709; NP 136
Buckenham Tofts (Buckenham-near-Tofts, Buckenham Parva) (parish), 25/709; TL838948; NP 136
Buckenham-near-Tofts (parish), 25/709; NP 136

Buckerell (parish), 9/238; ST124005; NP 176
Buckfastleigh (parish), 9/375; SX710670; NP 187
Buckholt (East and West Buckholt) (extra-parochial), 14/150; SU283325; NP 167, 168
Buckhorn Weston (parish), 10/21; ST757247; NP 166
Buckingham (division in Buckingham), 3/78; SP693343; NP 146
Buckingham (parish), 3/78-82; NP 145, 146
Buckingham Palace (division in St George Hanover Square), 24/36B; TQ290796; NP 160/1
Buckland (parish), 2/31; SU340985; NP 158
Buckland (parish), 3/174; SP902102; NP 146, 159
Buckland (parish), 13/32; SP067356; NP 144
Buckland (parish), 16/22; TL361334; NP 147, 148
Buckland (Buckland next Faversham) (parish), 19/157; TQ980618; NP 172
Buckland (parish), 19/372; TR308426; NP 173
Buckland (parish), 35/115; TQ225515; NP 170
Buckland Brewer (parish), 9/59; SS415189; NP 163, 174
Buckland Dinham (Buckland Denham) (parish), 32/120; ST750512; NP 166
Buckland Filleigh (parish), 9/108; SS481091; NP 175
Buckland in the Moor (parish), 9/377; SX725736; NP 175
Buckland Monachorum (parish), 9/359; SX500676; NP 175, 187
Buckland Newton (parish), 10/152-157; NP 178
Buckland Newton (tithing in Buckland Newton), 10/152; ST690050; NP 178
Buckland Ripers (parish), 10/261; SY644827; NP 178
Buckland St Mary (parish), 32/429; ST264139; NP 164
Buckland-tout-Saints (parish), 9/478; SX758460; NP 187
Bucklebury (Bucklebury and Hawkeridge) (tithing in Bucklebury), 2/161; SU552702; NP 158
Bucklebury (parish), 2/161-162; NP 158
Bucklesham (parish), 34/448; TM251415; NP 150
Buckminster (parish), 21/107-108; NP 122
Buckminster (township in Buckminster), 21/107; SK864224; NP 122
Bucknall (parish), 22/362; TF170690; NP 113
Bucknall (township in Stoke-on-Trent), 33/26; SJ915465; NP 110
Bucknall cum Bagnall (township in Stoke-on-Trent), 33/24-25; NP 110
Bucknall Eaves (division in Stoke-on-Trent), 33/25; SJ919481; NP 110
Bucknell (parish), 29/81; SP555251; NP 145
Bucknell (parish), 15/12, 31/407-408; NP 129
Bucknell (township in Bucknell), 31/407; SO350743; NP 129
Buckton (township in Kyloe parochial chapelry in Holy Island), 27/26; NU073385; NP 64
Buckton (township in Bridlington), 41/252; TA175732; NP 93
Buckton and Doxall (township in Bucknell), 15/12; SO380737; NP 129
Buckworth (parish), 17/43; TL150770; NP 134
Budbrooke (Budbrook) (parish), 37/169; SP252643; NP 131
Budby (township in Edwinstowe), 28/80; SK616699; NP 112
Buddington (hamlet in Bignor), 36/19; SU886235; NP 181
Budle (township in Bamburgh), 27/109; NU164350; NP 71
Budock (district in Budock), 6/181A; SW782320; NP 190
Budock (district in Budock), 6/181B; SW774341; NP 190
Budock (parish), 6/181A-B; NP 190
Buerhill, 20/439; NP 101
Buersil (Buerhill) (division in township of Castleton in Rochdale), 20/439; SD908111; NP 101
Buerton (township in Aldford), 5/366; SJ428603; NP 109
Buerton (township in Audlem), 5/270; SJ688428; NP 110
Bugbrooke (parish), 26/280; SP682575; NP 132, 133
Buglawton (township in Astbury), 5/234; SJ888638; NP 110
Bugsworth, 8/12; NP 102, 111
Bugthorpe (parish), 41/135; SE773579; NP 98
Buildwas (parish), 31/467; SJ638041; NP 119
Builth (Llanfair-in-Buallt) (parish), 45/14; SO040505; NP 141
Bulby (hamlet in Irnham), 22/682; TF042257; NP 123
Bulcamp (parish), 34/155; TM453763; NP 137
Bulcote (chapelry in Burton Joyce), 28/226; SK651446; NP 112, 121

Bulford (parish), 39/261; SU188442; NP 167
Bulk (township in Lancaster), 20/118; SD493633; NP 89
Bulkeley (township in Malpas), 5/335; SJ532543; NP 109
Bulkington (hamlet in Bulkington), 37/100; SP395867; NP 132
Bulkington (parish), 37/100-101; NP 132
Bulkington (tithing in Keevil), 39/140; ST947585; NP 167
Bulkworthy (parish), 9/57; SS389142; NP 163, 174, 175
Bullers Green (township in Morpeth), 27/412; NZ195865; NP 78
Bulley (parish), 13/142; SO759199; NP 143
Bullingham (Upper Bulingham, Over Bullinghope, Bullinghope) (parish), 15/186; SO506365; NP 142
Bullinghope (parish), 15/186; NP 142
Bullington (parish), 14/142; SU461419; NP 168
Bullington (chapelry in Goltho), 22/352; TF098769; NP 105
Bullock's Hall (township in Warkworth), 27/231; NZ244976; NP 71
Bulmer (parish), 12/48; TL842398; NP 149
Bulmer (parish), 42/647-649; NP 92
Bulmer (township in Bulmer), 42/649; SE702677; NP 92
Bulphan (Bulpham) (parish), 12/408; TQ640860; NP 161
Bulthey (division in Alberbury Upper Quarter township in Alberbury), 31/306; SJ316134; NP 118
Bulwell (parish), 28/181; SK539458; NP 112, 121
Bulwick (parish), 26/48; SP955940; NP 133, 134
Bulwick Short Leys (extra-parochial), 26/49; SP970926; NP 134
Bulworthy (district in Alverdiscott), 9/43B; SS510261; NP 163
Bumpstead Helion (parish), 12/26; TL655420; NP 148
Bunbury (parish), 5/300-311; NP 109, 110
Bunbury (township in Bunbury), 5/303; SJ571581; NP 109
Bungay, Holy Trinity (Bungay Trinity) (parish), 34/30; TM346890; NP 137
Bungay, St Mary (parish), 34/31; TM336899; NP 137
Bunny (parish), 28/274; SK585296; NP 121
Bunwell (parish), 25/749; TM131930; NP 136
Burbage (parish), 39/196; SU230609; NP 167
Burbage (township in Aston Flamville), 21/227A; SP442921; NP 132
Burcombe (parish), 39/325; SU071308; NP 167
Burcot (Burcott) (hamlet in Dorchester), 29/300; SU561967; NP 158
Burdon (township in Bishop Wearmouth), 11/70; NZ388513; NP 78, 85
Burdon, 11/335; NP 85
Bures Hamlet (hamlet in Bures St Mary), 12/95; TL897338; NP 149
Bures St Mary (hamlet in Bures St Mary), 34/495; TL920350; NP 149
Bures St Mary (parish), 12/95, 34/495; NP 149
Burfield (township in Clun), 31/389; SO267804; NP 128
Burford (hamlet in Burford), 29/157; SP261109; NP 144, 157
Burford (parish), 29/157-158; NP 144, 157
Burford (parish), 31/528, 538-543; NP 129, 130
Burford (township in Burford), 31/542; SO591691; NP 129, 130
Burgate (parish), 34/135; TM079751; NP 136
Burgedin (township in Guilsfield [Cegidfa]), 54/76; SJ238147; NP 117
Burgh (parish), 34/388; TM235523; NP 150
Burgh Apton (Bergh Apton) (parish), 25/576; TG311003; NP 126, 137
Burgh by Sands (parish), 7/103-108; NP 75, 76
Burgh Castle (parish), 34/1; TG482050; NP 126
Burgh cum Girsby (parish), 22/275; TF213862; NP 105
Burgh Head (township in Burgh by Sands), 7/104; NY330598; NP 75, 76
Burgh le Marsh (parish), 22/493; TF512652; NP 114
Burgh Marsh (area in Burgh by Sands), 7/106; NY315601; NP 75, 76
Burgh next Aylsham (parish), 25/211; TG219251; NP 126
Burgh on Bain (Burgh cum Girsby) (parish), 22/275; TF213862; NP 10
Burgh St Margaret (Burgh St Margaret and St Mary, Fleggburgh) (parish), 25/389; TG448141; NP 126
Burgh St Peter (parish), 25/627; TM482938; NP 137

Burgh West End (township in Burgh by Sands), 7/105; NY317587; NP 75
Burgham (tithing in Worplesden), 35/76A; TQ000530; NP 169
Burghclere (parish), 14/9; SU471593; NP 168
Burghfield (parish), 2/175; SU673690; NP 158, 169
Burghill (parish), 15/122A-B; NP 142
Burghill (township in Burghill), 15/122A; SO480440; NP 142
Burghwallis (division of Burghwallis township in Burghwallis), 43/650; SE533118; NP 103
Burghwallis (division of Burghwallis township in Owston), 43/651; SE523117; NP 103
Burghwallis (parish), 43/649-650; NP 103
Burghwallis (township in Burghwallis and Owston), 43/650-651; NP 103
Burham (parish), 19/443; TQ730623; NP 171
Buriton (parish), 14/245; SU740203; NP 181
Burland (township in Acton), 5/287; SJ620529; NP 109, 110
Burlescombe (parish), 9/138; ST065159; NP 164
Burleston (Burlestone) (parish), 10/303; SY777955; NP 178
Burley (division of Headingley township in Leeds), 43/501; SE278337; NP 96
Burley (extra-parochial), 14/307; SU212035; NP 179
Burley (parish), 30/13; SK883107; NP 122
Burley in Wharfedale (Burley) (township in Otley), 43/363; SE157488; NP 96
Burley Lodge (division in Burley Lodge extra-parochial, 14/306B; SU238052; NP 179
Burley Lodge (extra-parochial), 14/306A-B; NP 179
Burley Outer Rails Enclosure (division in Burley Lodge extra-parochial), 14/306A; SU232057; NP 179
Burley Walk (extra-parochial division in New Forest extra-parochial), 14/302D; SU208049; NP 179
Burley, 43/363; NP 96
Burlingham St Andrew (North Burlingham) (parish), 25/455; TG361102; NP 126
Burlingham St Edmund (South Burlingham) (parish), 25/457; TG372079; NP 126
Burlingham St Peter (North Burlingham) (parish), 25/456; TG372101; NP 126
Burlton (township in Loppington), 31/52; SJ459264; NP 118
Burmarsh (parish), 19/423; TR102321; NP 173, 184
Burmington (parish), 37/293; SP273373; NP 144, 145
Burn (township in Brayton), 43/452; SE602282; NP 97
Burnage (township in Manchester), 20/528; SJ865925; NP 101
Burnaston (township in Etwall), 8/254; SK297316; NP 121
Burnby (parish), 41/104; NP 98
Burnby (township in Burnby and Hayton), 41/104; SE839465; NP 98
Burneston (parish), 42/221-225; NP 91
Burneston (township in Burneston), 42/224; SE318851; NP 91
Burnett (parish), 32/47; ST664652; NP 156, 166
Burnham (division in Burnham), 3/222; SU940834; NP 159
Burnham (parish), 3/222-223; NP 159
Burnham (parish), 12/358; NP 162
Burnham (parish), 32/173; NP 165
Burnham Broome (division in Burnham Broome), 25/556; TG182073; NP 125
Burnham Broome (parish), 25/556-557; NP 125
Burnham Deepdale (parish), 25/9; TF809438; NP 125
Burnham Market (Burnham Westgate) (parish), 25/10; TF816412; NP 125
Burnham Norton (parish), 25/11; TF827438; NP 125
Burnham on Sea (Burnham) (parish), 32/173; ST325491; NP 165
Burnham Overy (parish), 25/12; TF851441; NP 125
Burnham Sutton (Sutton cum St Andrew, Burnham Sutton cum Burnham Ulph) (parish), 25/13; TF833410; NP 125
Burnham Thorpe (parish), 25/14; TF857412; NP 125
Burnham Westgate (parish), 25/10; NP 125
Burnham-on-Crouch (Burnham) (parish), 12/358; TQ975965; NP 162
Burnhope and Hamsteels, 11/149
Burniston (township in Scalby), 42/399; TA012922; NP 93
Burnley (township in Whalley), 20/276; SD850330; NP 95

Burnop and Hamsteels (Burnhope) (township in Lanchester), 11/149; NZ178451; NP 84, 85
Burnsall (Burnsal, Burnsall with Thorpe sub Montem) (township in Burnsall), 43/209; SE018505; NP 90, 95, 96
Burnsall (parish), 43/207-216; NP 90, 91, 95, 96
Burnsall and Thorpe Fell (common to Burnsall and Thorpe in Burnsall), 43/210; SE015598; NP 90, 96
Burntwood (township in St Michael), 33/266A; SK060100; NP 120
Burpham (parish), 36/217; TQ051095; NP 181, 182
Burradon (Borrowden, Burrowden) township in Alwinton), 27/182; NT902050; NP 71
Burradon (township in Earsdon), 27/487; NZ275729; NP 78
Burrell-cum-Cowling, 42/210; NP 91
Burrells (township in St Lawrence Appleby), 38/44; NY684177; NP 83
Burrill with Cowling (Burrell-cum-Cowling) (township in Bedale), 42/210; SE241876; NP 91
Burringham (township in Bottesford), 22/30; SE845087; NP 104
Burrington (parish), 9/88; SS629175; NP 163
Burrington (parish), 15/3; SO445725; NP 129
Burrington (parish), 32/70; ST482591; NP 165
Burrogh (parish), 21/266; NP 122
Burrough Green (parish), 4/143; TL626564; NP 135, 148
Burrough on the Hill (Burrow or Burrogh, Burrow on the Hill) (parish), 21/266; SK752107; NP 122
Burrow (parish), 21/266; NP 122
Burrow on the Hill (parish), 21/266; NP 122
Burrow with Burrow (Burrow) (township in Tunstall), 20/75; SD628768; NP 89
Burroway (extra-parochial), 29/174; SP303003; NP 158
Burrowden, 27/182; NP 71
Burscough (township in Ormskirk), 20/369; SD432122; NP 100
Bursledon (parish), 14/273; SU487102; NP 180
Burslem (parish), 33/19-21, 23; SJ862498; NP 110
Burslem (township in Burslem), 33/19; SJ862498; NP 110
Burstall (parish), 34/423; TM096445; NP 149, 150
Burstock (parish), 10/109; ST423026; NP 177
Burston (parish), 25/747; TM137840; NP 136, 137
Burstow (parish), 35/111; TQ320432; NP 170
Burstwick (parish), 41/423-426; NP 99
Burstwick and Skeckling (division in township of Burstwick and Skeckling in Burstwick), 41/424; TA225285; NP 99
Burstwick and Skeckling (township in Burstwick), 41/423-424; NP 99
Burtholme (division of Burtholme township in Lanercost), 7/32; NY567637; NP 76
Burtholme (division of Burtholme township in Lanercost), 7/33A; NY550640; NP 76
Burton (Bodecton) (parish), 36/73; SU970186; NP 181
Burton (Burton by Lincoln) (parish), 22/247; SK952742; NP 104, 113
Burton (parish), 5/483-484; NP 100, 109
Burton (parish), 55/107; SM987067; NP 151
Burton (township in Burton), 5/483; SJ319744; NP 100, 109
Burton (township in Tarvin), 5/392; SJ319744; NP 109
Burton (township in Bamburgh), 27/107; NU182326; NP 71
Burton (township in Gresford), 49/69; SJ350583; NP 109
Burton Agnes (parish), 41/261A-263, 270; NP 93, 99
Burton Agnes (township in Burton Agnes), 41/262; TA107627; NP 93, 99
Burton Bradstock (parish), 10/235; SY497896; NP 177
Burton by Lincoln (parish), 22/247; NP 104, 113
Burton Coggles (parish), 22/684; SK975260; NP 123
Burton Constable (division in township of West Newton and Burton Constable in Swine), 41/382; TA185371; NP 99
Burton cum Walden (West Burton) (township in Aysgarth), 42/143; SE004821; NP 90
Burton Dassett (parish), 37/262; SP384518; NP 145
Burton Extra (township in Burton upon Trent), 33/214B; SK240230; NP 120
Burton Fleming (North Burton) (parish), 41/170; TA086720; NP 93
Burton Hastings (parish), 37/102; SP419895; NP 132

Burton Hill (division in Malmsbury Eastern Registration Subdistrict of Burton Hill tything in St Paul Malmesbury), 39/33A; ST940867; NP 157
Burton Hill (division in Malmsbury Western Registration Subdistrict of Burton Hill tything in St Paul Malmesbury), 39/33B; ST933866; NP 157
Burton Hill (tything in St Paul Malmesbury), 39/33A-B; NP 157
Burton in Kendal (parish), 20/72, 38/127-129; NP 89
Burton in Kendal (parish), 38/127-129; NP 89
Burton in Kendal (township in Burton in Kendal), 38/129; SD532772; NP 89
Burton in Lonsdale (township in Thornton in Lonsdale), 43/266; SD658728; NP 90
Burton Joyce (parish), 28/226-227; NP 112, 121
Burton Joyce (township in Burton Joyce), 28/227; SK642441; NP 121
Burton Latimer (parish), 26/154; SP909748; NP 134
Burton Lazars (chapelry in Melton Mowbray), 21/75; SK779170; NP 122
Burton Leonard (parish), 43/147; SE333640; NP 91
Burton on the Wolds (township in Prestwold), 21/43; SK608212; NP 121
Burton Overy (parish), 21/321; SP679971; NP 132, 133
Burton Pedwardine (parish), 22/652; TF110428; NP 123
Burton Pidsea (parish), 41/422; TA253309; NP 99
Burton Salmon (township in Monk Fryston), 43/463; SE496277; NP 97
Burton upon Stather (parish), 22/21-22; NP 104
Burton upon Stather (township in Burton upon Stather), 22/21; SE886179; NP 104
Burton upon Trent (parish), 8/313, 33/212-215; NP 120
Burton upon Trent (township in Burton upon Trent), 33/214A; SK250230; NP 120
Burton upon Ure (Burton upon Yore) (township in Masham), 42/173; SE235810; NP 91
Burton upon Yore, 42/173; NP 91
Burtonwood (township in Warrington), 20/620; SJ578918; NP100
Burwardsley (Burdwardsley) (township in Bunbury), 5/311; SJ516564; NP 109
Burwarton (parish), 31/562; SO612850; NP 129, 130
Burwash (parish), 36/52; TQ665244; NP 183
Burwell (hamlet in Burwell), 4/48A; TL588665; NP 135
Burwell (parish), 4/48A-B; NP 135
Burwell (parish), 22/293; TF360800; NP 105
Bury (division in township of Bury in Bury), 20/431; SD820106; NP 101
Bury (division in township of Bury in Bury), 20/432; SD807098; NP 101
Bury (division in township of Bury in Bury), 20/433; SD812119; NP 101
Bury (division in township of Bury in Bury), 20/434; SD828120; NP 101
Bury (division in township of Bury outside Bury borough boundary in Bury), 20/411; SD829114; NP 101
Bury (parish), 17/24; TL290832; NP 134
Bury (parish), 20/408-434, 475; NP 95, 101
Bury (parish), 36/78; TQ004142; NP 181
Bury (township in Bury), 20/411, 431-434; NP 101
Bury St Edmunds, St James (parish), 34/226; TL858671; NP 136
Bury St Edmunds, St Mary (parish), 34/227; TL863633; NP 136
Burythorpe (division in parish and township of Burythorpe), 41/131; SE790648; NP 92
Burythorpe (parish and township), 41/130-131; NP 92
Buscot (parish), 2/37; SU229966; NP 157
Bushbury (parish), 33/309-310; NP 119
Bushbury (township in Bushbury), 33/310; SK921029; NP 119
Bushby (township in Thurnby), 21/253; SK660040; NP 121
Bushey (parish), 16/140; TQ135953; NP 159
Bushley (parish), 40/239; SO872345; NP 143
Bushwood (hamlet in Old Stratford), 37/201; SP178686; NP 131
Buslingthorpe (parish), 22/785; TF087852; NP 104
Bustabeck (Bustabeck-Bound) (township in Castle Sowerby), 7/152; NY375430; NP 83

Bustabeck-Bound, 7/152; NP 83
Butcombe (parish), 32/59; ST516621; NP 165
Buteland (township in parochial chapelry of Birtley in Chollerton), 27/367; NY882808; NP 77
Butleigh (parish), 32/206; ST518337; NP 165
Butlers Marston (parish), 37/279; SP318498; NP 145
Butley (parish), 34/378; TM378498; NP 150
Butley (township in Prestbury), 5/39; SJ901786; NP 101
Butsfield (East Butsfield, West Butsfield and Steely) (township in Lanchester), 11/161; NZ109449; NP 84, 85
Buttercrambe (township in Bossall), 42/663; SE726578; NP 92, 97
Butterlaw (township in Newburn), 27/535; NZ186693; NP 78
Butterleigh (parish), 9/155; SS972085; NP 176
Butterley Park (township in Pentrich), 8/195A; SK413512; NP 112
Buttermere (township in Brigham), 7/273; NY182164; NP 82
Buttermere (parish), 39/387; SU344608; NP 168
Butterton (township in Trentham), 33/64; SJ833424; NP 119
Butterwaite (division in township of Ecclesfield in Ecclesfield), 43/794; SK377944; NP 102
Butterwick (division in township of Butterwick and Oldacres in Sedgefield), 11/239; NZ391301; NP 85
Butterwick (division adjoining East Fen in Butterwick), 22/758B; TF373486; NP 114
Butterwick (division in Butterwick), 22/758A; TF388449; NP 114, 124
Butterwick (parish), 22/758A-C; NP 114, 124
Butterwick - East Fen (division in Butterwick), 22/758C; TF391577; NP 114
Butterwick (township in Foxholes), 41/176; SE989716; NP 93
Butterwick (township in Barton-le-Street), 42/633; SE730770; NP 92
Butterworth (township in Rochdale), 20/463-470; NP 101
Butterworth Freehold Side (division in Butterworth township in Rochdale), 20/463-464; NP 101
Butterworth Hall (subdivision in Butterworth Lord's Side division in Butterworth township in Rochdale), 20/467; SD937124; NP 101
Butterworth Lord's Side (division in Butterworth township in Rochdale), 20/465-470; NP 101
Buttolphs (parish), 36/109; NP 182
Buttsbury (parish), 12/293; TQ670970; NP 161
Buxhall (parish), 34/350; TL999572; NP 136, 149
Buxted (parish), 36/55; TQ497249; NP 183
Buxton (parish), 25/246; TG231226; NP 126
Buxton (township in Bakewell), 8/107; SK082715; NP 111
Bwlch (township in Llanwddyn), 54/23B; SJ022179; NP 117
Bwlch-Trewern (hamlet in), 53/1; SO326226; NP 142
Byards Leap (extra-parochial), 22/578; SK991499; NP 113
Bychton (township in Whitford), 50/40; SJ161798; NP 108
Byers Green (township in St Andrew Auckland), 11/207; NZ221338; NP 85
Byfield (parish), 26/265; SP513542; NP 132, 145
Byfleet (parish), 35/87; TQ058611; NP 169, 170
Byford (parish), 15/121; SO396432; NP 142
Bygrave (parish), 16/8; TL259356; NP 147
Byker (township in All Saints), 27/283; NZ278672; NP 78
Byland Abbey (township in Coxwold), 42/549; SE544791; NP 92
Bylaugh (parish), 25/342; TG035190; NP 125
Byley cum Yatehouse (Biley cum Yatehouses) (township in Middlewich), 5/194; SJ714685; NP 110
Byram with Pool (Byrome) (township in Brotherton), 43/465; SE501262
Byrome, 43/465; NP 97
Bystock (district in Colaton Raleigh), 9/303B; SY022835; NP 176
Bythorn (parish), 17/48; TL061761; NP 134
Byton (parish), 15/35; SO372636; NP 129
Bywell St Andrew (parish), 27/622-626
Bywell St Andrew (township in Bywell St Andrew), 27/625; NZ038619; NP 77
Bywell St Peter (parish), 27/627-639; NP 77
Bywell St Peter (township in Bywell St Peter), 27/632; NZ044625; NP 77

C

Caborn (parish), 22/99; TA140025; NP 104, 105
Cabourne (Caborn) (parish), 22/99; TA140025; NP 104, 105
Cabus (township in Garstang), 20/149; SD492498; NP 94
Caca Dutton, 49/74; NP 109
Cacca Dutton (Caca Dutton) (township in Holt), 49/74; SJ406516; NP 109
Cadbury (parish), 9/217; SS911051; NP 176
Caddington (division in Caddington), 1/129; TL069199; NP 147
Caddington (parish), 1/129, 16/154; NP 147
Caddington (division in Caddington), 16/154; TL056193; NP 147
Cadeby (parish), 21/167-168; NP 121
Cadeby (township in Cadeby), 21/168; SK426022; NP 121
Cadeby (township in Sprotbrough), 43/882; SE518005; NP 103
Cadeleigh (parish), 9/157; SS912087; NP 164, 176
Cadishead (division in township of Barton upon Irwell in Eccles), 20/541; SJ702937; NP 101
Cadnam (division in Minstead), 14/304D; SU293147; NP 180
Cadney cum Howsham (parish), 22/111; TA030042; NP 104
Cadoxton juxta Barry (parish), 51/176; ST133687; NP 154
Cadoxton Juxta Neath (parish), 51/11-19; NP 153
Caegwrle (township in Hope), 50/124; SJ304572; NP 109
Caeliber Isaf (township in Kerry [Llanfihangel-yng-Ngheri]), 54/181; SO220930; NP 128
Caeliber Uchaf (township in Kerry [Llanfihangel-yng-Ngheri]), 54/180; SO192922; NP 128
Caenby (parish), 22/223; TF001897; NP 104
Caerau (Cayra, Cairau) (parish), 51/148; ST135753; NP 154
Caerdydd (parishes), 51/10, 139-140; NP 154
Caereinion Fechan (township in Mallwyd), 54/124; SH832090; NP 116, 127
Caerfallwch (township in Northop), 50/17; SJ220690; NP 108
Caergybi (parish), 44/51
Caerhun (parish), 48/11; SH714692; NP 107
Caerleon (hamlet in Llangattock juxta Caerleon), 53/110; ST338906; NP 155
Caerleon ultra Pontem (hamlet in Christchurch), 53/132B; ST343901; NP 155
Caernarfon (Carnarvon) (borough in Llanbeblig), 48/30; SH493631; NP 106
Caerseddfan (township in Darowen), 54/126A; SH820020; NP 127
Caersws (township in Llanwnog), 54/156; SO030920; NP 128
Caerwent (hamlet in Caerwent), 53/101A; ST463913; NP 155
Caerwent (parish), 53/101A-B; NP 155
Caerwys (parish), 50/85-88; NP 108
Cainham (parish), 31/534A-B; NP 129
Cainham, 31/534B; NP 129
Cairau (parish), 51/148; NP 154
Caister (parish), 25/383; NP 126
Caister next Yarmouth (Caister, Caister-on-Sea) (parish), 25/383; TG511122; NP 126
Caister St Edmund (Caistor St Edmunds) (parish), 25/484; TG246037; NP 126
Caister-on-Sea (parish), 25/383; NP 126
Caistor (hamlet in Caistor), 22/103A; TA113012; NP 104
Caistor (parish), 22/102-105B; NP 104
Caistor Moor (division in Caistor), 22/103B; TA099014; NP 104
Caistor St Edmunds (parish), 25/484; NP 126
Caistron (township in Rothbury), 27/260; NT994004; NP 71
Cakemore (township in Halesowen), 40/13; SO985865; NP 130
Calbourne (division in Calbourne), 18/3A; SZ430885; NP 180
Calbourne (parish), 18/3A-B; NP 180
Calceby (parish), 22/323; TF391755; NP 105, 114
Calcethorpe (parish), 22/198; TF248884; NP 105
Calcoed, 50/32; NP 108
Calcot (Calcoed) (township in Holywell), 50/32; SJ167741; NP 108
Caldbeck (parish), 7/211-215; NP 82, 83
Caldbeck Fells (area in Caldbeck), 7/212; NY320350; NP 82, 83
Caldbeck Haltcliff (township in Caldbeck), 7/213; NY353373; NP 83
Caldbeck High (High Caldbeck) (township in Caldbeck), 7/215; NY308381; NP 82, 83

Caldbeck Low (Low Caldbeck) (township in Caldbeck), 7/214; NY318398; NP 82, 83
Caldbergh (Caldbridge) (division in township of Caldbergh in Coverham), 42/155A; SE107837; NP 90, 91
Caldbergh (township in Coverham), 42/154-155a; NP 90, 91
Caldbridge, 42/155A; NP 90, 91
Caldecote (Caldecot) (parish), 4/112; TL349577; NP 134, 135
Caldecote (hamlet in Northill), 1/68B; TL170460; NP 147
Caldecote (Caldecot) (parish), 16/3; TL236385; NP 147
Caldecote (Caldecot) (parish), 17/18; TL164883; NP 134
Caldecote (hamlet in Eynesbury), 17/109; TL226583; NP 134
Caldecote (Caldecot) (parish), 25/531; TF752036; NP 124, 125
Caldecote (parish), 37/63; SP351945; NP 132
Caldecott (township in Shocklach), 5/348; SJ431512; NP 109
Caldecott (parish), 16/3; NP 147
Caldecott (parish), 30/59; SP871940; NP 133
Calderbrook (division in township of Blatchinworth and Calderbrook in Rochdale), 20/461; SD940186; NP 101
Caldewgate (township in St Mary [Carlisle]), 7/97; NY378558; NP 76
Caldicot (Caldicott) (parish), 53/142; ST479888; NP 155
Caldon (parish), 33/110; NP 111
Caldwell (Cauldwell) (township in Stapenhill), 8/315B; SK258176; NP 120
Caldwell (division in township of Caldwell in Stanwick St John), 42/36; NZ160140; NP 85
Caldwell (township in Stanwick St John), 42/36-37; NP 84
Caldy (township in West Kirby), 5/457; SJ231854; NP 100
Caldy Island [Ynys Byr] (extra-parochial), 55/141; SN138966; NP 152
Calke (parish), 8/306; SK370220; NP 121
Callaly and Yetlington (Callaley) (township in Whittingham), 27/173; NU037093; NP 71
Callaughton (township in Much Wenlock), 31/454; SO621971; NP 130
Callington (parish), 6/61; SX360696; NP 186
Calloes (parish), 39/85; NP 157
Callow (parish), 15/185; SO500345; NP 142
Callow (township in Wirksworth), 8/152; SK268522; NP 111
Calne (parish), 39/111; SU001705; NP 157
Calow (township in Chesterfield), 8/71; SK411698; NP 112
Calshot Castle (extra-parochial), 14/337; SU488025; NP 180
Calstock (parish), 6/60; SX413706; NP 186, 187
Calstone Wellington (parish), 39/376; SU024676; NP 157
Calthorpe (parish), 25/142; TG180318; NP 126
Calthwaite (township in Hesket in the Forest), 7/166; NY464405; NP 83
Calton (township in Blore), 33/92B; SK106501; NP 111
Calton (township in Mayfield), 33/92A; SK104498; NP 111
Calton (township in Waterfall), 33/92C; SK100502; NP 111
Calton (township in Kirkby Malhamdale), 43/233; SD914594; NP 90, 95
Calveley (township in Bunbury), 5/305; SJ608594; NP 109, 110
Calver (township in Bakewell), 8/88; SK237744; NP 111
Calverhall (Corra) (township in Prees), 31/19A; SJ606371; NP 118, 119
Calverleigh (Hightleigh, Highley St Mary) (extra-parochial), 9/175; SS915145; NP 164
Calverley (division in township of Calverley with Farsley in Calverley), 43/512; SE202362; NP 96
Calverley (parish), 43/510-515; NP 96
Calverley with Farsley (township in Calverley), 43/512-513; NP 96
Calverton (parish), 3/19; SP798388; NP 146
Calverton (parish), 28/184; SK611508; NP 112
Calvington (township in Edgmond), 31/190; SJ701226; NP 119
Calwick (township in Ellastone), 33/99; SK128437; NP 111
Cam (parish), 13/314; ST750999; NP 156
Camberwell (division in St Giles Camberwell), 35/18; TQ333754; NP 170, 171
Camblesforth (township in Drax), 43/971A; SE638266; NP 97
Camblesforth and Carlton (allotment to Carlton and

Camblesforth jointly in Snaith and Drax), 43/971B; SE628282; NP 97
Cambo (township in Hartburn), 27/344; NZ018867; NP 77
Camboise (township in Bedlington), 27/430; NZ306837; NP 78
Camborne (parish), 6/167; SW636404; NP 189
Cambridge, All Saints (parish), 4/85; TL452589; NP 135/1
Cambridge, Catherine Hall (extra-parochial), 4/93E; TL447582; NP 135/1
Cambridge, Christ's College (extra-parochial), 4/93M; TL451585; NP 135/1
Cambridge, Clare Hall (extra-parochial), 4/93H; TL446584; NP 135/1
Cambridge, Corpus Christi College (extra-parochial), 4/93F; TL448582; NP 135/1
Cambridge, Downing College (extra-parochial), 4/93A; TL452579; NP 135/1
Cambridge, Emmanuel College (extra-parochial), 4/93; TL452583; NP 135/1
Cambridge, Gonville and Caius College (extra-parochial), 4/93K; TL447585; NP 135/1
Cambridge, Holy Trinity (parish), 4/86; TL451586; NP 135/1
Cambridge, Jesus College (extra-parochial), 4/93O; TL452589; NP 135/1
Cambridge, King's College (extra-parochial), 4/93G; TL447583; NP 135/1
Cambridge, Magdalen College (extra-parochial), 4/93R; TL447590; NP 135/1
Cambridge, Pembroke Hall (extra-parochial), 4/93C; TL449581; NP 135/1
Cambridge, Peterhouse (extra-parochial), 4/93B; TL449580; NP 135/1
Cambridge, Queen's College (extra-parochial), 4/93D; TL447581; NP 135/1
Cambridge, Sidney Sussex College (extra-parochial), 4/93N; TL450587; NP 135/1
Cambridge, St Andrew the Great (parish), 4/92; TL453582; NP 135/1
Cambridge, St Benedict (parish), 4/90; TL448582; NP 135/1
Cambridge, St Botolph (parish), 4/91; TL446581; NP 135/1
Cambridge, St Clement (parish), 4/83; TL448590; NP 135/1
Cambridge, St Edward (parish), 4/88; TL447583; NP 135/1
Cambridge, St Giles (parish), 4/81; TL429588; NP 135
Cambridge, St John's College (extra-parochial), 4/93Q; TL447588; NP 135/1
Cambridge, St Mary the Great (parish), 4/89; TL449584; NP 135/1
Cambridge, St Mary the Less (parish), 4/94; TL448576; NP 135/1
Cambridge, St Michael (parish), 4/87; TL446586; NP 135/1
Cambridge, St Peter (parish), 4/82; TL444590; NP 135
Cambridge, St Sepulchre (parish), 4/84; TL449588; NP 135/1
Cambridge, Trinity College (extra-parochial), 4/93P; TL446586; NP 135/1
Cambridge, Trinity Hall (extra-parochial), 4/93J; TL447585; NP 135/1
Camden Town (division in St Pancras), 24/44B; TQ296836; NP 160
Cameley (parish), 32/81; ST612578; NP 165, 166
Camerton (Cammerton) (township in Camerton), 7/248; NY038313; NP 82
Camerton (parish), 7/248-249; NP 82
Camerton (parish), 32/106; ST684576; NP 166
Camerton (division in township of Ryhill and Camerton in Burstwick), 41/425; TA220249; NP 99
Cammeringham (parish), 22/229; SK940822; NP 104
Cammerton, 7/248; NP 82
Campsall (parish), 43/643-648; NP 103
Campsall (township in Campsall), 43/647; SE532138; NP 103
Campsey Ash (parish), 34/369; TM330560; NP 137, 150
Campsfield (division in Kidlington), 29/199; SP469148; NP 145
Campton (parish), 1/85-86; NP 147
Campton (township in Campton), 1/85; TL127382; NP 147
Camrose (parish), 55/75; SM927203; NP 138, 151

Candlesby (parish), 22/422; TF457671; NP 114
Canewdon (parish), 12/370; TQ900946; NP 162
Canford Magna (parish), 10/192-196; NP 179
Cann (Shaston St Rumbold) (parish), 10/8; ST875217; NP 166
Cannington (division in Cannington), 32/222; ST257398; NP 165
Cannington (parish), 32/222-223; NP 165
Cannock (division in Cannock), 33/228B; SK010120; NP 119, 120
Cannock (parish), 33/228A-230; NP 119, 120
Cannon Fee (tithing in Crediton), 9/211D; (not located); NP 175
Canon Frome (parish), 15/160; SO653435; NP 143
Canon Pyon (Canon Pion) (parish), 15/107; SO465492; NP 142
Canongate (township in Alnwick), 27/199; NU182139; NP 71
Canons Ashby (hamlet in Canons Ashby), 26/273; SP571602; NP 145
Canons Ashby (parish), 26/273-274; NP 145
Canterbury, All Saints (parish), 19/244; TR149580; NP 173/1
Canterbury, Black Princes Chantry (extra-parochial), 19/245; TR150581; NP 173/1
Canterbury, Christchurch (extra-parochial), 19/256; TR151579; NP 173/1
Canterbury, Eastbridge Hospital (East Bridge Hospital) (extra-parochial), 19/255; TR148579; NP 173/1
Canterbury, Holy Cross (parish), 19/241A-B; NP 173/1
Canterbury, Holy Cross Westgate Without (division in Canterbury, Holy Cross), 19/241A; TR575142; NP 173/1
Canterbury, Holy Cross Westgate Without (division in Canterbury, Holy Cross), 19/241B; TR140576; NP 173/1
Canterbury, Longport (extra-parochial), 19/249B; TR155577; NP 173/1
Canterbury, Old Castle Precincts (extra-parochial), 19/242B; TR146574; NP 173/1
Canterbury, St Alphege (parish), 19/247; TR149581; NP 173/1
Canterbury, St Andrew (parish), 19/248; TR150579; NP 173/1
Canterbury, St Augustine (Canterbury, St Augustine's Monastry, Almonry and Precinct) (extra-parochial), 19/249A; TR155579; NP 173/1
Canterbury, St Dunstan (parish), 19/239; TR139586; NP 173
Canterbury, St George the Martyr (parish), 19/250; TR151576; NP 173/1
Canterbury, St Gregory the Great (parish), 19/257; TR154583; NP 173/1
Canterbury, St John's Hospital (extra-parochial), 19/242C
Canterbury, St Margaret (parish), 19/251; TR148577; NP 173/1
Canterbury, St Martin (parish), 19/260; TR174583; NP 173
Canterbury, St Mary Bredin (parish), 19/240; TR149562; NP 173
Canterbury, St Mary Bredman (parish), 19/252; TR149579; NP 173/1
Canterbury, St Mary Magdalen (parish), 19/253; TR151577; NP 173/1
Canterbury, St Mary Northgate (parish), 19/259; TR162589; NP 173
Canterbury, St Mildred (parish), 19/242A; TR142570; NP 173/1
Canterbury, St Paul (parish), 19/261; TR168570; NP 173
Canterbury, St Peter (parish), 19/243; TR147479; NP 173/1
Canterbury, Staplegate (extra-parochial), 19/246; TR150581; NP 173/1
Canterbury, The Arbishop's Palace Precincts (extra-parochial), 19/254; TR150580; NP 173/1
Canterbury, The White Friars (extra-parochial), 19/258; TR151576; NP 173/1
Cantley (parish), 25/468; TG380044; NP 126
Cantley (parish), 43/931; SE635020; NP 103
Cantlop (township in Berrington), 31/284; SJ519054; NP 118
Canton (hamlet in Llandaff [Llandaf]), 51/141; ST168756; NP 154
Cantref (Cantreff) (division in Cantref), 45/52A; SO035240; NP 141
Cantref (Cantreff) (parish), 45/52A-B; NP 141
Cantsfield (township in Tunstall), 20/78; SD627730; NP 89
Canwell (extra-parochial), 33/287; SK148003; NP 120, 131
Canwick (parish), 22/518; SK997694; NP 113
Capel (parish), 19/308; TQ637457; NP 171

Capel (parish), 35/169; TQ181410; NP 170
Capel St Andrew (parish), 34/436; TM355482; NP 150
Capel St Mary (Caple St Mary) (parish), 34/510; TM091374; NP 149, 150
Capel-Bettws-Lleucu, 46/51; NP 140
Capel-Betws-Lleucu (Bettws Leiki, Capel-Bettws-Lleucu) (township in Llandewi-Brefi), 46/51; SN612580; NP 140
Capel-Colman (parish), 55/10; SN216384; NP 139
Capel-le-Ferne (parish), 19/381; TR251393; NP 173
Capenhurst (township in Shotwick), 5/487; SJ368735; NP 109
Capesthorne (township in Prestbury), 5/64; SJ841728; NP 110
Capheaton (township in Kirkwhelpington), 27/382; NZ035800; NP 77
Caple St Mary (parish), 34/510; NP 149, 15
Car Colston (parish), 28/213; SK720425; NP 122
Carbrooke (parish), 25/541; TF951018; NP 125, 136
Carburton (chapelry in Edwinstowe), 28/79; SK605733; NP 112
Carden (township in Tilston), 5/341; SJ464531; NP 109
Cardeston (Cardiston) (parish), 31/310; SJ392121; NP 118
Cardiff St Johns [Caerdydd] (St John the Baptist, Cardiff) (parish), 51/140; ST181775; NP 154
Cardiff St Mary [Caerdydd] (St Mary, Cardiff) (division in Cardiff St Mary [Caerdydd]), 51/139; ST190753; NP 154
Cardiff St Mary [Caerdydd] (St Mary, Cardiff) (parish), 51/10, 139; NP 154
Cardigan St Mary [Aberteifi] (St Marys, Cardigan) (parish), 46/104; SN188476; NP 139
Cardington (parish), 1/54-55; NP 147
Cardington (township in Cardington), 1/54; TL097469; NP 147
Cardington (parish), 31/432-433E; NP 129
Cardington (township in Cardington), 31/433B; SO506952; NP 129
Cardinham (Cardynham) (parish), 6/52; SX121679; NP 185, 186
Cardynham, 6/52; NP 185, 186
Careby (parish), 22/701; TF028162; NP 123
Carew (parish), 55/144; SN051033; NP 151
Cargo (township in Stanwix), 7/71; NY367598; NP 76
Carham (parish), 27/3-36; NP 64
Carham (township in Carham), 27/30; NT805379; NP 64
Carhampton (hamlet in Carhampton), 32/237A; SS999420; NP 164
Carhampton (parish), 32/237A-B; NP 164
Carisbrooke (parish), 18/12; SZ480874; NP 180
Carisbrooke Castle, 18/13B; NP 180
Carkin (township in Gilling), 42/43; NZ172096; NP 85
Carlatton (extra-parochial), 7/63; NY530528; NP 76
Carlbury (division in township of Low Coniscliffe with Carlbury in Coniscliffe), 11/313; NZ216166; NP 85
Carlby (parish), 22/700; TF045146; NP 123
Carleton (township in St Cuthbert [Carlisle]), 7/79; NY443517; NP 76
Carleton (township in Poulton-le-Fylde), 20/172-173; NP 94
Carleton (parish), 25/579; NP 126, 137
Carleton (Carlton) (division in township of Carleton in Carleton), 43/322; SD967492; NP 95
Carleton (Carlton) (parish and township), 43/320-322; NP 95
Carleton (township in Pontefract), 43/623; SE470202; NP 97
Carleton Forehoe (parish), 25/555; TG092061; NP 125
Carleton Moor (common to divisions of Lothersdale and Carleton in township and parish of Carleton), 43/321; SD956476; NP 95
Carleton Rode (parish), 25/666; TM106930; NP 136
Carleton St Peter (Carleton) (parish), 25/579; TG344023; NP 126, 137
Carlton (division in township of Lofthouse with Carlton in Rothwell), 43/596; SE339271; NP 96
Carlton (parish), 1/24; SP965550; NP 133, 134, 146, 147
Carlton (parish), 34/260; TM378646; NP 137
Carlton (parish), 42/307; NZ505040; NP 85, 86, 92
Carlton (township in Redmarshall), 11/265; NZ398218; NP 85
Carlton (township in Market Bosworth), 21/150; SK391047; NP 121
Carlton (township in Gedling), 28/230; SK610418; NP 121

Carlton (township in Guiseley), 43/509; SE223428; NP 96
Carlton (township in Royston), 43/686; SE362099; NP 102
Carlton (township in Snaith), 43/970; SE647240; NP 97
Carlton Colville (parish), 34/21; TM511917; NP 137
Carlton cum Willingham (parish), 4/140; TL622540; NP 135, 148
Carlton Curlieu (parish), 21/291-292; NP 122, 133
Carlton Curlieu (township in Carlton Curlieu), 21/292; SP699968; NP 133
Carlton Highdale (township in Coverham), 42/151; SE020790; NP 90
Carlton Husthwaite (township in Husthwaite), 42/561; SE500767; NP 91, 92
Carlton in Lindrick (parish), 28/25A-B; NP 103
Carlton Islebeck, 42/531; NP 91
Carlton le Moorland (parish), 22/550; SK911572; NP 113
Carlton Miniott (Carlton Islebeck) (township in Thirsk), 42/531; SE398807; NP 91
Carlton Miniott (township in Kirby Knowle), 42/526; SE403804; NP 91
Carlton on Trent (township in Norwell), 28/132; SK786639; NP 112, 113
Carlton Scroop (Carlton Scroope) (parish), 22/791; SK940449; NP 113, 122, 123
Carlton Town (township in Coverham), 42/152; SE051844; NP 90
Carnaby (parish), 41/258-260; NP 93, 99
Carnaby (township in Carnaby), 41/260; TA148652; NP 93, 99
Carnarvon, 48/30; NP 106
Carnedd (township in Llandinam), 54/154; SO022909; NP 128
Carnforth (township in Warton), 20/69; SD500704; NP 89
Carnguwch (Carngiwch) (parish), 48/51; SH372423; NP 115
Carno (parish), 54/116-120; NP 117, 128
Caron (parish), 46/37-38F; NP 127, 140
Caron-uwch-clawdd (township in Caron), 46/37; SN769630; NP 127, 140
Carperby cum Thoresby (division in township of Carperby cum Thoresby in Aysgarth), 42/137; SD997910; NP 90
Carperby cum Thoresby (township in Aysgarth), 42/137-138; NP 90
Carr (division in township of Laughton en le Morthen in Laughton en le Morthen), 43/916; SK513907; NP 103
Carr House Green Common (division in Inskip with Sowerby township in St Michaels on Wyre), 20/160B; SD475370; NP 94
Carreghofa (township in Llanymynech), 54/1; SJ257207; NP 117
Carrington (township in Bowdon), 5/79; SJ742922; NP 101
Carrington (parish), 22/460; TF312534; NP 114
Carrs (extra-parochial), 42/603; SE673683; NP 92
Carrycoats (township in Throckington), 27/369; NY921811; NP 77
Carshalton (parish), 35/51; TQ276638; NP 170
Carsington (parish), 8/161; SK245532; NP 111
Carthorpe (township in Burneston), 42/225; SE302832; NP 91
Cartington (township in Rothbury), 27/247; NU041049; NP 71
Cartmel (parish), 20/57-60A, 61-64B; NP 89
Cartmel Fell (township in Cartmel), 20/57; SD405892; NP 89
Cartmel Townships Intermixed (intermixed lanmds in Cartmel), 20/64B; SD 421820; NP 89
Cartworth (division in township of Cartworth in Kirkburton), 43/737A; SE140075; NP 102
Cartworth (division in township of Cartworth in Kirkburton), 43/737B; SE131054; NP 102
Cartworth (township in Kirkburton), 43/737A-B; NP 102
Cas-Gwent (parish), 53/98A; NP 155
Cascob (parish), 56/26; SO212658; NP 128
Casewick (division in Deeping Fen of Casewick hamlet in Uffington), 22/723B; TF153167; NP 123
Casewick (division of Casewick hamlet in Uffington), 22/723B; TF076090; NP 123
Casewick (hamlet in Uffington), 22/723B, 723D; NP 123
Casnewydd, 53/124; NP 155
Cassington (hamlet in Cassington), 29/192; SP450110; NP 145, 158
Cassington (parish), 29/192-193; NP 145, 158

Cassio, Leavesden (hamlet in Watford), 16/132C; TQ090970; NP 160
Cassop (division in township of Cassop cum Quarrington in Kelloe), 11/104; NZ332394; NP 85
Cassop cum Quarrington (township in Kelloe), 11/103-104; NP 85
Castell Hendre (parish), 55/48; NP 138
Castellan (chapelry in Penrydd), 55/13B; SN192358; NP 139
Castelldwyran (hamlet in Cilymaenllwyd), 47/88; SN135186; NP 152
Casterton (township in Kirkby Lonsdale), 38/125; SD653806; NP 89
Castle (township in Castle Caereinion), 54/63; SJ162051; NP 117
Castle Acre (parish), 25/279; TF668246; NP 125
Castle Ashby (parish), 26/291; SP861592; NP 133
Castle Bigh, 55/49; NP 138
Castle Bolton (township in Wensley), 42/150; SE020925; NP 90
Castle Bromwich (township in Aston), 37/40; SP148891; NP 131
Castle Bytham (parish), 22/697A-699; NP 122, 123
Castle Bytham (township in Castle Bytham), 22/697A; SK976188; NP 122, 123
Castle Caereinion (parish), 54/58-64; NP 117
Castle Camps (division in Castle Camps), 4/154A; TL622428; NP 148
Castle Camps (parish), 4/154A-B; NP 148
Castle Carrock (parish), 7/62; NY548544; NP 76
Castle Carlton (parish), 22/299; TF396837; NP 105
Castle Cary (parish), 32/350; ST627312; NP 166
Castle Church (parish), 33/182; SJ922218; NP 119
Castle Combe (parish), 39/77; ST845772; NP 156
Castle Donington (parish), 21/14; SK437270; NP 121
Castle Dykes (extra-parochial), 22/500; SK974720; NP 113/1
Castle Eaton (parish), 39/9; SU156947; NP 157
Castle Eden (parish), 11/93; NZ422381; NP 85
Castle Frome (Castle Froome) (parish), 15/161; SO669454; NP 143
Castle Gresley (township in Church Gresley), 8/318; SK280180; NP 120, 121
Castle Green, Carmarthen (extra-parochial), 47/72; SN412199; NP 139
Castle Hedingham (parish), 12/51; TL787366; NP 149
Castle Inn (extra-parochial), 45/49; SO044287; NP 141
Castle Levington (township in Kirklevington), 42/274; NZ449106; NP 85
Castle Malwood Walk (division in Minstead), 14/304B; SU279126; NP 179, 180
Castle Precincts (extra-parochial), 11/117; NZ273423; NP 85
Castle Precincts (division in township of Pontefract in Pontefract), 43/625; SE461223; NP 97
Castle Pulverbatch (township in Church Pulverbatch), 31/335; SJ411023; NP 118
Castle Rising (parish), 25/175; TF668246; NP 124
Castle Sowerby (parish), 7/152-157; NP 83
Castle Street (township in St Mary [Carlisle]), 7/95; NY399559; NP 76/1
Castle Town Quarter (township in Rockcliff), 7/68; NY345630; NP 76
Castle Ward Within and Castle Foregate [Shrewsbury]n (extra-parochial), 31/246; SJ504146; NP 118
Castlebythe (Castle Bigh) (parish), 55/49; SN017287; NP 138
Castleford (parish), 43/617-618; NP 97
Castleford (township in Castleford), 43/617; SE432257; NP 97
Castleleavington, 42/274; NP 85
Castlemartin (parish), 55/156; SR910974; NP 151
Castlemorton (parish), 40/230; SO787402; NP 143
Castlethorpe (parish), 3/23; SP804436; NP 146
Castleton (parish), 8/30-31; NP 102, 111
Castleton (township in Castleton), 8/30; SK142828; NP 102, 111
Castleton (parish), 10/30; ST648168; NP 178
Castleton (division in township of Castleton in Rochdale), 20/441; SD885103; NP 101
Castleton (division within borough of Rochdale of division of township of Castleton in Rochdale), 20/442; SD895127; NP 101
Castleton (division within borough of Rochdale of Castleton division in township of Castleton in Rochdale), 20/443; SD901129; NP 101
Castleton (division within borough of Rochdale of Castleton division in township of Castleton in Rochdale), 20/444; SD911129; NP 101
Castleton (township in Rochdale), 20/438-444; NP 101
Castlewright (township in Mainstone), 54/196; SO273905; NP 128, 129
Castley (township in Leathley), 43/392; SE264463; NP 96
Caston (parish), 25/678; TL960977; NP 136
Castor (township in Castor), 26/22; TF129996; NP 123, 134
Castor, 26/22-25; NP 123, 134
Catcherside (township in Kirkwhelpington), 27/378; NY992880; NP 77
Catcliffe (township in Rotherham), 43/838; SK418882; NP 103
Catcott (chapelry in Moorlinch), 32/211; ST401402; NP 165
Caterham (parish), 35/96; TQ335555; NP 170
Catesby (Catesby Abbey) (parish), 26/246; SP530592; NP 132
Catfield (parish), 25/371; TG399215; NP 126
Catforth (division in township of Woodplumpton in St Michaels on Wyre), 20/161; SD77359; NP 94
Catfoss (township in Sigglesthorne), 41/365; TA144472; NP 99
Cathedine (parish), 45/85; SO151253; NP 141
Catherington (parish), 14/249; SU693137; NP 180, 181
Catherston Leweston (Catherston Lewston) (parish), 10/135; SY371942; NP 177
Catley Lane (subdivision of Spotland Further Side division in Spotland township in Rochdale), 20/447; SD875148; NP 101
Catmore (parish), 2/114; SU450804; NP 158
Caton with Littledale (township in Lancaster), 20/122; SD560620; NP 89, 94
Catsfield (parish), 36/173; TQ724137; NP 183, 184
Catshaw Vachery (division in township of Over Wyresdale in Lancaster), 20/131; SD555519; NP 94
Cattal (township in Hunsingore), 43/106; SE443544; NP 97
Catterall (township in Garstang), 20/153; SD489422; NP 94
Catterick (parish), 42/71-86; NP 91
Catterick (township in Catterick), 42/83; SE240972; NP 91
Catterlen (Catterlin) (township in Newton Regny), 7/192; NY477336; NP 83
Catterlin, 7/192; NP 83
Catterton (township in Tadcaster), 43/82; SE510455; NP 97
Catthorpe (parish), 21/350; SP552788; NP 132
Cattistock (parish), 10/120; ST591011; NP 177, 178
Catton (parish), 25/359; TG230121; NP 126
Catton (parish), 41/83-87; NP 97
Catton (township in Croxall), 8/324; SK216151; NP 120
Catton (township in Topcliffe), 42/244; SE377783; NP 91
Catton and Broadside (township in Allendale), 27/593; NY825575; NP 77
Catwick (parish), 41/397; TA133451; NP 99
Catworth (Great Catworth) (parish), 17/51A-B; TL084721; NP 134
Caughall (township in Backford), 5/495; SJ413707; NP 109
Cauldon (Caldon) (parish), 33/110; SK077495; NP 111
Cauldwell, 8/315B; NP 120
Caundle Bishop (parish), 10/48; NP 178
Caundle Marsh (parish), 10/47; ST682140; NP 178
Caundle Purse (parish), 10/27; NP 178
Caunton (parish), 28/142; SK741603; NP 112
Cause (township in Westbury), 31/319; SJ340079; NP 118
Causey Park (township in Hebburn parochial chapelry), 27/302; NZ181950; NP 71, 78
Cautley and Dowbiggin (division in township of Sedbergh in Sedbergh), 43/263; SD715945; NP 89, 90
Cavendish Square (division in St Marylebone), 24/45E; TQ286816; NP 160/1
Cavendish (parish), 34/340; TL800480; NP 149
Cavenham (parish), 34/206; TL760706; NP 136
Caversfield (parish), 29/3; SP583258; NP 145

Caversham (parish), 29/318; SU711778; NP 158, 159
Caverswall (parish), 33/39A-B; NP 110, 119
Caverswall (township in Caverswall), 33/39A; SJ950430; NP 110, 119
Cavill (Cavil) (division in township of Portington and Cavill in Eastrington), 41/15; SE771311; NP 98
Cawkwell (parish), 22/335; TF279801; NP 105
Cawood (parish), 43/447; SE570365; NP 97
Cawston (parish), 25/207; TG149240; NP 125, 126
Cawthorne (Cawthorn) (township in Middleton), 42/441; SE780900; NP 92
Cawthorne (parish), 43/710; SE280080; NP 102
Cawthorpe (hamlet in Bourne), 22/709B; TF190220; NP 123
Cawton (township in Gilling), 42/611; SE631767; NP 92
Caxton (parish), 4/114; TL304586; NP 134
Caynham (Cainham) (parish), 31/534A-B; NP 129
Caynham (Cainham) (township in Caynham), 31/534B; SO553733; NP 129
Caynton (township in Edgmond), 31/191; SJ702212; NP 119
Cayra (parish), 51/148; NP 154
Caythorpe (Caythorpe cum Friston) (parish), 22/601; SK939486; NP 113
Caythorpe (township in Lowdham), 28/188; SK687459; NP 112
Caythorpe (division in parish and township of Rudston), 41/243; TA117685; NP 93
Caythorpe (division in Rudston and Boynton), 41/243-244; NP 93
Caythorpe (division in township of Boynton in Boynton), 41/244; TA120687; NP 93
Cayton (township in Seamer), 42/407; TA060830; NP 93
Cefey-berin, 54/182; NP 128
Cefn (hamlet in Gelligaer), 51/75D; ST120970; NP 154
Cefn (township in Cilcain), 50/101; SJ188666; NP 108
Cefn Brith (township in Carno), 54/116; SH979004; NP 117, 128
Cefn Llyffiog (township in Meifod), 54/37; SJ173153; NP 117
Cefn-y-mynach (township in Kerry [Llanfihangel-yng-Ngheri]), 54/172; SO135868; NP 128
Cefnhafod (township in Llanidloes), 54/146; SN983840; NP 128
Cefnllys (parish), 56/38; SO100620; NP 128
Cefnpawl (township in Abbey-Cwmhir), 56/2A; SO030760; NP 128
Cefnyberin (Cefey-berin) (township in Kerry [Llanfihangel-yng-Ngheri]), 54/182; SO203915; NP 128
Cegidfa (parish), 54/73-81; NP 117
Ceidio (parish), 48/60; SH288380; NP 115
Ceidio Rhodogedio (Rhodogedio) (parish), 44/15; SH410841; NP 106
Ceirchiog (parish), 44/46; SH359758; NP 106
Cellan (parish), 46/74; SN625483; NP 139, 140
Cemmaes (township in Llanbadrig), 44/4; SH395935; NP 106
Cemmes (parish), 52/122-123; NP 116, 117
Cenarth (Kenarth) (parish), 47/40; SN290390; NP 139
Cenarth (township in St Harmon), 56/1A; SN970760; NP 128
Cenol (township in Llanfihangel Cwm-du), 45/82B; SO175255; NP 141
Cerne Abbas (parish), 10/150; ST664011; NP 178
Cerrigceinwen (parish), 44/42; SH430746; NP 106
Cerrigydrudion (Cerryg-y-drudion) (parish), 49/20; SH940495; NP 107, 108
Cerryg-y-drudion (parish), 49/20; NP 107, 108
Cestersover (hamlet in Monks Kirby), 37/112; SP505820; NP 132
Ceulan Maesmawr (Ceulan-y-Maes-Mawr) (township in Llanfihangel Genu'rglyn), 46/3; SN705900; NP 127
Ceulan-y-Maes-Mawr, 46/3; NP 127
Chaceley (Chaseley) (parish), 40/238; SO849306; NP 143
Chacombe (parish), 26/356; SP494436; NP 145
Chaddenwick (Chaddenwicke, Charnage) (tithing in Mere), 39/337; ST837331; NP 166
Chaddenwicke, 39/337; NP 166
Chadderton (township in Oldham), 20/483; SD900060; NP 101
Chadderton (parish), 33/73-74B; NP 110, 111
Chadderton (township in Chadderton), 33/74A; SK955505; NP 110

Chaddesden (parish), 8/278; SK382372; NP 121
Chaddesley Corbett (parish), 40/36; SO892750; NP 130
Chaddleworth (parish), 2/111; SU412788; NP 158
Chadshunt (parish), 37/260; SP349530; NP 145
Chadwell (division in Barking), 12/318; TQ468876; NP 161
Chadwell (parish), 12/427; TQ645778; NP 171
Chadwell (chapelry in Rothley), 21/55; SK777249; NP 122
Chadwell St Mary (Chadwell) (parish), 12/427; TQ645778; NP 171
Chadwick (subdivision of Spotland Further Side division in Spotland township in Rochdale), 20/445; SD874136; NP 101
Chaffcombe (parish), 32/487; ST354095; NP 177
Chagford (parish), 9/381; SX691861; NP 175
Chaigley (division in Aighton, Bailey and Chaigley township in Mitton), 20/231; SD670420; NP 95
Chailey (parish), 36/125; TQ390200; NP 182
Chalbury (parish), 10/171; SU013074; NP 179
Chaldon (parish), 35/95; TQ316548; NP 170
Chaldon Herring (East Chaldon) (parish), 10/278; SY784828; NP 178
Chale (parish), 18/27; SZ484787; NP 180
Chalfont St Giles (parish), 3/202; SU990940; NP 159
Chalfont St Peter (parish), 3/203; TQ008912; NP 159
Chalgrave (parish), 1/132; SP998266; NP 147
Chalgrove (division in Chalgrove), 29/286; SU639973; NP 158
Chalgrove (parish), 29/286-287; NP 158
Chalk (parish), 19/36; TQ677729; NP 171
Challacombe (parish), 9/11; SS690412; NP 163
Challock (parish), 19/451; TR000503; NP 172
Challow East, 2/93; NP 158
Chalton (division in Chalton), 14/246; SU728160; NP 181
Chalton (parish), 14/246-247; NP 181
Chalvington (parish), 36/190; TQ526102; NP 183
Chandlings Farm (extra-parochial), 2/10; SP507012; NP 158
Chapel (parish), 12/135; NP 149
Chapel Allerton (division in Chapel Allerton), 32/165; ST402495; NP 165
Chapel Allerton (parish), 32/165-166; NP 165
Chapel Allerton (township in Leeds), 43/503; SE303380; NP 96
Chapel Ascote (extra-parochial), 37/245; SP423572; NP 132
Chapel Brampton (parish), 26/189; SP727665; NP 133
Chapel Chorlton (township in Ecclleshall), 33/150A; SJ822372; NP 119
Chapel en le Frith (parish), 8/13A-C; NP 111
Chapel Haddesley (township in Birkin), 43/458; SE588263; NP 97
Chapel Hill (parish), 53/90; SO533000; NP 155
Chapel St Leonards (Mumby Chapel) (hamlet in Mumby), 22/409; TF559733; NP 114
Chapel Sucken (township in Millom), 7/324; SD145799; NP 88
Chapelgate (division in East Retford), 28/50A; SK706813; NP 103
Chapeltown (division in township of Ecclesfield in Ecclesfield), 43/790; SK354958; NP 102
Chappel (Chapel, Pontisbright) (parish), 12/135; TL894277; NP 149
Charborough (hamlet in Morden), 10/200B; SY921981; NP 178, 179
Chard (parish), 32/450; ST335079; NP 177
Chardstock (district in Chardstock), 9/145; ST305039; NP 177
Chardstock (parish), 9/145, 10/111
Chardstock (parish), 10/111; ST305039; NP 177
Charfield (parish), 13/353; ST721913; NP 156
Charing (parish), 19/294; TQ940495; NP 172
Charingworth (hamlet in Ebrington), 13/30; SP202395; NP 144
Charlbury (hamlet in Charlbury), 29/128; SP362202; NP 145
Charlbury (parish), 29/128-134; NP 145
Charlcombe (parish), 32/26; ST748672; NP 156
Charlcote, 37/220; NP 131
Charlecote (Charlcote) (hamlet in Charlecote), 37/220; SP268568; NP 131
Charlecote (Charlcote) (parish), 37/220-221; NP 131, 132
Charles (parish), 9/30; SS682337; NP 163

Charlesworth (township in Glossop), 8/3C; SK004929; NP 101, 102
Charleton (parish), 9/492; SX756427; NP 187
Charley (extra-parochial), 21/29; SK475145; NP 121
Charlinch (parish), 32/262; ST243376; NP 165
Charlton (hamlet in Wantage), 2/90; SU413880; NP 158
Charlton (tithing in Henbury), 13/380; ST582805; NP 155
Charlton (Charlton next Dover) (parish), 19/371; TR319424; NP 173, 173/1
Charlton (Charlton-next-Woolwich) (parish), 19/10; TQ416778; NP 171
Charlton (hamlet in King's Sutton), 26/361B; SP529359; NP 145
Charlton (township in Wrockwardine), 31/219; SJ600110; NP 118, 119
Charlton (hamlet in Singleton), 36/229; SU890125; NP 181
Charlton (division in Malmsbury Eastern Registration Subdistrict of Charlton in Charlton), 39/24A; ST984888; NP 157
Charlton (division in Malmsbury Western Registration Subdistrict of Charlton in Charlton), 39/24B; ST938897; NP 156, 157
Charlton (parish), 39/24A-B; NP 156, 157
Charlton (parish), 39/223; SU095535; NP 167
Charlton (hamlet in Cropthorne), 40/209; SP015442; NP 144
Charlton Abbots (parish), 13/111; SP030237; NP 144
Charlton Adam (parish), 32/340; ST540290; NP 165, 177
Charlton East (Charlton East Quarter) (township in Bellingham), 27/278; NY815855; NP 77
Charlton Horethorne (parish), 32/386; ST657235; NP 166
Charlton Kings (parish), 13/112; SO974205; NP 143
Charlton Marshall (parish), 10/180; ST885025; NP 178
Charlton Mackrell (parish), 32/341; ST529287; NP 165, 177
Charlton Musgrove (Charlton Musgrave) (parish), 32/358; ST721302; NP 166
Charlton on Otmoor (hamlet in Charlton on Otmoor), 29/115; SP571168; NP 145
Charlton on Otmoor (parish), 29/115-116; NP 145
Charlton West (Charlton West Quarter) (township in Bellingham), 27/277; NY795865; NP 77
Charlwood (parish), 35/172; TQ247414; NP 170
Charminster (parish), 10/220; SY679946; NP 178
Charmouth (parish), 10/134; SY359935; NP 177
Charnage, 39/337; NP 166
Charndon (hamlet in Twyford), 3/113; SP676238; NP 145, 146
Charnes (township in Eccleshall), 33/145; SJ799344; NP 119
Charney Basset (Charney) (chapelry in Longworth), 2/29; SU381948; NP 158
Charnock Richard (township in Standish), 20/376; SD552162; NP 100
Charsfield (parish), 34/528; TM250564; NP 137, 150
Chart Sutton (Chart-next-Sutton-Valence) (parish), 19/300; TQ795486; NP 172
Chart-next-Sutton-Valence (parish), 19/300; NP 172
Charter House (extra-parochial), 24/8; TQ319821; NP 160/1
Charter House (extra-parochial), 41/334; TA101293; NP 99/1
Charterhouse Hinton (parish), 32/91; NP 166
Charterhouse on Mendip (extra-parochial), 32/74; ST492556; NP 165
Chartham (parish), 19/146; TR106553; NP 172, 173
Chartley Holme (extra-parochial), 33/124; SK011298; NP 119, 120
Charwelton (parish), 26/248; SP535557; NP 132, 145
Chaseley (parish), 40/238; NP 143
Chastleton (parish), 29/49; SP248298; NP 144
Chatburn (township in Whalley), 20/245; SD772445; NP 95
Chatcull (township in Eccleshall), 33/146; SJ798341; NP 119
Chatham (division in Gillingham registration subdistrict in Chatham), 19/89B; TQ773642; NP 172
Chatham (division in Rochester registration subdistrict in Chatham), 19/89A; TQ754668; NP 172
Chatham), 19/89A; TQ754668; NP 172
Chathill (township in Ellingham), 27/122; NU185269; NP 71
Chatley (hamlet in Great Leighs), 12/213; TL732182; NP 148
Chatsworth (division in Edensor and Chatsworth township in Edensor), 8/79; SK268702; NP 111

Chatteris (division in Chatteris), 4/17; TL410860; NP 135
Chatteris (parish), 4/17-18; NP 135
Chatterley (township in Wolstanton), 33/18D; SJ840510; NP 110
Chattisham (parish), 34/480; TM092422; NP 149, 150
Chatton (parish), 27/69-76; NP 64, 70, 71
Chatton (township in Chatton), 27/76; NU085280; NP 71
Chatwall (township in Cardington), 31/433E; SO512977; NP 129
Chawleigh (Chawley) (parish), 9/123; SS711118; NP 175
Chawley (tithing in Cumnor), 2/3C; SP468051; NP 158
Chawley, 9/123; NP 175
Chawton (parish), 14/173; SU698370; NP 168, 169
Cheadle (parish), 5/25-30; NP 101
Cheadle (township in Cheadle), 33/71; SK015435; NP 110, 111, 120
Cheadle Bulkeley (division in Cheadle Bulkeley township in Cheadle), 5/28B; SJ883895; NP 101
Cheadle Bulkeley (division in Cheadle Bulkeley township in Cheadle), 5/29; SJ856886; NP 101
Cheadle Bulkeley (township in Cheadle), 5/28B-29; NP 101
Cheadle Moseley (division in Cheadle), 5/27; SJ872869; NP 101
Cheadle Moseley (division in Cheadle), 5/28A; SJ888899; NP 101
Cheadle Moseley (township in Cheadle), 5/27-28A; NP 101
Cheam (parish), 35/53; TQ246643; NP 170
Cheapsides (extra-parochial), 41/22F; SE840296; NP 98/1
Chearsley (parish), 3/156; SP717107; NP 146, 159
Chebsey (parish), 33/129-130; NP 119
Chebsey (township in Chebsey), 33/129; SJ866294; NP 119
Checkendon (parish), 29/313; SU658832; NP 158, 159
Checkley (parish), 33/113-114; NP 119, 120
Checkley (township in Checkley), 33/114; SK029394; NP 119, 120
Checkley cum Wrinehill (township in Wybunbury), 5/267; SJ736456; NP 110, 119
Chedburgh (Chedbury) (parish), 34/313; TL798580; NP 136
Chedbury (parish), 34/313; NP 136
Cheddar (division in Cheddar), 32/148; ST459531; NP 165
Cheddar (parish), 32/148-149; NP 165
Cheddington (parish), 3/136; SP918175; NP 146
Cheddington (parish), 10/105; NP 177
Cheddon Fitzpaine (parish), 32/312; ST235279; NP 165, 177
Chedgrave (parish), 25/582; TM361995; NP 137
Chedington (Cheddington) (parish), 10/105; ST487056; NP 177
Chediston (parish), 34/76; TM350780; NP 137
Chedworth (parish), 13/215; SP050120; NP 143, 15
Chedzoy (parish), 32/216; ST342369; NP 165
Cheeseburn Grange), 27/465; NZ095705; NP 77
Cheetham (township in Manchester), 20/508; SD844007; NP 101
Chelderton (parish), 39/262; NP 167
Cheldon (parish), 9/124; SS738138; NP 163, 175
Chelford (township in Prestbury), 5/65; SJ821735; NP 101, 110
Chell (township in Wolstanton), 33/17G; SJ880520; NP 110
Chellaston (parish), 8/297; SK382304; NP 121
Chellesworth (parish), 34/404; NP 149
Chellington (parish), 1/25; SP962462; NP 133, 134
Chelmarsh (parish), 31/553; SO725871; NP 130
Chelmondiston (parish), 34/520; TM205376; NP 150
Chelmorton (township in Bakewell), 8/105; SK110700; NP 111
Chelmsford (parish), 12/286; TL701059; NP 161
Chelsea (parish), 24/40A-C; NP 170
Chelsea North East (division in St Luke Chelsea), 24/40C; TQ278792; NP 170
Chelsea North West (division in St Luke Chelsea), 24/40B; TQ271782; NP 170
Chelsea South (division in St Luke Chelsea), 24/40A; TQ277781; NP 170
Chelsfield (parish), 19/444; TQ471636; NP 171
Chelsham (parish), 35/99; TQ385585; NP 171
Chelson Meadows (extra-parochial), 9/453; SX512547; NP 187
Chelston (Chilston) (district in Salcombe Regis), 9/299B; SY166923; NP 176
Chelston (parish), 26/148; NP 134
Chelsworth (Chellesworth) (parish), 34/404; TL984480; NP 149

Cheltenham (parish), 13/114; SO933223; NP 143
Chelveston cum Caldecott (Chelston) (parish), 26/148; SP993691; NP 134
Chelvey (parish), 32/490; ST472680; NP 165
Chelwood (parish), 32/84; ST633615; NP 166
Chenies (parish), 3/201; TQ016978; NP 159, 160
Chepstow [Cas-Gwent] (parish), 53/98A; ST537921; NP 155
Cherhill (parish), 39/377; SU044702; NP 157
Cherington (Cherrington) (parish), 13/305; ST913975; NP 156
Cherington (parish), 37/292; SP288371; NP 145
Cheriton (parish), 14/187; SU575278; NP 168
Cheriton (parish), 19/390; TR191362; NP 173
Cheriton (parish), 51/31; SS461931; NP 153
Cheriton (parish), 55/161; NP 151
Cheriton Bishop (parish), 9/322; SX757937; NP 175
Cheriton Fitzpaine (parish), 9/216; SS881069; NP 176
Cherrington (parish), 13/305; NP 156
Cherrington (township in Edgmond), 31/194; SJ669192; NP 119
Cherry Burton (North Burton) (parish), 41/222; SE980420; NP 98, 99
Cherry Hinton (parish), 4/104; TL481567; NP 135, 148
Cherry Orton, 17/5
Cherry Willingham (parish), 22/357; TF027721; NP 113
Chertsey (parish), 35/67; TQ031649; NP 169, 170
Cheselbourne (Chesilbourne) (parish), 10/210; ST759001; NP 178
Chesham (parish), 3/197; SP963029; NP 159
Chesham Bois (parish), 3/198; SU963998; NP 159
Cheshunt (parish), 16/118-120; NP 161
Cheshunt Street (hamlet in Cheshunt), 16/118; TL361034; NP 161
Chesilbourne (parish), 10/210; NP 178
Cheslyn Hay (extra-parochial), 33/231; SJ969077; NP 119
Chessington (parish), 35/39; TQ181628; NP 170
Chester Castle (extra-parochial), 5/511; SJ405658; NP 109/1
Chester Cathedral Precincts (extra-parochial), 5/509; SJ406665; NP 109/1
Chester le Street (parish), 11/34-51; NP 78, 85
Chester le Street (township in Chester le Street), 11/44; NZ272509; NP 78, 85
Chesterfield (parish), 8/70-77; NP 112
Chesterfield (township in Chesterfield), 8/75; SK382712; NP 111
Chesterhope (township in Corsenside), 27/214; NY897855; NP 77
Chesterton (parish), 4/77; TL463610; NP 135
Chesterton (tithing in Cirencester), 13/279; SP013005; NP 157
Chesterton (parish), 17/3; TL125952; NP 134
Chesterton (parish), 29/107; SP554213; NP 145
Chesterton (township in Wolstanton), 33/18A; SJ830495; NP 110
Chesterton (Great Chesterton) (hamlet in Chesterton), 37/255; SP351583; NP 132
Chesterton Parva, 37/256; NP 132
Cheswardine (parish), 31/182-185; NP 119
Cheswardine (township in Cheswardine), 31/183; SJ704301; NP 119
Cheswick (township in Ancroft parochial chapelry in Holy Island), 27/19; NU029462; NP 64
Chetnole (chapelry in Yetminster), 10/41; ST603082; NP 177, 178
Chettisham, 4/26; NP 135
Chettle (parish), 10/61; ST947139; NP 179
Chetton (parish), 31/557-558; NP 130
Chetton (township in Chetton), 31/557; SO678898; NP 130
Chetwode (parish), 3/86; SP642293; NP 145
Chetwynd (parish), 31/187; SJ723218; NP 119
Chetwynd Aston (township in Edgmond), 31/196; SJ757176; NP 119
Cheveley (parish), 4/148; TL672619; NP 135
Cheveley (hamlet in Enstone), 29/94; SP387236; NP 145
Chevening (parish), 19/193; TQ504543; NP 171
Chevet (township in Royston), 43/689; SE248151; NP 102
Chevington (parish), 34/314; TL792600; NP 136

Chew Magna (parish), 32/55; ST584618; NP 155, 165
Chew Stoke (parish), 32/56; ST559615; NP 165
Chewton Mendip (division in Chewton Mendip), 32/77; ST586518; NP 165, 166
Chewton Mendip (parish), 32/77-78; NP 165, 166
Chicheley (parish), 3/41; SP912467; NP 146
Chichester, All Saints (All Saints or The Pallast) (parish), 36/261; SU851046; NP 181/1
Chichester, Cathedral Close (Chichester, Precinct of the Close) (extra-parochial), 36/262; SU848048; NP 181/1
Chichester, Precinct of the Close (extra-parochial), 36/262; NP 181/1
Chichester, St Andrew (parish), 36/259; SU853059; NP 181/1
Chichester, St Bartholomew (parish), 36/252; SU855045; NP 181/1
Chichester, St James (extra-parochial), 36/255; SU861053; NP 181/1
Chichester, St John (Newtown or St John) (extra-parochial), 36/256; SU854047; NP 181/1
Chichester, St Martin (parish), 36/258; SU852049; NP 181/1
Chichester, St Olave (parish), 36/257; SU851049; NP 181/1
Chichester, St Pancras (parish), 36/253-254; NP 181/1
Chichester, St Pancras within the Liberty (division in Chichester, St Pancras), 36/254; SU856049; NP 181/1
Chichester, St Pancras without the Liberty (division in Chichester, St Pancras), 36/253; SU862038; NP 181/1
Chichester, St Peter the Great (Chichester, The Subdeanery) (parish), 36/251; SU859059; NP 181/1
Chichester, St Peter the Less (parish), 36/260; SU852051; NP 181/1
Chichester, The Subdeanery (parish), 36/251; NP 181/1
Chick St Osyth (parish), 12/169; NP 149, 150
Chickerell (West Chickerell) (parish), 10/262; SY648806; NP 178
Chicklade (parish), 39/279; ST910347; NP 166
Chickney (parish), 12/61; TL569285; NP 148
Chicksands (extra-parochial), 1/88; TL113396; NP 147
Chiddingfold (parish), 35/159; SU958349; NP 169, 181
Chiddingly (parish), 36/134; TQ549141; NP 183
Chiddingstone (parish), 19/200; TQ496455; NP 171
Chideock (parish), 10/137; SY421929; NP 177
Chidham (parish), 36/249; SU793045; NP 181
Chidlow (township in Malpas), 5/321; SJ504450; NP 109
Chieveley (parish), 2/129-134; NP 158
Chieveley (tithing in Chieveley), 2/129; SU472743; NP 158
Chignal Smealey (Little Chignal, Chignal Smeeley) (parish), 12/247; TL668117; NP 148
Chignal St James (Great Chignal) (parish), 12/246; TL675100; NP 148, 161
Chigwell (parish), 12/311; TQ443937; NP 161
Chilbolton (parish), 14/144; SU407381; NP 168
Chilcomb (parish), 14/192; SU505285; NP 168
Chilcombe (parish), 10/237; SY529912; NP 177
Chilcompton (parish), 32/114; ST644519; NP 166
Chilcote (township in Clifton Campville), 8/328; SK288112; NP 120, 121
Child Okeford (parish), 10/54; ST832133; NP 178
Child's Ercall (parish), 31/180; SJ675242; NP 119
Childer Thornton (township in Eastham), 5/434; SJ357777; NP 100
Childerditch (parish), 12/414; TQ615891; NP 161
Childerley (Childerly) (parish), 4/68; TL357615; NP 134, 135
Childrey (parish), 2/96; SU358863; NP 158
Childswickham (parish), 13/33; SP061395; NP 144
Childwall (parish), 20/643-653; NP 100
Childwall (township in Childwall), 20/652; SJ417892; NP 100
Chilfrome (Chilfroome) (parish), 10/121; SY578992; NP 177
Chilham (parish), 19/147; TR067538; NP 172
Chillenden (parish), 19/278; TR269538; NP 173
Chillesford (parish), 34/377; TM392522; NP 150
Chillingham (parish), 27/112-114; NP 71
Chillingham (township in Chillingham), 27/112; NU064256; NP 71

Chillington (parish), 32/485; ST393110; NP 177
Chilmark (parish), 39/284-285; NP 167
Chilmark (tithing in Chilmark), 39/285; ST971332; NP 167
Chilson, 29/132
Chilston, 9/299B; NP 176
Chilswell (tithing in Cumnor), 2/3D; SP493033; NP 158
Chilthorne Domer (parish), 32/465; ST526198; NP 177
Chilton (parish), 2/83; SU484856; NP 158
Chilton (parish), 3/157; SP680117; NP 145, 146
Chilton (parish), 34/488; TL893436; NP 149
Chilton (township in Merrington), 11/222; NZ295301; NP 85
Chilton (township in Atcham), 31/241; SJ527091; NP 118
Chilton Candover (parish), 14/133; SU592408; NP 168
Chilton Cantelo (parish), 32/395; ST571221; NP 177
Chilton Common (extra-parochial), 32/265; ST297400; NP 165
Chilton Foliat (Chilton Foliatt) (division in Chilton Foliat), 2/108; SU337710; NP 158
Chilton Foliat (Chilton Foliatt) (division in Chilton Foliat), 39/181; SU319716; NP 158
Chilton Foliat (parish), 2/108, 39/181; NP 158
Chilton super Polden, 32/213; NP 165
Chilton Trinity (parish), 32/264; ST299394; NP 165
Chilton upon Polden (Chilton super Polden) (chapelry in Moorlinch), 32/213; ST378408; NP 165
Chilvers Coton (parish), 37/68; SP340900; NP 132
Chilwell (township in Attenborough), 28/252; SK514366; NP 121
Chilworth (parish), 14/228; SU404184; NP 180
Chilworth (hamlet in Great Milton), 29/255; SP632041; NP 158
Chilworth (St Martha, St Martha-on-the-Hill) (parish), 35/137; TQ032477; NP 169, 170
Chimney (hamlet in Bampton), 29/173; SP360010; NP 158
Chimney Mill (Chimney Mills) (extra-parochial), 34/202; TL821698; NP 136
Chingford (parish), 12/308; TQ382939; NP 161
Chinley, Bugsworth and Bownside (Bugsworth, Brownside) (township in Glossop), 8/12; SK051833; NP 102, 111
Chinnor (division in Chinnor), 29/266A; SP759001; NP 159
Chinnor (parish), 29/266A-B; NP 159
Chipchase (township in Chollerton), 27/438; NY890760; NP 77
Chipnall (township in Cheswardine), 31/184; SJ734314; NP 119
Chippenham (parish), 4/44; TL666687; NP 135
Chippenham (parish), 39/80-82; NP 156, 157
Chippenham (tithing in Chippenham), 39/81; ST917742; NP 156
Chipping (township in Chipping), 20/230; SD607427; NP 95
Chipping Barnet (parish), 16/149; TQ240960; NP 160
Chipping Campden (hamlet in Chipping Campden), 13/27A; SP155395; NP 144
Chipping Campden (parish), 13/27A-D; NP 144
Chipping Lambourn (township in Lambourn), 2/107E; SU325790; NP 158
Chipping Norton (parish), 29/51-52; NP 145
Chipping Norton (township in Chipping Norton), 29/51; SP320264; NP 145
Chipping Ongar (parish), 12/275; TL555035; NP 161
Chipping Sodbury (parish), 13/348; ST821729; NP 156
Chipping Wycombe (High Wycombe) (division in Chipping Wycombe), 3/205; SU868930; NP 159
Chipping Wycombe (High Wycombe) (parish), 3/205-206; NP 159
Chipping Wycombe, 3/206; NP 159
Chipping Warden (parish), 26/271; SP505493; NP 145
Chippinghurst (hamlet in Cuddesdon), 29/248; SP597008; NP 158
Chipstable (parish), 32/290; ST044262; NP 164
Chipstead (parish), 35/92; TQ271559; NP 170
Chirbury (township in Chirbury), 31/361; SO261985; NP 128
Chirdon (township in Greystead), 27/361; NY715795; NP 76, 77

Chirk (parish), 49/96-100; NP 108, 117, 118
Chirk (township in Chirk), 49/98; SJ287381; NP 117, 118
Chirton (parish), 39/207A-B; NP 167
Chirton (township in Tynemouth), 27/497; NZ339681; NP 78
Chirton (tithing in Chirton), 39/207A; SU075553; NP 167
Chiselborough (parish), 32/461; ST473149; NP 177
Chisledon (parish), 39/95; SU184802; NP 157
Chislehampton (parish), 29/247; SU587992; NP 158
Chislehurst (Chiselhurst) (parish), 19/21; TQ444706; NP 171
Chislet (Chislett) (parish), 19/121; TR236653; NP 173
Chiswick (parish), 24/102; TQ208775; NP 170
Chisworth (township in Glossop), 8/5; SJ997918; NP 101, 102
Chithurst (parish), 36/8; SU837249; NP 181
Chitterne All Saints (parish), 39/243; ST993456; NP 167
Chitterne St Mary (parish), 39/244; ST986438; NP 167
Chittlehamholt (district in Chittlehampton), 9/69; SS649202; NP 163
Chittlehampton (district in Chittlehampton), 9/68; SS638252; NP 163
Chittlehampton (parish), 9/68-69; NP 163
Chittoe (tithing in Bishops Cannings), 39/132B; ST957673; NP 157
Chivelstone (parish), 9/489; SX787378; NP 187, 188
Chobham (parish), 35/70; SU970626; NP 169
Cholderton (Chelderton, West Cholderton) (parish), 39/262; SU221428; NP 167
Cholesbury (Choulesbury) (parish), 3/172; SP930070; NP 146
Chollerton, 27/438-444; NP 77
Chollerton (township in Chollerton), 27/444; NY945730; NP 77
Cholmondeley (township in Malpas), 5/333; SJ550517; NP 109
Cholmondeston (township in Acton), 5/295; SJ632584; NP 110
Cholsey (division in Cholsey), 2/71; SU590855; NP 158
Cholsey (township in South Moreton), 2/72; SU581877; NP 158
Cholsey (township), 2/71, 2/72; NP 158
Cholstrey (township in Leominster), 15/69; SO478585; NP 129
Cholswell (hamlet in Abingdon St Helen), 2/16A; SU480994; NP 158
Choppington (township in Bedlington), 27/428; NZ247847; NP 78
Chopwell (township in Ryton), 11/29; NZ110580; NP 77, 78
Chorley (parish), 20/336; SD585175; NP 100, 101
Chorley (township in Wilmslow), 5/70; SJ835782; NP 101
Chorley (township in Wrenbury), 5/280; SJ574506; NP 110
Chorley and Northwood (township in Stottesden), 31/574; SO696836; NP 130
Chorlton (township in Backford), 5/494; SJ406725; NP 109
Chorlton (township in Malpas), 5/326; SJ466477; NP 109
Chorlton (township in Wybunbury), 5/257; SJ729501; NP 110
Chorlton upon Medlock (township in Manchester), 20/521; SJ845965; NP 101
Chorlton-cum-Hardy (township in Manchester), 20/525; SJ819932; NP 101
Choseley (extra-parochial), 25/6; TF756407; NP 124, 125
Choulesbury (parish), 3/172; NP 146
Choulton (township in Lydbury North), 31/370; SO376883; NP 129
Chowley (township in Coddington), 5/357; SJ479558; NP 109
Chrishall (parish), 12/11; TL445381; NP 148
Christ Church (Christchurch Newgate-Street) (parish), 23/3; TQ319814; NP 160/2
Christ College (Christ's College) (extra-parochial), 45/50; SO042284; NP 141
Christchurch (Christchurch Twynham) (parish), 14/320; SZ160950; NP 179
Christchurch Newgate-Street (parish), 23/3; TQ319814; NP 160/2
Christchurch (division in St Marylebone), 24/45A; TQ289824; NP 160
Christchurch Spitalfields (parish), 24/61A-C; NP 160/1
Christchurch Southwark (parish), 35/1; TQ317802; NP 160/1
Christchurch (hamlet in Christchurch), 53/132A; ST338882; NP 155
Christchurch (parish), 53/132A-B; NP 155

Christian Malford (division in Christian Malford), 39/63; ST976798; NP 157
Christian Malford (parish), 39/63-64; NP 157
Christionydd Coed, 49/93; NP 108, 118
Christionydd Enrick (township in Ruabon), 49/92; SJ274441; NP 108, 117
Christleton (parish), 5/377-381; NP 109
Christleton (township in Christleton), 5/378; SJ451659; NP 109
Christon (parish), 32/153; ST382578; NP 165
Christow (parish), 9/402; SX825840; NP 175, 176
Chudleigh (parish), 9/400; SX880810; NP 176, 188
Chulmleigh (parish), 9/87; SS703160; NP 163, 175
Chunal (Chunall) (township in Glossop), 8/3D; SK033917; NP 102
Church (Church Kirk) (township in Whalley), 20/296; SD748297; NP 95
Church (division in St Matthew Bethnal Green), 24/63C; TQ339824; NP 160/1
Church (township in Llanddewi Ystradenny), 56/30B; SO120690; NP 128
Church (township in Llanfihangel Beguidy), 56/7; SO178782; NP 128
Church Aston (township in Edgmond), 31/195; SJ741178; NP 119
Church Brampton (parish), 26/188; SP717663; NP 133
Church Broughton (parish), 8/238; SK205335; NP 120
Church Coniston (division in township of Church Coniston in Ulverston), 20/9; SD287987; NP 88, 89
Church Coniston (township in Ulverston), 20/9-10; NP 88, 89
Church Coppenhall (township in Coppenhall), 5/245; SJ707574; NP 110
Church Eaton (parish), 33/22; SJ839169; NP 119
Church Enstone (hamlet in Enstone), 29/93; SP385255; NP 145
Church Fenton (Kirk Fenton) (parish), 43/444-446; NP 97
Church Fenton (Kirk Fenton) (township in Church Fenton), 43/444; SE520366; NP 97
Church Gresley (Gresley) (parish), 8/316-320, 332, 334; SK250195; NP 120, 121, 121/3
Church Gresley (township in Church Gresley), 8/319; SK294183; NP 120, 121
Church Honeybourne (Church Honeybourne with Poden) (parish), 40/226; SP122441; NP 144
Church Hulme (township in Sandbach), 5/213; SJ765672; NP 110
Church Icomb (Church Iccomb) (hamlet in Icomb), 13/3; SP216231; NP 144
Church Knowle (parish), 10/291-292B; NP 178, 179
Church Knowle (tithing in Church Knowle), 10/292A; SY940820; NP 178, 179
Church Langton (parish), 21/310; NP 133
Church Lawton (parish), 5/239; SJ820556; NP 110
Church Lawford (parish), 37/139; SP449757; NP 132
Church Lench (parish), 40/191-193; NP 144
Church Lench (township in Church Lench), 40/191; SP023513; NP 144
Church Minshull (parish), 5/298; SJ655607; NP 110
Church Oakley (parish), 14/54; SU572515; NP 168
Church Preen (parish), 31/434; SO542978; NP 129
Church Pulverbatch (parish), 31/335-338B; NP 118, 129
Church Pulverbatch (township in Church Pulverbatch), 31/338A; SJ432029; NP 118
Church Shocklach (township in Shocklach), 5/347; SJ441500; NP 109
Church Somershall (parish), 8/243; NP 120
Church Stoke (parish), 31/362-363, 54/187-194; NP 128, 129
Church Stoke (township in Church Stoke), 54/193; SO280946; NP 128, 129
Church Street (division in West Ham), 12/323; TQ402840; NP 161
Church Street (parish), 19/38; NP 171
Church Streetton (parish), 31/342; SO450940; NP 129
Church Town Quarter (township in Rockcliff), 7/69; NY372618; NP 76

Church Wilne (township in Wilne), 8/287; SK447319; NP 121
Churcham (hamlet in Churcham), 13/144; SO764182; NP 143
Churcham (parish), 13/143A-144; NP 143
Churchdown (hamlet in Churchdown), 13/201; SO880204; NP 143
Churchdown (parish), 13/201; NP 143
Churchill (parish), 29/136; SP279242; NP 144, 145
Churchill (parish), 32/69; ST455605; NP 165
Churchill (parish), 40/154; SO920537; NP 130
Churchill (parish), 40/260; SO874797; NP 130
Churchover (parish), 37/118; SP519802; NP 132
Churchstanton (parish), 9/142; ST195138; NP 164, 177
Churchstow (parish), 9/475; SX712453; NP 187
Churnham Street (tithing in Hungerford), 39/182; SU320680; NP 158, 168
Churston Ferrers (parish), 9/435; SX895559; NP 188
Churt and Pitfold (tithing in Frensham), 35/153; SU870380; NP 169, 181
Churton Bruera, 5/501; NP 109
Churton by Aldford (township in Aldford), 5/363; SJ423572; NP 109
Churton by Farndon (township in Farndon), 5/351; SJ418560; NP 109
Churton Heath (Churton on the Heath, Churton Bruera) (township in St Oswald Chester), 5/501; SJ440600; NP 109
Churton on the Heath, 5/501; NP 109
Churwell (township in Batley), 43/588; SE273296; NP 96
Chute (parish), 39/190; SU302542; NP 167, 168
Chute Forest (East and West Walks of the Forests of Chute and Wakeswood) (extra-parochial), 39/191; SU311517; NP 157
Cil-cowen (township in Llanllwchaiarn), 54/165; SO109943; NP 128
Cil-yr-ych (Kilyruch) (township in Llanfair Caereinion), 54/56; SJ121074; NP 117
Cilcain (parish), 50/99A-104; NP 108
Cilcennin (parish), 46/57; SN527601; NP 140
Cilfach-allt (Kilmachallt, Cilfach-alt) (township in Llanidloes), 54/141; SN967837; NP 128
Cilgerran (Kilgerran) (parish), 55/8; SN196415; NP 139
Cilgwrrwg (parish), 53/85; NP 155
Ciliau-Aeron (division in Llan Hundred in Ciliau-Aeron), 46/60A; SN503578; NP 140
Ciliau-Aeron (division in Troed-y-Taur Hundred in Ciliau-Aeron), 46/60B; SN490570; NP 139, 140
Ciliau-Aeron (parish), 46/60a-B; NP 139, 140
Cilowen (township in St Asaph [Llanelwy]), 50/78; SJ062738; NP 108
Cilrhedyn (division in Cilrhedyn), 47/41; SN310350; NP 139
Cilrhedyn (Kilrhedyn) (parish), 47/41, 55/12; NP 139
Cilwych (township in Llanfihangel Cwm-du), 45/82C; SO160210; NP 141
Cilybebyll (Kilybebell) (parish), 51/9; SN753053; NP 153
Cilycwm (parish), 47/2; SN740430; NP 140
Cilymaenllwyd (division in Cilymaenllwyd), 47/50; SN152234; NP 139
Cilymaenllwyd (parish), 47/50, 88, 55/80
Cippin (hamlet in St Dogmaels), 55/1; SN139478; NP 139
Cirencester (parish), 13/276-279; NP 157
Cirencester (tithing in Cirencester), 13/277; SP032022; NP 157
Citadel (extra-parochial), 41/336; TA105386; NP 99/1
City Road (division in St Luke), 24/48B; TQ323826; NP 160/1
Claife (township in Hawkshead), 20/44-45; NP 89
Claines (parish), 40/111A-112; NP 130, 143
Claines (township in Claines), 40/111A-B; NP 130, 143
Clanfield (parish), 14/250; SU706172; NP 181
Clanfield (parish), 29/163; SP294013; NP 157, 158
Clannaborough (parish), 9/209; SS736001; NP 175
Clapcot (division in Wallingford, All Hallows), 2/66B; SU602914; NP 158
Clapham (division in township of Clapham cum Newby in Clapham), 43/276; SD745695; NP 90

Clapham (parish), 1/34; TL038537; NP 134, 147
Clapham (parish), 35/20; TQ295749; NP 170
Clapham (parish), 36/215; TQ100068; NP 182
Clapham (parish), 42/275-279; NP 90
Clapham cum Newby (township in Clapham), 43/275-276; NP 90
Clapton (Clapton on the Hill) (parish), 13/225; SP162180; NP 144
Clapton (parish), 26/80; NP 134
Clapton (parish), 32/7; ST465736; NP 155
Clapton on the Hill (parish), 13/225; NP 144
Clapton-in-Gordano (Clapton) (parish), 32/7; ST465736; NP 155
Claragh (township in Llanbadarn fawr), 46/11B; SN607847; NP 127
Clarbeston (parish), 55/78; SN050210; NP 138
Clarborough (township in Clarborough), 28/48; SK735832; NP 103, 104
Clare (district in Tiverton), 9/160; SS903133; NP 164
Clare (parish), 34/338; TL764461; NP 148, 149
Clarendon Park (Clarendon) (extra-parochial), 39/385; SU187302; NP 167
Clareton (township in Allerton Mauleverer), 43/113; SE395595
Clarewood (township in Corbridge), 27/470; NZ025695; NP 77
Clarksfield (ward in Oldham-above-Town division in township of Oldham in Oldham), 20/493; SD946045; NP 101
Clase (hamlet in Llangyfelach), 51/6; SN660000; NP 153
Clase (township in St Harmon), 56/1B; SN960740; NP 128
Clatford (tithing in Preshute), 39/169; SU156690; NP 157
Clatford Park (extra-parochial), 39/176; SU162661; NP 157
Clattercot (Clattercote) (extra-parochial), 29/7; SP459491; NP 145
Clatworthy (parish), 32/277; ST052324; NP 164
Claughton cum Grange (township in Bidston), 5/447; SJ305891; NP 100
Claughton (parish), 20/90; SD569656; NP 89
Claughton (township in Garstang), 20/151; SD532428; NP 94
Claverdon (hamlet in Claverdon), 37/175; SP202643; NP 131
Claverdon (parish), 37/175-176; NP 131
Clavering (parish), 12/16; TL468322; NP 148
Claverley (parish), 31/480; SO790925; NP 130
Claverton (extra-parochial), 5/373; SJ405636; NP 109
Claverton (parish), 32/39; ST781640; NP 166
Clawrplwyf (hamlet in Mynyddislwyn), 53/70A; SO200000; NP 154
Clawton (parish), 9/193; SX346993; NP 174
Claxby (Claxby by Normanby) (parish), 22/160; TF109947; NP 104
Claxby (parish), 22/420; TF448718; NP 114
Claxby by Normanby (parish), 22/160; NP 104
Claxby Pluckacre (parish), 22/443; TF307644; NP 114
Claxton (parish), 25/578; TG336036; NP 126
Claxton (township in Greatham), 11/257; NZ476285; NP 85
Claxton (township in Bossall), 42/665; SE690601; NP 92, 97
Clay Coton (parish), 26/117; SP594772; NP 132
Clay Cross, 8/132; NP 111, 112
Clay Lane (subdivision of Spotland Further Side division in Spotland township in Rochdale), 20/446; SD859136; NP 101
Claybrooke (Claybrook) (parish), 21/233-237, 37/108; NP 132
Claybrooke Magna (Great Claybrooke) (township in Claybrooke), 21/234; SP489891; NP 132
Claybrooke Parva (Little Claybrooke) (parish), 21/235; SP490880; NP 132
Claydon (chapelry in Cropredy), 29/9; SP460503; NP 145
Claydon (parish), 34/395; TM140498; NP 150
Claygate (hamlet in Thames Ditton), 35/61; TQ152627; NP 170
Clayhanger (parish), 9/132; ST019235; NP 164
Clayhidon (parish), 9/141; ST160132; NP 164
Claylane (Clay Cross) (township in North Wingfield), 8/132; SK382631; NP 111, 112
Claypole (parish), 22/609; SK853498; NP 113
Claythorpe (chapelry in Belleau), 22/319; TF410795; NP 105
Clayton (parish), 36/101; TQ301164; NP 182
Clayton (township in Stoke-on-Trent), 33/37; SJ851433; NP 119

Clayton (township in Bradford), 43/530B; SE113313; NP 96
Clayton (township and parish of Clayton with Frickley), 43/874; SE458074; NP 103
Clayton Griffith (township in Trentham), 33/69; SJ849449; NP 110, 119
Clayton le Dale (township in Blackburn), 20/314; SD660335; NP 95
Clayton le Moors (township in Whalley), 20/295; SD746311; NP 95
Clayton West (township in High Hoyland), 43/712; SE259105; NP 102
Clayton with Frickley (parish and township), 43/873-874; NP 103
Clayton-le-Woods (township in Leyland), 20/332; SD569228; NP 94
Clayworth (parish), 28/13-14; NP 103
Clayworth (township in Clayworth), 28/13; SK731877; NP 103
Cleadon (division in township of Whitburn in Whitburn), 11/11; NZ389630; NP 78
Clearwell (hamlet in Newland), 13/163B; SO570080; NP 155
Cleasby (parish), 42/29; NZ253121; NP 85
Cleatham (township in Gainford), 11/301; NZ116183; NP 84, 85
Cleatham (township in Staindrop), 11/290; NZ120190; NP 84
Cleatham (township), 11/290, 301; NP 84, 85
Cleatham (township in Manton), 22/37; SE927013; NP 104
Cleator (parish), 7/304; NY023142; NP 82
Cleckheaton (division in township of Cleckheaton in Birstal), 43/543; SE183259; NP 96
Cleckheaton (township in Birstal), 43/542-544; NP 96
Clee (parish), 22/80-83; TA279076; NP 105
Clee (township in Clee), 22/81; TA294079; NP 105
Clee St Margaret (St Margaret Clee, St Margaret Clee Brown) (parish), 31/513; SO571843; NP 129
Clee Stanton, Clee Downton, Moor and Stoke St Milborough (township in Stoke St Milborough), 31/514A; SO580813; NP 129, 130
Cleethorpes (township in Clee), 22/82; TA301094; NP 105
Cleeton (township in Bitterley), 31/531B; SO603782; NP 129, 130
Cleeve (tithing in Ross-on-Wye), 15/253; SO590234; NP 142
Cleeve Prior (parish), 40/197; SO088490; NP 144
Clegg (subdivision in Butterworth Freehold Side division in Butterworth township in Rochdale), 20/463; SD940150; NP 101
Clegyrog (township in Llanbadrig), 44/5; SH387897; NP 106
Clehonger (parish), 15/194; SO465381; NP 142
Clemenston (parish), 51/117; NP 154
Clements Inn (division in St Clement Danes), 24/24; TQ307811; NP 160/1
Clenchwarton (division in Clenchwarton), 25/292A; TF588203; NP 124
Clenchwarton (division in Marshland fen in Clenchwarton), 25/292B; TF541111; NP 124
Clenchwarton (parish), 25/292A-B; NP 124
Clennel (township in Alwinton), 27/178; NT923077; NP 71
Clent (parish), 40/4; SO930795; NP 130
Cleobury Mortimer (parish), 31/547-548; NP 130
Cleobury North (parish), 31/561; SO619870; NP 129, 130
Clerkenwell (parish), 24/47A-D; NP 160/1
Cletterwood (township in Buttington), 54/92; SJ265085; NP 117, 118
Clevedon (parish), 32/10; ST410710; NP 155, 165
Cleveley (township in Cockerham or Garstang), 20/147B; SD498501; NP 94
Cleveload, 40/159B; NP 143
Clevelode (Cleveload) (hamlet in Powick), 40/159B; SO830470; NP 143
Clewer (parish), 2/221; SU946755; NP 159
Cley next the Sea (parish), 25/28; TG053433; NP 125
Cliburn (parish), 38/9; NY587251; NP 83
Cliddesden (parish), 14/99; SU642488; NP 168
Cliffe (Cliffe-at-Hoo) (parish), 19/39; TQ736766; NP 171, 172
Cliffe (township in Manfield), 42/31; NZ203150; NP 85
Cliffe cum Lund (Cliff cum Lund) (township in Hemingbrough), 41/48; SE665329; NP 97
Cliffe Pypard (parish), 39/90; SU075775; NP 157

Clifford (parish), 15/203; SO262444; NP 141, 142
Clifford Chambers (parish), 13/14; SP190498; NP 144
Clifford with Boston (township in Bramham), 43/90; SE423450; NP 97
Clifford's Inn (extra-parochial), 24/20; TQ312812; NP 160/1
Clifton (Clifton with Rocksavage, Rocksavage) (township in Runcorn), 5/161; SJ526802; NP 100
Clifton (Clifton-with-Glapton) (parish), 28/254; SK552341; NP 121
Clifton (division in township of Clifton with Salwick in Kirkham), 20/201; SD464302; NP 94
Clifton (division inside borough in township of Clifton in St Olave), 42/694; SE605631; NP 97
Clifton (division inside borough in township of Clifton in St Michael le Belfrey), 42/696; SE595530; NP 97
Clifton (division outside borough in township of Clifton in St Olave), 42/693; SE597543; NP 97
Clifton (division outside borough in township of Clifton in St Michael le Belfrey), 42/695; SE599536; NP 97
Clifton (division in parish and township of Conisbrough), 43/886; SK523963; NP 103
Clifton (hamlet in Deddington), 29/38; SP482326; NP 145
Clifton (parish), 1/93; TL164389; NP 147
Clifton (parish), 13/408; ST573733; NP 156
Clifton (parish), 38/1; NY542260; NP 83
Clifton (township in Eccles), 20/563; SD781030; NP 101
Clifton (township in St Olave and St Michael le Belfrey), 42/693-696; NP 97
Clifton (township in Dewsbury), 43/579; SE159232; NP 96
Clifton and Compton (Clifton) (township in Ashbourne), 8/180; SK170451; NP 111, 120
Clifton and Coldwell (township in Stannington), 27/421; NZ200820; NP 78
Clifton Campville (Clifton) (township in Clifton Campville), 33/277; SK259104; NP 120
Clifton Campville (parish), 33/275-277; NP 120
Clifton Hampden (parish), 29/244; SU541953; NP 158
Clifton Maybank (parish), 10/36; ST579132; NP 178
Clifton Reynes (parish), 3/35; SP911502; NP 146
Clifton upon Dunsmore (Clifton) (township in Clifton upon Dunsmore), 37/121; SP534762; NP 132
Clifton upon Dunsmore (parish), 37/119-122; NP 120
Clifton upon Teme (parish), 40/94; SO719616; NP 13
Clifton upon Ure, 42/182; NP 91
Clifton upon Yore (Clifton upon Ure) (township in Thornton Watlass), 42/182; SE219844; NP 91
Clifton with Rocksavage, 5/161; NP 100
Clifton with Salwick (township in Kirkham), 20/201, 202; NP 94
Clifton with Norwood (township in Fewston), 43/377; SE212428; NP 96
Clifton, 8/180; NP 111, 120
Clifton, 37/121
Clifton-with-Glapton (parish), 28/254; NP 121
Climping (parish), 36/287; TQ005019; NP 181
Clinch and Hartside (township in Ingram), 27/129; NU035147; NP 71
Clint (township in Ripley), 43/152; SE260605; NP 91, 96
Clippesby (parish), 25/390B; TG425150; NP 126
Clipsham (parish), 30/9; SK969157; NP 123
Clipston (parish), 26/107; SP706819; NP 133
Clipston (Clipstone) (township in Plumtree), 28/272; SK639334; NP 121
Clipstone (township in Edwinstowe), 28/83; SK594648; NP 112
Clipstone, 28/272
Clist Honiton, 9/280
Clist St George, 9/311
Clist St Lawrence,
Clist-Hydon, 9/244; NP 176
Clitheroe (township in Whalley), 20/244; SD745422; NP 95
Clive (Clive and Sansaw) (township in St Mary Shrewsbury), 31/247; SJ512244; NP 118
Clive (township in Middlewich), 5/205; SJ671653; NP 110
Cliviger (township in Whalley), 20/275; SD878286; NP 95

Clixby (chapelry in Caistor), 22/105A; TA100043; NP 104
Clixby - Caistor Moor (division in Caistor), 22/105B; TA095025; NP 104
Cloatley (Cloatly) (hamlet in Hankerton), 39/23B; ST983903; NP 157
Clocaenog (parish), 49/25A-B; NP 108
Clocaenog Issa (township in Clocaenog), 49/25A; SJ075545; NP 108
Clocaenog Ucha (township in Clocaenog), 49/25B; SJ020520; NP 108
Cloddiau (township in Kerry [Llanfihangel-yng-Ngheri]), 54/174; SO153910; NP 128
Clodock (parish), 15/208-209, 211-212; NP 141, 142
Cloffocks (extra-parochial), 7/250; NX999293; NP 82
Cloford (parish), 32/129; ST723438; NP 166
Clophill (parish), 1/84; TL089383; NP 147
Clopton (Clapton) (parish), 26/80; TL060802; NP 134
Clopton (hamlet in Mickleton), 13/20; SP172451; NP 144
Clopton (parish), 34/363; TM224546; NP 150
Close of Winchester (extra-parochial), 14/202B; NP 168/1
Closeworth (parish), 32/475; NP 177
Closworth (Closeworth) (parish), 32/475; ST562105; NP 177
Clothall (parish), 16/9; TL279315; NP 147
Clotherholme (township in Ripon), 43/182; SE286722; NP 91
Clotton Hoofield (Clotton Hoolfield) (township in Tarvin), 5/391; SJ521635; NP 109
Cloughton (township in Scalby), 42/400; TA007950; NP 93
Clovelly (parish), 9/50; SS315235; NP 174
Clowance (district in Stoke Damerel), 9/460; SX455545; NP 187/1
Clowne (Clown) (parish), 8/59; SK489752; NP 103, 112
Clun (parish), 31/385-401; NP 128, 129
Clun (parochial division in Clun), 31/400-401; NP 129
Clun (township in Clun), 31/401; SO301802; NP 129
Clunbury (Clunbury and Coston) (parish), 31/410; SO375805; NP 129
Clungunford (parish), 31/414; SO405785; NP 129
Clutton (parish), 32/83; ST627595; NP 166
Clutton (township in Farndon), 5/353; SJ467546; NP 109
Clydach (hamlet in Ystrad-dyfodwg), 51/66C; SS990930; NP 154
Clydey (parish), 55/11; SN248355; NP 139
Clyne, 51/53; NP 153
Clynnog-fawr (Clynog) (parish), 48/40; SH452485; NP 106, 115, 116
Clynog, 48/40; NP 106, 115, 116
Clyro (parish), 56/55A-B; NP 141
Clyro (township in Clyro), 56/55A; SO195455; NP 141
Clyst Hidon (Clist-Hydon) (parish), 9/244; ST042013; NP 176
Clyst Honiton (Clist Honiton, Honiton-Clist) (parish), 9/280; SX993934; NP 176
Clyst St George (Clist St George, St George Clist) (parish), 9/311; SX982892; NP 176
Clyst St Lawrence (Clist St Lawrence) (parish), 9/243; ST031001; NP 176
Clyst St Mary (St Mary Clist) (parish), 9/310; SX987902; NP 176
Clytha (hamlet in Llanarth), 53/27; SO376086; NP 155
Coal Aston (township in Dronfield), 8/48; SK367798; NP 111
Coal Hill (moor common to Laverton township and Galphay division in Kirkby Malzeard), 43/199; SE202711; NP 91
Coaley (parish), 13/313; SO772017; NP 156
Coanwood (township in Haltwhistle), 27/575; NY720680; NP 76, 77
Coat Yards (township in Netherwitton), 27/331; NZ083944; NP 71, 77
Coate (tithing in Swindon), 39/55; SU173834; NP 157
Coates (parish), 13/301; SO981008; NP 157
Coates (parish), 22/228; SK913833; NP 104
Coates (parish), 36/72; SU996178; NP 181
Coates (township in Barnoldswick), 43/313; SD878487; NP 95
Coatham Mundeville (township in Haughton le Skerne), 11/333; NZ273200; NP 85

Coatham Stob (division of Long Newton township in Long Newton), 11/340; NZ402162; NP 85
Coaton, 26/174; NP 132
Coats-a-Moor, 11/281; NP 85
Coatsawmoor, 11/281; NP 85
Coatsay Moor (Coats-a-Moor, Coatsawmoor) (township in Heighington), 11/281; NZ251209; NP 85
Coberley (Cubberley) (parish), 13/208; SO962165; NP 143
Cobham (parish), 19/52; TQ674685; NP 171
Cobham (parish), 35/59; TQ110600; NP 170
Cobholm Island (hamlet in Gorleston), 34/5; TG518077; NP 126
Cockayne Hatley (parish), 1/63; TL260496; NP 147
Cocken (township in Houghton-le-Spring), 11/61; NZ289476; NP 85
Cockerand Abbey (extra-parochial), 20/100; SD433544; NP 94
Cockerham (parish), 20/101-103 (& cf 20/145-147B); NP 94
Cockerham (township in Cockerham), 20/101; SD459509; NP 94
Cockerington St Leonard (parish), 22/187; NP 105
Cockermouth (township in Brigham), 7/267; NY126303; NP 82
Cockerton (township in Darlington), 11/319; NZ271167; NP 85
Cockfield (parish), 11/293-294; NP 84, 85
Cockfield (township in Cockfield), 11/293; NZ127242; NP 84, 85
Cockfield (parish), 34/347; TL907543; NP 149
Cocking (parish), 36/17; SU874176; NP 181
Cockington (parish), 9/433; SX894638; NP 188
Cocklaw (township in St John Lee), 27/447; NY965709; NP 77
Cockle Park (township in Hebburn parochial chapelry), 27/307; NZ199907; NP 78
Cockley Cley (All Saints and St Peters, Cockley Cley) (parish), 25/533; TF800046; NP 125
Cockshutt, 31/54; NP 118
Cockthorpe (parish), 25/23; TF985422; NP 125
Coddenham (division in Coddenham), 34/288; TM130548; NP 150
Coddenham (parish), 34/287-288; NP 136, 137, 150
Coddington (parish), 5/355-357; NP 109
Coddington (township in Coddington), 5/355; SJ444568; NP 109
Coddington (parish), 15/276; SO724423; NP 143
Coddington (parish), 28/147; SK838542; NP 113
Codecerney (parish), 53/131; NP 154, 155
Codekernew (Codecernew) (parish), 53/131; ST271839; NP 154, 155
Codford St Mary (parish), 39/246; ST986406; NP 167
Codford St Peter (parish), 39/245; ST967415; NP 167
Codicote (parish), 16/88; TL219187; NP 147
Codnor (parish), 8/197A-199; NP 112, 121
Codnor (township in Codnor), 8/197A; SK422492; NP 112
Codnor Park (extra-parochial), 8/196; SK434502; NP 112
Codsall (parish), 33/323-324; NP 119
Codsall (township in Codsall), 33/323; SJ864040; NP 119
Coed Christionyd (Christionydd Coed) (township in Ruabon), 49/93; SJ282414; NP 108, 118
Coed-Ffranc (Coedfrank) (hamlet in Cadoxton Juxta Neath), 51/13; SN715953; NP 153
Coed-rwg (township in Llantysilio), 49/101; SJ150450; NP 108
Coedana (parish), 44/31; SH429822; NP 106
Coedcanlas (parish), 55/109; SN013091; NP 151
Coedfrank, 51/13; NP 153
Coedlasson (township in Nantmel), 56/31C; SO030690; NP 128
Coelwn-Glynn (Upper Division) (township in Llanfigan), 45/54A; SO060180; NP 141
Coelwn-Penkelly (Lower Division, Pencelli) (township in Llanfigan), 45/54B; SO090250; NP 141
Coffinswell (parish), 9/416; SX895685; NP 188
Coffronydd, 54/65; NP 117
Cofton Hackett (Coston Hackett) (parish), 40/49; SP012755; NP 130, 131
Cogan (parish), 51/180; ST170708; NP 154
Cogden (division in township of Grinton in Grinton), 42/117; SE053970; NP 90
Cogenhoe (Cooknoe) (parish), 26/288; SP833607; NP 133

Cogges (Coggs) (parish), 29/181; SP373092; NP 145, 158
Coggeshall (Great Coggeshall) (parish), 12/131; TL840237; NP 149
Coggs (parish), 29/181; NP 145, 158
Cogshall (township in Great Budworth), 5/120; SJ635771; NP 101
Coity (Coyty), 51/89-80; NP 154
Coity (Coyty), 51/89-80; NP 154
Coity Higher (Coity, Higher Hamlet, Coyty Higher) (hamlet in Coity), 51/90; SS928818; NP 154
Coity Lower (Coity, Lower Hamlet, Coyty Lower) (hamlet in Coity), 51/89; SS907793; NP 154
Colan (Little Colan) (parish), 6/90; SW874605; NP 185
Colaton Raleigh (district in Colaton Raleigh), 9/303A; SY059879; NP 176
Colaton Raleigh (parish), 9/303A-B; NP 176
Colbatch, 31/379; NP 129
Colburn (township in Catterick), 42/81; SE200986; NP 91
Colby (parish), 25/139; TG221311; NP 126
Colby (township in St Lawrence Appleby), 38/37; NY657201; NP 83
Colchester St Leonard (parish), 12/153A; TL012248; NP 149
Colchester, All Saints (parish), 12/149; TM001053; NP 149/1
Colchester, Holy Trinity (parish), 12/151; TL987238; NP 149/1
Colchester, St Botolph (parish), 12/144; TM007241; NP 149
Colchester, St Giles (parish), 12/143; TL992221; NP 149
Colchester, St James (parish), 12/145; TM005257; NP 149
Colchester, St Martin (parish), 12/147; TL997252; NP 149/1
Colchester, St Mary at the Walls (parish), 12/142; TL981241; NP 149
Colchester, St Mary Magdalen (parish), 12/152; TL992249; NP 149/1
Colchester, St Michael Mile End (parish), 12/120; NP 149
Colchester, St Nicholas (parish), 12/148; TL999251; NP 149/1
Colchester, St Peter (parish), 12/146; TL993252; NP 149/1
Colchester, St Runwald (parish), 12/150; TM007253; NP 149/1
Cold Ashby (parish), 26/119; SP653768; NP 132
Cold Ashton (parish), 13/400; ST743722; NP 156
Cold Aston (parish), 13/102; NP 144
Cold Brayfield (parish), 3/33; SP927526; NP 146
Cold Cotes (division in township of Ingleton in Bentham), 43/272; SD715715; NP 90
Cold Dunghills (parish), 34/467; TM168444; NP 150/1
Cold Hanworth (parish), 22/252; TF030833; NP 104
Cold Hatton (township in High Ercall), 31/207; SJ630210; NP 119
Cold Hesledon (Hesledon) (township in Dalton-le-Dale), 11/87; NZ411467; NP 85
Cold Hiendly (division in Havercroft with Cold Hiendly township in Felkirk), 43/679; SE371141; NP 102
Cold Higham (parish), 26/277; SP657439; NP 132, 145
Cold Kirby (parish), 42/496; SE532842; NP 92
Cold Newton (township in Lowesby), 21/262; SK722061; NP 122
Cold Norton (parish), 12/340; TL843001; NP 162
Cold Norton (township in Chebsey), 33/130; SJ875317; NP 119
Cold Overton (parish), 21/268; SK810100; NP 122
Cold Weston (parish), 31/584; SO549833; NP 130
Coldbath House (extra-parochial), 22/509; SK986716; NP 113/1
Coldcoats (division in township of Little Mitton in Whalley), 20/243; SD757386; NP 95
Coldcoats (township in Ponteland), 27/522; NZ144742; NP 78
Coldcotes (division in township of Seacroft in Whitkirk), 43/479; SE356348; NP 96
Colden Magna, 41/372; NP 99
Colden Parva (parish), 41/374; NP 99
Colden Parva, 41/373; NP 99
Coldens Ambo (township in Mappleton and Colden Parva), 41/372-374; NP 99
Coldmeece (township in Eccleshall), 33/135; SJ853331; NP 119
Coldred (parish), 19/374; TR277472; NP 173
Coldrey (extra-parochial), 14/115; SU773436; NP 169
Coldridge (parish), 9/178; SS693065; NP 175

83

Coldsnouth and Thompson's Walls (township in Kirknewton), 27/57; NT861291; NP 70
Coldstead (hamlet in Stainton by Langworth), 22/260; TF099757; NP 104
Coldwaltham (parish), 36/82; TQ019166; NP 181, 182
Coldwell (township in Kirkwhelpington), 27/379; NZ002872; NP 77
Cole Park (division in Malmsbury Eastern Registration Subdistrict of Cole Park tything in St Paul Malmesbury), 39/28A; ST940852; NP 157
Cole Park (division in Malmsbury Western Registration Subdistrict of Cole Park tything in St Paul Malmesbury), 39/28B; ST927851; NP 156, 157
Cole Park (tything in St Paul Malmesbury), 39/28A-B; NP 156, 157
Colebatch (Colbatch) (township in Bishop's Castle), 31/379; SO300870; NP 129
Colebrooke (Colebrook) (parish), 9/210; SX760995; NP 175
Coleby (parish), 22/555; SK975605; NP 113
Coledale, 7/285; NP 82
Coleford (hamlet in Newland), 13/163C; SO575108; NP 142, 155
Coleham (division in Coleham township in St Julian Shrewsbury), 31/256; SJ503118; NP 118
Coleham (division in Coleham township in St Julian Shrewsbury), 31/257; Coleham (township in St Julian), 31/256-257; NP 118
Colemere (township in Ellesmere), 31/59; SJ428322; NP 118
Colemere (township in Ellesmere), 31/60; SJ429322; NP 118
Colemore (parish), 14/182; SU702306; NP 181
Coleorton (parish), 21/25; SK393171; NP 121
Colerne (parish), 39/118; ST821722; NP 156
Colesbourne (Colesborn) (parish), 13/211; SO999129; NP 143, 144
Coleshill (division in Coleshill), 2/38; SU245941; NP 157
Coleshill (hamlet in Amersham), 3/4; SU956947; NP 159
Coleshill (parish), 37/54; SP195885; NP 131
Coleshill (parish), 2/38, 39/4; NP 157
Coleshill (township in Holywell), 50/26-27; NP 109
Coleshill Fawr (division in Coleshill township in Holywell), 50/26; SJ227731; NP 108
Coleshill Fechan (division in Coleshill township in Holywell), 50/27; SJ229744; NP 108
Colethorp (hamlet in Standish), 13/262; SO821111; NP 143
Colkirk (parish), 25/157; TF930260; NP 125
College (Durham University) (extra-parochial), 11/119; NZ273420; NP 85
Collfryn (township in Llansantffraid), 54/2A; SJ215170; NP 117
Collier Row (division in Romford), 12/314A; TQ498902; NP 161
Collierley (Collierley and Pontop) (township in Lanchester), 11/155; NZ150539; NP 78, 84, 85
Collingbourne Ducis (parish), 39/194; SU245527; NP 167, 168
Collingbourne Kingston (parish), 39/195; SU240559; NP 167, 168
Collingham (parish), 43/92; SE395448; NP 96, 9
Collington (parish), 15/81; SO645602; NP 129
Collingtree (parish), 26/303; SP751551; NP 133, 146
Collow (hamlet in Legsby), 22/269; TF139838; NP 104
Collyweston (parish), 26/33; SK998025; NP 123
Colmworth (parish), 1/12; TL104590; NP 134
Coln Rogers (parish), 13/237; SP073090; NP 144, 157
Coln St Aldwyn (parish), 13/290; SP145075; NP 157
Coln St Dennis (parish), 13/236; SP082112; NP 144, 157
Colne (parish), 17/72; TL376768; NP 134, 135
Colne (township in Whalley), 20/266; SD915415; NP 95
Colne Engaine (parish), 12/126; TL851305; NP 149
Colney (parish), 25/491; TG178077; NP 126
Colsterdale (division in township of East Witton Without in East Witton), 42/163; SE134814; NP 91
Colsterworth (parish), 22/689-690; NP 122
Colsterworth with Woolsthorpe (township in Colsterworth), 22/689; SK927243; NP 122, 123
Colston Bassett (parish), 28/265; SK702328; NP 122

Colthorp, 2/153; NP 158, 168
Coltishall (parish), 25/250; TG279202; NP 126
Colton (division in township of Temple Newsham in Whitkirk), 43/482; SE369324; NP 96
Colton (parish), 25/621; TG106093; NP 125
Colton (parish), 33/192; SK055255; NP 120
Colton (township and parish), 20/50-56; NP 89
Colton (township in Bolton Percy), 43/64; SE545448; NP 97
Colton East (division in township of Colton in Colton), 20/53; SD329863; NP 89
Colton West (division in township of Colton in Colton), 20/54; SD305860; NP 88, 89
Colva (parish), 56/51; SO190450; NP 141
Colveston (Colvestone) (parish), 25/688; TL794957; NP 136
Colwall (parish), 15/277; SO750420; NP 143
Colwell and Great Swinburn (township in Chollerton), 27/441; NY955755; NP 77
Colwich (parish), 33/191A-B; NP 119, 120
Colwich (township in Colwich), 33/191A; SK015215; NP 119, 120
Colwick (parish), 28/231; SK610401; NP 121
Colwinston (Colwinstone) (parish), 51/111; SS944760; NP 154
Colworth (extra-parochial), 1/17; SP971603; NP 134
Colyton (parish), 9/290; SY234946; NP 176, 177
Comb, 39/256; NP 167
Combe (parish), 14/2; SU372606; NP 168
Combe (parish), 29/126; SP413159; NP 145
Combe (township in Presteigne), 15/38A; SO350632; NP 129
Combe Edge (township in Chapel en le Frith), 8/13A; SK050770; NP 111
Combe Florey (Coombeflorey) (parish), 32/295; ST152316; NP 164
Combe Hay (Combhay) (parish), 32/88; ST733603; NP 166
Combe Martin (Combmartin) (parish), 9/4; SS601471; NP 163
Combe Raleigh (Combrawleigh) (parish), 9/227; ST166023; NP 176
Combe St Nicholas (parish), 32/448; ST297120; NP 177
Combefields (parish), 37/142; SP411808; NP 132
Combeinteignhead (Combeintinhead) (parish), 9/412; SX890712; NP 188
Comberbach (Comberbatch) (township in Great Budworth), 5/122; SJ645775; NP 101
Comberton (parish), 4/109; TL389569; NP 135, 148
Combhay (parish), 32/88; NP 166
Combmartin, 9/4; NP 163
Combpyne (parish), 9/293; SY295926; NP 177
Combrawleigh, 9/227; NP 176
Combrook (chapelry in Kineton), 37/273; SP311515; NP 145
Combs (parish), 34/294; TM040560; NP 136, 149
Common to Barony and Evenwood and West Auckland (area in St Andrew Auckland), 11/199; NZ175281; NP 85
Common to Bradley, Helme Park and Thornley (area in Wolsingham), 11/184; NZ112378; NP 84
Common to Brandon and Byshottles and Brancepeth (area in Brancepeth), 11/135; NZ224363; NP 85
Common to Forest Quarter and Park Quarter (common in Stanhope), 11/173A; NY930409; NP 84
Commondale (township in Guisborough), 42/360; NZ658108; NP 86
Compton (Compton Parva) (parish), 2/119; SU522799; NP 158
Compton (parish), 14/231; SU463255; NP 168
Compton (parish), 35/142; SU959474; NP 169
Compton (parish), 36/235; SU774152; NP 181
Compton (tithing in Newent), 13/127B; SO730250; NP 143
Compton Abbas (parish), 10/10; ST873188; NP 178
Compton Abbas (parish), 10/143; NP 177
Compton Abdale (parish), 13/216; SP062163; NP 144
Compton Bassett (parish), 39/110; SU038726; NP 157
Compton Beauchamp (parish), 2/102; SU284857; NP 157, 158
Compton Bishop (parish), 32/161; ST410551; NP 165
Compton Chamberlayne (Compton Chamberlain) (parish), 39/327; SU029296; NP 167
Compton Dando (parish), 32/48; ST649640; NP 166

Compton Dundon (Compton Dunden) (parish), 32/207; ST487323; NP 165, 177
Compton Gifford (Compton Giffard, Effard) (tithing in Plymouth, Charles the Martyr), 9/454; SX492566; NP 187
Compton Greenfield (district in Compton Greenfield and Henbury), 13/381-382; NP 155
Compton Greenfield (parish), 13/382; ST569819; NP 155
Compton Greenfield (tithing in Henbury), 13/381; ST551835; NP 155
Compton Martin (parish), 32/73; ST547578; NP 165
Compton Parva (parish), 2/119; NP 158
Compton Pauncefoot (parish), 32/375; ST646257; NP 166
Compton Valence (Compton Vallence, East Compton) (parish), 10/226; SY589934; NP 177, 178
Compton Verney (parish), 37/259; SP325535; NP 145
Compton Wynyates (Compton Wyniates) (parish), 37/282; SP327423; NP 145
Conderton (hamlet in Overbury), 40/214; SO968374; NP 143
Condicote (parish), 13/81; SP145289; NP 144
Condover (parish), 31/286-287; NP 118
Condover (township in Condover), 31/286; SJ492059; NP 118
Coney Weston (parish), 34/99; TL959791; NP 136
Coneysthorpe (township in Barton-le-Street), 42/635; SE717719; NP 92
Coneythorpe (township in Goldsborough), 43/112; SE393591; NP 91, 96, 97
Congerstone (parish), 21/151; SK372050; NP 121
Congham (parish), 25/174; TF721238; NP 124, 125
Congleton (township in Astbury), 5/233; SJ862628; NP 110
Congresbury (parish), 32/68; ST434633; NP 165
Coningsby (division in Coningsby), 22/455A; TF233570; NP 114
Coningsby (parish), 22/455A-D; NP 114
Coningsby - Wildmore Fen (division in Coningsby), 22/455B; TF225546; NP 114
Coningsby - Wildmore Fen (division in Coningsby), 22/455C; TF263487; NP 114
Coningsby - Wildmore Fen (division in Coningsby), 22/455D; TF252516; NP 114
Conington (parish), 4/59; TL328662; NP 134
Conington (Connington) (parish), 17/30; TL182862; NP 134
Conisbrough (division in parish and township of Conisbrough), 43/884; SK514984; NP 103
Conisbrough (division of Conisbrough township in Wickersley), 43/848; SK478935; NP 103
Conisbrough (parish and township), 43/884-887; NP 103
Conisbrough (township in Wickersley and Conisbrough), 43/848, 884; NP 103
Conisbrough Common (common to divisions of Conisbrough and Clifton in parish and township of Conisbrough), 43/885; SK525979; NP 103
Conisbrough Parks (division in parish and township of Conisbrough), 43/887; SK507961; NP 103
Coniscliffe (parish), 11/313-317; NP 85
Conisholme (parish), 22/184; TF391943; NP 105
Coniston (township in Swine), 41/385; TA157353; NP 99
Coniston Cold (township in Gargrave), 43/230; SD895565; NP 95
Conistone (division in township of Conistone with Kilnsey in Burnsall), 43/216; SE005695; NP 90
Conistone with Kilnsey (township in Burnsall), 43/215-216; NP 90
Conock (tithing in Chirton), 39/207B; SU066566; NP 167
Cononley (township in Kildwick), 43/350; SD988472; NP 95, 96
Consall (township in Chadderton), 33/73; SJ982487; NP 110, 111
Conside and Knitsley (Conside with Knitsley, Conside-cum-Knitsley) (township in Lanchester), 11/159; NZ107491; NP 77, 84, 85
Constable (division in township of Lower Booths in Whalley), 20/285; SD809239; NP 95
Constable Burton (township in Finghall), 42/193; SE162908; NP 91
Constantine (parish), 6/174; SW734291; NP 190
Conway, 48/7

Conwil Cayo (parish), 47/3; NP 140
Conwil-Elvet (parish), 47/36; NP 139
Conwil-Gaio (Conwil Cayo) (parish), 47/3; SN670430; NP 140
Conwil-in-Elfet (parish), 47/36; NP 139
Conwill in Elvet (parish), 47/36; NP 139
Conwy (Conway) (parish), 48/7; SH770782; NP 107
Conwyl Elved (parish), 47/36; NP 139
Cookbury (parish), 9/103; SS385050; NP 174, 175
Cookham (division in Cookham), 2/209; SU885835; NP 159
Cookham, 2/209; SU885835; NP 159
Cookley (parish), 34/151; TM358752; NP 137
Cooknoe (parish), 26/288; NP 133
Cookridge (division in township of Adel cum Eccup in Adel), 43/397; SE253404; NP 96
Coole Pilate (township in Acton), 5/283; SJ653466; NP 110
Cooling (Cowling) (parish), 19/40; TQ759763; NP 171, 172
Coombe (Comb) (tithing in Enford), 39/256; SU168516; NP 167
Coombe Bissett (parish), 39/354; SU107250; NP 167
Coombe Keynes (parish), 10/281; SY851843; NP 178
Coombeflorey (parish), 32/295; NP 164
Coombes (Coombs) (parish), 36/212; TQ186070; NP 182
Copdock (parish), 34/389; TM114411; NP 150
Copeland Forest (extra-parochial), 7/308; NY105095; NP 82
Copford (parish), 12/140; TL928233; NP 149
Copgrove (parish), 43/148; SE350632; NP 91
Cople (parish), 1/56; TL107480; NP 147
Copmanthorpe (township in St Mary Bishophill (Junior)), 43/44; SE568462; NP 97
Coppenhall (parish), 5/244-245; NP 110
Coppenhall (township in Penkridge), 33/233; SJ908197; NP 119
Copping Sykes (extra-parochial), 22/745; TF228253; NP 114
Coppingford (parish), 17/41; TL163801; NP 134
Coppull (Coppul) (township in Standish), 20/378; SD564139; NP 100
Copston Magna (Great Copston) (hamlet in Monks Kirby), 37/110; SP460880; NP 132
Copt Hewick (township in Ripon), 43/193; SE345718; NP 91
Corbridge (parish), 27/468-477; NP 77
Corbridge (township in Corbridge), 27/473; NY992620; NP 77
Corby (Corby Glen) (township in Irnham), 22/683; SK997254; NP 123
Corby (parish), 26/91; SP892892; NP 133
Corby Glen (parish), 22/683; NP 123
Coreley (parish), 31/533; SO611746; NP 129, 130
Corfe (parish), 32/421; ST236188; NP 177
Corfe Castle (parish), 10/293; SY970820; NP 179
Corfe Mullen (parish), 10/191; SY979967; NP 179
Corfton (township in Diddlebury), 31/504A; SO495850; NP 129
Corhampton (parish), 14/235; SU588205; NP 168, 180
Corley (parish), 37/98; SP300854; NP 131, 132
Cornborough (division in township of Sheriff Hutton with Cornborough in Sheriff Hutton), 42/598; SE629668; NP 92
Cornbury Park (extra-parochial), 29/149; SP351181; NP 145
Cornelly (parish), 6/152; SW908445; NP 190
Corney (parish), 7/315; SD122918; NP 88
Cornforth (township in Bishop Middleham), 11/226; NZ313352; NP 85
Cornhill (chapelry in Norham), 27/17A-C; NP 64
Cornhill on Tweed (Cornhill) (division of Cornhill chapelry in Norham), 27/17C; NT862395; NP 64
Cornsay (township in Lanchester), 11/147; NZ141422; NP 84, 85
Cornwell (parish), 29/48; SP271273; NP 144, 145
Cornwood (parish), 9/366; SX609599; NP 187
Cornworthy (parish), 9/441; SX826546; NP 188
Corpusty (parish), 25/148; TG101295; NP 125
Corra, 31/19A; NP 118, 119
Corridge (township in Hartburn), 27/353; NZ065835; NP 77
Corringham (parish), 12/403; TQ712834; NP 161, 162
Corringham (parish), 22/140-146; NP 104
Corscombe (parish), 10/114; ST522046; NP 177
Corse (parish), 13/123; SO799285; NP 143
Corsenside (parish), 27/213-215; NP 77
Corsenside (township in Corsenside), 27/213; NY885895; NP 77
Corsham (parish), 39/115; ST873702; NP 156

85

Corsley (parish), 39/234; ST828463; NP 166
Corston (division in Malmsbury Eastern Registration Subdistrict of Corston tything in St Paul Malmesbury), 39/31A; ST921826; NP 156, 157
Corston (division in Malmsbury Western Registration Subdistrict of Corston tything in St Paul Malmesbury), 39/31B; ST918835; NP 156
Corston (parish), 32/46; ST685652; NP 156, 166
Corston (tything in St Paul Malmesbury), 39/31A-B; NP 156, 157
Corton (parish), 34/15; TM535980; NP 137
Corton (tithing in Boyton), 39/272; ST926386; NP 166, 167
Corton Denham (parish), 32/387; ST634223; NP 166, 178
Corwen (parish), 52/18; SJ090430; NP 108, 117
Coryton (parish), 9/340; SX463841; NP 175
Cosby (parish), 21/245; SP545944; NP 132
Cosford (township in Newbold on Avon), 37/123; SP498787; NP 132
Cosgrove (parish), 26/336; SP792428; NP 146
Cosheston (parish), 55/146; SN009038; NP 151
Cossall (parish), 28/245; SK485424; NP 121
Cossey (parish), 25/493; NP 126
Cossington (parish), 21/59; SK612136; NP 121
Cossington (parish), 32/218; ST366409; NP 165
Costessy (Cossey) (parish), 25/493; TG171115; NP 126
Costock (division in Costock), 28/287; SK576262; NP 121
Costock (parish), 28/287-289; NP 121
Coston (parish), 21/104A; SK852218; NP 122
Coston (parish), 25/553; TG063062; NP 125
Coston and Garthorpe (common to Coston and Garthorpe), 21/104B; SK825227; NP 122
Coston Hackett (parish), 40/49; NP 130, 131
Cotcliffe (township in Leake), 42/510B; SE419911; NP 91
Cote and Aston (hamlet in Bampton), 29/170; SP355025; NP 158
Cotehill, 7/44; NP 76, 83
Cotes (parish), 21/41; SK553213; NP 121
Cotes (township in Eccleshall), 33/137; SJ834351; NP 119
Cotesbach (Cottesbach) (parish), 21/346; SP537820; NP 132
Cotgrave (parish), 28/263; SK650350; NP 121
Cotham (extra-parochial), 22/70; TA153111; NP 104
Cotham (parish), 28/200; SK797470; NP 112, 113
Cothelstone (parish), 32/297; ST186317; NP 164, 165
Cothercott (township in Church Pulverbatch), 31/336A; SJ418028; NP 118, 129
Cotheridge (parish), 40/109; SO794550; NP 130, 143
Cotherstone (Cotherston) (division in township of Cotherstone in Romaldkirk), 42/8; NZ010185; NP 84
Cotherstone (township in Romaldkirk), 42/7-8; NP 84
Cotleigh (parish), 9/229; ST211032; NP 176, 177
Cotness (township in Howden), 41/10; SE803247; NP 98
Coton (Coaton) (hamlet in Ravensthorpe), 26/174; SP664719; NP 132
Coton (division in St Julian and St Mary Shrewsbury), 31/254A; SJ482141; NP 118
Coton (parish), 4/107; TL411587; NP 135
Coton in the Elms (township in Lullington), 8/326; SK245150; NP 120
Coton in the Clay (Coton) (township in Hanbury), 33/205; SK169290; NP 120
Coton, 33/205; NP 120
Cottam (chapelry in South Leverton), 28/45; SK822804; NP 104
Cottam (division in township of Lea, Ashton, Ingol and Cottam in Preston), 20/213; SD506315; NP 94
Cottam (township in Langtoft), 41/238; SE988634; NP 93, 98, 99
Cottenham (parish), 4/53; TL459687; NP 135
Cottered (parish), 16/26; TL321292; NP 147
Cotterstock (parish), 26/59; TL041912; NP 134
Cottesbach (parish), 21/346; NP 132
Cottesbrooke (Cottesbrook) (parish), 26/169; SP711745; NP 133
Cottesford (parish), 29/70; NP 145
Cottesmore (parish), 30/4-5; NP 122
Cottesmore (township in Cottesmore), 30/4; SK904140; NP 122
Cottingham (township in Cottingham), 26/92; SP856901; NP 133
Cottingham (parish), 41/305; TA044332; NP 98, 99

Cottingwood Common (area in Morpeth), 27/415; NZ200870; NP 78
Cottisford (Cottesford) (parish), 29/70; SP585315; NP 145
Cottles (extra-parochial), 39/122; ST846656; NP 156
Cotton (parish), 34/185; TM070668; NP 136
Cotton (township in Sandbach), 5/214; SJ746673; NP 110
Cotton (township in Ruyton of the Eleven Towns), 31/135; SJ379217; NP 118
Cotton (Upper and Lower Cotton) (township in Alton), 33/109; SK066476; NP 111, 120
Cotton Abbotts (Cotton Abbott) (township in Christleton), 5/379; SJ467649; NP 109
Cotton Edmunds (township in Christleton), 5/380; SJ471658; NP 109
Coughton (parish), 37/187; SP083603; NP 131
Coulsdon (parish), 35/47; TQ312586; NP 170
Coulston (parish), 39/229; NP 167
Coulton (township in Hovingham), 42/627; SE633740; NP 92
Cound (parish), 31/443-447; NP 118, 119
Coundon (hamlet in Coventry, Holy Trinity), 37/149; SP313813; NP 132
Coundon (township in St Andrew Auckland), 11/212; NZ240298; NP 85
Coundon Grange (township in St Andrew Auckland), 11/213; NZ230287; NP 85
Countesthorpe (township in Blaby), 21/248; SP585955; NP 132
Counthorpe (hamlet in Castle Bytham), 22/697B; SK993208; NP 123
Countisbury (parish), 9/9; SS761491; NP 163
Coupland (township in Kirknewton), 27/65; NT940310; NP 64, 70
Courage, 2/131; NP 158
Court (hamlet in Llanwenog), 46/83; SN496486; NP 140
Courteenhall (parish), 26/302; SP761537; NP 146
Cove (tithing in Yateley), 14/29; SU858548; NP 169
Covehithe (Northales, North Hales) (parish), 34/59; TM519811; NP 137
Coveney (hamlet in Coveney), 4/21; TL485828; NP 135
Coveney (parish), 4/21-22; NP 135
Covenham St Bartholomew (parish), 22/787; TF340952; NP 105
Covenham St Mary (parish), 22/788; TF349943; NP 105
Coventry, Holy Trinity (hamlet in Coventry, Holy Trinity), 37/147A; SP341798; NP 132
Coventry, Holy Trinity (parish), 37/147A-149, 154; NP 132
Coventry, St John the Baptist (division in Coventry, St Michael), 37/150; SP320790; NP 132
Coventry, St Michael (division in Coventry, St Michael), 37/152; SP348773; NP 132
Coventry, St Michael (parish), 37/150-152; NP 132
Coverham (division in township of Agglethorpe with Coverham in Coverham), 42/156; SE101866; NP 90, 91
Coverham (parish), 42/154-158; NP 90, 91
Coverham [unnamed division] (unnamed division in Coverham]), 42/155B; SE104858; NP 90
Covington (parish), 17/50; TL059714; NP 134
Cow Honeybourne (parish), 13/24; SP109437; NP 144
Cowbit (division in Cowbit), 22/730A; TF265170; NP 123
Cowbit (division in Pinchbeck North Fen in Cowbit), 22/730B; TF180270; NP 123
Cowbit (parish), 22/730A-B; NP 123
Cowbridge [Y Bont-faen] (parish), 51/123; SS994747; NP 154
Cowden (parish), 19/199; TQ465415; NP 171
Cowesby (parish), 42/521; SE460900; NP 91
Cowfold (parish), 36/95; TQ216228; NP 182
Cowlam (parish), 41/237; SE968657; NP 98
Cowley (hamlet in Brampford Speke), 9/250B; SX896957; NP 176
Cowley (parish), 13/209; SO946145; NP 143
Cowley (parish), 24/112; TQ055820; NP 160
Cowley (parish), 39/223; SP542043; NP 158
Cowley (township in Gnosall), 33/168; SJ807182; NP 119
Cowling (division in township of Cowling in Kildwick), 43/352; SE958443; NP 95
Cowling (parish), 19/40; NP 171, 172

Cowling (township in Kildwick), 43/352-354; NP 95
Cowlinge (parish), 34/323; TL715545; NP 135, 148
Cowney (township in Llangadfan), 54/26; SH986174; NP 117
Cowpe (Cowpe Lenches) (division in township of Cowpe Lench, New Hall Hey and Hall Carr in Bury), 20/408; SD838202; NP 95, 101
Cowpe Lench, New Hall Hey and Hall Carr (township in Bury), 20/408-410; NP 95
Cowpen (township in Horton parochial chapelry in Woodhorn), 27/478; NZ298814; NP 78
Cowpen Bewley (township in Billingham), 11/259; NZ499244; NP 85
Cowthorpe (parish), 43/105; SE438518; NP 97
Coxhoe (township in Kelloe), 11/102; NZ331362; NP 85
Coxlodge (township in Gosforth), 27/511; NZ237682; NP 78
Coxwold (parish), 42/548-559; NP 91, 92
Coxwold (township in Coxwold), 42/551; SE530771; NP 92
Coychurch (parish), 51/85-88; NP 154
Coychurch Higher (Coychurch, Higher Hamlet) (hamlet in Coychurch), 51/86; SS960850; NP 154
Coychurch Lower (Coychurch, Lower Hamlet, Lower Coychurch) (hamlet in Coychurch), 51/88; SS940798; NP 154
Coyty Higher, 51/90; NP 154
Coyty Lower, 51/89; NP 154
Crackenthorpe (township in St Michael Appleby or Bongate), 38/38; NY656229; NP 83
Crackpot (division in township of Grinton in Grinton), 42/111; SD965965; NP 90
Cracoe (township in Burnsall), 43/211; SD988602; NP 90, 95, 96
Cradley (parish), 15/158A-F; NP 143
Cradley (township in Halesowen), 40/18; SO941847; NP 130
Cradley - division no.1 (division in Cradley), 15/158A; SO713490; NP 143
Cradley - division no.2 (division in Cradley), 15/158B; SO707468; NP 143
Cradley - division no.3 (division in Cradley), 15/158C; SO729469; NP 143
Cradley - division no.4 (division in Cradley), 15/158D; SO753478; NP 143
Cradley - division no.5 (division in Cradley), 15/158E; SO749495; NP 143
Cradley - division no.6 (division in Cradley), 15/158F; SO733491; NP 143
Crai (Cray) (division outside Fforest-fawr in Devynock), 45/64A; SN900250; NP 140, 141
Craike, (parish), 42/1; SE 564710; NP 92
Crakehall (township in Bedale), 42/209; SE248897; NP 91
Crakehill (division in township of Eldmire with Crakehill in Topcliffe), 42/241; SE433741; NP 91
Crambe (parish), 42/654-655; NP 92
Crambe (township in Crambe), 42/655; SE731639; NP 92
Cramlington (chapelry in St Andrews), 27/640; NZ263767; NP 78
Cranage (township in Sandbach), 5/209; SJ749690; NP 110
Cranborne (Cranborne and Holwell) (tithing in Cranborne), 10/68A; SU062131; NP 179
Cranborne (parish), 10/68A-72; NP 179
Cranbrook (parish), 19/407; TQ777367; NP 171, 172, 183, 184
Cranfield (parish), 1/74; SP952423; NP 146, 147
Cranford (parish), 24/107; TQ102777; NP 160
Cranford St Andrew (parish), 26/156; SP928781; NP 133
Cranford St John (parish), 26/155; SP928762; NP 134
Cranham (parish), 12/417; TQ575868; NP 161
Cranham (parish), 13/257; SO898125; NP 143
Cranleigh (Cranley) (parish), 35/163; TQ064384; NP 169, 170, 182
Cranoe (parish), 21/296; SP760951; NP 133
Cransford (parish), 34/256; TM322648; NP 137
Crantock (parish), 6/131; SW805597; NP 185
Cranwell (parish), 22/579; TF024498; NP 113
Cranwich (Cranwick) (parish), 25/701; TL777945; NP 136
Cranworth (parish), 25/543; TF982047; NP 125
Craster (township in Embleton), 27/154; NU252190; NP 71

Craswall (Upper and Lower Crasswell) (chapelry in Clodock), 15/208; SO282359; NP 141, 142
Cratfield (parish), 34/146; TM307753; NP 137
Crathorne (parish), 42/288; NZ450080; NP 85
Crawcrook (township in Ryton), 11/31; NZ133639; NP 77, 78
Crawley (division in Crawley), 14/158; SU429348; NP 168
Crawley (hamlet in Witney), 29/178; SP340130; NP 145
Crawley (parish), 14/158-159; NP 168
Crawley (parish), 36/39; TQ273374; NP 170, 182
Crawley (township in Eglingham), 27/138; NU072168; NP 71
Crawshaw Booth (division in township of Higher Booths in Whalley), 20/287; SD818247; NP 95
Cray - Fforest-fawr (division within Fforest-fawr in Devynock), 45/64B; SN890200; NP 140, 141
Cray, 45/64A; NP 140, 141
Crayford (parish), 19/16; TQ520759; NP 171
Crayke (Craike) (parish), 42/1; SE 564710; NP 92
Creacombe (parish), 9/81; SS824193; NP 164
Credenhill (parish), 15/121; SO451438; NP 142
Crediton (parish), 9/211A-H; NP 175
Crediton Borough (tithing in Crediton), 9/211A; (not located); NP 175
Crediton Town (tithing in Crediton), 9/211B; SS837002; NP 176
Creech (tithing in Church Knowle), 10/291; SY924834; NP 178, 179
Creech St Michael (parish), 32/310; ST278267; NP 165, 177
Creed (district in Creed), 6/143; SW951485; NP 190
Creed (parish), 6/142-143; NP 190
Creeksea (Crixeth, Crixea) (parish), 12/359; TQ930971; NP 162
Creeting All Saints (parish), 34/289B; NP 149, 150
Creeting St Mary (parish), 34/289A; TM100657; NP 136, 149, 150
Creeting St Olave (parish), 34/289C; NP 149, 150
Creeting St Peter (Creeting St Peters, West Creeting) (parish), 34/290; TM092568; NP 136, 149
Cregrina (parish), 56/47; SO115521; NP 141
Creighton with Stramshall (township in Uttoxter), 33/119; SK080360; NP 120
Creslow (parish), 3/124; SP816217; NP 146
Cressage (township in Cound), 31/447; SJ588038; NP 118, 119
Cressing (parish), 12/189; TL789205; NP 149
Cresswell (township in Woodhorn), 27/328; NZ293931; NP 78
Creswell (extra-parochial), 33/176; SJ961361; NP 119
Cretingham (parish), 34/283; TM223603; NP 137
Crewe (township in Barthomley), 5/243; SJ737546; NP 110
Crewe (township in Farndon), 5/349; SJ424527; NP 109
Crewkerene (division in Crewkerene), 32/483B; ST428094; NP 177
Crewkerene (parish), 32/483A-C; NP 177
Criccieth (Crickieth) (parish), 48/78; SH506390; NP 115, 116
Criccin (township in Rhuddlan), 50/64; SJ034722; NP 108
Crich (parish), 8/144-146; NP 111
Crich (township in Crich), 8/144; SK347547; NP 111
Crick (hamlet in Caerwent), 53/101B; ST488898; NP 155
Crick (parish), 26/178; SP592725; NP 132
Crickadarn (parish), 45/8-9; NP 141
Crickadarn (township in Crickadarn), 45/8; SO074400; NP 141
Cricket Malberbie (parish), 32/452; ST360116; NP 177
Cricket St Thomas (parish), 32/488; ST373088; NP 177
Cricket, 31/64; NP 118
Crickett (Cricket) (township in Ellesmere), 31/64; SJ361346; NP 118
Crickheath (township in Oswestry), 31/114; SJ288230; NP 118
Crickhowell (parish), 45/81; SO211208; NP 141
Crickieth (parish), 48/78; NP 115, 116
Cricklade St Mary (parish), 39/12B; SU101938; NP 157
Cricklade St Sampson (parish), 39/12A; SU084922; NP 157
Cridling Park (division in township of Cridling Stubbs in Womersley), 43/634; SE519221; NP 97
Cridling Stubbs (township in Womersley), 43/634-635
Criggion (township in Alberbury), 54/87; SJ296147; NP 117, 118
Crigglestone (township in Sandal Magna), 43/693; SE319161; NP 102

87

Crimplesham (parish), 25/516; TF648040; NP 124
Cringleford (parish), 25/490; TG191058; NP 126
Cringles (division in township of Silsden in Kildwick), 43/345; SE050480; NP 96
Crinow (parish), 55/117; SN128143; NP 152
Cripton (hamlet in Winterborne Came), 10/249; SY703866; NP 178
Crixeth, Crixea (parish), 12/359; NP 162
Croes and Berwyn (township in Caron), 46/38E; SN720690; NP 140
Croes-llwybr (Croeslwbyr) (township in Llanidloes), 54/137; SN964966; NP 128
Croeslwbyr, 54/137; NP 128
Croft (Croft and Bamburgh Field) (parish), 22/494; TF530610; NP 114
Croft (division in township of Barton upon Irwell in Eccles), 20/547; SJ771961; NP 101
Croft (division in township of Southworth with Croft in Winwick), 20/601; SJ633937; NP 101
Croft (division in township of Croft in Croft), 42/56; NZ282088; NP 85
Croft (parish), 15/29-30; NP 129
Croft (parish), 21/214; SP514958; NP 132
Croft (parish), 42/54-57; NP 85
Croft (township in Croft), 15/29; SO450655; NP 129
Croft (township in Croft), 42/55-56; NP 85
Crofton (parish), 43/678; SE375183; NP 102
Crofton (township in Thursby), 7/138; NY303507; NP 75, 82
Crogen Iddon (township in Llangollen), 49/116; SJ236389; NP 117
Croglin, (parish), 7/173; NY595495; NP 83
Cromer (parish), 25/39; TG214416; NP 126
Cromford (township in Wirksworth), 8/148; SK296560; NP 111
Cromhall (parish), 13/354; ST697906; NP 156
Crompton (township in Oldham), 20/481; SD941096; NP 101
Cromwell (parish), 28/131; SK797615; NP 112, 113
Crondall (parish), 14/32A-34B; NP 169
Crondall and Swanthorpe (Crondall and Swanthrope) (tithing in Crondall), 14/32A; SU800490; NP 169
Crondon (Orsett Hamlet) (division in Orsett), 12/407; TL696010; NP 161
Cronkhill (township in Atcham), 31/240; SJ538082; NP 118
Cronton (township in Prescot), 20/626; SJ495885; NP 100
Crook (division in township of Great Mitton in Mitton), 43/289; SD710410; NP 95
Crook (township in Kendal), 38/103; SD449947; NP 89
Crook and Billy Row (township in Brancepeth), 11/145; NZ156375; NP 85
Crookdean (township in Kirkwhelpington), 27/375; NY978830; NP 77
Crookes (intermixed parts belonging to townships of Ecclesall Bierlow, Sheffield and Upper Hallam, in Sheffield), 43/822; SK325873; NP 102
Crookham (tithing in Crondall), 14/34A; SU803530; NP 169
Crookham (township in Ford), 27/37; NT903388; NP 64
Crookham, 2/153; NP 158, 168
Crookhouse (township in Kirknewton), 27/61; NT808318; NP 64
Croome D'Abitot (parish), 40/174; SO885448; NP 143
Cropredy (division in Cropredy), 29/11; SP458470; NP 145
Cropredy (parish), 29/9-13, 37/267; NP 145
Cropston (township in Thurcaston), 21/130; SK558107; NP 121
Cropthorne (hamlet in Cropthorne), 40/210; SP002442; NP 143
Cropthorne (parish), 40/209-211; NP 143, 144
Cropton (township in Middleton), 42/439; SE760900; NP 92
Cropwell Bishop (Great Cropwell) (parish), 28/264; SK677351; NP 121, 122
Cropwell Butler (township in Tythby), 28/222; SK679372; NP 121, 122
Crosby (division of Crosby township in Flixborough), 22/24A; SE888135; NP 104
Crosby (township in Crosscanonby), 7/226; NY073385; NP 82
Crosby (township in Flixborough and Frodingham), 22/24A-B; NP 104

Crosby (township in Frodingham), 22/24B; SE888123; NP 104
Crosby (township in Leake), 42/518; SE409907; NP 91
Crosby Cote (division in township of Thornton le Beans in North Otterington), 42/260; SE414916; NP 91
Crosby Garrett (parish), 38/52-53; NP 83, 84
Crosby Garrett (township in Crosby Garrett), 38/53; NY718084; NP 83, 84
Crosby Ravensworth (parish), 38/30-35; NP 83
Crosby Ravensworth (township in Crosby Ravensworth), 38/32; NY623146; NP 83
Crosby Ravensworth Fell ('Undivided moor' in Crosby Ravensworth), 38/31; NY605105; NP 83
Crosby upon Eden (parish), 7/23-26; MP 76
Croscombe (parish), 32/138; ST602453; NP 165, 166
Crosemere (Cockshutt) (township in Ellesmere), 31/54; SJ437295; NP 118
Crosland Half (division in township of Lockwood in Huddersfield), 43/766; SE125145; NP 102
Crosper (division in township of Spofforth with Stockeld in Spofforth), 43/99; SE365524; NP 96
Cross Canonby (township in Crosscanonby), 7/225; NY066393; NP 82
Crosscanonby (parish), 7/225-227; NP 82
Crossgate (division in township of Crossgate in St Oswald), 11/128; NZ271424; NP 85
Crossgate (division in township of Crossgate in St Oswald), 11/129; NZ263422; NP 85
Crossgate (township in St Oswald), 11/128-129; NP 85
Crosswayland Lodge (extra-parochial), 26/56; SP996921; NP 134
Crosthwaite (parish), 7/280-287; NP 82
Crosthwaite and Lyth (township in Heversham), 38/84; SD450900; NP 89
Croston (parish), 20/344-348; NP 94, 100
Croston (township in Croston), 20/346; SD484178; NP 100
Crostwick (parish), 25/218; NP 126
Crostwick (parish), 25/361; TG261157; NP 126
Crostwight (Crostwick) (parish), 25/218; TG336288; NP 126
Croughton (township in St Oswald Chester), 5/497; SJ415725; NP 109
Croughton (parish), 26/363; SP550333; NP 145
Crow Meole (township in St Chad Shrewsbury), 31/264; SJ468122; NP 118
Crowan (parish), 6/171; SW638343; NP 190
Crowcombe (parish), 32/257; ST138364; NP 164
Crowell (parish), 29/267; SU756987; NP 158
Crowfield (chapelry in Coddenham), 34/287; TM144575; NP 136, 137, 150
Crowhurst (parish), 35/105; TQ396471; NP 170
Crowhurst (parish), 36/171; TQ765121; NP 183, 184
Crowland (Croyland) (parish), 22/729; TF250110; NP 123
Crowle (division in township of Crowle in Crowle), 43/951; SE760140; NP 103, 104
Crowle (parish), 40/149; SO925565; NP 130, 143
Crowle (parish), 22/11-12, 43/951
Crowle (township in Crowle), 22/11; SE782127; NP 103, 104
Crowle (township in Crowle), 22/11, 43/951
Crowley (township in Great Budworth), 5/113; SJ664815; NP 101
Crowmarsh Gifford (parish), 29/303; SU628892; NP 158
Crown Farm (extra-parochial), 14/153; SU317305; NP 168
Crownthorpe (parish), 25/654; TG088030; NP 125, 136
Crowton (township in Weaverham), 5/165; SJ582742; NP 100, 109
Croxall (parish), 8/324-325, 33/221; NP 120
Croxall (township in Croxall), 8/325; SK207134; NP 120
Croxby (parish), 22/167; TF185986; NP 105
Croxdale (division in township of Sunderland Bridge in St Oswald), 11/126; NZ280380; NP 85
Croxden (parish), 33/112A-B; NP 120
Croxden with Great Yate (township in Croxden), 33/112A; SK065395; NP 120
Croxteth Park (extra-parochial), 20/642; SJ418949; NP 100

Croxton (parish), 4/65; TL252588; NP 134
Croxton (parish), 22/54; TA088128; NP 104
Croxton (parish), 25/714; TL875875; NP 136
Croxton (township in Middlewich), 5/196; SJ696678; NP 110
Croxton (township in Eccleshall), 33/144; SJ768315; NP 119
Croxton Kerrial (parish), 21/94; SK839288; NP 122
Croydon (Croydon cum Clapton) (parish), 4/121; TL307495; NP 147
Croydon (division in Croydon), 35/44A; TQ333664; NP 170
Croydon (parish), 35/44A-B; NP 170, 171
Croydon Crook, 35/44B; NP 170, 171
Croyland (parish), 22/729; NP 123
Crudgington (township in High Ercall), 31/208; SJ640180; NP 119
Crudwell (division in Malmsbury Eastern Registration Subdistrict in Crudwell), 39/19B; ST970932; NP 157
Crudwell (division in Malmsbury Western Registration Subdistrict in Crudwell), 39/19A; ST945932; NP 157
Crudwell (parish), 39/19A-B; NP 157
Crumpsall (township in Manchester), 20/509; SD843023; NP 101
Crundale (parish), 19/333; TR083488; NP 172
Crunwear (parish), 55/123; SN178103; NP 152
Crutch (extra-parochial), 40/56; SO902664; NP 130
Cruwys Morchard (parish), 9/158; SS875117; NP 164, 176
Crux Easton (parish), 14/65; SU426564; NP 168
Crychynen (township in St Asaph [Llanelwy]), 50/74; SJ049758; NP 108
Cubberley (parish), 13/208; NP 143
Cubbington (parish), 37/226; SP343681; NP 132
Cubert (parish), 6/132; SW785586; NP 185
Cubley (parish), 8/230; SK162382; NP 120
Cublington (parish), 3/125; SP841222; NP 146
Cuby (parish), 6/148; SW940451; NP 190
Cuckfield (parish), 36/97; TQ297255; NP 182
Cucklington (parish), 32/361; ST756273; NP 166
Cuckney (parish), 28/84-87; NP 112
Cuddesdon (Cuddesden) (hamlet in Cuddesdon), 29/250; SP602032; NP 158
Cuddesdon (parish), 29/248-251; NP 158
Cuddington (parish), 3/164; SP743111; NP 146, 159
Cuddington (township in Malpas), 5/325; SJ454465; NP 109
Cuddington (township in Weaverham), 5/168; SJ594722; NP 109, 110
Cuddington (parish), 35/54; TQ231633; NP 170
Cudham (parish), 19/68; TQ430588; NP 171
Cudworth (parish), 32/486; ST373107; NP 177
Cudworth (township in Royston), 43/684; SE390087; NP 102
Cuerdale (township in Blackburn), 20/324; SD595285; NP 95
Cuerden (township in Leyland), 20/333; SD560246; NP 94
Cuerdley (township in Prescot), 20/623; SJ544863; NP 100
Cugley (tithing in Newent), 13/127C; SO720230; NP 143
Culbone (Kitner, Kitnor) (parish), 32/244; SS825481; NP 164
Culcheth (division in township of Culcheth in Winwick), 20/597; SJ660960; NP 101
Culcheth (township in Winwick), 20/597-600; NP 101
Culford (parish), 34/116; TL836711; NP 136
Culgaith (township in Kirkland), 7/187; NY613299; NP 83
Culham (division in Culham), 29/243A; SU514958; NP 158
Culham (parish), 29/243A-B; NP 158
Cullercoats (township in Tynemouth), 27/494; NZ363715; NP 78
Cullompton (district in Cullompton), 9/152A; ST022061; NP 176
Cullompton (parish), 9/152A-C; NP 176
Culmington (parish), 31/517; SO480824; NP 129
Culmstock (parish), 9/139; ST100154; NP 164
Culpho (parish), 34/428; TM210493; NP 150
Culverlands and Tilford (tithing in Farnham), 35/147; SU874431; NP 169
Culverthorpe (chapelry in Haydor), 22/642; TF022402; NP 123
Culworth (parish), 26/329; SP536474; NP 145
Cumberwell (tithing in Great Bradford), 39/153B; ST822632; NP 166
Cumberworth (parish), 22/412; TF507731; NP 114

Cumberworth (division of Cumberworth township in Silkstone), 43/702; SE205085; NP 102/1
Cumberworth (division of Cumberworth township in High Hoyland), 43/703A; SE232106; NP 102/1
Cumberworth (township in High Hoyland and Silkstone) (parish), 43/702-703B; NP 102/1
Cumberworth and Cumberworth Half (intermixed division in townships of Cumberworth and Cumberworth Half in High Hoyland and Emley), 43/704B; SE247102; NP 102/1
Cumberworth Half (township in Emley and Kirkburton), 43/703B, 704A, 705; NP 102/1
Cumberworth Half (township in Emley), 43/704A; SE233112; NP 102/1
Cumberworth Half (township in Kirkburton), 43/705; SE225095; NP 102/1
Cumberworth Half and Cumberworth (intermixed division in townships of Cumberworth and Cumberworth Half in Emley and High Hoyland), 43/703B; SE246106; NP 102/1
Cumdivock (township in Dalston), 7/142; NY353498; NP 76, 82, 83
Cummersdale (township in St Mary [Carlisle]), 7/98A; NY379539; NP 76
Cumnor (parish), 2/3A-K; NP 158
Cumnor (township in Cumnor), 2/3E; SP462042; NP 158
Cumrew (parish), 7/64-65; NP 76, 83
Cumrew Inside (township in Cumrew), 7/65; NY561507; NP 76, 83
Cumrew Outside (township in Cumrew), 7/64; NY562526; NP 76
Cumwhinton and Coathill (Cotehill) (township in Wetheral), 7/44; NY459513; NP 76, 83
Cumwhitton (parish), 7/66-67; NP 76, 83
Cumwhitton (township in Cumwhitton), 7/66; NY506518; NP 76, 83
Cundall (parish), 42/571-573; NP 91
Cundall with Leckby (township in Cundall), 42/572; SE419728; NP 91
Cunscough (township in Halsall), 20/362; SD404028; NP 100
Curbar (township in Bakewell), 8/85; SK260750; NP 111
Curborough and Elmhurst (township in St Chad), 33/255; SK112122; NP 120
Curbridge (hamlet in Witney), 29/177; SP337090; NP 145, 158
Curdworth (parish), 37/29-31; NP 131
Curdworth (township in Curdworth), 37/29; SP180927; NP 131
Curland (parish), 32/431; ST274169; NP 177
Curridge (Courage) (tithing in Chieveley), 2/131; SU492722; NP 158
Curry Mallet (Curry Mallett) (parish), 32/414; ST329220; NP 177
Curry Rivel (Curry Rivell) (division in Curry Rivel), 32/333A; ST391241; NP 177
Curry Rivel (Curry Rivell) (parish); 32/333A, 407; NP 177
Cury (parish), 6/193; SW691213; NP 189, 190
Cusop (parish), 15/204; SO247414; NP 141
Cutcombe (parish), 32/248; SS913396; NP 164
Cutsdean (Cutsden) (chapelry in Bredon), 40/242; SP106308; NP 144
Cutsden, 40/242; NP 144
Cutslow, 29/203; NP 145, 158
Cutteslowe (Cutslow) (division in Woolvercot), 29/203; SP510110; NP 145, 158
Cuttridge (Cuttridge Farm) (district in Kenton), 9/390; SX872923; NP 176
Cuxham, 29/283; SU667953; NP 158
Cuxton (Cuxtone) (parish), 19/51; TQ704672; NP 171
Cuxwold (parish), 22/94; TA175009; NP 105
Cwm (parish), 50/66-67; NP 108
Cwm (township in Meifod), 54/39; SJ192148; NP 117
Cwm Du (hamlet in Llangynwyd), 51/59; SS857912; NP 153, 154
Cwmcarvan (Cwmcarvon) (parish), 53/55; SO474078; NP 155
Cwmrheidol (township in Llanbadarn fawr), 46/19; SN740800; NP 127
Cwmvoy (parish), 53/1-3, 15/210; NP 141, 142
Cydplwyf (township in Llanina), 46/64; SN401580; NP 139

Cyffic (Kiffig) (parish), 47/54; SN198141; NP 152
Cyffin (township in Llangadfan), 54/28; SJ022142; NP 117
Cyffylliog (Gwyffylliog, Gyffylliog) (parish), 49/26; SJ030560; NP 108
Cyfoeth-y-brenin (township in Llanfihangel Genu'rglyn), 46/5; SN612873; NP 127
Cyfronydd (Coffronydd) (township in Pool), 54/65; SJ141089; NP 117
Cylch Bychan (division in St Davids [Tyddewi]), 55/65; SM777262; NP 138
Cylch Gwaelod (division in St Davids [Tyddewi]), 55/63; SM741268; NP 138
Cylch Mawr (division in St Davids [Tyddewi]), 55/62; SM787283; NP 138
Cylch y Dre (division in St Davids [Tyddewi]), 55/64; SM759254; NP 138
Cymmau (township in Hope), 50/123; SJ295562; NP 109
Cynnill-mawr, 46/6; NP 127
Cynnull-mawr (Cynnill-mawr) (township in Llanfihangel Genu'rglyn), 46/6; SN660870; NP 127
Cynon (hamlet in Merthyr Tydfil), 51/74; SO120040; NP 154
Cynwyl Elfed (Conwill in Elvet, Conwil-in-Elfet, Conwil-Elvet, Conwyl Elved) (parish), 47/36; SN370305; NP 139
Cynynion (township in Oswestry), 31/102B; SJ247308; NP 117
Cysyllte (township in Llangollen), 49/107; SJ263408; NP 108, 117

D

Dacre (parish), 7/193-197; NP 83
Dacre (township in Dacre), 7/196; NY460267; NP 83
Dacre (township in Ripon), 43/160; SE174615; NP 91
Dadington (township in Hinckley), 21/223; SP403982; NP 132
Dagenham (parish), 12/315; TQ498844; NP 161
Daglingworth (Daglinworth) (parish), 13/240A; SO995050; NP 157
Dalbury (parish), 8/256; NP 120
Dalbury Lees (Dalbury) (parish), 8/256; SK266361; NP 120
Dalby (division in township of Dalby-cum-Skewsby in Dalby), 42/606; SE642708; NP 92
Dalby (parish), 22/418; TF410700; NP 114
Dalby (parish), 42/606-607; NP 92
Dalby-cum-Skewsby (township in Dalby), 42/606-607; NP 92
Dalderby (division in Dalderby), 22/379A; TF252662; NP 114
Dalderby (parish), 22/379A-B; NP 114
Dalderby - Wildmore Fen (division in Dalderby), 22/379B; NP 114
Dale (parish), 55/98A; SM806053; NP 151
Dale Abbey (chapelry in Dale Abbey), 8/282; SK439388; NP 121
Dale Abbey (parish), 8/282; NP 121
Dale Park (division in township of Satterthwaite in Hawkshead), 20/48; SD352925; NP 89
Dale Town (township in Hawnby), 42/499; SE530890; NP 92
Dalham (parish), 34/216; TL729617; NP 135, 136
Dallinghoo (Dallingho) (division in Dallinghoo), 34/366A; TM268550; NP 150
Dallinghoo (Dallingho) (parish), 34/366A-B; NP 150
Dallinghoo Weild (division in Dallinghoo), 34/366B; TM257541; NP 150
Dallington (parish), 26/234; SP737625; NP 133
Dallington (parish), 36/137B; TQ663192; NP 183
Dalston (parish), 7/141-6; NP 76, 82, 83
Dalston (township in Dalston), 7/141; NY364504; NP 76, 83
Dalton (division in township of Dalton in Rotherham), 43/845; SK460925; NP 103
Dalton (division of Dalton township in Thrybergh), 43/846; SK468935; NP 103
Dalton (township in Burton in Kendal), 20/72; SD550750; NP 89
Dalton (township in Dalton in Furness), 20/24-30; NP 88
Dalton (township in Wigan), 20/590; SD493083; NP 100
Dalton (township in Newburn), 27/531; NZ103729; NP 77
Dalton (township in Kirkby Ravensworth), 42/23; NY110087; NP 84, 85
Dalton (township in Topcliffe), 42/242; SE438762; NP 91
Dalton (township in Kirkheaton), 43/725; SE165175; NP 102

Dalton (township in Rotherham and Thrybergh), 43/845-846; NP 103
Dalton in Furness (parish), 20/24-30; NP 88
Dalton Piercy (township in Hart), 11/244; NZ465310; NP 85
Dalton Proper (division in township of Dalton in Dalton in Furness), 20/26; SD233731; NP 88
Dalton upon Tees, 42/57
Dalton-le-Dale (parish), 11/84-87; NP 85
Dalton-le-Dale (township in Dalton-le-Dale), 11/85; NZ414482; NP 85
Dalton-on-Tees (Dalton upon Tees) (township in Croft), 42/57; NZ308067; NP 85
Dalwood (chapelry in Stockland), 9/498; ST245998; NP 176
Damerham South (parish), 39/390; NP 179
Danbury (parish), 12/241; TL783051; NP 161, 162
Danby (parish), 42/361-363; NP 86, 92
Danby (township in Danby), 42/362; NZ710080; NP 86, 92
Danby Low Moor, Danby High Moor (common to Danby and Glaisdale townships in Danby), 42/361; NZ705045; NP 86, 92
Danby Wiske (42/67-68; NP 91
Danby Wiske (township in Danby Wiske), 42/67; SE322985; NP 91
Danthorpe (township in Humbleton), 41/408; TA244327; NP 99
Darcy Lever (township in Bolton le Moors), 20/399; SD741081; NP 101
Darenth (parish), 19/27; TQ566714; NP 171
Daresbury (township in Runcorn), 5/152; SJ585828; NP 100
Darfield (parish), 43/856-862; NP 102, 103
Darfield (township in Darfield), 43/859; SE407055; NP 102, 103
Dark Side (sub-division of Friars Mere Division in Saddleworth with Quick township in Rochdale), 43/739; SD972090; NP 101, 102
Darlaston (parish), 33/306; SO980970; NP 130, 131
Darlaston (township in Stone), 33/53; SJ881351; NP 119
Darley (Darley and Little Rowsley) (township in Darley), 8/121; SK284639; NP 111
Darley (parish), 8/120-121; NP 111
Darley Abbey (township in Derby St Alkmund), 8/275; SK351387; NP 121
Darlingscott (hamlet in Tredington), 40/254; SP239417; NP 144
Darlington (parish), 11/318-325
Darlington Borough (division in township of Darlington in Darlington), 11/321; NZ289144; NP 85
Darliston (township in Prees), 31/24; SJ578335; NP 118
Darlton (parish), 28/66; SK774729; NP 112
Darmsden (hamlet in Barking), 34/293; TM095529; NP 149, 150
Darnhall (township in Whitegate), 5/173; SJ649632; NP 110
Darowen (parish), 54/126A-B; NP 127
Darras Hall (township in Ponteland), 27/523; NZ151707; NP 78
Darrington (parish), 43/632-633; NP 97, 103
Darrington (township in Darrington), 43/632; SE488198; NP 97, 103
Darsham (parish), 34/162; TM418702; NP 137
Darsingham (parish), 25/92; NP 124
Dartford (parish), 19/24; TQ539739; NP 171
Dartington (parish), 9/372; SX775625; NP 187, 188
Dartmoor Forest (quarter in Lydford), 9/334; SX610770; NP 175
Dartmouth, St Petrox (parish), 9/484; SX878512; NP 188
Dartmouth, St Saviour (parish), 9/485; SX879508; NP 188
Darton (division in township of Darton in Darton), 43/707; SE314099; NP 102
Darton (parish), 43/706-709; NP 102
Darton (township in Darton), 43/707-708; NP 102
Datchet (parish), 3/238; SU992769; NP 159
Datchworth (parish), 16/84; TL270190; NP 147
Dauntsey (parish), 39/62; ST997821; NP 157
Davenham (parish), 5/180-192; NP 110
Davenham (township in Davenham), 5/188; SJ663707; NP 110
Davenport (township in Astbury), 5/228; SJ792664; NP 110
Daventry (hamlet in Daventry), 26/244A; SP580630; NP 132
Daventry (parish), 26/244A-B; NP 132
Davidstow (David Stowe) (parish), 6/27; SX160864; NP 186
Davington (parish), 19/109; TR004622; NP 172
Davy Hall (extra-parochial), 43/34; SE603519; NP 97/1

Davyhulme (division in township of Barton upon Irwell in Eccles), 20/546A; SJ752954; NP 101
Dawdon (township in Dalton-le-Dale), 11/86; NZ428483; NP 85
Dawley Magna (Great Dawley) (parish), 31/227-229; NP 119
Dawley Magna (Great Dawley) (township in Dawley Magna), 31/228; SJ686070; NP 119
Dawley Parva (Little Dawley) (township in Dawley Magna), 31/229; SJ678060; NP 119
Dawlish (parish), 9/394; SX953779; NP 188
Daylesford (parish), 40/250; SP251263; NP 144
Daywall (township in Whittington), 31/80; SJ296346; NP 117, 118
Deal (parish), 19/356; TR373525; NP 173
Dean (Nether and Upper Dean) (parish), 1/2; TL051682; NP 134
Dean (parish), 7/261-263; NP 82
Dean (township in Dean), 7/263; NY078258; NP 82
Dean Prior (parish), 9/374; SX701649; NP 187
Deane (parish), 14/95; SU554504; NP 168
Deane (parish), 20/564-573; NP 101
Deanham (township in Hartburn), 27/357; NZ035832; NP 77
Deanraw (township in parochial chapelry of Haydon in Warden), 27/595; NY811617; NP 77
Dearham (parish), 7/245-6; NP 82
Dearham (township in Dearham), 7/245; NY069363; NP 82
Debach (parish), 34/365; TM245545; NP 150
Debden (parish), 12/436; TL560327; NP 148
Debdon (township in Rothbury), 27/253; NU059039; NP 71
Debenham (parish), 34/248; TM174640; NP 136, 137
Debtling (parish), 19/170; NP 172
Decoy Pond (extra-parochial), 14/300C; SU358072; NP 180
Deddington (hamlet in Deddington), 29/37; SP473316; NP 145
Deddington (parish), 29/37-38; NP 145
Deddithorpe, 22/7; NP 104
Dedham (parish), 12/102; TM054322; NP 149
Dedworth (hamlet in New Windsor), 2/222; SU945773; NP 159
Deene (parish), 26/53-54; NP 133, 134
Deene (township in Deene), 26/53; SP933925; NP 133, 134
Deenethorpe (Deenthorpe) (hamlet in Deene), 26/54; SP960913; NP 133, 134
Deepdale (division in township of East Harlsey in East Harlsey), 42/318; SE415999; NP 91
Deepdale (division in township of Dent in Sedbergh), 43/256; SD720840; NP 89, 90
Deeping Fen (extra-parochial), 22/728A-B; NP 123
Deeping Fen [in Holland] (extra-parochial), 22/728B; TF200170; NP 123
Deeping Fen [in Kesteven] (extra-parochial), 22/728A; TF180150; NP 123
Deeping Gate (hamlet in Maxey), 26/17B; TF142089; NP 123
Deeping St James (parish), 22/727; TF168101; NP 123
Deerhurst (hamlet in Deerhurst), 13/53A; SO871295; NP 143
Deerhurst (parish)), 13/53A-D; NP 143
Deerhurst Walton (hamlet in Deerhurst), 13/53D; SO885272; NP 143
Defford (chapelry in St Andrew Pershore), 40/175; SO910433; NP 143
Deighton (township in Escrick), 41/73; SE633445; NP 97
Deighton (township in Northallerton), 42/267; NZ375020; NP 91
Deighton (division in township of Huddersfield in Huddersfield), 43/747; SE162194; NP 102
Delamere (parish), 5/401-404; NP 109
Delamere (township in Delamere), 5/401; SJ556677; NP 109
Dembleby (parish), 22/797; TF036379; NP 123
Denaby (Dennaby) (township in Mexborough), 43/868; SK480990; NP 103
Denbigh (Dinbych) (parish), 49/30; SJ060660; NP 108
Denbigh Walk (division of West Dean township in St Pauls, Forest of Dean), 13/155; SO641073; NP 143, 156
Denbury (parish), 9/420; SX828684; NP 188
Denby (parish), 8/206; SK398469; NP 112, 121
Denby (township in Penistone), 43/779; SE230080; NP 102
Denby Grange (division in township of Whitley Upper in Kirkheaton), 43/722; SE234159; NP 102

Denby Walk, 13/152; NP 143
Denchworth (parish), 2/49; SU379920; NP 158
Dendron (division in township of Aldingham in Aldingham), 20/34; SD243708; NP 88
Denford (parish), 26/143; TL004768; NP 134
Dengie (parish), 12/356; TM005005; NP 162
Denham (parish), 3/235; TQ036870; NP 159, 160
Denham (parish), 34/139; TM184738; NP 137
Denham (parish), 34/219; TL757623; NP 135, 136
Denholme (division in township of Thornton in Bradford), 43/528; SE069343; NP 96
Denio (parish), 48/54; NP 115
Dennaby, 43/868; NP 103
Dennington (parish), 34/169; TM285680; NP 137
Denny Lodge (extra-parochial), 14/300B; SU333056; NP 180
Denny Lodge Walk (extra-parochial division in New Forest registration subdistrict in New Forest extra-parochial), 14/302K; SU240060; NP 180
Denny Lodge Walk (extra-parochial division in Lymington registration subdistrict in New Forest extra-parochial), 14/302L; SU367057; NP 180
Denny Lodge Walk (in New Forest), 14/302K-L; NP 180
Denston (Denardiston) (parish), 34/321; TL764527; NP 149
Denstone (township in Alton), 33/106; SK094405; NP 120
Dent (township in Sedbergh), 43/255-259; NP 89, 90
Denton (hamlet in Cuddesdon), 29/249; SP594024; NP 158
Denton (parish), 17/20; TL171881; NP 134
Denton (parish), 19/35; TQ659729; NP 171
Denton (parish), 19/344; TR211462; NP 173
Denton (parish), 22/632A; SK863323; NP 122
Denton (parish), 25/629; TM280885; NP 137
Denton (parish), 26/290; SP837573; NP 133
Denton (parish), 36/332; TQ464028; NP 183
Denton (township in Gainford), 11/311; NZ216194; NP 85
Denton (township in Manchester), 20/533; SJ914949; NP 101
Denton (township in Otley), 43/362; SE145505; NP 96
Denver (parish), 25/520; TF595007; NP 124, 135
Denwick (township in Alnwick), 27/200; NU205145; NP 71
Deopham (parish), 25/658; TG050005; NP 125, 136
Depden (parish), 34/320; TL779563; NP 136, 149
Derby All Saints (parish), 8/271; SK353363; NP 121/2
Derby Hills (extra-parochial), 8/305; SK368241; NP 121
Derby St Alkmund (parish), 8/273-276; NP 121, 121/2
Derby St Alkmund (township in Derby St Alkmund), 8/273; SK347373; NP 121/2
Derby St Michael (parish), 8/269B, 272; NP 121, 121/2
Derby St Michael (township in Derby St Michael), 8/272; SK352366; NP 121/2
Derby St Peter (parish), 8/268-269A; NP 121
Derby St Peter (township in Derby St Peter), 8/269A; SK357354; NP 121
Derby St Werbergh (parish), 8/270; SK338358; NP 121
Deritend (township in Aston), 37/37; SP078861; NP 131
Derlwyn (township in Carno), 54/120; SJ960997; NP 128
Derrythorpe (Deddithorpe) (hamlet in Althorpe), 22/7; SE822087; NP 104
Dersingham (Darsingham) (parish), 25/92; TF702302; NP 124
Derwen (Derwen y Mal) (parish), 49/24; SJ071508; NP 108
Derwen y Mal (parish), 49/24; NP 108
Derwent (township in Hathersage), 8/39; SK192887; NP 102
Desborough (parish), 26/126; SP800835; NP 133
Desford (parish), 21/174-175; NP 121
Desford (township in Desford), 21/174; SK480032; NP 121
Desfurlong (division in township of Culcheth in Winwick), 20/599; SJ657941; NP 101
Detchant (township in Belford), 27/81; NU080360; NP 64
Dethenydd (township in Llandinam), 54/150; SO015835; NP 128
Dethick, Lea and Hollway (township in Ashover), 8/124; SK332574; NP 111
Detling (Debtling) (parish), 19/170; TQ802596; NP 172
Deuxhill (parish), 31/556; SO697870; NP 130
Devizes, St John the Baptist (parish), 39/135; ST994609; NP 167

91

Devizes, St Mary the Virgin (parish), 39/134; SU004614; NP 167
Devynock (parish), 45/64A-68; NP 140, 141, 153
Dewlish (parish), 10/209; SY774982; NP 178
Dewsall (parish), 15/188; SO483334; NP 142
Dewsbury (parish), 43/579-584; NP 96, 102
Dewsbury (township in Dewsbury), 43/581; SE238220; NP 96
Dexthorpe (hamlet in Well), 22/416; TF407721; NP 114
Dibden (parish), 14/301; SU409079; NP 180
Dicheat (parish), 32/201; ST618351; NP 165, 166
Dickleburgh (parish), 25/761; TM178828; NP 137
Didbrook (parish), 13/71-72; NP 144
Didbrook (township in Didbrook), 13/71; SP049318; NP 144
Didcot (Didcote) (hamlet in Beckford), 13/40; SP002356; NP 143, 144
Didcot (parish), 2/81; SU530905; NP 158
Didcote, 13/40; NP 143, 144
Diddington (parish), 17/101; TL192657; NP 134
Diddlebury (parish), 31/502-511; NP 129
Diddlebury (township in Diddlebury), 31/505; SO503856; NP 129
Didling (parish), 36/14; SU838187; NP 181
Didlington (parish), 25/689; TL789971; NP 136
Didmarton (parish), 13/343; ST827879; NP 156
Didnam (tithing in Shinfield), 2/186; SU710669; NP 169
Didsbury (township in Manchester), 20/527; SJ848912; NP 101
Digby (parish), 22/574; TF090550; NP 113
Digswell (parish), 16/155; TL245145; NP 147
Dihewid (parish), 46/69; NP 139, 140
Dihewyd (Dihewid) (parish), 46/69; SN497546; NP 139, 140
Dilham (parish), 25/236; TG332260; NP 126
Dilhorne (parish), 33/70A; NP 110, 119
Dilhorne (township in Dilhorne), 33/70A; SJ975435; NP 110, 119
Dillicar (township in Kendal), 38/113; SD617974; NP 89
Dillington (hamlet in East Dereham), 25/338; TF973152; NP 125
Dilston (division of Dilston township in Corbridge), 27/477A; NY975635; NP 77
Dilston (division of Dilston township in Corbridge), 27/477B; NY963604; NP 77
Dilston (township in Corbridge), 27/477A-B; NP 77
Dilton (tithing in Westbury), 39/232B; ST860490; NP 166
Dilworth (township in Ribchester), 20/225; SD627380; NP 95
Dilwyn (parish), 15/60; SO419545; NP 129, 142
Dinas (parish), 55/24; SN011389; NP 138
Dinas Mawddwy (township in Mallwyd), 52/32; SH830140; NP 116, 117
Dinbren (Dinbrin) (township in Llangollen), 49/105B; SJ214435; NP 108
Dinbrin, 49/105B; NP 108
Dinbych (parish), 49/30
Dinckley (township in Blackburn), 20/322; SD691360; NP 95
Dinder (parish), 32/139; ST588452; NP 165, 166
Dinedor (parish), 15/183; SO535370; NP 142
Dingestow (parish), 53/22; SO449106; NP 142, 155
Dingley (parish), 26/100; SP766882; NP 133
Dinham (hamlet in Llanvair-Discoed), 53/102; ST480920; NP 155
Dinmore (extra-parochial), 15/105; SO482509; NP 142
Dinmore (extra-parochial), 31/377; SO369891; NP 129
Dinnington, 27/514-520; NP 78
Dinnington (township in Dinnington), 27/517; NZ211722; NP 78
Dinnington (parish), 32/456; ST402125; NP 177
Dinnington (division of Dinnington township in Dinnington), 43/907; SK539849; NP 103
Dinnington (division of Dinnington township in Laughton en le Morthen), 43/908; SK528860; NP 103
Dinnington (parish), 43/906-907; NP 103
Dinnington (township in Dinnington and Laughton en le Morthen), 43/907-908; NP 103
Dinsdale (parish), 11/329; NP 85
Dinthill (township in St Alkmond Shrewsbury), 31/262B; SJ428129; NP 118
Dinting (township in Glossop), 8/3A; SK013943; NP 102
Dinton (Donnington) (parish), 3/165; SP778097; NP 146, 159
Dinton (parish), 39/290; SU015330; NP 167

Dippenhall (tithing in Crondall), 14/32B; SU801481; NP 169
Diptford (parish), 9/443; SX749557; NP 187
Dirham and Hinton (parish), 13/396; NP 156
Discoed (township in Presteigne [Llanandras]), 56/18; SO277648; NP 128, 129
Discove (tithing in Bruton), 32/197B; ST694434; NP 166
Diseworth (parish), 21/19; SK460240; NP 121
Dishforth (township in Topcliffe), 42/237; SE375725; NP 91
Dishley-cum-Thorpacre (parish), 21/37B-38; NP 121
Disley (Disley Stanley) (township in Stockport), 5/20; SJ983843; NP 101
Disley with Thorpe Acre (Dishley-cum-Thorpacre) (parish), 21/37B-38; NP 121
Disley with Thorpe Acre (Dishley-cum-Thorpacre) (township in Disley with Thorpe Acre), 21/38; SK510210; NP 121
Diss (parish), 25/746; TM124832; NP 136
Disserth (parish), 56/40A-B; NP 128, 141
Disserth (township in Disserth), 56/40A; SO040580; NP 128
Distington (parish), 7/257; NY019224; NP 82
Ditchampton (tithing in Wilton), 39/324B; SU092218; NP 167
Ditchburn (township in Eglingham), 27/146; NU137211; NP 71
Ditcheling (parish), 36/119; NP 182
Ditcheridge (parish), 39/119; NP 156
Ditchford (hamlet in Blockley), 40/246; SP215369; NP 144
Ditchingham (parish), 25/616; TM332921; NP 137
Ditchling (Ditcheling) (parish), 36/119; TQ328151; NP 182
Ditheringham (division in St Mary Shrewsbury), 31/254B; SJ492140; NP 118
Ditteridge (Ditcheridge) (parish), 39/119; ST818698; NP 156
Dittisham (parish), 9/482; SX853536; NP 188
Ditton (hamlet in Stoke Poges), 3/230; TQ003774; NP 159
Ditton (parish), 19/174; TQ713578; NP 171
Ditton (township in Prescot), 20/625; SJ498859; NP 100
Ditton Priors (parish), 31/560; SO618898; NP 129, 130
Ditton, 31/547; NP 130
Dixton (hamlet in Alderton), 13/43; SP983310; NP 143
Dixton (parish), 53/18; NP 142
Dixton Newton (Dixton) (division in Dixton Newton), 15/235; SO498163; NP 142
Dixton Newton (Dixton) (division in Dixton Newton), 53/18; SO532135; NP 142
Dixton Newton (parish), 15/235, 53/18; NP 142
Dixton, 15/235; NP 142
Dockenfield (extra-parochial), 14/118; SU825401; NP 169
Docker (township in Kendal), 38/115; SD560950; NP 89
Docking (division in Docking), 25/86; TF770370; NP 124, 125
Docking (parish), 25/86; NP 124, 125
Docklow (parish), 15/98; SO564575; NP 129
Dodbrooke (Dodbrook) (parish), 9/477; SX738439; NP 187
Dodcott cum Wilkesley (township in Acton), 5/282; SJ590450; NP 109, 118, 119
Dodcott cum Wilkesley (township in Audlem and Acton), 5/281-282; NP 109, 118, 119
Dodcott cum Wilkesley (Wilksley) (division of Dodcott cum Wilkesley township in Audlem), 5/281; SJ630420; NP 119
Doddenham (Dodenham) (parish), 40/107; SO745565; NP 130
Dodderhill (parish), 40/58A-59; NP 130
Dodderhill - In-Liberty (division in Dodderhill), 40/58B; SO900640; NP 130
Dodderhill - Out-Liberty (division in Dodderhill), 40/58A; SO930660; NP 130
Doddinghurst (parish), 12/332; TQ569982; NP 161
Doddington (parish), 4/13-16; NP 123, 124, 134, 135
Doddington township in Doddington), 4/13; TL378903; NP 135
Doddington (township in Wybunbury), 5/266; SJ712472; NP 110
Doddington (parish), 19/233; TQ942582; NP 172
Doddington (parish), 22/526-527; NP 113
Doddington (township in Doddington), 22/526; SK903700; NP 113
Doddington (parish), 27/47-51; NP 64, 71
Doddington (township in Doddington), 27/47; NU008344; NP 64
Doddington (Ditton) (township in Cleobury Mortimer), 31/547; SO647783; NP 130

Doddiscombsleigh (parish), 9/385; SX851870; NP 176
Dodenham (parish), 40/107; NP 130
Dodford (parish), 26/252; SP617609; NP 132
Dodington (parish), 13/394; ST747798; NP 156
Dodington (township in Whitchurch), 31/33; SJ528408; NP 118
Dodington (parish), 32/259; ST174402; NP 164
Dodleston (parish), 5/369-370, 50/16; NP 109
Dodleston (township in Dodleston), 5/370; SJ363614; NP 109
Dodworth (township in Silkstone), 43/697; SE312052; NP 102
Doehole (township in Ashover), 8/125; SK350590; NP 111
Doethie-Camddwr (Dothie-Camddwr, Doithie Carnddwr) (township in Llandewi-Brefi), 46/47; SN775525; NP 140
Doethie-pysgoiwr (Doithie Pysgottwr, Dothie-Piscottwr) (township in Llandewi-Brefi), 46/46; SN731524; NP 140
Dog Lane Liberty (township in Croxden), 33/112B; SK040400; NP 120
Dogdyke (division in Billinghay), 22/573A; TF200552; NP 113
Dogdyke (township in Billinghay), 22/573A-B; NP 114
Dogdyke - Wildmore Fen (division in Billinghay), 22/573B; TF213542; NP 114
Dogmersfield (parish), 14/38; SU774520; NP 169
Dogsthorpe (hamlet in Peterborough, St John the Baptist), 26/3; TF184006; NP 123, 134
Doithie Carnddwr, 46/47
Doithie Pysgottwr, 46/46; NP 140
Dolbenmaen (parish), 48/43; SH506436; NP 115, 116
Dolfor (township in Kerry [Llanfihangel-yng-Ngheri]), 54/169B; SO110863; NP 128
Dolforwyn (township in Bettws), 54/105; SO157958; NP 128
Dolgarrog (Dolgarog) (parish), 48/13; SH745658; NP 107
Dolgead (Dolged) (township in Llanfair Caereinion), 54/47; SJ085085; NP 117
Dolged, 54/47; NP 117
Dolgellau (Dolgelley) (parish), 52/29; SH766167; NP 116
Dolgelley (parish), 52/29
Dolgwden (township in Trefeglwys), 54/135; SN958895; NP 128
Dolton (parish), 9/113; SS572124; NP 175
Dolwar (township in Llanfihangel-yng-Ngwynfa), 54/33; SJ062143; NP 117
Dolwen (township in Llansantffraid), 54/4; SJ215196; NP 117
Dolwyddelan (Dolwyddelen, Dol-wyddelan) (parish), 48/20; SH721521; NP 107, 116
Doncaster (township in Doncaster), 43/938; SE580033; NP 103
Donhead St Andrew (parish), 39/342; ST924246; NP 166, 167, 178, 179
Donhead St Mary (parish), 39/341; ST902227; NP 166, 178, 179
Donington (parish), 22/736; TF207253; NP 123
Donington on Bain (Donnington on Bain) (parish), 22/341; TF246832; NP 105
Donington (parish), 31/472; SJ805052; NP 119
Donisthorpe (division of Donisthorpe township in Church Gresley), 8/332; SK313137; NP 121/3
Donisthorpe (division of Donisthorpe township in Seal), 8/331; SK313127; NP 121/3
Donisthorpe (division of Donisthorpe township in Measham), 8/330; SK316140; NP 121/3
Donisthorpe (township in Measham, Seal and Church Gresley), 8/330-332; SK316140; NP 121/3
Donisthorpe (township in Church Gresley, Measham and Seal), 8/330-332, 21/1; NP 121/3
Donisthorpe (township in Seal), 21/1; SK310130; NP 121/3
Donnington (parish), 3/165; NP 146, 159
Donnington (hamlet in Stow on the Wold), 13/88; SP190280; NP 144
Donnington (parish), 15/280; SO711341; NP 143
Donnington on Bain (parish), 22/341; NP 105
Donnington (parish), 36/265; SU851016; NP 181
Donyatt (parish), 32/447; ST337141; NP 177
Dorchester, All Saints (parish), 10/219; SY695504; NP 178, 178/1
Dorchester, Holy Trinity (Dorchester, Holy Trinity with Froome Whitfield) (parish), 10/217; SY698923; NP 178, 178/1
Dorchester, St Peter (parish), 10/218; SY692906; NP 178, 178/1

Dorchester (hamlet in Dorchester), 29/298; SU576957; NP 158
Dorchester (parish), 29/298-300; NP 158
Dordon (township in Polesworth), 37/18; SK273008; NP 120, 121, 131
Dore (township in Dronfield), 8/43; SK295815; NP 111
Dorking (parish), 35/120; TQ164478; NP 170
Dormington (parish), 15/169-170; NP 142
Dormington (township in Dormington), 15/169; SO587399; NP 142
Dormston (parish), 40/142; SO988562; NP 130
Dorn (hamlet in Blockley), 40/248; SP209339; NP 144
Dorney (parish), 3/221; SU927789; NP 159
Dorrington (parish), 22/584; TF101537; NP 113
Dorrington (township in Muckleston), 31/3; SJ726412; NP 119
Dorsington (parish), 13/10; SP134496; NP 144
Dorstone (parish), 15/205; SO314418; NP 141, 142
Dorton (parish), 3/152; SP682135; NP 145, 146
Dothie-Camddwr, 46/47
Dothie-Piscottwr, 46/46; NP 140
Dotton (extra-parochial), 9/302; SY082888; NP 176
Doulting (parish), 32/135; ST647427; NP 166
Dovaston (township in Kinnerley), 31/125; SJ349211; NP 118
Dovecote Hall (division in Thornton-le-Fen), 22/463B; TF277533; NP 114
Dovenby (township in Bridekirk), 7/244; NY102319; NP 82
Dover Castle (extra-parochial), 19/367; TR427417; NP 173, 173/1
Dover, St James the Apostle (parish), 19/369; TR324416; NP 173, 173/1
Dover, St Mary the Virgin (parish), 19/370; TR419415; NP 173, 173/1
Dovercourt (parish), 12/110; TM241309; NP 150
Doverdale (parish), 40/68; SO860660; NP 130
Doveridge (division in Doveridge), 8/242A; SK120340; NP 120
Doveridge (parish), 8/241-242B; NP 120
Doveridge (township in Doveridge), 8/241-242B; NP 120
Dowdeswell (parish), 13/213; SP001192; NP 143, 144
Dowland (parish), 9/116; SS579102; NP 175
Dowles (parish), 31/568; SO775770; NP 130
Dowlish Wake (parish), 32/454; ST377127; NP 177
Down Ampney (parish), 13/287; SU111973; NP 157
Down Hatherley (parish), 13/117; SO879227; NP 143
Down St Mary (parish), 9/180; SS743042; NP 175
Down Stonebeck, 43/206; NP 90, 91
Downe (Down) (parish), 19/69; TQ434617; NP 171
Downham (division in Wymondham), 25/650; TG114031; NP 125, 136
Downham (parish), 4/23; TL510872; NP 135
Downham (parish), 12/432; TQ730952; NP 161
Downham (township in Whalley), 20/258; SD798437; NP 95
Downham (township in Carham), 27/34; NT865342; NP 64
Downham Market (parish), 25/519; TF610030; NP 124
Downhead (parish), 32/130; ST696456; NP 166
Downholland (division in township of Downholland in Halsall), 20/358; SD363071; NP 100
Downholland (township in Halsall), 20/356-358; NP 100
Downholme (parish), 42/97-100; NP 90, 91
Downholme (township in Downholme), 42/97; SE116987; NP 90, 91
Downton (division in Downton), 39/368; SU189218; NP 167, 179
Downton (parish), 15/4; SO437748; NP 129
Downton (parish), 39/357, 368; NP 167, 179
Downton and Hopton (township in Stanton Lacy), 31/522; SO528800; NP 129
Dowsby (parish), 22/674-675; NP 123
Dowsby (township in Dowsby), 22/675; TF128295; NP 123
Doxford (township in Ellingham), 27/124; NU184233; NP 71
Doynton (parish), 13/399; ST722739; NP 156
Drainage Marsh (extra-parochial), 22/768; TF253347; NP 123
Drakelow (township in Church Gresley), 8/316; SK250195; NP 120
Draughton (parish), 26/165; SP766773; NP 133

93

Draughton (township in Skipton), 43/329; SE050520; NP 96
Drax (division in township of Drax in Drax), 43/972; SE670260; NP 97
Drax (parish), 43/971B-975; NP 97
Drax (township in Drax), 43/972-973; NP 97
Draycot (hamlet in Ickford), 29/256A; SP645057; NP 158
Draycot Cerne (parish), 39/66; ST933788; NP 156, 157
Draycot Foliat (Draycott Foliatt, Draycot Foliatt) (parish), 39/96; SU178777; NP 157
Draycot Moor (Draycott Moor, Southmoor) (hamlet in Longworth), 2/28; SU399981; NP 158
Draycott (township in Wilne), 8/288; SK436338; NP 121
Draycott (hamlet in Cheddar), 32/149; ST477509; NP 165
Draycott Foliatt (parish), 39/96; NP 157
Draycott in the Clay (township in Hanbury), 33/204; SK154287; NP 120
Draycott in the Moors (Draycot in the Moors) (parish), 33/115; SJ988400; NP
Draycott Moor, 2/28; NP 158
Drayton (Drayton St Leonard) (parish), 29/297; SU594968; NP 158
Drayton (division in Drayton), 32/333B; ST410238; NP 177
Drayton (hamlet in Daventry), 26/244B; SP560620; NP 132
Drayton (parish), 2/58; SU467942; NP 158
Drayton (parish), 25/353; TG185135; NP 126
Drayton (parish), 29/15; SP432416; NP 145
Drayton (parish), 32/333B, 407; NP 177
Drayton (township in Bringhurst), 21/306; SP825923; NP 133
Drayton Bassett (parish), 33/286; SK180002; NP 120, 131
Drayton Beauchamp (division in Drayton Beauchamp), 3/173; SP908108; NP 146, 159
Drayton Beauchamp (parish), 3/173, 16/152; NP 146, 159
Drayton in Hales (parish), 31/8-13, 33/158A-B; NP 119
Drayton Parslow (parish), 3/96; SP853290; NP 146
Drefor (township in Kerry [Llanfihangel-yng-Ngheri]), 54/176; SO168887; NP 128
Drewern (township in Glascwm), 56/42A; SO140560; NP 128, 141
Drewsteignton (parish), 9/324; SX722915; NP 175
Drewton (division in township of Drewton with Everthorpe in North Cave), 41/202; SE928333; NP 98
Drewton with Everthorpe (township in North Cave), 41/203; NP 98, 98/1
Driby (parish), 22/401; TF396742; NP 114
Driffield (parish), 13/298; SU075992; NP 157
Drigg (parish), 7/312; SD069998; NP 88
Drighlington (township in Birstal), 43/537; SE226288; NP 96
Dringhoe, Upton and Brough (township in Skipsea), 41/355; TA150550; NP 99
Dringhouses (township in St Mary Bishophill [Senior]), 43/45B; SE582495; NP 97
Drinkstone (parish), 34/301; TL959611; NP 136
Droitwich, St Andrew (parish), 40/62; SO893621; NP 130
Droitwich, St Nicholas (parish), 40/61; SO892633; NP 130
Droitwich, St Peter (parish), 40/63; SO902625; NP 130
Dronfield (parish), 8/43-49; NP 111
Dronfield (township in Dronfield), 8/47; SK344782; NP 111
Droxford (parish), 14/254; SU586158; NP 168, 180
Droylsden (township in Manchester), 20/517; SJ896989; NP 101
Drumburgh (township in Bowness-on-Solway), 7/109; NY254597; NP 75
Druridge (township in Widdrington parochial chapelry in Woodhorn), 27/313; NZ271959; NP 71, 78
Dry Doddington (parish), 22/610; SK850475; NP 113
Dry Drayton (parish), 4/70; TL378618; NP 135
Drybeck (township in St Lawrence Appleby), 38/45; NY667154; NP 83
Drypool (parish), 41/337-338; NP 99, 99/1
Drypool (township), 41/337; TA113289; NP 99/1
Duchy of Lancaster (extra-parochial), 24/27B; TQ306807; NP 160/1
Duckinfield, 5/10; NP 101
Duckington (township in Malpas), 5/338; SJ486517; NP 109

Ducklington (hamlet in Ducklington), 29/182; SP353072; NP 158
Ducklington (parish), 29/182; NP 158
Duddeston cum Nechells (township in Aston), 37/35; SP085881; NP 131
Duddington (parish), 26/34; SK991003; NP 123, 134
Duddo (township in Norham), 27/14; NT936426; NP 64
Duddo, 27/423; NP 78
Duddon (township in Tarvin), 5/393; SJ513654; NP 109
Dudleston (chapelry in Ellesmere), 31/66; SJ355375; NP 118
Dudley (parish), 40/258; SO940890; NP 130
Dudley Castle (extra-parochial), 40/259; SO947908; NP 130
Dudston (township in Chirbury), 31/357; SO243972; NP 128
Dues Hill (Dueshill) (township in Holystone), 27/189; NT960999; NP 71
Duffield (parish), 8/186-193; NP 111, 121
Duffield (township in Duffield), 8/189; SK343438; NP 111, 121
Duffryn (hamlet in Llanddetty), 45/74A; SO080140; NP 141
Duffryn (hamlet in Bassaleg), 53/119; ST290850; NP 154, 155
Dufton (parish), 38/8; NY738284; NP 83, 84
Duggleby (township in Kirby Grindalythe), 41/183C; SE877670; NP 93
Dukes Hagg (Dukers-Hagg) (township in Ovingham), 27/565; NZ111604; NP 77
Dukinfield (Duckinfield) (township in Stockport), 5/10; SJ950976; NP 101
Dulais Higher, 51/16; NP 153
Dulais Lower, 51/15; NP 153
Dulas (parish), 15/220; SO372295; NP 142
Dullingham (parish), 4/144; TL630573; NP 135
Duloe (parish), 6/100; SX227586; NP 186
Dulverton (parish), 32/283; SS904291; NP 164
Dulwich (hamlet in St Giles Camberwell), 35/19; TQ333733; NP 170
Dumbleton (parish), 13/37; SP021358; NP 144
Dummer (parish), 14/98; SU590458; NP 168
Dumplington (division in township of Barton upon Irwell in Eccles), 20/549; SJ770969; NP 101
Dunchideock (parish), 9/391; SX875880; NP 176
Dunchurch (parish), 37/130-131; NP 132
Dunchurch (township in Dunchurch), 37/130; SP480715; NP 132
Duncton (parish), 36/74; SU958170; NP 181
Dundraw, Kelsick and Wheyrigg (township in Bromfield), 7/132; NY203498; NP 75, 82
Dundry (parish), 32/17; ST561663; NP 155
Dungworth (division in township of Bradfield in Ecclesfield), 43/805; SK278898; NP 111
Dunham, 28/68; SK810748; NP 104, 112, 113
Dunham Massey (township in Bowdon), 5/81; SJ742887; NP 101
Dunham on the Hill (Dunham) (township in Thornton le Moors), 5/418; SJ469729; NP 109
Dunham, 5/418; NP 109
Dunholme (Dunholm) (parish), 22/254; TF023792; NP 104
Dunkenshaw Fell (division in township of Over Wyresdale in Lancaster), 20/124; SD579568; NP 94
Dunkerton (parish), 32/87; ST704593; NP 166
Dunkeswell (parish), 9/147; ST142076; NP 164, 176
Dunkeswick (township in Harewood), 43/401; SE302472; NP 96
Dunkirk (parish), 19/114; TR090600; NP 172, 173
Dunnerdale with Seathwaite (township in Kirkby Ireleth), 20/1; SD235995; NP 88
Dunnington (parish), 41/69-70; NP 97
Dunnington (township in Beeford), 41/350; TA151525; NP 99
Dunnington (township in Dunnington), 41/70; SE670515; NP 97
Dunnockshaw (township in Whalley), 20/290; SD818278; NP 95
Dunnockshaw Close (district in Whalley), 20/291; SD798381; NP 95
Duns Tew (parish), 29/59; SP452286; NP 145
Dunsborne Rouse (parish), 13/241; NP 157
Dunsby (parish), 22/677; TF121267; NP 123
Dunsfold (parish), 35/160; TQ005352; NP 169, 181
Dunsford (parish), 9/318; SX824896; NP 176
Dunstable (parish), 1/131; TL021217; NP 147

Dunstall (Dunstall and Bonsdale) (hamlet in Corringham), 22/145; SK891839; NP 104
Dunstall (township in Tamworth), 33/285D; SK190038; NP 120
Dunstall (township in Tatenhill), 33/218; SK185204; NP 120
Dunstall and Bonsdale, 22/145; NP 104
Dunstan (Dunston) (township in Embleton), Dunston, 27/153; NU243211; NP 71
Dunster (parish), 32/238; SS981437; NP 164
Dunston (parish), 22/560; TF045625; NP 113
Dunston (parish), 25/485; TG224024; NP 126, 137
Dunston (township in Penkridge), 33/234; SJ919178; NP 119
Dunterton (parish), 9/350; SX380793; NP 186
Duntisborne Abbotts (hamlet in Duntisborne Abbotts), 13/243; SO967083; NP 157
Duntisborne Abbotts (parish), 13/242-243; NP 157
Duntisborne Leer (hamlet in Duntisborne Abbotts), 13/242; SO973073; NP 157
Duntisborne Rouse (Dunsborne Rouse) (parish), 13/241; SO980060; NP 157
Duntish (tithing in Buckland Newton), 10/154; ST690065; NP 178
Dunton (parish), 1/66; TL240440; NP 147
Dunton (parish), 3/102; SP821143; NP 146
Dunton (parish), 12/409; TQ653887; NP 161, 162
Dunton (parish), 25/108; NP 125
Dunton (township in Curdworth), 37/30; SP192931; NP 131
Dunton Bassett (parish), 21/241; SP542905; NP 132
Dunton cum Doughton (Dunton) (parish), 25/108; TF880308; NP 125
Dunwich (parish), 34/159; TM470700; NP 137
Dunwood (extra-parochial), 14/222; SU312229; NP 168
Durham University, 11/119; NP 85
Durleigh (parish), 32/267; ST272362; NP 165
Durley (parish), 14/256; SU517168; NP 180
Durnford (parish), 39/301-306; NP 167
Durrington (parish), 36/301; TQ118058; NP 182
Durrington (parish), 39/264; SU136442; NP 167
Dursley (parish), 13/327; ST762978; NP 156
Durston (parish), 32/309; ST296279; NP 177
Durweston (parish), 10/163; ST846079; NP 178
Duston (parish), 26/235; SP728612; NP 133
Dutton (township in Great Budworth), 5/117; SJ588783; NP 100, 101
Dutton (township in Ribchester), 20/227; SD659377; NP 95
Dutton Differth (Dutton diffaeth, Dutton Diffeth) (township in Holt), 49/76; SJ410507; NP 109
Dutton y Bran (Dutton y Brain) (township in Holt), 49/75; SJ410512; NP 109
Duxbury (township in Standish), 20/385; SD585150; NP 100
Duxford (Duxford St John and Duxford St Peter) (parish), 4/180; TL467450; NP 148
Dwygyfylchi (parish), 48/9; SH730760; NP 107
Dwyrhiew, 54/114; NP 117, 128
Dwyriw (Dwyrhiew) (township in Manafon), 54/114; SJ082027; NP 117, 128
Dyffrun Ceidrych, 47/22; NP 140
Dyffryn (township in Meifod), 54/41; SJ148126; NP 117
Dyffryn Ceidrych (Dyffrun Ceidrych) (hamlet in Llangadog), 47/22; SN710220; NP 140
Dyffryn Clydach (hamlet in Cadoxton Juxta Neath), 51/12; SS734997; NP 153
Dyffryn-Elan (township in Llansantffraid-Cwmdeuddwr), 56/33B; SN880670; NP 127, 128
Dyffryn-Gwy (township in Llansantffraid-Cwmdeuddwr), 56/33A; SN960680; NP 128
Dyke (hamlet in Bourne), 22/709C; TF105225; NP 123
Dylais Higher (Upper Dylais, Dulais Higher) (hamlet in Cadoxton Juxta Neath), 51/16; SN815075; NP 153
Dylais Lower (Lower Dylais, Dulais Lower) (hamlet in Cadoxton Juxta Neath), 51/15; SN785035; NP 153
Dymchurch (parish), 19/424; TR102298; NP 173, 184
Dymock (parish), 13/129; SO710316; NP 143
Dynhille Issa, 49/84; NP 118
Dynhille Ucha, 49/85; NP 109, 118
Dynmynlle Isaf (Dynhille Issa) (township in Ruabon), 49/84; SJ327417; NP 118
Dynmynlle Ucha (Dynhille Ucha) (township in Ruabon), 49/85; SJ319433; NP 109, 118
Dyrham and Hinton (Dyrham cum Hinton, Dirham and Hinton) (parish), 13/396; ST737764; NP 156
Dyserth, 50/55-56; NP 108
Dytchley (division in Spelsbury), 29/98; SP387200; NP 145

E
Eachwick (township in Heddon on the Wall), 27/548; NZ111704; NP 77
Eagle (parish), 22/530A; SK882664; NP 113
Eagle Hall (extra-parochial), 22/529; SK866655; NP 113
Eagle Woodhouse (extra-parochial), 22/530B; SK880680; NP 113
Eaglesfield (township in Brigham), 7/266; NY099284; NP 82
Eaglesfield Abbey, 7/99
Eakring (parish), 28/136; SK679615; NP 112
Ealing (division in Ealing), 24/103A; TQ179812; NP 160, 170
Ealing (parish), 24/103A-B; NP 160, 170
Earby (division in township and parish of Thornton in Cravern), 43/316; SD912466; NP 95
Eardington (township in Quatford), 31/486; SO723908; NP 130
Eardisland (parish), 15/33; SO419589; NP 129
Eardisley (parish), 15/51; SO307503; NP 142
Eardiston (township in Ruyton of the Eleven Towns), 31/138; SJ365248; NP 118
Eardleyend (township in Audley), 33/42B; SJ795528; NP 110
Earith (hamlet in Bluntisham), 17/74; TL388756; NP 135
Earl Shilton (township in Kirkby Mallory), 21/171; SP473973; NP 121
Earl Soham (parish), 34/251; TM232630; NP 137
Earl Stoke (parish), 39/228; NP 167
Earl Stoneham (Earl Stonham, Stonham Earl) (parish), 34/243; TM101597; NP 136
Earl's Croome (parish), 40/222; SO872425; NP 143
Earl, 27/51; NP 71
Earldoms (extra-parochial), 39/369; SU247217; NP 167
Earle (Earl, Yearle) (township in Doddington), 27/51; NT979258; NP 71
Earley (division in Sonning), 2/204; SU744718; NP 159, 169
Earlham (parish), 25/407; TG199085; NP 126
Earls Barton (parish), 26/218; SP856634; NP 133
Earls Colne (parish), 12/134; TL860280; NP 149
Earlsdon (hamlet in Coventry, Holy Trinity), 37/147B; SP317778; NP 132
Earnestrey Park, 31/511; NP 129
Earnley (parish), 36/271; SZ822967; NP 181
Earnshill (parish), 32/409; ST384218; NP 177
Earnstrey Park (Earnestrey Park, Upper Parks) township in Diddlebury), 31/511; SO585875; NP 129
Earsdon (parish), 27/483-491; NP 78
Earsdon (township in Earsdon), 27/491; NZ311721; NP 78
Earsdon (township in Hebburn parochial chapelry), 27/304; NZ196939; NP 78
Earsdon Forest (township in Hebburn parochial chapelry), 27/303; NZ206952; NP 71, 78
Earsham (parish), 25/628; TM310894; NP 137
Earswick (division of Earswick township in Wigginton), 42/680; SE630580; NP 97
Earswick (division of Earswick township in Huntington), 42/681; SE630572; NP 97
Earswick (division of Earswick township in Strensall), 42/685; SE635574; NP 97
Earswick (township in Wigginton, Huntington and Strensall), 42/680-681, 685
Eartham (parish), 36/225; SU939095; NP 181
Easby (parish), 42/89-93; NP 91
Easby (township in Easby), 42/92; NZ194011; NP 91
Easby (township in Stokesley), 42/305; NZ578090; NP 86
Easby, 7/53; NP 76

Easebourne (parish), 36/20; SU899235; NP 181
Easedike (division in township and parish of Wighill), 43/70; SE476451; NP 97
Easenhall (hamlet in Monks Kirby), 37/116; SP461796; NP 132
Easington (division of Easington township in Easington), 1 1/90; NZ414440; NP 85
Easington (parish), 11/88-92; NP 85
Easington (township in Easington), 11/90-91; NP 85
Easington (parish), 13/285; NP 157
Easington (township in Belford), 27/84; NU122350; NP 64
Easington Grange (township in Belford), 27/83; NU116358; NP 64
Easington (parish), 29/284; SU661968; NP 158
Easington (parish), 41/445-446; NP 99, 105
Easington (township in Easington), 41/446; TA397190; NP 99, 105
Easington (division in Easington township in Easington), 42/368; NZ750180; NP 86
Easington (parish), 42/366-368; NP 86
Easington (township in Easington), 42/367-368; NP 86
Easington (township in Slaidburn), 43/280-281; NP 90, 95
Easingwold (parish), 42/566-567; NP 91, 92
Easingwold (township in Easingwold), 42/566; SE527686; NP 91, 92
East Acomb (township in Bywell St Peter), 27/631; NZ049638; NP 77
East Adderbury (township in Adderbury), 29/33; SP481361; NP 145
East Allington (parish), 9/480; SX778481; NP 187
East Allington (parish), 22/615; SK864406; NP 122
East and Middle Herrington (township in Houghton-le-Spring), 11/55; NZ358530; NP 78
East and West Duddoe (Duddo) (township in Stannington), 27/423; NZ188801
East and West Kenton, 27/512; NP 78
East and West Thirston with Shothaugh (township in Felton), 27/291; NZ187997; NP 71
East and West Walks of the Forests of Chute and Wakeswood (extra-parochial), 39/191; NP 157
East Anstey (parish), 9/79; SS864265; NP 164
East Ardsley (parish), 43/590; SE300248; NP 96
East Ayton (township in Seamer), 42/411; TA001855; NP 93
East Barkwith (parish), 22/343; TF172818; NP 105
East Barming (parish), 19/217; TQ725546; NP 171
East Barnet (parish), 16/150; TQ277952; NP 160
East Barsham (East Basham) (parish), 25/111; TF921333; NP 125
East Basham (parish), 25/111; NP 125
East Beckham (parish), 25/34; TG158403; NP 125, 126
East Bedfont (Bedfont) (parish), 24/123; TQ083736; NP 170
East Bergholt (parish), 34/507; TM085348; NP 149
East Bilney (parish), 25/270; TF952193; NP 125
East Blatchington (parish), 36/335; TQ483002; NP 183
East Bolton (division in township of Boldon in Boldon), 11/9; NZ364612; NP 78
East Bradenham (parish), 25/506; TF943088; NP 125
East Breary (division in township of Adel cum Eccup in Adel), 43/395; SE268428; NP 96
East Brent (parish), 32/168; ST358526; NP 165
East Bridge Hospital (extra-parochial), 19/255; NP 173/1
East Bridgford (parish), 28/212; SK702442; NP 112, 122
East Brunton (township in Gosforth), 27/507; NZ229708; NP 78
East Buckland (parish), 9/33; SS675315; NP 163
East Budleigh (parish), 9/305; SY055838; NP 176
East Butsfield, West Butsfield and Steely, 11/161; NP 84, 85
East Butterwick (division in Bottesford), 22/32; SE847066; NP 104
East Butterwick (division in Messingham), 22/33; SE839052; NP 104
East Butterwick (township in Bottesford and Messingham), 22/32-33; NP 104
East Camel (parish), 32/371; NP 166, 177
East Carleton (Carleton St Mary and Carleton St Peter) (parish), 25/564; TG177020; NP 126, 137

East Carlton (parish), 26/95; SP829893; NP 133
East Chadlington (chapelry in Charlbury), 29/133; SP335229; NP 145
East Chaldon (parish), 10/278; NP 178
East Challow (Challow East) (chapelry in Letcombe Regis), 2/93; SU382892; NP 158
East Chelborough (parish), 10/116; ST551057; NP 177
East Chevington (East Chivington) (township in Warkworth), 27/230; NZ248996; NP 71
East Chiltington (hamlet in Westmeston), 36/121; TQ346160; NP 183
East Chinnock (parish), 32/471; ST496134; NP 177
East Chisenbury (tithing in Enford), 39/252; SU156533; NP 167
East Chivington, 27/230; NP 71
East Clandon (parish), 35/126; TQ060520; NP 170
East Claydon (parish), 3/108; SP739252; NP 146
East Cliffe (extra-parochial), 19/368; TR427416; NP 173, 173/1
East Coker (parish), 32/473; ST538128; NP 177
East Compton (parish), 10/226; NP 177, 178
East Cottingwith (township in Aughton), 41/38; SE708420; NP 97
East Coulston (Coulston) (parish), 39/229; ST950530; NP 167
East Cowick (township in Snaith), 43/964B; SE662210; NP 97, 103
East Cowton (parish), 42/63; NZ317038; NP 85, 91
East Cranmore (parish), 32/133; ST689439; NP 166
East Dean (township in Trinity, Forest of Dean), 13/151-154; NP 143, 156
East Dean (parish), 14/219; SU278263; NP 167, 168
East Dean (parish), 36/227; SU915135; NP 181
East Denton (township in Newburn), 27/538; NZ199662; NP 78
East Dereham (division in East Dereham), 25/339; TF999131; NP 125
East Donyland (parish), 12/166; TM021214; NP 149
East Down (parish), 9/16; SS589415; NP 163
East Drayton (parish), 28/59; SK756773; NP 103, 112
East Farlam (township in Farlam), 7/57; NY602604; NP 76
East Farleigh (parish), 19/305; TQ738527; NP 171, 172
East Farndon (parish), 26/108; SP717850; NP 133
East Fen Chapel Allotment (extra-parochial), 22/467C; TF389572; NP 114
East Fen Royal Allotments (extra-parochial), 22/468A; TF412594; NP 114
East Ferry (division in Owston and Scotton), 22/4B, 22/36C; NP 104
East Ferry (division in Owston), 22/4B; SE820010; NP 104
East Ferry (division in Scotton), 22/36C; SK821997; NP 104
East Firsby (township in Firsby), 22/218; TF016857; NP 104
East Foreign Liberty and West Foreign Liberty and Town Liberty, 31/548
East Garston (parish), 2/109; SU366768; NP 158
East Garton, 41/411; NP 99
East Golcar (division in township of Golcar in Huddersfield), 43/754; SE102161; NP 102
East Graby (hamlet in Dowsby), 22/674; TF102300; NP 123
East Grimstead (tithing in West Dean), 39/365; SU228272; NP 167
East Grinstead (parish), 36/41; TQ409356; NP 171, 183
East Guildford (parish), 36/147; NP 184
East Guldeford (East Guildford) (parish), 36/147; TQ951214; NP 184
East Haddon (parish), 26/186; SP668678; NP 132, 133
East Hagbourne (East Hagborn) (division in Hagbourne), 2/79; SU532884; NP 158
East Halton (parish), 22/50; TA138204; NP 99, 104, 105
East Ham (parish), 12/325; TQ427832; NP 161
East Hamlet (East Hamlets) (township in Stanton Lacy), 31/520; SO526776; NP 129
East Hanney (tithing in township of East Hanney in West Hanney), 2/51; SU436936; NP 158
East Hanney (township in West Hanney), 2/51-52; NP 158
East Hanningfield (parish), 12/289; TL768015; NP 161, 162
East Hardwick (township in Pontefract), 43/622; SE648181; NP 97, 103

East Harling (parish), 25/734; TM002860; NP 136
East Harlsey (division in township of East Harlsey in East Harlsey), 42/316; SE430998; NP 91
East Harlsey (parish and township, 42/316-319; NP 91
East Harptree (parish), 32/76; ST564545; NP 165
East Hartburn (township in Stockton-on-Tees), 11/348; NZ419184; NP 85
East Hartford (township in Horton parochial chapelry in Woodhorn), 27/480; NZ266792; NP 78
East Hatley (parish), 4/119; TL295509; NP 147
East Hauxwell (township in Hauxwell), 42/191; SE172944; NP 91
East Heddon (township in Heddon on the Wall), 27/546; NZ141688; NP 77, 78
East Hendred (parish), 2/84; SU465875; NP 158
East Heslerton (township in West Heslerton), 41/156; SE932763; NP 93
East Hoathley (Easthothly, Easthoathly, East Hoathly) (parish), 36/133; TQ525168; NP 183
East Holme (parish), 10/284; SY904854; NP 178
East Horndon (parish), 12/412; TQ637896; NP 161
East Horsley (parish), 35/124; TQ099530; NP 170
East Hyde (hamlet in Luton), 1/124; TL126186; NP 147
East Ilsley (Market Ilsley) (parish), 2/118; SU493810; NP 158
East Keal (Easter Keal) (division in East Keal), 22/433A; TF378632; NP 114
East Keal (Easter Keal) (parish), 22/433A-B; NP 114
East Keal - East Fen (division in East Keal), 22/433B; TF380609; NP 114
East Kennett (East Kynett) (parish), 39/165; SU118665; NP 157, 167
East Keswick (township in Harewood), 43/405; SE358449; NP 96
East Kirkby (division in East Kirkby), 22/438A; TF330620; NP 114
East Kirkby (parish), 22/438A-B; NP 114
East Kirkby - West Fen (division in East Kirkby), 22/438B; TF326605; NP 114
East Knoyle (parish), 39/334; ST884317; NP 166
East Kynett (parish), 39/165; NP 157, 167
East Langdon (parish), 19/361; TR338463; NP 173
East Langton (township in Church Langton), 21/312; SP730929; NP 133
East Lavant (parish), 36/242; SU869099; NP 181
East Lavington (parish), 36/24; SU943176; NP 181
East Lavington (parish), 39/212-213; NP 167
East Lavington, 39/212; NP 167
East Layton (township in Stanwick St John), 42/35; NZ143107; NP 85
East Leake (Great Leke) (parish), 28/279; SK558268; NP 121
East Leicester Forest (extra-parochial), 21/177; SK529029; NP 121
East Lexham (parish), 25/276; TF860180; NP 125
East Lilburn (township in Eglingham), 27/132; NU044229; NP 71
East Lilling (division in township of Lillings Ambo in Sheriff Hutton), 42/602; SE655634; NP 92
East Lockinge (parish), 2/87; SU429862; NP 158
East Looe (chapelry in St Martin), 6/117; SX255535; NP 186
East Lulworth (parish), 10/280; SY856821; NP 178
East Lutton (division in township of Luttons Ambo in Weaverthorpe), 41/178; SE943693; NP 93
East Lydford (parish), 32/346; ST574308; NP 165, 177
East Maidstone (division in Maidstone), 19/218B; TQ778542; NP 172
East Malling (parish), 19/175; TQ699575; NP 171
East Marden (parish), 36/232; SU814145; NP 181
East Markham (parish), 28/65; SK742732; NP 103, 112
East Marton (division in township of Martons Both in Marton), 43/307; SD910515; NP 95
East Matfen (township in Stamfordham), 27/461; NZ050698; NP 77
East Meon (parish), 14/240; SU689223; NP 168, 180, 181
East Mersea (parish), 12/175; TM041146; NP 149

East Molesey (East Moulsey) (parish), 35/63; TQ145680; NP 170
East Moors (division in township of Helmsley in Helmsley), 42/492; SE603924; NP 92
East Morton, 11/84; NP 85
East Moulsey (parish), 35/63; NP 170
East Murton (Murton, East Morton) (township in Dalton-le-Dale), 11/84; NZ388469; NP 85
East Ness (township in Hovingham), 42/624; SE698788; NP 92
East Newton (East Newton and Ringborough) (division in township of Bewick and East Newton in Aldborough), 41/380; TA267374; NP 99
East Newton and Laysthorpe (township in Stonegrave), 42/622; SE641792; NP 92
East Norton (chapelry in Tugby), 21/281; SK788003; NP 122, 133
East Ogwell (parish), 9/418; SX834703; NP 188
East Orchard (Hartgrove or East Orchards) (parish), 10/14; ST836171; NP 178
East Peckham (parish), 19/212; TQ665494; NP 171
East Pennard (parish), 32/203; ST593370; NP 165, 166
East Plain (division in Cartmel), 20/64A; SD378752; NP 89
East Poringland (Great Poringland) (parish), 25/569; TG276015; NP 126, 137
East Portlemouth (parish), 9/490; SX758379; NP 187
East Preston (parish), 36/297; TQ071021; NP 182
East Pulham (division in Pulham), 10/94A; ST715095; NP 178
East Putford (parish), 9/58; SS376172; NP 163
East Quantoxhead (East Quantockshead) (parish), 32/232; ST133420; NP 164
East Quarter (division in township of Wolsingham in Wolsingham), 11/180; NZ098397; NP 84
East Rainham (parish), 25/164; NP 125
East Rainton (township in Houghton-le-Spring), 11/62; NZ334480; NP 78
East Ravendale (Great Ravendale) (parish), 22/170-171; NP 105
East Ravendale (Great Ravendale) (township in East Ravendale), 22/171; NP 105
East Raynham (East Rainham, Rainham St Mary) (parish), 25/164; TF886261; NP 125
East Retford (division in East Retford), 28/50B; SK705811; NP 103
East Retford (parish), 28/50A-B; NP 103
East Rounton (township in Rudby in Cleveland), 42/292; NZ432048; NP 85
East Rudham (division in East Rudham), 25/167; TF834289; NP 125
East Rudham (parish), 25/167-168; NP 125
East Ruston (parish), 25/221; TG358287; NP 126
East Scaleby (township in Scaleby), 7/22; NY461640; NP 76
East Scrafton (division in township of Caldbergh in Coverham), 42/154; SE090830; NP 90
East Shaftoe (township in Hartburn), 27/359; NZ059818; NP 77
East Shefford (parish), 2/137; SU386743; NP 158
East Shutford (township in Swalcliffe), 29/28; SP389401; NP 145
East Sleekburn (township in Bedlington), 27/431; NZ296835; NP 78
East Somerton (parish), 25/377; TG482198; NP 126
East Stockwith (township in Gainsborough), 22/128; SK793943; NP 104
East Stoke (parish), 10/283; SY872877; NP 178
East Stoke (division in East Stoke), 28/199C; SK789538; NP 112
East Stoke (parish), 28/199A-C; NP 112
East Stoke (township in East Stoke), 28/199B; SK760491; NP 112
East Stonehouse (parish), 9/461; SX465544; NP 187/1
East Stonesdale (division in township of Muker in Grinton), 42/127; NY901023; NP 90
East Stour (East Stower) (parish), 10/18; ST807236; NP 166
East Stower (parish), 10/18; NP 166

97

East Stratton (parish), 14/138; SU544401; NP 168
East Sunderland, 11/81; NP 78
East Sutton (parish), 19/298; TQ831486; NP 172
East Tanfield (township in Kirklington), 42/227; SE297788; NP 91
East Teignmouth (parish), 9/395; SX944743; NP 188
East Thickley (township in St Andrew Auckland), 11/219; NZ241257; NP 85
East Thornton (township in Hartburn), 27/350; NZ110870; NP 77
East Tilbury (parish), 12/430; TQ683779; NP 171
East Tisbury (parish), 39/332; ST959302; NP 167
East Tisted (parish), 14/176; SU700322; NP 168, 181
East Titherley (parish), 14/216; NP 167, 168
East Torrington (parish), 22/268; TF154838; NP 104, 105
East Tuddenham (parish), 25/497; TG086115; NP 125
East Tytherley (East Titherley) (parish), 14/216; SU299288; NP 167, 168
East Walton (parish), 25/281; TF747161; NP 124, 125
East Williamston (chapelry in Begelly), 55/127; SN104051; NP 152
East Winch (parish), 25/311; TF698164; NP 124
East Wittering (parish), 36/270; SZ808975; NP 181
East Witton (parish), 42/160-164; NP 91
East Witton Within (township in East Witton), 42/160; SE139816; NP 91
East Witton Without (division in township of East Witton Without in East Witton), 42/161; SE165845; NP 91
East Witton Without (township in East Witton), 42/161-163; NP 91
East Woodhay (parish), 14/6; SU421613; NP 168
East Woodyates (hamlet in Pentridge), 10/66; SU027201; NP 167, 179
East Worldham (parish), 14/124; SU751380; NP 169
East Worlington (parish), 9/126; SS775159; NP 163, 175
East Wretham (parish), 25/719; TL916906; NP 136
East Wykeham (parish), 22/200; TF229883; NP 105
Eastbourne (parish), 36/340; TV602987; NP 183
Eastbridge (parish), 19/420; TR078322; NP 184
Eastburn (East Burn) (township in Kirkburn), 41/232; SE993563; NP 98, 99
Eastbury and Bockhampton (tithing in Lambourn), 2/107C; SU350780; NP 158
Eastby (division in township of Embsay with Eastby in Skipton), 43/327; SE023545; NP 96
Eastchurch (parish), 19/100; TQ985702; NP 172
Eastcote (Eastcott) (tithing in Urchfont), 39/211; SU033549; NP 167
Eastcott, 39/211; NP 167
Eastcotts (township in Cardington), 1/55; TL080460; NP 147
Eastdean (parish), 36/339; TV562971; NP 183
Easter Keal (parish), 22/433A-B; NP 114
Eastergate (parish), 36/280; SU950051; NP 181
Easterton (tithing in Market Lavington), 39/213; SU038532; NP 167
Eastfield (hamlet in Peterborough, St John the Baptist), 26/4; TF202006; NP 123, 134
Eastham (hamlet in Eastham), 40/89; SO663680; NP 130
Eastham (parish), 5/428-435; NP 100, 109
Eastham (parish), 40/88-90; NP 130
Eastham (township in Eastham), 5/435; SJ360801; NP 100
Easthampstead (parish), 2/216; SU863663; NP 169
Easthams (tithing in Crewkerene), 32/483B; ST458099; NP 177
Easthoathly (parish), 36/133; NP 183
Easthope (parish), 31/435; SO565955; NP 129
Easthorpe (parish), 12/183; TL908213; NP 149
Easthorpe (division in township of Londesborough and Easthorpe in Londesborough), 41/191; SE888451; NP 98
Easthorpe (division in township of Appleton-le-Street in Appleton-le-Street), 42/637; SE733710; NP 92
Easthothly (parish), 36/133; NP 183
Eastington (parish), 13/270A-B; NP 156
Eastington (tithing in Eastington), 13/270A; SO784160; NP 156
Eastington (tithing in Northleach), 13/223; SP123127; NP 144
Eastleach Martin (parish), 13/293; SP205050; NP 157

Eastleach Turville (parish), 13/292; SP190066; NP 157
Eastling (parish), 19/234; TQ965564; NP 172
Eastnor (parish), 15/279; SO740370; NP 143
Eastoft (division in Crowle), 22/12; SE805146; NP 104
Eastoft (division of Eastoft township in Adlingfleet), 43/952; SE792164; NP 104
Eastoft (township in Crowle and Adlingfleet), 22/12, 43/952; NP 104
Easton (parish), 14/191; SU512308; NP 168
Easton (parish), 17/55; TL139709; NP 134
Easton (parish), 22/795; SK938265; NP 122, 123
Easton (parish), 25/495; TG138109; NP 125
Easton (parish), 34/280; TM285595; NP 137
Easton (township in Bridlington), 41/254; TA154691; NP 93
Easton Bavents (parish), 34/61; TM513781; NP 137
Easton Grey (parish), 39/37; ST881875; NP 156
Easton Maudit (parish), 26/369; SP889579; NP 133
Easton Neston (parish), 26/308; SP711502; NP 146
Easton on the Hill (parish), 26/32; TF019038; NP 123, 134
Easton Percy (Easton Piercy) (tithing in Kington St Michael), 39/69; ST882776; NP 156
Easton Piercy, 39/69; NP 156
Easton Royal (parish), 39/197; SU210600; NP 157
Easton-in-Gordano (St George) (parish), 32/4; ST515763; NP 155
Eastridge (tithing in Ramsbury), 39/180B; SU305735; NP 158
Eastrington (division in township of Eastrington in Eastrington), 41/17; SE805300; NP 98
Eastrington (parish), 41/15-21; NP 98, 98/1
Eastrington (township in Eastrington), 41/17-18; NP 98, 98/1
Eastrip (extra-parochial), 32/194; ST748463; NP 166
Eastrop (parish), 14/48; SU644518; NP 168
Eastrop (tithing in Highworth), 39/5C; SU208925; NP 157
Eastry (parish), 19/275; TR305543; NP 173
Eastville (parish), 22/462; TF414574; NP 114
Eastwell (parish), 19/292; TR011471; NP 172
Eastwell (parish), 21/97; SK775285; NP 122
Eastwick (parish), 16/71; TL431130; NP 148
Eastwick (township in Ellesmere), 31/68; SJ381373; NP 118
Eastwood (parish), 12/375; TQ850890; NP 162
Eastwood (township in Greasley), 28/177; SK463470; NP 112
Eathorpe (township in Wappenbury), 37/160; SP396691; NP 132
Eatington (parish), 37/276; NP 144, 145
Eaton (Eaton St Andrew) (parish), 25/408; TG210065; NP 126
Eaton (Eaton-under-Heywood) (parish), 31/427A-430; NP 129
Eaton (Eaton-under-Heywood) (township in Eaton), 31/427A; SO491888; NP 129
Eaton (parish), 21/96; SK793294; NP 122
Eaton (parish), 28/61; SK713780; NP 103
Eaton (township in Appleton), 2/4B; SP447031; NP 158
Eaton (township in Davenham), 5/182; SJ648704; NP 110
Eaton (township in Eccleston), 5/371; SJ403609; NP 109
Eaton (township in Prestbury), 5/59; SJ867657; NP 110
Eaton (township in Tarporley), 5/399; SJ569633; NP 109
Eaton (township in Lydbury North), 31/371; SO373891; NP 129
Eaton Bishop (parish), 15/196; SO441391; NP 142
Eaton Bray (parish), 1/140; SP982199; NP 147
Eaton Constantine (parish), 31/232; SJ597061; NP 118, 119
Eaton Hastings (parish), 2/36; SU260975; NP 157
Eaton Mascott (township in Berrington), 31/282; SJ540060; NP 118
Eaton Socon (parish), 1/11; TL152583; NP 134
Eaton upon Tern (township in Stoke upon Tern), 31/176; SJ653232; NP 119
Eaton-under-Heywood (parish), 31/427A-430; NP 129
Eaves (division in township of Woodplumpton in St Michaels on Wyre), 20/164; SD496371; NP 94
Eavestone (township in Ripon), 43/162; SE216682; NP 91
Ebberston (division of Ebberston township in Brompton), 42/419; SE914823; NP 92, 93
Ebberston (division of Ebberston township in Ebberston), 42/420; SE900860; NP 92
Ebberston (parish), 42/420; NP 92

Ebbesbourne Wake (Ebbesborne Wake) (parish), 39/346; ST991228; NP 167
Ebchester (parish), 11/164; NZ103551; NP 77
Ebnal (township in Whittington), 31/81; SJ321346; NP 118
Ebony (parish), 19/434; TQ919301; NP 184
Ebrington (hamlet in Ebrington), 13/29; SP183402; NP 144
Ebrington (parish), 13/28-30; NP 144
Ecchinswell (Itchingswell) (parish), 14/11; SU500587; NP 168
Eccles (Eccles next the Sea) (parish), 25/225; TG414288; NP 126
Eccles (parish), 20/541-563; NP 101
Eccles (parish), 25/672; TM011891; NP 136
Eccles next the Sea (parish), 25/225; TG414288; NP 126
Ecclesall Bierlow (township in Sheffield), 43/823; SK328842; NP 102, 111
Ecclesfield (parish), 43/787-821, 844; NP 102
Ecclesfield (township in Ecclesfield), 43/787-802, 844; NP 102
Eccleshall (parish), 33/131-150B; NP 119
Eccleshall (township in Eccleshall), 33/133; SJ830297; NP 119
Eccleshill (township in Blackburn), 20/304; SD705235; NP 95
Eccleshill (township in Bradford), 43/518; SE188360; NP 96
Eccleston (parish), 5/371-372; NP 109
Eccleston (township in Eccleston), 5/372; SJ402623; NP 109
Eccleston (division outside borough of St Helens of township of Eccleston in Prescot), 20/636; SJ480950; NP 100
Eccleston (division within borough of St Helens of township of Eccleston in Prescot), 20/635; SJ499948; NP 100
Eccleston (parish), 20/372-375; NP 100
Eccleston (township in Eccleston), 20/375; SD522173; NP 100
Eccleston (township in Prescot), 20/635-636; NP 100
Eccup (division in township of Adel cum Eccup in Adel), 43/396; SE287427; NP 96
Echelford (parish), 24/122; NP 170
Eckington (parish), 8/55A-B; NP 102, 103, 111
Eckington (township in Eckington), 8/55A; SK420800; NP 102, 103, 111
Eckington (parish), 36/191; NP 183
Eckington (parish), 40/219; SO930410; NP 143
Ecton (parish), 26/219; SP828633; NP 133
Edale (township in Castleton), 8/31; SK117858; NP 102, 111
Edburton (hamlet in Edburton), 36/114; TQ230110; NP 182
Edburton (parish), 36/114-115; NP 18
Edderton (township in Forden), 54/98; SJ232024; NP 117
Eddicliff (parochial division in Clun), 31/396-399; NP 128, 129
Eddicliff (township in Clun), 31/398; SO292648; NP 128
Eddisbury (township in Delamere), 5/403; SJ544700; NP 109
Eddlethorpe (township in Westow), 41/123; SE773663; NP 92
Eden-Owain (Edenowen) (township in Whitford), 50/37; SJ146772; NP 108
Edenbridge (parish), 19/197; TQ443460; NP 171
Edenhall (parish), 7/189; NY556317; NP 83
Edenham (parish), 22/705; TF050220; NP 123
Edenhope (township in Mainstone), 31/383; SO271889; NP 128, 129
Edenowen, 50/37; NP 108
Edensor (division in Edensor and Chatsworth township in Edensor), 8/80; SK243695; NP 111
Edensor (parish), 8/79-81; NP 111
Edensor and Chatsworth (township in Edensor), 8/79-80; NP 111
Edern (Edeyrn) (parish), 48/61; SH277399; NP 115
Edeyrn, 48/61; NP 115
Edgbaston (parish), 37/42; SP053847; NP 131
Edgcote (Edgcott) (parish), 26/330; SP510470; NP 145
Edgcott (parish), 3/115; SP672224; NP 145, 146
Edge (tithing in Painswick), 13/248; SO858102; NP 143, 156
Edge (township in Malpas), 5/328; SJ485502; NP 109
Edgefield (parish), 25/127; TG095348; NP 125
Edgeley (township in Whitchurch), 31/34; SJ554402; NP 118
Edgerley (township in Aldford), 5/364; SJ435579; NP 109
Edgerley (township in Kinnerley), 31/127; SJ350185; NP 118
Edgeworth (parish), 13/275; SO941063; NP 156, 157
Edgmond (parish), 31/188-196; NP 119
Edgmond (township in Edgmond), 31/192; SJ712192; NP 119
Edgton (parish), 31/412; SO387858; NP 129
Edgware (parish), 24/88; TQ192935; NP 160
Edgworth (township in Bolton le Moors), 20/394; SD743186; NP 95, 101
Edial (township in St Michael), 33/266C; SK079086; NP 120
Edingale (parish), 33/274; SK230120; NP 120
Edingley (parish), 28/161; SK672561; NP 112
Edingthorpe (parish), 25/48; TG315323; NP 126
Edington (township in Mitford), 27/411; NZ157827; NP 78
Edington (chapelry in Moorlinch), 32/212; ST391419; NP 165
Edington (parish), 39/230; ST937525; NP 166, 167
Edington, Hidden and Newtown (tithing in Hungerford), 2/140; SU351708; NP 158
Edith Weston (parish), 30/35; SK931051; NP 122
Edlaston and Wyaston (Edlaston) (parish), 8/226; SK180425; NP 120
Edlesborough (parish), 3/130; SP975185; NP 146, 147
Edleston (township in Acton), 5/286; SJ636508; NP 110
Edlingham (parish), 27/1901195; NP 71
Edlingham (township in Edlingham), 27/192; NU110080; NP 71
Edlington (parish), 22/369; TF219705; NP 113, 114
Edlington (parish), 43/921; SK543977; NP 103
Edmondbyers (division in parish and township of Edmondbyers), 11/167; NY985480; NP 77, 84
Edmondbyers (parish and township), 11/167-168; NP 77, 84
Edmondsham (division in Edmondsham), 10/71; SU068114; NP 179
Edmondsley (township in Chester le Street), 11/46; NZ229492; NP 78, 85
Edmondthorpe (parish), 21/110; SK865171; NP 122
Edmonton (parish), 24/83; TQ320937; NP 160, 161
Ednol (township in Old Radnor), 56/19; SO232647; NP 128
Edstaston (township in Wem), 31/40; SJ528328; NP 118
Edvin Loach (Edwin Loach) (parish), 15/94; SO664589; NP 130
Edvin Ralph (parish), 15/93; NP 130
Edwalton (parish), 28/256; SK595351; NP 121
Edwardstone (Edwardston) (parish), 34/486; TL942422; NP 149
Edwin Loach (parish), 15/94; NP 130
Edwinstowe (township in Edwinstowe), 28/81; SK626669; NP 112
Edwinstowe, 28/78-83; NP 112
Edworth (parish), 1/145; TL224412; NP 147
Edwyn Ralph (Edvin Ralph) (parish), 15/93; SO642580; NP 130
Efenechtyd (parish), 49/41; SJ108557; NP 108
Effard, 9/454; NP 187
Effingham (parish), 35/123; TQ115530; NP 170
Egdean (parish), 36/71; SU998207; NP 181
Egerton (parish), 19/295; TQ897467; NP 172
Egerton (township in Malpas), 5/334; SJ523515; NP 109
Egg Buckland (parish), 9/363A; SX504584; NP 187
Eggborough (Egborough) (township in Kellington), 43/642; SE578239; NP 97
Eggesford (parish), 9/122; SS684096; NP 175
Eggington (Egginton) (hamlet in Leighton Buzzard), 1/137; SP951247; NP 146, 147
Egginton (parish), 8/251; SK268283; NP 120, 121
Egginton, 1/137; NP 146, 147
Egglescliffe (parish), 11/341-344; NP 85
Egglescliffe (township in Egglescliffe), 11/344; NZ419142; NP 85
Eggleston (Egleston, Egglestone) (township in Middleton in Teesdale), 11/189B; NZ003272; NP 84
Egglestone Abbey (township in Startforth), 42/14; NZ062146; NP 84
Eggleton, 15/157
Egham (division in Egham registration subdistrict in Egham), 35/69A; SU992692; NP 159, 169, 170
Egham (division in Windsor registration subdistrict in Egham), 35/69B; TQ988723; NP 169
Egham (parish), 35/69A-B; NP 159, 169, 170
Egleston, 11/189B; NP 84
Egleton (Eggleton) (township in Bishops Frome), 15/157; SO637453; NP 143
Egleton (parish), 30/22; SK872072; NP 122

Eglingham (parish), 27/131-146; NP 71
Eglingham (township in Eglingham), 27/142; NU111193; NP 71
Egloshayle (parish), 6/47; SX025711; NP 185
Egloskerry (parish), 6/30; SX265869; NP 186
Eglwsilan (parish), 51/77-81; NP 154
Eglwys Eagle, 49/104; NP 108
Eglwys Fach (Eglwys-Vach, Eglwysbach) (division in Eglwys Fach), 49/4; SH810690; NP 108
Eglwys Fach (Eglwys-Vach, Eglwysbach) (parish), 48/15, 49/4; SH810690; NP 108
Eglwys Newydd, 46/20
Eglwys-Brewis (parish), 51/167; ST007690; NP 154
Eglwys-cymmin (parish), 47/56; NP 152
Eglwys-Vach (parish), 48/15, 49/4; NP 108
Eglwysael (parish), 44/56; NP 106
Eglwysbach (parish), 48/15, 49/4; NP 108
Eglwyscummin (Eglwys-cymmin, Eglwys-Cymmyn) (parish), 47/56; SN222110; NP 152
Eglwyseg (Eglwys Eagle) (township in Llangollen), 49/104; SJ215465; NP 108
Eglwysfair-a-churig (Eglwysfairacherig, Eglwysfairachyrig) (chapelry in Henllan Amgoed), 47/46; SN205275; NP 139
Eglwysilan (Eglwsilan) (parish), 51/77-81; NP 154
Eglwysrhos (parish), 48/5; SH793800; NP 107
Eglwyswrw (parish), 55/19; SN142385; NP 139
Egmanton (parish), 28/107; SK733688; NP 112
Egmere (parish), 25/80; TF896376; NP 125
Egremont (parish), 7/302; NY002114; NP 82
Egremont (parish), 47/87; SN097195; NP 139
Egton (division in township of Egton with Newland in Ulverston), 20/19; SD299832; NP 88, 89
Egton (township in Lythe), 42/376; NZ800040; NP 86, 92
Egton with Newland (township in Ulverston), 20/19-20; NP 88, 89
Eidda (township in Tir-Ifan (Ysbyty), 48/22; SH815475; NP 107, 116
Eirias (township in Llandrillo-yn-Rhos), 48/3; SH858779; NP 107
Eisey, 39/10A; NP 157
Elberton (parish), 13/360; ST601887; NP 156
Elcombe, Westlecot, Salthorp and Overtown (tithing in Wroughton), 39/94; SU117816; NP 157
Elcott (tithing in Preshute), 39/171; SU176702; NP 157
Elden (parish), 34/104; NP 136
Eldersfield (parish), 40/235; SO803317; NP 143
Eldmire (division in township of Eldmire with Crakehill in Topcliffe), 42/240; SE430750; NP 91
Eldon (township in St Andrew Auckland), 11/215; NZ245275; NP 85
Elerch (township in Llanbadarn fawr), 46/8; SN720870; NP 127
Elfenden (subdivision of Stacksteads division in Newchurch in Rossendale township in Whalley), 20/282; SD841222; NP 95
Elford (parish), 33/272; SK195105; NP 120
Elford (township in Bamburgh), 27/105; NU192306; NP 71
Elham (parish), 19/341; TR178446; NP 173
Eling (division in Eling), 14/299A; SU339130; NP 180
Eling (parish), 14/299A-C; NP 180
Elkington (parish), 26/118; SP626768; NP 132
Elksley (parish), 28/32; SK674756; NP 103, 112
Elkstone (parish), 13/210; SO973121; NP 143
Elland (division in township of Elland with Greetland in Halifax), 43/575; SE108206; NP 96, 102
Elland with Greetland (township in Halifax), 43/571, 574-575; NP 96, 102
Ellastone (Ellaston) (parish), 33/99-104; NP 111, 120
Ellastone (Ellaston) (township in Ellastone), 33/103; SK114434; NP 120
Ellel (township in Cockerham), 20/102; SD501547; NP 94
Ellenborough and Ewanrigg (Unerigg) (township in Dearham), 7/246; NY043354; NP 82
Ellenhall (parish), 33/171; SJ838258; NP 119
Ellenthorpe (Ellingthorpe) (township in Aldborough), 42/578; SE421671; NP 91
Ellerbeck (township in Osmotherley), 42/506; SE430970; NP 91

Ellerburn (parish), 42/422-426), NP 92, 92/1
Ellerburn (township in Ellerburn), 42/424; SE843843; NP 92, 92/1
Ellerby (township in Swine), 41/384; TA168380; NP 99
Ellerby (township in Lythe), 42/373; NZ800145; NP 86
Ellerker (township in Brantingham), 41/207; SE925295; NP 98
Ellerton (township in Cheswardine), 31/186; SJ718260; NP 119
Ellerton (parish), 41/39; NP 97
Ellerton Abbey (township in Downholme), 42/100; SE070965; NP 90
Ellerton Priory (township in Ellerton), 41/39; SE720400; NP 97
Ellerton-on-Swale (Ellerton-upon-Swale) (township in Catterick), 42/73; SE266979; NP 91
Ellerton-upon-Swale, 42/73; NP 91
Ellesborough (parish), 3/181; SP842067; NP 159
Ellesmere (township in Ellesmere), 31/73; SJ397353; NP 118
Ellesmere (parish), 31/53-74; NP 118
Ellingdon, 39/93; NP 157
Ellingham (parish), 14/317; SU160079; NP 179
Ellingham (parish), 25/618; TM362923; NP 137
Ellingham (parish), 27/121-126; NP 71
Ellingham (township in Ellingham), 27/121; NU160250; NP 71
Ellingstring (township in Masham), 42/168; SE179838; NP 91
Ellingthorpe, 42/578; NP 91
Ellington (parish), 17/56; TL161719; NP 134
Ellington (township in Woodhorn), 27/327; NZ275920; NP 78
Ellisfield (Illsfield) (parish), 14/102; SU640456; NP 168
Ellough, 34/48; TM455875; NP 137
Elloughton (parish), 41/211-213); NP 98
Elloughton (township in Elloughton), 41/212; SE952278; NP 98
Elm (parish), 4/9; TF455035; NP 124, 135
Elmbridge (township in Dodderhill), 40/59; SO892697; NP 130
Elmdon (parish), 12/9; TL470393; NP 148
Elmdon (parish), 37/79; SP169826; NP 131
Elmeley (parish), 43/703B, 704A-B, 713; NP 102, 102/1
Elmeley, 43/713; NP 102
Elmesthorpe (Elmsthorpe) (parish), 21/229; SP463958; NP 132
Elmington (hamlet in Oundle), 26/64; TL058891; NP 134
Elmire, 42/240; NP 91
Elmley (parish), 19/99; TQ942684; NP 172
Elmley Castle (parish), 40/212; SO985407; NP 143, 144
Elmley Lovett (parish), 40/33; SO868694; NP 130
Elmore (parish), 13/258; SO782153; NP 143
Elmsett (parish), 34/421; TM057471; NP 149
Elmstead (parish), 12/155; TM063240; NP 149
Elmsted (parish), 19/335; TR120456; NP 172, 173
Elmsthorpe (parish), 21/229; NP 132
Elmstone (parish), 19/133; TR258602; NP 173
Elmstone Hardwicke (Elmston Hardwick) (hamlet in Elmstone Hardwicke), 13/55; SO908273; NP 143
Elmstone Hardwicke (parish), 13/55-56; NP 143
Elmswell (parish), 34/235; TL992642; NP 136
Elmswell (Emswell) (division in township of Elmswell with Kelleythorpe in Great Driffield), 41/277; TA001588; NP 98, 99
Elmswell with Kelleythorpe (township in Great Driffield), 41/277-278; NP 98, 99
Elmton (parish), 8/61; SK510736; NP 103, 112
Elrington (township in parochial chapelry of Haydon in Warden), 27/597; NY866634; NP 77
Elsdon (Elsdon Ward) township in Elsdon), 27/241; NY950930; NP 70, 71, 77
Elsdon (parish), 27/237-242; NP 70, 71, 77
Elsenham (parish), 12/73; TL547251; NP 148
Elsfield (parish), 29/226; SP538101; NP 145, 158
Elsham (parish), 22/61; TA037126; NP 104
Elsing (parish), 25/343; TG051166; NP 125
Elslack (township in Broughton), 43/319; SD940490; NP 95
Elson (township in Ellesmere), 31/67; SJ381357; NP 118
Elstead (parish), 35/154; SU895425; NP 169
Elsted (parish), 36/11; SU815192; NP 181
Elsternwick, 41/407; NP 99
Elstob (township in Great Stainton), 11/271; NZ341237; NP 85

Elston (parish), 28/198; SK754474; NP 112
Elston (township in Preston), 20/222; SD600326; NP 94, 95
Elston Chapel (township in East Stoke), 28/199A; SK762482; NP 112
Elstow (parish), 1/53; TL052462; NP 147
Elstree (parish), 16/128; TQ196961; NP 160
Elstronwick (Elsternwick) (township in Humbleton), 41/407; TA230320; NP 99
Elswick (township in St Michaels on Wyre), 20/165; SD422384; NP 94
Elswick (township in St John), 27/647; NZ231638; NP 78
Elsworth (parish), 4/60; TL312630; NP 134
Eltham (parish), 19/18; TQ431743; NP 171
Eltisley (parish), 4/64; TL276598; NP 134
Elton (division in township of Elton in Bury), 20/422; SD791147; NP 101
Elton (division in township of Elton in Bury), 20/423; SD790110; NP 101
Elton (division in township of Elton in Bury), 20/424; SD80112; NP 101
Elton (division in township of Elton in Bury), 20/425; SD798088; NP 101
Elton (parish), 11/345; NZ395180; NP 85
Elton (parish), 15/20; SO457706; NP 129
Elton (parish), 17/13; TL946140; NP 134
Elton (parish), 28/217; SK770387; NP 122
Elton (township in Thornton le Moors), 5/416; SJ460754; NP 100, 109
Elton (township in Warmingham), 5/225; SJ727602; NP 110
Elton (township in Youlgreave), 8/116; SK219608; NP 111
Elton (township in Bury), 20/422-425; NP 101
Eltringham (township in Ovingham), 27/561; NZ077627; NP 77
Elvaston (parish), 8/295-296; NP 121
Elvaston (township in Elvaston), 8/296; SK410328; NP 121
Elveden (Elvedon, Elden) (parish), 34/104; TL815795; NP 136
Elvet (division in township of Elvet in St Oswald), 11/121; NZ281420; NP 85
Elvet (division in township of Elvet in St Oswald), 11/122; NZ272402; NP 85
Elvet (township in St Oswald), 11/121-123; NP 85
Elvetham (parish), 14/35; SU796570; NP 169
Elvington (parish and township), 41/82; SE647479; NP 97
Elwick (division of Elwick township in Belford), 27/79; NU110380; NP 64
Elwick (division of Elwick township in Belford), 27/80; NU107373; NP 64
Elwick (township in Hart), 11/243; NZ455332; NP 85
Elwick (township in Belford), 27/79-80; NP 64
Elwick Hall (parish), 11/242; NZ443297; NP 85
Elworthy (parish), 32/275; ST091336; NP 164
Ely College (extra-parochial), 4/28; TL541802; NP 135
Ely St Mary (division in Ely St Mary; includes Chettisham chapelry), 4/26; TL527799; NP 135
Ely St Mary (parish), 4/25-26, 29; NP 135
Ely Trinity (division in Ely Trinity), 4/27A; TL550813; NP 135
Ely Trinity (parish), 4/27A-B, 29; NP 135
Ely West Moor Fen (division in Ely St Mary and Ely Trinity), 4/29; TL575830; NP 135
Elyhaugh (township in Felton), 27/289; NZ156997; NP 71
Ember and Weston (hamlet in Thames Ditton), 35/62; TQ156661; NP 170
Emberton (parish), 32/113; NP 166
Emberton (division in Emberton), 3/36; SP897492; NP 146
Emberton (parish), 3/36-37; NP 146
Embleton (township in Brigham), 7/269; NY164299; NP 82
Embleton (township in Sedgefield), 11/241; NZ409304; NP 85
Embleton (parish), 27/147-156); NP 71
Embleton (township in Embleton), 27/150; NU226227; NP 71
Emborough (Emberrow, Emborrow) (parish), 32/113; ST614505; NP 166
Emborrow (parish), 32/113; NP 166
Embsay (division in township of Embsay with Eastby in Skipton), 43/326; SD999538; NP 95, 96
Embsay Moor (common to Embsay and Eastby divisions in Embsay with Eastby township in Skipton), 43/328; SE006547; NP 95, 96
Embsay with Eastby (township in Skipton), 43/326-328; NP 95, 96
Emington (Emmington) (parish), 29/265; SP741029; NP 159
Emley (Elmeley) (parish), 43/703B, 704A-B, 713; NP 102, 102/1
Emley (Elmeley) (township in Emley), 43/713; SE247129; NP 102
Emmanuel (township in Loughborough), 21/37A; SK533165; NP 121
Emmetts Vachery (division in township of Over Wyresdale in Lancaster), 20/133; SD574548; NP 94
Emmington (parish), 29/265; NP 159
Emneth (division in Emneth), 25/299A; TF501074; NP 124
Emneth (division in Marshland fen in Emneth), 25/299B; TF541057; NP 124
Emneth (parish), 25/299A-B; NP 124
Empingham (parish), 30/25; SK954083; NP 122, 123
Empshott (parish), 14/177; SU755316; NP 181
Emstrey (township in Atcham), 31/242; SJ519107; NP 118
Emswell, 41/277; NP 98, 99
Enborne (parish), 2/148; NP 158, 168
Enbourne (Enborne) (parish), 2/148; SU440652; NP 158, 168
Enchmarsh (township in Cardington), 31/433C; SO495970; NP 129
Endellion, 6/44; NP 185
Enderby (parish), 21/208; SP523996; NP 121, 132
Endon (township in Leek), 33/14; SJ920530; NP 110
Energlyn (hamlet in Eglwysilan), 51/80; ST157877; NP 154
Enfield (parish), 24/84; TQ320980; NP 160, 161
Enford (parish), 39/251-256); NP 167
Enford (tithing in Enford), 39/251; SU118510; NP 167
Englefield (parish), 2/168; SU624720; NP 158
English Bicknor (parish), 13/159; SO578151; NP 142, 143
English Frankton (township in Ellesmere), 31/55A; SJ452299; NP 118
English Street, Botchergate Ward (district in English Street township in St Mary [Carlisle]), 7/89; NY399558; NP 76/1
English Street, St Mary's Ward (district in English Street township in St Cuthbert [Carlisle]), 7/88; NY401559; NP 76/1
Englishcombe (parish), 32/42; ST717620; NP 166
Enmore (parish), 32/268; ST242352; NP 165
Ennerdale (township in St Bees), 7/289; NY141134; NP 82
Ensham (parish), 29/191; 145, 157
Enstone (parish), 29/91-96; NP 145
Entwistle (division in township of Briercliffe with Entwistle in Whalley), 20/273; SD895342; NP 95
Entwistle (township in Bolton le Moors), 20/393; SD721183; NP 95, 101
Enville (parish), 33/338; SO829878; NP 130
Epperstone (parish), 28/192; SK651495; NP 112
Epping (parish), 12/269-271; NP 161
Epping Street (hamlet in Epping), 12/269; TL450030; NP 161
Epping Upland (division of Epping Upland and Ryehill hamlet in Epping), 12/270; TL434042; NP 161
Epping Upland and Ryehill (hamlet in Epping), 12/270-271; NP 161
Eppleby (township in Gilling), 42/41; NZ143147; NP 85
Epsom (parish), 35/90; TQ205605; NP 170
Epwell (township in Swalcliffe), 29/26; SP358411; NP 145
Epworth (parish), 22/3; SE762039; NP 103, 104
Erbistock (division in Erbistock), 49/83; SJ340422; NP 118
Erbistock (division in Erbistock parish and township), 50/131; SJ358416; NP 118
Erbistock (parish and township), 49/83, 50/131; NP 118
Erddig (Erthig) (township in Gresford), 49/63; SJ326487; NP 109
Erdington (township in Aston), 37/32; SP118113; NP 131
Eriswell (parish), 34/111; TL751782; NP 135, 136
Erith (parish), 19/15; TQ494787; NP 161, 171
Erlas (township in Gresford), 49/64; SJ367507; NP 109
Erlestoke (Earl Stoke) (parish), 39/228; ST962534; NP 167
Ermington (parish), 9/449; SX622544; NP 187

101

Erpingham (parish), 25/140; TG198302; NP 126
Erringden (township in Halifax), 43/566; SE984252; NP 96
Erthig, 49/63; NP 109
Erwallo (township in Llangollen), 49/115; SJ222384; NP 117
Erwarton (Arwarton) (parish), 34/522; TM219349; NP 150
Eryholme (township in Gilling), 42/50; NZ330080; NP 85
Esclusam Below (township in Wrexham [Wrecsam]), 49/62; SJ313480; NP 109
Esclusham Above (township in Wrexham [Wrecsam]), 49/49; SJ285490; NP 108, 109
Escob and Castle (township in Llanwnog), 54/160; SO040940; NP 128
Escomb (parochial chapelry or township in St Andrew Auckland), 11/225; NZ184299; NP 85
Escrick (parish), 41/73-74; NP 97
Escrick (township in Escrick), 41/74; SE640415; NP 97
Esgair-maen (township in Llandinam), 54/149; SN997790; NP 128
Esh (Ashe, Ash) (township in Lanchester), 11/148; NZ196434; NP 85
Esher (parish), 35/60; TQ134639; NP 170
Esholt (township in Otley), 43/366; SE182405; NP 96
Eshott (Eshot) (township in Felton), 27/292; NY206977; NP 71
Eshton (township in Gargrave), 43/232A; SD926567; NP 95
Eskdale (chapelry in St Bees), 7/293; NY190035; NP 82
Eskdaleside (township in Whitby), 42/383; NZ870070; NP 86, 92
Eske (township in St John Beverley), 41/292; TA061431; NP 99
Eslington (township in Whittingham), 27/166; NU043123; NP 71
Espershields (Espershiels) (township in Bywell St Peter), 27/639; NZ003540; NP 77
Esse (parish), 12/34; NP 148, 149
Essendine (parish), 30/31; TF049126; NP 123
Essendon (parish), 16/123; TL273079; NP 147, 160
Essington (township in Bushbury), 33/309; SJ971038; NP 119, 120
Eston (parish), 42/335-336; NP 85, 86
Eston (township in Eston), 42/336; NZ552193; NP 86
Estyn (township in Hope), 50/125; SJ312579; NP 109
Etal (township in Ford), 27/42; NT945395; NP 64
Etchells, 5/7; NP 101
Etchells, 5/24; NP 101
Etchilhampton (tithing in All Cannings), 39/163; SU047603; NP 167
Etchingham (parish), 36/49; TQ708270; NP 183
Etherwick (division in township of Aldborough and Etherwick in Aldborough), 41/376; TA237372; NP 99
Eton (parish), 3/224; SU960782; NP 159
Eton College (extra-parochial), 3/225; SU967779; NP 159
Etterby (township in Stanwix), 7/73; NY388574; NP 76
Ettington (Eatington) (parish), 37/276; SP274483; NP 144, 145
Etton (parish), 26/20; TF137045; NP 123
Etton (parish), 41/223; SE956434; NP 98
Etwall (township in Etwall), 8/253; SK274319; NP 120, 121
Euny Redruth, 6/165; NP 189, 190
Euston (parish), 34/102; TL900790; NP 136
Euxton (township in Leyland), 20/334; SD553193; NP 94, 100
Evedon (parish), 22/592; TF095475; NP 113
Evenjobb (Evenjobb, Newcastle, Barland and Burfa) (township in Old Radnor), 56/21; SO270625; NP 128, 129
Evenley (Evenly) (parish), 26/364; SP582348; NP 145
Evenlode (parish), 40/249; SP223293; NP 144
Evenwood (division of Barony and Evenwood township in St Andrew Auckland), 11/196; NZ155245; NP 85
Evercreech (parish), 32/187; ST653392; NP 166
Everingham (parish), 41/100; SE818422; NP 98
Everleigh (Everley) (parish), 39/220; SU196546; NP 167
Everley (parish), 39/220; NP 167
Eversholt (parish), 1/110; SP987336; NP 147
Evershot (parish), 10/117; ST573045; NP 177
Eversley (division in Eversley), 14/25; SU783608; NP 169
Eversley (parish), 14/25; NP 169
Everthorpe (division in township of Drewton with Everthorpe in North Cave), 41/203; SE902317; NP 98, 98/1

Everton (parish), 1/60; TL193512; NP 147
Everton (parish), 28/4-6; NP 103
Everton (township in Walton on the Hill), 20/670; SJ360920; NP 100
Everton (township in Everton), 28/6; SK695925; NP 103
Evesham All Saints (parish), 40/206; SP042445; NP 144
Evesham St Lawrence (parish), 40/207; SP036544; NP 144
Evington (parish), 21/255; SK625030; NP 121
Ewart (township in Doddington), 27/49; NT952322; NP 64
Ewell (division in Ewell), 35/55; TQ222622; NP 170
Ewell (parish), 19/376; TR282498; NP 173
Ewell (parish), 35/55-56; NP 170
Ewelme (parish), 29/293; SU654914; NP 158
Ewenny (parish), 51/112; SS919773; NP 154
Ewesley (township in Netherwitton), 27/332; NZ061921; NP 77
Ewhurst (parish), 14/14; SU570572; NP 168
Ewhurst (parish), 35/164; TQ097391; NP 170, 182
Ewhurst (parish), 36/141; TQ790230; NP 184
Ewias Harold (parish), 15/225; NP 142
Ewloe Town (township in Hawarden), 50/7; SJ302656; NP 109
Ewloe Wood (township in Hawarden), 50/8; SJ276661; NP 108, 109
Ewshot (Ewshott) (tithing in Crondall), 14/33; SU821508; NP 169
Ewyas Harold (Ewias Harold) (parish), 15/225; SO389285; NP 142
Exbourne (parish), 9/205; SS603021; NP 175
Exbury (parish), 14/331; SZ432998; NP 180
Exelby, Leeming and Newton (township in Burneston), 42/221; SE308888; NP 91
Exeter, All Hallows Goldsmith Street (parish), 9/260; SX920927; NP 176/1
Exeter, All Hallows on the Walls (parish), 9/270; SX916924; NP 176/1
Exeter, Bedford Circus (precinct and chapelry in Exeter, Bedford Circus), 9/258; SX922927; NP 176/1
Exeter, Bradninch Precinct (extra-parochial), 9/256; SX921929; NP 176/1
Exeter, Castle Yard (extra-parochial), 9/255; SX921930; NP 176/1
Exeter, Cathedral Close (parish), 9/263; SX921925; NP 176/1
Exeter, Holy Trinity (parish), 9/275; SX922922; NP 176/1
Exeter, St David (parish), 9/254; SX916946; NP 176, 176/1
Exeter, St Edmund (parish), 9/271; SX915923; NP 176/1
Exeter, St George the Martyr (parish), 9/273; SX918923; NP 176/1
Exeter, St John (parish), 9/269; SX917924; NP 176/1
Exeter, St Kerrian (parish), 9/266; SX918926; NP 176/1
Exeter, St Lawrence (parish), 9/257; SX922928; NP 176/1
Exeter, St Leonard (parish), 9/276; SX926920; NP 176
Exeter, St Martin (parish), 9/262; SX920926; NP 176/1
Exeter, St Mary Arches (parish), 9/267; SX919925; NP 176/1
Exeter, St Mary Major (parish), 9/274; SX919923; NP 176/1
Exeter, St Mary Steps (parish), 9/272; SX918921; NP 176/1
Exeter, St Olave (parish), 9/268; SX918925; NP 176/1
Exeter, St Pancras (parish), 9/264; SX919927; NP 176/1
Exeter, St Paul (parish), 9/261; SX919928; NP 176/1
Exeter, St Petrock (parish), 9/265; SX919926; NP 176/1
Exeter, St Sidwell (parish), 9/277; SX928934; NP 176
Exeter, St Stephen (parish), 9/259; SX921927; NP 176/1
Exeter, St Thomas the Apostle (district in Exeter, St Thomas the Apostle), 9/253A; SX904932; NP 176
Exeter, St Thomas the Apostle (parish), 9/253A-B; NP 176
Exford (parish), 32/247; SS842394; NP 164
Exhall (parish), 37/99; SP342851; NP 132
Exhall (parish), 37/195; SP342851; NP 131, 144
Exminster (parish), 9/313; SX935879; NP 176
Exmoor Forest (extra-parochial), 32/246; SS770390; NP 163, 164
Exmouth (district in Littleham), 9/306B; SY002905; NP 176
Exmouth (district in Withycombe Raleigh), 9/307B; SY001912; NP 176
Exmouth, 9/306B, 9/307B; NP 176

Exning (parish), 34/214; TL626653; NP 135
Exton (parish), 14/236; SU606216; NP 168
Exton (parish), 30/12; SK923112; NP 122
Exton (parish), 32/279; SS936353; NP 164
Eyam (parish), 8/340-342; NP 111
Eyam (township in Eyam), 8/342; SK217774; NP 111
Eyam Woodland (township in Eyam), 8/341; SK233797; NP 111
Eydon (parish), 26/272; SP539502; NP 145
Eye (parish), 15/26; NP 129
Eye (parish), 26/11; TF235030; NP 123
Eye (parish), 34/138; TM153733; NP 136, 137
Eye and Dunsden (division in Sonning), 29/319; SU730780; NP 159
Eye, Morton and Ashton (township in Eye), 15/26; SO510640; NP 129
Eyesbatch (parish), 15/162; SO694483; NP 143
Eyeworth (Eyworth) (parish), 1/65; TL255453; NP 147
Eyeworth Walk (extra-parochial division in New Forest extra-parochial), 14/302B; SU223144; NP 179
Eyeworth Walk (Fritham) (division in Bramshaw), 14/305C; SU235140; NP 179
Eyeworth Walk (in New Forest and Bramshaw) 14/302B, 14/305C; NP 179
Eyford (parish), 13/78; SP142247; NP 144
Eyke (parish), 34/381; TM331505; NP 150
Eynesbury (hamlet in Eynesbury), 17/107; TL200577; NP 134
Eynesbury (parish), 17/107-110; NP 134
Eynsford (Eynesford) (parish), 19/59; TQ542657; NP 171
Eynsham (Ensham) (parish), 29/191; SP423101; NP 145, 157
Eysey (Eisey) (hamlet in Eysey), 39/10A; SU122946; NP 157
Eysey (Eisey) (parish), 39/10A-B; NP 157
Eythorne (parish), 19/349; TR282498; NP 173
Eyton (parish), 15/72; SO476618; NP 129
Eyton (township in Bangor-is-y-coed), 49/81; SJ358448; NP 109, 118
Eyton and Little Shrawardine (division in Alberbury Lower Quarter township in Alberbury), 31/297; SJ382145; NP 118
Eyton and Plowden (township in Lydbury North), 31/369; SO383873; NP 129
Eyton upon the Weald Moors (Eyton upon the Wildmoors) (parish), 31/215; SJ650150; NP 118
Eyton upon the Wildmoors (parish), 31/215; NP 118
Eyworth (parish), 1/65; NP 147

F
Faccombe (parish), 14/4; SU390577; NP 168
Faceby (township in Whorlton), 42/308; NZ498034; NP 85, 91, 92
Faddiley (township in Acton), 5/288; SJ581526; NP 109
Fadmoor (township in Kirkbymoorside), 42/474; SE669896; NP 92
Faenol (township in St Asaph [Llanelwy]), 50/68; SH989758; NP 108
Faenor, 45/73; NP 141, 154
Failsworth (township in Manchester), 20/513; SD900012; NP 101
Failworth (subdivision of Spotland Nearer Side division in Spotland township in Rochdale), 20/455; SD892139; NP 101
Fairburn (township in Ledsham), 43/467; SE467286; NP 97
Fairfield (township in Hope), 8/15; SK072744; NP 111
Fairfield (parish), 19/437; TQ970264; NP 184
Fairford (parish), 13/296; SP157019; NP 157
Fairhaugh (township in Alwinton), 27/176; NT880125; NP 70
Fairhurst (sub-division in Westnall with Waldershaigh division in township of Bradfield in Ecclesfield), 43/816; SK266946; NP 102
Fairlight (parish), 36/157; TQ863122; NP 184
Fairnley (township in Hartburn), 27/339; NZ006889; NP 77
Fairstead (Fairsted) (parish), 12/215; TL768167; NP 148, 149
Fairwood, 10/70; NP 179
Fakenham (parish), 25/160; TF932311; NP 125
Fakenham (Great Fakenham) (parish), 34/123; TL903763; NP 136

Falcott, 26/324; NP 145
Falcutt (Falcott) (hamlet in Wappenham), 26/324; SP594427; NP 145
Faldingworth (division in Faldingworth), 22/213A; TF057847; NP 104
Faldingworth (parish), 22/213A-B; NP 104
Faldingworth - Lissingleys (division in Faldingworth), 22/213B; TF085838; NP 104
Falfield and Morton (Falfield and Moorton) (tithing in Thornbury), 13/358D; ST655905; NP 156
Falkenham (parish), 34/450; TM300390; NP 150
Falkingham (parish), 22/663; NP 123
Fallibroome (Fallybroome) (township in Prestbury), 5/43; SJ892754; NP 101, 110
Fallodon (Falloden) (township in Embleton), 27/149; NU200231; NP 71
Fallowfield (township in St John Lee), 27/449; NY932682; NP 77
Fallowlees (township in Rothbury), 27/261; NZ014948; NP 71, 77
Fallybroome, 5/43; NP 101, 110
Falmer (parish), 36/206; TQ356086; NP 183
Falmouth (district in Falmouth), 6/179; SW808322; NP 190
Falmouth (parish), 6/179-180; NP 190
Falmouth - Borough (district in Falmouth), 6/180; SW809327; NP 190
Falsgrave (township in Scarborough), 42/402; TA028879; NP 93
Falstone (parish), 27/216-217; NP 70, 76, 77
Fangfoss (Fangfoss with Spittle) (parish), 41/114; SE760532; NP 98
Far Oxenhope (division in township of Haworth in Bradford), 43/524; SE038338; NP 96
Farcet (Farcett) (chapelry in Stanground), 17/10; TL233928; NP 134
Fareham (parish), 14/295; SU575075; NP 180
Farewell (parish), 33/254; SK079117; NP 120
Farforth cum Maidenwell (parish), 22/330; TF320792; NP 105
Faringdon (parish), 2/33-34; NP 157, 158
Faringdon (township in Faringdon), 2/33; SU293970; NP 157, 158
Faringdon (parish), 14/174; NP 168, 169, 181
Farington (township in Penwortham), 20/338; SD535245; NP 94
Farlam (parish), 7/57-58; NP 76
Farleigh (Farley) (parish), 35/98; TQ375607; NP 171
Farleigh Hungerford (Hungerford Farley) (parish), 32/92; ST799576; NP 166
Farleigh Wallop (parish), 14/100; SU619471; NP 168
Farlesthorpe (Farlstorpe) (parish), 22/414; TF483743; NP 105, 114
Farleton (township in Melling), 20/86; SD581672; NP 89
Farleton (township in Beetham), 38/130; SD535810; NP 89
Farley (chapelry in Alderbury), 39/362; SU225295; NP 167
Farley (division in Swallowfield), 2/188; SU752650; NP 169
Farley (parish), 35/98; NP 171
Farley (township in Alton), 33/108; SK070450; NP 111, 120
Farley Chamberlayne (parish), 14/211; SU396274; NP 168
Farley, Wyke and Bradley (township in Much Wenlock), 31/451; SJ640020; NP 119
Farlington (parish), 14/286; SU682066; NP 180, 181
Farlington (parish), 42/596; SE613677; NP 92
Farlow (township in Stottesden), 31/588; SO640805; NP 130
Farlsthorpe (parish), 22/414; NP 105, 114
Farmanby (township in Ellerburn), 42/423; SE828830; NP 92, 92/1
Farmborough (parish), 32/85; ST655605; NP 166
Farmcote (hamlet in Guiting Power), 13/68; SP059281; NP 144
Farmington (parish), 13/224; SP141148; NP 144
Farnborough (parish), 2/113; SU438820; NP 158
Farnborough (parish), 14/30; SU874550; NP 169
Farnborough (parish), 19/70; TQ441641; NP 171
Farnborough (parish), 37/265; SP439502; NP 145
Farndale East (Farndale East Side) (township in Lastingham), 42/461; SE675975; NP 92

103

Farndale High Quarter with Bransdale East Side, Farndale West Side or High Quarter, 42/473; NP 92
Farndale Low Quarter (township in Kirkbymoorside), 42/472; SE662936; NP 92
Farndale West (Farndale High Quarter with Bransdale East Side, Farndale West Side or High Quarter) (township in Kirkbymoorside), 42/473; SE640980; NP 92
Farndish (parish), 1/21; SP931635; NP 133
Farndon (parish), 5/349-353; NP 109
Farndon (parish), 28/152; SK775515; NP 112
Farndon (township in Farndon), 5/350; SJ419546; NP 109
Farne Islands (extra-parochial), 27/87; NU235375; NP 71
Farnham (parish), 10/62; ST952148; NP 179
Farnham (parish), 12/68; TL472246; NP 148
Farnham (parish), 34/273; TM371591; NP 137
Farnham (parish), 35/146-150; NP 169
Farnham (parish), 43/135-138; NP 91, 96
Farnham (township in Alwinton), 27/188C; NT971029; NP 71
Farnham (tithing in Farnham), 35/148; SU842471; NP 169
Farnham (township in Farnham), 43/135; SE352607; NP 91, 96
Farnham Royal (hamlet in Farnham Royal), 3/226; SU960840; NP 159
Farnham Royal (parish), 3/226-227B; NP 159
Farnham Tollard (tithing in Tolland Royal), 10/63; NP 179
Farnhill (township in Kildwick), 43/349; SE005466; NP 95, 96
Farnhurst (parish), 36/3; NP 181
Farningham (parish), 19/58; TQ557669; NP 171
Farnley (township in Leeds), 43/496; SE252312; NP 96
Farnley (township in Otley), 43/372; SE203476; NP 96
Farnley Tyas (township in Almondbury), 43/768; SE171133; NP 102
Farnsfield (parish), 28/163; SK640567; NP 112
Farnworth (township in Deane), 20/565; SD730058; NP 101
Farringdon (parish), 9/281; SY015913; NP 176
Farringdon (Faringdon) (parish), 14/174; SU703354; NP 168, 169, 181
Farringdon Gurney (parish), 32/494; ST632558; NP 166
Farsley (division in township of Calverley with Farsley in Calverley), 43/513; SE214351; NP 96
Farthinghoe (parish), 26/352; SP538399; NP 145
Farthingstone (Farthingston) (parish), 26/261; SP614552; NP 132, 145
Fartown (division in township of Huddersfield in Huddersfield), 43/748; SE145185; NP 102
Farway (parish), 9/287; SY176955; NP 176
Faugh and Fenton (township in Hayton), 7/49; NY512557; NP 76
Fauld (township in Hanbury), 33/206; SK185290; NP 120
Faulk Stapleford, 5/390; NP 109
Faulkbourne (Faulkbourn) (parish), 12/219; TL793166; NP 149
Faulsgreen (township in Prees), 31/23; SJ589323; NP 118, 119
Faversham (parish), 19/153-154; NP 172
Faversham In-Liberty (division in Faversham), 19/154; TR018613; NP 172
Faversham Out-Liberty (division in Faversham), 19/153; TR036604; NP 172
Fawcet-Forest, 38/109
Fawcett Forest (township in Kendal), 38/109; SD526036; NP 83, 89
Fawden, 27/513; NP 78
Fawdington (township in Cundall), 42/571; SE441730; NP 91
Fawdon (Fawden) (township in Gosforth), 27/513; NZ225693; NP 78
Fawdon (township in Ingram), 27/128; NU028152; NP 71
Fawfieldhead (township in Alstonfield), 33/85; SK080620; NP 111
Fawkham (parish), 19/56; TQ591671; NP 171
Fawler (hamlet in Sparsholt), 2/99; SU321885; NP 158
Fawler (hamlet in Charlbury), 29/129; SP377176; NP 145
Fawley (parish), 2/110; SU393809; NP 158
Fawley (parish), 3/211; SU755865; NP 159
Fawley (parish), 14/332; SU452027; NP 180
Fawley (township in Fownhope), 15/174B; SO582300; NP 142

Fawnog (hamlet in Llanwenog), 46/84; SN485509; NP 139, 140
Fawns (township in Kirkwhelpington), 27/380; NZ006853; NP 77
Fawsley (parish), 26/249; SP560566; NP 132
Faxfleet (township in South Cave), 41/204; SE861267; NP 98
Faxton (parish), 26/164; SP782858; NP 133
Fazakerley (township in Walton on the Hill), 20/674; SJ383963; NP 100
Fazeley (township in Tamworth), 33/285A; SK203021; NP 120
Fearby (township in Masham), 42/171; SE196814; NP 91
Fearnhead (division in township of Poulton with Fearnhead in Warrington), 20/616; SJ634910; NP 101
Featherstone (township in Haltwhistle), 27/576; NY680610; NP 76
Featherstone (township in Wolverhampton), 33/314; SJ935055; NP 119
Featherstone (parish), 43/613-616; NP 97, 103
Featherstone (township in Featherstone), 43/615; SE421213; NP 97
Feckenham (division in Feckenham), 40/136A; SP020617; NP 130, 131
Feckenham (division in Feckenham), 40/136B; SP033661; NP 131
Feckenham (parish), 40/136A-B; NP 130, 131
Feering (parish), 12/185; TL875212; NP 149
Feetham (division in township of Melbecks in Grinton), 42/110; SD997991; NP 90
Feizor (division in township of Lawkland in Clapham), 43/278; SD792678; NP 90
Felaws Houses (extra-parochial), 34/466; TM169445; NP 150/1
Felbrigg (parish), 25/37; TG201395; NP 126
Feliskirk, 42/536; NP 91
Felixkirk (Feliskirk) (parish), 42/536-539; NP 91, 92
Felixkirk (Feliskirk) (township in Felixkirk), 42/536; SE465841; NP 91
Felixstowe (Felixstow) (parish), 34/451; TM317366; NP 150
Felkington (township in Norham), 27/13; NT942445; NP 64
Felkirk (parish), 43/679-683; NP 102, 103
Felley (extra-parochial), 28/169; SK485515; NP 112
Felliscliffe (township in Hampsthwaite), 43/155A; SE233564; NP 96
Fellside (township in Whickham), 11/24; NZ195585; NP 78
Felmersham (hamlet in Felmersham), 1/26A; SP993577; NP 134
Felmersham (parish), 1/26A-B; NP 134
Felmingham (parish), 25/214; TG249290; NP 126
Felpham (parish), 36/285; SU964008; NP 181
Felsted (parish), 12/193; TL700206; NP 148
Felsham (parish), 34/348A; TL945565; NP 149, 150
Feltham (parish), 24/124; TQ103730; NP 170
Felthorpe (parish), 25/351; TG165177; NP 125, 126
Felton (parish), 15/150; SO575480; NP 142
Felton (parish), 27/271, 285-292; NP 71
Felton (parish), 32/18; NP 155, 156, 165
Felton (township in Felton), 27/288; NU164019; NP 71
Felton Butler (township in Great Ness), 31/130; SJ393175; NP 118
Feltwell (St Mary and St Nicholas in Feltwell, Feltwell St Mary and St Nicholas) (parish), 25/700; TL687910; NP 135, 136
Feltwell Anchor (extra-parochial), 25/698; TL632886; NP 135
Fen Ditton (parish), 4/96; TL497601; NP 135
Fen Drayton (parish), 4/58; TL340690; NP 134
Fencot and Murcot (Fencott and Murcott) (hamlet in Charlton on Otmoor), 29/116; SP588164; NP 145
Fenemere, Walford, Eyton, Yeaton and Prescott (Fennemere) (township in Baschurch), 31/147; SJ445208; NP 118
Fenham (township in Holy Island), 27/28; NU084407; NP 64
Fenham (township in St Andrew), 27/642; NZ220658; NP 78
Feniton (parish), 9/239; ST101001; NP 176
Fenn and Fern, 15/144
Fennemere, 31/147; NP 118
Fenny Bentley (parish), 8/172; SK177498; NP 111
Fenny Compton (parish), 37/263; SP421522; NP 145
Fenny Drayton (parish), 21/220; SP350962; NP 132

Fenny Stratford (division in Simpson), 3/65; SP883346; NP 146
Fenny Stratford (hamlet in Bletchley), 3/66; SP868343; NP 146
Fenny Stratford (in Simpson and Bletchley) 3/65-66; NP 146
Fenrother (township in Hebburn parochial chapelry), 27/306; NZ174918; NP 78
Fenstanton (Fen Stanton) (parish), 17/88; TL311769; NP 134
Fenton (parish), 22/608; SK884511; NP 113
Fenton (township in Kettlethorpe), 22/241; SK839773; NP 104
Fenton (township in Wooler), 27/53; NT971348; NP 64
Fenton Culvert (township in Stoke-on-Trent), 33/29; SJ898441; NP 119
Fenton Vivian (township in Stoke-on-Trent), 33/28; SJ898449; NP 110, 119
Fenwick (township in Kyloe parochial chapelry in Holy Island), 27/25; NU062403; NP 64
Fenwick (township in Stamfordham), 27/462; NZ055729; NP 77
Fenwick (township in Campsall), 43/643; SE596162; NP 103
Feock (parish), 6/162; SW816394; NP 190
Ferensby, 43/137; NP 91, 96
Fernham (hamlet in Shrivenham), 2/44; SU295918; NP 158
Fernhill (township in Whittington), 31/82; SJ319329; NP 118
Fernhurst (Farnhurst) (parish), 36/3; SU883273; NP 181
Fernilee (township in Hope), 8/14; SK022769; NP 111
Fernsby, 43/137; NP 91, 96
Ferrensby (Ferrinsby, Ferensby, Fernsby) (township in Farnham), 43/137; SE367602; NP 91, 96
Ferring (parish), 36/299; TQ094034; NP 182
Ferrinsby, 43/137; NP 91, 96
Ferry Corner (extra-parochial), 22/742; TF252482; NP 123
Ferry Fryston (intermixed lands in Ferry Fryston and Pontefract), 43/620; SE478234; NP 97
Ferry Fryston (parish), 43/619-620; NP 97
Ferry Fryston (township in Ferry Fryston), 43/619; SE460260; NP 97
Ferryhill (township in Merrington), 11/223; NZ286331; NP 85
Fersfield (parish), 25/740; TM068831; NP 136
Ferwig (parish), 46/100
Festiniog (parish), 52/3; NP 116
Fetcham (parish), 35/88; TQ148560; NP 170
Fewcot (hamlet in Stoke Lyne), 29/66C; SP541283; NP 145
Fewston (parish), 43/377-381; NP 91, 96
Fewston (township in Fewston), 43/378; SE182556; NP 96
Ffestiniog (Festiniog) (parish), 52/3; SH700440; NP 116
Fforest (hamlet in Llandingat), 47/16; SN773381; NP 140
Fforest (hamlet in Llanycrwys), 47/4A; SN640470; NP 140
Fiddington and Natton (hamlet in Ashchurch), 13/49; SO926316; NP 143
Fiddington (parish), 32/261; ST219403; NP 165
Field (township in Leigh), 33/117; SK027332; NP 120
Field Dalling (parish), 25/74; TG009389; NP 125
Field Head (division in township of Hawkshead and Monk Coniston with Skelwith in Hawkshead), 20/42; SD343994; NP 89
Fifehead Magdalen (parish), 10/22; ST773211; NP 166
Fifehead Neville (parish), 10/89; ST764108; NP 178
Fifield (hamlet in Benson), 29/302; SU628926; NP 158
Fifield (parish), 29/138; SP242191; NP 144
Fifield (tithing in Enford), 39/255; SU136500; NP 167
Fifield Bavant (Fifield Brabant) (parish), 39/347; SU009250; NP 167
Figheldean (parish), 39/258; SU165474; NP 167
Filby (parish), 25/385; TG477134; NP 126
Filey (parish), 41/165; TA/404-406
Filey (parish), 42/404-406; NP 93
Filey (township in Filey), 41/165; TA114812; NP 93
Filkins (hamlet in Broadwall), 29/159B; SP233051; NP 157
Filleigh (parish), 9/72; SS661278; NP 163
Filley, 6/156; NP 190
Fillingham (parish), 22/226; SK938858; NP 104
Fillongley (parish), 37/72; SP275865; NP 131, 132
Filton (parish), 13/387; ST602792; NP 155, 156
Fimber (township in Wetwang), 41/186; SE902609; NP 92, 98
Fincham (Fincham St Michael and Fincham St Martin) (parish), 25/514; TF693058; NP 124

Finchampstead (parish), 2/201; SU790638; NP 169
Finchingfield (parish), 12/56; TL692339; NP 148
Finchley (parish), 24/81; TQ263902; NP 160
Findern (township in Mickleover), 8/260; SK310304; NP 121
Findon (Finden) (parish), 36/214; TQ126091; NP 182
Finedon (Thingdon) (parish), 26/151; SP918715; NP 133
Fineshade, 26/36; SP980980; NP 134
Fingal, Fingall (parish), 42/193-196; NP 91
Fingal, Fingall, 42/195; NP 91
Fingest (parish), 3/208; SU788919; NP 159
Finghall (Fingal, Fingall) (parish), 42/193-196; NP 91
Finghall (Fingal, Fingall) (township in Finghall), 42/195; SE183198; NP 91
Fingland (township in Bowness-on-Solway), 7/110; NY263574; NP 75
Fingringhoe (parish), 12/172; TM034196; NP 149
Finmere (parish), 29/72; SP632332; NP 145
Finningham (parish), 34/133; TM063699; NP 136
Finningley (township in Finningley), 28/2; SK685995; NP 103
Finningley (parish), 28/1-2, 43/929-930; NP 103
Finsbury (division in St Luke), 24/48E; TQ326827; NP 160/1
Finsthwaite (division in township of Colton in Colton), 20/51; SD366877; NP 89
Finstock (hamlet in Charlbury), 29/130; SP363165; NP 145
Firbank (township in Kirkby Lonsdale), 38/118; SD616941; NP 89
Firbeck (township in Laughton en le Morthen), 43/913; SK564885; NP 103
Firby (township in Westow), 41/121; SE746665; NP 92
Firby (township in Bedale), 42/211; SE269862; NP 91
Firsby (parish), 22/218-219; NP 104
Firsby (parish), 22/485; TF460630; NP 114
Fishburn (township in Sedgefield), 11/231; NZ365321; NP 85
Fisher Street (township in St Mary [Carlisle]), 7/94; NY399561; NP 76/1
Fisherton Anger (parish), 39/321; SU136304; NP 167
Fisherton de la Mere (parish), 39/268; SU001389; NP 167
Fisherwick (township in St Michael), 33/263; SK178095; NP 120
Fishguard [Abergwaun] (parish), 55/31; SM962362; NP 138
Fishlake (parish), 43/948-949; NP 103
Fishlake (township in Fishlake), 43/948; SE652144; NP 103
Fishley (parish), 25/394; TG399115; NP 126
Fishtoft (division adjoining East Fen in Fishtoft), 22/756B; TF352463; NP 114
Fishtoft (division in Fishtoft), 22/756A; TF363427; NP 114, 124
Fishtoft (parish), 22/756A-C; TF363427; NP 114, 124
Fishtoft - West Fen (division in Fishtoft), 22/756C; TF315490; NP 114
Fishwick (township in Preston), 20/217; SD561293; NP 94
Fiskerton (parish), 22/358; TF063726; NP 113
Fiskerton (township in Rolleston), 28/157; SK730502; NP 112
Fitling (township in Humbleton), 41/409; TA250350; NP 99
Fittleton (parish), 39/257; SU185506; NP 167
Fittleworth (parish), 36/70; TQ012202; NP 181
Fitz (parish), 31/149; SJ445178; NP 118
Fitzhead (parish), 32/292; ST117286; NP 164
Fivehead (parish), 32/412; ST352229; NP 177
Fixby (township in Halifax), 43/576; SE126193; NP 96
Fladbury (hamlet in Fladbury), 40/184; SO992471; NP 143, 144
Fladbury (parish), 40/184-189; NP 143, 144
Flagg (township in Bakewell), 8/104; SK133687; NP 111
Flamborough (parish), 41/248; TA233702; NP 93
Flamstead (Flamsted) (parish), 16/92; TL072142; NP 147
Flasby (division in township of Flasby with Winterburn in Gargrave), 43/232B; SD951566; NP 95
Flasby with Winterburn (township in Gargrave), 43/232B-C; NP 95
Flashbrook (township in Adbaston), 33/162; SJ741252; NP 119
Flat Holm (division in Cardiff St Mary), 51/10; ST222649; NP 154
Flaunden (parish), 16/135; TL012001; NP 159
Flawborough (township in Staunton), 28/201; SK782432; NP 122
Flawith (township in Alne), 42/581; SE479655; NP 91

Flax Bourton (Bourton) (parish), 32/15; ST508694; NP 155, 165
Flaxby (township in Goldsborough), 43/111; SE402582; NP 96, 97
Flaxley (parish), 13/148; SO688158; NP 143
Flaxton (division of Flaxton township in Foston), 42/658; SE682631; NP 92
Flaxton (division of township in Bossall), 42/659; SE680618; NP 92
Flaxton (township in Foston and Bossall), 42/658-659; NP 92
Fleckney (parish), 21/326; SP643932; NP 132
Fledborough (Fledborough cum Woodcoates) (parish), 28/69; SK792720; NP 112, 113
Fleeceston, 41/162; NP 93
Fleet (division in Crondall), 14/34B; SU813545; NP 169
Fleet (division in Fleet), 22/777A; TF373222; NP 124
Fleet (parish), 10/260; SY633803; NP 178
Fleet (parish), 22/777A-B; NP 123, 124
Fleet Fen (division in Fleet), 22/777B; TF332132; NP 123, 124
Fleet Marston (parish), 3/143; SP778160; NP 146
Fleetham (township in Bamburgh), 27/99; NU199292; NP 71
Fleetwood (division in township of Thornton in Poulton-le-Fylde), 20/176; SD324463; NP 94
Fleggburgh (parish), 25/389; NP 126
Flemingston (Flemingstone) (parish), 51/168; ST018701; NP 154
Flempton (parish), 34/203; TL809698; NP 136
Fletching (parish), 36/57; TQ421253; NP 183
Fletton (parish), 17/8; TL194963; NP 134
Flimby (parish), 7/247; NY031338; NP 82
Flint (Y Fflint) (parish), 50/25; SJ245715; NP 108
Flintham (parish), 28/196; SK740460; NP 112, 122
Flinton (township in Humbleton), 41/406; TA216360; NP 99
Flitcham (parish), 25/171; TF723268; NP 124, 125
Flitteris Park (division in Oakham), 30/15; SK825085; NP 122
Flitton (division in Flitton), 1/106; TL052348; NP 147
Flitton (parish), 1/105-106; NP 147
Flitwick (parish), 1/108; TL032345; NP 147
Flixborough (parish), 22/23-24A; NP 104
Flixborough (township in Flixborough), 22/23; SE881149; NP 104
Flixton (Fleeceston) (township in Folkton), 41/162; TA038786; NP 93
Flixton (parish), 20/539-540; NP 101
Flixton (parish), 34/14; TM517956; NP 137
Flixton (parish), 34/526; TM317862; NP 137
Flixton (township in Flixton), 20/540; SJ742945; NP 101
Flockton (township in Thornhill), 43/721; SE240149; NP 102
Floore (parish), 26/253-254; NP 132
Floore, 26/253; NP 132
Flordon (parish), 25/604; TM190977; NP 137
Flore (Flower, Floore) (hamlet in Flore), 26/253; SP646612; NP 132
Flore (Flower, Floore) (parish), 26/253-254; NP 132
Flotterton (township in Rothbury), 27/249; NT994007; NP 71
Flower (parish), 26/253-254; NP 132
Flower, 26/253; NP 132
Flowton (parish), 34/422; TM080473; NP 149
Flyford Flavell (parish), 40/143; SO980540; NP 130, 143
Fobbing (parish), 12/401; TQ717852; NP 161
Fockerby (township in Adlingfleet), 43/954; SE839196; NP 98, 104
Foggathorpe (township in Bubwith), 41/26; SE762372; NP 97, 98
Foleshill (parish), 37/145; SP347828; NP 132
Folke (parish), 10/46; ST659127; NP 178
Folkestone (parish), 19/382-383; NP 173
Folkestone - Parish (division in Folkestone), 19/383; TR216374; NP 173
Folkestone - Town (division in Folkestone), 19/382; TR233364; NP 173
Folkingham (Falkingham) (parish), 22/663; TF074331; NP 123
Folkington (parish), 36/186; TQ575049; NP 183
Folksworth (parish), 17/16; TL149903; NP 134

Folkton (Folkton and East and West Flotmanby) (township in Folkton), 41/163; TA063788; NP 93
Folkton (parish), 41/162-163; NP 93
Follifoot (township in Spofforth), 43/100; SE335530; NP 96
Follithorpe (division in township of Walton in Walton), 43/74; SE456468; NP 97
Fonaby (in Caistor), 22/104; NP 104
Fonthill Bishop (parish), 39/283; ST942342; NP 166, 167
Fonthill Gifford (parish), 39/282; ST920315; NP 166, 167
Fontmell Magna (parish), 10/12-13; NP 166, 178
Fontmell Magna (tithing in Fontmell Magna), 10/12; ST860173; NP 178
Foolow (township in Eyam), 8/340; SK193776; NP 111
Foots Cray (parish), 19/22; TQ463724; NP 171
Forcett (township in Gilling), 42/42; NZ173117; NP 85
Ford (division in township of Orrell and Ford in Sefton), 20/688; SJ340990; NP 100
Ford (division in Alberbury Lower Quarter township in Alberbury), 31/295; SJ402129; NP 118
Ford (division in Ford), 31/294; SJ415130; NP 118
Ford (Fordsbridge, The Ford) (extra-parochial), 15/103; SO514554; NP 129, 142
Ford (parish), 27/37-42; NP 64
Ford (parish), 36/288; SU998035; NP 181
Ford (tithing in Idmiston), 39/310A; NP 167
Ford (township in Bishop Wearmouth), 11/72; NZ362570; NP 78
Ford (township in Ford), 27/40; NT953372; NP 64
Ford (township in Ford and Alberbury) 31/294-295; NP 118
Ford Common (lands common to Ford and Etal townships in Ford), 27/41; NT960385; NP 64
Forden (Fordon) (township in Hunmanby), 41/168; TA045755; NP 93
Forden (parish), 54/97A-103; NP 117, 128
Forden (township in Forden), 54/101; SO231999; NP 117, 128
Fordham (parish), 4/43; TL514739; NP 135
Fordham (parish), 12/123; TL930280; NP 149
Fordham (parish), 25/521; TL595995; NP 124, 135
Fordingbridge (parish), 14/312; SU155139; NP 179
Fordington (parish), 10/245; SY687898; NP 178
Fordington, 22/417; NP 114
Fordon, 41/168; NP 93
Fordsbridge (extra-parochial), 15/103; NP 129, 142
Fordwich (division inside Canterbury municipal boundary in Fordwich), 19/138B; TR182582; NP 173
Fordwich (division outside Canterbury municipal boundary in Fordwich), 19/138A; TR181595; NP 173
Fordwich (parish), 19/138A-B; NP 173
Fore Fen (division in Wigtoft), 22/767B; TF260410; NP 123
Foreign Liberty (East Foreign Liberty and West Foreign Liberty and Town Liberty) (township in Cleobury Mortimer), 31/548; SO686753; NP 130
Foreign of Tenbury (Tenbury Foreign with Kyrewood) (township in Tenbury), 40/82; SO600673; NP 129, 130
Foremark (parish), 8/302-303; SK347265; NP 121
Foremark (township in Foremark), 8/303; SK334253; NP 121
Forest (hamlet in Talgarth), 45/86B; SO180290; NP 141
Forest (township in Westbury), 31/317; SJ309082; NP 118
Forest and Frith (township in Middleton in Teesdale), 11/188A; NY839324; NP 84
Forest of Bowland (Lower Division) (division in township of Forest of Bowland (Lower Division) township in Whalley), 43/285; SD669468; NP 95
Forest of Bowland (Lower Division) (township in Whalley), 43/285-287; NP 95
Forest Quarter (township in Stanhope), 11/170; NY846394; NP 84
Foresthill (parish), 29/234; SP578077; NP 158
Formby (division in township of Formby in Walton on the Hill), 20/676A; SD298082; NP 100
Formby (township in Walton on the Hill), 20/675-677; NP 100
Forncett St Mary (parish), 25/646; TM168952; NP 137
Forncett St Peter (parish), 25/647; TM150931; NP 136, 137
Fornham All Saints (parish), 34/199; TL838670; NP 136

Fornham St Genevieve (parish), 34/200; TL844687; NP 136
Fornham St Martin (parish), 34/198; TL862671; NP 136
Forrabury (parish), 6/22A; SX100915; NP 185
Forsbrook (township in Dilhorne), 33/70B; SJ965415; NP 110
Forscote (parish), 32/103; NP 166
Forthampton (parish), 13/52; SO852326; NP 143
Forthington, 22/417; NP 114
Forton (parish), 33/167; SJ764207; NP 119
Forton (township in Cockerham or Garstang), 20/145; SD484511; NP 94
Foscote (Foxcott, Foscott) (parish), 3/76; SP722358; NP 146
Fosdyke (division in Fosdyke), 22/771A; TF318332; NP 123
Fosdyke - Holland Fen (division in Fosdyke), 22/771B; TF244492; NP 114
Fosdyke), 22/771A-B; NP 114, 123
Fosham and Carlton (township in Aldborough), 41/378; TA215387; NP 99
Foston (parish), 21/249; SP605954; NP 132
Foston (parish), 22/616; SK861429; NP 122
Foston (parish), 42/656-658; NP 92
Foston (township in Scropton), 8/245; SK188318; NP 120
Foston (township in Foston), 42/656; SE696648; NP 92
Foston on the Wolds (parish), 41/265-268; NP 99
Foston on the Wolds (township in Foston on the Wolds), 41/267; TA101554; NP 99
Fotherby (parish), 22/192; TF312918; NP 105
Fotheringay (parish), 26/43; TL067976; NP 123
Fotherington, 22/417; NP 114
Foulby (township in Wragby), 43/671; SE398178; NP 103
Foulden (parish), 25/690; TL770992; NP 124, 125, 135, 136
Foulk Stapleford (Faulk Stapleford) (township in Tarvin), 5/390; SJ487628; NP 109
Foulmire (parish), 4/178; NP 148
Foulness (parish), 12/382; TR010924; NP 162
Foulridge (division in township of Foulridge in Whalley), 20/267; SD893427; NP 95
Foulridge (township in Whalley), 20/267-268; NP 95
Foulsham (parish), 25/197; TG040249; NP 125
Fountains Earth (township in Kirkby Malzeard), 43/204; SE130720; NP 90, 91
Four Towers (extra-parochial), 32/355; ST738332; NP 166
Fourstones (township in Warden), 27/607; NY890680; NP 77
Fovant (parish), 39/328; SU005288; NP 167
Fowberry (township in Chatton), 27/74; NU032287; NP 64, 71
Fowey (parish), 6/124; SX113523; NP 186, 190
Fowlmere (Foulmire) (parish), 4/178; TL420448; NP 148
Fownhope (parish), 15/174A-B; NP 142, 143
Fownhope (township in Fownhope), 15/174A; SO584350; NP 142, 143
Foxcote (Foscote) (parish), 32/103; ST718552; NP 166
Foxcott, 3/76; NP 146
Foxcotte (Foxcott) (division in Andover), 14/72; SU343573; NP 168
Foxearth (parish), 12/40; TL836448; NP 149
Foxhall (parish), 34/447; TM225441; NP 150
Foxhill (division in township of Barton upon Irwell in Eccles), 20/545; SJ740970; NP 101
Foxholes (division in township of Foxholes with Boythorpe in Foxholes), 41/174; TA016731; NP 93
Foxholes (parish), 41/174-176; NP 93
Foxholes with Boythorpe (township in Foxholes), 41/174-175; NP 93
Foxley (parish), 25/266; TG041221; NP 125
Foxley (parish), 39/36; ST891859; NP 157
Foxt (division of Foxt township in Checkley), 33/113; SK037482; NP 111
Foxt (division of Foxt township in Ipstones), 33/75C; SK032488; NP 111
Foxt (township in Ipstones and Checkley) 33/75, 113
Foxton (division in township of Foxton and Shotton in Sedgefield), 11/235; NZ359249; NP 85
Foxton (division in township of Thimbleby in Osmotherley), 42/505; SE426958; NP 91

Foxton (parish), 4/162; TL416480; NP 148
Foxton (parish), 21/222; SP709903; NP 133
Foxton and Shotton (township in Sedgefield), 11/234-235; NP 85
Foy (parish), 15/246; SO611287; NP 142, 143
Fradley (township in Alrewas), 33/222B; SK160130; NP 120
Fradswell (township in Colwich), 33/191B; SJ992312; NP 1119, 120
Fraisthorpe (township in Carnaby), 41/259; TA150620; NP 99
Framfield (parish), 36/131; TQ505194; NP 183
Framingham Earl (parish), 25/570; TG274023; NP 126, 137
Framingham Pigot (parish), 25/571; TG279040; NP 126
Framlingham (parish), 34/255; TM285635; NP 137
Frampton (parish), 10/225; SY623940; NP 178
Frampton (division in Frampton), 22/764A; TF326392; NP 123, 124
Frampton (parish), 22/764A-B; NP 123, 124
Frampton - Holland Fen (division in Frampton), 22/764B; TF279435; NP 123
Frampton Cotterell (parish), 13/391; ST620824; NP 156
Frampton Mansell (hamlet in Sapperton), 13/303; SO923013; NP 156, 157
Frampton upon Severn (parish), 13/269; SO754066; NP 156
Framsden (parish), 34/284; TM206595; NP 137
Framwellgate (division in township of Framwellgate in St Oswald), 11/130; NZ272454; NP 85
Framwellgate (division in township of Framwellgate in St Oswald), 11/131; NZ270430; NP 85
Framwellgate (township in St Oswald), 11/130-131; NZ270430; NP 85
Frankby (township in West Kirby), 5/458; SJ242865; NP 100
Frankley (parish), 40/39; SO990800; NP 130
Frankton (parish), 37/133; SP421705; NP 132
Frankton, 31/88; NP 118
Frankwell (township in St Chad Shrewsbury), 31/268; SJ480132; NP 118
Frant (division in Frant), 19/206; TQ601381; NP 171
Frant (division in Frant), 36/45; TQ589362; NP 171, 183
Frant (parish), 19/206, 36/45; NP 171, 183
Frating (parish), 12/156; TM087227; NP 149, 150
Freasley and Quarry Hill (township in Polesworth), 37/12; SP244998; NP 120, 131
Freckenham (parish), 34/210; TL680720; NP 135
Freckleton (township in Kirkham), 20/200A; SD432295; NP 94
Freeby (chapelry in Melton Mowbray), 21/76; SK203204; NP 122
Freefolk (Freefolk Manor) (parish), 14/61; SU489461; NP 168
Freeford (extra-parochial), 33/269; SK139074; NP 120
Freeford (township in St Michael), 33/268; SK130071; NP 120
Freeholders Quarter (township in Longhorsley), 27/295; NZ132938; NP 71, 78
Freethorpe (parish), 25/466; TG409053; NP 126
Fremington (parish), 9/39; SS516296; NP 163
Fremington (division in township of Reeth in Grinton), 42/103A; NZ032008; NP 90
Frenchay and Hambrook (tithing in Winterbourne), 13/390; ST638776; NP 156
Frensham (parish), 35/152-153; NP 169, 181
Frensham (tithing in Frensham), 35/152; SU840420; NP 169
Frenze (parish), 25/757; TM140800; NP 136
Fresden (tithing in Highworth), 39/5D; SU228928; NP 157
Freshford (parish), 32/90; ST782600; NP 166
Freshwater (parish), 18/7; SZ345872; NP 180
Fressingfield (parish), 34/80; TM269773; NP 137
Freston (parish), 34/518; TM170384; NP 150
Fretherne (parish), 13/267; SO739090; NP 143, 156
Frettenham (parish), 25/253; TG246184; NP 126
Freystrop (parish), 55/90; SM957118; NP 151
Friars Mere (division in Saddleworth with Quick township in Rochdale), 43/738-739; NP 101, 102
Frickley (division in township and parish of Clayton with Frickley), 43/873; SE463084; NP 103
Fridaythorpe (parish), 41/187; SE877599; NP 92, 98

Friern Barnet (Fryern Barnet) (parish), 24/82; TQ276924; NP 160
Friesden (hamlet in Pitstone), 3/134; TL018111; NP 147
Friesthorpe (Fristhorpe) (parish), 22/212; TF069829; NP 104
Frieston (division adjoining East Fen in Frieston), 22/757B; TF363482; NP 114
Frieston (Freiston) (division in Frieston), 22/757A; TF378438; NP 114, 124
Frieston (Freiston) (parish), 22/757A-C; NP 114, 124
Frieston - West Fen (division in Frieston), 22/757C; TF323562; NP 114
Frilford (township in Marcham), 2/55; SU435972; NP 158
Frilsham (parish), 2/163; SU548735; NP 158
Frimley (hamlet in Ash), 35/72; SU891588; NP 169
Frindsbury (parish), 19/47; TQ748710; NP 171, 172
Fring (parish), 25/99; TF741345; NP 124, 125
Fringford (parish), 29/75; SP588274; NP 145
Frinsted (Frinstead) (parish), 19/228; TQ893564; NP 172
Frinton (parish), 12/163; TM223198; NP 150
Frisby (township in Galby), 21/290; SK709018; NP 122
Frisby on the Wreak (parish), 21/116; SK699267; NP 122
Friskney (parish), 22/478; TF364547; NP 114
Fristhorpe (parish), 22/212; NP 104
Friston (parish), 36/338; TV549985; NP 183
Frith Bank (division in Sibsey), 22/469A; TF314479; NP 114
Frith Bank - Wildmore Fen (division in Sibsey), 22/469B; TF290490; NP 114
Fritham, 14/305C; NP 179
Frithelstock (parish), 9/60; SS453186; NP 163
Friths (extra-parochial), 22/752; NP 123
Frithville (parish), 22/464; TF303503; NP 114
Frittenden (parish), 19/317; TQ817409; NP 172
Fritton (parish), 25/640; TM229931; NP 137
Fritton (parish), 34/8; TG467005; NP 126, 137
Fritwell (parish), 29/65; SP530297; NP 145
Frocester (parish), 13/312; SP783032; NP 156
Frodesley (parish), 31/441; SJ510005; NP 118, 129
Frodingham (parish), 22/24B-27; NP 104
Frodingham (township in Frodingham), 22/26; SE891109; NP 104
Frodsham (parish), 5/405-412; NP 100, 109
Frodsham Lordship (Frodsham) (township in Frodsham), 5/409; SJ515765; NP 100, 109
Frodsham Township (Frodsham) (township in Frodsham), 5/408; SJ509785; NP 100, 109
Froggatt (township in Bakewell), 8/86; SK248771; NP 111
Frolesworth (Frowlesworth) (parish), 21/243; SP504906; NP 132
Frome (Frome Selwood) (parish), 32/124; ST777462; NP 166
Frome St Quintin (parish), 10/119; ST602028; NP 177, 178
Frome Vauchurch (Froome Vauchurch) (parish), 10/146; SY594974; NP 177, 178
Froome Bishop (parish), 15/156-157; NP 143
Froome Bishop, 15/156; NP 143
Froome Whitfield, 10/217; NP 178, 178/1
Frostenden (parish), 34/63; TM480813; NP 137
Frosterley (township in Stanhope), 11/176; NY028376; NP 84
Frostrow and Soolbank (division in township of Sedbergh in Sedbergh), 43/262; SD670925; NP 89
Frotherley (township in Bywell St Peter), 27/635; NZ030570; NP 77
Frowlesworth (parish), 21/243; NP 132
Froxfield (parish), 14/241; SU714272; NP 168, 181
Froxfield (parish), 39/183; SU290688; NP 157, 158
Froyle (parish), 14/114; SU754439; NP 169
Fryern Barnet (parish), 24/82; NP 160
Fryerning (parish), 12/296; TL632010; NP 161
Fryton (township in Hovingham), 42/631; SE687747; NP 92
Fugglestone St Peter (parish), 39/322; SU117317; NP 167
Fulbeck (parish), 22/600A; SK950600; NP 113
Fulbourn (Fulbourn All Saints and St Vigors) (parish), 4/102; TL525553; NP 135, 148
Fulbrook (parish), 29/154; SP258135; NP 144
Fulbrook (parish), 37/214; SP245604; NP 131

Fulfen (Fulfin) (township in St Michael), 33/262; SK144094; NP 120
Fulfin, 33/262; NP 120
Fulford (parish), 41/64-66; NP 97
Fulford (township in Stone), 33/61; SJ958383; NP 119
Fulham (parish), 24/41; TQ250770; NP 170
Fulking (hamlet in Edburton), 36/115; TQ243118; NP 182
Full Sutton (parish), 41/115; SE744554; NP 98
Fullaway (tithing in All Cannings), 39/164; SU034591; NP 167
Fulletby (parish), 22/383; TF296732; NP 114
Fulmer (parish), 3/233; SU998857; NP 159
Fulmodeston cum Croxton (Fulmodeston with Croxton, Fulmodestone-cum-Croxton) (parish), 25/152; TF992301; NP 125
Fulnetby (chapelry in Rand), 22/261; TF093796; NP 104
Fulshaw (township in Wilmslow), 5/71; SJ839802; NP 101
Fulstone (township in Kirkburton), 43/733; SE185080; NP 102
Fulstow (parish), 22/180; TF332973; NP 105
Fulwell (township in Monkwearmouth), 11/13; NZ395598; NP 78
Fulwood (extra-parochial), 28/95; SK470570; NP 112
Fulwood (township in Lancaster), 20/137; SD549322; NP 94
Fundenhall (parish), 25/609; TM147963; NP 137
Funtington (parish), 36/239; SU814073; NP 181
Furneaux Pelham (parish), 16/62; TL438273; NP 148
Furnivals Inn (extra-parochial), 24/12; TQ312817; NP 160/1
Furtho (parish), 26/337; SP737427; NP 146
Furzy Park and Portfield (extra-parochial), 55/163; SM935150; NP 151
Fwthog (township in Cwmvoy), 15/210; SO277252; NP 141, 142
Fyfield (parish), 2/25; SU415985; NP 158
Fyfield (parish), 12/277; TL564074; NP 161
Fyfield (parish), 14/76; SU296481; NP 168
Fyfield (parish), 39/203; SU146596; NP 157
Fylingdales (township in Whitby), 42/389; NZ947037; NP 93
Fylingdales Moor (common to Hawsker with Stainsacre and Fylingdales townships in Whitby), 42/388; SE910980; NP 92, 93

G
Gaddesby (parish), 21/121; SK689135; NP 121, 122
Gagingwell (hamlet in Enstone), 29/92; SP403249; NP 145
Gainford (division in township of Gainford in Gainford), 11/303; NZ180170; NP 85
Gainford (parish), 11/296-312; NP 84, 85
Gainford (township in Gainford), 11/302-303; NP 85
Gainsborough (division in Gainsborough), 22/131; SK817896; NP 104
Gainsborough (parish), 22/127-131; NP 104
Gainsborough (township in Gainsborough), 22/127, 131; NP 104
Galby (parish), 21/289-290; NP 122, 133
Galby (township in Galby), 21/289; SK698009; NP 122, 133
Gallowhill (township in Bolam), 27/388; NZ105815; NP 77
Gallt Melyd (parish), 50/53-54; NP 108
Gallt Melyd, 50/54
Galphay (division in Azerley township in Ripon and Kirkby Malzeard), 43/197-198; NP 91
Galphay (division in Azerley township in Kirkby Malzeard), 43/198; SE255730; NP 91
Galphay (division in township of Azerley in Ripon), 43/197; SE259718; NP 91
Gamblesby (township in Addingham), 7/178; NY636405; NP 83
Gamblesby, 7/120; NP 75
Gambleside (division in township of Newchurch in Rossendale in Whalley), 20/279; SD837273; NP 95
Gamlingay (parish), 4/117; TL248528; NP 147
Gamston (parish), 28/62; SK710763; NP 103, 112
Gamston (township in West Bridgford), 28/258; SK603371; NP 121
Ganarew (parish), 15/262; SO532165; NP 142
Ganstead (township in Swine), 41/389; TA149338; NP 99
Ganthorpe (township in Terrington), 42/652; SE688701; NP 92
Ganton (parish), 41/158; SE987764; NP 93
Garboldisham (parish), 25/733; TM005823; NP 136
Garendon Park (extra-parochial), 21/351; SK499197; NP 121

Garford (chapelry in Marcham), 2/56; SU426955; NP 158
Garforth (parish), 43/474; SE410330; NP 96, 97
Gargrave (parish), 43/229-232C; NP 95
Gargrave (township in Gargrave), 43/231; SD926542; NP 95
Garmondsway Moor (extra-parochial), 11/230; NZ345345; NP 85
Garneddwen (township in Ysceifiog), 50/93; SJ174701; NP 108
Garrigill (township in Alston), 7/177; NY740420; NP 83
Garrison Side (extra-parochial), 41/335; TA104290; NP 99/1
Garriston (township in Hauxwell), 42/192; SE158924; NP 91
Garsdale (division in township of Sedbergh in Sedbergh), 43/264; SD750915; NP 90
Garsdon (parish), 39/25; ST974878; NP 157
Garsington (parish), 29/240; SP578024; NP 158
Garstang 9parish), 20/143-156; NP 94
Garstang (township in Garstang), 20/155; SD491456; NP 94
Garston (township in Childwall), 20/650; SJ395850; NP 100
Garth (hamlet in Merthyr Tydfil), 51/72; SO057090; NP 141, 154
Garth (township in Guilsfield [Cegidfa]), 54/80; SJ204102; NP 117
Garth and Ystrad (township in Llandewi-Brefi), 46/44; SN654559; NP 140
Garth-gelin, 54/106; NP 128
Garth-Gynyd (hamlet in Gelligaer), 51/75C; ST130980; NP 154
Garth-Helyn, 54/169A; NP 128
Garthbeibo (parish), 54/24; SH945155; NP 117
Garthbrengy (parish), 45/37; SO050336; NP 141
Garthele, 46/50
Gartheli (Garthele, Garthely) (township in Llandewi-Brefi), 46/50; SN586559; NP 140
Garthelin (Garth-Helyn) (township in Kerry [Llanfihangel-yng-Ngheri]), 54/169A; SO098952; NP 128
Garthely, 46/50
Garthgellin (Garth-gelin) (township in Bettws), 54/106; SO138960; NP 128
Garthorpe (parish), 21/105; SK833209; NP 122
Garthorpe (township in Luddington), 22/14; SE853187; NP 98, 104
Garton (division in Garton with Grimston township in Roos), 41/410; TA286349; NP 99
Garton (East Garton) (division in Garton with Grimston township in Garton), 41/411; TA271345; NP 99
Garton (parish), 41/411-412; NP 99
Garton on the Wolds (parish), 41/236; SE970600; NP 98
Garton with Grimston (township in Roos and Garton), 41/410-411
Garveston (Garvestone) (parish), 25/548; TG027085; NP 125
Garway (parish), 15/233; SO468226; NP 142
Gasper (hamlet in Stourton), 32/356; ST762320; NP 166
Gasthorpe (parish), 25/732; TL981817; NP 136
Gatcombe (parish), 18/31; SZ486854; NP 180
Gate (sub-division in Bradfield division in township of Bradfield in Ecclesfield), 43/810; SK293927; NP 102
Gate Burton (parish), 22/134; SK842832; NP 104
Gate Fulford (division inside borough in township of Gate Fulford in Fulford), 41/66; SE608502; NP 97
Gate Fulford (division outside borough in township of Gate Fulford in Fulford), 41/65; SE621483; NP 97
Gate Fulford (township in Fulford), 41/65-66; NP 97
Gate Helmsley (parish), 42/667; SE693557; NP 97
Gateford (township in Worksop), 28/28; SK571814; NP 103
Gateforth (township in Brayton), 43/453; SE563287; NP 97
Gateley (parish), 25/192; TF961252; NP 125
Gatenby (township in Burneston), 42/222; SE328875; NP 91
Gatesend (parish), 25/106; NP 125
Gateshead (parish), 11/23; NZ256618; NP 78
Gatton (parish), 35/93; TQ275526; NP 170
Gaunt's Earthcott (tithing in Almondsbury), 13/368; ST636843; NP 156
Gautby (parish), 22/365; TF172722; NP 113
Gawcott (chapelry in Buckingham), 3/82; SP677322; NP 146
Gawsworth (parish), 5/66; SJ889702; NP 110
Gaydon (parish), 37/261; SP367541; NP 132, 145
Gayhurst (Gothurst) (parish), 3/45; SP845549; NP 146

Gayles (township in Kirkby Ravensworth), 42/24; NZ116067; NP 84, 85
Gayton (parish), 25/283; TF640207; NP 124, 125
Gayton (parish), 26/306; SP705546; NP 133, 146
Gayton (parish), 33/125; SJ982290; NP 119
Gayton (township in Heswall), 5/474; SJ276805; NP 100
Gayton le Marsh (parish), 22/317; TF434851; NP 105
Gayton le Wold (parish), 22/277; TF244856; NP 105
Gayton Thorpe (parish), 25/282; TF751185; NP 124, 125
Gaywood (parish), 25/288; TF640207; NP 124
Gazeley (hamlet in Gazeley), 34/217; TL727646; NP 135
Gazeley (parish), 34/218; NP 135, 136
Gedding (parish), 34/525; TL948581; NP 136
Geddington (parish), 26/133; SP891826; NP 133
Gedgrave (extra-parochial), 34/375; TM408488; NP 150
Gedling (parish), 28/228-230; NP 121
Gedling (township in Gedling), 28/228; SK619432; NP 121
Gedney (division in Gedney), 22/778; TF410240; NP 124
Gedney (parish), 22/779; NP 123, 124
Gedney Hill (hamlet in Gedney), 22/779; TF344124; NP 123, 124
Geldeston (parish), 25/622; TM396921; NP 137
Gelli Loveday (township in Ysceifiog), 50/90; SJ150740; NP 108
Gelligaer (parish), 51/75A-E; NP 154
Gelligason (township in Llanfair Caereinion), 54/55; SJ106049; NP 117
Gellydhg (hamlet in Merthyr Tydfil), 51/71; SO036506; NP 154
Geltsdale (Gertsdale) (extra-parochial), 7/61; NY600530; NP 76
Gembling (township in Foston on the Wolds), 41/266; TA110570; NP 99
George Nympton (Nympton St George) (parish), 9/74; SS708238; NP 163
Georgeham (parish), 9/21; SS459401; NP 163
Germansweek (parish), 9/200; SX442944; NP 175
Germoe (parish), 6/197; SW586298; NP 189
Gerrans (parish), 6/157; SW872350; NP 190
Gertsdale, 7/61; NP 76
Gestingthorpe (parish), 12/50; TL810380; NP 149
Gibbet Hills (extra-parochial), 22/739A; TF210430; NP 123
Gidleigh (Gidley) (parish), 9/382; SX654876; NP 175
Giggleswick (parish), 43/247-252; NP 90, 95
Giggleswick (township in Giggleswick), 43/248; SD798642; NP 90
Gil (Keel) (township in Meifod), 54/40; SJ180141; NP 117
Gilberdyke (division in township of Eastrington in Eastrington), 41/19A; SE825295; NP 98/1
Gilberdyke (township in Eastrington), 41/19A-E; NP 98/1
Gilcrux (parish), 7/229; NY112378; NP 82
Gildersome (township in Batley), 43/586; SE247290; NP 96
Gildingwells (township in Laughton en le Morthen), 43/912; SK557854; NP 103
Gileston (parish), 51/170; ST015669; NP 154
Gillamoor (township in Kirkbymoorside), 42/471; SE681901; NP 92
Gilligate, 11/112-113; NP 85
Gilling (Gilling East) (township in Gilling), 42/612; SE610763; NP 92
Gilling (Gilling West) (division in township of Gilling in Gilling), 42/47; NZ186053; NP 85, 91
Gilling (Gilling West) (parish), 42/38-53; NP 84, 85, 91
Gilling (parish), 42/610-612; NP 92
Gilling (township in Gilling), 42/46-47; NP 85, 91
Gilling East, 42/612; NP 92
Gillingham (division in Gillingham), 10/1; ST799269; NP 166
Gillingham (parish), 10/1-2; NP 166
Gillingham (division in Gillingham), 19/90; TQ776684; NP 172
Gillingham (parish), 19/90-92; NP 172
Gillingham All Saints (parish), 25/624; TM419919; NP 137
Gillingham St Mary (parish), 25/623; TM410930; NP 137
Gilmonby (township in Bowes), 42/11; NY995117; NP 84
Gilmorton (parish), 21/344; SP565876; NP 132
Gilraes (Gilroe, Gilroes) (extra-parochial), 21/185; SK565064; NP 121
Gilroe (extra-parochial), 21/185; NP 121

Gilston (parish), 16/70; TL442134; NP 148
Gimingham (parish), 25/44; TG285371; NP 126
Gipping (hamlet in Stowmarket), 34/240; TM073632; NP 136
Girrick (division in township of Moorsholm cum Girrick in Skelton), 42/351; NZ708127; NP 86
Girsby (Grisby) (township in Sockburn), 42/59; NZ360085; NP 85
Girton (parish), 4/79; TL421617; NP 135
Girton (parish), 28/115; SK825670; NP 113
Gisborough, 42/359; NP 86
Gisborough, (parish), 42/356-360; NP 86
Gisburn (parish), 43/297-304
Gisburn (township in Gisburn), 43/298B; SD830490; NP 95
Gisburn Forest (township in Gisburn), 43/300; SD775545; NP 95
Gisleham (parish), 34/56; TM515885; NP 137
Gislingham (parish), 34/134; TM072719; NP 136
Gissing (parish), 25/754; TM150855; NP 136, 137
Gittisham (parish), 9/237; SY139980; NP 176
Givendale (township in Ripon), 43/174-175; NP 91
Gladestry (parish), 56/52; SO230546; NP 128, 141
Glaisdale (township in Danby), 42/363; NZ765075; NP 86, 92
Glan Honddu (township in Llandefaelog-fach), 45/35; SO024327; NP 141
Glandford (parish), 25/70; TG043411; NP 125
Glanford Brigg, 22/63; NP 104
Glanton (township in Whittingham), 27/167; NU064148; NP 71
Glanvilles Wootton (Wootton Glanville) (parish), 10/95; ST683086; NP 178
Glapthorn (parish), 26/58; TL022902; NP 134
Glapwell (township in Bolsover), 8/63; SK478662; NP 112
Glasbury (division in Glasbury), 45/1; SO185392; NP 141
Glasbury (division in Glasbury), 56/62; SO167403; NP 141
Glasbury (parish), 45/1-3, 56/62; NP 141
Glascoed (hamlet in Usk [Brynbuga]), 53/64B; SO332017; NP 155
Glascwm (Glascomb) (parish), 56/42A-B; NP 128, 141
Glass Houghton (township in Castleford), 43/618; SE438245; NP 97
Glassonby (township in Addingham), 7/179; NY579387; NP 83
Glassthorpe (hamlet in Floore), 26/254; SP670615; NP 132
Glaston (parish), 30/52; SK901004; NP 122, 133
Glastonbury (St Benedict and St John, Glastonbury) (parish), 32/182; ST500385; NP 165
Glatton (district in Glatton), 17/21; TL151868; NP 134
Glatton (parish), 17/21-22; NP 134
Glazebrook (division in township of Rixton with Glazebrook in Warrington), 20/611; SJ695919; NP 101
Glazeley (parish), 31/555; SO706875; NP 130
Gleaston (division in township of Aldingham in Aldingham), 20/32; SD262706; NP 88
Glemsford (parish), 34/150; TL830480; NP 149
Glen Parva (Little Glenn) (township in Aylestone), 21/206; SP570989; NP 132
Glendon (parish), 26/136; SP851823; NP 133
Glenfield (parish), 21/178-180; NP 121
Glenfield (township in Glenfield), 21/179; SK538061; NP 121
Glenfield Frith (extra-parochial), 21/183; SK547057; NP 121
Glentham (parish), 22/151; TF000910; NP 104
Glentworth (parish), 22/225; SK941880; NP 104
Glewstone (Glewston) (township in), 15/257; SO562219; NP 142
Glinton (parish), 26/15; TF152054; NP 123
Globe Street (extra-parochial), 34/473; NP 150/1
Globwll (township in Llanfyllin), 49/121; SJ125185; NP 117
Glooston (parish), 21/295; SP750962; NP 133
Glororum (township in Bamburgh), 27/108; NU168333; NP 71
Glossop (parish), 8/1-12; NP 101, 102, 111
Glossop Dale (township in Glossop), 8/3E; SK080930; NP 102
Gloster Hill (township in Warkworth), 27/224; NU252045; NP 71
Gloucester, College Precincts (parish), 13/181; SO831188; NP 143/1
Gloucester, Holy Trinity (parish), 13/182; SO830186; NP 143/1
Gloucester, Kingholm St Catherine (hamlet in Gloucester, Kingholm St Catherine), 13/186B; SO839201; NP 143/1
Gloucester, Kingholm St Catherine (parish), 13/186A-B; NP 143/1
Gloucester, St Aldate (parish), 13/184; SO833185; NP 143/1
Gloucester, St Catherine (hamlet in Gloucester, St Catherine), 13/186A; SO839193; NP 143/1
Gloucester, St John the Baptist (parish), 13/185; SO836189; NP 143/1
Gloucester, St Mary de Crypt (parish), 13/183; SO830185; NP 143/1
Gloucester, St Mary de Grace (parish), 13/189; SO831186; NP 143/1
Gloucester, St Michael (division in Gloucester, St Michael), 13/188A; SO833183; NP 143/1
Gloucester, St Michael (parish), 13/188A-B; NP 143/1
Gloucester, St Nicholas (parish), 13/180; SO822188; NP 143/1
Gloucester, St Owen (parish), 13/187; SO827183; NP 143/1
Glusburn (township in Kildwick), 43/348; SD997451; NP 95, 96
Glympton (parish), 29/100; SP423212; NP 145
Glyn (Glynn) (division outside Fforest-fawr in Devynock), 45/66A; SN970230; NP 141
Glyn (hamlet in Llanelli), 47/83C; SN600030; NP 152
Glyn - Fforest-fawr (division Fforest-fawr in Devynock), 45/66B; SN973197; NP 141
Glyn Ceiriog (township in Llansantfraid Glyn Ceiriog), 49/119; SJ175375; NP 117
Glyn-fach (township in Llanigon), 45/90; SO255325; NP 141
Glyncorrwg (Glyn-corwg) (hamlet in Glyncorrwg), 51/56; SS877993; NP 153
Glyncorrwg (Glyn-corwg) (parish), 51/55-56; NP 153
Glynde (parish), 36/193; TQ456097; NP 183
Glynharren, 54/143; NP 127, 128
Glynhayren (Glynharren) (township in Llanidloes), 54/143; SN902858; NP 127, 128
Glynn, 45/66A-B; NP 141
Glyntawe (division in Devynock), 45/68; SN850130; NP 140, 141, 153
Glyntraian (township in Llangollen), 49/118; SJ223357; NP 117
Glyntrefnant (township in Trefeglwys), 54/132; SN917927; NP 127, 128
Gnosall (parish), 33/168-170; NP 119
Gnosall (township in Gnosall), 33/169; SJ834212; NP 119
Goadby (parish), 21/283; SP752987; NP 133
Goadby Marwood (parish), 21/98; SK777264; NP 122
Goathill (parish), 32/384; ST674171; NP 178
Goathland (township in Pickering), 42/430; NZ847003; NP 92
Goathurst (parish), 32/299; ST259343; NP 165
Godalming (parish), 35/141; SU979426; NP 169
Goddington (parish), 29/77; NP 145
Godington (Goddington) (parish), 29/77; SP636269; NP 145
Godley (township in Mottram), 5/7; SJ965949; NP 101
Godmanchester (parish), 17/85; TL248696; NP 134
Godmanstone (parish), 10/222; SY654971; NP 178
Godmersham (parish), 19/290; TR068507; NP 172
Godsfield (extra-parochial), 14/134; SU599373; NP 168
Godshill (parish), 18/25; SZ526804; NP 180
Godshill [east part] (extra-parochial), 14/313B; SU178153; NP 179
Godshill [west part] (extra-parochial), 14/313A; SU172152; NP 179
Godstone (parish), 35/108; TQ359488; NP 170, 171
Goetre (township in Kerry [Llanfihangel-yng-Ngheri]), 54/178; SO180923; NP 128
Gogoyan (township in Llandewi-Brefi), 46/49; SN634544; NP 140
Golant, 6/96; NP 185, 186
Golborne (township in Winwick), 20/594; SJ609983; NP 100, 101
Golborne Bellow (Golbourn Bellow) (township in Tattenhall), 5/360; SJ474596; NP 109
Golborne David (Golbourn David) (township in Handley), 5/362; SJ456600; NP 109
Golcar (township in Huddersfield), 43/754-755; NP 102
Goldcliff (parish), 53/152; ST370830; NP 155

Golden Grove (township in Llanasa), 50/49B; SJ087814; NP 108
Golden Hill (township in Wolstanton), 33/17J; SJ852533; NP 110
Golden Square (division in St James Westminster), 24/37B; TQ293810; NP 160/1
Goldhanger (parish), 12/232; TL900087; NP 162
Golding (township in Cound), 31/445; SJ542037; NP 118
Goldington (parish), 1/44; TL067518; NP 147
Goldsborough (township in Lythe), 42/379B; NZ839146; NP 86
Goldsborough (parish), 43/110-112; NP 91, 96, 97
Goldsborough (township in Goldsborough), 43/110; SE386560; NP 96
Goldshaw Booth (township in Whalley), 20/255; SD809388; NP 95
Goldstone (township in Cheswardine), 31/182; SJ707283; NP 119
Goldthorpe (division in township and parish of Bolton upon Dearne), 43/864; SE465040; NP 103
Golftyn (township in Northop), 50/19; SJ280696; NP 108, 109
Golon (township in Abbey-Cwmhir), 56/2B; SO050710; NP 128
Goltho (parish), 22/351-352; NP 105
Goltho (township in Goltho), 22/351; TF118771; NP 105
Gomeldon (tithing in Idmiston), 39/310B; SU180360; NP 167
Gomersal (township in Birstal), 43/538; SE210267; NP 96
Gonalston (Gonalstone) (parish), 28/191; SK682476; NP 112
Good Easter (parish), 12/250; TL634120; NP 161
Gooderstone (parish), 25/532; TF779995; NP 125, 135, 136
Goodleigh (parish), 9/27; SS599346; NP 163
Goodmanham (parish), 41/194; SE906438; NP 98
Goodmans Fields (division in St Mary Whitechapel), 24/60B; TQ340810; NP 160/1
Goodnestone (Goodnestone next Faversham) (parish), 19/111; TR043615; NP 172
Goodnestone (Goodnestone next Wingham) (parish), 19/279; TR262548; NP 173
Goodrich (parish), 15/256; NP 142
Goodrich (township in Goodrich), 15/256; SO572192; NP 142
Goodshaw Booth (division in township of Higher Booths in Whalley), 20/288; SD806265; NP 95
Goodworth Clatford (parish), 14/89; SU364421; NP 168
Goole (township in Snaith), 43/960; SE745195; NP 97, 98, 104
Goosepool (division of Middleton St George township in Long Newton), 11/338; NZ368142; NP 85
Goosey (chapelry in Stanford in the Vale), 2/47; SU366926; NP 158
Goosnagh (division in township of Goosnagh with Newsham in Kirkham), 20/207; SD565405; NP 94
Goosnagh with Newsham (township in Kirkham), 20/206-207; NP 94
Goostrey cum Barnshaw (township in Sandbach), 5/210; SJ775712; NP 110
Gop (township in Newmarket [Trelawnyd]), 50/51; SJ082793; NP 108
Gopsall (Gopsall Hall) (extra-parochial), 21/144; SK349067; NP 121
Goresland (township in Monks Kirby), 21/238; SP491866; NP 132
Goring (Goring-by-Sea) (parish), 36/300; TQ109030; NP 182
Goring (parish), 29/315; SU630802; NP 158
Gorleston (hamlet in Gorleston), 34/3; TG525038; NP 126, 137
Gorleston (parish), 34/3-5; NP 126, 137
Gorton (township in Manchester), 20/519; SJ884962; NP 101
Gorwith, 46/48; NP 140
Gorwydd (Gorwith) (township in Llandewi-Brefi), 46/48; SN672528; NP 140
Gosbeck (parish), 34/360; TM156562; NP 137, 150
Gosberton (parish), 22/733; TF220320; NP 123
Gosfield (parish), 12/87; TL774297; NP 149
Gosford (hamlet in Kidlington), 29/200; SP501129; NP 145
Gosforth (parish), 7/310; NY080040; NP 82, 88
Gosforth (parish), 27/507-513; NP 78
Gosport (division in Alverstoke), 14/293; SU618002; NP 180
Goswell Street (division in St James Clerkenwell), 24/47D; TQ316827; NP 160/1
Goswick (township in Holy Island), 27/27; NU052448; NP 64

Gotham (division in Edmondsham), 10/72; SU081106; NP 179
Gotham (parish), 28/278; SK540300; NP 121
Gotherington (hamlet in Bishop's Cleeve), 13/61; SO962292; NP 143
Gothurst (parish), 3/45; NP 146
Goudhurst (parish), 19/314; TQ720363; NP 171, 172, 183
Goulceby (parish), 22/337; TF252788; NP 105
Goulton (division in township of Potto in Whorlton), 42/309; NZ480040; NP 91
Gourton (township in Wrexham [Wrecsam]), 49/57; SJ372521; NP 109
Gowdall (township in Snaith), 43/969; SE622222; NP 97
Gowthorpe (division in township of Youlthorpe with Gowthorpe in Bishop Wilton), 41/113; SE756545; NP 98
Goxhill (parish), 22/49; TA114228; NP 99, 104
Goxhill (parish), 41/363; TA182445; NP 99
Goytre (Goytrey) (parish), 53/46; SO318053; NP 155
Graby (hamlet in Aslackby), 22/673; TF095297; NP 123
Grade (parish), 6/190; SW713148; NP 190
Graffham (parish), 36/23; SU924176; NP 181
Grafham (Graffham) (parish), 17/94; TL158687; NP 134
Grafton (division in township of Marton with Grafton in Marton), 43/127; SE412632; NP 91
Grafton (township in Tilston), 5/34; SJ446515; NP 109
Grafton (township in Hereford, St Martin), 15/133; SO496365; NP 142
Grafton (township in Little Faringdon), 29/161; SP269004; NP 157
Grafton Flyford (parish), 40/148; SO962565; NP 130, 143
Grafton Manor (parish), 40/55; SO937697; NP 130
Grafton Regis (parish), 26/311; SP756468; NP 146
Grafton Underwood (parish), 26/139; SP923804; NP 133
Graig (hamlet in Bassaleg), 53/118; ST260870; NP 154, 155
Graig (township in Newmarket [Trelawnyd]), 50/50; SJ097794; NP 108
Graig (township in Tremeirchion), 50/83; SJ093727; NP 108
Graig (township in Kerry [Llanfihangel-yng-Ngheri]), 54/168; SO096884; NP 128
Grain (St James, Grain; St James, Isle of Grain) (parish), 19/44; TQ877759; NP 172
Grainsby (parish), 22/175; TF283996; NP 105
Grainthorpe (parish), 22/183; TF380970; NP 105
Grampound (district in Creed), 6/142; SW937484; NP 190
Grampound (district in Probus), 6/141; SW920483; NP 190
Grampound (district), 6/141-142; NP 190
Grampound, 2/7; NP 158
Granby (Granby and Sutton) (parish), 28/218; SK758366; NP 122
Grandborough (parish), 3/105; SP768252; NP 146
Grandborough (Grandbor') (parish), 37/236; SP482658; NP 132
Grandpont (Grampound) (tithing in St Aldate), 2/7; SP518050; NP 158
Grange (hamlet in Gillingham), 19/92; TQ793680; NP 172
Grange (hamlet in Llangeler), 47/37; SN405370; NP 139
Grange (township in West Kirby), 5/454; SJ229878; NP 100
Grange de Lings (extra-parochial), 22/249; SK984776; NP 104
Grange Lane (division in township of Ecclesfield in Ecclesfield), 43/795; SK379945; NP 102
Grange Leys (division in Costock), 28/288; SK577281; NP 121
Gransmoor (township in Burton Agnes), 41/263; TA125597; NP 99
Granston [Treopert] (parish), 55/35; SM903333; NP 138
Grantchester (parish), 4/106; TL429564; NP 135, 148
Grantham (borough in Grantham), 22/626; SK908354; NP 122
Grantham (parish), 22/624-627; NP 122
Grantley (township in Ripon), 43/188; SE233700; NP 91
Grappenhall (parish), 5/109-110; NP 101
Grappenhall (township in Grappenhall), 5/109; SJ638861; NP 101
Grasby (division in Grasby), 22/106A; TA092052; NP 104
Grasby (parish), 22/106A-B; NP 104
Grasby - Caistor Moor (division in Grasby), 22/106B; TA083033; NP 104
Grasmere (parish), 38/76-79; NP 82, 83, 89

Grasmere (township in Grasmere), 38/77; NY328091; NP 82, 83
Grassington (township in Linton), 43/217; SE018668; NP 90
Grassthorpe (township in Marnham), 28/112; SK802677; NP 112, 113
Grateley (Grately) (parish), 14/85; SU274416; NP 167, 168
Gratton (township in Youlgreave), 8/115; SK206612; NP 111
Gratwich (parish), 33/123; SK030311; NP 120
Graveley (parish), 4/63; TL255645; NP 134
Graveley (Graveley cum Chisfield) (parish), 16/50; TL242277; NP 147
Gravelhunger (township in Muckleston), 31/1; SJ742248; NP 119
Graveney (parish), 19/112; TR044636; NP 172
Gravesend (parish), 19/32; TQ643733; NP 171
Gray's Inn Lane (division in St Pancras), 24/44F; TQ305825; NP 160/1
Grayingham (parish), 22/120; Sk937959; NP 104
Grayrigg (township in Kendal), 38/112; SD588979; NP 89
Grays (Grays Thurrrock) (parish), 12/425; TQ628781; NP 161, 171
Grays Inn (extra-parochial), 24/15; TQ310818; NP 160/1
Graythwaite (division in township of Satterthwaite in Hawkshead), 20/49; SD370918; NP 89
Grazeley (tithing in Sulhampstead Abbots), 2/172; SU688676; NP 158, 169
Greasborough (township in Rotherham), 43/842; SK421953; NP 103
Greasby (township in West Kirby), 5/459; SJ255872; NP 100
Greasley (parish), 28/171-177; NP 112, 121
Greasley (township in Greasley), 28/173; SK498470; NP 112
Great Abington (parish), 4/157; TL525475; NP 148
Great Addington (parish), 26/153; SP953749; NP 133, 134
Great Alne (parish), 37/186; SP116602; NP 131
Great Amwell (parish), 16/112; TL370120; NP 147, 160
Great and Little Birch (parish), 12/182; NP 149
Great and Little Singleton (township in Kirkham), 20/187-189; NP 94
Great and Little Snarehill (extra-parochial), 25/717; TL886818; NP 136
Great and Little Berwick and Newton (Almond Park, Great and Little Berwick and Newton) (township in St Mary Shrewsbury), 31/252; SJ479158; NP 118
Great and Little Wollascot, 31/250; NP 118
Great and Little Hampton (parish), 40/208; SP026448; NP 144
Great and Little Preston (township in Kippax), 43/472; SE401294; NP 96
Great Ashfield (parish), 34/189; TM003671; NP 136
Great Aycliffe (township in Aycliffe), 11/276; NZ276233; NP 85
Great Ayton (township in Ayton), 42/330; NZ560110; NP 86
Great Baddow (parish), 12/287; TL725035; NP 161
Great Badminton (parish), 13/344; ST805825; NP 156
Great Bardfield (parish), 12/79; TL683296; NP 148
Great Barford (parish), 1/42; TL120526; NP 147
Great Barlow (township in Staveley), 8/50; SK335750; NP 111
Great Barrington (parish), 13/227; SP210140; NP 144, 157
Great Barr (township in Aldridge), 33/301; SP065975; NP 131
Great Barton (parish), 34/196; TL891669; NP 136
Great Barugh (township in Barughs Ambo township in Kirby Misperton), 42/448; SE750787; NP 92
Great Bavington (township in Kirkwhelpington), 27/373; NY981801; NP 77
Great Bealings (parish), 34/430; TM238488; NP 150
Great Beats (extra-parochial), 22/746; TF221530; NP 114
Great Bedwyn (Great Bedwin) (parish), 39/185-186; NP 157, 158, 167, 168
Great Bedwyn (Great Bedwin) (tithing in Great Bedwyn), 39/185; SU266640; NP 157, 158, 167, 168
Great Bentley (parish), 12/158; TM114213; NP 149, 150
Great Billing (parish), 26/220; SP811631; NP 133
Great Bircham (parish), 25/98; TF765313; NP 124, 125
Great Blakenham (parish), 34/396; TM117504; NP 149, 150
Great Blencow (Blencow) (township in Dacre), 7/193; NY447334; NP 83

Great Bolas (Bolas Magna) (parish), 31/175; SJ660215; NP 119
Great Bolton (Eastern) (division in township of Great Bolton in Bolton-le-Moors), 20/405B; SD721082; NP 101
Great Bolton (township in Bolton-le-Moors), 20/405A-B; NP 101
Great Bolton (Western) (division in township of Great Bolton in Bolton-le-Moors), 20/405A; SD712090; NP 101
Great Bookham (parish), 35/121; TQ136537; NP 170
Great Boughton (township in St Oswald Chester), 5/504; SJ427662; NP 109
Great Bowden (township in Great Bowden), 21/314; SP739891; NP 133
Great Bradley (parish), 34/324; TL677534; NP 135, 148
Great Bradford (parish), 39/124, 151A-155; NP 156, 166
Great Bramshill (tithing in Eversley), 14/26A; SU750610; NP 169
Great Braxted (parish), 12/222; TL858156; NP 149
Great Brickhill (parish), 3/98; SP901309; NP 146
Great Bricett (Bricett) (parish), 34/355; TM039506; NP 149
Great Bromley (parish), 12/117; TM089253; NP 149, 150
Great Broughton (township in Bridekirk), 7/241; NY066320; NP 82
Great Broughton (division in township of Broughton in Kirkby), 42/323; NZ550060; NP 86, 92
Great Budworth (township in Great Budworth), 5/123; SJ659779; NP 101
Great Budworth, 5/111-140, 142-145; NP 100, 101
Great Burdon (township in Haughton le Skerne), 11/335; NZ322161; NP 85
Great Burstead (hamlet in Great Burstead), 12/334A; TQ690930; NP 161
Great Burstead (parish), 12/334A-B; NP 161
Great Busby (township in Stokesley), 42/303; NZ522056; NP 85, 86, 92
Great Canford, Middle Division (division in Canford Magna), 10/193; SZ033963; NP 179
Great Canford, Western Division (division in Canford Magna), 10/192; SZ004961; NP 179
Great Canfield (parish), 12/197; TL589186; NP 148
Great Carleton (division in Carleton township in Poulton-le-Fylde), 20/173; SD338402; NP 94
Great Carlton (parish), 22/300; TF425866; NP 105
Great Casterton (parish), 30/28; TF001109; NP 123
Great Catworth (parish), 17/51A-B; NP 134
Great Chalfield (parish), 39/125; ST860635; NP 156, 166
Great Chart (parish), 19/323; TQ974415; NP 172
Great Chesterford (parish), 12/4; TL523442; NP 148
Great Chesterton, 37/255
Great Cheverell (parish), 39/227; ST977534; NP 167
Great Chignal (parish), 12/246; NP 148, 161
Great Chishall (parish), 12/13; TL423400; NP 148
Great Clacton (parish), 12/167; TM177165; NP 150
Great Claybrooke, 21/234; NP 132
Great Clifton (township in Workington), 7/253; NY041291; NP 82
Great Coates (parish), 22/77; TA239107; NP 105
Great Coggeshall (parish), 12/131; NP 149
Great Comberton (parish), 40/217; SO957424; NP 143
Great Copston, 37/110
Great Corby (township in Wetheral), 7/46; NY484537; NP 76
Great Cornard (parish), 34/493; TL900402; NP 149
Great Corringham (hamlet in Corringham), 22/141; SK872918; NP 104
Great Cowden (Colden Magna) (division in township of Coldens Ambo in Mappleton), 41/372; TA226427; NP 99
Great Coxwell (parish), 2/35; SU268944; NP 158
Great Cransley (parish), 26/161; SP822762; NP 133
Great Creaton (parish), 26/191; NP 133
Great Creeton (Great Creaton) (parish), 26/191; SP709724; NP 133
Great Cressingham (parish), 25/683; TF852018; NP 125, 136
Great Cropwell (parish), 28/264; NP 121, 122
Great Crosby (township in Sefton), 20/689; SJ319996; NP 100
Great Dalby (parish), 21/114; SK748140; NP 122
Great Dawley (parish), 31/227-229; NP 119
Great Dawley, 31/228; NP 119

Great Doddington (parish), 26/210; SP880650; NP 133
Great Driffield (parish), 41/275-278; NP 98, 99
Great Driffield (township in Great Driffield), 41/275; TA026596; NP 99
Great Dromonby (division in township of Kirkby in Kirkby), 42/321; NZ532058; NP 85, 86, 92
Great Dunham (parish), 25/330; TF868150; NP 125
Great Dunmow (parish), 12/195; TL628218; NP 148
Great Durnford (tithing in Durnford), 39/303; SU141373; NP 167
Great Easby (Easby) (township in Brampton), 7/53; NY537626; NP 76
Great Easton (Great Eiston) (parish), 12/76; TL620260; NP 148
Great Easton (township in Bringhurst), 21/304; SP847937; NP 133
Great Eccleston (township in St Michaels on Wyre), 20/166; SD435401; NP 94
Great Edstone (parish), 42/467-468; NP 92
Great Edstone (township in Great Edstone), 42/467; SE710830; NP 92
Great Eiston (parish), 12/76; TL620260; NP 148
Great Ellingham (parish), 25/663; TM021972; NP 136
Great Elm (hamlet in Great Elm), 32/121; ST748493; NP 166
Great Elm (parish), 32/121-122; NP 166
Great Eppleton (township in Houghton-le-Spring), 11/67; NZ369484; NP 85
Great Eversden (parish), 4/125; TL362534; NP 135, 147, 148
Great Everdon (hamlet in Great Everdon), 26/259; SP590580; NP 132
Great Everdon (parish), 26/259-260; NP 132
Great Fakenham (parish), 34/123; NP 136
Great Finborough (parish), 34/296; TM016570; NP 136, 149
Great Fransham (parish), 25/333; TF906133; NP 125
Great Gaddesden (parish), 16/96; TL042122; NP 147, 159, 160
Great Gidding (parish), 17/34; TL121838; NP 134
Great Givendale (division parish and township of Great Givendale), 41/109; SE815544; NP 98
Great Givendale (parish and township), 41/108-109; NP 98
Great Givendale (division in township of Givendale in Ripon), 43/174; SE340685; NP 91
Great Glemham (parish), 34/276; TM332620; NP 137
Great Glen (parish), 21/322-323; NP 121, 132
Great Glen (township in Great Glen), 21/322; SP658981; NP 132
Great Gonerby (parish), 22/619; SK897392; NP 122
Great Gransden (parish), 17/113; TL274568; NP 134, 147
Great Greenford (parish), 24/97; NP 160
Great Grimsby (parish), 22/79A; TA262088; NP 105
Great Habton (township in Kirby Misperton), 42/452; SE760769; NP 92
Great Hadham (parish), 16/74; NP 148
Great Hale (parish), 22/654-655; NP 123
Great Hale (township in Great Hale), 22/654; TF167427; NP 123
Great Hallingbury (parish), 12/199; TL511196; NP 148
Great Hampden (parish), 02/241; SP851021; NP 159
Great Hanwood (Hanwood) (parish), 31/293; SJ445103; NP 118
Great Harborough (parish), 37/117; NP 132
Great Hardres (parish), 19/288; NP 173
Great Harrowden (Harrowden Magna) (parish), 26/209; SP887707; NP 133
Great Harwood (township in Blackburn), 20/310; SD730330; NP 95
Great Haseley (parish), 29/258-261; NP 158
Great Haseley (township in Great Haseley), 29/258; SP643018; NP 158
Great Hatfield (division in Great Hatfield township in Sigglesthorne), 41/368; TA195425; NP 99
Great Hatfield (division in Great Hatfield township in Mappleton), 41/369; TA197437; NP 99
Great Hatfield (township in Sigglesthorne and Mappleton), 41/368-369
Great Hautbois (Hautbois Magna) (parish), 25/248; TG264212; NP 126
Great Heaton (township in Prestwich), 20/495; SD834045; NP 101

Great Heck (township in Snaith), 43/967; SE592212; NP 97, 103
Great Henny (parish), 12/46; TL871379; NP 149
Great Hinton (Hinton) (tithing in Steeple Ashton), 39/143; ST902590; NP 166
Great Holcombe (division in Newington), 29/289; SU611971; NP 158
Great Holland (parish), 12/164; TM216191; NP 150
Great Horkesley (Great Horksley) (parish), 12/99; TL977312; NP 149
Great Hormead (parish), 16/59; TL404302; NP 148
Great Horton (division in township of Horton in Bradford), 43/531; SE138317; NP 96
Great Horwood (parish), 3/91-92; NP 146
Great Horwood (township in Great Horwood), 3/91; SP766311; NP 146
Great Houghton (parish), 26/285; SP795584; NP 133
Great Houghton (township in Darfield), 43/862; SE439071; NP 103
Great Hucklow (township in Hope), 8/24; SK175776; NP 111
Great Hutton (Hutton Long Villiers, Hutton Magna) (township in Gilling), 42/45; NZ126118; NP 84, 85
Great Ilford (hamlet in Barking), 12/319; TQ445881; NP 161
Great Kelk (township in Foston on the Wolds), 41/265; TA101586; NP 99
Great Kimble (parish), 3/183; SP821061; NP 159
Great Kyre (parish), 40/86; NP 129, 130
Great Langton (Langton-upon-Swale) (parish), 42/69-70; NP 91
Great Langton (Langton-upon-Swale) (township in Great Langton), 42/70; SE302971; NP 91
Great Leighs (hamlet in Great Leighs), 12/212; TL732152; NP 148
Great Leighs (parish), 12/212-213; NP 148
Great Leke (parish), 28/279; NP 121
Great Limber (parish), 22/98; TA130070; NP 104, 105
Great Linford (parish), 3/50; SP857412; NP 146
Great Livermere (parish), 34/119; TL888712; NP 136
Great Longstone and Holme (Great Longstone) (township in Bakewell), 8/89; SK199734; NP 111
Great Lumley (township in Chester le Street), 11/48; NZ297489; NP 78
Great Malvern (parish), 40/168-169; NP 143
Great Malvern (township in Great Malvern), 40/168; SO800455; NP 143
Great Maplestead (parish), 12/89; TL817345; NP 149
Great Marlow (Marlow) (parish), 3/214; SU841881; NP 159
Great Marsden (division in township of Great Marsden and Little Marsden in Whalley), 20/265; SD878374; NP 95
Great Marsden and Little Marsden (township in Whalley), 20/264-265; NP 95
Great Marton (division in Marton township in Poulton-le-Fylde), 20/171; SD333329; NP 94
Great Massingham (parish), 25/181; TF790205; NP 125
Great Mearley (division in Mearley township in Whalley), 20/248; SD770408; NP 95
Great Melton (Melton St Mary and All Saints) (parish), 25/560; TG135064; NP 125
Great Meols (Great Meolse) (township in West Kirby), 5/451; SJ241909; NP 100
Great Milton (parish), 29/252-255; NP 158
Great Milton (township in Great Milton), 29/252; SP631029; NP 158
Great Missenden (parish), 3/196; SP900015; NP 159
Great Mitton (division in Great Mitton township in Mitton), 43/290; SD718398; NP 95
Great Mitton (township in Mitton), 43/289-290; NP 95
Great Mollington (township in Backford), 5/491; SJ381710; NP 109
Great Mongeham (parish), 19/354; TR354512; NP 173
Great Moorsholm (division in township of Moorsholm cum Girrick in Skelton), 42/350; NZ690130; NP 86
Great Munden (parish), 16/54; TL357238; NP 147, 148
Great Musgrave (parish), 38/51; NY776169; NP 84
Great Ness (Great Ness and Hopton) (township in Great Ness), 31/134; SJ390196; NP 118

113

Great Ness (parish), 31/130-134; NP 118
Great Ness and Hopton, 31/134; NP 118
Great Neston (township in Neston), 5/478; SJ295784; NP 100
Great Oakley (parish), 12/113; TM195275; NP 150
Great Oakley (parish), 26/131; SP871859; NP 133
Great Ormside (township in Ormside), 38/49; NY695157; NP 83
Great Orton (township in Orton), 7/140B; NY332547; NP 75, 76
Great Ouseburn (parish), 43/125; SE449619; NP 91
Great Oxenden (parish), 26/106; SP736836; NP 133
Great Packington (parish), 37/76; SP235840; NP 131
Great Parndon (parish), 12/262A; TL435085; NP 148, 161
Great Paxton (parish), 17/104; TL213633; NP 134
Great Plumpton (division in township of Westby with Plumptons in Kirkham), 20/185; SD384334; NP 94
Great Plumstead (parish), 25/451; TG300098; NP 126
Great Ponton (parish), 22/633B; SK925301; NP 122, 123
Great Poringland (parish), 25/569; TG276015; NP 126, 137
Great Poston, 31/510; NP 129
Great Raveley (Raveley) (parish), 17/28; TL250811; NP 134
Great Ravendale (parish), 22/170-171; NP 105
Great Ravendale, 22/171; NP 105
Great Redisham (parish), 34/45; TM404855; NP 137
Great Ribston (division in township of Great Ribston and Walshford in Hunsingore), 43/109; SE402545; NP 96
Great Ribston and Walshford (township in Hunsingore), 43/108-109; NP 96
Great Ringstead (St Peter and St Andrew) (parish), 25/3; NP 124
Great Rissington (parish), 13/226; SP200175; NP 144
Great Rollright (parish), 29/45; SP322313; NP 145
Great Rowsley, 8/95; NP 111
Great Ryburgh (parish), 25/155; TF949272; NP 125
Great Ryle (township in Whittingham), 27/165; NU020127; NP 71
Great Saling (parish), 12/82; TL707250; NP 148
Great Salkeld (parish), 7/182; NY540355; NP 83
Great Salterns (extra-parochial), 14/288; SU672021; NP 180
Great Sampford (parish), 12/57; TL640360; NP 148
Great Sandal (parish), 43/691-694; NP 96, 102
Great Sankey (township in Prescot), 20/621; SJ577888; NP 100
Great Saughall (township in Shotwick), 5/488; SJ369713; NP 109
Great Saxham (parish), 34/221; TL789638; NP 136
Great Sheepey (parish), 21/159-160; NP 121, 132
Great Sheepey, 21/159; NP 121, 132
Great Shefford (parish), 2/138; NP 158
Great Shelford (parish), 4/131; TL463533; NP 148
Great Sherston (parish), 39/39; NP 156
Great Shurdington (Shurdington Magna) (parish), 13/205; SO923189; NP 143
Great Singleton (division in township of Great and Little Singleton in Kirkham), 20/187; SD382380; NP 94
Great Smeaton (42/60-62); NP 85, 91
Great Smeaton (township in Great Smeaton), 42/62; NZ342050; NP 85, 91
Great Snoring (parish), 25/112; TF945346; NP 125
Great Somerford (Broad Somerford) (parish), 39/46; ST955825; NP 156, 157
Great Soudley (Great Sowdley) (township in Cheswardine), 31/185; SJ730284; NP 119
Great Sowdley, 31/185; NP 119
Great Stainton (parish), 11/270-271; NP 85
Great Stainton (Stainton le Street) (township in Great Stainton), 11/270; NZ335220; NP 85
Great Stainforth (division in township of Stainforth in Giggleswick), 43/251; SD838698; NP 90
Great Stambridge (parish), 12/373; TQ910917; NP 162
Great Stanney (township in Stoke), 5/426; SJ406753; NP 100, 109
Great Stanmore (parish), 24/90; TQ168922; NP 160
Great Staughton (parish), 17/98A-B; NP 134
Great Steeping (parish), 22/484; TF443644; NP 114
Great Stretton (township in Great Glen), 21/323; SK657006; NP 121, 132

Great Strickland (township in Morland), 38/15; NY568232; NP 83
Great Stukeley (parish), 17/64; TL223742; NP 134
Great Sturton (parish), 22/347; TF211768; NP 105
Great Sugnall (Sugnall Magna, Sugnall) (township in Eccleshall), 33/143; SJ799309; NP 119
Great Sutton (township in Eastham), 5/429; SJ381752; NP 100, 109
Great Sutton (township in Diddlebury), 31/508; SO517830; NP 129
Great Tew (parish), 29/55; SP398284; NP 145
Great Tey (parish), 12/136; TL884252; NP 149
Great Thirkleby (division in township of Thirkleby in Thirkleby), 42/542; SE469788; NP 91
Great Thornham (parish), 34/183; NP 136
Great Thurlow (parish), 34/327; TL672510; NP 148
Great Timble (township in Fewston), 43/379; SE169532; NP 96
Great Torrington (parish), 9/91; SS501204; NP 163
Great Tosson and Ryehill (Ryehall, Rye-Hill) (township in Rothbury), 27/257; NZ022922; NP 71
Great Totham (parish), 12/234; TL865110; NP 149, 162
Great Trefgarn (parish), 55/54; NP 138
Great Urswick (division in township of Great Urswick in Urswick), 20/39; SD273748; NP 88
Great Urswick (towsnship in Urswick), 20/35-40; NP 88, 89
Great Usworth (township in Usworth in Washington), 11/22; NZ297585; NP 78
Great Wakering (parish), 12/380; TQ953878; NP 162
Great Waldingfield (parish), 34/414; TL910440; NP 149
Great Walsingham (parish), 25/76; TF940377; NP 125
Great Waltham (parish), 12/210; TL692150; NP 148
Great Warford (township in Alderley), 5/69; SJ812778; NP 101
Great Warley (parish), 12/416; TQ590900; NP 161
Great Washbourne (parish), 13/41; SO994348; NP 143, 144
Great Weldon (hamlet in Great Weldon), 26/89; SP934892; NP 133
Great Weldon (parish), 26/89-90; NP 133
Great Welnetham (parish), 34/308; TL879592; NP 136
Great Wenham (Wenham Magna) (parish), 34/508; TM068393; NP 149
Great Whelnetham (Great Welnetham) (parish), 34/308; TL879592; NP 136
Great Whittington (township in Corbridge), 27/468; NZ006709; NP 77
Great Wigborough (parish), 12/227; TL969147; NP 149
Great Wilbraham (parish), 4/101; TL550565; NP 135, 148
Great Wishford (Wishford Magna) (parish), 39/294; SU072353; NP 167
Great Witcombe (Great Witcomb, Whitcomb Magna) (parish), 13/204; SO912145; NP 143
Great Witchingham (parish), 25/261; TG100198; NP 125
Great Witley (parish), 40/101; SO761650; NP 130
Great Wolford (Great Woolford) (hamlet in Great Wolford), 37/294; SP250343; NP 144
Great Wolford (Great Woolford) (parish), 37/294-295; NP 144
Great Woolstone (parish), 3/55; SP868385; NP 146
Great Woolton, 20/644
Great Woolford (parish), 37/294-295; NP 144
Great Wratting (parish), 34/331; TL686486; NP 148
Great Wymondley (parish), 16/32; TL218294; NP 147
Great Wyrley (township in Cannock), 33/230; SK991068; NP 119, 120
Great Yarmouth (parish), 25/463A-B; NP 126
Great Yarmouth - Northern (division in Great Yarmouth), 25/463B; TG538094; NP 126
Great Yarmouth - Southern (division in Great Yarmouth), 25/463A; TG529061; NP 126
Great Yeldham (parish), 12/53; TL760382; NP 148, 149
Greater Poston (Great Poston) (township in Diddlebury), 31/510; SO550821; NP 129
Greatford (parish), 22/715-716; NP 123
Greatford (township in Greatford), 22/715; TF096123; NP 123
Greatham (parish), 11/255-257; NP 85
Greatham (township in Greatham), 11/256; NZ498281; NP 85

Greatham (parish), 14/178; SU776302; NP 181
Greatham (parish), 36/81; TQ037155; NP 181, 182
Greatham Hospital Lands (extra-parochial), 11/255; NZ488269; NP 85
Greatworth (parish), 26/353; SP556421; NP 145
Green (division in St Matthew Bethnal Green), 24/63B; TQ356832; NP 160/1
Green (sub-division in Westnall with Waldershaigh division in township of Bradfield in Ecclesfield), 43/820; SK253981; NP 102
Green Hammerton (township in Whixley), 43/117; SE468569; NP 97
Green Moor (extra-parochial), 53/150; ST396855; NP 155
Greenbank Vachery (division in township of Over Wyresdale in Lancaster), 20/129; SD528543; NP 94
Greencroft (township in Lanchester), 11/154; NZ157500; NP 78, 84, 85
Greenfield (Maes-Glas) (township in Holywell), 50/34; SJ191775; NP 108
Greenford (Great Greenford) (parish), 24/97; TQ152843; NP 160
Greenhalgh (division in township of Greenhalgh with Thistleton in Kirkham), 20/194; SD407358; NP 94
Greenhalgh with Thistleton (township in Kirkham), 20/193-194; NP 94
Greenham (chapelry in Thatcham), 2/154; SU494651; NP 158, 168
Greenham (tithing in Crewkerene), 32/483C; ST398042; NP 177
Greenhill and Redhill (extra-parochial), 22/124; SK815953; NP 104
Greenhow (township in Ingleby Greenhow), 42/325A; NZ582041; NP 86, 92
Greenleighton (township in Hartburn), 27/336; NZ032925; NP 77
Greenoak (division in township of Bellasize in Eastrington), 41/20C; SE812280; NP 98/1
Greens and Glantlees (township in Felton), 27/285; NU142053; NP 77
Greens Norton (parish), 26/316; SP668502; NP 145
Greenside (township in Ryton), 11/30; NZ142619; NP 77, 78
Greenstead (Grinstead) (parish), 12/153B; TM028250; NP 149
Greensted (Greenstead) (parish), 12/274; TL534028; NP 161
Greenwich (parish), 19/5-7; NP 171
Greenwich East (division in Greenwich), 19/7; TQ398783; NP 171
Greenwich West (division in Greenwich), 19/5; TQ380771; NP 171
Greenwich, Royal Hospital (division in Greenwich), 19/6; TQ395778; NP 171
Greet (Greete) (division in Burford), 31/537; SO563710; NP 129
Greet (Greete) (division in Greet), 31/536; SO575710; NP 129
Greet (Greete) (parish), 31/536; NP 129
Greet (township in Greet and Burford), 31/536-537; NP 129
Greetham (parish), 22/390; TF308709; NP 114
Greetham (parish), 30/10; SK940144; NP 122, 123
Greetland (division in township of Elland with Greetland in Halifax), 43/574; SE079214; NP 96
Greetwell (parish), 22/356; TF008721; NP 113
Greinton (Grenton) (parish), 32/209; ST414357; NP 165
Grendon (parish), 26/217; SP880608; NP 133
Grendon (parish), 37/19-20; NP 121, 131, 132
Grendon (township in Grendon), 37/19; SK292004; NP 121, 131, 132
Grendon Bishop (parish), 15/95; SO595564; NP 129, 130
Grendon Underwood (parish), 3/116; SP685209; NP 145, 146
Grendon Warren (extra-parochial), 15/147; SO597548; NP 129, 142
Grenoside (division in township of Ecclesfield in Ecclesfield), 43/788; SK332944; NP 102
Grenton (parish), 32/209; NP 165
Gresford (township in Gresford), 49/66; SJ349544; NP 109
Gresford (parish), 49/63-71, 50/129; NP 109
Gresham (parish), 25/60; TG167385; NP 125, 126
Gressenhall (parish), 25/337; TF957150; NP 125
Gressingham (township in Lancaster), 20/121; SD568695; NP 89

Greta Mills and Briery Cottage (extra-parochial), 7/279; NY287242; NP 82
Gretton (parish), 26/52; SP896934; NP 133
Gretton (township in Cardington), 31/432; SO517946; NP 129
Gretton (township in Rushbury and Cardington), 31/431-432; NP 129
Gretton (township in Rushbury), 31/431; SO521949; NP 129
Grewell (parish), 14/40; NP 169
Grewelthorpe (township in Kirkby Malzeard), 43/203; SE215765; NP 91
Grey's Forest (township in Kirknewton), 27/58; NT880240; NP 70
Greysouthern (township in Brigham), 7/264; NY069288; NP 82
Greystead (parish), 27/360361; NP 76, 77
Greystoke (parish), 7/198-210; NP 82, 83
Greystoke (township in Greystoke), 7/200; NY417313; NP 83
Greystonegill (division in township of Bentham in Bentham), 43/270; SD690692; NP 89, 90
Greywell (Grewell) (parish), 14/40; SU716513; NP 169
Gribthorpe (township in Bubwith), 41/33; SE760356; NP 97, 98
Griff Grange (extra-parochial), 8/158; SK246555; NP 111
Grimblethorpe (extra-parochial), 22/199; TF240870; NP 105
Grimley (parish), 40/104; SO820602; NP 130
Grimmer (township in Worthen), 31/329; SJ348034; NP 118
Grimoldby (parish), 22/287; TF396883; NP 105
Grimsargh (division in Grimsargh with Brockholes in Preston), 20/221; SD587340; NP 94
Grimsargh with Brockholes (township in Preston), 20/219-221; NP 94
Grimsbury (hamlet in Warkworth), 26/360; SP461418; NP 145
Grimsby (Great Grimsby) (parish), 22/79A; TA262088; NP 105
Grimshill (parish), 31/160; NP 118
Grimston (parish), 21/67; SK688215; NP 121, 122
Grimston (parish), 25/179; TF718218; NP 124, 125
Grimston (township in Dunnington), 41/69; SE655502; NP 97
Grimston (Grimstone) (township in Gilling), 42/610; SE618743; NP 92
Grimston (township in Kirkby Wharfe), 43/437; SE492412; NP 97
Grimthorpe (division in parish and township of Great Givendale), 41/108; SE814529; NP 98
Grindale (township in Bridlington), 41/251; TA138715; NP 93
Grindleton (township in Mitton), 43/293-294; NP 95
Grindleybrook (township in Whitchurch), 31/37; SJ523422; NP 118
Grindlow (township in Hope), 8/25; SK185776; NP 111
Grindon (division in Grindon), 33/77A; SK090540; NP 111
Grindon (parish), 11/262-263; NP 85
Grindon (parish), 33/77A-B; NP 111
Grindon (township in Grindon), 11/262; NZ407253; NP 85
Grindon (township in Norham), 27/15; NT916445; NP 64
Grindon (township in Grindon), 33/77B; SK080550; NP 111
Gringley on the Hill (parish), 28/10; SK735920; NP 103, 104
Grinsdale (parish), 7/100; NY364576; NP 76
Grinshill (Grimshill) (parish), 31/160; SJ522230; NP 118
Grinton (division in township of Grinton in Grinton), 42/116; SE043967; NP 90
Grinton (parish), 42/-128; NP 84, 90
Grinton (township in Grinton), 43/111-118; NP 90
Grisby, 42/59; NP 85
Gristhorpe (division in township of Gristhorpe in Filey), 42/405; TA090824; NP 93
Gristhorpe (township in Filey), 42/404-405; NP 93
Griston (parish), 25/679; TL943992; NP 136
Grittenham (tithing in Brinkworth), 39/50; SU026823; NP 157
Grittleton (parish), 39/72; ST862802; NP 156
Grizedale (division in township of Satterthwaite in Hawkshead), 20/46; SD330940; NP 89
Groby (township in Ratby), 21/132B; SK524076; NP 121
Gronant (township in Llanasa), 50/48; SJ093831; NP 108
Grondre (hamlet in Cilymaenllwyd), 55/80; SN115186; NP 139, 152
Grosmont (parish), 53/7; SO395232; NP 142

115

Groton (parish), 34/485; TL966427; NP 149
Grove (parish), 3/128; SP919225; NP 146
Grove (parish), 28/53; SK744800; NP 103, 104
Grove (township in Wantage), 2/89; SU401905; NP 158
Groveley Wood (extra-parochial), 39/293; SU052342; NP 167
Grundisburgh (parish), 34/390; TM215514; NP 150
Grunty Fen (extra-parochial), 4/30; TL498769; NP 135
Grwyne-fawr (township in Talgarth), 45/88; SO260250; NP 141
Grwyne-fechan (township in Talgarth), 45/87; SO230250; NP 141
Gueldale (township in Leake), 42/517; SE431901; NP 91
Guestling (parish), 36/155; TQ848151; NP 184
Guestwick (parish), 25/198; TG055275; NP 125
Guilden Down (township in Clun), 31/400; SO310830; NP 129
Guilden Morden (parish), 4/170; TL276422; NP 147
Guilden Sutton (Sutton-Guilden) (parish), 5/382; SJ448680; NP 109
Guildford St Nicholas (parish), 35/130A-B; NP 169, 169/1
Guildford, Holy Trinity (parish), 35/135; TQ002493; NP 169/1
Guildford, House of Correction (extra-parochial), 35/134; SU998493; NP 169
Guildford, St Mary (Guildford, St Mary-the-Virgin) (parish), 35/132; SU995494; NP 169/1
Guildford, The Friary, 35/131; NP 169/1
Guilsborough (hamlet in Guilsborough), 26/170; SP679736; NP 132, 133
Guilsborough (parish), 26/170-172; NP 132, 133
Guilsfield [Cegidfa]) (parish), 54/73-81; NP 117
Guisborough (Gisborough) (parish), 42/356-360; NP 86
Guisborough (Gisborough) (township in Guisborough), 42/359; NZ618158; NP 86
Guiseley (parish), 43/505-509; NP 96 (parish), 43/505-509; NP 96
Guiseley (township in Guiseley), 43/508; SE192428; NP 96
Guist (parish), 25/194; TG001261; NP 125
Guiting Power (Guyting Power) (division in Guiting Power), 13/77; SP096245; NP 144
Guiting Power (Guyting Power) (parish), 13/68, 77; NP 144
Gulval (parish), 6/207; SW479339; NP 189
Gumfreston (parish), 55/136; SN103022; NP 152
Gumley (parish), 21/317; SP679899; NP 132, 133
Gummershay (tithing in Stalbridge), 10/26B; ST760180; NP 178
Gunby (division in township of Breighton and Gunby in Bubwith), 41/29; SE720350; NP 97
Gunby (parish), 22/488; TF473662; NP 114
Gunby (parish), 22/692; SK910210; NP 122
Gungrog Fawr (township in Pool), 54/72; SJ243100; NP 117
Gunhouse, 22/20; NP 104
Gunnerside with Lodge Green (division in township of Melbecks in Grinton), 42/107; SD945985; NP 90
Gunnerton (township in Chollerton), 27/439; NY914762; NP 77
Gunness (Gunhouse) (township in West Halton), 22/20; SE845115; NP 104
Gunthorpe (parish), 25/121; TG013351; NP 125
Gunthorpe (township in Paston), 26/10; TF184301; NP 123
Gunthorpe (township in Lowdham), 28/189; SK682448; NP 112, 121
Gunthorpe (hamlet in Oakham), 30/19; SK870057; NP 122
Gunthwaite (township in Penistone), 43/780; SE238066; NP 102
Gunton (parish), 25/136; TG232338; NP 126
Gunton (parish), 34/16; TM542957; NP 137
Gunwalloe (parish), 6/194; SW661221; NP 189
Gussage All Saints (parish), 10/76; SU006125; NP 179
Gussage St Michael (parish), 10/77; ST990130; NP 179
Guston (parish), 19/366; TR326439; NP 173
Guyson, 27/212; NP 71
Guyting Power, 13/77
Guyzance (Guyson) (extra-parochial), 27/212; NU 211041
Gwaenynog (township in Llanfair Caereinion), 54/45; SJ077111; NP 117
Gwaenysgor (parish), 50/52; SJ083819; NP 108
Gwarafog (township in Llanlleonfel), 45/27; SN958480; NP 141
Gwastedin (township in Nantmel), 56/31A; SN985665; NP 128

Gwehelog (Gwehellog) (hamlet in Usk [Brynbuga]), 53/63; SO385031; NP 155
Gwenddwr (parish), 45/10; SO050435; NP 141
Gwennap (parish), 6/164; SW742415; NP 189, 190
Gwenthrew (township in Kerry [Llanfihangel-yng-Ngheri]), 54/179; SO190890; NP 128
Gwern Howel (extra-parochial), 49/19; NP 107, 108
Gwern Hywel (Gwerni Hywel, Gwern Howel, Gwerni Howel) (extra-parochial), 49/19 SH859496; NP 107, 108
Gwern-y-bwch (township in Cemmes), 54/123; SH876039; NP 116, 117
Gwern-y-go (township in Kerry [Llanfihangel-yng-Ngheri]), 54/183; SO213913; NP 128
Gwernafield (township in Mold), 50/107; SJ206651; NP 108
Gwerneigron, 50/72; NP 108
Gwerneirin (township in Llandinam), 54/152; SO012890; NP 128
Gwernesgob (township in Kerry [Llanfihangel-yng-Ngheri]), 54/171; SO122869; NP 128
Gwernesney (parish), 53/79; ST418022; NP 155
Gwernglefryd (township in St Asaph [Llanelwy]), 50/73; SJ036751; NP 108
Gwerni Howel (extra-parochial), 49/19; NP 107, 108
Gwerni Hywel (extra-parochial), 49/19; NP 107, 108
Gwernigron (Gwerneigron) (township in St Asaph [Llanelwy]), 50/72; SJ028768; NP 108
Gwernospin (township in Chirk), 49/100; SJ268387; NP 117
Gwersyllt (township in Gresford), 49/67; SJ318538; NP 108
Gwespyr (township in Llanasa), 50/47; SJ111828; NP 108
Gwestydd (township in Llanllwchaiarn), 54/166A; SO123933; NP 128
Gwillim (hamlet in Llanwenog), 46/82A; SN492467; NP 139, 140
Gwinear (parish), 6/170; SW611371; NP 189
Gwithian (parish), 6/168; SW591409; NP 189
Gwlad (hamlet in Llangeler), 47/38; SN378372; NP 139
Gwnnws (parish), 46/34-35; NP 127
Gwnnws Issa (Lower Gwnnws) (township in Gwnnws), 46/34; SN700703; NP 127
Gwredog (extra-parochial), 44/16; SH404864; NP 106
Gwsaney, 50/108; NP 108
Gwyddelwern (parish), 52/16; SJ075470; NP 108
Gwydir, 48/18; NP 107
Gwydyr (Gwydir) (township in Llanwrst), 48/18; SH740560; NP 107
Gwyffylliog (parish), 49/26; NP 108
Gwynfe Quarter Bach, 47/21; NP 140, 153
Gwynfil (township in Llandewi-Brefi), 46/42; SN627588; NP 140
Gwysaney (Gwsaney) (township in Mold), 50/108; SJ226661; NP 108
Gwytherin (parish), 49/12; SH875607; NP 107, 108
Gyffin (Gyfin) (parish), 48/8; SH769759; NP 107
Gyffylliog, 49/26; NP 108
Gyfin, 48/8; NP 107

H

Habberley (parish), 31/334; SJ390029; NP 118
Habblesthorpe (Applethorpe) (parish), 28/43; SK796823; NP 104
Habergham Eaves (township in Whalley), 20/278; SD830310; NP 95
Habrough (Haburgh) (parish), 22/72; TA152141; NP 104, 105
Haburgh (parish), 22/72; NP 104, 105
Haccombe (parish), 9/413; SX895700; NP 188
Hacconby (Haconby) (hamlet in Hacconby), 22/706A; TF130255; NP 123
Hacconby (Haconby) (parish), 22/706A-B; NP 123
Haceby (parish), 22/640; TF030361; NP 123
Hacheston (parish), 34/529; TM306584; NP 137, 150
Hackensall (division in township of Preesall with Hackensall in Lancaster), 20/140; SD355478; NP 94
Hacketts-Broughton (parish), 40/153; NP 130
Hackford (Hackford next Reepham, Hackford-by-Reepham) (parish), 25/264; TG085227; NP 125
Hackford (parish), 25/659; TG056026; NP 125, 136

Hackforth (township in Hornby), 42/199; SE245933; NP 91
Hackington (St Stephen) (parish), 19/141; TR152602; NP 173
Hackleton (hamlet in Piddington), 26/293; SP815552; NP 133, 146
Hackness (parish), 42/391-395; NP 92, 93
Hackness (township in Hackness), 42/392; SE953923; NP 93
Hackney (division in St John at Hackney), 24/75; TQ358853; NP 160, 161
Hackney Road (division in St Matthew Bethnal Green), 24/63A; TQ344831; NP 160/1
Hackthorn (parish), 22/251; SK999821; NP 104
Hackwell (parish), 12/367; NP 162
Haconby (parish), 22/706A-B; NP 123
Haconby, 22/706A; NP 123
Haddenham (parish), 3/163; SP737087; NP 146, 159
Haddenham (parish), 4/37; TL442748; NP 135
Haddington (division in Aubourn), 22/538; SK918632; NP 113
Haddington (division in South Hykeham), 22/537; SK905633; NP 113
Haddington (township in South Hykeham and Aubourn), 22/537-538; NP 113
Haddiscoe (parish), 25/588; TM446970; NP 137
Haddon (parish), 17/12; TL135930; NP 134
Hadfield (township in Glossop), 8/2; SK020960; NP 102
Hadleigh (parish), 12/388; TQ810869; NP 162
Hadleigh (parish), 34/482; TM033433; NP 149
Hadleigh Hamlet (hamlet in Boxford), 34/483; TL976418; NP 149
Hadley (parish), 24/86; NP 160
Hadley (tithing in Lambourn), 2/107B; SU330760; NP 158
Hadlow (parish), 19/210; TQ625492; NP 171
Hadnall (township in Myddle), 31/157; SJ518198; NP 118
Hadstock (parish), 12/1; TL563448; NP 148
Hadston (Hadstone) (township in Warkworth), 27/229; NU266005; NP 71
Hadzor (parish), 40/134; SO918620; NP 130
Hagbourne (parish), 2/79-80; NP 158
Haggerston East (Haggerstone East) (division in St Leonard Shoreditch), 24/62F; TQ341837; NP 160/1
Haggerston West (Haggerstone West) (division in St Leonard Shoreditch), 24/62E; TQ336835; NP 160/1
Haggerston (township in Ancroft parochial chapelry in Holy Island), 27/21; NU035435; NP 64
Hagley (parish), 40/26; SO909805; NP 130
Hagnaby (division in Hagnaby), 22/437A; TF344621; NP 114
Hagnaby (parish), 22/437A-B; TF344621; NP 114
Hagnaby - West Fen (division in Hagnaby), 22/437B; TF331597; NP 114
Hagworthingham (parish), 22/450; TF351698; NP 114
Haigh (township in Wigan), 20/584; SD593089; NP 100, 101
Haighton (township in Preston), 20/210; SD565345; NP 94
Hail Weston (parish), 17/99; TL154624; NP 134
Haile (Hale) (parish), Hale, 7/306; NY043095; NP 82
Hailes (parish), 13/69; SP048303; NP 144
Hailey (hamlet in Witney), 29/179; SP360120; NP 145
Hailsham (parish), 36/182; TQ597085; NP 183
Hainford (Haynford) (parish), 25/254; TG230187; NP 126
Hainton (parish), 22/273; TF188849; NP 105
Haisthorpe (township in Burton Agnes), 41/261A; TA132642; NP 93, 99
Halam (parish), 28/160; SK672542; NP 112
Halberton (parish), 9/154; ST003114; NP 164, 176
Haldenby (township in Adlingfleet), 43/953; SE819179; NP 104
Hale (parish), 14/308; SU190182; NP 179
Hale (township in Bowdon), 5/85; SJ794859; NP 101
Hale (township in Childwall), 20/647; SJ465825; NP 100
Hale Fen (extra-parochial), 4/34; TL480810; NP 135
Hale, 7/306; NP 82
Hales (parish), 25/591; TM381963; NP 137
Halesowen (parish), 40/5-19; NP 130, 131
Halesowen (township in Halesowen), 40/10; SO968838; NP 130
Halesworth (parish), 34/75; TM386774; NP 137
Halewood (township in Childwall), 20/646; SJ460850; NP 100

Halford (chapelry in Bromfield), 31/421; SO440835; NP 129
Halford (parish), 37/285; SP268456; NP 144
Halghton (township in Hanmer), 50/138; SJ432411; NP 118
Halifax (parish), 43/546-577; NP 95, 96, 101, 102
Halifax (township in Halifax), 43/552; SE086250; NP 96
Halkyn (Halkin), 50/105-106; NP 108
Hall End and Delves (township in Polesworth), 37/13; SK253007; NP 120, 131
Hall Field (extra-parochial), 12/437; TL765395; NP 149
Hallaton (parish), 21/298; SP782972; NP 133
Hallgarth (division of Pittington township in Pittington), 11/110; NZ328439; NP 85
Halling (parish), 19/83; TQ694646; NP 171
Hallington (parish), 22/280; TF299858; NP 105
Hallington (township in St John Lee), 27/445; NY990760; NP 77
Halliwell (township in Deane), 20/572; SD685125; NP 101
Halloughton (parish), 28/194; SK685515; NP 112
Hallow (parish), 40/110A-B; NP 130, 143
Halmer End (township in Audley), 33/42D; SJ795490; NP 110
Halnaby (division in township of Croft in Croft), 42/55; NZ258077; NP 85
Halsall (parish), 20/355-362; NP 100
Halsall (township in Halsall), 20/355; SD350120; NP 100
Halse (hamlet in Brackley St Peter), 26/347; SP566403; NP 145
Halse (parish), 32/293; ST138284; NP 164
Halsham (parish), 41/417; TA279275; NP 99
Halstead (Halsted) (parish), 12/127; TL815300; NP 149
Halstead (Halsted) (parish), 19/72; TQ486615; NP 171
Halstead (township in Tilton), 21/272; SK754061; NP 122
Halsted (parish), 19/72; NP 171
Halstock (parish), 10/104; ST530081; NP 177
Halston (extra-parochial), 31/89; SJ341313; NP 118
Haltemprice (extra-parochial), 41/306; TA042310; NP 99
Halten (parish), 3/177; NP 146, 159
Haltham (division in Haltham), 22/449A; TF253639; NP 114
Haltham (parish), 22/449A-B; NP 114
Haltham - Wildmore Fen (division in Haltham), 22/449B; TF241548; NP 114
Halton (division in township of Temple Newsham in Whitkirk), 43/481; SE348331; NP 96
Halton (Halten) (parish), 3/177; SP882094; NP 146, 159
Halton (parish), 20/97-98; NP 89
Halton (parish), 22/19-20; NP 98, 104
Halton (township in Runcorn), 5/158; SJ535823; NP 100
Halton (township in Halton), 20/97; SD522665; NP 89
Halton (township in Corbridge), 27/472; NZ003681; NP 77
Halton (township in Chirk), 49/96; SJ312393; NP 118
Halton East (township in Skipton), 43/330; SE041541; NP 96
Halton Gill (township in Arncliffe), 43/227; SD865755; NP 90
Halton Holegate (division in Halton Holegate), 22/425A; TF417650; NP 114
Halton Holegate (parish), 22/425A-B; NP 114
Halton Holegate - East Fen (division in Halton Holegate), 22/425B; TF423612; NP 114
Halton Shields (township in Corbridge), 27/471; NZ015688; NP 77
Haltwhistle (parish), 27/574-586; NP 76, 77
Haltwhistle (township in Haltwhistle), 27/583; NY702651; NP 76
Halvergate (parish), 25/461; TG435065; NP 126
Halwell (parish), 9/442; SX781535; NP 187, 188
Halwell, 9/191; NP 174, 175
Halwill (Halwell) (parish), 9/191; SX432989; NP 174, 175
Ham (parish), 19/274; TR329548; NP 173
Ham (parish), 39/386; SU333624; NP 158, 168
Ham (tithing in Berkeley), 13/321; ST660980; NP 156
Ham and Bargham (tithing in Angmering), 36/296; TQ058035; NP 182
Ham with Hatch (hamlet in Kingston upon Thames), 35/33; TQ190717; NP 170
Hamble (Hamblerice) (parish), 14/272; SU478067; NP 180
Hambleden (Hambledon) (parish), 3/212; SU783880; NP 159
Hambledon (parish), 14/251; SU655148; NP 168, 180
Hambledon (parish), 35/158; SU967386; NP 169

Hambleton (township in Kirkham), 20/190; SD378424; NP 94
Hambleton (parish), 30/23; SK900071; NP 122
Hambleton (township in Brayton), 43/455; SE552312; NP 97
Hameringham (parish), 22/387; TF307667; NP 114
Hamerton (parish), 17/40; TL130792; NP 134
Hamfallow (tithing in Berkeley), 13/317; SO612092; NP 156
Hamlet of St Thomas (hamlet in Haverfordwest, St Thomas), 55/88; SM938134; NP 151
Hammersmith (parish), 24/42A-C; NP 160, 170
Hammerwich (township in St Michael), 33/267; SK063072; NP 120
Hammoon (parish), 10/53; ST815140; NP 178
Hamphall Stubbs (township in South Kirkby), 43/657; SE497111; NP 103
Hampnett (parish), 13/220; SP097156; NP 144
Hampole (township in Adwick le Street), 43/655; SE510100; NP 103
Hampreston (hamlet in Hampreston), 10/174A; SU070005; NP 179
Hampreston (parish), 10/174A-B; NP 179
Hampstead Marshall (parish), 2/147; NP 158, 168
Hampstead Norreys (Hampstead Norris) (parish), 2/126; SU520750; NP 158
Hampstead (parish), 24/43; TQ261851; NP 160
Hampsthwaite (parish), 43/154-157; NP 91, 96
Hampsthwaite (township in Hampsthwaite), 43/154; SE261580; NP 96
Hampton (hamlet in Hampton), 24/129; TQ142700; NP 170
Hampton (parish), 24/129-130; NP 170
Hampton (township in Malpas), 5/329; SJ510495; NP 109
Hampton Bishop (township in Hampton Bishop), 15/137; SO558378; NP 142
Hampton Charles (hamlet in Bockleton), 15/77; SO608609; NP 129
Hampton Gay (parish), 29/121; SP496163; NP 145
Hampton in Arden (hamlet in Hampton in Arden), 37/81A; SP198810; NP 131
Hampton in Arden (parish), 37/81A-82, 84-85; NP 131
Hampton Lovett (Hampton Lovet) (parish), 40/57; SO885658; NP 130
Hampton Lucy (hamlet in Hampton Lucy), 37/215; SP243579; NP 131
Hampton Lucy (parish), 37/215-216; NP 131
Hampton Poyle (parish), 29/120; SP508152; NP 145
Hampton Wafer (extra-parochial), 15/97; SO574564; NP 129
Hampton Wick (hamlet in Hampton), 24/130; TQ168689; NP 170
Hampton Wood (township in Ellesmere), 31/71; SJ429385; NP 118
Hamsey (parish), 36/197; TQ402127; NP 183
Hamstall Ridware (parish), 33/198; SK110194; NP 120
Hamstead Marshall (Hampstead Marshall) (parish), 2/147; SU415668; NP 158, 168
Hamsterley (township in St Andrew Auckland), 11/193; NZ118301; NP 84, 85
Hamsterley Common (common to Hamsterley, South Bedburn and Lynesack and Softley in St Andrew Auckland), 11/190; NZ055315; NP 84
Hamworthy (parish), 10/198; SY990910; NP 179
Hanborough (parish), 29/190; SP427138; NP 145
Hanbury (parish), 33/200-208; NP 120
Hanbury (parish), 40/135; SO956622; NP 130
Hanbury (township in Hanbury), 33/207; SK182278; NP 120
Hanbury Park (division in Tutbury), 33/209B; SK172269; NP 120
Hanbury Woodend (township in Hanbury), 33/208; SK172272; NP 120
Hanby (hamlet in Lenton), 22/667; TF028320; NP 123
Hanby, 22/421; NP 114
Hanchurch (township in Trentham), 33/65; SJ841410; NP 119
Handforth (division in Handsforth cum Bosden township in Cheadle), 5/26; SJ864835; NP 101
Handforth cum Bosden (township in Cheadle), 5/25-26; NP 101
Handley (parish), 5/361-362; NP 109
Handley (Sixpenny Handley) (parish), 10/64; ST983571; NP 179

Handley (township in Handley), 5/361; SJ463582; NP 109
Handley (township in Towcester), 26/315; SP673471; NP 145, 146
Handsworth (parish), 33/303; NP 131
Handsworth (township in Handsworth), 33/303; SP050900; NP 131
Handsworth (parish), 43/834; SK407858; NP 102, 103, 111
Hanford (extra-parochial), 10/58; ST849113; NP 178
Hanford (township in Trentham), 33/67; SJ873425; NP 119
Hanging Grimston (division in parish and township of Kirby Underdale), 41/138C; SE799598; NP 98
Hanging Houghton (hamlet in Lamport), 26/168; SP743736; NP 133
Hangleton (parish), 36/210; TQ265080; NP 182
Hanham (chapelry in Bitton), 13/403; ST647706; NP 156
Hankelow (township in Audlem), 5/272; SJ667458; NP 110, 119
Hankerton (division in Malmsbury Eastern Registration Subdistrict of Hankerton in Hankerton), 39/23A; ST967919; NP 157
Hankerton (parish), 39/23A-C; NP 157
Hanley (township in Stoke-on-Trent), 33/35; SJ889476; NP 110
Hanley Castle (Hanley Swan) (parish), 40/171; SO810430; NP 143
Hanley Child (Lower Hanley) (chapelry in Eastham), 40/88; SO650652; NP 130
Hanley Swan (parish), 40/171; SO810430; NP 143
Hanley William (Upper Hanley) (parish), 40/91; SO673660; NP 130
Hanlith (township in Kirkby Malhamdale), 43/237; SD909612; NP 90, 95
Hanmer (parish), 50/138-143; NP 118
Hanmer (township in Hanmer), 50/139; SJ458392; NP 118
Hannah cum Hagnaby (parish), 22/310; TF490800; NP 105
Hannington (division in Hannington), 14/57; SU536567; NP 168
Hannington (parish), 14/56-57; NP 168
Hannington (parish), 26/201; SP817709; NP 133
Hannington (parish), 39/8; SU177937; NP 157
Hanover Square (division in St George Hanover Square), 24/36D; TQ285808; NP 160
Hanslope (parish), 3/25; SP800470; NP 146
Hanson Grange (township in Thorpe), 8/176; SK157540; NP 111
Hanthorpe (hamlet in Morton), 22/707; TF082238; NP 123
Hanwell (parish), 24/105; TQ157812; NP 160, 170
Hanwell (parish), 29/14; SP441435; NP 145
Hanwood (parish), 31/293; NP 118
Hanworth (parish), 24/125; TQ118719; NP 170
Hanworth (parish), 25/135; TG206349; NP 126
Happisburgh (Hasbro') (parish), 25/222; TG383299; NP 126
Hapsford (township in Thornton le Moors), 5/417; SJ471745; NP 100, 109
Hapton (parish), 25/610; TM182966; NP 137
Hapton (township in Whalley), 20/292; SD802307; NP 95
Harberton (parish), 9/371; SX774584; NP 187
Harbledown (parish), 19/143; TR118582; NP 173
Harborne (parish), 33/345; NP 131
Harborne (township in Harborne), 33/345; SP026842; NP 131
Harborough, 21/315; NP 133
Harborough Magna (Great Harborough) (parish), 37/117; SP484798; NP 132
Harbottle (township in Holystone), 27/187; NT937041; NP 71
Harbridge (parish), 14/315; SU126089; NP 179
Harbury (parish), 37/254; SP368602; NP 132
Harby (parish), 21/84; SK751304; NP 122
Harby (township in North Clifton), 28/119; SK884719; NP 113
Harcourt (township in Stanton upon Hine Heath), 31/203; SJ568248; NP 118
Harden (division in township and parish of Thornton in Cravern), 43/315; SD922447; NP 95
Harden (division in township of Bingley in Bingley), 43/358; SE087387; NP 96
Hardenhuish (parish), 39/83; ST910748; NP 156
Hardham (parish), 36/83; TQ042175; NP 181, 182
Hardham with Newton, 20/169; NP 94

Hardhorn with Newton (Hardham with Newton) (township in Poulton-le-Fylde), 20/169; SD351370; NP 94
Hardingham (parish), 25/552; TG041048; NP 125
Hardingstone (parish), 26/284; SP760583; NP 133
Hardington (parish), 32/101; ST743528; NP 166
Hardington Mandeville (parish), 32/478; ST505105; NP 177
Hardley (parish), 25/583; TG383006; NP 126, 137
Hardmead (parish), 3/38; SP937475; NP 146
Hardshaw within Windle (division in township of Windle in Prescot), 20/633; SJ514957; NP 100
Hardwick (Hardwicke) (hamlet in Hardwick), 3/140; SP805190; NP 146
Hardwick (Hardwicke) (parish), 3/140-141; NP 146
Hardwick (Hardwicke) (parish), 4/110; TL371584; NP 135
Hardwick (township in Torksey), 22/239; SK873758; NP 104, 113
Hardwick (parish), 25/638; TM225897; NP 137
Hardwick (parish), 26/205; SP843697; NP 133
Hardwick (Hardwicke) (hamlet in Ducklington), 29/183; SP381577; NP 158
Hardwick (parish), 29/67; SP576297; NP 145
Hardwick (township in Ellesmere), 31/63; SJ371340; NP 118
Hardwick (extra-parochial), 34/228; TL850620; NP 136
Hardwick (Hardwicke) (hamlet in Abergavenny [Y Fenn]), 53/36; SO313124; NP 142
Hardwicke (parish), 4/110; NP 135
Hardwicke (parish), 13/260; SO792127; NP 143
Hardwicke (township in Myddle), 31/156B; SJ518213; NP 118
Hardy Flatts (extra-parochial), 42/646; SE726667; NP 92
Hareby (division in Hareby), 22/439A; TF339658; NP 114
Hareby (parish), 22/439A-B; NP 114
Hareby - West Fen (division in Hareby), 22/439B; TF312600; NP 114
Harefield (parish), 24/94; TQ061895; NP 160
Harehope (Hareup, Harup) (township in Eglingham), 27/141; NU090204; NP 71
Harescombe (Harescomb) (parish), 13/253; SO839098; NP 143, 156
Haresfield (parish), 13/261; SO809101; NP 143, 156
Hareup, 27/141
Harewood (parish), 15/243; SO532272; NP 142
Harewood (parish), 43/399-406; NP 96
Harewood (township in Harewood), 43/402; SE325445; NP 96
Harford (parish), 9/367; SX639586; NP 187
Hargham (parish), 25/670; TM022915; NP 136
Hargrave (parish), 26/146; TL032710; NP 134
Hargrave (parish), 34/315; TL772598; NP 136
Harkerside (division in township of Grinton in Grinton), 42/114; SE024984; NP 90
Harkerside Moor (division in township of Grinton in Grinton), 42/118; SE027971; NP 90
Harkstead (parish), 34/521; TM198350; NP 150
Harlaston (township in Clifton Campville), 33/275; SK217099; NP 120
Harlaxton (parish), 22/71; SK887332; NP 122
Harlech, 52/8; NP 116
Harlescott (township in St Alkmond Shrewsbury and St Mary Shrewsbury), 31/253; SJ503163; NP 118
Harleston (chapelry in Redenhall), 25/636; TM242831; NP 137
Harleston (parish), 34/298; TM019608; NP 136
Harlestone (parish), 26/238; SP702646; NP 132, 133
Harlethorpe, 41/27; NP 97, 98
Harley (division of Harley, Wigwig and Homer township in Much Wenlock), 31/449; SJ593012; NP 118
Harley (parish), 31/448; SJ593012; NP 118, 119, 129, 130
Harley, Wigwig and Homer (township in Much Wenlock), 31/449-450; NP 118, 119
Harlington (parish), 1/118; TL043304; NP 147
Harlington (parish), 24/113; TQ089784; NP 160, 170
Harlow (parish), 12/259; TL480110; NP 148, 161
Harlow Hill (township in Ovingham), 27/551; NZ080682; NP 77
Harlthorpe (Harletorpe) (township in Bubwith), 41/27; SE745372; NP 97, 98

Harlton (parish), 4/127; TL386528; NP 148
Harmby (township in Spennithorne), 42/187; SE113905; NP 91
Harmondsworth (parish), 24/115; TQ071767; NP 170
Harmston (parish), 22/556; SK975625; NP 113
Harnage (township in Cound), 31/446; SJ561031; NP 118
Harnham (township in Bolam), 27/392; NZ071810; NP 77
Harnhill (parish), 13/281; SP060007; NP 157
Harold Wood (Harrold's Wood) (hamlet in Romford), 12/314C; TQ533917; NP 161
Haroldslea, 35/109B
Haroldston St Issells (Harroldston St Issells) (parish), 55/89; SM956139; NP 151
Haroldston West (Harroldston West, West Harroldston) (parish), 55/93; SM879149; NP 151
Harome (township in Helmsley), 42/489; SE652819; NP 92
Harpenden (parish), 16/91; TL126138; NP 147
Harpford (parish), 9/285; SY088905; NP 176
Harpham (township in Burton Agnes), 41/270; TA095620; NP 99
Harpley (parish), 25/170; TF789261; NP 125
Harpole (parish), 26/237; SP690610; NP 132, 133
Harpsden (Harpsden cum Bolney) (parish), 29/322; SU750803; NP 159
Harpswell (parish), 22/224; SK920893; NP 104
Harpton and Wolfpits (Upper Harpton) (township in Old Radnor), 56/24; 56/25
Harpurhey (township in Manchester), 20/511; SD859015; NP 101
Harraby (township in St Cuthbert [Carlisle]), 7/84; NY421545; NP 76
Harraton (township in Chester le Street), 11/51; NZ295540; NP 78
Harrietsham (parish), 19/226; TQ869532; NP 172
Harrington (parish), 7/256; NX991238; NP 82
Harrington (parish), 22/397; TF365715; NP 114
Harrington (parish), 26/125; SP776804; NP 133
Harringworth (parish), 26/51; SP923957; NP 133
Harrold (parish), 1/23; SP936572; NP 133, 146
Harrold's Wood, 12/314C; NP 161
Harroldston St Issells, 55/89; NP 151
Harrop (division in township of Forest of Bowland (Lower Division) in Whalley, 43/287; SD742495; NP 95
Harrow on the Hill (parish), 24/91; TQ150890; NP 160
Harrowby (township in Grantham), 22/624; SK935361; NP 122
Harrowden Magna (parish), 26/209; NP 133
Harrowden Parva (parish), 26/199; NP 133
Harrowsley (Haroldslea) (division in Horne), 35/109B; TQ302427; NP 170
Harston (parish), 4/129; TL427507; NP 148
Harston (parish), 21/93; SK841316; NP 122
Harswell (parish), 41/101; SE830410; NP 98
Hart (parish), 11/243-248; NP 85
Hart (township in Hart), 11/246; NZ471349; NP 85
Hartburn (parish), 27/336-359; NP 77
Hartburn (township in Hartburn), 27/348; NZ087863; NP 77
Hartburn Grange (township in Hartburn), 27/346; NZ060862; NP 77
Hartest (parish), 34/344; TL835525; NP 149
Hartfield (parish), 36/42A-B; NP 171, 183
Hartfield - North Division (division in Hartfield), 36/42A; TQ470380; NP 171
Hartfield - South Division (division in Hartfield), 36/42B; TQ465325; NP 171, 183
Hartford (township in Great Budworth), 5/143; SJ642722; NP 110
Hartford (parish), 17/79; TL258734; NP 134
Hartforth (division in township of Gilling in Gilling), 42/46; 166068; NP 85
Hartgrave (tithing in Fontmell Magna), 10/13; ST837193; NP 166, 178
Hartgrove or East Orchards (parish), 10/14; NP 178
Harthill (parish), 5/340; SJ503551; NP 109
Harthill (Hartle) (township in Bakewell), 8/96; SK225635; NP 111
Harthill (parish), 43/899-900; NP 103, 103/1

119

Harthill with Woodall (township in Harthill), 43/900; SK491809; NP 103
Harting (parish), 36/10; NP 181
Hartington (parish), 8/108; NP 111
Hartington (township in Hartburn), 27/338; NZ010896; NP 77
Hartington Hall (township in Hartburn), 27/340; NZ020880; NP 77
Hartishead, 43/580; NP 96
Hartland (parish), 9/51; SS259228; NP 174
Hartle, 8/96; NP 111
Hartlebury (parish), 40/31-32; NP 130
Hartlebury (township in Hartlebury), 40/32; SO838708; NP 130
Hartlepool (parish and township), 11/249; NZ527340; NP 85
Hartley (parish), 19/55; TQ611672; NP 171
Hartley (township in Earsdon), 27/490; NZ336748; NP 78
Hartley (township in Kirkby Stephen), 38/61; NY799078; NP 84, 90
Hartley Dummer (division in Shinfield), 2/185; SU703682; NP 169
Hartley Mauditt (parish), 14/122; SU746361; NP 169
Hartley Wespall (Hartley Westpall) (parish), 14/43; SU700580; NP 169
Hartley Westpall (parish), 14/43; NP 169
Hartley Wintney (parish), 14/36; SU763566; NP 169
Hartleyburn (township in Haltwhistle), 27/574; NY652598; NP 76
Hartlington (township in Burnsall), 43/208; SE044630; NP 90, 96
Hartlip (parish), 19/446; TQ835639; NP 172
Hartoft (township in Middleton), 42/438; SE750950; NP 92
Harton (township in Jarrow), 11/3; NZ371648; NP 78
Harton (township in Bossall), 42/660; SE694618; NP 92
Hartpury (parish), 13/139; SO790240; NP 143
Harts Grounds (extra-parochial), 22/743; TF202528; NP 113, 114
Hartshead (division in township of Ashton under Lyne in Ashton under Lyne), 20/538; SD960010; NP 101
Hartshead (Hartishead) (township in Dewsbury), 43/580; SE181222; NP 96
Hartsheath (township in Mold), 50/119; SJ283612; NP 108
Hartshill (township in Mancetter), 37/62; SP335946; NP 132
Hartshorn (parish), 8/309; SK325210; NP 121
Hartsop and Patterdale (township in Barton), 38/28; NY390140; NP 83
Hartwell (parish), 3/167; SP800125; NP 146
Hartwell (parish), 26/298; SP789498; NP 146
Hartwell Lodge (extra-parochial in Salcey Forest), 26/297; SP791514; NP 146
Hartwith cum Winsley (township in Kirkby Malzeard), 43/194; SE221626; NP 91
Harup, 27/141
Harvington (parish), 40/194; SP056492; NP 144
Harwell (parish), 2/82; SU494890; NP 158
Harwell (township in Everton), 28/5; SK678913; NP 103
Harwich (St Nicholas; Harwich, St Nicholas) (parish), 12/111; TM261326; NP 150
Harwood (township in Bolton le Moors), 20/397; SD744122; NP 101
Harwood (township in Hartburn), 27/337; NY998918; NP 77
Harwood Dale (township in Hackness), 42/391; SE953967; NP 92, 93
Harworth (parish), 28/17; SK640930; NP 103
Hasbro' (parish), 25/222; NP 126
Hasbury (township in Halesowen), 40/6; SO958835; NP 130
Hascombe (parish), 35/161; TQ008384; NP 169, 170
Haselbech (Haselbeich, Haselbeech) (parish), 26/122; SP704773; NP 133
Haselbeich (parish), 26/122; NP 133
Haselbury Bryan (parish), 10/90; ST749089; NP 178
Haselbury Plucknett (parish), 32/479; ST486108; NP 177
Haseley (parish), 37/91; SP235695; NP 131
Haselor (parish), 37/199; SP123574; NP 131
Haselour (Haslour) (extra-parochial), 33/273; SK205108; NP 120
Hasfield (parish), 13/121; SO828276; NP 143

Hasguard (parish), 55/100; SM850100; NP 151
Hasingham (Hassingham) (parish), 25/469; TG370059; NP 126
Haskayne (division in township of Downholland in Halsall), 20/357; SD349078 NP 100
Hasketon (parish), 34/387; TM250505; NP 150
Hasland (township in Chesterfield), 8/76; SK395690; NP 111, 112
Haslingden (township in Whalley), 20/300; SD777229; NP 95
Haslingfield (parish), 4/128; TL409528; NP 148
Haslington (township in Barthomley), 5/242; SJ747566; NP 110
Haslour (extra-parochial), 33/273; NP 120
Hassall (Little Hassall) (township in Sandbach), 5/219; SJ769577; NP 110
Hassop (township in Bakewell), 8/93; SK224718; NP 111
Hastingleigh (parish), 19/334; TR096446; NP 172, 173
Hastings, All Saints (parish), 36/159; TQ835104; NP 184, 184/1
Hastings, Holy Trinity (Priory) (parish), 36/163; TQ814099; NP 184, 184/1
Hastings, St Andrew (parish), 36/162; TQ819099; NP 184/1
Hastings, St Clement (parish), 36/160; TQ828102; NP 184, 184/1
Hastings, St Mary at the Castle (parish), 36/161; TQ804111; NP 184, 184/1
Hastings, St Mary Magdalene (division in Hastings, St Mary Magdalene), 36/165; TQ806094; NP 184, 184/1
Hastings, St Mary Magdalene, 36/165-166; NP 184, 184/1
Hastings, St Michael on the Rock (parish), 36/164; TQ814094; NP 184
Haston (township in Myddle), 31/156A; SJ512205; NP 118
Haswell (township in Easington), 11/89; NZ371433; NP 85
Hatch Beauchamp (parish), 32/416; ST303204; NP 177
Hatcham (hamlet in St Paul Deptford), 35/21; TQ357769; NP 171
Hatcliffe (parish), 22/168B; TF214001; NP 105
Hatfield (parish), 15/76; SO586594; NP 129
Hatfield (Bishops Hatfield) (parish), 16/105; TL230090; NP 147, 160
Hatfield (parish), 43/944-946; NP 103
Hatfield (township in Hatfield), 43/946; SE663095; NP 103
Hatfield Broad Oak (Kings Hatfield, Hatfield Regis) (parish), 12/198; TL545165; NP 148
Hatfield Hill and Brush House (division in township of Ecclesfield in Ecclesfield), 43/798; SK362918; NP 102
Hatfield Peverel (parish), 12/218; TL794119; NP 149, 161
Hatfield Regis (parish), 12/198; NP 148
Hatford (parish), 2/32; SU336954; NP 158
Hatherleigh (parish), 9/186; SS548052; NP 175
Hathern (Hatherne) (parish), 21/21; SK499220; NP 121
Hatherop (parish), 13/291; SP164048; NP 157
Hathersage (parish), 8/37-42; NP 102, 111
Hathersage (township in Hathersage), 8/42; SK253807; NP 111
Hatherton (township in Wybunbury), 5/262; SJ682474; NP 110
Hatherton (township in Wolverhampton), 33/312; SJ952099; NP 119
Hatley St George (parish), 4/118; TL280515; NP 147
Hattersley (township in Mottram), 5/6; SJ979940; NP 101
Hatton (hamlet in Hatton), 37/170; SP237668; NP 131
Hatton (parish), 22/348; TF175765; NP 105, 114
Hatton (parish), 37/170-172; NP 131
Hatton (township in Runcorn), 5/153; SJ602821; NP 100, 101
Hatton (township in Waverton), 5/375; SJ474613; NP 109
Hatton (township in Marston on Dove), 8/247; SK210310; NP 120
Hatton (township in Eaton), 31/427B; SO470900; NP 129
Hatton (township in Shifnal), 31/223D; SJ760050; NP 119
Haugh (), 20/468; SD945113; NP 101
Haugh (extra-parochial), 22/402; TF417758; NP 105, 114
Haugham (parish), 22/291; TF338816; NP 105
Haughley (parish), 34/237; TM030628; NP 136
Haughmond Demesne (extra-parochial), 31/244; SJ542168; NP 118
Haughton (township in Bunbury), 5/307; SJ590564; NP 109, 110

120

Haughton (township in Haughton le Skerne), 11/331; NZ310155; NP 85
Haughton (township in Manchester), 20/534; SJ932948; NP 101
Haughton (township in Simondburn), 27/436; NY918725; NP 77
Haughton (Houghton) (parish), 28/76; SK680726; NP 112
Haughton (township in West Felton), 31/92; SJ374268; NP 118
Haughton (parish), 33/96; SJ865205; NP 119
Haughton le Skerne (parish), 11/330-336; NP 85
Haulgh (township in Bolton-le-Moors), 20/400; SD727087; NP 101
Haunton (township in Clifton Campville), 33/276; SK232097; NP 120
Hautbois Magna (parish), 25/248; NP 126
Hautbois Parva (parish), 25/247; NP 126
Hauxley (township in Warkworth), 27/227; NU279031; NP 71
Hauxton (parish), 4/130; TL439518; NP 148
Hauxwell (parish), 42/189-192; NP 91
Havant (parish), 14/282; SU724081; NP 181
Haven Bank (extra-parochial), 22/749; TF249504; NP 114
Havengore (extra-parochial), 12/381; TQ979887; NP 162
Haverah Park (extra-parochial), 43/153; SE247541; NP 96
Haverbrack (township in Beetham), 38/131; SD489806; NP 89
Havercroft (division in Havercroft with Cold Hiendly township in Felkirk), 43/680; SE384132; NP 102
Havercroft with Cold Hiendly (township in Felkirk), 43/679-680; NP 102
Haverfordwest, St Martin (division in Haverfordwest, St Martin), 55/86; SM940163; NP 151
Haverfordwest, St Martin (parish), 55/86, 98B; NP 151
Haverfordwest, St Mary [Hwlffordd] (parish), 55/87; SM952156; NP 151
Haverfordwest, St Thomas (division in Haverfordwest, St Thomas), 55/88; SM941151; NP 151
Havergate Island (extra-parochial), 34/376; TM413474; NP 150
Haverhill (division in Haverhill), 12/27; TL679449; NP 148
Haverhill (division in Haverhill), 34/334; TL657456; NP 148
Haverhill (parish), 12/27, 34/334; NP 148
Haverholme Priory (extra-parochial), 22/590; TF111496; NP 113
Havering atte Bower (Havering) (parish), 12/313; TQ510930; NP 161
Haveringland (parish), 25/257; TG159202; NP 125, 126
Haversham (parish), 3/24; SP825433; NP 146
Haverthwaite (division in township of Colton in Colton), 20/52; SD345847; NP 89
Hawarden (Penarlag) (parish), 50/1-15; NP 109
Hawarden (Penarlag) (township in Hawarden), 50/5; SJ316658; NP 109
Hawcoat (division of Dalton township in Dalton in Furness), 20/28-30; NP 88
Hawcoat (part of Hawcoat division in Dalton township in Dalton in Furness), 20/28; SD203712; NP 88
Hawerby cum Beesby (parish), 22/177; TF261964; NP 105
Hawes (township in Aysgarth), 42/133; SD860900; NP 90
Hawick (township in Kirkharle), 27/384; NY952828; NP 77
Hawkchurch (parish), 10/112-113; NP 177
Hawkedon (parish), 34/342; TL799530; NP 149
Hawkesbury (parish), 13/340A-F; NP 156
Hawkesbury (tithing in Hawkesbury), 13/340A; ST770870; NP 156
Hawkesbury Upton (tithing in Hawkesbury), 13/340C; ST780870; NP 156
Hawkesdale (township in Dalston), 7/144; NY352471; NP 83
Hawkhill (township in Lesbury), 27/202; NU222129; NP 71
Hawkhurst (division in Hawkhurst), 19/408; TQ754309; NP 183, 184
Hawkhurst (division in Hawkhurst), 36/346; TQ729299; NP 183
Hawkhurst (parish), 19/408, 36/346; NP 183
Hawkinge (parish), 19/384; TR230400; NP 173
Hawkley (parish), 14/180; SU752294; NP 181
Hawkridge (parish), 32/282; SS844318; NP 164
Hawkshead (division in township of Hawkshead and Monk Coniston with Skelwith in Hawkshead), 20/43; SD352965; NP 89
Hawkshead (parish), 20/41-49; NP 89

Hawkshead and Monk Coniston with Skelwith (township in Hawkshead), 20/41-43; NP 89
Hawkstone Park (township in Hodnet), 31/166; SJ583306; NP 118
Hawkswick (township in Arncliffe), 43/224; SD955710; NP 90
Hawksworth (parish), 28/209; SK753434; NP 122
Hawksworth (township in Otley), 43/364; SE161422; NP 96
Hawkwell (Hackwell) (parish), 12/367; TQ854918; NP 162
Hawkwell (township in), 27/463; NZ072714; NP 77
Hawley and Minley (tithing in Yateley), 14/28; SU834572; NP 169
Hawling (parish), 13/105; SP070225; NP 144
Hawn (township in Halesowen), 40/11; SO961841; NP 130
Hawnby (parish), 42/499-502; NP 91, 92
Hawnby (township in Hawnby), 42/501B; SE540927; NP 92
Hawnes (parish), 1/70; NP 147
Haworth (division in township of Haworth in Bradford), 43/526; SE016364; NP 95, 96
Haworth (township in Bradford), 43/524-527; NP 95, 96
Hawridge (parish), 3/171; SP948062; NP 159
Hawserle Demesne (township in Worthen), 31/333; SJ383022; NP 118, 129
Hawsker with Stainsacre (township in Whitby), 42/386; NZ918088; NP 86
Hawstead (parish), 34/309; TL855590; NP 136, 149
Hawthorn (township in Easington), 11/88; NZ416457; NP 85
Hawthornthwaite Vachery (division in township of Over Wyresdale in Lancaster), 20/132; SD571522; NP 94
Hawthorpe (hamlet in Irnham), 22/681; TF049277; NP 123
Hawthorpe with Bulby (township in Irnham), 22/681-682; NP 123
Hawton (parish), 28/150; SK795504; NP 112, 113
Haxby (township in Wigginton), 42/679; SE610595; NP 97
Haxey (parish), 22/2; SK764998; NP 103, 104
Hay (parish), 45/92A-B
Hay-on-Wye [Y Gelli Gandryll] (division inside town of Hay in Hay-on-Wye [Y Gelli Gandryll]), 45/92B; SO230425; NP 141
Hay-on-Wye [Y Gelli Gandryll] (Hay) (division outside town of Hay in Hay-on-Wye [Y Gelli Gandryll]), 45/92A; SO223407; NP 141
Haydock (township in Winwick), 20/609; SJ562970; NP 100
Haydon (parish), 10/28; ST672155; NP 178
Haydon (parochial chapelry in Warden), 27/595-602B; NP 77
Haydon Bridge (North Side) (township in parochial chapelry of Haydon in Warden), 27/601; NY841645; NP 77
Haydon Bridge (South Side) (township in parochial chapelry of Haydon in Warden), 27/600; NY843641; NP 77
Haydor (parish), 22/641-643; NP 123
Haydor (township in Haydor), 22/641; TF001387; NP 123
Hayes (division in Hayes), 24/108; TQ105810; NP 160, 170
Hayes (division in Alberbury Lower Quarter township in Alberbury), 31/301; SJ352155; NP 118
Hayes (parish), 19/66; TQ404664; NP 171
Hayes (parish), 24/108-109; NP 160, 170
Hayfield (township in Glossop), 8/11; SK023858; NP 102, 111
Haynes (Hawnes) (parish), 1/70; TL088413; NP 147
Haynford (parish), 25/254; NP 126
Hays Haw Fell (division in township of Over Wyresdale in Lancaster), 20/130; SD539521; NP 94
Hayscastle (parish), 55/72; SM912251; NP 138
Hayton (parish), 7/49-51; NP 76
Hayton (parish), 28/36; SK723843; NP 103
Hayton (parish), 41/97-98, 104; NP 98
Hayton (township in Hayton), 7/50; NY516579; NP 76
Hayton (township in Hayton), 41/97; SE821453; NP 98
Hayton and Mealo (Melay) (township in Aspatria), 7/223; NY103415; NP 82
Haywards Field (extra-parochial), 13/75; NP 14
Haywood (parish), 15/187; SO482362; NP 142
Haywood Oaks (extra-parochial), 28/164; SK600550; NP 112
Hazeleigh (parish), 12/342; TL836039; NP 162
Hazeley Heath (tithing in Heckfield), 14/24; SU753586; NP 169
Hazelridge, 27/71; NP 64, 70

Hazelrigg (Hazelridge) (township in Chatton), 27/71; NU058326; NP 64, 70
Hazelwood (division in township of Stutton with Hazelwood in Tadcaster), 43/87; SE457401; NP 97
Hazlebache, 8/22; NP 111
Hazlebadge (Hazlebache) (township in Hope), 8/22; SK172798; NP 111
Hazleton (hamlet in Hazleton), 13/217; SP082179; NP 144
Hazleton (parish), 13/217-218; NP 144
Hazlewood (township in Duffield), 8/190; SK331457; NP 111, 121
Hazlewood (parish), 34/265; TM441590; NP 137
Hazlewood with Storiths (township in Skipton), 43/333; SE094557; NP 96
Hazon and Hartlaw (township in Shilbottle), 27/211; NU195051; NP 71
Heacham (parish), 25/89; TF683379; NP 124
Headbourne Worthy (Headbourn Worthy) (parish), 14/161; SU471335; NP 168
Headcorn (parish), 19/318; TQ834442; NP 172
Headingley (division of Headingley township in Leeds), 43/502; SE272370; NP 96
Headingley (township in Leeds) 53/500-502; NP 96
Headington (parish), 29/224; SP548069; NP 158
Headlam (township in Gainford), 11/305; NZ183190; NP 85
Headley (division in King's Norton), 40/42; SP065760; NP 131
Headley (parish), 14/119; SU822370; NP 169
Headley (parish), 35/117; TQ200542; NP 170
Headon (parish), 28/60; SK749773; NP 103, 104
Heage (township in Duffield), 8/192; SK369505; NP 111
Healaugh (division in township of Reeth in Grinton), 42/104; SE018999; NP 90
Healaugh (parish), 43/81; SE495465; NP 97
Healey (Healy) (township in Bywell St Peter), 27/634; NZ006578; NP 77
Healey (subdivision of Spotland Nearer Side division in Spotland township in Rochdale), 20/454; SD888154; NP 101
Healey and Combhill (township in Netherwitton), 27/333; NZ079920; NP 77
Healey with Sutton (Healey with Suttons) (township in Masham), 42/167; SE160800; NP 91
Healeyfield (township in Lanchester), 11/163; NZ069484; NP 85
Healing (parish), 22/76; TA213101; NP 105
Healy, 27/634; NP 77
Heanor (township in Codnor), 8/198; SK441466; NP 112, 121
Heanton Punchardon (parish), 9/23; SS509352; NP 163
Heap (division in township of Heap in Bury), 20/428; SD866115; NP 101
Heap (division in township of Heap in Bury), 20/430; SD815500; NP 101
Heap (township in Bury), 20/426-430, 475; NP 101
Heapey (Heapy) (township in Leyland), 20/330; SD610196; NP 94, 95, 100, 101
Heapham (parish), 22/138; SK885885; NP 104
Heath (parish), 8/68; SK446670; NP 112
Heath (township in Stoke St Milborough), 31/515; SO557857; NP 129
Heath and Reach (hamlet in Leighton Buzzard), 1/135; SP932287; NP 146
Heath and Jay (township in Bucknell), 31/408; SO384758; NP 129
Heath Charnock (township in Standish), 20/386; SD610150; NP 100, 101
Heather (parish), 21/140; SK391109; NP 121
Heatherslaw and Flodden (township in Ford), 27/38; NT922363; NP 64
Heathfield (parish), 32/316; ST162267; NP 164
Heathfield (parish), 36/53; TQ604213; NP 183
Heathpool (township in Kirknewton), 27/59; NT891281; NP 70
Heathwaite (division in township of Kirkby Ireleth in Kirkby Ireleth), 20/5; SD241859; NP 88
Heathylee (township in Alstonfield), 33/82; SK040640; NP 111
Heaton (division in township of Heaton with Oxcliffe in Lancaster), 20/111; SD436598; NP 89, 94

Heaton (division of Cornhill chapelry in Norham), 27/17A; NT894407; NP 64
Heaton (township in Deane), 20/571; SD670110; NP 101
Heaton (township in All Saints), 27/284; NZ271660; NP 78
Heaton (township in Leek), 33/5; SJ960620; NP 110
Heaton (township in Bradford), 43/520; SE135355; NP 96
Heaton Norris (township in Manchester), 20/531; SJ878912; NP 101
Heaton with Oxcliffe (township in Lancaster), 20/110-111; NP 89, 94
Heavitree (parish), 9/278; SX945929; NP 176
Hebburn (Hebron) (parochial chapelry), 27/302-308; NP 71, 78
Hebburn, 27/113; NP 71
Hebburn, 27/308; NP 78
Hebburn, Monkton and Jarrow (township in Jarrow), 11/4-6; NP 78
Hebden (township in Linton), 43/218; SE040650; NP 90
Hebron (Hebburn) (township in Hebburn parochial chapelry), 27/308; NZ195886
Heckfield (township), 14/21; NP 169
Heckfield (tithing in Heckfield), 14/21; SU723608; NP 169
Heckingham (parish), 25/592; TM388989; NP 137
Heckington (parish), 22/653; TF160450; NP 113, 123
Heckmondwike (township in Birstal), 43/539; SE218240; NP 96
Heddington (parish), 39/131; SU003663; NP 157
Heddon on the Wall (parish), 27/545-550; NP 77, 78
Heddon on the Wall (township in Heddon on the Wall), 27/545; NZ136669; NP 78
Hedenham (parish), 25/614; TM310930; NP 137
Hedgeley (township in Eglingham), 27/139; NU065175; NP 71
Hedgerley (parish), 3/228; SU977872; NP 159
Hedgerley Dean (hamlet in Farnham Royal), 3/227A; SU967878; NP 159
Hedley (township in Chester le Street), 11/36; NZ217565; NP 78
Hedley on the Hill (Hedley) (township in Ovingham), 27/566; NZ088594; NP 77
Hedley Woodlands (Hedley Woodside) (township in Ovingham), 27/567; NZ099573; NP 77
Hedley, 27/566; NP 77
Hedleyhope (township in Brancepeth), 11/146; NZ152407; NP 85
Hedon (parish), 41/427; TA189285; NP 99
Hedsor (parish), 3/217; SU911863; NP 159
Hedworth (division in township of Hebburn, Monkton and Jarrow in Jarrow), 11/4; NZ328622; NP 78
Heeley (division in township of Nether Hallam in Sheffield), 43/825; SK361847; NP 102, 111
Heene (parish), 36/303; TQ134027; NP 182
Heigham (parish), 25/406; TG217088; NP 126
Heighington (division of Heighington township in Heighington), 11/280; NZ239223; NP 85
Heighington (parish), 11/279-285; NP 85
Heighington (township in Washingborough), 22/520; TF047691; NP 113
Helhoughton (parish), 25/166; TF852262; NP 125
Helions Bumpstead (parish), 4/154B, 12/26; NP 148
Helions Bumpstead (Bumpstead Helion) (parish), 12/26; TL655420; NP 148
Hellaby (division in township of Stainton cum Hellaby in Stainton), 43/920B; SK503927; NP 103
Helland, 6/49; SX078707; NP 185, 186
Hellesdon (division in Hellesdon), 25/357; TG203119; NP 126
Hellesdon (hamlet in Hellesdon), 25/358; TG213105; NP 126
Hellesdon (parish), 25/357-358; NP 126
Hellidon (parish), 26/247; SP512585; NP 132
Hellifield (division in township of Hellifield in Long Preston), 43/242; SD870566; NP 95
Hellifield (township in Long Preston), 43/2420243; NP 95
Hellingly (parish), 36/135; TQ586131; NP 183
Hellington (parish), 25/575; TG 126, 137
Helmdon (parish), 26/325; SP588441; NP 145
Helmingham (parish), 34/285; TM187577; NP 137, 150

122

Helmington (division of Hunwick and Helmington township in St Andrew Auckland), 11/205; NZ186336; NP 85
Helmington Row (township in Brancepeth), 11/144; NZ181356; NP 85
Helmsley (division in township of Helmsley in Helmsley), 42/493; SE610860; NP 92
Helmsley (parish), 42/482-493; NP 92
Helmsley (township in Helmsley), 42/492-493; NP 92
Helperby (township in Brafferton), 42/568; SE452698; NP 91
Helperthorpe (parish), 41/180; SE956700; NP 93
Helpringham (parish), 22/656; TF147400; NP 123
Helpston (Helpstone) (parish), 26/19; TF122048; NP 123
Helsby (township in Frodsham), 5/410; SJ489758; NP 100, 109
Helsington (township in Kendal), 38/93; SD507897; NP 89
Helston (chapelry in Wendron), 6/173; SW660274; NP 189
Helton (township in Askham), 38/20; NY501214; NP 83
Hemblington (parish), 25/454; TG347116; NP 126
Hemel Hempstead (Hemel Hempsted) (parish), 16/139; TL055075; NP 159, 160
Hemingbrough (parish), 41/45-53; NP 97
Hemingbrough (township in Hemingbrough), 41/47; SE680305; NP 97
Hemingby (parish), 22/368; TF249751; NP 105, 114
Hemingford Abbots (Hemingford Abbotts) (parish), 17/86; TL277697; NP 134
Hemingford Grey (parish), 17/87; TL295693; NP 134
Hemingstone (parish), 34/359; TM152523; NP 150
Hemington (Hemmington) (township in Lockington), 21/15; SK462292; NP 121
Hemington (parish), 26/69; TL098851; NP 134
Hemington (parish), 32/102; ST739545; NP 166
Hemley (parish), 34/444; TM285427; NP 150
Hemlington (township in Stainton), 42/281; NZ499143; NP 85
Hemmington, 21/15
Hempholme (township in Leven), 41/345; TA086501; NP 99
Hempnall (parish), 25/612; TM250936; NP 137
Hempstead (Hempsted) (parish), 12/25; TL646386; NP 148
Hempstead (parish), 25/65; TG105371; NP 125
Hempstead (parish), 25/224; TG405281; NP 126
Hempsted (parish), 12/25; NP 148
Hempsted (parish), 13/194; SO813170; NP 143
Hempston Arundell, 9/427; NP 188
Hempton (hamlet in Deddington), 29/39; SP448317; NP 145
Hempton (parish), 25/161; TF907290; NP 125
Hempton and Patchway (tithing in Almondsbury), 13/369; ST617826; NP 156
Hemsby (parish), 25/379; TG490171; NP 126
Hemswell (parish), 22/150; SK938907; NP 104
Hemsworth (parish), 43/665; SE426141; NP 103
Hemyock (parish), 9/140; ST136129; NP 164
Hen-didley (township in Llanllwchaiarn), 54/164; SO097923; NP 128
Henbury (parish), 13/374-381; NP 155
Henbury (tithing in Henbury), 13/379; ST564788; NP 155
Henbury with Pexall (township in Prestbury), 5/53; SJ869728; NP 110
Hencott (Hencott Grange and Hencott Stye) (township in St Alkmond Shrewsbury), 31/261; SJ487182; NP 118
Henderskelfe (township in Bulmer), 42/648; SE710700; NP 92
Hendon (parish), 24/131; TQ222900; NP 160
Hendre Denny (hamlet in Eglwysilan), 51/79; ST135885; NP 154
Hendre Ergill (township in Halkyn), 50/105; SJ190700; NP 108
Hendrebiffa (township in Mold), 50/112; SJ214638; NP 108
Hendrehen Llan, 54/78; NP 117
Heneglwys (parish), 44/43; SH422761; NP 106
Henfield (parish), 36/106; TQ209157; NP 182
Henfriniw, 46/62
Henfrynw (Henfriniw, Henfynyw) (parish), 46/62; SN458611; NP 139
Henfynyw, 46/62
Hengoed (hamlet in Llanelli), 47/83A; SN490060; NP 153
Hengoed (hamlet in Gelligaer), 51/75E; ST130970; NP 154

Hengrave (parish), 34/201; TL821682; NP 136
Hengynwith-fach, 54/139; NP 128
Hengynwydd (Hengynwith-fach) (township in Llanidloes), 54/139; SN984862; NP 128
Hengynwydd (township in Llandinam), 54/148; SN992844; NP 128
Henham (hamlet in Henham), 12/62; TL545285; NP 148
Henham (hamlet in Wangford), 34/65; TM449778; NP 137
Henham (parish), 12/62-63; NP 148
Henheads (township in Whalley), 20/299; SD788259; NP 95
Henhull (township in Acton), 5/291; SJ641534; NP 110
Heniarth (township in Llanfair Caereinion), 54/49; SJ112082; NP 117
Henley (parish), 34/393; TM162516; NP 150
Henley (township in Bitterley), 31/530; SO544759; NP 129
Henley (township in Stanton Lacy), 31/521C; SO545767; NP 129
Henley in Arden (township in Wootton Wawen), 37/178; SP149658; NP 131
Henley-on-Thames (parish), 29/308; SU753836; NP 159
Henllan (division outside borough of Denbigh in Henllan), 49/29B; SJ005655; NP 108
Henllan (division within borough of Denbigh in Henllan), 49/29A; SJ050680; NP 108
Henllan (parish), 46/89; SN356410; NP 139
Henllan (parish), 49/29A-B; NP 108
Henllan Amgoed (parish), 47/46, 52; NP 139
Henllan Amgoed (township in Henllan Amgoed), 47/52; SN180200; NP 139
Henlle (township in Whittington), 31/83; SJ325332; NP 118
Henllis (parish), 53/114; NP 154
Henllys (Henllis) (parish), 53/114; ST260958; NP 154
Henllys (township in Llanfihangel Genu'rglyn), 46/4; SN627897; NP 127
Henlow (parish), 1/94; TL180378; NP 147
Hennock (parish), 9/403; SX843805; NP 176, 188
Henry's Moat (Castell Hendre) (parish), 55/48; SN050287; NP 138
Hensall (township in Snaith), 43/968; SE598231; NP 97
Henshaw (township in Haltwhistle), 27/581; NY760700; NP 77
Hensingham (chapelry in St Bees), 7/295; NX992161; NP 82
Hensington (hamlet in Bladon), 29/195; SP453171; NP 145
Henstead (hamlet in Henstead), 34/53; TM489858; NP 137
Henstead (parish), 34/53-54; NP 137
Henstridge (parish), 32/382; ST723204; NP 166, 178
Henthorn (division in township of in Whalley), 20/242; SD727396; NP 95
Hentland (parish), 15/244; SO533262; NP 142
Henton (division in Chinnor), 29/266B; SP763024; NP 159
Henwick, 2/153; NP 158, 168
Henwood (tithing in Cumnor), 2/3F; SP473030; NP 158
Heol-wermood (hamlet in Merthyr Tydfil), 51/73; SO062060; NP 141, 154
Hepburn (Hebburn) (township in Chillingham), 27/113; NU077237; NP 71
Hepple (township in Rothbury), 27/243; NT979009; NP 71, 77
Hepple Demesne (township in Rothbury), 27/244; NY987992; NP 71
Hepscott (township in Morpeth), 27/417; NZ227841; NP 78
Heptonstall (township in Halifax), 43/558; SD945305; NP 95
Hepworth (parish), 34/129; TL986750; NP 136
Hepworth (township in Kirkburton), 43/734; SE170060; NP 102
Herberts Walk (division of East Dean township in Trinity, Forest of Dean), 13/151; SO642162; NP 143
Herbrainstone (parish), 55/101; NP 151
Herbrandston (Herbrainstone) (parish), 55/101; SM870075; NP 151
Hereford, All Saints (parish), 15/128; SO520410; NP 142/1
Hereford, St John the Baptist (parish), 15/130; SO511398; NP 142/1
Hereford, St Martin (parish), 15/132-134; NP 142, 142/1
Hereford, St Martin (township in Hereford, St Martin), 15/132; SO506383; NP 142/1

Hereford, St Nicholas (parish), 15/127; SO497399; NP 142, 142/1
Hereford, St Owen (parish), 15/131; SO518392; NP 142/1
Hereford, St Peter (parish), 15/129; SO514402; NP 142/1
Hermitage (parish), 10/98; ST650076; NP 178
Herne (parish), 19/118; TR172664; NP 173
Hernehill (parish), 19/113; NP 172, 173
Hernhill (Hernehill) (parish), 19/113; TR072620; NP 172, 173
Herringfleet (parish), 34/9; TM475985; NP 137
Herringswell (parish), 34/211; TL718697; NP 135
Herstmonceaux (parish), 36/194; TQ635114; NP 183
Hertford, All Saints (division in Hertford, All Saints), 16/108; TL327125; NP 147
Hertford, All Saints (parish), 16/108-110; NP 147, 148, 160
Hertford, St Andrew (parish), 16/107; TL300130; NP 147
Hertford, St John (parish), 16/111; TL341109; NP 147, 160
Hertingfordbury (parish), 16/106; TL297115; NP 147
Hesketh with Becconsall (parish), 20/352; SD433229; NP 94
Heskin (township in Eccleston), 20/374; SD527151; NP 100
Hesledon, 11/87; NP 85
Hesleyhurst (township in Rothbury), 27/263; NZ086983; NP 71
Heslington St Lawrence (township in St Lawrence), 41/67; SE630490; NP 97
Heslington St Paul (parish and township), 41/68; SE628505; NP 97
Hessay (township in Moor Monkton), 43/52; SE521532; NP 97
Hessett (parish), 34/303; TL938610; NP 136
Hessle (parish), 31/317-318; NP 99
Hessle (township in Hessle), 41/318; TA042268; NP 99
Hessle (township in Wragby), 43/667; SE430179; NP 103
Hest (division in township of Slyne with Hest in Bolton-le-Sands), 20/94; SD469663; NP 89
Heston, 24/106; TQ134772; NP 160
Heswall (parish), 5/473-474; NP 100
Heswall (township in Heswall), 5/473; SJ262821; NP 100
Hethe (parish), 29/69; SP591291; NP 145
Hethel (parish), 25/606; TG163009; NP 136, 137
Hethersett (parish), 25/562; TG155045; NP 125, 126
Hethersgill (township in Kirklinton), 7/20; NY475675; NP 76
Hett (township in Merrington), 11/224; NZ287361; NP 85
Hetton (division in township of Hetton with Bordley in Burnsall), 43/213; SD953597; NP 90, 95
Hetton (township in Chatton), 27/69; NU030342; NP 64
Hetton (township in Chatton), 27/72; NU030342; NP 64, 71
Hetton with Bordley (township in Burnsall), 43/213-214; NP 90, 95
Hetton-le-Hole (township in Houghton-le-Spring), 11/65; NZ352470; NP 78
Heugh (township in Stamfordham), 27/464; NZ082733; NP 77
Heveningham (parish), 34/166; TM342722; NP 137
Hever (parish), 19/198; TQ475448; NP 171
Heversham (division of Heversham with Milnthorpe township in Heversham), 38/86; SD495830; NP 89
Heversham (parish), 38/84-91; NP 89
Heversham with Milnthorpe, 38/86-87
Hevingham (parish), 25/256; TG195205; NP 126
Hewelsfield (parish), 13/166; SO572021; NP 155
Heworth (chapelry in Jarrow), 11/7; NZ291616; NP 78
Heworth (township in St Cuthbert), 42/675; SE625533; NP 97
Heworth (township in St Olave), 42/674; SE633533; NP 97
Heworth (township in St Olave, St Cuthbert and St Saviour), 42/674-677; NP 97
Heworth (township in St Saviour), 42/676; SE635547; NP 97
Heworth (township in St Saviour), 42/677; SE613632; NP 97
Hexham (parish), 27/610-617; NP 77
Hexham (township in Hexham), 27/610; NY920638; NP 77
Hexhamshire High Quarter (township in Hexham), 27/616; NY905515; NP 77, 84
Hexhamshire Low Quarter (township in Hexham), 27/612; NY923601; NP 77
Hexhamshire Middle Quarter (township in Hexham), 27/614; NY910580; NP 77
Hexhamshire Stinted Pasture [no. 1] (township in Hexham), 27/613; NY876578; NP 77

Hexhamshire Stinted Pasture [no. 2] (township in Hexham), 27/615; NY892525; NP 77
Hexhamshire Stinted Pasture [no. 3] (township in Hexham), 27/617; NY898482; NP 84
Hexhamshire West Quarter (township in Hexham), 27/611; NY879616; NP 77
Hexton (parish), 16/43; TL106302; NP 147
Heybridge (parish), 12/235; TL860083; NP 162
Heydon (parish), 12/12; TL431408; NP 148
Heydon (parish), 25/204; TG113276; NP 125
Heyhouses (extra-parochial), 20/236; SD786376; NP 95
Heyop (parish), 56/91-B; NP 128
Heyop (township in Heyop), 56/9A; SO240750; NP 128
Heysham (parish), 20/99; SD417612; NP 89, 94
Heyshott (parish), 36/22; SU898181; NP 181
Heytesbury (parish), 39/239; ST928425; NP 166, 167
Heythrop (Heythrop and Dunthorp) (parish), 29/53; SP355276; NP 145
Hibaldstow (parish), 22/117; SE973023; NP 104
Hickleton (parish), 43/876; SE482053; NP 103
Hickling (parish), 25/230; TG415235; NP 126
Hickling (parish), 28/297; SK682283; NP 121, 122
Hidcote Bartrim (hamlet in Mickleton), 13/19; SP179430; NP 144
Hidcote Boyce (hamlet in Ebrington), 13/28; SP174414; NP 144
High Abbotside (township in Aysgarth), 42/132; SD840930; NP 90
High and Low Brunton, 27/148; NP 71
High and Low Highlaws (High and Low Highley) (township in Mitford), 27/401; NZ178890; NP 78
High and Low Highley, 27/401; NP 78
High and Low Trewhitt (township in Rothbury), 27/246; NU004051; NP 71
High and Low Bishopside (township in Ripon), 43/161; SE180668; NP 91
High Angerton (township in Hartburn), 27/347; NZ088852; NP 77
High Barton (township in Barton), 38/25; NY474242; NP 83
High Bickington (parish), 9/67; SS595198; NP 163
High Blackhall (Blackhall High Quarter, High Blackwell) (township in St Cuthbert [Carlisle]), 7/81; NY402502; NP 76
High Blackwell, 7/81; NP 76
High Bolton (Bolton High Hide Quarter) (township in Bolton), 7/217; NY249398; NP 82
High Bray (parish), 9/31; SS702363; NP 163
High Buston (township in Warkworth), 27/218; NU234088; NP 71
High Caldbeck, 7/215; NP 82, 83
High Callerton (township in Ponteland), 27/525; NZ163702; NP 78
High Catton (township in Catton), 41/86; SE730530; NP 97
High Conyscliffe (division in township of High Coniscliffe in Coniscliffe), 11/317; NZ232159; NP 85
High Crosby (township in Crosby upon Eden), 7/26; NY457598; NP 76
High Cross (division in Tottenham), 24/79A; TQ340910; NP 160, 161
High Easter (parish), 12/208; TL625150; NP 148
High Ellington (Over Ellington) (township in Masham), 42/169; SE194833; NP 91
High Ercall (parish), 31/206-213; NP 118, 119
High Ercall (township in High Ercall), 31/209; SJ602172; NP 118, 119
High Forest (township in Allendale), 27/590B; NY850475; NP 84
High Green and Mortomley (division in township of Ecclesfield in Ecclesfield), 43/787; SK339975; NP 102
High Halden (Halden) (parish), 19/405; TQ899374; NP 172
High Halstow (parish), 19/41; TQ783761; NP 172
High Ham (parish), 32/208; ST428310; NP 165, 177
High Hatton (High Hatton and Booley) (township in Stanton upon Hine Heath), 31/204; SJ606249; NP 118
High Hoyland (parish), 43/703A-B, 704B, 711-712; NP 102, 102/1
High Hoyland (township in High Hoyland), 43/711; SE275106; NP 102

High Hunsley (hamlet in Rowley), 41/216C; SE950346; NP 98
High Ireby (township in Ireby), 7/220; NY239361; NP 82
High Laver (parish), 12/258; TL522092; NP 148, 161
High Leigh (township in Rostherne), 5/92; SJ691837; NP 101
High Littleton (parish), 32/109; ST644577; NP 166
High Melton (Melton on the Hill) (parish), 43/877; SE513025; NP 103
High Mowthorpe (division in township of Kirby Grindalythe in Kirby Grindalythe), 41/183A; SE889689; NP 92, 93
High Offley (parish), 33/163; SJ777261; NP 119
High Ongar (High Onger) (parish), 12/283; TL580030; NP 161
High Roding (High Roothing) (parish), 12/207; TL602170; NP 148
High Roothing (parish), 12/207; NP 148
High Santon (Upper Santon) (township in Appleby), 22/42; SE932118; NP 104
High Sedbergham (township in Sedbergham), 7/151; NY348441; NP 82, 83
High Thornton (division in township of Bishop Thornton in Ripon), 43/165; SE246641; NP 91
High Toynton (Toynton Supra) (division in High Toynton), 22/385A; TF284700; NP 114
High Toynton (Toynton Supra) (parish), 22/385A-B; NP 114
High Toynton - Wildmore Fen (division in High Toynton), 22/385B; TF254556; NP 114
High Walton (township in Walton), 7/35; NY530668; NP 76
High Warden and Walwick Grange (township in Warden), 27/606; NY903687; NP 77
High Worsall (chapelry in Northallerton), 42/268; NZ383080; NP 85
High Wycombe (Chipping Wycombe) (borough in Chipping Wycombe), 3/206; SU883923; NP 159
High Wycombe (parish), 3/205-206; NP 159
High Wycombe, 3/205; NP 159
Higham (hamlet in Gazeley), 34/218; TL747663; NP 135, 136
Higham (Higham or Church Street) (parish), 19/38; TQ719731; NP 171
Higham (parish), 34/504; TM036361; NP 149
Higham (township in Shirland and Higham), 8/136; SK391585; NP 111
Higham Dykes (township in Ponteland), 27/528; NZ135755; NP 77, 78
Higham Ferrers (parish), 26/149; SP970687; NP 133, 134
Higham Gobion (parish), 1/121; TL099325; NP 147
Higham on the Hill (parish), 21/221; SP379958; NP 132
Higham Park (extra-parochial), 26/214; SP990641; NP 134
Higham with West Close Booth (township in Whalley), 20/254; SD815370; NP 95
Highampton (parish), 9/188; SS494036; NP 175
Highburton (division in township of Kirkburton in Kirkburton), 43/727; SE201144; NP 102
Highclere (parish), 14/7; SU446600; NP 168
Higher Bebington (Higher Bebbington) (township in Bebington), 5/440; SJ319850; NP 100
Higher Booths (township in Whalley), 20/287-289; NP 95
Higher Division (division in township of Worsley in Eccles), 20/559; SD741025; NP 101
Higher Irlam (division in township of Barton upon Irwell in Eccles), 20/543; SJ721958; NP 101
Higher Kinnerton (township in Dodleston), 50/16; SJ330615; NP 109
Higher Laleston (hamlet in Laleston), 51/95A; SS865820; NP 153
Higher Lowick (division in township of Lowick in Ulverston), 20/16; SD286861; NP 88
Higher Newcastle, 51/93; NP 153, 154
Higher Odcombe (parish), 32/470C; ST506160; NP 177
Higher Subberthwaite (division in township of Subberthwaite in Ulverston), 20/13; SD266874; NP 88
Higher Walton, 5/148; NP 100
Higher Weaver (district in Cullompton), 9/152C; ST053043; NP 176
Higher Whitley (township in Great Budworth), 5/115; SJ618804; NP 101

Highfields (division in Costock), 28/289; SK599276; NP 121
Highhead, 7/146; NP 83
Highlands Park (township in Tatenhill), 33/217B; SK191219; NP 120
Highlaws (township in Hartburn), 27/352; NZ076839; NP 77
Highleadon (hamlet in 13/137; SO770236; NP 143
Highleadon (parish), 13/137-138; NP 143
Highley (Higley) (parish), 31/552; SO740834; NP 130
Highley St Mary, 9/175; NP 164
Highlight (extra-parochial), 51/175; ST100697; NP 154
Highlow (township in Hope), 8/28; SK222802; NP 111
Highnam (hamlet in Churcham), 13/143A; SO793211; NP 143
Hightleigh, 9/175; NP 164
Highway (parish), 39/378; SU050741; NP 157
Highweek (parish), 9/410; SX843724; NP 188
Highworth (parish), 39/5A-6; NP 157
Highworth (tithing in Highworth), 39/5A; SU195925; NP 157
Higley (parish), 31/552; NP 130
Hilbeck, 38/54
Hilborough (parish), 25/684; TF815008; NP 125, 136
Hilbre (division in St Oswald Chester), 5/496; SJ184881; NP 100
Hildenley (township in Appleton-le-Street), 42/638; SE749709; NP 92
Hildersham (parish), 4/136; TL544482; NP 148
Hilderstone (township in Stone), 33/58; SJ952349; NP 119
Hilderthorpe (division in township of Hilderthorpe with Wilsthorpe in Bridlington), 41/256; TA171652; NP 93, 99
Hilderthorpe with Wilsthorpe (township in Bridlington), 41/256-257; NP 93, 99
Hilfield, 10/149; NP 178
Hilgay (division in Hilgay), 4/185; TL620890; NP 135
Hilgay (division in Hilgay), 25/693; TL598968; NP 135
Hilgay (parish), 4/185, 25/693; NP 135
Hill (parish), 13/357; ST647956; NP 156
Hill (The Hill) (township in Halesowen), 40/12; SO975848; NP 130
Hill and Moor (hamlet in Fladbury), 40/185; SO983481; NP 143, 144
Hill Chorlton (township in Eccleshall), 33/150B; SJ800395; NP 119
Hill Croome (parish), 40/221; SO885310; NP 143
Hill Deverill (parish), 39/275; ST862400; NP 166
Hill Top (division of Hill Top township in Wragby), 43/666; SE420170; NP 103
Hill Top (division of Hill Top township in Wragby), 43/668; SE422181; NP 103
Hill Top (township in Wragby), 43/666, 668; NP 103
Hill Walk (division in Lyndhurst), 14/303B; SU302064; NP 180
Hillam (township in Monk Fryston), 43/461; SE516286; NP 97
Hillbeck (township in Brough), 38/54; NY802175; NP 84
Hillend (tithing in Cumnor), 2/3G; SP466065; NP 158
Hillesden (Hillsden) (parish), 3/88; SP685291; NP 145, 146
Hillfarence (parish), 32/325; ST175248; NP 164
Hillfield (Hilfield) (chapelry in Sydling St Nicholas), 10/149; ST635061; NP 178
Hillhampton (hamlet in Martley), 40/96B; SO775660; NP 130
Hillingdon (parish), 24/110-111; TQ068825; NP 160, 170
Hillingdon (township in Hillingdon), 24/110; TQ068825; NP 160, 170
Hillington (Hellington) (parish), 25/575; TG315029; NP 126, 137
Hillington (parish), 25/173; TF726254; NP 124, 125
Hillmarton (parish), 39/89; NP 157
Hillmorton (parish), 37/129; SP534739; NP 132
Hillsden (parish), 3/88; NP 145, 146
Hillsley (tithing in Hawkesbury), 13/340F; ST769897; NP 156
Hilmarton (Hillmarton) (parish), 39/89; SU032761; NP 157
Hilperton (parish), 39/146; ST874596; NP 166
Hilston (parish), 41/415; TA286335; NP 99
Hilton (parish), 10/159; ST770039; NP 178
Hilton (parish), 17/89; TL286658; NP 134
Hilton (parish), 42/287; NZ465113; NP 85
Hilton (township in Marston on Dove), 8/250; SK252311; NP 120
Hilton (township in Staindrop), 11/287; NZ173223; NP 85
Hilton (township in Wolverhampton), 33/313; SJ953025; NP 119

Hilton (township in St Michael Appleby or Bongate), 38/43; NY762216; NP 83, 84
Himbleton (parish), 40/132; SO943591; NP 130
Himley (parish), 33/332; SO885913; NP 130
Hincaster (township in Heversham), 38/89; SD513848; NP 89
Hinckley (parish), 21/223-226, 37/66; NP 132
Hinckley (township in Hinckley), 21/226; SP423925; NP 132
Hinderclay (parish), 34/94; TM025769; NP 136
Hinderwell (parish), 42/369-370; NP 86
Hinderwell (township in Hinderwell), 42/370; NZ793172; NP 86
Hindford (township in Whittington), 31/84; SJ332330; NP 118
Hindley (township in Wigan), 20/582; SD623043; NP 100, 101
Hindlip (parish), 40/129; SO880581; NP 130
Hindolveston (parish), 25/150; TG038293; NP 125
Hindon (parish), 39/280; ST908331; NP 166
Hindringham (parish), 25/75; TF978368; NP 125
Hingham (parish), 25/660; TM021018; NP 125, 136
Hinstock (parish), 31/181; SJ695269; NP 119
Hintlesham (parish), 34/481; TM084435; NP 149, 150
Hinton (parish), 39/99; NP 157
Hinton (tithing in Berkeley), 13/316; SO686024; NP 156
Hinton (township in Whitchurch), 31/39; SJ531436; NP 118
Hinton Ampner (parish), 14/186; SU614273; NP 168
Hinton Blewitt (parish), 32/80; ST593563; NP 165, 166
Hinton Charterhouse (Charterhouse Hinton) (parish), 32/91; ST773586; NP 166
Hinton in the Hedges (parish), 26/350; SP564368; NP 145
Hinton Martell (Hinton Martel) (parish), 10/172; SU008056; NP 179
Hinton on the Green (parish), 13/34; SP092402; NP 144
Hinton Parva (Stanbridge) (parish), 10/176; SU001044; NP 179
Hinton St Mary (parish), 10/24; ST787165; NP 178
Hinton St George (parish), 32/457; ST419124; NP 177
Hinton Waldrist (parish), 2/30; SU373985; NP 158
Hinton, 39/143; NP 166
Hints (parish), 33/288; SK158029; NP 120
Hinxhill (parish), 19/453; TR044432; NP 172
Hinxton (parish), 4/181; TL499459; NP 148
Hinxworth (parish), 16/2; TL238403; NP 147
Hippenscombe (parish), 39/189; SU307562; NP 168
Hipperholme (division in township of Hipperholme cum Brighouse), 43/547; SE137255; NP 96
Hipperholme cum Brighouse (township in Halifax), 43/546-547; NP 96
Hipswell (division in township of Hipswell in Catterick), 42/78; SE175985; NP 91
Hipswell (township in Catterick), 42/78-79; NP 91
Hirnant (parish), 54/21; SJ050230; NP 117
Hirst (township in Woodhorn), 27/322; NZ281879; NP 78
Hirst Courtney (Hurst Courtney) (township in Birkin), 43/456; SE616246; NP 97
Hisland (township in Oswestry), 31/110; SJ314274; NP 118
Histon (parish), 4/75; TL434642; NP 135
Hitcham (parish), 3/220; SU918832; NP 159
Hitcham (parish), 34/351; TL987525; NP 149
Hitchenden (parish), 3/195; NP 159
Hitchin (hamlet in Hitchin), 16/35; TL180295; NP 147
Hitchin (parish), 16/35-39; NP 147
Hittisleigh (parish), 9/323; SX734954; NP 175
Hive (division in township of Gilberdyke in Eastrington), 41/19B; SE823309; NP 98/1
Hixon (township in Stowe), 33/190; SK002258; NP 119, 120
Hoath (parish), 19/120; TR209649; NP 173
Hob Lench, 40/188; NP 144
Hobarris (township in Clun), 31/394; SO310780; NP 129
Hobthorin (township in Clun), 31/392; SO308757; NP 129
Hoby (parish), 21/64; SK670180; NP 121, 122
Hockenhall, 5/388; NP 109
Hockenhull (Hockenhall, Hockenhull Stapleford) (township in Tarvin), 5/388; SJ482659; NP 109
Hockenhull Stapleford, 5/388; NP 109
Hockering (parish), 25/586; TG080138; NP 125
Hockerton (parish), 28/139; SK702575; NP 112

Hockham (Great Hockham) (division in Hockham), 25/723; TL951926; NP 136
Hockham (parish), 25/723-724; NP 136
Hockleton (township in Chirbury), 31/354; SO277997; NP 117, 128, 129
Hockley (parish), 12/363; TQ826942; NP 162
Hockliffe (parish), 1/134; SP963269; NP 146, 147
Hockwold cum Wilton (parish), 25/703; TL703877; NP 135, 136
Hockworthy (parish), 9/133; ST030202; NP 164
Hoddesdon (hamlet in Broxbourne), 16/115; TL360090; NP 160, 161
Hodgeston (parish), 55/143; SS034998; NP 151
Hodnell (Hodnel) (extra-parochial), 37/246; SP424566; NP 132
Hodnet (parish), 31/165-173; NP 118, 119
Hodnet (township in Hodnet), 31/170; SJ614284; NP 118, 119
Hodre (township in Clun), 31/393; SO325770; NP 129
Hodsock (township in Blyth), 28/19; SK612855; NP 103
Hoe (Hoo) (parish), 25/340; TF992163; NP 125
Hoff and Row (township in St Lawrence Appleby), 38/36; NY665175; NP 83
Hoggeston (parish), 3/103; SP805245; NP 146
Hoghton (township in Leyland), 20/327; SD627258; NP 95
Hognaston (parish), 8/160; SK237507; NP 111
Hogshaw (Hogshaw with Fulbrook) (parish), 3/119; SP744228; NP 146
Hogsthorpe (parish), 22/411; TF534710; NP 114
Hogstow (township in Worthen), 31/332A; SJ356005; NP 118, 129
Holbeach (division in Holbeach), 22/776A; TF360260; NP 123, 124
Holbeach (parish), 22/776A-B; NP 123, 124
Holbeach Drove (division in Holbeach), 22/776B; TF327127; NP 123
Holbeck (extra-parochial), 22/392; TF314728; NP 114
Holbeck (township in Norton Cuckney), 28/87; SK540730; NP 112
Holbeck (township in Leeds), 43/494; SE293324; NP 96
Holbeton (parish), 9/470; SX600482; NP 187
Holborn, 27/46; NP 64
Holbrook (Holbrooke) (township in Duffield), 8/193; SK366446; NP 111, 121
Holbrook (parish), 34/517; TM170360; NP 150
Holburn (Holborn) (township in Lowick), 27/46; NU047360; NP 64
Holcombe (parish), 32/116; ST670503; NP 166
Holcombe Burnell (parish), 9/319; SX842912; NP 176
Holcombe Rogus (parish), 9/137; ST065190; NP 164
Holcot (Holcut), 1/76; SP947393; NP 146, 147
Holcot (parish), 26/202; SP798695; NP 133
Holcroft (division in township of Culcheth in Winwick), 20/598; SJ677947; NP 101
Holcut (parish), 1/76; NP 146, 147
Holdenby (parish), 26/187; SP695678; NP 132, 133
Holdenhurst (parish), 14/319; SZ098937; NP 179
Holdfast (hamlet in Ripple), 40/224; SO846378; NP 143
Holdgate (Holgate) (parish), 31/498B; NP 129
Holdgate (Holgate) (township in Holdgate), 31/498B; SO565890; NP 129
Holdingham (hamlet in New Sleaford), 22/596; TF053470; NP 113
Holdshott (tithing in Heckfield), 14/22; SU741599; NP 169
Holdworth (sub-division in Bradfield division in township of Bradfield in Ecclesfield), 43/808; SK295905; NP 102
Hole (in Clee), 22/82; NP 105
Holegate, 43/42; NP 97
Holford (parish), 32/230; ST164400; NP 164
Holgate (Holegate) (township in St Mary Bishophill (Junior)), 43/42; SE583512; NP 97
Holgate (parish), 31/498B; NP 129
Holkham (parish), 25/15; TF888428; NP 125
Hollacombe (parish), 9/102; SS378027; NP 174, 175
Holland Meadow (extra-parochial), 20/349; SD467151; NP 100
Holland Ward, 8/184; NP 111, 120

Hollanden (hamlet in Leigh), 19/203B; TQ566499; NP 171
Hollesley (parish), 34/438; TM360450; NP 150
Holleth (township in Cockerham or Garstang), 20/146; SD478523; NP 94
Hollin Ward, 8/184; NP 111, 120
Hollingbourne (Hollingbourn) (parish), 19/225; TQ846556; NP 172
Hollinghill (township in Rothbury), 27/262; NZ050968; NP 71, 77
Hollington (township in Longford), 8/235; SK229396; NP 120
Hollington (parish), 36/170; TQ785119; NP 184
Hollingworth (township in Mottram), 5/3; SJ999977; NP 101, 102
Hollinhope Common (common to Frosterley, Bishopley and Newlandside divisions in Stanhope), 11/173B; NY980345; NP 84
Hollinsclough (township in Alstonfield), 33/83; SK055665; NP 111
Hollowell (hamlet in Guilsborough), 26/171; SP689719; NP 132, 133
Hollym, 41/436-438; NP 99
Hollym (township in Hollym), 41/436; TA346249; NP 99
Holm-Lacy (parish), 15/182; NP 142
Holme (chapelry in Glatton), 17/22; TL215889; NP 134
Holme (parish), 28/128; SK810585; NP 112, 113
Holme (township in Bottesford), 22/31; SE913067; NP 104
Holme (township in Burton in Kendal), 38/128; SD532792; NP 89
Holme (township in Pickhill), 42/249; SE356821; NP 91
Holme (township in Almondbury), 43/776; SE104053; NP 102
Holme Abbey (township in Holme Cultram), 7/124; NY155500; NP 75, 82
Holme Cultram (parish), 7/122-126; NP 75, 82
Holme Demesne (division in township of Stirton with Thorlby in Skipton), 43/323; SD965545; NP 95
Holme East Waver (township in Holme Cultram), 7/122; NY205535; NP 75, 82
Holme Hale (parish), 25/508; TF891070; NP 125
Holme Island (extra-parochial), 20/64B; SD423789; NP 89
Holme Lacy (Holm-Lacy) (parish), 15/182; SO552346; NP 142
Holme Low (township in Holme Cultram), 7/123; NY137537; NP 75, 82
Holme next the Sea (parish), 25/4; TF710433; NP 124
Holme on the Wolds (parish), 41/225; SE942466; NP 98
Holme Pierrepont (parish), 28/259-261; NP 121
Holme Pierrepont (township in Holme Pierrepont), 28/261; SK628384; NP 121
Holme Side (division in township of Slaithwaite in Huddersfield), 43/758; SE057137; NP 102
Holme St Cuthbert (township in Holme Cultram), 7/125; NY117488; NP 75, 82
Holme upon Spalding Moor (parish), 41/25; SE825365; NP 98
Holmer (division inside Hereford municipal boundary in Holmer), 15/125A; SO512427; NP 142
Holmer (division inside Hereford municipal boundary in Holmer), 15/125B; SO508417; NP 142
Holmer (parish), 15/125A-126; NP 142
Holmes Common (extra-parochial), 22/498; SK969712; NP 113/1
Holmesfield (township in Dronfield), 8/45; SK300770; NP 111
Holmpton (division of Holmpton township in Hollym), 41/438; TA362226; NP 99
Holmpton (division of Holmpton township in Holmpton), 41/439; TA367223; NP 99
Holmpton, 41/439; NP 99
Holmpton (township in Hollym and Holmpton), 41/438-439; NP 99
Holmside (township in Lanchester), 11/152; NZ205497; NP 78, 84, 85
Holmsley Walk (extra-parochial division in New Forest extra-parochial), 14/302F; SU218007; NP 179
Holne (parish), 9/376; SX698696; NP 175, 187
Holnest (parish), 10/96; ST650098; NP 178
Holsworthy (parish), 9/96; SS346062; NP 174
Holt (division in Wimborne Minster), 10/175B; SU030050; NP 179

Holt (parish), 25/66; TG082386; NP 125
Holt (parish), 40/103-102; NP 130
Holt (parish), 49/72-77; NP 109
Holt (tithing in Great Bradford), 39/153A; ST858620; NP 166
Holt (township in Holt), 40/103; SO815630; NP 130
Holt (township in Holt), 49/72; SJ394531; NP 109
Holt Parks (township in Gresford), 49/71; SJ382545; NP 109
Holt, 21/307; NP 133
Holtby (division in township of Ainderby Mires with Holtby township in Hornby), 42/197; SE271920; NP 91
Holtby (parish), 42/668-669; NP 97
Holtby (township in Holtby), 42/668; SE667539; NP 97
Holton (Holton St Peter) (parish), 34/71; TM402783; NP 137
Holton (parish), 29/235; SP603067; NP 158
Holton (parish), 32/378; ST684268; NP 166
Holton cum Beckering (Holton with Beckering) (parish), 22/266; TF118810; NP 104
Holton le Clay (parish), 22/86; TA290023; NP 105
Holton le Moor (chapelry in Caistor), 22/102; TF082978; NP 104
Holton St Mary (parish), 34/505; TM056371; NP 149
Holton St Peter (parish), 34/71; NP 137
Holverston (parish), 25/574; TG304030; NP 126
Holwell (hamlet in Broadwall), 29/159C; SP225088; NP 157
Holwell (parish), 1/99; TL171336; NP 147
Holwell (parish), 10/299; ST700110; NP 178
Holwell (township in Ab Kettleby), 21/80; SK735236; NP 122
Holwick (township in Romaldkirk), 42/3; NY910260; NP 84
Holy Cross and St Giles, Shrewsbury (parish), 31/255; SJ511126; NP 118
Holy Cross Pershore (parish), 40/182-183B; NP 143
Holy Cross Pershore (township in Holy Cross Pershore), 40/182; SO940475; NP 143
Holy Island (parish), 27/18-29
Holy Island (township in Holy Island), 27/29; NU126433; NP 64
Holy Oakes, 21/303 ; NP 133
Holy Tinity Kingston upon Hull), 41/326-333B; NP 99/1
Holy Trinity Chester (parish), 5/519-521; NP 109, 109/1
Holy Trinity Chester (township in Holy Trinity Chester), 5/519; SJ400660; NP 109/1
Holy Trinity Chester (township in Holy Trinity Chester), 5/521; SJ389664; NP 109
Holy Trinity (division in Wareham, Holy Trinity), 10/287; SY923872; NP 178
Holy Trinity (Holy Trinity-the-Less) (parish), 23/76; TQ323809; NP 160/2
Holy Trinity-the-Less (parish), 23/76; TQ323809; NP 160/2
Holy Trinity (Holy Trinity Minories) (parish), 24/56; TQ337811; NP 160/1
Holy Trinity Goodramgate, 43/11; NP 97/1
Holy Trinity Micklegate, 43/27; NP 97/1
Holy Trinity, Kings Court, 43/9; NP 97/1
Holybourne (division in Holybourne), 14/125; SU729418; NP 169
Holybourne (parish), 14/125-126; NP 169
Holyfield (hamlet in Waltham Holy Cross), 12/266; TL389021; NP 161
Holyhead (Caergybi) (parish), 44/51; SH240810; NP 106
Holyoaks (Holy Oakes) (township in Stoke Dry), 21/303; SP845960; NP 133
Holystone (parish), 27/185-188B, 188D-189; NP 70, 71
Holystone (township in Holystone), 27/188A; NT955026; NP 71
Holystone Common (area in Holystone), 27/188D; NT925015; NP 71
Holywell (hamlet in Castle Bytham), 22/698; TF000158; NP 123
Holywell (division in St Leonard Shoreditch), 24/62A; TQ331820; NP 160/1
Holywell (township in Earsdon), 27/489; NZ314742; NP 78
Holywell (parish), 29/207; SP518070; NP 158, 158/1
Holywell (Treffynnon) (parish), 50/26-34; NP 108
Holywell (Treffynnon) (township in Holywell), 50/33; SJ182752; NP 108
Holywell cum Needingworth (Holywell with Needingworth) (parish), 17/75; TL340720; NP 134, 135

Holywell cum Aunby (chapelry in Castle Bytham), 22/698-699; NP 123
Holywell Row (division in Mildenhall), 34/110D; TL710770; NP 135
Home (hamlet in Ystrad-dyfodwg), 51/66B; SS970960; NP 154
Homersfield (parish), 34/33; NP 137
Homington (parish), 39/355; SU128249; NP 167
Honeychurch (parish), 9/183; SS626062; NP 175
Honiley (Honity) (parish), 37/92; SP245722; NP 131
Honing (parish), 25/217; TG327280; NP 126
Honingham (parish), 25/496; TG110116; NP 125
Honington (parish), 22/605; SK945435; NP 122, 123
Honington (parish), 34/121; TL902742; NP 136
Honington (parish), 37/286; SP271423; NP 144, 145
Honiton (parish), 9/236; SY162994; NP 176, 177
Honiton-Clist,
Honity (parish), 37/92; NP 131
Honley (township in Almondbury), 43/772; SE132108; NP 102
Hoo (parish), 25/340; NP 125
Hoo (parish), 34/368; TM258587; NP 137
Hoo (St Werneth) (parish), 19/46; TQ791728; NP 172
Hood Grange (division in township of Kilburn in Kilburn), 42/544; SE506821; NP 91, 92
Hooe (parish), 36/177; TQ685094; NP 183
Hook (hamlet in Kingston upon Thames), 35/36; TQ173638; NP 170
Hook (township in Snaith), 43/961; SE745197; NP 97, 98, 103
Hook Norton (parish), 29/43; SP357338; NP 145
Hooke (Hook) (parish), 10/124; ST553004; NP 177
Hoole (parish), 5/422; NP 109
Hoon (township in Marston on Dove), 8/248; SK225310; NP 120
Hoose (township in West Kirby), 5/452; SJ221893; NP 100
Hooton (township in Eastham), 5/432; SJ372790; NP 100
Hooton Levitt (township in Maltby), 43/917; SK527913; NP 103
Hooton Pagnell (parish), 43/871-872; NP 103
Hooton Pagnell (township in Hooton Pagnell), 43/872; SE485085; NP 103
Hooton Roberts (parish), 43/888; SK482973; NP 103
Hope (Hope All Saints) (parish), 19/429; TR058263; NP 184
Hope (parish), 8/14-29; NP 102, 111
Hope (parish), 50/120-127; NP 108, 109
Hope (township in Hope), 8/17; SK172838; NP 102, 111
Hope (township in Worthen), 31/331; SJ337017; NP 118
Hope (township in Barningham), 42/18; NZ030080; NP 84
Hope (township in Buttington), 54/93; SJ257069; NP 117
Hope Bagot (Hope Baggot) (parish), 31/544; SO589738; NP 129
Hope Bowdler (parish), 31/426; SO471928; NP 129
Hope Mansel (Hope Mansell) (parish), 15/219; SO626196; NP 143
Hope Owen (township in Hope), 50/126; SJ306601; NP 109
Hope under Dinmore (parish), 15/104; SO497525; NP 129, 142
Hope Woodlands (Woodlands) (township in Hope), 8/16; SK131912; NP 102
Hopesay (parish), 31/411; SO391825; NP 129
Hoppen (township in Bamburgh), 27/106; NU162305; NP 71
Hopperton (division in township of Allerton Mauleverer with Hopperton in Allerton Mauleverer), 43/115; SE419566; NP 97
Hopsford (hamlet in Withybrook), 37/106; SP422842; NP 132
Hopton (Hopton on Sea) (parish), 34/6; TG523004; NP 137
Hopton (parish), 34/97; TL990793; NP 136
Hopton (township in Wirksworth), 8/151; SK261539; NP 111
Hopton and Espley (township in Hodnet), 31/171; SJ603266; NP 118, 119
Hopton and Coton (township in Stafford St Mary), 33/180; SJ940250; NP 119
Hopton Cangeford (parish), 31/516; SO552805; NP 129
Hopton Castle (parish), 31/409; SO358772; NP 129
Hopton Isaf (township in Church Stoke), 54/189; SO234908; NP 128
Hopton on Sea (parish), 34/6; NP 137
Hopton Uchaf (township in Church Stoke), 54/188; SO224901; NP 128

Hopton Wafers (parish), 31/587; SO636766; NP 130
Hopwas (township in Tamworth), 33/283; SK174043; NP 120
Hopwas Hays (township in Tamworth), 33/282; SK174056; NP 120
Hopwell (township in Wilne), 8/285; SK438344; NP 121
Hopwood (township in Middleton), 20/478; SD870089; NP 101
Horbling (parish), 22/658; TF130353; NP 123
Horbury (township in Wakefield), 43/605; SE295183; NP 102
Hordle (parish), 14/323; SZ273954; NP 179, 180
Hordley (parish), 31/90-91; NP 118
Hordley (township in Hordley), 31/90; SJ385305; NP 118
Horfield (parish), 13/386; ST597770; NP 155, 156
Horham (parish), 34/141; TM211722; NP 137
Horkstow (Horkstowe) (parish), 22/57; SE988185; NP 104
Horley (parish), 29/127; SP412444; NP 145
Horley (parish), 35/173; TQ286449; NP 170
Horn (parish), 30/11; SK953118; NP 122, 123
Hornblotton (parish), 32/202; ST595336; NP 165, 166
Hornby (parish), 42/197-201; NP 91
Hornby (township in Melling), 20/85; SD593697; NP 89
Hornby (township in Great Smeaton), 42/61; NZ367052; NP 85, 91
Hornby (township in Hornby), 42/200; SE222933; NP 91
Horncastle (division in Horncastle), 22/381A; TF263691; NP 114
Horncastle (parish), 22/381A-B; NP 114
Horncastle - Wildmore Fen (division in Horncastle), 22/381B; TF249524; NP 114
Hornchurch (parish), 12/327A-B; NP 161
Horncliffe (township in Norham), 27/8; NT936498; NP 64
Horncliffe Loanend, 27/7; NP 64
Horndon on the Hill (parish), 12/405; TQ669837; NP 161
Horne (division in Horne), 35/109A; TQ344428; NP 170, 171
Horne (Horne with Harrowsley) (parish), 35/109A-B; NP 170, 171
Horninghold (parish), 21/301; SP812974; NP 133
Horninglow (township in Burton upon Trent), 33/213; SK238248; NP 120
Horningsea (parish), 4/97; TL497629; NP 135
Horningsham (parish), 39/389; ST815419; NP 166
Horningsheath (parish), 34/225; NP 136
Horningtoft (parish), 25/191; TF937233; NP 125
Hornington (division in township of Bolton Percy in Bolton Percy), 43/61; SE518415; NP 97
Hornsea (division in township of Hornsea and Hornsea Burton in Hornsea), 41/361; TA194477; NP 99
Hornsea (parish), 41/361-362; NP 99
Hornsea and Hornsea Burton (township in Hornsea), 41/361-362; NP 99
Hornsea Burton (division in township of Hornsea and Hornsea Burton in Hornsea), 41/362; TA210466; NP 99
Hornsey (parish), 24/80; TQ297887; NP 160
Hornton (parish), 29/325; SP389449; NP 145
Horringer (Horningsheath) (parish), 34/225; TL832620; NP 136
Horseheath (parish), 4/152; TL613471; NP 148
Horseley (township in Eccleshall), 33/142; SJ804284; NP 119
Horsell (parish), 35/79; SU995597; NP 169
Horsemonden (parish), 19/313; NP 171
Horsenden (Horsendon) (parish), 3/190; SP800018; NP 159
Horsepath (parish), 29/239; SP575048; NP 158
Horsey (Horsey-next-the-Sea) (parish), 25/229; TG457228; NP 126
Horsford (parish), 25/354; TG200160; NP 126
Horsforth (township in Guiseley), 43/505; SE238388; NP 96
Horsham (parish), 36/36; TQ178311; NP 170, 182
Horsham St Faith (parish), 25/356; TG216141; NP 126
Horsington (parish), 22/371; TF185678; NP 113, 114
Horsington (parish), 32/380; ST707247; NP 166
Horsley (parish), 8/207-209; NP 111, 112, 121
Horsley (parish), 13/331; ST832983; NP 156
Horsley (township in Horsley), 8/209; SK381439; NP 112, 121
Horsley (township in Ovingham), 27/556; NZ095662; NP 77
Horsley Woodhouse (township in Horsley), 8/207; SK397447; NP 112, 121

Horsmonden (Horsemonden) (parish), 19/313; TQ706401; NP 171
Horstead (parish), 25/251; TG267186; NP 126
Horsted Keynes (parish), 36/58; TQ385283; NP 183
Horton (parish), 3/237; TQ014760; NP 159
Horton (parish), 10/73; SU045070; NP 179
Horton (parish), 13/350; ST760847; NP 156
Horton (parish), 26/295; SP829537; NP 133, 146
Horton (parochial chapelry in Woodhorn), 27/478-482; NP 78
Horton (parish), 33/2A-B; NP 110
Horton (township in Tilston), 5/345; SJ455492; NP 109
Horton (township in Chatton), 27/70; NU028310; NP 64, 71
Horton (township in Horton parochial chapelry in Woodhorn), 27/482; NZ289786; NP 78
Horton (township in Wem), 31/46; SJ487297; NP 118
Horton (township in Bradford), 43/531-532; NP 96
Horton and Horton Hay (township in Horton), 33/2A; SJ935585; NP 110
Horton cum Peel (Horton cum Peele) township in Tarvin), 5/394; SJ496691; NP 109
Horton cum Studley (hamlet in Beckley), 29/231; SP593124; NP 145
Horton Grange (township in Dinnington), 27/514; NZ197762; NP 78
Horton in Ribblesdale (parish), 43/253-254; NP 90
Horton in Ribblesdale: Lower Division (division in parish and township of Horton in Ribblesdale), 43/253; SD815725; NP 90
Horton in Ribblesdale: Upper Division (division in parish and township of Horton in Ribblesdale), 43/254; SD795780; NP 90
Horton Kirby (parish), 19/57; TQ570682; NP 171
Horton near Gisburn (Horton) (township in Gisburn), 43/304; SD862510; NP 95
Horton, 43/304; NP 95
Horwich (township in Deane), 20/573; SD650120; NP 101
Horwood (parish), 9/42; SS509275; NP 163
Hose (parish), 21/83; SK739291; NP 122
Hotham (parish), 41/199; SE878341; NP 98
Hothersall (division in township of Alston and Hothersall in Ribchester), Alston and Hothersall (township in Ribchester), 20/223-224; NP 94, 95
Hothfield (parish), 19/322; TQ965444; NP 172
Hothorpe (hamlet in Theddingworth), 26/111; SP671845; NP 132, 133
Hoton (parish), 21/40; SK572227; NP 121
Hough (township in Wybunbury), 5/258; SJ710502; NP 110
Hough on the Hill (parish), 22/606; SK911471; NP 113, 122
Hougham (Huffam) (parish), 19/380; TR288401; NP 173
Hougham (parish), 22/617; SK896449; NP 113, 122
Houghton (township in Stanwix), 7/78; NY409605; NP 76
Houghton (parish), 14/154; SU338336; NP 168
Houghton (parish), 17/111; TL292729; NP 134
Houghton (division in township of Houghton, Middleton and Arbury in Winwick), 20/604; SJ620910; NP 101
Houghton (parish), 25/102; TF792285; NP 125
Houghton (parish), 28/76; NP 112
Houghton (parish), 36/220; TQ003111; NP 181
Houghton and Close House (township in Heddon on the Wall), 27/550; NZ122622; NP 77, 78
Houghton Conquest (parish), 1/72; TL018239; NP 147
Houghton le Side (township in Gainford), 11/312; NZ219157; NP 85
Houghton next Walsingham (parish), 25/78; NP 125
Houghton on the Hill (parish), 21/286; SK680035; NP 121, 122
Houghton on the Hill (parish), 25/536; TF869052; NP 125
Houghton Regis (parish), 1/130; TL018239; NP 147
Houghton St Giles (Houghton next Walsingham, Houghton-in-the-Hole) (parish), 25/78; TF923357; NP 125
Houghton Winterborne (parish), 10/161; NP 178
Houghton, Middleton and Arbury (township in Winwick), 20/603-605; NP 101
Houghton, 31/211; NP 118
Houghton-in-the-Hole (parish), 25/78; NP 125
Houghton-le-Spring (parish), 11/52-69; NP 78, 85
Houghton-le-Spring (township in Houghton-le-Spring), 11/68; NZ342499; NP 78, 85
Hound (parish), 14/271; SU470092; NP 180
Hove (parish), 36/312; TQ291050; NP 182
Hoveringham (parish), 28/190; SK709469; NP 112
Hoveton St John (parish), 25/364; TG318172; NP 126
Hoveton St Peter (parish), 25/365; TG317193; NP 126
Hovingham (parish), 42/624-631; NP 92
Hovingham (township in Hovingham), 42/626; SE662755; NP 92
How Bound (township in Castle Sowerby), 7/157; NY372376; NP 83
How Caple (parish), 15/176; SO607306; NP 142, 143
Howden (parish), 41/1-14B, 43/976; NP 97, 98
Howden (parish), 41/1-14B, 43/976; NP 97, 98
Howden (township in Howden), 41/4; SE749283; NP 97, 98
Howdon Pans (township in Wallsend), 27/502; NZ325665; NP 78
Howe (parish), 25/599; TM269995; NP 137
Howe (township in Pickhill), 42/247; SE352800; NP 91
Howell (parish), 22/587; TF151465; NP 113, 123
Howgill and Bland (division in township of Sedbergh in Sedbergh), 43/261; SD645965; NP 89
Howgrave (division in township of Nunwick with Howgrave in Kirklington), 42/229; SE317801; NP 91
Howick (hamlet in Itton), 53/94; ST503955; NP 155
Howick (parish), 27/157; NU247178; NP 71
Howick (township in Penwortham), 20/339; SD505278; NP 94
Howsham (township in Scrayingham), 41/119; SE750630; NP 92
Howtel (Howtell) (township in Kirknewton), 27/54; NU900338; NP 64
Howton (parish), 15/228; NP 142
Hoxne (parish), 34/83; TM195760; NP 137
Hoxton New Town (division in St Leonard Shoreditch), 24/62C; TQ316830; NP 160/1
Hoxton Old Town (division in St Leonard Shoreditch), 24/62D; TQ329834; NP 160/1
Hoyland Nether (Nether Hoyland) (township in Wath upon Dearne), 43/855; SE371002; NP 102
Hoyland Swaine (township in Silkstone), 43/701; SE258045; NP 102
Hubberston (Hubberstone) (parish), 55/103; SM889064; NP 151
Huby (township in Sutton-on-the-Forest), 42/589; SE558642; NP 92
Hucclecote (hamlet in Churchdown), 13/200; SO873180; NP 143
Huckerby (hamlet in Corringham), 22/146; SK902938; NP 104
Hucking (parish), 19/168; TQ839589; NP 172
Hucknall Huthwaite, 28/97
Hucknall Torkard (Hucknall) (parish), 28/180; SK529483; NP 112
Hucknall under Huthwaite, 28/97
Hudan (Hydon) (township in Castle Caereinion), 54/59; SJ157071; NP 117
Huddersfield (division in township of Huddersfield in Huddersfield), 43/749; SE144168; NP 102
Huddersfield (parish), 43/746-759, 765-766; NP 96, 102
Huddersfield (township in Huddersfield), 43/746-750; NP 102
Huddington (parish), 40/131; SO938578; NP 130
Huddleston (division in township of in Sherburn in Elmet), 43/426; SE467338; NP 97
Huddleston cum Lumby (township in Sherburn in Elmet), 43/426-427; NP 97
Hudnall (division in Little Gaddesden), 16/95B; TL012124; NP 147
Hudspen (hamlet in Pitcombe), 32/353; ST651316; NP 166
Hudswell (division of Hudswell township in Catterick), 42/80; SE141997; NP 91
Hudswell (township in Catterick and Easby), 42/80, 93; NP 91
Huffam (parish), 19/380; NP 173
Huffley (township in Battlefield), 31/245B; SJ494170; NP 118
Huggate (parish), 41/188; SE890560; NP 98
Hugglescote (Hugglescote and Donnington) (township in Ibstock), 21/138; SK431126; NP 121

129

Hughenden (Hughendon, Hitchenden) (parish), 3/195; SU865973; NP 159
Hughley (parish), 31/436; SO572980; NP 129
Hugil, 38/106
Hugill (township in Kendal), 38/106; SD442995; NP 89
Huish (parish), 9/114; SS538110; NP 175
Huish (parish), 39/202; SU149642; NP 157, 1667
Huish Champflower (parish), 32/288; ST037293; NP 164
Huish Episcopi (division in Huish Episcopi), 32/334A; ST426279; NP 165, 177
Huish Episcopi (division in Huish Episcopi), 32/334B; ST417256; NP 177
Huish Episcopi (parish), 32/334A-C; NP 165, 177
Hulam (township in Monk Hesleden), 11/95; NZ442369; NP 85
Hulcott (parish), 3/170; SP859133; NP 146
Hulland (township in Ashbourne), 8/183; SK244467; NP 111
Hulland Ward (Holland Ward, Hollin Ward) (township in Ashbourne), 8/184; SK272467; NP 111, 120
Hulland Ward Intakes (township in Ashbourne), 8/185; SK269458; NP 111, 120
Hullavington (parish), 39/43-44; NP 156
Hullavington (tithing in Hullavington), 39/44; ST891824; NP 156
Hulme (division in township of in Winwick), 20/606; SJ603917; NP 100, 101
Hulme (township in Manchester), 20/522; SJ830970; NP 101
Hulme Walfield (township in Astbury), 5/232; SJ849652; NP 110
Hulne Park (township in Alnwick), 27/201; NU163158; NP 71
Hulse (township in Great Budworth), 5/132; SJ709727; NP 110
Hulver Street (hamlet in Henstead), 34/54; TM473867; NP 137
Humber (parish), 15/99-100; NP 129, 142
Humber (township in Humber), 15/99; SO541563; NP 129, 142
Humber Ward (division in Holy Trinity Kingston upon Hull), 31/333A-B; NP 99/1
Humber Ward (division in parish and township of St Mary Kingston upon Hull), 41/325; TA100282; NP 99/1
Humber Ward (east part of ward in parish and township of Holy Tinity Kingston upon Hull), 41/333B; TA101283; NP 99/1
Humber Ward (west part of ward in parish and township of Holy Tinity Kingston upon Hull), 41/333A; TA998283; NP 99/1
Humbershoe (hamlet in Studham), 1/144; TL056169; NP 147
Humberstone (parish), 21/256; SK628065; NP 121
Humberston (Humberstone) (parish), 22/84; TA312053; NP 105
Humbleton (township in Doddington), 27/50; NT971285; NP 64, 71
Humbleton (parish), 41/405-409; NP 99
Humbleton (township in Humbleton), 41/405; TA224345; NP 99
Humburton (division in township of Milby in Kirby Hill), 42/576; SE399681; NP 91
Humby (Little Humby) (hamlet in Ropsley), 22/637; TF001327; NP 123
Humshaugh (township in Simonburn), 27/435; NY911717; NP 77
Huncoat (township in Whalley), 20/293; SD779229; NP 95
Huncote (township in Narborough), 21/212; SP517989; NP 121, 132
Hunderthwaite (township in Romaldkirk), 42/6; NY950195; NP 84
Hundle Houses (extra-parochial), 22/456; TF252549; NP 114
Hundleby 9parish), 22/431A-B; TF331589; NP 114
Hundleby (division in Hundleby), 22/431A; TF389662; NP 114
Hundleby - West Fen (division in Hundleby), 22/431B; TF331589; NP 114
Hundon (in Caistor), 22/104; NP 104
Hundon (parish), 34/329; TL740490; NP 148, 149
Hungate and Risplith (division in township of Sawley in Ripon), 43/164; SE241688; NP 91
Hungerford (tithing in Hungerford), 2/139; SU348681; NP 158
Hungerford Farley (parish), 32/92; NP 166
Hungerford (parish), 2/139-141, 39/182; NP 158, 168
Hungerton (parish), 21/258-261; NP 121, 122
Hungerton (township in Hungerton), 21/260; SK688072; NP 121, 122
Hungry Bentley (Bentley) (township in Longford), 8/231; SK180385; NP 120

Hunmanby (parish), 41/168-169; NP 93
Hunmanby (township in Hunmanby), 41/169; TA100750; NP 93
Hunningham (parish), 37/161; SP382676; NP 132
Hunnington (township in Halesowen), 40/7; SO968816; NP 130
Hunsdon (parish), 16/72; TL413133; NP 148
Hunshelf (township in Penistone), 43/784; SE271001; NP 102
Hunsingore (parish), 43/107-109; NP 96
Hunsingore (township in Hunsingore), 43/107; SE430543; NP 97
Hunslet (township in Leeds), 43/493; SE308313; NP 96
Hunsonby and Winskill (Winskel) (township in Addingham), 7/181; NY585355; NP 83
Hunstanton (parish), 25/1; TF690420; NP 124
Hunstanworth (parish), 11/169; NY940470; NP 84
Hunsterton (township in Wybunbury), 5/269; SJ699454; NP 110, 119
Hunston (parish), 34/190; TL979678; NP 136
Hunston (parish), 36/264; SU863014; NP 181
Hunsworth (township in Birstal), 43/541; SE186284; NP 96
Huntingdon, All Saints (parish), 17/81; TL238718; NP 134
Huntingdon, St Benedict (parish), 17/80; TL239718; NP 134
Huntingdon, St John (parish), 17/82; TL234724; NP 134
Huntingdon, St Mary (parish), 17/83; TL231712; NP 134
Huntingfield (parish), 34/149; TM337744; NP 137
Huntington (township in St Oswald Chester), 5/503; SJ423634; NP 109
Huntington (parish), 15/46; SO257530; NP 141
Huntington (township in Holmer), 15/126; SO484419; NP 142
Huntington (township in Cannock), 33/229; SJ970130; NP 119
Huntington (parish), 42/681-683; NP 97
Huntington (township in Huntington), 42/682; SE620557; NP 97
Huntley (parish), 13/135; SO717194; NP 143
Hunton (chapelry in Crawley), 14/159; SU493417; NP 168
Hunton (parish), 19/304; TQ723500; NP 171
Hunton (township in Hornby), 42/202; SE191927; NP 91
Hunton (township in Patrick Brompton), 42/203; SE189919; NP 91
Huntsham (parish), 9/134; SS995199; NP 164
Huntsham (township in Goodrich), 15/258; SO562172; NP 142
Huntshaw (parish), 9/64; SS509234; NP 163
Huntspill (parish), 32/174; ST329452; NP 165
Huntwick (extra-parochial), 43/675; SE409193; NP 103
Hunwick (division of Hunwick and Helmington township in St Andrew Auckland), 11/204; NZ187327; NP 85
Hunwick and Helmington (township in St Andrew Auckland), 11/204-205; NP 85
Hunworth (parish), 25/124; TG070351; NP 125
Hurcot (tithing in Somerton), 32/338B; ST508298; NP 165, 177
Hurdley (township in Church Stoke), 54/194; SO298942; NP 128
Hurdsfield (township in Prestbury), 5/46; SJ932748; NP 101, 110
Hurleston (township in Acton), 5/292; SJ618547; NP 110
Hurley (parish), 2/207; SU822818; NP 159
Hursley (parish), 14/210; SU423249; NP 168
Hurst (parish), 2/194-197; NP 159, 169
Hurst (parish), 19/398; TR076345; NP 172, 184
Hurst Courtney, 43/456; NP 97
Hurstbourne Priors (parish), 14/92; SU436483; NP 168
Hurstbourne Tarrant (parish), 14/67; SU376537; NP 168
Hurstley (township in Letton), 15/55; SO352487; NP 142
Hurstpierpoint (parish), 36/102; TQ282177; NP 182
Hurworth (parish), 11/326-327; NP 85
Hurworth (township in Hurworth), 11/326; NZ302109; NP 85
Husbands Bosworth (parish), 21/340; SP642835; NP 132
Husborne Crawley (Husborn Crawley) (parish), 1/78; SP959363; NP 146, 147
Hussington (parish), 31/347, 54/198; NP 129
Hussington, 54/198; NP 129
Husthwaite (parish), 42/560-561; NP 91, 92
Husthwaite (township in Husthwaite), 42/560; SE518736; NP 91, 92
Huthwaite (Hucknall Huthwaite, Hucknall under Huthwaite) (township in Sutton in Ashfield), 28/97; SK467592; NP 112
Huttoft (parish), 22/407; TF523777; NP 105
Hutton (parish), 12/333; TQ632945; NP 161
Hutton (parish), 32/154; ST349587; NP 165

Hutton (township in Penwortham), 20/340; SD490270; NP 94
Hutton Bonville (township in Birkby), 42/66; NZ350001; NP 91
Hutton Buscel (Hutton Bushel) (parish), 42/412-413; NP 93
Hutton Buscel (Hutton Bushel) (township in Hutton Buscel), 42/413; SE970850; NP 93
Hutton Bushel, 42/413; NP 93
Hutton Conyers (extra-parochial), 42/235; SE345741; NP 91
Hutton Cranswick (parish), 41/279-281; NP 99
Hutton Cranswick (township in Hutton Cranswick), 41/280; TA025525; NP 99
Hutton Hang (township in Finghall), 42/194; SE169887; NP 91
Hutton Henry (township in Monk Hesleden), 11/97; NZ417359; NP 85
Hutton in the Forest (parish), 7/161-167; NP 83
Hutton in the Forest (township in Hutton in the Forest), 7/161; NY458377; NP 83
Hutton John (township in Greystoke), 7/203; NY416276; NP 83
Hutton Long Villiers, 42/45
Hutton Lowcross (township in Guisborough), 42/358; NZ597142; NP 86
Hutton Magna, 42/45
Hutton Mulgrave (township in Lythe), 42/377; NZ835101; NP 86
Hutton near Rudby, 42/291; NP 85, 91
Hutton Roof (township in Greystoke), 7/210; NY373345; NP 83
Hutton Roof (township in Kirkby Lonsdale), 38/126; SD566784; NP 89
Hutton Rudby (Hutton near Rudby) (township in Rudby in Cleveland), 42/291; NZ458052; NP 85, 91
Hutton Sessay (division in Allertonshire Hundred in township of Hutton Sessay in Sessay), 42/562; SE472765; NP 91
Hutton Sessay (division in Birdforth Hundred in township of Hutton Sessay in Sessay), 42/563; SE464762; NP 91
Hutton Sessay (township in Sessay), 42/562-563; NP 91
Hutton Soil (township in Greystoke), 7/202; NY416276; NP 83
Hutton Wandesley (township in Long Marston), 43/67; SE512501; NP 97
Hutton-le-Hole (township in Lastingham), 42/463; SE705895; NP 92
Huttons Ambo (parish), 42/645; SE750697; NP 92
Huxham (parish), 9/248; SX951977; NP 176
Huxley (township in Waverton), 5/376; SJ505616; NP 109
Huyton (division in township of Huyton with Roby in Huyton), 20/639; SJ459888; NP 100
Huyton (parish), 20/638-641; NP 100
Huyton with Roby (township in Huyton), 20/639-640; NP 100
Hyde (township in Stockport), 5/11; SJ952944; NP 101
Hyde (township in Leominster), 15/65; SO457552; NP 129, 142
Hydes Pastures (township in Hinckley), 37/66; SP399924; NP 132
Hydon, 54/59; NP 117
Hylton (township in Monkwearmouth), 11/17; NZ352585; NP 78
Hylton Grove (division in township of Boldon in Boldon), 11/8B; NZ333599; NP 78
Hyssington (Hussington) (division in Hyssington), 54/198; SO322958; NP 129
Hyssington (Hussington) (parish), 31/347, 54/198; NP 129
Hythe (Hythe, St Leonard; St Leonards, Hythe) (parish), 19/391; TR154344; NP 173

I

Ibberton (parish), 10/88; ST788080; NP 178
Ible (township in Wirksworth), 8/150A; SK252572; NP 111
Ibsley (parish), 14/316; SU167100; NP 179
Ibstock (parish), 21/138-139; NP 121
Ibstock (township in Ibstock), 21/139; SK420100; NP 121
Ibstone (division in Ibstone), 3/209; SU763923; NP 159
Ibstone (division in Ibstone), 29/275; SU753928; NP 159
Ibworth (division in Hannington), 14/56; SU567543; NP 168
Ickburgh (Igborough) (parish), 25/687; TL813960; NP 136
Ickenham (parish), 24/95; TQ090851; NP 160
Ickford (hamlet in Ickford), 3/160; SP651075; NP 158
Ickford (parish), 3/160, 29/256A; NP 158
Ickham (Ickham and Well) (parish), 19/263; TR222570; NP 173

Ickleford (parish), 16/40; TL184332; NP 147
Icklesham (parish), 36/149; TQ899169; NP 184
Ickleton (parish), 4/182; TL483428; NP 148
Icklingham All Saints (parish), 34/113; TL787747; NP 136
Icklingham St James (Icklingham, St James and All Saints) (parish), 34/112; TL762748; NP 135, 136
Icklingham, St James and All Saints (parish), 34/112-113; NP 135, 136
Ickornshaw (division in township of Cowling in Kildwick), 43/353; SE958418; NP 95
Ickworth (parish), 34/224; TL813612; NP 136
Icomb (parish), 13/3, 94; SP216231; NP 144
Idbury (parish), 29/137; SP23720; NP 144, 145
Iddesleigh (parish), 9/117; SS575075; NP 175
Iddinshall (township in St Oswald Chester), 5/499; SJ532624; NP 109
Ide (parish), 9/316; SX885897; NP 176
Ideford (parish), 9/399; SX886769; NP 188
Iden (parish), 36/145; TQ920248; NP 184
Idle (township in Calverley), 43/510; SE173382; NP 96
Idlicote (parish), 37/284; SP288440; NP 144, 145
Idmiston (parish), 39/310A-E; NP 167
Idmiston (tithing in Idmiston), 39/310C; SU195375; NP 167
Idridgehay (division in township of Idridgehay and Alton in Wirksworth), 8/154; SK287486; NP 111
Idridgehay and Alton (township in Wirksworth), 8/153-154; NP 111
Idstock and Beere (Idstock and Beere with Habergen, Idstock and Beer) (hamlet in Cannington), 32/223; ST226416; NP 165
Idstone (tithing in Ashbury), 2/106; SU260840; NP 157, 158
Idsworth (chapelry in Chalton), 14/247; SU740133; NP 181
Iffley (division in Iffley), 29/222; SP529036; NP 158
Iffley (parish), 29/221-222; SP529036; NP 158
Ifield (parish), 19/34; NP 171
Ifield (parish), 36/38; TQ246374; NP 170
Iford (parish), 36/318; TQ398067; NP 183
Ifton (parish), 53/144; ST465881; NP 155
Ifton Rhyn (township in St Martin), 31/76; SJ320370; NP 118
Ightenhill (Ightonhill Park) (township in Whalley), 20/277; SD821342; NP 95
Ightfield (parish), 31/27-28; NP 118, 119
Ightfield (township in Ightfield), 31/28; SJ595385; NP 118, 119
Ightham (parish), 19/185; TQ589562; NP 171
Iken (parish), 34/372; TM416558; NP 137, 150
Ilam (parish), 33/91; SK123523; NP 111
Ilchester (parish), 32/401; ST509228; NP 177
Ilderton (parish), 27/115-120; NP 71
Ilderton (township in Ilderton), 27/118; NT990200; NP 71
Ilebrewers (parish), 32/410; NP 177
Ilfracombe (parish), 9/2; SS514461; NP 163
Ilkeston (parish), 8/200; SK466419; NP 112
Ilketshall, St Andrew (parish), 34/44; TM383862; NP 137
Ilketshall, St John (St Johns Ilketshall) (parish), 34/43; TM362875; NP 137
Ilketshall, St Lawrence (parish), 34/42; TM371851; NP 137
Ilketshall, St Margaret (St Margaret in Ilketshall) (parish), 34/41; TM352855; NP 137
Ilkley (parish), 43/337-342; NP 96
Ilkley (township in Ilkley), 43/342; SE112468; NP 96
Illey (township in Halesowen), 40/8; SO982818; NP 130
Illington (parish), 25/725; TL943896; NP 136
Illmire, 3/188; NP 159
Illogan (Illogen) (parish), 6/166; SW672421; NP 189
Illsfield (parish), 14/102; NP 168
Illston on the Hill (Ilston) (township in Carlton Curlieu), 21/291; SP710992; NP 122, 133
Ilmer (Illmire) (parish), 3/188; SP762057; NP 159
Ilmington (parish), 13/18, 37/299; NP 144
Ilmington (hamlet in Ilmington), 37/299; SP211428; NP 144
Ilminster (parish), 32/446; ST362147; NP 177
Ilsington (parish), 9/406; SX790757; NP 175, 188
Ilston (parish), 51/42; SS551910; NP 153
Ilston, 21/291; NP 122, 133

131

Ilton (division in township of Ilton cum Pott in Masham), 42/166; SE192788; NP 91
Ilton (parish), 32/435; ST355175; NP 177
Ilton cum Pott (township in Masham), 42/165-166; NP 91
Imber (parish), 39/242; ST966483; NP 167
Immingham (parish), 22/73; TA178142; NP 105
Impington (parish), 4/78; TL451628; NP 135
in Kirkby Malzeard), 43/194-206; NP 90, 91
Ince (Stoke with Ince) (parish), 5/413; SJ446767; NP 100, 109
Ince Blundall (township in Sefton), 20/680; SD320039; NP 100
Ince in Makerfield (Ince within Makerfield) (township in Wigan), 20/586; SD598044; NP 100, 101
Ingardine and The Lowe (township in Stottesden), 31/570; SO628810; NP 130
Ingarsby (township in Hungerton), 21/258; SK688053; NP 121, 122
Ingatestone (parish), 12/295; TQ633993; NP 161
Ingbirchworth (township in Penistone), 43/778; SE220056; NP 102
Ingerthorpe (township in Ripon), 43/169; SE294662; NP 91
Ingestre (parish), 33/187; SJ940248; NP 119
Ingham (parish), 22/227; SK948838; NP 104
Ingham (parish), 25/232; TG399261; NP 126
Ingham (parish), 34/117; TL852720; NP 136
Ingleby (township in Foremark), 8/302; SK347265; NP 121
Ingleby Arncliffe (division in Ingleby Arncliffe township in Arncliffe), 42/315; NZ443006; NP 91
Ingleby Arncliffe (township in Arncliffe), 42/314-315; NP 91
Ingleby Barwick (township in Stainton), 42/276; NZ442139; NP 85
Ingleby Greenhow (parish), 42/325A-326; NP 86, 92
Ingleby Greenhow (township in Ingleby Greenhow), 42/325B; NZ588064; NP 86, 92
Inglesham (division of Inglesham hamlet formerly in Berkshire in Inglesham), 39/2A; ST207980; NP 157
Inglesham (division of Inglesham hamlet in Inglesham), 39/2B; SU205985; NP 157
Inglesham (hamlet in Inglesham), 39/2A-B; NP 157
Inglesham (parish), 39/2A-3; NP 157
Ingleton (township in Staindrop), 11/286; NZ171205; NP 85
Ingleton (township in Bentham), 43/274; NP 89, 90
Ingleton and Moorgarth (division in township of Ingleton in Bentham), 43/271; SD700725; NP 89, 90
Ingleton Fells (division in township of Ingleton in Bentham), 43/274; SD755795; NP 90
Ingoe (township in Stamfordham), 27/458; NZ045775; NP 77
Ingol (division in township of Lea, Ashton, Ingol and Cottam in Preston), 20/212; SD513322; NP 94
Ingoldisthorpe (parish), 25/91; TF683325; NP 124
Ingoldmells (parish), 22/491; TF562690; NP 114
Ingoldsby (parish), 22/650; TF008302; NP 123
Ingon (hamlet in Hampton Lucy), 37/216; SP213576; NP 131
Ingram (parish), 27/127-130; NP 71
Ingram (township in Ingram), 27/127; NU005155; NP 71
Ingrave (parish), 12/411; TQ633926; NP 161
Ingthorpe Grange (division in township of Martons Both in Marton), 43/306; SD894520; NP 95
Ingworth (parish), 25/141; TG194301; NP 126
Inkberrow (parish), 40/137; SP020580; NP 130, 131
Inkpen (parish), 2/145; SU362638; NP 158, 168
Inner Temple (extra-parochial), 24/17B; TQ312810; NP 160/1
Inskip (division in township of Inskip with Sowerby in St Michaels on Wyre), 20/160A; SD456380; NP 94
Inskip with Sowerby (township in St Michaels on Wyre), 20/159-160B; NP 94
Instow (parish), 9/40; SS488305; NP 163
Intermixed lands in North Curry and Stoke St Gregory, 32/332B; ST359261; NP 177
Intwood (parish), 25/489; TG193042; NP 126
Inwardleigh (parish), 9/203; SX560985; NP 175
Inworth (parish), 12/223; TL879169; NP 149
Ipersbridge (extra-parochial), 14/329; SU423029; NP 180
Iping (parish), 36/7; SU851247; NP 181

Ipley (extra-parochial), 14/300A; SU376060; NP 180
Ipplepen (district in Ipplepen), 9/422; SX842661; NP 188
Ipplepen (parish), 9/422-423; NP 188
Ippollitts (parish), 16/34; NP 147
Ipsden (parish), 29/312; SU650850; NP 158, 159
Ipsley (parish), 37/183; SP058658; NP 131
Ipstones (parish), 33/75A-C; NP 111
Ipstones (township in Ipstones), 33/75A; SK020500; NP 111
Ipswich, George Street (Globe Street) (extra-parochial), 34/473; TM165443; NP 150/1
Ipswich, Shire Hall Yard (extra-parochial), 34/468; TM168445; NP 150/1
Ipswich, St Clement (parish), 34/464; TM181431; NP 150
Ipswich, St Helen (parish), 34/465; TM176445; NP 150/1
Ipswich, St Lawrence (parish), 34/471B; TM164445; NP 150/1
Ipswich, St Margaret (parish), 34/463; TM171457; NP 150
Ipswich, St Mary at the Elms (parish), 34/472; TM160445; NP 150/1
Ipswich, St Mary at the Quay (parish), 34/469; TM166441; NP 150/1
Ipswich, St Mary at the Tower (parish), 34/471A; TM164447; NP 150/1
Ipswich, St Mary Stoke (parish), 34/477; TM145425; NP 150
Ipswich, St Matthew (parish), 34/476; TM145454; NP 150
Ipswich, St Nicholas (parish), 34/474; TM162443; NP 150/1
Ipswich, St Peter (parish), 34/475; TM161440; NP 150/1
Ipswich, St Stephen (parish), 34/470; TM165444; NP 150/1
Irby (division of Irby township in Woodchurch), 5/470; SJ362846; NP 100
Irby (parish), 22/486; NP 114
Irby (township in Thurstaston), 5/471; SJ255851; NP 100
Irby (township in Woodchurch and Thurstaston), 5/470-471
Irby in the Marsh (Irby) (parish), 22/486; TF470630; NP 114
Irby upon Humber (parish), 22/92; TA201044; NP 105
Irchester (parish), 26/211; SP922657; NP 133
Ireby (parish), 7/219-220; NP 82
Ireby (township in Thornton in Lonsdale), 20/79; SD652750; NP 89
Ireton Wood (township in Kirk Ireton), 8/159C; SK279483; NP 111
Irmingland (parish), 25/146; TG130293; NP 125
Irnham (parish), 22/680-682; NP 123
Irnham (township in Irnham), 22/680; TF029262; NP 123
Iron Acton (parish), 13/366; ST678843; NP 156
Ironshill (division in Eling), 14/299B; SU393100; NP 180
Irstead (parish), 25/370; TG363201; NP 126
Irthington (parish), 7/37-40; NP 76
Irthington (township in Irthington), 7/39; NY494612; NP 76
Irthlingborough (parish), 26/150; SP945708; NP 133, 134
Irton (parish), 7/311; NP 88
Irton (township in Seamer), 42/410; TA008846; NP 93
Irton, Santon and Melthwaite (township in Irton), 7/311; NY114015; NP 88
Isan-dre (Issaynre) (township in Llanbadarn fawr), 46/14; SN597811; NP 127
Iscoed (township in Mapas), 50/144; SJ492426; NP 109, 118
Iscoyd, 50/144; NP 109, 118
Isell (parish), 7/235-237; NP 82
Isell Old Park (township in Isell), 7/235; NY196341; NP 82
Isfield (parish), 36/128; TQ451185; NP 183
Isglan (township in Whitford), 50/35; SJ173786; NP 108
Isham (parish), 26/198; SP884738; NP 133
Ishlawrcoed (hamlet in Bedwellty), 53/69C; SO180010; NP 154
Islan (township in Cwm), 50/67; SJ061768; NP 108
Isle Abbotts (parish), 32/413; ST350200; NP 177
Isle Brewers (Ilebrewers) (parish), 32/410; ST372206; NP 177
Isle of Harty (St Thomas, Isle of Harty) (parish), 19/103; TR020670; NP 172
Isle of Walney (sub-division of Hawcoat division of Dalton township in Dalton in Furness), 20/29-30; NP 88
Islebeck (division in township of Bagby with Islebeck in Kirby Knowle), 42/525; SE449777; NP 91

Isleham (parish), 4/42; TL637754; NP 135
Isles of Scilly (parish), 6/217-222; NP 189
Isleworth (parish), 24/126; TQ157760; NP 170
Isley Walton (township in Kegworth), 21/18; SK425250; NP 121
Islington - East (division in St Mary Islington), 24/46B; TQ319854; NP 160
Islington - West (division in St Mary Islington), 24/46A; TQ308844; NP 160
Islip (parish), 26/84; SP982790; NP 134
Islip (parish), 29/119; SP529137; NP 145
Isombridge (township in High Ercall), 31/213; SJ610140; NP 118, 119
Issayndre, 46/14; NP 127
Isygarreg (township in Machynlleth), 54/129; SN735985; NP 127
Itchen Abbas (parish), 14/164; SU538345; NP 168
Itchen Stoke (Itchen Stoke with Abbotstone) (parish), 14/165; SU562345; NP 168
Itchingfield (parish), 36/65; TQ130282; NP 182
Itchingswell (parish), 14/11; NP 168
Itchington (hamlet in Tytherington), 13/364B; ST660870; NP 156
Itonfield (township in Hesket in the Forest), 7/163; NY434441; NP 83
Itterby (in Clee), 22/82; NP 105
Itteringham (parish), 25/144; TG150310; NP 125, 126
Itton (hamlet in Itton), 53/95; ST490953; NP 155
Itton (partish), 53/94-95; NP 155
Ivegill (Highhead) (township in Dalston), 7/146; NY406441; NP 83
Ivelet and Calvert House (division in township of Muker in Grinton), 42/128; SD918996; NP 90
Iver (parish), 3/236; TQ034812; NP 159
Ivestone (Ivestone) (township in Lanchester), 11/160; NZ131509; NP 77, 78, 84, 85
Ivinghoe (parish), 3/131; SP956160; NP 146, 147
Ivington (township in Leominster), 15/66; SO474553; NP 129, 142
Ivonbrook Grange (Ivenbrook Grange, Grange Mill) (township in Wirksworth), 8/150B; SK242583; NP 111
Ivychurch (parish), 19/430; TQ999251; NP 184
Iwade (parish), 19/96; TQ896692; NP 172
Iwerne Courtney (Iwerne Courtney with Farringdon; Iwerne Courtney or Shroton) (parish), 10/55; ST861124; NP 178
Iwerne Minster (parish), 10/57; ST872145; NP 178
Ixworth (parish), 34/194; TL935711; NP 136
Ixworth Thorpe (parish), 34/125; TL921726; NP 136

J

Jacobstow (parish), 6/8; SX204955; NP 174
Jacobstowe (Jacobstow), 9/204; SS581014; NP 175
Jarrow (division of Hebburn, Monkton and Jarrow township in Jarrow), 11/6; NZ316645; NP 78
Jarrow (parish), 11/1-7; NP 78
Jefferston (parish), 55/133; NP 151, 152
Jeffreston (parish), 55/133; NP 151, 152
Jeffreyston (Jefferston, Jeffreston) (parish), 55/133; SN072062; NP 151, 152
Jesmond (township in St Andrew), 27/641; NZ259660; NP 78
Jevington (parish), 36/185; TQ565020; NP 183
Johnby (township in Greystoke), 7/199; NY415335; NP 83
Johnston (Johnstone) (parish), 55/91; SM935115; NP 151
Joint Lordship (township in Worthen), 31/332B; SO363992; NP 118, 129
Jordanston (Jordanstone) (parish), 55/36; SM921331; NP 138

K

Kaber (township in Kirkby Stephen), 38/60; NY834096; NP 84
Kattern (parish), 32/30; NP 156
Kea (parish), 6/161; SW802421; NP 190
Keadby (township in Althorpe), 22/9; SE827123; NP 104
Kearsley (Kersley) (township in Deane), 20/564; SD752048; NP 101
Kearsley (township in Stamfordham), 27/454; NZ028755; NP 77
Keckwick (Kekewick) (township in Runcorn), 5/151; SJ572829; NP 100

Keddington (parish), 22/285; TF344897; NP 105
Kedington (division in Kedington), 12/29; TL700450; NP 148
Kedington (division in Kedington), 34/335; TL709468; NP 148
Kedington (parish), 12/29, 34/335; NP 148
Kedleston (parish), 8/217; SK309404; NP 121
Keelby (parish), 22/74; TA165095; NP 105, 105
Keele (parish), 33/41; SJ810453; NP 110
Keenley (township in Allendale), 27/594; NY800570; NP 77
Keevil (division in Keevil), 39/141; ST925583; NP 166, 167
Keevil (parish), 39/140-141; NP 166, 167
Kegworth (parish), 21/17; NP 121
Kegworth (township in Kegworth), 21/17; SK482270; NP 121
Keinton Mandeville (parish), 32/344; ST550303; NP 165, 177
Keisby (township in Lenton), 22/669; TF045295; NP 123
Kekewick, 5/151; NP 100
Kelby (chapelry in Haydor), 22/643; TF015415; NP 123
Keld and Thorns (division in township of Muker in Grinton), 42/124; NY900000; NP 90
Kelfield (township in Stillingfleet), 41/58; SE597390; NP 97
Kelham (parish), 28/145; SK772561; NP 112, 113
Kelleythorpe (division in township of Elmswell with Kelleythorpe in Great Driffield), 41/278; TA008565; NP 98, 99
Kelling (parish), 25/30; TG092240; NP 125
Kelloe (parish), 11/99-104; NP 85
Kelloe (township in Kelloe), 11/101; NZ355368; NP 85
Kelloweys (parish), 39/85; NP 157
Kelly (parish), 9/348; SX403818; NP 175, 186
Kelmarsh (parish), 26/123; SP732797; NP 133
Kelmscot (Kelmscott) (township in Broadwall), 29/160; SU253995; NP 157
Kelsale (parish), 34/259; TM383657; NP 137
Kelsall (Kelsall on the Hill) (township in Tarvin), 5/386; SJ522683; NP 109
Kelshall (Kelshal) (parish), 16/12; TL320370; NP 147
Kelstern (hamlet in Kelstern), 22/197; TF253903; NP 105
Kelstern (parish), 22/196-197; NP 105
Kelsterton (township in Northop), 50/22; SJ273700; NP 108, 109
Kelston (parish), 32/22; ST701671; NP 156
Kelston (township in Llanasa), 50/49A; SJ102821; NP 108
Kelvedon (parish), 12/186; TL854187; NP 149
Kelvedon Hatch (parish), 12/299; TQ565995; NP 161
Kemberton (parish), 31/224; SJ730045; NP 119
Kemble (parish), 39/18; ST989975; NP 157
Kempley (parish), 13/130; SO671308; NP 143
Kempsey (parish), 40/158; SO862492; NP 143
Kempsford (parish), 13/297; SU166982; NP 157
Kempshott (division in Winslade with Kempshott), 14/103; SU598476; NP 168
Kempston (parish), 1/51; TL022473; NP 147
Kempstone (parish), 25/331; TF883171; NP 125
Kemsing (parish), 19/187; TQ560589; NP 171
Kenardington (Kennardington) (parish), 19/415; TQ971320; NP 184
Kenarth (parish), 47/40; NP 139
Kenchester (parish), 15/119; SO440423; NP 142
Kencot (Kencott) (parish), 29/164; SP254053; NP 157
Kendal (parish), 38/92-117; NP 83, 89
Kendal (township in Kendal), 38/97; SD522923; NP 89
Kenderchurch (Howton) (parish), 15/228; SO416296; NP 142
Kenfig (Kenfigg) (parish), 51/99; SS800820; NP 153
Kenilworth (parish), 37/93; SP278728; NP 131, 132
Kenley (township in Stanton Lacy), 31/437; SO569996; NP 129
Kenn (district in Kenn), 9/387; SX904852; NP 176
Kenn (parish), 9/317, 387; NP 176
Kenn (parish), 32/61; ST416690; NP 165
Kennardington (parish), 19/415; NP 184
Kennerleigh (parish), 9/171; SS819075; NP 176
Kennett (parish), 4/45; TL694678; NP 135
Kenninghall (parish), 25/736; TM050852; NP 136
Kennington (division of Kennington township in Sunningwell), 2/12; SP523025; NP 158
Kennington (township in Radley), 2/13C; SP525015; NP 158
Kennington (township in Sunningwell and Radley), 2/12, 13C; NP 158

133

Kennington (parish), 19/452; TR024446; NP 172
Kennington First (division in Lambeth), 35/13A; TQ307774; NP 170
Kennington Second (division in Lambeth), 35/13B; TQ311769; NP 170
Kennythorpe (township in Langton), 41/129; SE790660; NP 92
Kensington (parish), 24/39A-B; TQ246805; NP 160, 170
Kensington Town (division in Kensington), 24/39A; TQ246805; NP 160, 170
Kenstone (township in Hodnet), 31/167B; SJ590280; NP 118
Kenswick (extra-parochial), 40/106; SO788587; NP 130
Kensworth (parish), 16/153; TL027194; NP 147
Kent Road (division in St George the Martyr Southwark), 35/9A; TQ330790; NP 170
Kentbury (parish), 2/143; NP 158, 168
Kentchurch (parish), 15/226; SO421267; NP 142
Kentford (parish), 34/212; TL709668; NP 135
Kentisbeare (parish), 9/151; ST070085; NP 164, 176
Kentisbury (parish), 9/15; SS626436; NP 163
Kentish Town (division in St Pancras), 24/44A; TQ295855; NP 160
Kentmere (township in Kendal), 38/107; NY455055; NP 83, 89
Kenton (district in Kenton), 9/389; SX945830; NP 176, 188
Kenton (East and West Kenton) (township in Gosforth), 27/512; NZ220676; NP 78
Kenton (parish), 9/389-390; NP 176, 188
Kenwick (township in Ellesmere), 31/74; SJ421308; NP 118
Kenwick Park (township in Ellesmere), 31/55B; SJ406296; NP 118
Kenwick Wood (township in Ellesmere), 31/56; SJ402286; NP 118
Kenwyn (parish), 6/136; SW800460; NP 190
Kenyon (township in Winwick), 20/596; SJ632957; NP 101
Kepwick (township in Over Silton), 42/512; SE477917; NP 91
Kerdiston (parish), 25/201; TG081241; NP 125
Keresley (hamlet in Coventry, St Michael), 37/151; SP318835; NP 132
Kermincham (township in Swettenham), 5/222; SJ800685; NP 110
Kersall (township in Kneesall), 28/104; SK716622; NP 112
Kersey (parish), 34/419; TL998438; NP 149
Kersley, 20/564; NP 101
Kesgrave (parish), 34/446; TM225454; NP 150
Kessingland (parish), 34/57; TM528868; NP 137
Keston (parish), 19/67; TQ416635; NP 171
Keswick (parish), 25/487; TG211042; NP 126
Keswick (township in Crosthwaite), 7/285; NY263234; NP 82
Ketsby (hamlet in South Ormsby cum Ketsby), 22/326; TF358770; NP 105
Kettering (parish), 26/158; SP863784; NP 133
Ketteringham (parish), 25/563; TG163027; NP 125, 126, 136, 137
Kettlebaston (parish), 34/405; TL966502; NP 149
Kettleburgh (parish), 34/281; TM265611; NP 137
Kettleshulme (township in Prestbury), 5/36; SJ989788; NP 101
Kettlestone (parish), 25/115; TF966315; NP 125
Kettlethorpe (parish), 22/239-241; NP 104
Kettlethorpe (township in Kettlethorpe), 22/240; SK845759; NP 104
Ketton (division in of Brafferton in Aycliffe), 11/278; NZ312202; NP 85
Ketton (parish), 30/33; SK973053; NP 123
Kevencalolog (Kevengalolog) (township in Bettws-y-crwyn), 31/402; SO211852; NP 128
Kevengalolog, 31/402
Kew (parish), 35/30; TQ188733; NP 170
Kewstoke (parish), 32/64; ST339638; NP 165
Kexby (township in Upton), 22/136; SK876858; NP 104
Kexby (township in Catton), 41/83; SE693505; NP 97
Keyham (township in Rothley), 21/53; SK677601; NP 121, 122
Keyingham (parish), 41/431; TA239243; NP 99
Keymer (parish), 36/100; TQ315175; NP 182
Keynsham (parish), 32/20; ST658677; NP 156
Keysoe (parish), 1/8; TL073627; NP 134

Keyston (parish), 17/49; TL040743; NP 134
Keythorpe (district in Tugby), 21/280; SP772991; NP 122, 133
Keyworth (parish), 28/291; SK614303; NP 121
Kibblesworth (township in Chester le Street), 11/38; NZ239558; NP 78
Kibworth Beauchamp (parish), 21/318-319; NP 132, 133
Kibworth Beauchamp (township in Kibworth Beauchamp), 21/319; SP676938; NP 132, 133
Kibworth Harcourt (township in Kibworth Beauchamp), 21/320; SP684950; NP 132, 133
Kidbrooke (Kidbrook) (parish), 19/9; TQ412760; NP 171
Kidderminster (borough in Kidderminster), 40/28; SO832769; NP 130
Kidderminster (parish), 40/28-30; NP 130
Kidderminster Foreign (division in Kidderminster), 40/29; SO815765; NP 130
Kiddington (division in Kiddington), 29/89; SP413224; NP 145
Kiddington (parish), 29/89-90; NP 145
Kidland (extra-parochial), 27/175; NT860140; NP 70, 71
Kidlington (division in Kidlington), 29/197; SP493142; NP 145
Kidlington (parish), 29/197-201; NP 145
Kidwelly (parish), 47/80; NP 152
Kidwelly Park (hamlet in Kidwelly), 47/80; SN400090; NP 152
Kiffig (parish), 47/54; NP 152
Kilbourn, 8/208; NP 111
Kilburn (division in township of Kilburn in Kilburn), 42/543; SE512804; NP 91, 92
Kilburn (Kilbourn, Kilbourne) (township in Horsley), 8/208; SK374462; NP 111
Kilburn (parish), 42/543-547; NP 91, 92
Kilburn (township in Kilburn), 42/543-544; NP 91, 92
Kilby (parish), 21/327; SP624949; NP 132
Kildale (parish), 42/327; NZ630090; NP 86
Kilham (township in Kirknewton), 27/55; NT881326; NP 64, 70
Kilkhampton (parish), 6/2; SS250109; NP 174
Killam (division in parish and township of Killam), 41/241; TA050655; NP 93, 99
Killam (parish and township), 41/240-241; NP 93, 99
Killamarsh (parish), 8/57; SK458807; NP 103
Killerby (township in Heighington), 11/308; NZ197200; NP 85
Killerby (township in Catterick), 42/74; SE268970; NP 91
Killingholme (parish), 22/51-52; NP 99, 104, 105
Killington (township in Kirkby Lonsdale), 38/119; SD606895; NP 89
Killingworth (township in Longbenton), 27/504; NZ280713; NP 78
Kilmersdon (parish), 32/117; ST692516; NP 166
Kilmeston (Kilmiston) (parish), 14/238; SU592257; NP 168
Kilmington (parish), 9/232; SY268985; NP 177
Kilmington (parish), 32/193; ST783367; NP 166
Kilmiston (parish), 14/238; NP 168
Kilnsea (division in parish and township of Kilnsea), 41/447; TA415163; NP 105
Kilnsea (parish and township of), 41/447-448; NP 105
Kilnwick (parish), 41/285-288; NP 98,99
Kilnwick (township in Kilnwick), 41/286; TA004493; NP 98, 99
Kilnwick Percy (parish), 41/105; SE830500; NP 98
Kilpeck (parish), 15/230; SO442298; NP 142
Kilpin (township in Howden), 41/7; SE770271; NP 98
Kilsby (parish), 26/179; SP566712; NP 132
Kilton (parish), 32/229; ST163427; NP 164
Kilton (township in Skelton), 42/352; NZ679139; NP 86
Kilton (township in Skelton), 42/353; NZ695175; NP 86
Kilve (parish), 32/231; ST150432; NP 164
Kilverstone (parish), 25/718; TL900950; NP 136
Kilvington (parish), 28/203-204; NP 122
Kilvington (township in Kilvington), 28/203; SK800429; NP 122
Kilybebell (parish), 51/9; NP 153
Kimberley (parish), 25/554; TG072043; NP 125
Kimberley (township in Greasley), 28/176; SK500446; NP 112, 121
Kimblesworth (Kimbleworth) (extra-parochial), 11/134; NZ255467; NP 85
Kimbolton (parish), 15/73; SO529614; NP 129

134

Kimbolton (hamlet in Kimbolton), 17/96; TL100680; NP 134
Kimbolton (parish), 17/95-97; NP 134
Kimcote and Walton (Kincote) (parish), 21/335C; SP600870; NP 132
Kimmeridge (parish), 10/294; SY923786; NP 178, 179
Kimmerston (Kimmerston and Broomridge) (township in Ford), 27/39; NT960360; NP 64
Kimpton (parish), 14/77; SU277479; NP 167, 168
Kimpton (parish), 16/89; TL171183; NP 147
Kincote (parish), 21/335C; NP 132
Kinderton cum Hulme (township in Middlewich), 5/200; SJ723659; NP 110
Kineton (parish), 37/272-273; NP 145
Kineton (township in Kineton), 37/272; SP343506; NP 145
Kinfare (parish), 33/341; NP 130
King Stanley (parish), 13/310; NP 156
King's Brompton (parish), 32/285; SS960311; NP 164
King's Caple (parish), 15/267; SO564290; NP 142
King's Cliffe (King's Cliff) (parish), 26/38; TL008974; NP 123, 134
King's Langley (parish), 16/137; TL060027; NP 159, 160
King's Newnham (Newnham Regis) (parish), 37/140; SP451777; NP 132
King's Norton (parish), 21/287-288; NP 121, 122
King's Norton (township in King's Norton), 21/287; SK683002; NP 121, 122
King's Norton (parish), 40/41-44; NP 130, 131
King's Nympton (parish), 9/86; SS691204; NP 163
King's Pyon (parish), 15/61; SO431503; NP 142
King's Ripton (parish), 17/65-66; NP 134
King's Ripton (district in King's Ripton), 17/66; TL261765; NP 134
King's Stanley (King Stanley) (parish), 13/310; SO821032; NP 156
King's Standing (division in Tutbury), 33/209C; SK151241; NP 120
King's Sutton (hamlet in King's Sutton), 26/361A; SP499362; NP 145
King's Sutton (parish), 26/361A-B; SP499362; NP 145
King's Walden (parish), 16/45; TL158232; NP 147
King's Worthy (parish), 14/162; SU493342; NP 168
Kingerby (parish), 22/157; TF048921; NP 104
Kingham (parish), 29/50; SP262250; NP 144
Kingkerswell, 9/430; NP 188
Kingmoor (extra-parochial), 7/70; NY391589; NP 76
Kings Areley (parish), 40/72; NP 130
Kings Barns (division in Beeding), 36/111; TQ189119; NP 182
Kings Bromley (parish), 33/225; SK115155; NP 120
Kings Bromley Hays (extra-parochial), 33/224; SK128149; NP 120
Kings Hatfield (parish), 12/198; NP 148
Kings Lynn - Chequer Ward (division in Lynn St Margaret), 25/289D; TF616202; NP 124/1
Kings Lynn - Jews Lane Ward (division in Lynn St Margaret), 25/289C; TF618203; NP 124/1
Kings Lynn - Kettlewell Ward (division in Lynn St Margaret), 25/289B; TF620293; NP 124/1
Kings Lynn - New Conduit Ward (division in Lynn St Margaret), 25/289F; TF618201; NP 124/1
Kings Lynn - North End Ward (division in Lynn St Margaret), 25/289A; TF620204; NP 124/1
Kings Lynn - Paradise Ward (division in Lynn St Margaret), 25/289E; TF622201; NP 124/1
Kings Lynn - Sedgeford Lane Ward (division in Lynn St Margaret), 25/289H; TF621199; NP 124/1
Kings Lynn - Stonegate Ward (division in Lynn St Margaret), 25/289J; TF620197; NP 124/1
Kings Lynn - Trinity Hall Ward (division in Lynn St Margaret), 25/289G; TF617199; NP 124/1
KIngs Marsh (extra-parochial), 5/354; SJ430546; NP 109
Kings Meaburn (township in Morland), 38/11; NY633206; NP 83
Kings Somborne (parish), 14/155; SU363307; NP 168
Kings Weston (tithing in Henbury), 13/378; ST541778; NP 155

Kingsbridge (parish), 9/476; SX734444; NP 187
Kingsbury (parish), 24/87; TQ207889; NP 160
Kingsbury Episcopi (division in Kingsbury Episcopi), 32/406; ST421206; NP 177
Kingsbury Episcopi (parish), 32/406-407; NP 177
Kingsbury (parish), 37/24-25; SP228962; NP 120, 131
Kingsbury (township in Kingsbury), 37/24; SP228962; NP 131
Kingsclere (parish), 14/12; SU527588; NP 168
Kingscote (parish), 13/332; ST819965; NP 156
Kingsdon (parish), 32/339; ST519261; NP 177
Kingsdown (division in Kingsdown), 19/75; TQ570630; NP 171
Kingsdown (parish), 19/75, 188; NP 171
Kingsdown (parish), 19/161; TQ922589; NP 172
Kingsey (division in Kingsey), 3/186; SP755067; NP 159
Kingsey (parish), 3/186, 29/263; NP 159
Kingsholm St Mary (division in Gloucester, St Mary de Lode), 13/177B; SO827198; NP 143
Kingskerswell (Kingkerswell) (parish), 9/430; SX881672; NP 188
Kingsland (parish), 15/32; SO447613; NP 129
Kingsley (township in Frodsham), 5/406; SJ550752; NP 100, 109
Kingsley (parish), 14/120; SU791384; NP 169
Kingsley (parish), 33/72A-B; NP 110, 111, 120
Kingsley (township in Kingsley), 33/72A; SK010470; NP 110, 111, 120
Kingsmead (division in Bath, St Peter and St Paul), 32/36B; ST744651; NP 156/1
Kingsnorth (parish), 19/402; TR003391; NP 172
Kingsteignton (parish), 9/398; SX866745; NP 188
Kingsthorpe (parish), 26/228; SP755633; NP 133
Kingston (parish), 4/124; TL342546; NP 134, 135, 147, 148
Kingston (parish), 9/471; SX632479; NP 187
Kingston (division in Portsea), 14/289A; SU650020; NP 180
Kingston (Kingstone) (parish), 18/26; SZ474812; NP 180
Kingston (Kingstone) (parish), 19/342; TR190507; NP 173
Kingston (parish), 32/313; NP 165, 177
Kingston (Kingstone) (parish), 33/122; SK057291; NP 120
Kingston (parish), 36/205; NP 183
Kingston (parish), 36/298; TQ084020; NP 182
Kingston (Chesterton Parva) (hamlet in Chesterton), 37/256; SP363567; NP 132
Kingston Bagpuize (parish), 2/26; SU407984; NP 158
Kingston by Sea (parish), 36/309; TQ226062; NP 182
Kingston Deverill (parish), 39/277; ST842370; NP 166
Kingston Lisle (chapelry in Sparsholt), 2/98; SU325870; NP 158
Kingston near Lewes (Kingston) (parish), 36/205; TQ397080; NP 183
Kingston Russell (parish), 10/240; SY581903; NP 177
Kingston Seymour (parish), 32/62; ST393672; NP 165
Kingston St Mary (Kingston) (parish), 32/313; ST212296; NP 165, 177
Kingston upon Soar (parish), 28/281; SK507279; NP 121
Kingston upon Thames (division in Kingston upon Thames), 35/34; TQ183692; NP 170
Kingston upon Thames (parish), 35/33-36; NP 170
Kingstone Winslow (hamlet in Ashbury), 2/105; SU269855; NP 157, 158
Kingstone (parish), 15/197; SO428356; NP 142
Kingstone (parish), 18/26; NP 180
Kingstone (parish), 32/455; ST391134; NP 177
Kingstone (parish), 33/122; NP 120
Kingswear (parish), 9/437; SX885511; NP 188
Kingswinford (parish), 33/339; SO900880; NP 130
Kingswood (hamlet in Ludgershall), 3/149; SP689184; NP 146
Kingswood (township in Delamere), 5/404; SJ529728; NP 109
Kingswood (parish), 13/5; ST742907; NP 156
Kingswood and Buttonoak (township in Stottesden), 31/569; SO751775; NP 130
Kingswood (division in Ewell), 35/56; TQ251544; NP 170
Kingthorpe (township in Pickering), 42/433; SE840865; NP 92
Kington (parish), 15/41A-D; NP 128, 129, 141, 142
Kington (parish), 40/141; SO992553; NP 130, 131, 143, 144

Kington (tithing in Thornbury), 13/358B; ST620905; NP 156
Kington Langley (tithing in Kington St Michael), 39/68; ST922771; NP 156, 157
Kington Magna (parish), 10/20; ST759226; NP 166
Kington St Michael (parish), 39/67-69; NP 156, 157
Kington St Michael (tithing in Kington St Michael), 39/67; ST901772; NP 156
Kington, 15/7; NP 129
Kingwater (township in Lanercost), 7/28; NY640730; NP 76
Kingweston (parish), 32/342; ST529308; NP 165, 177
Kinlet (parish), 31/551; SO735800; NP 130
Kinnerley (Kinnerley and Argoed) (township in Kinnerley), 31/124; SJ333204; NP 118
Kinnerley (parish), 31/120-127; NP 118
Kinnerley and Argoed, 31/124; NP 118
Kinnersley (parish), 15/53; SO344497; NP 142
Kinnersley (parish), 31/201; SJ665170; NP 119
Kinniside (Kinnyside) (township in St Bees), 7/290; NY080120; NP 82
Kinnyside, 7/290
Kinoulton (parish), 28/266; SK687304; NP 121
Kinsham (township in Presteigne), 15/38B; SO358645; NP 129
Kinson (Kingstone) (tithing in Canford Magna), 10/194; SZ066953; NP 179
Kintbury (Kintsbury, Kentbury) (parish), 2/143; SU380667; NP 158, 168
Kinton (Kington) (township in Leintwardine), 15/7; SO412751; NP 129
Kinton (township in Great Ness), 31/133; SJ363195; NP 118
Kinvaston (township in Wolverhampton), 33/311; SJ910116; NP 119
Kinver (Kinfare) (parish), 33/341; SO861849; NP 130
Kinwalsey (hamlet in Hampton in Arden), 37/81B; SP255855; NP 131
Kiplin (township in Catterick), 42/71; SE285975; NP 91
Kirby Bedon (Kirby Bedon St Andrew and Kirby Bedon St Mary) (parish), 25/480; TG283055; NP 126
Kirby Bellars (parish), 21/115; SK722259; NP 122
Kirby Cane (parish), 25/619; TM371938; NP 137
Kirby Frith (extra-parochial), 21/182; SK537050; NP 121
Kirby Grindalythe (Kirbygrindalyth) (division in township of Kirby Grindalythe in Kirby Grindalythe), 41/182; SE912670; NP 92, 93, 98
Kirby Grindalythe (Kirbygrindalyth) (parish), 41/181-183C
Kirby Grindalythe (township in Kirby Grindalythe), 41/182-183B
Kirby Hill (Kirkby-on-the-Moor) (parish), 42/236, 574-577; NP 91
Kirby Hill (township in Kirby Hill or Kirkby-on-the-Moor), 42/574; SE393697; NP 91
Kirby Knowle (42/522-526); NP 91
Kirby Knowle (township in Kirby Knowle), 42/522; SE468872; NP 91
Kirby Misperton (parish), 42/448-453; NP 92
Kirby Misperton (township in Kirby Misperton), 42/450; SE778793; NP 92
Kirby Moorside, (parish), 42/469-474; NP 92
Kirby Muxloe (township in Glenfield), 21/178; SK520043; NP 121
Kirby Sigston (Kirkby Sigston) (parish), 42/508-510A; NP 91
Kirby Sigston (Kirkby Sigston) (township in Kirby Sigston), 42/509; SE423946; NP 91
Kirby Thore (parish), 38/4-6; NP 83
Kirby Thore (township in Kirby Thore), 38/5; NY643627; NP 83
Kirby Underdale (division in parish and township of Kirby Underdale), 41/136; SE802579; NP 98
Kirby Underdale (parish and township), 41/136-138C; NP 92, 98
Kirby Wiske (parish), 42/253-255B; NP 91
Kirby Wiske (township in Kirby Wiske), 42/253; SE364848; NP 91
Kirby-le-Soken (parish), 12/161; TM219208; NP 150
Kirdford (parish), 36/31; TQ007283; NP 181, 182
Kirk Ella (division in township of Kirk Ella in Kirk Ella), 41/308; TA028298; NP 99, 99/1

Kirk Ella (division in Wold Ings in township of Kirk Ella in Kirk Ella), 41/319; TA070276; NP 99/1
Kirk Ella (parish), 31/307-312, 319-321; NP 98, 99, 99/1
Kirk Ella (township in Kirk Ella), 31/308-309; NP 99, 99/1
Kirk Hallam (parish), 8/201; NP 121
Kirk Hallam (township in Kirk Hallam), 8/201; SK456403; NP 121
Kirk Ireton (parish), 8/159A-C; NP 111
Kirk Ireton (township in Kirk Ireton), 8/159A; SK269495; NP 111
Kirk Langley (parish), 8/215-216; NP 120, 121
Kirk Langley (township in Kirk Langley), 8/215; SK482384; NP 120, 121
Kirkandrews Middle (Middle Quarter) (township in Kirkandrews upon Esk), 7/12; NY365716; NP 76
Kirkandrews Nether (Nether Quarter) (township in Kirkandrews upon Esk), 7/13; NY345685; NP 76
Kirkandrews upon Eden (parish), 7/101; NY352574; NP 76
Kirkandrews upon Esk (parish), 7/10-13; NP 76
Kirkbampton (parish), 7/114-117; NP 75
Kirkbampton (township in Kirkbampton), 7/116; NY302566; NP 75
Kirkbride (parish), 7/113; NY230555; NP 75
Kirkburn (parish), 41/231-235; NP 98, 99
Kirkburn (township in Kirkburn), 41/234; SE975555; NP 98
Kirkby (Kirby in Cleveland), 42/322; NZ538059; NP 86, 92
Kirkby (Kirby in Cleveland, Kirkby in Cleveland) (division in township of Kirkby in Kirkby), 42/322; NP 86, 92
Kirkby (parish), 42/320-324; 85, 86, 92
Kirkby (township in Walton on the Hill), 20/675; SJ421982; NP 100
Kirkby (township in Kirkby), 42/320-322; NP 85, 86, 92
Kirkby cum Osgodby (parish), 22/158; TF082921; NP 104
Kirkby Fleetham (parish), 42/215; SE280945; NP 91
Kirkby Green (parish), 22/569; TF087579; NP 113
Kirkby Hill (Kirkby Ravensworth or Kirkby on the Hill) (parish), 42/21-27; NP 84, 85, 90, 91
Kirkby Hill (Kirkby Ravensworth or Kirkby on the Hill) (township in Kirkby Ravensworth), 42/25; NZ135063; NP 85
Kirkby in Ashfield (parish), 28/167; SK505558; NP 112
Kirkby Ireleth (parish), 20/1-7; NP 88
Kirkby Kendal (parish), 38/92-117; NP 83, 89
Kirkby Kendal, 38/97
Kirkby la Thorpe (parish), 22/593; TF100453; NP 113, 123
Kirkby Lonsdale (parish), 38/118-126; NP 89
Kirkby Lonsdale (township in Kirkby Lonsdale), 38/123; SD598800; NP 89
Kirkby Mallory (parish), 21/170-171; NP 121, 132
Kirkby Mallory (township in Kirkby Mallory), 21/170; SK454003; NP 121, 132
Kirkby Moor (division in township of Kirkby Ireleth in Kirkby Ireleth), 20/4; SD268901; NP 88
Kirkby on Bain (parish), 22/451; NP 114
Kirkby on Bain (township in Kirkby on Bain), 22/451; TF232630; NP 114
Kirkby on the Hill (parish), 42/21-27; NP 84, 85, 90, 91
Kirkby on the Hill, 42/25; NP 85
Kirkby Ravensworth (parish), 42/21-27; NP 84, 85, 90, 91
Kirkby Ravensworth, 42/25; NP 85
Kirkby Sigston (parish), 42/508-510A; NP 91
Kirkby Sigston, 42/509; NP 91
Kirkby Stephen (parish), 38/58-67; NP 83, 84, 90
Kirkby Stephen (township in Kirkby Stephen), 38/65; NY763077; NP 84
Kirkby Underwood (parish), 22/678; TF071272; NP 123
Kirkby-on-the-Moor (parish), 42/236, 574-577; NP 91
Kirkby-on-the-Moor, 42/574; NP 91
Kirkbymoorside (Kirby Moorside) (division in township of Kirkbymoorside in Kirkbymoorside), 42/470; SE697866; NP 92
Kirkbymoorside (Kirby Moorside) (parish), 42/469-474; NP 92
Kirkbymoorside (Kirby Moorside) (township), 42/469-470; NP 92
Kirkcambeck (extra-parochial), 7/9; NY532694; NP 76
Kirkdale (township in Walton on the Hill), 20/671; SJ347935; NP 100
Kirkdale (parish), 42/475-481; NP 92

Kirkham (extra-parochial), 41/120; SE735657; NP 92
kirkham (parish), 20/181-208; NP 94
Kirkham (township in Kirkham), 20/196; SD413320; NP 94
Kirkharle (parish), 27/383-384; NP 77
Kirkharle (township in Kirkharle), 27/383; NZ015815; NP 77
Kirkhaugh (parish), 27/570; NY699495; NP 76, 77, 83
Kirkheaton (extra-parochial), 27/385; NY031776; NP 77
Kirkland (parish), 7/185-187; NP 83
Kirkland (township in Garstang), 20/154; SD478438; NP 94
Kirkland (township in Kendal), 38/96; SD517921; NP 89
Kirkland and Blencarn (township in Kirkland), 7/186; NY660320; NP 83
Kirkleatham (division in township of Kirkleatham in Kirkleatham), 42/342; NZ593227; NP 86
Kirkleatham (parish and township), 42/341-342; NP 86
Kirkleavington (parish), 42/271-274; NP 85
Kirkleavington, 42/273; NP 85
Kirklevington (Kirkleavington) (parish), 42/271-274; NP 85
Kirklevington (Kirkleavington) (township in Kirklevington), 42/273; NZ428097; NP 85
Kirkley (Kirtley) (parish), 34/19; TM539915; NP 137
Kirkley (township in Ponteland), 27/529; NZ150764; NP 77, 78
Kirklington (parish), 28/138; SK679585; NP 112
Kirklington (parish), 42/226-230; NP 91
Kirklington cum Upsland (township in Kirklington), 42/226; SE319811; NP 91
Kirklinton (parish), 7/18-20; NP 76
Kirklinton Middle (Middle Quarter) (township in Kirklinton), 7/19; NY428653; NP 76
Kirknewton (parish), 27/54-68; NP 64, 70, 71
Kirknewton (township in Kirknewton), 27/63; NT912285; NP 64, 70, 71
Kirkoswald (parish), 7/172; NP 83
Kirkoswald (township in Kirkoswald), 7/171; NY600520; NP 83
Kirkstead (division in Kirkstead), 22/377A; TF194618; NP 113, 114
Kirkstead (parish), 22/377A-C; NP 113, 114
Kirkstead - Wildmore Fen (division in Kirkstead), 22/377B; NP 114
Kirkstead - Wildmore Fen (division in Kirkstead), 22/377C; TF269503; NP 114
Kirkton (parish), 28/73; NP 112
Kirkwhelpington (parish), 27/373-382; NP 77
Kirkwhelpington (township in Kirkwhelpington), 27/377; NY999850; NP 77
Kirmington (parish), 22/67; TA102108; NP 104
Kirmond le Mire (parish), 22/164; TF183920; NP 105
Kirstead (parish), 25/597; TM298973; NP 137
Kirtley (parish), 34/19; NP 137
Kirtling (parish), 4/150; TL690570; NP 135, 148
Kirtlington (parish), 29/106; SP502204; NP 145
Kirton (division in Kirton), 22/765A; TF305381; NP 123
Kirton (Kirkton) (parish), 28/73; SK695699; NP 112
Kirton (parish), 22/765A-C, 765E, 766; NP 114, 123
Kirton (parish), 34/449; TM283407; NP 150
Kirton - Holland Fen (division in Kirton), 22/765B; TF272423; NP 123
Kirton - Holland Fen (division in Kirton), 22/765C; TF243471; NP 114, 123
Kirton in Lindsey (Kirton Lindsey) (parish), 22/119; SK938983; NP 104
Kirton Lindsey (parish), 22/119; NP 104
Kislingbury (parish), 26/281; SP703585; NP 133
Kitner, Kitnor (parish), 32/244; NP 164
Kittesford (parish), 32/319; NP 164
Kittisford (Kittesford) (parish), 32/319; ST078226; NP 164
Knaith (parish), 22/133; SK837845; NP 104
Knaptoft (parish), 21/334-335B, 336; NP 132
Knaptoft (township in Knaptoft), 21/335A; SP628883; NP 132
Knapton (parish), 25/49; TG302338; NP 126
Knapton (township in Wintringham), 41/153; SE885765; NP 92, 93
Knapwell (parish), 4/66; TL331617; NP 134

Knaresdale, 27/571; NP 76, 83
Knarsdale (Knaresdale) (parish), 27/571; NY660520; NP 76, 83
Knawston (parish), 21/269; NP 122
Knayton with Brawith (township in Leake), 42/520; SE437880; NP 91
Knebworth (parish), 16/47; TL230210; NP 147
Knedlington (division of Knedlington township in Howden), 41/1; SE732272; NP 97
Kneesall (Kneesal) (township in Kneesall), 28/103; SK705640; NP 112
Kneesall (parish), 28/103-104; NP 112
Kneesworth (hamlet in Bassingbourn), 4/173; TL351428; NP 147, 148
Kneeton (parish), 28/211; SK719469; NP 122
Knelson (parish), 51/36; SS461896; NP 153
Knettishall (parish), 34/100; TL960801; NP 136
Knight Thorpe (township in Disley with Thorpe Acre), 21/37B; SK510190; NP 121
Knight's Enham (parish), 14/70; SU360478; NP 168
Knightley (township in Gnosall), 33/170; SJ810240; NP 119
Knightley (township in Leicester, St Margaret), 21/194; SK602018; NP 121
Knighton (township in Mucklestone), 33/154; SJ731399; NP 119
Knighton on Teme (division of Knighton on Teme township in Lindridge), 40/80A; SO636702; NP 130
Knighton on Teme (division of Knighton on Teme township in Lindridge), 40/80B; SO646688; NP 130
Knighton on Teme (township in Lindridge), 40/80A-B; NP 130
Knights Fee (division in parish and township of Walkington), 41/220; TA005369; NP 98, 99
Knightwick (parish), 40/162; SO728551; NP 130, 143
Knill (parish), 15/268; SO293613; NP 129
Knipton (parish), 21/92; SK822315; NP 122
Kniveton (parish), 8/173; SK208498; NP 111
Knockholt (parish), 19/71; TQ469595; NP 171
Knockin (parish), 31/580; SJ342222; NP 118
Knodishall (Knoddishall) (parish), 34/267; TM420610; NP 137
Knoll (division of Brockhampton and Knoll tything in Buckland Newton), 10/156; ST700043; NP 178
Knoll and Bassett House (extra-parochial), 21/211; SP488998; NP 121, 132
Knolton (township in Overton), 50/132; SJ362403; NP 118
Knook (parish), 39/240; ST952433; NP 167
Knossington (Knawston) (parish), 21/269; SK804079; NP 122
Knott Lanes (division in township of Ashton under Lyne in Ashton under Lyne), 20/537; SD939023; NP 101
Knotting (parish), 1/6; TL005625; NP 134
Knowbury (township in Caynham), 31/534A; SO587752; NP 129
Knowl End (township in Audley), 33/42C; SJ775510; NP 110
Knowle (hamlet in Hampton in Arden), 37/82; SP185755; NP 131
Knowle (tithing in Crediton), 9/211H; (not located); NP 175
Knowle St Giles (parish), 32/451; ST345112; NP 177
Knowlton (parish), 19/276; TR281536; NP 173
Knowsley (township in Huyton), 20/638; SJ445945; NP 100
Knowstone (parish), 9/80; SS832227; NP 163, 164
Knuckshadwell (Mainstone and Knuckshadwell) (township in Mainstone), 31/384A; SO272878; NP 128
Knutsford (parish), 5/102-106; NP 101, 110
Knutsford Inferior (Nether Knutsford) (township in Knutsford), 5/102; SJ755787; NP 101
Knutsford Superior (Over Knutsford) (township in Knutsford), 5/103; SJ767779; NP 101
Knutton (township in Wolstanton), 33/18B; SJ823473; NP 110
Kyloe (parochial chapelry in Holy Island), 27/22-26; NP 64
Kyloe (township in Kyloe parochial chapelry in Holy Island), 27/24; NU052399; NP 64
Kynaston (township in Kinnerley), 31/126; SJ356205; NP 118
Kynaston and Rushall (hamlet in Much Marcle), 15/283; SO643350; NP 143
Kyo (township in Lanchester), 11/153; NZ174528; NP 78, 84, 85
Kyre (parish), 40/86; NP 129, 130

Kyre Magna (Kyre, Kyre Wyard, Great Kyre) (parish), 40/86; SO629639; NP 129, 130
Kyre Parva (Little Kyre) (hamlet in Stoke Bliss), 40/87; SO642627; NP 130
Kyre Wyard (parish), 40/86; NP 129, 130

L

Laceby (parish), 22/91; TA222062; NP 105
Lach Dennis (Lache Dennis) (township in Great Budworth), 5/131; SJ714715; NP 110
Lackenby (division in township of Wilton in Wilton), 42/338; NZ565195; NP 86
Lackford (parish), 34/205; TL790700; NP 136
Lacock (parish), 39/114; ST915690; NP 156, 157
Lacon (township in Wem), 31/41A; SJ537313; NP 118
Ladbroke (Ladbrooke) (parish), 37/244; SP420589; NP 132
Ladbrooke (parish), 37/244; NP 132
Ladock (parish), 6/129; SW890514; NP 185, 190
Lady Cross Walk (division in Boldre), 14/326B; SU358028; NP 180
Lady Halton (township in Bromfield), 31/423A; SO474746; NP 129
Lady St Mary Within (division inside borough in Wareham, Lady St Mary), 10/285A; SY922873; NP 178
Lady St Mary Without (Worgret) (Wareham, Lady St Mary), 10/285B; SY905870; NP 178
Laindon (parish), 12/398; TQ687899; NP 161
Laindon Hills (Langdon) (parish), 12/399; TQ680870; NP 161
Lainston (Lainstone) (extra-parochial), 14/209; SU443317; NP 168
Laira Green (extra-parochial), 9/363B; SX504557; NP 187
Lake (tithing in Wilsford), 39/299; SU121391; NP 167
Lakenham (parish), 25/409; TG232068; NP 126
Lakenheath (parish), 34/109; TL727827; NP 135, 136
Laleham (parish), 24/118; TQ056668; NP 170
Laleston (parish), 51/95A-B; SS865820; NP 153
Lamarsh (parish), 12/93; TL888358; NP 149
Lamas (parish), 25/244; TG248229; NP 126
Lambcroft (hamlet in Kelstern), 22/196; TF262922; NP 105
Lamberhurst (division in Lamberhurst), 19/312; TQ669368; NP 171, 183
Lamberhurst (division in Lamberhurst), 36/47; TQ672355; NP 171, 183
Lamberhurst (parish), 19/312, 36/47; NP 171, 183
Lambeth (parish), 35/11A; TQ312802; NP 160/1, 170
Lambeth Church First (division in Lambeth), 35/12A; TQ305783; NP 170
Lambeth Church Second (division in Lambeth), 35/12B; TQ312789; NP 170
Lambeth Palace (extra-parochial), 35/10; TQ307792; NP 160/1
Lambley (parish), 28/186; SK625455; NP 112, 121
Lambley (township in Lambley), 27/573; NY672580; NP 76
Lambley, 27/572-573; NP 76
Lambourn (parish), 2/107A-E; NP 158
Lambourne (parish), 12/312; TQ480960; NP 161
Lambrigg (township in Kendal), 38/114; SD589957; NP 89
Lambton (township in Chester le Street), 11/50; NZ298521; NP 78
Lamerton (district in Lamerton), 9/338; SX442768; NP 175
Lamesley (chapelry in Chester le Street), 11/39; NZ245590; NP 78
Lamonby (township in Skelton), 7/158; NY416361; NP 83
Lamorran (parish), 6/153; SW883432; NP 190
Lampeter (division in Lampeter Pont Stephan), 46/75; SN560485; NP 140
Lampeter Pont Stephan (parish), 46/75-76; NP 140
Lampha, 51/113
Lamphay, 51/113; NP 154
Lamplugh (parish), 7/260; NY093210; NP 82
Lamport (hamlet in Lamport), 26/167; SP753750; NP 133
Lamport (parish), 26/167-168; NP 133
Lamyatt (parish), 32/199; ST656358; NP 166
Lancaster (parish), 20/104-146; NP 89, 94, 95
Lancaster (township in Lancaster), 20/109; SD480612; NP 89

Lancaster Castle (district in Lancaster), 20/108; SD473619; NP 89
Lancelynsbury, 17/108
Lanchester (Lanchester Proper) (township in Lanchester), 11/151; NZ157474; NP 78, 84, 85
Lanchester (parish), 11/147-163; NP 77, 78, 84, 85
Lancing (parish), 36/306; TQ194051; NP 182
Landbeach (parish), 4/52; TL474657; NP 135
Landburgh (township in Burgh by Sands), 7/107; NY303582; NP 75
Landcross (parish), 9/62; SS462239; NP 163
Landewednack (parish), 6/191; SW701135; NP 189, 190
Landford (parish), 39/371; SU264198; NP 167, 179
Landican (township in Woodchurch), 5/465; SJ283856; NP 100
Landkey (parish), 9/28; SS598323; NP 163
Landmoth-cum-Catto (township in Leake), 42/513; SE428926; NP 91
Landrake (parish), 6/104; SX364613; NP 186
Lands common to all townships in Sowerby parish (area in Castle Sowerby), 7/155; NY380395; NP 83
Lands common to Tarrant Monkton and Tarrant Launceston, 10/167B; ST862031; NP 178
Lands common to Newport and Debden, 12/21; TL530347; NP 148
Landulph (parish), 6/107; SX426300; NP 186, 187
Landwade (parish), 4/183; TL623680; NP 135
Lane End (township in Stoke-on-Trent), 33/30; SJ912441; NP 119
Laneast (parish), 6/29; SX235850; NP 186
Laneham (parish), 28/57; SK802764; NP 104
Lanercost (parish), 7/27-33; NP 76
Langan (parish), 51/104; NP 154
Langar (parish), 28/219; SK731343; NP 122
Langdale (township in Grasmere), 38/76; NY288058; NP 82, 83, 88, 89
Langdale (township in Orton), 38/69; NY659014; NP 83, 90
Langdon (parish), 12/399; NP 161
Langdon Wyke (Wykedown, Temple Ruckley) (tithing in Preshute), 39/105; SU136726; NP 157
Langenhoe (parish), 12/173; TM019174; NP 149
Langford (parish), 1/95; TL196401; NP 147
Langford (parish), 12/237; TL838090; NP 162
Langford (parish), 25/686; TL825978; NP 136
Langford (parish), 28/127; SK825575; NP 113
Langford (parish), 29/5; NP 157
Langford (tithing in Langford), 29/5; SP241023; NP 157
Langford Budville (parish), 32/322; ST106228; NP 164
Langham (parish), 12/101; TM024318; NP 149
Langham (parish), 25/25; TG008412; NP 125
Langham (parish), 30/14; SK843111; NP 122
Langham (parish), 34/193; TL979699; NP 136
Langley (division in Rogate), 36/9B; SU814296; NP 181
Langley (hamlet in Claverdon), 37/176; SP192625; NP 131
Langley (Langley without Wychwood Forest) (hamlet in Shipton under Wychwood), 29/143; SP302154; NP 145
Langley (parish), 3/234; NP 159, 160
Langley (parish), 12/15; TL438345; NP 148
Langley (parish), 19/222; TQ799516; NP 172
Langley (parish), 25/581; TG366026; NP 126, 137
Langley (township in Lanchester), 11/150; NZ205471; NP 84, 85
Langley (township in parochial chapelry of Haydon in Warden), 27/596; NY839628; NP 77
Langley (township in Halesowen), 40/14B; SO996984; NP 130, 131
Langley and Ruckley, 31/438; NP 118, 129
Langley Burrell (parish), 39/84; ST935756; NP 156, 157
Langley Marish (Langley) (parish), 3/234; TQ010825; NP 159, 160
Langley Priory (extra-parochial), 21/13; SK436236; NP 121
Langley without Wychwood Forest, 29/143; NP 145
Langley Wood (extra-parochial), 39/388; SU224204; NP 167
Langleydale with Shotton (township in Staindrop), 11/292; NZ067237; NP 84
Langonoyd Lower, 51/61; NP 153, 154

Langonoyd Middle (parish), 51/60
Langport (Langport Eastover) (parish), 32/335; ST420269; NP 177
Langrick Ferry (extra-parochial), 22/472; TF263471; NP 114
Langrick Ville (parish), 22/465A-B; NP 114
Langridge (parish), 32/25; ST740695; NP 156
Langrigg and Mealrigg (township in Bromfield), 7/129; NY162560; NP 82
Langriville (Langrick Ville) (division in Langriville), 22/465A; TF270490; NP 114
Langriville (Langrick Ville) (parish), 22/465A-B; NP 114
Langrville (division in West Fen in Langriville), 22/465B; TF299476; NP 114
Langthorne (township in Bedale), 42/214; SE254912; NP 91
Langthorpe (Langthorp) (township in Kirby Hill), 42/575; SE380677; NP 91
Langtoft (parish), 22/712; TF132126; NP 123
Langtoft (township in Langtoft), 41/239; TA004669; NP 93, 99
Langton (parish), 22/374; TF233687; NP 114
Langton (parish), 22/400; NP 114
Langton (parish), 41/128-129; NP 92
Langton (township in Gainford), 11/304; NZ160195; NP 85
Langton (township in Langton), 41/128; SE807678; NP 92
Langton by Spilsby (Langton) (parish), 22/400; TF151765; NP 114
Langton by Wragby (Langton) (parish), 22/349; TF151765; NP 104, 105, 113
Langton Herring (parish), 10/259; SY614821; NP 178
Langton Long Blandford (parish), 10/166; ST903056; NP 178
Langton Matravers (parish), 10/296; SY998788; NP 179
Langton Woodhouse (extra-parochial), 22/350; TF141761; NP 104
Langton-upon-Swale (parish), 42/69-70; NP 91
Langton-upon-Swale, 42/70; NP 91
Langtree (parish), 9/93; SS454150; NP 163, 175
Langtree (division in township of Standish in Standish), 20/379; SD560111; NP 100
Langwathby (parish), 7/188; NY577336; NP 83
Langwith (township in Wheldrake), 41/71; SE660480; NP 97
Lanhydrock (parish), 6/75; SX085638; NP 185, 186
Lanivet (parish), 6/77; SX040640; NP 185
Lanlivery (parish), 6/74; SX081593; NP 185, 186
Lanreath (parish), 6/99; SX180580; NP 186
Lansallos (parish), 6/122; SX188520; NP 186
Lansbury [T], 17/108
Lansdown (division in Walcot), 32/34A; ST754663; NP 156/1
Lanslingbury (Lancelynsbury, Lansbury) (hamlet in Eynesbury), 17/108; TL211586; NP 134
Lanteglos (Lanteglos by Camelford) (parish), 6/25; SX101837; NP 185, 186
Lanteglos (Lanteglos by Fowey) (parish), 6/123; SX148521; NP 186
Lanton (township in Kirknewton), 27/62; NT930320; NP 64
Lantwit Lower, 51/52; NP 153
Lantwit Major (parish), 51/165; NP 154
Lanwarne (parish), 15/240; NP 142
Lapal (Lappall) (township in Halesowen), 40/9; SO980830; NP 130
Lapford (parish), 9/176; SS734091; NP 163, 175
Lapley (parish), 33/241-242; NP 119
Lapley (township in Lapley), 33/241; SJ870126; NP 119
Lappall, 40/9; NP 130
Lapworth (parish), 37/88; SP170710; NP 131
Larbreck (division in township of Little Eccleston with Larbreck in Kirkham), 20/191; SD404403; NP 94
Lark Stoke (hamlet in Ilmington), 13/18; SP193437; NP 144
Larkton (township in Malpas), 5/337; SJ502517; NP 109
Larling (parish), 25/673; TL973892; NP 136
Lartington (township in Romaldkirk), 42/9; NY970165; NP 84
Lasborough (parish), 13/338; ST828932; NP 156
Lasham (parish), 14/129; SU675428; NP 168, 169
Laskill Pasture (township in Helmsley), 42/486; SE577917; NP 92

Lassington (parish), 13/141; SO799210; NP 143
Lastingham (parish), 42/460-466; NP 92
Lastingham (township in Lastingham), 42/465; SE739902; NP 92
Latchford (township in Grappenhall), 5/110; SJ622872; NP 101
Latchford and Lobb (hamlet in Great Haseley), 29/260; SP662017; NP 158
Latchingdon (Latchingdon cum Lawling) (parish), 12/348; TQ893993; NP 162
Lathbury (parish), 3/44; SP872458; NP 146
Lathom (division in township of Lathom in Ormskirk), 20/366; SD460090; NP 100
Lathom (township in Ormskirk), 20/366-367; NP 100
Latton (parish), 12/260; TL468095; NP 148, 161
Latton (parish), 39/13; SU089966; NP 157
Laugharne (division in Laugharne), 47/63; SN300100; NP 152
Laugharne (parish), 47/62-63; NP 152
Laugharne (township in Laugharne), 47/62; SN262122; NP 152
Laughton (parish), 21/338; SP662890; NP 132
Laughton (parish), 22/122-123; NP 104
Laughton (parish), 22/679; TF072312; NP 123
Laughton (township in Laughton), 22/122; SK850970; NP 104
Laughton (parish), 36/192; TQ502130; NP 183
Launcells (parish), 6/5; SS252062; NP 174
Launceston, St Mary Magdalen (parish), 6/33; SX334831; NP 186
Launceston, St Thomas the Apostle (district in Launceston, St Thomas the Apostle), 6/35; SX295844; NP 186
Launceston, St Thomas the Apostle (parish), 6/34-35; NP 186
Launde (extra-parochial), 21/276; SK792042; NP 122
Launton (parish), 29/78; SP611233; NP 145
Lavendon (parish), 3/32; SP926542; NP 133, 146
Lavenham (parish), 34/408; TL912502; NP 149
Lavernock (parish), 51/182; ST182686; NP 154
Laversdale (township in Irthington), 7/37; NY471620; NP 76
Laverstock (parish), 39/382; SU169322; NP 167
Laverstoke (parish), 14/60; SU495485; NP 168
Laverton (parish), 32/100; ST778531; NP 166
Lavington (parish), 22/667-670; NP 123
Lavington, 22/668; NP 123
Lawford (parish), 12/103; TM090310; NP 149, 150
Lawhitton (parish), 6/32; SX359826; NP 186
Lawrence Weston (tithing in Henbury), 13/377; ST543788; NP 155
Lawshall (parish), 34/345; TL866546; NP 136, 149
Lawton (township in Diddlebury), 31/506; SO519840; NP 129
Laxfield (parish), 34/145; TM292723; NP 137
Laxton (Lexington) (township in Laxton), 28/105; SK723670; NP 112
Laxton (parish), 26/50; TL950966; NP 133, 134
Laxton (parish), 28/105-106; NP 112
Laxton (township in Howden), 41/13; SE790260; NP 98
Layer Breton (parish), 12/180; TL945186; NP 149
Layer de la Haye (Layer-de-la-Hay) (parish), 12/179; TL970190; NP 149
Layer Marney (parish), 12/181; TL933173; NP 149
Layham (parish), 34/502; TM020404; NP 149
Laysters (parish), 15/74; SO565630; NP 129
Layston (parish), 16/58; TL372292; NP 147, 148
Laytham (township in Aughton), 41/37; SE753401; NP 97, 98
Layton (division in township of Sedgefield in Sedgefield), 11/233; NZ384272; NP 85
Layton with Warbreck (township in Bispham), 20/179; SD310360; NP 94
Lazenby (division in township of Wilton in Wilton), 42/339; NZ570200; NP 86
Lazenby (township in Northallerton), 42/262; SE346987; NP 91
Lazonby (parish), 7/168-9; NP 83
Lazonby (township in Lazonby), 7/169; NY518409; NP 83
Lea (division in township of Lea, Ashton, Ingol and Cottam in Preston), 20/214; SD489308; NP 94
Lea (parish), 15/264-265; SO658213; NP 143
Lea (parish), 22/132; SK831867; NP 104

Lea (The Leigh) (extra-parochial), 13/373; ST586818; NP 155
Lea (township in Backford), 5/492; SJ388718; NP 109
Lea (township in Wybunbury), 5/264; SJ714488; NP 110
Lea and Cleverton (parish), 39/48; ST965861; NP 157
Lea and Oakley (township in Bishop's Castle), 31/378; SO349889; NP 129
Lea Hall (township in Bradbourne), 8/166; SK194519; NP 111
Lea Marston (parish), 37/55; SP202931; NP 131
Lea Newbold (township in St Oswald Chester), 5/500; SJ438589; NP 109
Lea, Ashton, Ingol and Cottam (township in Preston), 20/212-215; NP 94
Leadbrook Major (township in Northop), 50/21; SJ265702; NP 108
Leadbrook Minor (township in Northop), 50/23; SJ257710; NP 108
Leaden Roding (Leaden Roothing) (parish), 12/205; TL594132; NP 148
Leadenham (parish), 22/546; SK949523; NP 113
Leafield (Leafield without Wychwood Forest) (chapelry in Shipton under Wychwood), 29/144; SP321148; NP 145
Leafield without Wychwood Forest, 29/144
Leagram (division in township of Bowland with Leagram in Whalley), 20/239; SD634439; NP 95
Leagrave (Leegrave) (hamlet in Luton), 1/127; TL059238; NP 147
Leake (Old Leake) (division in Leake), 22/761A; TF396516; NP 114
Leake (parish), 22/761A-C; NP 114
Leake (parish), 42/510B, 513-520; NP 91
Leake (township in Leake), 42/514; SE429912; NP 91
Leake - East Fen (division in Leake), 22/761B; TF583571; NP 114
Leamington Hastings (parish), 37/235; SP458669; NP 132
Leamington Priors (Royal Leamington Spa) (parish), 37/164; SP321653; NP 132
Leamington Spa, 37/164; NP 132
Learchild (township in Edlingham), 27/193; NU100107; NP 71
Learmouth (township in Carham), 27/32; NT857367; NP 64
Leasingham (parish), 22/580-581; NP 113
Leasingham (South Leasingham) (township in Leasingham), 22/580; TF062487; NP 113
Leather Market (division in St Mary Magdalen Bermondsey), 35/6C; TQ330797; NP 170
Leatherhead (parish), 35/89; TQ169567; NP 170
Leaton (township in St Mary Shrewsbury), 31/251; SJ471187; NP 118
Leaton and Sedsall (division in Doveridge township in Doveridge), 8/241; SK109367; NP 120
Leaveland (parish), 19/236; NP 172
Leavening (township in Acklam), 41/132; SE786631; NP 92
Lebberston (township in Filey), 42/406; TA077823; NP 93
Lechlade (division in Lechlade), 13/4; SP213013; NP 157
Lechlade (division in Lechlade), 13/295; SP205005; NP 157
Lechlade (parish), 13/4, 295; NP 157
Leck (township in Tunstall), 20/76; SD660780; NP 89, 90
Leckford (parish), 14/145; SU386370; NP 168
Leckhampstead (chapelry in Chieveley), 2/134; SU439764; NP 158
Leckhampstead (parish), 3/16; SP730376; NP 146
Leckhampton (parish), 13/207; SO942193; NP 143
Leckwith (parish), 51/149; ST157745; NP 154
Leconfield (parish), 41/284; NP 99
Leconfield and Arram (township in Leconfield), 41/284; TA028437; NP 99
Ledbury (borough in Ledbury), 15/278B; SO709376; NP 143
Ledbury (division outside Ledbury borough in Ledbury), 15/278A; SO703384; NP 143
Ledbury (parish), 15/278A-C; NP 143
Ledsham (township in Neston), 5/482; SJ356748; NP 100
Lee (parish), 02/242; SP869046; NP 159
Lee (parish), 19/19; TQ401736; NP 171
Lee (township in Ellesmere), 31/58; SJ404323; NP 118
Lee Brockhurst (parish), 31/164; SJ549275; NP 118

Lee Chapel (extra-parochial), 12/400; TQ691881; NP 161
Lee Fell (division in township of Over Wyresdale in Lancaster), 20/125; SD565568; NP 94
Lee Ward (township in Rothbury), 27/267; NZ073987; NP 71
Leebotwood (parish), 31/341; SO479995; NP 118, 129
Leece (division in township of Aldingham in Aldingham), 20/33; SD246689; NP 88
Leeds (parish), 19/223; TQ820531; NP 172
Leegrave, 1/127; NP 147
Leek (parish), 33/3-14; NP 110
Leek and Lowe (township in Leek), 33/11; SJ990550; NP 110, 111
Leek Wootton (parish), 37/166; SP290690; NP 131, 132
Leekfrith (township in Leek), 33/7; SJ990610; NP 110, 111
Leemailing (township in Bellingham), 27/279; NY830820; NP 77
Lees, 5/208; NP 110
Leese (Lees) (township in Sandbach), 5/208; SJ732685; NP 110
Leeswood (township in Mold), 50/117; SJ262609; NP 108
Leftwich (township in Davenham), 5/183; SJ660724; NP 110
Legbourne (parish), 22/289; TF370850; NP 105
Legsby (hamlet in Legsby), 22/271; TF140860; NP 104, 105
Legsby (parish), 22/269-271; NP 104, 105
Leicester Abbey (extra-parochial), 21/192; SK576064; NP 121
Leicester Frith (extra-parochial), 21/186; SK558068; NP 121
Leicester, All Saints (parish), 21/196; SK584048; NP 121/4
Leicester, Black Friars (extra-parochial), 21/197; SK581047; NP 121/4
Leicester, Castle View (extra-parochial), 21/201; SK582042; NP 121/4
Leicester, St Leonard with Abbeygate and Woodgate (parish), 21/195; SK581055; NP 121/4
Leicester, St Margaret (parish), 21/193-194; NP 121
Leicester, St Margaret (township in Leicester, St Margaret), 21/193; SK593050; NP 121
Leicester, St Martin (parish), 21/198; SK586044; NP 121/4
Leicester, St Mary (parish), 21/203-204; NP 121
Leicester, St Mary (township in Leicester, St Mary), 21/203; SK575035; NP 121
Leicester, St Nicholas (parish), 21/199; SK581045; NP 121/4
Leicester, The Newarke (extra-parochial), 21/202; SK583040; NP 121/4
Leicester, White Augustine Friars (extra-parochial), 21/200; SK581043; NP 121/4
Leigh (chapelry in Yetminster), 10/42; ST619075; NP 178
Leigh (chapelry in Ashton Keynes), 39/14B; SU062925; NP 157
Leigh (Leigh next Tonbridge) (division in Leigh), 19/203A; TQ538468; NP 171
Leigh (Leigh next Tonbridge) (parish), 19/203A-B; NP 171
Leigh (parish), 13/54; SO877252; NP 143
Leigh (parish), 20/574-580; NP 101
Leigh (parish), 32/131; NP 166
Leigh (parish), 33/116-117; NP 119, 120
Leigh (parish), 35/171; TQ224463; NP 170
Leigh (parish), 40/160-161; SO797515; NP 130, 143
Leigh (township in Worthen), 31/328; SJ336038; NP 118
Leigh (township in Leigh), 33/116; SK016356; NP 119, 120
Leigh (township in Leigh), 40/161; SO773510; NP 130, 143
Leigh and Woolley (tithing in Great Bradford), 39/152A; ST835625; NP 166
Leigh Delamere (parish), 39/71; ST872788; NP 156
Leigh upon Mendip (Leigh) (parish), 32/131; ST691477; NP 166
Leigh-on-Sea (Leigh) (parish), 12/387; TQ837867; NP 162
Leighfield (Leigh-Field Forest) (extra-parochial), 30/41; SK820040; NP 122
Leighton (township in Nantwich), 5/247; SJ681578; NP 110
Leighton (township in Neston), 5/475; SJ284794; NP 100
Leighton (parish), 17/44; TL112855; NP 134
Leighton (parish), 31/231; SJ615058; NP 118, 119
Leighton Buzzard (parish), 1/135-139; NP 146, 147
Leighton Buzzard (township in Leighton Buzzard), 1/136; SP926248; NP 146
Leinthall Starkes (Leinthall Starks) (parish), 15/19; SO435698; NP 129
Leintwardine (parish), 15/5-11; NP 129

Leintwardine (township in Leintwardine), 15/8; SO404741; NP 129
Leire (parish), 21/242; SP525906; NP 132
Leiston (parish), 34/262; TM458628; NP 137
Lelley (township in Preston), 41/403; TA218324; NP 99
Lelley Dale (extra-parochial), 41/404; TA213338; NP 99
Lemmington (township in Edlingham), 27/191; NU118111; NP 71
Lenborough (Lenbro') (hamlet in Buckingham), 3/81; SP700311; NP 146
Lench (division in township of Cowpe Lench, New Hall Hey and Hall Carr in Bury), 20/409; SD826215; NP 95
Lenham (parish), 19/229; TQ901521; NP 172
Lenton (Lavington) (parish), 22/667-670; NP 123
Lenton (Lavington) (township in Lenton), 22/668; TF041307; NP 123
Lenton (parish), 28/240; SK551393; NP 121
Lentworth Vachery (division in township of in Lancaster), 20/127; SD543552; NP 94
Leominster (parish), 15/65-70; NP 129, 142
Leominster (township in Leominster), 15/70; SO496592; NP 129
Leonard Stanley (parish), 13/311; SO801037; NP 156
Leppington (township in Scrayingham), 41/118; SE761615; NP 92, 98
Lesbury (parish), 27/202-206; NP 71
Lesbury (township in Lesbury), 27/203; NU245121; NP 71
Lesnewth (parish), 6/20; SX135899; NP 174, 186
Lesser Poston (Little Poston) (township in Munslow), 31/501B; SO539823; NP 129
Lessingham (parish), 25/223; TG389283; NP 126
Letchworth (parish), 16/31; TL215315; NP 147
Letcombe Bassett (Upper Letcombe) (parish), 2/95; SU369835; NP 158
Letcombe Regis (Letcombe) (township in Letcombe Regis), 2/92; SU383844; NP 158
Letcombe Regis (parish), 2/92-94; NP 158
Letheringham (parish), 34/367; TM273576; NP 137, 150
Letheringsett (parish), 25/68; TG060392; NP 125
Letton (parish), 15/54-55; NP 142
Letton (parish), 25/542; TF976060; NP 125
Letton (township in Letton), 15/54; SO336470; NP 142
Leveland (Leaveland) (parish), 19/236; TR004549; NP 172
Leven (parish), 41/344-345; NP 99
Leven (township in Leven), 41/344; TA088457; NP 99
Levens (township in Heversham), 38/85; SD488859; NP 89
Levenshulme (township in Manchester), 20/530; SJ879942; NP 101
Leverington (hamlet in Leverington), 4/3; TF425110; NP 124
Leverington (parish), 4/3-4; NP 123, 124
Leverton (division in Leverton), 22/760A; TF406478; NP 114, 123
Leverton (parish), 22/760A-C; NP 114, 123
Leverton - East Fen (division in Leverton), 22/760B; TF386556; NP 114
Leverton - West Fen (division in Leverton), 22/760C; TF325574; NP 114
Levington (parish), 34/456; TM238398; NP 150
Levisham (parish), 42/428; SE832921; NP 92
Lew (hamlet in Bampton), 29/169; SP337062; NP 158
Lewannick (parish), 6/37; SX274800; NP 186
Lewes Castle (extra-parochial), 36/200; TQ415102; NP 183/1
Lewes, All Saints (parish), 36/201; TQ418102; NP 183/1
Lewes, St Ann (Lewes, St Peter and St Mary Westout) (parish), 36/198; TQ390097; NP 183
Lewes, St John sub Castro (Lewes, St John under the Castle) (parish), 36/199; TQ408107; NP 183
Lewes, St John under the Castle (parish), 36/199; NP 183
Lewes, St Michael (parish), 36/203; TQ414100; NP 183/1
Lewes, St Peter and St Mary Westout (parish), 36/198; NP 183
Lewes, St Thomas in the Cliffe (parish), 36/202; TQ421103; NP 183
Leweston (extra-parochial), 10/44; ST637123; NP 178
Lewisham (division in Lewisham), 19/3; TQ376733; NP 170, 171
Lewisham (parish), 19/3-4, 8; NP 170, 171

Lewisham - Lee (division in Lewisham), 19/8; TQ390763; NP 171
Lewknor (parish), 3/3, 29/273-274; NP 159
Lewknor (township in Lewknor), 29/273; SU717973; NP 159
Lewknor Uphill (division in Lewknor), 3/3; SU812900; NP 159
Lewknor Uphill (township in Lewknor), 3/3, 29/273-274; NP 159
Lewknor Uphill (township in Lewknor), 29/274; SU740950; NP 159
Lewtrenchard (parish), 9/341; SX474859; NP 175
Lexden (parish), 12/121; TL972254; NP 149
Lexington (parish), 28/105-106; NP 112
Lexington, 28/105
Leybourne (parish), 19/177; TQ686591; NP 171
Leyburn (township in Wensley), 42/147; SE108912; NP 90, 91
Leyland (parish), 20/327-335; NP 94, 95, 100, 101
Leyland (township in Leyland), 20/335; SD531220; NP 94
Leysdown (Leysdown-on-Sea) (parish), 19/102; TR028699; NP 172
Leyton (Low Leyton) (parish), 12/321; TQ388875; NP 161
Lezant (district in Lezant), 6/58A; SX343788; NP 186
Lezant (parish), 6/58A-B; NP 186
Leziate (parish), 25/285; TF688198; NP 124
Liberty of Glasshouse Yard (extra-parochial), 24/49; TQ321820; NP 160/1
Liberty of Norton Folgate (extra-parochial), 24/64B; TQ334820; NP 160/1
Liberty of Saffron Hill (extra-parochial), 24/9; TQ314818; NP 160/1
Liberty of the Rolls (extra-parochial), 24/16; TQ311813; NP 160/1
Liberty of the Tower (extra-parochial), 24/2; TQ335807; NP 160/1
Liberty of the Sluice (division in Bexhill), 36/179; TQ682062; NP 183
Liddiard Millicent (parish), 39/57; NP 157
Liddiard Tregooze (parish), 39/58; NP 157
Liddington (parish), 39/97; SU204812; NP 157
Lidgate (parish), 34/318; TL725575; NP 136
Lidlington (parish), 1/80; SP987393; NP 147
Lidsing (hamlet in Gillingham), 19/91; TQ789629; NP 172
Lidstone (hamlet in Enstone), 29/96; SP349257; NP 145
Lifton (parish), 9/344; SX387849; NP 175, 186
Lighthorne (parish), 37/257; SP337558; NP 132, 145
Lilbourne (parish), 26/116; SP567768; NP 132
Lilford-cum-Wigsthorpe (parish), 26/74; TL042827; NP 134
Lillesbourn Priory (extra-parochial), 34/458; TM198412; NP 150
Lilleshall (parish), 31/199; SJ725148; NP 119
Lilley (parish), 16/44; TL120270; NP 147
Lillings Ambo (township in Sheriff Hutton), 42/601-602; NP 91
Lillingstone Dayrell (parish), 3/8; SP693405; NP 146
Lillingstone Lovell (division formerly in Oxfordshire in Lillingstone Lovell), 3/1; SP712405; NP 146
Lillingstone Lovell (division in Lillingstone Lovell), 3/7; SP720424; NP 146
Lillingstone Lovell (parish), 3/1, 7; NP 146
Lillington (parish), 10/43A-B; NP 178
Lillington Inner (division in Lillington), 10/43A; ST626127; NP 178
Lillington Outer (division in Lillington), 10/43B; ST628105; NP 178
Lillington (parish), 37/163; SP328673; NP 132
Lilstock (parish), 32/228; ST179445; NP 164
Lilwall, Pembers Oak and Chickward (township in Kington), 15/41C; SO535285; NP 128, 129, 141, 142
Limbury and Biscot (Limbury and Biscott) (hamlet in Luton), 1/122; TL072241; NP 147
Limehouse (parish), 24/69; NP 160/1
Limington (parish), 32/466; ST542217; NP 177
Limpenhoe (parish), 25/465; TG399032; NP 126, 137
Limpley Stoke (tithing in Great Bradford), 39/154B; ST779613; NP 166
Limpsfield (parish), 35/103; TQ420515; NP 171

141

Linbriggs (Linbridge, Linbrig) (township in Alwinton), 27/177; NT888090; NP 70, 71
Linby (Lyndby) (parish), 28/56; SK539510; NP 112
Linch (parish), 36/15; SU862276; NP 181
Linchmere (parish), 36/4; SU878303; NP 181
Lincoln Castle (extra-parochial), 22/501; SK975719; NP 113/1
Lincoln St Benedict (parish), 22/513; SK975711; NP 113/1
Lincoln St Botolph (parish), 22/517; SK972700; NP 113/1
Lincoln St Margaret in the Close (parish), 22/508; SK980718; NP 113/1
Lincoln St Mark (parish), 22/515; SK973708; NP 113/1
Lincoln St Martin (parish), 22/511; SK972715; NP 113/1
Lincoln St Mary le Wigford (parish), 22/514; SK976709; NP 113/1
Lincoln St Mary Magdalen in the Bail (parish), 22/506B; SK978719; NP 113/1
Lincoln St Michael on the Mount (parish), 22/506A; SK976715; NP 113/1
Lincoln St Nicholas (parish), 22/502; SK972728; NP 113
Lincoln St Paul (parish), 22/505; SK975721; NP 113/1
Lincoln St Peter at Arches (parish), 22/512; SK975713; NP 113/1
Lincoln St Peter at Gowts (parish), 22/516; SK975704; NP 113/1
Lincoln St Peter in Eastgate (parish), 22/504; SK982721; NP 113/1
Lincoln St Swithin (parish), 22/510; SK981712; NP 113/1
Lincolns Inn (extra-parochial), 24/14; TQ309815; NP 160/1
Lindale and Martin (division of Above Town township in Dalton in Furness), 20/25; SD246760; NP 88
Lindfield (parish), 36/98; TQ362251; NP 182, 183
Lindhurst (extra-parochial), 28/99; SK572578; NP 112
Lindridge (parish), 40/78-80B; NP 130
Lindridge (township in Lindridge), 40/79; SO681696; NP 130
Lindsell (parish), 12/77; TL644276; NP 148
Lindsey (parish), 34/418; TL982450; NP 149
Linemouth, 27/326; NP 78
Lineside (Lyneside Quarter) (township in Arthuret), 7/17; NY389659; NP 76
Ling (parish), 25/345; NP 125
Lingen (parish), 15/15; SO362676; NP 129
Lingfield (parish), 35/106; TQ404429; NP 171
Lingwood (parish), 25/471; TG362086; NP 126
Linkenholt (parish), 14/3; SU369581; NP 168
Linkinhorne (parish), 6/57; SX294730; NP 186
Linley (parish), 31/462; SO692986; NP 119, 130
Linshiels (Linsheeles) (township in Holystone), 27/185; NT850070; NP 70, 71
Linslade (parish), 3/127; SP907251; NP 146
Linstead (parish), 19/159; NP 172
Linstead Magna (parish), 34/147; TM319764; NP 137
Linstead Parva (parish), 34/148; TM330777; NP 137
Linstock (township in Stanwix), 7/76; NY430593; NP 76
Linthorpe (township in Middlesbrough), 42/283; NZ495185; NP 85
Linton (division in township of Balkholme in Howden), 41/14B; SE799288; NP 98
Linton (division in township of Wintringham in Wintringham), 41/152; SE900715; NP 92, 93
Linton (hamlet in Churcham), 13/143C; SO800193; NP 143
Linton (parish), 4/156; TL564474; NP 148
Linton (parish), 15/249; SO656250; NP 143
Linton (parish), 19/303; TQ749497; NP 171, 172
Linton (township in Church Gresley), 8/317; SK273172; NP 120, 121
Linton (township in Bromyard), 15/89; SO680535; NP 143
Linton upon Ouse (township in Newton upon Ouse), 42/586; SE495610; NP 91, 92, 97
Linwood (hamlet in Blankney), 22/563; TF122608; NP 113
Linwood (Lynwode) (parish), 22/209; TF113864; NP 104
Lipwood (township in parochial chapelry of Haydon in Warden), 27/602A; NY825665; NP 77
Liscard (township in Wallasey), 5/445; SJ310929; NP 100

Lisfane (parish), 51/136; NP 154
Liskeard (district in Liskeard), 6/69B; SX232637; NP 186
Liskeard (parish), 6/69A-B; NP 186
Liskeard Borough (district in Liskeard), 6/69A; SX251653; NP 186
Lisleburn (township in Corsenside), 27/215; NY920860; NP 77
Liss (Lyss) (parish), 14/179; SU783275; NP 181
Lissett (township in Beeford), 41/351; TA139578; NP 99
Lissington (parish), 22/210; TF109833; NP 104
Liston (parish), 12/42; TL851449; NP 149
Lisvane (Lisfane) (parish), 51/136; ST190837; NP 154
Litcham (parish), 25/275; TF876187; NP 125
Litchborough (parish), 26/276; SP636544; NP 132, 145
Litchfield (parish), 14/63; SU469541; NP 168
Litchurch (township in Derby St Peter), 8/268; SK361347; NP 121
Litherland (township in Sefton), 20/686; SJ337975; NP 100
Litlington (parish), 4/171; TL317421; NP 147
Litlington (Littlington) (parish), 36/328; TQ536009; NP 183
Little Abingdon (parish), 4/135; TL532500; NP 148
Little Addington (parish), 26/152; SP958735; NP 133, 134
Little Amwell (division in Hertford, All Saints), 16/110; TL351124; NP 147, 148
Little Asby (township in Asby), 38/47; NY698096; NP 83
Little Ashby (parish), 21/240; NP 132
Little Ayton (division in township of Little Ayton in Ayton), 42/328; NZ567099; NP 86
Little Ayton (township in Ayton), 42/328-329; NZ567099; NP 85, 86
Little Baddow (hamlet in Little Baddow), 12/242; TL765075; NP 161, 162
Little Baddow (parish), 12/242-243; NP 161, 162
Little Badminton (tithing in Hawkesbury), 13/340B; ST797847; NP 156
Little Bampton (township in Kirkbampton), 7/115; NY268554; NP 75
Little Barford (parish), 1/38; TL188565; NP 147
Little Barlow (township in Dronfield), 8/49; SK324762; NP 111
Little Bardfield (parish), 12/78; TL659309; NP 148
Little Barrington (parish), 13/228; SP210113; NP 144, 157
Little Barningham (Barningham Parva) (parish), 25/129; TG136332; NP 125, 126
Little Barton (parish), 34/208; NP 135
Little Barugh (division in Barughs Ambo township in Kirby Misperton), 42/449; SE758798; NP 92
Little Bavington (township in Throckington), 27/372; NY992785; NP 77
Little Beats (extra-parochial), 22/748; TF232521; NP 114
Little Bealings (parish), 34/431; TM232473; NP 150
Little Bedwyn (Little Bedwin) (parish), 39/184; SU295653; NP 157, 158, 167, 168
Little Bentley (parish), 12/116; TM120250; NP 150
Little Berkhampstead (parish), 16/122; TL293093; NP 147, 160
Little Billing (parish), 26/221; SP801624; NP 133
Little Birch (parish), 15/270; SO518311; NP 142
Little Bittering (parish), 25/273; TF942172; NP 125
Little Blakenham (parish), 34/397; TM103485; NP 149, 150
Little Blencow (township in Greystoke), 7/198; NY448332; NP 83
Little Bolton (township in Bolton-le-Moors), 20/403-404; NP 101
Little Bolton, Higher End (division in township of Little Bolton in Bolton-le-Moors), 20/403; SD700132; NP 101
Little Bolton, Lower End (division in township of Little Bolton in Bolton-le-Moors), 20/404; SD716100; NP 101
Little Bolas (township in Hodnet), 31/173; SJ642227; NP 119
Little Bookham (parish), 35/122; TQ125539; NP 170
Little Bowland (division in township of Bowland with Leagram in Whalley), 20/238; SD641463; NP 95
Little Bowden (hamlet in Little Bowden), 26/104; SP744863; NP 133
Little Bowden (parish), 26/104-105; NP 133
Little Braxted (parish), 12/221; TL839140; NP 149
Little Bramshill (tithing in Eversley), 14/26B; SU760595; NP 169
Little Bradley (parish), 34/325; TL688524; NP 148

Little Brickhill (parish), 3/99; SP908326; NP 146
Little Bricett (hamlet in Offton), 34/401; TM050500; NP 149
Little Broughton (township in Bridekirk), 7/243; NY084332; NP 82
Little Bromley (parish), 12/118; TM101283; NP 149, 150
Little Bromwich (township in Aston), 37/39; SP118876; NP 131
Little Broughton (division in township of Broughton in Kirkby), 42/324; NZ561069; NP 86, 92
Little Budworth (parish), 5/179; SJ598657; NP 110
Little Burstead (parish), 12/410; TQ668906; NP 161
Little Busby (township in Stokesley), 42/304; NZ509052; NP 85, 92
Little Callerton (township in Ponteland), 27/524; NZ155719; NP 78
Little Canfield (parish), 12/196; TL591209; NP 148
Little Carleton (division in Carleton township in Poulton-le-Fylde), 20/172; SD330385; NP 94
Little Carlton (parish), 22/298; TF393855; NP 105
Little Casterton (parish), 30/29; TF021095; NP 122
Little Catworth (chapelry in Stow), 17/52; TL104727; NP 134
Little Cawthorpe (parish), 22/292; TF359832; NP 105
Little Chart (parish), 19/321; TQ946459; NP 172
Little Chalfield (extra-parochial), 39/123; ST848640; NP 166
Little Chester (division inside borough in Little Chester township in Derby St Alkmund), 8/274B; SK362364; NP 121
Little Chester (division outside borough in Little Chester township in Derby St Alkmund), 8/274A; SK361377; NP 121
Little Chester (township in Derby St Alkmund), 8/274A-B; SK362364; NP 121
Little Chesterford (parish), 12/5; TL524418; NP 148
Little Cheverell (parish), 39/226; ST986532; NP 167
Little Chignal (parish), 12/247; NP 148
Little Chishall (parish), 12/14; TL411389; NP 148
Little Clacton (parish), 12/168; TM172190; NP 150
Little Claybrooke, 21/235; NP 132
Little Clifton (township in Workington), 7/254; NY055281; NP 82
Little Coates (parish), 22/78; TA249091; NP 105
Little Coggeshall (parish), 12/132; TL840216; NP 149
Little Colan, 6/90; NP 185
Little Compton (parish), 37/303; SP257306; NP 144, 145
Little Comberton (parish), 40/216; SO970430; NP 143
Little Corby (township in Wetheral), 7/48; NY478576; NP 76
Little Corringham (hamlet in Corringham), 22/140; SK870910; NP 104
Little Cornard (parish), 34/494; TL902382; NP 149
Little Cowarne (Little Cowarn) (parish), 15/148; SO605510; NP 142, 143
Little Cowden (Colden Parva) (division in township of Coldens Ambo in Mappleton), 41/373; TA233413; NP 99
Little Cowden (Colden Parva) (division in township of Coldens Ambo in Colden Parva), 41/374; TA241409; NP 99
Little Coxwell (township in Faringdon), 2/34; SU282933; NP 157, 158
Little Creech (extra-parochial), 14/277B; SU640110; NP 180
Little Cressingham (parish), 25/682; TL867990; NP 136
Little Creaton (parish), 26/192; NP 133
Little Creeton (Little Creaton) (parish), 26/192; SP717717; NP 133
Little Crosby (township in Sefton), 20/690; SD314019; NP 100
Little Dalby (parish), 21/113; SK775135; NP 122
Little Dawley, 31/229; NP 119
Little Dean (parish), 13/161; SO671138; NP 143
Little Dean Walk (Denby Walk) (division of East Dean township in Trinity, Forest of Dean), 13/152; SO660160; NP 143
Little Dewchurch (parish), 15/180; SO546317; NP 142
Little Drayton (township in Drayton in Hales), 31/11; SJ665338; NP 119
Little Driffield (township in Great Driffield), 41/276; TA009579; NP 99
Little Dromonby (division in township of Kirkby in Kirkby), 42/320; NZ528057; NP 85, 86, 92
Little Dunmow (parish), 12/194; TL658218; NP 148
Little Dunham (parish), 25/329; TF861132; NP 125

Little Durnford (tithing in Durnford), 39/306; SU133347; NP 167
Little Easton (parish), 12/75; TL604235; NP 148
Little Eaton (township in Derby St Alkmund), 8/276; SK360421; NP 121
Little Eccleston (division in township of Little Eccleston with Larbreck in Kirkham), 20/192; SD412400; NP 94
Little Eccleston with Larbreck (township in Kirkham), 20/191-192; NP 94
Little Edstone (township in Sinnington), 42/459; SE710859; NP 92
Little Ellingham (parish), 25/662; TM002990; NP 136
Little Elm (hamlet in Great Elm), 32/122; ST710477; NP 166
Little Eppleton (township in Houghton-le-Spring), 11/66; NZ366471; NP 78
Little Eversden (parish), 4/126; TL377531; NP 148
Little Faringdon (Little Farringdon) (tithing in Little Faringdon), 29/6; SP228014; NP 157
Little Faringdon (parish), 29/6, 161-162; NP 157, 158
Little Finborough (parish), 34/295; TM020550; NP 149
Little Fransham (parish), 25/334; TF905121; NP 125
Little Gaddesden (division in Little Gaddesden), 16/95A; SP998137; NP 147
Little Gidding (parish), 17/38; TL135824; NP 134
Little Givendale (division in parish and township of Millington), 41/107; SE825535; NP 98
Little Glenn, 21/206
Little Glemham (parish), 34/277; TM346588; NP 137
Little Gransden (parish), 4/116; TL282541; NP 134, 147
Little Grimsby (parish), 22/191; TF331932; NP 105
Little Gringley (North Retford) (township in Clarborough), 28/47; SK731811; NP 103, 104
Little Habton (township in Kirby Misperton), 42/453; SE749776; NP 92
Little Hadham (parish), 16/66; TL440220; NP 148
Little Hallingbury (parish), 12/200; TL509171; NP 148
Little Hale (township in Great Hale), 22/655; TF162410; NP 123
Little Hampden (parish), 02/24O; SP863036; NP 159
Little Harwood (township in Blackburn), 20/316; SD698299; NP 95
Little Harrowden (Harrowden Parva) (parish), 26/199; SP870715; NP 133
Little Harle (township in Kirkwhelpington), 27/381; NZ012831; NP 77
Little Hassall, 5/219; NP 110
Little Haseley (township in Great Haseley), 29/259; SP637003; NP 158
Little Hatfield (township in Sigglesthorne), 41/367; TA174432; NP 99
Little Hautbois (Hautbois Parva) (parish), 25/247; TG263210; NP 126
Little Heaton (township in Prestwich), 20/494; SD837055; NP 101
Little Henny (parish), 12/47; TL860385; NP 149
Little Hereford (township in Little Hereford), 15/22; SO553696; NP 129
Little Hereford), 15/22-23; NP 129
Little Hinton (Hinton) (parish), 39/99; SU230830; NP 157
Little Hockham (division in Hockham), 25/724; TL941910; NP 136
Little Holland (parish), 12/165; TM202163; NP 150
Little Hoole (township in Much Hoole), 20/342; SD481238; NP 94
Little Horwood (parish Little Horwood), 3/93; SP795308; NP 146
Little Horkesley (Little Horksley) (parish), 12/98; TL959323; NP 149
Little Hormead (parish), 16/63; TL399285; NP 148
Little Horsted (parish), 36/130; TQ473178; NP 183
Little Houghton (division in township of Worsley in Eccles), 20/556; SD764002; NP 101
Little Houghton (parish), 26/286; SP811591; NP 133
Little Houghton (township in Longhoughton), 27/158; NU229166; NP 71
Little Hucklow (township in Hope), 8/23; SK161786; NP 111

Little Hulton (Red Hulton) (township in Deane), 20/566; SD722038; NP 101
Little Humby, 22/637; NP 123
Little Hutton (division in Barforth township in Gilling), 42/39; NY141131; NP 85
Little Ilford (parish), 12/326; TQ427860; NP 161
Little Kelk (extra-parochial), 41/264; TA098602; NP 99
Little Kimble (parish), 3/182; SP825072; NP 159
Little Kyre, 40/87; NP 130
Little Langley (township in Acton Burnell), 31/439; SJ554007; NP 118, 129
Little Langford (parish), 39/292; SU042359; NP 167
Little Langton (township in Great Langton), 42/69; SE312958; NP 91
Little Laver (parish), 12/255; TL545095; NP 148, 161
Little Lawford (township in Newbold on Avon), 37/125; SP475771; NP 132
Little Leake (division in township of Nether Silton in Leake), 42/516; SE437912; NP 91
Little Leigh (township in Great Budworth), 5/119; SJ616768; NP 100, 101
Little Leighs (parish), 12/214; TL715171; NP 148
Little Lever (township in Bolton-le-Moors), 20/406; SD754072; NP 101
Little Linford (parish), 3/46; SP841445; NP 146
Little Livermere (parish), 34/118; TL872728; NP 136
Little Longstone (township in Bakewell), 8/91; SK183723; NP 111
Little Lumley (township in Chester le Street), 11/49; NZ295510; NP 78
Little Malvern (parish), 40/229; SO772403; NP 143
Little Maplestead (parish), 12/90; TL830340; NP 149
Little Marlow (parish), 3/215; SU878888; NP 159
Little Marcle (parish), 15/281; SO671369; NP 143
Little Marsden (division in township of Great Marsden and Little Marsden in Whalley), 20/264; SD860368; NP 95
Little Marton (division in township of Marton in Poulton-le-Fylde), 20/170; SD348335; NP 94
Little Massingham (parish), 25/180; TF792241; NP 125
Little Mearley (division in Mearley township in Whalley), 20/247; SD781415; NP 95
Little Melton (parish), 25/561; TG160070; NP 125, 126
Little Meols (Little Meolse) (township in West Kirby), 5/453; SJ215884; NP 100
Little Milton (hamlet in Great Milton), 29/253; SP618011; NP 158
Little Missenden (parish), 3/199; SU910982; NP 159
Little Mitton (township in Whalley), 20/241-243; NP 95
Little Mollington (township in St Mary on the Hill, Chester), 5/527; SJ393692; NP 109/1
Little Mongeham (parish), 19/353; TR327499; NP 173
Little Moorsholm (division in township of Moorsholm cum Girrick in Skelton), 42/349; NZ684163; NP 86
Little Munden (parish), 16/53; TL335219; NP 147, 148
Little Musgrave (township in Crosby Garrett), 38/52; NY750132; NP 83, 84
Little Neston (township in Neston), 5/479; SJ308773; NP 100
Little Ness (township in Baschurch), 31/141; SJ413198; NP 118
Little Oakley (parish), 12/112; NM219288; NP 150
Little Oakley (parish), 26/132; SP892856; NP 133
Little Oxenden (hamlet in Little Bowden), 26/105; SP728841; NP 133
Little Packington (parish), 37/77; SP515852; NP 131
Little Palgrave (Palgrave Parva) (parish), 25/327; TF832136; NP 125
Little Parndon (parish), 12/262B; TL445110; NP 148, 161
Little Paxton (parish), 17/103; TL180630; NP 134
Little Petherick (parish), 6/86; SW916701; NP 185
Little Plumpton (division in township of Westby with Plumptons in Kirkham), 20/184; SD381328; NP 94
Little Plumstead (parish), 25/452; TG306118; NP 126
Little Ponton (parish), 22/633A; SK934322; NP 122, 123
Little Poringland (parish), 25/568; NP 126, 137
Little Poston, 31/501B; NP 129

Little Preston (hamlet in Preston Capes), 26/263; SP588542; NP 132, 145
Little Raveley (parish), 17/27; TL257757; NP 134
Little Rissington (parish), 13/96; SP192198; NP 144
Little Rollright (parish), 29/46; SP292303; NP 145
Little Ryburgh (parish), 25/154; TF966280; NP 125
Little Ryle (township in Whittingham), 27/172; NU021107; NP 71
Little Salkeld (township in Addingham), 7/180; NY580370; NP 83
Little Sampford (New Sampford) (parish), 12/58; TL653333; NP 148
Little Sankey (division in township of Warrington in Warrington), 20/619; SJ592880; NP 100, 101
Little Saughall (township in Shotwick), 5/489; SJ373692; NP 109
Little Saxham (parish), 34/222; TL801637; NP 136
Little Shelford (parish), 4/132; TL454504; NP 148
Little Shelsey (parish), 40/93; NP 130
Little Singleton (division in township of in Kirkham), 20/188; SD372398; NP 94
Little Smeaton (township in Birkby), 42/64; NZ350030; NP 91
Little Snoring (parish), 25/113; TF959328; NP 125
Little Sodbury (parish), 13/349; ST759831; NP 156
Little Somborne (parish), 14/156; SU382334; NP 168
Little Somerford (parish), 39/47; ST967844; NP 157
Little St John (extra-parochial), 5/508; SJ403667; NP 109/1
Little Staughton (parish), 1/10; TL099623; NP 134
Little Stanney (township in Stoke), 5/425; SJ412743; NP 100, 109
Little Stainton (township in Bishopton), 11/269; NZ343200; NP 85
Little Stambridge (parish), 12/374; TQ888920; NP 162
Little Stanmore (Whitchurch) (parish), 24/89; TQ182922; NP 160
Little Steeping (division in Little Steeping), 22/483A; TF437677; NP 114
Little Steeping (parish), 22/483A-B; TF437677; NP 114
Little Steeping - East Fen (division in Little Steeping), 22/483B; TF438617; NP 114
Little Stoneham (Little Stonham) (parish), 34/244; TM115611; NP 136
Little Stretton (township in King's Norton), 21/288; SK668002; NP 121, 132
Little Strickland (township in Morland), 38/16; NY563207; NP 83
Little Stukeley (parish), 17/63; TL209752; NP 134
Little Sugnall (Sugnall Parva) (township in Eccleshall), 33/140; SJ809317; NP 119
Little Sutton (township in Eastham), 5/433; SJ365766; NP 100, 109
Little Sutton (township in Diddlebury), 31/509; SO512824; NP 129
Little Swinburn (township in Chollerton), 27/442; NY947772; NP 77
Little Tarbock (division in township of Tarbock in Huyton), 20/641; SJ473854; NP 100
Little Tew (parish), 29/54; SP377288; NP 145
Little Tey (parish), 12/137; TL892237; NP 149
Little Thetford (Thetford) (hamlet in Stretham), 4/40; TL532753; NP 135
Little Thirkleby (division in township of Thirkleby in Thirkleby), 42/541; SE483768; NP 91
Little Thorpe (division in township of Easington in Easington), 11/91; NZ412424; NP 85
Little Thornham (parish), 34/182; NP 136
Little Thurrock (parish), 12/426; TQ630778; NP 161, 171
Little Thurlow (parish), 34/326; TL671511; NP 148
Little Torrington (parish), 9/92; SS489167; NP 163, 174
Little Tosson (township in Rothbury), 27/258; NU008008; NP 71
Little Totham (parish), 12/233; TL885104; NP 149, 162
Little Urswick (division in township of sub-division of Little Urswick division of Great Urswick township in Urswick), 20/38; SD261738; NP 88
Little Urswick (division of Great Urswick township in Urswick), 20/36-38; NP 88
Little Usworth (division in township of Usworth in Washington), 11/21; NZ318584; NP 78

Little Wakering (parish), 12/379; TQ938887; NP 162
Little Waltham (parish), 12/211; TL721126; NP 148
Little Walsingham (parish), 25/77; TF932368; NP 125
Little Waldingfield (parish), 34/415; TL930450; NP 149
Little Warley (parish), 12/415; TQ601895; NP 161
Little Washbourne (hamlet in Overbury), 13/1; SP989334; NP 143, 144
Little Waxham (hamlet in Waxham), 25/228; TG474228; NP 126
Little Weeton, 41/216D; NP 98
Little Weighton (Little Weeton) (hamlet in Rowley), 41/216D; SE979338; NP 98
Little Weldon (hamlet in Great Weldon), 26/90; SP919902; NP 133
Little Welnetham (parish), 34/307; NP 136
Little Weltenham (parish), 34/307; NP 136
Little Wenlock (parish), 31/230; SJ650070; NP 119
Little Wenham (parish), 34/509; TM085398; NP 149
Little Whelnetham (Little Weltenham, Little Welnetham) (parish), 34/307; TL890600; NP 136
Little Whittington (township in Corbridge), 27/469; NY990695; NP 77
Little Wigborough (Little Wigborow) (parish), 12/228; TL983147; NP 149
Little Wigston, 21/233; NP 132
Little Wilbraham (parish), 4/100; TL550585; NP 135
Little Wittenham (parish), 2/63; SU565933; NP 158
Little Witchingham (parish), 25/260; TG120205; NP 125
Little Witley (township in Holt), 40/102; SO782633; NP 130
Little Wolstone (parish), 3/56; NP 146
Little Wolford (hamlet in Great Wolford), 37/295; SP266350; NP 144
Little Woolstone (Little Wolstone) (parish), 3/56; SP870396; NP 146
Little Woolton (township in Childwall), 20/645; SJ431892; NP 100
Little Wratting (parish), 34/332; TL690473; NP 148
Little Wymondley (parish), 16/33; TL221274; NP 147
Little Yarmouth with West Town, 34/4
Little Yeldham (parish), 12/52; TL776393; NP 149
Littleborough (parish), 28/44; SK822831; NP 104
Littlebourne (Littlebourn) (parish), 19/262; TR201578; NP 173
Littlebredy (parish), 10/241; SY589888; NP 177, 178
Littlebury (parish), 12/7; TL508393; NP 148
Littlecott (Littlecot) (tithing in Enford), 39/253; SU160525; NP 167
Littleham (district in Littleham), 9/306A; SY029809; NP 176
Littleham (parish), 9/48; SS438237; NP 163
Littleham (parish), 9/306A-B; NP 176
Littlehampton (parish), 36/293; TQ035022; NP 181, 182
Littlehempston (Hempston Arundell) (parish), 9/427; SX816631; NP 188
Littlemoor, 29/220; NP 158
Littlemoor, 29/221
Littlemore (Littlemoor) (division in Iffley), 29/221; SP549032; NP 158
Littlemore (Littlemoor) (division in Oxford, St Mary the Virgin), 29/220; SP546028; NP 158
Littlemore (Littlemoor) (in Oxford, St Mary the Virgin and Iffley), 29/220-221; NP 158
Littleover (township in Mickleover), 8/261; SK329336; NP 121
Littleport (parish), 4/24; TL583878; NP 135
Littleton (township in Christleton), 5/381; SJ443669; NP 109
Littleton upon Severn (parish), 13/365; ST597903; NP 155, 156
Littleton (parish), 14/160; SU457328; NP 168
Littleton (parish), 24/119; TQ070695; NP 170
Littleton (tithing in Steeple Ashton), 39/144B; ST912602; NP 166
Littleton Drew (parish), 39/73; ST837803; NP 156
Littleton Pannet (tithing in West Lavington), 39/225; ST998537; NP 167
Littleworth (extra-parochial), 13/191; SO830181; NP 143/1
Littlington (parish), 36/328; NP 183
Litton (parish), 32/79; ST592545; NP 165, 166
Litton (township in Tideswell), 8/35; SK167750; NP 111
Litton Cheney (parish), 10/238; SY551917; NP 177
Liverpool (parish and township), 20/654-665
Liverpool - Abercromby (ward in township and parish of Liverpool), 20/663; SJ359898; NP 100
Liverpool - Castle Street (ward in township and parish of Liverpool), 20/658; SJ343905; NP 100
Liverpool - Exchange (ward in township and parish of Liverpool), 20/656; SJ343908; NP 100
Liverpool - Great George Street (ward in township and parish of Liverpool), 20/661; SJ349893; NP 100
Liverpool - Lime Street (ward in township and parish of Liverpool), 20/664; SJ350907; NP 100
Liverpool - Pitt Street (ward in township and parish of Liverpool), 20/660; SJ348896; NP 100
Liverpool - Rodney (ward in township and parish of Liverpool), 20/662; SJ353898; NP 100
Liverpool - Scotland (ward in township and parish of Liverpool), 20/654; SJ343920; NP 100
Liverpool - St Anne (ward in township and parish of Liverpool), 20/665; SJ352911; NP 100
Liverpool - St Paul (ward in township and parish of Liverpool), 20/657; SJ349909; NP 100
Liverpool - St Peter (ward in township and parish of Liverpool), 20/659; SJ346902; NP 100
Liverpool - Vauxhall (ward in township and parish of Liverpool), 20/655; SJ339913; NP 100
Liverton (township in Easington), 42/366; NZ712155; NP 86
Livesey (township in Blackburn), 20/307; SD660250; NP 95
Llai, 49/68
Llampha (Lampha, Lamphay) (hamlet in St Brides Major), 51/113; SS926758; NP 154
Llan (township in Llandegla), 49/47; SJ202519; NP 108
Llan (township in Tremeirchion), 50/81; SJ080730; NP 108
Llan-eurgain (parish), 50/17-24; NP 108, 109
Llan-eurgain, 50/18; NP 108
Llan-fechan (parish), 45/17; NP 141
Llan-y-wern (parish), 45/43; SO101290; NP 141
Llanaelhaearn (Llanaelhaiarn) (parish), 48/49; SH399451; NP 115
Llanafan (Llanavan) (parish), 46/33; SN698728; NP 127
Llanafan-fawr (parish), 45/21-22C; NP 128, 141
Llanafan-fawr - first division (division in Llanafan-fawr), 45/22A; SN960550; NP 128
Llanafan-fawr - second division (township in Llanafan-fawr), 45/22B; SN940570; NP 128
Llanafan-fawr - third division (township in Llanafan-fawr), 45/22C; SN910570; NP 128
Llanafan-fechan (Llanavanfechan, Llan-fechan) (parish), 45/17; SN970500; NP 141
Llanallgo (parish), 44/35; SH505855; NP 106
Llanarmon (parish), 48/47; SH426392; NP 115
Llanarmon Dyffryn Ceiriog (parish), 49/121; SJ140330; NP 117
Llanarmon Mynydd-mawr (parish), 49/130; SJ135287; NP 117
Llanarmon yn ial (Llanarmon) (division in Llanarmon yn ial township in Llanarmon yn ial), 50/128; SJ221539; NP 108
Llanarmon yn ial (parish), 49/46, 50/128; NP 108
Llanarmon, 50/128; NP 108
Llanarmon-yn-Ial (Llanarmon) (division in Llanarmon-yn-Ial), 49/46; SJ190560; NP 108
Llanarth (parish), 46/68; SN442554; NP 139
Llanarthney (parish), 47/75; SN550180; NP 139, 140, 153
Llanasa, 50/43-49B; NP 108
Llanavan (parish), 46/33; NP 127
Llanavanfechan (parish), 45/17; NP 141
Llanbadarn fawr (parish), 46/8-19; NP 127
Llanbadarn odyn (parish), 46/39; NP 140
Llanbadarn-odwyn (parish), 46/39; SN646611; NP 140
Llanbado (parish), 44/18; SH377870; NP 106
Llanbadrig (parish), 44/4-5; NP 106
Llanbardarn-trefeglwys (parish), 46/53; SN545635; NP 127, 140
Llanbeblig (division in Llanbeblig), 48/31; SH522597; NP 106
Llanbeblig (parish), 48/30-31; NP 106

Llanbedr (Llanbedr-ystradwy) (parish), 45/80; SO248215; NP 141
Llanbedr (parish), 49/36; NP 108
Llanbedr-Dyffryn-Clwyd (Llanbedr) (parish), 49/36; SJ148600; NP 108
Llanbedr-ystradwy (parish), 45/80
Llanbedr-y-cennin (Llanbedr) (parish), 48/12; SH753693; NP 107
Llanbedrgoch (parish), 44/37; SH515805; NP 106
Llanbedrog (parish), 48/56; SH325325; NP 115
Llanberis (Llanberris) (parish), 48/33; SH579599; NP 106, 107, 116
Llanbeulan (parish), 44/45; SH372755; NP 106
Llanbleiddian (parish), 51/122; NP 154
Llanblethian (Llanbleiddian) (parish), 51/122; ST008750; NP 154
Llanboidy (parish), 47/47; SN220240; NP 139, 152
Llancarfan (Llancarvan) (parish), 51/154; ST054712; NP 154
Llancarvan (parish), 51/154; NP 154
Llanchydd (parish), 49/38; NP 108
Llancillo (Llancillow) (parish), 15/222; SO366256; NP 142
Llanclys (township in Llanyblodwel), 31/117; SJ281242; NP 117, 118
Llancynfelyn (parish), 46/1; SN658925; NP 127
Llandaff [Llandaf] (hamlet in Llandaff [Llandaf]), 51/142; ST144778; NP 154
Llandaff [Llandaf] (parish), 51/141-142; NP 154
Llandawke (parish), 47/64; SN280110; NP 152
Llanddaniel (parish), 44/73; NP 106
Llanddaniel Fab (Llanddaniel) (parish), 44/73; SH495702; NP 106
Llanddarog (parish), 47/76; SN510150; NP 153
Llanddausaint (parish), 44/25; NP 106
Llanddeiniol (Llanddinol) (parish), 46/25; SN568720; NP 127
Llanddeiniolen (Llanddeniolen) (parish), 48/28; SH560650; NP 106, 107
Llanddetty (parish), 45/74A-B; NP 141
Llanddeusant (Llanddausaint) (parish), 44/25; SH345853; NP 106
Llanddeusant (Llanthoysaint) (parish), 47/20; SN776230; NP 140
Llanddew (parish), 45/44; SO069308; NP 141
Llanddewi Abergwesyn (Llanddewi Abergwessin) (parish), 45/24; SN821560; NP 127, 140, 141
Llanddewi (Llandewi, Llandewy) (parish), 51/35; SS450880; NP 153
Llanddewi'r Cwm, 45/13; NP 141
Llanddewi-Cwm (Llanddewi'r Cwm) (parish), 45/13; SO045487; NP 141
Llanddinol, 46/25; NP 127
Llanddoged (Llanddoget) (parish), 49/14; SH793635; NP 107
Llanddoget (parish), 49/14; NP 107
Llanddona (parish), 44/62; SH563793; NP 106
Llanddowror (Llandouror, Llandowror) (parish), 47/57; SN242140; NP 152
Llanddulas (Llandulas) (parish), 49/6; SH908781; NP 108
Llanddyfnan (parish), 44/38; SH490790; NP 106
Llandebie (parish), 47/27; NP 140
Llandefaelog-fach (parish), 45/35-36; NP 141
Llandefaelog-tre'r-graig (parish), 45/40; SO121302; NP 141
Llandefaelog-Tre-Graig (parish), 45/40; NP 141
Llandefaelog (parish), 47/78; NP 152
Llandefailog (parish), 47/78; NP 152
Llandefalle (Llandefalley) (parish), 45/7; SO104370; NP 141
Llandefalley (parish), 45/7
Llandefeilog (Llandefailog, Llandefaelog) (parish), 47/78; SN414133; NP 152
Llandefodwg (parish), 51/65; NP 154
Llandegai (parish), 48/26; SH620650; NP 106, 107
Llandegfan (parish), 44/68; SH571745; NP 106
Llandegla (parish), 49/47-48; NP 108
Llandegwning (parish), 48/67; SH269294; NP 115
Llandeilo-Talybont (Llandilo-Talybont) (parish), 51/3; SN600035; NP 153

Llandelio'r Fan (Llandilofane) (parish), 45/32; SN890370; NP 140, 141
Llandesilio (parish), 44/70; NP 106
Llandewi (parish), 51/35; NP 153
Llandewi-Aberarth (Llandewy Aberarth) (parish), 46/55; SN480631; NP 127, 139, 140
Llandewi-Brefi (parish), 46/41-51; NP 127, 140
Llandewy (parish), 51/35; NP 153
Llandewy Aberarth (parish), 46/55; NP 127, 139, 140
Llandilo Fawr (division in Llandilo Subdistrict in Llandilo Fawr), 47/24; SN640240; NP 140
Llandilo Fawr (division in Llandybie Subdistrict in Llandilo Fawr), 47/25; SN678165; NP 140, 153
Llandilo Fawr (parish), 47/24-25; NP 140, 153
Llandilo-abercowin (parish), 47/67; SN315139; NP 152
Llandilo-Talybont (parish), 51/3; NP 153
Llandilofane (parish), 45/32; NP 140, 141
Llandingat (parish), 47/15; NP 140
Llandisilio-Gogo, 46/66
Llandissiliogogo, 46/66
Llandissilio East (division in), 47/49; SN135235; NP 139
Llandough (Llandough-juxta-Penarth, Llandough juxta Cardiff) (parish), 51/150; ST168730; NP 154
Llandough (parish), 51/160; SS991725; NP 154
Llandough juxta Cardiff (parish), 51/150; NP 154
Llandough-juxta-Penarth (parish), 51/150; NP 154
Llandouror, 47/57; NP 152
Llandovery (borough in Llandingat), 47/17; SN770350; NP 140
Llandow (parish), 51/118; SS943730; NP 154
Llandrillo-yn-Rhos (division in Llandrillo-yn-Rhos), 49/1; SH840785; NP 107
Llandrillo-yn-Rhos (parish), 48/2A-3, 49/1; NP 107
Llandrygarn (Llandrygarn with Gwyndu) (parish), 44/29; SH390797; NP 106
Llandudno (parish), 48/6; SH781825; NP 107
Llandudwen (parish), 48/62; SH277372; NP 115
Llandugwydd, 46/97; NP 139
Llandulas (New Church Hir Abbot) (parish), 45/31; SN877414; NP 140, 141
Llandulas (parish), 49/6; NP 108
Llandwrog (parish), 48/38; SH497543; NP 106
Llandybie (Llandebie) (parish), 47/27; SN620150; NP 140
Llandyfeisant (Llandyfeysant) (parish), 47/29; SN612228; NP 140
Llandyfeysant (parish), 47/29; NP 140
Llandyfodwg (Llandefodwg) (parish), 51/65; SS955905; NP 154
Llandyfriog (parish), 46/93; SN330418; NP 139
Llandyfrydog (parish), 44/13; SH445860; NP 106
Llandygwydd (Llandugwydd, Llandygwidd) (parish), 46/97; SN258440; NP 139
Llandynog (parish), 49/32; NP 108
Llandyrnog (parish), 49/32; SJ109659; NP 108
Llandysilio (Llandesilio) (parish), 44/70; SH550727; NP 106
Llandyssil (parish), 46/86; NP 139
Llandyssiliogogo (Llandissiliogogo, Llandisilio-Gogo) (parish), 46/66; SN390520; NP 139
Llandyssul (Llandyssil) (parish), 46/86; SN440450; NP 139
Llanedarn (parish), 51/137; NP 154
Llanedeyrn (Llanedarne, Llanedarn) (parish), 51/137; ST204810; NP 154
Llanedi (Llanedy) (parish), 47/85; SN591073; NP 153
Llanedwen (parish), 44/72; SH512692; NP 106
Llanegwad (parish), 47/32; SN515255; NP 140
Llaneilian (division in Llaneilian), 44/9; SH468916; NP 106
Llaneilian (parish), 44/9-10; NP 106
Llanelian-yn-Rhos (Llanetian-yn-Rhos) (parish), 49/2; SH868750; NP 107, 108
Llanelidan (parish), 49/43; SJ110500; NP 108
Llanelieu (parish), 45/89; SO205325; NP 141
Llanelli (Llanelly) (borough in Llanelli), 47/83D; SN505005; NP 153
Llanelli (Llanelly) (parish), 47/83A-E; NP 153
Llanelly (parish), 45/77; SO230135; NP 141

Llanelly, 47/83D; NP 153
Llanengan (parish), 48/66; SH300268; NP 115
Llanerch-Aeron (division in Llan Hundred in Llanerch-Aeron), 46/61B; SN484597; NP 139, 140
Llanerch-Aeron (division in Troed-y-Taur Hundred in Llanerch-Aeron), 46/61A; SN478583; NP 140
Llanerch-Aeron (Llanerch-ayron) (parish), 46/61A-B; NP 139, 140
Llanerchymedd (parish), 44/14; SH419840; NP 106
Llanetian-yn-Rhos (parish), 49/2; NP 107, 108
Llaneugrad (parish), 44/34; SH486837; NP 106
Llanfabon (Llanvabon) (parish), 51/76; ST120942; NP 154
Llanfachraeth (Llanvachraeth, Llanfachreth) (parish), 44/23; SH315835; NP 106
Llanfaelog (Llanvaeloy) (parish), 44/53; SH342735; NP 106
Llanfaelrhys (parish), 48/76; SH219268; NP 115
Llanfaes (Llanvaes) (parish), 44/66; SH600777; NP 106, 107
Llanfaes, 45/51A; NP 141
Llanfaethlu (Llanfaethly) (parish), 44/21; SH312871; NP 106
Llanfaglan (parish), 48/37; SH465605; NP 106
Llanfair Dyffryn Clwyd (Llanfair) (parish), 49/42; SJ150540; NP 108
Llanfair Orllwyn (parish), 46/88; SN379421; NP 139
Llanfair Pwyllgwyngyll (parish), 44/71; SH538718; NP 106
Llanfair Treflygen (Llanfairtrefligen, Llanfair-Tref-Helygen) (parish), 46/92; SN341437; NP 139
Llanfair Talhaiarn (parish), 49/11; SH905665; NP 107, 108
Llanfair Waterdine (parish), 31/405; SO253773; NP 128, 129
Llanfair y Cwmmwd (Llanfair yn y cwmwd, Llanfairynycwmmwd) (parish), 44/77; SH448668; NP 106
Llanfair yn y cwmwd (parish), 44/77; NP 106
Llanfair-ar-y-bryn (parish), 47/1A-D; NP 140
Llanfair-Clydogau (Llanfairclydogan) (parish), 46/73; SN628518; NP 140
Llanfair-in-Buallt, 45/14; NP 141
Llanfair-is-gaer (parish), 48/29; SH515660; NP 106
Llanfair-mathafarn-eithaf (parish), 44/36; SH500822; NP 106
Llanfair-Tref-Helygen (parish), 46/92; NP 139
Llanfair-yn-neubwll (parish), 44/49; NP 106
Llanfairfechan (parish), 48/23; SH698736; NP 107
Llanfairtrefligen (parish), 46/92; NP 139
Llanfairyneubwll (Llanfair-yn-neubwll) (parish), 44/49; SH299779; NP 106
Llanfairynghornwy (Llanfair y'nghornwy) (parish), 44/1; SH310918; NP 106
Llanfallteg East (division in Llanfallteg), 47/51; SN163203; NP 139
Llanfechell (parish), 44/3; SH359912; NP 106
Llanfedw (Llanfedwy) (hamlet in Michaelstone-y-Vedw), 51/135; ST230850; NP 154
Llanfeigan (parish), 45/54A-B; NP 141
Llanferres (parish), 49/37; SJ188612; NP 108
Llanffinan (parish), 44/39; SH492758; NP 106
Llanfflewyn (parish), 44/19; SH353878; NP 106
Llanfigael (Llanvigael, Llanfugail) (parish), 44/24; SH329835; NP 106
Llanfigan (Llanvigan, Llanfeigan) (parish), 45/54A-B; NP 141
Llanfihanel Bachellaeth (parish), 48/57; SH306349; NP 115
Llanfihangel din silwy, 44/63; NP 106, 107
Llanfihangel Esgeifiog (parish), 44/59; SH483728; NP 106
Llanfihangel yn Nhowyn (Llanfihangel-yn-Howyn) (parish), 44/48; SH320771
Llanfihangel-tyn-Sylwy (Llanfihangel din silwy) (parish), 44/63; SH588815; NP 106, 107
Llanfihangel-yn-Howyn (parish), 44/48; NP 106
Llanfihangel Abergwesyn (Llanfihangel Abergwessin) (parish), 45/25; SN865560; NP 127, 128, 140, 141
Llanfihangel Cwm-du (parish), 45/82A-D; NP 141
Llanfihangel Fechan (township in Llandefaelog-fach), 45/36; SO047363; NP 141
Llanfihangel Nant Bran (Llanfihangel-nant-brane, Llanfihangel-Nant-Bryn) (parish), 45/33; SN943353; NP 141
Llanfihangel Tal-y-llyn (parish), 45/42; SO115285; NP 141

Llanfihangel-Brynpabuan (Llanvihangel Brynpabuan) (parish), 45/20; NP 128, 141
Llanfihangel-Brynpabuan (Llanvihangel Brynpabuan) (township in Llanfihangel-Brynpabuan), 45/20; SN985565; NP 128, 141
Llanfihangel Genu'rglyn (Llanvihangel Geneurglyn, Llanfihangel-Geneur-Glynn) (parish), 46/2-7; NP 127
Llanfihangel-Geneur-Glynn (parish), 46/2-7; NP 127
Llanfihangel-Iledrod (parish), 46/30; NP 127
Llanfihangel-y-creuddyn (Llanfihangle y Croddyn, Llanfihangel-y-Croyddin) (parish), 46/20-21; NP 127
Llanfihangel-y-Croyddin (parish), 46/20-21; NP 127
Llanfihangel-Ystrad (parish), 46/59; SN535543; NP 140
Llanfihangle y Croddyn (parish), 46/20-21; NP 127
Llanfihangel Aberbythych (parish), 47/28; SN590185; NP 140
Llanfihangel-Abercowin (Llanfihangel Aberconrn) (parish), 47/61; SN305165; NP 152
Llanfihangel-ar-arth (parish), 47/8; SN450360; NP 140
Llanfihangel-Cilfargen (parish), 47/31; SN598266; NP 140
Llanfihangel-Rhos-y-corn (parish), 47/10; SN535345; NP 140
Llanfihangel-y-pennant (parish), 48/42; SH543453; NP 116
Llanfihangel Glyn Myfyr (Llanfihangel Glyn y Myfyr) (parish), 49/23; SH980490; NP 108
Llanfihangel (parish), 51/161; NP 154
Llanfilo (Llanvillo) (parish), 45/39; SO112318; NP 141
Llanfinangel Tre'r Beirdd (parish), 44/33; SH460836; NP 106
Llanforda (township in Oswestry), 31/101; SJ266289; NP 118
Llanfrynach (parish), 45/53A-B; NP 141
Llanfrynach - Lower Division (division in Llanfrynach), 45/53A; SO070250; NP 141
Llanfrynach - Upper Division (division in Llanfrynach), 45/53B; SO040190; NP 141
Llanfugail (parish), 44/24; NP 106
Llanfwrog (parish), 44/22; SH301846; NP 106
Llanfwrog (parish), 49/40; SJ105573; NP 108
Llanfynydd (parish), 47/11; SN570290; NP 140
Llangadock (Llangattock) (parish), 42/21-23; NP 140
Llangadwaladr (Eglwysael) (parish), 44/56; SH378676; NP 106
Llangadwaladr (parish), 49/120; SJ182303; NP 117
Llangaffo (parish), 44/75; SH451699; NP 106
Llangain (parish), 47/73; SN386159; NP 152
Llangamarch, 45/29-30; NP 140, 141
Llangan (Langan, Llanganna, Llan-gan) (parish), 51/104; SS954777; NP 154
Llangan East (division in Llangan), 47/53; SN200200; NP 139, 152
Llanganhafal (parish), 49/35; NP 108
Llanganna (parish), 51/104; NP 154
Llanganten (parish), 45/18; SO003514; NP 141
Llangarron (Llangarren) (parish), 15/237; SO528208; NP 142
Llangasty-Talyllyn (Llangasty tall y llyn) (parish), 45/84; SO130250; NP 141
Llangathen (parish), 47/30; SN585223; NP 140
Llangattock (parish), 45/76A-B; NP 141
Llangedwyn (Llangedwin) (parish), 49/131; SJ191241; NP 117
Llangefni (parish), 44/41; SH465765; NP 106
Llangeinor (parish), 51/64; SS920900; NP 154
Llangeinwen (parish), 44/78; SH452653; NP 106
Llangeitho (parish), 46/40; SN619620; NP 127, 140
Llangeler (Llangeller) (parish), 47/37-38; NP 139
Llangelynin (parish), 48/10; SH777740; NP 107
Llangendeirne (Llangyndeyrn) (parish), 47/77; SN465125; NP 152, 153
Llangennech (parish), 47/86; SN556024; NP 153
Llangenney (parish), 45/78; NP 141
Llangennith (parish), 51/33; SS436915; NP 153
Llangenny (Llangenney) (parish), 45/78; SO244180; NP 141
Llangerniew (parish), 49/13
Llangernyw (Llangerniew) (parish), 49/13; SH862668; NP 107, 108
Llangevelach (parish), 51/4-7; NP 153
Llangian (parish), 48/65; SH300303; NP 115
Llanginning (parish), 47/59; NP 139, 152

147

Llangiwg (Llanguicke) (parish), 51/8; SN730090; NP 153
Llangldwen (parish), 47/48; SN170275; NP 139
Llangoed (parish), 44/64; SH610807; NP 106, 107
Llangoedmor (Llangoedmore) (parish), 46/102; SN218460; NP 139
Llangollen Abbott (township in Llangollen), 49/109; SJ230423; NP 108
Llangollen Fawr (township in Llangollen), 49/111; SJ212419; NP 108
Llangollen Fechan (township in Llangollen), 49/108; SJ239412; NP 108
Llangollen, 49/104-118; NP 108, 117
Llangorse (parish), 45/41; SO144280; NP 141
Llangranog (parish), 46/67; NP 139
Llangranog (Llangrannog) (parish), 46/67; SN338537; NP 139
Llangristiolus (parish), 44/58; SH439729; NP 106
Llangrwyddon (parish), 46/28; NP 127
Llanguby (parish), 46/72; NP 140
Llanguicke (parish), 51/8; NP 153
Llangunllo (parish), 46/90; NP 139
Llangunnog (parish), 47/69; NP 139, 152
Llangunnor (parish), 47/74; SN465182; NP 139, 140, 152, 153
Llangwm (parish), 49/21; SH980450; NP 108, 117
Llangwnnadl (Llangwnnadle~) (parish), 48/72; SH194334; NP 115
Llangwsterin (Llangwstenin, Llangwstennin) (parish), 48/4; SH812794; NP 107
Llangwyfan (parish), 44/54; SH337709; NP 106
Llangwyfan (parish), 49/34; SJ122653; NP 108
Llangwyllog (parish), 44/32; SH436795; NP 106
Llangwyryfon (Llangrwyddon, Llanygwyryfon) (parish), 46/28; SN609701; NP 127
Llangybi (Llanguby, Llangyby) (parish), 46/72; SN609531; NP 140
Llangybi (parish), 48/48; SH427419; NP 115
Llangyby (parish), 46/72; NP 140
Llangyfelach (Llangevelach) (parish), 51/4-7; NP 153
Llangyndeyrn (parish), 47/77; NP 152, 153
Llangynhafal (Llanganhafal) (parish), 49/35; SJ133633; NP 108
Llangynidir (parish), 45/75A-B; NP 141, 154
Llangynin (Llanginning) (parish), 47/59; SN252197; NP 139, 152
Llangynllo (Llangunllo) (parish), 46/90; SN363451; NP 139
Llangynnog (Llangunnog) (parish), 47/69; SN352162; NP 139, 152
Llangynog (parish), 45/12; SO023460; NP 141
Llangynwyd (parish), 51/58; NP 153, 154
Llangynwyd Higher (Llanonoyd Higher) (hamlet in Llangynwyd), 51/58; SS857945; NP 153, 154
Llangynwyd Lower (Langonoyd Lower) (hamlet in Llangynwyd), 51/61; SS873853; NP 153, 154
Llangynwyd Middle (Langonoyd Middle, Middle Llangynwyd) (hamlet in Llangynwyd), 51/60; SS862880; NP 153, 154
Llanhamlach (parish), 45/45; SO090278; NP 141
Llanharan (Llanharran) (parish), 51/84; ST020738; NP 154
Llanharran (parish), 51/84; NP 154
Llanharry (Llanhary) (parish), 51/107; ST011709; NP 154
Llanhary (parish), 51/107; NP 154
Llanidan (parish), 44/74; SH475680; NP 106
Llaniestyn (Llaniestin) (parish), 44/76; SH588794; NP 106, 107
Llaniestyn (parish), 48/64; SH261348; NP 115
Llanigon (parish), 45/90-91; NP 141
Llanigon (township in Llanigon), 45/91; SO235365; NP 141
Llanilar (parish), 46/22-23; NP 127
Llanilid (parish), 51/106; SS982715; NP 154
Llanilltern (chapelry in Llanilltern), 51/127; ST098800; NP 154
Llanina (parish), 46/63-64; NP 139
Llanina (township in Llanina), 46/63; SN416596; NP 139
Llanio (township in Llandewi-Brefi), 46/43; SN648575; NP 140
Llanishen (parish), 51/131; ST177818; NP 154
Llanithog (extra-parochial), 15/227; SO430265; NP 142
Llanllawddog (parish), 47/34; SN464292; NP 139, 140
Llanllechid (parish), 48/25; SH656658; NP 107
Llanlleonfel (Llanlleonvel) (parish), 45/27-28; NP 141

Llanlleonfel (Llanlleonvel) (township in Llanlleonfel), 45/28; SN931509; NP 141
Llanllibio (parish), 44/26; SH332822; NP 106
Llanllwchaiaen (Llanllwchaiarn) (parish), 46/65; SN385575; NP 139
Llanllwni (Llanllwny) (parish), 47/7; SN500400; NP 140
Llanlyfni (division in Llanlyfni), 48/39A; SH500500; NP 106, 115, 116
Llanlyfni), 48/39A-B; NP 106, 115, 116
Llanmadoc (Llanmadock, Llanmadog) (parish), 51/32; SS445942; NP 153
Llanmaes (parish), 51/166; SS988700; NP 154
Llanmihangel (Llanfihangel) (parish), 51/161; SS980720; NP 154
Llannefydd (Llannevydd) (parish), 49/9; SH985705; NP 108
Llannevydd (parish), 49/9
Llannon (Llanon) (parish), 47/84; SN555085; NP 153
Llannor (parish), 48/52; SH353372; NP 115
Llanon (parish), 47/84; NP 153
Llanonoyd Higher, 51/58; NP 153, 154
Llanpumsaint (parish), 47/35; SN430290; NP 139
Llanraeadr (division inside borough of Denbigh in Llanraeadr), 49/27B; SJ064646; NP 108
Llanraeadr (division outside borough of Denbigh in Llanraeadr), 49/27A; SJ035615; NP 108
Llanraeadr (Llanraiadr in Cinmerch, Llanraiadr in Kinmerch, Llanraiadr) (parish), 49/27A-B; NP 108
Llanraiadr (parish), 49/27A-B; NP 108
Llanraiadr in Cinmerch, (parish), 49/27A-B; NP 108
Llanraiadr in Kinmerch, (parish), 49/27A-B; NP 108
Llanrhaeadr-ym-Mochnant [Llanrhaiadr ym Mochnant] (parish), 49/132A-139; NP 117
Llanrhaiadr ym Mochnant (parish), 49/132A-139, 54/19; NP 117
Llanrhidian (parish), 51/27; NP 153
Llanrhidian Higher (Upper Hamlet of Llanrhidian) (hamlet in Llanrhidian), 51/27; SS548945; NP 153
Llanrhidian Lower (Llanrhidian Lower Division) (hamlet in Llanrhidian), 51/28; SS498922; NP 152, 153
Llanrhuddlad, 44/20; NP 106
Llanrhwdrys (parish), 44/2; SH336920; NP 106
Llanrhychwyn (parish), 48/17; SH750610; NP 107
Llanrhydd (Llanchydd) (parish), 49/38; SJ142577; NP 108
Llanrhyddlad (Llanrhuddlad) (parish), 44/20; SH325892; NP 106
Llanrhystid-haminiog, 46/27; NP 127
Llanrhystyd (Llanrhystyd-mefenydd) (parish), 46/26-27; NP 127
Llanrhystyd-haminiog (Llanrhystid-haminiog) (township in Llanrhystyd), 46/27; SN565675; NP 127
Llanrhystyd-mefenydd (township in Llanrhystyd), 46/26; SN570700; NP 127
Llanrothal (Llanrothall) (parish), 15/234; SO481186; NP 142
Llanrug (parish), 48/32; SH539625; NP 106
Llansadurnen (Llansadwrnen) (parish), 47/65; SN278095; NP 152
Llansadwrn (parish), 44/69; SH550760; NP 106
Llansadwrn (parish), 47/13; SN685315; NP 140
Llansaintffraed, 45/83; NP 141
Llansaintffraid (parish), 46/54; NP 127
Llansamlet Higher (hamlet in Llansamlet), 51/20; SS700985; NP 153
Llansamlet Lower (hamlet in Llansamlet), 51/21; SS680950; NP 153
Llansan Sior (parish), 49/8; NP 108
Llansanffraid Glan Conwy (Llansantffraid Glan Conway) (parish), 49/3; SH812748; NP 107
Llansannan (parish), 49/10; SH940630; NP 108
Llansannor (parish), 51/109; SS992794; NP 154
Llansantffraed (Llansaintffraed) (parish), 45/83; SO125235; NP 141
Llansantffraid (Llansaintffraid) (parish), 46/54; SN534658; NP 127
Llansantffraid Glan Conway (parish), 49/3
Llansantfraid Glyn Ceiriog (parish), 49/119; SJ175375; NP 117
Llansawel (parish), 47/89; SN595365; NP 139

Llansilin (parish), 31/115, 49/122-129; NP 117
Llansilin (parish), 31/115, 49/122-129; NP 117
Llansilin (township in Llansilin), 49/125; SJ214286; NP 117
Llanspyddid (Llanspythid, Llanspyddyd) (township in Llanspyddid), 45/56; SO007279; NP 141
Llanspyddid (Llanspythid, Llanspyddyd) (parish), 45/55-57; SO007279; NP 141
Llanspythid (parish), 45/55-57; SO007279; NP 141
Llanspythid, 45/56; NP 141
Llanstephan (parish), 47/68; SN340112; NP 152
Llanthoysaint (parish), 47/20; NP 140
Llantrisaint (parish), 51/83; ST040870; NP 154
Llantrisant (Llantrisaint) (parish), 44/17; SH374834; NP 106
Llantrisant (Llantrisaint) (parish), 51/83; ST040870; NP 154
Llantrithyd (parish), 51/157; ST039728; NP 154
Llantwit Fardre (Llantwit Vardre) (parish), 51/82; ST085860; NP 154
Llantwit Higher (Clyne) (hamlet in Llantwit juxta Neath), 51/53; SS815995; NP 153
Llantwit juxta Neath (parish), 51/52-54; NP 153
Llantwit Lower (Lantwit Lower, Lower Llantwit) (hamlet in Llantwit juxta Neath), 51/52; SS780980; NP 153
Llantwit Major (Lantwit Major) (parish), 51/165; SS970690; NP 154
Llantwit Vardre (parish), 51/82; NP 154
Llantysilio (parish), 49/101-103; NP 108
Llanvachraeth (parish), 44/23; NP 106
Llanvaeloy (parish), 44/53; NP 106
Llanvaes, 44/66; NP 106, 107
Llanvair vechan (parish), 48/23; NP 107
Llanveynoe (Llanveynol) (chapelry in Clodock), 15/209; SO300306; NP 141, 142
Llanveynol, 15/209; NP 141, 142
Llanvigael (parish), 44/24; NP 106
Llanvigan (parish), 45/54A-B; NP 141
Llanvihangel Brynpabuan (parish), 45/20; NP 128, 141
Llanvihangel Brynpabuan, 45/20; NP 128, 141
Llanvihangel Geneurglyn (parish), 46/2-7; NP 127
Llanvillo (parish), 45/39; NP 141
Llanvithyn (extra-parochial), 51/156; ST055730; NP 154
Llanwarne (Lanwarne) (parish), 15/240; SO496278; NP 142
Llanwenllwyfo (division in Llanwenllwyfo), 44/11; SH477895; NP 106
Llanwenllwyfo (parish), 44/10-11; NP 106
Llanwinio (parish), 47/45; SN245265; NP 139
Llanwnda (parish), 48/36; SH500580; NP 106
Llanwnen, 46/77; NP 139, 140
Llanwnnen (Llanwnen) (parish), 46/77; SN520484; NP 139, 140
Llanwonno (parish), 51/69; ST040948; NP 154
Llanwrda (parish), 47/14; SN715352; NP 140
Llanwrst (parish), 48/18, 49/15; NP 107
Llanwrst (township in Llanwrst), 49/15; SH825575; NP 107
Llanwrthwl (parish), 45/23A-B; NP 127, 128
Llanwrthwl - Lower Division (division in Llanwrthwl), 45/23B; SN960630; NP 127, 128
Llanwrthwl - Upper Division (division in Llanwrthwl), 45/23A; SN900600; NP 127, 128
Llanwrtyd (parish), 45/26; SN863478; NP 140, 141
Llanwrytyd (parish), 45/26; NP 140, 141
Llanyblodwel), 31/116-117; NP 117, 118
Llanybyther (Llanbydder) (parish), 47/6; SN540400; NP 140
Llanychaiarn (parish), 46/24; SN579761; NP 127
Llanychan (parish), 49/143; SJ119615; NP 108
Llanycrwys (parish), 47/4A-B; NP 140
Llanygwyryfon (parish), 46/28; NP 127
Llanymynech (parish), 31/118-119; NP 117, 118, 54/1
Llanynghenedl (parish), 44/50; SH300800; NP 106
Llanynis (parish), 45/16; SN999497; NP 141
Llanynys (parish), 49/142; SJ100605; NP 108
Llanystumdwy (Llanystymdwy) (parish), 48/46; SH477400; NP 115
Llay (Llai) (township in Gresford), 49/68; SJ332560; NP 109
Llechchylched (parish), 44/47; SH340760; NP 106

Llechcynfarwy (Llechcynvarwy, Llechcynfarwdd) (parish), 44/28; SH385815; NP 106
Llechryd (parish), 46/103; SN206439; NP 139
Llechwedd (hamlet in Llanwenog), 46/81A; SN489449; NP 139, 140
Lledrod (township in Llansilin), 49/124; SJ224306; NP 117
Llorau Isaf (township in Llansilin), 49/129; SJ169273; NP 117
Llorau Ucha (township in Llansilin), 49/122; SJ162303; NP 117
Llwynegrin (township in Mold), 50/109; SJ241654; NP 108
Llwyntydmon (township in Llanymynech), 31/118; SJ212205; NP 117, 118
Llygan y llan (township in Halkyn), 50/106; SJ206716; NP 108
Llyntaff (hamlet in Eglwysilan), 51/77; ST090910; NP 154
Llys dan hunedd (township in Cilcain), 50/103; SJ181683; NP 108
Llys y coed (township in Cilcain), 50/100; SJ168668; NP 108
Llysdinam (township in Llanafan-fawr), 45/21; SN999583; NP 141
Llysfaen (division formerly in Denbighshire in Llysfaen), 48/2B; SH872783; NP 107
Llysfaen (parish), 48/1; SH893776; NP 107, 108
Llysfaen (township in Llandrillo-yn-Rhos), 48/2A; SH872779; NP 107
Llyswen (parish), 45/6; SO127384; NP 141
Llysworney (parish), 51/120; SS962742; NP 154
Llywel (parish), 45/61-63B; SN845215; NP 140, 141, 153
Loanend (Horncliffe Loanend) (township in Norham), 27/7; NT944511; NP 64
Lobthorpe (hamlet in North Witham), 22/695; SK951205; NP 122, 123
Lockeridge (tithing in Overton), 39/167; SU149677; NP 157
Lockerley (parish), 14/220; SU300255; NP 167, 168
Locking (parish), 32/155; ST363606; NP 165
Lockington (parish), 21/15-16; NP 121
Lockington (township in Lockington), 21/16; SK471289; NP 121
Lockington (division of Lockington township in Kilnwick), 41/288; TA989469; NP 98, 99
Lockington (division of Lockington township in Lockington), 41/289; TA002465; NP 98, 99
Lockington (parish), 41/289-290; NP 98, 99
Lockington (township in Kilnwick and Lockington), 41/288-289; NP 98, 99
Lockton (township in Middleton), 42/436; SE860930; NP 92
Loddington (hamlet in Maidstone), 19/219; TQ761491; NP 172
Loddington (parish), 21/277; SK789024; NP 122
Loddington (parish), 26/160; SP807780; NP 133
Loddiswell (parish), 9/446; SX720497; NP 187
Loddon (parish), 25/593; TM360970; NP 137
Loders (division in Loders), 10/228A; SY504937; NP 177
Loders (parish), 10/228A-B; NP 177
Lodge on the Wolds (extra-parochial), 28/268; SK652311; NP 121
Lodsworth (parish), 36/26; SU928244; NP 181
Lofthouse (parish and township), 42/364-365; NP 86
Lofthouse, 42/364; NP 86
Loftsome (division in township of Wressle and Loftsome in Wressle), 41/43; Wressle and Loftsome (township in Wressle), 41/43, 44; NP 97
Loftus (Lofthouse) (division in township of Loftus in Loftus), 42/364; NZ728183; NP 86
Loftus (parish and township), 42/364-365; NP 86
Lolworth (parish), 4/69; TL364637; NP 135
Londesborough (division in township of Londesborough and Easthorpe in Londesborough), 41/190; SE872457; NP 98
Londesborough and Easthorpe (township), 41/190-191; NP 98
Londesborough, 41/190-191; NP 98
London Road (division in St George the Martyr Southwark), 35/9C; TQ316791; NP 170
Londonthorpe (parish), 22/792; SK944378; NP 122, 123
Long Ashton (parish), 32/2; ST544706; NP 155, 165
Long Bennington (parish), 22/612; SK030447; NP 113, 122
Long Bredy (parish), 10/239; SY567909; NP 177
Long Buckby (parish), 26/185; SP631673; NP 132

149

Long Clawston (parish), 21/82; SK723273; NP 122
Long Compton (hamlet in Long Compton), 37/297; SP288332; NP 144, 145
Long Compton (parish), 37/297, 301; NP 144, 145
Long Crendon (parish), 3/162; SP695087; NP 145, 146, 158, 159
Long Crichel (Long Crichell) (parish), 10/79; ST970104; NP 179
Long Ditton (division in Long Ditton), 35/37; TQ174655; NP 170
Long Ditton (parish), 35/37-38; NP 170
Long Eaton (township in Sawley), 8/290; SK497329; NP 121
Long Houghton (Longhoughton) (parish), 27/158-160
Long Itchington (parish), 37/232; SP409553; NP 132
Long Lawford (township in Newbold on Avon), 37/126; SP468756; NP 132
Long Marston (Marston Sicca) (parish), 13/13; SP161481; NP 144
Long Marston (hamlet in Long Marston), 16/147; SP892162; NP 146
Long Marston (parish), 16/147, 152; NP 146
Long Marton (parish), 38/7A, 7B; NP 83
Long Marton (township in Long Marton), 38/7A; NY690290; NP 83, 84
Long Melford (parish), 34/412; TL867470; NP 149
Long Newnton (parish), 39/21; ST909930; NP 156, 157
Long Newton (division of Long Newton township in Long Newton), 11/339; NZ379159; NP 85
Long Newton (parish), 11/338-340; NP 85
Long Newton (township in Long Newton), 11/339-340; NP 85
Long Riston (parish), 41/395-396; NP 99
Long Riston (township in Long Riston), 41/396; TA125425; NP 99
Long Sleddale (township in Kendal), 38/108; NY498032; NP 83, 89
Long Stow (Stow Longa) (district in Stow), 17/53; TL112711; NP 134
Long Sutton (parish), 14/113; SU750468; NP 169
Long Sutton (Sutton in Holland) (hamlet in Sutton St Mary), 22/783; TF445223; NP 124
Long Sutton (parish), 32/337; ST464261; NP 177
Long Whatton (parish), 21/20; SK478233; NP 121
Long Wittenham (parish), 2/62; SU550934; NP 158
Longbenton (parish), 27/503-506; NP 78
Longbenton (township in Longbenton), 27/505; NZ280686; NP 78
Longborough (parish), 13/87; SP183293; NP 144
Longbridge Deverill (parish), 39/274; ST861418; NP 166
Longbridge (division in King's Norton), 40/41; SP007776; NP 130, 131
Longburton (parish), 10/45; ST645129; NP 178
Longcott (Longcot) (township in Shrivenham), 2/43; SU272910; NP 157, 158
Longden (township in Pontesbury), 31/290; SJ451058; NP 118
Longdon (parish), 33/253; SK078138; NP 120
Longdon (parish), 40/237; SO836354; NP 143
Longdon on Tern (Longdon upon Tern) (parish), 31/214; SJ624155; NP 119
Longdon upon Tern (parish), 31/214; NP 119
Longfield (parish), 19/54; TQ618685; NP 171
Longfleet (tithing in Canford Magna), 10/196; SZ018924; NP 179
Longford (parish), 8/231-235; NP 120
Longford (township in Longford), 8/234; SK218374; NP 120
Longford (hamlet in Gloucester, St Mary de Lode), 13/175; SO834208; NP 143
Longford (parish), 31/581; SJ720170; NP 119
Longford (township in Moreton Say), 31/14; SJ643332; NP 119
Longframlington (parochial chapelry in Felton), 27/271; NU132023; NP 71
Longham (hamlet in Hampreston), 10/174B; SZ065980; NP 179
Longham (parish), 25/336; TF938158; NP 125
Longhirst (township in Bothal), 27/316; NZ223891; NP 78
Longhope (parish), 13/133A-B; NP 143
Longhope - Lower Division (division in Longhope), 13/133B; SO688188; NP 143

Longhope - Upper Division (division in Longhope), 13/133A; SO686204; NP 143
Longhorsley (parish), 27/293-301; NP 71, 78
Longhorsley Moor (common to Bigges, Freeholders and Riddells Quarters in Longhorsley), 27/296; NZ159926; NP 78
Longhoughton (Long Houghton) (township in Longhoughton), 27/159; NU240150; NP 71
Longney (parish), 13/259; SO762130; NP 143
Longnor (parish), 31/442; SJ490007; NP 118, 129
Longnor (township in Alstonfield), 33/84; SK091651; NP 111
Longparish (parish), 14/91; SU425447; NP 168
Longridge (township in Norham), 27/6; NT954498; NP 64
Longsdon (township in Leek), 33/12; SJ953553; NP 110
Longshaws (township in Longhorsley), 27/298; NZ122885; NP 78
Longsleddale, 38/108
Longslow (township in Drayton in Hales), 31/10; SJ659353; NP 119
Longstanton All Saints (parish), 4/71; TL393670; NP 135
Longstanton St Michael (parish), 4/72; TL399655; NP 135
Longstock (parish), 14/147; SU348375; NP 168
Longstowe (parish), 4/115; TL306546; NP 134, 147
Longstreet (tithing in Enford), 39/254; SU165522; NP 167
Longthorpe (hamlet in Peterborough, St John the Baptist), 26/6; TF162984; NP 123, 134
Longton (township in Penwortham), 20/341; SD490250; NP 94
Longton Lane End (township in Stoke-on-Trent), 33/31; SJ901431; NP 119
Longtown (Longtown Quarter) (township in Arthuret), 7/14; NY382681; NP 76
Longtown (chapelry in Clodock), 15/211; SO345285; NP 142
Longwitton (township in Hartburn), 27/342; NZ073888; NP 77
Longworth (hamlet in Longworth), 2/27; SU390990; NP 158
Longworth (parish), 2/27-29; NP 158
Longworth (township in Bolton le Moors), 20/391; SD684163; NP 101
Looe Island, 6/120; NP 186
Loose (parish), 19/302; TQ761522; NP 171, 172
Lopen (parish), 32/442; ST424147; NP 177
Loppington (parish), 31/50-52; NP 118
Loppington (township in Loppington), 31/50; SJ470294; NP 118
Lorbottle (township in Whittingham), 27/174; NU047070; NP 71
Lords House (subdivision in Butterworth Lord's Side division in Butterworth township in Rochdale), 20/469; SD959141; NP 101
Lorton (parochial chapelry), 2/274-276; NP 82
Lorton (township in Lorton parochial chapelry in Brigham), 7/275; NY179257; NP 82
Loscoe (township in Codnor), 8/197B; SK417477; NP 112
Lostford (township in Hodnet), 31/169; SJ623318; NP 119
Lostock (division in township of Barton upon Irwell in Eccles), 20/546B; SJ777957; NP 101
Lostock (township in Bolton-le-Moors), 20/407A; SD656083; NP 101
Lostock Graham (township in Great Budworth), 5/134; SJ693743; NP 101, 110
Lostwithiel (parish), 6/73; SX105600; NP 185, 186
Loton (division in Alberbury Lower Quarter township in Alberbury), 31/300; SJ353152; NP 118
Loughborough (parish), 21/35-37A; NP 121
Loughborough (township in Loughborough), 21/35; SK540180; NP 121
Loughor (borough in Loughor), 51/1; SS579080; NP 153
Loughor (division outside borough in Loughor), 51/2; ST575965; NP 153
Loughor (parish), 51/1-2; NP 153
Loughton (parish), 3/54; SP837381; NP 146
Loughton (parish), 12/307; TQ428968; NP 161
Loughton (township in Chetton), 31/558; SO611830; NP 129, 130
Lound (parish), 34/11; TM510996; NP 137
Lound (township in Sutton), 28/35; SK689867; NP 103
Louth (borough in Louth), 22/283; TF332872; NP 105
Louth (parish), 22/283-284; NP 105

Louth Park (township in Louth), 22/284; TF354882; NP 105
Love Clough (division in township of Higher Booths in Whalley), 20/289; SD873273; NP 95
Love Lane (division in township of Castleton in Rochdale), 20/440; SD916117; NP 101
Lovington (parish), 32/348; ST595314; NP 165, 166
Low Abbotside (township in Aysgarth), 42/131; SE022914; NP 90
Low Angerton (township in Hartburn), 27/351; NZ096835; NP 77
Low Blackhall (Blackhall Low Quarter, Low Blackwell) (township in St Cuthbert [Carlisle]), 7/82; NY404526; NP 76
Low Blackwell, 7/82; NP 76
Low Bolton (Bolton Low Quarter, Bolton Wood and Quarry Hill) (township in Bolton), 7/218; NY244440; NP 82
Low Buston (township in Warkworth), 27/219; NU235075; NP 71
Low Caldbeck, 7/214; NP 82, 83
Low Catton (township in Catton), 41/87; SE712528; NP 97
Low Coniscliffe (division in township of Low Coniscliffe with Carlbury in Coniscliffe), 11/314; NZ249149; NP 85
Low Crosby (township in Crosby upon Eden), 7/25; NY446596; NP 76
Low Dinsdale (township in Dinsdale), 11/329; NZ337116; NP 85
Low Ellington (Nether Ellington) (township in Masham), 42/170; SE201828; NP 91
Low Forest (township in Allendale), 27/590A; NY845510; NP 77, 84
Low House (subdivision in Butterworth Lord's Side division in Butterworth township in Rochdale), 20/466; SD928132; NP 101
Low Ireby (township in Ireby), 7/219; NY227396; NP 82
Low Keekle (extra-parochial), 7/303; NY006147; NP 82
Low Leyton (parish), 12/321; NP 161
Low Mowthorpe (division in township of Kirby Grindalythe in Kirby Grindalythe), 41/183B; SE890660; NP 92, 93, 98
Low Oulton (Oulton Low, Oultonlowe) (township in Over), 5/177; SJ611635; NP 109, 110
Low Row (division in township of Melbecks in Grinton), 42/109; SD975984; NP 90
Low Sedbergham (township in Sedbergham), 7/150; NY340410; NP 83
Low Toynton (division in Low Toynton), 22/384A; TF278761; NP 114
Low Toynton (parish), 22/384A-B; TF278761; NP 114
Low Toynton - Wildmore Fen (division in Low Toynton), 22/384B; TF255549; NP 114
Low Walton (township in Walton), 7/34; NY521644; NP 76
Low Winder (township in Barton), 38/24; NY492250; NP 83
Low Worsall (township in Kirklevington), 42/272; NZ383080; NP 91
Lowdham (parish), 29/187-189; NP 112, 121
Lowdham (township in Lowdham), 28/187; SK658462; NP 112, 121
Lower Allithwaite (township in Cartmel), 20/62; SD384774; NP 89
Lower Bebington (Lower Bebbington) (township in Bebington), 5/441; SJ335846; NP 100
Lower Beeding (chapelry in Beeding), 36/113; TQ220290; NP 182
Lower Benefield (hamlet in Benefield), 26/55B; SP982873; NP 134
Lower Boddington (Lower Bodington) (parish), 26/268; SP480520; NP 145
Lower Bodington (parish), 26/268; NP 145
Lower Booths (township in Whalley), 20/284-286; NP 95
Lower Boveney, 3/223; NP 159
Lower Brockhampton (division in Brockhampton), 15/86; SO692562; NP 130
Lower Bullingham (township in Hereford, St Martin), 15/134; SO515376; NP 142
Lower Claife (division in township of Claife in Hawkshead), 20/45; SD376958; NP 89
Lower Cound (township in Cound), 31/443; SJ561059; NP 118
Lower Coychurch, 51/88; NP 154
Lower Darwen (township in Blackburn), 20/303; SD682246; NP 95

Lower Division (division in township of Worsley in Eccles), 20/560; SD760020; NP 101
Lower Division [Brecon], 45/46; NP 141
Lower Division, 45/54B
Lower Down (township in Lydbury North), 31/376; SO329843; NP 129
Lower Dyffrin Honddu (hamlet in Merthyr Cynog), 45/34A; SO015356; NP 141
Lower Dylais, 51/15; NP 153
Lower Elkstone (township in Alstonfield), 33/87; SK063585; NP 111
Lower Gravenhurst (parish), 1/104; TL110348; NP 147
Lower Gwnnws, 46/34; NP 127
Lower Halstow (parish), 19/95; TQ868677; NP 172
Lower Hamlet of Michaelstone, 51/48; NP 153
Lower Hanley, 40/88; NP 130
Lower Hardres (parish), 19/287; TR154524; NP 173
Lower Harpton (township in Old Radnor), 15/40; SO274590; NP 128, 129
Lower Hayton (township in Stanton Lacy), 31/523; SO503810; NP 129
Lower Heyford (parish), 29/85; SP499241; NP 145
Lower Holker (includes Flookburgh and Cark) (township in Cartmel), 20/63; SD363760; NP 89
Lower Irlam (division in township of Barton upon Irwell in Eccles), 20/542; SJ709945; NP 101
Lower Kinnerton (township in Dodleston), 5/369; SJ350624; NP 109
Lower Laleston (hamlet in Laleston), 51/95B; SS875800; NP 153, 154
Lower Lea (division in Lea), 15/265; SO658230; NP 143
Lower Lemington (parish), 13/6B; SP219347; NP 144
Lower Llanbadarn Y-Greuddyn (Lower Llanbadarn-y-Croyddin) (township in Llanbadarn fawr), 46/16; SN615780; NP 127
Lower Llanbadarn-y-Croyddin, 46/16; NP 127
Lower Llanfihangel-y-creuddyn (Lower Llanfihangle y Croddyn) (township in Llanfihangel-y-creuddyn), 46/21; SN670750; NP 127
Lower Llanfihangle y Croddyn, 46/21; NP 127
Lower Llanilar (township in Llanilar), 46/23; SN600740; NP 127
Lower Llantwit, 51/52; NP 153
Lower Lledrod (township in Llanfihangel-lledrod), 46/30; SN642687; NP 127
Lower Lowick (division in township of Lowick in Ulverston), 20/17A; SD295855; NP 88, 89
Lower Milcote (hamlet in Weston upon Avon), 13/7; SP173523; NP 144
Lower Millom, 7/323; NP 88
Lower Mitton (Lower Mitton with Stourport) (township in Kidderminster), 40/30; SO800721; NP 130
Lower Myddfai (hamlet in Myddfai), 47/19A; SN760310; NP 140
Lower Newcastle, 51/94; NP 154
Lower Penn (township in Penn), 33/328; SO870970; NP 130
Lower Peover, 5/128; NP 101, 110
Lower Quarter (division in township of Kirkby Ireleth in Kirkby Ireleth), 20/7; SD231813; NP 88
Lower Radbourn (extra-parochial), 37/248; SP439569; NP 132
Lower Sapey (Sapey Pitchard) (parish), 40/95; SO687611; NP 130
Lower Shuckburgh (parish), 37/240; SP488626; NP 132
Lower Slaughter (parish), 13/98; SP167223; NP 144
Lower Subberthwaite (division in township of Subberthwaite in Ulverston), 20/14; SD276853; NP 88
Lower Swell (parish), 13/79; SP163258; NP 144
Lower Tockington (tithing in Almondsbury), 13/372; ST566843; NP 155
Lower Tooting (parish), 35/24; NP 170
Lower Tottenham (division in Tottenham), 24/79B; TQ335890; NP 160, 161
Lower Vaenor (Lower Vainor) (township in Llanbadarn fawr), 46/12; SN593828; NP 127
Lower Vainor, 46/12; NP 127
Lower Walton, 5/147; NP 100

151

Lower Whitley (township in Great Budworth), 5/116; SJ613790; NP 100, 101
Lower Winchendon (parish), 3/155; SP726125; NP 146
Lower Withington (township in Prestbury), 5/61; SJ813700; NP 110
Lowesby (parish), 21/262-263; NP 122
Lowesby (township in Lowesby), 21/263; SK726080; NP 122
Lowestoft (parish), 34/18; TM541937; NP 137
Loweswater (township in St Bees or parochial chapelry), 7/288; NY131201; NP 82
Lowgate Ward (division in parish and township of Holy Tinity Kingston upon Hull), 41/328-329; NP 99/1
Lowgate Ward (part of division in parish and township of Holy Tinity Kingston upon Hull), 41/328; TA102292; NP 99/1
Lowgate Ward (part of division in parish and township of Holy Tinity Kingston upon Hull), 41/329; TA102288; NP 99/1
Lowick (parish), 26/85; SP976809; NP 134
Lowick (parish), 27/44-47; NP 64
Lowick (township in Ulverston), 20/16-17C; NP 88, 89
Lowick (township in Lowick), 27/45; NU022390; NP 64
Lowick Common (division in township of Lowick in Ulverston), 20/17B; SD291849; NP 88
Lowside (township in Whickham), 11/25; NZ236610; NP 78
Lowside Quarter (township in St Bees), 7/301; NY002076; NP 82
Lowther (parish), 38/18; NY534228; NP 83
Lowthorpe (parish), 41/269; TA081593; NP 99
Lowton (township in Winwick), 20/595; SJ620980; NP 100, 101
Loxbeare (Loxbear) (parish), 9/166; SS910157; NP 164
Loxhore (parish), 9/13; SS623383; NP 163
Loxley (parish), 37/275; SP258523; NP 144
Loxley (township in Uttoxter), 33/121A; SK052317; NP 120
Loxton (parish), 32/159; ST373555; NP 165
Loynton (township in Norbury), 33/165; SJ789255; NP 119
Lubbesthorpe (township in Aylestone), 21/207; SK540012; NP 121, 132
Lubenham (parish), 21/316; SP709879; NP 132, 133
Luccombe (Luckham) (parish), 32/241; SS902445; NP 164
Lucker (township in Bamburgh), 27/97; NU152297; NP 71
Luckham (parish), 32/241; NP 164
Luckington (parish), 39/41; ST831837; NP 156
Lucton (parish), 15/31; SO437642; NP 129
Ludborough (parish), 22/179; TF296960; NP 105
Luddenham (parish), 19/108; TQ990639; NP 172
Luddesdown (parish), 19/82; TQ671647; NP 171
Luddington (district in Luddington), 17/35; TL102828; NP 134
Luddington (parish), 17/35, 26/70
Luddington (parish), 22/13-14; NP 98, 104
Luddington (township in Luddington), 22/13; SE826153; NP 104
Luddington in the Brook (Luddington) (division in Luddington in the Brook), 26/70; TL110848; NP 134
Luddington in the Brook (parish), 17/35, 26/70; TL110848; NP 134
Luddington (Luddington and Dodwell) (hamlet in Old Stratford), 37/206; SP168531; NP 144
Luddington and Dodwell, 37/206; NP 144
Ludford (division in Ludford), 15/286; SO512736; NP 129
Ludford (division in Ludford), 31/526; SO535840; NP 129
Ludford (parish), 15/286, 31/526; NP 129
Ludford Magna (parish), 22/201; TF213897; NP 105
Ludford Parva (parish), 22/202; TF189893; NP 105
Ludgershall (hamlet in Ludgershall), 3/148; SP661185; NP 145, 146
Ludgershall (parish), 3/148-149; NP 145, 146
Ludgershall (Ludgarshall) (parish), 39/192; SU276509; NP 167, 168
Ludgvan (parish), 6/206; SW505331; NP 189
Ludham (parish), 25/372; TG388184; NP 126
Ludworth (township in Glossop), 8/6; SJ982908; NP 101, 102
Ludworth (division in township of Shadforth in Pittington), 11/107; NZ371411; NP 85
Luffield Abbey (extra-parochial), 3/6; SP668428; NP 145
Luffincott (Luffincot) (parish), 9/195; SX336939; NP 174

Lufton (parish), 32/470A; ST517168; NP 177
Lugwardine (parish), 15/71; SO555405; NP 142
Lullingstaine, 19/74; NP 171
Lullingstone (Lullingstone and Lullingstaine) (parish), 19/74; TQ516650; NP 171
Lullington (parish), 8/326-327; NP 120
Lullington (township in Lullington), 8/327; SK248128; NP 120
Lullington (parish), 32/99; ST783522; NP 166
Lullington (parish), 36/327; TQ537022; NP 183
Lulsley (township in Suckley), 40/165; SO724551; NP 130, 143
Lund (parish), 41/226; SE942479; NP 98
Lundy Island (extra-parochial), 9/101; SS135455; NP 174
Lunedale (township in Romaldkirk), 42/2; NY870220; NP 84
Lunt (township in Sefton), 20/682; SD350018; NP 100
Luppitt (parish), 9/146; ST172058; NP 176
Lupton (township in Kirkby Lonsdale), 38/122; SD574825; NP 89
Lurgashall (parish), 36/28; SU932285; NP 181
Lusby (division in Lusby), 22/440A; TF342680; NP 114
Lusby - West Fen (division in Lusby), 22/440B; TF341589; NP 114
Lusby, 22/440A-B; NP 114
Lustleigh (parish), 9/405; SX770820; NP 175
Luston (township in Eye), 15/27; SO488628; NP 129
Lutley (township in Halesowen), 40/19; SO943828; NP 130
Luton (parish), 1/122-127; NP 147
Luton (township in Luton), 1/126; TL088208; NP 147
Lutterworth (parish), 21/345; SP539843; NP 132
Lutton (district in Lutton), 17/19; TL119871; NP 134
Lutton (division in Lutton), 26/62; TL117878; NP 134
Lutton (parish), 17/19, 26/62; NP 134
Lutton (Sutton St Nicholas) (hamlet in Sutton St Mary), 22/782; TF446255; NP 124
Luttons Ambo (township in Weaverthorpe), 41/178-179; NP 93
Luxborough (parish), 32/251; SS977380; NP 164
Luxulyan (Luxulian) (parish), 6/94; SX045588; NP 185
Lydbury North (North Lydbury) (parish), 31/369-376; NP 129
Lydbury North (township in Lydbury North), 31/373; SO352860; NP 129
Lydd (parish), 19/442; TR050203; NP 184
Lydden (parish), 19/375; TR254452; NP 173
Lyddington (Liddington) (parish), 30/56; SP870970; NP 133
Lydeard St Lawrence (parish), 32/273; ST129318; NP 164
Lydford (Old Lydford) (district in Lydford), 9/333; SX534855; NP 175
Lydford (parsh), 9/333-334; NP 175
Lydham (division in Lydham), 31/365; SO339906; NP 129
Lydiard Millicent (Liddiard Millicent) (parish), 39/57; SU093858; NP 157
Lydiard Tregoze (Liddiard Tregooze) (parish), 39/58; SU095839; NP 157
Lydiate (township in Halsall), 20/359; SD372050; NP 100
Lydlinch (parish), 10/51; ST743127; NP 178
Lydney (parish), 13/170-171; NP 155, 156
Lydney (tithing in Lydney), 13/171; SO639036; NP 156
Lye (township in Old Swinford), 40/21; SO923843; NP 130
Lyford (chapelry in West Hanney), 2/53; SU399943; NP 158
Lyham (township in Chatton), 27/73; NU070310; NP 64
Lyme Handley (township in Prestbury), 5/35; SJ967817; NP 101
Lyme Regis (parish), 10/133; SY344933; NP 177
Lyminge (parish), 19/340; TR146419; NP 173
Lymington (parish), 14/325; SZ322954; NP 180
Lyminster (Leominster) (division in Lyminster), 36/290; TQ025048; NP 181, 182
Lyminster (Leominster) (parish), 36/290-291; NP 181, 182
Lymm (parish), 5/108; SJ685872; NP 101
Lympne (parish), 19/421; TR107355; NP 172, 173
Lympsham (parish), 32/169; ST339550; NP 165
Lympstone (Lympston) (parish), 9/308; SY010842; NP 176
Lyncombe and Widcombe (parish), 32/38; ST748630; NP 156, 166
Lyndby (parish), 28/56; NP 112
Lyndhurst (division in Lyndhurst), 14/303A; SU301075; NP 180
Lyndhurst (parish), 14/303A-B; NP 180

Lyndon (parish), 30/37; SK912042; NP 122
Lyneham (hamlet in Shipton under Wychwood), 29/142; SP284206; NP 144, 145
Lyneham (parish), 39/61; SU026787; NP 157
Lynemouth (Linemouth, Lynmouth) (township in Woodhorn), 27/326; NP 78
Lynesack and Softley (township in St Andrew Auckland), 11/192; NZ097264; NP 84
Lyneside Quarter, 7/17; NP 76
Lynford (parish), 25/706; TL818920; NP 136
Lyng (Ling) (parish), 25/345; TG077169; NP 125
Lyng (parish), 32/308; ST325288; NP 165, 177
Lynmouth, 27/326; NP 78
Lynn St Margaret (parish), 25/289A-J; NP 124/1
Lynsted (Linstead) (parish), 19/159; TQ950608; NP 172
Lynt (tithing in Coleshill), 39/4; SU210959; NP 157
Lynton (parish), 9/8; SS712469; NP 163
Lynwode (parish), 22/209; NP 104
Lyonshall (parish), 15/45; SO331561; NP 129, 142
Lytchett Matravers (parish), 10/190; SY941957; NP 178, 179
Lytchett Minster (Lytchet Minster) (parish), 10/199; SY961934; NP 178, 179
Lytham (parish), 20/180; SD345290; NP 94
Lythe (parish), 42/371-379B; NP 86, 92
Lythe (township in Lythe), 42/379A; NZ850130; NP 86
Lythwood (township in Condover), 31/287; SJ470080; NP 118

M

Mabe (parish), 6/175; SW754333; NP 190
Mablethorpe St Mary (parish), 22/307; TF495845; NP 105
Mablethorpe St Peter (parish), 22/306; TF490860; NP 105
Macclesfield (division of Macclesfield township in Prestbury), 5/48; SJ938729; NP 110
Macclesfield (division of Macclesfield township in Prestbury), 5/49; SJ901735; NP 101, 110
Macclesfield (township in Prestbury), 5/48-49; NP 101, 110
Macclesfield Forest (township in Prestbury), 5/47; SJ973729; NP 101, 110
Macefen (township in Malpas), 5/330; SJ516470; NP 109
Machen, 51/134, 53/116-117; NP 154
Machen Lower (hamlet in Machen), 53/117; ST240890; NP 154
Machen Upper (hamlet in Machen), 53/116; ST200900; NP 154
Machynlleth (township in Machynlleth), 54/128; SH748002; NP 127
Mackworth (parish), 8/213-214; NP 121
Mackworth (township in Mackworth), 8/214; SK311378; NP 121
Maddington (parish), 39/267; SU052434; NP 167
Madehurst (parish), 36/222; SU982101; NP 181
Madeley (parish), 31/225; SJ692040; NP 119
Madeley (parish), 33/45A-B; NP 110, 119
Madeley (township in Madeley), 33/45A; SJ770440; NP 110, 119
Madingley (parish), 4/80; TL400605; NP 135
Madley (parish), 15/198; SO410390; NP 142
Madresfield (parish), 40/170; SO809474; NP 143
Madron (district in Madron), 6/209; SW442316; NP 189
Madron (parish), 6/208-209; NP 189
Maenan (Maenau) (township in Eglwys Fach), 48/15; SH798665; NP 107
Maenau, 48/15; NP 107
Maenclochog (division in Maenclochog), 55/41; SN084292; NP 138, 139
Maenclochog (parish), 55/41-42; NP 138, 139
Maenefa (township in Tremeirchion), 50/79; SJ081745; NP 108
Maenllwyd (township in Kerry [Llanfihangel-yng-Ngheri]), 54/175; SO163922; NP 128
Maentwrog (parish), 52/4; SH700400; NP 116
Maer (parish), 33/46-47; NP 119
Maer (township in Maer), 33/47; SJ787386; NP 119
Maerway Lane (township in Maer), 33/46; SJ764398; NP 119
Maes y groes (township in Cilcain), 50/99A; SJ172636; NP 108
Maes yr Uchan (township in Llantysilio), 49/103; SJ200450; NP 108, 117
Maes-Glas, 50/34; NP 108
Maes-Llanysten (township in Llangadfan), 54/31; SH959112; NP 117
Maesbrook-isaf (Maesbrook Issa) (township in Kinnerley), 31/122; SJ303212; NP 118
Maesbrook-uchaf (township in Kinnerley), 31/121; SJ302212; NP 118
Maesbury (township in Oswestry), 31/112; SJ308256; NP 118
Maescar (division in Devynock), 45/65; SN947266; NP 141
Maesgwyn (township in Nantmel), 56/31B; SO020670; NP 128
Maesmawr (township in Penstrowed), 54/162; SO068906; NP 128
Maesmynis (parish), 45/15; SO008472; NP 141
Maestregomer (township in Trefeglwys), 54/133; SN971916; NP 128
Mag Lordship (division in township of South Crosland in Almondbury), 43/769; SE130130; NP 102
Magdalen Laver (parish), 12/257; TL510080; NP 161
Magdalen Place (extra-parochial), 11/114; NZ281430; NP 85
Maghull (township in Halsall), 20/360; SD375020; NP 100
Magor (division in Magor), 53/148; ST422874; NP 155
Magor (parish), 53/148-149; NP 155
Maiden Bradley (division in Maiden Bradley), 39/276; ST808392; NP 166
Maiden Bradley (parish), 32/192, 39/276; NP 166
Maiden House (extra-parochial), 22/600B; SK982502; NP 113
Maiden Newton (parish), 10/147; SY611969; NP 177, 178
Maidenhead (borough in Cookham and Bray), 2/210-211; NP 159
Maidenhead (division in Bray), 2/211; SU888803; NP 159
Maidenhead (division in Cookham), 2/210; SU888815; NP 159
Maidford (parish), 26/275; SP610527; NP 145
Maids' Moreton (parish), 3/77; SP705352; NP 146
Maidstone (parish), 19/218A-218; NP 171, 172
Maidwell (parish), 26/166; SP742770; NP 133
Mainsforth (township in Bishop Middleham), 11/228; NZ313316; NP 85
Mainstone and Knuckshadwell, 31/384A; NP 128
Mainstone (parish), 31/383-384B, 54/196; NP 128, 129
Maisemore (parish), 13/140; SO812219; NP 143
Maker (district in Maker), 6/112A; SX430530; NP 187
Maker (district in Maker), 6/112B; SX411532; NP 187
Maker (parish), 6/112A-113; NP 187
Malborough (parish), 9/496; SX712385; NP 187
Malborough in the Vines (extra-parochial), 40/60; SO902636; NP 130
Malden (parish), 35/40; TQ216669; NP 170
Maldon All Saints (parish), 12/345; TL848070; NP 162
Maldon St Mary (St Mary-in-Maldon) (parish), 12/346; TL859058; NP 162
Maldon St Peter (St Peter-in-Maldon) (parish), 12/344; TL838065; NP 162
Malham (township in Kirkby Malhamdale), 43/239; SD897640; NP 95
Malham Moor (township in Kirkby Malhamdale), 43/240; SD880690; NP 95
Malins Lee (township in Dawley Magna), 31/227; SJ695087; NP 119
Mallerstang (township in Kirkby Stephen), 38/63; NY784001; NP 84, 90
Mallwyd (parish), 52/31-32, 54/124; NP 116, 117
Mallwyd (township in Mallwyd), 52/31; SH888133; NP 116, 117
Malpas (parish), 5/316-339, 50/144; NP 109, 118
Malpas (parish), 53/122; ST304908; NP 155
Malpas (township in Malpas), 5/324; SJ491472; NP 109
Malswick (tithing in Newent), 13/127D; SO745245; NP 143
Maltby (division in Maltby township in Maltby), 43/918; SK533921; NP 103
Maltby (parish), 43/917-919; NP 103
Maltby (township in Stainton), 42/278; NZ477146; NP 85
Maltby (township in Maltby), 43/918-919; NP 103
Maltby le Marsh (parish), 22/313; TF472816; NP 105
Malton (parish), 42/642-644; NP 92
Mamble (parish), 40/77; SO691714; NP 130

Mamhead (parish), 9/392; SX933805; NP 176, 188
Mamhilad (parish), 53/47; SO305039; NP 155
Manaccan (parish), 6/183; SW756248; NP 190
Manafon (Manavon) (parish), 54/112-114; NP 117, 128
Manafon-gaenog (township in Manafon), 54/113; SJ137036; NP 117
Manafon-llan (township in Manafon), 54/112; SJ111026; NP 117
Manaton (parish), 9/379; SX725808; NP 175
Manavon (parish), 54/112-114; NP 117, 128
Manby (parish), 22/288; TF405870; NP 105
Mancetter (parish), 37/59-62; NP 132
Mancetter (township in Mancetter), 37/60; SP324963; NP 132
Manchester (parish), 20/500-534; NP 101
Manchester (township in Manchester), 20/500-504; NP 101
Manchester - Ancoats (division in township of Manchester in Manchester), 20/500; SJ858986; NP 101
Manchester - Deansgate (division in township of Manchester in Manchester), 20/501; SJ836978; NP 101
Manchester - London Road (division in township of Manchester in Manchester), 20/502; SJ850980; NP 101
Manchester - Market Street (division in township of Manchester in Manchester), 20/503; SJ837982; NP 101
Manchester - St George (division in township of Manchester in Manchester), 20/504; SD854001; NP 101
Mancot (township in Hawarden), 50/6; SJ320670; NP 109
Manea (chapelry in Coveney), 4/22; TL492911; NP 135
Manfield (parish), 42/30-31; NP 85
Manfield (township in Manfield), 42/30; NZ228128; NP 85
Mangotsfield (parish), 13/406; ST655768; NP 156
Manley (township in Frodsham), 5/412; SJ501721; NP 109
Manlled (township in Llanidloes), 54/136; SN937883; NP 128
Manmoel (hamlet in Bedwellty), 53/69A; SO170050; NP 154
Manningford Abbots (parish), 39/219; SU148579; NP 167
Manningford Bohun (tithing in Wilsford), 39/216; SU138574; NP 167
Manningford Bruce (parish), 39/218; SU144575; NP 167
Manningham (township in Bradford), 43/519; SE148342; NP 96
Mannington (parish), 25/145; TG134321; NP 125
Manningtree (parish), 12/104; TM105319; NP 150
Manor and Rake (township in Hawarden), 50/4; SJ347653; NP 109
Manorbeer (parish), 55/142; NP 151, 152
Manorbier (Manorbeer) (parish), 55/142; SS061986; NP 151, 152
Manordeifi (Manordivy) (parish), 55/9; SN234408; NP 139
Manordivy (parish), 55/9; NP 139
Manorial allotment common to townships of Cartington, Debdon, Mount Healy, Rothbury and Pauperhaugh (in Rothbury), 27/248; NU072052; NP 71
Manorowen (parish), 55/32; SM935345; NP 138
Mansell Gamage (parish), 15/110; SO400449; NP 142
Mansell Lacy (Mansel Lacy) (parish), 15/117; SO426452; NP 142
Mansergh (township in Kirkby Lonsdale), 38/121; SD603842; NP 89
Mansfield (parish), 28/92; SK530610; NP 112
Mansfield Woodhouse (parish), 28/91; SK547635; NP 112
Mansriggs (township in Ulverston), 20/21; SD289805; NP 88
Manston (parish), 10/25; ST813157; NP 178
Manthorpe (hamlet in Witham on the Hill), 22/703; TF073159; NP 123
Manthorpe cum Little Gonerby (township in Grantham), 22/625; SK912372; NP 122
Manton (parish), 22/37-38; NP 104
Manton (parish), 30/38; SK884044; NP 122
Manton (tithing in Preshute), 39/170; SU167688; NP 157
Manton (township in Manton), 22/38; SE932038; NP 104
Manuden (parish), 12/67; TL480270; NP 148
Maperton (parish), 32/377; ST674270; NP 166
Maplebeck (parish), 28/141; SK708609; NP 112
Mapledurham (parish), 29/317; SU684770; NP 158, 159
Mapledurwell (Mappledurwell) (parish), 14/105; SU685516; NP 168, 169

Mapleton (Mappleton) (parish), 8/171; SK169477; NP 111
Maplewell (township in Barrow upon Soar), 21/50; SK524131; NP 121
Mapperley (township in Kirk Hallam), 8/202; SK429431; NP 121
Mapperton (parish), 10/125; SY511996; NP 177
Mappledurwell (parish), 14/105; NP 168, 169
Mappleton (parish), 8/171; NP 111
Mappleton (division in township of Mappleton in Mappleton), 41/371; TA219439; NP 99
Mappleton (parish), 31/370-372; NP 99
Mapplewell (division in township of Darton in Darton), 43/708; SE328098; NP 102
Mappowder (parish), 10/93; ST733069; NP 178
Marazion (Market Jew) (chapelry in St Hilary), 6/199A; SW528309; NP 189
Marbury (parish), 5/312-313; NP 109, 118
Marbury (township in Great Budworth), 5/137; SJ656761; NP 101
Marbury with Quoisley (township in Marbury), 5/313; SJ564456; NP 109, 118
March (chapelry in Doddington), 4/15; TL400969; NP 123, 124, 134, 135
March Baldon (parish), 29/245; NP 158
Marcham (parish), 2/54-56; NP 158
Marcham (township in Marcham), 2/54; SU457977; NP 158
Marchamley (township in Hodnet), 31/167A; SJ599303; NP 118, 119
Marchington (township in Hanbury), 33/202; SK135308; NP 120
Marchington Woodlands (township in Hanbury), 33/201; SK106291; NP 120
Marchweil (parish), 49/82A-B; NP 109, 118
Marchweil (township in Marchweil), 49/82A; SJ358478; NP 109, 118
Marcross (parish), 51/163; SS930691; NP 154
Marden (parish), 15/142-143; NP 142
Marden (parish), 19/315; TQ746449; NP 171, 172
Marden (parish), 39/214; SU085560; NP 167
Marden (township in Marden), 15/142; SO531480; NP 142
Marefield (township in Tilton), 21/271; SK750079; NP 122
Mareham le Fen (division in Mareham le Fen), 22/447A; TF277603; NP 114
Mareham le Fen (parish), 22/447A-B; NP 114
Mareham le Fen - West Fen (division in Mareham le Fen), 22/447B; TF281585; NP 114
Mareham on the Hill (division in Mareham on the Hill), 22/386A; TF288678; NP 114
Mareham on the Hill (parish), 22/386A-B; NP 114
Mareham on the Hill - Wildmore Fen (division in Mareham on the Hill), 22/386B; TF261541; NP 114
Maresfield (parish), 36/56; TQ456278; NP 183
Marfleet (parish), 41/401; TA143298; NP 99
Marford and Hoseley (township in Gresford), 50/129; SJ360550; NP 109
Margam (parish), 51/62; SS810880; NP 153
Margaret Marsh (parish), 10/16; ST826196; NP 166, 178
Margaret Roding (Margaret Roothing) (parish), 12/251; TL597117; NP 148
Margaretting (parish), 12/433; TL677022; NP 161
Margate (St John the Baptist) (parish), 19/127; TR353696; NP 173
Marham (parish), 25/323; TF722097; NP 124, 125
Marham (parish), 26/21; NP 123
Marhamchurch (parish), 6/6; SS229031; NP 174
Marholm (Marham, Marholme) (parish), 26/21; TF147023; NP 123
Mariansleigh (Maryansleigh) (parish), 9/85; SS748217; NP 163
Marishes (The Marishes) (township in Pickering), 42/434; SE813781; NP 92
Mark (parish), 32/175; ST364482; NP 165
Markby (parish), 22/311; TF489788; NP 105
Markeaton (township in Mackworth), 8/213; SK330382; NP 121
Markenfield Hall (Markingfield Hall) (township in Ripon), 43/168; SE288671; NP 91

Market Bosworth (parish), 21/150, 163-166; NP 121, 132
Market Bosworth (township in Market Bosworth), 21/163; SK401029; NP 121
Market Deeping (division in Market Deeping), 22/726A; TF133106; NP 123
Market Deeping (parish), 22/726A-B; NP 123
Market Deeping - Deeping Fen (division in Market Deeping), 22/726B; TF159126; NP 123
Market Drayton (township in Drayton in Hales), 31/9; SJ676346; NP 119
Market Harborough (Harborough) (township in Great Bowden), 21/315; SP732875; NP 133
Market Ilsley (parish), 2/118; NP 158
Market Jew, 6/199A; NP 189
Market Lavington (East Lavington) (parish), 39/212-213; NP 167
Market Lavington (East Lavington) (tithing in Market Lavington), 39/212; SU026529; NP 167
Market Overton (parish), 30/6; SK891167; NP 122
Market Rasen (parish), 22/208; TF113886; NP 104
Market Stainton (parish), 22/339; TF230800; NP 105
Market Warsop (parish), 28/89-90; NP 112
Market Warsop (township in Market Warsop), 28/89; SK572678; NP 112
Market Weighton (division in township of Market Weighton and Arras in Market Weighton), 41/193A; SE878412; NP 98
Market Weighton (parish), 41/192-193B; NP 98
Market Weighton and Arras (township in Market Weighton), 41/193A-B; NP 98
Market Weighton Canal (extra-parochial), 41/22E; SE857302; NP 98/1
Market Weston (Weston Market) (parish), 34/96; TL989779; NP 136
Marketshall (Markshall) (parish), 25/486; TG227043; NP 126
Markfield (parish), 21/134; SK487098; NP 121
Markham Clinton (West Markham) (parish), 28/71; SK714723; NP 112
Markingfield Hall, 43/167; NP 91
Markington with Wallerthwaite (township in Ripon), 43/167; SE272656; NP 91
Marks Tey (parish), 12/138; TL907232; NP 149
Marksbury (parish), 32/86; ST662621; NP 166
Markshall (parish), 12/133; TL841255; NP 149
Marland (division in township of Castleton in Rochdale), 20/438; SD876116; NP 101
Marland Peters, 9/109; NP 175
Marlborough St Mary (parish), 39/174; SU191694; NP 157
Marlborough St Peter and St Paul (Marlborough St Peter) (parish), 39/173; SU187691; NP 157
Marldon (parish), 9/429; SX872636; NP 188
Marlesford (parish), 34/278; TM327587; NP 137, 150
Marleston (Martleston) (tithing in Bucklebury), 2/162; SU532719; NP 158
Marlingford (parish), 25/675; TG131091; NP 125
Marloes (parish Marloes), 55/97; SM795082; NP 151
Marlow (parish), 3/214; NP 159
Marlow (township in Leintwardine), 15/6; SO422773; NP 129
Marlston cum Lache (township in St Mary on the Hill, Chester), 5/524; SJ381631; NP 109
Marnham (parish), 28/110-112; NP 112, 113
Marnham (township in Marnham), 28/110; SK807701; NP 112, 113
Marnhull (parish), 10/23; ST787188; NP 166, 178
Marple (township in Stockport), 5/19A; SJ958874; NP 101
Marr (parish), 43/878; SE516051; NP 103
Marrick (parish), 42/101; NZ060010; NP 90, 91
Marrington (township in Chirbury), 31/359; SO271970; NP 128, 129
Marros (parish), 47/55; SN202086; NP 152
Marsden (division in Marsden township in Huddersfield), 43/759; SE027123; NP 101, 102
Marsden (division in Marsden township in Almondbury), 43/760; SE050100; NP 102
Marsden (township in Huddersfield and Almondbury), 43/759-760

Marsh (division in township of Huddersfield in Huddersfield), 43/750; SE133167; NP 102
Marsh and Wigmore (township in Westbury), 31/314; SJ343111; NP 118
Marsh Baldon (Baldon Marsh, March Baldon) (parish), 29/245; SU565990; NP 158
Marsh Gibbon (parish), 3/114; SP647222; NP 145
Marsham (parish), 25/208; TG190238; NP 126
Marshaw Fell (division in township of Over Wyresdale in Lancaster), 20/134; SD605525; NP 94, 95
Marshchapel (parish), 22/182; TF370990; NP 105
Marshfield (parish), 13/401; ST782737; NP 156
Marshfield (parish), 53/130; ST255828; NP 154
Marshwood (parish), 10/130; SY401984; NP 177
Marske (Marske in Cleveland) (parish), 42/346-347; NP 86
Marske (Marske in Cleveland) (township in Marske), 42/346; NZ635218; NP 86
Marske (parish), 42/96; NZ102021; NP 91
Marston (parish), 22/618; SK891422; NP 113, 122
Marston (parish), 29/225; SP523092; NP 145, 158
Marston (township in Great Budworth), 5/136; SJ671764; NP 101
Marston (township in Stafford St Mary), 33/178; SJ922282; NP 119
Marston (tithing in Potterne), 39/139; ST969565; NP 167
Marston Bigot (division in Frome registration subdistrict in Marston Bigot), 32/127B; ST764496; NP 166
Marston Bigot (division in Nunney registration subdistrict in Marston Bigot), 32/127A; ST765435; NP 166
Marston Bigot (parish), 32/127A-B; NP 166
Marston Magna (division in Marston Magna), 32/391; ST597224; NP 166, 177
Marston Magna (parish), 32/391-392; NP 166, 177
Marston Maisey (parish), 39/11; NP 157
Marston Meysey (Marston Maisey) (parish), 39/11; SU134975; NP 157
Marston Moretaine (Marston Mortaine) (parish), 1/73; SP995420; NP 147
Marston Montgomery (parish), 8/343; SK135380; NP 120
Marston on Dove (Marston upon Dove) (parish), 8/247-250; NP 120
Marston on Dove (Marston upon Dove) (township in Marston on Dove), 8/249; SK235296; NP 120
Marston St Lawrence (Marston St Lawrance) (parish), 26/354; SP542433; NP 145
Marston Trussell (parish), 26/110; SP691852; NP 132, 133
Marston upon Dove (parish), 8/247-250; NP 120
Marston upon Dove, 8/249; NP 120
Marstow (extra-parochial), 15/271; SO558195; NP 142
Marstow (parish), 15/260; SO552198; NP 142
Marsworth (division in Marsworth), 3/135; SP924150; NP 146
Marsworth (parish), 3/135, 16/148; NP 146
Marsworth (division in Marsworth), 16/148; SP879168; NP 146
Marthall cum Warford (Marthall and Little Warford) (township in Rostherne), 5/98; SJ806771; NP 101, 110
Martham (parish), 25/375; TG454186; NP 126
Marthwaite (division in township of Sedbergh in Sedbergh), 43/260; SD643921; NP 89
Martin (division in Martin), 22/376A; TF232661; NP 114
Martin (Merton) (hamlet in Timberland), 22/564; TF113599; NP 113
Martin (parish), 22/376A-C; NP 114
Martin (parish), 39/351; SU064202; NP 167, 179
Martin - Wildmore Fen (division in Martin), 22/376B; TF266500; NP 114
Martin Dales (hamlet in Timberland), 22/565; TF170622; NP 113
Martin Hussingtree (parish), 40/66; SO882602; NP 130
Martindale (township in Barton), 38/27; NY432170; NP 83
Martinhoe (parish), 9/6; SS670479; NP 163
Martinscroft (division in township of Woolston with Martinscroft in Warrington), 20/613; SJ661898; NP 101
Martinsthorpe (parish), 30/39; SK865045; NP 122
Martlesham (parish), 34/432; TM259461; NP 150
Martleston, 2/162; NP 158

155

Martletwy (parish), 55/110; SN038107; NP 151
Martley (parish), 40/96A-B; NP 130
Martley (township in Martley), 40/96A; SO752600; NP 130
Martock (parish), 32/404; ST463210; NP 177
Marton (division in township of Marton in Marton), 42/285; NZ517158; NP 85, 86
Marton (division in township of Marton with Grafton in Marton), 43/126; SE418617; NP 91
Marton (parish), 22/236; SK848818; NP 104
Marton (parish), 37/233; SP412681; NP 132
Marton (parish and township), 42/285-286; NP 85, 86
Marton (parish), 43/126-127; NP 91
Marton (parish), 43/305-307; NP 95
Marton (township in Over), 5/176; SJ622666; NP 110
Marton (township in Prestbury), 5/60; SJ848682; NP 110
Marton (township in Whitegate), 5/172; SJ611684; NP 109, 110
Marton (township in Poulton-le-Fylde), 20/170-171; NP 94
Marton (township in Chirbury), 31/351; SJ279028; NP 117, 118
Marton (township in Swine), 41/383; TA179372; NP 99
Marton (township in Sinnington), 42/457; SE737834; NP 92
Marton in the Forest (division in township of Marton in the Forest in Marton in the Forest), 42/594; SE598688; NP 92
Marton in the Forest (parish and township), 42/594-595; NP 92
Marton le Moor (township in Topcliffe and Kirby Hill), 42/236; SE370705; NP 91
Marton with Grafton (township in Marton), 43/126-127; NP 91
Martons Both (township in Marton), 43/305-307; NP 95
Martyr Worthy (parish), 14/163; SU516343; NP 168
Marwood (parish), 9/18; SS549385; NP 163
Marwood (township in Gainford), 11/296; NZ030200; NP 84
Mary Tavy (parish), 9/336; SX507805; NP 175
Maryansleigh, 9/85; NP 163
Marygate (division in St Olave), 43/40; SE598521; NP 97/1
Maryport (township in Crosscanonby), 7/228; NY040370; NP 82
Marystow (parish), 9/347; SX436846; NP 175
Masham (parish), 42/164-175; NP 91
Masham (township in Masham), 42/172; SE216812; NP 91
Masham Moor (common to townships in Masham and to Colsterdale township in East Witton), 42/164; SE110800; NP 91
Mashbury (parish), 12/248; TL651119; NP 148
Mason (township in Dinnington), 27/516; NZ219734; NP 78
Masters Close (extra-parochial), 27/568; NZ087631; NP 77
Matching (parish), 12/202; TL522118; NP 148
Mathern (Matherne) (parish), 53/99; ST512919; NP 155
Mathon (parish), 40/167; SO748458; NP 143
Mathry (parish), 55/58; SM885315; NP 138
Matlask (Matlaske) (parish), 25/125; TG151348; NP 125, 126
Matley (township in Mottram), 5/8; SJ975963; NP 101
Matlock (parish), 8/123; SK302595; NP 111
Matson (parish), 13/196; SO844057; NP 143
Matterdale (township or chapelry in Greystoke), 7/205; NY373233; NP 83
Mattersey (parish), 28/15; SK690885; NP 103
Mattingley (hamlet in Heckfield), 14/23; SU723583; NP 169
Mattinshall, 25/498; NP 125
Mattishall (Mattinshall) (parish), 25/498; TG048110; NP 125
Mattishall Burgh (parish), 25/499; TG050122; NP 125
Maugersbury (hamlet in Stow on the Wold), 13/89; SP200241; NP 144
Maulden (parish), 1/83; TL058393; NP 147
Maulds Meaburn (township in Crosby Ravensworth), 38/34; NY630165; NP 83
Maunby (township in Kirby Wiske), 42/254; SE353870; NP 91
Mautby (parish), 25/384; TG489114; NP 126
Mavesyn Ridware (parish), 33/196; SK078190; NP 120
Mavis Enderby (division in Mavis Enderby), 22/435A; TF362667; NP 114
Mavis Enderby (parish), 22/435A-B; NP 114
Mavis Enderby - West Fen (division in Mavis Enderby), 22/435B; TF321582; NP 114
Mawdesley (township in Croston), 20/347; SD492152; NP 100
Mawgan (Mawgan in Meneage) (parish), 6/187; SW700245; NP 189, 190
Mawgan in Pyder, 6/88; NP 185

Mawnan (parish), 6/182; SW778287; NP 190
Mawr (hamlet in Llangyfelach), 51/4; SN655055; NP 153
Mawsley (parish), 26/163; SP802767; NP 133
Maxey (parish), 26/17A-B; NP 123
Maxey (township in Maxey), 26/17A; TF126080; NP 123
Maxstoke (division in Maxstoke), 37/75A; SP236866; NP 131
Maxstoke (parish), 37/75A-B; NP 131
Maxstoke Castle (division in Maxstoke), 37/75B; SP229994; NP 131
Mayfair (division in St George Hanover Square), 24/36C; TQ286803; NP 160/1
Mayfield (parish), 33/92A, 97-98; SK150455; NP 111, 120
Mayfield (township in Mayfield), 33/98; SK150455; NP 111, 120
Mayfield (parish), 36/54; TQ579264; NP 183
Mayland (parish), 12/350; TL922010; NP 162
Meadowtown (township in Worthen), 31/330; SJ318008; NP 118
Meaford (township in Stone), 33/56; SJ892360; NP 119
Meare (parish), 32/177; ST459422; NP 165
Mearley (township in Whalley), 20/247-248; NP 95
Mears Ashby (parish), 26/206; SP842667; NP 133
Measham (township in Measham), 8/337; SK334114; NP 121
Measham), 8/330, 333, 337; SK334114; NP 121, 121/3
Meathop and Ulpha (township in Beetham), 38/133; SD 442813; NP 89
Meaux (township in Wawne), 41/342; TA092402; NP 99
Meavy (parish), 9/358; SX540663; NP 187
Mechlas (township in Cilcain), 50/102; SJ201671; NP 108
Medbourne (Medbourn) (parish), 21/307-308; NP 133
Medbourne (Medbourn) (township in Medbourne), 21/308; SP802930; NP 133
Medlam (hamlet in Revesby), 22/458; TF311562; NP 114
Medlar with Wesham (township in Kirkham), 20/195; SD420338; NP 94
Medmenham (parish), 3/213; SU812860; NP 159
Medomsley (township in Lanchester), 11/157; NZ124546; NP 77, 78, 84, 85
Medstead (Medsted) (parish), 14/171; SU652365; NP 168
Medwalther and Creigbyther (township in Llanfihangel Beguidy), 56/6; SO140820; NP 128
Meeching (parish), 36/333; NP 183
Meeridge (township in Ipstones), 33/75B; SK050520; NP 111
Meering (Mering) (extra-parochial), 28/114; SK814655; NP 113
Meesden (parish), 16/19; TL432325; NP 148
Meeth (parish), 9/115; SS542081; NP 175
Meidrim (Mydrim) (parish), 47/60; SN300210; NP 152
Meifod (parish), 54/35-43; NP 117
Meilltyrne (parish), 48/70; NP 115
Melay, 7/223; NP 82
Melbecks (township in Grinton), 42/106-110; NP 90
Melbecks Moor (common to the divisions in Melbecks township in Grinton), 42/106; NY953007; NP 90
Melbourn (Melbourne) (parish), 4/175; TL388434; NP 148
Melbourne (parish), 8/300; SK391255; NP 121
Melbourne (township in Thornton), 41/78; SE750430; NP 97, 98
Melbury Abbas (parish), 10/9; ST882201; NP 166, 178
Melbury Bubb (parish), 10/101; ST599056; NP 177, 178
Melbury Osmond (parish), 10/103; ST572081; NP 177
Melbury Sampford (parish), 10/118; ST576062; NP 177
Melchbourne (Melchbourn) (parish), 1/5; TL029655; NP 134
Melchet (extra-parochial), 39/370; SU272221; NP 167, 168
Melcombe Horsey (parish), 10/158; ST746027; NP 178
Melcombe Regis (parish), 10/266; SY678808; NP 178
Meldon (parish), 27/399; NZ116840; NP 77
Meldreth (parish), 4/176; TL373462; NP 148
Meliden (Gallt Melyd) (parish), 50/53-54; NP 108
Meliden (Gallt Melyd) (township in Meliden), 50/54; SJ060812; NP 108
Melindwr (township in Llanbadarn fawr), 46/18; SN720820; NP 127
Meline (parish), 55/18; SN129358; NP 139
Melinog Fach or Melinog Fawr, 54/6-7; NP 117
Melinog [Melinog Fach or Melinog Fawr], (township in Llansantffraid), 54/6; SJ231208; NP 117

Melinog [Melinog Fach or Melinog Fawr], (township in Llansantffraid), 54/7; SJ240213; NP 117
Melkridge (township in Haltwhistle), 27/580; NY735670; NP 76, 77
Melksham (parish), 39/127-128; NP 156, 157, 166, 167
Melksham (tithing in Melksham), 39/127; ST924637; NP 156, 157, 166, 167
Melling (division in township of Melling with Wrayton in Melling), 20/83; SD604711; NP 89
Melling (division in township of Melling in Halsall), 20/361; SD391011; NP 100
Melling (parish), 20/81-89; NP 89, 94, 95
Melling with Wrayton (township in Melling), 20/82-83; NP 89
Mellington (township in Church Stoke), 54/192; SO267924; NP 128, 129
Mellis (parish), 34/136; TM098745; NP 136
Mellor (township in Glossop), 8/7; SJ984882; NP 101, 102
Mellor (township in Blackburn), 20/317; SD653307; NP 95
Mells (parish), 32/119; ST720493; NP 166
Melmerby (parish), 7/183; NY644382; NP 83
Melmerby (township in Coverham), 42/158; SE071859; NP 90
Melmerby (township in Wath), 42/234; SE343767; NP 91
Melsonby (parish), 42/32; NZ193088; NP 85
Meltham (township in Almondbury), 43/771; SE090100; NP 102
Melton (parish), 34/434; TM282506; NP 150
Melton (township in Welton), 41/215; SE971259; NP 98
Melton Constable (Melton Constable with Little Burgh annexed, Melton Constable with Burgh Parva) (parish), 25/119; TG039323; NP 125
Melton Mowbray (parish), 21/72-76; NP 122
Melton Mowbray (township in Melton Mowbray), 21/74; SK752190; NP 122
Melton on the Hill, (parish), 43/877; NP 103
Melton Ross (parish), 22/66; TA069117; NP 104
Melton St Mary and All Saints (parish), 25/560; NP 125
Meltonby (division in township of Yapham cum Meltonby in Pocklington), 41/95; SE805505; NP 98
Meltonby and Yapham (township in Pocklington), 41/94-95; NP 98
Melverley (parish), 31/128; SJ330173; NP 118
Membury (parish), 9/230; ST277032; NP 177
Mendham (division in Mendham), 25/634; TM260827; NP 137
Mendham (division in Mendham), 34/34; TM279826; NP 137
Mendham (parish), 25/634, 34/34; NP 137
Mendlesham (parish), 34/242; TM101651; NP 136
Menethorpe (township in Westow), 41/124; SE772679; NP 92
Menheniot (parish), 6/68; SX288638; NP 186
Menston (Menstone) (township in Otley), 43/367; SE170437; NP 96
Menthorpe (division in township of Menthorpe in Hemingbrough), 41/53; SE694346; NP 97
Menthorpe (division in township of Menthorpe in Skipwith), 41/54; SE687342; NP 97
Menthorpe (township in Hemingbrough and Skipwith), 41/52-54; NP 97
Mentmore (parish), 3/137; SP908208; NP 146
Menutton (township in Clun), 31/395; SO300775; NP 129
Menwith with Darley (township in Hampsthwaite), 43/156; SE197577; NP 91, 96
Meole (township in Meole Brace), 31/274; SJ481111; NP 118
Meole Brace (Brace Meole) (parish), 31/274-277; SJ481111; NP 118
Meonstoke (parish), 14/252; SU632196; NP 168, 180
Meopham (parish), 19/81; TQ646650; NP 171
Mepal (parish), 4/20; TL437817; NP 135
Meppershall (parish), 1/102; TL143373; NP 147
Mercaston (township in Mugginton), 8/219; SK276418; NP 120, 121
Mere (parish), 22/557; TF007650; NP 113
Mere (tithing in Mere), 39/336A; ST815325; NP 166
Mere (township in Rostherne), 5/95; SJ725821; NP 101
Mere), 39/336A-337; NP 166
Meredydd (township in St Asaph), 49/140; SJ002730; NP 108

Merevale (division in Merevale), 21/158; SK311018; NP 121, 132
Merevale (parish), 21/158, 37/21; NP 121, 132
Merevale (division in Merevale, 37/21; SP295975; NP 131, 132
Mereworth (parish), 19/183; TQ653541; NP 171
Meriden (parish), 37/96; SP252828; NP 131
Mering (extra-parochial), 28/114; NP 113
Merrington (parish), 11/221-224; NP 85
Merrington (township in Merrington), 11/221; NZ267314; NP 85
Merriott (parish), 32/458; ST445135; NP 177
Merrow (parish), 35/128; TQ030508; NP 169, 170
Mersham (Mershem) (parish), 19/327; TR048390; NP 172
Merstham (parish), 35/94; TQ293546; NP 170
Merston (parish), 36/276; SU897023; NP 181
Merther (parish), 6/154; SW867448; NP 190
Merthyr (parish), 47/70; SN354211; NP 139
Merthyr Cynog (parish), 45/34A-D; NP 141
Merthyr Dovan (parish), 51/174; NP 154
Merthyr Dyfan (Merthyr Dovan) (parish), 51/174; ST112691; NP 154
Merthyr Mawr (parish), 51/103; SS870772; NP 153, 154
Merthyr Tydfil (parish), 51/70-74; NP 154
Merton (parish), 9/111; SS526134; NP 163, 175
Merton (parish), 25/680; TL912987; NP 136
Merton (parish), 29/110; SP583183; NP 145
Merton (parish), 35/41; TQ242686; NP 170
Merton, 22/564
Meshaw (parish), 9/83; SS764188; NP 163
Messing (parish), 12/184; TL897183; NP 149
Messingham (parish), 22/33-34; NP 104
Messingham (township in Messingham), 22/34; SE875043; NP 104
Metfield (parish), 34/77; TM297802; NP 137
Metham (township in Howden), 41/11; SE812247; NP 98, 98/1
Metheringham (parish), 22/561; TF085625; NP 113
Methley (parish), 43/631; SE390265; NP 97
Methwold (parish), 25/692; TL685952; NP 135, 136
Mettingham (parish), 34/29; TM364900; NP 137
Metton (parish), 25/56; TG199372; NP 126
Mevagissey (parish), 6/145; SX013453; NP 190
Mewith (division in township of Bentham in Bentham), 43/269; SD682670; NP 89, 90
Mexborough (Mexbrough) (parish), 43/867-868; NP 103
Mexborough (Mexbrough) (township in Mexborough), 43/867; SE485005; NP 103
Meyllteryn (Meilltyrne) (parish), 48/70; SH242328; NP 115
Meynell Langley (township in Kirk Langley), 8/216; SK287401; NP 120, 121
Meysey Hampton (Maisey Hampton) (parish), 13/288; SP120005; NP 157
Michael Church (parish), 32/302; NP 165, 177
Michaelchurch Escley (Michaelchurch Eskley) (parish), 15/207; SO310357; NP 142
Michaelchurch on Arrow (Michaelchurch upon Arrow) (parish), 56/53; SO241509; NP 141
Michaelstow (parish), 6/41; SX080790; NP 185
Michaelston Higher (Michaelstone Higher) (hamlet in Michaelston super Avon), 51/49; SS830970; NP 153
Michaelston le Pit (parish), 51/151; ST150730; NP 154
Michaelston Lower (Lower Hamlet of Michaelstone) (hamlet in Michaelston super Avon), 51/48; SS788932; NP 153
Michaelston super Avon (Michaelstown super Avan) (parish), 41/48-49; NP 153
Michaelston-super-Ely (parish), 51/147; ST115762; NP 154
Michaelstone Higher, 51/49; NP 153
Michaelstone-y-Vedw (parish), 51/135, 53/129; NP 154
Michaelstone-y-Vedw (hamlet in Michaelstone-y-Vedw), 53/129; ST241845; NP 154
Micheldever (parish), 14/139; SU520390; NP 168
Michelmersh (Mitchelmersh) (parish), 14/213; SU346266; NP 168
Mickfield (parish), 34/246; TM138621; NP 136, 137
Mickle Trafford (township in Plemstall), 5/421; SJ448698; NP109

Mickleby (township in Lythe), 42/374; NZ807130; NP 86
Micklefield (township in Sherburn in Elmet), 43/424; SE442332; NP 97
Mickleham (parish), 35/119; TQ172529; NP 170
Micklehurst (township in Mottram), 5/1; SE010010; NP 101, 102
Mickleover (parish), 8/259; NP 121
Mickleover (township in Mickleover), 8/259; SK306343; NP 121
Micklethwaite (Micklethwaite Grange) (extra-parochial), 43/93; SE402472; NP 97
Mickleton (hamlet in Mickleton), 13/21; SP162435; NP 144
Mickleton (parish), 13/19-21; NP 144
Mickleton (township in Romaldkirk), 42/4; NY938212; NP 84
Micklewaite (division in township of Bingley in Bingley), 43/360; SE125415; NP 96
Mickley (division in township of Azerley in Kirkby Malzeard), 43/195; SE255665; NP 91
Mickley (township in Ovingham), 27/562; NZ074610; NP 77
Mickley (township in Prees), 31/22; SJ612328; NP 119
Mid Lavant (parish), 36/241; SU586085; NP 181
Middle (hamlet in Ystrad-dyfodwg), 51/66A; SS930990; NP 154
Middle (parish), 31/152-157; NP 118
Middle Aston (township in Steeple Aston), 29/61; SP476272; NP 145
Middle Chinnock (parish), 32/460; ST474134; NP 177
Middle Claydon (West Claydon) (parish), 3/109; SP714250; NP 146
Middle Division (division in township of Heap in Bury), 20/429; SD844108; NP 101
Middle division (in Pool), 54/68; NP 117
Middle Hulton (township in Deane), 20/567; SD702053; NP 101
Middle Linthwaite (division in township of Linthwaite in Almondbury), 43/763; SE095135; NP 102
Middle Llangynwyd (parish), 51/60
Middle Quarter, 7/12; NP 76
Middle Quarter, 7/19; NP 76
Middle Quarter (township in Hartington), 8/109; SK112654; NP 111
Middle Quarter (division in township of Kirkby Ireleth in Kirkby Ireleth), 20/6; SD239834; NP 88
Middle Quarter (division in township of Bentham in Bentham), 43/268; SD663705; NP 89
Middle Raisin (parish), 22/207A-B; NP 104, 104/1
Middle Raisin, 22/207A; NP 104
Middle Rasen (Middle Raisin) (division in Middle Rasen), 22/207A; TF092892; NP 104
Middle Rasen (Middle Raisin) (parish), 22/207A-B; NP 104
Middle Rasen - Lissingleys (division in Middle Rasen), 22/207B; TF091843; NP 104/1
Middle Shitlington, 43/716; NP 102
Middle Sitlington (Middle Shitlington) (division in township of Sitlington in Thornhill), 43/716; SE270175; NP 102
Middle Temple (extra-parochial), 24/17A; TQ311810; NP 160/1
Middle Tottenham (division in Tottenham), 24/79C; TQ320890; NP 160
Middle, 31/152; NP 118
Middleham (parish), 42/159; SE120873; NP 91
Middlehope (township in Diddlebury), 31/502; SO498885; NP 129
Middlemead (hamlet in Little Baddow), 12/243; TL785074; NP 162
Middlesborough, 42/284; NP 85
Middlesbrough (Middlesborough) (township in Middlesbrough), 42/284; NZ495200; NP 85
Middlesbrough (parish), 42/283-284; NP 85
Middlesceugh and Braithwaite (township in St Mary [Carlisle]), 7/98C; NY410415; NP 83
Middlestone (township in St Andrew Auckland), 11/211; NZ250310; NP 85
Middlethorpe (township in St Mary Bishophill [Senior]), 43/45C; SE601488; NP 97
Middleton Keynes (parish), 3/57; NP 146
Middleton (division in Middleton and Smerill township in Youlgreave), 8/112; SK183624; NP 111

Middleton (Middleton by Wirksworth) (township in Wirksworth), 8/149; SK273560; NP 111
Middleton and Smerill (township in Youlgreave), 8/112-113; NP 111
Middleton by Wirksworth, 8/149; NP 111
Middleton in Teesdale (parish), 11/188A-189B; NP 84
Middleton in Teesdale (township in Middleton in Teesdale), 11/189A; NY958291; NP 84
Middleton St George (division in parish and township of Middleton St George in Middleton St George), 11/337; NZ358132; NP 85
Middleton St George (township), 11/337-338; NP 85
Middleton (parish), 12/45; TL872396; NP 149
Middleton on the Hill (parish), 15/24; SO550650; NP 129
Middleton (Myddleton) (division in township of Houghton, Middleton and Arbury in Winwick), 20/603; SJ621926; NP 101
Middleton (parish), 20/472-480; NP 101
Middleton (township in Lancaster), 20/113; SD421595; NP 89, 94
Middleton (township in Middleton), 20/479; SD864066; NP 101
Middleton (parish), 25/310; TF662160; NP 124
Middleton (township in Cottingham), 26/93; SP844889; NP 133
Middleton Cheney (hamlet in Middleton Cheney), 26/357A; SP508413; NP 145
Middleton Cheney (parish), 26/357A-B; NP 145
Middleton Malzor (parish), 26/304; NP 133, 146
Middleton (township in Belford), 27/82; NU100350; NP 64
Middleton Hall (township in Ilderton), 27/115; NT988252; NP 71
Middleton South (South Middleton) (township in Hartburn), 27/354; NZ052832; NP 77
Middleton (parish), 29/83; NP 145
Middleton Stoney (Middleton) (parish), 29/83; SP529233; NP 145
Middleton (township in Bitterley), 31/532; SO540780; NP 129
Middleton (township in Chirbury), 31/348; SO302988; NP 128, 129
Middleton (township in Oswestry), 31/109; SJ317288; NP 118
Middleton Scriven (parish), 31/566; SO673877; NP 130
Middleton (parish), 34/161; TM420677; NP 137
Middleton (Middleton-on-Sea) (parish), 36/286; SU982001; NP 181
Middleton (parish), 37/26; SP182974; NP 131
Middleton (township in Kirkby Lonsdale), 38/120; SD643863; NP 89
Middleton on the Wolds (parish), 41/227; SE930490; NP 98
Middleton (parish), 42/436-444; NP 982
Middleton and Aislaby (undivided moor common to Middleton and Aislaby townships in Middleton), 42/443; SE756984; NP 92
Middleton Quernhow (township in Wath), 42/233; SE337790; NP 91
Middleton Tyas (Middleton Tyas with Kneeton) (township in Middleton Tyas), 42/88; NZ228058; NP 85, 91
Middleton Tyas (parish), 42/87-88; NP 85, 91
Middleton upon Leven, 42/289
Middleton (township in Ilkley), 43/341; SE115505; NP 96
Middleton (township in Rothwell), 43/592; SE306287; NP 96
Middleton-on-Leven (Middleton upon Leven) (township in Rudby in Cleveland), 42/289; NZ275095; NP 85
Middletown (township in Alberbury), 54/89; SJ305125; NP 118
Middlewich (parish), 5/193-207; NP 110
Middlewich (township in Middlewich), 5/197; SJ704662; NP 110
Middlezoy (parish), 32/304; ST372332; NP 165, 177
Middop (Midhope) (township in Gisburn), 43/298A; SD843448; NP 95
Middridge (Midridge) (township in St Andrew Auckland), 11/217; NZ261258; NP 85
Middridge Grange (township in St Andrew Auckland), 11/218; NZ244245; NP 85
Midgeholme (division of Burtholme township in Lanercost), 7/33B; NY639595; NP 76
Midgeholme (extra-parochial), 7/59; NY607571; NP 76
Midgeholme and Halton Lee West Fell (extra-parochial), 7/60; NY631576; NP 76

Midgham (chapelry in Thatcham), 2/155; SU558672; NP 158
Midgley (division in township of Sitlington in Thornhill), 43/714; SE265149; NP 102
Midgley (township in Halifax), 43/556; SE022282; NP 96
Midhope (sub-division in Westnall with Waldershaigh division in township of Bradfield in Ecclesfield), 43/821; SK210980; NP 102
Midhope, 43/298A; NP 95
Midhurst (parish), 36/18; SU882218; NP 181
Midley (parish), 19/440; TR014221; NP 184
Midloe (extra-parochial), 17/100; TL163651; NP 134
Midridge, 11/217; NP 85
Midsomer Norton (parish), 32/107; ST668548; NP 166
Midville (parish), 22/461; TF370575; NP 114
Milborne Port (Milbourne Port) (parish), 32/383; ST675196; NP 166, 178
Milborne St Andrew (parish), 10/208; SY797979; NP 178
Milborne Stileham (hamlet in Bere Regis), 10/203; SY812973; NP 178
Milbourne (township in Ponteland), 27/526; NZ118741; NP 77, 78
Milbourne Grange (township in Ponteland), 27/527; NZ115758; NP 77
Milbourne (Milbourn, Mitbourn) (division in Malmsbury Eastern Registration Subdistrict of Milbourne tything in St Paul Malmesbury), 39/26A; ST944877; NP 157
Milbourne (Milbourn, Mitbourn) (division in Malmsbury Western Registration Subdistrict of Milbourne tything in St Paul Malmesbury), 39/26B; ST934878; NP 157
Milburn (township in Kirby Thore), 38/6; NY696316; NP 83, 84
Milby (division in township of Milby in Aldborough), 42/577; SE403678; NP 91
Milby (township in Kirby Hill and Aldborough), 42/576-577; NP 91
Milcombe (Milcomb) (chapelry in Bloxham), 29/31; SP408348; NP 145
Milcote (division in Weston upon Avon), 37/207; SP188527; NP 144
Milcote (hamlet in Weston upon Avon), 13/7, 37/207; NP 144
Milden (parish), 34/416; TL952458; NP 149
Mildenhall (parish), 34/110A-D; NP 135
Mildenhall High Town (division in Mildenhall), 34/110A; TL710750; NP 135
Mildenhall (Minall) (parish), 39/179; SU214704; NP 157
Mile End (Colchester, St Michael Mile End; Mile End, St Michael), 12/120; TL999274; NP 149
Mile End New Town (division in Christchurch Spitalfields), 24/61A; TQ339818; NP 160/1
Mile End New Town (division in St Dunstan Stepney), 24/65C; TQ342819; NP 160/1
Mile End New Town (division in St Mary Whitechapel), 24/60E; TQ340817; NP 160/1
Mile End Old Town Lower (division in St Dunstan Stepney), 24/65A; TQ360822; NP 160/1
Mile End Old Town Upper (division in St Dunstan Stepney), 24/65B; TQ352815; NP 160/1
Mileham (parish), 25/274; TF920190; NP 125
Milfield (township in Kirknewton), 27/66; NT930339; NP 64
Milford (parish), 14/324; SZ300935; NP 179, 180
Milford (tithing in Salisbury, St Martin), 39/316; SU149308; NP 167
Milland (division in Trotton), 36/341; SU831285; NP 181
Milland (extra-parochial), 14/205; SU483286; NP 168
Millbrook (parish), 1/81; TL014385; NP 147
Millbrook (parish), 14/297; SU394140; NP 180
Millenheath (township in Prees), 31/20; SJ581354; NP 118
Millichope (township in Eaton), 31/429; SO524894; NP 129
Millington (township in Rostherne), 5/93; SJ729847; NP 101
Millington (division in parish and township of Millington), 41/106; SE838538; NP 98
Millington (parish and township), 41/106-107; NP 98
Millmeece (township in Eccleshall), 33/136; SJ838332; NP 119
Millom (parish), 7/319-327; NP 88.

Millom Above (Upper Millom) (township in Millom), 7/322; SD179837; NP 88
Millom Below (Lower Millom) (township in Millom), 7/323; SD167807; NP 88
Millthorpe (hamlet in Aslackby), 22/672; TF130306; NP 123
Milnthorpe (division of Heversham with Milnthorpe township in Heversham), 38/87; SD501819; NP 89
Milson (parish), 31/545; SO641730; NP 130
Milstead (Milsted) (parish), 19/162; TQ908580; NP 172
Milsted (parish), 19/162; NP 172
Milston (Milston and Brigmerston) (parish), 39/260; SU194466; NP 167
Milton (hamlet in Adderbury), 29/35; SP449348; NP 145
Milton (Milton next Sittingbourne) (parish), 19/104; TQ910658; NP 172
Milton (Milton-next-Gravesend) (parish), 19/33; TQ653731; NP 171
Milton (Middleton Malzor) (parish), 26/304; SP727558; NP 133, 146
Milton (Milton under Wychwood) (township in Shipton under Wychwood), 29/141; SP258173; NP 144
Milton (parish), 2/59; SU485915; NP 158
Milton (parish), 4/76; TL478631; NP 135
Milton (parish), 14/322; SZ244952; NP 179
Milton (parish), 19/145; TR123555; NP 173
Milton Abbot (Milton Abbott) (parish), 9/351; SX422800; NP 175
Milton Abbas (parish), 10/160; ST805015; NP 178
Milton Bryan (Milton Bryant) (parish), 1/114; SP975304; NP 147
Milton Clevedon (parish), 32/200; ST669370; NP 166
Milton Damerel (parish), 9/95; SS387109; NP 174, 175
Milton Ernest (Milton Erness) (parish), 1/33; TL021561; NP 134, 147
Milton Keynes (Middleton Keynes) (parish), 3/57; SP892387; NP 146
Milton Lilbourne (Milton Lilborne) (parish), 39/199; SU188605; NP 167
Milton under Wychwood, 29/141; NP 144
Milverton (parish), 32/317; ST105253; NP 164
Milverton (parish), 37/165; SP308672; NP 132
Milwich (parish), 33/126; SJ978330; NP 119, 120
Min-y-llyn, 54/102; NP 117
Minall (parish), 39/179; NP 157
Minchinhampton (parish), 13/307; SO873011; NP 156
Mindrum (township in Carham), 27/35; NT835335; NP 64
Midtown (parish), 31/368; NP 174
Minehead (parish), 32/89; SS948470; NP 164
Minera (township in Wrexham [Wrecsam]), 49/50; SJ267526; NP 108, 109
Minety (Minty) (division formerly in Gloucestershire in Minety), 39/1A; SU023912; NP 157
Minety (Minty) (division in Minety), 39/1B; SU009911; NP 157
Minety (Minty) (parish), 39/1A-B; NP 157
Miningsby (division in Miningsby), 22/442A; TF321641; NP 114
Miningsby (parish), 22/442A-B; NP 114
Miningsby - West Fen (division in Miningsby), 22/442B; TF311582; NP 114
Minsden and Langley (Missenden) (hamlet in Hitchin), 16/39; TL206231; NP 147
Minshull Vernon (township in Middlewich), 5/207; SJ682606; NP 110
Minskip (township in Aldborough), 43/132; SE390647; NP 91
Minstead (division in Minstead), 14/304A; SU287106; NP 179, 180
Minstead (parish), 14/304A-D; NP 179, 180
Minster (Minster in Sheppey) (parish), 19/97; TQ942719; NP 172
Minster (Minster in Thanet) (parish), 19/237; TR324645; NP 173
Minster (parish), 6/21; SX112880; NP 174, 185, 186
Minster Lovell (parish), 29/151; SP322112; NP 145, 158
Minster Yard (extra-parochial), 43/3; SE603523; NP 97/1
Minster Yard with Bedern (Beddern) (extra-parochial), 43/4; SE604523; NP 97/1
Minsterley (township in Westbury), 31/322; SJ368048; NP 118

Minsterworth (parish), 13/145; SO789171; NP 143
Mint Yard (extra-parochial), 43/39; SE601520; NP 97/1
Minterne Magna (Mintern Magna) (parish), 10/99; ST662059; NP 178
Minterne Parva (tithing in Buckland Newton), 10/153; ST670045; NP 178
Minting (parish), 22/366; TF178738; NP 105, 113
Mintlyn (parish), 25/287; TF659189; NP 124
Minty, 39/1A-B; NP 157
Minwear (Minwere) (parish), 55/111; SN049129; NP 151
Minworth (township in Curdworth), 37/31; SP152917; NP 131
Mirfield (parish), 43/578; SE208198; NP 96, 102
Miserden (Miserdine) (parish), 13/247; SO918092; NP 143, 156, 157
Missenden, 16/39; NP 147
Misson (parish), 28/3; SK690965; NP 103
Misterton (parish), 21/343; SP570840; NP 132
Misterton (parish), 28/7-8; NP 103, 104
Misterton (township in Misterton), 28/7; SK757949; NP 103, 104
Misterton (parish), 32/481; ST457080; NP 177
Mistley (parish), 12/105; TM112300; NP 150
Mitbourn, 39/26A-B; NP 157
Mitcham (parish), 35/43; TQ282689; NP 170
Mitchel Troy (parish), 53/20; SO500100; NP 142, 155
Mitcheldean (Mitchell-Dean) (parish), 13/150; SO665193; NP 143
Mitchell-Dean (parish), 13/150; NP 143
Mitchelmersh (parish), 14/213; NP 168
Mitford (parish), 27/401-411; NP 77, 78
Mitford (township in Mitford), 27/408; NZ168848; NP 78
Mitton (division in township of Little Mitton in Whalley), 20/241; SD722386; NP 95
Mitton (parish), 43/288-294; NP 95
Mitton (township in Penkridge), 33/238; SJ880150; NP 119
Mixbury (parish), 29/71; SP610334; NP 145
Moat (Moat Quarter) (township in Kirkandrews upon Esk), 7/11; NY409741; NP 76
Mobberley (parish), 5/101; SJ792807; NP 101
Moccas (parish), 15/201; SO356427; NP 142
Mochdre (Mochtre) (parish), 54/163; SO065862; NP 128
Mochtre, 54/163; NP 128
Modbury (parish), 9/448; SX664518; NP 187
Moddershall (township in Stone), 33/59; SJ930370; NP 119
Modrydd (hamlet in Llanspyddid), 45/55; SO004230; NP 141
Moelfeliarth (township in Llangadfan), 54/25; SH958182; NP 117
Moelfeliarth (township in Llangadfan), 54/27; SJ001124; NP 117
Moelfre (township in Llansilin), 49/128; SJ196286; NP 117
Moggerhanger (Muggerhanger) (hamlet in Blunham), 1/41; TL144497; NP 147
Moilgrove (parish), 55/20; NP 139
Molash (Moldash) (parish), 19/148; TR028256; NP 172
Mold (Yr Wyddgrug) (parish), 50/107-119; NP 108
Mold (Yr Wyddgrug) (township in Mold), 50/111; SJ238640; NP 108
Moldash (parish), 19/148; NP 172
Molescroft (Molscroft) (township in St John Beverley), 41/296; TA025411; NP 99
Molesden (township in Mitford), 27/409; NZ143842; NP 78
Molesworth (parish), 17/47; TL072770; NP 134
Molland (parish), 9/77; SS811283; NP 163, 164
Mollington (chapelry in Cropredy), 29/10, 37/267; NP 145
Mollington (division in Cropredy), 29/10; SP444479; NP 145
Mollington (chapelry in Cropredy), 29/10, 37/267; NP 145
Mollington (division in Cropredy), 37/267; SP431473; NP 145
Molscroft, 41/296; NP 99
Monachlog-ddu (parish), 55/45
Monewden (parish), 34/364; TM238584; NP 137, 150
Moneylaws (township in Carham), 27/33; NT880358; NP 64
Mongewell (parish), 29/310; SU648868; NP 158, 159
Monington (parish), 55/5; SN137443; NP 139
Monk Bretton (Monk Burton) (township in Royston), 43/685; SE370076; NP 102
Monk Burton, 43/685; NP 102

Monk Fryston (parish), 43/461-463; NP 97
Monk Fryston (township in Monk Fryston), 43/462; SE511298; NP 97
Monk Hesleden (Monk-Hesleton) (township in Monk Hesleden), 11/94; NZ459383; NP 85
Monk Sherborne (Monk Sherbourne, West Sherborne) (parish), 14/51; SU605560; NP 168
Monk Soham (parish), 34/252; TM210655; NP 137
Monken Hadley (Hadley) (parish), 24/86; TQ258972; NP 160
Monkhill (division in township of Pontefract in Pontefract), 43/626; SE462227; NP 97
Monkhopton (parish), 31/495; SO620930; NP 129, 130
Monkland (parish), 15/64; SO451579; NP 129
Monkleigh (parish), 9/61; SS455218; NP 163
Monknash (parish), 51/162; SS921705; NP 154
Monkokehampton (parish), 9/185; SS584055; NP 175
Monkridge (Monkridge Ward) (township in Elsdon), 27/242; NY935895; NP 77
Monkroyd and Barnside (division in township of Foulridge in Whalley), 20/268; SD931418; NP 95
Monks Coppenhall (township in Coppenhall), 5/244; SJ697557; NP 110
Monks Eleigh (parish), 34/417; TL970475; NP 149
Monks Horton (parish), 19/395; TR124400; NP 173
Monks House (extra-parochial), 27/86; NU204335; NP 64
Monks Kirby (hamlet in Monks Kirby), 37/111; SP471849; NP 132
Monks Kirby (parish), 21/238, 37/110-116; NP 132
Monks Liberty (extra-parochial), 22/496; SK992712; NP 113
Monks Risborough (parish), 3/184; SP851049; NP 159
Monks Risbridge (extra-parochial), 34/328; TL714507; NP 148
Monkseaton (township in Tynemouth), 27/492; NZ343719; NP 78
Monksilver (parish), 32/254; ST070378; NP 164
Monkswood (parish), 53/48; SO347029; NP 155
Monkton (division in Hebburn, Monkton and Jarrow township in Jarrow), 11/5; NZ325634; NP 78
Monkton (division inside borough of Pembroke in Monkton), 55/151; SM977013; NP 151
Monkton (division outside borough of Pembroke in Monkton), 55/152; SM950000; NP 151
Monkton (parish), 9/228; ST188025; NP 176, 177
Monkton (parish), 19/124; TR284652; NP 173
Monkton (parish), 55/151-152; NP 151
Monkton Combe (parish), 32/40; ST774623; NP 166
Monkton Deverill (parish), 39/278; ST866358; NP 166
Monkton Farleigh (parish), 39/121; ST809649; NP 156, 166
Monkwearmouth (parish), 11/13-18; NP 78
Monkwearmouth (township in Monkwearmouth), 11/14; NZ401585; NP 78
Monkwearmouth Shore (township in Monkwearmouth), 11/15; NZ402581; NP 78
Monmouth [Trefynwy] (parish), 53/17; SO500130; NP 142
Monnington on Wye (Monnington upon Wye) (parish), 15/113; SO370438; NP 142
Montacute (parish), 32/464; ST497171; NP 177
Montford (parish), 31/148; SJ420162; NP 118
Montgomery (Trefaldwyn) (parish), 54/186; SO220970; NP 128
Monton (division in township of Barton upon Irwell in Eccles), 20/554; SJ776996; NP 101
Monxton (parish), 14/86; SU309433; NP 168
Monyash (township in Bakewell), 8/99; SK148665; NP 111
Moor (moor, common to Grewelthorpe and Kirkby Malzeard townships in Kirkby Malzeard), 43/202; SE179748; NP 91
Moor (township in Hawarden), 50/10; SJ328663; NP 109
Moor Crichel (Moore Crichell) (parish), 10/78; ST988090; NP 179
Moor Monkton (parish), 43/51-52; NP 97
Moor Monkton (township in Moor Monkton), 43/51; SE513561; NP 97
Moor Town (township in Brandesburton), 41/347; TA110503; NP 99
Moor, 5/150; NP 100

Moorby (division in Moorby), 22/444A; TF291644; NP 114
Moorby (parish), 22/444A-B; NP 114
Moorby - Wildmore Fen (division in Moorby), 22/444B; TF239552; NP 114
Moore (Moor) (township in Runcorn), 5/150; SJ575850; NP 100
Moore Crichell (parish), 10/78; NP 179
Moorgreen (township in Greasley), 28/172; SK483481; NP 112
Moorhay Lodge (extra-parochial), 26/46; SP996930; NP 134
Moorhouse (Moor-House) (township in Burgh by Sands), 7/103; NY326567; NP 75, 76
Moorhouse (township in Houghton-le-Spring), 11/63; NZ310459; NP 85
Moorhouse (township in Laxton), 28/106; SK753668; NP 112
Moorhouses (hamlet in Revesby), 22/457; TF282567; NP 114
Moorlinch (hamlet in Moorlinch), 32/210; ST402365; NP 165
Moorlinch (parish), 32/210-215; ST402365; NP 165
Moorsbarrow cum Parme (township in Middlewich), 5/202; SJ746650; NP 110
Moorsholm cum Girrick (township in Skelton), 42/349-351; NP 86
Moorsley (township in Houghton-le-Spring), 11/64; NZ343461; NP 85
Moorwenstow (Moorwinstow) (parish), 6/1; SS231149; NP 174
Moorwinstow, 6/1; NP 174
Moorwood (division in township of Bradfield in Ecclesfield), 43/806; SK242873; NP 102
Moot Hall (extra-parochial), 27/272; NZ251638; NP 78/1
Morborne (Morborn) (parish), 17/14; TL139915; NP 134
Morchard Bishop (Morchards Bishop) (parish), 9/181; SS774075; NP 163, 175, 176
Morcott (parish), 30/48; SK920010; NP 122, 133
Morden (division in Morden), 10/200A; SY907930; NP 178, 179
Morden (parish), 10/200A-B; NP 178, 179
Morden (parish), 35/42; TQ251675; NP 170
Morden, 11/236; NP 85
Mordiford (parish), 15/173; SO581384; NP 142
Mordon (Morden) (township in Sedgefield), 11/236; NZ331265; NP 85
More (The More) (parish), 31/364; SO340940; NP 129
Morebath (parish), 9/131; SS960252; NP 164
Moreby (division in township of Stillingfleet and Moreby in Stillingfleet), 41/60; SE603428; NP 97
Moreleigh (Morley) (parish), 9/444; SX753527; NP 187
Moresby (township in Moresby), 7/325; NX999201; NP 82
Morestead (parish), 14/234; SU519262; NP 168
Moreton (parish), 10/276; SY796891; NP 178
Moreton (parish), 12/256; TL544073; NP 161
Moreton (township in Hanbury), 33/203; SK150299; NP 120
Moreton Above (township in Ruabon), 49/89; SJ288468; NP 108, 109
Moreton Above (township in Ruabon), 49/90; SJ279456; NP 108, 109, 118
Moreton Anglicorum (township in Ruabon), 49/87; SJ326454; NP 109, 118
Moreton Below (township in Ruabon), 49/86; SJ314453; NP 109, 118
Moreton Corbet (parish), 31/163; SJ546240; NP 118
Moreton cum Alcumlow (township in Astbury), 5/236; SJ843596; NP 110
Moreton cum Lingham (township in Bidston), 5/449; SJ261902; NP 100
Moreton in Marsh (Moreton in the Marsh) (parish), 13/86; SP210318; NP 144
Moreton in the Marsh (parish), 13/86; NP 144
Moreton Jeffries (Morton Jeffreys, Moreton Jeffreys) (parish), 15/152; SO606482; NP 142, 143
Moreton Morrell (parish), 37/258; SP310555; NP 132, 145
Moreton on Lugg (Morton on Lugg) (parish), 15/123; SO502462; NP 142
Moreton Pinkney (Moreton Pinckney) (parish), 26/328; SP568488; NP 145
Moreton Say (parish), 31/14-18; NP 119
Moreton Say (township in Moreton Say), 31/16; SJ636349; NP 119

Moreton Valence (parish), 13/264; SO787087; NP 143, 156
Moretonhampstead (parish), 9/383; SX758869; NP 175
Morfodion (township in Llanidloes), 54/140; SN977854; NP 128
Morice (district in Stoke Damerel), 9/457; SX451549; NP 187/1
Morland (parish), 38/10-17; NP 83
Morland (township in Morland), 38/13; NY602228; NP 83
Morley (parish), 8/204-205; NP 112, 121
Morley (township in Morley), 8/204; SK398412; NP 121
Morley (township in Batley), 43/587; SE260270; NP 96
Morley St Botolph (parish), 25/657; TG062000; NP 136
Morley St Peter (parish), 25/656; TM063987; NP 136
Morley, 9/444; NP 187
Morningthorpe (Mourningthorpe) (parish), 25/641; TM218929; NP 137
Morpeth (parish), 27/412-420; NP 78
Morpeth (township in Morpeth), 27/414; NZ199866; NP 78
Morpeth Castle (township in Morpeth), 27/416; NZ209856; NP 78
Morralee (township in parochial chapelry of Haydon in Warden), 27/598; NY805640; NP 77
Morrell Roding (Morrell Roothing) (hamlet in White Roding), 12/204; TL566149; NP 148
Morrick, 27/225; NP 71
Morston (parish), 25/24; TG006437; NP 125
Mortehoe (Morthoe) (parish), 9/1; SS468435; NP 163
Morthoe, 9/1; NP 163
Mortimer West End (tithing in Stratfield Mortimer), 14/1; SU635640; NP 168
Mortlake (parish), 35/29; TQ197755; NP 170
Morton (extra-parochial), 22/533; SK886640; NP 113
Morton (hamlet in Morton), 22/708; TF130240; NP 123
Morton (Morton Grange) (township in Houghton-le-Spring), 11/59; NZ316499; NP 78, 85
Morton (parish), 8/134; NP 111, 112
Morton (parish), 22/707-708; NP 123
Morton (parish), 28/158; SK722515; NP 112
Morton (township in Morton), 8/134; SK410608; NP 111, 112
Morton (township in Gainsborough), 22/130; SK919809; NP 104
Morton (township in Oswestry), 31/113; SJ304241; NP 118
Morton (township in Ormesby), 42/332; NZ552149; NP 86
Morton (township in Bingley), 43/361; SE090430; NP 96
Morton Bagot (parish), 37/181; SP111645; NP 131
Morton Jeffreys (parish), 15/152; NP 142, 143
Morton on Lugg (parish), 15/123; NP 142
Morton on the Hill (Morton) (parish), 25/348; TG124162; NP 125
Morton Palms (township in Haughton le Skerne), 11/330; NZ333149; NP 85
Morton Tinmouth (Morton, Morton Tynemouth) (township in Gainford), 11/306; NZ188210; NP 85
Morton upon Swale, 42/218; NP 91
Morton-on-Swale (Morton upon Swale) (township in Ainderby Steeple), 42/218; SE324907; NP 91
Morvah (parish), 6/210; SW411353; NP 189
Morval (parish), 6/102; SX280580; NP 186
Morvil (Morville) (parish), 55/40; SN044313; NP 138
Morville (parish), 31/492-493; NP 130
Morville (township in Morville), 31/492; SO674944; NP 130
Morwick (division in township of Barwick in Elmet in Barwick in Elmet), 43/416; SE362371; NP 96
Morwick (Morrick) (township in Warkworth), 27/225; NU232037; NP 71
Mosedale (township in Caldbeck), 7/211; NY340330; NP 82, 83
Moseley (division in King's Norton), 40/44; SP071819; NP 131
Moss (township in Campsall), 43/644; SE600138; NP 103
Moss Side (township in Manchester), 20/523; SD840958; NP 101
Moss-houses and Waltham-Hill, 20/8; NP 88
Mossdale Moor (undivided moor, common to Hawes and Bainbridge townships in Aysgarth), 42/134A; SD800900; NP 90
Mosser (township in Brigham), 7/271; NY118243; NP 82
Mosterton (parish), 10/107; ST455058; NP 177
Moston (township in St Mary on the Hill, Chester), 5/526; SJ401703; NP 109
Moston (township in Warmingham), 5/226; SJ725619; NP 110

Moston (township in Manchester), 20/512; SD880020; NP 101
Moston (township in Stanton upon Hine Heath), 31/202; SJ568261; NP 118
Motcombe (parish), 10/4; ST847255; NP 166
Motherby and Gill (township in Greystoke), 7/201; NY433293; NP 83
Mottingham (extra-parochial), 19/20; TQ420724; NP 171
Mottisfont (parish), 14/215; SU320272; NP 168
Mottistone (Mottiston) (parish), 18/9; SZ409836; NP 180
Mottram (Mottram in Longdendale) (parish), 5/1-9; NP 101, 102
Mottram (Mottram in Longdendale) (township in Mottram), 5/5; SJ994952; NP
Mottram St Andrew (township in Prestbury), 5/41; SJ880786; NP 101
Mouldsworth (township in Tarvin), 5/384; SJ503707; NP 109
Moulsford (parish), 2/121; SU577833; NP 158
Moulsoe (parish), 3/48; SP908417; NP 146
Moulton (parish), 22/773; TF305235; NP 123
Moulton (parish), 25/460; TG402068; NP 126
Moulton (parish), 26/225; SP779670; NP 133
Moulton (parish), 34/213; TL690649; NP 135
Moulton (township in Davenham), 5/181; SJ655692; NP 110
Moulton (township in Middleton Tyas), 42/87; NZ250040; NP 85, 91
Moulton Park (extra-parochial), 26/224; SP769646; NP 133
Moulton St Michael (parish), 25/751; TM169902; NP 137
Moundsley (division in King's Norton), 40/43; SP065785; NP 131
Mount Bures (parish), 12/96; TL910320; NP 149
Mount Healey (township in Rothbury), 27/266; NU069006; NP 71
Mount, 46/101; NP 139
Mountfield (parish), 36/138; TQ734205; NP 183, 184
Mountnessing (parish), 12/294; TQ649966; NP 161
Mounton (parish), 53/97; ST512931; NP 155
Mounton (parish), 55/113; SN081125; NP 151, 152
Mountsorrel, North End (township in Barrow upon Soar), 21/51; SK576150; NP 121
Mountsorrel, South End (township in Rothley), 21/52B; SK585145; NP 121
Mourningthorpe (parish), 25/641; NP 137
Mousehold Heath, 25/405; TG241101; NP 126
Mousen (Mowson) (township in Bamburgh), 27/92; NU122320; NP 64
Mown Rakes (extra-parochial), 22/741; TF448212; NP 114, 123
Mowsley (chapelry in Knaptoft), 21/336; SP644885; NP 132
Mowson, 27/92; NP 64
Mowthorpe (division in township of Terrington with Wiganthorpe in Terrington), 42/651; SE683689; NP 92
Moydog (township in Castle Caereinion), 54/60; SJ167081; NP 117
Moylgrove (Moilgrove) (parish), 55/20; SN120440; NP 139
Mucclestone (parish), 31/1-4, 33/153-157; NP 119
Much Birch (parish), 15/241; SO506304; NP 142
Much Cowarne (parish), 15/163; SO626470; NP 142, 143
Much Dewchurch (parish), 15/189; SO475310; NP 142
Much Hadham (Great Hadham) (parish), 16/74; TL433189; NP 148
Much Hoole (parish), 20/342-343; NP 94
Much Hoole (township in Much Hoole), 20/343; SD474223; NP 94
Much Marcle (hamlet in Much Marcle), 15/284; SO650326; NP 143
Much Wenlock (parish), 31/449-454, 456-457; NP 118, 119
Much Wenlock (Wenlock) (township in Much Wenlock), 31/452; SO621998; NP 119, 129, 130
Much Woolton (Great Woolton) (division in township of Much Woolton in Childwall), 20/644; SJ427862; NP 100
Much Woolton (township in Childwall), 20/643-644; NP 100
Muchelney (parish), 32/405; ST435246; NP 177
Mucking (parish), 12/431; TQ682810; NP 161, 171
Muckleston (Mucclestone) (parish), 31/1-4, 33/153-157; NP 119
Mucklestone (Mucclestone, Muckleston) (township in Mucklestone), 33/15; SJ731373; NP 119

Mucklewick (township in Hyssington), 31/347; SO330964; NP 129
Muckton (parish), 22/294; TF378818; NP 105
Mudford (parish), 32/394; ST571199; NP 177
Muggerhanger, 1/41
Mugginton (parish), 8/218-221; NP 120, 121
Mugginton (township in Mugginton), 8/220; SK291441; NP 120, 121
Muggleswick (parish), 11/165-166; NP 77, 84
Muggleswick (township in Muggleswick), 11/166; NZ069466; NP 84
Muker (division in township of Muker in Grinton), 42/121; SD902965; NP 90
Muker (township in Grinton), 42/119-128; NP 84, 90
Mulbarton (parish), 25/565; TG198008; NP 126, 137
Mullion (parish), 6/192; SW683174; NP 189, 190
Mumby (parish), 22/410-411; NP 105, 114
Mumby (township in Mumby), 22/410; TF520740; NP 105, 114
Muncaster (parish), 7/313; SD120971; NP 88
Mundesley (parish), 25/45; TG305366; NP 126
Mundford (parish), 25/702; TL802930; NP 136
Mundham (parish), 25/594; TM333971; NP 137
Mundon (parish), 12/347; TL887032; NP 162
Mungrisdale (township or chapelry in Greystoke), 7/207; NY343296; NP 82, 83
Munlyn (Min-y-llyn) (township in Forden), 54/102; SJ214007; NP 117
Munsley (parish), 15/275; SO664408; NP 143
Munslow (parish), 31/501A-B; NP 129
Munslow (township in Munslow), 31/501A; SO523880; NP 129
Mursley (parish), 3/94; SP819290; NP 146
Murston (parish), 19/105; TQ926654; NP 172
Murton (extra-parochial), 42/498; SE535875; NP 92
Murton (township in Tynemouth), 27/495; NZ330708; NP 78
Murton (township in St Michael Appleby or Bongate), 38/42; NY744238; NP 83, 84
Murton (township in Osbaldwick), 42/672; SE651526; NP 97
Murton, 11/84; NP 85
Musbury (parish), 9/291; SY284950; NP 177
Musbury (township in Bury), 20/413-415; NP 101
Musbury Heights (division in township of Musbury in Bury), 20/414; SD756220; NP 101
Musbury Park (division in township of Musbury in Bury), 20/413; SD772206; NP 95, 101
Muscoates (division in Muscoates township Kirkdale), 42/476A; SE691803; NP 92
Muscoates (township in Kirkdale), 42/476A-B; 92
Musden Grange (extra-parochial), 33/93; SK121503; NP 111
Musden Head (division in township of Musbury in Bury), 20/415; SD758204; NP 101
Muston (parish), 21/90; SK827382; NP 122
Muston (parish), 41/164; TA097798; NP 93
Mutford (parish), 34/22; TM484885; NP 137
Mwnt (Mount) (parish), 46/101; SN210517; NP 139
Myddfai (parish), 47/19A-B; NP 140
Myddle (Middle) (parish), 31/152-157; NP 118
Myddle (Middle) (township in Myddle), 31/152; SJ461241; NP 118
Myddleton, 20/603; NP 101
Mydrim, 47/60; NP 152
Myerscough (township in Lancaster), 20/136; SD500390; NP 94
Mylor (parish), 6/178; SW804363; NP 190
Mynachlog-ddu (Monachlog-ddu) (parish), 55/45; SN145305; NP 139
Mynachty (hamlet in Llanycrwys), 47/4B; SN620440; NP 140
Myndtown (Mindtown) (parish), 31/368; SO389893; NP 129
Mynyddislwyn (parish), 53/70A-C; NP 154
Mynyddmaen (hamlet in Mynyddislwyn), 53/70B; ST190990; NP 154
Mystyrrhoes-Howdy (township in Llanddewi Ystradenny), 56/30A; SO090690; NP 128
Mythe (The Mythe) (extra-parochial), 21/161; SP313993; NP 132

Myton (division in parish and township of Holy Tinity Kingston upon Hull), 41/326-327; NP 99/1
Myton upon Swale (parish), 42/579; NP 91
Myton-on-Swale (Myton upon Swale) (parish), 42/579; SE447668; NP 91

N

Naburn (division of Naburn township in Acaster Malbis), 41/62; SE609457; NP 97
Naburn (division of Naburn township in Naburn), 41/63; SE603452; NP 97
Naburn (township in Acaster Malbis and Naburn), 41/62-63
Nackington (parish), 19/286; TR155548; NP 173
Nacton (parish), 34/457; TM213406; NP 150
Nafferton (township in Ovingham), 27/555; NZ065660; NP 77
Nafferton (parish), 41/272-273; NP 99
Nafferton (township in Nafferton), 41/272; TA055590; NP 99
Nafford and Birlingham (parish), 40/218; NP 143
Nailsea (parish), 32/12; ST461699; NP 155, 165
Nailstone (parish), 21/147-149; NP 121
Nailstone (township in Nailstone), 21/147; SK419072; NP 121
Nannerch (parish), 49/33; 50/96-98; NP 108
Nant Prestatyn (township in Meliden), 50/53; SJ070828; NP 108
Nant-ddu (chapelry in Cantref), 45/52B; SO005165; NP 141
Nant-y-meichaid (township in Meifod), 54/35; SJ147172; NP 117
Nantcwnlle (parish), 46/52; SN580597; NP 140
Nantforch (township in Castle Caereinion), 54/58; SJ144066; NP 117
Nantglyn (parish), 49/28; SH978586; NP 108
Nantmel (parish), 56/31A-C; NP 128
Nantmor (township in Beddgelert), 52/1; SH625475; NP 116
Nantwich (parish), 5/247-251; NP 110
Nantwich (township in Nantwich), 5/250; SJ651522; NP 110
Nappa (township in Gisburn), 43/302; SD860528; NP 95
Napton on the Hill (parish), 37/241; SP462611; NP 132
Narberth (parish), 55/114-116; NP 151, 152
Narberth North (division in Narberth), 55/115; SN108148; NP 151, 152
Narberth South (division in Narberth), 55/116; SN110120; NP 152
Narborough (parish), 21/212-213; NP 121, 132
Narborough (township in Narborough), 21/213; SP535981; NP 121, 132
Narborough (Narburgh) (parish), 25/324; TF752113; NP 124, 125
Narburgh (parish), 25/324; NP 124, 125
Narford (parish), 25/325; TF774127; NP 125
Narthalam (township in Llanfyllin), 54/15; SJ102190; NP 117
Naseby (parish), 26/120; SP685785; NP 132, 133
Nash (extra-parochial), 51/121; SS962730; NP 154
Nash (hamlet in Whaddon), 3/74; SP778343; NP 146
Nash (parish), 53/153; ST350840; NP 155
Nash (parish), 55/145, 147; NP 151
Nash (township in Burford), 31/541A; SO590710; NP 129, 130
Nassington (parish), 26/42; TF046963; NP 123
Nateby (township in Garstang), 20/156; SD465455; NP 94
Nateby (township in Kirkby Stephen), 38/62; NY791060; NP 84, 90
Nately Scures (parish), 14/107; SU706532; NP 169
Natland (township in Kendal), 38/92; SD524895; NP 89
Naughton (parish), 34/98; TM026486; NP 149
Naunton (parish), 13/104; SP120230; NP 144
Naunton Beauchamp (parish), 40/144; SO966524; NP 143
Navenby (parish), 22/552; SK984578; NP 113
Navestock (parish), 12/301; TQ540970; NP 161
Naworth (township in Brampton), 7/54; NY552617; NP 76
Nawton (township in Kirkdale), 42/479; SE653857; NP 92
Nayland (parish), 34/498; TL965345; NP 149
Nazeing (parish), 12/264; TL403062; NP 161
Near Oxenhope (division in township of Haworth in Bradford), 43/525; SE021354; NP 95, 96
Neasham (township in Hurworth), 11/327; NZ334107; NP 85
Neat Enstone (hamlet in Enstone), 29/95; SP368247; NP 145

Neath (parish), 51/51; SS757970; NP 153
Neath Higher (hamlet in Cadoxton Juxta Neath), 51/17; SN875080; NP 153, 154
Neath Lower (hamlet in Cadoxton Juxta Neath), 51/19; SN805020; NP 153
Neath Middle (hamlet in Cadoxton Juxta Neath), 51/18; SN840060; NP 153
Neatham (tithing in Holybourne), 14/126; SU744404; NP 169
Neatishead (parish), 25/369; TG337197; NP 126
Necton (parish), 25/509; TF882100; NP 125
Nedging (hamlet in Nedging), 34/402; TM008490; NP 149
Needham (parish), 25/767; TM223817; NP 137
Needham Market (hamlet in Barking), 34/292; TM089548; NP 149
Neen Savage (parish), 31/549; SO682782; NP 130
Neen Sollars (parish), 31/546; SO660720; NP 130
Neenton (parish), 31/559; SO643883; NP 130
Nefyn (Nevin) (parish), 48/59; SH307406; NP 115
Neithrop (township in Banbury), 29/17; SP446406; NP 145
Nempnett Thrubwell (Nempnett) (parish), 32/58; ST525615; NP 165
Nenthead (township in Alston), 7/176; NY780440; NP 83
Nercwys (Nerquis) (township in Mold), 50/115; SJ228598; NP 108
Nerquis, 50/115; NP 108
Nesbit (township in Doddington), 27/48; NT988342; NP 64
Nesbitt (Nesbit or Nesbit Hall) (township in Hart), 11/248; NZ456367
Nesbitt (Nesbit) (township in Stamfordham), 27/467; NZ080698; NP 77
Nesfield (division in township of Nesfield with Langbar in Ilkley), 43/339; SE098501; NP 96
Nesfield with Langbar (township in Ilkley), 43/337-340; NP 96
Ness (township in Neston), 5/480; SJ308759; NP 100, 109
Neston (parish), 5/475-482; NP 100
Neswick (township in Bainton), 41/230; SE981532; NP 98
Nether Abner (division in Marston Magna), 32/392; ST592210; NP 166
Nether Alderley (township in Alderley), 5/68; SJ839758; NP 101, 110
Nether and Upper Dean (parish), 1/2; NP 134
Nether Bradfield (sub-division in Bradfield division in township of Bradfield in Ecclesfield), 43/812; SK230930; NP 102
Nether Broughton (parish), 21/69; SK697252; NP 122
Nether Cerne (parish), 10/221; SY668984; NP 178
Nether Compton (parish), 10/33; ST602171; NP 178
Nether Denton (parish), 7/55; NY601629; NP 76
Nether Ellington, 42/170; NP 91
Nether Exe (parish), 9/219; SS938002; NP 176
Nether Graveship (township in Kendal), 38/95; SD512916; NP 89
Nether Haddon (division in township of Over and Nether Haddon in Bakewell), 8/97; SK232661; NP 111
Nether Hallam (division in township of Nether Hallam in Sheffield), 43/824; SK332887; NP 102
Nether Hallam (township in Sheffield), 43/824-825; NP 102, 111
Nether Heyford (parish), 26/256; SP657586; NP 132
Nether Hoyland, 43/855; NP 102
Nether Kellet (township in Bolton-le-Sands), 20/92; SD502682; NP 89
Nether Knutsford,
Nether Langwith (township in Norton Cuckney), 28/86; SK542705; NP 112
Nether Padley (township in Bakewell), 8/87; SK251783; NP 111
Nether Peover (township in Great Budworth), 5/129; SJ733737; NP 110
Nether Poppleton (township in Nether Poppleton), 43/49; SE561548; NP 97
Nether Quarter (township in Hartington), 8/111; SK164592; NP 111
Nether Shitlington, 43/717; NP 102
Nether Silton (division in township of Nether Silton in Leake), 42/515; SE463923; NP 91

Nether Silton (township in Leake), 42/515-516; NP 91
Nether Sitlington (Nether Shitlington) (division in township of Sitlington in Thornhill), 43/717; SE284169; NP 102
Nether Staveley (township in Kendal), 38/104; SD458972; NP 89
Nether Stavely, 38/104
Nether Stowey (parish), 32/260; ST197397; NP 164, 165
Nether Wallop (parish), 14/148; SU291363; NP 167, 168
Nether Warden (township in Warden), 27/605; NY912667; NP 77
Nether Wasdale (chapelry in St Bees), 7/291; NY140085; NP 82, 88
Nether Whitacre (parish), 37/56; SP232927; NP 131
Nether Worton (parish), 29/58; SP430302; NP 145
Nether Wyresdale (township in Garstang), 20/148; SD524498; NP 94
Netheravon (Netherhaven) (parish), 39/259; SU127478; NP 167
Netherbury (parish), 10/139; SY467976; NP 177
Netherby (Netherby Quarter) (township in Arthuret), 7/15; NY404716; NP 76
Nethercote (hamlet in Warkworth), 26/359; SP471414; NP 145
Nethercott (township in Tackley), 29/103; SP484214; NP 145
Netherhampton (parish), 39/323; SU106293; NP 167
Netherhaven (parish), 39/259; NP 167
Netherpool (township in Eastham), 5/431; SJ391782; NP 100
Netherseal (township in Seal), 21/5; SK278135; NP 120, 121
Netherthong (township in Almondbury), 43/773; SE139097; NP 102
Netherton (township in Sefton), 20/684; SJ362995; NP 100
Netherton (township in Bedlington), 27/433; NZ236820; NP 78
Netherton North Side (township in Alwinton), 27/184; NT994080; NP 71
Netherton South Side (township in Alwinton), 27/183; NT995072; NP 71
Netherton (hamlet in Cropthorne), 40/211; SP000415; NP 143, 144
Netherwitton (parish), 27/329-335; NP 71, 77
Netherwitton (township in Netherwitton), 27/335; NZ104908; NP 77
Netherwood (township in Thornbury), 15/79; SO637607; NP 130
Netley (township in Stapleton), 31/289; SJ465018; NP 118
Netteswell (parish), 12/261; TL460095; NP 148, 161
Nettlebed (parish), 29/306; SU702871; NP 159
Nettlecombe (parish), 32/253; ST053376; NP 164
Nettleden (chapelry in Pitstone), 3/133; TL001112; NP 147, 159
Nettleham (parish), 22/256; TF004752; NP 104, 113
Nettlestead (Nettlested) (parish), 19/213; TQ679512; NP 171
Nettlestead (parish), 34/398; TM091498; NP 149, 150
Nettleton (parish), 22/101; TF115989; NP 104
Nettleton (parish), 39/74; ST824792; NP 156
Netton (tithing in Durnford), 39/304; SU141365; NP 167
Nevendon (parish), 12/394; TQ731904; NP 161
Nevern (parish), 55/22; SN090370; NP 138, 139
Nevill Holt (Holt) (township in Medbourne), 21/307; SP823940; NP 133
Nevin (parish), 48/59; NP 115
New Accrington (township in Whalley), 20/298; SD771274; NP 95
New Alresford (parish), 14/168; SU584323; NP 168
New Bewick (township in Eglingham), 27/134; NU062202; NP 71
New Brentford (parish), 24/104; TQ168779; NP 170
New Buckenham (parish), 25/668; TM093903; NP 136
New Church Hir Abbot (parish), 45/31; NP 140, 141
New Fishbourne (New Fishborne) (parish), 36/247; SU842049; NP 181
New Forest (extra-parochial), 14/302A-M; NP 179, 180
New Forest (township in Kirkby Ravensworth), 42/22; NZ062052; NP 84, 90
New Hall (division in township of Barton upon Irwell in Eccles), 20/551; SJ754976; NP 101
New Hall Hey and Hall Carr (division in township of Cowpe Lench, New Hall Hey and Hall Carr in Bury), 20/410; SD814224; NP 95
New Hampton (extra-parochial), 15/96; SO586576; NP 129
New Hutton (township in Kendal), 38/116; SD570910; NP 89
New Inn (extra-parochial), 24/25; TQ307810; NP 160/1
New Leake (division in Leake), 22/761C; TF396558; NP 114
New Malton St Leonard (township in Malton), 42/643; SE788716; NP 92
New Malton St Michael (township in Malton), 42/642; SE785717; NP 92
New Marton (township in Ellesmere), 31/65; SJ339346; NP 118
New Moat (parish), 55/47; SN065245; NP 138, 139
New Moor (township in Bothal), 27/319; NZ262887; NP 78
New Parks (extra-parochial), 21/184; SK560055; NP 121
New Radnor (parish), 56/25; SO215614; NP 128
New Romney (parish), 19/428; TR045251; NP 184
New Sampford (parish), 12/58; NP 148
New Sawcock (division in township of East Harlsey in East Harlsey), 42/319; NZ401998; NP 91
New Shoreham (parish), 36/308; TQ215052; NP 182
New Sleaford (parish), 22/595-596; NP 113
New Sleaford (township in New Sleaford), 22/595; TF072467; NP 113
New Street and Davy Gate, 43/34; NP 97/1
New Village (extra-parochial), 41/22A; SE855295; NP 98/1
New Village (extra-parochial), 41/22C; SE862298; NP 98/1
New Windsor (division in New Windsor), 2/223; SU964750; NP 159, 169
New Windsor (parish), 2/22-2232; NP 159, 169
New Woodhouse (township in Whitchurch), 31/36; SJ589422; NP 118, 119
Newall (township in Davenham), 5/192; SJ700712; NP 110
Newall with Clifton (township in Otley), 43/371; SE197476; NP 96
Newark (hamlet in Peterborough, St John the Baptist), 26/5; TF210007; NP 123, 134
Newark-on-Trent (Newark-upon-Trent, Newark) (parish), 28/151; SK805545; NP 112, 113
Newbald and Dunston (township in Chesterfield), 8/74; SK365735; NP 111
Newball (hamlet in Stainton by Langworth), 22/259; TF087759; NP 104, 113
Newbiggen, 27/619; NP 77, 78
Newbiggen, 42/142; NP 90
Newbiggin (township in Dacre), 7/194; NY462300; NP 83
Newbiggin (division in township of Redworth in Heighington), 11/284; NZ220240; NP 85
Newbiggin (township in Bishopton), 11/268; NZ362186; NP 85
Newbiggin (township in Middleton in Teesdale), 11/188B; NY912299; NP 84
Newbiggin (Newbiggen) (township in Shotley), 27/619; NY933501; NP 77, 78
Newbiggin (Newbiggin-by-the-Sea) (township in Woodhorn), 27/325; NZ316883; NP 78
Newbiggin (township in Newburn), 27/537; NZ202683; NP 78
Newbiggin (parish), 38/3; NY636286; NP 83
Newbiggin (division in township of Gristhorpe in Filey), 42/404; TA103819; NP 93
Newbiggin (Newbiggen) (township in Aysgarth), 42/142; SD995848; NP 90
Newbold Astbury (township in Astbury), 5/235; SJ849608; NP 110
Newbold on Avon (Newbold upon Avon) (township in Newbold on Avon), 37/124; SP481779; NP 132
Newbold on Avon (parish), 37/123-126; NP 132
Newbold Pacey (parish), 37/223; SP305578; NP 131, 132
Newbold Revel (hamlet in Monks Kirby), 37/115; SP443802; NP 132
Newbold upon Avon (parish), 37/123-126; NP 132
Newbold upon Avon, 37/124
Newbold Verdon (parish), 21/169A-B; NP 121
Newbold Verdon (township in Newbold Verdon), 21/169A; SK446040; NP 121
Newbold, Armscote and Talton (hamlet in Tredington), 40/256; SP243457; NP 144
Newboro' with Thoney Lanes, 33/200; NP 120

Newborough (parish), 26/12; TF206051; NP 123
Newborough (Newboro' with Thoney Lanes) (township in Hanbury), 33/200; SK133257; NP 120
Newborough (Niwbwrch) (parish), 44/79; SH420655; NP 106
Newbottle (township in Houghton-le-Spring), 11/57; NZ335514; NP 78, 85
Newbottle (parish), 26/362; SP521370; NP 145
Newbourne (Newbourn) (parish), 34/268; TM270430; NP 150
Newbrough (parochial chapelry in Warden), 27/603A-604; NP 77
Newbrough (township in parochial chapelry of Newbrough in Warden), 27/604; NY860690; NP 77
Newbrough, 42/554; NP 91
Newburgh (division in township of Lathom in Ormskirk), 20/367; SD479101; NP 100
Newburgh (Newbrough) (township in Coxwold), 42/554; SE551769; NP 91
Newburn (parish), 27/531-544; NP 77, 78
Newburn (township in Newburn), 27/541; NZ160660; NP 78
Newburn Hall (township in Newburn), 27/542; NZ180650; NP 78
Newbury (parish), 2/151; SU465660; NP 158, 168
Newby (division of Newby township in Seamer), 42/298; NZ511113; NP 85
Newby (division of Newby township in Stokesley), 42/299; NZ511121; NP 85
Newby (division in township of Clapham cum Newby in Clapham), 43/275; SD720690; NP 90
Newby (township in Irthington), 7/40; NY482592; NP 76
Newby (township in Morland), 38/14; NY578198; NP 83
Newby (township in Scalby), 42/397; TA028895; NP 93
Newby (township in Seamer and Stokesley), 42/298-299; NP 85
Newby Wiske (division in township of Newby Wiske in Kirby Wiske), 42/255B; SE362881; NP 91
Newby Wiske (township in Kirby Wiske), 42/255A-B
Newby with Mulwith (township in Ripon), 43/172; SE356677; NP 91
Newcastle (parochial division in Clun), 31/385-387; NP 128, 129
Newcastle under Lyme (division in Stoke-on-Trent), 33/32; SJ844460; NP 110
Newcastle under Lyme (parish), 33/40; SJ847460; NP 110
Newcastle (parish), 51/93; NP 153, 154
Newcastle Higher (Higher Newcastle) (hamlet in Newcastle), 51/93; SS881830; NP 153, 154
Newcastle Lower (Lower Newcastle) (hamlet in Newcastle), 51/94; SS895798; NP 154
Newchurch (parish), 18/19A-B; NP 180
Newchurch - North (division in Newchurch), 18/19A; SZ574888; NP 180
Newchurch - South (division in Newchurch), 18/19B; SZ556817; NP 180
Newchurch (parish), 19/419; TR054311; NP 184
Newchurch in Rossendale (township in Whalley), 20/279-283; NP 95
Newchurch (parish), 47/43; SN390240; NP 139
Newchurch (parish), 53/86-88; NP 155
Newchurch East (division in Newchurch), 53/88; ST490980; NP 155
Newchurch West (division in Newchurch), 53/86; ST428955; NP 155
Newchurch West (division in Newchurch), 53/87; ST463969; NP 155
Newchurch West (township in Newchurch), 53/86-87; NP 155
Newchurch (parish), 56/54; SO210500; NP 141
Newdigate (parish), 35/170; TQ209415; NP 170
Newenden (parish), 19/412; TQ842280; NP 184
Newent (division in Newent), 13/127E; SO725260; NP 143
Newent (parish), 13/127A-E; SO705253; NP 143
Newfield (township in St Andrew Auckland), 11/206; NZ205335; NP 85
Newhall (division of Newhall township in Audlem), 5/274; SJ643442; NP 110, 119
Newhall (division of Newhall township in Wrenbury), 5/275; SJ615455; NP 109, 110, 119
Newhall (township in Wrenbury and Audlem), 5/274-275; NP 110, 119

Newham (division in township of Marton in Marton), 42/286; NZ511143; NP 85
Newham (township in Bamburgh), 27/98; NU176291; NP 71
Newham (township in Whalton), 27/398; NZ106766; NP 77
Newhaven (Meeching) (parish), 36/333; TQ443011; NP 183
Newhay (division in township of Drax in Drax), 43/973; SE663308; NP 97
Newholm cum Dunsley (township in Whitby), 42/380; NZ861109; NP 86
Newick (parish), 36/126; TQ421208; NP 183
Newington Bagpath (parish), 13/333; ST816948; NP 156
Newington (Newington next Hythe) (parish), 19/389; TR180383; NP 173
Newington (parish), 19/447; TQ860645; NP 172
Newington (division in Newington), 29/288; SU615961; NP 158
Newington (parish), 29/288-290; NP 158, 159
Newland (chapelry in Great Malvern), 40/169; SO800492; NP 143
Newland (division in Hurst), 2/194; SU768685; NP 169
Newland (division in township of Egton with Newland in Ulverston), 20/20; SD310810; NP 88, 89
Newland (division in township of Eastrington in Eastrington), 41/18; SE806290; NP 98/1
Newland (hamlet in Newland), 13/163A; SO553095; NP 142, 155
Newland (parish), 13/163A-164; NP 142, 155, 156
Newland (township in Drax), 43/975; SE698254; NP 97
Newland with Woodhouse Moor (extra-parochial), 43/609; SE369221; NP 96
Newland, St Lawrence (parish), 12/352; NP 162
Newlands (township in Crosthwaite), 7/283; NY220190; NP 82
Newlands (township in Bywell St Peter), 27/638; NZ080553; NP 77
Newlandside (division in township of Newlandside and Bishopley in Stanhope), 11/174; NY995379; NP 84
Newlandside and Bishopley (township in Stanhope), 11/174-175; NP 84
Newlyn East (Newlyn) (parish), 6/130; SW839564; NP 185, 190
Newmarket (Trelawnyd) (parish), 50/50-51; NP 108
Newmarket, 4/147, 34/215
Newmarket, All Saints (parish), 4/147; TL642631; NP 135
Newmarket, St Mary (parish), 34/215; TL639634; NP 136
Newminster Abbey (township in Morpeth), 27/413; NZ189860; NP 78
Newnes (township in Ellesmere), 31/62; SJ382341; NP 118
Newnham (parish), 13/173; SO683113; NP 143, 155
Newnham (parish), 14/41; SU709539; NP 169
Newnham (parish), 16/4; TL248376; NP 147
Newnham (parish), 19/232; TQ948570; NP 172
Newnham (parish), 26/251; SP585603; NP 132
Newnham Murren (parish), 29/304; SU657870; NP 158, 159
Newnham Regis (parish), 37/140; NP 132
Newport (Newport-Wallingfen) (township in Eastrington), 41/21; SE855315; NP 98/1
Newport (parish), 12/20; TL519341; NP 148
Newport (parish), 18/14; SZ500892; NP 180
Newport (parish), 31/582; SJ747192; NP 119
Newport (parish), 55/23; SN054378; NP 138
Newport Pagnell (parish), 3/47; SP882432; NP 146
Newport [Casnewydd] (borough in St Woollos), 53/124; ST310880; NP 155
Newsham (division in township of Goosnagh with Newsham in Kirkham), 20/206; SD511359; NP 94
Newsham (division in township of Temple Newsham in Whitkirk), 43/483; SE357312; NP 96
Newsham (extra-parochial), 22/68; TA131134; NP 104
Newsham (Newsome, Newsholme) (division in parish and township of Bempton), 41/247; TA189717; NP 93
Newsham (township in Egglescliffe), 11/341; NZ380120; NP 85
Newsham (township in Earsdon), 27/484; NZ312793; NP 78
Newsham (township in Barningham), 42/20; NZ101103; NP 84
Newsham (township in Kirkby Ravensworth), 42/21; NZ090090; NP 84

Newsham with Breckenbrough (township in Kirby Wiske), 42/256; SE384843; NP 91
Newsholme (division in township of Newsholme and Brind in Wressle), 41/42; SE725301; NP 97
Newsholme and Brind (township in Wressle), 41/41-42; NP 97
Newsholme (Newsome) (township in Gisburn), 43/301; SD840515; NP 95
Newsholme, 41/247; NP 93
Newsome (division in township of Spofforth with Stockeld in Spofforth), 43/98; SE372510; NP 96
Newsome, 41/247; NP 93
Newsome, 43/301; NP 95
Newstead (extra-parochial), 22/110; TA001049; NP 104
Newstead (township in Bamburgh), 27/88; NU141268; NP 71
Newstead Priory (extra-parochial), 28/166; SK535535; NP 112
Newthorpe (township in Sherburn in Elmet), 43/428; SE465321; NP 97
Newtimber (parish), 36/117; TQ273122; NP 182
Newton (chapelry in Clodock), 15/212; SO340340; NP 142
Newton (division in Newton and Biggin township in Clifton upon Dunsmore), 37/119; SP526782; NP 132
Newton (division in township of Hellifield in Long Preston), 43/243; SD850570; NP 95
Newton (Newton by Daresbury) (township in Runcorn), 5/154; SJ589812; NP 100
Newton (Newton by Frodsham) (township in Frodsham), 5/407; SJ529752; NP 100, 109
Newton (Newton in Cleveland) (township in Newton), 42/337; NZ570130; NP 86
Newton (parish), 4/2; TF428140; NP 124
Newton (parish), 4/161; TL437494; NP 148
Newton (parish), 22/798; TF054363; NP 123
Newton (parish), 26/134; SP878839; NP 133
Newton (parish), 34/487; TL922410; NP 149
Newton (parish), 51/102; NP 153
Newton (parish), 55/112; NP 151
Newton (township in Malpas), 5/318; SJ465455; NP 109
Newton (township in Middlewich), 5/198; SJ708657; NP 110
Newton (township in Mottram), 5/9; SJ954961; NP 101
Newton (township in Prestbury), 5/40; SJ881809; NP 101
Newton (township in St Oswald Chester), 5/505; SJ416679; NP 109
Newton (township in Tattenhall), 5/359; SJ499601; NP 109
Newton (township in Croft), 15/30; SO503440; NP 142
Newton (township in Manchester), 20/514; SD874001; NP 101
Newton (township in Bywell St Peter), 27/628; NZ030650; NP 77
Newton (township in Meole Brace), 31/275; SJ462106; NP 118
Newton (township in Myddle), 31/151; SJ482224; NP 118
Newton (township in Westbury), 31/321; SJ382086; NP 118
Newton (township in Blithfield), 33/194; SK042258; NP 120
Newton (township in Pickering), 42/432; SE808908; NP 92
Newton (township in Slaidburn), 43/284; SD690500; NP 95
Newton and Biggin (township in Clifton upon Dunsmore), 37/119-120; NP 120
Newton Bewley (township in Billingham), 11/258; NZ465261; NP 85
Newton Blossomville (parish), 3/34; SP922512; NP 146
Newton Bromswold (parish), 26/213; SP993655; NP 134
Newton by Daresbury, 5/154; NP 100
Newton by Frodsham, 5/407; NP 100, 109
Newton by Toft (Newton next Toft) (parish), 22/216; TF053870; NP 104
Newton by Castle Acre (Newton next Castle Acre) (parish), 25/278; TF833152; NP 125
Newton Cap (township in St Andrew Auckland), 11/203; NZ189311; NP 85
Newton cum Larton (Newton) (township in West Kirby), 5/455; SJ238878; NP 100
Newton Ferrers (parish), 9/468; SX569496; NP 187
Newton Flotman (parish), 25/603; TM212988; NP 137
Newton Grange (township in Ashbourne), 8/177; SK163538; NP 111
Newton Grange (division in township of Oswaldkirk in Oswaldkirk), 42/618; SE618798; NP 92

Newton Hall (township in Bywell St Peter), 27/629; NZ042652; NP 77
Newton Harcourt (township in Wistow), 21/324; SP638973; NP 132
Newton in Makerfield (Newton within Makerfield, Newton le Willows) (township in Winwick), 20/608; SJ590950; NP 100, 101
Newton in Cleveland, 42/337; NP 86
Newton Kyme (division in township of Newton Kyme cum Toulston in Newton Kyme), 43/72; SE462448; NP 97
Newton Kyme (parish), 43/72-73; NP 97
Newton Kyme cum Toulston (township in Newton Kyme), 43/72-73; NP 97
Newton le Willows, 20/608; NP 100, 101
Newton le Wold (parish), 22/172; NP 105
Newton Linford (parish), 21/32; SK516102; NP 121
Newton Longville (parish), 3/95; SP848314; NP 146
Newton Moor (Newton-on-the-Moor) (township in Shilbottle), 27/210; NU173053; NP 71
Newton Morrell (Newton Morrel) (township in Gilling), 42/52; NZ242096; NP 85
Newton Mulgrave (township in Lythe), 42/372; NZ777140; NP 86
Newton next Toft (parish), 22/216; NP 104
Newton next Castle Acre (parish), 25/278; NP 125
Newton North (Newton) (parish), 55/112; SN068134; NP 151
Newton Nottage (Newton) (parish), 51/102; SS830782; NP 153
Newton Park (township in Mitford), 27/405; NZ157868; NP 78
Newton Poppleford (hamlet in Aylesbeare), 9/283B; SY072891; NP 176
Newton Purcell (parish), 29/74; SP612299; NP 145
Newton Regny (Newton) (township in Newton Regny), 7/191; NY483313; NP 83
Newton Regny (parish), 7/191-2; NP 83
Newton Regis (parish), 37/2; SK280080; NP 120, 121
Newton Solney (parish), 8/312; SK283428; NP 120, 121
Newton St Cyres (district in Newton St Cyres), 9/252A; SX877976; NP 176
Newton St Petrock (parish), 9/94; SS413126; NP 174, 175
Newton St Faith (hamlet in Newton St Faith), 25/355; TG228168; NP 126
Newton St Loe (parish), 32/44; ST704644; NP 156, 166
Newton Tony (Newton Toney) (parish), 39/307; SU224402; NP 167
Newton Tracey (parish), 9/38; SS530272; NP 163
Newton Underwood (township in Mitford), 27/406; NZ146860; NP 78
Newton Unthank and Newton Bocheston (township in Ratby), 21/133; SK489050; NP 121
Newton upon Trent (parish), 22/242; SK832740; NP 104
Newton upon Derwent (township in Wilberfoss), 41/89; SE739496; NP 97
Newton upon Ouse (parish), 42/586-588; NP 91, 92, 97
Newton upon Ouse (township in Newton upon Ouse), 42/587; SE522607; NP 92, 97
Newton Valence (parish), 14/175; SU712336; NP 169, 181
Newton with Docker (division in township of Whittington in Whittington), 20/74; SD586745; NP 89
Newton with Scales (township in Kirkham), 20/200B; SD347307; NP 94
Newton within Makerfield, 20/608; NP 100, 101
Newton, 5/455; NP 100
Newton, 7/38; NP 76
Newton, 7/191; NP 83
Newton-by-the-Sea (township in Embleton), 27/147; NU235232; NP 71
Newton-le-Willows (division in township of Newton-le-Willows township in Patrick Brompton), 42/206; SE215890; NP 91
Newton-le-Willows (township in Patrick Brompton), 42/205-206; NP 91
Newton-on-the-Moor, 27/210; NP 71
Newtown (division in Calbourne), 18/3B; SZ423907; NP 180
Newtown (Newton) (township in Irthington), 7/38; NY494647; NP 76
Newtown (Newtown-near-Newbury) (parish), 14/8; SU475633; NP 168

Newtown (township in Chillingham), 27/114; NU036262; NP 71
Newtown (township in Rothbury), 27/256; NZ038996; NP 71
Newtown (township in Baschurch), 31/146; SJ429227; NP 118
Newtown (township in Wem), 31/47; SJ494301; NP 118
Newtown (Y Drenewydd) (parish), 54/167; SO115910; NP 128
Newtown or St John) (extra-parochial), 36/256; SU854047; NP 181/1
Nibthwaite (division in township of Colton in Colton), 20/55; SD298895; NP 88, 89
Nicholaston (parish), 51/40; SS512885; NP 153
Nicholforest (township in Kirkandrews upon Esk), 7/10; NY462781; NP 76
Nidd (parish), 43/149; SE303958; NP 91, 96
Nidon (extra-parochial), 32/408; ST391200; NP 177
Ninfield (parish), 36/176; TQ704119; NP 183
Niton (parish), 18/28; SZ505766; NP 180
Nitsley Fell (common to all divisions in Wolsingham except Helme Park and Thornley), 11/186; NZ095341; NP 84
Niwbwrch (parish), 44/79; NP 106
Nixons (township in Bewcastle), 7/2; NY560800; NP 76
No Man's Heath (extra-parochial), 37/1; SK291089; NP 121
No Man's Land (extra-parochial), 5/19B; SJ974865; NP 101
No Man's Land (extra-parochial), 36/344; SU997243; NP 181
No Mans Land (extra-parochial), 14/193A; SU4507297; NP 168
Noak Hill (hamlet in Romford), 12/314D; TQ550930; NP 161
Nobold (township in Meole Brace), 31/276; SJ472101; NP 118
Nocton (parish), 22/559; TF073647; NP 113
Noctorum (township in Woodchurch), 5/462; SJ286879; NP 100
Noddfa (township in Darowen), 54/126B; SH850000; NP 127
Noke (parish), 29/229; SP550130; NP 145
Nolton (parish), 55/92; SM875173; NP 138, 151
Noneley (township in Loppington), 31/51; SJ480280; NP 118
Nonington (parish), 19/280; TR254519; NP 173
Nook (township in Bellingham), 27/281; NY860840; NP 77
Norbreck (division in township of Bispham with Norbreck in Bispham), 20/177; SD315415; NP 94
Norbury (parish), 31/366-367; NP 129
Norbury (parish), 33/164-166; NP 119
Norbury (township in Marbury), 5/312; SJ557476; NP 109
Norbury (township in Stockport), 5/22; SJ929860; NP 101
Norbury (township in Norbury), 31/366; SO365926; NP 129
Norbury (township in Norbury), 33/166; SJ791229; NP 119
Norbury and Roston (parish), 8/229; SK135409; NP 120
Norham (parish), 27/6-17C; NP 64
Norham (township in Norham), 27/11; NT907466; NP 64
Norham Mains (township in Norham), 27/10; NT917487; NP 64
Norland (division of Elland with Greetland township in Halifax), 43/571; SE067224; NP 96
Norley (township in Frodsham), 5/405; SJ565729; NP 100, 109
Normacot (Normicott) (township in Stone), 33/62; SJ937414; NP 119
Normanby (parish), 22/222; NP 104
Normanby (township in Burton upon Stather), 22/22; SE883168; NP 104
Normanby (division in Normanby township in Normanby), 42/447; SE743813; NP 92
Normanby (parish), 42/445-447; NP 92
Normanby (township in Eston), 42/355; NZ540188; NP 85, 86
Normanby (township in Normanby), 42/446-447; NP 92
Normanby by Stow (Normanby) (hamlet in Stow), 22/235B; SK882930; NP 104
Normanby le Wold (Normanby on the Wolds) (parish), 22/161; TF123958; NP 104, 105
Normanby next Spital (parish), 22/222; NP 104
Normanby on the Wolds (parish), 22/161; NP 104, 105
Normanby, 22/235B; NP 104
Normanby-by-Spital (Normanby next Spital, Normanby) (parish), 22/222; SK999882; NP 104
Normandy (hamlet in Ash), 35/74; SU926524; NP 169
Normanton (parish), 8/262; SK348328; NP 121
Normanton le Heath (township in Nailstone), 21/149; SK382127; NP 121
Normanton Turville (township in Thurlaston), 21/210; SP492985; NP 121, 132
Normanton (parish), 22/602; SK963468; NP 113
Normanton on Soar (Normanton upon Soar) (parish), 28/284; SK526240; NP 121
Normanton on the Wolds (Normanton on the Woulds) (township in Plumtree), 28/271; SK620321; NP 121
Normanton upon Soar (parish), 28/284; NP 121
Normanton upon Trent (parish), 28/109; SK793688; NP 112
Normanton (parish), 30/34; SK938061; NP 122, 123
Normanton (hamlet in Durnford), 39/301; SU121411; NP 167
Normanton (parish), 43/610-612; NP 96
Normanton (township in Normanton), 43/611; SE389224; NP 96, 97
Normicott, 33/62; NP 119
North Ambersham (tithing in Steep), 36/1; SU910284; NP 181
North and Middle Littleton (parish), 40/198; SP088471; NP 144
North Anston (division in township of Anston in Anston cum Membris), 43/904; SK523846; NP 103
North Aston (township in Steeple Aston), 29/62; SP478290; NP 145
North Baddesley (parish), 14/227; SU400207; NP 168, 180
North Bailey (St Mary le Bow) (parish), 11/118; NZ275421; NP 85
North Barningham (Barningham Norwood) (parish), 25/61; TG150372; NP 125, 126
North Barrow (parish), 32/367; ST603295; NP 165, 166, 177
North Barsham (North Basham) (parish), 25/79; TF905335; NP 125
North Basham (parish), 25/79; NP 125
North Bedburn (township in St Andrew Auckland), 11/194; NZ135350; NP 84, 85
North Bemfleet (parish), 12/392; NP 161, 162
North Benfleet (North Bemfleet) (parish), 12/392; TQ764904; NP 161, 162
North Biddick (division in township of Usworth in Washington), 11/19; NZ313548; NP 78
North Bierley (township in Bradford), 43/534-535
North Bierley - East Division (division in township of North Bierley in Bradford), 43/535; SE176291; NP 96
North Bierley - West Division (division in township of North Bierley in Bradford), 43/534; SE147288; NP 96
North Bovey (parish), 9/380; SX716833; NP 175
North Bradley (parish), 39/158-159; NP 16
North Bradley (tithing in North Bradley), 39/159; ST855540; NP 166
North Brentor (district in Lamerton), 9/337; SX483820; NP 175
North Brewham (parish), 32/195; ST720372; NP 166
North Burlingham (parish), 25/455; NP 126
North Burlingham (parish), 25/456-457; NP 126
North Burton (parish), 41/222; NP 98, 99
North Burton, 41/170; NP 93
North Cadbury (parish), 32/364; ST637281; NP 166
North Carlton (parish), 22/245; SK947777; NP 104
North Carlton (township in Carlton in Lindrick), 28/25A; SK590840; NP 103
North Cave (parish), 41/200-203; NP 98, 98/1
North Cave (township in North Cave), 41/201; SE885325; NP 98
North Cerney (parish), 13/238; SP030080; NP 143, 144, 157
North Charford (parish), 14/310; SU170200; NP 167, 179
North Charlton (township in Ellingham), 27/125; NU158226; NP 71
North Cheriton (parish), 32/379; ST698258; NP 166
North Claines (division in township of Claines in Claines), 40/111B; SO857583; NP 130
North Clifton (parish), 28/116-119; NP 113
North Clifton (township in North Clifton), 28/116; SK830720; NP 113
North Cliffe (North Cliff) (township in Sancton), 41/196; SE862375; NP 98
North Coates (North Coats, North Cotes) (parish), 22/181; TF358011; NP 105
North Coats (parish), 22/181; NP 105
North Cockerington (parish), 22/188; TF380909; NP 105
North Collingham (parish), 28/125; SK836618; NP 113
North Cotes (parish), 22/181; NP 105

167

North Cove (parish), 34/24; TM466899; NP 137
North Cowton (township in Gilling), 42/48; NZ282043; NP 85, 91
North Crawley (parish), 3/40; SP932442; NP 146, 147
North Cray (parish), 19/23; TQ490718; NP 171
North Creake (parish), 25/83; TF843382; NP 125
North Curry (division in North Curry), 32/332A; ST315245; NP 177
North Curry (parish), 32/332A-B; NP 177
North Dalton (parish), 41/228; SE929522; NP 98
North Deighton (township in Kirk Deighton), 43/103; SE393517; NP 96, 97
North Dissington (township in Newburn), 27/532; NZ124726; NP 77, 78
North Duffield (township in Skipwith), 41/55; SE686373; NP 97
North Elkington (parish), 22/193; TF289908; NP 105
North Elmham (parish), 25/193; TF979222; NP 125
North Elmsall (township in South Kirkby), 43/660; SE470123; NP 103
North End (extra-parochial), 12/36B; TL790390; NP 149
North Fambridge (parish), 12/361; TQ852978; NP 162
North Ferriby (division in North Ferriby township in North Ferriby), 41/316; TA987264; NP 98, 99, 99/1
North Ferriby (division in township in Kirk Ella), 41/321; TA074275; NP 99/1
North Ferriby (parish), 41/313-316; NP 98, 99, 99/1
North Ferriby (township in North Ferriby and Kirk Ella), 41/316, 321; NP 98, 99, 99/1
North Forty Foot Drain (extra-parochial), 22/739B; NP 123
North Frodingham (parish), 41/348; TA103523; NP 99
North Gosforth (township in Gosforth), 27/509; NZ249708; NP 78
North Grimston (parish), 41/145; SE838665; NP 92
North Hales (parish), 34/59; NP 137
North Hallow (division in Hallow), 40/110A; SO813576; NP 130
North Hamlet (extra-parochial), 13/179; SO825189; NP 143/1
North Hayling (parish), 14/284; SU727029; NP 181
North Hill (Northill) (parish), 6/56; SX268765; NP 186
North Hinksey (division in North Hinksey), 2/6A; SP498045; NP 158
North Hinksey (parish), 2/6A-B; NP 158
North Holme (township in Great Edstone), 42/468; SE703811; NP 92
North Hornchurch (division in Hornchurch), 12/327A; TQ540890; NP 161
North Huish (parish), 9/369; SX716558; NP 187
North Hykeham (parish), 22/535; SK947662; NP 113
North Kelsey (division in North Kelsey), 22/112A; TA037013; NP 104
North Kelsey (parish), 22/112A-B; NP 104
North Kelsey - Caistor Moor (division in North Kelsey), 22/112B; TA081021; NP 104
North Killingholme (township in Killingholme), 22/51; TA148178; NP 99, 104, 105
North Kilvington (township in Thornton-le-Street), 42/528; SE426858; NP 91
North Kilworth (parish), 21/341; SP615839; NP 132
North Kyme (township in South Kyme), 22/585; TF162522; NP 113
North Leigh (parish), 29/189; SP386129; NP 145
North Leverton (parish), 28/42; SK787822; NP 104
North Lopham (parish), 25/741; TM040828; NP 136
North Lord's Land (division in township of Dent in Sedbergh), 43/258; SD703883; NP 89, 90
North Luffenham (parish), 30/36; SK943032; NP 122, 123
North Lynn (parish), 25/291; TF612214; NP 124
North Marden (parish), 36/233; SU806162; NP 181
North Marston (parish), 3/120; SP772227; NP 146
North Meols (parish), 20/353-354; NP 94, 100
North Meols (township in North Meols), 20/353; SD365185; NP 94, 100
North Middleton (township in Hartburn), 27/355; NZ060850; NP 77
North Middleton (township in Ilderton), 27/116; NT981238; NP 71

North Milford (division in township of Kirkby Wharfe in Kirkby Wharfe), 43/439; SE502392; NP 97
North Mimms (parish), 16/125; TL231042; NP 160
North Molton (parish), 9/32; SS737320; NP 163
North Moreton (parish), 2/74; SU560904; NP 158
North Mundham (parish), 36/275; SU873009; NP 181
North Muskham (parish), 28/129-130; NP 112, 113
North Muskham (township in North Muskham), 28/129; SK793597; NP 112, 113
North Myton (ward in Myton division in parish and township of Holy Tinity Kingston upon Hull), 41/326; TA082291; NP 99/1
North Newbald (parish), 41/197-198; NP 98
North Newbald (township in North Newbald), 41/197; SE921372; NP 98
North Newington (township in Broughton), 29/20; SP414404; NP 145
North Newnton (North Newnton and Hilcott) (parish), 39/217; SU116578; NP 167
North Nibley (parish), 13/324; ST734958; NP 156
North Ockendon (parish), 12/418; TQ588849; NP 161
North Ormsby (Nun Ormsby) (parish), 22/195; TF283930; NP 105
North Otterington (parish), 42/259-261; NP 91
North Otterington (township in North Otterington), 42/261; SE365903; NP 91
North Owersby (parish), 22/155; TF063950; NP 104
North Perrott (parish), 32/480; ST476091; NP 177
North Pertherwin, 9/346; NP 174, 186
North Petherwin (North Pertherwin) (parish), 9/346; SX268910; NP 174, 186
North Petherton (division in Middlezoy registration sub-district in North Petherton), 32/301B; ST324345; NP 165
North Petherton (division in North Petherton registration sub-district in North Petherton), 32/301A; ST297318; NP 165, 177
North Petherton (parish), 32/301A-B; NP 165, 177
North Pickenham (parish), 25/534; TF860065; NP 125
North Piddle (parish), 40/147; SO968545; NP 130, 143
North Poorton (parish), 10/141; SY519985; NP 177
North Rauceby (parish), 22/599; TF012472; NP 113
North Redditch (division of Redditch township in Tardebigge), 40/50A; SP030685; NP 131
North Reston (parish), 22/297; TF384837; NP 105
North Retford, 28/47
North Rode (township in Prestbury), 5/58; SJ888668; NP 110
North Runcton (parish), 25/309A; TF640170; NP 124
North Savernake (extra-parochial), 39/177; SU192673; NP 157
North Scale (division of Isle of Walney Sub-Division of Hawcoat Division of Dalton township in Dalton in Furness), 20/29; SD177698; NP 88
North Scarle (parish), 22/531; SK850670; NP 113
North Seaton (township in Woodhorn), 27/321; NZ298866; NP 78
North Sheffield (division of Sheffield in Sheffield), 43/828; SK348882; NP 102
North Shields (township in Tynemouth), 27/498; NZ357682; NP 78
North Shoebury (parish), 12/383; TQ940866; NP 162
North Side (district in Great Staughton), 17/98A; TL137660; NP 134
North Skirlaugh (North Skirlaugh, Rowton and part of Arnold) (township in Swine), 41/393; TA135402; NP 99
North Somercotes (parish), 22/185; TF421975; NP 105
North Stainley with Sleningford (Steninford, Sleningford) (township in Ripon), 43/191; SE295755; NP 91
North Stoke (parish), 22/793; TF919284; NP 122
North Stoke (parish), 29/311; SU618862; NP 158
North Stoke (parish), 32/23; ST706688; NP 156
North Stoke (parish), 36/218; TQ032109; NP 181, 182
North Stoneham (parish), 14/229; SU433179; NP 168, 180
North Sunderland (township in Bamburgh), 27/103; NU213313; NP 71
North Tamerton (parish), 6/11; SX301970; NP 174
North Tanton (division in township of Stokesley in Stokesley), 42/300; NZ521109; NP 85

North Tawton (district in North Tawton), 9/206; SS670015; NP 175
North Tawton (parish), 9/206-207; NP 175
North Tedworth (parish), 39/193; NP 167
North Thoresby (parish), 22/176; TF294985; NP 105
North Tidworth (North Tedworth) (parish), 39/193; SU236499; NP 167
North Tuddenham (parish), 25/500; TG061137; NP 125
North Walsham (parish), 25/215; TG280300; NP 126
North Waltham (parish), 14/96; SU563465; NP 168
North Weald Bassett (parish), 12/272; TL498051; NP 161
North Wheatley (parish), 28/37; SK765869; NP 103, 104
North Widcombe (Widcombe) (tithing in Chewton Mendip), 32/78; ST579578; NP 165
North Willingham (parish), 22/203; TF162888; NP 104, 105
North Wingfield (parish), 8/128; NP 111, 112
North Wingfield (township in North Wingfield), 8/130; SK417656; NP 112
North Witham (parish), 22/694-695; NP 122, 123
North Witham (township in North Witham), 22/694; SK929214; NP 122
North Wood (extra-parochial), 12/37; TL791396; NP 149
North Woolwich [East] (division in Woolwich), 19/13B; TQ442809; NP 161, 171
North Woolwich [West] (division in Woolwich), 19/13A; TQ429800; NP 161, 171
North Wootton (parish), 10/29; ST654147; NP 178
North Wootton (parish), 25/176; TF641251; NP 124
North Wootton (parish), 32/184; ST562418; NP 165
North Wraxall (parish), 39/76; ST819752; NP 156
Northales (parish), 34/59; NP 137
Northallerton (division in township of Northallerton in Northallerton), 42/265; SE372942; NP 91
Northallerton (parish), 42/262-269; NP 85, 91
Northallerton (township in Northallerton), 42/264-265; NP 91
Northalt (parish), 24/96; NP 160
Northam (parish), 9/45; SS446293; NP 163
Northampton, All Saints (parish), 26/232; SP754598; NP 133
Northampton, St Andrew's Priory (parish), 26/230; SP761614; NP 133
Northampton, St Giles (parish), 26/231; SP768605; NP 133
Northampton, St Peter (parish), 26/233; SP749604; NP 133
Northampton, St Sepulchre (parish), 26/229; SP753610; NP 133
Northaw (parish), 16/124; TL290027; NP 160
Northaw (parish), 24/96; NP 160
Northborough (parish), 26/16; TF156082; NP 123
Northbourne (division in Northbourne), 19/272; TR329524; NP 173
Northbourne (parish), 19/272, 277; NP 173
Northchapel (parish), 36/29; SU955293; NP 181
Northchurch (Berkhampstead St Mary) (parish), 16/141; SP969081; NP 147, 159
Northcott (hamlet in Boyton), 9/196; SX341928; NP 174
Northcourt (hamlet in Abingdon St Helen), 2/17; SU508978; NP 158, 158/1
Northen Etchells, 5/74; NP 101
Northen, 5/75; NP 101
Northenden (Northen) (parish), 5/74-75; NP 101
Northenden (Northen) (township in Northenden), 5/75; SJ824903; NP 101
Northenden Etchells (Etchells, Northen Etchells) (township in Northenden), 5/74; SJ829872; NP 101
Northfield (parish), 40/40; SO030818; NP 130, 131
Northfleet (parish), 19/31; TQ631716; NP 171
Northgate (division in township of Wakefield in Wakefield), 43/608; SE334208; NP 96, 102
Northiam (parish), 36/142; TQ828244; NP 184
Northill (hamlet in Northill), 1/68A; TL143456; NP 147
Northill (parish), 1/68A-C; NP 147
Northington (parish), 14/166; SU553372; NP 168
Northleach (parish), 13/222-223; SP123127; NP 144
Northleach (tithing in Northleach), 13/222; SP123127; NP 144
Northleigh (parish), 9/288; SY197968; NP 176, 177

Northlew (parish), 9/189; SX500999; NP 175
Northmoor (parish), 29/186; SP442027; NP 158
Northolme (parish), 22/481; NP 114
Northolt (Northalt, Northaw) (parish), 24/96; TQ130840; NP 160
Northop (Llan-eurgain) (parish), 50/17-24; NP 108, 109
Northop (Llan-eurgain) (township in Northop), 50/18; SJ250686; NP 108
Northorpe (parish), 22/121; SK895967; NP 104
Northover (parish), 32/400; ST523238; NP 177
Northowram (township in Halifax), 43/549; SE099276; NP 96
Northrepps (parish), 25/41; TG243392; NP 126
Northscleugh with Moorgate (township in Cumwhitton), 7/67; NY532491; NP 76, 83
Northway and Newton (hamlet in Ashchurch), 13/48; SO924337; NP 143
Northwich (township in Great Budworth), 5/144; SJ659739; NP 110/1
Northwich Castle (township in Great Budworth), 5/145; SJ652736; NP 110/1
Northwick and Redwick (tithing in Henbury), 13/375; ST552865; NP 155
Northwick (hamlet in Blockley), 40/244; SP164365; NP 144
Northwold (parish), 25/691; TL730977; NP 136
Northwood (division in Northwood), 18/1A; SZ484939; NP 180
Northwood (parish), 18/1A-B; NP 180
Northwood (township in Ellesmere), 31/70; SJ407382; NP 118
Northwood (township in Wem), 31/48; SJ478331; NP 118
Norton (division in parish and township of Norton), 41/127; SE801712; NP 92
Norton (Norton Colepare) (parish), 39/45; ST888841; NP 156
Norton (Norton and Lenchwick) (parish), 40/195; SP035477; NP 144
Norton (parish), 8/54; SK359820; NP 111
Norton (parish), 11/346; NZ431218; NP 85
Norton (parish), 13/118; SO856244; NP 143
Norton (parish), 16/6; TL225346; NP 147
Norton (parish), 19/158; TQ969603; NP 172
Norton (parish), 26/243; SP603639; NP 132
Norton (parish), 34/191; TL965560; NP 136
Norton (parish), 40/157; NP 143
Norton (parish), 41/125-127; NP 92
Norton (parish), 56/16; SO303676; NP 129
Norton (township in Runcorn), 5/156; SJ555834; NP 100
Norton (township in Bromyard), 15/88; SO668570; NP 130, 143
Norton (township in Norton Cuckney), 28/84; SK578718; NP 112
Norton (township in Campsall), 43/646; SE547153; NP 103
Norton and Lenchwick (parish), 40/195; NP 144
Norton Bavant (division in Longbridge Deverill Registration Subdistrict in Norton Bavant), 39/238; ST919449; NP 166, 167
Norton Bavant (division in Warminster Registration Subdistrict in Norton Bavant), 39/235; ST812445; NP 166
Norton Bavant (parish), 39/235, 238; NP 166, 167
Norton Caines (parish), 33/252; NP 120
Norton Canon (parish), 15/56; SO375480; NP 142
Norton Canes (Norton Caines, Norton under Cannock) (parish), 33/252; SK021075; NP 120
Norton Colepare (parish), 39/45; NP 156
Norton Conyers (township in Wath), 42/231; SE313768; NP 91
Norton Cuckney (parish), 28/84-87; NP 112
Norton Cuckney (township in Norton Cuckney), 28/85; SK565703; NP 112
Norton Disney (parish), 22/541; SK880595; NP 113
Norton Fitzwarren (parish), 32/315; ST192265; NP 164, 177
Norton Hawkfield (parish), 32/54; ST594654; NP 155, 156, 166
Norton in Hales (parish), 31/5; SJ698392; NP 119
Norton in the Moors (parish), 33/15-16; NP 110
Norton in the Moors (township in Norton in the Moors), 33/15; SJ900525; NP 110
Norton juxta Twycross (parish), 21/143A-B; NP 121
Norton juxta Twycross (township in Norton juxta Twycross), 21/143A; SK321070; NP 121
Norton juxta Kempsey (Norton) (parish), 40/157; SO882512; NP 143

Norton Lindsey (parish), 37/211; SP234629; NP 131
Norton Malreward (parish), 32/53; ST607655; NP 155, 156, 166
Norton Mandeville (parish), 12/282; TL590048; NP 161
Norton St Philip (parish), 32/94; ST776561; NP 166
Norton Subcourse (Norton Subcorse) (parish), 25/584; TM410996; NP 137
Norton sub Hamdon (Norton under Hamdon) (parish), 32/462; ST477161; NP 177
Norton under Hamdon (parish), 32/462; NP 177
Norton under Cannock (parish), 33/252; NP 120
Norton-le-Clay (township in Cundall), 42/573; SE400710; NP 91
Norwell (parish), 28/132-134; NP 112, 113
Norwell (township in Norwell), 28/133; SK770623; NP 112
Norwell Woodhouse (township in Norwell), 28/134; SK731630; NP 112
Norwich - All Saints (parish), 25/418; TG231080; NP 126/1
Norwich - Castle (extra-parochial), 25/422; TG232085; NP 126/1
Norwich - St Andrew (parish), 25/427; TG231087; NP 126/1
Norwich - St Augustine (parish), 25/444; TG228095; NP 126/1
Norwich - St Benedict (parish), 25/433; TG224089; NP 126/1
Norwich - St Clement (parish), 25/410; TG230102; NP 126
Norwich - St Edmund (parish), 25/442; TG233091; NP 126/1
Norwich - St Ethelred (parish), 25/415; TG236079; NP 126/1
Norwich - St George Colegate (parish), 25/436; TG230090; NP 126/1
Norwich - St George Tombland (parish), 25/425; TG233088; NP 126/1
Norwich - St Giles (parish), 25/432; TG225085; NP 126/1
Norwich - St Gregory (parish), 25/429; TG228087; NP 126/1
Norwich - St Helen (parish), 25/440; TG238091; NP 126/1
Norwich - St James (hamlet in Norwich, St James), 25/441A; TG235093; NP 126/1
Norwich - St John Maddermarket (parish), 25/428; TG229087; NP 126/1
Norwich - St John Sepulchre (parish), 25/416; TG234079; NP 126/1
Norwich - St John Timberhill (parish), 25/421; TG232082; NP 126/1
Norwich - St Julian (parish), 25/414; TG235081; NP 126/1
Norwich - St Lawrence (parish), 25/430; TG227087; NP 126/1
Norwich - St Margaret (parish), 25/431; TG227089; NP 126/1
Norwich - St Martin at Oak (parish), 25/446; TG226095; NP 126/1
Norwich - St Martin at Palace (parish), 25/439; TG235091; NP 126/1
Norwich - St Mary at Coslany (parish), 25/445; TG228091; NP 126/1
Norwich - St Michael at Coslany (parish), 25/435; TG228090; NP 126/1
Norwich - St Michael at Plea (parish), 25/426; TG232087; NP 126/1
Norwich - St Michael at Thorn (parish), 25/417; TG233081; NP 126/1
Norwich - St Paul (parish), 25/443; TG232095; NP 126/1
Norwich - St Peter Hungate (parish), 25/447; TG232089; NP 126/1
Norwich - St Peter Mancroft (parish), 25/420; TG229084; NP 126/1
Norwich - St Peter per Mountergate (parish), 25/423; TG235084; NP 126/1
Norwich - St Peter Southgate (parish), 25/413; TG238077; NP 126/1
Norwich - St Saviour (parish), 25/437; TG232092; NP 126/1
Norwich - St Simon & St Jude (parish), 25/438; TG233090; NP 126/1
Norwich - St Stephen (parish), 25/419; TG229081; NP 126/1
Norwich - St Swithun (parish), 25/434; TG226089; NP 126/1
Norwich - The Close (extra-parochial), 25/424; TG237088; NP 126/1
Norwich - Town Close, 25/448; TG221070; NP 126/1
Norwich, St James (parish), 25/441A-B; NP 126/1
Norwood (division in Hayes), 24/109; TQ132803; NP 160, 170
Norwood (division in Lambeth), 35/15; TQ320720; NP 170

Noseley (extra-parochial), 21/352; SP733986; NP 133
Nostell (extra-parochial), 43/674; SE402174; NP 102, 103
Notgrove (parish), 13/103; SP112198; NP 144
Nottingham Castle (extra-parochial in Standard Hill extra-parochial), 28/238; SK564393; NP 121/1
Nottingham, St Mary (parish), 28/233A; SK582407; NP 121/1
Nottingham, St Mary, Ann's Ward (division in Nottingham, St Mary), 28/233B; SK578412; NP 121/1
Nottingham, St Mary, Byron Ward (division in Nottingham, St Mary), 28/233A; SK582407; NP 121/1
Nottingham, St Mary, Castlec Ward (division in Nottingham, St Mary), 28/233G; SK572390; NP 121/1
Nottingham, St Mary, Exchange Ward (division in Nottingham, St Mary), 28/233F; SK577390; NP 121/1
Nottingham, St Mary, Park Ward (division in Nottingham, St Mary), 28/233D; SK567400; NP 121/1
Nottingham, St Mary, Sherwood Ward (division in Nottingham, St Mary), 28/233C; SK568407; NP 121/1
Nottingham, St Mary, St Mary Ward (division in Nottingham, St Mary), 28/233E; SK580394; NP 121/1
Nottingham, St Nicholas (division in Nottingham, St Nicholas), 28/235; SK571397; NP 121/1
Nottingham, St Peter (parish), 28/234A-C; NP 121/1
Nottingham, St Peter, Castle Ward (division in Nottingham, St Peter), 28/234A; SK573396; NP 121/1
Nottingham, St Peter, Exchange Ward (division in Nottingham, St Peter), 28/234B; SK574397; NP 121/1
Nottingham, St Peter, Park Ward (division in Nottingham, St Peter), 28/234C; SK572398; NP 121/1
Notton (township in Royston), 43/688; SE347125; NP 102
Novington (hamlet in Westmeston), 36/122; TQ370133; NP 183
Nowton (parish), 34/229; TL864612; NP 136
Nuffield (parish), 29/305; SU670880; NP 158, 159
Nun Monkton (parish), 43/120; SE492578; NP 97
Nun Ormsby (parish), 22/195; NP 105
Nunburnholme (parish), 41/102-103; NP 98
Nunburnholme (township in Nunburnholme), 41/103; SE856483; NP 98
Nuneaton (parish), 37/65; SP364922; NP 132
Nuneham Courtenay (Nuneham Courtney) (parish), 29/242; SU545991; NP 158
Nunkeeling (parish), 41/358; NP 99
Nunney (parish), 32/128; ST742450; NP 166
Nunnington (division of Nunnington township in Nunnington), 42/619; SE667793; NP 92
Nunnington (division of Nunnington township in Stonegrave), 42/620; SE668787; NP 92
Nunnington (parish), 42/619; NP 92
Nunnington (township in Nunnington and Stonegrave), 42/619-620; NP 92
Nunnykirk (township in Netherwitton), 27/334; NZ084924; NP 77
Nunridge, 27/403; NP 77, 78
Nunriding (Nunridge) (township in Mitford), 27/403; NZ134875; NP 77, 78
Nunslands (township in Weobley), 15/59; SO380537; NP 129, 142
Nunstainton (division of Woodham township in Aycliffe), 11/275; NZ312289; NP 85
Nunthorpe (township in Ayton), 42/331; NZ540140; NP 85, 86
Nunton and Bodenham (tithing in Downton), 39/357; SU151246; NP 167
Nunwick (division in township of Nunwick with Howgrave in Kirklington), 42/230; SE309794; NP 91
Nunwick (township in Simondburn), 27/437; NY888736; NP 77
Nunwick with Howgrave (township in Kirkington and Ripon), 42/229-230, 43/192; NP 91
Nunwick with Howgrave (Nunwick) (township in Ripon), 43/192; SE322752; NP 91
Nursling (parish), 14/298; SU375160; NP 180
Nursted (parish), 19/53; TQ643684; NP 171
Nutfield (parish), 35/112; TQ309488; NP 170
Nuthall (parish), 28/178-179; NP 112, 121
Nuthall (township in Nuthall), 28/179; SK515445; NP 112, 121

Nuthampstead (hamlet in Barkway), 16/17; TL410350; NP 148
Nuthurst (parish), 36/63; TQ188263; NP 182
Nuthurst (hamlet in Hampton in Arden), 37/85; SP150710; NP 131
Nutley (parish), 14/101; SU609444; NP 168
Nutwith and Roomer Common (in Masham), 42/175; SE221779; NP 91
Nyland cum Batcombe (parish), 32/147; ST461507; NP 165
Nymet Rowland (parish), 9/177; SS715083; NP 175
Nymet Tracey, 9/208; NP 175
Nympsfield (Nymphsfield) (parish), 13/330; SO809003; NP 156
Nympton St George, 9/74; NP 163
Nynehead (parish), 32/323; ST144233; NP 164

O

Oadby (parish), 21/251; SK628002; NP 121, 132
Oake (parish), 32/324; ST159253; NP 164
Oaken (township in Codsall), 33/324; SJ854027; NP 119
Oakenheadwood (division in township of Lower Booths in Whalley), 20/286; SD800228; NP 95
Oakenshaw (division in township of Cleckheaton in Birstal), 43/544; SE174274; NP 96
Oakford (parish), 9/129; SS895222; NP 164
Oakham (parish), 30/15-19; NP 122
Oakham Lord's Hold (division in Oakham), 30/18; SK859081; NP 122
Oakham, Dean's Hold (division in Oakham), 30/16; SK858092; NP 122
Oakington (hamlet in Oakington), 4/73; TL406643; NP 135
Oakington (parish), 4/73-74; NP 135
Oakley (parish), 1/32; TL011540; NP 134, 147
Oakley (parish), 3/158; SP642112; NP 145, 158
Oakley (parish), 34/84; TM163773; NP 136, 137
Oakley (tithing in Cirencester), 13/276; SO990026; NP 157
Oakley (township in Croxall), 33/221; SK193133; NP 120
Oakley (township in Mucklestone), 33/157; SJ709371; NP 119
Oakmere (township in Delamere), 5/402; SJ577696; NP 109
Oaksey (division formerly in Gloucestershire in Oaksey), 39/79B; ST998920; NP 157
Oaksey (division in Oaksey), 39/79A; ST992935; NP 157
Oaksey (parish), 39/79A-B; NP 157
Oakthorpe (township in Church Gresley), 8/334; SK328134; NP 121
Oakthorpe (township in Measham), 8/333; SK323122; NP 121
Oakthorpe (township in Measham, Church Gresley and Stretton en le Field), 8/333-335; NP 121
Oakthorpe (township in Stretton en le Field), 8/335; SK316125; NP 121
Oare (hamlet in Chieveley), 2/130; SU496747; NP 158
Oare (parish), 19/110; TR010638; NP 172
Oare (parish), 32/245; SS809464; NP 163, 164
Oborne (parish), 10/32; ST651191; NP 178
Oby (parish), 25/391B; TG411141; NP 126
Occaney (division in township of Walkingham Hill with Occaney in South Stainley), 43/143; SE353619; NP 91
Occlestone (township in Middlewich), 5/203; SJ697638; NP 110
Occold (parish), 34/176; TM160707; NP 136, 137
Ockbrook (parish), 8/281; SK423359; NP 121
Ockham (parish), 35/85; TQ077569; NP 170
Ockley (parish), 35/168; TQ155394; NP 170
Ocle Pychard (Ocle Pitchard) (parish), 15/151; SO582462; NP 142
Octon (division in parish and township of Thwing), 41/172; TA030700; NP 93
Odd Rode (township in Astbury), 5/238; SJ829579; NP 110
Oddingley (parish), 40/130; SO915590; NP 130
Oddington (parish), 13/92; SP224254; NP 144
Oddington (parish), 29/117; SP549153; NP 145
Odell (parish), 1/22; TL960590; NP 133, 134
Odestone, 21/146; NP 121
Odiham (parish), 14/39; SU741510; NP 169
Odstock (parish), 39/356; SU137147; NP 167
Odstone (Odestone) (township in Shackerstone), 21/146; SK392078; NP 121

Odstone (tithing in Ashbury), 2/104; SU274862; NP 157, 158
Offchurch (parish), 37/162; SP367656; NP 132
Offcote and Underwood (Offcote Underwood) (township in Ashbourne), 8/178; SK190480; NP 111
Offcote Underwood, 8/178; NP 111
Offenham (parish), 40/196; SP062455; NP 144
Offerton (township in Stockport), 5/17; SJ924889; NP 101
Offerton (township in Hope), 8/27; SK209813; NP 111
Offerton (township in Houghton-le-Spring), 11/54; NZ344556; NP 78
Offham (parish), 19/182; TQ656575; NP 171
Offley (parish), 16/42; TL145265; NP 147
Offleyholes (hamlet in Hitchin), 16/37; TL168263; NP 147
Offord Cluny (Offord Cluney) (parish), 17/91; TL229673; NP 134
Offord D'Arcy (Offord Darcey, Offord Darcy) (parish), 17/92; TL228658; NP 134
Offton (hamlet in Offton), 34/400; TM056492; NP 149
Offton (parish), 34/400-401; NP 149
Offwell (parish), 9/235; SY189988; NP 176, 177
Ogbourne St Andrew (Ogbourn St Andrew) (parish), 39/104; SU166736; NP 157
Ogbourne St George (parish), 39/103; SU202749; NP 157
Ogbury (hamlet in Durnford), 39/302; SU147387; NP 167
Ogle (township in Whalton), 27/397; NZ138786; NP 77, 78
Oglethorpe (division in township of Bramham cum Oglethorpe in Bramham), 43/89; Bramham cum Oglethorpe (township in Bramham), 43/88-89; NP 97
Ogley Hay (extra-parochial), 33/293; SK064059; NP 120
Okeford Fitzpaine (parish), 10/85; ST800108; NP 178
Okehampton (parish), 9/329; SX573943; NP 175
Okeover (parish), 33/95; SK158486; NP 111
Old (Wold) (parish), 26/195; SP791736; NP 133
Old Accrington (township in Whalley), 20/297; SD759292; NP 95
Old Alresford (parish), 14/167; SU600357; NP 168
Old and New Kington (township in Kington), 15/41A; SO295565; NP 128, 129, 141, 142
Old Artillery Ground (extra-parochial), 24/64A; TQ335817; NP 160/1
Old Bewick (township in Eglingham), 27/133; NU100230; NP 71
Old Bolingbroke (division in Old Bolingbroke), 22/436A; TF350650; NP 114
Old Bolingbroke (parish), 22/436A-B; TF350650; NP 114
Old Bolingbroke - West Fen (division in Old Bolingbroke), 22/436B; TF302574; NP 114
Old Brentford (chapelry in Ealing), 24/103B; TQ180780; NP 170
Old Buckenham (parish), 25/667; TM069919; NP 136
Old Byland (parish), 42/497; SE545860; NP 92
Old Castle (extra-parochial), 39/314; NP 167
Old Cleeve (parish), 32/236; ST035395; NP 164
Old Crosland (division in township of Lockwood in Huddersfield), 43/765; SE132158; NP 102
Old Dalby (parish), 21/68; SK665235; NP 121
Old Durham (division in township of St Oswald in St Oswald), 11/124; NZ292419; NP 85
Old Hurst (parish), 17/68; TL300767; NP 134
Old Hutton with Holmescales, 38/117
Old Hutton with Holmscales (township in Kendal), 38/117; SD560887; NP 89
Old Hutton, 38/117
Old Laund Booth (township in Whalley), 20/263B; SD837374; NP 95
Old Leake, 22/761A; NP 114
Old Lindley (division in township of Stainland with Old Lindley in Halifax), 43/573; SE094190; NP 102
Old Lydford, 9/333; NP 175
Old Malton (township in Malton), 42/644; SE793737; NP 92
Old Marton (township in Whittington), 31/85; SJ352343; NP 118
Old Moor (township in Bothal), 27/315; NZ246900; NP 78
Old Newton (parish), 34/238; TM055625; NP 136
Old Park (township in St Andrew Auckland), 11/209; NZ233326; NP 85
Old Radnor (parish), 56/19-24, 15/40; NP 128
Old Radnor and Burlingjobb (township in Old Radnor), 56/23; SO257583; NP 128

171

Old Romney (parish), 19/439; TR025244; NP 184
Old Sarum (Old Castle) (extra-parochial), 39/314; SU137326; NP 167
Old Shoreham (parish), 36/307; TQ216073; NP 182
Old Sleaford (parish), 22/594; TF078447; NP 113, 123
Old Sodbury (parish), 13/347; ST749818; NP 156
Old Somerby (Somerby) (parish), 22/635; SK963337; NP 122
Old Stratford (division in Old Stratford), 37/202A; SP188553; NP 131, 144
Old Stratford (division in Old Stratford), 37/203; SP168572; NP 131
Old Stratford (parish), 37/201-204; NP 131, 144
Old Street (division in St Luke), 24/48A; TQ320826; NP 160/1
Old Swinford (parish), 33/340, 40/20-24; NP 130
Old Warden (parish), 1/69; TL140442; NP 147
Old Weston (parish), 17/45; TL097778; NP 134
Old Windsor (division in Egham Registration Subdistrict of Old Windsor in Old Windsor), 2/225B; SU965715; NP 169
Old Windsor (division in Windsor Registration Subdistrict of Old Windsor in Old Windsor), 2/225A; SU982740; NP 159, 169
Old Windsor (parish), 2/225A-B; NP 159, 169
Old Withington (township in Prestbury), 5/62; SJ820720; NP 110
Oldacres (division in township of Butterwick and Oldacres in Sedgefield), 11/240; NZ391285; NP 85
Oldberrow (Oldborough) (parish), 40/46; SP112670; NP 131
Oldborough (parish), 40/46; NP 131
Oldbury (parish), 31/489; SO707918; NP 130
Oldbury (township in Mancetter), 37/61; SP308947; NP 132
Oldbury (township in Halesowen), 40/14A; SO986891; NP 130
Oldbury on the Hill (parish), 13/342; ST812882; NP 156
Oldbury upon Severn (tithing in Thornbury), 13/358C; ST615925; NP 155, 156
Oldcastle (township in Malpas), 5/316; SJ461447; NP 109, 118
Oldcastle (parish), 53/4; SO323244; NP 142
Oldcott (township in Wolstanton), 33/17C; SJ860560; NP 110
Oldham (parish), 20/481-493; NP 101
Oldham (township in Oldham), 20/486-493
Oldham - Mumps (ward in Oldham-above-Town division in township of Oldham in Oldham), 20/490; SD936043; NP 101
Oldham - St James (ward in Oldham-above-Town division in township of Oldham in Oldham), 20/491; SD950070; NP 101
Oldham - St Marys (ward in Oldham-below-Town division in township of Oldham in Oldham), 20/488; SD925055; NP 101
Oldham - St Peter (ward in Oldham-below-Town division in township of Oldham in Oldham), 20/489; SD926040; NP 101
Oldham - Waterhead (Waterhead Mill Ward) (ward in Oldham-above-Town division in township of Oldham in Oldham), 20/492; SD943056; NP 101
Oldham - Werneth (ward in Oldham-below-Town division in township of Oldham in Oldham), 20/486; SD918036; NP 101
Oldham - Westwood (ward in Oldham-below-Town division in township of Oldham in Oldham), 20/487; SD915052; NP 101
Oldham-above-Town division in township of Oldham in Oldham), 20/490-493; NP 101
Oldham-below-Town (division in township of Oldham in Oldham), 20/489; NP 101
Oldland (hamlet in Bitton), 13/404; ST660730; NP 156
Oldridge (chapelry in Exeter, St Thomas the Apostle), 9/253B; SX830960; NP 176
Oldstead (township in Kilburn), 42/545; SE533809; NP 92
Oldton (parish), 34/17; NP 137
Ollerset (Ollersett) (township in Glossop), 8/10A; SK028858; NP 102, 111
Ollerton (township in Knutsford), 5/104; SJ781762; NP 101, 110
Ollerton (township in Edwinstowe), 28/82; SK658674; NP 112
Ollerton (township in Stoke upon Tern), 31/177; SJ649249; NP 119
Olmstead (division in Helions Bumpstead or Castle Camps), 4/154B; TL634419; NP 148
Olney (hamlet in Olney), 3/29; SP884427; NP 146
Olney (parish), 3/29-31; NP 133, 146
Olney Park Farm (hamlet in Olney), 3/30; SP834438; NP 146

Olveston (hamlet in Olveston), 13/361; ST592868; NP 156
Olveston (parish), 13/361-362; NP 156
Ombersley (parish), 40/69; SO845645; NP 130
Ompton (parish), 28/102; SK690654; NP 112
Onecote (township in Leek), 33/9; SK040560; NP 110
Onehouse (parish), 34/297; TM020595; NP 137
Onesacre (sub-division in Westnall with Waldersheigh division in township of Bradfield in Ecclesfield), 43/817; SK293936; NP 102
Onibury (parish), 31/415A-B; NP 129
Onibury (township in Onibury), 31/415A; SO460798; NP 129
Onley (hamlet in Barby), 26/181; SP517707; NP 132
Onley (township in Moreton Say), 31/17; SJ631363; NP 119
Onneley (township in Madeley), 33/45B; SJ750430; NP 110
Onslow (township in St Chad Shrewsbury), 31/267; SJ445130; NP 118
Onston (township in Weaverham), 5/169; SJ592737; NP 109
Oole (in Clee), 22/82; NP 105
Openshaw (township in Manchester), 20/518; SJ885973; NP 101
Orby (Orby in the Marsh) (parish), 22/489; TF503673; NP 114
Orchard Portman (parish), 32/420; ST246206; NP 177
Orchardleigh (parish), 32/98; ST774510; NP 166
Orcheston St George (parish), 39/249; SU068460; NP 167
Orcheston St Mary (parish), 39/248; SU054470; NP 167
Orcop (parish), 15/231; SO463263; NP 142
Ord (township in Tweedmouth), 27/5; NT977501; NP 64
Ordsall (parish), 28/52; SK711799; NP 103
Ore (parish), 36/158; TQ822125; NP 184
Oreton (township in Stottesden), 31/571; SO657797; NP 130
Orford (division in township of Warrington in Warrington), 20/617; SJ614904; NP 101
Orford (extra-parochial), 22/166; TF193953; NP 105
Orford (parish), 34/374; TM430502; NP 150
Orgarswick (parish), 19/425; TR084306; NP 184
Orgreave (township in Alrewas), 33/222C; SK150160; NP 120
Orgreave (township in Rotherham), 43/837; SK425865; NP 103
Orlestone (parish), 19/417; TR001345; NP 172, 184
Orleton (hamlet in Eastham), 40/90; SO693670; NP 130
Orleton (parish), 15/25; SO487673; NP 129
Orlingbury (parish), 26/200; SP851721; NP 133
Ormesby (parish), 42/332-334; NP 85, 86
Ormesby (township in Ormesby), 42/334; NZ528180; NP 85, 86
Ormesby St Margaret (parish), 25/382A; TG497148; NP 126
Ormesby St Michael (parish), 25/381; TG477151; NP 126
Ormside, 38/49; NP 83
Ormskirk (parish), 20/370-371; NP 100
Ormskirk (township in Ormskirk), 20/368; SD421082; NP 100
Orpington (parish), 19/62; TQ461666; NP 171
Orrell (division in township of Orrell and Ford in Sefton), 20/687; SJ350970; NP 100
Orrell (township in Wigan), 20/588; SD540055; NP 100
Orrell and Ford (township in Sefton), 20/687-688; NP 100
Orsett (division in Orsett), 12/406; TQ641823; NP 161
Orsett (parish), 12/406-407; NP 161
Orsett Hamlet, 12/407; NP 161
Orston (parish), 28/205; SK774411; NP 122
Ortner Vachery (division in township of Over Wyresdale in Lancaster), 20/128; SD536553; NP 94
Orton (chapelry in Rothwell), 26/129; SP803791; NP 133
Orton (parish), 7/140A-B; NP 75, 76
Orton (parish), 38/69-75; NP 83, 84, 90
Orton (township in Wombourne), 33/334; SO868950; NP 130
Orton (township in Orton), 38/71; NY620080; NP 83
Orton Longueville (parish), 17/6; TL168950; NP 134
Orton on the Hill (parish), 21/157; SK319045; NP 121
Orton Waterville (parish), 17/5; TL153957; NP 134
Orwell (parish), 4/164; TL360496; NP 147, 148
Osbaldeston (Osbaldestone) (township in Blackburn), 20/319; SD643337; NP 95
Osbaldwick (parish), 42/672-673; NP 97
Osbaldwick (township in Osbaldwick), 42/673; SE635522; NP 97
Osbaston (township in Cadeby), 21/167; SK442042; NP 121

Osbaston (township in Kinnerley), 31/120; SJ321227; NP 118
Osberton, Scofton and Rayton (township in Worksop), 28/30; SK631802; NP 103
Osbournby (parish), 22/648; TF078380; NP 123
Osgathorpe (parish), 21/24; SK432197; NP 121
Osgodby (division in township of Thirkleby in Thirkleby), 42/540; SE493806; NP 91
Osgodby (township in Lenton), 22/670; TF017283; NP 123
Osgodby (township in Hemingbrough), 41/50; SE649342; NP 97
Osgodby (township in Seamer), 42/408; TA053844; NP 93
Osleston and Thurvaston (Thurvaston, Osleston and Cropper) (township in Sutton on the Hill), 8/236; SK244366; NP 120
Osmaston (Osmaston next Derby) (parish), 8/267; SK368333; NP 121
Osmaston (parish), 8/227; SK196438; NP 120
Osmington (parish), 10/270; SY733827; NP 178
Osmondthorpe (division in township of Temple Newsham in Whitkirk), 43/480; SE332328; NP 96
Osmotherley (township in Ulverston), 20/18; SD277812; NP 88
Osmotherley (parish), 42/503-507; NP 91
Osmotherley (township in Osmotherley), 42/503; SE472977; NP 91
Osney Hill (extra-parochial), 29/180; SP382116; NP 145
Ospringe (parish), 19/155; TQ989590; NP 172
Ossendike (division in township of Ryther cum Ossendike in Ryther), 43/442; SE540390; NP 97
Ossett (township in Dewsbury), 43/584; SE279201; NP 96, 102
Ossington (parish), 28/135; SK757647; NP 112
Oswaldkirk (division in township of Oswaldkirk in Oswaldkirk), 42/617; SE620784; NP 92
Oswaldkirk (parish), 42/616-618; NP 92
Oswaldkirk (township in Oswaldkirk), 42/617-618; NP 92, 92/1
Oswaldtwistle (township in Whalley), 20/302; SD740260; NP 95
Oswestry (township in Oswestry), 31/100; SJ292297; NP 117, 118
Oswestry), 31/100-114; NP 117, 118
Otford (parish), 19/189; TQ526586; NP 171
Otham (parish), 19/221; TQ795535; NP 172
Othery (parish), 32/305; ST382317; NP 165, 177
Otley (parish), 34/362; TM205555; NP 137, 150
Otley (parish), 43/362-374; NP 96
Otley (township in Otley), 43/368; SE208448; NP 96
Otney Mead (division in Culham), 29/243B; SU496944; NP 158
Otterbourne (parish), 14/230; SU461225; NP 168
Otterburn (Otterburn Ward) (township in Elsdon), 27/239; NY890950; NP 70, 71, 77
Otterburn (township in Kirkby Malhamdale), 43/234; SD884577; NP 95
Otterden (parish), 19/231; TQ939538; NP 172
Otterford (parish), 32/428; ST230144; NP 164
Otterham (parish), 6/17; SX164912; NP 174, 186
Otterhampton (parish), 32/224; ST246430; NP 165
Otterton (parish), 9/301; SY092857; NP 176
Ottery St Mary (parish), 9/284A; SY096949; NP 176
Ottringham (parish), 41/432; TA267239; NP 99
Oughterby (district in Oughterby township in Kirkbampton), 7/117; NY299556; NP 75
Oughterside and Allerby (township in Aspatria), 7/224; NY098395; NP 82
Oughton (division in township of Seaton Carew in Seaton Carew), 11/253; NZ494290; NP 85
Oulston (township in Coxwold), 42/556; SE553739; NP 91
Oulton (division in township of Oulton cum Woodlesford in Rothwell), 43/598; SE360280; NP 96
Oulton (Oldton, Owlton) (parish), 34/17; TM514940; NP 137
Oulton (parish), 25/205; TG146283; NP 125, 126
Oulton (township in Wigton), 7/136; NY247514; NP 75
Oulton (township in Stone), 33/60; SJ909363; NP 119
Oulton cum Woodlesford (township in Rothwell), 43/597A, 598; NP 96
Oulton Low (Oultonlowe), 5/177; NP 109, 110

Oundle (hamlet in Oundle), 26/65; TL022883; NP 134
Oundle (parish), 26/63-65; NP 134
Ousby (parish), 7/184; NY655359; NP 83
Ousden (parish), 34/317; TL736583; NP 135, 136
Ouseby, 22/53; NP 104
Ousefleet (township in Whitgift), 43/956; SE835225; NP 98, 104
Ousethorpe (Ousthorpe) (township in Pocklington), 41/93; SE816514; NP 98
Ousthorpe, 41/93; NP 98
Ouston (township in Chester le Street), 11/41; NZ262548; NP 78
Ouston (township in Stamfordham), 27/466; NZ073704; NP 77
Out Newton (township in Easington), 41/445; TA382218; NP 99
Out Rawcliffe (township in St Michaels on Wyre), 20/167; SD406434; NP 94
Outchester (township in Bamburgh), 27/93; NU140333; NP 64
Outney Common (extra-parochial), 34/32A; TM325906; NP 137
Outseats (township in Hathersage), 8/41; SK230840; NP 102, 111
Outwell (division in Outwell), 4/10; TF507041; NP 124
Outwell (division in Outwell), 25/695; TF522042; NP 124
Outwell (parish), 4/10, 25/695; NP 124
Outwood (division in township of Pilkington in Prestwich), 20/499; SD772050; NP 101
Ovenden (Ovendon) (township in Halifax), 43/553; SE065285; NP 96
Over (division in Almondsbury), 13/370; ST600823; NP 155, 156
Over (division in Almondsbury), 13/371; ST583827; NP 155
Over (hamlet in Churcham), 13/143B; SO812195; NP 143
Over (parish), 4/56; TL383712; NP 135
Over (parish), 5/175-178; NP 109, 110
Over (township in Over), 5/175; SJ639657; NP 109, 110
Over (township in Whitegate), 5/174; SJ645691; NP 110
Over Alderley (township in Alderley), 5/67; SJ868762; NP 101, 110
Over and Nether Haddon (township in Bakewell), 8/97-98; NP 111
Over Bullinghope (parish), 15/186; NP 142
Over Compton (parish), 10/34; ST587173; NP 178
Over Darwen (township in Blackburn), 20/305; SD690210; NP 95, 101
Over Dinsdale (township in Sockburn), 42/58; NZ358107; NP 85
Over Ellington, 42/169; NP 91
Over Haddon (division in township of Over and Nether Haddon in Bakewell), 8/98; SK191664; NP 111
Over Helmsley, 42/666; NP 97
Over Hulton (township in Deane), 20/568; SD680050; NP 101
Over Kellet (township in Bolton-le-Sands), 20/91; SD534708; NP 89
Over Knutsford,
Over Norton (hamlet in Chipping Norton), 29/52; SP315288; NP 145
Over Peover, 5/99; NP 110
Over Shitlington, 43/715; NP 102
Over Silton (parish), 42/511-512; NP 91
Over Silton (township in Over Silton), 42/511; SE455935; NP 91
Over Sitlington (Over Shitlington) (division in township of Sitlington in Thornhill), 43/715; SE256167; NP 102
Over Staveley (township in Kendal), 38/105; SD475995; NP 89
Over Stavely, 38/105
Over Stowey (parish), 32/258; ST177378; NP 164, 165
Over Tabley, 5/97; NP 101
Over Wallop (parish), 14/149; SU272393; NP 167, 168
Over Whitacre (parish), 37/57; SP258914; NP 131
Over Worton (parish), 29/57; SP433286; NP 145
Over Wyresdale (township in Lancaster), 20/123-134; NP 94, 95
Overbury (parish), 13/1-2, 40/213-215; NP 143, 144
Overbury (hamlet in Overbury), 40/213; SO958373; NP 143
Overchurch, 5/460; NP 100
Overpool (township in Eastham), 5/430; SJ386772; NP 100
Overseal (township in Seal), 21/6; SK292157; NP 121
Oversley (hamlet in Arrow), 37/190; SP097563; NP 131, 144
Overstone (parish), 26/203; SP803663; NP 133
Overstrand (parish), 25/40; TG238411; NP 126

173

Overthorpe (hamlet in Middleton Cheney), 26/357B; SP484418; NP 146
Overton (Overton and Sunderland) (township in Lancaster), 20/112; SD431579; NP 94
Overton (parish), 14/59; SU514500; NP 168
Overton (parish), 39/166-168; SU118622; NP 167
Overton (parish), 42/687-689; NP 97
Overton (parish), 50/132-134; NP 118
Overton (township in Malpas), 5/327; SJ473487; NP 109
Overton (township in Overton), 42/688; SE549568; NP 97
Overton Foreign (township in Overton), 50/134; SJ382420; NP 118
Overton Heath (extra-parochial), 39/175; SU167652; NP 157, 167
Overton Villa (township in Overton), 50/133; SJ370420; NP 118
Overy (hamlet in Dorchester), 29/299; SU584938; NP 158
Oving (parish), 3/121; SP790223; NP 146
Oving (parish), 36/246; SU904042; NP 181
Ovingdean (parish), 36/315; TQ356040; NP 182, 183
Ovingham (parish), 27/551-567; NP 77
Ovingham (township in Ovingham), 27/558; NZ089646; NP 77
Ovingham, 42/40; NP 84, 85
Ovington (parish), 12/35; TL768424; NP 149
Ovington (parish), 14/189; SU554295; NP 168
Ovington (parish), 25/539; TF925031; NP 125, 136
Ovington (township in Ovingham), 27/560; NZ073640; NP 77
Ovington (Ovingham) (township in Gilling), 42/40; NZ135145; NP 84, 85
Owermoigne (parish), 10/274; SY772852; NP 178
Owle (in Clee), 22/82; NP 105
Owlpen (parish), 13/329; ST802987; NP 156
Owlton (parish), 34/17; NP 137
Owmby (division in Searby), 22/107A; TA080051; NP 104
Owmby (parish), 22/221; SK997872; NP 104
Owmby - Caistor Moor (division in Searby), 22/107B; TA073037; NP 104
Owslebury (Owlesbury) (parish), 14/233; SU515224; NP 168, 180
Owsthorpe (division in township of Gilberdyke in Eastrington), 41/19C; SE809312; NP 98/1
Owston (Owston and Newbold) (parish), 21/270; SK773079; NP 122
Owston (Owston Ferry) (township in Owston), 22/4A; SE810015; NP 104
Owston (parish), 22/4A-5; NP 104
Owston (parish), 43/651-653; NP 103
Owston (township in Owston), 43/653; SE560105; NP 103
Owston Ferry, 22/4A; NP 104
Owstwick (division in Owstwick township in Garton), 41/412; TA273335; NP 99
Owstwick (division in Owstwick township in Roos), 41/413; TA270326; NP 99
Owstwick (township in Garton and Roos), 41/412-413; NP 99
Owthorne (parish), 41/418-421; NP 99
Owthorne (township in Owthorne), 41/419; TA335280; NP 99
Owthorpe (parish), 28/267; SK668327; NP 121, 122
Oxborough (parish), 25/530; TF741017; NP 124, 125, 135, 136
Oxcliffe (division in township of Heaton with Oxcliffe in Lancaster), 20/110; SD446621; NP 89
Oxcombe (Oxcomb) (parish), 22/331; TF313772; NP 105
Oxenbold, 31/496; NP 129
Oxenhall (parish), 13/128; SO705274; NP 143
Oxenton (parish), 13/45; SP953318; NP 144
Oxenwood (tithing in Shalbourne), 2/144B; SU318592; NP 168
Oxey Mead, Pixey Mead, West Mead (common to Begbroke and Yarnton), 29/196B; SP477105; NP 145
Oxford, All Saints (parish), 29/211A; SP515062; NP 158/1
Oxford, All Souls College (extra-parochial), 29/218L; SP517063; NP 158/1
Oxford, Balliol College (extra-parochial), 29/218Y; SP513065; NP 158/1
Oxford, Brasenose College (extra-parochial), 29/218P; SP515063; NP 158/1
Oxford, Christchurch College (extra-parochial), 29/218R; SP517057; NP 158/1
Oxford, Corpus Christi College (extra-parochial), 29/218B; SP516060; NP 158/1
Oxford, Exeter College (extra-parochial), 29/218W; SP515064; NP 158/1
Oxford, Jesus College (extra-parochial), 29/218V; SP514063; NP 158/1
Oxford, Lincoln College (extra-parochial), 29/218Q; SP515063; NP 158/1
Oxford, Magdalen College (extra-parochial), 29/218D; SP521062; NP 158/1
Oxford, Magdalen Hall (extra-parochial), 29/218J; SP522063; NP 158/1
Oxford, Merton College (extra-parochial), 29/218A; SP517061; NP 158/1
Oxford, New College (extra-parochial), 29/218H; SP518064; NP 158/1
Oxford, New Inn Hall (extra-parochial), 29/218U; SP511062; NP 158/1
Oxford, Oriel College (extra-parochial), 29/218N; SP516062; NP 158/1
Oxford, Pembroke College (extra-parochial), 29/218S; SP513060; NP 158/1
Oxford, Queens College (extra-parochial), 29/218F; SP518063; NP 158/1
Oxford, St Alban Hall (extra-parochial), 29/218C; NP 158/1
Oxford, St Aldate (parish), 29/212; SP514058; NP 158/1
Oxford, St Clement (parish), 29/208; SP537061; NP 158
Oxford, St Ebbe (parish), 29/213; SP511059; NP 158/1
Oxford, St Edmund Hall (extra-parochial), 29/218E; SP519063; NP 158/1
Oxford, St Giles (parish), 29/206; SP510080; NP 145, 158
Oxford, St John (parish), 29/209; SP518061; NP 158/1
Oxford, St John's College (extra-parochial), 29/218Z; SP513066; NP 158/1
Oxford, St Martin (parish), 29/211B; SP513062; NP 158/1
Oxford, St Mary Magdalene (parish), 29/217; SP512065; NP 158/1
Oxford, St Mary the Virgin (division in Oxford, St Mary the Virgin), 29/219; SP516062; NP 158/1
Oxford, St Mary the Virgin (parish), 29/219-220; NP 158, 158/1
Oxford, St Mary's Hall (extra-parochial), 29/218M; SP516062; NP 158/1
Oxford, St Michael (parish), 29/216; SP513063; NP 158/1
Oxford, St Peter in the East (parish), 29/210; SP522062; NP 158/1
Oxford, St Peter le Bailey (parish), 29/215; SP511062; NP 158/1
Oxford, St Thomas (parish), 29/214; SP502061; NP 158/1
Oxford, Trinity College (extra-parochial), 29/218X; SP514066; NP 158/1
Oxford, University College (extra-parochial), 29/218G; SP517062; NP 158/1
Oxford, Wadham College (extra-parochial), 29/218K; SP516066; NP 158/1
Oxford, Worcester College (extra-parochial), 29/218T; SP509065; NP 158/1
Oxhey (hamlet in Watford), 16/132B; TQ110940; NP 160
Oxhill (parish), 37/280; SP318458; NP 145
Oxhill and Scarth Lees (division in township of Whorlton in Whorlton), 42/312; NZ456013; NP 91
Oxnead (parish), 25/245; TG231245; NP 126
Oxney (division in township of Darlington in Darlington), 11/325; NZ284109; NP 85
Oxney (parish), 19/362; TR355466; NP 173
Oxnop (division in township of Muker in Grinton), 42/120; SD929957; NP 90
Oxshott (Oxshot) (hamlet in Stoke D'Abernon), 35/58B; TQ151602; NP 170
Oxspring (township in Penistone), 43/783; SE266027; NP 102
Oxted (parish), 35/104; TQ394515; NP 171
Oxton (parish), 28/162; SK631530; NP 112

Oxton (township in Woodchurch), 5/463; SJ300877; NP 100
Oxton (township in Tadcaster), 43/83; SE506430; NP 97
Oxwich (parish), 51/39; SS495865; NP 152, 153
Oxwick (parish), 25/190; TF914251; NP 125
Oystermouth (parish), 51/45; SS605893; NP 153
Ozleworth (parish), 13/326; ST792936; NP 156

P

Packington (division in Derbyshire of Packington), 8/339; SK352148; NP 121
Packington (parish), 8/339, 21/2; NP 121
Packington (parish), 8/339, 21/2A-B; NP 121
Packington (township in Packington), 21/2A; SK370145; NP 121
Packington (township in Weeford), 33/290; SK158058; NP 120
Packwood (parish), 37/87; SP164734; NP 131
Padbury (parish), 3/89; SP722305; NP 146
Paddington (parish), 24/38A-B; NP 160
Paddington, St John (division in Paddington), 24/38B; TQ824235; NP 160
Paddington, St Mary (division in Paddington), 24/38A; TQ250806; NP 160
Paddlesworth (parish), 19/179; TQ685621; NP 171
Paddlesworth (parish), 19/388; TR198402; NP 173
Padfield (township in Glossop), 8/1; SK095975; NP 102
Padiham (township in Whalley), 20/253; SD795353; NP 95
Padstow (parish), 6/82; SW906753; NP 185
Padworth (parish), 2/169; SU618663; NP 158, 168
Page Bank (division in township of Stockley in Brancepeth), 11/142B; NZ231357; NP 85
Pagham (Paglesham) (parish), 36/274; SZ895993; NP 181
Paghill (division in township of Paull in Paull), 41/429; TA203223; NP 99
Paglesham (parish), 12/371; TQ930930; NP 162
Paglesham (parish), 36/274; NP 181
Paignton (Painton) (parish), 9/434; SX872603; NP 188
Pailton (hamlet in Monks Kirby), 37/113; SP474819; NP 132
Painton, 9/434; NP 188
Painshaw (township in Houghton-le-Spring), 11/53; NZ326536; NP 78
Painsthorpe (division in parish and township of Kirby Underdale), 41/137; SE824583; NP 98
Painswick (parish), 13/248-251; NP 143, 156
Pakefield (parish), 34/20; TM534894; NP 137
Pakenham (parish), 34/195; TL927689; NP 136
Palgrave (parish), 34/88; TM110782; NP 136
Pallathorpe (division in township of Bolton Percy in Bolton Percy), 43/62; SE515427; NP 97
Palling (Palling-near-the-Sea, Sea Palling) (parish), 25/226; TG423269; NP 126
Pallion (division in township of Bishop Wearmouth in Bishop Wearmouth), 11/73; NZ375577; NP 78
Pamber (parish), 14/17; SU617597; NP 168
Pamington (hamlet in Ashchurch), 13/46; S0942327; NP 143
Pampisford (parish), 4/158; TL504483; NP 148
Pancrasweek (Pancraswike) (parish), 9/97; SS299078; NP 174
Panfield (parish), 12/84; TL736252; NP 148
Pangbourne (Pangbourn) (parish), 2/166; SU619760; NP 158
Pannal (parish), 43/382; SE285530; NP 96
Pant-y-Groes (hamlet in St Dogmaels), 55/3; SN131461; NP 139
Panteague (parish), 53/72; NP 154, 155
Panteg (Panteague) (parish), 53/72; ST300985; NP 154, 155
Panton (parish), 22/345; TF172795; NP 105
Panxworth (parish), 25/398; TG344131; NP 126
Papcastle (township in Bridekirk), 7/240; NY105321; NP 82
Papplewick (parish), 28/298; SK560510; NP 121
Papworth Everard (Papworth Everd, Papworth St Everard) (parish), 4/61; TL288623; NP 135
Papworth St Agnes (division in Papworth St Agnes), 4/62; TL268646; NP 135
Papworth St Agnes (district in Papworth St Agnes), 17/90; TL273650; NP 134
Papworth St Agnes (parish), 4/62, 17/90; NP 134
Paracombe, 9/7; NP 163

Parbold (township in Eccleston), 20/372; SD500110; NP 100
Parc Grace Dieu (extra-parochial), 53/13; SO446132; NP 142
Parcel-canol (township in Llanbadarn fawr), 46/10; SN652818; NP 127
Parham (parish), 34/279; TM310610; NP 137
Parham (parish), 36/85; TQ060139; NP 182
Park (division in township of Sheffield in Sheffield), 43/831; SK375862; NP 102, 111
Park (hamlet in Eglwysilan), 51/78; ST120910; NP 154
Park End (township in Audley), 33/42G; SJ780480; NP 110
Park End Walk (division of West Dean township in St Pauls, Forest of Dean), 13/156; SO600080; NP 142, 143, 155, 156
Park House (extra-parochial), 14/80; SU231436; NP 167
Park Leys (extra-parochial), 28/143; SK732575; NP 112
Park Quarter (division in township of Wolsingham in Wolsingham), 11/178; NZ060420; NP 84
Park Quarter (township in Stanhope), 11/172; NY930379; NP 84
Parkham (parish), 9/49A; SS387216; NP 163, 174
Parkhold (township in Ledbury), 15/278C; NP 143
Parkhurst Forest (extra-parochial), 18/2; SZ478910; NP 180
Parkstone (tithing in Canford Magna), 10/195; SZ048905; NP 179
Parlington (township in Aberford), 43/422; SE421359; NP 97
Parr (township in Prescot), 20/631; SJ533962; NP 100
Parracombe (Paracombe) (parish), 9/7; SS667446; NP 163
Parson Drove (chapelry in Leverington), 4/4; TF378087; NP 123, 124
Partington (township in Bowdon), 5/80; SJ719914; NP 101
Partington, 41/16
Partney (parish), 22/429; TF410681; NP 114
Parton (township in Moresby), 7/326; NX978206; NP 82
Parton and Micklethwaite (township in Thursby), 7/137; NY281508; NP 75, 82
Partrishow (parish), 45/79
Parwich (parish), 8/168; SK182560; NP 111
Passenham (parish), 26/335; SP767403; NP 146
Paston (parish), 25/46; TG319341; NP 126
Paston (parish), 26/7-10; NP 123
Paston (township in Paston), 26/7; TF191206; NP 123
Paston, 27/56; NP 64, 70
Patcham (parish), 36/208; TQ304090; NP 182
Patching (parish), 36/216; TQ087082; NP 182
Patney (parish), 39/208; SU073591; NP 167
Patrick Brompton (parish), 42/203-208; NP 91
Patrick Brompton (township in Patrick Brompton), 42/207-208; NP 91
Patrick Brompton East (division in township of Patrick Brompton in Patrick Brompton), 42/208; SE228909; NP 91
Patrick Brompton West (division in township of Patrick Brompton in Patrick Brompton), 42/207; SE212908; NP 91
Patrington (Pattrington) (parish), 41/435; TA313223; NP 99, 105
Patrishow (Partrishow) (parish), 45/79; SO275225; NP 141, 142
Patrixbourne (Patrixbourn) (parish), 19/283; TR186549; NP 173
Patterdale with Hartsop, 38/28
Pattesley (Pattisley) (parish), 25/189; TF899246; NP 125
Pattingham (parish), 31/479, 33/326; NP 130
Pattingham (parish), 33/326; SO825985; NP 119, 130
Pattishall (parish), 26/289; SP673544; NP 132, 133, 145, 146
Pattishull (parish), 33/325; SJ804004; NP 119, 130
Pattisley (parish), 25/189; NP 125
Pattiswick (parish), 12/130; TL816240; NP 149
Patton (township in Kendal), 38/99; SD550968; NP 89
Pattrington, 41/435; NP 99, 105
Paul (parish), 6/212; SW458268; NP 189
Paulerspury (parish), 26/313; SP720464; NP 146
Paull (division in township of Paull in Paull), 41/428; TA181268; NP 99
Paull (parish), 41/428-430; NP 99
Paull (township in Paull), 41/428-429; NP 99
Paulton (parish), 32/110; ST655564; NP 166
Pauntley (parish), 13/126; SO746293; NP 143
Pauperhaugh (township in Rothbury), 27/265; NZ103991; NP 71
Pavenham (parish), 1/27; SP997557; NP 134, 147

Pawlett (parish), 32/221; ST294435; NP 165
Pawston (Paston) (township in Kirknewton), 27/56; NT847315; NP 64, 70
Paxford (hamlet in Blockley), 40/245; SP190378; NP 144
Payhembury (parish), 9/240; ST089017; NP 176
Paythorne (township in Gisburn), 43/299; SD822518; NP 95
Peak Forest (extra-parochial), 8/32; SK108795; NP 111
Peakirk (parish), 26/14; TF170062; NP 123
Peals, 27/181; NP 71
Peasemore (parish), 2/115; SU461774; NP 158
Peasenhall (parish), 34/165; TM348691; NP 137
Peasmarsh (parish), 36/144; TQ882228; NP 184
Peatling Magna (parish), 21/329; SP598926; NP 132
Peatling Parva (parish), 21/332; SP590899; NP 132
Peaton (township in Diddlebury), 31/507A; SO533843; NP 129
Pebmarsh (parish), 12/91; TL853336; NP 149
Pebworth (hamlet in Pebworth), 13/11; SP130470; NP 144
Pebworth (parish), 13/11-12; NP 144
Peckforton (township in Bunbury), 5/310; SJ539567; NP 109
Peckham (hamlet in St Giles Camberwell), 35/17; TQ349762; NP 170, 171
Peckleton (parish), 21/172-173; NP 121, 132
Peckleton (township in Peckleton), 21/172; SK470010; NP 121, 132
Peckleton-cum-Tooley (parish), 21/172-173; NP 121, 132
Pedmore (parish), 40/25; SO 911821; NP 130
Peels (Peals) (township in Alwinton), 27/181; NT946053; NP 71
Pegswood (township in Bothal), 27/317; NZ220872; NP 78
Peldon (parish), 12/176; TL993163; NP 149
Pelham's Lands (extra-parochial), 22/744; TF225515; NP 114
Pelsall (township in Wolverhampton), 33/315; SJ021040; NP 120
Pelton (township in Chester le Street), 11/43; NZ254526; NP 78
Pelynt (parish), 6/121; SX209550; NP 186
Pemberton (township in Wigan), 20/587; SD559047; NP 100
Pembrey (Pembre) (parish), 47/82; SN425035; NP 152
Pembridge (parish), 15/44; SO378575; NP 129, 142
Pembroke, St Mary [Penfro] (St Mary, Pembroke) (parish), 55/150; SM989025; NP 151
Pembroke, St Michael [Penfro] (St Michael, Pembroke) (parish), 55/149; SR999999; NP 151
Pembryn (parish), 46/56; NP 139
Pembury (parish), 19/310; TQ634406; NP 171
Pen Uchair Plwyf (township in Ysceifiog), 50/92; SJ172720; NP 108
Pen-y-clawdd (parish), 53/54; SO450080; NP 155
Pen-y-gelli (township in Kerry [Llanfihangel-yng-Ngheri]), 54/177; SO179910; NP 128
Pen-y-llawd (township in Chirk), 49/99; SJ281403; NP 108, 117, 118
Penallt (Penalt) (parish), 53/19; SO520090; NP 142, 155
Penallt (township in Llangattock), 45/76A; SO180140; NP 141
Penally [Penalum] (parish), 55/139; SS104996; NP 152
Penalt (parish), 53/19; NP 142, 155
Penalum (parish), 55/139; NP 152
Penarlag (parish), 50/1-15; NP 109
Penarlag, 50/5; NP 109
Penarth (parish), 51/181; ST187711; NP 154
Penarth (township in Meifod), 54/36; SJ153156; NP 117
Penbedw (township in Nannerch), 49/33; SJ155685; NP 108
Penbiddle, 53/6; NP 142
Penbidwal (Penbiddle) (hamlet in Llanvihangel Crucorney), 53/6; SO341227; NP 142
Penboyr (parish), 47/39; SN345375; NP 139
Penbryn (parish), 46/56; SN325500; NP 139
Penbuallt (township in Llangamarch), 45/30; SN915455; NP 140, 141
Pencarreg (parish), 47/5; SN590440; NP 140
Pencelli, 45/54B
Pencoed (hamlet in Coychurch), 51/87; SS960820; NP 154
Pencombe (parish), 15/146; SO580530; NP 142, 143
Pencoyd (parish), 15/239; SO514268; NP 142
Penderry (hamlet in Llangyfelach), 51/5; SS624987; NP 153

Penderyn (parish), 45/72; SN980090; NP 141, 154
Pendine (parish), 47/66; SN233086; NP 152
Pendlebury (township in Eccles), 20/562; SD797016; NP 101
Pendleton (township in Eccles), 20/561; SJ803996; NP 101
Pendleton (township in Whalley), 20/249; SD768389; NP 95
Pendleton Hall (extra-parochial), 20/235; SD759402; NP 95
Pendock (parish), 40/236; SO815341; NP 143
Pendomer (parish), 32/477; ST523104; NP 177
Pendoylan (parish), 51/125; ST056771; NP 154
Penegoes (parish), 54/127; SN830950; NP 127
Penfro (St Michael, Pembroke) (parish), 55/149; NP 151
Penge (division in Battersea), 35/22; TQ348701; NP 170, 171
Pengwern (township in Llangollen), 49/114; SJ216407; NP 108, 117
Pengwern (township in St Asaph [Llanelwy]), 50/70; SJ016758; NP 108
Penhow (parish), 53/105; ST408913; NP 155
Penhurst (parish), 36/174; TQ698169; NP 183
Penistone (parish), 43/777-784; NP 102
Penistone (township in Penistone), 43/781; SE247027; NP 102
Penketh (township in Prescot), 20/622; SJ562877; NP 100
Penkhall (township in Stoke-on-Trent), 33/36A; SJ875448; NP 110, 119
Penkridge (parish), 33/233-240; NP 119
Penkridge (township in Penkridge), 33/235; SJ925140; NP 119
Penley (township in Ellesmere), 50/137; SJ407403; NP 118
Penllech (parish), 48/71; SH220350; NP 115
Penlline (parish), 51/110; NP 154
Penllyn (Penlline, Pen-llin) (parish), 51/110; SS978767; NP 154
Penmachno (parish), 48/21; SH779497; NP 107, 116
Penmaen (parish), 51/41; SS529888; NP 153
Penmain (hamlet in Mynyddislwyn), 53/70C; ST200980; NP 154
Penmark (parish), 51/171; ST062678; NP 154
Penmon (parish), 44/65; SH624801; NP 107
Penmorfa (parish), 48/41; SH540420; NP 115, 116
Penmynydd (parish), 44/60; SH519739; NP 106
Penn (parish), 3/204; SP921940; NP 159
Penn (parish), 33/328-329; NP 130
Penn-y-caer (township in Castle Caereinion), 54/61; SJ184082; NP 117
Pennal (parish), 52/38A-B; NP 127
Pennal - Lower (division in Pennal), 52/38B; SH710020; NP 127
Pennal - Upper (division in Pennal), 52/38A; SH725045; NP 127
Pennant (Lower Pennant) (parish), 54/20; SJ025265; NP 117
Pennant (township in Llanfihangel Beguidy), 56/8; SO206756; NP 128
Pennard (parish), 51/43; SS566888; NP 153
Pennington (parish), 20/23; SD260780; NP 88
Pennington (Penington) (township in Leigh), 20/579; SJ652988; NP 101
Pennycross (Weston Peverel, Weston Peverell) (chapelry in Plymouth St Andrew), 9/462; SX476576; NP 187/1
Penpont (township in Llanspyddid), 45/57; SN975277; NP 141
Penrhos (parish), 48/55; SH351342; NP 115
Penrhos (parish), 53/24; SO406128; NP 142
Penrhos Lligwy (Penrhos Llugwy, Penrhoslligwy, Rhos Lligwy) (parish), 44/12; SH487866; NP 106
Penrhos Llugwy (parish), 44/12; NP 106
Penrhoslligwy (parish), 44/12; NP 106
Penrice (parish), 51/38; SS487877; NP 152, 153
Penrith (township in Penrith), 7/190; NY520320; NP 83
Penrith, 55/13A; NP 139
Penrydd (parish), 55/13A-B; NP 139
Penrydd (Penrith) (division in Penrydd), 55/13A; SN210344; NP 139
Penryn (borough in St Gluvias), 6/177; SW778348; NP 190
Penryndeudraeth (division in Llandecwyn), 52/5; SH604383; NP 116
Pensax (chapelry in Lindridge), 40/78; SO730685; NP 130
Pensby (township in Woodchurch), 5/468; SJ266835; NP 100
Penselwood (parish), 32/357; ST757311; NP 166
Pensham (township in St Andrew Pershore), 40/178; SO943440; NP 143

Penshurst (parish), 19/202; TQ527423; NP 171
Pensthorpe (parish), 25/159; TF953298; NP 125
Penstrowed (parish), 54/162; NP 128
Penterry (parish), 53/91; ST521989; NP 155
Pentlow (parish), 12/39; TL810450; NP 149
Pentney (parish), 25/313; TF721134; NP 124, 125
Penton Mewsey (parish), 14/73; SU336476; NP 168
Pentonville (division in St James Clerkenwell), 24/47C; TQ309822; NP 160/1
Pentraeth (parish), 44/61; SH529781; NP 106
Pentre (township in Rhuddlan), 50/61; SJ037792; NP 108
Pentrefoelas (Pentrevoelas) (parish), 49/16; SH885545; NP 107, 108
Pentregaer (township in Oswestry), 31/102A; SJ236291; NP 117
Pentrevoelas (parish), 49/16; NP 107, 108
Pentrich (division of Pentrich township in Pentrich), 8/194A; SK391526; NP 111, 112
Pentrich (parish), 8/194A, 195B; NP 111, 112
Pentrich (township in Pentrich), 8/194a, 195B; NP 111, 112
Pentridge (division in Pentridge), 10/67; SU035183; NP 179
Pentridge (parish), 10/66-67; NP 167, 179
Pentrobin (township in Hawarden), 50/12; SJ304637; NP 109
Pentrych (parish), 51/128; ST098828; NP 154
Pentrych (township in Llanfair Caereinion), 54/51; SJ041068; NP 117
Penwortham (parish), 20/337-341; NP 94
Penwortham (township in Penwortham), 20/337; SD524276; NP 94
Penygroes (division in Llanlyfni), 48/39B; SH470530; NP 106, 115, 116
Penzance (chapelry in Madron), 6/208; SW470306; NP 189
Peopleton (parish), 40/145; SO949509; NP 143
Peover Inferior (Lower Peover) (township in Great Budworth), 5/128; SJ746745; NP 101, 110
Peover Superior (Over Peover) (township in Rostherne), 5/99; SJ778739; NP 110
Peper Harow (Pepper-Harrow) (parish), 35/156; SU923434; NP 169
Peplow (township in Hodnet), 31/172; SJ634241; NP 119
Pepper Gowt (extra-parochial), 22/751; TF308472; NP 114
Pepper-Harrow (parish), 35/156; NP 169
Perivale (parish), 24/98; TQ170835; NP 160
Perlethorpe (township in Edwinstowe), 28/78; SK650720; NP 112
Perranarworthal (parish), 6/163; SW775395; NP 190
Perranuthnoe (parish), 6/200; SW546299; NP 189
Perranzabuloe (parish), 6/133; SW778528; NP 185, 190
Perridge (Perridge Farm) (district in Kenn), 9/317; SX865902; NP 176
Perry Barr (township in Handsworth), 33/302; SP068947; NP 131
Perry Hill (tithing in Worplesden), 35/76B; SU970530; NP 169
Pershall (township in Eccleshall), 33/141; SJ809312; NP 119
Pertenhall (parish), 1/9; TL088653; NP 134
Pertwood (parish), 39/380; ST895359; NP 166
Peter Tavy (parish), 9/335; SX512780; NP 175
Peterborough (division in Peterborough, St John the Baptist), 4/8B; TF241003; NP 123, 134
Peterborough - Boroughbury (township in Peterborough, St John the Baptist), 26/2; TF188986; NP 134
Peterborough - Precinct (extra-parochial), 26/1; TL194987; NP 134
Peterborough, St John the Baptist (parish), 4/8B, 26/2-6; NP 123, 134
Peterchurch (parish), 15/206; SO339389; NP 142
Peters Marland (Marland Peters) (parish), 9/109; SS483129; NP 175
Petersfield (parish), 14/243-244; NP 181
Petersfield (tithing in Petersfield), 14/243; SU747234; NP 181
Petersham (parish), 35/32; TQ189729; NP 170
Peterston super Montem (Peterstone super Montem) (chapelry in Coychurch), 51/85; SS995845; NP 154
Peterston-super-Ely (Peterstone super Ely) (parish), 51/126; ST079779; NP 154

Peterstone Wentlooge (Peterstone, Peterstone Wentloog) (parish), 53/126; ST270810; NP 154, 155
Peterstow (parish), 15/259; SO557242; NP 142
Petham (parish), 19/289; TR123527; NP 173
Petrockstowe (Petrockstow) (parish), 9/110; SS516098; NP 175
Petsoe End (Petsoe Manor) (division in Emberton), 3/37; SP920490; NP 146
Pett (division in Guestling hundred in Pett), 36/156A; TQ895147; NP 184
Pett (division in Winchelsea Liberty in Pett), 36/156B; TQ915165; NP 184
Pett (parish), 36/156A-B; NP 184
Pettaugh (parish), 34/286; TM168597; NP 137
Petterill Crooks (Petteril Crooks) (township in Hesket in the Forest), 7/164; NY433471; NP 83
Pettistree (parish), 34/384; TM301546; NP 150
Petton (parish), 31/53; SJ439262; NP 118
Petworth (parish), 36/30; SU986224; NP 181
Pevensey (parish), 36/180; TQ650067; NP 183
Pewsey (parish), 39/200; SU162596; NP 167
Pewsham (extra-parochial), 39/113; ST936708; NP 156, 157
Philadelphia (area in Tynemouth), 27/386; NZ334705; NP 78
Phillack (parish), 6/169; SW574378; NP 189
Philleigh (Filley) (parish), 6/156; SW872395; NP 190
Philley (tithing in Hawkchurch), 10/113; SY362998; NP 177
Pibsbury (division in Huish Episcopi), 32/334C; ST442267; NP 177
Pickering (parish), 42/430-434; NP 92
Pickering (township in Pickering), 42/431; SE800850; NP 92
Pickhill (parish), 42/247-252B; NP 91
Pickhill (township in Bangor-is-y-coed), 49/78; SJ395472; NP 109
Pickhill with Roxby (township in Pickhill), 42/251; SE345835; NP 91
Pickmere (township in Great Budworth), 5/125; SJ697777; NP 101
Pickstock (township in Edgmond), 31/188; SJ729239; NP 119
Pickthorn (township in Stottesden), 31/576; SO661845; NP 130
Pickwell with Leisthorpe (Pickwell and Leesthorpe) (parish), 21/112; SK792122; NP 122
Pickworth (parish), 22/666; TF042331; NP 123
Pickworth (parish), 30/27; SK992137; NP 122
Picton (township in Plemstall), 5/423; SJ433709; NP 109
Picton (township in Kirklevington), 42/271; NZ415075; NP 91
Picton (township in Llanasa), 50/45; SJ129820; NP 108
Piddinghoe (parish), 36/329; TQ422021; NP 183
Piddington (hamlet in Piddington), 26/294; SP803533; NP 133, 146
Piddington (parish), 26/293-294; NP 133, 146
Piddington (parish), 29/114; SP637171; NP 145
Piddlehinton (Puddlehinton) (parish), 10/212; SY715973; NP 178
Piddletrenthide (parish), 10/211; SY706997; NP 178
Pidley cum Fenton (parish), 17/70; TL332786; NP 134
Piecombe (parish), 36/118; NP 182
Piercebridge (Piers Bridge, Pierse Bridge) (township in Gainford), 11/310; NZ203168; NP 85
Piers Bridge, 11/310; NP 85
Pierse Bridge, 11/310; NP 85
Pigdon (township in Mitford), 27/402; NZ149885; NP 78
Pightlestone, Pightleshorne (parish), 3/132-134; NP 146, 147, 159
Pightlestone, Pightleshorne, 3/132
Pilham (Pilham with Gilby) (parish), 22/126; SK868935; NP 104
Pilkington (division in township of Pilkington in Prestwich), 20/498; SD791062; NP 101
Pilkington (township in Prestwich), 20/496-499; NP 101
Pillaton (parish), 6/66; SX384640; NP 186, 187
Pillerton Hersey (parish), 37/278; SP302491; NP 145
Pillerton Priors (parish), 37/277; SP299477; NP 145
Pilleth (parish), 56/12; SO256692; NP 128
Pilling (township in Garstang), 20/143; SD420470; NP 94
Pilling Lane (division in township of Preesall with Hackensall in Lancaster), 20/142; SD377487; NP 94

Pilsdon (parish), 10/128; ST414006; NP 177
Pilsgate (township in Barnack), 26/29B; TF063058; NP 123
Pilsley (township in Edensor), 8/81; SK237709; NP 111
Pilsley (township in North Wingfield), 8/131; SK419627; NP 112
Pilsworth (division in township of Pilsworth in Middleton), 20/476; SD811084; NP 101
Pilsworth (division in township of Pilsworth in Middleton), 20/477; SD840090; NP 101
Pilton (parish), 9/25; SS553348; NP 163
Pilton (parish), 26/75; TL006853; NP 134
Pilton (parish), 30/47; SK903030; NP 122
Pilton (parish), 32/185; ST589413; NP 165, 166
Pimperne (parish), 10/82; ST899097; NP 178
Pinchbeck (division in Pinchbeck), 22/732A; TF210260; NP 123
Pinchbeck (division in Spalding Fen and Deeping Fen in Pinchbeck), 22/732B; TF223189; NP 123
Pinchbeck (parish), 22/732A-B; NP 123
Pinchingthorpe (township in Guisborough), 42/357; NZ579147; NP 86
Pinhoe (parish), 9/246; SX956944; NP 176
Pinley (township in Rowington), 37/174; SP213658; NP 131
Pinner (parish), 24/92; TQ125895; NP 160
Pinnock and Hyde (township in Didbrook), 13/72; SP078282; NP 144
Pinvin (chapelry in St Andrew Pershore), 40/181; SO963490; NP 143
Pinxton (division in Pinxton), 8/141; SK454553; NP 112
Pinxton (division in Pinxton), 28/96; SK465563; NP 112
Pinxton (parish), 8/141, 28/96; NP 112
Pipe and Lyde (Pipe-cum-Lyde) (parish), 15/124; SO509440; NP 142
Pipe Ridware (parish), 33/197; SK093183; NP 120
Pipe-cum-Lyde (parish), 15/124; NP 142
Pipehill (township in St Michael), 33/265; SK096084; NP 120
Pipton (township in Glasbury), 45/2; SO149372; NP 141
Pirbright (parish), 35/77; SU931557; NP 169
Pirton (parish), 16/41; TL149317; NP 147
Pirton (parish), 40/173; SO888469; NP 143
Pishill (parish), 29/282; SU719896; NP 159
Pistill (parish), 48/51; NP 115
Pistyll (Pistill) (parish), 48/51; SH348428; NP 115
Pitchcombe (parish), 13/252; SO852083; NP 156
Pitchcott (Pitchcot) (parish), 3/122; SP778198; NP 146
Pitchford (parish), 31/285; SJ528040; NP 118
Pitcombe (parish), 32/352; NP 166
Pitcombe (township in Pitcombe), 32/352; ST685328; NP 166
Pitminster (parish), 32/422; ST215190; NP 164, 177
Pitney (parish), 32/336; ST550173; NP 165, 177
Pitsea (parish), 12/395; TQ737881; NP 161
Pitsford (parish), 26/226; SP752676; NP 133
Pitstone (Pightlestone, Pightleshorne) (division in Pitstone), 3/132; SP947149; NP 146, 147
Pitstone (Pightlestone, Pightleshorne) (parish), 3/132-134; NP 146, 147, 159
Pitt (district in Tiverton), 9/161; SS966173; NP 164
Pittington (division of Pittington township in Pittington), 11/111; NZ324448; NP 85
Pittington (parish), 11/107-111; NP 85
Pittington (township in Pittington), 11/110-111; NP 85
Pittleworth (hamlet in Broughton), 14/152; SU329291; NP 168
Pitton (chapelry in Alderbury), 39/361; SU215315; NP 167
Pitton and Farley (39/361-362); NP 167
Pixley (township in Pixley), 15/274; SO660389; NP 143
Plainmeller, 27/577; NP 76, 77
Plaish (township in Cardington), 31/433A; SO529963; NP 129
Plaistow (division in West Ham), 12/324; TQ409815; NP 161
Plaitford (parish), 39/372; SU278218; NP 167, 168, 179, 180
Plashetts and Tynehead (township in Falstone), 27/216; NY660960; NP 70, 76, 77
Plawsworth (township in Chester le Street), 11/47; NZ259481; NP 85
Playden (parish), 36/146; TQ931227; NP 184
Playford (parish), 34/429; TM216476; NP 150
Pleasington (township in Blackburn), 20/325; SD642272; NP 95

Pleasley (parish), 8/66; SK513661; NP 112
Plegdon (hamlet in Henham), 12/63; TL549271; NP 148
Plemstall (Plemondstall) (parish), 5/420-421, 423; NP 109
Plemstall (Plemondstall) (township in Hoole), 5/422; SJ429681; NP 109
Plenmeller (Plainmeller) (township in Haltwhistle), 27/577; NY731615; NP 76, 77
Pleshey (parish), 12/249; TL661142; NP 148
Plessey and Shotton (township in Stannington), 27/426; NZ218777; NP 78
Plompton (parish), 36/123; NP 182, 183
Plompton (Plumpton) (township in Spofforth), 43/101; SE362544; NP 96
Ploughland (township in Welwick), 41/441; TA335212; NP 99, 105
Pluckley (Pluckley and Pevington) (parish), 19/320; TQ925446; NP 172
Plumbland (parish), 7/230; NY144390; NP 82
Plumley (township in Great Budworth), 5/127; SJ722753; NP 101, 110
Plumpton (parish), 26/327; SP600488; NP 145
Plumpton (Plompton) (parish), 36/123; TQ362155; NP 182, 183
Plumpton Earle (Plumpton Maurice) (district in Plympton Earls), 9/452; SX547557; NP 187
Plumpton Street (township in Hesket in the Forest), 7/167; NY483368; NP 83
Plumpton Wall (township in Lazonby), 7/168; NY496392; NP 83
Plumpton, 43/101; NP 96
Plumstead (parish), 19/14; TQ455787; NP 161, 171
Plumstead (parish), 25/130; TG128349; NP 125, 126
Plumtree (Plumptree) (parish), 28/270-272; NP 121
Plumtree (Plumptree) (township in Plumtree), 28/270; SK620338; NP 121
Plungar (parish), 21/86; SK772334; NP 122
Plush (tithing in Buckland Newton), 10/157; ST728032; NP 178
Plymouth St Andrew (district in Plymouth St Andrew), 9/463; SX477552; NP 187/1
Plymouth St Andrew (parish), 9/462-463; NP 187/1
Plymouth, Charles the Martyr (district in Plymouth, Charles the Martyr), 9/454, 464; NP 187
Plymouth, Charles the Martyr (parish), 9/464; SX493548; NP 187
Plympton Maurice, 9/452; NP 187
Plympton St Mary (parish), 9/451; SX559575; NP 187
Plymstock (parish), 9/465; SX518527; NP 187
Plymtree (parish), 9/224; ST060033; NP 176
Pockley (township in Helmsley), 42/491; SE625895; NP 92
Pocklington (parish), 41/93-96; NP 98
Pocklington (township in Pocklington), 41/96; SE810490; NP 98
Pockthorne (hamlet in Norwich, St James), 25/441B; TG235094; NP 126/1
Podimore (Podymore Milton, Puddimore) (parish), 32/369; ST545253; NP 177
Podington (Puddington) (parish), 1/20; SP949620; NP 133, 134
Podmore (township in Eccleshall), 33/149; SJ784359; NP 119
Podymore Milton (parish), 32/369; ST545253; NP 177
Pointington (parish), 32/388; NP 166, 178
Pointon (hamlet in Sempringham), 22/661; TF123313; NP 123
Polebrook (hamlet in Polebrook), 26/67; TL080870; NP 134
Polebrook (parish), 26/67-68; NP 134
Polesworth (parish), 37/12-18; NP 120, 121, 131
Polesworth (township in Polesworth), 37/14; SK263019; NP 120, 131
Poling (parish), 36/292; TQ045051; NP 182
Pollard's Lands (township in St Andrew Auckland), 11/202; NZ212305; NP 85
Pollington (township in Snaith), 43/966; SE612202; NP 97, 103
Polshot (parish), 39/136; NP 167
Polstead (parish), 34/500; TL990390; NP 149
Poltimore (parish), 9/247; SX965972; NP 176
Ponsonby (parish), 7/309; NY055055; NP 82, 88
Pontefract (division in township of Pontefract in Pontefract), 43/624; SE460220; NP 97, 103
Pontefract (township in Pontefract), 43/624-627, 629; NP 97

178

Pontefract Park (division in township of Pontefract in Pontefract), 43/629; SE442225; NP 97
Pontefract Park (township in Pontefract), 43/628; SE437220; NP 97
Ponteland (parish), 27/521-530; NP 77, 78
Ponteland (township in Ponteland), 27/530; NZ121735; NP 77, 78
Pontesbury (parish), 31/290-292; NP 118
Pontesbury (township in Pontesbury), 31/292A; SJ410080; NP 118
Pontfaen (parish), 55/27; SN035333; NP 138
Pontisbright (parish), 12/135; NP 149
Pool (township in Otley), 43/369; SE240448; NP 96
Pool Foot (division in township of Great and Little Singleton in Kirkham), 20/189; SD381393; NP 94
Pool Meadow (extra-parochial), 13/178; SO823192; NP 143/1
Pool Middle (Welshpool, Y Trallwng) (township in Pool), 54/68; SJ224076; NP 117
Pool Upper (township in Pool), 54/66; SJ206049; NP 117
Poole (St James, Poole) (parish), 10/197; SZ011905; NP 179
Poole (township in Acton), 5/293; SJ638554; NP 110
Poole Keynes (parish), 39/17; SU005952; NP 157
Pooley (township in Polesworth), 37/15; SK255030; NP 120
Poolton cum Seacombe, 5/444; NP 100
Poolton cum Spittle, 5/438; NP 100
Popham (parish), 14/97; SU557440; NP 168
Poplar (parish), 24/70; NP 161, 171
Porchester (parish), 14/296; NP 180
Porlock (parish), 32/243; SS852466; NP 164
Port Meadow (extra-parochial), 29/204B; SP494084; NP 145
Port-Eynon (parish), 51/37; SS459860; NP 152, 153
Portbury (parish), 32/5; ST496753; NP 155
Portchester (Porchester) (parish), 14/296; SU616057; NP 180
Porters Close (extra-parochial), 11/115; NZ281428; NP 85
Portgate (township in St John Lee), 27/451A; NY980688; NP 77
Porthkerry (parish), 51/172; ST082667; NP 154
Portington (Partington) (division in township of Portington and Cavill in Eastrington), 41/16; SE785310; NP 98
Portington and Cavill (Partington and Cavil) (township in Eastrington), 41/15-16; NP 98
Portinscales (Coledale), (township in Crosthwaite), 7/284; NY246229; NP 82
Portisham (parish), 10/256; SY622858; NP 178
Portishead (parish), 32/6; ST462757; NP 155
Portland (parish), 10/263; SY689711; NP 178
Porton (chapelry in Idmiston), 39/310E; SU207359; NP 167
Portscuett, (parish), 53/143; NP 155
Portsea (parish), 14/289A-C; NP 180, 180/2
Portsea Town (division in Kingston registration subdistrict in Portsea), 14/289C; SU654983; NP 180
Portsea Town (division in Portsea), 14/289B; SU631005; NP 180/2
Portskewet (parish), 53/143; NP 155
Portskewett (Portskewett and Southbrook, Portscuett, Portskewet) (parish), 53/143; ST505885; NP 155
Portskewett and Southbrook (parish), 53/143; NP 155
Portslade (Portslade-by-Sea) (parish), 36/211; TQ252078; NP 182
Portsmouth (division in Kingston registration subdistrict in Portsmouth), 14/290B; SU641006; NP 180/2
Portsmouth (division in Landport registration subdistrict in Portsmouth), 14/290C; SU641003; NP 180/2
Portsmouth (parish), 14/290A-C; NP 180/2
Portsmouth Town (division in Portsmouth), 14/290A; SZ632995; NP 180/2
Portswood (division of Portswood tithing outside municipal boundary in South Stoneham), 14/262; SU428142; NP 180
Portswood (division of Portswood tithing inside municipal boundary in South Stoneham), 14/263; SU439156; NP 180
Portswood (tithing in South Stoneham), 14/262-263; NP 180
Posenhall (extra-parochial), 31/465; SJ659011; NP 119
Poslingford (parish), 34/339; TL770490; NP 149
Postling (parish), 19/393; TR145390; NP 173
Postwick (parish), 25/476; TG295080; NP 126

Potovens, 43/600; NP 96
Potsgrove (parish), 1/112; SP947302; NP 146, 147
Pott (division in township of Ilton cum Pott in Masham), 42/165; SE145775; NP 91
Pott Shrigley (township in Prestbury), 5/34; SJ946805; NP 101
Potter Hanworth (parish), 22/558; TF070670; NP 113
Potter Heigham (parish), 25/373; TG426200; NP 126
Potter Newton (township in Leeds), 43/504; SE319358; NP 96
Potterne (parish), 39/137-139; NP 167
Potterne (tithing in Potterne), 39/137; ST998585; NP 167
Potters Marston (township in Barwell), 21/215; SP500962; NP 132
Potterspury (hamlet in Potterspury), 26/338; SP757430; NP 146
Potterspury (parish), 26/338-339B; NP 146
Potterspury Lodge (hamlet in Potterspury), 26/339B; SP748448; NP 146
Potto (division in township of Potto in Whorlton), 42/310; NZ466033; NP 91
Potto (township in Whorlton), 42/309-310; NP 91
Potton (parish), 1/61; TL130496; NP 147
Poughill (parish), 6/3; SS218080; NP 174
Poughill (parish), 9/169; SS854086; NP 164, 176
Poughley (tithing in township of East Hanney in West Hanney), 2/52; SU417939; NP 158
Poulshot (Polshot) (parish), 39/136; ST967599; NP 167
Poulton (division in township of Poulton with Fearnhead in Warrington), 20/615; SJ632898; NP 101
Poulton (parish), 13/286; SP106013; NP 157
Poulton (parish), 19/378; TR277418; NP 173
Poulton (township in Pulford), 5/367; SJ400590; NP 109
Poulton cum Seacombe (Poolton cum Seacombe) (township in Wallasey), 5/444; NP 100
Poulton cum Spital (Poolton cum Spittle) (township in Bebington), 5/438; SJ332824; NP 100
Poulton le Sands (division in Poulton, Bare and Torrisholme township in Lancaster), 20/114; SD438642; NP 89
Poulton with Fearnhead (township in Warrington), 20/616; NP 101
Poulton, 20/168; NP 94
Poulton, Bare and Torrisholme (township in Lancaster), 20/114-116; NP 89
Poulton-le-Fylde (parish), 20/168-176; NP 94
Poulton-le-Fylde (Poulton) (township in Poulton-le-Fylde), 20/168; SD353393; NP 94
Pounden (hamlet in Twyford), 3/112; SP642252; NP 145
Poundstock (parish), 6/7; SX202998; NP 174
Powderham (parish), 9/388; SX958851; NP 176
Powerstock (Powerstock with West Milton) (parish), 10/140; SY520959; NP 177
Powick (hamlet in Powick), 40/159A; SO830510; NP 143
Powick (parish), 40/159A-C; SO830510; NP 143
Pownall Fee (township in Wilmslow), 5/73; SJ834826; NP 101
Poxwell (parish), 10/271; SY737844; NP 178
Poynings (parish), 36/116; TQ260121; NP 182
Poyntington (Pointington) (parish), 32/388; ST645205; NP 166, 178
Poynton (township in Prestbury), 5/51; SJ923839; NP 101
Poynton (township in High Ercall), 31/210; SJ567176; NP 118
Prebend and Priestgate (division in township of Darlington in Darlington), 11/322; NZ291147; NP 85
Prebend End (division in Buckingham), 3/80; SP696331; NP 145, 146
Precinct of Bridewell (extra-parochial), 24/4; TQ316810; NP 160/1
Precinct of Old Tower (extra-parochial), 24/3; TQ336808; NP 160/1
Precinct of St Katherine (extra-parochial), 24/58; TQ338804; NP 160/1
Prees (parish), 31/19a-26; NP 118, 119
Prees (township in Prees), 31/25; SJ555335; NP 118
Preesall (division in township of Preesall with Hackensall in Lancaster), 20/141; SD368472; NP 94
Preesall with Hackensall (township in Lancaster), 20/140-142; NP 89

Prendergast (parish), 55/85; SM959176; NP 151
Prendwick (township in Alnham), 27/162; NT999129; NP 71
Prenton (township in Woodchurch), 5/464; SJ303860; NP 100
Prescot (parish), 20/621-637; NP 100
Prescot (Prescott) (extra-parochial), 29/8; SP479481; NP 145
Prescot (township in Prescot), 20/637; SJ467927; NP 100
Prescott (extra-parochial), 13/63; SO987287; NP 143
Preshute (parish), 39/105, 169-172; NP 157
Preshute (tithing in Preshute), 39/172; SU193684; NP 157
Pressen (township in Carham), 27/36; NT832348; NP 64
Prestbury (parish), 5/32-65; NP 101, 110
Prestbury (township in Prestbury), 5/42; SJ895767; NP 101
Prestbury (parish), 13/113; SO972241; NP 143, 144
Presteigne (borough), 56/17A-18; NP 128, 129
Presteigne - Broad Street and Horeford (wards in borough and parish of Presteigne [Llanandras]), 56/17B; SO330640; NP 129
Presteigne - High Street and St David Street (wards in borough and parish of Presteigne [Llanandras]), 56/17A; SO300650; NP 128, 129
Presteigne [Llanandras] (parish), 15/36-39, 56/17-18, 63; NP 128, 129
Presthope (township in Much Wenlock), 31/456; SO580970; NP 129
Preston (division in Tarrant Rushton), 10/169B; ST941047; NP 178, 179
Preston (hamlet in Hitchin), 16/38; TL182245; NP 147
Preston (Preston and Sutton Poyntz) (parish), 10/269; SY698831; NP 178
Preston (parish), 13/132; SO675349; NP 143
Preston (parish), 13/280; SP047011; NP 157
Preston (Preston next Wingham, Preston-by-Wingham) (parish), 19/134; TR247609; NP 173
Preston (Preston-next-Faversham) (parish), 19/152; TR021596; NP 172
Preston (parish), 20/209-222; NP 94
Preston (parish), 30/45; SK872028; NP 122
Preston (parish), 31/200; NP 119
Preston (parish), 34/406; TL940507; NP 149
Preston (parish), 36/313; TQ306062; NP 182
Preston (parish), 41/402-403; NP 99
Preston (township in Preston), 20/216; SD541299; NP 94
Preston (township in Ellingham), 27/123; NU186252; NP 71
Preston (township in Tynemouth), 27/496; NZ346696; NP 78
Preston (township in Preston), 41/402; TA178307; NP 99
Preston Bagot (Preston Baggot) (parish), 37/229; SP172658; NP 131
Preston Bisset (parish), 3/87; SP659285; NP 145
Preston Candover (parish), 14/132; SU612420; NP 168
Preston Capes (hamlet in Preston Capes), 26/262; SP570543; NP 132, 145
Preston Capes (parish), 26/262; NP 132, 145
Preston Deanery (parish), 26/368; SP792548; NP 133, 146
Preston Gubbals (parish), 31/150; SJ480207; NP 118
Preston Montford (township in St Alkmond Shrewsbury), 31/262A; SJ430140; NP 118
Preston next Wingham (parish), 19/134; NP 173
Preston on the Hill (township in Runcorn), 5/155; SJ575806; NP 100
Preston on Wye (parish), 15/199; SO385415; NP 142
Preston Patrick (township in Burton in Kendal), 38/127; SD553841; NP 89
Preston Plucknett (parish), 32/468; ST538166; NP 177
Preston Quarter (township in St Bees), 7/297; NX976137; NP 82
Preston Richard (township in Heversham), 38/88; SD532846; NP 89
Preston St Mary (Preston) (parish), 34/406; TL940507; NP 149
Preston upon Stour (parish), 13/15; SP203489; NP 144
Preston upon the Weald Moors (Preston) (parish), 31/200; SJ677153; NP 119
Preston Wynne (Preston Wynn) (township in Withington), 15/139; SO558467; NP 142
Preston, 42/148; NP 90

Preston-by-Wingham (parish), 19/134; NP 173
Preston-le-Skerne (township in Aycliffe), 11/272; NZ213335; NP 85
Preston-on-Tees (Preston, Preston-upon-Tees) (township in Stockton-on-Tees), 11/349; NZ426162; NP 85
Preston-under-Scar (Preston) (township in Wensley), 42/148; SE069925; NP 90
Prestwich (parish), 20/471, 494-499; SD817033; NP 101
Prestwich (parish), 20/471; SD817033; NP 101
Prestwich-cum-Oldham (parish), 20/471, 481-499; NP 101
Prestwick (township in Dinnington), 27/519; NZ183720; NP 78
Prestwick Carr (area in Dinnington), 27/520; NZ192738; NP 78
Prestwold (parish), 21/42-43; NP 121
Prestwold (township in Prestwold), 21/42; SK575215; NP 121
Prestwood (township in Ellastone), 33/104; SK102421; NP 120
Priddy (parish), 32/145; ST520517; NP 165
Priest Hutton (township in Warton), 20/71; SD538739; NP 89
Priestweston (township in Chirbury), 31/360; SO287973; NP 128, 129
Primethorpe (township in Broughton Astley), 21/244B; SP522931; NP 132
Princes Risborough (parish), 3/189; SP815015; NP 159
Princethorpe (township in Stretton-on-Dunsmore), 37/135; SP399707; NP 132
Prinknash Park (extra-parochial), 13/198; SO880134; NP 143
Priors Dean (parish), 14/181; SU728297; NP 181
Priors Halton (township in Bromfield), 31/423B; SO495750; NP 129
Priors Hardwick (parish), 37/250; SP463565; NP 132, 145
Priors Heys (extra-parochial), 5/395; SJ515661; NP 109
Priors Marston (parish), 37/251; SP489572; NP 132
Priors, 9/162; NP 164, 176
Priorslee (township in Shifnal), 31/223B; SJ702103; NP 119
Prisk and Killey (township in Llangattock), 45/76B; SO210170; NP 141
Prisk and Carvan, 46/45; NP 140
Priston (parish), 32/497; ST689612; NP 166
Prittlewell (parish), 12/386; TQ876868; NP 162
Privett (parish), 14/184; SU674275; NP 168, 181
Probus (district in Probus), 6/140; SW900479; NP 190
Probus (parish), 6/140-141; NP 190
Provosts Fee (division in parish and township of Walkington), 41/219; SE972364; NP 98, 99
Prudhoe (township in Ovingham), 27/563; NZ102622; NP 77
Prudhoe Castle (township in Ovingham), 27/564; NZ100637; NP 77
Pryors (Priors) (district in Tiverton), 9/162; SS932105; NP 164, 176
Prysau (township in Ysceifiog), 50/91; SJ164730; NP 108
Prysc and Carfan (Prisk and Carvan) (township in Llandewi-Brefi), 46/45; SN690560; NP 140
Publow (parish), 32/50; ST625641; NP 156, 166
Puckington (parish), 32/437A; ST377189; NP 177
Pucklechurch (parish), 13/397; ST693770; NP 156
Puddimore (parish), 32/369; ST545253; NP 177
Pudding Norton (parish), 25/158; TF923280; NP 125
Puddington (parish), 1/20; NP 133, 134
Puddington (township in Burton), 5/484; SJ335736; NP 100, 109
Puddington (parish), 9/168; SS835110; NP 164, 176
Puddlehinton (parish), 10/212; NP 178
Puddletown (Piddletown) (parish), 10/213; SY745941; NP 178
Pudleston (Pudlestone) (parish), 15/75; SO560599; NP 129
Pudsey (division in township of Pudsey in Calverley), 43/514; SE223327; NP 96
Pudsey (township in Calverley), 43/514-515; NP 96
Pulborough (parish), 36/68; TQ059206; NP 182
Pulford (parish), 5/367-368; NP 109
Pulford (township in Pulford), 5/368; SJ379598; NP 109
Pulham (parish), 10/94A-B; NP 178
Pulham St Mary Magdalene (parish), 25/762; TM198871; NP 137
Pulham St Mary the Virgin (parish), 25/763; TM215859; NP 137
Pulley (township in Meole Brace), 31/277; SJ479095; NP 118

Pulloxhill (parish), 1/107; TL066337; NP 147
Pumney (division in Abingdon St Helen), 2/19; SU531978; NP 158
Puncheston (parish), 55/39; SN006302; NP 138
Punchknowle (parish), 10/258; SY538872; NP 177
Purdis Farm (extra-parochial), 34/460; TM211428; NP 150
Purfleet (division in West Thurrock), 12/434; TQ550787; NP 171
Puriton (parish), 32/220; ST324421; NP 165
Purleigh (parish), 12/341; TL840020; NP 162
Purley (parish), 2/179A; SU660763; NP 158
Purlogue (township in Clun), 31/391; SO282763; NP 128, 129
Purse Caundle (Caundle Purse) (parish), 10/27; ST695173; NP 178
Purston Jaglin (township in Featherstone), 43/616; SE433198; NP 97, 103
Purton (hamlet in Purton), 39/51A; SU080875; NP 157
Purton (parish), 39/51A-B; SU080875; NP 157
Pusey (parish), 2/48; SU364964; NP 158
Putley (parish), 15/273; NP 143
Putley (township in Putley), 15/273; SO646374; NP 143
Putney (parish), 35/27; TQ227742; NP 170
Puttenham (parish), 16/146; SP888147; NP 146
Puttenham (parish), 35/144; SU922468; NP 169
Puxton (parish), 32/67; ST405631; NP 165
Pwll-y-wrach (hamlet in Talgarth), 45/86C; SO180320; NP 141
Pwllan (township in Tregynon), 54/109; SJ112986; NP 117, 128
Pwllcrochan (Pwllcrochon) (parish), 55/153; SM922029; NP 151
Pwllheli (borough in Denio), 48/54; SH372358; NP 115
Pycombe, 36/118; NP 182
Pyecombe (Pycombe, Piecombe) (parish), 36/118; TQ296125; NP 182
Pyle (parish), 51/98; SS827812; NP 153
Pylle (parish), 32/186; ST613390; NP 165, 166
Pyrford (parish), 35/84; TQ041590; NP 169, 170
Pyrton (parish), 29/280; SU687957; NP 158, 159
Pytchley (parish), 26/197; SP855747; NP 133
Pyworthy (parish), 9/100; SS314028; NP 174

Q

Quadring (parish), 22/735; TF220340; NP 123
Quainton (parish), 3/117-118; NP 146
Quainton (township in Quainton), 3/117; SP744201; NP 146
Quarles (parish), 25/16; TF883391; NP 125
Quarley (parish), 14/83; SU258424; NP 167, 168
Quarlton (township in Bolton le Moors), 20/395; SD744144; NP 101
Quarmby (division in township of Lindley cum Quarmby in Huddersfield), 43/751; SE114169; NP 102
Quarndon (parish), 8/212; SK331404; NP 121
Quarnford (township in Alstonfield), 33/81; SK017667; NP 110, 111
Quarrendon (parish), 3/142; SP792165; NP 146
Quarries (common to Ampleforth Birdforth, Ampleforth St Peter and Ampleforth Oswaldkirk in Ampleforth and Oswaldkirk), 42/616; SE597793; NP 92/1
Quarrington (division in township of Cassop cum Quarrington in Kelloe), 11/103; NZ318378; NP 85
Quarrington (parish), 22/597; TF058445; NP 113
Quarry Hill, 7/218; NP 82
Quarter Bach (Gwynfe Quarter Bach) (hamlet in Llangadog), 47/21; SN745160; NP 140, 153
Quatford (parish), 31/485-486; NP 130
Quatford (township in Quatford), 31/485; SO743908; NP 130
Quatt (parish), 31/483-484; NP 130
Quatt Jarvis (township in Quatt), 31/483; SO753893; NP 130
Quatt Malvern (township in Quatt), 31/484; SO750880; NP 130
Quedgeley (hamlet in Quedgeley), 13/256A; SO815136; NP 143
Quedgeley (parish), 13/256A-B; NP 143
Queen Camel (East Camel) (parish), 32/371; ST590254; NP 166, 177
Queen Charlton (parish), 32/49; ST633668; NP 156
Queenborough (parish), 19/98; TQ912722; NP 172
Queenhill (hamlet in Ripple), 40/225; SO855370; NP 143
Quenby (township in Hungerton), 21/259; SK704062; NP 122
Quendon (parish), 12/64; TL519312; NP 148
Queniborough (parish), 21/120; SK651120; NP 121
Quenington (parish), 13/289; SP134039; NP 157
Quernmore (township in Lancaster), 20/120; SD526606; NP 89, 94
Quethiock (parish), 6/67; SX325640; NP 186
Quick Mere (division in Saddleworth with Quick township in Rochdale), 43/740-742B; NP 101
Quick Mere - Lower Division (division of sub-division of Quick Mere Division in Saddleworth with Quick township in Rochdale), 43/742A; SD973037; NP 101
Quick Mere - Lower Division (division of sub-division of Quick Mere Division in Saddleworth with Quick township in Rochdale), 43/742B; SD977028; NP 101
Quick Mere - Lower Division (sub-division of Quick Mere Division in Saddleworth with Quick township in Rochdale), 43/742A-B; SD973037; NP 101
Quick Mere - Middle Division (sub-division of Quick Mere Division in Saddleworth with Quick township in Rochdale), 43/741; SD962051; NP 101
Quick Mere - Upper Division (sub-division of Quick Mere Division in Saddleworth with Quick township in Rochdale), 43/740; SD971071; NP 101
Quidenham (parish), 25/735; TM026872; NP 136
Quinton (hamlet in Quinton), 13/16; SP183470; NP 144
Quinton (parish), 13/16-17; NP 144
Quinton (parish), 26/301; SP779541; NP 133, 146
Quorndon (township in Barrow upon Soar), 21/46; SK560160; NP 121

R

Raby (township in Neston), 5/477; SJ315798; NP 100
Raby with Keverstone (township in Staindrop), 11/291; NZ118221; NP 84, 85
Rackenford (parish), 9/128; SS856188; NP 164
Rackham (hamlet in Amberley), 36/80; TQ048135; NP 182
Rackheath (parish), 25/402; TG279136; NP 126
Racton (parish), 36/237; SU782096; NP 181
Radbourne (Radburn) (parish), 8/258; SK287362; NP 120, 121
Radburn (parish), 8/258; NP 120, 121
Radcliffe (division in parish and township of Radcliffe in Radcliffe), 20/435; SD785083; NP 101
Radcliffe (division in parish and township of Radcliffe in Radcliffe), 20/436; SD772101; NP 101
Radcliffe (division in parish and township of Radcliffe in Radcliffe), 20/437; SD794093; NP 101
Radcliffe (parish), 20/435-437; NP 101
Radcliffe on Trent (parish), 28/262; SK655395; NP 121
Radclive (parish), 3/83; SP679340; NP 145, 146
Radcot (Radcott) (hamlet in Little Faringdon), 29/162; SU283996; NP 157, 158
Raddington (parish), 32/289; ST024265; NP 164
Radford (hamlet in Enstone), 29/91; SP406237; NP 145
Radford (hamlet in Coventry, Holy Trinity), 37/148; SP812329; NP 132
Radford (parish), 28/241; SK553404; NP 121
Radford Semele (parish), 37/228; SP351636; NP 132
Radipole (parish), 10/267; SY667816; NP 178
Radley (division in Radley), 2/13A; SU522993; NP 158
Radley (parish), 2/13A-C; NP 158
Radnage (parish), 3/193; SU791970; NP 159
Radnor (township in Astbury), 5/230; SJ840645; NP 110
Radstock (parish), 32/105; ST690552; NP 166
Radstone (parish), 26/345; SP594404; NP 145
Radway (parish), 37/271; SP369487; NP 145
Radwell (hamlet in Felmersham), 1/26B; TL005575; NP 134
Radwell (parish), 16/5; TL238360; NP 147
Radwinter (parish), 12/24; TL610376; NP 148
Radyr (parish), 51/129; ST128803; NP 154
Ragdale (parish), 21/65; SK669203; NP 121
Raglan (Ragland) (parish), 53/52; SO413071; NP 155
Ragnall (parish), 28/67; SK788735; NP 112, 113

Rainford (township in Prescot), 20/632; SD485005; NP 100
Rainham (parish), 12/421; TQ541829; NP 161, 171
Rainham (parish), 19/93; TQ815659; NP 172
Rainham St Margaret (parish), 25/165; NP 125
Rainham St Martin (parish), 25/186; NP 125
Rainham St Mary (parish), 25/164; NP 125
Rainhill (township in Prescot), 20/629; SJ497905; NP 100
Rainow (township in Prestbury), 5/37; SJ365768; NP 101
Rainton with Newby (township in Topcliffe), 42/238; SE373753; NP 91
Raisbeck (township in Orton), 38/70; NY657071; NP 83
Raisdale (division in township of Bilsdale Midcable in Helmsley), 42/485; NZ535015; NP 92
Raithby (division in Raithby), 22/432A; TF374673; NP 114
Raithby (parish), 22/432A-B; TF374673; NP 114
Raithby - West Fen (division in Raithby), 22/432B; TF319591; NP 114
Raithby cum Maltby (parish), 22/282; TF316848; NP 105
Rame (parish), 6/114; SX427501; NP 187
Rampisham (parish), 10/123; ST556025; NP 177
Rampton (parish), 4/54; TL424684; NP 135
Rampton (parish), 28/55; SK798782; NP 104
Ramsbury (parish), 39/180A-D; NP 157, 158
Ramsbury Town (tithing in Ramsbury), 39/180C; SU275715; NP 157
Ramsden (township in Shipton under Wychwood), 29/145; SP350150; NP 145
Ramsden Bellhouse (parish), 12/336; TQ713950; NP 161
Ramsden Crays (parish), 12/335; TQ705936; NP 161
Ramsey (parish), 12/109; TM210334; NP 150
Ramsey (parish), 17/23; TL280870; NP 134
Ramsey Island (division in St Davids [Tyddewi]), 55/67; SM702239; NP 138
Ramsgate (parish), 19/130; TR381649; NP 173
Ramsgreave (township in Blackburn), 20/315; SD678315; NP 95
Ramsholt (parish), 34/441; TM317415; NP 150
Ramshope (extra-parochial), 27/236; NT735055; NP 70
Ramshorn (township in Ellastone), 33/102; SK091442; NP 111, 120
Ranby (parish), 22/338; TF233782; NP 105
Rand (parish), 22/261-262; NP 104
Rand (township in Rand), 22/262; TF107788; NP 104
Rand Grange (Rands Grange) (township in Bedale), 42/213A; SE258892; NP 91
Randwick (parish), 13/272; SO828068; NP 156
Rangemore (township in Tatenhill), 33/217C; SK169222; NP 120
Rangeworthy (chapelry in Thornbury), 13/359; ST689860; NP 156
Ranskill (township in Blyth), 28/21; SK656880; NP 103
Ranton (Ronton) (parish), 33/173; SJ850240; NP 119
Ranton Abbey (extra-parochial), 33/172; SJ837241; NP 119
Ranworth (parish), 25/399; TG353147; NP 126
Rapsthorpe and Burdale (township in Wharram Percy), 41/140; SE867624; NP 92
Raskelf (township in Easingwold), 42/567; SE485705; NP 91, 92
Rastrick (township in Halifax), 43/577; SE140216; NP 96, 102
Ratby (parish), 21/132A-133; NP 121
Ratby (township in Ratby), 21/132A; SK505065; NP 121
Ratchwood (township in Bamburgh), 27/89; NU143283; NP 71
Ratcliff (hamlet in St Dunstan, Stepney), 24/66; TQ359810; NP 160/1
Ratcliff upon Soar) (parish), 28/277; NP 121
Ratcliffe Culey (township in Sheepy Magna), 21/160; SP340997; NP 121, 132
Ratcliffe on the Wreak (parish), 21/62; SK633148; NP 121
Ratcliffe upon Soar (Ratcliff upon Soar) (parish), 28/277; SK507302; NP 121
Rathmell (township in Giggleswick), 43/247; SD791606; NP 90, 95
Ratley and Upton (parish), 37/270; SP378469; NP 145
Ratlinghope (parish), 31/343-344; NP 118
Ratlinghope (township in Ratlinghope), 31/343; SO411965; NP 118

Rattery (parish), 9/373; SX746624; NP 187
Rattlesden (parish), 34/302; TL972582; NP 136, 149
Raughton and Gatesgill (township in Dalston), 7/145; NY400465; NP 83
Raunds (parish), 26/145; TL006736; NP 134
Raveley, 17/28
Raven Meols (division in township of Formby in Walton on the Hill), 20/676B; SD284067; NP 100
Ravenfield (parish), 43/889; SK488948; NP 103
Raveningham (parish), 25/590; TM402965; NP 137
Ravenscroft (township in Middlewich), 5/195; SJ703676; NP 110
Ravensdale Park (township in Mugginton), 8/221; SK277439; NP 120, 121
Ravensden (parish), 1/35; TL070550; NP 134, 147
Ravensthorpe (hamlet in Ravensthorpe), 26/173; SP668704; NP 132
Ravensthorpe), 26/173; SP668704; NP 133
Ravenstone (parish), 3/27; SP846505; NP 146
Ravenstone (parish), 21/3; SK402139; NP 121
Ravenstonedale (parish), 38/68; NY710020; NP 83, 84, 89, 90
Ravensworth (township in Chester le Street), 11/37; NZ231584; NP 78
Ravensworth (township in Kirkby Ravensworth), 42/27; NZ146086; NP 85
Raventhorpe (township in Appleby), 22/41; SE937076; NP 104
Raw (township in Rothbury), 27/264; NZ090995; NP 71
Rawcliffe (division of Rawcliffe township in St Michael le Belfry), 42/691; SE587546; NP 97
Rawcliffe (division of Rawcliffe township in St Olave), 42/692; SE580550; NP 97
Rawcliffe (township in St Olave and St Michael le Belfry), 42/691-692
Rawcliffe (township in Snaith), 43/963; SE697216; NP 97
Rawdon (township in Guiseley), 43/506; SE213392; NP 96
Rawmarsh (parish), 43/850; SK440964; NP 103
Rawreth (parish), 12/364; TQ783932; NP 162
Rawtenstall (division in township of Lower Booths in Whalley), 20/284; SD814229; NP 95
Raydon (parish), 34/503; TM052355; NP 149
Rayleigh (parish), 12/365; TQ806910; NP 162
Rayne (parish), 12/83; TL723233; NP 148
Reach (division of Reach hamlet in Burwell), 4/48B; TL567662; NP 135
Reach (division of Reach hamlet in Swaffham Prior), 4/49A; TL566660; NP 135
Reach (hamlet in Burwell and Swaffham Prior), 4/48B-49A; NP 135
Read (township in Whalley), 20/251; SD765355; NP 95
Reagill (township in Crosby Ravensworth), 38/35; NY602175; NP 83
Rearsby (parish), 21/119; SK653142; NP 121
Reaveley (township in Ingram), 27/130; NU015175; NP 71
Rectory (division in St Marylebone), 24/45D; TQ282815; NP 160/1
Reculver (parish), 19/119; TR213682; NP 173
Red Hulton, 20/566; NP 101
Redberth (Redburth) (parish), 55/134; SN088038; NP 151, 152
Redbourn (parish), 16/97; TL105115; NP 147, 160
Redbourne (parish), 22/116; SK987992; NP 104
Redburth (parish), 55/134; NP 151, 152
Redcar (division of Redcar township in Marske), 42/345; NZ609251; NP 86
Redcar (division of Redcar township in Upleatham), 42/344; NZ608248; NP 86
Redcar (township in Upleatham and Marske), 42/344-345; NP 86
Reddish (township in Manchester), 20/532; SJ895933; NP 101
Redditch (township in Tardebigge), 40/50A-B; NP 131
Rede (Reed) (parish), 34/312; TL802562; NP 136, 149
Redenhall (division in Redenhall), 25/635; TM252854; NP 137
Redenhall, 25/635-636; NP 137
Redgrave (hamlet in Redgrave), 34/90; TM052781; NP 136
Redgrave (parish), 34/90; NP 136
Redisham (Great Redisham) (parish), 34/45; TM404855; NP137

Redland (division in Bristol, St James and St Paul), 13/409A; ST582748; NP 155
Redlingfield (parish), 34/140; TM187706; NP 137
Redlynch (tithing in Bruton), 32/197C; ST700430; NP 166
Redmarley D'Abitot (Redmarley D'Abitott) (parish), 40/233; SO763313; NP 143
Redmarshall (parish), 11/264-266; NP 85
Redmarshall (township in Redmarshall), 11/266; NZ385207; NP 85
Redmere (extra-parochial), 25/699; TL642864; NP 135
Redmile (parish), 21/88; SK795355; NP 122
Redmire (township in Wensley), 42/149; SE052930; NP 90
Rednal (township in West Felton), 31/93; SJ370282; NP 118
Redruth (Euny Redruth) (parish), 6/165; SW701430; NP 189, 190
Redwick (chapelry in Magor), 53/149; ST412846; NP 155
Redworth (division in township of Redworth in Heighington), 11/283; NZ243236; NP 85
Redworth (township in Heighington), 11/28-2853; NP 85
Reed (parish), 16/15; TL365375; NP 148
Reedham (parish), 25/464; TG426033; NP 126, 137
Reedley Hallows (extra-parochial), 20/237; SD830360; NP 95
Reedness (township in Whitgift), 43/958; SE792221; NP 98, 104
Reepham (Repham) (parish), 22/355; TF040743; NP 104, 113
Reepham (Reifham St Mary) (parish), 25/202; TG104234; NP 125
Reeth (division in township of Reeth in Grinton), 42/103B; SE032996; NP 90
Reeth (township in Grinton), 42/103A-105; NP 90
Reeth High Moor (common to Healaugh and Reeth divisions in Reeth in Grinton), 42/105; NY993006; NP 90
Regent's Park (division in St Pancras), 24/44C; TQ283835; NP 160
Regilbury (extra-parochial), 32/492; ST527634; NP 166
Reifham St Mary (parish), 25/202; NP 125
Reigate (parish), 35/113-114; NP 170
Reigate Borough (division in Reigate), 35/114; TQ253502; NP 170
Reigate Foreign (division in Reigate), 35/113; TQ259500; NP 170
Reighton (Righton) (parish), 41/166; TA130750; NP 93
Reilth (township in Mainstone), 31/384B; SO286871; NP 129
Reinden (extra-parochial), 19/385; TR219415; NP 173
Remenham (parish), 2/206; SU776835; NP 159
Rempstone (parish), 28/286; SK580245; NP 121
Rendcomb (Rendcombe) (parish), 13/214; SP022105; NP 143, 144, 157
Rendham (parish), 34/258; TM354654; NP 137
Rendlesham (parish), 34/380; TM339531; NP 150
Renhold (parish), 1/43; TL098524; NP 147
Renishaw (township in Eckington), 8/55B; SK448785; NP 103
Rennington (township in Embleton), 27/155; NU208181; NP 71
Renwick (parish), 7/174; NY613452; NP 83
Repham (parish), 22/355; NP 104, 113
Repps with Bastwick (parish), 25/374; TG423173; NP 126
Repton (parish), 8/310; NP 120, 121
Repton (township in Repton), 8/311; SK315255; NP 121
Resolven (hamlet in Llantwit juxta Neath), 51/54; SN855020; NP 153, 154
Rest Park (division in township of Sherburn in Elmet in Sherburn in Elmet), 43/432; SE540332; NP 97
Rettendon (parish), 12/338; TQ780970; NP 162
Revelstoke (parish), 9/469; SX548467; NP 187
Revesby (division in Revesby), 22/446A; TF302618; NP 114
Revesby (parish), 22/446A-D, 457-458; NP 114
Revesby - West Fen (division in Revesby), 22/446B; TF274568; NP 114
Revesby - West Fen (division in Revesby), 22/446C; TF309593; NP 114
Rewe (parish), 9/220-221; NP 176
Rewe (tithing in Rewe), 9/220; SS946008; NP 176
Reydon (parish), 34/62; TM494781; NP 137
Reymerston (parish), 25/546; TG018060; NP 125

Reynalton (Reynalston) (parish), 55/129; SN090089; NP 152
Reynoldston (parish), 51/30; SS479898; NP 152, 153
Rhanberfedd, 50/120; NP 108, 109
Rhanberfydd (Rhanberfedd) (township in Hope), 50/120; SJ292589; NP 108, 109
Rhandir-Abbot (hamlet in Llanfair-ar-y-bryn), 47/1D; SN830470; NP 140
Rhandir-Canol (hamlet in Llanfair-ar-y-bryn), 47/1B; SN800430; NP 140
Rhandir-Isaf (hamlet in Llanfair-ar-y-bryn), 47/1A; SN800400; NP 140
Rhandir-Uchaf (hamlet in Llanfair-ar-y-bryn), 47/1C; SN800470; NP 140
Rhayadyr (Rhayadyr ar Gwy) (parish), 56/32; SN972681; NP 128
Rhayadyr ar Gwy, 56/32; NP 128
Rhetescyn, 54/74; NP 117, 118
Rhigos (hamlet in Ystrad-dyfodwg), 51/67; SN930050; NP 154
Rhinefield Walk (division in Brockenhurst), 14/327C; SU285035; NP 179, 180
Rhinefield Walk (extra-parochial division in Lyndhurst registration subdistrict in New Forest extra-parochial), 14/302E; SU265050; NP 179
Rhinefield Walk (extra-parochial division in New Forest extra-parochial), 14/302J; SU260002; NP 179, 180
Rhinefield Walk (in New Forest and Brockenhurst), 14/302E, 302J, 327C; NP 179, 180
Rhiston (township in Church Stoke), 31/362; SO254953; NP 128
Rhiw (parish), 48/77; SH228278; NP 115
Rhiw-hiriaeth, 54/53; NP 117
Rhiwabon (parish), 49/84-95; NP 108, 109, 118
Rhiwabon, 49/88; NP 109, 118
Rhiwhiriaeth (Rhewhirieth, Rhiw-hiriaeth) (township in Llanfair Caereinion), 54/53; SJ062050; NP 117
Rhiwlas (township in Llansilin), 49/123; SJ201328; NP 117
Rhiwnachor (township in Llanfyllin), 54/16; SJ078192; NP 117
Rhiwrhad (township in St Harmon), 56/1C; SO000720; NP 128
Rhiwsion (hamlet in Llanwenog), 46/81B; SN503467; NP 140
Rhodogedio, 44/15; NP 106
Rhos Lligwy (parish), 44/12; NP 106
Rhos y mynach, 44/10; NP 106
Rhos-Goch (township in Worthen), 54/94; SJ283069; NP 117, 118
Rhos-mynach (Rhos y mynach) (district in Llaneilian and Llanwenllwyfo), 44/10; SH487910; NP 106
Rhosaflo (township in Llanfair Caereinion), 54/52; SJ067068; NP 117
Rhosbeiro, 44/6; SH394914; NP 106
Rhoscilly, 51/34; NP 153
Rhoscolyn (parish), 44/52; SH273759; NP 106
Rhoscrowther (parish), 55/154; SM915015; NP 151
Rhosdie, 46/29; NP 127
Rhosferig (Rhosferrig) (hamlet in Llanfihangel-Brynpabuan), 45/19; SO021521; NP 141
Rhossili (Rossilly, Rhoscilly) (parish), 51/34; SS422881; NP 153
Rhostie (Rhosdie) (parish), 46/29; SN637724; NP 127
Rhuddlan (parish), 50/57-65; NP 108
Rhugantin, 31/403; NP 128
Rhulen (parish), 56/49; SO138498; NP 141
Rhuthun (parish), 49/39; NP 108
Rhwngowy Clydach, 51/7; NP 153
Rhyd (township in Dyserth), 50/56; SJ052806; NP 108
Rhyd-y-cwm (Rhugantin) (township in Bettws-y-crwyn), 31/403; SO172822; NP 128
Rhyd-y-gwern (Rhydgwern) (hamlet in Machen), 51/134; ST212882; NP 154
Rhyddlan-issa (hamlet in Llanwenog), 46/80; SN478429; NP 139, 140
Rhyddlan-ucha (hamlet in Llanwenog), 46/79; SN502436; NP 140
Rhydescyn (Rhetescyn) (township in Guilsfield [Cegidfa]), 54/74; SJ276152; NP 117, 118
Rhydfaes (township in Llandinam), 54/151; SN996875; NP 128

Rhydgwern, 51/134; NP 154
Rhydorddwy (township in Rhuddlan), 50/57; SJ036813; NP 108
Rhydyboithan (hamlet in Eglwysilan), 51/81; ST130850; NP 154
Rhyl (township in Rhuddlan), 50/62; SJ001811; NP 108
Rhyllan (township in St Asaph [Llanelwy]), 50/75; SJ054744; NP 108
Rhymney [Rhymni] (Rumney) (parish), 53/127; ST220790; NP 154
Rhymni (parish), 53/127; NP 154
Rhyndwyclydach (Rhwngowy Clydach) (hamlet in Llangyfelach), 51/7; SN697097; NP
Rhysgog (township in Llangollen), 49/112; SJ182438; NP 108
Rhysgog (township in Llanfyllin), 54/10; SJ162181; NP 117
Rhysnant (township in Llandrinio), 54/84; SJ256177; NP 117
Ribbesford (parish), 40/73-74; NP 130
Ribbesford (township in Ribbesford), 40/73; SO779729; NP 130
Ribbleton (township in Preston), 20/219; SD571319; NP 94
Ribbleton Moor (common to Ribbleton and Brockholes in Preston), 20/218; SD569312; NP 94
Ribby with Wrea (township in Kirkham), 20/197; SD402313; NP 94
Ribchester (parish), 20/223-227; NP 94, 95
Ribchester (township in Ribchester), 20/226; SD643365; NP 95
Ribton (township in Bridekirk), 7/242; NY054312; NP 82
Riby (parish), 22/97; TA182078; NP 105
Riccall (parish), 41/57; SE627375; NP 97
Richards Castle (division in Richards Castle), 15/1; SO488690; NP 129
Richards Castle (parish), 15/1, 31/535; NP 129
Richards Castle (township in Richards Castle), 31/535; SO500710; NP 129
Richmond (West Sheen) (parish), 35/31; TQ184759; NP 170
Richmond (parish), 42/95; NZ158018; NP 91
Rickerby (township in Stanwix), 7/75; NY419573; NP 76
Rickergate (township in St Mary [Carlisle]), 7/87; NY408560; NP 76
Rickinghall Inferior (parish), 34/93; TM030740; NP 136
Rickinghall Superior (parish), 34/92; TM044736; NP 136
Rickling (parish), 12/65; TL503310; NP 148
Rickmansworth (parish), 16/133; TL050950; NP 159, 160
Ricknall (division of Woodham township in Aycliffe), 11/273; NZ292257; NP 85
Riddells Quarter (township in Longhorsley), 27/294; NZ155939; NP 71, 78
Riddlesworth (parish), 25/731; TL963816; NP 136
Ridgacre (township in Halesowen), 40/15; SP006846; NP 130, 131
Ridge (parish), 16/126; TL211010; NP 160
Ridge (tithing in Chilmark), 39/284; ST958328; NP 167
Ridgewell (Ridgwell) (parish), 12/32; TL735410; NP 148, 149
Ridgmont (parish), 1/79; SP976373; NP 147
Ridgmont (division in township of Burstwick and Skeckling in Burstwick), 41/423; TA242289; NP 99
Ridgwell (parish), 12/32; NP 148, 149
Riding (township in Bywell St Andrew), 27/623; NZ008611; NP 77
Ridley (parish), 19/79; TQ621646; NP 171
Ridley (township in Bunbury), 5/309; SJ552544; NP 109
Ridley (township in Haltwhistle), 27/579; NY779623; NP 77
Ridley (township in Holt), 49/73; SJ395402; NP 109
Ridlington (parish), 25/219; TG348311; NP 126
Ridlington (parish), 30/40; SK842055; NP 122
Rievaulx (township in Helmsley), 42/487; SE583957; NP 92
Righton, 41/166; NP 93
Rigsby with Ailby (parish), 22/403; TF432761; NP 105, 114
Rigton (township in Kirkby Overblow), 43/384; SE281498; NP 96
Rillington (parish), 41/149-150; NP 92
Rillington (township in Rillington), 41/149; SE840753; NP 92
Rilstone, 43/212; NP 91
Rimington (Rimmington) (township in Gisburn), 43/297; SD817459; NP 95
Rimmington, 43/297; NP 95
Rimpton (Rympton) (parish), 32/390; ST610216; NP 166, 178

Rimswell (township in Owthorne), 41/421; TA313286; NP 99
Ringland (parish), 25/349; TG133137; NP 125
Ringmer (parish), 36/195; TQ456134; NP 183
Ringmore (parish), 9/472; SX648470; NP 187
Ringsash, 9/119; NP 163, 175
Ringsfield (parish), 34/46; TM402872; NP 137
Ringshall (parish), 34/353; TM040525; NP 149
Ringstead (Great Ringstead (St Peter and St Andrew)) (parish), 25/3; TF714403; NP 124
Ringstead (parish), 26/144; SP986749; NP 134
Ringwood (parish), 14/318; SU158041; NP 179
Ringwould (Ringwold) (parish), 19/363; TR369479; NP 173
Ripe (Eckington) (parish), 36/191; TQ511104; NP 183
Ripley (chapelry in Send), 35/83; TQ056552; NP 170
Ripley (parish), 43/150-152; NP 91, 96
Ripley (township in Pentrich), 8/194B; SK397500; NP 111, 112
Ripley (township in Ripley), 43/150; SE282610; NP 91, 96
Riplingham (hamlet in Rowley), 41/216B; SE966322; NP 98
Riplingham, 41/216A; NP 98
Riplington (township in Whalton), 27/395; NZ116820; NP 77
Ripon (parish), 43/158-193, 197; NP 91
Ripon (township in Ripon), 43/178; SE312712; NP 91
Rippingale (parish), 22/676; TF117284; NP 123
Ripple (division in Barking), 12/317; TQ468837; NP 161
Ripple (hamlet in Ripple), 40/223; SO872395; NP 143
Ripple (parish), 19/358; TR353494; NP 173
Ripple (parish), 40/223-225; NP 143
Risbury (division in Humber), 15/100; SO552557; NP 142
Risbury (division in Stoke Prior), 15/101; SO548548; NP 129, 142
Risbury (township in Humber and Stoke Prior), 15/100-101; NP 142
Risby (hamlet in Walesby), 22/205; TF142913; NP 104, 105
Risby (parish), 34/204; TL798669; NP 136
Risby (township in Roxby-cum-Risby), 22/44; SE923143; NP 104
Risby (township in Rowley), 41/217; TA008353; NP 98, 99
Risca (parish), 53/115; ST240920; NP 154
Rise (parish), 41/398; TA156421; NP 99
Riseholme (parish), 22/248; SK982752; NP 104
Riseley (Risley) (parish), 1/7; TL040630; NP 134
Riselip (parish), 24/93; NP 160
Rishangles (parish), 34/175; TM164687; NP 136, 137
Rishton (township in Blackburn), 20/309; SD722299; NP 95
Rishworth (township in Halifax), 43/569; SE007164; NP 101, 102
Risley (division in township of Culcheth in Winwick), 20/600; SJ928665; NP 101
Risley (township in Wilne), 8/284; SK457364; NP 121
Ritton Colt Park (township in Netherwitton), 27/330; NZ077937; NP 71, 77
Ritton White House (township in Netherwitton), 27/329; NZ058945; NP 71, 77
Rivenhall (parish), 12/187; TL823186; NP 149
River (parish), 19/377; TR294434; NP 173
River Green (extra-parochial), 27/400; NZ131840; NP 77, 78
Riverhead (division in Sevenoaks), 19/192; TQ514548; NP 171
Rivington (township in Bolton le Moors), 20/387; SD640140; NP 101
Rixton (division in township of Rixton with Glazebrook in Warrington), 20/612; SJ681905; NP 101
Rixton with Glazebrook (township in Warrington), 20/611-612; NP 101
Road (parish), 32/96; ST812536; NP 166
Roade (parish), 26/300; SP763512; NP 146
Roath (parish), 51/138; ST200776; NP 154
Robeston Wathen (chapelry in Narberth), 55/114; SN085115; NP 151, 152
Robeston West (parish), 55/102; SM883092; NP 151
Roborough (parish), 9/89; SS574174; NP 163
Roby (division in township of Huyton with Roby in Huyton), 20/640; SJ431903; NP 100
Roch (parish), 55/73; SM879207; NP 138

184

Rochdale (parish), 20/438-470, 43/738-745B; NP 101, 102
Rochdale (parish), 20/438-470, 43/738-745A-B; NP 95, 101, 102
Roche (parish), 6/93; SW992602; NP 185
Rochester (Rochester Ward) (township in Elsdon), 27/238; NT820010; NP 70, 71, 77
Rochester (parish), 33/105; SK110392; NP 111
Rochester, Cathedral Precinct (extra-parochial), 19/87; TQ742685; NP 171/1
Rochester, St Margaret (division inside Rochester borough in Rochester, St Margaret), 19/88A; TQ736664; NP 171, 172
Rochester, St Margaret (division outside the Rochester borough in Rochester, St Margaret (parish), 19/88A-B; NP 171, 172
Rochester, St Margaret), 19/88A-B; NP 171, 172
Rochester, St Nicholas (parish), 19/86; TQ746686; NP 171/1
Rochford (parish), 12/366; TQ865905; NP 162
Rochford (parish), 40/2; SO632677; NP 130
Rock (division of Rock and Henley township in Stanton Lacy), 31/521B; SO532757; NP 129
Rock (parish), 40/75; SO740720; NP 130
Rock (township in Embleton), 27/151; NU193205; NP 71
Rock and Henley (township in Stanton Lacey), 51/521B-C; NP 129
Rockbeare (parish), 9/282; SY039941; NP 176
Rockbourne (Rockbourn) (parish), 14/314; SU112189; NP 167, 179
Rockcliff (parish), 7/68-69
Rockfield (parish), 53/16; SO475152; NP 142
Rockhampton (parish), 13/356; ST651935; NP 156
Rockingham (parish), 26/367; SP870913; NP 133
Rockland All Saints (parish), 25/676A; TL994964; NP 136
Rockland All Saints (parish), 25/676B; TL990955; NP 136
Rockland St Mary (parish), 25/478; TG320045; NP 126
Rockland St Peter (parish), 25/677; TL982982; NP 136
Rocksavage, 5/161; NP 100
Rodbaston (township in Penkridge), 33/236; SJ920118; NP 119
Rodborough (parish), 13/308; SO850040; NP 156
Rodbourne (Rodbourn) (tithing in St Paul Malmesbury), 39/32; ST934832; NP 156, 157
Rodbourne Cheney (parish), 39/56; SU137874; NP 157
Rodd, Nash and Little Brampton (township in Presteigne), 15/39; SO313621; NP 129
Roddam (township in Ilderton), 27/120; NU022197; NP 71
Rodden (parish), 32/126; ST799477; NP 166
Roden (township in High Ercall), 31/212; SJ570160; NP 118
Rodhuish (hamlet in Carhampton), 32/237B; ST012399; NP 164
Rodington (parish), 31/236; SJ581146; NP 118, 119
Rodmarton (parish), 13/304; ST947978; NP 156, 157
Rodmell (parish), 36/319; TQ413056; NP 183
Rodmersham (parish), 19/160; TQ919608; NP 172
Rodney Stoke (parish), 32/146; ST479499; NP 165
Rodsley (township in Longford), 8/232; SK202401; NP 120
Roeburndale (township in Melling), 20/89; SD611622; NP 89, 94, 95
Roecliffe (township in Aldborough), 43/133; SE371656; NP 91
Roel (Rowell) (extra-parochial), 13/67; SP064248; NP 144
Rofford (division in Chalgrove), 29/287; SU628985; NP 158
Rogate (division in Rogate), 36/9A; SU805251; NP 181
Rogate (parish), 36/9A-B; NP 181
Rogerstone (hamlet in Bassaleg), 53/120; ST270890; NP 154, 155
Roggett (parish), 53/145; NP 155
Roggiett (parish), 53/145; NP 155
Rogiet (Roggett, Roggiett) (parish), 53/145; ST455879; NP 155
Rokeby (parish), 42/15; NZ079139; NP 84
Rollesby (parish), 25/380; TG450160; NP 126
Rolleston (Rollstone) (township in Billesdon), 21/284; SK703003; NP 122, 133
Rolleston (parish), 28/156-157; NP 112
Rolleston (township in Rolleston), 28/156; SK750524; NP 112
Rolleston on Dove (parish), 33/210-211; NP 120
Rolleston on Dove (Rolleston) (township in Rolleston on Dove), 33/210; SK235274; NP 120

Rolleston, 33/210; NP 120
Rollestone, 21/284; NP 122, 133
Rollestone (Rollstone) (parish), 39/266; SU090444; NP 167
Rollstone (parish), 39/266; NP 167
Rolston (Rowlston, Rowlstone) (division in township of Mappleton in Mappleton), 41/370; TA210450; NP 99
Rolvenden (parish), 19/411; TQ849309; NP 184
Romaldkirk (parish), 42/2-8; NP 84
Romaldkirk (township in Romaldkirk), 42/5; NY975215; NP 84
Romanby (township in Northallerton), 42/263; SE373923; NP 91
Romansleigh (parish), 9/84; SS736197; NP 163
Romford (hamlet in Romford), 12/314B; TQ514892; NP 161
Romford (parish), 12/314A-D; NP 161
Romiley (township in Stockport), 5/18; SJ949909; NP 101
Romsey (parish), 14/224-225; NP 168, 180
Romsey Extra (division in Romsey), 14/224; SU359201; NP 168, 180
Romsey Intra (division in Romsey), 14/225; SU349213; NP 168
Romsley (township in Alveley), 31/482; SO784836; NP 130
Romsley (township in Halesowen), 40/5; SO958795; NP 130
Ronton (parish), 33/173; NP 119
Rook Barugh (division in township of Normanby in Normanby), 42/446; SE726826; NP 92
Rookwith (township in Thornton Watlass), 42/184; SE208868; NP 91
Roomhill (parish), 19/441, 36/148; NP 184
Roos (parish), 41/410, 413-414; NP 99
Roos (township in Roos), 41/414; TA288305; NP 99
Roosdown, 9/294; NP 177
Rope (township in Wybunbury), 5/253; SJ692528; NP 110
Ropley (parish), 14/172; SU650323; NP 168
Ropsley (parish), 22/636-637; SK992351; NP 123
Ropsley (township in Ropsley), 22/636; SK992351; NP 123
Rorrington (township in Chirbury), 31/349; SJ303005; NP 118, 129
Rose Ash (parish), 9/82; SS791209; NP 163, 164
Roseacre (division in township of Treales, Roseacre and Wharles in Kirkham), 20/205; SD439639; NP 94
Rosedale East (Rosedale East Side) (township in Middleton), 42/437; SE715985; NP 92
Rosedale West (Rosedale West Side) (township in Lastingham), 42/462; SE708968; NP 92
Roseden (Rosedon) (township in Ilderton), 27/119; NU038214; NP 71
Rosemarket (parish), 55/106; SM954088; NP 151
Rosley (township in Westward), 7/148; NY320460; NP 82, 83
Rosliston (Rostliston) (parish), 8/321; SK249163; NP 120
Ross (borough in Ross-on-Wye), 15/252; SO608242; NP 142, 143
Ross (township in Belford), 27/78; NU135375; NP 64
Ross Foreign (division in Ross-on-Wye), 15/254; SO579223; NP 142
Ross-on-Wye (parish), 15/252-254; NP 142, 143
Rossall Up and Down (township in St Chad Shrewsbury), 31/272; SJ457162; NP 118
Rossington (parish), 43/926; SK623988; NP 103
Rostherne (parish), 5/89, 91-100; NP 101, 110
Rostherne (township in Rostherne), 5/94; SJ745840; NP 101
Rostliston (parish), 8/321; NP 120
Rothbury (parish), 27/243-267; NP 71, 77
Rothbury (township in Rothbury), 27/254; NU068025; NP 71
Rotherby (parish), 21/117; SK682162; NP 121, 122
Rotherfield Greys (parish), 29/309; SU725831; NP 159
Rotherfield Peppard (parish), 29/321; SU714816; NP 159
Rotherfield (parish), 36/44; TQ546311; NP 171, 183
Rotherham (parish), 43/836-843, 845; NP 102, 103
Rotherham (township in Rotherham), 43/843; SK437927; NP 103
Rothersthorpe (parish), 26/282; SP717572; NP 133
Rotherwick (parish), 14/42; SU718562; NP 169
Rothley (parish), 21/52A-55; NP 121
Rothley (township in Rothley), 21/52A; SK582131; NP 121
Rothley (township in Hartburn), 27/341; NZ046894; NP 77

Rothley Temple (extra-parochial), 21/56; SK579124; NP 121
Rothwell (parish), 22/100; TF152991; NP 104
Rothwell (Rowell) (hamlet in Rothwell), 26/127; SP822810; NP 133
Rothwell (Rowell) (parish), 26/127-129; NP 133
Rothwell (division in township of Rothwell in Rothwell), 43/594; SE347282; NP 96
Rothwell (parish), 43/591-598; NP 96
Rothwell (township in Rothwell), 43/593-595; NP 96
Rothwell Haigh (division in township of Rothwell in Rothwell), 43/593; SE333297; NP 96
Rotsea (township in Hutton Cranswick), 41/281; TA071514; NP 99
Rottingdean (parish), 36/316; TQ377029; NP 182, 183
Rottington (township in St Bees), 7/299; NX955129; NP 82
Roudham (parish), 25/726; TL949877; NP 136
Rougham (parish), 25/182; TF826205; NP 125
Rougham (parish), 34/231; TL912633; NP 136
Roughdown (parish), 14/330; SU431022; NP 180
Roughlee Booth (township in Whalley), 20/260; SD842403; NP 95
Roughside, 11/168; NP 77, 84
Roughton (division in Roughton), 22/378A; TF246650; NP 114
Roughton (parish), 22/378A-B; NP 114
Roughton (parish), 25/55; TG220376; NP 126
Roughton - Wildmore Fen (division in Roughton), 22/378B; TF249528; NP 114
Roulston (parish), 22/570; TF083565; NP 113
Roundhay (township in Barwick in Elmet), 43/415; SE334373; NP 96
Roundhay Grange (division in township of Shadwell in Thorner), 43/411; SE349372; NP 96
Roundway, 39/133; NP 167
Rous Lench (Rouse Lench) (parish), 40/139; SP013542; NP 131, 144
Rousdon (Rousdon St Pancras, Roosdown) (extra-parochial), 9/294; SY295905; NP 177
Rousham (parish), 29/86; SP473238; NP 145
Routh (parish), 41/343; TA090427; NP 99
Row Bound (township in Castle Sowerby), 7/156; NY396387; NP 83
Rowberrow (parish), 32/150; ST457581; NP 165
Rowde (parish), 39/129; ST982622; NP 157, 167
Rowell (extra-parochial), 13/67; NP 14
Rowell, 26/127-129; NP 133
Rowington (parish), 32/498; NP 164
Rowington (parish), 37/173-174; NP 131
Rowington (township in Rowington), 37/173; SP202683; NP 131
Rowland (township in Bakewell), 8/92; SK213720; NP 111
Rowlands Marsh (extra-parochial), 22/467D; NP 114
Rowlestone (Rowlstone) (parish), 15/221; SO375270; NP 142
Rowley (parish), 41/216A-218
Rowley (Riplingham) (hamlet in Rowley), 41/216A; SE974327; NP 98
Rowley (township in Muggleswick), 11/165; NZ077497; NP 77, 84
Rowley Regis (parish), 33/343; SO967877; NP 130
Rowlston (Rowlstone), 41/370
Rowlstone (parish), 15/221; NP 142
Rowner (parish), 14/294; SU585015; NP 180
Rowsley (Great Rowsley) (township in Bakewell), 8/95; SK252658; NP 111
Rowston (Roulston) (parish), 22/570; TF083565; NP 113
Rowton (division in Alberbury Lower Quarter township in Alberbury), 31/298; SJ377129; NP 118
Rowton (township in Christleton), 5/377; SJ442643; NP 109
Rowton (township in Stokesay), 31/418; SO426808; NP 129
Rowton and Ellerdine (township in High Ercall), 31/206; SJ640182; NP 119
Roxby (township in Roxby-cum-Risby), 22/45; SE941172; NP 104
Roxby (township in Hinderwell), 42/369; NZ757141; NP 86
Roxby-cum-Risby (parish), 22/44-45; NP 104

Roxham (parish), 25/523; TL637999; NP 124, 135
Roxholm (hamlet in Leasingham), 22/581; TF053502; NP 113
Roxton (parish), 1/37; TL140551; NP 134, 147
Roxwell (parish), 12/281; TL640090; NP 148, 161
Royal Leamington Spa, 37/164; NP 132
Royalty Farm (extra-parochial), 22/740; TF209423; NP 123
Roydon (division in Harlow hundred in Roydon), 12/263A; TL412097; NP 148, 161
Roydon (division in Waltham hundred in Roydon), 12/263B; TL419081; NP 161
Roydon, 12/263A; NP 148, 161
Roydon (parish), 25/178; TF692229; NP 124
Roydon (parish), 25/745; TM097807; NP 136
Royds Green (division in township of Rothwell in Rothwell), 43/595; SE355265; NP 96
Royston (division in Royston), 4/174; TL535407; NP 148
Royston (division in Royston), 16/14; TL362404; NP 148
Royston (parish), 4/174, 16/14; NP 148
Royston (Roystone) (parish), 43/684-690; NP 102
Royston (Roystone) (township in Royston), 43/687; SE359113; NP 102
Royton (township in Oldham), 20/482; SD925075; NP 101
Royton (township in Bangor-is-y-coed), 49/80; SJ369458; NP 109, 118
Ruabon (Rhiwabon) (parish), 49/84-95; NP 108, 109, 118
Ruabon (Rhiwabon) (township in Ruabon), 49/88; SJ303438; NP 109, 118
Ruabon Mountain (township in Ruabon), 49/91; SJ255465; NP 108, 117
Ruan Major (parish), 6/188; SW715185; NP 189, 190
Ruan Minor (parish), 6/189; SW717159; NP 189, 190
Ruanlanihorne (Ruan Lanyhorne) (parish), 6/151; SW900425; NP 190
Ruardean (parish), 13/160; SO621177; NP 142, 143
Ruckinge (parish), 19/401; TR019342; NP 172, 184
Ruckland (parish), 22/329; TF339783; NP 105
Ruckley and Langley (Langley and Ruckley) (township in Acton Burnell), 31/438; SJ537001; NP 118, 129
Rudbaxton (parish), 55/76; SM970200; NP 138, 151
Rudby (Rudby in Cleveland) (township in Rudby in Cleveland), 42/290; NZ477079; NP 85
Rudby in Cleveland (parish), 42/289-296; NP 85, 91
Rudchester (township in Ovingham), 27/552; NZ113675; NP 77
Ruddington (parish), 28/255; SK573330; NP 121
Ruddry, 51/133; NP 154
Rudford (hamlet in Highleadon), 13/138; SO776211; NP 143
Rudge (tithing in Crediton), 9/211E; SX852979; NP 176
Rudge (township in Pattingham), 31/479; SO807976; NP 130
Rudgwick (parish), 36/33; TQ084320; NP 170, 182
Rudheath Lordship (township in Davenham), 5/185; SJ691711; NP 110
Rudheath Township (township in Davenham), 5/184; SJ690730; NP 110
Rudry (Ruddry) (parish), 51/133; ST181865; NP 154
Rudston (division in parish and township of Rudston), 41/242; TA090680; NP 93
Rudston (parish), 41/242-243; NP 93
Rudyard (township in Leek), 33/6; SJ958598; NP 110
Rufford (parish), 20/350; SD451162; NP 100
Rufford (parish), 28/100; SK620610; NP 112
Rufforth (parish), 43/53; SE538504; NP 97
Ruffside (Roughside) (division in parish and township of Edmondbyers), 11/168; NY995505; NP 77, 84
Rugby (parish), 37/128; SP508748; NP 132
Rugeley (parish), 33/227; SK038162; NP 119, 120
Ruishton (parish), 32/330; ST267240; NP 177
Ruislip (Riselip) (parish), 24/93; TQ100880; NP 160
Rumboldswyke (parish), 36/263; SU872037; NP 181
Rumburgh (parish), 34/73; TM353813; NP 137
Rumney (parish), 53/127; NP 154
Rumworth (township in Deane), 20/570; SD695078; NP 101
Runcorn (parish), 5/146-164; NP 100-101
Runcorn (township in Runcorn), 5/159; SJ512826; NP 100

Runcton Holme (parish), 25/317; TF616094; NP 124
Runhall (parish), 25/551; TG057072; NP 125
Runham (parish), 25/387; TG471105; NP 126
Runnington (Rowington) (parish), 32/498; ST124221; NP 164
Runswick (tithing in Farnham), 35/149; SU835485; NP 169
Runton (parish), 25/38; TG196422; NP 126
Runwell (parish), 12/337; TQ760960; NP 161, 162
Ruscombe (parish), 2/215; SU804763; NP 159
Rushall (parish), 25/764; TM204863; NP 137
Rushall (parish), 33/308; SP023999; NP 120, 131
Rushall (parish), 39/222; SU128562; NP 167
Rushbrooke (parish), 34/230; TL888618; NP 136
Rushbury (parish), 31/430; NP 129
Rushbury (township in Rushbury), 31/430; SO525918; NP 129
Rushden (parish), 16/25; TL311319; NP 147
Rushden (parish), 26/212; SP963662; NP 133, 134
Rushford (division in Rushford), 25/729; TL923820; NP 136
Rushford (parish), 25/729, 34/101; NP 136
Rushford (division in Rushford), 34/101; TL932807; NP 136
Rushmere (parish), 34/55; TM495875; NP 137
Rushmere St Andrew (Rushmere) (hamlet in Rushmere St Andrew), 34/461; TM204452; NP 150
Rushmere St Andrew (Rushmere) (parish), 43/461-462; NP 150
Rushmere, 34/461; NP 150
Rushock (parish), 40/34; SO885711; NP 130
Rusholme (Rushulme) (township in Manchester), 20/529; SJ861953; NP 101
Rushton (parish), 26/130; SP838841; NP 133
Rushton (township in Tarporley), 5/398; SJ588631; NP 109, 110
Rushton Green (township in Burslem), 33/21; SJ872488; NP 110
Rushton James (township in Leek), 33/3; SJ926612; NP 110
Rushton Spencer (township in Leek), 33/4; SJ935621; NP 110
Ruskington (parish), 22/582; TF097515; NP 113
Rusland (division in township of Colton in Colton), 20/50; SD350892; NP 89
Rusper (parish), 36/37; TQ208365; NP 170, 182
Rustington (parish), 36/294; TQ055021; NP 182
Ruston Parva (parish), 41/271; TA066618; NP 99
Ruswarp (township in Whitby), 42/381; NZ886102; NP 86
Ruswick (division in township of Newton-le-Willows township in Patrick Brompton), 42/205; SE198896; NP 91
Ruthin (Rhuthun) (parish), 49/39; SJ122585; NP 108
Ruyton of the Eleven Towns (parish), 31/135-140; NP 118
Ruyton of the Eleven Towns (Ruyton, Ruyton-XI-Towns) (township in Ruyton of the Eleven Towns), 31/140; SJ385229; NP 118
Ryal (township in Stamfordham), 27/459; NZ012745; NP 77
Ryarsh (parish), 19/180; TQ670591; NP 171
Rycote (division in Great Haseley), 29/261; SP669039; NP 158
Rydal and Loughrigg (township in Grasmere), 38/78; NY363063; NP 83, 89
Rydall, 38/78
Ryddalt, 49/95; NP 109, 118
Rye (parish), 36/151; TQ915212; NP 184
Ryehill (division of Epping Upland and Ryehill hamlet in Epping), 12/271; TL454058; NP 161
Ryhall (parish), 30/30; TF036110; NP 123
Ryhill (division in township of Ryhill and Camerton in Burstwick), 41/426; TA223264; NP 99
Ryhill (township in Wragby), 43/672; SE389148; NP 102, 103
Ryhill and Camerton (township in Burstwick), 41/425-426; NP 99
Ryhope (township in Bishop Wearmouth), 11/79; NZ408532; NP 78
Rylstone (Rilston, Rilstone) (township in Burnsall), 43/212; SD970586; NP 91
Ryme Intrinseca (Ryme Intrinsica) (parish), 10/39; ST578109; NP 177
Rymer (extra-parochial), 34/122; TL875758; NP 136
Rympton (parish), 32/390; NP 166, 178
Rymsdallt (Ryddalt) (township in Ruabon), 49/95; SJ298423; NP 109, 118
Ryston (parish), 25/522; TF624012; NP 124, 137
Ryther (division in township of Ryther cum Ossendike in Ryther), 43/443; SE548378; NP 97
Ryther (parish), 43/441-443; NP 97
Ryther cum Ossendike (township in Ryther), 43/442-443; NP 97
Ryton (parish), 11/28-33
Ryton (parish), 31/470; SJ764030; NP 119
Ryton (township in Ryton), 11/32; NZ156644; NP 78
Ryton (township in Kirby Misperton), 42/451; SE782763; NP 92
Ryton on Dunsmore (parish), 37/136; SP386734; NP 132

S

Sacombe (Sacomb) (parish), 16/79; TL332191; NP 147, 148
Sadberge (township in Haughton le Skerne), 11/336; NZ346170; NP 85
Saddington (parish), 21/337; SP657917; NP 132
Saddlewood (tithing in Hawkesbury), 13/340E; ST810900; NP 156
Saddleworth with Quick township in Rochdale), 43/738-745A-B; NP 101, 102
Saffron Walden (parish), 12/6; TL550400; NP 148
Saham Toney (parish), 25/538; TF908038; NP 125, 136
Saighton (township in St Oswald Chester), 5/502; SJ442621; NP 109
St Agnes (district in Isles of Scilly), 6/222; SV881080; NP 189
St Agnes (parish), 6/134; SW724485; NP 189, 190
St Alban (St Alban Wood-street) (parish), 23/10; TQ323815; NP 160/2
St Alban Wood-street (parish), 23/10; TQ323815; NP 160/2
St Albans (parish), 16/100; TL146070; NP 160
St Aldate, 2/7, 29/212
St Alkmond (township in St Alkmond Shrewsbury), 31/260; SJ491122; NP 118
St Alkmond Shrewsbury (parish), 31/260-262B; NP 118
St Allen (parish), 6/138; SW818514; NP 190
St Alphage (St Alphage Sion College) (parish), 23/9; TQ324816; NP 160/2
St Alphage Sion College (parish), 23/9; TQ324816; NP 160/2
St Andrew the Less (parish), 4/95; TL463581; NP 135
St Andrew Auckland (parish), 11/190-219, 225; NP 84
St Andrew Auckland (South Church) (township in St Andrew Auckland), 11/200; NZ216276
St Andrew by the Wardrobe (parish), 23/32; TQ319808; NP 160/2
St Andrew Hubbard (parish), 23/87; TQ330808; NP 160/2
St Andrew Undershaft (parish), 23/52; TQ332811; NP 160/2
St Andrew Holborn (parish), 24/21A-C; NP 160/1
St Andrew Holborn above the Bars, Eastern (division in), 24/21C; TQ311819; NP 160/1
St Andrew Holborn above the Bars, Western (division in St Andrew Holborn), 24/21B; TQ308817; NP 160/1
St Andrew Holborn below the Bars (division in St Andrew Holborn), 24/21A; TQ313815; NP 160/1
St Andrew (township in St Andrew), 27/643; NZ240658; NP 78
St Andrew Liberty (extra-parochial), 32/142; ST554461; NP 165
St Andrew Pershore (chapelry in St Andrew Pershore), 40/177; SO938453; NP 143
St Andrew Pershore (parish), 40/175-181; NP 143
St Andrew (parish), 43/12; SE606520; NP 97/1
St Andrews (parish), 27/640-643; NP 78
St Andrews (parish), 51/178; NP 154
St Andrews Major (St Andrews) (parish), 51/178; ST153708; NP 154
St Andrews Minor (Clemenston) (parish), 51/117; SS926733; NP 154
St Anne (St Anne Blackfriars) (parish), 23/1; TQ317810; NP 160/2
St Anne and St Agnes (St Anne and St Agnes Aldersgate) (parish), 23/4; TQ321814; NP 160/2
St Anne Blackfriars (parish), 23/1; TQ317810; NP 160/219.1.2
St Anne Limehouse (parish), 24/69; TQ367811; NP 160/1
St Anne Soho (parish), 24/31; TQ297810; NP 160/1
St Antholin (parish), 23/67; TQ325810; NP 160/2
St Anthony in Roseland (parish), 6/158; SW862323; NP 190
St Anthony, 6/184; NP 190
St Anthony-in-Meneage (St Anthony) (parish), 6/184; SW780245; NP 190

St Arvans (hamlet in St Arvans), 53/92; ST520960; NP 155
St Arvans Grange (hamlet in St Arvans), 53/93; ST506966; NP 155
St Arvans, 53/92; NP 155
St Asaph (Llanelwy), 49/140-141, 50/68-78; NP 108
St Athan (St Athans) (parish), 51/169; ST020680; NP 154
St Aubyns (district in Stoke Damerel), 9/458; SX450544; NP 187/1
St Augustine (St Augustine Watling-street) (parish), 23/36; TQ322811; NP 160/2
St Augustine Watling-street (parish), 23/36; TQ322811; NP 160/2
St Austell (parish), 6/126; SX020550; NP 185, 190
St Bartholomew (St Bartholomew by the Royal Exchange) (parish), 23/2; TQ328812; NP 160/2
St Bartholomew by the Royal Exchange (parish), 23/2; TQ328812; NP 160/2
St Bartholomew the Great (parish), 24/51; TQ320817; NP 160/1
St Bartholomew the Less (parish), 24/52; TQ319816; NP 160/1
St Bees (parish), 7/288-301; NP 82
St Bees (township in St Bees), 7/300; NX978115; NP 82
St Benedict and St John, Glastonbury (parish), 32/182; NP 165
St Benet (St Benet Gracechurch-street) (parish), 23/58; TQ329809; NP 160/2
St Benet (St Benet Pauls Wharf) (parish), 23/33; TQ320809; NP 160/2
St Benet Fink (parish), 23/19; TQ329812; NP 160/2
St Benet Gracechurch-street (parish), 23/58; TQ329809; NP 160/2
St Benet Sherehog (parish), 23/46; TQ325811; NP 160/2
St Blazey (parish), 6/125; SX060539; NP 185, 190
St Botolph (St Botolph Billingsgate) (parish), 23/94; TQ330806; NP 160/2
St Botolph Billingsgate (parish), 23/94; TQ330806; NP 160/2
St Botolph Aldersgate (parish), 24/50; TQ321816; NP 160/1
St Botolph without Aldgate (division in St Botolph without Aldgate), 24/55; TQ336812; NP 160/1
St Botolph without Aldgate (division in St Botolph without Aldgate), 24/57; TQ340806; NP 160/1
St Botolph without Aldgate (parish), 24/55, 57; TQ340806; NP 160/1
St Botolph without Bishopsgate (parish), 24/54; TQ333816; NP 160/1
St Breock (parish), 6/80; SW980700; NP 185
St Breward (Simonward) (parish), 6/40; SX126786; NP 185, 186
St Briavels (parish), 13/165; SO562145; NP 155
St Bride (St Bridget) (parish), 24/5; TQ315812; NP 160/1
St Bride's Minor (hamlet in St Bride's Minor), 51/91; SS930850; NP 154
St Bride's super Ely (parish), 51/144; ST100778; NP 154
St Bride's Netherwent (hamlet in St Bride's Netherwent), 53/141; ST438903; NP 155
St Bride's Netherwent (parish), 53/140-141; NP 155
St Brides Major (hamlet in St Brides Major), 51/114; SS892747; NP 153, 154
St Brides Major (parish), 51/113-115; NP 153, 154
St Brides Wentlooge (St Brides Wentllooge) (parish), 53/125; ST296827; NP 154, 155
St Brides (parish), 55/96; SM809105; NP 151
St Bridget Beckermet (St Bridget Beckermont) (parish), 7/307; NY049068; NP 82, 88
St Bridget Chester (division in St Bridget Chester), 5/516; SJ405661; NP 109/1
St Bridget Chester (parish), 5/516-517; NP 109/1
St Bridget Chester (township in St Bridget Chester), 5/517; SJ415659; NP 109/1
St Bridget (parish), 24/5; NP 160/1
St Budeaux (parish), 9/362; SX461592; NP 187
St Burian, 6/213; NP 189
St Buryan (St Burian) (parish), 6/213; SW414252; NP 189
St Catherine (Kattern) (parish), 32/30; ST770701; NP 156
St Chad (parish), 33/256; NP 120

St Chad (Stowe) (township in St Chad), 33/256; SK114105; NP 120
St Chad (township in St Chad Shrewsbury), 31/263; SJ487125; NP 118
St Chad Shrewsbury (Shrewsbury St Chad the Bishop) (parish), 31/263-268, 270-273B; NP 118
St Christopher (St Christopher le Stocks) (parish), 23/21; TQ327811; NP 160/2
St Christopher le Stocks (parish), 23/21; TQ327811; NP 160/2
St Clears (parish), 47/58; SN251168; NP 152
St Cleather, 6/28; NP 186
St Cleer (parish), 6/55; SX248703; NP 186
St Clement (parish), 6/160; SW847455; NP 190
St Clement (St Clement East-Cheap) (parish), 23/61; TQ328808; NP 160/2
St Clement East-Cheap (parish), 23/61; TQ328808; NP 160/2
St Clement Danes (division in St Clement Danes), 24/23A; TQ308812; NP 160/1
St Clement Danes (division in St Clement Danes), 24/23B; TQ310809; NP 160/1
St Clement Danes (parish), 24/23A-C; TQ308812; NP 160/1
St Clement Danes, Holywell Ward (division in St Clement Danes), 24/23C; NP 160/1
St Clement (parish), 40/122; SO841549; NP 130, 143
St Clether (St Cleather) (parish), 6/28; SX193845; NP 186
St Columb Major (parish), 6/87; SW921634; NP 185
St Columb Minor (St Minor Columb) (parish), 6/89; SW840617; NP 185
St Cross or St George South Elmham, St Cross South Elmham (parish), 34/35; NP 137
St Crux (parish), 43/14; SE606517; NP 97/1
St Cuthbert [Carlisle] (parish), 7/79-86; NP 76
St Cuthbert in Thetford (parish), 25/716; NP 136
St Cuthbert In (division in Wells, St Cuthbert), 32/141; ST543459; NP 165
St Cuthbert in Wells (parish), 32/140-141; NP 165, 166
St Cuthbert Out (division in Wells, St Cuthbert), 32/140; ST555465; NP 165, 166
St Cuthbert (parish), 42/675, 43/8; NP 97/1
St Cuthbert (division), 43/8; SE611522; NP 97/1
St Davids [Tyddewi] (parish), 55/62-67; NP 138
St Decumans (Williton) (parish), 32/235; ST072416; NP 164
St Denis in Walmgate, 43/17; NP 97/1
St Dennis (parish), 6/92; SW952580; NP 185
St Dennis (St Denis in Walmgate) (parish), 43/17; SE607516; NP 97/1
St Devereux (parish), 15/190; SO450321; NP 142
St Dionis Backchurch (parish), 23/57; TQ331810; NP 160/2
St Dogmaels (St Dogmells) (parish), 55/1-4; NP 139
St Dogwells (parish), 55/55; SM959275; NP 138
St Dominick (parish), 6/65; SX401674; NP 185, 186
St Donat's (parish), 51/164; SS942692; NP 154
St Dunstan in the East (parish), 23/89; TQ332807; NP 160/2
St Dunstan in the West (parish), 24/65; TQ313812; NP 160/1
St Dunstan Stepney (parish), 24/65A-C, 66; NP 160/1
St Edmund the King and Martyr (parish), 23/60; TQ328810; NP 160/2
St Edrens, 55/57; NP 138
St Edrins (St Edrens) (parish), 55/57; SM894285; NP 138
St Elvis (parish), 55/69; SM821243; NP 138
St Endellion (Endellion) (parish), 6/44; SX001799; NP 185
St Enoder (parish), 6/91; SW899565; NP 185, 190
St Erme (parish), 6/139; SW848514; NP 190
St Erney (parish), 6/105; SX372582; NP 186
St Erth (parish), 6/201; SW566344; NP 189
St Ervan (parish), 6/85; SW896700; NP 185
St Ethelburga (parish), 23/16; TQ332814; NP 160/2
St Eval (parish), 6/84; SW866698; NP 185
St Ewe (parish), 6/144; SW982468; NP 190
St Fagans (parish), 51/143; ST121777; NP 154
St Faith the Virgin (parish), 23/30; TQ320812; NP 160/2
St Faith under St Pauls (St Faith the Virgin) (parish), 23/30; TQ320812; NP 160/2

St Florence (parish), 55/135; SN079014; NP 151, 152
St Gabriel (St Gabriel Fenchurch-street) (parish), 23/56; TQ332809; NP 160/2
St Gabriel Fenchurch-street (parish), 23/56; TQ332809; NP 160/2
St Gennis, 6/18; NP 174
St Gennys (St Gennis) (parish), 6/18; SX160964; NP 174
St George Clist,
St George (St George Botolph-lane) (parish), 23/93; TQ330807; NP 160/2
St George Botolph-lane (parish), 23/93; TQ330807; NP 160/2
St George Bloomsbury (parish), 24/30; TQ301819; NP 160/1
St George Hanover Square (parish), 24/36A-D; NP 160, 160/1
St George in the East (parish), 24/68A-C; NP 160/1
St George the Martyr (parish), 24/22; TQ305819; NP 160/1
St George (parish), 32/4; NP 155
St George Ward (division in Walsall), 33/298; SP006973; NP 130, 131
St George South Elmham (parish), 34/35; NP 137
St George (division in St Giles Camberwell), 35/16; TQ348772; NP 170, 171
St George the Martyr Southwark (parish), 35/9A-C; NP 170
St George (Llansan Sior) (parish), 49/8; SH972753; NP 108
St George (parish), 43/20; SE608514; NP 97/1
St George's Island (Looe Island) (extra-parochial), 6/120; SX257514; NP 186
St Georges (parish), 51/146; ST102755; NP 154
St Germans (parish), 6/103; SX331569; NP 186
St Giles (Gilligate) (division in township of St Giles in St Giles), 11/113; NZ286429
St Giles (Gilligate) (parish and township in St Giles), 11/112-113
St Giles (St Giles-in-the-Suburbs) (parish), 43/2; SE602526; NP 97/1
St Giles Camberwell (parish), 35/16-19; TQ348772; NP 170, 171
St Giles in the Wood (parish), 9/90; SS534193; NP 163
St Giles in Blaston, 21/300; NP 133
St Giles in the Fields (parish), 24/29A-B; NP 160/1
St Giles in the Fields North (division in St Giles in the Fields), 24/29B; TQ298816; NP 160/1
St Giles in the Fields South (division in St Giles in the Fields), 24/29A; TQ306813; NP 160/1
St Giles on the Heath (parish), 9/197; SX359912; NP 174, 186
St Giles Reading (division in St Giles Reading), 2/182; SU723730; NP 159, 169
St Giles Reading (parish), 2/182-183; NP 159, 169
St Giles without Cripplegate (parish), 24/53; TQ324818; NP 160/1
St Gluvias (district in St Gluvias), 6/176; SW785349; NP 190
St Gluvias (parish), 6/176-177; NP 190
St Goran (St Gorran) (parish), 6/146; SW997425; NP 190
St Gregory by St Pauls (parish), 23/31; TQ320811; NP 160/2
St Gyles or Sarr (parish), 19/122; NP 173
St Harmon (parish), 56/1A-C; NP 128
St Helen (division in Abingdon St Helen), 2/14; SU492961; NP 158, 158/1
St Helen (St Helen Bishopgate) (parish), 23/17; TQ332813; NP 160/2
St Helen (on the Walls) (parish), 43/10, 22; NP 97/1
St Helen (Stonegate) (parish), 43/36; SE602519; NP 97/1
St Helen Auckland (township in St Andrew Auckland), 11/198; NZ198262; NP 85
St Helen Bishopgate (parish), 23/17; TQ332813; NP 160/2
St Helen on the Walls (division in St Helen on the Walls), 43/10; SE607521; NP 97/1
St Helen on the Walls (division in St Helen on the Walls), 43/22; SE619519; NP 97/1
St Helens (parish), 18/20; SZ619912; NP 180
St Hilary (district in St Hilary), 6/198; SW553318; NP 189
St Hilary (parish), 6/198-199; NP 189
St Hilary (parish), 51/158; ST015728; NP 154
St Ippollitts (Ippollitts) (parish), 16/34; TL195266; NP 147
St Ishmael (parish), 47/79; SN371095; NP 152
St Ishmael's (parish), 55/99; SM833078; NP 151

St Issells (parish), 55/126; SN132072; NP 152
St Issey (parish), 6/81; SW934704; NP 185
St Ive (parish), 6/63; SX316682; NP 186
St Ives (parish), 6/203; SW505400; NP 189
St Ives (parish), 17/76; TL313722; NP 134
St James (St James Dukes-place) (parish), 23/54; TQ334812; NP 160/2
St James (division in St Mary Magdalen Bermondsey), 35/6A; TQ342793; NP 170, 171
St James (Southbroom, Roundway) (chapelry in Bishops Cannings), 39/133; SU012630; NP 167
St James Clerkenwell (division in St James Clerkenwell), 24/47A; TQ316822; NP 160/1
St James Clerkenwell (parish), 24/47A-D; NP 160/1
St James Dukes-place (parish), 23/54; TQ334812; NP 160/2
St James Garlickhithe (parish), 23/77; TQ324808; NP 160/2
St James South Elmham (parish), 34/38; NP 137
St James Westminster (parish), 24/37A-C; NP 160/1
St James's Palace (division in St Martin in the Fields), 24/32D; TQ293800; NP 160/1
St James's Square (division in St James Westminster), 24/37A; TQ295804; NP 160/1
St James, Poole (parish), 10/197; NP 179
St James, Grain (parish), 19/44; NP 172
St James, Isle of Grain (parish), 19/44; NP 172
St John (district in St John), 6/111A; SX404521; NP 186, 187
St John (district in St John), 6/111B; SX407534; NP 187
St John (division in St George in the East), 24/68C; TQ346803; NP 160/1
St John (division in St Marylebone), 24/45B; TQ267831; NP 160
St John (Delpike) (parish), 43/6; SE605522; NP 97/1
St John (Micklegate) (parish), 43/28; SE601516; NP 97/1
St John (parish), 6/111A-B; NP 186, 187
St John (parish), 27/645-648; NP 78/1
St John (parish), 51/22; NP 153
St John (township in St John), 27/645; NZ246640; NP 78/1
St John at Hackney (parish), 24/73-77; NP 160, 161
St John Baptist Savoy (extra-parochial), 24/27A; TQ306808; NP 160/1
St John Beckermet (St John's Beckermont) (parish), 7/305; NY019085; NP 82
St John Beverley (parish), 41/291-300; NP 99
St John Bredwardine (division inside city of Worcester in St John Bredwardine), 40/123; SO837548; NP 130, 143
St John Bredwardine (division outside city of Worcester in St John Bredwardine), 40/124; SO820548; NP 130, 143
St John Bredwardine (parish), 40/123-124; NP 130, 143
St John Hampstead (parish), 24/43; TQ261851; NP 160
St John Horsleydown (parish), 35/5; TQ335799; NP 160/1
St John Lee (parish), 27/445-453; NP 77
St John Newport (parish), 22/503; SK975728; NP 113/1
St John near Swansea (parish), 51/22; NP 153
St John of Wapping (parish), 24/59; TQ342805; NP 160/1
St John the Baptist Chester (parish), 5/514; SJ415667; NP 109/1
St John the Baptist (parish), 19/127; NP 173
St John the Baptist (St John the Baptist Walbrook) (parish), 23/66; TQ326809; NP 160/2
St John the Baptist Walbrook (parish), 23/66; TQ326809; NP 160/2
St John the Evangelist (parish), 23/38; TQ322811; NP 160/2
St John the Evangelist Westminster (parish), 24/35; TQ299786; NP 170
St John the Baptist, Southover (parish), 36/204; TQ417092; NP 183
St John the Baptist, Cardiff (parish), 51/140; NP 154
St John Waterloo - Waterloo Road First (division in Lambeth), 35/11A; TQ312802; NP 160/1
St John Waterloo - Waterloo Road Second (division in Lambeth), 35/11B; TQ310798; NP 160/1
St John Zachary (parish), 23/6; TQ322814; NP 160/2
St John, 7/286; NP 82, 83
St Johns (district in Stoke Damerel), 9/459; SX457542; NP187/1

St Johns Castlerigg and Wythburn (St John) (township in Crosthwaite), 7/286; NY320190; NP 82, 83
St Johns Ilketshall (parish), 34/43; NP 137
St Julian (division in St Julian Shrewsbury), 31/258; SJ494124; NP 118
St Julian (division in St Julian Shrewsbury), 31/259; SJ488092; NP 118
St Julian (parish), 31/256-259; NP 118
St Juliot (St Juliott) (parish), 6/19; SX135920; NP 174
St Just (St Just in Penwith) (parish), 6/215; SW375315; NP 189
St Just in Roseland (parish), 6/159; SW853360; NP 190
St Katherine Coleman (parish), 23/55; TQ334810; NP 160/2
St Katherine Cree (St Katherine Cree-Church) (parish), 23/53; TQ334811; NP 160/2
St Kaynne near Looe, 6/116; NP 186
St Keverne (parish), 6/185; SW770200; NP 190
St Kew (parish), 6/43; SX022769; NP 185
St Keyne (parish), 6/101; SX243609; NP 186
St Kingsmark (extra-parochial), 53/98B; ST525943; NP 155
St Lawrence Reading (parish), 2/181; SU722739; NP 159
St Lawrence Newland (Newland, St Lawrence) (parish), 12/352; TL959042; NP 162
St Lawrence (parish), 18/30; SZ540769; NP 180
St Lawrence (parish), 19/129; TR362662; NP 173
St Lawrence Jewry (parish), 23/26; TQ324813; NP 160/2
St Lawrence Pountney (parish), 23/83; TQ327808; NP 160/2
St Lawrence Ludlow (parish), 31/525; SO512748; NP 129
St Lawrence Appleby (parish), 38/36-37, 39-40, 44-45; NP 83
St Lawrence (parish), 41/67, 43/21; NP 97, 97/1
St Lawrence (township in St Lawrence), 43/21; SE608510; NP 97/1
St Lawrences (parish), 55/56; SM912272; NP 138
St Leonards (hamlet in Aston Clinton), 3/176; SP906078; NP 159
St Leonards, Hythe (parish), 19/391; NP 173
St Leonard (St Leonard Eastcheap) (parish), 23/86; TQ329807; NP 160/2
St Leonard (St Leonard Foster-lane) (parish), 23/5; TQ322813; NP 160/2
St Leonard Eastcheap (parish), 23/86; TQ329807; NP 160/2
St Leonard Foster-lane (parish), 23/5; TQ322813; NP 160/2
St Leonard (division in St Leonard Shoreditch), 24/62B; TQ333824; NP 160/1
St Leonard Shoreditch (parish), 24/62A-F; NP 160/1
St Leonards (division in St Leonards), 36/167; TQ795088; NP 184/1
St Leonards (division in St Leonards), 36/168; TQ792096; NP 184
St Leonards (hamlet in Hastings, St Mary Magdalene), 36/166; TQ800099; NP 184/1
St Leonards (hamlet in Hastings, St Mary Magdalene and St Leonards), 36/166, 36/167; NP 184/1
St Leonards (parish), 36/167-168; NP 184, 184/1
St Levan (parish), 6/214; SW378232; NP 189
St Luke (parish), 24/48A-E; NP 160/1
St Luke Chelsea (parish), 24/40A-C; NP 170
St Lythans (St Lythians) (parish), 51/153; ST101721; NP 154
St Lythians (parish), 51/153; NP 154
St Mabyn (parish), 6/48; SX056727; NP 185
St Magnus the Martyr (parish), 23/96; TQ329807; NP 160/2
St Margarets (St Margaret) (parish), 15/213; SO352340; NP 142
St Margaret (parish), 16/113; NP 148
St Margaret's at Cliffe (St Margaret's at Cliff, St Margarets) (parish), 19/364; TR366447; NP 173
St Margarets (parish), 19/364; NP 173
St Margaret (St Margaret Lothbury) (parish), 23/22; TQ327813; NP 160/2
St Margaret (St Margaret New Fish-street) (parish), 23/95; TQ329807; NP 160/2
St Margaret Lothbury (parish), 23/22; TQ327813; NP 160/2
St Margaret Moses (parish), 23/37; TQ322810; NP 160/2
St Margaret New Fish-street (parish), 23/95; TQ329807; NP 160/2

St Margaret Pattens (parish), 23/88; TQ331808; NP 160/2
St Margaret Westminster (division in St Margaret Westminster), 24/33A; TQ298798; NP 160/1, 160, 170
St Margaret Westminster (division in St Margaret Westminster), 24/33B; TQ287807; NP 160, 170
St Margaret Clee (St Margaret Clee Brown) (parish), 31/513; NP 129
St Margaret in Ilketshall (parish), 34/41; NP 137
St Margaret South Elmham (parish), 34/36; NP 137
St Margaret (St Margaret Walmgate) (parish), 43/16; SE609516; NP 97/1
St Margaret Walmgate, 43/16; NP 97/1
St Margaret's Island (extra-parochial), 55/140o; SS121972; NP 152
St Mark Kennington (ecclesiastical district in Lambeth), 13A-B; NP 170
St Martha, St Martha-on-the-Hill (parish), 35/137; NP 169, 170
St Martin (parish), 6/116-117; NP 186
St Martin (St Kaynne near Looe) (district in St Martin), 6/116; SX282552; NP 186
St Martin (St Martin in Meneage) (parish), 6/186; SW734239; NP 190
St Martin Chester (parish), 5/518; SJ403660; NP 109/1
St Martin Within (division inside borough in Wareham, St Martin), 10/286A; SY925878; NP 178, 179
St Martin Without (division outside borough in Wareham, St Martin), 10/286B; SY935895; NP 178, 179
St Martin (St Martin Ludgate) (parish), 23/2; TQ316812; NP 160/2
St Martin Ludgate (parish), 23/2; TQ316812; NP 160/2
St Martin Orgar (parish), 23/84; TQ328808; NP 160/2
St Martin Outwich (parish), 23/18; TQ330812; NP 160/2
St Martin Pomroy (parish), 23/25; TQ325812; NP 160/2
St Martin Vintry (parish), 23/78; TQ325808; NP 160/2
St Martin in the Fields (division in Charing Cross Registration Subdistrict in St Martin in the Fields), 24/32A; TQ300804; NP 160/1
St Martin in the Fields (division in Long Acre Registration Subdistrict in St Martin in the Fields), 24/32B; TQ302810; NP 160/1
St Martin in the Fields (parish), 24/32A-D; NP 160/1
St Martin in the Fields, Verge of the Palaces of St James and Whitehall (division in St Martin in the Fields), 24/32C; TQ297800; NP 160/1
St Martin (parish), 31/76-78; NP 117, 118
St Martin Beverley (parish), 41/303; TA039392; NP 99
St Martin (Coney Street) (St Martin-le-Grand) (parish), 43/35; SE602518; NP 97/1
St Martin (cum Gregory) (St Martin Micklegate with St Gregory) (parish), 43/30; SE599516; NP 97/1
St Martin Micklegate with St Gregory, 43/30; NP 97/1
St Martin's (district in Isles of Scilly), 6/218; SV929158; NP 189
St Martin-le-Grand, 43/35; NP 97/1
St Martins (extra-parochial), 42/94; NZ180002; NP 91
St Mary (Castlegate) (parish), 43/25; SE605513; NP 97/1
St Mary (district in St Mary [Carlisle]), 7/93; NY399559; NP 76/1
St Mary (division in St George in the East), 24/68A; TQ344810; NP 160/1
St Mary (division in St Marylebone), 24/45C; TQ277814; NP 160
St Mary (division in St Mary Newington), 35/8C; TQ319784; NP 170
St Mary (Islington), 24/46A-B; NP 160
St Mary (parish), 33/258; SK118094; NP 120
St Mary (St Mary Abchurch) (parish), 23/63; TQ327809; NP 160/2
St Mary (St Mary Aldermanbury) (parish), 23/11; TQ324814; NP 160/2
St Mary Abchurch (parish), 23/63; TQ327809; NP 160/2
St Mary Aldermanbury (parish), 23/11; TQ324814; NP 160/2
St Mary Aldermary (parish), 23/68; TQ324810; NP 160/2
St Mary and St Nicholas in Feltwell (parish), 25/700; TL687910; NP 135, 136
St Mary at Hill (parish), 23/92; TQ330807; NP 160/2

St Mary Beverley (parish), 41/301; TA023392; NP 99
St Mary Bishophill (Junior) (division in St Mary Bishophill (Junior)), 43/26; SE600514; NP 97/1
St Mary Bishophill (Junior) (division in St Mary Bishophill (Junior)), 43/41; SE590520; NP 97/1
St Mary Bishophill (Junior) (parish), 43/26, 41-44; NP 97, 97/1
St Mary Bishophill (Junior) (township in St Mary Bishophill (Junior)), 43/26, 41; NP 97/1
St Mary Bishophill (Senior) (division in township of St Mary Bishophill in St Mary Bishophill (Senior)), 43/24A; SE599515; NP 97/1
St Mary Bishophill (Senior) (division in township of St Mary Bishophill in St Mary Bishophill (Senior)), 43/24B; SE594490; NP 97/1
St Mary Bishophill (Senior) (parish), 43/24A-B, 45A-C; NP 97, 97/1
St Mary Bishophill (Senior) (township in St Mary Bishophill (Senior)), 43/24A-B, 45A; NP 97, 97/1
St Mary Bishophill [Senior] (division outside city boundary in township of St Mary Bishophill in St Mary Bishophill [Senior]), 43/45A; SE590505; NP 97
St Mary Bourne (parish), 14/66; SU415515; NP 168
St Mary Bothaw (parish), 23/65; TQ326809; NP 160/2
St Mary Bulverhythe (St Mary Bulverhithe) (parish), 36/169; TQ772083; NP 184
St Mary Church (parish), 51/159; ST004713; NP 154
St Mary Clist, 9/310; NP 176
St Mary Colechurch (parish), 23/45; TQ325811; NP 160/2
St Mary Cray (parish), 19/60; TQ492676; NP 171
St Mary de Lode (parish), 13/174-177B, 195; NP 143
St Mary Extra (parish), 14/270; SU445105; NP 180
St Mary Hill (parish), 51/105; SS962790; NP 154
St Mary Hoo (St Marys Hoo) (parish), 19/42; TQ803774; NP 172
St Mary in the Marsh (St Mary, Romney Marsh) (parish), 19/427; TR075281; NP 184
St Mary in the Borough (hamlet in Kidwelly), 47/81; SN420075; NP 152
St Mary Kingston upon Hull (parish and township), 41/324-325; NP 99/1
St Mary le Bow, 11/118; NP 85
St Mary le Bow (parish), 23/43; TQ324811; NP 160/2
St Mary le Strand (division in city of Westminster in St Mary le Strand), 24/26A; TQ308808; NP 160/1
St Mary le Strand (division in Hundred of Ossulton in St Mary le Strand), 24/26B; TQ307809; NP 160/1
St Mary le Strand (parish), 24/26A-B; NP 160/1
St Mary Magdalen (St Mary Magdalen Milk-street) (parish), 23/41; TQ324813; NP 160/2
St Mary Magdalen (St Mary Magdalen Old Fish-street) (parish), 23/35; TQ321810; NP 160/2
St Mary Magdalen Old Fish-street (parish), 23/35; TQ321810; NP 160/2
St Mary Magdalen (division in St Mary Magdalen Bermondsey), 35/6B; TQ333794; NP 170
St Mary Magdalen Bermondsey (parish), 35/6A-C; NP 170, 171
St Mary Mounthaw (parish), 23/73; TQ321809; NP 160/2
St Mary Newington (parish), 35/8A-C; NP 170
St Mary on the Hill, Chester (township in St Mary on the Hill, Chester), 5/522; SJ403658; NP 109/1
St Mary on the Hill, Chester (township in St Mary on the Hill, Chester), 5/523; SJ400650; NP 109
St Mary on the Hill (Chester), 5/522-527; NP 109, 109/1
St Mary Reading (parish), 2/180A-B; NP 159, 169
St Mary Reading (tithing in St Mary Reading), 2/180A; SU705733; NP 159, 169
St Mary Rotherhithe (parish), 35/7; TQ358795; NP 161, 171
St Mary Shrewsbury (parish), 31/247-254B; NP 118
St Mary Somerset (parish), 23/74; TQ321808; NP 160/2
St Mary Stoke Newington (parish), 24/78; TQ331866; NP 160
St Mary Stratford (parish), 24/72; TQ372837; NP 161
St Mary the Less, 11/120; NP 85
St Mary Ward (division in parish and township of St Mary Kingston upon Hull), 41/324; TA100288; NP 99/1

St Mary Whitechapel (parish), 24/60A-E; NP 160/1
St Mary Woolchurch (St Mary Woolchurch-Haw) (parish), 23/48; TQ328811; NP 160/2
St Mary Woolnoth (parish), 23/49; TQ327810; NP 160/2
St Mary [Carlisle] (parish), 7/87-98A-C
St Mary's (district in Isles of Scilly), 6/217; SV920111; NP 189
St Mary, Cardiff (parish), 51/10, 139; NP 154
St Mary, Pembroke, 55/150; NP 151
St Mary, Romney Marsh (parish), 19/427; NP 184
St Marychurch (parish), 9/431; SX914665; NP 188
St Marylebone (parish), 24/45A-F; NP 160, 160/1
St Marys Truro, 6/137; NP 190
St Marys, Cardigan, 46/104; NP 139
St Matthew (St Matthew Friday-street) (parish), 23/39; TQ322812; NP 160/2
St Matthew Friday-street (parish), 23/39; TQ322812; NP 160/2
St Matthew Bethnal Green (parish), 24/63A-D; NP 160/1
St Matthew Brixton (division in Lambeth), 35/14; TQ315750; NP 170
St Maughans (parish), 53/15; SO465198; NP 142
St Maurice (St Maurice in the Suburbs) (parish), 43/7; SE608525; NP 97/1
St Mawgan in Pyder (Mawgan in Pyder, St Mawgan) (parish), 6/88; SW872659; NP 185
St Mellion (parish), 6/64; SX368665; NP 186
St Mellons (parish), 53/128; ST234811; NP 154
St Merryn (parish), 6/83; SW874737; NP 185
St Mewan (parish), 6/127; SW990526; NP 185, 190
St Michael Caerhays (St Michael Carhayes) (parish), 6/147; SW965423; NP 190
St Michael Carhayes, 6/147
St Michael Penkevil (St Michael Penkivel) (parish), 6/155; SW860415; NP 190
St Michael's Mount (extra-parochial), 6/199B; SW515299; NP 189
St Michael Chester (extra-parochial), 5/512; SJ406661; NP 109/1
St Michael (division in Basingstoke), 14/46; SU644521; NP 168
St Michael (division inside borough of St Albans in St Michael), 16/98A; TL138071; NP 160
St Michael (division outside the borough of St Albans in St Michael), 16/98B; TL118078; NP 147, 160
St Michael (parish), 16/98A-B; NP 147, 160
St Michaels on Wyre (parish), 20/157-167; NP 94
St Michaels in Blaston, 21/299; NP 133
St Michael (St Michael Cornhill) (parish), 23/50; TQ328811; NP 160/2
St Michael (St Michael Crooked-lane) (parish), 23/85; TQ328807; NP 160/2
St Michael (St Michael Queenhithe) (parish), 23/75; TQ323808; NP 160/2
St Michael (St Michael Wood-street) (parish), 23/7; TQ322815; NP 160/2
St Michael (St Michael Wood-street) (parish), 23/27; TQ323813; NP 160/2
St Michael Bassishaw (parish), 23/12; TQ325814; NP 160/2
St Michael Crooked-lane (parish), 23/85; TQ328807; NP 160/2
St Michael le Querne (parish), 23/29; TQ321812; NP 160/2
St Michael Paternoster Royal (parish), 23/79; TQ325809; NP 160/2
St Michael Queenhithe (parish), 23/75; TQ323808; NP 160/2
St Michael Wood-street (parish), 23/7; TQ322815; NP 160/2
St Michael Wood-street (parish), 23/27; TQ323813; NP 160/2
St Michael (Michael Church, St Michael-church) (parish), 32/302; ST301302; NP 165, 177
St Michael (parish), 33/260-268; NP 120
St Michael (township in St Michael), 33/260; SK123084; NP 120
St Michael South Elmham (parish), 34/39; NP 137
St Michael Appleby or Bongate (parish), 38/38, 41-43; NP 83, 84
St Michael (Spurriergate) (parish), 43/29; SE603517; NP 97/1
St Michael le Belfrey (division in St Michael le Belfrey), 43/1; SE592526; NP 97/1

St Michael le Belfrey (division in St Michael le Belfrey), 43/37; SE603521; NP 97/1
St Michael le Belfrey (parish), 42/691, 695-696, 43/1, 37; NP 97, 97/1
St Michael, Pembroke (parish), 55/149; NP 151
St Mildred (St Mildred Bread-street) (parish), 23/70; TQ323810; NP 160/2
St Mildred (St Mildred Poultry) (parish), 23/23; TQ326811; NP 160/2
St Mildred Bread-street (parish), 23/70; TQ323810; NP 160/2
St Mildred Poultry (parish), 23/23; TQ326811; NP 160/2
St Minor Columb, 6/89; NP 185
St Minver (parish), 6/45-56; NP 185
St Minver Highlands (district in St Minver), 6/45; SW962772; NP 185
St Minver Lowlands (district in St Minver), 6/46; SW942764; NP 185
St Neot (parish), 6/54; SX191701; NP 186
St Neots (parish), 17/106; TL207607; NP 134
St Nicholas Shaldon, ; NP 188
St Nicholas (parish), 11/116; NZ275428; NP 85
St Nicholas (parish), 12/111; NP 150
St Nicholas in the Castle (parish), 18/13A-B; NP 18
St Nicholas Within Newport Borough (Carisbrooke Castle) (division in St Nicholas in the Castle), 18/13A; SZ486877; NP 180
St Nicholas Without Newport Borough (Carisbrooke Castle) (division in St Nicholas in the Castle), 18/13B; SZ455882; NP 180
St Nicholas at Wade (parish), 19/123; TR266676; NP 173
St Nicholas Deptford (parish), 19/2; TQ371780; NP 171
St Nicholas Acon (parish), 23/62; TQ328810; NP 160/2
St Nicholas Cole Abbey (parish), 23/72; TQ322809; NP 160/2
St Nicholas Olave (parish), 23/71; TQ322809; NP 160/2
St Nicholas (parish), 27/644; NZ248636; NP 78/1
St Nicholas South Elmham (parish), 34/37B; NP 137
St Nicholas (division in Guildford St Nicholas), 35/130A; SU992493; NP 169/1
St Nicholas Beverley (parish), 41/302; TA038400; NP 99
St Nicholas (parish), 51/145; ST091741; NP 154
St Nicholas (St Nicholas in the Suburbs) (parish), 43/18; SE618511; NP 97/1
St Nicholas in the Suburbs, 43/18; NP 97/1
St Nicholas (parish), 55/34; SM905360; NP 138
St Olave (parish), 5/513; SJ407660; NP 109/1
St Olave (St Olave Hart Street, St Olave Hart-street with St Nicholas in the Shambles) (parish), 23/90; TQ336808; NP 160/2
St Olave (St Olave Old Jewry) (parish), 23/24; TQ326812; NP 160/2
St Olave (St Olave Silver-street) (parish), 23/8; TQ323816; NP 160/2
St Olave (parish), 42/674, 692-694; NP 97, 97/1
St Olave Hart-street with St Nicholas in the Shambles (parish), 23/90; TQ336808; NP 160/2
St Olave Silver-street (parish), 23/8; TQ323816; NP 160/2
St Olave Southwark (parish), 35/4; TQ330802; NP 160/1
St Oswald Chester (parish), 5/496-507; NP 100, 109, 109/1
St Oswald Chester (township in St Oswald Chester), 5/507; SJ402671; NP 109/1
St Oswald (parish), 11/121-132B; NP 85
St Osyth (Chick St Osyth, St Osyth Chich) (parish), 12/169; TM124157; NP 149, 150
St Pancras (St Pancrass Soper Lane) (parish), 23/44; TQ325811; NP 160/2
St Pancrass Soper Lane (parish), 23/44; TQ325811; NP 160/2
St Pancras (parish), 24/44A-F; NP 160, 160/1
St Paul (division in St George in the East), 24/68B; TQ349811; NP 160/1
St Paul Covent Garden (parish), 24/28; TQ304809; NP 160/1
St Paul Deptford (division in St Paul Deptford), 19/1; TQ368770; NP 171
St Paul Deptford (parish), 19/1, 35/21; NP 171
St Paul Hammersmith (division in Hammersmith), 24/42A; TQ232790; NP 170
St Paul Malmesbury (division in Malmsbury Western Registration Subdistrict of St Paul Malmesbury tything in St Paul Malmesbury), 39/27B; ST932871; NP 157
St Paul Malmesbury (parish), 39/26A-30A, 31-33B; NP 156, 157
St Paul Malmesbury (St Paul Malmsbury) (division in Malmsbury Eastern Registration Subdistrict of St Paul Malmesbury tything in St Paul Malmesbury), 39/27A; ST934871; NP 157
St Paul Malmesbury (tything in St Paul Malmesbury), 39/27A-B; NP 157
St Paul Shadwell (parish), 24/67; TQ343807; NP 160/1
St Paul's Walden (parish), 16/46; TL182212; NP 147
St Paul's Cray (parish), 19/61; TQ472692; NP 171
St Pauls, Forest of Dean (parish), 13/155-158; NP 142, 143, 155, 156
St Peter (St Peter, Thanet) (parish), 19/128; TR385686; NP 173
St Peter (St Peter Cornhill) (parish), 23/51; TQ330811; NP 160/2
St Peter (St Peter near Pauls Wharf) (parish), 23/34; TQ321809; NP 160/2
St Peter (The Little) (parish), 43/32; SE603518; NP 97/1
St Peter and St Nicholas in Thetford (parish), 25/715; NP 136
St Peter and St Paul (parish), 32/36A-B; NP 156/1
St Peter Chester (parish), 5/510; SJ405663; NP 109/1
St Peter Hammersmith (division in Hammersmith), 24/42B; TQ223788; NP 170
St Peter Hammersmith (division in Hammersmith), 24/42C; TQ226804; NP 160, 170
St Peter le Poer Bread-street (parish), 23/15; TQ329813; NP 160/2
St Peter le Poor (St Peter le Poer Bread-street) (parish), 23/15; TQ329813; NP 160/2
St Peter le Willows (parish), 43/19; SE610514; NP 97/1
St Peter near Pauls Wharf (parish), 23/34; TQ321809; NP 160/2
St Peter South Elmham (parish), 34/40; NP 137
St Peter the Great (parish), 40/125A-126; NP 130, 143
St Peter Westcheap (parish), 23/40; TQ323812; NP 160/2
St Peter Walworth (division in St Mary Newington), 35/8B; TQ328781; NP 170
St Peter, Carmarthen (parish), 47/71; SN400202; NP 139, 152
St Peter-in-Maldon (parish), 12/344; NP 162
St Peters (hamlet in St Peters), 16/101; TL166057; NP 160
St Peters (parish), 16/101-103; NP 160
St Peters, Bengeworth (parish), 40/205; NP 143
St Petrox (parish), 55/159; SR970965; NP 151
St Pierre (parish), 53/100; ST508902; NP 155
St Pinnock (parish), 6/70; SX200624; NP 186
St Sampson (Golant) (parish), 6/96; SX112566; NP 185, 186
St Sampson (parish), 43/5; SE604518; NP 97/1
St Saviour Southwark (parish), 35/2; TQ323802; NP 160/1
St Saviour (division), 43/15; SE607518; NP 97/1
St Saviour (parish), 42/676-677, 43/15; NP 97, 97/1
St Sepulchre (division in Middlesex in St Sepulchre), 24/7; TQ317820; NP 160/1
St Sepulchre (division in the City of London Without the Walls in St Sepulchre), 24/6; TQ317816; NP 160/1
St Sepulchre (parish), 24/6-7; NP 160/1
St Stephens (St Stephen's by Launceston, St Stephen) (parish), 6/31; SX320860; NP 186
St Stephens (St Stephens by Saltash) (district in St Stephens), 6/108; SX408589; NP 186, 187
St Stephens (St Stephens by Saltash) (parish), 6/108-109; SX408589; NP 186, 187
St Stephens in Brannel (St Stephens in Branwell) (parish), 6/128; SW955545; NP 185, 190
St Stephens (parish), 16/99; TL140030; NP 160
St Stephen (parish), 19/141; NP 173
St Stephen (St Stephen Coleman-street) (parish), 23/13; TQ327815; NP 160/2

St Stephen (St Stephen Walbrook) (parish), 23/47; TQ326810; NP 160/2
St Stephen Coleman-street (parish), 23/13; TQ327815; NP 160/2
St Stephen Walbrook (parish), 23/47; TQ326810; NP 160/2
St Swithin (St Swithin London Stone) (parish), 23/64; TQ327810; NP 160/2
St Swithin London Stone (parish), 23/64; TQ327810; NP 160/2
St Teath (parish), 6/24; SX059821; NP 185
St Thomas Street (hamlet in Launceston, St Thomas the Apostle), 6/34; SX330848; NP 185
St Thomas the Apostle, 6/35; NP 186
St Thomas the Apostle, 9/253A-B; NP 176
St Thomas the Apostle, 9/253A; NP 176
St Thomas the Apostle (parish), 23/80; TQ324809; NP 160/2
St Thomas in Pensford (parish), 32/51; ST618637; NP 166
St Thomas Southwark (parish), 35/3; TQ328800; NP 160/1
St Thomas, Isle of Harty (parish), 19/103; NP 172
St Tudy (parish), 6/42; SX075761; NP 185
St Twinnels (parish), 55/158; NP 151
St Twynnells (St Twinnels, St Twinell, St Twynnell) (parish), 55/158; SR950967; NP 151
St Vedast (St Vedast Foster-lane) (parish), 23/28; TQ322812; NP 160/2
St Vedast Foster-lane (parish), 23/28; TQ322812; NP 160/2
St Veep (parish), 6/97; SX142559; NP 186
St Wenn (parish), 6/79; SW965656; NP 185
St Weonards (St Weonard) (parish), 15/232; SO488240; NP 142
St Werneth (parish), 19/46; NP 172
St Wilfred (parish), 43/38; SE601520; NP 97/1
St Winnow (parish), 6/72; SX125603; NP 186
St Woollos (hamlet in St Woollos), 53/123; ST309874; NP 155
St Woollos (parish), 53/123-124; NP 155
Saintbury (parish), 13/25; SP116402; NP 144
Salcey Forest (extra-parochial), 26/296-297; NP 146
Salcey Lodge (extra-parochial in Salcey Forest), 26/296; SP801511; NP 146
Salcombe Regis (district in Salcombe Regis), 9/299A; SY146888; NP 176
Salcombe Regis (parish), 9/299A-B; NP 176
Salcott (parish), 12/225; TL951135; NP 149
Sale (township in Ashton upon Mersey), 5/76; SJ793915; NP 101
Saleby with Thoresthorpe (parish), 22/405; TF458782; NP 105
Salehurst (parish), 36/50; TQ742251; NP 183, 184
Salesbury (township in Blackburn), 20/313; SD679347; NP 95
Salford (parish), 1/75; SP930400; NP 146
Salford (parish), 29/47; SP285285; NP 144, 145
Salford (township in Manchester), 20/505-506; NP 101
Salford - Greengate (division in township of Salford in Manchester), 20/505; SJ830990; NP 101
Salford - Regent Road (division in township of Salford in Manchester), 20/506; SJ818974; NP 101
Salford Priors (parish), 37/192; SP062522; NP 144
Salhouse (parish), 25/401; TG303150; NP 126
Salisbury, St Edmund (parish), 39/320; SU147202; NP 167
Salisbury, St Martin (division in Salisbury, St Martin), 39/317; SU138197; NP 167
Salisbury, St Martin (parish), 39/316-317; NP 167
Salisbury, St Thomas (parish), 39/319; SU143200; NP 167
Salisbury, The Close (extra-parochial), 39/318; SU142196; NP 167
Sall (Salle) (parish), 25/203; TG104255; NP 125
Salle (parish), 25/203; NP 125
Salmonby (parish), 22/393; TF324734; NP 114
Salperton (parish), 13/106; SP080202; NP 144
Salt and Enson (township in Stafford St Mary), 33/179; SJ952275; NP 119
Saltash (chapelry in St Stephens), 6/109; SX428589; NP 187
Saltby (parish), 21/101; SK855265; NP 122
Salter and Eskett (parish), 7/259; NY060170; NP 82
Salterforth (township in Barnoldswick), 43/312; SD890450; NP 95

Salterton (tithing in Durnford), 39/305; SU137357; NP 167
Saltfleet cum Skidbrook (parish), 22/789; NP 105
Saltfleetby All Saints (parish), 22/303; TF455904; NP 105
Saltfleetby St Clement (parish), 22/302; TF460918; NP 105
Saltfleetby St Peter (Saltfleetby St Peters) (parish), 22/301; TF432893; NP 105
Saltford (parish), 32/21; ST685674; NP 156
Salthouse (parish), 25/29; TG072433; NP 125
Saltley and Washwood Heath (township in Aston), 37/36; SP101879; NP 131
Saltmarsh (extra-parochial), 15/87; SO670580; NP 130
Saltmarshe (township in Howden), 41/9; SE783244; NP 98, 98/1
Saltney (township in Hawarden), 50/14; SJ340670; NP 109
Saltney Meads (common to Whitchurch, Purley, Sulham), 2/179B; SU645770; NP 158
Salton (parish), 42/454-455; NP 92
Salton (township in Salton), 42/455; SE720804; NP 92
Saltwick (township in Stannington), 27/422; NZ175801; NP 78
Saltwood (parish), 19/392; TR151364; NP 173
Salwarpe (Salwarp) (parish), 40/65; SO887613; NP 130
Salwick (division in township of Clifton with Salwick in Kirkham), 20/202; SD472328; NP 94
Sambourn (parish), 37/184; SP063624; NP 131
Samford Spiney, 9/355; NP 175, 187
Samlesbury (township in Blackburn), 20/321; SD609297; NP 94, 95
Sampford Arundel (parish), 32/427; ST108185; NP 164
Sampford Brett (parish), 32/234; ST086403; NP 164
Sampford Courtenay (Sampford Courtnay) (parish), 9/328; SX627896; NP 175
Sampford Courtnay, 9/328; NP 175
Sampford Peverell (parish), 9/136; ST035143; NP 164
Sampford Spiney (Samford Spiney) (parish), 9/355; SX530718; NP 175, 187
Samson (district in Isles of Scilly), 6/221; SV877126; NP 189
Sancreed (parish), 6/211; SW419301; NP 189
Sancton (parish), 41/195-196; NP 98
Sancton and Houghton (township in Sancton), 41/195; SE904398; NP 98
Sand Hutton (township in Bossall), 42/664; SE695585; NP 97
Sand Hutton (township in Thirsk), 42/530; SE386818; NP 91
Sandal Magna (Great Sandal) (parish), 43/691-694; NP 96, 102
Sandal Magna (Great Sandal) (township in Sandal Magna), 43/692; SE342181; NP 96, 102
Sandbach (parish), 5/208-220; NP 110
Sandbach (township in Sandbach), 5/216; SJ757608; NP 110
Sanden Fee (tithing in Hungerford), 2/141; SU333670; NP 158, 168
Sanderstead (parish), 35/46; TQ337614; NP 170, 171
Sandford (township in Abingdon St Helen), 2/16B; SP472000; NP 158
Sandford (parish), 9/212; SS815040; NP 175, 176
Sandford (Sandford-on-Thames) (parish), 29/241; SP545015; NP 158
Sandford (township in Prees), 31/21; SJ601334; NP 118, 119
Sandford (township in West Felton), 31/97; SJ342233; NP 118
Sandford Orcas (parish), 32/389; ST621202; NP 166, 178
Sandford St Martin (Sandford) (parish), 29/56; SP420273; NP 145
Sandhoe (Sandoe) (township in St John Lee), 27/450; NY973670; NP 77
Sandhurst (parish), 2/217; SU857622; NP 169
Sandhurst (parish), 13/119; SO828638; NP 143
Sandhurst (parish), 19/409; TQ800284; NP 184
Sandiacre (parish), 8/289; SK473365; NP 121
Sandleford Priory (extra-parochial), 2/152; SU472644; NP 158, 168
Sandoe, 27/450; NP 77
Sandon (parish), 12/288; TL754038; NP 161, 162
Sandon (parish), 16/11; TL322342; NP 147
Sandon (parish), 33/127; SJ957306; NP 119
Sandridge (parish), 16/104; TL168102; NP 147, 160

193

Sandringham (parish), 25/96; TF695287; NP 124
Sandwich, St Bartholomew's Hospital (extra-parochial), 19/269; TR330575; NP 173, 173/1
Sandwich, St Clement (parish), 19/270; TR339576; NP 173, 173/1
Sandwich, St Mary (parish), 19/267; TR327577; NP 173, 173/1
Sandwich, St Peter (parish), 19/268; TR328583; NP 173, 173/1
Sandwith (township in St Bees), 7/298; NY956146; NP 82
Sandy (hamlet in Sandy), 1/58; TL182496; NP 147
Sandy (parish), 1/58-59; NP 147
Santon (Santon House) (parish), 25/707; TL830887; NP 136
Santon Downham (parish), 34/106; TL820857; NP 136
Santon House (parish), 25/707; NP 136
Sapcote (parish), 21/231; SP487932; NP 132
Saperton (parish), 13/302-303; NP 156, 157
Saperton, 13/302; NP 156, 157
Sapey Pitchard (parish), 40/95; NP 130
Sapiston (parish), 34/124; TL925755; NP 136
Sapley (hamlet in King's Ripton), 17/65; TL245748; NP 134
Sapperton (Saperton) (hamlet in Sapperton), 13/302; SO945020; NP 156, 157
Sapperton (Saperton) (parish), 13/302-303; NP 156, 157
Sapperton (parish), 22/638; TF022335; NP 123
Saredon (township in Shareshill), 33/251; SJ953080; NP 119
Sarnesfield (parish), 15/57; SO371509; NP 142
Sarratt (parish), 16/134; TQ034996; NP 159, 160
Sarre (St Gyles or Sarr) (parish), 19/122; TR262652; NP 173
Sarsden (parish), 29/135; SP290230; NP 144, 145
Sascott (township in Pontesbury), 31/292B; SJ431123; NP 118
Satley (township in Lanchester), 11/162A; NZ119432; NP 84, 85
Satley and Butsfield (intermixed parts of townships in Lanchester), 11/162B; NZ125469; NP 84, 85
Satron (division in township of Muker in Grinton), 42/119; SD943967; NP 90
Satterleigh (parish), 9/71; SS667225; NP 163
Satterthwaite (division in township of Satterthwaite in Hawkshead), 20/47; SD332921; NP 89
Satterthwaite (township in Hawkshead), 20/46-49; NP 89
Saughall Massie (Saughan Massie, Saughall Massey) (township in Bidston), 5/450; SJ247891; NP 100
Saughan Massie, 5/450; NP 100
Saul (parish), 13/266; SO751096; NP 143, 156
Saundby (parish), 28/12; SK786884; NP 104
Saunderton (parish), 3/191; SU801998; NP 159
Sausthorpe (parish), 22/430; TF387690; NP 114
Sawbridgeworth (parish), 16/69; TL470153; NP 148
Sawdon (township in Brompton), 42/416; SE938853; NP 92, 93
Sawley (division in township of Sawley in Ripon), 43/163; SE250670; NP 91
Sawley (extra-parochial), 43/296; SD785465; NP 95
Sawley (parish), 8/290-292; NP 121
Sawley (township in Sawley), 8/292; SK473315; NP 121
Sawley (township in Ripon), 43/163-164; NP 91
Sawston (parish), 4/159; TL482499; NP 148
Sawtry All Saints (parish), 17/32; TL165840; NP 134
Sawtry St Andrew (parish), 17/31; TL175839; NP 134
Sawtry St Judith (parish), 17/33; TL187814; NP 134
Saxby (parish), 21/106; SK822198; NP 122
Saxby (parish), 22/58; NP 104
Saxby (Saxby in Aslacoe) (parish), 22/220; SK998862; NP 104
Saxby All Saints (Saxby) (parish), 22/58; SE992167; NP 104
Saxby in Aslacoe (parish), 22/220; SK998862; NP 104
Saxelby (parish), 21/70; SK699217; NP 121
Saxelby (parish), 22/243; NP 104, 113
Saxilby (Saxelby) (parish), 22/243; SK896761; NP 104, 113
Saxlingham (parish), 25/71; TG035397; NP 125
Saxlingham Nethergate (parish), 25/602B; TM240965; NP 137
Saxlingham Thorpe (parish), 25/602A; TM220975; NP 137
Saxmundham (parish), 34/271; TM386630; NP 137
Saxondale (township in Shelford), 28/224; SK684402; NP 121, 122
Saxtead (Saxted) (parish), 34/254; TM258654; NP 137
Saxthorpe (parish), 25/128; TG117313; NP 125

Saxton (parish), 43/434-436; NP 97
Saxton cum Scarthingwell (township in Saxton), 43/435; SE478379; NP 97
Scackleton (township in Hovingham), 42/628; SE645728; NP 92
Scaftworth (township in Everton), 28/4; SK670925; NP 103
Scagglethorpe (township in Settrington), 41/147; SE834726; NP 92
Scalby (parish), 42/396-401; NP 93
Scalby (township in Blacktoft), 41/24; SE849269; NP 98
Scalby (township in Scalby), 42/398; TA008907; NP 93
Scaldwell (parish), 26/194; SP769726; NP 133
Scale Park (division of Kettlewell with Starbotton township in Kettlewell), 43/221; SD981748; NP 90
Scaleby (parish), 7/21-22; NP 76
Scalford (parish), 21/79; SK759239; NP 122
Scaling Dam (division in township of Easington in Easington), 42/367; NZ739127; NP 86
Scalthwaite-rig, 38/98
Scalthwaiterigg Hay, 38/98
Scalthwaiterigg, Hay and Hutton-i-the-Hay (township in Kendal), 38/98; SD550920; NP 89
Scamblesby (parish), 22/334; TF280780; NP 105
Scammonden (township in Huddersfield), 43/756; SE042157; NP 102
Scampston (township in Rillington), 41/150; SE858762; NP 92
Scampton (parish), 22/233; SK943795; NP 104
Scarborough (parish), 42/402-403; NP 93
Scarborough (township in Scarborough), 42/403; TA042878; NP 93
Scarcliff (parish), 8/64; SK489688; NP 112
Scarcroft (township in Thorner), 43/410; SE379414; NP 96
Scargill (township in Barningham), 42/17; NZ020100; NP 84
Scarisbrick (division in township of Scarisbrick in Ormskirk), 20/370; SD395125; NP 100
Scarisbrick (township in Ormskirk), 20/370-371; NP 100
Scarning (parish), 25/505; TF958117; NP 125
Scarrington (parish), 28/214; SK736414; NP 122
Scartho (parish), 22/786; TA267061; NP 105
Scattergate (township in St Lawrence Appleby), 38/39; NY674198; NP 83
Scawby (parish), 22/118; SE972051; NP 104
Scawsby (division in parish and township of Brodsworth), 43/880; SE540050; NP 103
Scawton (parish), 42/494; SE560830; NP 92
Scholes (division in township of Barwick in Elmet in Barwick in Elmet), 43/417; SE382365; NP 96
Scholes (division in township of Cleckheaton in Birstal), 43/542; SE168257; NP 96
Scholes (division in township of Wooldale in Kirkburton), 43/735A-B; NP 102
Scholes (subdivision of Scholes division in township of Wooldale in Kirkburton), 43/735A; SE160073; NP 102
Scholes (subdivision of Scholes division in township of Wooldale in Kirkburton), 43/735B; SE143052; NP 102
School Aycliffe (township in Heighington), 11/279; NZ262240; NP 85
Sco Ruston (South Ruston) (parish), 25/249; TG281219; NP 126
Scole (Osmondeston) (parish), 25/758; TM148795; NP 136, 137
Scopwick (parish), 22/568; TF065580; NP 113
Scorbrough (parish), 41/283; TA025460; NP 98, 99
Scorton (township in Catterick), 42/85; NZ258007; NP 91
Scosthorp (township in Kirkby Malhamdale), 43/236; SD886602; NP 90, 95
Scot Willoughby (parish), 22/647; NP 123
Scotby (township in Wetheral), 7/43; NY435553; NP 76
Scotch Street, Rickergate Ward (township in St Mary [Carlisle]), 7/92; NY400562; NP 76/1
Scotch Street, St Cuthbert Ward (district in Scotch Street township in St Mary [Carlisle]), 7/90; NY401560; NP 76/1
Scotch Street, St Mary Ward (district in Scotch Street township in St Mary [Carlisle]), 7/91; NY400561; NP 76/1
Scotforth (township in Lancaster), 20/119; SD490590; NP 89, 94
Scothern (Scothorn) (parish), 22/255; TF035775; NP 104

Scott Willoughby (Scot Willoughby) (parish), 22/647; TF056380; NP 123
Scotter (parish), 22/35; SE871012; NP 104
Scotton (division in Scotton), 22/36A; SK893989; NP 104
Scotton (parish), 22/36A-C; NP 104
Scotton (township in Catterick), 42/77; SE178965; NP 91
Scotton (township in Farnham), 43/136; SE331593; NP 91, 96
Scotton Common (division in Scotton), 22/36B; SK860995; NP 104
Scottow (Scottowe) (parish), 25/241; TG274234; NP 126
Scoulton (parish), 25/661; TF981010; NP 125, 136
Scrafield (parish), 22/389; TF303689; NP 114
Scraptoft (parish), 21/257; SK653057; NP 121
Scratby (parish), 25/382B; TG513155; NP 126
Scrayingham (parish), 41/117-119; NP 92, 98
Scrayingham (township in Scrayingham), 41/117; SE743598; NP 92, 98
Scredington (parish), 22/651; TF104404; NP 123
Scremby (parish), 22/423; TF443680; NP 114
Scremerston (township in Ancroft parochial chapelry in Holy Island), 27/18; NU010485; NP 64
Screnwood (township in Alnham), 27/164; NT990095; NP 71
Screveton (parish), 28/210; SK735440; NP 112, 122
Scrivelsby (division in Scrivelsby), 22/380A; TF272659; NP 114
Scrivelsby (parish), 22/380A-B; NP 114
Scrivelsby - Wildmore Fen (division in Scrivelsby), 22/380B; TF261513; NP 114
Scriven with Tentergate (division outside the borough of Knaresborough in township of Scriven with Tentergate in Knaresborough), 43/141B; SE350590; NP 96
Scriven with Tentergate (division within borough of Knaresborough in township of Scriven with Tentergate in Knaresborough), 43/141A; SE343573; NP 96
Scriven with Tentergate (township in Knaresborough), 43/141A-B; NP 96
Scrooby (parish), 28/16; SK651906; NP 103
Scropton (township in Scropton), 8/246; SK199308; NP 120
Scropton (division in Scropton), 33/216; SK142212; NP 120
Scropton (parish), 8/245-246, 33/216; NP 120
Scruton (parish), 42/216; SE304916; NP 91
Sculcoates (parish), 41/322-323; NP 99, 99/1
Sculcoates - East (division in parish and township of Sculcoates), 41/323; TA099294; NP 99, 99/1
Sculcoates - West (division in parish and township of Sculcoates), 41/322; TA090289; NP 99, 99/1
Sculthorpe (parish), 25/109; TF889312; NP 125
Scunthorpe (township in Frodingham), 22/25; SE888112; NP 104
Sea Palling (parish), 25/226; NP 126
Seaborough (parish), 32/482; ST433064; NP 177
Seabridge (township in Stoke-on-Trent), 33/38; SJ837437; NP 110, 119
Seacourt (extra-parochial), 2/2; SU480075; NP 158
Seacroft (division in township of Seacroft in Whitkirk), 43/478; SE352354; NP 96
Seacroft (township in Whitkirk), 43/479-478; NP 96
Seaford (Sutton cum Seaford) (parish), 36/336; TV502990; NP 183
Seagrave (parish), 21/61; SK618172; NP 121
Seagry (parish), 39/65; ST952811; NP 157
Seaham (parish), 11/82-83; NP 78, 85
Seaham (township in Seaham), 11/82; NZ413504; NP 78, 85
Seal (parish), 8/331, 21/1, 21/5-7; NP 121, 121/3
Seal (parish), 19/186; TQ564549; NP 171
Seal with Tongham (parish), 35/145; NP 169
Sealand (township in Hawarden), 50/3; SJ340690; NP 109
Seale (Seal with Tongham) (parish), 35/145; SU894474; NP 169
Seamer (parish), 42/297-298; NP 85
Seamer (parish), 42/407-411; NP 93
Seamer (township in Seamer), 42/297; NZ505095; NP 85
Seamer (township in Seamer), 42/409; TA024846; NP 93
Searby (division in Searby), 22/108A; TA072059; NP 104
Searby (parish), 22/107A-108B; NP 104

Searby - Caistor Moor (division in Searby), 22/108B; TA085028; NP 104
Seasalter (parish), 19/115; TR091644; NP 172, 173
Seaton (parish), 9/296-297; NP 177
Seaton (parish), 30/57-58; NP 122, 133
Seaton (tithing in Seaton), 9/296; SY245910; NP 177
Seaton (township in Camerton), 7/249; NY017314; NP 82
Seaton (township in Seaton), 30/57; SP905982; NP 122, 133
Seaton and Wassand (township in Sigglesthorne), 41/364; TA170470; NP 99
Seaton Carew (division in township of Seaton Carew in Seaton Carew), 11/254; NZ519293; NP 85
Seaton Carew (parish), 11/250-254; NP 85
Seaton Carew (township in Seaton Carew), 11/253-254; NP 85
Seaton Delaval (township in Earsdon), 27/485; NZ319768; NP 78
Seaton Ross (parish), 41/99; SE778402; NP 98
Seaton with Slingsby (township in Seaham), 11/83; NZ384487; NP 78, 85
Seavington St Mary (Sevington St Mary) (parish), 32/444; ST402147; NP 177
Seavington St Michael (parish), 32/443; ST414152; NP 177
Seckington (parish), 37/4; SK263069; NP 120
Sedbergh (parish), 43/255-264; NP 89, 90
Sedbergh (township of Sedbergh in Sedbergh), 43/260-264; NP 89, 90
Sedbergham (parish), 7/150-151; NP 82, 83
Sedgebarrow (parish), 40/261; SP015385; NP 144
Sedgebrook (parish), 22/629; SK848380; NP 122
Sedgefield (division in township of Sedgefield in Sedgefield), 11/232; NZ358294; NP 85
Sedgefield (parish), 11/231-241; NP 85
Sedgefield (township in Sedgefield), 11/231-233; NP 85
Sedgeford (parish), 25/88; TF717366; NP 124
Sedghill (parish), 39/339; ST863281; NP 166
Sedgley (parish), 33/330; SO920935; NP 130
Sedgwick (township in Heversham), 38/90; SD517869; NP 89
Sedlescombe (Sedlescomb) (parish), 36/140; TQ785193; NP 184
Seend (chapelry in Melksham), 39/128; ST940610; NP 166, 167
Seer Green (chapelry in Farnham Royal), 3/227B; SU971928; NP 159
Seething (parish), 25/596; TM316970; NP 137
Sefton (parish), 20/680-690; NP 100
Sefton (township in Sefton), 20/683; SJ346999; NP 100
Seghill (township in Earsdon), 27/486; NZ286748; NP 78
Seighford (parish), 33/174; SJ881250; NP 119
Selattyn (Sylattyn) (parish), 31/79; SJ273322; NP 117, 118
Selborne (parish), 14/121; SU768342; NP 169, 181
Selby (parish), 43/449; SE595328; NP 97
Selby's Forest (township in Kirknewton), 27/68; NT930230; NP 70, 71
Sellack (parish), 15/245; SO562273; NP 142
Sellindge (Sellinge) (parish), 19/396; TR102381; NP 172, 173
Selling (parish), 19/151; TR041569; NP 172
Selmeston (Simpston) (parish), 36/189; TQ513076; NP 183
Selsdon (Croydon Crook) (division in Croydon), 35/44B; TQ353621; NP 170, 171
Selsey (parish), 36/273; SZ860944; NP 181
Selside and Whitwell (township in Kendal), 38/110; NY530000; NP 89
Selston (parish), 28/168; SK464525; NP 112
Selworthy (parish), 32/240; SS916467; NP 164
Semer (Seamer) (parish), 34/403; TL999466; NP 149
Semington (Sernington) (chapelry in Steeple Ashton), 39/144A; ST894603; NP 166
Semley (parish), 39/340; ST888267; NP 166
Sempringham (hamlet in Sempringham), 22/660; TF135325; NP 123
Sempringham (parish), 22/660-662; NP 123
Send (division in Send), 35/82; TQ031544; NP 169, 170
Send (parish), 35/82; NP 169, 170
Sennen (parish), 6/216; SW363255; NP 189

Senny (division outside Fforest-fawr in Devynock), 45/67A; SN940210; NP 141
Senny - Fforest-fawr (division within Fforest-fawr in Devynock), 45/67B; SN916188; NP 141
Serjeant's Inn (Serjeant's Inn Fleet Street) (extra-parochial), 24/19A; TQ313811; NP 160/1
Serjeant's Inn (Serjeant's Inn Chancery Lane) (extra-parochial), 24/19B; TQ312811; NP 160/1
Sernington, 39/144A; NP 166
Sessay (parish), 42/562-564; NP 91
Sessay (township in Sessay), 42/564; SE464747; NP 91
Sesswick (township in Bangor-is-y-coed), 49/79; SJ382463; NP 109
Setchey (Setch) (parish), 25/309B; TF642139; NP 124
Setmurthy (township in Brigham), 7/268; NY165322; NP 82
Settle (township in Giggleswick), 43/249; SD840625; NP 90
Settrington (parish), 41/146-147; NP 92
Settrington (township in Settrington), 41/146; SE843697; NP 92
Seven Acres (extra-parochial), 22/747; TF225528; NP 114
Sevenhampton (parish), 13/110; SP030220; NP 143, 144
Sevenhampton (tithing in Highworth), 39/5E; SU208903; NP 157
Sevenoaks (township in Great Budworth), 5/121; SJ639787; NP 101
Sevenoaks (division in Sevenoaks), 19/190; TQ534542; NP 171
Sevenoaks (parish), 19/190-192; NP 171
Severn Stoke (parish), 40/172; SO856440; NP 143
Sevington (parish), 19/326; TR033402; NP 172
Sewardstone (hamlet in Waltham Holy Cross), 12/267; TQ405989; NP 161
Sewerby cum Marton (township in Bridlington), 41/253; TA199698; NP 93
Sewstern (Sewsterne) (chapelry in Buckminster), 21/108; SK884210; NP 122
Sexhow (township in Rudby in Cleveland), 42/293; NZ486060; NP 85, 91
Sezincote (parish), 13/82; SP173310; NP 144
Shabbington (parish), 3/161; SP670075; NP 158, 159
Shackerstone (parish), 21/145-146; NP 121
Shackerstone (township in Shackerstone), 21/145; SK338097; NP 121
Shaddingfield (parish), 34/50; NP 137
Shadforth (division of Shadforth township in Pittington), 11/108; NZ345409; NP 85
Shadforth (township in Pittington), 11/107-108; NP 85
Shadingfield (Shaddingfield) (parish), 34/50; TM430844; NP 137
Shadoxhurst (parish), 19/403; TQ977375; NP 172
Shadwell (township in Clun), 31/397; SO278849; NP 128, 129
Shadwell (division in township of Shadwell in Thorner), 43/412; SE335398; NP 96
Shadwell (township in Thorner), 43/411-413; NP 96
Shaftesbury, Holy Trinity (Shaston, Holy Trinity with St Martin and St Lawrence) (parish), 10/6; ST866232; NP 166
Shaftesbury, St James (Shaston St James) (parish), 10/5A-B; NP 166, 178
Shaftesbury, St James (Shaston St James) (division in Shaftesbury, St James), 10/5A; ST848216; NP 166, 178
Shaftesbury, St Peter (parish), 10/7; ST867228; NP 166
Shafton (township in Felkirk), 43/683; SE395108; NP 102
Shakerley (division in township of Tyldesley with Shakerley in Leigh), 20/575; SD691026; NP 101
Shalbourne (Shalbourn) (division in Shalbourne tithing in Shalbourne), 2/144A; SU318649; NP 158, 168
Shalbourne (Shalbourn) (division in Shalbourne), 39/188; SU308622; NP 157
Shalbourne (Shalbourn) (parish), 2/144A-B, 39/188; NP 157
Shalden (parish), 14/128; SU699420; NP 169
Shaldeston (parish), 3/12; NP 145
Shaldon (St Nicholas Shaldon) (parish), 9/41; SX927719
Shalfleet (parish), 18/4; SZ397889; NP 180
Shalford (parish), 12/85; TL720280; NP 148
Shalford (parish), 35/136; TQ006469; NP 169
Shalstone (Shalston, Shaldeston, Shalstone with Old Wick) (parish), 3/12; SP640362; NP 145

Shamblehurst (Townhill) (tithing in South Stoneham), 14/258; SU482140; NP 180
Shangton (Shankton and Shangton) (parish), 21/293; SP719971; NP 133
Shanklin (parish), 18/23; SZ578804; NP 180
Shankton and Shangton (parish), 21/293; NP 133
Shap (parish), 38/29; NY540110; NP 83, 89
Shapwick (Shapwicke) (parish), 10/177; ST954032; NP 178, 179
Shapwick (parish), 32/178; ST422391; NP 165
Shardlaw and Great or Far Wilne, 8/293; NP 121
Shardlow and Great Wilne (township in Aston upon Trent), 8/293; SK443307; NP 121
Shareshill (parish), 33/250-251; NP 119
Shareshill (township in Shareshill), 33/250; SJ948062; NP 119
Sharlston (township in Warmfield), 43/676; SE390192; NP 102, 103
Sharnbrook (parish), 1/16; SP999599; NP 134
Sharnford (parish), 21/232; SP480910; NP 132
Sharow (township in Ripon), 43/180; SE328720; NP 91
Sharpenhoe (hamlet in Streatley), 1/119B; TL062302; NP 147
Sharperton (township in Alwinton), 27/188B; NT968042; NP 71
Sharples (township in Bolton le Moors), 20/389-390; NP 101
Sharples Higher End (division in township of Sharples in Bolton le Moors), 20/389; SD670160; NP 101
Sharples Lower End (division in township of Sharples in Bolton le Moors), 20/390; SD714124; NP 101
Sharrington (parish), 25/72; TG031370; NP 125
Shaston St James (parish), 10/5A-B; NP 166, 178
Shaston St Rumbold (parish), 10/8; NP 166
Shaston, Holy Trinity with St Martin and St Lawrence (parish), 10/6; NP 166
Shaugh Prior (Shaugh) (parish), 9/365; SX572639; NP 187
Shavington cum Gresty (township in Wybunbury), 5/254; SJ705526; NP 110
Shavington (township in Adderley), 31/7; SJ630390; NP 119
Shaw (Shaw-cum-Donnington) (parish), 2/150; SU474696; NP 158
Shaw Mere (ivision in Saddleworth with Quick township in Rochdale), 43/743A-744; NP 101
Shaw Mere - Lower Division (division of sub-division of Shaw Mere Division in Saddleworth with Quick township in Rochdale), 43/743A; SD990040; NP 101
Shaw Mere - Lower Division (division of sub-division of Shaw Mere Division in Saddleworth with Quick township in Rochdale), 43/743B; SD990050; NP 101
Shaw Mere - Lower Division (sub-division of Shaw Mere Division in Saddleworth with Quick township in Rochdale), 43/743A-B; SD990050; NP 101
Shaw Mere - Upper Division (sub-division of Shaw Mere Division in Saddleworth with Quick township in Rochdale), 43/744; SD982062; NP 101
Shaw-cum-Donnington (parish), 2/150; NP 158
Shawbury (parish), 31/161-162; NP 118
Shawbury (township in Shawbury), 31/161; SJ565206; NP 118
Shawdon and Woodhouse (township in Whittingham), 27/168; NU095145; NP 71
Shawell (parish), 21/347; SP545802; NP 132
Shearsby (chapelry in Knaptoft), 21/334; SP630910; NP 132
Shebbear (Shebbeare) (parish), 9/107; SS439106; NP 175
Sheen (parish), 33/80; SK112613; NP 111
Sheephall (parish), 16/48; NP 147
Sheeping Moors (common to St Andrews Major and Cadoxton juxta Barry), 51/177; ST135685; NP 154
Sheepscombe (Shepscomb) (tithing in Painswick), 13/249; SO890100; NP 143, 156
Sheepshed (parish), 21/22; NP 121
Sheepstor (parish), 9/357; SX579672; NP 187
Sheepwash (parish), 9/187; SS480074; NP 175
Sheepy Magna (Great Sheepey) (parish), 21/159-160; NP 121, 132
Sheepy Magna (Great Sheepey) (township in Sheepy Magna), 21/159; SK327016; NP 121, 132
Sheepy Parva (parish), 21/162; SK336013; NP 121

Sheering (parish), 12/201; TL503142; NP 148
Sheet (tithing in Petersfield), 14/244; SU765239; NP 181
Sheffield (parish), 43/822-833; NP 102, 111
Sheffield (township in Sheffield), 43/827-831
Sheffield Park (division in township of Sheffield in Sheffield), 43/830; SK348870; NP 102
Shefford (township in Campton), 1/86; TL141390; NP 147
Shefford Hardwick (extra-parochial), 1/87; TL141398; NP 147
Sheinton (parish), 31/468; SJ614036; NP 119
Sheldon (parish), 9/148; ST118084; NP 164, 176
Sheldon (parish), 37/53; SP158862; NP 131
Sheldon (township in Bakewell), 8/101; SK171692; NP 111
Sheldwich (parish), 19/150; TR015563; NP 172
Shelf (township in Halifax), 43/548; SE123281; NP 96
Shelfanger (parish), 25/739; TM100839; NP 136
Shelford (parish), 28/224-225; NP 121, 122
Shelford (township in Shelford), 28/225; SK671418; NP 121, 122
Shell (extra-parochial), 40/133; SO950600; NP 130
Shelland (parish), 34/299; TM003604; NP 136
Shelley (division in township of Shelley in Kirkburton), 43/730; SE210110; NP 102
Shelley (parish), 12/276; TL554050; NP 161
Shelley (parish), 34/501; TM019382; NP 149
Shelley (township in Kirkburton), 43/729-730; NP 102
Shelley Lane End (division in township of Shelley in Kirkburton), 43/729; SE215125; NP 102
Shellingford (parish), 2/45; SU313933; NP 158
Shellow Bowells (parish), 12/280; TL601080; NP 161
Shelsey Walsh (parish), 40/93; NP 130
Shelsley Beauchamp (parish), 40/97-98; NP 130
Shelsley Beauchamp (township in Shelsley Beauchamp), 40/97; SO740633; NP 130
Shelsley Kings (township in Shelsley Beauchamp), 40/98; SO723651; NP 130
Shelsley Walsh (Shelsey Walsh, Little Shelsey) (parish), 40/93; SO721631; NP 130
Shelswell (parish), 29/73; SP610309; NP 145
Shelton (parish), 1/3; TL029696; NP 134
Shelton (parish), 25/639; TM237906; NP 137
Shelton (parish), 28/207; SK779445; NP 112, 122
Shelton (township in Stoke-on-Trent), 33/34; SJ878468; NP 110
Shelton and Oxon (township in St Chad Shrewsbury), 31/271; SJ464132; NP 118
Shelve (parish), 31/346; SO332988; NP 118, 129
Shelvock (Shelvoke) (township in Ruyton of the Eleven Towns), 31/137; SJ372242; NP 118
Shelvoke, 31/137; NP 118
Shenington (parish), 29/1; SP368432; NP 145
Shenley (parish), 3/71-72; NP 146
Shenley (parish), 16/127; TQ200997; NP 160
Shenley Brook End (hamlet in Shenley), 3/70; SP837354; NP 146
Shenley Church End (township in Shenley), 3/71; SP820366; NP 146
Shenstone (parish), 33/292; SK099035; NP 120, 131
Shenton (township in Market Bosworth), 21/164; SP385999; NP 121, 132
Shephall (Sheephall) (parish), 16/48; TL260230; NP 147
Shepherdswell (parish), 19/347; NP 173
Shepley (township in Kirkburton), 43/731; SE192098; NP 102
Shepperton (parish), 24/120; TQ079672; NP 170
Shepreth (parish), 4/177; TL394479; NP 148
Shepscomb, 13/249; NP 143, 156
Shepshed (Sheepshed) (parish), 21/22; SK470180; NP 121
Shepton Beauchamp (parish), 32/440; ST404174; NP 177
Shepton Mallet (parish), 32/136; ST625445; NP 165, 166
Shepton Montague (parish), 32/354; ST693315; NP 166
Sheraton (township in Monk Hesleden), 11/96; NZ441354; NP 85
Sherborne (parish), 10/31; ST633168; NP 178
Sherborne (parish), 13/230; SP172148; NP 144
Sherborne St John (parish), 14/49; SU630560; NP 168
Sherborne (Sherbourne) (parish), 37/212; SP256619; NP 131
Sherbourne (parish), 37/212; NP 131
Sherburn (township in Pittington), 11/109; NZ323422; NP 85
Sherburn (parish), 41/157; SE958759; NP 93
Sherburn House (extra-parochial), 11/106; NZ319409; NP 85
Sherburn in Elmet (division in township of Sherburn in Elmet in Sherburn in Elmet), 43/430; SE495335; NP 97
Sherburn in Elmet (parish), 43/424-434; NP 97
Sherburn in Elmet (township in Sherburn in Elmet), 43/430-433; NP 97
Shere (parish), 35/165; TQ082461; NP 170
Shereford (parish), 25/163; TF892291; NP 125
Sherfield English (parish), 14/221; SU293232; NP 167, 168, 180
Sherfield on Loddon (Sherfield upon Loddon) (parish), 14/44; SU678569; NP 168, 169
Sherford (parish), 9/479; SX772444; NP 187
Sheriff Hales (division in Sheriff Hales), 31/198; SJ749132; NP 119
Sheriff Hales (parish), 31/197-198, 33/247; NP 119
Sheriff Hales (township in Sheriff Hales), 33/247; SJ772130; NP 119
Sheriff Hutton (division in township of Sheriff Hutton with Cornborough in Sheriff Hutton), 42/599; SE653667; NP 92
Sheriff Hutton Moor and Lilling Green (intermixed between Sheriff Hutton township and West Lilling division in Sheriff Hutton), 42/600; SE642527; NP 92
Sheriff's Lench (hamlet in Church Lench), 40/193; SP020490; NP 144
Sheringham (Sherringham) (parish), 25/32; TG143420; NP 125, 126
Sherington (Sherrington) (parish), 3/42; SP889465; NP 146
Shermanbury (parish), 36/317; TQ221194; NP 182
Shernborne (Shernborn) (parish), 25/147; TF724320; NP 124
Sherringham (parish), 25/32; NP 125, 126
Sherrington (parish), 39/270; ST954376; NP 167
Sherston Magna (Great Sherston) (parish), 39/39; ST850865; NP 156
Sherston Parva (Sherston Pinkney) (parish), 39/38; ST868868; NP 156
Sherston Pinkney (parish), 39/38; NP 156
Sherwood Villa (district in Newton St Cyres), 9/252B; SX862962; NP 176
Shevington (township in Standish), 20/381; SD542090; NP 100
Sheviock (parish), 6/115; SX365550; NP 186
Shiffnal, 31/223A; NP 119
Shifford (chapelry in Bampton), 29/171; SP373023; NP 158
Shifnal (Shiffnal) (parish), 31/223A-D; NP 119
Shifnal (Shiffnal) (township in Shifnal), 31/223A; SJ755085; NP 119
Shilbottle (parish), 27/207-211; NP 71
Shilbottle (township in Shilbottle), 27/207; NU190085; NP 71
Shildon (township in St Andrew Auckland), 11/214; NZ225263; NP 85
Shilling Okeford (parish), 10/84; ST830103; NP 178
Shillingford (Shillingford St George) (parish), 9/315; SX905880; NP 176
Shillingstone (Shilling Okeford) (parish), 10/84; ST830103; NP 178
Shillington (Shitlington) (parish), 1/100; TL133337; NP 147
Shilton (parish), 29/4; SP260087; NP 157
Shilton (parish), 37/104; SP404844; NP 132
Shilvington (township in Morpeth), 27/419; NZ160809; NP 78
Shimpling (parish), 25/755; TM157831; NP 136, 137
Shimpling (Shimpling Thorne) (parish), 34/410; TL863514; NP 149
Shincliffe (township in St Oswald), 11/125; NZ296399; NP 85
Shinfield (division in Shinfield), 2/184; SU733678; NP 169
Shinfield (parish), 2/184-186; NP 169
Shingay (parish), 4/167; TL308468; NP 147
Shingham (parish), 25/449; TG772053; NP 125
Shinglewell or Ifield (parish), 19/34; NP 171
Shipbourne (Shipborne) (parish), 19/209; TQ592522; NP 171
Shipbrook (Shipbrooke) (township in Davenham), 5/187; SJ674713; NP 110

Shipdham (parish), 25/504; TF964074; NP 125
Shipham (parish), 32/151; ST443576; NP 165
Shiplake (parish), 29/320; SU745786; NP 159
Shipley (parish), 36/64; TQ141227; NP 182
Shipley (township in Codnor), 8/199; SK446443; NP 112, 121
Shipley (township in Eglingham), 27/144; NU142182; NP 71
Shipley (township in Bradford), 43/521; SE139375; NP 96
Shipmeadow (parish), 34/28; TM380898; NP 137
Shippon (township in Abingdon St Helen), 2/15; SU482980; NP 158
Shipston on Stour (Shipton on Stour) (parish), 40/252; SP252403; NP 144
Shipton (parish), 14/79; NP 167
Shipton (parish), 31/497; SO564921; NP 129
Shipton (Shipton Thorpe) (township in Market Weighton), 41/192; SE847429; NP 98
Shipton (township in Overton), 42/687; SE549593; NP 97
Shipton Bellinger (Shipton) (parish), 14/79; SU240454; NP 167
Shipton Gorge (parish), 10/234; SY503916; NP 177
Shipton Lee (hamlet in Quainton), 3/118; SP728212; NP 146
Shipton Moyne (parish), 13/336; ST890900; NP 156
Shipton Olliffe (parish), 13/107; SP048185; NP 144
Shipton on Cherwell (parish), 29/122; SP472172; NP 145
Shipton on Stour (parish), 40/252; NP 144
Shipton Sollers (Shipton Sollars) (parish), 13/108; SP047197; NP 144
Shipton Thorpe, 41/192; NP 98
Shipton-under-Wychwood (parish), 29/140-146; NP 144, 145
Shipton-under-Wychwood (township in Shipton-under-Wychwood), 29/140; SP281172; NP 144, 145
Shirburn (parish), 29/276; SU702959; NP 159
Shirehampton (tithing in Westbury upon Trym), 13/385; ST525775; NP 155
Shirenewton (parish), 53/96; ST470940; NP 155
Shireoaks (Shireoaks and Haggonfield) (township in Worksop), 28/27; SK560801; NP 103
Shireshead (township in Cockerham or Garstang), 20/147A; SD499517; NP 94
Shirland (township in Shirland and Higham), 8/137; SK402584; NP 111, 112
Shirland and Higham (parish), 8/136-137; NP 111, 112
Shirley (parish), 8/223-225; NP 120
Shirley (township in Shirley), 8/223; SK216417; NP 120
Shirwell (Shirwill) (parish), 9/17; SS588375; NP 163
Shitlington (parish), 1/100; NP 147
Shitlington High Quarter (township in Wark), 27/362; NY780790; NP 76, 77
Shitlington Low Quarter (township in Wark), 27/363; NY828802; NP 77
Shitlington (township in Thornhill), 43/714-717; NP 102
Shitterton (tithing in Bere Regis), 10/204; SY843934; NP 178
Shobdon (parish), 15/34; SO403622; NP 129
Shobrooke (Shobrook) (parish), 9/214; SS873009; NP 176
Shoby (extra-parochial), 21/66; SK678203; NP 121, 122
Shocklach (parish), 5/346-248; NP 109
Shocklach Oviatt (township in Shocklach), 5/346; SJ433481; NP 109
Sholden (parish), 19/355; TR352545; NP 173
Shopland (parish), 12/377; TQ904888; NP 162
Shordley (township in Hope), 50/127; SJ324593; NP 109
Shoreditch (parish), 24/62A-F; NP 160/1
Shoreham (parish), 12/349; NP 16
Shoreham (parish), 19/73; TQ520621; NP 171
Shoreswood (township in Norham), 27/12; NT944463; NP 64
Shorncote (parish), 39/15; SU028968; NP 157
Shorne (Shorne and Merston) (parish), 19/37; TQ694715; NP 171
Shorston (township in Bamburgh), 27/104; NU202328; NP 71
Shortflatt (township in Bolam), 27/391; NZ089805; NP 77
Shorthampton (Chilson, Shorthampton or Chilson) (chapelry in Charlbury), 29/132; SP318198; NP 145
Shorwell (parish), 18/11; SZ457822; NP 180
Shotatton (township in Ruyton of the Eleven Towns), 31/136; SJ368229; NP 118

Shotesham All Saints (Shotisham All Saints) (parish), 25/600; TM259982; NP 137
Shotesham St Mary (Shotisham St Mary) (parish), 25/601; TM239986; NP 137
Shotisham All Saints (parish), 25/600; NP 137
Shotisham St Mary (parish), 25/601; NP 137
Shotley (parish), 34/523; TM238359; NP 150
Shotley High Quarter (township in Shotley), 27/620; NY953521; NP 77, 78
Shotley Low Quarter (township in Shotley), 27/621; NZ062525; NP 77
Shotley, 27/619-621; NP 77, 78
Shotover (extra-parochial), 29/238; SP575065; NP 158
Shottesbrook (parish), 2/127; SU845769; NP 159, 169
Shotteswell (parish), 37/268; SP424456; NP 145
Shottisham (parish), 34/442; TM323447; NP 150
Shottle and Postern (township in Duffield), 8/187; SK312486; NP 111
Shotton (division in township of Foxton and Shotton in Sedgefield), 11/234; NZ375265; NP 85
Shotton (township in Easington), 11/92; NZ420400; NP 85
Shotton (township in Hawarden), 50/15; SJ303680; NP 109
Shotwick (parish), 5/485-489; NP 109
Shotwick (township in Shotwick), 5/485; SJ342727; NP 109
Shotwick Park (extra-parochial), 5/490; SJ351715; NP 109
Shouldham (parish), 25/322; TF686089; NP 124
Shouldham Thorpe (parish), 25/321; TF658083; NP 124
Shrawardine (parish), 31/129; SJ390161; NP 118
Shrawley (parish), 40/70; SO801651; NP 130
Shrewley (hamlet in Hatton), 37/172; SP221672; NP 131
Shrewton (parish), 39/250; SU086462; NP 167
Shripple (tithing in Idmiston), 39/310D; NP 167
Shrivenham (parish), 2/39-44; NP 157, 158
Shrivenham (tithing in Shrivenham), 2/39; SU237888; NP 157
Shropham (parish), 25/674; TL983926; NP 136
Shudy Camps (parish), 4/153; TL624451; NP 148
Shuff Fen (extra-parochial), 22/750; TF302466; NP 114
Shurdington Magna (parish), 13/205; SO923189; NP 143
Shurlach (township in Davenham), 5/186; SJ676726; NP 110
Shustoke (hamlet in Shustoke), 37/73; SP230905; NP 131
Shustoke (parish), 37/73-74; NP 131, 132
Shute (parish), 9/233; SY251970; NP 177
Shutlanger (Shuttlehanger) (hamlet in Stoke Bruerne), 26/309; SP726493; NP 146
Shuttington (parish), 37/5; SK252055; NP 120
Shuttlehanger, 26/309; NP 146
Shuttleworth (district in division in township of Walmersley-cum-Shuttleworth in Bury), 20/419A; SD828186; NP 95, 101
Shuttleworth (district in division in township of Walmersley-cum-Shuttleworth in Bury), 20/419B; SD792179; NP 101
Shuttleworth (division in township of Walmersley-cum-Shuttleworth in Bury), 20/419A-B; NP 101
Sibbertoft (parish), 26/112; SP682823; NP 132, 133
Sibertswold (Sibertswould, Shepherdswell) (parish), 19/347; TR255480; NP 173
Sibford Ferris (township in Swalcliffe), 29/24; SP362374; NP 145
Sibford Gower (township in Swalcliffe), 29/25; SP353387; NP 145
Sible Hedingham (parish), 12/88; TL765340; NP 148, 149
Sibsey (division in Sibsey), 22/475A; TF356512; NP 114
Sibsey (division in West Fen in Sibsey), 22/475D; TF323505; NP 114
Sibsey - West Fen (division in Sibsey), 22/475B; TF353488; NP 114
Sibsey - West Fen (division in Sibsey), 22/475C; TF360492; NP 114
Sibsey Willows (division in Sibsey), 22/474; TF338472; NP 114
Sibsey), 22/469A-B, 474-475D; NP 114
Sibson (parish), 21/152-155; NP 121, 132
Sibson (township in Sibson), 21/152; SK355021; NP 121
Sibson cum Stibbington (parish), 17/1; TL089977; NP 134
Sibthorpe (parish), 28/208; SK765454; NP 112, 122
Sibton (parish), 34/164; TM369693; NP 137

Sibton Carwood (parish), 31/413; SO414832; NP 129
Sicklinghall (division in township of Sicklinghall in Kirkby Overblow), 43/389; SE366480; NP 96
Sicklinghall (township in Kirkby Overblow), 43/389-390; NP 96
Sidbury (parish), 9/286; SY142926; NP 176
Sidbury (parish), 31/567; SO689856; NP 130
Siddington (township in Prestbury), 5/63; SJ846707; NP 110
Siddington (parish), 13/300; SU030990; NP 157
Siddle (division in township of East Harlsey in East Harlsey), 42/317; NZ422107; NP 91
Side (parish), 13/245; NP 143
Side Ings (extra-parochialSide Ings), 42/604; SE657698; NP 92
Sidestrand (parish), 25/42; TG263398; NP 126
Sidlesham (parish), 36/272; SZ848975; NP 181
Sidmonton (parish), 14/10; NP 168
Sidmouth (parish), 9/300; SY121889; NP 176
Sigglesthorne (parish), 31/364-368; NP 99
Sigglesthorne (township in Sigglesthorne), 41/366; TA157452; NP 99
Silchester (parish), 14/18; SU637616; NP 168
Sileby (parish), 21/60; SK607158; NP 121
Silfield (division in Wymondham), 25/651; TG125010; NP 125, 136
Silian (parish), 46/70; SN567514; NP 140
Silio (township in Llantysilio), 49/102; SJ175465; NP 108
Silk Willoughby (parish), 22/644; TF058427; NP 123
Silkstone (parish), 43/695-702; NP 102, 102/1
Silkstone (township in Silkstone), 43/700; SE290050; NP 102
Silksworth (township in Bishop Wearmouth), 11/71; NZ375541; NP 78
Silpho (township in Hackness), 42/394; SE967921; NP 93
Silsden (division in township of Silsden in Kildwick), 43/344; SE042465; NP 96
Silsden (township in Kildwick), 20/342-345, 351; NP 95, 96
Silsden Moor (division in township of Silsden in Kildwick), 43/351; SE035475; NP 96
Silsoe (hamlet in Flitton), 1/105; TL083351; NP 147
Silt Pits (extra-parochial), 22/467B; NP 114
Silton (parish), 10/3; ST779296; NP 166
Silverdale (township in Warton), 20/65; SD469759; NP 89
Silverstone (parish), 26/342; SP670440; NP 145, 146
Silverton (parish), 9/222; SS960044; NP 176
Silvington (parish Silvington), 31/565; SO620800; NP 130
Simmondley (township in Glossop), 8/3B; SK020935; NP 102
Simonburn (parish), 27/434-427; NP 77
Simonburn, 27/434; NP 77
Simondburn (parish), 27/434-427; NP 77
Simondburn (Simonburn) (township in Simondburn), 27/434; NY845725; NP 77
Simonstone (township in Whalley), 20/252; SD776346; NP 95
Simonswood (extra-parochial), 20/678; SJ433006; NP 100
Simonward, 6/40; NP 185, 186
Simpson (division in Simpson), 3/64; SP877355; NP 146
Simpson (parish), 3/64-65; NP 146
Simpston (parish), 36/189; NP 183
Sinderby (township in Pickhill), 42/250; SE342816; NP 91
Sinfin and Arleston (township in Barrow upon Trent), 8/264; SK340300; NP 121
Sinfin Moor (extra-parochial), 8/266; SK357308; NP 121
Singleborough (hamlet in Great Horwood), 3/92; SP765320; NP 146
Singleton (hamlet in Singleton), 36/228; SU880150; NP 181
Singleton (parish), 36/228-229; NP 181
Singlewell (Shinglewell or Ifield) (parish), 19/34; TQ657706; NP 171
Sinnington (area in Sinnington), 42/456; SE724833; NP 92
Sinnington (parish), 42/456-459; NP 92
Sinnington (township in Sinnington), 42/458; SE740860; NP 92
Sion Hill (division in Walcot), 32/34C; ST744658; NP 156/1
Sisland (parish), 25/595; TM342987; NP 137
Siston (parish), 13/405; ST682750; NP 156
Sithney (parish), 6/195; SW645289; NP 189
Sitlington (township in Thornhill), 43/714-717; NP 102

Sittingbourne (parish), 19/163; TQ910631; NP 172
Sixhills (parish), 22/272; TF171869; NP 104, 105
Sixpenny Handley (parish), 10/64; ST983167; NP 179
Skeeby (township in Easby), 42/90; NZ203027; NP 91
Skeffington (parish), 21/278; SK747027; NP 122
Skeffling (parish), 41/444; TA372195; NP 99, 105
Skegby (parish), 28/93; SK495612; NP 112
Skegby (township in Marnham), 28/111; SK779701; NP 112
Skegness (parish), 22/495; TF560628; NP 114
Skelbrooke (township in South Kirkby), 43/656; SE508126; NP 103
Skelden (Skelding) (township in Ripon), 43/189; SE212701; NP 91
Skellingthorpe (parish), 22/525; SK934910; NP 113
Skellow (township in Owston), 43/652; SE534101; NP 103
Skelmersdale (township in Ormskirk), 20/365; SD478060; NP 100
Skelsmergh (township in Kendal), 38/100; SD526963; NP 89
Skelton (division of Skelton township in Overton), 42/689; SE578578; NP 97
Skelton (division of Skelton township in Skelton), 42/690; SE569567; NP 97
Skelton (parish), 7/158-160; NP 83
Skelton (parish), 42/690; NP 97
Skelton (Skelton in Cleveland) (parish), 42/347-355; NP 86
Skelton (Skelton in Cleveland) (township in Skelton), 42/347; NZ658188; NP 86
Skelton (township in Skelton), 7/159; NY440350; NP 83
Skelton (township in Howden), 41/8; SE772255; NP 98, 98/1
Skelton (township in Overton and Skelton), 42/689-690
Skelton (township in Ripon), 43/173; SE368686; NP 91
Skelwith (division in township of Hawkshead and Monk Coniston with Skelwith in Hawkshead), 20/41; NY345025; NP 89
Skendleby (parish), 22/419; TF433702; NP 114
Skenfrith (Skenfreth) (parish), 53/10; SO440200; NP 142
Sker (extra-parochial), 51/100; SS802792; NP 153
Skerne (parish), 41/274; TA046552; NP 99
Skerton (township in Lancaster), 20/117; SD473636; NP 89
Sketchley (township in Aston Flamville), 21/227B; SP424921; NP 132
Skewsby (division in township of Dalby-cum-Skewsby in Dalby), 42/607; SE630710; NP 92
Skeyton (parish), 25/243; TG246261; NP 126
Skidbrooke with Saltfleet Haven (Saltfleet cum Skidbrook) (parish), 22/789; TF452941; NP 105
Skidby (parish), 41/304; TA006338; NP 98, 99
Skiddaw Forest (extra-parochial), 7/278; NY281294; NP 82
Skilgate (parish), 32/286; SS984273; NP 164
Skillington (parish), 22/688; SK899258; NP 123
Skinburness Marsh (common to the three townships in Holme Cultram), 7/126; NY150552; NP 75
Skinnand (parish), 22/549; SK974569; NP 113
Skinningrove (township in Skelton), 42/354; NZ711199; NP 86
Skiplam (township in Kirkdale), 42/480; SE652888; NP 92
Skipsea (parish), 41/354-357; NP 99
Skipsea (township in Skipsea), 41/356; TA178548; NP 99
Skipton (parish), 43/323-334; NP 95, 96
Skipton (township in Skipton), 43/325; SD999511; NP 95, 96
Skipton upon Swale, 42/246; NP 91
Skipton-on-Swale (Skipton upon Swale) (township in Topcliffe), 42/246; SE374800; NP 91
Skipwith (parish), 41/54-56; NP 97
Skipwith (township in Skipwith), 41/56; SE657387; NP 97
Skirbeck (division in Skirbeck), 22/754A; TF349466; NP 114, 123, 124
Skirbeck (parish), 22/754A; TF349466; NP 114, 123, 124
Skirbeck - East Fen (division in Skirbeck), 22/754B; TF334478; NP 114
Skirbeck - Holland Fen (division in Skirbeck), 22/754C; TF310439; NP 123
Skirbeck Quarter (hamlet in Skirbeck), 22/755; TF332423; NP 123
Skircoat (township in Halifax), 43/551; SE082238; NP 96

Skirlington (division in parish and township of Atwick), 41/359A; TA182527; NP 99
Skirmage (extra-parochial), 31/585; SO556828; NP 130
Skirpenbeck (parish), 41/116; SE745575; NP 98
Skirwith (township in Kirkland), 7/185; NY640330; NP 83
Skokholm Island (extra-parochial), 55/98C; SM736050; NP 151
Skomer Island (division in Haverfordwest, St Martin), 55/98B; SM725095; NP 151
Skutterskelfe (division in township of Skutterskelfe in Rudby in Cleveland), 42/294; NZ480070; NP 85
Skutterskelfe (township in Rudby in Cleveland), 42/294-296; NP 85
Slade Hooton (division in township of Laughton en le Morthen in Laughton en le Morthen), 43/915; SK526896; NP 103
Slaidburn (parish), 43/280-285; NP 90, 95
Slaidburn (township in Slaidburn), 43/282; SD700540; NP 95
Slaithwaite (township in Huddersfield), 43/757-758
Slaley (parish), 27/618; NY963573; NP 77
Slapton (parish), 3/129; SP931207; NP 146
Slapton (parish), 9/487; SX810466; NP 188
Slapton (parish), 26/321; SP639472; NP 146
Slaugham (parish), 36/62; TQ256286; NP 182
Slaughterford (parish), 39/117; ST848742; NP 156
Slawston (parish), 21/297; SP773943; NP 133
Sleagill (township in Morland), 38/12; NY601195; NP 83
Sleap (township in Myddle), 31/153B; SJ484258; NP 118
Sleap (township in Wem), 31/44; SJ486267; NP 118
Slebech (parish), 55/82; SN029142; NP 151
Sledmere (parish), 41/184; SE940640; NP 92, 93, 98
Sledwick (division in township of Whorlton in Gainford), 11/300A; NZ097156; NP 84
Sleegill (division in township of Hipswell in Catterick), 42/79; NZ168002; NP 91
Sleep (Sleep and part of Smallford) (hamlet in St Peters), 16/103; TL196081; NP 160
Sleights Moor (common to Eskdaleside and Ugglebarnby townships in Whitby), 42/384; NZ860043; NP 86, 92
Slimbridge (parish), 13/315; SO733035; NP 156
Slindon (parish), 36/224; SU961100; NP 181
Slindon (township in Eccleshall), 33/138; SJ829332; NP 119
Slinfold (parish), 36/34; TQ120315; NP 182
Slingsby (parish), 42/632; SE704750; NP 92
Slipton (parish), 26/140; SP948799; NP 133, 134
Sloley (parish), 25/239; TG298241; NP 126
Slyne (division in township of Slyne with Hest in Bolton-le-Sands), 20/95; SD465655; NP 89
Slyne with Hest (township in Bolton-le-Sands), 20/94-96; NP 89
Smalesmouth (township in Greystead), 27/360; NY700800; NP 76, 77
Smallburgh (parish), 25/235; TG340240; NP 126
Smalley (township in Morley), 8/205; SK413447; NP 112, 121
Smallfield (sub-division in Bradfield division in township of Bradfield in Ecclesfield), 43/813; SK235945; NP 102
Smallwood (township in Astbury), 5/237; SJ807609; NP 110
Smardale (township in Kirkby Stephen), 38/67; NY739076; NP 83, 84, 90
Smarden (parish), 19/319; TQ882427; NP 172
Smeeth (parish), 19/328; TR074394; NP 172
Smeeton Westerby (township in Kibworth Beauchamp), 21/318; SP679921; NP 132, 133
Smerill (division in Middleton and Smerill township in Youlgreave), 8/113; SK194608; NP 111
Smethcote (township in Myddle), 31/155; SJ502214; NP 118
Smethcott (parish), 31/339A-B; NP 129
Smethcott and Picklescott (township in Smethcott), 31/339A; SJ448001; NP 118, 129
Smethwick (township in Harborne), 33/344; SP020860; NP 131
Smisby (parish), 8/307; SK352197; NP 121
Snailwell (parish), 4/46; TL653668; NP 135
Snainton (chapelry in Brompton), 42/418; SE925835; NP 92, 93
Snaith (parish), 43/960-971B; NP 97, 98, 103, 104
Snaith (township in Snaith), 43/964A; SE642222; NP 97, 103

Snape (division in township of Scarisbrick in Ormskirk), 20/371; SD376139; NP 100
Snape (division in township of Snape in Well), 42/178; SE260840; NP 91
Snape (parish), 34/269; TM400590; NP 137, 150
Snape (township in Well), 42/178-179; NP 91
Snapethorpe (division in township of Alverthorpe with Thornes in Wakefield), 43/602; SE308198; NP 96, 102
Snarestone (Snareston) (parish), 21/142; SK351103; NP 121
Snarford (parish), 22/253; TF053825; NP 104
Snargate (parish), 19/432; TQ983289; NP 184
Snave (parish), 19/418; TR016301; NP 184
Snead (parish), 54/197; SO310927; NP 129
Sneaton (parish), 42/390; NZ900040; NP 86, 92, 93
Sneinton (Snenton) (parish), 28/232; SK591398; NP 121
Snelland (parish), 22/263; TF073806; NP 104
Snelsmore (tithing in Chieveley), 2/132; SU474717; NP 158
Snelson (township in Rostherne), 5/100; SJ804740; NP 110
Snelston (parish), 8/228; SK158428; NP 120
Snenton (parish), 28/232; NP 121
Snetterton (parish), 25/671; TM000909; NP 136
Snettisham (parish), 25/90; TF700340; NP 124
Sneyd (township in Burslem), 33/20; SJ874502; NP 110
Snibston (township in Packington), 21/2B; SK411131; NP 121
Snilesworth (township in Hawnby), 42/501A; SE520960; NP 91, 92
Snitter (township in Rothbury), 27/252; NU020040; NP 71
Snitterby (parish), 22/154; SK990046; NP 104
Snitterfield (parish), 37/209; SP216598; NP 131
Snitton (township in Bitterley), 31/529; SO562752; NP 129
Snodland (parish), 19/84; TQ695626; NP 171
Snoreham (Shoreham) (parish), 12/349; TQ881997; NP 162
Snorscomb (Snorscombe) (hamlet in Great Everdon), 26/260; SP595560; NP 132
Snowshill (parish), 13/31; SP112335; NP 144
Snydale (township in Normanton), 43/612; SE400208; NP 96
Soberton (parish), 14/253; SU617145; NP 180
Sock Dennis (Sock Dennis and Sock Wyndham) (extra-parochial), 32/402; ST515215; NP 177
Sockbridge and Tirril (township in Barton), 38/23; NY504263; NP 83
Sockburn (parish), 11/328, 42/58-59; NP 85
Sockburn (township), 11/328, 42/58-59; NZ350077; NP 85
Sockburn, 11/328, 42/58-59; NP 85
Soham (parish), 4/41; TL589751; NP 135
Sokeholme, 28/90
Solihull (parish), 37/80; SP145795; NP 131
Sollars Hope (parish), 15/177; 618328; NP 143
Sollers Hope (Sollars Hope, Sollershope) (parish), 15/177; SO618328; NP 143
Solport (township in Stapleton), 7/7; NY470730; NP 76
Somerby (hamlet in Corringham), 22/142; SK851895; NP 104
Somerby (parish), 21/267; SK775105; NP 122
Somerby (parish), 22/109; TA064064; NP 104
Somerby (parish), 22/635; SK963337; NP 122
Somerford (Somerford Radnor) (township in Astbury), 5/229; SJ823645; NP 110
Somerford Booths (township in Astbury), 5/231; SJ832662; NP 110
Somerford Radnor, 5/229; NP 110
Somerford Keynes (parish), 39/16; SU019960; NP 157
Somerleyton (parish), 34/12; TM451971; NP 137
Somers Town (division in St Pancras), 24/44D; TQ296829; NP 160
Somersal Herbert (Church Somershall, Somershall Herbert) (parish), 8/243; SK136349; NP 120
Somersby (parish), 22/394; TF342729; NP 114
Somershall Herbert (parish), 8/243; NP 120
Somersham (parish), 17/71; TL363787; NP 134
Somersham (parish), 34/399; TM084481; NP 149
Somerton (parish), 29/64; SP504281; NP 145
Somerton (division in Somerton), 32/338A; ST484286; NP 165, 177

Somerton (parish), 32/338A-B; NP 165, 177
Somerton (parish), 34/343; TL812530; NP 149
Somerton Castle (hamlet in Boothby Graffoe), 22/553; SK949590; NP 113
Sompting (parish), 36/213; TQ163065; NP 182
Sonning (parish), 2/202-204, 29/319; NP 159, 169
Sonning Town (division in Sonning), 2/202; SU763762; NP 159
Sontley (Soutley) (township in Marchweil), 49/82B; SJ330470; NP 109, 118
Sookholme (Sokeholme) (township in Market Warsop), 28/90; SK544658; NP 112
Soothill (township in Dewsbury), 43/582-534; NP 96
Soper's Farm (division in Walcot), 32/34D; ST742683; NP 156
Sopley (parish), 14/321; SZ161985; NP 179
Sopworth (parish), 39/40; ST829863; NP 156
Sotby (parish), 22/346; TF202788; NP 105
Sotherton (parish), 34/70; TM429793; NP 137
Sotterley (parish), 34/51; TM463847; NP 137
Sotwell (parish), 2/65; SU587912; NP 158
Soughton (township in Northop), 50/24; SJ257668; NP 108
Soulbury (parish), 3/100; SP889269; NP 146
Soulby (township in Dacre), 7/197; NY465250; NP 83
Soulby (township in Kirkby Stephen), 38/58; NY743113; NP 84
Souldern (parish), 29/63; SP512308; NP 145
Souldrop (Souldrope) (parish), 1/18; SP978615; NP 134
Soulton (township in Wem), 31/41B; SJ549301; NP 118
Sound (township in Wrenbury), 5/277; SJ620489; NP 110
Sourton (parish), 9/330; SX526915; NP 175
South Acre (parish), 25/326; TF806132; NP 125
South Ambersham (tithing in Steep), 36/2; SU916210 ; NP 181
South Anston (division in township of Anston in Anston cum Membris), 43/905; SK527827; NP 103
South Anston (division in township of Anston in Dinnington), 43/906; SK521823; NP 103
South Bailey (St Mary the Less) (parish), 11/120; NZ273419; NP 85
South Barrow (parish), 32/366; ST600280; NP 166, 177
South Bedburn (township in St Andrew Auckland), 11/191; NZ090310; NP 84
South Bemfleet (parish), 12/390; NP 162
South Benfleet (South Bemfleet) (parish), 12/390; TQ781866; NP 162
South Bersted (parish), 36/277-278; NP 181
South Bersted (township in South Bersted), 36/277; SU931010; NP 181
South Biddick (Biddick Waterville) (township in Houghton-le-Spring), 11/52; NZ314529; NP 78
South Blyth (township in Earsdon), 27/483; NZ318802; NP 78
South Bradon (parish), 32/436; ST366191; NP 177
South Bramwith (division in township of Stainforth in Hatfield), 43/944; SE629109; NP 103
South Brent (parish), 9/370; SX713599; NP 187
South Brent (parish), 32/172; NP 165
South Brewham (South Bruham) (parish), 32/196; ST730348; NP 166
South Bruham (parish), 32/196; NP 166
South Burlingham (parish), 25/457; NP 126
South Cadbury (parish), 32/374; ST631256; NP 166
South Carlton (parish), 22/246; SK952762; NP 104, 113
South Carlton (township in Carlton in Lindrick), 28/25B; SK590820; NP 103
South Cave (parish), 41/204-206; NP 98
South Cave (township in South Cave), 41/206; SE918309; NP 98
South Cerney (parish), 13/299; SU057971; NP 157
South Charford (parish), 14/309; SU170192; NP 179
South Charlton (township in Ellingham), 27/126; NU164202; NP 71
South Church, 11/200; NP 85
South Claines (division in township of Claines in Claines), 40/111A; SO842565; NP 130, 143
South Clifton (township in North Clifton), 28/117; SK834704; NP 113

South Cliffe (South Cliff) (township in North Cave), 41/200; SE869358; NP 98
South Cockerington (Cockerington St Leonard) (parish), 22/187; TF385985; NP 105
South Collingham (parish), 28/126; SK840590; NP 113
South Common (extra-parochial), 22/497; SK978697; NP 113
South Cove (parish), 34/60; TM502804; NP 137
South Cowton (township in Gilling), 42/49; NZ299018; NP 91
South Creake (parish), 25/82; TF861357; NP 125
South Crosland (division in township of South Crosland in Almondbury), 43/770; SE114124; NP 102
South Crosland (township in Almondbury), 43/769-770; NP 102
South Croxton (parish), 21/124; SK681102; NP 121, 122
South Dalton (parish), 41/224; SE959453; NP 98
South Damerham (Damerham South) (parish), 39/390; SU096165; NP 179
South Dissington (township in Newburn), 27/533; NZ135707; NP 77, 78
South Duffield (township in Hemingbrough), 41/51; SE679338; NP 97
South Elkington (parish), 22/279; TF296887; NP 105
South Elmham, All Saints (All Saints South Elmham) (parish), 34/37A; TM341825; NP 137
South Elmham, St Cross (St Cross or St George South Elmham, St Cross South Elmham) (parish), 34/35; TM300838; NP 137
South Elmham, St James (St James in Southelmham, St James South Elmham) (parish), 34/38; TM321811; NP 137
South Elmham, St Margaret (St Margaret in Southelmham, St Margaret South Elmham) (parish), 34/36; TM313840; NP 137
South Elmham, St Mary (Homersfield) (parish), 34/33; TM291851; NP 137
South Elmham, St Michael (St Michael in Southelmham, St Michael South Elmham) (parish), 34/39; TM342833; NP 137
South Elmham, St Nicholas (St Nicholas South Elmham) (parish), 34/37B; TM330828; NP 137
South Elmham, St Peter (St Peter in Southelmham, St Peter South Elmham) (parish), 34/40; TM335852; NP 137
South Elmsall (township in South Kirkby), 43/658; SE477110; NP 103
South Fambridge (parish), 12/369; TQ859950; NP 162
South Ferriby (parish), 22/46; SE990204; NP 98, 99, 104
South Fields (district in Leicester, St Mary), 21/204; SK588033; NP 121
South Frodingham (township in Owthorne), 41/420; TA315264; NP 99
South Gosforth (township in Gosforth), 27/510; NZ250680; NP 78
South Hackney (division in St John at Hackney), 24/73; TQ353840; NP 160, 161
South Hallow (division in Hallow), 40/110B; SO834562; NP 130, 143
South Hamlet (extra-parochial), 13/192; SO828178; NP 143/1
South Hanningfield (parish), 12/290; TQ735985; NP 161, 162
South Harting (Harting) (parish), 36/10; SU785194; NP 181
South Hayling (parish), 14/285; SZ722998; NP 181
South Heighton (parish), 36/331; TQ462038; NP 183
South Hiendly (township in Felkirk), 43/681; SE398127; NP 102, 103
South Hill (parish), 6/62; SX335715; NP 186
South Hinksey (division in South Hinksey), 2/8B; SP518033; NP 158
South Hinksey (South Hincksey) (division in South Hinksey), 2/8A; SP511041; NP 158
South Hinksey (South Hincksey) (parish), 2/8A-B; NP 158
South Holme (township in Hovingham), 42/625; SE702775; NP 92
South Hornchurch (division in Hornchurch), 12/327B; TQ524742; NP 161
South Huish (parish), 9/495; SX692407; NP 187
South Hykeham (parish), 22/536-537; NP 113
South Hykeham (township in South Hykeham), 22/536; SK642937; NP 113

South Kelsey (parish), 22/113; TF047988; NP 104
South Killingholme (township in Killingholme), 22/52; TA158162; NP 104, 105
South Kilvington (parish), 42/533-535; NP 91
South Kilvington (township in South Kilvington), 42/535; SE442841; NP 91
South Kilworth (parish), 21/342; SP600820; NP 132
South Kirkby (parish), 43/656-660; NP 103
South Kirkby (township in South Kirkby), 43/659; SE450110; NP 103
South Kyme (parish), 22/585-586; NP 113
South Kyme (township in South Kyme), 22/586; TF177498; NP 113
South Leasingham, 22/580; NP 113
South Leigh (parish), 29/188; SP391083; NP 145, 158
South Leverton (parish), 28/45-46; NP 104
South Leverton (township in South Leverton), 28/46; SK780805; NP 104
South Linton (township in Woodhorn), 27/314; NZ256917; NP 78
South Littleton (parish), 40/199; SP092460; NP 144
South Lopham (parish), 25/742; TM044808; NP 136
South Lord's Land (division in township of Dent in Sedbergh), 43/257; SD690860; NP 89
South Luffenham (parish), 30/49; SK943018; NP 122, 123
South Lynn (All Saints, Kings Lynn) (parish), 25/307; TF621185; NP 124
South Malling (parish), 36/196; TQ431105; NP 183
South Marston (tithing in Highworth), 39/5F; SU193877; NP 157
South Middleton (township in Ilderton), 27/117; NT993229; NP 71
South Middleton, 27/354; NP 77
South Milford (township in Sherburn in Elmet), 43/429; SE490315; NP 97
South Milton (parish), 9/494; SX696426; NP 187
South Mimms (parish), 24/85; TQ232999; NP 160
South Molton (parish), 9/73; SS698266; NP 163
South Moreton (parish), 2/73-74; NP 158
South Moreton (township in South Moreton), 2/73; SU561885; NP 158
South Muskham (parish), 28/144; SK771575; NP 112, 113
South Myton (ward in Myton division in parish and township of Holy Tinity Kingston upon Hull), 41/327; TA087281; NP 99/1
South Newbald (township in North Newbald), 41/198; SE926358; NP 98
South Newington (parish), 29/41; SP410324; NP 145
South Newton (parish), 39/295; SU096347; NP 167
South Normanton (parish), 8/140; SK441566; NP 112
South Ockendon (parish), 12/419; TQ600830; NP 161
South Ormsby (hamlet in South Ormsby cum Ketsby), 22/325; TF365750; NP 105, 114
South Ormsby cum Ketsby (parish), 22/325-326; NP 105, 114
South Otterington (parish), 42/257; SE378878; NP 91
South Owersby (parish), 22/156; TF063937; NP 104
South Perrott (parish), 10/106; ST472066; NP 177
South Petherwin (parish), 6/36; SX310819; NP 186
South Petherton (parish), 32/441; ST434169; NP 177
South Pickenham (parish), 25/535; TF846041; NP 125
South Pool (parish), 9/491; SX770407; NP 187
South Quarter (township in Wolsingham), 11/187; NZ055357; NP 84
South Rainham (parish), 25/186; NP 125
South Rauceby (parish), 22/598; TF023450; NP 113, 123
South Raynham (South Rainham, Rainham St Martin) (parish), 25/186; TF877237; NP 125
South Redditch (division of Redditch township in Tardebigge), 40/50B; SO038672; NP 131
South Reston (parish), 22/296; TF404830; NP 105
South Runcton (parish), 25/318; TF636088; NP 124
South Ruston (parish), 25/249; NP 126
South Savernake with Brimslade and Cadley (extra-parochial), 39/178; SU213660; NP 157, 167
South Scarle (parish), 28/123-124; NP 113
South Scarle (township in South Scarle), 28/123; SK850642; NP 113

South Sheffield (division in township of Sheffield in Sheffield), 43/829; SK358868; NP 102
South Shields (township in Jarrow), 11/1; NZ360670; NP 78
South Shoebury (parish), 12/384; TQ939851; NP 162
South Side (district in Great Staughton), 17/98B; TL120630; NP 134
South Skirlaugh (township in Swine), 41/392; TA146392; NP 99
South Somercotes (parish), 22/186; TF418933; NP 105
South Stainley (parish), 43/143-146; NP 91, 96
South Stainley (township in South Stainley), 43/146; SE303625; NP 91
South Stoke (parish), 22/794; SK924277; NP 122, 123
South Stoke (South Stoke with Woodcott) (parish), 29/314; SU635825; NP 158
South Stoke (parish), 32/41; ST751612; NP 166
South Stoke (parish), 36/219; TQ022090; NP 181, 182
South Stoneham (parish), 14/258-263; NP 180
South Sydenham, 9/352; NP 175, 186
South Tanton (division in township of Stokesley in Stokesley), 42/301; NZ524105; NP 85, 86
South Tawton (parish), 9/327; SX666949; NP 175
South Tedworth (parish), 14/78; NP 167
South Thoresby (parish), 22/322; TF407769; NP 105
South Tidworth (South Tedworth) (parish), 14/78; SU236477; NP 167
South Walsham St Lawrence (parish), 25/396; TG344136; NP 126
South Walsham St Mary (parish), 25/397; TG358129; NP 126
South Warnborough (parish), 14/112; SU724464; NP 169
South Weald (hamlet in South Weald), 12/329; TQ573942; NP 161
South Weald (parish), 12/329-330; NP 161
South Weston (parish), 29/277; SU701983; NP 159
South Wheatley (parish), 28/38; SK765853; NP 103, 104
South Willingham (parish), 22/274; TF201837; NP 105
South Wingfield (parish), 8/143; SK377552; NP 111
South Witham (parish), 22/693; SK922195; NP 122
South Wootton (parish), 25/177; TF645231; NP 124
South Wraxall (tithing in Great Bradford), 39/152B; ST835645; NP 156, 166
Southam (parish), 37/243; SP422617; NP 132
Southam with Brockhampton (hamlet in Bishop's Cleeve), 13/58; SO980255; NP 143, 144
Southampton Common (extra-parochial), 14/264; SU416146; NP 180
Southampton, All Saints (parish), 14/267; SU420115; NP 180/1
Southampton, Holy Rood (parish), 14/268; SU420112; NP 180/1
Southampton, St John (parish), 14/269A; SU419111; NP 180/1
Southampton, St Laurence (parish), 14/266; SU418125; NP 180/1
Southampton, St Mary (parish), 14/265; SU426120; NP 180/1
Southampton, St Michael (parish), 14/269B; SU419113; NP 180/1
Southbroom, 39/133; NP 167
Southburgh (parish), 25/545; TG001050; NP 125
Southburn (township in Kirkburn), 41/231; SE988545; NP 98, 99
Southchurch (parish), 12/385; TQ910860; NP 162
Southcoates (township in Drypool), 41/338; TA121306; NP 99
Southcote (Southcot) (tithing in St Mary Reading), 2/180B; SU692735; NP 158, 169
Southease (parish), 36/321; TQ423048; NP 183
Southernby (Southernby-Bound) (township in Castle Sowerby), 7/154; NY362398; NP 83
Southernby-Bound, 7/154
Southerndown (hamlet in St Brides Major), 51/115; SS882738; NP 153, 154
Southery (parish), 25/694; TL612952; NP 135
Southey (division in township of Ecclesfield in Ecclesfield), 43/799; SK343917; NP 102
Southfleet (parish), 19/30; TQ611709; NP 171
Southill (parish), 1/89-92; NP 147
Southill (township in Southill), 1/89; TL138417; NP 147
Southleigh (parish), 9/289; SY200930; NP 176, 177

Southminster (parish), 12/357; TQ980990; NP 162
Southmoor, 2/28; NP 158
Southoe (parish), 17/102; TL187644; NP 134
Southolt (parish), 34/173; TM200690; NP 137
Southorpe (extra-parochial), 22/147; SK892950; NP 104
Southorpe (Southorpe with Walcot) (township in Barnack), 26/28; TF085925; NP 123
Southowram (township in Halifax), 43/550; SE116236; NP 96
Southrepps (parish), 25/53; TG258366; NP 126
Southrey (hamlet in Bardney), 22/360; TF133672; NP 113
Southrop (parish), 13/294; SP195030; NP 157
Southtown (Little Yarmouth with West Town) (hamlet in Gorleston), 34/4; TG519067; NP 126
Southwell (parish), 28/159; SK698536; NP 112
Southwell Park (extra-parochial), 34/316; TL758602; NP 135, 136
Southwick (township in Monkwearmouth), 11/16; NZ381591; NP 78
Southwick (parish), 14/279; SU637091; NP 180
Southwick (parish), 26/57; TL023921; NP 134
Southwick (parish), 36/310; TQ244061; NP 182
Southwick (tithing in North Bradley), 39/158; ST833550; NP 166
Southwold (parish), 34/158; TM501759; NP 137
Southwood (parish), 25/467; TG394054; NP 126
Southworth (division in township of Southworth with Croft in Winwick), 20/602; SJ624933; NP 100, 101
Southworth with Croft (township in Winwick), 20/601-602; NP 100, 101
Soutley, 49/82B; NP 109, 118
Sowber Hill (division in township of Newby Wiske in Kirby Wiske), 42/255A; SE352893; NP 91
Sowerby (division in township of Inskip with Sowerby in St Michaels on Wyre), 20/159; SD475385; NP 94
Sowerby (division in Sowerby township in Halifax), 43/567; SE025235; NP 95, 96
Sowerby (township in Thirsk), 42/532; SE435801; NP 91
Sowerby (township in Halifax), 43/564-565, 567; NP 95, 96
Sowerby-under-Cotcliffe (Sowerby under Catcliffe) (township in Kirby Sigston), 42/510A; SE410935; NP 91
Sowton (parish), 9/279; SX979920; NP 176
Soyland (township in Halifax), 43/568; SE010200; NP 95, 96, 101, 102
Spalding (division in Pinchbeck North Fen in Spalding), 22/731B; TF178242; NP 123
Spalding (division in Spalding), 22/731A; TF250220; NP 123
Spalding (parish), 22/731A-B; NP 123
Spaldington (division of Spaldington township in Aughton), 41/34; SE770335; NP 97, 98
Spaldington (division of Spaldington township in Bubwith), 41/35; SE754338; NP 97, 98
Spaldington (township in Aughton and Bubwith), 41/34-35; NP 97, 98
Spaldwick (parish), 17/54; TL117721; NP 134
Spalford (township in North Clifton), 28/118; SK839691; NP 113
Spanby (parish), 22/796; TF102379; NP 123
Sparchford (township in Diddlebury), 31/504B; SO494829; NP 129
Sparham (parish), 25/344; TG071195; NP 125
Sparkford (parish), 32/365; ST608265; NP 166, 177
Sparsholt (division in Sparsholt), 2/97; SU340872; NP 158
Sparsholt (parish), 2/97-99; NP 158
Sparsholt (parish), 14/157; SU431309; NP 168
Spaunton (township in Lastingham), 42/464; SE723887; NP 92
Spaunton Moor (ommon to townships of Appleton le Moors, Hutton le Hole, Lastingham, Rosedale West, and Spaunton in Lastingham), 42/460; SE703948; NP 92
Spaxton (parish), 32/269; ST216354; NP 164, 165
Speckington (hamlet in Yeovilton), 32/398; ST559236; NP 177
Speech House Walk (division of East Dean township in Trinity, Forest of Dean), 13/153; SO634133; NP 143
Speech House Walk (division of West Dean township in St Pauls, Forest of Dean), 13/157; SO622107; NP 143, 155

Speen (parish), 2/149; SU450680; NP 158
Speeton (township in Bridlington), 41/250; TA156742; NP 93
Speke (division in township of Speke in Childwall), 20/648; SJ432831; NP 100
Speke (township in Childwall), 20/648-649; NP 100
Speke Demesne (division in township of Speke in Childwall), 20/649; SJ419826; NP 100
Speldhurst (parish), 19/205; TQ553396; NP 171
Spelsbury (division in Spelsbury), 29/97; SP361225; NP 145
Spennithorne (parish), 42/186-188; NP 90, 91
Spennithorne (township in Spennithorne), 42/186; SE147887; NP 91
Spernall (Spernal) (parish), 37/185; SP096623; NP 131
Spetchley (parish), 40/151; SO895540; NP 130, 143
Spetisbury (Spettisbury) (parish), 10/304; ST899014; NP 178
Spexhall (parish), 34/72; TM381811; NP 137
Spilsby (division in Spilsby), 22/428A; TF403659; NP 114
Spilsby (parish), 22/428A-B; NP 114
Spilsby - East Fen (division in Spilsby), 22/428B; TF375600; NP 114
Spindlestone (Spindleston) (township in Bamburgh), 27/94; NU152338; NP 71
Spital (Spittle) (township in Ovingham), 27/554; NZ079669; NP 77
Spital (Spittle) (township in Tweedmouth), 27/3; NU004513; NP 64
Spital Hill (Spittle Hill) (township in Mitford), 27/410; NZ175862; NP 78
Spitalfields (division in Christchurch Spitalfields), 24/61B; TQ337819; NP 160/1
Spitalfields (parish), 24/61A-C; NP 160/1
Spittal (parish), 55/53; SM988230; NP 138
Spittle 27/554; NP 77
Spittle Boughton (extra-parochial), 5/515; SJ419664; NP 109/1
Spittle Hill, 27/410
Spittle, 27/3; NP 64
Spittlegate, Houghton and Walton (township in Grantham), 22/627; SK924342; NP 122
Spixworth (parish), 25/360; TG241148; NP 126
Spoad (township in Clun), 31/387; SO254811; NP 128
Spofforth (division in township of Spofforth with Stockeld in Spofforth), 43/97; SE345500; NP 97
Spofforth (parish), 43/94-102; NP 96, 97
Spofforth with Stockeld (township in Spofforth), 43/96-99; NP 96, 97
Spondon (parish), 8/279; NP 121
Spondon (township in Spondon), 8/280; SK403363; NP 121
Spoonbed (tithing in Painswick), 13/250; SO868112; NP 143, 156
Sporle (Sporle with Palgrave) (parish), 25/328; TF849111; NP 125
Spotland (township in Rochdale), 20/445-455; NP 95, 101
Spotland Further Side (division in Spotland township in Rochdale), 20/445-449; NP 101
Spotland Nearer Side (division in Spotland township in Rochdale), 20/454-455; NP 101
Spratton (parish), 26/190; SP729699; NP 133
Spreyton (parish), 9/326; SX704967; NP 175
Spridlington (parish), 22/217; TF001842; NP 104
Springfield (parish), 12/244; TL728084; NP 161
Springhill (township in Tweedmouth), 27/4; NT996505; NP 64
Springthorpe (parish), 22/139; SK880899; NP 104
Sproatley (parish), 41/400; TA191240; NP 99
Sproston (township in Middlewich), 5/201; SJ735666; NP 110
Sprotbrough (Sprotborough) (parish), 43/881-882; NP 103
Sprotbrough (Sprotborough) (township in Sprotbrough), 43/881; SE543028; NP 103
Sproughton (division in Sproughton), 34/478A; TM124442; NP 150
Sproughton (division in Sproughton), 34/478B; TM138430; NP 150
Sproughton (parish), 34/478A-B; NP 150
Sprowston (parish), 25/404; TG253121; NP 126

203

Sproxton (parish), 21/103; SK860245; NP 122
Sproxton (township in Helmsley), 42/488; SE606816; NP 92
Spurn (division in parish and township of Kilnsea), 41/448; TA403112; NP 105
Spurstow (township in Bunbury), 5/308; SJ568557; NP 109
Sputty Ystradmeurig (parish), 46/32; NP 127
Sputty Ystwyth, 46/36; NP 127
Stackpole Bosher (parish), 55/160; NP 151
Stackpole Elidor (Cheriton) (parish), 55/161; SR991969; NP 151
Stackrow Divisions (township in Barton), 38/26B; NY455215; NP 83
Stacksteads (division in Newchurch in Rossendale township in Whalley), 20/282-283; NP 95
Staddlethorpe (division in township of Gilberdyke in Eastrington), 41/19D; SE833294; NP 98/1
Stadhampton (parish), 29/323; SU603994; NP 158
Stadmorslow (township in Wolstanton), 33/17E; SJ870555; NP 110
Staffield (township in Kirkoswald), 7/172; NY569459; NP 83
Stafford St Mary (parish), 33/177-181; NP 119
Stafford St Mary (township in Stafford St Mary), 33/181; SJ920240; NP 119
Stagsden (parish), 1/30; SP980490; NP 147
Stain (Stane) (hamlet in Withern with Stain), 22/316; TF469849; NP 105
Stainborough (township in Silkstone), 43/698; SE320032; NP 102
Stainburn (township in Workington), 7/252; NY029287; NP 82
Stainburn (township in Kirkby Overblow), 43/383; SE251493; NP 96
Stainby (parish), 22/691; SK912228; NP 122
Staindrop (parish), 11/286-292; NP 84, 85
Staindrop (township in Staindrop), 11/289; NZ115206; NP 84, 85
Staines (parish), 24/117; TQ033717; NP 159, 169, 170
Stainfield (hamlet in Hacconby), 22/706B; TF080250; NP 123
Stainfield (parish), 22/353; TF110729; NP 113
Stainforth (township in Giggleswick), 43/251-252; NP 90
Stainforth (division in township of Stainforth in Hatfield), 43/945; SE644115; Stainforth (township in Hatfield), 43/944-945; NP 103
Staininghall (Stanninghall) (parish), 25/252; TG255178; NP 126
Stainland (division in township of Stainland with Old Lindley in Halifax), 43/572; SE078192; NP 96, 102
Stainland with Old Lindley (township in Halifax), 43/572-573; NP 102
Stainmore (township in Brough), 38/56; NY855137; NP 84
Stainsby (division in township of Stainton in Stainton), 42/279; NZ468165; NP 85
Stainton (township in Dacre), 7/195; NY493285; NP 83
Stainton (township in Stanwix), 7/72; NY378576; NP 76
Stainton (in Urswick), 20/36; SD244731; NP 88
Stainton (township in Heversham), 38/91; SD529872; NP 89
Stainton (division in township of Stainton in Stainton), 42/280; NZ480140; NP 85
Stainton (parish), 42/276-281; NP 85
Stainton (township in Downholme), 42/99; SE100960; NP 90, 91
Stainton (township in Stainton), 42/279-280; NP 85
Stainton (division in township of Stainton cum Hellaby in Stainton), 43/920A; SK550940; NP 103
Stainton (parish), 43/920A-B; NP 103
Stainton (parish), 55/104; NP 151
Stainton and Streatlam, 11/298; NP 84
Stainton by Langworth (hamlet in Stainton by Langworth), 22/258; TF069787; NP 104
Stainton by Langworth (parish), 22/258-260; NP 104
Stainton cum Hellaby (township in Stainton), 43/920A-B; NP 103
Stainton Dale (township in Scalby), 42/401; SE985995; NP 93
Stainton Farm (township in Millom), 7/327; SD142943; NP 88
Stainton le Street, 11/270; NP 85
Stainton le Hole (parish), 22/163; NP 104, 105
Stainton le Vale (Stainton le Hole) (parish), 22/163; TF169942; NP 104, 105
Stalbridge (parish), 10/26A-D; NP 178

Stalbridge (tithing in Stalbridge), 10/26A; ST735180; NP 178
Stalbridge Weston (tithing in Stalbridge), 10/26C; ST720165; NP 178
Stalham (parish), 25/234; TG371251; NP 126
Stalisfield (parish), 19/450; TQ964530; NP 172
Stallingborough (parish), 22/75; TA200120; NP 105
Stalmine (division in township of Stalmine with Staynall in Lancaster), 20/138; SD383409; NP 94
Stalmine with Staynall (township in Lancaster), 20/138-139; NP 94
Stambourne (parish), 12/55; TL715385; NP 148
Stamford (township in Embleton), 27/152; NU223199; NP 71
Stamford All Saints (Stamford All Saints with St Peters) (parish), 22/718; TF017075; NP 123
Stamford Bridge East (township in Catton), 41/85; SE725553; NP 97
Stamford Bridge with Scoreby (Stamford Bridge West with Scoreby) (township in Catton), 41/84; SE696337; NP 97
Stamford Hill (chapelry in St John at Hackney), 24/77; TQ343871; NP 160, 161
Stamford St George (Stamford St George with St Paul annexed) (parish), 22/719; TF041074; NP 123
Stamford St John (Stamford St John with St Clements) (parish), 22/720; TF024073; NP 123
Stamford St Mary (parish), 22/722; TF030070; NP 123
Stamford St Michael (Stamford St Michael with St Stephens and St Andrews) (parish), 22/721; TF033074; NP 123
Stamford, St Martin Baron (parish), 26/30-31; NP 123
Stamford, St Martin Baron (township in Stamford, St Martin Baron), 26/30; TF040058; NP 123
Stamford, 31/189; NP 119
Stamfordham, 27/454-466; NP 77
Stanage (township in Brampton Bryan), 56/15; SO331717; NP 129
Stanah (division in township of Thornton in Poulton-le-Fylde), 20/174; SD352417; NP 94
Stanbridge (hamlet in Leighton Buzzard), 1/138; SP959237; NP 146, 147
Stanbridge (parish), 10/176; NP 179
Stanbury (division in township of Haworth in Bradford), 43/527; SD985365; NP 95, 96
Stancil with Wellingley (division in township of Stancil with Wellingley and Wilsic in Tickhill), 43/925; SK600960; NP 103
Stancil with Wellingley and Wilsic (township in Tickhill), 43/924-925; NP 103
Standard Hill (extra-parochial), 28/237; SK570396; NP 121/1
Standen and Standen Hey (extra-parochial), 20/234; SD736396; NP 95
Standerwick (parish), 32/495; ST814510; NP 166
Standford (Stamford) (township in Edgmond), 31/189; SJ707229; NP 119
Standish (hamlet in Standish), 13/263; SO801085; NP 143, 156
Standish (parish), 13/262-263; NP 143
Standish (division in township of Standish in Standish), 20/380; SD561095; NP 100
Standish (parish), 20/376-386; NP 100, 101
Standish (township in Standish), 20/379-380; NP 100
Standlake (parish), 29/185; SP393033; NP 158
Standlynch (parish), 39/384; SU196239; NP 167
Standon (parish), 16/75; TL383210; NP 148
Standon (parish), 33/151; SJ814351; NP 119
Stane, 22/316; NP 105
Stanfield (parish), 25/272; TF938216; NP 125
Stanford (division in hamlet of Stanford in Southill), 1/91; TL165410; NP 147
Stanford (hamlet in Southill), 1/90-91; NP 147
Stanford (Standford) (parish), 19/394; TR124379; NP 173
Stanford (parish), 25/710; TL856937; NP 136
Stanford (Stanford on Avon) (township in Stanford on Avon), 26/115; SP601793; NP 133
Stanford (parish), 28/285; NP 121
Stanford Bishop (parish), 15/155; SO685519; NP 143
Stanford Dingley (parish), 2/164; SU570725; NP 158

204

Stanford in the Vale (division in Stanford in the Vale), 2/46; SU344934; NP 158
Stanford in the Vale (parish), 2/46-47; NP 158
Stanford on Avon (parish), 21/348, 26/115
Stanford on Avon, 26/115
Stanford on Soar (Stanford, Stanford upon Soar) (parish), 28/285; SK547232; NP 121
Stanford on Teme (Stanford) (parish), 40/92; SO708652; NP 130
Stanford Rivers (parish), 12/300; TL524013; NP 161
Stanford upon Soar (parish), 28/285; NP 121
Stanford-le-Hope (parish), 12/404; TQ690830; NP 161
Stanfordbury (division in hamlet of Stanford in Southill), 1/90; TL149401; NP 147
Stanghow (township in Skelton), 42/348; NZ662141; NP 86
Stanground North (division in Stanground), 4/184; TL219977; NP 134
Stanground (district in Stanground), 17/9; TL210960; NP 134
Stanground (parish), 4/184, 17/9-10; NP 134
Stanhoe (parish), 25/85; TF800372; NP 125
Stanhope (parish), 11/17—176; NP84
Stanhope Quarter (township in Stanhope), 11/171; NY962426; NP 84
Stanley (division in township of Tanfield in Chester le Street), 11/35; NZ203532; NP 78
Stanley (division in township of Stanley cum Wrenthorpe in Wakefield), 43/599; SE331233; NP 96
Stanley (township in Spondon), 8/279; SK418405; NP 121
Stanley (township in Leek), 33/13; SJ934524; NP 110
Stanley and Nethermore (tithing in Chippenham), 39/80; ST943724; NP 156, 157
Stanley cum Wrenthorpe (in Wakefield), 43/599-600
Stanley Pontlarge (parish), 13/64; SO996298; NP 143, 144
Stanlow (extra-parochial), 5/414; SJ425765; NP 100
Stanmer (parish), 36/207; TQ338101; NP 182, 183
Stanningfield (parish), 34/346; TL880563; NP 136, 149
Stanninghall (parish), 25/252; NP 126
Stannington (parish), 27/421-427; NP 78
Stannington (township in Stannington), 27/424; NZ217798; NP 78
Stannington (division in township of Bradfield in Ecclesfield), 43/803; SK302884; NP 102
Stansfield (parish), 34/341; TL782525; NP 149
Stansfield (township in Halifax), 43/559-562; NP 95
Stansfield Moor (common to all divisions of Stansfield township in Halifax), 43/562; SE927278; NP 95
Stansfield: Lower Third (division in township of Stansfield in Halifax), 43/559; SE962278; NP 95
Stansfield: Middle Third (division in township of Stansfield in Halifax), 43/560; SE952257; NP 95
Stansfield: Upper Third (division in township of Stansfield in Halifax), 43/561; SE928261; NP 95
Stanstead Mountfitchet (Stansted Mountfitchet) (hamlet in Stanstead Mountfitchet), 12/70; TL522248; NP 148
Stanstead Mountfitchet (Stansted Mountfitchet) (parish), 12/70-71; NP 148
Stanstead Abbotts (parish), 16/117; TL395121; NP 148, 160
Stanstead St Margarets (St Margaret) (parish), 16/113; TL370115; NP 148
Stansted (Stansted) (parish), 19/78; TQ607617; NP 171
Stanstead (parish), 34/411; TL843499; NP 149
Stansted Mountfitchet (hamlet in Stanstead Mountfitchet), 12/70; TL522248; NP 148
Stansty (township in Wrexham [Wrecsam]), 49/54; SJ322521; NP 109
Stanthorne (township in Davenham), 5/190; SJ687660; NP 110
Stanton (parish), 13/74; SP066342; NP 144
Stanton (parish), 26/88; SP913868; NP 133
Stanton (township in Youlgreave), 8/119; SK250640; NP 111
Stanton (township in Longhorsley), 27/297; NZ137901; NP 78
Stanton (township in Ellastone), 33/100; SK124463; NP 111, 120
Stanton All Saints (parish), 34/127A; TL960740; NP 136
Stanton and Newhall (township in Stapenhill), 8/315A; SK279203; NP 120, 121

Stanton by Bridge (parish), 8/301; SK368263; NP 121
Stanton by Dale (Stanton juxta Dale Abbey) (parish), 8/283; SK466385; NP 121
Stanton Drew (parish), 32/52; ST607626; NP 155, 166
Stanton Fitzwarren (parish), 39/7; SU178900; NP 157
Stanton Harcourt (parish), 29/187; SP417067; NP 158
Stanton juxta Dale Abbey (parish), 8/283; NP 121
Stanton Lacy (parish), 31/518-524; NP 129
Stanton Lacy (township in Stanton Lacy), 31/519; SO503792; NP 129
Stanton Long (Stanton, Brockton, Weston, Oxenbold) (parish), 31/496; SO582919; NP 129
Stanton on Arrow (parish), 15/43; NP 129
Stanton on the Wolds (parish), 28/292; SK640305; NP 121
Stanton Prior (parish), 32/45; ST682632; NP 166
Stanton St Gabriel (parish), 10/136; SY389929; NP 177
Stanton St John (parish), 29/233; SP583096; NP 145, 158
Stanton St John (parish), 34/127B; TL970730; NP 136
Stanton St Bernard (Staunton St Bernard) (parish), 39/205; SU097630; NP 157, 167
Stanton St Quintin (parish), 39/70; ST917803; NP 156, 157
Stanton under Bardon (township in Thornton), 21/137; SK462104; NP 121
Stanton upon Hine Heath (parish), 31/202-205; NP 118
Stanton upon Hine Heath (Stanton) (township in Stanton upon Hine Heath), 31/205; SJ582236; NP 118
Stanton, 31/205; NP 118
Stanton, 31/496; NP 129
Stantonbury (parish), 3/51; SP839417; NP 146
Stanwardine in the Fields (township in Baschurch), 31/144B; SJ415240; NP 118
Stanwardine in the Wood (township in Baschurch), 31/144B; SJ427272; NP 118
Stanway (parish), 12/141; TL952236; NP 149
Stanway (parish), 13/73; SP073317; NP 144
Stanwell (parish), 24/116; TQ053740; NP 159, 170
Stanwick (parish), 26/147; SP986709; NP 134
Stanwick St John (parish), 42/33A-37; NP 84-5
Stanwick St John (township in Stanwick St John), 42/34; NZ193125; NP 85
Stanwix (township in Stanwix), 7/74; NY405574; NP 76
Stanwix, 7/71-78; NP 76
Stapeley (township in Wybunbury), 5/260; SJ672508; NP 110
Stapenhill (parish), 8/314-315B; NP 120, 121
Stapenhill (township in Stapenhill), 8/314; SK258214; NP 120, 121
Staple (Staple-next-Wingham) (parish), 19/265; TR274567; NP 173
Staple Fitzpaine (parish), 32/430; ST257178; NP 177
Staple Inn (extra-parochial), 24/13; TQ311815; NP 160/1
Stapleford (parish), 4/133; TL487524; NP 148
Stapleford Abbots (parish), 12/302; TQ503957; NP 161
Stapleford Tawney (parish), 12/303; TQ515993; NP 161
Stapleford (parish), 16/81; TL308168; NP 147
Stapleford (parish), 21/111; SK807171; NP 122
Stapleford (parish), 22/542; SK872569; NP 113
Stapleford (parish), 28/249; SK490372; NP 121
Stapleford (parish), 39/296; SU079380; NP 167
Staplegrove (parish), 32/314; ST211272; NP 164, 177
Staplehurst (parish), 19/316; TQ782430; NP 172
Stapleton (parish), 7/5-8; NP 76
Stapleton (township in Stapleton), 7/6; NY509702; NP 76
Stapleton (parish), 13/407; ST626764; NP 156
Stapleton (township in Presteigne), 15/37; SO330655; NP 129
Stapleton Farm (division in township of Slyne with Hest in Bolton-le-Sands), 20/96; SD483658; NP 89
Stapleton (township in Barwell), 21/217; SP433997; NP 121, 132
Stapleton (parish), 31/288; NP 118
Stapleton (township in Stapleton), 31/288; SJ462038; NP 118
Stapleton (township in Croft), 42/54; NZ260110; NP 85
Stapleton (township in Gilling), 42/53; NZ271111; NP 85

205

Stapleton (township in Darrington), 43/633; SE506194; NP 97, 103
Starbotton (division of Kettlewell with Starbotton township in Kettlewell), 43/223; SD950750; NP 90
Starston (parish), 25/637; TM234857; NP 137
Startforth (parish), 42/13-14; NP 84
Startforth (township in Startforth), 42/13; NZ045143; NP 84
Statfold (parish), 33/279; NP 120
Stathern (parish), 21/85; SK769313; NP 122
Staunton (parish), 13/162; SO550122; NP 142
Staunton (parish), 28/201-202; NP 112, 113, 122
Staunton (township in Staunton), 28/202; SK807443; NP 112, 113, 122
Staunton (parish), 40/234; SO780290; NP 143
Staunton Harold (township in Breedon on the Hill), 21/10; SK384210; NP 121
Staunton on Arrow (Stanton on Arrow) (parish), 15/43; SO354612; NP 129
Staunton on Wye (Staunton upon Wye) (parish), 15/111; SO360460; NP 142
Staunton St Bernard (parish), 39/205; NP 157, 167
Staveley (parish), 8/51; NP 111, 112
Staveley (township in Staveley), 8/51; SK428753; NP 111, 112
Staveley (detached) (township in Cartmel), 20/59B; SD410826; NP 89
Staveley (township in Cartmel), 20/58; SD385957; NP 89
Staveley (parish), 43/134; SE371628; NP 91
Staverton (parish), 9/425; SX776654; NP 187, 188
Staverton (parish), 13/116; SO898230; NP 143
Staverton (parish), 26/245; SP537613; NP 132
Staverton (tithing in Trowbridge), 39/150; ST859602; NP 166
Stawell (hamlet in Moorlinch), 32/214; ST363381; NP 165
Stawley (parish), 32/320; ST064223; NP 164
Staxton (township in Willerby), 41/161; TA022785; NP 93
Stayley (township in Mottram), 5/2; SJ981989; NP 101
Staynall (division in township of Stalmine with Staynall in Lancaster), 20/139; SD360440; NP 94
Staythorpe (township in Averham), 28/154; SK754539; NP 112
Steane (parish), 26/351; SP545381; NP 145
Stearsby (division in township of Brandsby-cum-Stearsby in Brandsby), 42/608; SE610715; NP 92
Stebbing (parish), 12/81; TL673251; NP 148
Stedham (parish), 36/6; SU859246; NP 181
Stedham (parish), 36/25; SU859246; NP 181
Steep (division in Steep), 14/242; SU746258; NP 181
Steep (parish), 14/242, 36/1-2; NP 181
Steeple (parish), 10/290; SY908818; NP 178
Steeple (parish), 12/351; TL933034; NP 162
Steeple Aston (parish), 29/60-62; NP 145
Steeple Aston (township in Steeple Aston), 29/60; SP475257; NP 145
Steeple Ashton (parish), 39/142-145; NP 166, 167
Steeple Ashton (tithing in Steeple Ashton), 39/142; ST906562; NP 166, 167
Steeple Barton (parish), 29/87; SP456242; NP 145
Steeple Bumpstead (parish), 12/30; TL689408; NP 148
Steeple Claydon (parish), 3/110; SP701265; NP 145, 146
Steeple Gidding (parish), 17/39; TL140812; NP 134
Steeple Langford (parish), 39/289; SU038380; NP 167
Steeple Morden (parish), 4/169; TL298412; NP 147
Steepleton Iwerne (Steepleton Preston) (parish), 10/59; ST881121; NP 178
Steepleton Preston (parish), 10/59; NP 178
Steeton (township in Bolton Percy), 43/63; SE525443; NP 97
Steeton with Eastburn (township in Kildwick), 43/356; SE029438; NP 96
Stella (township in Ryton), 11/33; NZ172636; NP 78
Stelling (parish), 19/337; TR148476; NP 173
Stelling (township in Bywell St Peter), 27/630; NZ049656; NP 77
Stelling Minnis (extra-parochial), 19/338; TR147464; NP 173
Stembridge (extra-parochial), 51/119; SS945741; NP 154
Stenigot (parish), 22/340; TF255815; NP 105
Stepney (parish), 24/65A-C; NP 160/1

Steppingley (parish), 1/109; TL012357; NP 147
Sternfield (parish), 34/270; TM393615; NP 137
Stert (chapelry in Urchfont), 39/209A; SU045595; NP 167
Stetchworth (parish), 4/145; TL641583; NP 135
Stevenage (parish), 16/49; TL240245; NP 147
Steventon (parish), 1/28; NP 147
Steventon (parish), 2/57; SU456923; NP 158
Steventon (parish), 14/94; SU542469; NP 168
Stevington (Steventon) (parish), 1/28; SP984529; NP 147
Stewkley (parish), 3/101; SP848258; NP 146
Stewton (parish), 22/286; TF361867; NP 105
Steyning (parish), 36/107; TQ175125; NP 182
Steynton (Stainton) (parish), 55/104; SM910100; NP 151
Stibbard (parish), 25/153; TF985280; NP 125
Stickford (division in Stickford), 22/477A; TF351598; NP 114
Stickford (parish), 22/477A-B; NP 114
Stickford - East Fen (division in Stickford), 22/477B; TF366593; NP 114
Stickland Winterborne (parish), 10/162; NP 178
Stickney (division in Stickney), 22/476A-D; TF352569; NP 114
Stickney (division in Stickney), 22/476D; TF349544; NP 114
Stickney (parish), 22/476A-D; NP 114
Stickney - East Fen (division in Stickney), 22/476C; TF359580; NP 114
Stickney - West Fen (division in Stickney), 22/476B; TF336567; NP 114
Stidd (extra-parochial), 20/228; SD654361; NP 95
Stiffkey (parish), 25/21; TF971431; NP 125
Stifford (parish), 12/424; TQ604803; NP 161, 171
Stillingfleet (division in township of Stillingfleet and Moreby in Stillingfleet), 41/59; SE598409; NP 97
Stillingfleet (parish), 41/58-60, 43/58; NP 97
Stillingfleet and Moreby (township in Stillingfleet), 41/59-60; NP 97
Stillingfleet (parish), 41/58-60, 43/58; NP 97
Stillington (township in Redmarshall), 11/264; NZ361234; NP 85
Stillington (parish), 42/593; SE571678; NP 92
Stilton (parish), 17/17; TL172894; NP 134
Stinchcombe (parish), 13/323; ST734981; NP 156
Stinsford (Stintsford) (parish), 10/216; SY718921; NP 178
Stintsford (parish), 10/216; NP 178
Stirchley (parish), 31/226; SJ705069; NP 119
Stirton with Thorlby (township in Skipton), 43/323, 324; NP 95
Stistead (Stisted) (parish), 12/129; TL800252; NP 149
Stitt and Gatten (township in Ratlinghope), 31/344; SO393985; NP 118, 129
Stittenham (township in Sheriff Hutton), 42/597; SE682670; NP 92
Stivichall (parish), 37/153; SP330765; NP 132
Stixwould (parish), 22/361; TF174653; NP 113
Stoborough (division in Wareham, Holy Trinity), 10/288; SY948843; NP 178, 179
Stobswood (township in Ulgham parochial chapelry in Morpeth), 27/309; NZ230947; NP 71, 78
Stock (parish), 12/292; TQ687981; NP 161
Stock and Bradley (chapelry in Fladbury), 40/189; SO987619; NP 130
Stock Gayland (parish), 10/50; ST721131; NP 178
Stockbridge (parish), 14/146; SU366352; NP 168
Stockbury (parish), 19/167; TQ842612; NP 172
Stockdalewath (Stockdalewath-Bound) (township in Castle Sowerby), 7/153; NY388436; NP 83
Stockdalewath-Bound, 7/153; NP 83
Stockeld (division in township of Spofforth with Stockeld in Spofforth), 43/96; SE379494; NP 96
Stockerston (Stockerstone) (parish), 21/302; SP832978; NP 133
Stockham (township in Runcorn), 5/157; SJ550807; NP 100
Stocking Pelham (parish), 16/61; TL450290; NP 148
Stockland (district in Stockland), 9/497; ST238034; NP 176
Stockland (parish), 9/497-498; NP 176
Stockland Bristol (parish), 32/225; ST240435; NP 165
Stockleigh English (Stockley English) (parish), 9/170; SS845070; NP 176

Stockleigh Pomeroy (Stockley Pomeroy) (parish), 9/215; SS880039; NP 176
Stockley (division in township of Stockley in Brancepeth), 11/142A; NZ221369; NP 85
Stockley (township in Brancepeth), 11/142A-B; NP 85
Stocklinch Ottersey (parish), 32/439; ST386169; NP 177
Stocklinch St Magdalen (Stocklinch Magdalen) (parish), 32/438; ST384175; NP 177
Stockport (division in Stockport township in Stockport), 5/15; SJ907903; NP 101
Stockport (division in Stockport township in Stockport), 5/16; SJ903889; NP 101
Stockport (parish), 5/10-19A, 20-24; NP 101
Stockport (township in Stockport), 5/15-16; NP 101
Stockport Etchells (Etchells) (township in Stockport), 5/24; SJ848871; NP 101
Stocks (township in Ellesmere), 31/72; SJ421362; NP 118
Stocksfield Hall (township in Bywell St Andrew), 27/626; NZ056615; NP 77
Stockton (township in Malpas), 5/317; SJ477451; NP 109
Stockton (Stockton-upon-Tees) (township in Stockton-on-Tees), 11/347; NZ443196; NP 85
Stockton (parish), 25/620; TM389939; NP 137
Stockton (parish), 31/477; SO727996; NP 119, 130
Stockton (township in Chirbury), 31/352; SJ269016; NP 118
Stockton (parish), 37/242; SP437637; NP 132
Stockton (parish), 39/269; ST972373; NP 167
Stockton (parish), 40/99; NP 130
Stockton on Teme (Stockton) (parish), 40/99; SO714674; NP 130
Stockton on the Forest (parish), 42/671; SE663572; NP 97
Stockton-on-Tees (parish), 11/347-349; NP 85
Stockwood (parish), 10/102; ST589079; NP 177
Stodday (division of Ashton with Stodday township in Lancaster), 20/106; SD469587; NP 94
Stodmarsh (parish), 19/137; TR215610; NP 173
Stody (parish), 25/123; TG058348; NP 125
Stogumber (parish), 32/255; ST098369; NP 164
Stogursey (parish), 32/226; ST213441; NP 164, 165
Stoke (district in Stoke Damerel), 9/455; SX465559; NP 187, 187/1
Stoke (parish), 5/424-427; NP 100, 109
Stoke (parish), 19/45; TQ832750; NP 172
Stoke (parish), 37/146; SP356794; NP 132
Stoke (Stoke with Ince) (township in Stoke), 5/424; SJ421737; NP 109
Stoke (township in Acton), 5/294; SJ619564; NP 110
Stoke (township in Hathersage), 8/38; SK237765; NP 111
Stoke (township in Burford), 31/539; SO560709; NP 129
Stoke Abbott (parish), 10/127; ST441005; NP 177
Stoke Albany (parish), 26/102; SP806872; NP 133
Stoke Ash (parish), 34/180; TM119701; NP 136
Stoke Bardolph (township in Gedling), 28/229; SK640415; NP 121
Stoke Bishop (tithing in Westbury upon Trym), 13/384; ST561754; NP 155
Stoke Bliss (parish), 15/269, 40/87; NP 130
Stoke Bliss (township in Stoke Bliss), 15/269; SO656630; NP 130
Stoke Bruerne (Stoke Bruern) (hamlet in Stoke Bruerne), 26/310; SP746500; NP 146
Stoke Bruerne (Stoke Bruern) (parish), 26/309-310; NP 146
Stoke by Clare (Stoke juxta Clare) (parish), 34/337; TL735445; NP 148, 149
Stoke by Nayland (parish), 34/499; TL987357; NP 149
Stoke Canon (parish), 9/249; SX937975; NP 176
Stoke Charity (parish), 14/140; SU485376; NP 168
Stoke Climsland (parish), 6/59; SX368743; NP 186, 187
Stoke D'Abernon (Stoke D'Albernon) (division in Stoke D'Abernon), 35/58A; TQ137596; NP 170
Stoke D'Abernon (Stoke D'Albernon) (parish), 35/58a-B; NP 170
Stoke Damerel (parish) 09/455-460; NP 187, 187/1
Stoke Doyle (parish), 26/66; TL021862; NP 134

Stoke Dry (parish), 21/303, 30/55; NP 133
Stoke Dry (township in Stoke Dry), 30/55; SP853969; NP 133
Stoke Edith (parish), 15/168, 171; NP 142, 143
Stoke Edith (township in Stoke Edith), 15/168; SO601402; NP 142, 143
Stoke Ferry (parish), 25/528; TL700995; NP 124, 135
Stoke Fleming (parish), 9/486; SX851495; NP 188
Stoke Gabriel (parish), 9/438; SX856576; NP 188
Stoke Gifford (parish), 13/388; ST621803; NP 156
Stoke Goldington (parish), 3/26; SP832493; NP 146
Stoke Golding (township in Hinckley), 21/224; SP400970; NP 132
Stoke Hammond (parish), 3/97; SP877300; NP 146
Stoke Holy Cross (parish), 25/567; TG242019; NP 126, 137
Stoke Lacy (parish), 15/153; SO623507; NP 142
Stoke Lane (Stoke St Michael) (parish), 32/132; ST662473; NP 166
Stoke Lyne (hamlet in Stoke Lyne), 29/66A; SP565285; NP 145
Stoke Lyne (parish), 29/66A-C; NP 145
Stoke Mandeville (parish), 3/179; SP833107; NP 146, 159
Stoke Newington (parish), 24/78; NP 160
Stoke Orchard (hamlet in Bishop's Cleeve), 13/59; SO927287; NP 143
Stoke Pero (parish), 32/242; SS866433; NP 164
Stoke Poges (hamlet in Stoke Poges), 3/229; SU980832; NP 159
Stoke Poges (parish), 3/229-230; NP 159
Stoke Prior (township in Stoke Prior), 15/102; SO529559; NP 129, 142
Stoke Prior) (parish, 15/101-102; NP 129, 142
Stoke Prior (parish), 40/53; SO968679; NP 130
Stoke Rivers (parish), 9/29; SS645350; NP 163
Stoke St Gregory (division in Stoke St Gregory), 32/307; ST358278; NP 165, 177
Stoke St Gregory (parish), 32/307, 332B; NP 165, 177
Stoke St Milborough (parish), 31/514A-515; NP 129, 130
Stoke St Mary (parish), 32/419; ST264223; NP 177
Stoke St Michael (parish), 32/132; NP 166
Stoke sub Hamdon (Stoke under Hamdon) (parish), 32/463; ST476175; NP 177
Stoke Talmage (parish), 29/279; SU679989; NP 158, 159
Stoke Trister (parish), 32/360; ST734288; NP 166
Stoke under Hamdon (parish), 32/463; NP 177
Stoke upon Tern (parish), 31/176-179; NP 119
Stoke upon Tern (Stoke upon Terne) (township in Stoke upon Tern), 31/178; SJ646277; NP 119
Stoke Wake (parish), 10/92; ST758066; NP 178
Stoke with Ince, 5/413; NP 100, 109
Stoke with Ince, 5/424
Stoke-next-Guildford (parish), 35/129; SU999511; NP 169
Stoke-on-Trent (parish), 33/24-32, 34-38; NP 110
Stokeham (parish), 28/58; SK780770; NP 104
Stokeinteignhead (parish), 9/414; SX926701; NP 188
Stokenchurch (parish), 29/268; SU775952; NP 158
Stokenham (parish), 9/488; SX802418; NP 187, 188
Stokesay (parish), 31/417-420; NP 129
Stokesay (Stokesay and Newton) (township in Stokesay), 31/419; SO432817; NP 129
Stokesay and Newton, 31/419; NP 129
Stokesby with Herringby (parish), 25/388; TG440108; NP 126
Stokesley (division in township of Stokesley in Stokesley), 42/302; NZ526087; NP 85, 86
Stokesley (parish), 42/299-306; NP 85, 86, 92
Stokesley (township in Stokesley), 42/300-302; NP 85, 86
Ston Easton (Stone Easton) (parish), 32/112; ST625536; NP 166
Stonar (parish), 19/131; TR331598; NP 173
Stondon Massey (parish), 12/298; TL582008; NP 161
Stone (chapelry in Berkeley), 13/322; ST682956; NP 156
Stone (parish), 3/166; SP793111; NP 146, 159
Stone (parish), 19/436; TQ935274; NP 184
Stone (parish), 33/52-62; SJ895328; NP 119
Stone (parish), 40/35; SO857745; NP 130

Stone (Stone next Faversham) (parish), 19/156; TQ986610; NP 172
Stone (Stone-near-Dartford) (parish), 19/28; TQ580736; NP 171
Stone (township in Stone), 33/57; SJ912341; NP 119
Stone Allerton (division in Chapel Allerton), 32/166; ST399508; NP 165
Stone Easton (parish), 32/112; NP 166
Stonebeck Down (Down Stonebeck) (township in Kirkby Malzeard), 43/206; SE100700; NP 90, 91
Stonebeck Up (Upper Stonebeck) (township in Kirkby Malzeard), 43/205; SE050755; NP 90, 91
Stoneferry (division in township of Sutton in Sutton), 41/340; TA102318; NP 99
Stonegrave (parish), 42/620-623; NP 92
Stonegrave (township in Stonegrave), 42/621; SE658778; NP 92
Stonehouse (parish), 13/271; SO815055; NP 156
Stonelands (extra-parochial), 29/150; SP276099; NP 157
Stoneleigh (parish), 37/94; SP315755; NP 131, 132
Stonely (hamlet in Kimbolton), 17/95; TL116670; NP 134
Stoneraise (township in Westward), 7/147B; NY270450; NP 82
Stonesby (parish), 21/102; SK825242; NP 122
Stonesfield (parish), 29/99; SP398185; NP 145
Stoneton (parish), 26/267; SP461549; NP 132, 145
Stoney Middleton (township in Hathersage), 8/37; SK216750; NP 111
Stoney Stanton (parish), 21/230; SP494945; NP 132
Stoney Stretton (Stony Stretton) (township in Westbury), 31/312; SJ383096; NP 118
Stonham Aspal (Stonham Aspall) (parish), 34/245; TM140600; NP 136
Stonham Earl (parish), 34/243; NP 136
Stonton Wyville (parish), 21/294; SP739959; NP 133
Stony Stratford East Side (parish), 3/21; SP788407; NP 146
Stony Stratford West Side (parish), 3/20; SP787403; NP 146
Stony Stratford (parish), 39/353; NP 167
Stony Stretton, 31/312; NP 118
Stoodleigh (parish), 9/167; SS915192; NP 164
Stopham (parish), 36/69; TQ028194; NP 181, 182
Stopsley (hamlet in Luton), 1/123; TL108235; NP 147
Storeton (township in Bebington), 5/439; SJ304842; NP 100
Storkhill and Sandholme (township in St John Beverley), 41/295; TA049419; NP 99
Storrington (parish), 36/86; TQ080141; NP 182
Storrs (division in township of Bradfield in Ecclesfield), 43/804; SK292898; NP 102
Storthwaite (township in Thornton), 41/77; SE721442; NP 97
Storwood, 41/77
Stotfold (parish), 1/98; TL212362; NP 147
Stotfold (Statfold) (parish), 33/279; SK234071; NP 120
Stotfold (extra-parochial), 43/875; SE472063; NP 103
Stott Hill (division in township of Cowling in Kildwick), 43/354; SE978418; NP 95
Stottesden (parish), 31/569-577, 588; NP 130
Stottesden, Duddlewick and Hinton (township in Stottesden), 31/575; SO663827; NP 130
Stoughton (parish), 21/252; SK648008; NP 121
Stoughton (parish), 36/236; SU786107; NP 181
Stoulton (parish), 40/156; SO910503; NP 143
Stour Provost (Stower Provost) (parish), 10/17; ST814213; NP 166
Stourbridge (township in Old Swinford), 40/22; SO901842; NP 130
Stourmouth (parish), 19/135; TR260629; NP 173
Stourpaine (Stourpain) (parish), 10/83; ST878104; NP 178
Stourton (hamlet in Whichford), 37/291; SP302358; NP 145
Stourton (hamlet in Stourton), 39/338; ST778343; NP 166
Stourton (parish), 32/356, 39/338; NP 166
Stourton Caundle (parish), 10/49; ST709149; NP 178
Stoven (parish), 34/67; TM448822; NP 137
Stow (parish), 17/53-54; NP 134
Stow (Stowe) (parish), 22/234A-235C; NP 104
Stow (Stowe) (township in Stow, 22/235A; SK892820; NP 104
Stow (Stowe) (parish), 31/406; SO308737; NP 129

Stow Bardolph (parish), 25/517; TF595075; NP 124
Stow Bedon (parish), 25/721; TL955961; NP 136
Stow cum Quy (parish), 4/98; TL520606; NP 135
Stow Fen (extra-parochial), 34/32B; TM327884; NP 137
Stow Maries (Stowe Maries) (parish), 12/362; TQ831982; NP 162
Stow on the Wold (hamlet in Stow on the Wold), 13/90; SP191258; NP 144
Stow on the Wold (parish), 13/88-90; NP 144
Stow Park (division in Stow), 22/235C; SK864800; NP 104
Stow Wood (parish), 29/228; NP 145, 158
Stowe (hamlet in Stowe), 3/14; SP675375; NP 145, 146
Stowe (parish), 3/2, 14; P675375; NP 145, 146
Stowe (parish), 22/234A-235C; NP 104
Stowe (parish), 22/713; TF104111; NP 123
Stowe (parish), 33/189-190; NP 119, 120
Stowe (township in Stowe), 33/189; SJ025275; NP 119, 120
Stowe Maries (parish), 12/362; NP 162
Stowe Nine Churches (parish), 26/257; SP638570; NP 132
Stowe, 33/256; NP 120
Stowell (parish), 13/221; SP091134; NP 144
Stowell (parish), 32/385; ST682219; NP 166
Stower Provost (parish), 10/17; NP 166
Stowey (parish), 32/82; ST595599; NP 165, 166
Stowford (parish), 9/343; SX418868; NP 175, 186
Stowick (tithing in Henbury), 13/376; ST548808; NP 155
Stowlangtoft (parish), 34/192; TL959685; NP 136
Stowmarket (hamlet in Stowmarket), 34/239; TM046586; NP 136
Stowmarket (parish), 34/239-240; NP 136
Stowood (Stow Wood) (parish), 29/228; SP556101; NP 145, 158
Stowting (Stouting) (parish), 19/339; TR124426; NP 173
Stowupland (parish), 34/241; TM078598; NP 136
Stradbroke (Stradbrooke) (parish), 34/144; TM250740; NP 137
Stradishall (parish), 34/322; TL742528; NP 148, 149
Stradsett (parish), 25/515; TF665056; NP 124
Stragglethorpe (parish), 22/545; SK907524; NP 113
Stranton (division in township of Stranton in Seaton Carew), 11/250; NZ506318; NP 85
Stranton (township in Seaton Carew), 11/250-51; NP 85
Stratfield Mortimer (parish), 2/191-192, 14/1; NP 158, 168, 169
Stratfield Mortimer (tithing in Stratfield Mortimer), 2/191; SU670640; NP 158, 168, 169
Stratfield Saye, 2/190, 14/19; NP 169
Stratfield Saye (division in Stratfield Saye), 14/19; SU680615; NP 168, 169
Stratfield Turgis (parish), 14/20; SU696600; NP 168, 169
Stratford (division in West Ham), 12/322; TQ387847; NP 161
Stratford (parish), 24/72; NP 161
Stratford St Andrew (parish), 34/274; TM351604; NP 137
Stratford St Mary (parish), 34/506; TM053347; NP 149
Stratford St Avon, 37/202B
Stratford St Anthony(parish), 39/353; NP 167
Stratford sub Castle (Stratford under the Old Castle) (parish), 39/315; SU135330; NP 167
Stratford Toney (Stony Stratford, Stratford St Anthony, Stratford Tony) (parish), 39/353; SU095251; NP 167
Stratford under the Old Castle (parish), 39/315; NP 167
Stratford-upon-Avon (Stratford on Avon) (borough in Old Stratford), 37/202B; SP201549; NP 131, 144
Stratton (parish), 6/4; SS230060; NP 174
Stratton (parish), 10/223; SY650946; NP 178
Stratton (parish), 13/240B; SP010037; NP 157
Stratton Audley (parish), 29/76; SP614268; NP 145
Stratton Baskerville (parish), 37/67; NP 132
Stratton Hall (extra-parochial), 34/455; TM248387; NP 150
Stratton St Mary (parish), 25/643; TM200913; NP 137
Stratton St Michael (parish), 25/642; TM204938; NP 137
Stratton Strawless (parish), 25/255; TG213203; NP 126
Stratton St Margaret (parish), 39/53; ST169873; NP 157
Stratton-on-the-Fosse (parish), 32/115; ST661504; NP 166
Streat (Street) (parish), 36/124; TQ351152; NP 182, 183
Streatham (parish), 35/23; TQ301721; NP 170

Streatlam and Stainton (township in Gainford), 11/298; NZ080195; NP 84
Streatley (hamlet in Streatley), 1/119A; TL077280; NP 147
Streatley (parish), 1/119A-B; NP 147
Streatley (parish), 2/122; SU578803; NP 158
Street (parish), 32/181; ST485359; NP 165
Street (parish), 36/124; NP 182, 183
Streethay (township in St Michael), 33/261; SK140109; NP 120
Strelley (parish), 28/244; SK501423; NP 121
Strensall (parish), 42/684-686; NP 97
Strensall (township in Strensall), 42/686; SE680610; NP 97
Strensham (parish), 40/220; SO901398; NP 143
Stretford (parish), 15/63; SO443565; NP 129
Stretford (township in Manchester), 20/524; SJ799952; NP 101
Strethall (parish), 12/8; TL491409; NP 148
Stretham (division in Stretham), 4/39; TL514739; NP 135
Stretham (parish), 4/39-40; NP 135
Stretton (township in Great Budworth), 5/112; SJ626822; NP 101
Stretton (township in Tilston), 5/342; SJ444530; NP 109
Stretton (township in North Wingfield), 8/133; SK382613; NP 111, 112
Stretton (parish), 30/8; SK946165; NP 122, 123
Stretton (chapelry in Penkridge), 33/240; SJ885115; NP 119
Stretton (township in Burton upon Trent), 33/212; SK260260; NP 120
Stretton Baskerville (Stratton Baskerville) (parish), 37/67; SP411915; NP 132
Stretton en le Field (parish), 8/329, 335; NP 121
Stretton en le Field (township in Stretton en le Field), 8/329; SK304110; NP 121
Stretton Grandison (parish), 15/164; SO636438; NP 143
Stretton on the Fosse (parish), 37/300; NP 144
Stretton Sugwas (parish), 15/120; SO462425; NP 142
Stretton under Fosse (Stretton under Foss) (hamlet in Monks Kirby), 37/114; SP446816; NP 132
Stretton-on-Dunsmore (parish), 37/134-135; NP 132
Stretton-on-Dunsmore (Stretton-on-Dunsmoor) (township in Stretton-on-Dunsmore), 37/134; SP419729; NP 132
Stretton-on-Fosse (Stretton on the Fosse, Stretton on the Foss) (parish), 37/300; SP448818; NP 144
Strickland Kettle (township in Kendal), 38/102; SD494953; NP 89
Strickland Roger (township in Kendal), 38/101; SD507971; NP 89
Stringston (parish), 32/227; ST167421; NP 164
Strixton (parish), 26/216; SP904616; NP 133
Strood (parish), 19/48-50; NP 171, 171/1
Strood Extra (division in Strood), 19/50; TQ722688; NP 171
Strood Intra (division in Strood), 19/48; TQ738693; NP 171/1
Strood Media (division in Strood), 19/49; TQ732698; NP 171
Stroud (parish), 13/273; SO872151; NP 156
Stroud (tithing in Cumnor), 2/3H; SP448074; NP 158
Stroud End (tithing in Painswick), 13/251; SO863074; NP 156
Stroxton (parish), 22/632B; SK902313; NP 122
Strubby with Woodthorpe (parish), 22/314; TF453819; NP 105
Strumpshaw (parish), 25/472; TG347070; NP 126
Stubbs (division in township of Cridling Stubbs in Womersley), 43/635; SE516213; NP 97
Stublach (Stublach and Lees) (township in Middlewich), 5/193; SJ717704; NP 110
Stubton (parish), 22/607; SK878491; NP 113
Stuchbury (Stutchbury) (parish), 26/333; SP570437; NP 145
Studdon (township in Allendale), 27/591; NY835535; NP 77
Studham (division in Studham), 1/143; TL014168; NP 147
Studham (division in Studham), 16/94; TL020142; NP 147
Studham (parish), 1/143-144, 16/94; NP 147
Studholme (district in Oughterby township in Kirkbampton), 7/114; NY260561; NP 75
Studland (parish), 10/297; SZ025835; NP 179
Studley (hamlet in Beckley), 29/232; SP602140; NP 145
Studley (parish), 37/182; SP086651; NP 131
Studley (tithing in Trowbridge), 39/149; ST851568; NP 166
Studley Magna, 43/184
Studley Parva, 43/183; NP 91
Studley Roger (Studley Parva) (township in Ripon), 43/183; SE287710; NP 91
Studley Royal (Studley Magna) (township in Ripon), 43/184; SE282693; NP 91
Stuntney (chapelry in Ely Trinity), 4/27B; TL577786; NP 135
Sturmer (Sturmere) (parish), 12/28; TL692442; NP 148
Sturminster Marshall (parish), 10/189; SY946995; NP 178, 179
Sturminster Newton (Sturminster Newton Castle and Bagber) (parish), 10/52; ST777138; NP 178
Sturry (parish), 19/140; TR175610; NP 173
Sturston (township in Ashbourne), 8/181; SK192463; NP 111
Sturston (parish), 25/712; TL875935; NP 136
Sturton (township in Stow), 22/234A; SK895809; NP 104
Sturton Grange (township in Warkworth), 27/220; NU216063; NP 71
Sturton Grange (Sturton) (township in Aberford), 43/423; SE425335; NP 97
Sturton le Steeple (parish), 28/41; SK786840; NP 104
Stuston (parish), 34/86; TM135780; NP 136
Stutton (division in township of Stutton with Hazelwood in Tadcaster), 43/86; SE481415; NP 97
Stutton (parish), 34/515; TM145345; NP 150
Stutton with Hazelwood (township in Tadcaster), 43/86-87; NP 97
Stych and Woodlands (township in Moreton Say), 31/18; SJ636374; NP 119
Stydd (township in Shirley), 8/225; SK175400; NP 120
Styford (township in Bywell St Andrew), 27/622; NZ020630; NP 77
Styrrup (township in Blyth), 28/18; SK608895; NP 103
Subberthwaite (township in Ulverston), 20/13-14; NP 88
Suckley (parish), 40/164-166; NP 130, 143
Suckley (township in Suckley), 40/164; SO723519; NP 143
Sud Meadow (extra-parochial), 13/193; SO816186; NP 143
Sudborough (parish), 26/86; SP964829; NP 133, 134
Sudbourne (Sudborne) (parish), 34/373; TM430530; NP 150
Sudbrook (hamlet in Ancaster), 22/603; SK973451; NP 113, 123
Sudbrooke (parish), 22/257; TF039761; NP 104, 113
Sudbury (parish), 8/244; SK161336; NP 120
Sudbury, All Saints (parish), 34/491; TL868411; NP 149
Sudbury, St Bartholomew (parish), 34/489; TL873430; NP 149
Sudbury, St Gregory (parish), 34/490; TL875422; NP 149
Sudbury, St Peter (parish), 34/492; TL874413; NP 149
Sudeley Manor (parish), 13/66; SP040260; NP 144
Suet Carr (division in township of Sutton-on-the-Forest in Sutton-on-the-Forest), 42/591; SE599624; NP 92
Suffield (parish), 25/138; TG238313; NP 126
Suffield-cum-Everley (township in Hackness), 42/395; SE986898; NP 93
Sugley (township in Newburn), 27/543; NZ187646; NP 78
Sugnall Magna, 33/143
Sugnall Parva, 33/140; NP 119
Sugnall, 33/143
Sulby (parish), 26/113; SP662809; NP 132
Sulehay (extra-parochial), 26/41B; TL045982; NP 123
Sulgrave (parish), 26/323; SP567459; NP 145
Sulham (parish), 2/178A; SU646740; NP 158
Sulhampstead Abbots (parish), 2/171-172; NP 158, 169
Sulhampstead Abbots (tithing in Sulhampstead Abbots), 2/171; SU643689; NP 158
Sulhampstead Bannister (parish), 2/173-174; NP 158, 169
Sulhampstead Bannister - Lower End (division in Sulhampstead Bannister), 2/174; SU679672; NP 158, 169
Sulhampstead Bannister - Upper End (division in Sulhampstead Bannister), 2/173; SU639686; NP 158
Sullington (parish), 36/87; TQ101130; NP 182
Sully (parish), 51/179; ST150680; NP 154
Summer Lodge (division in township of Grinton in Grinton), 42/112; SD962952; NP 90
Summerfield (division in Docking), 25/87; TF748384; NP 124, 125

Summerhouse (township in Gainford), 11/309; NZ205193; NP 85
Sun Side (division in township of Slaithwaite in Huddersfield), 43/757; SE070160; NP 102
Sunbury (parish), 24/121; TQ102693; NP 170
Sunderland (township in Isell), 7/236; NY179358; NP 82
Sunderland (parish), 11/80-81; NP 78
Sunderland Bridge (division in township of Sunderland Bridge in St Oswald), 11/127; NZ271371; NP 85
Sunderland Bridge (township in St Oswald), 11/126-127; NP 85
Sunderland [East Sunderland] (division in township of Sunderland in Sunderland), 11/81; NZ408575; NP 78
Sunderland [West Sunderland] (division in township of Sunderland in Sunderland), 11/80; NZ404573; NP 78
Sunderlandwick (township in Hutton Cranswick), 41/279; TA015550; NP 99
Sundon (parish), 1/128; TL051274; NP 147
Sundridge (parish), 19/194; TQ557669; NP 171
Sunk Island (parish), 41/434; TA270190; NP 99, 105
Sunley Court (division in Muscoates township in Kirkdale), 42/476B; SE686815; NP 92
Sunninghill (parish), 2/220; SU932688; NP 169
Sunningwell (division in Sunningwell), 2/11; SP498005; NP 158
Sunningwell (parish), 2/11; SP498005; NP 158
Surbiton (hamlet in Kingston upon Thames), 35/35; TQ201679; NP 170
Surfleet (parish), 22/734; TF257297; NP 123
Surlingham (Surlingham St Mary and Surlingham St Saviour) (parish), 25/477; TG317058; NP 126
Surnant (township in Llanwnog), 54/158; SO014936; NP 128
Surrendell (tithing in Hullavington), 39/43; ST867823; NP 156
Sustead (parish), 25/57; TG187369; NP 126
Sutcombe (parish), 9/54; SS352115; NP 174
Suton (division in Wymondham), 25/653; TM093995; NP 125, 136
Sutterby (parish), 22/399; TF386723; NP 114
Sutterton (division in Sutterton), 22/769A; TF279356; NP 123
Sutterton (parish), 22/769A-B; NP 113, 114, 123
Sutterton - Holland Fen (division in Sutterton), 22/769B; TF223473; NP 113,
Sutton (division in parish and township of Norton), 41/126; SE789708; NP 92
Sutton (division of Sutton township in Burghwallis), 43/649; SE550122; NP 103
Sutton (division of Sutton township in Campsall), 43/648; SE545130; NP 103
Sutton (hamlet in Castor), 26/24; TL098992; NP 123, 134
Sutton (parish), 1/62; TL220475; NP 147
Sutton (parish), 4/36; TL425790; NP 135
Sutton (parish), 12/376; TQ890893; NP 162
Sutton (parish), 25/231; TG386237; NP 126
Sutton (parish), 28/34-35; NP 103
Sutton (parish), 31/278; SJ501102; NP 118
Sutton (parish), 34/435; TM305465; NP 150
Sutton (parish), 35/52; TQ259647; NP 170
Sutton (parish), 36/76; SU974151; NP 181
Sutton (Sutton Weaver) (township in Runcorn), 5/162; SJ544796; NP 100
Sutton (Sutton-by-Dover) (parish), 19/359; TR334493; NP 173
Sutton (Sutton-on-Hull) (division in parish and township of Sutton), 41/339; TA117330; NP 99
Sutton (Sutton-on-Hull) (parish and township), 41/339-340; NP 99
Sutton (tithing in Woking), 35/81; TQ004544; NP 169
Sutton (township in Middlewich), 5/199; SJ701646; NP 110
Sutton (township in Prestbury), 5/54; SJ941703; NP 110
Sutton (township in Prescot), 20/630; SJ520930; NP 100
Sutton (township in Sutton), 28/34; SK691844; NP 103
Sutton (township in Drayton in Hales), 31/12; SJ660315; NP 119
Sutton (township in West Felton), 31/94; SJ357262; NP 118
Sutton (township in Tenbury), 40/84; SO615660; NP 129, 130
Sutton (township in Holt), 49/77; SJ409488; NP 109
Sutton (township in Brotherton), 43/464; SE500250; NP 97
Sutton (township in Kildwick), 43/355; SE001432; NP 95, 96

Sutton (township in Campsall and Burghwallis), 43/648-9; NP 103
Sutton at Hone (parish), 19/26; TQ533699; NP 171
Sutton Bassett (parish), 26/99; SP771899; NP 133
Sutton Benger (parish), 39/86; ST947784; NP 156, 157
Sutton Bingham (parish), 32/476; ST545107; NP 177
Sutton Bonington St Ann (Sutton Bonnington St Ann) (parish), 28/283; SK514250; NP 121
Sutton Bonington St Michael (Sutton Bonnington St Michael) (parish), 28/282; SK505259; NP 121
Sutton Bonnington St Ann (parish), 28/283; NP 121
Sutton Bonnington St Michael (parish), 28/282; NP 121
Sutton Cheney (township in Market Bosworth), 21/165; SK414003; NP 121, 132
Sutton Coldfield (parish), 37/27; SP130950; NP 120, 131
Sutton Courteney (parish), 2/60-62; NP 158
Sutton Courteney (Sutton Courtney) (township in Sutton Courteney), 2/60; SU508930; NP 158
Sutton cum Duckmanton (parish), 8/69; SK441704; NP 112
Sutton cum St Andrew (parish), 25/13; NP 125
Sutton cum Seaford (parish), 36/336; NP 183
Sutton cum Howgrave, 42/228; NP 91
Sutton Grange (township in Ripon), 43/190; SE281739; NP 91
Sutton Howgrave (Sutton cum Howgrave) (township in Kirklington), 42/228; SE320790; NP 91
Sutton in the Elms (township in Broughton Astley), 21/244C; SP526940; NP 132
Sutton in Holland, 22/783; NP 124
Sutton in the Marsh (parish), 22/309; NP 105
Sutton in Ashfield (parish), 28/97-98; NP 112
Sutton in Ashfield (township in Sutton in Ashfield), 28/98; SK500590; NP 112
Sutton le Marsh (Sutton in the Marsh, Sutton on Sea) (parish), 22/309; TF517806; NP 105
Sutton Maddock (parish), 31/469; SJ724021; NP 119
Sutton Mallet (Sutton Mallett) (chapelry in Moorlinch), 32/215; ST374371; NP 165
Sutton Mandeville (parish), 39/329; ST986279; NP 167
Sutton Montis (Sutton Montague) (parish), 32/373; ST625245; NP 166
Sutton on the Hill (parish), 8/236-237B; NP 120
Sutton on the Hill (township in Sutton on the Hill), 8/237A; SK240335; NP 120
Sutton on Sea (parish), 22/309; NP 105
Sutton on Trent (Sutton upon Trent) (parish), 28/113; SK789658; NP 112, 113
Sutton Poyntz, 10/269; NP 178
Sutton St Michael (parish), 15/141; SO526260; NP 142
Sutton St Nicholas (parish), 15/140; SO540450; NP 142
Sutton St Edmund (division in Sutton St Mary), 22/780A; TF362118; NP 123, 124
Sutton St Edmund (hamlet in Sutton St Mary), 22/780A-B; NP 123, 124
Sutton St Edmund - Commons in Long Sutton (division in Sutton St Mary), 22/780B; TF452228; NP 124
Sutton St James (division in Sutton St Mary), 22/781A; TF388178; NP 124
Sutton St James (hamlet in Sutton St Mary), 22/781A-B; NP 124
Sutton St James - Commons in Long Sutton (division in Sutton St Mary), 22/781B; TF206448; NP 124
Sutton St Mary (parish), 22/780A-783; NP 123, 124
Sutton St Nicholas, 22/782; NP 124
Sutton under Brailes (parish), 37/302; SP308373; NP 145
Sutton upon Trent (parish), 28/113; NP 112, 113
Sutton upon Derwent (division in township of Sutton upon Derwent in Sutton upon Derwent), 41/81; SE712468; NP 97
Sutton upon Derwent (parish and township), 41/80-81; NP 97
Sutton Valence (parish), 19/299; TQ811478; NP 172
Sutton Veny (parish), 39/273; ST904408; NP 166
Sutton Waldron (parish), 10/56; ST869159; NP 178
Sutton Weaver, 5/162; NP 100
Sutton Wick (township in Sutton Courtney), 2/61A; SU488957; NP 158
Sutton-Guilden (parish), 5/382; NP 109

Sutton-on-Hull, 41/339
Sutton-on-the-Forest (division in township of Sutton-on-the-Forest in Sutton-on-the-Forest), 42/590; SE582637; NP 92
Sutton-on-the-Forest (parish), 42/589-592; NP 92
Sutton-on-the-Forest (township in Sutton-on-the-Forest); 42/590-592; NP 92
Sutton-under-Whitestonecliffe (township in Felixkirk), 42/539; SE482028; NP 91, 92
Swaby (parish), 22/324; TF386776; NP 105
Swadlincote (township in Church Gresley), 8/320; SK299202; NP 121
Swaffham (division in Saham Toney registration subdistrict in Swaffham), 25/510B; TF830100; NP 125
Swaffham (division in Swaffham registration subdistrict in Swaffham), 25/510A; TF805085; NP 125
Swaffham (parish), 25/510A-B; NP 125
Swaffham Bulbeck (parish), 4/50; TL569609; NP 135
Swaffham Prior (hamlet in Swaffham Prior), 4/49B; TL566648; NP 135
Swaffham Prior (parish), 4/49A-B; NP 135
Swafield (parish), 25/50; TG286331; NP 126
Swainby (division in Swainby with Allerthorpe township in Pickhill), 42/252A; SE339856; NP 91
Swainby with Allerthorpe (township in Pickhill), 42/252A-B
Swainsthorpe (parish), 25/566; TG221008; NP 126, 137
Swainswick (parish), 32/28; ST756689; NP 156
Swalcliffe (parish), 29/23-28; NP 145
Swalcliffe (Swaleclife) (township in Swalcliffe), 29/23; SP380380; NP 145
Swaleclife (Swalecliff) (parish), 19/117; TR141654; NP 173
Swallow (parish), 22/95; TA173037; NP 105
Swallowcliffe (Swallowclift) (parish), 39/330; ST971269; NP 167
Swallowfield (parish), 2/187-189; NP 169
Swallowfield East (division in Swallowfield), 2/189; SU740647; NP 169
Swallowfield West (division in Swallowfield), 2/187; SU718645; NP 169
Swalwell (township in Whickham), 11/26; NZ210620; NP 78
Swanage (parish), 10/298; SZ013809; NP 179
Swanbourne (parish), 3/104; SP798269; NP 146
Swanington (Swannington) (parish), 25/258; TG139190; NP 125
Swanland (township in Kirk Ella and North Ferriby), 41/312, 314, 315; NP 98, 99
Swanland (township in Kirk Ella), 41/312; TA001269; NP 98, 99
Swanland (township in North Ferriby), 41/314; TA001289; NP 98, 99, 99/1
Swannington (township in Whitwick), 21/27; SK415163; NP 121
Swannington (parish), 25/258; NP 125
Swanscombe (parish), 19/29; TQ601742; NP 171
Swansea Higher (division in Swansea [Abertawe]), 51/25; SS618948; NP 153
Swansea Lower (division in Swansea [Abertawe]), 51/26; SS612927; NP 153
Swansea Town (division in Swansea [Abertawe]), 51/24; SS648932; NP 153
Swansea [Abertawe] (parish), 51/23-26; NP 153
Swansea, St John (St John, St John near Swansea) (parish), 51/22; SS665948; NP 153
Swansea, St Thomas (hamlet in Swansea [Abertawe]), 51/23; SS671932; NP 153
Swanton Abbot (Swanton Abbott) (parish), 25/242; TG263264; NP 126
Swanton Morley (parish), 25/341; TG018172; NP 125
Swanton Novers (parish), 25/118; TG017321; NP 125
Swarby (parish), 22/645; TF048407; NP 123
Swardeston (parish), 25/488; TG205028; NP 126
Swarkestone (Swarkeston) (parish), 8/298; SK376289; NP 121
Swarland (township in Felton), 27/286; NU162026; NP 71
Swarraton (parish), 14/135; SU577369; NP 168
Swaton (parish), 22/657; TF138377; NP 123
Swavesey (parish), 4/57; TL371674; NP 134, 135
Swayfield (parish), 22/696; SK988228; NP 123
Swaythorpe (division in parish and township of Killam), 41/240; TA042687; NP 93

Sweeney (township in Oswestry), 31/107; SJ288266; NP 117, 118
Sweethope (township in Throckington), 27/370; NY952816; NP 77
Sweffling (parish), 34/275; NP 137
Swefling (Sweffling) (parish), 34/275; TM342639; NP 137
Swell (parish), 32/411; ST366236; NP 177
Swepstone (parish), 21/141; SK370100; NP 121
Swerford (parish), 29/44; SP370308; NP 145
Swettenham (parish), 5/222-223; NP 110
Swettenham (township in Swettenham), 5/223; SJ811671; NP 110
Swilland (parish), 34/391; TM194526; NP 150
Swillington (parish), 43/475; SE382304; NP 96
Swimbridge (Swymbridge) (parish), 9/35; SS621299; NP 163
Swinbrook (Swinbrooke) (parish), 29/153; SP282120; NP 144, 145
Swincombe (parish), 29/292; NP 158, 159
Swinden (township in Gisburn), 43/303; SD869539; NP 95
Swinden, 43/387; NP 96
Swinderby (parish), 22/532; SK871625; NP 113
Swindon (parish), 13/57; SO932251; NP 143
Swindon (parish), 39/54-55; NP 157
Swindon (Swinden) (division in township of Kirkby Overblow with Swindon in Kirkby Overblow), 43/387; SE312483; NP 96
Swindon (township in Wombourne), 33/336; SO853907; NP 130
Swindon (tithing in Swindon), 39/54; SU159837; NP 157
Swine (parish), 41/382-394; NP 99
Swine (township in Swine), 41/390; TA135361; NP 99
Swinecoats (extra-parochial), 22/470; TF294502; NP 114
Swinefleet (township in Whitgift), 43/959; SE776194; NP 98, 104
Swineshead (parish), 17/116; TL060657; NP 134
Swineshead (division in Swineshead), 22/738A; TF325405; NP 123
Swineshead (parish), 22/738A-C; NP 123
Swineshead - Holland Fen (division in Swineshead), 22/738C; TF211521; NP 114, 123
Swineshead - The Rakes (division in Swineshead), 22/738B; TF218443; NP 114, 123
Swinethorpe (extra-parochial), 22/528; SK873688; NP 113
Swinfen (township in Weeford), 33/291; SK133060; NP 120
Swinford (tithing in Cumnor), 2/3J; SP446084; NP 158
Swinford (parish), 21/349; SP565796; NP 132
Swingfield (parish), 19/386; TR224433; NP 173
Swinhoe (township in Bamburgh), 27/100; NU217283; NP 71
Swinhope (Swinhop) (parish), 22/169; TF221960; NP 105
Swinney (township in Barrow), 31/461; SJ700999; NP 119, 130
Swinton (division in township of Worsley in Eccles), 20/555; SD780010; NP 101
Swinton (township in Appleton-le-Street), 42/640; SE760730; NP 92
Swinton (township in Wath upon Dearne), 43/851; SK458983; NP 103
Swinton with Warthermarske (Swinton) (township in Masham), 42/174; SE209789; NP 91
Swinton, 42/174; NP 91
Swithland (parish), 21/34; SK556131; NP 121
Swydd, Graig and Tynlan (township in Llandegley), 56/37; SO140630; NP 128
Swymbridge, 9/35; NP 163
Swyncombe (Swincombe) (parish), 29/292; SU688898; NP 158, 159
Swynnerton (parish), 33/49-50; SJ840370; NP 119
Swynnerton (township in Swynnerton), 33/49; SJ840370; NP 119
Swyre (parish), 10/236; SY522886; NP 177
Sycharth (township in Llansilin), 49/126; SJ202256; NP 117
Sychtyn (township in Llansilin), 31/115; SJ231268; NP 117
Syde (Side) (parish), 13/245; SO956111; NP 143
Sydenham (chapelry in Lewisham), 19/4; TQ360720; NP 170, 171
Sydenham (parish), 29/264; SP727023; NP 159
Sydenham Damerel (South Sydenham) (parish), 9/352; SX418765; NP 175, 186

Syderstone (parish), 25/105; TF841335; NP 125
Sydling St Nicholas (division in Sydling St Nicholas), 10/148; ST631003; NP 178
Sydling St Nicholas (parish), 10/148-149; NP 178
Sydmonton (Sidmonton) (parish), 14/10; SU488586; NP 168
Syerscote (township in Tamworth), 33/280; SK226071; NP 120
Syerston (parish), 28/197; SK748472; NP 112
Syke Mouth (division in Kirton), 22/765E; TF258438; NP 123
Sykehouse (township in Fishlake), 43/949; SE640170; NP 103
Sylattyn (parish), 31/79; NP 117, 118
Syleham (parish), 34/82; TM212783; NP 137
Symmondsbury (parish), 10/138; NP 177
Symondsbury (Symmondsbury) (parish), 10/138; SY445936; NP 177
Syningwaite (division in township of Bilton in Bilton), 43/78; SE460488; NP 97
Syresham (parish), 26/343; SP622417; NP 145
Sysonby (chapelry in Melton Mowbray), 21/73; SK739200; NP 122
Syston (parish), 21/58; SK631112; NP 121
Syston (parish), 22/621; SK934408; NP 122, 123
Sywell (parish), 26/204; SP822677; NP 133
Tabley Inferior (township in Great Budworth), 5/126; SJ723778; NP 101
Tabley Superior (Over Tabley) (township in Rostherne), 5/97; SJ724793; NP 101
Tachbrook Mallory (hamlet in Bishop's Tachbrook), 37/225B; SP326616; NP 132

T

Tackley (parish), 29/102-105; NP 145
Tackley (township in Tackley), 29/102; SP469208; NP 145
Tacolneston (parish), 25/648; TM143951; NP 136, 137
Tadcaster (parish), 43/82-87; NP 97
Tadcaster East (township in Tadcaster), 43/84; SE494438; NP 97
Tadcaster West (township in Tadcaster), 43/85; SE472431; NP 97
Taddington and Priestcliffe (township in Bakewell), 8/103; SK144711; NP 111
Tadley (parish), 14/16; SU597608; NP 168
Tadlow (parish), 4/120; TL280481; NP 147
Tadmarton (parish), 29/29; SP399372; NP 145
Taf (hamlet in Merthyr Tydfil), 51/70; SO065005; NP 154
Takeley (parish), 12/74; TL565223; NP 148
Tal-y-garth (township in Llangollen), 49/117; SJ256388; NP 108, 117
Talachddu (parish), 45/38; SO075335; NP 141
Talar (township in St Asaph [Llanelwy]), 50/71; SJ026743; NP 108
Talaton (parish), 9/241; SY072986; NP 176
Talbenny (parish), 55/95; SM837116; NP 151
Talgarth (parish), 45/86A; NP 141
Talgarth Borough (hamlet in Talgarth), 45/86A; SO155338; NP 141
Talke (township in Audley), 33/42A; SJ825530; NP 110
Talkin (township in Hayton), 7/51; NY557568; NP 76
Talland (district in Talland), 6/119; SX230524; NP 186
Talland (parish), 6/118-119; NP 186
Tallentire (township in Bridekirk), 7/238; NY108359; NP 82
Talley (parish), 47/12; SN634317; NP 140
Tallington (division in Tallington), 22/724A; TF094089; NP 123
Tallington (division in Tallington), 22/724B; TF142159; NP 123
Tallington (parish), 22/724A-B; NP 123
Talworth, 35/38
Talyllyn (parish), 52/33; SH750110; NP 116, 127
Tamar (district in Stoke Damerel), 9/456; SX452554; NP 187/1
Tamerton Foliot (Tamerton Foliott) (parish), 9/361; SX481626; NP 187
Tamhorn (extra-parochial), 33/271; SK175069; NP 120
Tamworth (division in Tamworth township in Tamworth), 33/284; SK203041; NP 120
Tamworth (parish), 33/280-285E, 37/6-11; NP 120
Tamworth (township), 33/284, 37/9; NP 120
Tamworth (division in Tamworth), 37/9; SK209041; NP 120
Tamworth (township in Tamworth), 37/8; SK211044; NP 120
Tamworth Castle (township in Tamworth), 37/10; SK212022; NP 120
Tandridge (parish), 35/107; TQ377487; NP 170, 171
Tanfield (chapelry division of Tanfield township in Chester le Street), 11/34; NZ174557; NP 78
Tanfield (township in Chester le Street), 11/34-35; NP 78
Tangley (parish), 14/69; SU336530; NP 168
Tangmere (parish), 36/245; SU903062; NP 181
Tankersley (parish), 43/785-786; NP 102
Tankersley (township in Tankersley), 43/786; SK347995; NP 102
Tannington (parish), 34/171; TM245675; NP 137
Tanshelf (division in township of Pontefract in Pontefract), 43/627; SE450217; NP 97
Tansley (township in Crich), 8/146; SK325604; NP 111
Tansor (parish), 26/60; TL068900; NP 134
Tansterne (township in Aldborough), 41/377; TA222372; NP 99
Tanworth (Tanworth-in-Arden) (parish), 37/86; SP127734; NP 131
Taplow (parish), 3/219; SU909820; NP 159
Tapton (township in Chesterfield), 8/73; SK396720; NP 111, 112
Tarbock (division in township of Tarbock in Huyton), 20/641A; SJ460880; NP 100
Tardebigge (parish), 40/1, 50A-52; NP 130, 131
Tarent Rushton (parish), 10/169A-B; NP 178, 179
Tarleton (parish), 20/351; SD430200; NP 94, 100
Tarnacre (Tarnicar) (division in Upper Rawcliffe with Tarnacre township in St Michaels on Wyre), 20/157; SD452423; NP 94
Tarnbrook (division in township of Over Wyresdale in Lancaster), 20/123; SD601564; NP 94, 95
Tarporley (parish), 5/397-400; NP 109, 110
Tarporley (township in Tarporley), 5/400; SJ553626; NP 109
Tarraby (township in Stanwix), 7/77; NY411583; NP 76
Tarrant Crawford (parish), 10/178; ST922031; NP 178, 179
Tarrant Gunville (parish), 10/60; ST818138; NP 178, 179
Tarrant Hinton (parish), 10/81; ST934112; NP 178, 179
Tarrant Keyneston (Tarrant Keinston, Tarrant Keynston) (parish), 10/179; ST930043; NP 178, 179
Tarrant Launceston (division in Tarrant Launceston), 10/80; ST935093; NP 178, 179
Tarrant Launceston (parish), 10/80, 167B; NP 178, 179
Tarrant Monkton (division in Tarrant Monkton), 10/167A; ST940080; NP 178, 179
Tarrant Monkton (parish), 10/167A-B; NP 178, 179
Tarrant Rawston (parish), 10/168; ST934066; NP 178, 179
Tarrant Rushton (Tarent Rushton) (division in Tarrant Rushton), 10/169A; ST951065; NP 179
Tarrant Rushton (Tarent Rushton) (parish), 10/169A-B; NP 178, 179
Tarretburn (township in Bellingham), 27/276; NY798912; NP 77
Tarring Neville (parish), 36/330; TQ445040; NP 183
Tarrington (parish), 15/167; SO621403; NP 143
Tarset (West Tarset) (township in Thorneyburn), 27/274; NY750950; NP 70, 77
Tarvin (parish), 5/384-394; NP 109
Tarvin with Oscroft (Tarvin) (township in Tarvin), 5/387; SJ499667; NP 109
Tasburgh (parish), 25/611; TM208960; NP 137
Tasley (parish), 31/490; SO697938; NP 130
Tatenhill (parish), 8/323, 33/217A-220; NP 120
Tatenhill (Tatenhill and Callingwood) (township in Tatenhll), 33/217A; NP 120
Tatham (parish), 20/80; SD658658; NP 89
Tathwell (parish), 22/290; TF314820; NP 105
Tatsfield (parish), 35/102; TQ422563; NP 171
Tattenhall (parish), 5/358-360; NP 109
Tattenhall (township in Tattenhall), 5/358; SJ501583; NP 109
Tattenhoe (parish), 3/72; SP832335; NP 146
Tatterford (parish), 25/107; TF864295; NP 125
Tattersett (Gatesend) (parish), 25/106; TF852300; NP 125
Tattershall (parish), 22/453-454B; NP 114

Tattershall (township in Tattershall), 22/453; TF208578; NP 113, 114
Tattershall Thorpe (division in Tattershall), 22/454A; TF218603; NP 113, 114
Tattershall Thorpe (township in Tattershall), 22/454A-B; NP 114
Tattershall Thorpe - Wildmore Fen (division in Tattershall), 22/454B; TF244531; NP 114
Tattingstone (parish), 34/516; TM138372; NP 150
Tatton (township in Rostherne), 5/96; SJ756817; NP 101
Taunton St James (division inside Taunton borough in Taunton St James), 32/328A; ST228252; NP 177
Taunton St James (division outside Taunton borough in Taunton St James), 32/328B; ST231267; NP 177
Taunton St James (parish), 32/328A-B; NP 177
Taunton St Mary Magdalen (division inside Taunton borough in Taunton St Mary Magdalen), 32/329A; ST234240; NP 177
Taunton St Mary Magdalen (division outside Taunton borough in Taunton St Mary Magdalen), 32/329B; ST248237; NP 177
Taunton St Mary Magdalen (parish), 32/329A-B; NP 177
Taverham (parish), 25/352; TG162147; NP 125, 126
Tavistock (parish), 9/353; SX471745; NP 175, 187
Tawestock, 9/37; NP 163
Tawstock (Tawestock) (parish), 9/37; SS552284; NP 163
Taxal (parish), 5/30-31; NP 101, 110, 111
Taxal (township in Taxal), 5/31; SK005760; NP 101, 110, 111
Taynton (parish), 13/134; SO730217; NP 143
Taynton (parish), 29/155; SP232147; NP 144
Tealby (Tevilby) (parish), 22/204; TF155905; NP 104, 105
Tebay (township in Orton), 38/75; NY616029; NP 83, 89
Tedburn St Mary (parish), 9/321; SX810941; NP 175, 176
Teddesley Hay (extra-parochial), 33/232; SJ959158; NP 119
Teddington (parish), 24/128; TQ157712; NP 170
Teddington (hamlet in Overbury), 40/215; SO959334; NP 143
Tedmore (township in West Felton), 31/95; SJ361256; NP 118
Tedstone Delamere (parish), 15/83; SO699590; NP 130
Tedstone Wafer (parish), 15/82; SO675597; NP 130
Teeton (hamlet in Guilsborough), 26/172; SP698702; NP 133
Teffont Evias (Teffont Ewyas) (parish), 39/286; ST987310; NP 167
Teffont Magna (parish), 39/287; ST992336; NP 167
Teigh (parish), 30/2; SK866658; NP 122
Teigngrace (parish), 9/409; SX850741; NP 188
Tellisford (Telsford) (parish), 32/93; ST797557; NP 166
Telscombe (parish), 36/320; TQ399024; NP 183
Telsford (parish), 32/93; NP 166
Telych (hamlet in Llandingat), 47/18; SN787335; NP 140
Temple (division in township of West Witton in West Witton), 42/144; SE032886; NP 90
Temple (parish), 6/51; SX146733; NP 186
Temple Bruer (extra-parochial), 22/576B; TF007538; NP 113
Temple Coombe (parish), 32/381; NP 166
Temple Grafton (parish), 37/196; SP129536; NP 131, 144
Temple Guiting (parish), 13/76; SP103277; NP 144
Temple Hall (division in Sibson), 21/155; SK362031; NP 121
Temple High Grange (extra-parochial), 22/576A; TF026575; NP 113
Temple Hirst (Temple Hurst) (township in Birkin), 43/457; SE605255; NP 97
Temple Newsham (township in Whitkirk), 43/480-483; NP 96
Temple Normanton (township in Chesterfield), 8/70; SK419676; NP 112
Temple Ruckley, 39/105; NP 157
Temple Sowerby (township in Kirby Thore), 38/4; NY613268; NP 83
Templeton (parish), 9/159; SS877149; NP 164
Tempsford (parish), 1/39; TL176543; NP 134, 147
Tenbury (parish), 40/81-84; NP 129, 130
Tenbury (township in Tenbury), 40/81; SO592678; NP 129, 130
Tenbury Foreign with Kyrewood, 40/82; NP 129, 130
Tenby (parish), 55/137-138; NP 152
Tenby St Mary - In-Liberty (borough in Tenby), 55/138; SN129009; NP 152

Tenby St Mary - Out-Liberty (division outside borough in Tenby [Dinbych-y-pysgod]), 55/137; SN129028; NP 152
Tendring (parish), 12/115; TM145245; NP 150
Tenterden (parish), 19/413; TQ890328; NP 172, 184
Terling (parish), 12/216; TL768149; NP 148, 149
Terrington St Clement (division in Marshland fen in Terrington St Clement), 25/293B; TF529098; NP 124
Terrington St Clement (division in Terrington St Clement), 25/293A; TF540200; NP 124
Terrington St Clement (parish), 25/293A-B; NP 124
Terrington St John (division in Terrington St John), 25/294A; TF533144; NP 124
Terrington St John (divisionin Marshland fen in Terrington St John), 25/294B; TF547096; NP 124
Terrington St John (parish), 25/294A-B; TF533144; NP 124
Terrington (parish), 42/650-652; NP 92
Terrington with Wiganthorpe (Terrington with Wigganthorpe) (division in township of Terrington with Wiganthorpe in Terrington), 42/650; SE665703; NP 92
Terrington with Wiganthorpe (township in Terrington), 42/650-651; NP 92
Terwick (parish), 36/343; SU823325; NP 181
Testerton (parish), 25/156; TF936273; NP 125
Teston (parish), 19/215; TQ704536; NP 171
Tetbury (parish), 13/335; ST883928; NP 156
Tetchill (township in Ellesmere), 31/57; SJ384321; NP 118
Tetcott (parish), 9/194; SX345962; NP 174
Tetford (parish), 22/332; TF337752; NP 105, 114
Tetney (parish), 22/85; TA325020; NP 105
Tetsworth (parish), 29/271; SP683019; NP 158, 159
Tettenhall (parish), 33/321-322; NP 119, 130
Tettenhall (township in Tettenhall), 33/321; SJ870010; NP 119, 130
Tettenhall Wood (township in Tettenhall), 33/322; SJ872989; NP 119, 130
Tetton (township in Warmingham), 5/227; SJ720631; NP 110
Tetworth (parish), 17/115; TL220540; NP 134
Teversal (Teversall) (parish), 28/94; SK476620; NP 112
Teversham (parish), 4/103; TL501578; NP 135
Tevilby (parish), 22/204; TF155905; NP 104, 105
Tewin (parish), 16/83; TL271146; NP 147
Tewkesbury (parish), 13/51; SO890319; NP 143
Teynham (parish), 19/107; TQ964638; NP 172
Thakeham (parish), 36/88; TQ109180; NP 182
Thame (parish), 29/262; SP700050; NP 158, 159
Thames Ditton (parish), 35/61-62; NP 170
Thanington (parish), 19/238; TR135558; NP 173
Tharston (parish), 25/645; TM185945; NP 137
Thatcham (parish), 2/153-155; NP 158, 168
Thatcham (Thatcham, Henwick, Colthorp, Awbery Street, Crookham) (tithing in Thatcham), 2/153; SU522675; NP 158, 168
Thatcham, 2/153; NP 158, 168
Thavies Inn (extra-parochial Thavies Inn), 24/10; TQ314815; NP 160/1
Thaxted (parish), 12/59; TL615305; NP 148
The Abbey (extra-parochial), 48/14; SH782662; NP 107
The Adventurers Hall Wood (division in Chatteris), 4/18; TL387808; NP 135
The Birch (township in Ellesmere), 31/61; SJ402336; NP 118
The Castle (York Castle) (extra-parochial), 43/23; SE605515; NP 97/1
The Cathedral Close of St Davids [Tyddewi] (extra-parochial), 55/66; SM751254; NP 138
The Close of the Collegiate Church of St Peter (extra-parochial), 24/34; TQ301794; NP 160/1, 170
The Close (extra-parochial), 33/257; SK116097; NP 120
The Ford (extra-parochial), 15/103; NP 129, 142
The Friary (extra-parochial), 33/259; SK115093; NP 120
The Friary (extra-parochial), 35/131; SU994496; NP 169/1
The Friths (extra-parochial), 22/752; TF292421; NP 123
The Gumber (extra-parochial), 36/223; SU962120; NP 181
The Hill, 40/12; NP 130

The Island (division in Gloucester, St Mary de Lode), 13/177A; SO826192; NP 143/1
The Isle (division in township of Bradbury in Sedgefield), 11/238; NZ302268; NP 85
The Lawn, 22/499; SK973719; NP 113/1
The Leigh (extra-parochial), 13/373; NP 155
The Marishes, 42/434; NP 92
The Mint and St Nicholas Hospital (extra-parochial), 19/144; TR127579; NP 173
The More (parish), 31/364
The Mythe, 21/161
The Vern (Fenn and Fern, Venn and Vern) (tithing in Bodenham), 15/144; SO526504; NP 142
The Vineyard (extra-parochial), 15/135; SO527391; NP 142/1
The Withens (division in township of Sowerby in Halifax), 43/564; SE974222; NP 95
The Yelds (extra-parochial), 31/279; SJ465145; NP 118
Theakston (township in Burneston), 42/223; SE309863; NP 91
Theale (division in Tilehurst), 2/177; SU641713; NP 158
Thearne (township in St John Beverley), 41/300; TA079361; NP 99
Thearne and Woodmansey (lands common to Tearne township and Woodmansey Woodmansey and Beverley Parks township in St John Beverly), 41/299; TA070362; NP 99
Theberton (parish), 34/261; TM432653; NP 137
Theddingworth (division in Theddingworth), 21/339; SP665866; NP 132, 133
Theddingworth (parish), 21/339, 26/111; NP 132, 133
Theddlethorpe All Saints (West Theddlethorpe) (parish), 22/304; TF463882; NP 105
Theddlethorpe St Helen (East Theddlethorpe) (parish), 22/305; TF480870; NP 105
Thelbridge (parish), 9/174; SS806134; NP 163, 164
Thelnetham (parish), 34/95; TM0033768; NP 136
Thelsford (hamlet in Charlecote), 37/221; SP280575; NP 131, 132
Thelveton (Thelton) (parish), 25/756; TM155812; NP 136, 137
Thelwall (township in Runcorn), 5/146; SJ653871; NP 101
Themelthorpe (parish), 25/200; TG061245; NP 125
Thenford (parish), 26/355; SP523422; NP 145
Theobald Street (hamlet in Aldenham), 16/130; TQ181988; NP 160
Therfield (parish), 16/13; TL345368; NP 147, 148
Thetford St Cuthbert (St Cuthbert in Thetford) (parish), 25/716; TL877832; NP 136
Thetford St Peter (St Peter and St Nicholas in Thetford) (parish), 25/715; TL852855; NP 136
Thetford St Mary (parish), 34/105; TL840830; NP 136
Thetford, 4/40
Theydon Bois (Thoydon Bois) (parish), 12/306; TQ453990; NP 161
Theydon Garnon (Theydon Gernon, Thoydon Garnon) (parish), 12/305; TL473012; NP 161
Theydon Mount (Thoydon Mount) (parish), 12/304; TL492002; NP 161
Thickley (division in township of Redworth in Heighington), 11/285; NZ210250; NP 85
Thimbleby (division in Thimbleby), 22/373A; TF241704; NP 114
Thimbleby (parish), 22/373A-B; NP 114
Thimbleby - Wildmore Fen (division in Thimbleby), 22/373B; TF228538; NP 114
Thimbleby (division in township of Thimbleby in Osmotherley), 42/504; SE452952; NP 91
Thimbleby (division in Osmotherley), 42/504-505); NP 91
Thingdon (parish), 26/151; NP 133
Thingwall (township in Woodchurch), 5/466; SJ280847; NP 100
Thingwall (division in township of Much Woolton in Childwall), 20/643; SJ413900; NP 100
Thirkleby (township in Kirby Grindalythe), 41/181; SE925689; NP 93
Thirkleby (parish and township), 42/540-542; NP 91
Thirlby (township in Felixkirk), 42/538; SE490840; NP 91, 92

Thirlwall (township in Haltwhistle), 27/585; NY655680; NP 76
Thirn (township in Thornton Watlass), 42/183; SE221856; NP 91
Thirsk (parish), 42/529-532; NP 91
Thirsk (township in Thirsk), 42/529; SE418828; NP 91
Thirtleby (township in Swine), 41/386; TA172349; NP 99
Thistleton (division in township of Greenhalgh with Thistleton in Kirkham), 20/193; SD404381; NP 94
Thistleton (parish), 30/7; SK920180; NP 122
Thixendale (township in Wharram Percy), 41/139; SE846607; NP 92, 98
Tholthorpe (township in Alne), 42/580; SE478674; NP 91
Thomas Close (township in Hutton in the Forest), 7/162; NY430400; NP 83
Thomley (division in Waterperry), 29/236B; SP631089; NP 158
Thompson (parish), 25/720; TL922969; NP 136
Thonock (division of Gainsborough township in Gainsborough), 22/127; SK829904; NP 104
Thoralby (township in Aysgarth), 42/140A; SD983860; NP 90
Thoraldby (division in township of Skutterskelfe in Rudby in Cleveland), 42/295; NZ492071; NP 85
Thoresway (parish), 22/162; TF162967; NP 104, 105
Thorganby (parish), 22/168A; TF205976; NP 105
Thorganby (division in township of Thorganby and West Cottingwith in Thorganby), 41/75; SE681411; NP 97
Thorganby (parish), 41/75-76; NP 97
Thorganby and West Cottingwith (township in Thorganby), 41/75-76; NP 97
Thorlby (division in township of Stirton with Thorlby in Skipton), 43/324; SD969527; NP 95
Thorley (parish), 16/68; TL475190; NP 148
Thorley (parish), 18/5; SZ373879; NP 180
Thormanby (parish), 42/565; SE493744; NP 91, 92
Thornaby (township in Stainton), 42/277; NZ455165; NP 85
Thornage (parish), 25/67; TG052371; NP 125
Thornborough (parish), 3/75; SP746335; NP 146
Thornborough, 42/534; NP 91
Thornbrough (township in Corbridge), 27/476; NZ016650; NP 77
Thornbrough (Thornborough) (township in South Kilvington), 42/534; SE437850; NP 91
Thornbury (parish), 9/104; SS387080; NP 174, 175
Thornbury (borough in Thornbury), 13/358A; ST635900; NP 156
Thornbury (parish), 13/358A-359; ST689860; NP 155, 156
Thornbury (parish), 15/78-79; NP 130
Thornbury (township in Thornbury), 15/78; SO628599; NP 130
Thornbury (township in Forden), 54/103; SO211993; NP 117, 128
Thornby (parish), 26/121; SP674758; NP 132, 133
Thorncombe (parish), 10/300; ST364035; NP 177
Thorncote (hamlet in Northill), 1/68C; TL151476; NP 147
Thorndon (Thorndon All Saints) (parish), 34/177; TM148688; NP 136, 137
Thorne (parish), 32/469; ST523181; NP 177
Thorne (parish), 43/950; SE710150; NP 103, 104
Thorne St Margaret (parish), 32/321; ST097204; NP 164
Thorner (township in Thorner), 43/414; SE377400; NP 96, 97
Thornes (tithe-free division in township of Alverthorpe with Thornes in Wakefield), 43/603; SE318195; NP 96, 102
Thornes (titheable division in township of Alverthorpe with Thornes in Wakefield), 43/604; SE328198; NP 96, 102
Thorney (parish), 4/7; TF290050; NP 123, 124, 134
Thorney (parish), 28/120-122; NP 113
Thorney (township in Thorney), 28/121; SK860730; NP 113
Thorneyburn (parish), 27/274-275; NP 70, 77
Thorneyburn (township in Thorneyburn), 27/275; NY761875; NP 77
Thornfalcon (Thorn Faulcon, Thorne Falcon, Thorn Falcon) (parish), 32/331; ST283235; NP 177
Thornford (parish), 10/37; ST610133; NP 177, 178
Thorngrafton (township in Haltwhistle), 27/582; NY761663; NP 77
Thorngumbald (township in Paull), 41/430; TA204254; NP 99
Thornham (Thurnham) (parish), 19/169; TQ813580; NP 172
Thornham (township in Middleton), 20/480; SD900090; NP 101

Thornham (parish), 25/5; TF740428; NP 124, 125
Thornham Magna (Great Thornham) (parish), 34/183; TM102713; NP 136
Thornham Parva (Little Thornham) (parish), 34/182; TM106728; NP 136
Thornhaugh (parish), 26/40; TF063005; NP 123, 134
Thornhill (township in Hope), 8/19; SK196836; NP 102, 111
Thornhill (tithing in Stalbridge), 10/26D; ST740150; NP 178
Thornhill (parish), 43/714-721; NP 102
Thornhill (township in Thornhill), 43/718; SE246186; NP 102
Thornholme (township in Burton Agnes), 41/261B; TA113642; NP 93, 99
Thornley (division in township of Wolsingham in Wolsingham), 11/183; NZ114371; NP 84
Thornley (division in township of Wolsingham in Wolsingham), 11/185; NZ127370; NP 85
Thornley (township in Kelloe), 11/100; NZ361391; NP 85
Thornley with Wheatley (township in Chipping), 20/229; SD631404; NP 95
Thornset (Thornsett) (township in Glossop), 8/9; SK005886; NP 101, 102
Thornthorpe (division in parish and township of Burythorpe), 41/130; SE787672; NP 92
Thornthwaite (township in Crosthwaite), 7/281; NY214264; NP 82
Thornthwaite and Padside (township in Hampsthwaite), 43/157; SE140605; NP 91, 96
Thornton (parish), 3/17; SP759366; NP 146
Thornton (division in township of Thornton in Poulton-le-Fylde), 20/175; SD333432; NP 94
Thornton (township in Poulton-le-Fylde), 20/174-176; NP 94
Thornton (township in Sefton), 20/681; SD338015; NP 100
Thornton (parish), 21/135-137; NP 121
Thornton (township in Thornton), 21/135; SK472072; NP 121
Thornton (parish), 22/375; TF241679; NP 114
Thornton (township in Norham), 27/9; NT952477; NP 64
Thornton (township in Thornton), 41/79; SE761451; NP 97, 98
Thornton le (division in township and parish of Thornton in Cravern), 43/317; SD905488; NP 95
Thornton (division in township of Thornton in Bradford), 43/529; SE095325; NP 96
Thornton (township in Bradford), 43/528-529; NP 96
Thornton Bridge (Thornton Briggs) (township in Brafferton), 42/570; SE421704; NP 91
Thornton Briggs, 42/570; NP 91
Thornton Curtis (parish), 22/56; TA072181; NP 104
Thornton Dale (division in Thornton Dale), 42/427; SE850840; NP 92, 92/1
Thornton Dale (parish), 42/425-427; NP 92, 92/1
Thornton Dale and Ellerburn (intermixed lands in Thornton Dale and Ellerburn), 42/426; SE820815; NP 92, 92/1
Thornton Dale, Farmanby and Ellerburn (quarries common to the townships of Thornton Dale, Farmanby and Ellerburn in Thornton Dale and Ellerburn), 42/425; SE835835; NP 92, 92/1
Thornton Hough (township in Neston), 5/476; SJ307812; NP 100
Thornton Hall (division in township of Low Coniscliffe with Carlbury in Coniscliffe), 11/315; NZ241168; NP 85
Thornton in Lonsdale (parish), 20/79, 43/265-266; NP 89, 90
Thornton in Cravern (parish and township), 43/314-317; NP 95
Thornton in Lonsdale (parish), 20/79, 43/265-266; NP 89, 90
Thornton in Lonsdale (township in Thornton in Lonsdale), 43/265; SD700775; NP 89, 90
Thornton le Moors (parish), 5/415-419; NP 100, 109
Thornton le Moors (Thornton) (township in Thornton le Moors), 5/415; SJ438744; NP 100, 109
Thornton le Moor (parish), 22/114; TF048962; NP 104
Thornton le Beans (division in township of Thornton le Beans in North Otterington), 42/259; SE399901; NP 91
Thornton le Beans (township in North Otterington), 42/259-260; NP 91
Thornton le Moor (township in North Otterington), 42/258; SE388898; NP 91
Thornton Riseborough (Thornton Risebrough) (township in Normanby), 42/445; SE749828; NP 92

Thornton Rust (township in Aysgarth), 42/140B; SD977886; NP 90
Thornton Steward (parish), 42/185; SE178872; NP 91
Thornton Watlass (parish), 42/181-184; NP 91
Thornton Watlass (township in Thornton Watlass), 42/181; SE232861; NP 91
Thornton, 5/415; NP 100, 109
Thornton-le-Fen (parish), 22/463B; NP 114
Thornton-le-Fen (parochial township in Thornton-le-Fen), 22/463; TF276503; NP 114
Thornton-le-Clay (township in Foston), 42/657; SE678644; NP 92
Thornton-le-Street (parish), 42/527-528; NP 91
Thornton-le-Street (township in Thornton-le-Street), 42/527; SE406859; NP 91
Thornton-on-the-Hill (division in township of Thornton-on-the-Hill-cum-Baxby in Coxwold), 42/558; SE534737; NP 91
Thornton-on-the-Hill-cum-Baxby (township in Coxwold), 42/558-559; NP 91
Thornville (township in Whixley), 43/118; SE452548; NP 97
Thoroton (parish), 28/206; SK762426; NP 122
Thorp Arch (division in Walton), 43/76; SE452487; NP 97
Thorp Arch (township in Thorp Arch), 43/91; SE433464; NP 97
Thorp Arch (township in Walton and Thorp Arch), 43/76, 91.
Thorp Audlin, 43/662; NP 103
Thorp Perrow (division in township of Snape in Well), 42/179; SE268857; NP 91
Thorp, 43/591
Thorpe (hamlet in Thorpe next Norwich), 25/450A; TG248087; NP 126
Thorpe (parish), 8/170, 176; NP 111
Thorpe (parish), 28/299; SK770497; NP 121
Thorpe (parish), 35/68; TQ028689; NP 169, 170
Thorpe (Thorp, Thorpe on the Hill) (township in Rothwell), 43/591; SE312270; NP 96
Thorpe (township in Thorpe), 8/170; SK158509; NP 111
Thorpe (township in Howden), 41/5; SE761308; NP 98
Thorpe Abbots (parish), 25/765; TM191798; NP 137
Thorpe Achurch (parish), 26/79; TL027819; NP 134
Thorpe Arnold (parish), 21/78; SK772210; NP 122
Thorpe Audlin (Thorp Audlin) (township in Badsworth), 43/662; SE482160; NP 103
Thorpe Bassett (parish), 41/148; SE861729; NP 92
Thorpe Brantingham (township in Brantingham), 41/210; SE952308; NP 98
Thorpe Bulmer (township in Hart), 11/247; NZ469364; NP 85
Thorpe by Water (township in Seaton), 30/58; SP891971; NP 133
Thorpe Constantine (parish), 33/278; SK255086; NP 120
Thorpe in the Fallows (parish), 22/231; NP 104
Thorpe in the Glebe (parish), 28/294; SK610260; NP 121
Thorpe in Balne (township in Barnby Dun), 43/942A; SE600100; NP 103
Thorpe Langton (township in Church Langton), 21/313; SP746918; NP 133
Thorpe le Fallows (West Thorpe, Thorpe in the Fallows) (parish), 22/231; SK916904; NP 104
Thorpe le Street (township in Nunburnholme), 41/102; SE838440; NP 98
Thorpe Lubenham (extra-parochial), 26/109; SP704866; NP 133
Thorpe Malsor (parish), 26/159; SP837789; NP 133
Thorpe Mandeville (parish), 26/331; SP530448; NP 145
Thorpe Market (parish), 25/54; TG238356; NP 126
Thorpe Marsh (lands disputed between Barnby Dun and Thorpe in Balne townships in Barnby Dun), 43/942B; SE600080; NP 103
Thorpe Morieux (parish), 34/348B; TL940536; NP 149
Thorpe next Haddiscoe (parish), 25/587; TM435982; NP 137
Thorpe next Norwich (Thorpe St Andrew) (parish), 25/450A-B; NP 126
Thorpe next Norwich (Thorpe St Andrew) (division in Thorpe next Norwich), 25/450B; TG268097; NP 126
Thorpe on the Hill (parish), 22/534; SK910652; NP 113
Thorpe on the Hill, 43/591

Thorpe Parva (parish), 25/759; TM162793; NP 137
Thorpe Salvin (parish), 43/901; SK531807; NP 103
Thorpe Satchville (chapelry in Twyford), 21/265; SK735121; NP 122
Thorpe St Peter (division in Thorpe St Peter), 22/482A; TF475610; NP 114
Thorpe St Peter (parish), 22/482A-B; NP 114
Thorpe St Peter - East Fen (division in Thorpe St Peter), 22/482B; TF428600; NP 114
Thorpe St Andrew (parish), 25/450A-B; NP 126
Thorpe Stapleton (township in Whitkirk), 43/484; SE341306; NP 96
Thorpe Tilney (hamlet in Timberland), 22/567; TF140580; NP 113
Thorpe Underwood (hamlet in Rothwell), 26/128; SP793813; NP 133
Thorpe Underwoods (Thorpe Underwood) (township in Little Ouseburn), 43/122; SE470595; NP 97
Thorpe Willoughby (township in Brayton), 43/454; SE576311; NP 97
Thorpe-le-Soken (parish), 12/160; TM181222; NP 150
Thorpe-le-Willows (township in Kilburn), 42/546; SE578772; NP 92
Thorpland (hamlet in Wallington cum Thorpland), 25/319; TF613079; NP 124
Thorrington (parish), 12/157; TM097197; NP 149, 150
Thorverton (parish), 9/218; SS931032; NP 176
Thowthorpe (division in township of Marton in the Forest in Marton in the Forest), 42/595; SE617667; NP 92
Thoydon Bois (parish), 12/306; NP 161
Thoydon Garnon (parish), 12/305; NP 161
Thoydon Mount (parish), 12/304; NP 161
Thrandeston (parish), 34/87; TM118763; NP 136
Thrapston (parish), 26/83; TL009781; NP 134
Threapwood (extra-parochial), 5/315; SJ443455; NP 109, 118
Threapwood (extra-parochial), 50/145; SJ439456; NP 109, 118
Three Farms (township in Eccleshall), 33/134; SJ848313; NP 119
Threekingham (Threekingham with Stow) (parish), 22/664; TF091358; NP 123
Threlkeld (township or chapelry in Greystoke), 7/206; NY331262; NP 82, 83
Threshfield (township in Linton), 43/220; SD970640; NP 90
Threxton (parish), 25/681; TL888994; NP 136
Thrigby (parish), 25/386; TG458124; NP 126
Thrimby (township in Morland), 38/17; NY548200; NP 83
Thringston (Thringstone) (township in Whitwick), 21/28; SK421181; NP 121
Thrintoft (township in Ainderby Steeple), 42/217; SE320942; NP 91
Thriplow (parish), 4/179; TL439463; NP 148
Thrislington (township in Bishop Middleham), 11/227; NZ309332; NP 85
Throapham (division in township of Throapham with Thwaites in Laughton en le Morthen), 43/909; SK534872; NP 103
Throapham with Thwaites (township in Laughton en le Morthen), 43/909-910; NP 103
Throcking (parish), 16/23; TL345302; NP 147, 148
Throckington (parish), 27/369-372; NP 77
Throckington (township in Throckington), 27/371; NY956794; NP 77
Throckley (township in Newburn), 27/544; NZ152670; NP 78
Throckmorton (chapelry in Fladbury), 40/187; SO977499; NP 143
Throp Hill (Thropple) (township in Mitford), 27/404; NZ127859; NP 77, 78
Thropple, 27/404; NP 77, 78
Thropton (township in Rothbury), 27/251; NU030023; NP 71
Throston (township in Hart), 11/245; NZ492338; NP 85
Throwleigh (Throwley) (parish), 9/325; SX680896; NP 175
Throwley (parish), 19/235; TQ991549; NP 172
Throxenby (township in Scalby), 42/396; TA014890; NP 93
Thrumpton (parish), 28/276; SK518312; NP 121

Thrunscoe (township in Clee), 22/83; TA309075; NP 105
Thrunton (township in Whittingham), 27/171; NU084096; NP 71
Thrup (hamlet in Kidlington), 29/198; SP472159; NP 145
Thrupp and Wick (division in Radley), 2/13B; SU520970; NP 158
Thruscross (township in Fewston), 43/381; SE125585; NP 91, 96
Thrush House Farm (division in township of Sutton-on-the-Forest in Sutton-on-the-Forest), 42/592; SE589651; NP 92
Thrushelton (Thurshelton) (parish), 9/342; SX454885; NP 175
Thrussington (parish), 21/63; SK647173; NP 121
Thruxton (parish), 14/81; SU267450; NP 167, 168
Thruxton (parish), 15/192; SO439344; NP 142
Thrybergh (parish), 43/846-847; NP 103
Thrybergh (township in Thrybergh), 43/847; SK467953; NP 103
Thundersley (parish), 12/389; TQ794889; NP 162
Thundridge (parish), 16/76; TL373169; NP 147, 148
Thurcaston (parish), 21/129-131; NP 121
Thurcaston (township in Thurcaston), 21/129; SK572105; NP 121
Thurgarton (parish), 25/58; TG181356; NP 126
Thurgarton (parish), 28/193; SK690490; NP 112
Thurgoland (township in Silkstone), 43/699; SE290020; NP 102
Thurlaston (parish), 21/209-210; NP 121, 132
Thurlaston (township in Thurlaston), 21/209; SP502995; NP 121, 132
Thurlaston (township in Dunchurch), 37/131; SP465697; NP 132
Thurlbear (Thurlbeer) (parish), 32/418; ST263208; NP 177
Thurlby (parish), 22/540; SK898615; NP 113
Thurlby (parish), 22/710; TF109167; NP 123
Thurleigh (parish), 1/14; TL056582; NP 134
Thurlestone (Thurleston) (parish), 9/474; SX680440; NP 187
Thurloxton (parish), 32/300; ST276303; NP 165, 177
Thurlstone (township in Penistone), 43/777; SE188028; NP 102
Thurlton (parish), 25/585; TM424990; NP 137
Thurmaston North (township in Barkby), 21/128; SK615093; NP 121
Thurmaston South (township in Belgrave), 21/190; SK613084; NP 121
Thurnby (parish), 21/253-254; NP 121
Thurnby (township in Thurnby), 21/254; SK640041; NP 121
Thurne (parish), 25/392; TG405158; NP 126
Thurnham (parish), 19/169; NP 172
Thurnham (township in Cockerham), 20/103; SD456544; NP 94
Thurnham (township in Lancaster), 20/104; SD450555; NP 94
Thurnham (township), 20/103-104; NP 94
Thurning (district in Thurning), 17/36; TL083824; NP 134
Thurning (parish), 17/36, 26/71; NP 134
Thurning (parish), 25/149; TG300076; NP 125
Thurning (division in Thurning), 26/71; TL082828; NP 134
Thurnscoe (parish), 43/863; SE459063; NP 103
Thursby (parish), 7/137-139; NP 75, 76, 82, 83
Thursby (township in Thursby), 7/139; NY326505; NP 75, 76, 82, 83
Thursfield (township in Wolstanton), 33/17D; SJ860550; NP 110
Thursford (parish), 25/116; TF985342; NP 125
Thurshelton, 9/342; NP 175
Thursley (parish), 35/155; SU901371; NP 169, 181
Thurstaston (parish), 5/471-472; NP 100
Thurstaston (township in Thurstaston), 5/472; SJ244842; NP 100
Thurston (parish), 34/232; TL930654; NP 136
Thurstonland (township in Kirkburton), 43/732; SE174111; NP 102
Thurton (parish), 25/580; TG337004; NP 137
Thurvaston, Osleston and Cropper, 8/236; NP 120
Thuxton (parish), 25/549; TG040078; NP 125
Thwaite (division in township of Muker in Grinton), 42/122; SD876978; NP 90
Thwaite (parish), 25/615; TM335950; NP 137
Thwaite (parish), 34/179; TM115680; NP 136
Thwaite (Thwaite All Saints) (parish), 25/133; TG192331; NP 126
Thwaite All Saints (parish), 25/133; NP 126

Thwaites (township in Millom), 7/321; SD189881; NP 88
Thwaites (division in township of Throapham with Thwaites in Laughton en le Morthen), 43/910; SK544876; NP 103
Thwing (division in parish and township of Thwing), 41/171; TA057708; NP 93
Thwing (parish and township), 41/171-172; NP 93
Tibberton (parish), 13/136; SO752217; NP 143
Tibberton (parish), 15/216; NP 142
Tibberton (township in Edgmond), 31/193; SJ689198; NP 119
Tibberton (parish), 40/150; SO907570; NP 130
Tibbiston (parish), 33/331; NP 130
Tibenham (parish), 25/748; TM125893; NP 136
Tibshelf (parish), 8/138; SK439607; NP 112
Tibthorpe (township in Kirkburn), 41/235; SE948568; NP 98
Ticehurst (parish), 36/48; TQ679302; NP 183
Tichborne (Titchborne) (parish), 14/188; SU564287; NP 168
Tickencote (parish), 30/26; SK980098; NP 123
Tickenham (parish), 32/11; ST456719; NP 155
Tickenhurst (division in Northbourne), 19/277; TR289544; NP 173
Tickhill (parish), 43/923-925; NP 103
Tickhill (township in Tickhill), 43/923; SK590930; NP 103
Ticklerton (township in Eaton), 31/428; SO485907; NP 129
Ticknall (parish), 8/304; SK351236; NP 121
Tickton with Hull Bridge (township in St John Beverley), 41/293; TA065417; NP 99
Tid St Giles (parish), 4/1; NP 124
Tidcombe (district in Tiverton), 9/163; SS983139; NP 164
Tidcombe (parish), 39/187; SU307569; NP 167, 168
Tiddington (hamlet in Albury), 29/256B; SP647045; NP 158
Tidenham (parish), 13/167; SO555965; NP 155
Tideswell (parish), 8/33-36; NP 111
Tideswell (township in Tideswell), 8/34; SK150765; NP 111
Tidmarsh (parish), 2/167; SU632746; NP 158
Tidmington (parish), 40/251; SP254385; NP 144
Tiertreff (township in Meifod), 54/43; SJ126129; NP 117
Tiffield (parish), 26/307; SP707521; NP 146
Tilbrook (parish), 1/1; TL080697; NP 134
Tilbury (parish), 12/33; NP 148, 149
Tilbury Fort, 12/428; TQ651752; NP 171
Tilbury juxta Clare (Tilbury) (parish), 12/33; TL758405; NP 148, 149
Tilehurst (division in Tilehurst), 2/176; SU669733; NP 158, 159, 169
Tilehurst (parish), 2/176-177; NP 158, 159, 169
Tilley (township in Wem), 31/43; SJ511272; NP 118
Tillingham (parish), 12/354; TM010038; NP 162
Tillington (township in Burghill), 15/122B; SO465455; NP 142
Tillington (extra-parochial), 33/175; SJ913255; NP 119
Tillington (parish), 36/27; SU951227; NP 181
Tillmouth (division of Cornhill chapelry in Norham), 27/17B; NT875420; NP 64
Tilmanstone (parish), 19/352; TR299515; NP 173
Tilney All Saints (division in Marshland fen in Tilney All Saints), 25/300B; TF540097; NP 124
Tilney All Saints (division in Tilney All Saints), 25/300A; TF566186; NP 124
Tilney All Saints (parish), 25/300A-B; NP 124
Tilney cum Islington (division in Marshland fen in Tilney cum Islington), 25/302B; TF543105; NP 124
Tilney cum Islington (division in Tilney cum Islington), 25/302A; TF582161; NP 124
Tilney cum Islington (parish), 25/302B; NP 124
Tilney St Lawrence (parish), 25/301; TF552140; NP 124
Tilshead (parish), 39/247; SU025479; NP 167
Tilsop (township in Burford), 31/541B; SO607730; NP 130
Tilstock (township in Whitchurch), 31/31; SJ531371; NP 118
Tilston (parish), 5/341-345; NP 109
Tilston (township in Tilston), 5/344; SJ463511; NP 109
Tilstone (township in Bunbury), 5/301; SJ569595; NP 109
Tilsworth (parish), 1/133; SP983243; NP 147
Tiltey (parish), 12/60; TL594266; NP 148
Tilton (Tilton on the Hill) (parish), 21/271-274; NP 122

Tilton (Tilton on the Hill) (township in Tilton), 21/273; SK752050; NP 122
Tilts (division in township of Langthwaite with Tilts in Doncaster), 43/936; SE574094; NP 103
Tilty (Tiltey) (parish), 12/60; TL594266; NP 148
Timberland (hamlet in Timberland), 22/566; TF144591; NP 113
Timberland (parish), 22/564-567; NP 113
Timberscombe (parish), 32/250; SS952416; NP 164
Timberth (township in Chirbury), 31/358; SO255968; NP 128
Timble Great, 43/379; NP 96
Timble Little, 43/374; NP 96
Timperley (township in Bowdon), 5/83; SJ784888; NP 101
Timsbury (parish), 14/226; SU352249; NP 168
Timsbury (parish), 32/108; ST666589; NP 166
Timworth (parish), 34/197; TL869691; NP 136
Tincleton (parish), 10/215; SY774921; NP 178
Tingewick (parish), 3/84; SP656326; NP 145
Tingrith (parish), 1/116; TL004324; NP 147
Tinsley (township in Rotherham), 43/839; SK400900; NP 102, 103
Tintagel (parish), 6/23; SX070874; NP 185
Tintern Parva (Little Tintern) (parish), 53/89; SO525010; NP 155
Tintinhull (parish), 32/403; ST498202; NP 177
Tintwistle (township in Mottram), 5/4; SK017976; NP 102
Tinwell (parish), 30/32; SK992072; NP 123
Tipton (Tibbiston) (parish), 33/331; SO960930; NP 130
Tir Evan (parish), 48/22, 49/18; NP 107
Tir-Ifan (Tir Evan, Ysbyty, Yspytty) (division in Tir-Ifan), 48/22, 49/18; SH835455; NP 107
Tir-Ifan (Tir Evan, Ysbyty, Yspytty) (parish), 48/22, 49/18; SH835455; NP 107
Tir-y-coed (township in Kinnerley), 31/123; SJ325192; NP 118
Tir-y-mynach (township in Llanfihangel Genu'rglyn), 46/7; SN678857; NP 127
Tirley, 13/122; SO837288; NP 143
Tirymynach (township in Guilsfield [Cegidfa]), 54/73; SJ260125; NP 117
Tisbury (former parish), 39/331-333; NP 166, 167
Tissington (parish), 8/169; SK174522; NP 111
Titchfield (parish), 14/275; SU520060; NP 180
Titchmarsh (parish), 26/82; TL032794; NP 134
Titchwell (parish), 25/7; TF758433; NP 124
Tithby (Tythby) (parish), 28/221; NP 121, 122
Tithby (Tythby) (township in Tithby), 28/221; SK701371; NP 122
Titherington,
Titley (parish), 15/42; SO321605; NP 129
Titlington (township in Eglingham), 27/143; NU110160; NP 71
Titsey (parish), 35/101; TQ410552; NP 171
Tittenhanger (hamlet in St Peters), 16/102; TL188058; NP 160
Tittenley (township in Audlem), 5/273; SJ649387; NP 119
Tittensor (township in Stone), 33/55; SJ870380; NP 119
Tittesworth (township in Leek), 33/8; SK005585; NP 110, 111
Tittleshall (Tittleshall cum Godwick) (parish), 25/187; TF898213; NP 125
Tiverton (township in Bunbury), 5/300; SJ543610; NP 109
tiverton (parish), 9/160-164; NP 164, 176
Tivetshall St Margaret (parish), 25/752; TM172876; NP 137
Tivetshall St Mary (parish), 25/753; TM171852; NP 137
Tixall (parish), 33/186; SJ976230; NP 119
Tixover (parish), 30/50; SK974009; NP 123, 134
Tockenham (parish), 39/60; SU041800; NP 157
Tocketts (township in Guisborough), 42/356; NZ622178; NP 86
Tockholes (township in Blackburn), 20/306; SD662222; NP 95, 101
Tockwith (township in Bilton), 43/80; SE466529; NP 97
Todber (parish), 10/305; ST802202; NP 166, 178
Todburn (township in Longhorsley), 27/300; NZ121951; NP 71, 78
Toddington (parish), 1/115; TL015285; NP 147
Toddington (parish), 13/70; SP037333; NP 144
Todenham (parish), 13/6A; SP235350; NP 144
Todmorden (division in township of Todmorden and Walsden in Rochdale), 20/459; SD912248; NP 95, 101

217

Todmorden and Walsden (township in Rochdale), 20/459-460; NP 95, 101
Todridge (township in Hartburn), 27/356; NZ059857; NP 77
Todwick (parish), 43/902; SK491848; NP 103
Toft (parish), 4/111; TL364563; NP 134, 135, 148
Toft (township in Knutsford), 5/105; SJ756760; NP 101, 110
Toft and Lound (hamlet in Witham on the Hill), 22/704; TF072180; NP 123
Toft Monks (parish), 25/589; TM428953; NP 137
Toft next Newton (parish), 22/215; TF038872; NP 104
Toftrees (Tofttrees) (parish), 25/162; TF901273; NP 125
Togston (township in Warkworth), 27/228; NU261019; NP 71
Tolland (parish), 32/274; ST107321; NP 164
Tolland Royal (division in Tolland Royal), 39/344; ST938178; NP 167, 179
Tolland Royal (parish), 10/63, 39/344; 167, 179
Tollard Farnham (Farnham Tollard) (tithing in Tolland Royal), 10/63; ST952159; NP 179
Toller Fratrum (parish), 10/145; SY579976; NP 177
Toller Porcorum (parish), 10/142; SY556981; NP 177
Tollerton (parish), 28/269; SK616351; NP 121
Tollerton (township in Alne), 42/583; SE522647; NP 92
Tollesbury (parish), 12/229; TL960107; NP 149, 162
Tolleshunt D'Arcy (parish), 12/230; TL929112; NP 149, 162
Tolleshunt Knights (parish), 12/224; TL918144; NP 149
Tolleshunt Major (Beckingham) (parish), 12/231; TL899120; NP 149, 162
Tolpuddle (parish), 10/207; SY790945; NP 178
Tolworth (Talworth) (hamlet in Long Ditton), 35/38; TQ198658; NP 170
Tomson (parish), 10/186; NP 178
Tonbridge (division in Tonbridge), 19/208; TQ592457; NP 171
Tonbridge (parish), 19/207-208; NP 171
Tong (parish), 31/473; SJ804078; NP 119
Tong (township in Birstal), 43/536; SE210308; NP 96
Tonge (parish), 19/164; TQ938634; NP 172
Tonge (township in Bolton-le-Moors), 20/401-402; NP 101
Tonge (township in Oldham), 20/484; SD881058; NP 101
Tonge Higher End (division in township of Tonge in Bolton-le-Moors), 20/402; SD729110; NP 101
Tonge Lower End (division in township of in Bolton-le-Moors), 20/401; SD732095; NP 101
Tongue (extra-parochial), 41/22D; SE856264; NP 98/1
Tooley (township in Peckleton), 21/173; SK479001; NP 121, 132
Toot Baldon (parish), 29/246; SP568002; NP 158
Tooting Graveney (Lower Tooting) (parish), 35/24; TQ276713; NP 170
Topcliffe (parish), 42/236-246; NP 91
Topcliffe (township in Topcliffe), 42/243; SE405773; NP 91
Topcroft (parish), 25/631; TM270920; NP 137
Toppesfield (parish), 12/54; TL735367; NP 148, 149
Topsham (parish), 9/312; SX960889; NP 176
Torbryan (Torbrian) (parish), 9/421; SX812691; NP 187, 188
Torkington (township in Stockport), 5/21; SJ943872; NP 101
Torksey (parish), 22/237-239; NP 104
Torksey (township in Torksey), 22/238; SK852786; NP 104
Tormarton (parish), 13/346; ST777792; NP 156
Tormoham (Tormoham with Torquay) (parish), 9/432; SX918643; NP 188
Torpenhow (parish), 7/231-234; NP 82
Torpenhow and Whitrigg (township in Torpenhow), 7/233; NY205381; NP 82
Torquay, 9/432; NP 188
Torrisholme (division in Poulton, Bare and Torrisholme township in Lancaster), 20/116; SD453636; NP 89
Tortington (parish), 36/289; TQ005057; NP 181
Tortworth (parish), 13/355; ST702932; NP 156
Torver (township in Ulverston), 20/11; SD284938; NP 88
Torworth (township in Blyth), 28/22; SK652862; NP 103
Toseland (parish), 17/105; TL237622; NP 134
Tosside (extra-parochial), 43/241; SD780560; NP 95
Tostock (parish), 34/234; TL955638; NP 136
Tothill (parish), 22/318; TF417816; NP 105
Totley (township in Dronfield), 8/44; SK309797; NP 111

Totnes (parish), 9/440; SX798600; NP 187, 188
Toton (township in Attenborough), 28/250; SK507343; NP 121
Tottenham (parish), 24/79A-D; NP 160, 161
Tottenham Court (division in St Pancras), 24/44E; TQ296822; NP 160/1
Tottenhill (parish), 25/315; TF640113; NP 124
Totteridge (parish), 16/151; TQ242943; NP 160
Totternhoe (parish), 1/141; SP995207; NP 147
Totterton (township in Lydbury North), 31/372; SO360882; NP 129
Tottington Higher End (township in Bury), 20/412; SD790195; NP 95, 101
Tottington Lower End (township in Bury), 20/416-418; NP 101
Tottington Lower End, Higher End (division in township of Tottington Lower End in Bury), 20/416; SD772159; NP 101
Tottington Lower End, Higher End (division in township of Tottington Lower End in Bury), 20/418; SD792163; NP 101
Tottington Lower End, Lower End (division in township of Tottington Lower End in Bury), 20/417; SD473131; NP 101
Tottington (parish), 25/711; TL897958; NP 136
Toulston (division in township of Newton Kyme cum Toulston), 43/73; SE453438; NP 97
Towcester (parish), 26/314-315; NP 145, 146
Towcester (township in Towcester), 26/314; SP689483; NP 145, 146
Towednack (parish), 6/204; SW486376; NP 189
Tower of London (The Tower) (extra-parochial), 24/1; TQ336806; NP 160/1
Towersey (parish), 3/187; SP738048; NP 159
Town (All Fours) (district in Tiverton), 9/164; SS946108; NP 164, 176
Town (division in St Matthew Bethnal Green), 24/63D; TQ347825; NP 160/1
Town Barningham (Barningham Winter) (parish), 25/62; TG147357; NP 125, 126
Town Quarter (township in Hartington), 8/110; SK132608; NP 111
Town Quarter (division in township of Wolsingham in Wolsingham), 11/181; NZ074372; NP 84
Towngreen, 25/649A
Townhill, 14/258
township in Darlington), 11/320-323, 325; NP 85
township in Middleton), 42/444; SE784860; NP 92
Townstal (Townstall) (parish), 9/483; SX859516; NP 188
Towthorpe (township in Wharram Percy), 41/141; SE902634; NP 92, 98
Towthorpe (division of Towthorpe township in Huntington), 42/683; SE634587; NP 97
Towthorpe (division of Towthorpe township in Strensall), 42/684; SE641593; NP 97
Towthorpe (township in Huntington and Strensall), 42/683-684
Towton (township in Saxton), 43/436; SE483393; NP 97
Towyn (parish), 52/37; NP 127
Toxteth Park (division in Toxteth Park extra-parochial), 20/666; SJ379878; NP 100
Toxteth Park (division in Toxteth Park extra-parochial), 20/667; SJ359883; NP 100
Toxteth Park (extra-parochial), 20/666-667; NP 100
Toyd Farm and Allenford (extra-parochial), 39/352; SU088108; NP 167
Toynton All Saints (division in Toynton All Saints), 22/427A; TF392633; NP 114
Toynton All Saints (parish), 22/427A-B; TF392633; NP 114
Toynton All Saints - East Fen (division in Toynton All Saints), 22/427B; TF393612; NP 114
Toynton St Peter (division in Toynton St Peter), 22/426A; TF408631; NP 114
Toynton St Peter (parish), 22/426A-C; NP 114
Toynton St Peter - East Fen (division in Toynton St Peter), 22/426B; TF402612; NP 114
Toynton St Peter - Wildmore Fen (division in Toynton St Peter), 22/426C; TF283503; NP 114
Toynton Supra (parish), 22/385A-B; NP 114

Trafford Hill (division in township of Aislaby in Egglescliffe), 11/342; NZ376109; NP 85
Traian-glas (Trayanglaes) (division outside Fforest-fawr in Llywel), 45/63A; SN860280; NP 140, 141
Traian-glas - Fforest-fawr (division within Fforest-fawr in Llywel), 45/63B; SN845215; NP 140, 153
Traian-mawr (division in Llywel), 45/62A; SN870320; NP 140, 141
Trallong (parish), 45/60; SN955303; NP 141
Tranby (division in Kirk Ella township in Kirk Ella), 41/309; TA017269; NP 99
Tranmere (Tranmore) (township in Bebington), 5/442; SJ321869; NP 100
Tranmore, 5/442; NP 100
Tranwell and High Church (township in Morpeth), 27/418; NZ190838; NP 78
Trawden (division in township of Trawden in Whalley), 20/271; SD918367; NP 95
Trawden (township in Whalley), 20/269-271; NP 95
Trawscoed (township in Crickadarn), 45/9; SO082355; NP 141
Trawsffynydd (parish), 52/11; SH730350; NP 116
Trawsgoed (township in Carno), 54/118; SN952952; NP 128
Trayanglaes, 45/63A; NP 140, 141
Tre Brys (extra-parochial), 49/17; SH880508; NP 107, 108
Tre Cwm (township in Nannerch), 50/97; SJ146684; NP 108
Tre Llan (township in Nannerch), 50/98; SJ164696; NP 108
Tre Llan, 50/38; NP 108
Tre-cefel (township in Caron), 46/38D; SN700590; NP 140
Tre-derwen fawr (Tre Derwen) (township in Llansantffraid), 54/2C; SJ217196; NP 117
Tre-lan (township in Cilcain), 50/99B; SJ168655; NP 108
Tre-wan, 49/132A
Tre-wern (Tre-wan) (township in Llanrhaeadr-ym-Mochnant [Llanrhaiadr ym Mochnant]), 49/132A; SJ100300; NP 117
Tre-wylan (township in Llansantffraid), 54/2D; SJ227179; NP 117
Treabbot (township in Whitford), 50/42; SJ104799; NP 108
Treales (division in township of Treales, Roseacre and Wharles in Kirkham), 20/203; SD448336; NP 94
Treales, Roseacre and Wharles (township in Kirkham), 20/203-205; NP 94
Treborough (parish), 32/252; ST005364; NP 164
Trebrodier (township in Bettws-y-crwyn), 31/404; SO195815; NP 128
Trebrys bach (township in Llanrhaeadr-ym-Mochnant [Llanrhaiadr ym Mochnant]), 49/134; SJ254262; NP 117
Trebrys Fawr (township in Llanrhaeadr-ym-Mochnant [Llanrhaiadr ym Mochnant]), 49/139; SJ147230; NP 117
Trebydan, 54/81; NP 117
Trecastle (division in Llywel), 45/62B; SN885295; NP 140, 141
Trecastle (township in Dyserth), 50/55; SJ067798; NP 108
Trecoed (township in Disserth), 56/40B; SO050550; NP 128, 141
Trederwen (township in Llandrinio), 54/85; SJ258168; NP 117
Tredington (hamlet in Tredington), 40/253; SP252427; NP 144
Tredington (parish), 40/253-256; SP252427; NP 144
Tredunnock (Tredynog) (parish), 53/107; ST363943; NP 155
Tredynog (parish), 53/107; NP 155
Treeton (parish), 43/892-894, 898; NP 103, 103/1
Treeton (township in Treeton), 43/893; SK439880; NP 103
Tref-lynn (township in Caron), 46/38B; SN680620; NP 127, 140
Tref-y-Clawdd (parish), 56/14
Tref-y-coed (hamlet in Lampeter Pont Stephan), 46/76; SN542473; NP 140
Trefaldwyn, 54/186; NP 128
Trefardclawdd, 31/104; NP 117
Trefdraeth (parish), 44/57; SH410700; NP 106
Trefecca (hamlet in Talgarth), 45/86D; SO150320; NP 141
Trefechan (township in Nannerch), 50/96; SJ141689; NP 108
Trefedwyn (township in Caerwys), 50/87; SJ136746; NP 108
Trefeglwys (parish), 54/131-135; NP 127, 128
Trefeiliw (township in Llanrhaeadr-ym-Mochnant [Llanrhaiadr ym Mochnant]), 49/135; SJ152249; NP 117

Trefeirig (township in Llanbadarn fawr), 46/9; SN700830; NP 127
Treffgarne (Great Trefgarn, Trefgarn) (parish), 55/54; SM951239; NP 138
Treffrith (township in Ysceifiog), 50/89; SJ135710; NP 108
Treffynnon (parish), 50/26-34; NP 108
Treffynnon, 50/33; NP 108
Trefgarn (parish), 55/54; NP 138
Trefilan (parish), 46/58; SN547587; NP 140
Treflach (township in Oswestry), 31/106; SJ270257; NP 118
Treflan (Trefllan) (township in Kerry [Llanfihangel-yng-Ngheri]), 54/170; SO130899; NP 128
Treflis (hamlet in Llangamarch), 45/29; SN920480; NP 140, 141
Trefllan, 54/170; NP 128
Treflyn (township in Llanidloes), 54/138; SN987887; NP 128
Treflys (Tref-llys) (parish), 48/45; SH535380; NP 116
Trefnamlechen (township in Pool), 54/70; SJ219088; NP 117
Trefnanney (township in Meifod), 54/38; SJ218157; NP 117
Trefnant (division in Alberbury Upper Quarter township in Alberbury), 31/309; SJ302102; NP 118
Trefoileu (township in Llanrhaeadr-ym-Mochnant [Llanrhaiadr ym Mochnant]), 49/138; SJ154232; NP 117
Trefonen (Trefonnen) (township in Oswestry), 31/105; SJ249255; NP 117
Trefonnen, 31/105; NP 117
Trefor (division in Llangollen), 49/105A; SJ233434; NP 108
Trefor-clawdd (Trefardclawdd) (township in Oswestry), 31/104; SJ261277; NP 117
Trefriw (parish), 48/16; SH778632; NP 107
Trefyddbychain (township in Llandegla), 49/48; SJ218508; NP 108
Trefynwy (parish), 53/17; NP 142
Tregaian (Tregayan) (parish), 44/40; SH463800; NP 106
Tregare (parish), 53/23; SO420107; NP 142, 155
Tregavethan (extra-parochial), 6/135; SW777479; NP 190
Tregayan (parish), 44/40; NP 106
Tregony (Tregoney, Tregony, St James) (parish), 6/149; SW925449; NP 190
Tregoyd and Felindre, 45/3
Tregoyd and Velindre (Tregoyd and Felindre) (township in Glasbury), 45/3; SO200360; NP 141
Tregynon (parish), 54/109; NP 117, 128
Trehelig (township in Pool), 54/67; SJ218034; NP 117
Trelan (township in Whitford), 50/38; SJ143779; NP 108
Trelan Isaf (township in Ysceifiog), 50/94; SJ154708; NP 108
Trelawnyd (parish), 50/50-51; NP 108
Treleach-ar-Bettws (parish), 47/44; NP 139
Trelech (parish), 47/44; NP 139
Trelech-ar-Bettws (Treleach-ar-Bettws, Trelech) (parish), 47/44; SN292276; NP 139
Trellech (Trellock, Trelleck) (hamlet in Trellech), 53/57; SO500040; NP 155
Trellech (Trellock, Trelleck) (parish), 53/57-59; NP 155
Trellech Grange (Trelleck Grange) (hamlet in Trellech), 53/59; SO489019; NP 155
Trellech Town (Trellock Town, Trelleck Town) (hamlet in Trellech), 53/58; SO500054; NP 155
Trelleck (parish), 53/57-59; NP 155
Trelleck Grange, 53/59; NP 155
Trelleck Town, 53/58; NP 155
Trelleck, 53/57; NP 155
Trellewelyn (township in Rhuddlan), 50/59; SJ026807; NP 108
Trellock (parish), 53/57-59; NP 155
Trellock Town, 53/58; NP 155
Trellock, 53/57; NP 155
Trellynian (township in Cilcain), 50/104; SJ182697; NP 108
Trelogan (township in Llanasa), 50/44; SJ127806; NP 108
Trelydan (Trebydan) (township in Guilsfield [Cegidfa]), 54/81; SJ226099; NP 117
Trelystan (township in Worthen), 54/95; SJ266041; NP 117, 118
Tremain (parish), 46/98; SN228492; NP 139
Tremaine (Tremayne) (parish), 6/13; SX230900; NP 174, 186
Tremeirchion (parish), 50/79-83; NP 108

Tremostyn (township in Whitford), 50/41; SJ130790; NP 108
Trench (township in Ellesmere), 31/69; SJ394374; NP 118
Treneglos (parish), 6/15; SX203880; NP 174, 186
Trenholme (division in Ingleby Arncliffe township in Arncliffe), 42/314; NZ439028; NP 91
Trenholme (division in township of Whorlton in Whorlton), 42/313; NZ446026; NP 91
Trent (parish), 32/393; ST596193; NP 166, 177, 178
Trentham (parish), 33/64; NP 110, 119
Trentham (township in Trentham), 33/66; SJ868408; NP 119
Trentishoe (parish), 9/5; SS634476; NP 163
Treopert (parish), 55/35; SM903333; NP 138
Trepenal, 31/119; NP 118
Treprennal (Trepenal) (township in Llanymynech), 31/119; SJ283218; NP 118
Trerdre (township in Caerwys), 50/88; SJ128727; NP 108
Tresco (district in Isles of Scilly), 6/219; SV893149; NP 189
Tresham and Kilcott (tithing in Hawkesbury), 13/340D; ST790890; NP 156
Tresmeer (parish), 6/14; SX235879; NP 186
Treswell (parish), 28/54; SK790795; NP 104
Tretire with Michaelchurch (parish), 15/238; SO518248; NP 142
Tretower (township in Llanfihangel Cwm-du), 45/82D; SO190210; NP 141
Treuddyn (Tryddyn) (township in Mold), 50/116; SJ250570; NP 108
Trevalga (parish), 6/22B; SX093890; NP 185, 186
Treverward (parochial division in Clun), 31/388-395; NP 128, 129
Trevethin (Trevethin with Pontypool) (parish), 53/67; SO265050; NP 154, 155
Treville (parish), 15/191; SO434328; NP 142
Trevor Issa (township in Llangollen), 49/106; SJ262427; NP 108
Trevor Uchaf (Trevor Ucha) (township in Llangollen), 49/110; SJ232424; NP 108
Trewaelod (township in Llanasa), 50/46; SJ116839; NP 108
Trewalchmai (parish), 44/44; SH398754; NP 106
Trewarlett (district in Lezant), 6/58B; SX330801; NP 186
Trewen (Trewenn) (parish), 6/38; SX261839; NP 186
Trewern (township in Buttington), 54/91; SJ272118; NP 117, 118
Trewern and Gwaithla (township in Llanfihangel-nant-Melan), 56/27; SO211568; NP 128
Trewick (township in Bolam), 27/387; NZ111802; NP 77
Trewythen (township in Llandinam), 54/153; SO003902; NP 128
Treyford (parish), 36/13; SU824182; NP 181
Trimdon (parish), 11/98; NZ375343; NP 85
Trimingham (parish), 25/43; NP 126
Trimley St Martin (parish), 34/454; TM265368; NP 150
Trimley St Mary (parish), 34/453; TM279361; NP 150
Trimmingham (Trimingham) (parish), 25/43; TG279388; NP 126
Tring (parish), 16/145; SP919124; NP 146, 159
Trinity (division in St Mary Newington), 35/8A; TQ324794; NP 170
Trinity (Goodramgate) (Holy Trinity Goodramgate) (parish), 43/11; SE605520; NP 97/1
Trinity (Kings Court) (Holy Trinity, Kings Court) (parish), 43/9; SE605519; NP 97/1
Trinity (Micklegate) (Holy Trinity Micklegate) (parish), 43/27, 48; NP 97/1
Trinity (Micklegate) (Holy Trinity Micklegate) (township), 43/27; SE596512; NP 97/1
Trinity Ward (division in parish and township of Holy Tinity Kingston upon Hull), 41/331; TA099106; NP 99/1
Trinity, Forest of Dean (parish), 13/151-154; NP 143, 156
Tritlington (township in Hebburn parochial chapelry), 27/305; NZ202925; NP 78
Troedyraur (parish), 46/91; SN318457; NP 139
Troston (parish), 34/120; TL896727; NP 136
Trostrey (parish), 53/51; SO370047; NP 155
Trotterscliffe (parish), 19/80; NP 171
Trottiscliffe (Trotterscliffe) (parish), 19/80; TQ644603; NP 171
Trotton (parish), 36/12, 341; NP 181
Trotton (Trotton cum Tuxlith) (division in Trotton), 36/12; SU825254; NP 181

Trough (township in Stapleton), 7/8; NY482748; NP 76
Troughend (Troughend Ward) (township in Elsdon), 27/237; NY800970; NP 70, 77
Troutbeck (township in Windermere), 38/81; NY415055; NP 83, 89
Troutsdale (township in Brompton), 42/417; SE890920; NP 92, 93
Trowbridge (division in Trowbridge), 39/148; ST861582; NP 156
Trowell (parish), 28/246; SK494401; NP 121
Trowle (tithing in Great Bradford), 39/155; ST833590; NP 166
Trowse (parish), 25/411; NP 126
Trowse Millgate, Carrow and Bracondale (hamlet in Trowse), 25/412; TG241074; NP 126/1
Trowse Newton (hamlet in Trowse), 25/411; TG253070; NP 126
Trull (parish), 32/423; ST200219; NP 177
Trumfleet (division in township of and parish of Kirk Sandall), 43/941B; SE602119; NP 103
Trumpington (parish), 4/105; TL448550; NP 135, 148
Trunch (parish), 25/52; TG286351; NP 126
Truro (St Marys Truro, Truro, St Mary) (parish), 6/137; SW825450
Trusham (parish), 9/401; SX854822; NP 176
Trusley (parish), 8/257; SK256363; NP 120
Trusthorpe (parish), 22/308; TF502821; NP 105
Tryddyn, 50/116; NP 108
Trysull (Trysull and Seisdon) (parish), 33/327; SO845945; NP 130
Tubney (parish), 2/23; SU440995; NP 158
Tuddenham (Tuddenham St Martin) (parish), 34/427; TM183487; NP 150
Tuddenham (Tuddenham St Mary) (parish), 34/207; TL740718; NP 135, 136
Tuddenham St Martin (parish), 34/427; NP 150
Tuddenham St Mary (parish), 34/207; TL740718; NP 135, 136
Tudeley (Tudely) (parish), 19/309; TQ629448; NP 171
Tudhoe (township in Brancepeth), 11/141; NZ263355; NP 85
Tudweiliog (Tydweiliog) (parish), 48/63; SH240373; NP 115
Tuffley (hamlet in St Mary de Lode), 13/195; SO831151; NP 143
Tufton (parish), 14/93; SU468454; NP 168
Tugby (parish), 21/279-280; NP 122, 133
Tugby (township in Tugby), 21/279; SK760010; NP 122, 133
Tugford (parish), 31/500; SO549876; NP 129
Tughall (township in Bamburgh), 27/101; NU213266; NP 71
Tumby (division in Kirkby on Bain), 22/452A; TF252600; NP 114
Tumby (township in Kirkby on Bain), 22/452A-B; NP 114
Tumby - Wildmore Fen (division in Kirkby on Bain), 22/452B; TF262568; NP 114
Tunbridge Wells (division in Tonbridge), 19/207; TQ588400; NP 171
Tunstall (division in township of Stranton in Seaton Carew), 11/251; NZ489322; NP 85
Tunstall (township in Bishop Wearmouth), 11/78; NZ390537; NP 78
Tunstall (parish), 19/164; TQ897614; NP 172
Tunstall (Tunstal) (parish), 20/75-78; NP 89, 90
Tunstall (Tunstal) (township in Tunstall), 20/77; SD615739; NP 89
Tunstall (parish), 25/393; TG425085; NP 126
Tunstall (township in Adbaston), 33/160; SJ772278; NP 119
Tunstall (township in Wolstanton), 33/17H; SJ858518; NP 110
Tunstall (parish), 34/371; TM375550; NP 150
Tunstall (parish), 41/416; TA305317; NP 99
Tunstall (division in township of Little Ayton in Ayton), 42/329; NZ527121; NP 85, 86
Tunstall (township in Catterick), 42/76; SE213961; NP 91
Tunstead (subdivision of Stacksteads division in Newchurch in Rossendale township in Whalley), 20/281; SD854223; NP 95
Tunstead (parish), 25/238; TG306226; NP 126
Tunworth (parish), 14/333; SU675488; NP 168, 169
Tupholme (parish), 22/364; TF149697; NP 113
Tupsley (township in Hampton Bishop), 15/136; SO535395; NP 142
Tupton (township in North Wingfield), 8/129; SK398657; NP 111, 112

Tur Langton (township in Church Langton), 21/310; SP714948; NP 133
Turkdean (parish), 13/219; SP110175; NP 144
Turleyholes Moss (division in township of Sowerby in Halifax), 43/565; SE984218; NP 95, 96
Turnastone (parish), 15/214; SO349365; NP 142
Turnditch (township in Duffield), 8/186; SK297463; NP 111
Turners Puddle (parish), 10/205; SY827918; NP 178
Turnhill (extra-parochial), 42/435; SE750988; NP 92
Turnworth (parish), 10/87; ST815080; NP 178
Turton (township in Bolton le Moors), 20/392; SD719152; NP 101
Turvey (parish), 1/29; SP951521; NP 146, 147
Turville (parish), 3/210; SU750910; NP 159
Turweston (parish), 3/10; SP607734; NP 145
Tushingham cum Grindley (township in Malpas), 5/331; SJ527453; NP 109, 118
Tusmore (parish), 29/68; SP565307; NP 145
Tutbury (division in Tutbury), 33/209A; SK205275; NP 120
Tutbury (parish), 33/209A-C; NP 120
Tutnall and Cobley (township in Tardebigge), 40/1; SP013704; NP 131
Tuttington (parish), 25/212; TG229271; NP 126
Tuxford (parish), 28/70; SK736709; NP 112
Tweedmouth (parish), 27/2-5; NP 64
Tweedmouth (township in Tweedmouth), 27/2; NT994516; NP 64
Twemlow (township in Sandbach), 5/212; SJ781688; NP 110
Twerton (Twiverton) (parish), 32/43; ST726641; NP 156, 166
Twickenham (parish), 24/127; TQ159735; NP 170
Twigmoor (township in Manton), 22/39; SE935065; NP 104
Twigworth (hamlet in Gloucester, St Mary de Lode), 13/174; SO845221; NP 143
Twineham (parish), 36/103; TQ252199; NP 182
Twinstead (Twinsted) (parish), 12/92; TL857363; NP 149
Twisel, 27/16; NP 64
Twistleton (division in township of Ingleton in Bentham), 43/273; SD720770; NP 89, 90
Twiston (township in Whalley), 20/259; SD813438; NP 95
Twitchen (parish), 9/76; SS783306; NP 163, 164
Twiverton (parish), 32/43; NP 156, 166
Twizell (township in Morpeth), 27/420; NZ165785; NP 78
Twizell (Twisel) (township in Norham), 27/16; NT905426; NP 64
Twycross (parish), 21/156; SK343043; NP 121
Twyford (hamlet in Twyford), 3/111; SP666259; NP 145, 146
Twyford (hamlet in Colsterworth), 22/690; SK943233; NP 122
Twyford (parish), 3/111-113; NP 145, 146
Twyford (parish), 14/232; SU490244; NP 168
Twyford (parish), 25/195; TG015245; NP 125
Twyford (township in Twyford), 21/264; SK730100; NP 122
Twyford (township in West Felton), 31/99; SJ343266; NP 118
Twyford Abbey (extra-parochial), 24/99; TQ194832; NP 160
Twyford and Stenson (township in Barrow upon Trent), 8/263; SK325297; NP 121
Twyning (parish), 13/125; SO896369; NP 143
Twywell (parish), 26/141; SP949782; NP 133, 134
Tyberton (Tibberton) (parish), 15/216; SO380390; NP 142
Tybroughton (township in Hanmer), 50/142; SJ466423; NP 118
Tyd St Mary (parish), 22/784; NP 124
Tydd St Giles (Tid St Giles) (parish), 4/1; TF426160; NP 124
Tydd St Mary (Tyd St Mary) (parish), 22/784; TF423180; NP 124
Tyddewi (parish), 55/62-67; NP 138
Tydweiliog (parish), 48/63
Tyersall (division in Pudsey township in Calverley), 43/515; SE200325; NP 96
Tyldesley (division in township of Tyldesley with Shakerley in Leigh), 20/576; SD704019; NP 101
Tyldesley with Shakerley (township in Leigh), 20/576; NP 101
Tyneham (parish), 10/302; SY880817; NP 178
Tynemouth (parish), 27/386, 492-499; NP 78
Tynemouth (township in Tynemouth), 27/499; NZ361699; NP 78
Tyringham with Filgrave (Tyringham-cum-Filgrave) (parish), 3/43; SP869480; NP 146

Tyrley, 33/158A; NP 119
Tysoe (parish), 37/281; SP345450; NP 145
Tythby (parish), 28/221; NP 121, 122
Tythby, 28/221
Tythegston (parish), 51/97; NP 153
Tythegston Higher (hamlet in Tythegston), 51/97; SS852822; NP 153
Tythegston Lower (Tythegstone Lower) (hamlet in Tythegston), 51/96; SS857794; NP 153
Tytherington (Titherington) (township in Prestbury), 5/45; SJ917755; NP 101, 110
Tytherington (hamlet in Tytherington), 13/364A; ST665875; NP 156
Tytherington (parish), 13/364A-B; NP 156
Tytherton Calloes (parish), 39/85; NP 157
Tytherton Kellaway (parish) (Calloes, Kelloweys, Tytherton Kellaways, Tytherton Kelways, Tytherton Calloes), 39/85; ST950757; NP 157
Tytherton Kellaways (parish), 39/85; NP 157
Tytherton Kelways (parish), 39/85; NP 157
Tytherton Lucas (tithing in Chippenham), 39/82; ST953741; NP 157
Tythrop (division in Kingsey), 29/263; SP740070; NP 159
Tywardreath (parish), 6/95; SX090542; NP 185, 186, 190
Tywyn (Towyn) (parish), 52/37; SH645005; NP 127

U

Ubbeston (parish), 34/167; TM320722; NP 137
Ubley (parish), 32/72; ST525573; NP 165
Uchan-dre (Uchanyndre) (township in Llanbadarn fawr), 46/15; SN606809; NP 127
Uchanyndre, 46/15; NP 127
Ucheldre (township in Bettws), 54/107; SO134980; NP 128
Uckerby (township in Catterick), 42/86; NZ249026; NP 91
Uckfield (parish), 36/129; TQ470211; NP 183
Uckington (hamlet in Elmstone Hardwicke), 13/56; SO921253; NP 143
Udimore (parish), 36/152; TQ883190; NP 184
Uffculme (parish), 9/149; SS083117; NP 164, 176
Uffington (parish), 2/21, 100-101; NP 158
Uffington (township in Uffington), 2/100; SU310880; NP 158
Uffington (division in Deeping Fen of Uffington township in Uffington), 22/723C; TF150157; NP 123
Uffington (division of Uffington township in Uffington), 22/723A; TF060085; NP 123
Uffington (parish), 22/723A-D; NP 123
Uffington (township in Uffington), 22/723A, 723C; NP 123
Uffington (parish), 31/243; SJ592092; NP 118
Ufford (parish), 26/26-27; NP 123
Ufford (parish), 34/383; TM293523; NP 150
Ufford (tithing in Crediton), 9/211F; (not located); NP 175
Ufford (township in Ufford), 26/26; TF097039; NP 123
Ufton (parish), 37/231; SP379621; NP 132
Ufton Nervet (Ufton) (parish), 2/170; SU625682; NP 158
Ugborough (parish), 9/368; SX673570; NP 187
Uggeshall (parish), 34/66; TM458808; NP 137
Ugglebarnby (township in Whitby), 42/385; NZ881066; NP 86, 92
Ughill (sub-division in Bradfield division in township of Bradfield in Ecclesfield), 43/807; SK250905; NP 102
Ugley (parish), 12/72; TL518285; NP 148
Ugthorpe (township in Lythe), 42/375; NZ795108; NP 86
Ulceby (Ouseby) (parish), 22/53; TA108148; NP 104
Ulceby (parish) (Ulceby with Fotherington otherwise Fordington otherwise Forthington), 22/417; TF421728; NP 114
Ulcombe (Ulcomb) (parish), 19/297; TQ853487; NP 172
Uldale (parish), 7/216; NY267349; NP 82
Uley (parish), 13/328; ST788981; NP 156
Ulgham (parochial chapelry in Morpeth), 27/309-311; NP 71, 78
Ulgham (township in Ulgham parochial chapelry in Morpeth), 27/310; NZ230925; NP 78
Ulgham Grange (township in Ulgham parochial chapelry in Morpeth), 27/311; NZ245923; NP 71, 78

Ullenhill (chapelry in Wootton Wawen), 37/179; SP131676; NP 131
Ulleskelf (township in Kirkby Wharfe), 43/440; SE521389; NP 97
Ullesthorpe (township in Claybrooke), 21/236; SP510872; NP 132
Ulley (division of Ulley township in Aston with Aughton), 43/895; SK466868; NP 103
Ulley (division of Ulley township in Treeton), 43/894; SK469879; NP 103
Ulley (township in Treeton and Aston with Aughton), 43/894-895; NP 103
Ullingswick (parish), 15/149; SO591500; NP 142, 143
Ullock (township in Dean), 7/262; NY083245; NP 82
Ulnaby (division in township of High Coniscliffe in Coniscliffe), 11/316; NZ228171; NP 85
Ulnes Walton (township in Croston), 20/345; SD509201; NP 94
Ulpha (township in Millom), 7/320; SD212972; NP 82, 88
Ulrome (division of Ulrome township in Barmston), 41/353; TA174580; NP 99
Ulrome (division of Ulrome township in Skipsea), 41/354; TA165570; NP 99
Ulrome (township in Barmston and Skipsea), 41/354
Ulshaw Bridge (division in township of East Witton Without in East Witton), 42/162; SE150873; NP 91
Ulting (parish), 12/238; TL810091; NP 162
Ulverscroft (extra-parochial), 21/31; SK495124; NP 121
Ulverston (Ulverstone) (parish), 20/9-22; NP 88, 89
Ulverston (Ulverstone) (township in Ulverston), 20/22; SD293773; NP 89
Uncleby (division in parish and township of Kirby Underdale), 41/138A; SE813593; NP 92, 98
Underbarrow and Bradleyfield (township in Kendal), 38/94; SD481924; NP 89
Undermillbeck (township in Windermere), 38/83; SD414959; NP 89
Underskiddaw (township in Crosthwaite), 7/280; NY269258; NP 82
Undivided moor (common to Coldsnouth and Thompson's Walls, Grey's Forest and Westnewton in Kirknewton), 27/60B; NT868292; NP 70
Undivided moor, common to townships of High Barton, Sockbridge and Low Winder (township in Barton), 38/26A; NY470217; NP 83
Undivided Land (common to Llanrhidian, Penmaen, Nicholaston, Penrice, Reynoldston), 51/29; SS509891; NP 153
Undy (parish), 53/147; ST439871; NP 155
Unerigg, 7/246
Unstone (township in Dronfield), 8/46; SK373776; NP 111
Unsworth (division in township of Pilkington in Prestwich), 20/497; SD824069; NP 101
Unthank (township in Skelton), 7/160; NY446364; NP 83
Unthank (township in Alnham), 27/163; NU014112; NP 71
Uny Lelant (parish), 6/202; SW525375; NP 189
Up Cerne (parish), 10/100; ST648033; NP 178
Up Eldon (extra-parochial), 14/214; NP 168
Up Exe (tithing in Rewe), 9/221; SX943024; NP 176
Up Hatherley (parish), 13/206; SO920200; NP 143
Up Marden (parish), 36/234; SU783134; NP 181
Up Nately (parish), 14/108; SU702517; NP 169
Up-Waltham (parish), 36/226; NP 181
Upavon (Uphaven) (parish), 39/221; SU132544; NP 167
Upchurch (parish), 19/94; TQ852689; NP 172
Upham (parish), 14/55; SU533207; NP 168
Uphaven (parish), 39/221; NP 167
Uphill (parish), 32/157; ST323590; NP 165
Upholland (township in Wigan), 20/589; SD515050; NP 100
Upleadon (parish), 13/124; SO762268; NP 143
Upleatham (parish), 42/343-344; NP 86
Upleatham (township in Upleatham), 42/343; NZ632195; NP 86
Uplowman (parish), 9/135A-B; NP 164
Uplowman (tithing in Uplowman), 9/135A; ST012166; NP 164
Uplyme (parish), 9/292; SY320935; NP 177
Upminster (parish), 12/328; TQ560868; NP 161

Upottery (parish), 9/143; ST208083; NP 164, 176, 177
Upper Allithwaite (township in Cartmel), 20/59A; SD410830; NP 89
Upper and Nether Hesket (township in Hesket in the Forest), 7/165; NY480560; NP 83
Upper and Lower Crasswell, 15/208; NP 141, 142
Upper and Lower Cotton, 33/109; NP 111, 120
Upper and Lower Broniarth (township in Guilsfield [Cegidfa]), 54/77; SJ190135; NP 117
Upper Arley (Arley) (parish), 33/342; SO770805; NP 130
Upper Beeding (division in Upper Beeding tithing in Beeding), 36/110; TQ210104; NP 182
Upper Beeding (tithing in Beeding), 36/110, 112; NP 170, 182
Upper Benefield (hamlet in Benefield), 26/55A; SP979893; NP 133, 134
Upper Boddington (Upper Bodington) (parish), 26/266; SP477537; NP 132, 145
Upper Bodington (parish), 26/266; NP 132, 145
Upper Broughton (parish), 28/296; SK672259; NP 121, 122
Upper Bulingham (parish), 15/186; NP 142
Upper Claife (division in township of Claife in Hawkshead), 20/44; SD278996; NP 89
Upper Clatford (parish), 14/88; SU348428; NP 168
Upper Cound (township in Cound), 31/444; SJ552042; NP 118
Upper Cwmvoy (hamlet in Cwmvoy), 53/3; SO282280; NP 141, 142
Upper Cwmyoy, 53/3; NP 141, 142
Upper Denton (township in Upper Denton), 7/56; NY619652; NP 76
Upper Division, 45/54A
Upper division (in Pool), 54/66-67; NP 117
Upper Dunsforth with Branton (Upper Dunsforth cum Branton Green) (township in Aldborough), 43/128; SE438630; NP 91
Upper Dyffrin Honddu (hamlet in Merthyr Cynog), 45/34B; SO005405; NP 141
Upper Dylais, 51/16; NP 153
Upper Easington (division in township of Easington in Slaidburn), 43/280; SD735570; NP 90, 95
Upper Ecclesfield (division in township of Ecclesfield in Ecclesfield), 43/792; SK346932; NP 102
Upper Eldon (Up Eldon) (extra-parochial), 14/214; SU366278; NP 168
Upper Elkstone (township in Alstonfield), 33/86; SK052586; NP 111
Upper Gravenhurst (parish), 1/103; TL113362; NP 147
Upper Grindleton (division in township of Grindleton in Mitton), 43/294; SD751514; NP 95
Upper Gwnnws (township in Gwnnws), 46/35; SN758682; NP 127
Upper Hallam (township in Sheffield), 43/826; SK280850; NP 102, 111
Upper Hamlet of Llanrhidian, 51/27; NP 153
Upper Hanley (parish), 40/91; NP 130
Upper Hardres (Great Hardres) (parish), 19/288; TR154498; NP 173
Upper Harpton, 56/24; NP 128
Upper Hayton (township in Stanton Lacy), 31/524; SO515811; NP 129
Upper Helmsley (Over Helmsley) (parish), 42/666; SE695568; NP 97
Upper Heyford (parish), 26/255; SP669593; NP 132
Upper Heyford (parish), 29/84; SP504261; NP 145
Upper Holker (township in Cartmel), 20/61; SD353707; NP 89
Upper Inglesham (hamlet in Inglesham), 39/3; SU201962; NP 157
Upper Kempley (township in Ightfield), 31/27; SJ598360; NP 118, 119
Upper Kinsham (parish), 15/16; SO358657; NP 129
Upper Lambourn (tithing in Lambourn), 2/107D; SU307810; NP 158
Upper Langwith (parish), 8/65; SK509680; NP 112
Upper Lea (division in Lea), 15/264; SO658213; NP 143
Upper Letcombe (parish), 2/95; NP 158

222

Upper Linthwaite (division in township of Linthwaite in Almondbury), 43/762; SE083132; NP 102
Upper Llanbadarn Y-Greuddyn (Upper Llanbadarn-y-Croyddin) (township in Llanbadarn fawr), 46/17; SN675790; NP 127
Upper Llanbadarn-y-Croyddin, 46/17; NP 127
Upper Llanfihangel-y-creuddyn (Upper Llanfihangle y Croddyn, Upper Llanfihangel-y-Croyddin, Eglwys Newydd) (township in Llanfihangel-y-creuddyn), 46/20; SN790780; NP 127
Upper Llanfihangel-y-Croyddin, 46/20
Upper Llanfihangle y Croddyn, 46/20
Upper Llanilar (township in Llanilar), 46/22; SN660730; NP 127
Upper Llangunllo (Upper Llangynllo) (township in Llangunllo), 56/10B; SO200730; NP 128
Upper Llangynllo, 56/10B
Upper Lledrod (township in Llanfihangel-lledrod), 46/31; SN685660; NP 127
Upper Lowick (division in township of Lowick in Ulverston), 20/17C; SD276839; NP 88
Upper Millom, 7/322; NP 88
Upper Mitton (township in Hartlebury), 40/31; SO813723; P 130
Upper Myddfai (hamlet in Myddfai), 47/19B; SN800300; NP 140
Upper Norncott (township in Stoke St Milborough), 31/514B; SO567861; NP 129
Upper Parks, 31/511; NP 129
Upper Penn (township in Penn), 33/329; SO898949; NP 130
Upper Poppleton (division of township in St Mary Bishophill (Junior)), 43/43; SE548536; NP 97
Upper Poppleton (parish), 43/49-50; NP 97
Upper Poppleton (township in Nether Poppleton), 43/50; SE557542; NP 97
Upper Poppleton (township in St Mary Bishophill (Junior) and in Nether Poppleton), 43/43, 50.
Upper Quarter (township in Hartington), 8/108; SK030710; NP 111
Upper Radbourn (extra-parochial), 37/249; SP448581; NP 132
Upper Rawcliffe (division in township of in St Michaels on Wyre), 20/158; SD448419; NP 94
Upper Rawcliffe with Tarnacre (township in St Michaels on Wyre), 20/157-158; NP 94
Upper Santon, 22/42; NP 104
Upper Sapey (parish), 15/224; SO687642; NP 130
Upper Shire Green and Wincobank (division in township of Ecclesfield in Ecclesfield), 43/797; SK379916; NP 102
Upper Shuckburgh (parish), 37/239; SP501615; NP 132
Upper Slaughter (parish), 13/99; SP151232; NP 144
Upper Soothill (division in township of Soothill in Dewsbury), 43/582; SE262232; NP 96
Upper Stondon (parish), 1/101; TL152352; NP 147
Upper Stonebeck, 43/205; NP 90, 91
Upper Swell (parish), 13/80; SP162271; NP 144
Upper Swinford (township in Old Swinford), 40/24; SO900830; NP 130
Upper Sylfaen (township in Castle Caereinion), 54/62; SJ177070; NP 117
Upper Tockington (hamlet in Olveston), 13/362; ST609861; NP 156
Upper Trefnant (township in Castle Caereinion), 54/64; SJ179046; NP 117
Upper Treverward (township in Clun), 31/390; SO273783; NP 128, 129
Upper Vaenor (Upper Vainor) (township in Llanbadarn fawr), 46/11A; SN617821; NP 127
Upper Vainor, 46/11A; NP 127
Upper Waltham (Up-Waltham) (parish), 36/226; SU941135; NP 181
Upper Whitley (division in township of Upper Whitley in Kirkheaton), 43/723; SE214159; NP 102
Upper Winchendon (parish), 3/154; SP742139; NP 146
Upperby (township in St Cuthbert [Carlisle]), 7/83; NY409537; NP 76
Upperthong (township in Almondbury), 43/774; SE080055; NP 102

Uppingham (parish), 30/54; SP860998; NP 122, 133
Uppington (parish), 31/234; SJ592092; NP 118, 119
Uppington (township in Alberbury), 54/90; SJ285100; NP 117, 118
Upsall (township in South Kilvington), 42/533; SE452862; NP 91
Upsall (Upsil) (township in Ormesby), 42/333; NZ560160; NP 86
Upshire (hamlet in Waltham Holy Cross), 12/268; TQ405995; NP 161
Upsil, 42/333; NP 86
Upton (chapelry in Castor), 26/25; TF105008; NP 123, 134
Upton (hamlet in Blewbury), 2/78; SU509862; NP 158
Upton (hamlet in Nash), 55/145; SN020050; NP 151
Upton (Overchurch) (parish), 5/460; SJ269884; NP 100
Upton (parish), 17/42; TL171788; NP 134
Upton (parish), 22/136-137; NP 104
Upton (parish), 25/395; TG393127; NP 126
Upton (parish), 26/236; SP714605; NP 133
Upton (parish), 28/155; SK733546; NP 112
Upton (parish), 32/287; ST000301; NP 164
Upton (township in Prestbury), 5/44; SJ902748; NP 101, 110
Upton (township in St Mary on the Hill, Chester), 5/525; SJ411693; NP 109
Upton (township in Little Hereford), 15/23; SO551662; NP 129
Upton (township in Sibson), 21/153; SP365995; NP 121, 132
Upton (township in Upton), 22/137; SK868871; NP 104
Upton (township in Badsworth), 43/663; SE478140; NP 103
Upton and Signet (Upton and Signett) (hamlet in Burford), 29/158; SP238118; NP 144, 157
Upton Bishop (parish), 15/248; SO648276; NP 143
Upton Cressett (parish), 31/494; SO651921; NP 130
Upton cum Chalvey (parish), 3/231; SU979795; NP 159
Upton Grey (Upton Gray) (parish), 14/109; SU702480; NP 169
Upton Hellions (parish), 9/213; SS846027; NP 176
Upton Lovell (parish), 39/241; ST958424; NP 167
Upton Magna (parish), 31/237; SJ552131; NP 118
Upton Noble (parish), 32/190; ST713393; NP 166
Upton Pyne (parish), 9/251; SX611975; NP 176
Upton Scudamore (parish), 39/233; ST864476; NP 166
Upton Snodsbury (parish), 40/146; SO944540; NP 130, 143
Upton St Leonard (parish), 13/197; SO867141; NP 143
Upton upon Severn (parish), 40/227; SO831399; NP 143
Upton Warren (parish), 40/54; SO910685; NP 130
Upton Weaver (district in Cullompton), 9/152B; ST050054; NP 176
Upway (parish), 10/255; NP 178
Upwell (division in Upwell township in Upwell), 4/11; TL485980; NP 124, 135
Upwell (division in Upwell township in Upwell), 25/696; TL530990; NP 124, 135
Upwell (parish), 4/11-12, 25/696-697; NP 124, 135
Upwell (township in Upwell), 4/11, 25/696; NP 124, 135
Upwey (Upway) (parish), 10/255; SY661853; NP 178
Upwood (parish), 17/25; TL256832; NP 134
Urchfont (parish), 39/209A-211; NP 167
Urchfont (tithing in Urchfont), 39/210; SU043563; NP 167
Urmston (township in Flixton), 20/539; SJ773944; NP 101
Urpeth (township in Chester le Street), 11/42; NZ244540; NP 78
Urswick (parish), 20/35-40; NP 88, 89
Ushlawrcoed (hamlet in Bedwellty), 53/69B; SO130030; NP 154
Usk [Brynbuga] (hamlet in Usk [Brynbuga]), 53/64A; SO380005; NP 155
Usk [Brynbuga] (parish), 53-63-64B; NP 155
Usselby (parish), 22/159; TF097938; NP 104
Usworth (township in Washington), 11/18, 21, 22; NP 78
Utkinton (township in Tarporley), 5/397; SJ558650; NP 109
Uton (tithing in Crediton), 9/211C; (not located); NP 175
Utterby (parish), 22/194; TF312939; NP 105
Uttoxter (parish), 33/119-121B; NP 120
Uttoxter (township in Uttoxter), 33/120; SK092336; NP 120
Uttoxter Woodlands (township in Uttoxter), 33/121B; SK090305; NP 120
Uwch y mynydd isaf (township in Hope), 50/121; SJ282575; NP 108, 109

Uwch y mynydd uchaf (township in Hope), 50/122; SJ260555; NP 108, 109
Uwchglan (township in Whitford), 50/36; SJ156763; NP 108
Uwchlan (township in Cwm), 50/66; SJ082772; NP 108
Uwchlaw-r-coed (township in Llanwnog), 54/159; SN995965; NP 128
Uwchygarreg (township in Machynlleth), 54/130; SN780940; NP 127
Uxbridge (township in Hillingdon), 24/111; TQ054842; NP 160
Uzmaston (parish), 55/84; SM980159; NP 151

V

Vainor (township in Llansantffraid-Cwmdeuddwr), 56/31D; SN990700; NP 128
Van (hamlet in Bedwas), 51/132; ST169873; NP 154
Vange (parish), 12/402; TQ731878; NP 161
Varchoel (township in Guilsfield [Cegidfa]), 54/75; SJ232122; NP 117
Vaultershome (tithing in Maker), 6/113; SX439515; NP 187
Vaynor (Faenor) (parish), 45/73; SO035115; NP 141, 154
Vaynor-Glare (township in Glascwm), 56/42B; SO150530; NP 128, 141
Venn and Vern, 15/144
Venn Ottery (parish), 9/284B; SY072912; NP 176
Vennington (township in Westbury), 31/315; SJ332097; NP 118
Venny-fach (township in Brecon, St John the Evangelist), 45/48; SO012297; NP 141
Vernham's Dean (parish), 14/68; SU350570; NP 168
Verwick (parish), 46/100
Verwig (parish), 46/100
Verwood (Fairwood) (division in Cranborne), 10/70; SU095076; NP 179
Veryan (parish), 6/150; SW932410; NP 190
Virginstow (parish), 9/198; SX383932; NP 174, 175, 186
Virley (parish), 12/226; TL945149; NP 149
Vivod (township in Llangollen), 49/113; SJ192420; NP 108, 117
Vo (hamlet in Llanddetty), 45/74B; SO110210; NP 141
Vorlan (hamlet in Maenclochog), 55/42; SN084263; NP 138
Vowchurch (parish), 15/215; SO376363; NP 142
Vro (township in Llangynidr), 45/75B; SO130130; NP 141, 154

W

Waberthwaite (parish), 7/314; SD117940; NP 88
Waborne, (parish), 25/31; NP 125
Wabourne (parish), 25/31; NP 125
Wackerfield (township in Staindrop), 11/288; NZ154219; NP 85
Wacton (Wacton Magna et Parva) (parish), 25/644; TM184908; NP 137
Wacton (township in Bromyard), 15/92; SO619572; NP 130
Waddesdon (Waddesden) (parish), 3/144-146; NP 146
Waddesdon (Waddesden) (township in Waddesdon), 3/144; SP755166; NP 146
Waddingham (parish), 22/115; TK993965; NP 104
Waddington (parish), 22/522; SK980650; NP 113
Waddington (township in Mitton), 43/291; SD724448; NP 95
Waddingworth (parish), 22/363; TF181711; NP 113
Wadenhoe (parish), 26/76; TL0040839; NP 134
Wadhurst (parish), 36/46; TQ630320; NP 171, 183
Wadsley (division in township of Ecclesfield in Ecclesfield), 43/802; SK323902; NP 102
Wadsley Bridge (division in township of Ecclesfield in Ecclesfield), 43/801; SK333912; NP 102
Wadsworth (township in Halifax), 43/557; SD970320; NP 95, 96
Wadworth (parish), 43/922; SK575970; NP 103
Waghen (parish), 41/341-342; NP 99
Waghen, 41/341; NP 99
Wainfleet All Saints (parish), 22/480; TF473597; NP 114
Wainfleet St Mary (parish), 22/479; TF498576; NP 114
Wainfleet St Thomas (Northolme) (parish), 22/481; TF499593; NP 114
Waingraves (division in Pentrich), 8/195B; SK414490; NP 112
Waitby (township in Kirkby Stephen), 38/66; NY752072; NP 84, 90

Waithe (parish), 22/174; TA282005; NP 105
Waithwith Grange (division in township of Hudswell in Easby), 42/93; SE151981; NP 91
Wakefield (parish), 43/599-608; NP 96, 102
Wakefield (township in Wakefield), 43/606-608; NP 96, 102
Wakeley (Wakely) (extra-parochial), 16/55; TL341268; NP 147, 148
Wakely (extra-parochial), 16/55; NP 147, 148
Wakerley (parish), 26/35; TF953986; NP 123, 133, 134
Wakes Colne (parish), 12/124; TL896301; NP 149
Walberswick (parish), 34/157; TM481748; NP 137
Walberton (parish), 36/282; SU968059; NP 181
Walborough (township in Holy Cross Pershore), 40/183B; SO901483; NP 143
Walbottle (township in Newburn), 27/540; NZ177676; NP 78
Walbridge, 27/455; NP 77
Walburn (township in Downholme), 42/98; SE120960; NP 91
Walby (township in Crosby upon Eden), 7/24; NY436604; NP 76
Walcot (division in Walcot), 32/34B; ST758659; NP 156/1
Walcot (hamlet in Billinghay), 22/571; TF153573; NP 113
Walcot (parish), 22/665; TF061349; NP 123
Walcot (parish), 32/34A-D; NP 156, 156/1
Walcot (township in Chirbury), 31/355; SO262998; NP 117, 128
Walcot (township in Wellington), 31/217; SJ592121; NP 118
Walcot (Walcott) (hamlet in Charlbury), 29/131; SP344196; NP 145
Walcot cum Membris (township in Holy Cross Pershore), 40/183A; SO930485; NP 143
Walcott (Walcot) (parish), 25/220; TG361318; NP 126
Walcott, 29/131; NP 145
Walden Stubbs (township in Womersley), 43/638; SE555170; NP 97
Waldershare (division in Cornilo Hundred in Waldershare), 19/351; TR307484; NP 173
Waldershare (division in Eastry Hundred in Waldershare), 19/350; TR296488; NP 173
Waldershare (parish), 19/350-351; NP 173
Walditch (parish), 10/233; SY483927; NP 177
Waldridge (township in Chester le Street), 11/45; NZ254499; NP 78
Waldringfield (parish), 34/443; TM278445; NP 150
Waldron (parish), 36/132; TQ558195; NP 183
Wales (division in township of Wales in Wales), 43/897; SK469830; NP 103/1
Wales (division in township of Wales in Treeton), 43/898; SK475830; NP 103/1
Wales (division in township of Wales in Harthill), 43/899; SK497832; NP 103/1
Wales (parish), 43/897; SK469830; NP 103/1
Wales (township in Wales, Treeton and Harthill), 43/897-899; NP 103/1
Walesby (parish), 22/205-206; NP 104, 105
Walesby (parish), 28/75; SK683706; NP 112
Walesby and Otby (hamlet in Walesby), 22/206; TF135925; NP 105
Walford (parish), 15/255; SO601203; NP 142
Walford, Letton and Newton (township in Leintwardine), 15/11; SO381707; NP 129
Walgherton (township in Wybunbury), 5/263; SJ693488; NP 110
Walgrave (parish), 26/196; SP806723; NP 133
Walker (township in Longbenton), 27/506; NZ290650; NP 78
Walkeringham (parish), 28/9; SK768927; NP 103, 104
Walkerith (township in Gainsborough), 22/129; SK792930; NP 104
Walkern (parish), 16/28; TL292262; NP 147
Walkhampton (parish), 9/356; SX565725; NP 175, 187
Walkingham Hill (township division in township of Walkingham Hill with Occaney), 43/144; SE344618; NP 91
Walkingham Hill with Occaney (township in South Stainley), 43/143-144; NP 91
Walkington (parish), 41/219-220; NP 98, 99
Walkmill (township in Warkworth), 27/235; NU227044; NP 71
Wall (township in St John Lee), 27/448; NY923697; NP 77

224

Wall (township in St Michael), 33/264; SK100067; NP 120
Wallasea Island (extra-parochial), 12/372; TQ939946; NP 162
Wallasey (parish), 5/444-446; NP 100
Wallasey (township in Wallasey), 5/446; SJ285925; NP 100
Wallerscote (Wallerscoat) (township in Weaverham), 5/167; SJ638737; NP 110
Wallingford Castle Precincts (extra-parochial), 2/68; SU610897; NP 158, 158/3
Wallingford, St Leonard (parish), 2/70; SU599891; NP 158, 158/3
Wallingford, St Mary More (parish), 2/67; SU603898; NP 158, 158/3
Wallingford, St Peter (parish), 2/69; SU606893; NP 158, 158/3
Wallington (parish), 16/10; TL290340; NP 147
Wallington (hamlet in Wallington cum Thorpland), 25/320; TF633076; NP 124
Wallington cum Thorpland (parish), 25/319-320; NP 124
Wallington Demesne (township in Hartburn), 27/345; NZ027848; NP 77
Wallington (hamlet in Beddington), 35/50; TQ288648; NP 170
Wallingwells (extra-parochial), 28/26; SK567842; NP 103
Wallop (township in Westbury), 31/318; SJ318072; NP 118
Wallridge (Walbridge, Walridge) (township in Stamfordham), 27/455; NZ053771; NP 77
Wallsend (parish), 27/500-502; NP 78
Wallsend (township in Wallsend), 27/500; NZ304669; NP 78
Walltown (township in Haltwhistle), 27/586; NY700673; NP 76
Walmer (parish), 19/357; TR374504; NP 173
Walmersley (district in division in township of Walmersley-cum-Shuttleworth in Bury), 20/420; SD808146; NP 101
Walmersley (district in division in township of Walmersley-cum-Shuttleworth in Bury), 20/421; SD790150; NP 101
Walmersley (division in township of Walmersley-cum-Shuttleworth in Bury), 20/420-421; NP 101
Walmersley-cum-Shuttleworth (township in Bury), 20/419A-421; NP 95, 101
Walmsgate (parish), 22/327; TF363780; NP 105
Walpole (parish), 34/152; TM371739; NP 137
Walpole St Andrew (division in Marshland fen in Walpole St Andrew), 25/295B; TF547072; NP 124
Walpole St Andrew (division in Walpole St Andrew), 25/295A; TF508190; NP 124
Walpole St Andrew (parish), 25/295A-B; NP 124
Walpole St Peter (division in Marshland fen in Walpole St Peter), 25/296B;
Walpole St Peter (division in Walpole St Peter), 25/296A; TF515138; NP 124
Walpole St Peter (parish), 25/296A-B; NP 124
Walridge, 27/455; NP 77
Walsall (borough in Walsall), 33/299; SP016983; NP 131
Walsall (parish), 33/294-299; NP 120
Walsall and Shefield (township in Walsall), 33/294; SK043033; NP 120
Walsall Foreign (division in Walsall), 33/296; SP002998; NP 119, 120, 130, 131
Walsden (division in township of Todmorden and Walsden in Rochdale), 20/460; SD929213
Walsgrave on Sowe (parish), 37/143; SP383817; NP 132
Walsham le Willows (parish), 34/131; TM010712; NP 136
Walshford (division in township of Great Ribston and Walshford in Hunsingore), 43/108; SE418533; NP 96
Walsoken (division in Marshland fen in Walsoken), 25/298B; TF532073; NP 124
Walsoken (division in Walsoken), 25/298A; TF495095; NP 124
Walsoken (parish), 25/298A-B; TF532073; NP 124
Walsworth (hamlet in Hitchin), 16/36; TL200303; NP 147
Walterstone (parish), 15/223; SO340250; NP 142
Waltham (parish), 19/336; TR115484; NP 172, 173
Waltham (parish), 22/88; TA270037; NP 105
Waltham Abbey (township in Waltham Holy Cross), 12/265; TL379004; NP 161
Waltham Cross (hamlet in Cheshunt), 16/119; TL353012; NP 160, 161
Waltham Holy Cross (parish), 12/265-268; NP 161
Waltham on the Wolds (parish), 21/99; SK800245; NP 122
Waltham St Lawrence (Waltham St Laurence) (parish), 2/214; SU832753; NP 159, 169
Walthamstow (parish), 12/309; TQ372898; NP 161
Walton (division in township of Walton in Walton), 43/75; SE446480; NP 97
Walton (parish), 3/62; SP898365; NP 146
Walton (parish), 7/34-36; NP 76
Walton (parish), 12/162; NP 150
Walton (parish), 32/180; ST462362; NP 165
Walton (parish), 34/452; TM292355; NP 150
Walton (parish), 43/74-76; NP 97
Walton (township in Chesterfield), 8/77; SK357691; NP 111
Walton (township in Paston), 26/8; TF168018; NP 123
Walton (township in Eccleshall), 33/131; SJ859276; NP 119
Walton (township in Stone), 33/52; SJ895328; NP 119
Walton (township in Walton), 43/74-75; NP 97
Walton (township in Sandal Magna), 43/691; SE364165; NP 102
Walton (Walton D'Eville and Walton Maudit) (hamlet in Wellesbourne Hastings), 37/274; SP291526; NP 144, 145
Walton and Womaston (township in Old Radnor), 56/22; SO261605; NP 128
Walton Cardiff (parish), 13/50; SO905323; NP 143
Walton D'Eville and Walton Maudit, 37/274; NP 144, 145
Walton East (parish), 55/52; SN024231; NP 138
Walton in Knaptoft (township in Knaptoft), 21/335B; SP610870; NP 132
Walton Inferior (Lower Walton) (township in Runcorn), 5/147; SJ599861; NP 100
Walton le Soken (Walton, Walton on the Naze) (parish), 1 2/162; TM253221; NP 150
Walton Moss (area in Walton), 7/36; NY509669; NP 76
Walton on the Naze (parish), 12/162; NP 150
Walton on the Hill (parish), 20/668-677; NP 100
Walton on the Hill (township in Walton on the Hill), 20/672; SJ368945; NP 100
Walton on the Wolds (parish), 21/44; SK600198; NP 121
Walton on the Hill (parish), 35/116; TQ220550; NP 170
Walton Superior (Higher Walton) (township in Runcorn), 5/148; SJ599849; NP 100
Walton upon Trent (parish), 8/322; SK223174; NP 120
Walton upon Thames (parish), 35/65; NP 170
Walton West (parish), 55/94; SM871134; NP 151
Walton, Prescott and Bagginswood (township in Stottesden), 31/572; SO672812; NP 130
Walton-in-Gordano (parish), 32/9; ST425735; NP 155
Walton-le-Dale (township in Blackburn), 20/323; SD572268; NP 94, 95
Walton-on-Thames (Walton upon Thames) (parish), 35/65; TQ108650; NP 170
Walwen (township in Holywell), 50/30; SJ206764; NP 108
Walwick (township in Warden), 27/608; NY897706; NP 77
Walwins Castle (parish), 55/162; NP 151
Walworth (township in Heighington), 11/282; NZ236192; NP 85
Walwyn's Castle (Walwins Castle, Walwyn Castle) (parish), 55/162; SM881115; NP 151
Wambrook (parish), 10/110; ST282081; NP 177
Wampool (township in Aikton), 7/121; NY247558; NP 75
Wanborough (extra-parochial), 35/143; SU934489; NP 169
Wanborough (parish), 39/98; SU215824; NP 157
Wandsworth (All Saints, Wandsworth) (parish), 35/25; TQ259738; NP 170
Wangford (hamlet in Wangford), 34/64; TM470789; NP 137
Wangford (parish), 34/64-65; NP 137
Wangford (Wangford near Brandon) (parish), 34/108; TL762832; NP 135, 136
Wanlip (parish), 21/57; SK591109; NP 121
Wansford (parish), 26/366; TF080000; NP 123, 134
Wansford (township in Nafferton), 41/273; TA063563; NP 99
Wanstead (parish), 12/320; TQ410880; NP 161
Wanstrow (parish), 32/189; ST707419; NP 166
Wantage (parish), 2/88-91; NP 158

Wantage (township in Wantage), 2/88; SU400855; NP 158
Wantisden (parish), 34/379; TM361527; NP 150
Wapley and Codrington (Wapley cum Codrington) (parish), 13/393; ST724791; NP 156
Wapley, 42/365; NP 86
Waplington (township in Barmby Moor), 41/92; SE772466; NP 97
Wappenbury (parish), 37/159-160; NP 132
Wappenbury (township in Wappenbury), 37/159; SP379699; NP 132
Wappenham (hamlet in Wappenham), 26/322; SP631454; NP 145
Wappenham (parish), 26/322-324; NP 145
Wapping (parish), 24/59; NP 160/1
Warbleton (parish), 36/136; TQ629179; NP 183
Warblington (parish), 14/283; SU744071; NP 181
Warborough (parish), 29/296; SU601934; NP 158
Warboys (parish), 17/69; TL334817; NP 134, 135
Warbstow (parish), 6/16; SX199911; NP 174, 186
Warburton (parish), 5/107; SJ710895; NP 101
Warcop (parish), 38/50; NY750170; NP 83
Warden (parish), 19/101; TR019718; NP 172
Warden (parish), 27/595-608; NP 77
Warden Law (township in Houghton-le-Spring), 11/69; NZ369503; NP 78
Wardington (chapelry in Cropredy), 29/12; SP490456; NP 145
Wardle (division in township of Wuerdale in Rochdale), 20/458; SD912172; NP 95, 101
Wardle (township in Bunbury), 5/306; SJ603572; NP 109
Wardleworth (township in Rochdale), 20/456; SD901147; NP 101
Wardley (parish), 30/60; SK839003; NP 122, 133
Wardlow (division in Wardlow township in Hope), 8/29; SK179745; NP 111
Wardlow (division of Wardlow township in Bakewell), 8/90; SK183748; NP 111
Wardlow (township in Hope and Bakewell), 8/29, 90; NP 111
Wardour (parish), 39/331; ST944276; NP 166, 167
Ware (parish), 16/77; TL375155; NP 147, 148
Wareham, Holy Trinity (parish), 10/287-288; NP 178, 179
Wareham, Lady St Mary (parish), 10/285A-B; NP 178
Wareham, St Martin (parish), 10/286A-B; NP 178, 179
Warehorne (parish), 19/416; TQ989331; NP 172, 184
Warenford (township in Bamburgh), 27/90; NU134281; NP 71
Warenton (township in Bamburgh), 27/91; NU102307; NP 64, 71
Waresley (parish), 17/114; TL242549; NP 134
Warfield (parish), 2/219; SU877715; NP 159, 169
Wargrave (parish), 2/205; SU796803; NP 159
Warham All Saints (parish), 25/20; TF953431; NP 125
Warham St Mary (Warham St Mary Magdalen and St Mary the Virgin) (parish), 25/19; TF940428; NP 125
Wark (parish), 27/362-365; NP 76, 77
Wark (township in Wark), 27/365; NY848777; NP 77
Wark (Wark and Sunnilaws) (township in Carham), 27/31; NT827377; NP 64
Wark and Sunnilaws, 27/31; NP 64
Warkleigh (parish), 9/70; SS644227; NP 163
Warksburn (township in Wark), 27/364; NY780750; NP 76, 7
Warkton (parish), 26/138; SP903801; NP 133
Warkworth (hamlet in Warkworth), 26/358; SP487398; NP 145
Warkworth (parish), 26/358-360; NP 145
Warkworth (parish), 27/218-235; NP 71
Warkworth (township in Warkworth), 27/223; NU243053; NP 71
Warlaby (township in Ainderby Steeple), 42/220; SE349906; NP 91
Warleggan (Warleggon) (parish), 6/53; SX155685; NP 186
Warley (township in Halifax), 43/554-555; NP 96
Warley - Lower Division (division in township of Warley in Halifax), 43/555; SE050250; NP 96
Warley - Upper Division (division in township of Warley in Halifax), 43/554;SE035295; NP 96
Warley Salop (township in Halesowen), 40/16; SP008856; NP 130, 131

Warley Wighorn (township in Halesowen), 40/17; SO999836; NP 130
Warlingham (parish), 35/97; TQ354586; NP 170, 171
Warmfield (parish), 43/677; NP 96, 102
Warmfield with Heath (township in Warmfield), 43/677; SE368205; NP 96, 102
Warmingham (parish), 5/224-227; NP 110
Warmingham (township in Warmingham), 5/224; SJ707605; NP 110
Warminghurst (parish), 36/89; TQ120171; NP 182
Warmington (parish), 26/61; TL083911; NP 134
Warmington (parish), 37/269; SP405482; NP 145
Warminster (parish), 39/236; ST874455; NP 166
Warmsworth (parish), 43/883; SE547005; NP 103
Warmwell (parish), 10/272; SY749861; NP 178
Warndon (parish), 40/128; SO885565; NP 130, 143
Warnford (parish), 14/237; SU616236; NP 168
Warnham (parish), 36/35; TQ151343; NP 170, 182
Warningcamp (tithing in Lyminster), 36/291; TQ043071; NP 181, 182
Warpsgrove (parish), 29/285; SU647982; NP 158
Warren (parish), 55/157; SR935967; NP 151
Warren House (extra-parochial), 34/459; TM195428; NP 150
Warrington (hamlet in Olney), 3/31; SP897446; NP 133, 146
Warrington (division in township of Warrington in Warrington), 20/618; SJ615882; NP 100, 101
Warrington (parish), 20/611-619; NP 100, 101
Warrington, (township in Warrington), 20/617-619; NP 100, 101
Warsill (township in Ripon), 43/158; SE229653; NP 91
Warslow (township in Alstonfield), 33/88; SK080590; NP 111
Warter (parish), 41/189; SE865513; NP 98
Warthill (parish), 42/670; NP 97
Warthill (Warthill Copyhold) (township in Warthill), 42/670; SE674553; NP 97
Warthill (Warthill Freehold) (township in Holtby), 42/669; SE674556; NP 97
Wartling (parish), 36/181; TQ666110; NP 183
Wartnaby (chapelry in Rothley), 21/54; SK711226; NP 122
Warton (parish), 20/65-71; NP 89
Warton (township in Kirkham), 20/199; SD405282; NP 94
Warton (township in Rothbury), 27/250; NU009029; NP 71
Warton (township in Polesworth), 37/17; SK282038; NP 120, 121
Warton with Lindeth (township in Warton), 20/68; SD487724; NP 89
Warwick (parish), 7/41-42; NP 76
Warwick (township in Warwick), 7/41; NY456579; NP 76
Warwick Bridge (township in Wetheral), 7/47; NY482562; NP 76
Warwick, St Mary (parish), 37/168; SP279646; NP 131, 132
Warwick, St Nicholas (parish), 37/167; SP297648; NP 131, 132
Wasdale (township in St Bees), 7/292; NY195090; NP 82, 88
Washbrook (parish), 34/479; TM107425; NP 149, 150
Washfield (parish), 9/165; SS931169; NP 164
Washford Pyne (parish), 9/173; SS811109; NP 163, 164, 175, 176
Washingborough (parish), 22/519-520; NP 113
Washingborough (township in Washingborough), 22/519; TF018702; NP 113
Washingley (parish), 17/15; TL130890; NP 134
Washington (parish), 11/18-22; NP 78
Washington (township in Washington), 11/20; NZ304566; NP 78
Washington (parish), 36/91; TQ128132; NP 182
Wasing (parish), 2/157; SU575642; NP 158, 168
Wasperton (parish), 37/222; SP278595; NP 131, 132
Wass (division of Wass township in Coxwold), 42/548; SE555810; NP 92
Wass (division of Wass township in Coxwold), 42/550; SE567776; NP 92
Wass (division of Wass township in Kilburn), 42/547; SE555795; NP 92
Wass (township in Kilburn and Coxwold), 42/547-548, 550
Watchfield (township in Shrivenham), 2/40; SU243911; NP 157
Water Eaton (hamlet in Bletchley), 3/67; SP871322; NP 146

Water Eaton (hamlet in Kidlington), 29/201; SP511119; NP 145
Water Eaton (township in Penkridge), 33/239; SJ903109; NP 119
Water Eaton (hamlet in Eysey), 39/10B; SU136936; NP 157
Water Fulford (township in Fulford), 41/64; SE606479; NP 97
Water Newton (parish), 17/2; TL105960; NP 134
Water Orton (township in Aston), 37/41; SP180910; NP 131
Water Stratford (parish), 3/13; SP656353; NP 145
Waterbeach (parish), 4/51; TL507681; NP 135
Watercombe (extra-parochial), 10/273; SY760860; NP 178
Waterden (parish), 25/81; TF889362; NP 125
Waterfall (parish), 33/76, 92C; NP 111
Waterfall (township in Waterfall), 33/76; SK081516; NP 111
Watergall (extra-parochial), 37/252; SP423551; NP 132, 145
Waterhead (division of Waterhead in Lanercost), 7/29; NY615680; NP 76
Waterhead (township in Lanercost), 7/30; NY622662; NP 76
Wateringbury (parish), 19/214; TQ685536; NP 171
Waterlooville (Waterloo) (extra-parochial), 14/280; SU683101; NP 180, 181
Watermillock (township or chapelry in Greystoke), 7/204; NY407213; NP 83
Waterperry (division in Waterperry), 29/236A; SP622077; NP 145, 158
Waterperry (parish), 29/236A-B; NP 145, 158
Waters Upton (parish), 31/174; SJ639199; NP 119
Waterstock (parish), 29/237; SP638058; NP 158
Watford (hamlet in Watford), 16/132A; TQ111965; NP 160
Watford (parish), 16/132A-C; NP 160
Watford (parish), 26/184; SP608696; NP 132
Wath (parish), 42/231-234; NP 91
Wath (township in Hovingham), 42/630; SE676743; NP 92
Wath (township in Wath), 42/232; SE325775; NP 91
Wath upon Dearne (parish), 43/851-855; NP 102, 103
Wath upon Dearne (township in Wath upon Dearne), 43/852; SE431008; NP 103
Watlass Moor (intermixed in Snape division and in Well township in Well), 42/180; SE240834; NP 91
Watlington (parish), 25/316; TF620110; NP 124
Watlington (parish), 29/281; SU700930; NP 158, 159
Watnall Cantelupe (township in Greasley), 28/175; SK505455; NP 112, 121
Watnall Chaworth (township in Greasley), 28/174; SK410470; NP 112
Wattisfield (parish), 34/130; TM009738; NP 136
Wattisham (parish), 34/352; TM011519; NP 149
Wattlefield (division in Wymondham), 25/652; TM112982; NP 136
Wattlesborough (division in Alberbury Lower Quarter township in Alberbury), 31/303; SJ352127; NP 118
Watton (parish), 25/540; TF921008; NP 125, 136
Watton (parish), 41/282; TA031501; NP 98, 99
Watton (Watton at Stone) (parish), 16/80; TL302190; NP 147
Wauldby (township in Elloughton), 41/213; SE971298; NP 98
Waupley (Wapley) (division in township of Loftus in Loftus), 42/365; NZ730140; NP 86
Wavendon (parish), 3/59-61; NP 146
Wavendon (Wavenden) (division in Wavendon), 3/59; SP818371; NP 146
Wavendon Heath (division in Wavendon), 3/61; SP930345; NP 146
Waverley (extra-parochial), 35/151; SU863453; NP 169
Waverton (parish), 5/374-376; NP 109
Waverton (township in Waverton), 5/374; SJ463637; NP 109
Waverton (township in Wigton), 7/133; NY225475; NP 75, 82
Wavertree (township in Childwall), 20/653; SJ398888; NP 100
Wawne (Wawn, Waghen) (parish), 41/341-342; NP 99
Wawne (Wawn, Waghen) (township in Wawne), 41/341; TA096372; NP 99
Waxham (division in Waxham), 25/227; TG442351; NP 126
Waxham (parish), 25/227-228; NP 126
Waxholme (township in Owthorne), 41/418; TA320301; NP 99
Waybourne (parish), 25/31; NP 125

Wayford (parish), 32/484; ST401062; NP 177
Weald (division in Sevenoaks), 19/191; TQ528510; NP 171
Weald (hamlet in Eynesbury), 17/110; TL232599; NP 134
Weald (hamlet in Bampton), 29/168; SP310020; NP 158
Wear Gifford, 9/63; NP 163
Weardley (township in Harewood), 43/399; SE299446; NP 96
Weare (division in Weare), 32/163; ST408524; NP 165
Weare (parish), 32/163-164; NP 165
Weare Gifford (Wear Gifford) (parish), 9/63; SS481229; NP 163
Weasenham All Saints (parish), 25/183; TF852212; NP 125
Weasenham St Peter (parish), 25/184; TF846227; NP 125
Weaveley (Weiveley) (hamlet in Tackley), 29/105; SP459188; NP 145
Weaver (township in Middlewich), 5/206; SJ662639; NP 110
Weaverham (parish), 5/165-170; NP 100, 101, 109, 110
Weaverham Lordship (township in Weaverham), 5/170; SJ617737; NP 101, 110
Weaverham Township (township in Whitegate), 5/171; SJ609704; NP 109, 110
Weaverthorpe (parish), 41/177; SE972705; NP 93
Weaverthorpe (township in Weaverthorpe), 41/177; NP 93
Webheath (township in Tardebigge), 40/51; SP008669; NP 130, 131
Weddicar (Wheddicar, Weddiker~) (township in St Bees), 7/294; NY018184; NP 82
Weddiker, 7/294
Weddington (parish), 37/64; SP368938; NP 132
Wedgwood (township in Wolstanton), 33/17F; SJ872538; NP 110
Wedhampton (tithing in Urchfont), 39/209B; SU060573; NP 167
Wedmore (parish), 32/176; ST438480; NP 165
Wednesbury (parish), 33/305; SO987953; NP 130, 131
Wednesfield (township in Wolverhampton), 33/318; SO958006; NP 119, 130
Weedon (hamlet in Hardwick), 3/141; SP819176; NP 146
Weedon Bec (Weedon Beck) (parish), 26/258; SP621582; NP 132
Weedon Lois (Weedon Loys) (parish), 26/326; SP596466; NP 145
Weeford (parish), 33/289-291; NP 120
Weeford (township in Weeford), 33/289; SK133030; NP 120
Week St Lawrence (parish), 32/63; NP 165
Week St Mary (parish), 6/9; SX240972; NP 174
Weeke (Week) (parish), 14/208; SU466302; NP 168
Weekley (parish), 26/137; SP882812; NP 133
Weel (township in St John Beverley), 41/294; TA067399; NP 99
Weeley (parish), 12/159; TM152217; NP 150
Weelsby (township in Clee), 22/80; TA279076; NP 105
Weethley (parish), 37/191; SP053554; NP 131, 144
Weeting (Weeting All Saints) (division in Weeting), 25/704; TL780900; NP 136
Weeton (township in Welwick), 41/443; TA355201; NP 99, 105
Weeton (township in Harewood), 43/400; SE280470; NP 96
Weeton with Preese (township in Kirkham), 20/186; SD378353; NP 94
Weetslade (Weetsleet) (township in Longbenton), 27/503; NZ250730; NP 78
Weetsleet, 27/503; NP 78
Weetwood (township in Chatton), 27/75; NU015287; NP 71
Weiveley, 29/105; NP 145
Welbeck (extra-parochial), 28/31; SK575740; NP 103, 112
Welborne (parish), 25/501; TG068099; NP 125
Welbourn (parish), 22/547; SK977537; NP 113
Welburn (township in Bulmer), 42/647; SE728678; NP 92
Welburn (township in Kirkdale), 42/477; SE680842; NP 92
Welbury (parish), 42/269; NZ400012; NP 91
Welby (chapelry in Melton Mowbray), 21/72; SK726211; NP 122
Welby (parish), 22/623; SK974382; NP 123
Welch Whittle (township in Standish), 20/377; SD546147; NP 100
Welchampton (parish), 31/75; NP 118
Welches Dam (parish), 4/19; TL452858; NP 135
Welcombe (Welcomb) (parish), 9/52; SS238182; NP 174

227

Welford (hamlet in Welford), 13/9; SP145509; NP 144
Welford (parish), 2/136; SU409727; NP 158
Welford (parish), 13/9, 37/213; NP 144
Welford (parish), 26/114; SP639798; NP 132
Welham (division in parish and township of Norton), 41/125; SE782697; NP 92
Welham (parish), 21/309; SP759926; NP 133
Well (hamlet in Well), 22/415; TF443738; NP 105, 114
Well (parish), 42/177-180; NP 91
Well (township in Well), 42/177; SE264814; NP 91
Well), 22/415-416; NP 105, 114
Welland (parish), 40/228; SO797403; NP 143
Wellesborough, 21/154; NP 121
Wellesbourne Hastings (hamlet in Wellesbourne Hastings), 37/219; SP286555; NP 131, 132, 145
Wellesbourne Hastings (parish), 37/219, 274; SP286555; NP 131, 132, 144, 145
Wellesbourne Mountford (parish), 37/218; SP266548; NP 131, 144, 145
Wellhaugh (township in Falstone), 27/217; NY650850; NP 76, 77
Wellingborough (parish), 26/208; SP886682; NP 133
Wellingham (parish), 25/185; TF871222; NP 125
Wellingore (parish), 22/548; SK980555; NP 113
Wellington (parish), 15/106; SO494484; NP 142
Wellington (parish), 31/216; NP 118, 119
Wellington (township in Wellington), 31/216; SJ665115; NP 119
Wellington (parish), 32/426; ST135194; NP 164
Wellow (extra-parochial), 22/79B; TA271088; NP 105
Wellow (parish), 14/223; SU314204; NP 168, 180
Wellow (parish), 28/101; SK677663; NP 112
Wellow (parish), 32/89; ST733578; NP 166
Wells next the Sea (parish), 25/18; TF916432; NP 125
Wellsborough (Wellesborough) (division of Wellsborough and Temple Hall hamlet in Sibson), 21/154; SK370023; NP 121
Wellsborough and Temple Hall (hamlet in Sibson), 21/154-155; NP 121
Welney (chapelry in Upwell), 25/697, 4/12; NP 135
Welney (division in Welney chapelry in Upwell), 4/12; TL519935; NP 135
Welney (division in Upwell), 25/697; TL540950; NP 135
Welsh Bicknor (parish), 15/266; SO585179; NP 142, 143
Welsh Frankton (Frankton) (township in Whittington), 31/88; SJ362321; NP 118
Welsh Newton (parish), 15/236; SO507180; NP 142
Welsh St Donats (parish), 51/124; ST030760; NP 154
Welsh Town (township in Pool), 54/71; SJ228078; NP 117
Welshampton (Welchampton) (parish), 31/75; SJ440359; NP 118
Welshpool, 54/68; NP 117
Welton (parish), 22/250; TF009802; NP 104
Welton (parish), 26/279; SP583663; NP 132
Welton (parish), 41/214-215; NP 98
Welton (township in Ovingham), 27/553; NZ069675; NP 77
Welton (township in Welton), 41/214; SE965275; NP 98
Welton le Marsh (Welton, Boothby and Hanby) (parish), 22/421; TF474689; NP 114
Welton le Wold (Welton on the Wold) (parish), 22/278; TF273870; NP 105
Welton on the Wold (parish), 22/278; NP 105
Welton, 22/421; NP 114
Welwick (parish), 41/440; NP 99, 105
Welwick (township in Welwick), 41/442; TA343210; NP 99, 105
Welwick Thorpe (township in Welwick), 41/440; TA329217; NP 99, 105
Welwyn (parish), 16/85; TL240170; NP 147
Wem (parish), 31/40-49; NP 118
Wem (township in Wem), 31/45; SJ508288; NP 118
Wembdon (parish), 32/263; ST284393; NP 165
Wembury (parish), 9/467; SX519496; NP 187
Wemworthy (parish), 9/120; SS673112; NP 163, 175
Wendens Ambo (parish), 12/19; TL510364; NP 148
Wendlebury (parish), 29/109; SP562192; NP 145

Wendling (parish), 25/335; TF931136; NP 12
Wendon Lofts (parish), 12/10; TL460380; NP 148
Wendover (parish), 3/180; SP881065; NP 159
Wendron (district in Wendron), 6/172; SW694322; NP 189, 190
Wendron (parish), 6/172-173; NP 189, 190
Wendy (parish), 4/166; TL326471; NP 147
Wenham Magna (parish), 34/508; NP 149
Wenhaston (Winhaston and Mells) (parish), 34/154; TM402759; NP 137
Wenlock, 31/452; NP 119, 129, 130
Wennington (parish), 12/422; TQ537807; NP 161, 171
Wennington (hamlet in Abbots Ripton), 17/62B; TL235795; NP 134
Wennington (township in Melling), 20/81; SD624705; NP 89
Wensley (parish), 42/146-150; NP 90, 91
Wensley (township in Wensley), 42/146; SE085900; NP 90, 91
Wensley and Snitterton (township in Darley), 8/120; SK266610; NP 111
Wentnor (parish), 31/345; SO388940; NP 129
Wentworth (division in Wentworth), 4/32A; TL482787; NP 135
Wentworth (parish), 4/32A-C; NP 135
Wentworth - Byall Fen (division in Wentworth), 4/32C; TL466783; NP 135
Wentworth - The Wash (division in Wentworth), 4/32B; TL462841; NP 135
Wentworth (township in Wath upon Dearne), 43/854; SK399975; NP 102, 103
Wenvoe (parish), 51/152; ST124720; NP 154
Weobley (parish), 15/58-59; SO394512; NP 142
Weobley (township in Weobley), 15/58; SO394512; NP 142
Wepre (township in Northop), 50/20; SJ274687; NP 108
Wereham (parish), 25/526; TF679014; NP 124, 135
Werneth (township in Stockport), 5/12; SJ955963; NP 101
Werrington (parish), 9/345; SX332886; NP 174, 186
Werrington (township in Paston), 26/9; TF167037; NP 123
Wervin (township in St Oswald Chester), 5/498; SJ425722; NP 109
Wessington (township in Crich), 8/145; SK374573; NP 111
West Acklam (Acklam in Cleveland) (parish and township), 42/282; NZ480178; NP 85
West Acomb (Acomb) (township in St John Lee), 27/451B; NY938667; NP 77
West Acre (parish), 25/280; TF782170; NP 125
West Adderbury (township in Adderbury), 29/34; SP469343; NP 145
West Allen High (township in Allendale), 27/588; NY785500; NP 77, 84
West Allen Low (township in Allendale), 27/589; NY 784525; NP 77, 84
West Allington (parish), 22/614; SK847402; NP 122
West Alvington (parish), 9/493; SX723428; NP 187
West Anstey (parish), 9/78; SS846280; NP 164
West Ardsley (parish), 43/589; SE277259; NP 96
West Ashby (division in West Ashby), 22/382A; TF263732; NP 114
West Ashby (parish), 22/382A-B; TF263732; NP 114
West Ashby - Wildmore Fen (division in West Ashby), 22/382B; TF259529; NP 114
West Ashton (tithing in Steeple Ashton), 39/145; ST884558; NP 166
West Auckland (township in St Andrew Auckland), 11/197; NZ177256; NP 85
West Ayton (Hutton Bushel) (township in Hutton Buscel), 42/412; SE985851; NP 93
West Bagborough (parish), 32/271; ST165340; NP 164
West Barkwith (parish), 22/344; TF154805; NP 104, 105
West Barming (parish), 19/216; TQ708545; NP 171
West Barsham (parish), 25/110; TF899337; NP 125
West Beckham (parish), 25/33; TG143397; NP 125, 126
West Bergholt (parish), 12/122; TL957282; NP 149
West Bilney (parish), 25/312; TF700150; NP 124
West Blatchington (parish), 36/209; TQ279075; NP 182

West Boldon (division in township of Boldon in Boldon), 11/8A; NZ324606; NP 78
West Bolton (division in township of Carperby cum Thoresby in Aysgarth), 42/138; SD995925; NP 90
West Bradenham (parish), 25/507; TF918091; NP 125
West Bradford (township in Mitton), 43/292; SD738462; NP 95
West Bradley (parish), 32/204; ST557368; NP 165
West Breary (division in township of Arthington in Adel), 43/394; SE261421; NP 96
West Bretton (division of West Bretton township in Sandal Magna), 43/694; SE280142; NP 102
West Bretton (division of West Bretton township in Silkstone), 43/695; SE280130; NP 102
West Bretton (township in Sandal Magna and Silkstone), 43/694-695; NP 102
West Bridgerule, 9/99; NP 174
West Bridgford (West Bridgeford) (parish), 28/257; NP 121
West Bridgford (West Bridgeford) (township in West Bridgford), 28/257; SK588374; NP 121
West Bromwich (parish), 33/304A-B; NP 130, 131
West Bromwich North-East (division in West Bromwich), 33/304B; SP010930; NP 130, 131
West Bromwich South-West (division in West Bromwich), 33/304A; SP000910; NP 130, 131
West Broughton (division in Doveridge township in Doveridge), 8/242B; SK140327; NP 120
West Broughton, 20/2; NP 88
West Brunton (township in Gosforth), 27/508; NZ211704; NP 78
West Buckland (parish), 9/34; SS657322; NP 163
West Buckland (parish), 32/425; ST171198; NP 164
West Burton (parish), 28/40; SK792860; NP 104
West Burton, 42/143; NP 90
West Butterwick (township in Owston), 22/5; SE828052; NP 104
West Camel (parish), 32/370; ST571252; NP 177
West Chadlington (tithing in Charlbury), 29/134; SP317229; NP 145
West Challow (chapelry in Letcombe Regis), 2/94; SU363887; NP 158
West Chelborough (parish), 10/115; ST541051; NP 177
West Chevington (West Chivington) (township in Warkworth), 27/232; NZ230977; NP 71
West Chickerell (parish), 10/262; NP 178
West Chiltington (parish), 36/67; TQ095203; NP 182
West Chinnock (parish), 32/459; ST467135; NP 177
West Chivington, 27/232; NP 71
West Cholderton (parish), 39/262; NP 167
West Cilrhedyn (division in Cilrhedyn), 55/12; SN282334; NP 139
West Clandon (parish), 35/127; TQ045518; NP 169, 170
West Claydon (parish), 3/109; NP 146
West Cliffe (parish), 19/365; TR344444; NP 173
West Coatham (division in township of Kirkleatham in Kirkleatham), 42/341; NZ570230; NP 86
West Coker (parish), 32/472; ST520139; NP 177
West Compton (Compton Abbas) (parish), 10/143; SY561953; NP 177
West Cottingwith (division in township of Thorganby and West Cottingwith in Thorganby), 41/76; SE684427; NP 97
West Cowes (division in Northwood), 18/1B; SZ496964; NP 180
West Cowick (township in Snaith), 43/964C; SE650215; NP 97
West Cranmore (parish), 32/134; ST668433; NP 166
West Creeting (parish), 34/290; NP 136, 149
West Dean (township in St Pauls, Forest of Dean), 13/155-158; NP 142, 143, 155, 156
West Dean (division in West Dean), 14/218; SU266280; NP 167
West Dean (parish), 36/230; SU849141; NP 181
West Dean (division in West Dean tithing in West Dean), 39/364; SU248282; NP 167
West Dean (parish), 14/218, 39/364-365; NP 167
West Dean (tithing in West Dean), 39/364-365; SU248282; NP 167
West Deeping (parish), 22/725; TF119096; NP 123
West Denton (township in Newburn), 27/539; NZ190657; NP 78
West Derby (chapelry in Walton on the Hill), 20/668-669; NP 100
West Derby (division in chapelry of West Derby in township of Walton on the Hill), 20/668; SJ369904; NP 100
West Derby (division in chapelry of West Derby in township of Walton on the Hill), 20/669; SJ400930; NP 100
West Dereham (parish), 25/525; TF662015; NP 124, 135
West Dowlish (parish), 32/453; ST365130; NP 177
West Down (parish), 9/20; SS515423; NP 163
West Drayton (parish), 24/114; TQ061790; NP 160, 170
West Drayton (parish), 28/63; SK702746; NP 103, 112
West Ella (division in West Ella township in Kirk Ella), 41/311; TA012289; NP 99, 99/1
West Ella (township in Kirk Ella and North Ferriby), 41/311, 313; NP 99, 99/1
West Ella (township in North Ferriby), 41/313; TA006293; NP 99, 99/1
West End (hamlet in Loders), 10/228B; SY458950; NP 177
West End (tithing in Worplesden), 35/76C; SU950510; NP 169
West Farlam (township in Farlam), 7/58; NY563583; NP 76
West Farleigh (parish), 19/306; TQ713526; NP 171
West Felton (parish), 31/92; NP 118
West Felton (township in West Felton), 31/96; SJ338251; NP 118
West Fen (extra-parochial), 4/35; TL508824; NP 135
West Fen Chapel Allotment (extra-parochial), 22/467A; TF302564; NP 114
West Firle (parish), 36/323; TQ479076; NP 183
West Firsby (township in Firsby), 22/219; SK985849; NP 104
West Golcar (division in township of Golcar in Huddersfield), 43/755; SE087152; NP 102
West Grimstead (parish), 39/366; SU212270; NP 167
West Grinstead (West Grinsted) (parish), 36/94; TQ176205; NP 182
West Grinton (division in township of Grinton in Grinton), 42/115; SE038983; NP 90
West Hackney (division in St John at Hackney), 24/74; TQ332842; NP 160
West Hackney (division in St John at Hackney), 24/76; TQ338859; NP 160
West Haddesley (township in Birkin), 43/459; SE557268; NP 97
West Haddon (parish), 26/175; SP666680; NP 132, 133
West Hagbourne (West Hagbourn) (division in Hagbourne), 2/80; SU507882; NP 158
West Hall (division in township of Nesfield with Langbar in Ilkley), 43/340; SE086501; NP 96
West Hallam (parish), 8/203; SK438414; NP 121
West Halton (township in West Halton), 22/19; SE905200; NP 98, 104
West Halton (township in Long Preston), 43/244; SD833544; NP 95
West Ham (parish), 12/322-324; NP 161
West Hamlets (township in Stanton Lacy), 31/518; SO480800; NP 129
West Hanney (parish), 2/50-53; SU436936; NP 158
West Hanney (township in West Hanney), 2/50; SU401928; NP 158
West Hanningfield (parish), 12/291; TL731003; NP 161
West Hardwick (township in Wragby), 43/669; SE416186; NP 103
West Harle (township in Kirkwhelpington), 27/374; NY982822; NP 77
West Harling (parish), 25/730; TL958842; NP 136
West Harlsey (township in Osmotherley), 42/507; SE410980; NP 91
West Harnham (parish), 39/359; SU124290; NP 167
West Harptree (parish), 32/75; ST545552; NP 165
West Harroldston, 55/93; NP 151
West Hartford (township in Horton parochial chapelry in Woodhorn), 27/481; NZ251791; NP 78
West Hatch (parish), 32/417; ST287212; NP 177
West Hauxwell (township in Hauxwell), 42/190; SE158943; NP 91
West Heddon (township in Heddon on the Wall), 27/547; NZ122688; NP 77, 78
West Hendred (parish), 2/85; SU449877; NP 158

West Herrington (township in Houghton-le-Spring), 11/56; NZ344532; NP 78
West Heslerton (parish), 41/155-156; NP 93
West Heslerton (township in West Heslerton), 41/155; SE912762; NP 93
West Hoathly (West Hoathley) (parish), 36/59; TQ359322; NP 182, 183
West Horndon (parish), 12/413; TQ628889; NP 161
West Horsley (parish), 35/125; TQ082527; NP 170
West Houses (extra-parochial), 22/471; TF336547; NP 114
West Hyde (hamlet in Luton), 1/125; TL108182; NP 147
West Hythe (parish), 19/422; TR134334; NP 173
West Ilsley (parish), 2/117; SU470825; NP 158
West Ings (area in Kirkdale), 42/475; SE689848; NP 92
West Itchenor (parish), 36/268; SU795008; NP 181
West Keal (division in West Keal), 22/434A; TF360628; NP 114
West Keal (parish), 22/434A-B; NP 114
West Keal (parish), 22/434A-D; NP 114
West Keal - East Fen (division in West Keal), 22/434B; TF368611; NP 114
West Keal - East Fen (division in West Keal), 22/434C; TF369601; NP 114
West Keal - West Fen (division in West Keal), 22/434D; TF332580; NP 114
West Kilrehedyn, 55/12; NP 139
West Kington (parish), 39/75; ST799771; NP 157
West Kirby (parish), 5/451-459; NP 100
West Kirby (township in West Kirby), 5/456; SJ217864; NP 100
West Knighton (parish), 10/252; SY728876; NP 178
West Knoyle (parish), 39/335; ST854326; NP 166
West Langdon (parish), 19/360; TR325472; NP 173
West Langton (township in Church Langton), 21/311; SP710930; NP 133
West Lavington (parish), 36/21; SU891202; NP 181
West Lavington (Bishops Lavington) (parish), 39/224-225; NP 167
West Lavington (Bishops Lavington) (tithing in West Lavington), 39/224; SU004520; NP 167
West Layton (township in Gilling), 42/44; NZ157107; NP 85
West Leake (parish), 28/280; SK528272; NP 121
West Leicester Forest (extra-parochial), 21/176; SK496016; NP 121
West Lexham (parish), 25/277; TF843175; NP 125
West Lilburn (township in Eglingham), 27/131; NU024248; NP 71
West Lilling (division in township of Lillings Ambo in Sheriff Hutton), 42/601; SE647642; NP 92
West Littleton (parish), 13/395; ST762762; NP 156
West Lockinge (hamlet in Wantage), 2/91; SU421877; NP 158
West Looe (district in Talland), 6/118; SX251535; NP 186
West Lulworth (parish), 10/279; SY823812; NP 178
West Lutton (division in township of Luttons Ambo in Weaverthorpe), 41/179; SE934696; NP 93
West Lydford (parish), 32/345; ST564319; NP 165, 177
West Lynn (West Lynn St Peter) (parish), 25/290; TF602189; NP 124
West Maidstone (division in Maidstone), 19/218A; TQ749552; NP 171, 172
West Malling (parish), 19/176; TQ677566; NP 171
West Markham (parish), 28/71; NP 112
West Marton (division in township of Martons Both in Marton), 43/305; SD892505; NP 95
West Matfen (township in Stamfordham), 27/460; NZ031715; NP 77
West Meon (parish), 14/239; SU646246; NP 168, 180
West Mersea (parish), 12/174; TM024142; NP 149
West Molesey (West Moulsey) (parish), 35/64; TQ133683; NP 170
West Monkton (parish), 32/311; ST258276; NP 165, 177
West Moor (common to Barrington, Drayton, Curry Rivel, Kingsbury Episcopi), 32/407; ST405214; NP 177
West Moulsey (parish), 35/64; NP 170
West Ness (township in Stonegrave), 42/623; SE687787; NP 92

West Newton (township in Bromfield), 7/128; NY132438; NP 82
West Newton (parish), 25/95; TF695278; NP 124
West Newton (division in township of West Newton and Burton Constable in Aldborough), 41/381; TA202377; NP 99
West Newton and Burton Constable (township in Aldborough and Swine), 41/381-382; NP 99
West Ogwell (parish), 9/419; SX821701; NP 188
West Orchard (parish), 10/15; ST826166; NP 178
West Overton (township in Overton), 39/166; SU133676; NP 157, 167
West Park (division in St Paul Malmesbury), 39/29; ST915844; NP 156
West Parley (parish), 10/173; SU091008; NP 179
West Peckham (parish), 19/211; TQ637527; NP 171
West Pennard (parish), 32/183; ST556386; NP 165
West Poringland (Little Poringland) (parish), 25/568; TG260008; NP 126, 137
West Pulham (division in Pulham), 10/94B; ST708082; NP 178
West Putford (parish), 9/55; SS353155; NP 163
West Quantoxhead (West Quantockshead) (parish), 32/233; ST113416; NP 164
West Rainham (parish), 25/165; NP 125
West Rainton (township in Houghton-le-Spring), 11/60; NZ317471; NP 85
West Rasen (parish), 22/214; TF058898; NP 104
West Ravendale (chapelry in East Ravendale), 22/170; TF227997; NP 105
West Raynham (West Rainham, Rainham St Margaret) (parish), 25/165; TF856248; NP 125
West Retford (parish), 28/51; SK694817; NP 103
West Rounton (parish), 42/270; NZ414036; NP 85, 91
West Row (division in Mildenhall), 34/110B; TL670760; NP 135
West Rudham (parish), 25/169; TF814274; NP 125
West Scaleby (township in Scaleby), 7/21; NY436627; NP 76
West Scrafton (township in Coverham), 42/153; SE075817; NP 90
West Shaftoe (township in Hartburn), 27/358; NZ043819; NP 77
West Sheen (parish), 35/31; NP 170
West Shefford (Great Shefford) (parish), 2/138; SU380755; NP 158
West Sheffield (division in township of Sheffield in Sheffield), 43/827; SK329863; NP 102
West Sherborne (parish), 14/51; NP 168
West Shutford (township in Swalcliffe), 29/27; SP373404; NP 145
West Sleekburn (township in Bedlington), 27/429; NZ271845; NP 78
West Somerton (parish), 25/376; TG470198; NP 126
West Stafford (parish), 10/251; SY723895; NP 178
West Stockwith (township in Misterton), 28/8; SK786956; NP 104
West Stoke (parish), 36/240; SU828087; NP 181
West Stones Dale (division in township of in Grinton), 42/126; NY880040; NP 84, 90
West Stour (West Stower) (parish), 10/19; ST778223; NP 166
West Stow (parish), 34/114; TL808732; NP 136
West Stower (parish), 10/19; NP 166
West Sunderland, 11/80; NP 78
West Tanfield (parish), 42/176; SE265793; NP 91
West Tarring (parish), 36/302; TQ130043; NP 182
West Tarset, 27/274; NP 70, 77
West Teignmouth (parish), 9/396; SX935735; NP 188
West Theddlethorpe (parish), 22/304; TF463882; NP 105
West Thornton (township in Hartburn), 27/349; NZ094867; NP 77
West Thorney (parish), 36/250; SU756026; NP 181
West Thorpe (parish), 22/231; NP 104
West Thurrock (division in West Thurrock), 12/423; TQ580780; NP 161, 171
West Thurrock (parish), 12/423, 434; NP 161, 171
West Tilbury (parish), 12/429; TQ662775; NP 171
West Tisbury (parish), 39/333; ST912287; NP 166, 167
West Tisted (parish), 14/183; SU660293; NP 168, 181

West Tofts (parish), 25/708; TL841911; NP 136
West Torrington (parish), 22/267; TF139813; NP 104, 105
West Tytherley (parish), 14/217; SU275304; NP 167, 168
West Walton (division in Marshland fen in West Walton), 25/297B; TF539087; NP 124
West Walton (division in West Walton), 25/297A; TF491130; NP 124
West Walton (parish), 25/297A-B; NP 124
West Wellow (parish), 39/373; SU293198; NP 168, 180
West Whelpington (township in Kirkwhelpington), 27/376; NY962850; NP 77
West Wickham (parish), 4/151; TL613491; NP 148
West Wickham (parish), 19/65; TQ395646; NP 171
West Willoughby, 22/604; NP 123
West Winch (parish), 25/308; TF629142; NP 124
West Wittering (parish), 36/269; SZ786986; NP 181
West Witton (division in township of West Witton in West Witton), 42/145; SE057878; NP 90
West Witton (parish), 42/144-145; NP 90
West Witton (township in West Witton), 42/144-145; NP 90
West Woodhay (parish), 2/146; SU392630; NP 168
West Woodyates (extra-parochial), 10/65; SU018192; NP 167, 179
West Worldham (parish), 14/123; SU737372; NP 169
West Worlington (parish), 9/125; SS760152; NP 163, 175
West Wratting (parish), 4/138; TL592524; NP 148
West Wretham (parish), 25/713; TL892905; NP 136
West Wycombe (parish), 3/207; SU926942; NP 159
Westbere (parish), 19/139; TR198610; NP 173
Westborough (parish), 22/611; SK857457; NP 113, 122
Westbourne (Westbourn) (parish), 36/238; SU775072; NP 181
Westbury (parish), 3/11; SP665401; NP 145
Westbury (parish), 31/312; NP 118
Westbury (township in Westbury), 31/313; SJ361092; NP 118
Westbury (parish), 32/144; NP 165
Westbury (parish), 39/231-232C; NP 166
Westbury (tithing in Westbury), 39/232A; ST870520; NP 166
Westbury Leigh (tithing in Westbury), 39/232C; ST860500; NP 166
Westbury on Severn (Westbury upon Severn) (parish), 13/146; SO730150; NP 143
Westbury upon Severn (parish), 13/146; NP 143
Westbury upon Trym (parish), 13/383-385; NP 155
Westbury upon Trym (tithing in Westbury upon Trym), 13/383; ST572772; NP 155
Westbury-sub-Mendip (Westbury) (parish), 32/144; ST499488; NP 165
Westby (division in township of Westby with Plumptons in Kirkham), 20/181-183; NP 94
Westby (hamlet in Bassingthorpe), 22/686; SK971288; NP 123
Westby (sub-division of Westby division in township of Westby with Plumptons in Kirkham), 20/183; SD383319; NP 94
Westby with Plumptons (township in Kirkham), 20/181-185; NP 94
Westcot Barton (Barton-Westcott) (parish), 29/88; SP434268; NP 145
Westcote (parish), 13/95; SP222207; NP 144
Westcott (hamlet in Waddesdon), 3/145; SP720170; NP 146
Westdean (parish), 36/337; TV529991; NP 183
Westerdale (division in township of Westerdale in Stokesley), 42/306B; NZ660040; NP 86, 92
Westerdale (township in Stokesley), 42/305-306; NP 86, 92
Westerfield (division inside Ipswich municipal boundary in Westerfield), 34/426A; TM172473; NP 150
Westerfield (division outside Ipswich municipal boundary in Westerfield), 34/426B; TM176481; NP 150
Westerfield (parish), 34/426A-B; NP 150
Westerham (parish), 19/196; TQ450525; NP 171
Westerleigh (parish), 13/392; ST682802; NP 156
Westerton (township in St Andrew Auckland), 11/210; NZ235313; NP 85
Westfa (hamlet in Llanelli), 47/83B; SN500040; NP 153
Westfield (extra-parochial), 19/77; TQ597639; NP 171

Westfield (parish), 25/503; TF995098; NP 125
Westfield (parish), 36/154; TQ808157; NP 184
Westgate (township in St John), 27/646; NZ241641; NP 78
Westgate (division in township of Wakefield in Wakefield), 43/606; SE328201; NP 96
Westhall (parish), 34/69; TM412815; NP 137
Westham (parish), 36/183; TQ625046; NP 183
Westhampnett (parish), 36/243; SU879074; NP 181
Westhay (extra-parochial), 26/37; TF001997; NP 123, 134
Westhide (township in Stoke Edith), 15/171; SO589439; NP 142
Westhope (township in Diddlebury), 31/503; SO475861; NP 129
Westhorpe (parish), 34/132; TM042694; NP 136
Westhoughton (township in Deane), 20/569; SD650060; NP 101
Westington (hamlet in Chipping Campden), 13/27D; SP140480; NP 144
Westleigh (parish), 9/41; SS479279; NP 163
Westleigh (township in Leigh), 20/580; SD645010; NP 101
Westleton (parish), 34/160; TM445685; NP 137
Westley (parish), 34/223; TL827647; NP 136
Westley (Westley, Winsley, Lake Hurst and The Hem) (township in Westbury), 31/320; SJ362070; NP 118
Westley Waterless (parish), 4/142; TL607565; NP 135, 148
Westley, Winsley, Lake Hurst and The Hem, 31/320; NP 118
Westlinton (township in Kirklinton), 7/18; NY395633; NP 76
Westmeston (parish), 36/120-122; NP 182
Westmeston (Westmeston cum Chiltington) (division in Westmeston), 36/120; TQ342149; NP 182
Westmill (parish), 16/57; TL368266; NP 147, 148
Westminster Abbey (The Close of the Collegiate Church of St Peter) (extra-parochial), 24/34; TQ301794; NP 160/1, 170
Westmorland (county) [unchanged in 1844], 38/1-135
Westnall with Waldershaigh (division in Bradfield township in Ecclesfield), 43/815-821; NP 102
Westnewton (township in Kirknewton), 27/60A; NT895303; NP 64, 70, 71
Westoe (township in Jarrow), 11/2; NZ362655; NP 78
Weston (hamlet in Long Compton), 37/301; SP281356; NP 144, 145
Weston (parish), 16/29; TL264300; NP 147
Weston (parish), 22/772; TF285235; NP 123
Weston (parish), 28/108; SK770680; NP 112
Weston (parish), 32/24; ST725669; NP 156, 166
Weston (parish), 34/47; TM428870; NP 137
Weston (parish), 43/375-376; NP 96
Weston (township in Runcorn), 5/160; SJ506807; NP 100
Weston (township in Wybunbury), 5/256; SJ738522; NP 110
Weston (township in Burford), 31/540; SO588720; NP 129
Weston (township in Clun), 31/388; SO276806; NP 129
Weston (township in Weston), 43/376; SE185484; NP 96
Weston (Weston and Wixhill under Redcastle) (chapelry in Hodnet), 31/165; SJ566285; NP 118
Weston and Wixhill under Redcastle, 31/165; NP 118
Weston Bampfylde (Weston Bamfylde) (parish), 32/372; ST614253; NP 166, 177
Weston Beggard (parish), 15/172; SO582418; NP 142
Weston Birt (parish), 13/337; ST863893; NP 156
Weston by Welland (parish), 26/98; SP774914; NP 133
Weston Colville (parish), 4/139; TL613531; NP 135, 148
Weston Corbett (extra-parochial), 14/110; SU684470; NP 168, 169
Weston Cotton (township in Oswestry), 31/108; SJ288275; NP 118
Weston Coyney (township in Caverswall), 33/39; SJ935440; NP 110, 119
Weston Favell (parish), 26/222; SP788623; NP 133
Weston Jones (township in Norbury), 33/164; SJ767238; NP 119
Weston Longville (parish), 25/346; TG107159; NP 125
Weston Lullingfields (township in Baschurch), 31/145; SJ421251; NP 118
Weston Madoc (township in Church Stoke), 54/187; SO231944; NP 128
Weston Market (parish), 34/96; NP 136
Weston Patrick (parish), 14/111; SU695455; NP 169

Weston Peverel, 9/462; NP 187/1
Weston Rhyn (township in St Martin), 31/77; SJ282358; NP 117, 118
Weston Sub-edge (parish), 13/22; SP130400; NP 144
Weston Turville (parish), 3/178; SP856113; NP 146, 159
Weston Underwood (parish), 3/28; SP865510; NP 146
Weston Underwood (township in Mugginton), 8/218; SK300428; NP 121
Weston under Penyard (parish), 15/251; SO640230; NP 143
Weston under Lizard (Weston under Liziard) (parish), 33/248; SJ808109; NP 119
Weston under Wetherley (Weston under Weatherley) (parish), 37/158; SP362693; NP 132
Weston upon Trent (parish), 8/299; SK402283; NP 121
Weston upon Avon (hamlet in Weston upon Avon), 13/8; SP165508; NP 144
Weston upon Avon (parish), 13/7-8, 37/207; NP 144
Weston upon Trent (parish), 33/188; SJ979271; NP 119
Weston Zoyland (parish), 32/303; ST360340; NP 165
Weston, 31/496; NP 129
Weston-in-Gordano (parish), 32/8; ST442743; NP 155
Weston-on-the-Green (parish), 29/108; SP539187; NP 145
Weston-super-Mare (parish), 32/156; ST327616; NP 165
Westoning (parish), 1/117; TL033324; NP 147
Westow (parish), 41/121-124; NP 92
Westow (township in Westow), 41/122; SE760650; NP 92
Westport (division in St Paul Malmesbury), 39/30A; ST932880; NP 156, 157
Westport St Mary (parish), 39/34; ST920862; NP 156, 157
Westrill and Starmore (township in Stanford on Avon), 21/348; SP582806; NP 132
Westrop (tithing in Highworth), 39/5B; SU202928; NP 157
Westville (parish), 22/459; TF292537; NP 114
Westward (parish), 7/147A-B-149; NP 82, 83
Westward Icomb (Westward Iccomb) (hamlet in Icomb), 13/94; SP223214; NP 144
Westwell (parish), 19/293; TQ979476; NP 172
Westwell (parish), 29/156; SP220100; NP 144, 157
Westwick (hamlet in Oakington), 4/74; TL423665; NP 135
Westwick (township in Gainford), 11/299; NZ082161; NP 84
Westwick (parish), 25/240; TG280260; NP 126
Westwick (township in Ripon), 43/171; SE351665; NP 91
Westwood (parish), 39/156; ST809593; NP 166
Westwood Park (extra-parochial), 40/67; SO875640; NP 130
Wether Fell (undivided moor, common to Bainbridge, Countersett and Marsett in Bainbridge township and Buttersett in Hawes township in Aysgarth), 42/134B; SD877871; NP 90
Wetheral (parish), 7/43-48; NP 76
Wetheral (township in Wetheral), 7/45; NY461535; NP 76
Wetherby (township in Spofforth), 43/94; SE413487; NP 96, 97
Wetherden (parish), 34/236; TM011641; NP 136
Wetheringsett cum Brockford (parish), 34/178; TM133653; NP 136, 137
Wethersfield (parish), 12/86; TL736307; NP 148, 149
Wettenhall (township in Over), 5/178; SJ622614; NP 109, 110
Wetton (parish), 33/78; SJ102552; NP 111
Wetwang (parish), 41/184-185; NP 92, 98
Wetwang (township in Wetwang), 41/185; SE928591; NP 98
Wexcombe (tithing in Great Bedwyn), 39/186; SU273584; NP 167, 168
Wexham (parish), 3/232; SU995827; NP 159
Weybourne (Wabourne, Waborne, Waybourne) (parish), 25/31; TG115428; NP 125
Weybread (parish), 34/79; TM242809; NP 137
Weybridge (parish), 35/66; TQ076644; NP 170
Weyhill (parish), 14/74; SU320480; NP 168
Weymouth (chapelry in Wyke Regis), 10/265; SY677786; NP 178
Whaddon (parish), 3/73-74; NP 146
Whaddon (parish), 4/165; TL350468; NP 147, 148
Whaddon (parish), 13/255; SO833137; NP 143
Whaddon (parish), 39/147; ST878612; NP 166

Whaddon (township in Whaddon), 3/73; SP807337; NP 146
Whaley cum Yeardsley, 5/30; NP 101, 111
Whalley (parish), 20/238-302, 43/285-287; NP 95
Whalley (township in Whalley), 20/240; SD736367; NP 95
Whalton (parish), 27/395-398; NP 77, 78
Whalton (township in Whalton), 27/396; NZ132814; NP 77, 78
Whaplode (division in Whaplode), 22/774; TF328232; NP 123
Whaplode (parish), 22/774-775; NP 123
Whaplode Drove (hamlet in Whaplode), 22/775; TF318312; NP 123
Wharles (division in township of Treales, Roseacre and Wharles in Kirkham), 20/204; SD449356; NP 94
Wharnley (township in parochial chapelry of Newbrough in Warden), 27/603B; NY880665; NP 77
Wharram le Street (parish), 41/144; SE865660; NP 92
Wharram Percy (parish), 41/139-142; NP 92, 98
Wharram Percy (township in Wharram Percy), 41/142; SE854639; NP 92
Wharton (township in Kirkby Stephen), 38/64; NY767042
Wharton, 5/180; NP 110
Whashton (township in Kirkby Ravensworth), 42/26; NZ145060; NP 85, 91
Whatborough (township in Tilton), 21/274; SK776060; NP 122
Whatcote (parish), 37/283; SP301444; NP 145
Whatcroft (township in Davenham), 5/191; SJ687695; NP 110
Whateley (township in Kingsbury), 37/25; SP220992; NP 120, 131
Whatfield (parish), 34/420; TM025465; NP 149
Whatley (parish), 32/123; ST736473; NP 166
Whatlington (parish), 36/139; TQ763193; NP 183, 184
Whatmore (division of Boraston and Whatmore township in Burford), 31/538; SO568715; NP 129
Whatton (parish), 28/215-216; NP 122
Whatton (township in Whatton), 28/216; SK745388; NP 122
Wheatacre (Wheatacre All Saints) (parish), 25/626; TM465950; NP 137
Wheatenhurst (Whitminster) (parish), 13/265; SO772085; NP 143, 156
Wheatfield (parish), 29/278; SU699999; NP 159
Wheathampstead (Whethampstead) (parish), 16/90; TL162148; NP 147
Wheathill (parish), 31/564; SO606810; NP 129, 130
Wheathill (parish), 32/347; ST584310; NP 165, 177
Wheatley (hamlet in Cuddesdon), 29/251; SP601050; NP 158
Wheatley (division in township of Long Sandall with Wheatley in Doncaster), 43/939; SE592054; NP 103
Wheatley Booth (division in Barley with Wheatley Booth township in Whalley), 20/257; SD830412; NP 95
Wheatley Lane (township in Whalley), 20/263A; SD840380; NP 95
Wheaton Aston (township in Lapley), 33/242; SJ847126; NP 119
Wheddicar, 7/294
Wheeldale (extra-parochial), 42/429; SE785975; NP 92
Wheelock (township in Sandbach), 5/220; SJ753585; NP 110
Wheelton (township in Leyland), 20/329; SD613211; NP 94, 95, 101
Wheldrake (parish), 41/71-72; NP 97
Wheldrake (township in Wheldrake), 41/72; SE665450; NP 97
Whenby (parish), 42/605; SE630693; NP 92
Whepstead (parish), 34/310; TL832582; NP 136, 149
Wherstead (parish), 34/512; TM153407; NP 150
Wherwell (parish), 14/90; SU377405; NP 168
Whessoe (township in Haughton le Skerne), 11/332; NZ283184; NP 85
Wheston (township in Tideswell), 8/36; SK132765; NP 111
Whethampstead (parish), 16/90; NP 147
Whetstone (parish), 21/246; SP557957; NP 132
Whettleton (township in Stokesay), 31/420; SO443822; NP 129
Whicham (parish), 7/318; SD144843; NP 88
Whichford (hamlet in Whichford), 33/290; SP321348; NP 145
Whichford (parish), 33/290-291; NP 145
Whickham (parish), 11/24-27; NP 78
Whickham (township in Whickham), 11/27; NZ210610; NP 78

Whilton (parish), 26/242; SP629647; NP 132
Whimple (parish), 9/242; SY047970; NP 176
Whin Fell (township in Brigham), 7/272; NY136256; NP 82
Whinbergh (parish), 25/547; ; NP 125
Whinburgh (Whinbergh) (parish), 25/547; TG007083; NP 125
Whinfell (township in Kendal), 38/111; SD565992; NP 89
Whinnetley (township in parochial chapelry of Haydon in Warden), 27/599; NY811659; NP 77
Whippingham (parish), 18/15; SZ523927; NP 180
Whipsnade (division in Whipsnade), 1/142; TL020177; NP 147
Whipsnade (parish), 1/142, 16/93; NP 147
Whipsnade (division in Whipsnade), 16/93; TL039143; NP 147
Whisby (township in Doddington), 22/527; SK908674; NP 113
Whissendine (parish), 30/1; SK822142; NP 122
Whissonsett (parish), 25/188; TF911232; NP 125
Whistley (Whistley in Hurst) (division in Hurst), 2/196; SU798730; NP 169
Whiston (division of Whiston township in Whiston), 43/835; SK452903; NP 103
Whiston (division of Whiston township in Rotherham), 43/836; SK480895; NP 103
Whiston (parish), 26/289; SP848603; NP 133
Whiston (parish), 43/835; NP 103
Whiston (township in Prescot), 20/628; SJ471907; NP 100
Whiston (township in Kingsley), 33/72B; SK040470; NP 111, 120
Whiston (township in Penkridge), 33/237; SJ891136; NP 119
Whiston (township in Whiston and Rotherham), 43/835-836; NP 103
Whistones (tithing in Claines), 40/112; SO845556; NP 130/1
Whitaside (division in township of Grinton in Grinton), 42/113; SD995967; NP 90
Whitbatch (township in Stanton Lacy), 31/521A; SO514773; NP 129
Whitbeck (parish), 7/317; SD119859; NP 88
Whitbourne (parish), 15/84; SO713564; NP 130, 143
Whitburn (division in township of Whitburn in Whitburn), 11/10; NZ360639; NP 78
Whitburn (division in township of Whitburn in Whitburn), 11/12; NZ406618; NP 78
Whitburn (parish and township), 11/10-12; NP 78
Whitby (division in Whitby township in Eastham), 5/428; SJ397761; NP 100, 109
Whitby (division in Whitby township in Stoke), 5/427; SJ403762; NP 100
Whitby (parish), 42/380-389; NP 86, 92, 93
Whitby (township in Stoke and Eastham), 5/427-428; NP 100, 109
Whitby (township in Whitby), 42/387; NZ898110; NP 86
Whitchester (township in Heddon on the Wall), 27/549; NZ100683; NP 77
Whitchurch (division in Whitchurch), 2/178B; SU644766; NP 158
Whitchurch (parish), 2/178B, 179B, 29/316; NP 158
Whitchurch (parish), 3/123; SP795203; NP 146
Whitchurch (parish), 5/314, 31/29-31/39; NP 109, 118
Whitchurch (parish), 9/354; SX514733; NP 175
Whitchurch Canonicorum (parish), 10/131; SY396955; NP 177
Whitchurch (parish), 14/62; SU468495; NP 168
Whitchurch (parish), 15/261; SO550170; NP 142
Whitchurch (parish), 24/89; TQ182922; NP 160
Whitchurch (Whitchurch), 29/316; SU642778; NP 158
Whitchurch (parish), 31/29-39; NP 118, 119
Whitchurch (township in Whitchurch), 31/38; SJ522415; NP 118
Whitchurch (Felton) (parish), 32/18; ST603679; NP 155, 156, 165
Whitchurch (parish), 37/298; SP225475; NP 144
Whitchurch (parish), 51/130; ST147807; NP 154
Whitchurch (Whitchurch in Dewsland) (parish), 55/68; SM805255; NP 138
Whitcliffe with Littlethorpe (Whitcliffe with Thorpe) (township in Ripon), 43/176; SE300690; NP 91
Whitcomb Magna (parish), 13/204; NP 143
Whitcombe (parish), 10/250; SY713872; NP 178
Whitcott Evan (township in Clun), 31/386; SO276816; NP 128, 129

Whitcott Keysett (township in Clun), 31/396; SO284828; NP 129
Whitcott Keysett and Newcastle (township in Clun), 31/385; SO252482; NP 128, 129
White Colne (parish), 12/125; TL880300; NP 149
White Ladies Aston (parish), 40/155; SO922523; NP 143
White Notley (parish), 12/190; TL781186; NP 149
White Roding (White Roothing and Morrell, White Roothing) (hamlet in White Roding), 12/203; TL565137; NP 148
White Roding (White Roothing) (parish), 12/203-204; NP 148
White Roothing (parish), 12/203-204; NP 148
White Roothing and Morrell, 12/203; NP 148
White Waltham (parish), 2/213; SU860775; NP 159
Whitechapel (parish), 24/60A-E; NP 160/1
Whitechapel Church (division in St Mary Whitechapel), 24/60C; TQ341814; NP 160/1
Whitechapel North (division in St Mary Whitechapel), 24/60D; TQ343817; NP 160/1
Whitechurch (Whitchurch in Kemes) (parish), 55/17; SN160352; NP 139
Whitechurch (Whitchurch in Dewsland) (parish), 55/68; NP 138
Whitechurch in Kemes (parish), 55/17
Whitecross Street (division in St Luke), 24/48C; TQ323822; NP 160/1
Whitecross Street (division in St Luke), 24/48D; TQ324822; NP 160/1
Whitefield (division in township of Pilkington in Prestwich), 20/496; SD806055; NP 101
Whitefriars Ward (division in parish and township of Holy Tinity Kingston upon Hull), 41/330; TA099107; NP 99/1
Whitegate (parish), 5/171-174; NP 109, 110
Whitehaven (township in St Bees), 7/296; NX975182; NP 82
Whitehill (Wighthill) (hamlet in Tackley), 29/104; SP475190; NP 145
Whitelackington (parish), 32/445; ST382162; NP 177
Whiteparish (parish), 39/367; SU239238; NP 167
Whiteside Law (township in Chollerton), 27/443; NY979757; NP 77
Whitestaunton (parish), 32/449; ST276104; NP 177
Whitestone (parish), 9/320; SX863942; NP 176
Whitestone Cote (extra-parochial), 42/495; SE510835; NP 92
Whitfield (township in Glossop), 8/4; SK045937; NP 102
Whitfield (parish), 19/373; TR305459; NP 173
Whitfield (parish), 26/344; SP603395; NP 145
Whitfield (parish), 27/569; NY750550; NP 76, 77, 84
Whitfield, 13/53C; NP 143
Whitford (parish), 50/35-42; NP 108
Whitford Garn (township in Whitford), 50/39; SJ143786; NP 108
Whitgift (parish), 43/956-956; NP 98, 104
Whitgift (township in Whitgift), 43/957; SE812212; NP 98, 104
Whitgreave (township in Stafford St Mary), 33/177; SJ899289; NP 119
Whitkirk (parish), 43/476-484; NP 96
Whitle (township in Glossop), 8/8; SJ998865; NP 101, 102
Whitley (division in township of Ecclesfield in Ecclesfield), 43/791; SK350946; NP 102
Whitley (hamlet in St Giles Reading), 2/183; SU720706; NP 169
Whitley (tithing in Cumnor), 2/3K; SP444046; NP 158
Whitley (township in Tynemouth), 27/493; NZ354725; NP 78
Whitley (township in Kellington), 43/641; SE560210; NP 97, 103
Whitley and Welbatch (township in St Chad Shrewsbury), 31/266; SJ457089; NP 118
Whitley Lower (division in township of Whitley Lower in Thornhill), 43/719; ; NP 102
Whitley Ridge Walk (division in Brockenhurst), 14/327B; SU317038; NP 180
Whitley Ridge Walk (extra-parochial division in New Forest extra-parochial), 14/302M; SU324042; NP 180
Whitley Ridge Walk (in New Forest and Brockenhurst), 14/302M, 327B; NP 180
Whitley Upper (township in Kirkheaton), 43/722-723; NP 102
Whitlingham (parish), 25/481; TG274073; NP 126
Whitminster (parish), 13/265; NP 143, 156
Whitmore (parish), 33/48; SJ807413; NP 119
Whitnage (tithing in Uplowman), 9/135B; ST024160; NP 164

233

Whitnash (parish), 37/227; SP331623; NP 132
Whitney (Whitney-on-Wye) (parish), 15/48; SO275476; NP 141, 142
Whitney-on-Wye (parish), 15/48; NP 141, 142
Whitridge (township in Hartburn), 27/343; NZ061877; NP 77
Whitsbury (parish), 39/383; SU122105; NP 167, 179
Whitson (Witson) (parish), 53/151; ST377855; NP 155
Whitstable (parish), 19/116; TR122647; NP 172, 173
Whitstone (parish), 6/10; SX269986; NP 174
Whittingham (township in Kirkham), 20/208; SD575365; NP 94
Whittingham (parish), 27/165-174; NP 71
Whittingham (township in Whittingham), 27/170; NU073115; NP 71
Whittington (parish), 8/52; SK386751; NP 103, 111, 112
Whittington (parish), 13/109; SP014209; NP 143, 144
Whittington (division in township of Whittington in Whittington), 20/73; SD597768; NP 89
Whittington (township and parish), 20/73-74; NP 89
Whittington (parish), 31/80; NP 117, 118
Whittington (township in Whittington), 31/86; SJ325305; NP 118
Whittington (parish), 33/270; SK159060; NP 120
Whittington (township in Grendon), 37/20; SP299990; NP 132
Whittington (chapelry in Worcester, St Peter the Great), 40/126; SO880530; NP 143
Whittle (division in township of Heap in Bury), 20/475; SD844078; NP 101
Whittle (township in Ovingham), 27/559; NZ078657; NP 77
Whittle (township in Shilbottle), 27/209; NU182067; NP 71
Whittle-le-Woods (township in Leyland), 20/331; SD581209; NP 94, 100
Whittlebury (parish), 26/341; SP709435; NP 145, 146
Whittlesey (Whittlesey St Mary and Whittlesey St Andrew) (parish), 4/8A; TL295962; NP 123, 124, 134, 135
Whittlesford (parish), 4/160; TL467480; NP 148
Whittleswick (division in township of Barton upon Irwell in Eccles), 20/548; SJ782974; NP 101
Whittlewood Forest (extra-parochial), 26/340; SP733433; NP 146
Whitton (parish), 22/16; SE907237; NP 98
Whitton (parish), 56/13; SO276677; NP 128, 129
Whitton (township in Grindon), 11/263; NZ380237; NP 85
Whitton (township in Rothbury), 27/255; NU058003; NP 71
Whitton (township in Burford), 31/528; SO574731; NP 129
Whitton (township in Westbury), 31/316; SJ344090; NP 118
Whitton and Trippleton (township in Leintwardine), 15/9; SO417730; NP 129
Whitton cum Thurlston (parish), 34/425; TM155479; NP 150
Whittonditch (tithing in Ramsbury), 39/180D; SU295725; NP 158
Whittonstall (township in Bywell St Peter), 27/637; NZ070564; NP 77
Whitwell (parish), 8/60; SK528770; NP 103, 112
Whitwell (parish), 18/29; SZ520782; NP 180
Whitwell (parish), 25/263; TG087214; NP 125
Whitwell (parish), 30/24; SK922088; NP 122
Whitwell (township in Catterick), 42/72; NZ287992; NP 91
Whitwell and Selside, 38/110
Whitwell House (extra-parochial), 11/105; NZ312399; NP 85
Whitwell-on-the-Hill (extra-parochial), 42/653; SE721657; NP 92
Whitwick (parish), 21/26-28; NP 121
Whitwick (township in Whitwick), 21/26; SK448156; NP 121
Whitwood (township in Featherstone), 43/613; SE410252; NP 96, 97
Whitworth (parish), 11/220; NZ242343; NP 85
Whitworth (division in Spotland township in Rochdale), 20/450-453; NP 95, 101
Whitworth Higher End (subdivision of Whitworth division in Spotland township in Rochdale), 20/452; SD889212; NP 95, 101
Whitworth Lower End (subdivision of Whitworth division in Spotland township in Rochdale), 20/453; SD882184; NP 95, 101
Whixall (township in Prees), 31/26; SJ505348; NP 118
Whixley (parish), 43/116-118; NP 97
Whixley (township in Whixley), 43/116; SE443581; NP 97
Whorlton (division in township of Whorlton in Gainford), 11/300B; NZ109160; NP 84

Whorlton (township in Gainford), 11/300A-B; NP 84
Whorlton (township in Newburn), 27/536; NZ191681; NP 78
Whorlton (division in township of Whorlton in Whorlton), 42/311; NZ490010; NP 91, 92
Whorlton (parish), 42/308-313; NP 85, 91, 92
Whorlton (township in Whorlton), 42/311-313; NP 91, 92
Wibtoft (township in Claybrooke), 37/108; SP477872; NP 132
Wichenford (parish), 40/105; SO780598; NP 130
Wichling (Witchling) (parish), 19/230; TQ916552; NP 172
Wichnor, 33/220; NP 120
Wick (parish), 51/116; SS929720; NP 154
Wick (Wick near Pershore) (chapelry in St Andrew Pershore), 40/179; SO962452; NP 143
Wick and Abson (Wick cum Abson) (parish), 13/398; ST710730; NP 156
Wick cum Abson (parish), 13/398; NP 156
Wick near Pershore, 40/179; NP 143
Wick Rissington (Wyck Rissington) (parish), 13/97; SP190216; NP 144
Wick St Lawrence (Week St Lawrence) (parish), 32/63; ST371653; NP 165
Wicken (parish), 4/47; TL553719; NP 135
Wicken (parish), 26/334; SP750388; NP 146
Wicken Bonant (parish), 12/18; NP 148
Wicken Bonhunt (Wickham Bonhunt, Wicken Bonant) (parish), 12/18; TL502334; NP 148
Wickenby (parish), 22/211A-C; TF090820; NP 104, 104/1
Wickenby (Wickenby cum Westlaby) (division in Wickenby), 22/211A; TF090820; NP 104
Wickenby ('extra-parochial' in Wickenby), 22/211C; TF078836; NP 104/1
Wickenby - Lissingleys (division in Wickenby), 22/211B; TF089839; NP 104/1
Wickersley (parish), 43/848-849; NP 103
Wickersley (township in Wickersley), 43/849; SK482909; NP 103
Wickford (parish), 12/393; TQ752938; NP 161, 162
Wickham (parish), 14/276; SU571117; NP 180
Wickham Bishops (parish), 12/236; TL834115; NP 149, 162
Wickham Bonhunt (parish), 12/18; NP 148
Wickham Forest (extra-parochial), 14/277A; SU591104; NP 180
Wickham Market (parish), 34/531; TM299599; NP 137, 150
Wickham Skeith (parish), 34/184; TM095699; NP 136
Wickham St Paul (parish), 12/49; TL830368; NP 149
Wickham, 29/18
Wickhambreux (parish), 19/136; TR231608; NP 173
Wickhambrook (parish), 34/319; TL750564; NP 135, 136, 148, 149
Wickhamford (parish), 40/203; SP067414; NP 144
Wickhampton (parish), 25/462; TG441050; NP 126
Wicklewood (parish), 25/655; TM077016; NP 125, 136
Wickmere (Wickmore) (parish), 25/131; TG169338; NP 125, 126
Wickmore (parish), 25/131; NP 125, 126
Wicks Ufford (hamlet in Rushmere), 34/462; TM193456; NP 150
Wickwar (parish), 13/352; ST707882; NP 156
Widcombe, 32/78
Widdington (parish), 12/22; TL535322; NP 148
Widdington (township in Little Ouseburn), 43/121; SE492596; NP 91, 97
Widdrington (parochial chapelry in Woodhorn), 27/312-313; NP 71, 78
Widdrington (township in Widdrington parochial chapelry in Woodhorn), 27/312; NZ245960; NP 71, 78
Widecombe in the Moor (Widecombe in the Moor) (parish), 9/378; SX703754; NP 175, 187
Widford (parish), 12/285; TL693053; NP 161
Widford (parish), 16/73; TL420160; NP 148
Widford (parish), 29/2; SP271129; NP 144
Widley (parish), 14/291; SU659072; NP 180
Widmerpool (parish), 28/293; SK638280; NP 121
Widnes (township in Prescot), 20/624; SJ512872; NP 100
Widworthy (parish), 9/234; SY215987; NP 176, 177
Wield (parish), 14/335; SU632395; NP 168
Wig (township in Llanwnog), 54/157; SO001928; NP 128
Wigan (parish), 20/581-593; NP 100, 101

Wigan (township in Wigan), 20/585; SD582065; NP 100, 101
Wigfair (township in St Asaph), 49/141; SJ028719; NP 108
Wiggenhall St German (Wiggenhall St Germans) (parish), 25/305; TF587129; NP 124
Wiggenhall St Mary Magdalen (parish), 25/303; TF580084; NP 124
Wiggenhall St Mary the Virgin (parish), 25/306; TF586150; NP 124
Wiggenhall St Peter (Wiggenhall St Peters) (parish), 25/304; TF600120; NP 124
Wiggington (Wigginton) (parish), 29/42; SP388334; NP 145
Wigginton (parish), 16/144; SP943093; NP 146, 147, 159
Wigginton (parish), 29/42; NP 145
Wigginton (township in Tamworth), 33/281; SK201064; NP 120
Wigginton (township in Wigginton), 42/678; SE593583; NP 97
Wigglesworth (township in Long Preston), 43/245; SD800565; NP 95
Wiggold (tithing in Cirencester), 13/278; SP045050; NP 157
Wiggonby (township in Aikton), 7/118; NY301530; NP 75
Wiggonholt (parish), 36/84; TQ059169; NP 182
Wighill (division in township and parish of Wighill), 43/71; SE473471; NP 97
Wighill (township and parish), 43/70-71; NP 97
Wightfield (Whitfield) (hamlet in Deerhurst), 13/53C; SO870287; NP 143
Wighthill, 29/104; NP 145
Wighton (parish), 25/17; TF925400; NP 125
Wightwizzle (Wightwistle) (sub-division in Westnall with Waldershaigh division in township of Bradfield in Ecclesfield), 43/815; SK228956; NP 102
Wigland (township in Malpas), 5/320; SJ495447; NP 109, 118
Wigmore (parish), 15/17; SO405685; NP 129
Wigsley (township in Thorney), 28/120; SK858700; NP 113
Wigston Magna (parish), 21/250; SP610985; NP 121, 132
Wigston Parva (Little Wigston) (township in Claybrooke), 21/233; SP467900; NP 132
Wigtoft (division in Wigtoft), 22/767A; TF262361; NP 123
Wigtoft (parish), 22/767A-C; NP 123
Wigtoft - Holland Fen (division in Wigtoft), 22/767C; TF247428; NP 123
Wigton (parish), 7/133-136; NP 75, 82
Wigton (township in Wigton), 7/135; NY253482; NP 75, 82
Wigton (township in Harewood), 43/404; SE322407; NP 96
Wigwig and Homer (division of Harley, Wigwig and Homer township in Much Wenlock), 31/450; SJ608015; NP 119
Wike (division in township of Wike in Bardsey), 43/407; SE332418; NP 96
Wike (division in township of Wike in Harewood), 43/406; SE329425; NP 96
Wike (township in Harewood and Bardsey), 43/406-407; NP 96
Wike (Wyke) (township in Birstal), 43/545; SE155267; NP 96
Wikey, 31/139; NP 118
Wilberfoss (parish), 41/88-89; NP 97, 98
Wilberfoss (township in Wilberfoss), 41/88; SE733510; NP 97, 98
Wilbraston (parish), 26/96; SP821878; NP 133
Wilburton (parish), 4/38; TL484736; NP 135
Wilby (parish), 25/669; TM043897; NP 136
Wilby (parish), 26/207; SP862665; NP 133
Wilby (parish), 34/143; TM242718; NP 137
Wilcot (parish), 39/201; SU145620; NP 167
Wilcote (parish), 29/205; SP371149; NP 145
Wilcott and Nesscliff (township in Great Ness), 31/132; SJ378188; NP 118
Wilcrick (parish), 53/139; ST410880; NP 155
Wild House (subdivision in Butterworth Freehold Side division in Butterworth township in Rochdale), 20/464; SD930138; NP 101
Wildboarclough (township in Prestbury), 5/55; SJ989692; NP 110
Wilden (parish), 1/36; TL099552; NP 134, 147
Wilderley (township in Church Pulverbatch), 31/337; SJ438019; NP 118
Wilderley Hill (township in Church Pulverbatch), 31/336B; SO424999; NP 118, 129

Wildmore Fen Chapel Allotment (extra-parochial), 22/466; TF249533; NP 114
Wildmore Fen Manorial Allotment (extra-parochial), 22/468B; TF251510; NP 114
Wildon Grange (township in Coxwold), 42/552; SE511775; NP 91, 92
Wildsworth (township in Laughton), 22/123; SK812970; NP 104
Wilfholme (division in township of Beswick in Kilnwick), 41/287B; TA052478; NP 99
Wilford (division in Wilford), 28/239A; SK565382; NP 121
Wilford (division in Wilford), 28/239B; SK572367; NP 121
Wilford (parish), 28/239A-B; NP 121
Wilksby (division in Wilksby), 22/445A; TF290628; NP 114
Wilksby (parish), 22/445A-B; NP 114
Wilksby - Wildmore Fen (division in Wilksby), 22/445B; TF244543; NP 114
Wilksley, 5/281; NP 119
Willand (parish), 9/153; ST034105; NP 164, 176
Willaston (division of Willaston township in Nantwich), 5/251; SJ665533; NP 110
Willaston (division of Willaston township in Wybunbury), 5/252; SJ671524; NP 110
Willaston (township in Nantwich and Wybunbury), 5/251-252; NP 110
Willaston (township in Neston), 5/481; SJ671524; NP 100
Willaston (township in Prees), 31/19B; SJ606357; NP 119
Willen (parish), 3/49; SP878410; NP 146
Willenhall (township in Wolverhampton), 33/317; SO969991; NP 119, 130
Willenhall (hamlet in Coventry, Holy Trinity), 37/154; SP371763; NP 132
Willerby (division in township of Willerby in Kirk Ella), 41/307; TA007309; NP 99
Willerby (division in township of Willerby in Kirk Ella), 41/320; TA070282; NP 99/1
Willerby (parish), 41/159-161; NP 93
Willerby (township in Kirk Ella), 41/307, 320; NP 99
Willerby (township in Willerby), 41/160; TA009784; NP 93
Willersey (parish), 13/26; SP105392; NP 144
Willersley (parish), 15/50; SO309471; NP 142
Willesborough (parish), 19/325; TR030422; NP 172
Willesden (parish), 24/100; TQ222848; NP 160
Willesley (parish), 8/338; SK339151; NP 121
Willey (parish), 31/463; SO674994; NP 119, 130
Willey (parish), 37/109; SP492852; NP 132
Willey (township in Presteigne), 15/36; SO330680; NP 129
Willian (parish), 16/30; TL228312; NP 147
Willingale Doe (parish), 12/279; TL594065; NP 161
Willingale Spain (parish), 12/278; TL608060; NP 161
Willingdon (parish), 36/184; TQ597027; NP 183
Willingham (parish), 4/55; TL416700; NP 135
Willingham (Willingham by Stow) (parish), 22/135; SK880841; NP 104
Willingham by Stow (parish), 22/135; NP 104
Willingham (parish), 34/49; TM442850; NP 137
Willington (parish), 1/57; TL121489; NP 147
Willington (extra-parochial), 5/396; SJ536661; NP 109
Willington (parish), 8/252; SK293287; NP 121
Willington (township in Brancepeth), 11/143; NZ201351; NP 85
Willington (township in Wallsend), 27/501; NZ327678; NP 78
Willington (hamlet in Barcheston), 37/288; SP278393; NP 144, 145
Willington (township in Hanmer), 50/143; SJ450428; NP 109, 118
Willisham (parish), 34/356; TM071505; NP 149
Willitoft (division of Willitoft township in Bubwith), 41/31; SE742350; NP 97
Willitoft (division of Willitoft township in Aughton), 41/32; SE749344; NP 97
Willitoft (township in Bubwith and Aughton), 41/31, 32; NP 97
Williton, 32/235; NP 164
Willoughby Waterless (parish), 21/330; SP578921; NP 132
Willoughby (West Willoughby) (hamlet in Ancaster), 22/604; SK970429; NP 123

235

Willoughby with Sloothby (parish), 22/413; TF483712; NP 114
Willoughby on the Wolds (Willoughby on the Woulds) (parish), 28/295; SK640250; NP 121
Willoughby (parish), 37/237; SP522678; NP 132
Willoughton (parish), 22/149; SK934927; NP 104
Wills Pastures (extra-parochial), 37/247; SP433561; NP 132
Willshamstead (parish), 1/71; NP 147
Willstone (Wilson) (township in Cardington), 31/433D; SO491952; NP 129
Wilmington (parish), 19/25; TQ526717; NP 171
Wilmington (township in Chirbury), 31/350; SJ298019; NP 118
Wilmington (parish), 36/187; TQ552058; NP 183
Wilmslow (parish), 5/70-73; NP 101
Wilne (parish), 8/284-288; NP 121
Wilnecote (township in Tamworth), 37/11; SK228012; NP 120, 131
Wilpshire (township in Blackburn), 20/312; SD691327; NP 95
Wilsden (township in Bradford), 43/522-523; NP 96
Wilsden - Lower Division (division in township of Wilsden in Bradford), 43/522; SE083360; NP 96
Wilsden - Upper Division (division in township of Wilsden in Bradford), 43/523; SE067357; NP 96
Wilseck, 43/924; NP 103
Wilsford (parish), 39/215-216; NP 167
Wilsford (parish), 39/298-299; NP 167
Wilsford (tithing in Wilsford), 39/215; SU092545; NP 167
Wilsford (tithing in Wilsford), 39/298; SU121403; NP 167
Wilshamstead (parish), 1/71; NP 147
Wilsic (Wilseck, Wilsick) (division in township of Stancil with Wellingley and Wilsic in Tickhill), 43/924; SK567955; NP 103
Wilson, 31/433D; NP 129
Wilstead (Wilshamstead, Willshamstead) (parish), 1/71; TL070438; NP 147
Wilsthorpe (township in Sawley), 8/291; SK475340; NP 121
Wilsthorpe (township in Greatford), 22/716; TF088143; NP 123
Wilsthorpe (division in township of Hilderthorpe with Wilsthorpe in Bridlington), 41/257; TA170643; NP 99
Wilstrop (township in Kirk Hammerton), 43/69; SE488547; NP 97
Wilton (division in township of Wilton in Wilton), 42/340; NZ585200; NP 86
Wilton (parish), 39/324A-B; NP 167
Wilton (parish and township), 42/338-340; NP 86
Wilton (tithing in Wilton), 39/324A; SU100210; NP 167
Wilton (township in Ellerburn), 42/422; SE863824; NP 92
Wilverley Walk (extra-parochial division in Lymington registration district in New Forest extra-parochial), 14/302G; SU244009; NP 179
Wilverley Walk (extra-parochial division in New Forest registration district in New Forest extra-parochial), 14/302H; SZ265995; NP 179
Wilverley Walk (in New Forest), 14/302G-H; NP 179
Wily (parish), 39/288; NP 167
Wimbish (Wimbish cum Thunderley) (parish), 12/23; TL584360; NP 148
Wimbledon (parish), 35/26; TQ239711; NP 170
Wimblingswold (parish), 19/346; NP 173
Wimblington (hamlet in Doddington), 4/14; TL445915; NP 135
Wimbolds Trafford (township in Thornton le Moors), 5/419; SJ449726; NP 109
Wimboldsley (township in Middlewich), 5/204; SJ682636; NP 110
Wimborne Minster (division in Wimborne Minster), 10/175A; SU010024; NP 179
Wimborne Minster (parish), 10/175A-B; SU010024; NP 179
Wimborne St Giles (parish), 10/75; SU026142; NP 179
Wimbotsham (parish), 25/518; TF622047; NP 124
Wimeswold (parish), 21/39; NP 121
Wimpole (parish), 4/123; TL340508; NP 147, 148
Wincanton (parish), 32/359; ST720270; NP 166
Winceby (parish), 22/388; TF319683; NP 114
Wincham (township in Great Budworth), 5/135; SJ682755; NP 101, 110

Winchcombe (Winchcomb) (parish), 13/65; SP022295; NP 143, 144
Winchelsea (Winchelsea, St Thomas the Apostle) (parish), 36/150; TQ905172; NP 184
Winchester, Cathedral Yard (extra-parochial), 14/202A; SU482293; NP 168/1
Winchester, Morley's College (extra-parochial), 14/202C; SU482294; NP 168/1
Winchester, St Batholomew Hyde (parish), 14/194; SU482310; NP 168
Winchester, St Cross Hospital Precinct (extra-parochial), 14/206; SU746278; NP 168
Winchester, St Faith (parish), 14/207; SU466281; NP 168
Winchester, St John (parish), 14/199; SU488295; NP 168/1
Winchester, St Lawrence (parish), 14/196; SU481294; NP 168/1
Winchester, St Mary Kalender (parish), 14/197; SU482296; NP 168/1
Winchester, St Mary's College (parish), 14/204B; SU482289; NP 168/1
Winchester, St Maurice (parish), 14/198; SU484295; NP 168/1
Winchester, St Michael (parish), 14/204A; SU481289; NP 168/1
Winchester, St Peter Cheesehill (parish), 14/200; SU488291; NP 168/1
Winchester, St Peter Colebrook (parish), 14/201; SU485291; NP 168/1
Winchester, St Swithin (parish), 14/203; SU481291; NP 168/1
Winchester, St Thomas (parish), 14/195; SU478296; NP 168/1
Winchester, The Close (Close of Winchester) (extra-parochial), 14/202B; SU483291; NP 168/1
Winchfield, 14/37; SU768541; NP 169
Wincle (township in Prestbury), 5/56; SJ956662; NP 110
Windermere (parish), 38/80-83; NP 83, 89
Windle (division in township of Windle in Prescot), 20/634; SJ508972; NP 100
Windle (township in Prescot), 20/633-634; NP 100
Windlesham (parish), 35/71; SU930635; NP 169
Windlestone (Windleston) (township in St Andrew Auckland), 11/216; NZ267287; NP 85
Windley (township in Duffield), 8/188; SK318441; NP 111, 121
Windrush (parish), 13/229; SP188122; NP 144, 157
Windsor Castle - Guard House (extra-parochial), 2/224C; NP 159
Windsor Castle - Lower Ward (extra-parochial), 2/224A; SU969770; NP 159
Windsor Castle - Upper Ward (extra-parochial), 2/224B; SU971770; NP 159
Winestead (parish), 41/433; TA301243; NP 99
Winewall (division in township of Trawden in Whalley), 20/270; SD920392; NP 95
Winfarthing (parish), 25/738; TM107864; NP 136
Winford (parish), 32/57; ST542638; NP 155, 165
Winforton (parish), 15/49; SO295470; NP 142
Winfrith Newburgh (parish), 10/277; SY810850; NP 178
Wing (parish), 3/126; SP878221; NP 146
Wing (parish), 30/46; SK895027; NP 122
Wingate (township in Kelloe), 11/99; NZ392360; NP 85
Wingates (township in Longhorsley), 27/301; NZ100950; NP 71, 78
Wingerworth (parish), 8/127; SK373672; NP 111
Wingfield (parish), 34/81; TM229771; NP 137
Wingfield (parish), 39/157; ST818573; NP 166
Wingham (parish), 19/264; TR247572; NP 173
Wingrave (Wingrave with Rowsham) (parish), 3/138; SP867186; NP 146
Winhaston and Mells (parish), 34/154; NP 137
Winkburn (parish), 28/140; SK710585; NP 112
Winkfield (parish), 2/218A-B; NP 159, 169
Winkfield - North District (division in Winkfield), 2/218A; SU915725; NP 159, 169
Winkfield - South District (division in Winkfield), 2/218B; SU900672; NP 169

Winkleigh (parish), 9/118; SS631091; NP 175
Winksley (township in Ripon), 43/187; SE247712; NP 91
Winlaton (township in Ryton), 11/28; NZ169606; NP 78
Winmarleigh (township in Garstang), 20/144; SD463475; NP 94
Winnall (Winnal) (parish), 14/193B; SU496300; NP 168
Winnersh (division in Hurst), 2/195; SU780706; NP 159, 169
Winnington (township in Great Budworth), 5/140; SJ646743; NP 110
Winnington (division in Alberbury Upper Quarter township in Alberbury), 31/308; SJ318110; NP 118
Winnington (township in Mucklestone), 33/155; SJ736386; NP 119
Winsbury (township in Chirbury), 31/356; SO241986; NP 128
Winscales (township in Workington), 7/255; NY035259; NP 82
Winscombe (parish), 32/152; ST416577; NP 165
Winsford (Wharton) (township in Davenham), 5/180; SJ664670; NP 110
Winsford (parish), 32/280; SS885356; NP 164
Winsham (parish), 32/489; ST374067; NP 177
Winshill (township in Burton upon Trent), 8/313; SK268233; NP 121
Winskel, 7/181; NP 83
Winslade (division in Winslade with Kempshott), 14/104; SU661487; NP 168
Winslade with Kempshott (parish), 14/103-104; NP 168
Winsley (tithing in Great Bradford), 39/154A; ST795615; NP 166
Winslow (parish), 3/106; SP770275; NP 146
Winslow (township in Bromyard), 15/91; SO634544; NP 130, 143
Winson (chapelry in Bibury), 13/235; SP088074; NP 157
Winstanley (township in Wigan), 20/593; SD542041; NP 100
Winster (township in Youlgreave), 8/117; SK239602; NP 111
Winston (parish), 34/249; TM178615; NP 137
Winston (Winstone) (parish and township), 11/295; NZ127174; NP 84, 85
Winstone (parish), 13/244; SO962094; NP 143, 157
Winterborne, 2/133; NP 158
Winterborne Abbas (parish), 10/242; NP 177, 178
Winterborne Came (Winterbourne Came) (division in Winterborne Came), 10/248; SY698875; NP 178
Winterborne Came (Winterbourne Came) (parish), 10/248-249; NP 178
Winterborne Clenston (Winterborne Clenstone) (parish), 10/182; ST838030; NP 178
Winterborne Herringstone (parish), 10/247; SY686873; NP 178
Winterborne Houghton (Houghton Winterborne) (parish), 10/161; ST809050; NP 178
Winterborne Kingston (parish), 10/184; SY862987; NP 178
Winterborne Monkton (Winterborne Monckton) (parish), 10/246; SY676875; NP 178
Winterborne St Martin (Winterbourne Martin, Winterbourne St Martin) (parish), 10/244; SY648886; NP 178
Winterborne Steepleton (parish), 10/243; NP 177, 178
Winterborne Stickland (Stickland Winterborne) (parish), 10/162; ST834052; NP 178
Winterborne Thomson (parish), 10/186; NP 178
Winterborne Tomson (Tomson, Winterbone Thomson) (parish), 10/186; SY885986; NP 178
Winterborne Whitechurch (Winterborne Whitchurch) (parish), 10/183; ST843004; NP 178
Winterborne Zelston (Winterborne Zelstone) (parish), 10/187; SY897977; NP 178
Winterborne Earls (parish), 39/313; NP 167
Winterborne Gunner (parish), 39/311; NP 167
Winterborne Stoke (parish), 39/265; NP 167
Winterbourn, 2/133; NP 158
Winterbourne (Winterbourn, Winterborne) (chapelry in Chieveley), 2/133; SU454730; NP 158
Winterbourne Abbas (Winterborne Abbas) (parish), 10/242; SY607908; NP 177, 178
Winterbourne Came (parish), 10/248-249; NP 178
Winterbourne Martin (parish), 10/244; SY648886; NP 178
Winterbourne St Martin (parish), 10/244; SY648886; NP 178
Winterbourne Steepleton (Winterborne Steepleton) (parish), 10/243; SY619893; NP 177, 178
Winterbourne (parish), 13/389-390; NP 156
Winterbourne (tithing in Winterbourne), 13/389; ST648805; NP 156
Winterbourne Bassett (parish), 39/106; SU102749; NP 157
Winterbourne Dauntsey (Winterborne Dauntsey) (parish), 39/312; SU177345; NP Winterborne Dauntsey (parish), 39/312; NP 167
Winterbourne Earls (Winterborne Earls) (parish), 39/313; SU176339; NP 167
Winterbourne Gunner (Winterborne Gunner) (parish), 39/311; SU182350; NP 167
Winterbourne Monkton (Winterbourne Monckton) (parish), 39/108; SU103722; NP 157
Winterbourne Stoke (Winterborne Stoke) (parish), 39/265; SU085417; NP 167
Winterburn (division in township of Flasby with Winterburn in Gargrave), 43/232C; SD933593; NP 95
Wintering ham (Wintringham) (parish), 22/17; SE941217; NP 98
Winterings (division in township of Melbecks in Grinton), 42/108; SD948993; NP 90
Wintersett (Winterset) (township in Wragby), 43/673; SE384158; NP 102
Winterslow (parish), 39/363; SU237334; NP 167
Winterton (parish), 22/18; SE940191; NP 98, 104
Winterton (parish), 25/378; TG491205; NP 126
Winthorpe (parish), 22/492; TF554652; NP 114
Winthorpe (parish), 28/146; SK815565; NP 112
Winton (division in township of in Eccles), 20/553; SJ760990; NP 101
Winton (township in Kirkby Stephen), 38/59; NY814089; NP 84
Winton, Stank and Hallikeld (township in Kirby Sigston), 42/508; SE407965; NP 91
Wintringham (parish), 22/17; NP 98
Wintringham (41/151-153); NP 92, 93
Wintringham (division in township of Wintringham in Wintringham), 41/151; SE884735; NP 92, 93
Wintringham (township in Wintringham), 41/151-152; NP 92, 93
Winwick (district in Winwick), 17/37; TL101806; NP 134
Winwick (division in township of Winwick with Hulme in Winwick), 20/607; SJ600937; NP 100, 101
Winwick (division in Winwick), 26/81; TL101804; NP 134
Winwick (parish), 17/37, 26/81; NP 134
winwick (parish), 20/594-610; NP 100, 101
Winwick (parish), 26/176; SP623745; NP 132
Winwick with Hulme (township in Winwick), 20/606-607; NP 100, 101
Wirksworth (parish), 8/147-157; NP 111
Wirksworth (township in Wirksworth), 8/147; SK289539; NP 111
Wirswall (township in Whitchurch), 5/314; SJ544445; NP 109, 118
Wisbech (Wisbech St Peters, Wisbeach St Peters) (parish), 4/5; TF430055; NP 124
Wisbech St Mary (Wisbeach St Mary) (parish), 4/6; TF391052; NP 123, 124
Wisborough Green (parish), 36/32; TQ050277; NP 181, 182
Wiseton (Wyseton) (township in Clayworth), 28/14; SK715900; NP 103
Wishaw (parish), 37/28; SP176950; NP 131
Wishford Magna (parish), 39/294; NP 167
Wisley (parish), 35/86; TQ068585; NP 170
Wispington (parish), 22/370; TF204716; NP 113, 114
Wissett (parish), 34/74; TM365793; NP 137
Wissington (Wiston) (parish), 34/497; TL958335; NP 149
Wistanstow (parish), 31/424; SO430865; NP 129
Wistanswick (township in Stoke upon Tern), 31/179; SJ663288; NP 119
Wistaston (parish), 5/246; SJ682541; NP 110
Wiston (parish), 34/497; NP 149
Wiston (parish), 36/92; TQ154141; NP 182
Wiston (parish), 55/77; SN015185; NP 138, 151
Wistow (parish), 17/26; TL278815; NP 134

237

Wistow (parish), 21/324-325; NP 132
Wistow (parish), 43/448; SE600355; NP 97
Wistow (township in Wistow), 21/325; SP643951; NP 132
Wiswell (township in Whalley), 20/250; SD750373; NP 95
Witcham (division in Witcham), 4/33A; TL466808; NP 135
Witcham (parish), 4/25, 33A-D; NP 135
Witcham - Byall Fen (division in Witcham), 4/33C; TL472879; NP 135
Witcham - Coveney Byall Fen (division in Witcham), 4/33B; TL476843; NP 135
Witcham - Meadlands (division in Witcham), 4/33D; TL441836; NP 135
Witcham Gravel (common to Ely St Mary and Witcham), 4/25; TL463828; NP 135
Witchampton (parish), 10/170; ST984066; NP 179
Witchford (division in Witchford), 4/31A; TL503799; NP 135
Witchford (parish), 4/31A-C; NP 135
Witchford - Byall Fen (division in Witchford), 4/31C; TL463883; NP 135
Witchford - The Wash (division in Witchford), 4/31B; TL460836; NP 135
Witham (parish), 12/220; TL820150; NP 149, 162
Witham Friary (parish), 32/191; ST750400; NP 166
Witham on the Hill (parish), 22/702-704; NP 123
Witham on the Hill (township in Witham on the Hill), 22/702; TF051168; NP 123
Withcall (parish), 22/281; TF279835; NP 105
Withcote (parish), 21/275; SK799059; NP 122
Witheridge (parish), 9/127; SS823162; NP 163, 164
Witherley (parish), 21/218-219; NP 132
Witherley (township in Witherley), 21/219; SP330980; NP 132
Withern (hamlet in Withern with Stain), 22/315; TF440830; NP 105
Withern with Stain (parish), 22/315-316; NP 105
Withernsea (township in Hollym), 41/437; TA353265; NP 99
Withernwick (parish), 41/399; TA198409; NP 99
Withersdale (parish), 34/78; TM281804; NP 137
Withersfield (parish), 34/333; TL650484; NP 148
Witherslack (township in Beetham), 38/132; SD442838; NP 89
Withiel (parish), 6/78; SW998650; NP 185
Withiel Florey (parish), 32/278; SS990343; NP 164
Withington (parish), 13/212; SP018162; NP 143, 144
Withington (township in Withington), 15/138; SO562432; NP 142
Withington (township in Manchester), 20/526; SJ850930; NP 101
Withington (parish), 31/235; SJ581128; NP 118
Withnell (township in Leyland), 20/328; SD640220; NP 95, 101
Withybrook (hamlet in Withybrook), 37/107; SP445846; NP 132
Withybrook (parish), 37/106-107; NP 132
Withycombe Raleigh (parish), 9/307A-B; NP 176
Withycombe Raleigh (Withycombe Rawleigh) (district in Withycombe Raleigh), 9/307A; SY018827; NP 176
Withycombe (parish), 32/496; ST006411; NP 164
Withyham (parish), 36/43; TQ506341; NP 171, 183
Withypool (parish), 32/281; SS836355; NP 164
Witley (parish), 35/157; SU935397; NP 169, 181
Witnesham (parish), 34/392; TM183510; NP 150
Witney (hamlet in Witney), 29/176; SP357098; NP 145, 158
Witney (parish), 29/176-179; NP 145, 158
Witson (parish), 53/151; NP 155
Witterage Green (township in Myddle), 31/153A; SJ481242; NP 118
Wittering (parish), 26/39; TF048023; NP 123
Wittersham (parish), 19/435; TQ894275; NP 184
Witton (parish), 25/216; TG331310; NP 126
Witton (parish), 25/475; TG314095; NP 126
Witton (township in Blackburn), 20/318; SD658278; NP 95
Witton (township in Aston), 37/33; SP084914; NP 131
Witton cum Twambrook (Witton cum Twambrooks) (township in Great Budworth), 5/142; SJ665741; NP 110
Witton Gilbert (parish), 11/133; NZ236462; NP 85
Witton le Wear (parish), 11/350; NZ 152319; NP 85
Witton Shields (township in Longhorsley), 27/299; NZ122632; NP 78
Witton, 17/78
Wiveliscombe (parish), 32/291; ST079287; NP 164
Wivelsfield (parish), 36/99; TQ348211; NP 182, 183
Wivenhoe (parish), 12/154; TM040234; NP 149
Wiverton Hall (extra-parochial), 28/220; SK718368; NP 122
Wiveton (parish), 25/27; TG040428; NP 125
Wix (parish), 12/107; TM158288; NP 150
Wixford (parish), 37/194; SP096542; NP 131, 144
Wixoe (parish), 34/336; TL714436; NP 148
Woburn (parish), 1/111; SP950333; NP 146, 147
Wokefield (tithing in Stratfield Mortimer), 2/192; SU675656; NP 158
Woking (division in Woking), 35/80; SU987572; NP 169, 170
Woking (parish), 35/80-81; NP 169, 170
Wokingham (division in Wokingham), 2/198; SU823710; NP 169
Wokingham (parish), 2/198-200; NP 169
Wokingham South (division in Wokingham), 2/199; SU814674; NP 169
Wokingham Town (division in Wokingham), 2/200; SU811687; NP 169
Wolborough (Wolborough with Newton Abbot) (parish), 9/411; SX861703; NP 188
Wold (parish), 26/195; SP791736; NP 133
Wold Ings (division in township of North Ferriby in North Ferriby), 41/315; TA066287; NP 99/1
Wold Newton (Newton le Wold) (parish), 22/172; TF240968; NP 105
Wold Newton (parish), 41/173; TA044735; NP 93
Woldingham (parish), 35/100; TQ374554; NP 171
Wolfendenen-in-Newchurch (division in Newchurch in Rossendale township in Whalley), 20/283; SD835240; NP 95
Wolferlow (parish), 15/80; SO668618; NP 130
Wolferton (Woolferton, Wolverton) (parish), 25/93; TF660283; NP 124
Wolfhampcote (Wolfhamcote) (parish), 37/238; SP513642; NP 132
Wollascot (Great and Little Wollascot) (township in St Mary Shrewsbury), 31/250; SJ481186; NP 118
Wollaston (parish), 26/215; SP908632; NP 133
Wollaston (division in Alberbury Upper Quarter township in Alberbury), 31/307; SJ327126; NP 118
Wollaston (township in Old Swinford), 40/23; SO889848; NP 130
Wollaton (parish), 28/247; SK525398; NP 121
Wollerton (township in Hodnet), 31/168; SJ618302; NP 118, 119
Wollescote (township in Old Swinford), 40/20; SO925835; NP 130
Wolsingham (parish), 11/177-187; NP 84, 85
Wolsingham (township in Wolsingham), 11/178, 180-183; NP 84
Wolsingham North Moor (common to all the divisions in Wolsingham except Bradley, Helme Park and Thornley), 11/179; NZ085408; NP 84
Wolsingham Park Moor (common to Frosterley division and to all the divisions in Wolsingham except Helme Park), 11/177; NZ030410; NP 84
Wolstanton (parish), 33/17A-18D; SJ860570; NP 110
Wolstanton (township in Wolstanton), 33/18C; SJ855480; NP 110
Wolstaston, 31/340; NP 129
Wolstenholme and Cheesden (subdivision of Spotland Further Side division in Spotland township in Rochdale), 20/449; SD846161; NP 101
Wolston (parish), 37/137-138; NP 132
Wolston (township in Wolston), 37/137; SP424750; NP 132
Wolterton (parish), 25/143; TG160320; NP 125, 126
Wolverhampton (parish), 33/311-320B; NP 119, 130
Wolverhampton Eastern (division in Wolverhampton), 33/320B; SO925980; NP 119, 130
Wolverhampton Western (division in Wolverhampton), 33/320; SO904984; NP 119, 130
Wolverley (township in Wem), 31/49; SJ468315; NP 118
Wolverley (parish), 40/27; SO840800; NP 130
Wolverton (parish), 3/22; SP808402; NP 146
Wolverton (Woolveston) (parish), 14/13; SU552576; NP 168
Wolverton (parish), 25/93; NP 124

Wolverton (parish), 32/95; NP 166
Wolverton (parish), 37/210; SP214624; NP 131
Wolvesnewton (Woolvesnewton) (parish), 53/84; ST461997; NP 155
Wolvey (parish), 37/103; SP430880; NP 132
Wolviston (Woolviston) (township in Billingham), 11/261; NZ440256; NP 85
Wombleton (township in Kirkdale), 42/478; SE672817; NP 92
Wombourne (Wombourn) (parish), 33/334-336; NP 130
Wombourne (Wombourn) (township in Wombourne), 33/335; SO873928; NP 130
Wombridge (parish), 31/222; SJ695110; NP 119
Wombwell (township in Darfield), 43/858; SE395027; NP 102, 103
Womenswold (Wimblingswold) (parish), 19/346; TR234500; NP 173
Womersley (parish), 43/634-638; NP 97, 103
Womersley (township in Womersley), 43/636; SE542194; NP 97, 103
Wonastow (parish), 53/21; SO476113; NP 142
Wonersh (parish), 35/139; TQ035435; NP 169, 170
Wonston (parish), 14/141; SU469394; NP 168
Wooburn (parish), 3/216; SU911885; NP 159
Wood, 19/126; NP 173
Wood Dalling (parish), 25/199; TG089273; NP 125
Wood Eaton (parish), 29/227; SP531118; NP 145
Wood Enderby (division in Wood Enderby), 22/448A; TF274632; NP 114
Wood Enderby (parish), 22/448A-B; NP 114
Wood Enderby - Wildmore Fen (division in Wood Enderby), 22/448B; TF242539; NP 114
Wood Green (division in Tottenham), 24/79D; TQ305905; NP 160
Wood Norton (parish), 25/151; TG013280; NP 125
Wood Walton (Woodwalton) (parish), 17/29; TL220826; NP 134
Woodbank (township in Shotwick), 5/486; SJ346723; NP 109
Woodbastwick (parish), 25/400; TG330150; NP 126
Woodbatch (township in Bishop's Castle), 31/380; SO300886; NP 129
Woodborough (parish), 28/185; SK627478; NP 112
Woodborough (parish), 39/391; SU111605; NP 167
Woodbridge (parish), 34/433; TM266486; NP 150
Woodbury (parish), 9/309; SY012873; NP 176
Woodchester (parish), 13/309; SO833021; NP 156
Woodchurch (parish), 5/461-470; NP 100
Woodchurch (township in Woodchurch), 5/461; SJ278869; NP 100
Woodchurch (parish), 19/414; TQ941354; NP 172, 184
Woodcote (township in Sheriff Hales), 31/197; SJ772162; NP 119
Woodcote and Horton (Woodcott and Horton) (township in St Chad Shrewsbury), 31/265; SJ450119; NP 118
Woodcott (Woodcote) (township in Wrenbury), 5/278; SJ609483; NP 110
Woodcott (parish), 14/64; SU440550; NP 168
Woodcott and Horton, 31/265; NP 118
Woodditton (parish), 4/146; TL657601; NP 135
Wooden (township in Lesbury), 27/204; NU237097; NP 71
Woodend (hamlet in Blakesley), 26/318; SP626490; NP 145
Woodford (township in Prestbury), 5/50; SJ889825; NP 101
Woodford (parish), 12/310; TQ408918; NP 161
Woodford (parish), 26/142; SP962763; NP 133, 134
Woodford (parish), 39/300; SU115368; NP 167
Woodford Grange (extra-parochial), 33/333; SO859935; NP 130
Woodford Halse (parish), 26/264; SP543531; NP 132, 145
Woodgreen (extra-parochial), 14/311B; SU167172; NP 179
Woodhall (division in Woodhall), 22/372A; TF208659; NP 113, 114
Woodhall (parish), 22/372A-B; NP 113, 114
Woodhall (division in township of Brackenholme with Woodhall in Hemingbrough), 41/45; SE698319; NP 97
Woodhall (division in township of Sicklinghall in Kirkby Overblow), 43/390; SE362468; NP 96

Woodhall - Wildmore Fen (division in Woodhall), 22/372B; TF262500; NP 114
Woodham (division of Woodham township in Aycliffe), 11/274; NZ289276; NP 85
Woodham (hamlet in Waddesdon), 3/146; SP697182; NP 146
Woodham (township in Aycliffe), 11/273-5; NP 85
Woodham Ferrers (Woodham Ferris) (parish), 12/339; TQ798995; NP 162
Woodham Mortimer (parish), 12/240; TL818050; NP 162
Woodham Walter (parish), 12/239; TL810070; NP 162
Woodhorn (parish), 27/312-314, 321-328, 478-482
Woodhorn (township in Woodhorn), 27/323; NZ296892; NP 78
Woodhorn Demesne (township in Woodhorn), 27/324; NZ308883; NP 78
Woodhouse Lane (subdivision of Spotland Further Side division in Spotland township in Rochdale), 20/448; SD858163; NP 101
Woodhouse (chapelry in Barrow upon Soar), 21/47; SK542155; NP 121
Woodhouse Eaves (township in Barrow upon Soar), 21/49; SK517143; NP 121
Woodhouse Farm (hamlet in Corringham), 22/143; SK847908; NP 104
Woodhouse (township in Shilbottle), 27/208; NU213081; NP 71
Woodhouse Hall (extra-parochial), 28/88; SK550735; NP 112
Woodhouse (extra-parochial), 31/586; SO650770; NP 130
Woodhouse (division in township of Sutton upon Derwent in Sutton upon Derwent), 41/80; SE732470; NP 97
Woodhouses (township in Mayfield), 33/97; SK147471; NP 111
Woodhouses (township in St Michael), 33/266B; SK084096; NP 120
Woodhurst (parish), 17/77; TL317760; NP 134
Woodland (chapelry in Ipplepen), 9/423; SX791689; NP 187, 188
Woodland (tithing in Crediton), 9/211G; (not located); NP 175
Woodland (township in Cockfield), 11/294; NZ053257; NP 84
Woodland (hamlet in Kingsdown), 19/188; TQ569606; NP 171
Woodland (division in township of Kirkby Ireleth in Kirkby Ireleth), 20/3; SD247897; NP 88
Woodlands (parish), 10/74; SU039088; NP 179
Woodlands (tithing in Mere), 39/336B; ST814312; NP 166
Woodlands, 8/16; NP 102
Woodleigh (parish), 9/445; SX745508; NP 187
Woodlesford (division in township of Oulton cum Woodlesford in Rothwell), 43/597A; SE368291; NP 96
Woodley and Sandford (division in Sonning), 2/203; SU767733; NP 159, 160
Woodluston (township in Forden), 54/99; SJ226017; NP 117
Woodmancote (hamlet in Bishop's Cleeve), 13/62; SO978273; NP 143
Woodmancott (parish), 14/137; SU576423; NP 168
Woodmancote (parish), 36/105; TQ237160; NP 182
Woodmansey (division in township of Woodmansey and Beverley Parks in St John Beverley), 41/298; TA056379; NP 99
Woodmansey and Beverley Parks (township in St John Beverley), 41/297-298; NP 99
Woodmansterne (parish), 35/48; TQ278600; NP 170
Woodnesborough (parish), 19/266; TR304571; NP 173
Woodnewton (parish), 26/44; TL037945; NP 134
Woodplumpton (division in township of Woodplumpton in St Michaels on Wyre), 20/163; SD504352; NP 94
Woodplumpton (township in St Michaels on Wyre), 20/161-164; NP 94
Woodrising (parish), 25/544; TF989031; NP 125, 136
Woodseaves (township in Drayton in Hales), 31/13; SJ682302; NP 119
Woodsetts (township in Anston cum Membris), 43/903; SK554835; NP 103
Woodsfield (hamlet in Powick), 40/159C; SO810490; NP 143
Woodsford (parish), 10/275; SY765898; NP 178
Woodside (township in Westward), 7/149; NY320480; NP 82, 83
Woodside (hamlet in Cheshunt), 16/120; TL332034; NP 160, 161

Woodside (Woodside Ward) (township in Elsdon), 27/240; NY930980; NP 71
Woodside (township in Shifnal), 31/223C; SJ730070; NP 119
Woodside Quarter (township in Wigton), 7/134; NY248472; NP 75, 82
Woodstock (parish), 29/124; SP444168; NP 145
Woodston (Woodstone) (parish), 17/7; TL182960; NP 134
Woodthorpe (township in North Wingfield), 8/128; SK383649; NP 111, 112
Woodthorpe (township in Loughborough), 21/36; SK542172; NP 121
Woodton (parish), 25/613; TM285950; NP 137
Wookey (parish), 32/143; ST506459; NP 165
Wool (parish), 10/282; SY842868; NP 178
Woolaston (Woolastone) (parish), 13/168; ST585995; NP 155, 156
Woolavington (parish), 32/219; ST349421; NP 165
Woolbeding (parish), 36/5; SU872234; NP 181
Wooldale (subdivision of Wooldale division in township of Wooldale in Kirkburton), 43/736A; SE150083; NP 102
Wooldale (subdivision of Wooldale division in township of Wooldale in Kirkburton), 43/736B; SE160090; NP 102
Wooldale (township in Kirkburton), 43/735A-736B
Wooler (parish), 27/52-53; NP 64, 71
Wooler (township in Wooler), 27/52; NT980270; NP 64, 71
Woolfardisworthy (parish), 9/49B; SS333202; NP 174
Woolfardisworthy (parish), 9/172; SS812090; NP 164, 175, 176
Woolferton (parish), 25/93; NP 124
Woolhampton (parish), 2/160; SU575672; NP 158
Woolhope (parish), 15/175; SO616361; NP 142, 143
Woolland (parish), 10/91; ST777071; NP 178
Woolley (parish), 17/57; TL152742; NP 134
Woolley (parish), 32/27; ST748685; NP 156
Woolley (township in Royston), 43/690; SE320128; NP 102
Woolpit (parish), 34/300; TL981619; NP 136
Woolsington (township in Dinnington), 27/518; NZ197710; NP 78
Woolstanwood (township in Nantwich), 5/248; SJ673563; NP 110
Woolstaston (Wolstaston) (parish), 31/340; SO455986; NP 129
Woolsthorpe (parish), 22/631; SK834346; NP 122
Woolston (division in township of Woolston with Martinscroft in Warrington), 20/614; SJ648893; NP 101
Woolston (township in West Felton), 31/98; SJ323240; NP 118
Woolston with Martinscroft (township in Warrington), 20/613-614; NP 101
Woolstone (township in Uffington), 2/101; SU294876; NP 158
Woolstone (parish), 13/44; SO961302; NP 143
Woolstrop (hamlet in Quedgeley), 13/256B; SO799144; NP 143
Woolvercot (division in Woolvercot), 29/202; SP492099; NP 145, 158
Woolvercot (parish), 29/202-203; NP 145, 158
Woolverstone (parish), 34/519; TM188382; NP 150
Woolverton (Wolverton) (parish), 32/95; ST792542; NP 166
Woolvesnewton (parish), 53/84; NP 155
Woolveston (parish), 14/13; NP 168
Woolviston, 11/261; NP 85
Woolwich (parish), 19/11-13B; NP 161, 171
Woolwich Arsenal (division in Woolwich), 19/12; TQ440792; NP 161, 171
Woolwich Dockyard (division in Woolwich), 19/11; TQ429786; NP 171
Wooperton (township in Eglingham), 27/135; NU043198; NP 71
Woore (township in Muckleston), 31/2; SJ725425; NP 119
Wooton (township in Oswestry), 31/111; SJ338276; NP 118
Wootton (parish), 1/52; TL010444; NP 147
Wootton (parish), 2/5; SP481018; NP 158
Wootton (parish), 18/16; SZ543926; NP 180
Wootton (parish), 19/345; TR235465; NP 173
Wootton (parish), 22/55; TA073152; NP 104
Wootton (parish), 26/283; SP756573; NP 133
Wootton (parish), 29/101; SP441202; NP 145
Wootton (township in Onibury), 31/415B; SO451781; NP 129
Wootton (township in Eccleshall), 33/132; SJ828273; NP 119
Wootton (township in Ellastone), 33/101; SK104456; NP 111, 120
Wootton Bassett (parish), 39/59; SU064821; NP 157
Wootton Courtney (parish), 32/249; SS930430; NP 164
Wootton Fitzpaine (Wotton Fitzpaine) (parish), 10/132; SY362957; NP 177
Wootton Glanville (parish), 10/95; NP 178
Wootton Rivers (parish), 39/198; SU198631; NP 167
Wootton St Lawrence (parish), 14/53; SU586522; NP 168
Wootton Wawen (Waves Wootton) (parish), 37/177-180; NP 131
Wootton Wawen (Waves Wootton) (township in Wootton Wawen), 37/177; SP152263; NP 131
Worcester Walk (division of West Dean township in St Pauls, Forest of Dean), 13/158; SO600130; NP 142, 143
Worcester, All Saints (parish), 40/114; SO847549; NP 130/1
Worcester, College Precincts (extra-parochial), 40/118; SO850545; NP 130/1
Worcester, St Alban (parish), 40/116; SO849547; NP 130/1
Worcester, St Andrew (parish), 40/115; SO848548; NP 130/1
Worcester, St Helen (parish), 40/119; SO850547; NP 130/1
Worcester, St Martin (inside city of Worcester in Worcester, St Martin), 40/127A; SO859548; NP 130, 143
Worcester, St Martin (outside city of Worcester in Worcester, St Martin), 40/127B; SO876550; NP 130, 143
Worcester, St Martin (parish), 40/127A-B; NP 130, 143
Worcester, St Michael Bredwardine (parish), 40/117; SO849546; NP 130/1
Worcester, St Nicholas (parish), 40/113; SO848552; NP 130/1
Worcester, St Peter the Great (division inside city of Worcester in Worcester, St Peter the Great), 40/125A; SO856536; NP 143
Worcester, St Peter the Great (division outside the city of Worcester in Worcester, St Peter the Great), 40/125B; SO863525; NP 130
Worcester, St Swithun (parish), 40/120; SO850549; NP 130/1
Worcester, The Blockhouse (parish), 40/121; SO853548; NP 130/1
Wordwell (parish), 34/115; TL832731; NP 136
Worfield (parish), 31/478; SO760960; NP 130
Worgret, 10/285B; NP 178
Workington (parish), 7/251-255; NP 82
Workington (township in Workington), 7/251; NY001277; NP 82
Worksop (parish), 28/27-30; NP 103, 112
Worksop (Worksop and Radford) (township in Worksop), 28/29; SK600770; NP 103, 112
Worlaby (parish), 22/60; TA011137; NP 104
Worlaby (parish), 22/328; TF333771; NP 105
Worle (parish), 32/65; ST359619; NP 165
Worleston (township in Acton), 5/297; SJ656551; NP 110
Worlingham (parish), 34/25; TM450900; NP 137
Worlington (parish), 34/209; TL693730; NP 135
Worlingworth (parish), 34/172; TM230690; NP 137
Wormbridge (parish), 15/229; SO420311; NP 142
Wormegay (parish), 25/314; TF671125; NP 124
Wormesley (parish), 15/108; NP 142
Wormhill (township in Tideswell), 8/33; SK113754; NP 111
Wormingford (parish), 12/97; TL936319; NP 149
Worminghall (parish), 3/159; SP639095; NP 145, 158
Wormington (parish), 13/36; SP044363; NP 144
Wormleighton (parish), 37/264; SP446539; NP 132, 145
Wormley (parish), 16/116; TL350060; NP 160, 161
Wormshill (parish), 19/227; TQ877575; NP 172
Wormsley (Wormesley) (parish), 15/108; SO430480; NP 142
Wornditch (hamlet in Kimbolton), 17/97; TL095684; NP 134
Worplesden (parish), 35/75-76C; NP 169
Worrall (sub-division in Bradfield division in township of Bradfield in Ecclesfield), 43/809; SK309919; NP 102
Worsbrough (township in Darfield), 43/856; SE351030; NP 102
Worsley (division in township of Worsley in Eccles), 20/557; SJ741999; NP 101
Worsley (township in Eccles), 20/555-560; NP 101
Worsley (township in Leeds), 43/497; SE278323; NP 96

Worstead (parish), 25/237; TG304266; NP 126
Worsthorne with Hurstwood (township in Whalley), 20/274; NP 95
Worston (extra-parochial), 33/90; SJ879279; NP 119
Worston (township in Whalley), 20/246; SD779428; NP 95
Worth (parish), 19/271; TR358571; NP 173
Worth (parish), 36/40A-C; NP 170, 171, 182
Worth (township in Prestbury), 5/32; SJ933832; NP 101
Worth - East Division (division in Worth), 36/40C; TQ350375; NP 170, 171
Worth - Middle Division (division in Worth), 36/40B; TQ318367; NP 170, 182
Worth - North-West Division (division in Worth), 36/40A; TQ286359; NP 170, 182
Worth Matravers (parish), 10/295; SY974776; NP 179
Wortham (parish), 34/89; TM082783; NP 136
Worthen (parish), 31/323; NP 118, 129
Worthen (parish), 31/323-333, 54/94-96; NP 117, 118
Worthen (township in Worthen), 31/325; SJ324049; NP 118
Worthenbury (township in Worthenbury), 50/136; SJ420460; NP 109, 118
Worthing (parish), 25/268; TF999197; NP 125
Worthing (township in Broadwater), 36/305; TQ155029; NP 182
Worthington (township in Standish), 20/382; SD577117; NP 100
Worthington (township in Breedon on the Hill), 21/11; SK403193; NP 121
Worting (parish), 14/52; SU600514; NP 168
Wortley (township in Tankersley), 43/785; SK313987; NP 102
Worton (hamlet in Cassington), 29/193; SP461117; NP 145, 158
Worton (tithing in Potterne), 39/138; ST981569; NP 167
Wortwell (parish), 25/633; TM277849; NP 137
Wothersome (township in Bardsey), 43/409; SE400425; NP 96, 97
Wotherton (township in Chirbury), 31/353; SJ282004; NP 117, 118, 128, 129
Wothorpe (hamlet in Stamford, St Martin Baron), 26/31; TF031052; NP 123
Wotton (parish), 35/167; TQ135445; NP 170
Wotton Fitzpaine (parish), 10/132; NP 177
Wotton St Mary Without (hamlet in Gloucester, St Mary de Lode), 13/176; SO854205; NP 143
Wotton Underwood (parish), 3/147; SP692168; NP 145, 146
Wotton under Edge (Wootton under Edge) (parish), 13/325; ST770940; NP 156
Woughton on the Green (parish), 3/69; SP867374; NP 146
Wouldham (parish), 19/85; TQ723642; NP 171
Wrabness (parish), 12/108; TM174312; NP 150
Wragby (parish), 22/265; TF133781; NP 104
Wragby (parish), 43/666-673; NP 103
Wragby (township in Wragby), 43/670; SE414173; NP 103
Wraisbury (parish), 3/239; NP 159, 169
Wramplingham (parish), 25/559; TG116060; NP 125
Wrangle (division in Wrangle), 22/762A; TF430520; NP 114
Wrangle (parish), 22/762A; TF430520; NP 114
Wrangle - East Fen (division in Wrangle), 22/762B; TF424543; NP 114
Wrawby (parish), 22/62-63; NP 104
Wrawby (township in Wrawby), 22/62; TA020090; NP 104
Wraxall (parish), 10/122; ST568007; NP 177
Wraxall (parish), 32/13; ST500720; NP 155
Wray (division in township of Wray with Botton in Melling), 20/87; SD605670; NP 89
Wray with Botton (township in Melling), 20/87-88; NP 89
Wraysbury (Wraisbury, Wyrardisbury) (parish), 3/239; TQ007737; NP 159, 169
Wrayton (division in township of Melling with Wrayton in Melling), 20/82; SD611719; NP 89
Wreay (township in St Mary [Carlisle]), 7/98B; NY427490; NP 76
Wrecclesham and Bourne (Wrecklesham) (tithing in Farnham), 35/150; SU852448; NP 169
Wrecklesham, 35/150; NP 169
Wrecsam (parish), 49/49-62, 50/130; NP 109
Wreighill (township in Rothbury), 27/245; NT980020; NP 71
Wrelton (township in Middleton), 42/440; SE764860; NP 92
Wrenbury (parish), 5/275-280; NP 109, 110, 119
Wrenbury cum Frith (township in Wrenbury), 5/279; SJ586484; NP 109, 110
Wreningham (parish), 25/607; TM149989; NP 136, 137
Wrentham (parish), 34/52; TM491831; NP 137
Wrenthorpe (Wrenthorpe or Potovens) (division in township of Stanley cum Wrenthorpe in Wakefield), 43/600; SE320230; NP 96
Wrentnall (township in Church Pulverbatch), 31/338B; SJ421037; NP 118
Wressle (Wressell) (division in township of Wressle and Loftsome in Wressle), 41/44; SE714328; NP 97
Wressle (Wressell) (parish), 41/41-44; NP 97, 98
Wrestlingworth (parish), 1/64; TL260471; NP 147
Wretton (parish), 25/527; TL686998; NP 124, 135
Wrexham (Wrecsam) (parish), 49/49-62, 50/130; NP 108, 109
Wrexham Abbot (township in Wrexham [Wrecsam]), 49/60; SJ330498; NP 109
Wrexham Regis (township in Wrexham [Wrecsam]), 49/61; SJ330500; NP 109
Wrickton, Newton, Overton and Walkerslow (Wricton) (township in Stottesden), 31/577; SO653863; NP 130
Wricton, 31/577; NP 130
Wrightington (township in Eccleston), 20/373; SD528120; NP 100
Wrington (parish), 32/60; ST487638; NP 165
Writhlington (parish), 32/104; ST702541; NP 166
Writtle (parish), 12/284; TL650050; NP 161
Wrockwardine (township in Wrockwardine), 31/218; SJ622122; NP 118, 119
Wrockwardine Wood (township in Wrockwardine), 31/221; SJ703120; NP 118
Wrockwardine), 31/218; SJ622122; NP 118, 119
Wroot (parish), 22/1; SE720020; NP 103
Wropton (township in Forden), 54/100; SJ242007; NP 117, 128
Wrotham (parish), 19/184; TQ621571; NP 171
Wroughton (Ellingdon) (tithing in Wroughton), 39/93; SU135805; NP 157
Wroughton (parish), 39/93-94; NP 157
Wroxall (parish), 37/90; SP227720; NP 131
Wroxeter (parish), 31/233; SJ586076; NP 118, 119
Wroxham (parish), 25/362; TG300170; NP 126
Wroxton (division in Wroxton), 29/21; SP411428; NP 145
Wroxton (parish), 29/21-22; NP 145
Wuerdale (division in township of Wuerdale in Rochdale), 20/457; SD918158; NP 101
Wuerdale (township in Rochdale), 20/457-458; NP 95, 101
Wyberton (division in Wyberton), 22/763A; TF408328; NP 123, 124
Wyberton (parish), 22/763A-B; NP 123, 124
Wyberton - Holland Fen (division in Wyberton), 22/763B; TF297435; NP 123
Wybunbury (parish), 5/252-269; NP 110, 119
Wybunbury (township in Wybunbury), 5/259; SJ691504; NP 110
Wychnor (Wichnor) (township in Tatenhill), 33/220; SK177165; NP 120
Wychough (township in Malpas), 5/319; SJ485453; NP 109, 118
Wychwood Forest (division in Shipton under Wychwood), 29/146; SP320160; NP 145
Wyck Rissington (parish), 13/97; NP 144
Wycliffe (parish), 42/28; NZ115135; NP 84
Wycoller (division in township of Trawden in Whalley), 20/269; SD951388; NP 95
Wydal (division in Revesby), 22/446D; TF362546; NP 114
Wyddial (Widdial) (parish), 16/21; TL375319; NP 148
Wye (parish), 19/332; TR057463; NP 172
Wyfordby (Wyfordby cum Brentingby) (parish), 21/77; SK789200; NP 122
Wyham cum Cadeby (Wyham with Cadeby) (parish), 22/178; TF270950; NP 105
Wyke (tithing in Worplesden), 35/75; SU915505; NP 169

Wyke Champflower (chapelry in Bruton), 32/198; ST661447; NP 166
Wyke Regis (division in Wyke Regis), 10/264; SY665780;NP178
Wyke Regis (parish), 10/264-265; NP 178
Wyke, 43/545; NP 96
Wykedown, 39/105; NP 157
Wykeham (parish), 42/414; SE953857; NP 93
Wyken (parish), 37/144; SP368803; NP 132
Wykey (Wikey) (township in Ruyton of the Eleven Towns), 31/139; SJ385250; NP 118
Wykham (Wickham) (township in Banbury), 29/18; SP440382; NP 145
Wykin (hamlet in Hinckley), 21/225; SP405950; NP 132
Wylam (township in Ovingham), 27/557; NZ116648; NP 77
Wyldecoat (tithing in Hawkchurch), 10/112; ST337004; NP 177
Wylye (Wily) (parish), 39/288; SU009370; NP 167
Wymering (parish), 14/287; SU653055; NP 180
Wymeswold (Wimeswold) (parish), 21/39; SK615235; NP 121
Wymington (parish), 1/19; SP958642; NP 133, 134
Wymondham (parish), 21/109; SK858188; NP 122
Wymondham (parish), 25/649A-653; NP 125, 136
Wymondham - Market Green (division in Wymondham), 25/649B; TG112013; NP 136
Wymondham - Town Green (Towngreen) (division in Wymondham), 25/649A; TG108018; NP 136
Wynford Eagle (parish), 10/144; SY578959; NP 177
Wyrardisbury (parish), 3/239; NP 159, 169
Wyre Piddle (chapelry in Fladbury), 40/186; SO967478; NP 143
Wysall (parish), 28/290; SK276607; NP 121
Wyseton, 28/14; NP 103
Wytham (parish), 2/1; SP469901; NP 145, 158
Wythop (township in Lorton parochial chapelry in Brigham), 7/276; NY198289; NP 82
Wyton (township in Swine), 41/387; TA176334; NP 99
Wyton (Witton) (parish), 17/78; TL278738; NP 134
Wyverstone (parish), 34/187; TM036679; NP 136
Wyville cum Hungerton (parish), 22/630; SK883291; NP 122

Y

Y Bont-faen (parish), 51/123; NP 154
Y Drenewydd (parish), 54/167; NP 128
Y Fenn (parish), 53/36-38; NP 141, 142
Y Ferwig (Verwig, Verwick, Ferwig) (parish), 46/100; SN180500; NP 139
Y Fflint, 50/25; NP 108
Y Gelli Gandryll (parish), 45/92A-B
Y Trallwng, 54/68; NP 117
Yaddlethorpe (township in Bottesford), 22/29B; SE883070; NP 104
Yafforth (township in Danby Wiske), 42/68; SE327946; NP 91
Yalding (parish), 19/307; TQ698479; NP 171
Yanwath and Eamont Bridge (township in Barton), 38/22; NY519270; NP 83
Yanworth (hamlet in Hazleton), 13/218; SP074142; NP 144
Yapham (division in township of Yapham cum Meltonby in Pocklington), 41/94; SE780510; NP 98
Yapham cum Meltonby, 41/94-95; NP 98
Yapton (parish), 36/284; SU977030; NP 181
Yarborough (parish), 22/790; NP 105
Yarburgh (Yarborough) (parish), 22/790; TF353932; NP 105
Yarcombe (parish), 9/144; ST245090; NP 177
Yardley (parish), 16/27; NP 147
Yardley (parish), 40/45; SP118830; NP 131
Yardley Gobion (hamlet in Potterspury), 26/339A; SP765451; NP 146
Yardley Hastings (parish), 26/292; SP862561; NP 133, 146
Yarkhill (parish), 15/165; SO610430; NP 142, 143
Yarlet (extra-parochial), 33/128; SJ914293; NP 119
Yarlington (parish), 32/363; ST659288; NP 166
Yarlside (division in township of Dalton in Dalton in Furness), 20/27; SD228695; NP 88
Yarm (parish), 42/275; NZ420120; NP 85
Yarmouth (parish), 18/6; SZ356896; NP 180

Yarnfield (hamlet in Maiden Bradley), 32/192; ST745482; NP 166
Yarnfield (township in Swynnerton), 33/50; SJ868331; NP 119
Yarnscombe (parish), 9/65; SS554229; NP 163
Yarnton (division in Yarnton), 29/196A; SP477120; NP 145
Yarpole (parish), 15/28; SO472657; NP 129
Yarwell (parish), 26/41A; TL044982; NP 134
Yate (parish), 13/351; ST715849; NP 156
Yate and Pickup Bank (township in Whalley), 20/301; SD721231; NP 95
Yateley (parish), 14/27-29; NP 169
Yateley (Yately) (tithing in Yateley), 14/27; SU822598; NP 169
Yatesbury (parish), 39/109; SU071716; NP 157
Yattendon (parish), 2/125; SU545752; NP 158
Yatton (parish), 32/493; ST433672; NP 165
Yatton (township in Much Marcle), 15/285; SO630309; NP 143
Yatton Keynell (parish), 39/78; ST865762; NP 156
Yaverland (parish), 18/22; SZ614858; NP 180
Yawthorpe (hamlet in Corringham), 22/144; SK896923; NP 104
Yaxham (parish), 25/502; TG017105; NP 125
Yaxley (parish), 17/11; TL190920; NP 134
Yaxley (parish), 34/137; TM121740; NP 136
Yazor (parish), 15/109; SO405475; NP 142
Yeadon (township in Guiseley), 43/507; SE202406; NP 96
Yealand Conyers (township in Warton), 20/67; SD502744; NP 89
Yealand Redmayne (township in Warton), 20/66; SD500763; NP 89
Yealmpton (parish), 9/450; SX586530; NP 187
Yeardsley cum Whaley (Whaley with Yeardsley, Whaley cum Yeardsley) (township in Taxal), 5/30; SK002822; NP 101, 111
Yearle, 27/51; NP 71
Yearsley (township in Coxwold), 42/555; SE585747; NP 91
Yeaveley (township in Shirley), 8/224; SK185407; NP 120
Yeavering (township in Kirknewton), 27/64; NT928295; NP 64, 71
Yedingham (parish), 41/154; SE900790; NP 92, 93
Yelden (parish), 1/4; TL011665; NP 134
Yeldersley (Yieldersley) (township in Ashbourne), 8/182; SK215445; NP 111
Yelford (parish), 29/184; SP357049; NP 158
Yelling (parish), 17/117; TL261617; NP 134
Yelvertoft (parish), 26/177; SP592753; NP 132
Yelverton (parish), 25/572; TG292029; NP 126, 137
Yeovil (parish), 32/467; ST554155; NP 177
Yeovilton (division in Yeovilton), 32/397; ST554233; NP 177
Yeovilton (parish), 32/397-399; NP 177
Yerbeston (parish), 55/131; SN063090; NP 151
Yetminster (parish), 10/40-42; NP 177, 178
Yetminster (tithing in Yetminster), 10/40; ST594103; NP 177, 178
Yew Tree Farm, 40/64; SO902617; NP 130
Yews (division in Maltby township in Maltby), 43/919; SK567904; NP 103
Yieldersley, 8/182; NP 111
Ynys Enlli, 48/75; NP 115
Ynysawdre (hamlet in St Bride's Minor), 51/92; SS900845; NP 154
Ynyscynhaiarn (parish), 48/44; SH524440; NP 116
Ynysymond (hamlet in Cadoxton Juxta Neath), 51/11; SN726018; NP 153
Yokefleet (township in Howden), 41/12; SE825253; NP 98, 98/1
Yoreton, 31/158; NP 118
York Castle, 43/23; NP 97/1
Yorton (Yoreton) (township in Broughton), 31/158; SJ503229; NP 118
Youlgreave (parish), 8/112-119; NP 111
Youlgreave (township in Youlgreave), 8/114; SK200645; NP 111
Youlthorpe (division in township of Youlthorpe with Gowthorpe in Bishop Wilton), 41/112; SE764556; NP 98
Youlthorpe with Gowthorpe (township in Bishop Wilton), 41/112-113; NP 98

Youlton (township in Alne), 42/584; SE498635; NP 91
Yoxall (parish), 33/199; SK140201; NP 120
Yoxford (parish), 34/163; TM391691; NP 137
Yr Wyddgrug (parish), 50/107-119; NP 108
Yr Wyddgrug, 50/111; NP 108
Yrer-uan (township in Llanrhaeadr-ym-Mochnant [Llanrhaiadr ym Mochnant]), 49/132B; SJ131255; NP 117
Ysbyty (parish), 48/22, 49/18; NP 107
Ysbyty Ystwyth (Sputty Ystwyth) (parish), 46/36; SN774703; NP 127
Yscawen (township in Rhuddlan), 50/63; SJ022787; NP 108
Ysceifiog (parish), 50/89-95; NP 108
Yscir-vawr (hamlet in Merthyr Cynog), 45/34C; SN985355; NP 141
Yscir-vechan (hamlet in Merthyr Cynog), 45/34D; SN960390; NP 141
Ysclydach (hamlet in Llywel), 45/61; SN913308; NP 141
Ysgeirieth (township in Trefeglwys), 54/131; SN860905; NP 127, 128
Ysgubor-y-coed (township in Llanfihangel Genu'rglyn), 46/2; SN712948; NP 127
Ysgwyddgwyn (hamlet in Gelligaer), 51/75B; ST120980; NP 154
Yspytty (parish), 48µ/22, 49/18; NP 107
Yspytty-Ystrad-Meiric (parish), 46/32; NP 127
Ystrad (hamlet in Llandingat), 47/15; SN751343; NP 140
Ystrad Meurig (Sputty Ystradmeurig, Yspytty-Ystrad-Meiric) (parish), 46/32; SN711681; NP 127
Ystrad-dyfodwg (parish), 51/66A-67; NP 154
Ystradfellte (division outside Fforest-fawr in Ystradfellte), 45/71B; SN950160; NP 141
Ystradfellte (Ystradfelty) (parish), 45/71A-B; NP 141, 153, 154
Ystradfellte - Fforest-fawr (division within Fforest-fawr in Ystradfellte), 45/71A; SN895135; NP 141, 153, 154
Ystradgunlais (parish), 45/69-70; SN800214; NP 140, 153
Ystradgunlais Higher, 45/69
Ystradgunlais Lower, 45/70; NP 140, 153
Ystradgynlais (parish), 45/69-70; SN800214; NP 140, 153
Ystradgynlais Higher (Ystradgunlais Higher) (division in Ystradgynlais), 45/69; SN850130; NP 141, 153
Ystradgynlais Lower (Ystradgunlais Lower) (division in Ystradgynlais), 45/70; SN800214; NP 140, 153
Ystradhynod (township in Llanidloes), 54/144; SN882878; NP 127, 128
Ystradowen (parish), 51/108; ST061781; NP 154
Ystymeolwyn (township in Meifod), 54/42; SJ142107; NP 117
Ystyn-alla (township in Llansilin), 49/127; SJ200272; NP 117

Z
Zeal Monachorum (parish), 9/179; SS715041; NP 175
Zeals (tithing in Mere), 39/336C; ST780320; NP 166
Zennor (parish), 6/205; SW452378; NP 189